BASIC HANDBOOK

OF

Child Psychiatry

VOLUME ONE

BASIC HANDBOOK
OF
Child Psychiatry

Joseph D. Noshpitz / Editor-in-Chief

VOLUME ONE

Development

JUSTIN D. CALL, JOSEPH D. NOSHPITZ,
RICHARD L.COHEN, AND IRVING N. BERLIN

EDITORS

Basic Books, Inc., Publishers / New York

To all those

who strive to ease the pain

and better the lives of troubled children

these books are dedicated

Library of Congress Cataloging in Publication Data
Main entry under title:

Basic handbook of child psychiatry.

Includes bibliographies and indexes.
CONTENTS: v. 1. Development.—
1. Child psychiatry. I. Noshpitz, Joseph D.
RJ499.B33   618.9′28′9   78–7082
ISBN: 0–465–00589–6

CONTENTS

SECTION ONE / Normal Development

SECTION TWO / Varieties of Development

PART D   THE CHILD WITH SEVERE HANDICAPS

SECTION THREE   /   Assessment

PART A   THE APPROACH TO ASSESSMENT

PART B   DIRECT EXAMINATION OF THE CHILD

PART C   SPECIAL DIAGNOSTIC TECHNIQUES

Contents

PART D   CASE FORMULATION AND MANAGEMENT

PART E   SPECIAL APPLICATIONS

CONTRIBUTORS

PAUL L. ADAMS, M.D.
Professor of Psychiatry, University of Louisville, Louisville, Kentucky.

BESSE-LEE ALLNUTT, M.D.
Assistant Professor of Child Psychiatry, University of Cincinnati; Medical Director, Millcreek Psychiatric Center for Children, Cincinnati, Ohio.

CAROLYN L. ATTNEAVE, PH.D.
Adjunct Professor of Psychiatry and Behavioral Sciences, University of Washington, Seattle, Washington.

HAROLD BALIKOV, M.D.
Assistant Clinical Professor, University of Illinois; Member of Faculty, Child Analytic Section, Chicago Institute of Psychoanalysis; Instructor of Child Psychiatry, Michael Reese Hospital, Professor and Lecturer, University of Chicago, Chicago, Illinois.

DOROTHY J. BECKER, M.D.
Assistant Professor of Pediatrics, Children's Hospital of Pittsburgh, Pittsburgh, Pennsylvania.

IRVING N. BERLIN, M.D.
Professor of Psychiatry and Director of Division of Child Psychiatry, Department of Psychiatry, School of Medicine, University of New Mexico, Albuquerque, New Mexico.

NORMAN R. BERNSTEIN, M.D.
Professor of Psychiatry, University of Illinois, Chicago, Illinois.

JUSTIN D. CALL, M.D.
Professor and Chief of Child and Adolescent Psychiatry, Department of Psychiatry and Human Behavior, School of Medicine, University of California at Irvine; Analyzing and Supervising Instructor, Los Angeles Psychoanalytic Society and Institute, Los Angeles, California.

JEAN E. CARLIN, M.D., PH.D.
Clinical Professor of Psychiatry and Assistant Chairman, Department of Psychiatry, University of California at Irvine; Associate Dean, College of Medicine, University of California, Irvine, California.

FORTUNATO G. CASTILLO, M.D.
Research Psychotherapist, The Hampstead Child Therapy Course and Clinic, London, England.

DONALD J. COHEN, M.D.
Associate Professor of Pediatrics, Psychiatry and Psychology, Yale University School of Medicine and the Child Study Center, New Haven, Connecticut.

RICHARD L. COHEN, M.D.
Executive Director, Pittsburgh Child Guidance Center, Pittsburgh, Pennsylvania.

GEORGE COLOMBEL, M.D.
Assistant Professor of Child Psychiatry, Department of Psychiatry, College of Medicine, University of Cincinnati, Cincinnati, Ohio.

C. KEITH CONNERS, PH.D.
Professor of Psychiatry, University of Pittsburgh School of Medicine, Pittsburgh, Pennsylvania.

MAUREEN DENNIS, PH.D.
Scientist, Research Institute, The Hospital for Sick Children, Toronto, Ontario.

ISRAEL M. DIZENHUZ, M.D.
Associate Professor of Child Psychiatry, Director of Psychiatry, Jewish Hospital, Cincinnati, Ohio.

ALLAN L. DRASH, M.D.
Professor of Pediatrics, Children's Hospital of Pittsburgh, Pittsburgh, Pennsylvania.

Contributors

JAN DRUCKER, PH.D.
Member, Psychology Faculty, Sarah Lawrence College, Bronxville, New York.

GEORGE EDINGTON, M.A.
Member, Workshop Institute for Living Learning, New York, New York.

BERNICE T. EIDUSON, PH.D.
Professor, Department of Psychiatry, UCLA School of Medicine, Los Angeles, California.

ROBERT N. EMDE, M.D.
Professor of Psychiatry, University of Colorado Medical School, Denver; Adjunct Associate Professor of Psychology, University of Denver, Denver, Colorado.

CARL B. FEINSTEIN, M.D.
Assistant Professor, Department of Psychiatry, George Washington University, Washington, D.C.; Director of Out-Patients, Department of Psychiatry, Children's Hospital, National Medical Center, Washington, D.C.

ELEANOR GALENSON, M.D.
Clinical Professor of Psychiatry, Albert Einstein College of Medicine, New York; Clinical Professor of Psychiatry, Mount Sinai School of Medicine, New York.

HERBERT J. GOLDINGS, M.D.
Training and Supervising Analyst, Psychoanalytic Institute of New England East and Boston Psychoanalytic Institute; Co-Director, Institute for Continuing Education in Child Psychiatry, Newton, Massachusetts.

FEDOR HAGENAUER, M.D.
Associate Professor of Child Psychiatry, Department of Psychiatry, University of Cincinnati, Cincinnati, Ohio.

VIVIAN THACKABERRY HARWAY, PH.D.
Associate Professor of Clinical Child Psychiatry, (Psychology), University of Pittsburgh School of Medicine; Director, Consultation and Education Program, Pittsburgh Child Guidance Center, Pittsburgh, Pennsylvania.

CHRISTOPH M. HEINICKE, PH.D.
Professor, Department of Psychiatry, University of California, Los Angeles, California.

PETER B. HENDERSON, M.D.
Associate Professor of Clinical Child Psychiatry and Director of Residency Training in General and Child Psychiatry, Western Psychiatric Institute and Clinic, University of Pittsburgh School of Medicine, Pittsburgh, Pennsylvania.

JAMES M. HERZOG, M.D.
Clinical Instructor, Department of Psychiatry, Harvard Medical School, Boston; Director, Infant Follow-up Clinic and the Clinic for Young Children and Parents, Children's Hospital Medical Center, Boston, Massachusetts.

F. ROBERT HOLTER, M.D.
Assistant Professor, Division of Child and Adolescent Psychiatry, State University of New York, Upstate Medical Center, Syracuse, New York.

R. RODNEY HOWELL, M.D.
Professor of Pediatrics, Texas Medical Center, University of Texas Medical School, Houston, Texas.

JOHN P. KEMPH, M.D.
Vice President for Academic Affairs, Dean of the Medical Faculty, and Professor, Department of Psychiatry, Medical College of Ohio at Toledo, Ohio.

MARCEL KINSBOURNE, M.D.
Professor of Pediatrics, Professor of Psychology, University of Toronto School of Medicine; Senior Staff Physician, Hospital for Sick Children, Toronto, Ontario.

NANCY M. KLEIN, M.A.
Director, Child Development Program, and Assistant Clinical Professor of Nursing, UCLA Center for Health Sciences, Los Angeles, California.

JULES M. KLUGER, M.D.
Clinical Instructor, University of Colorado, Denver; Part-time Consultant, La Rasa Medical Health Center, Denver, Colorado.

RUTH L. LaVIETES, M.D.
Clinical Professor of Psychiatry and Director of Child and Adolescent Psychiatry, New York Medical College, New York; Chief, Task Force on Child Psychiatry and Family Practice, American Psychiatric Association.

LEONARD E. LAWRENCE, M.D.
Associate Professor of Child and Adolescent Psychiatry, University of Texas Health Science Center, San Antonio, Texas.

DAVID R. LEAVERTON, M.D.
Director, Division of Child and Adolescent Psychiatry, Albany Medical College; Chief of Service, Child and Adolescent Psychiatry, Capital District Psychiatric Center, Albany, New York.

Contributors

PEGGY B. LEAVITT, B.A.
Director, Child Development Program, Los Angeles Heart Institute, St. Vincent's Medical Center, Los Angeles, California.

LEAH LEVINGER, PH.D.
Supervisor in Diagnostic Testing, Montefiore Hospital, Bronx, New York.

VIOLA G. LEWIS, M.A.
Instructor in Medical Psychology, Department of Psychiatry and Behavioral Sciences, Johns Hopkins University School of Medicine and Hospital, Baltimore, Maryland.

LEONARD M. LINDE, M.D.
Clinical Professor of Pediatrics (Cardiology), School of Medicine, University of California at Los Angeles; Chief, Pediatric Cardiology, Los Angeles Heart Institute, St. Vincent's Medical Center, Los Angeles, California.

MAX G. MAGNUSSEN, PH.D.
Professor of Clinical Child Psychiatry (Psychology), University of Pittsburgh, Pittsburgh, Pennsylvania.

CARL P. MALMQUIST, M.D.
Professor of Criminal Justice and Law, University of Minnesota, Minneapolis, Minnesota.

JOSEPH MARCUS, M.D.
Professor of Child Psychiatry and Director of Programs in Child Psychiatry, University of Chicago, Chicago, Illinois.

DAVID R. METCALF, M.D.
Associate Professor, Department of Psychiatry, University of Colorado Medical Center, Denver, Colorado.

ROBERT MILLER, M.D.
Assistant Clinical Professor of Psychiatry, Albert Einstein College of Medicine, New York, New York.

JOHN MONEY, PH.D.
Professor of Medical Psychology, Department of Psychiatry and Behavioral Sciences, and Associate Professor of Pediatrics, Johns Hopkins University School of Medicine and Hospital, Baltimore, Maryland.

CHARLEEN M. MOORE, PH.D.
Assistant Professor of Pediatrics and Director of Cytogenetics, Texas Medical Center, University of Texas Medical School, Houston, Texas.

C. JANET NEWMAN, M.D.
Staff Child Psychiatrist, Children's Psychiatric Center, Cincinnati; Associate Professor of Child Psychiatry, University of Cincinnati, Cincinnati, Ohio.

JOSEPH D. NOSHPITZ, M.D.
Professor of Psychiatry, George Washington University, Washington, D.C.; Professor of Psychiatry and Director of Education and Training, Department of Psychiatry, Children's Hospital, National Medical Center, Washington, D.C.

DANIEL OFFER, M.D.
Chairman, Department of Psychiatry, Michael Reese Hospital and Medical Center, Chicago; Professor of Psychiatry, Pritzker School of Medicine, University of Chicago, Chicago, Illinois.

ANNE C. PETERSEN, PH.D.
Director, Laboratory for the Study of Adolescence, and Research Associate (Assistant Professor), Department of Psychiatry, University of Chicago, Chicago, Illinois.

GLORIA JOHNSON POWELL, M.D.
Associate Professor, Child Psychiatry/Mental Retardation Division, Department of Psychiatry, UCLA Center for Health Sciences, Los Angeles, California.

SALLY PROVENCE, M.D.
Professor of Pediatrics, Yale University Child Study Center, New Haven, Connecticut.

JOSEPH REIDY, M.D.
Associate Professor of Psychiatry, Johns Hopkins University, Baltimore, Maryland.

JOHN B. REINHART, M.D.
Professor of Pediatrics and Child Psychiatry, University of Pittsburgh, School of Medicine; Director, Division of Behavioral Science, Children's Hospital of Pittsburgh, Pittsburgh, Pennsylvania.

JULIUS B. RICHMOND, M.D.
Assistant Secretary for Health and Surgeon General of the Public Health Service, Washington, D.C.

JEAN ROBINSON, M.D.
Resident I, Department of Psychiatry, University of Colorado Medical School, Denver, Colorado.

KENNETH S. ROBSON, M.D.
Associate Professor of Psychiatry, Tufts University School of Medicine, Boston; Director of Training in Child Psychiatry, New England Medical Center Hospital, Boston, Massachusetts.

HERMAN ROIPHE, M.D.
Professor of Psychiatry, Mount Sinai Medical School, New York, New York.

Contributors

MICHAEL B. ROTHENBERG, M.D.
Professor of Psychiatry and Pediatrics; Director, Child Psychiatry, Pediatrics Liaison Services, University of Washington, School of Medicine, Seattle, Washington.

MARSHALL D. SCHECHTER, M.D.
Professor and Director, Division of Child and Adolescent Psychiatry, State University of New York, Upstate Medical Center, Syracuse, New York.

HILDE S. SCHLESINGER, M.D.
Assistant Clinical Professor, University of California at Berkeley; Consultant at University of California at San Francisco Center on Deafness; Project Director, Mental Health Services for the Deaf, Berkeley, California.

JOHN E. SCHOWALTER, M.D.
Director of Training and Professor of Pediatrics and Psychiatry, Yale University Child Study Center, New Haven, Connecticut.

JEFFREY S. SCHWAM, M.D.
Assistant Clinical Professor, Department of Psychiatry, University of Cincinnati School of Medicine, Cincinnati, Ohio.

ALBERTO C. SERRANO, M.D.
Professor of Psychiatry and Pediatrics, University of Texas Health Science Center, San Antonio; Director, Community Guidance Center, San Antonio, Texas.

CATHERINE B. SHAPIRO, M.S.
Ph.D. candidate in Clinical Psychology, New York University, New York, New York.

JON A. SHAW, M.D.
Chief, Child and Adolescent Psychiatry, Department of Psychiatry, Walter Reed Army Medical Center, Washington, D.C.; Associate Clinical Professor of Psychiatry, Georgetown University Medical Center, Washington, D.C.

WILEY R. SMITH, JR., M.D.
Assistant Clinical Professor of Child Psychiatry, Department of Psychiatry, University of Cincinnati, Cincinnati, Ohio.

BARBARA SNYDERMAN, PH.D.
Clinical Assistant Professor of Child Psychiatry (Psychology), University of Pittsburgh School of Medicine, Pittsburgh, Pennsylvania.

ALBERT J. SOLNIT, M.D.
Sterling Professor of Pediatrics and Psychiatry, Director, Child Study Center, Yale University School of Medicine, New Haven, Connecticut.

JEANNE SPURLOCK, M.D.
Deputy Medical Director and Director of Minority Affairs Office, American Psychiatric Association, Washington, D.C.

MICHAEL H. STONE, M.D.
Associate Clinical Professor of Psychiatry, Cornell Medical School, Department of Psychiatry, Westchester Division, White Plains, New York.

HELEN TUCKER, M.D.
Assistant Clinical Professor of Child Psychiatry, Department of Psychiatry, University of Cincinnati, Cincinnati, Ohio.

MARIA KROCKER TUSKAN, M.D.
Assistant Professor, Department of Psychiatry, University of Cincinnati School of Medicine, Cincinnati, Ohio.

SIDNEY WERKMAN, M.D.
Professor of Psychiatry, University of Colorado School of Medicine, Denver, Colorado.

VIRGINIA NICHOLS WILKING, M.D.
Chief, Division of Child Psychiatry, Harlem Hospital Center, New York; Associate Professor of Clinical Psychiatry, Columbia University, New York.

BRADFORD WILSON, PH.D.
Member of Faculty and Administrator, Workshop Institute for Living Learning, New York.

BURTON N. WIXEN, M.D.
Associate Clinical Professor, Department of Psychiatry, University of California, Los Angeles, California.

J. GERALD YOUNG, M.D.
Assistant Professor of Pediatrics and Psychiatry, Yale University School of Medicine and the Child Study Center, New Haven, Connecticut.

JOEL P. ZRULL, M.D.
Professor and Chairman, Department of Psychiatry, Medical College of Ohio at Toledo, Ohio.

PREFACE

Child psychiatry is now in its seventieth year. It has passed through an early phase of clinic practice, a later period of intense concern with inpatient care, and, most recently, a move into the universities. In the course of this evolution child psychiatry has advanced from a set of unique skills and techniques to an ever more complex scientific endeavor. It involves a basic science dimension, a wide array of specialized practices, and an increasingly intricate universe of research. Along with these have come an extensive literature, now international in scope, and an ever-widening impact on the culture generally and on medicine and psychiatry in particular.

So rapidly has this growth proceeded that it has heretofore been difficult to find any single work that embraced the full complexity of the development of child psychiatry. The emphasis of most authors has been on specialized aspects of the field; only a few have attempted more comprehensive efforts in the form of textbooks, and some of these have tended to be rather brief surveys of major topics. As a result, teachers and residents in the many training programs and individual practitioners in the communities have long felt the need for an additional book—comprehensive in its scope—in which the array of topics would be sufficiently exhaustive and in which the study of each area would be examined in enough depth to satisfy student, scholar, and practitioner alike. It was the pressure to fill this need that brought forth the idea of the *Basic Handbook of Child Psychiatry*. The same sense of urgency led the more than 250 contributors and the six editors to commit time, energy, and industry to the accomplishment of this task. And it was in response to these pressures that the authors, editors, and publisher worked together for six years to produce these volumes. If their undertaking succeeds in its intent, the *Handbook* should provide a

primary reference source for many of the questions and needs that arise within the discipline. It is with this hope that the *Basic Handbook* is presented.

The arrangement of materials in these volumes speaks for something of the logic of the discipline of child psychiatry. To begin with there is an account of the first basic science of the field, a detailing of *child development*. This is followed by a series of brief descriptions (the sort of statements that can be read quickly in connection with individual clinical cases) of different *varieties of child development*. Next comes a recounting of one of the major subdisciplines of child psychiatry, the *nature of assessment*, a section written in large part by Dr. Richard L. Cohen. These three topics comprise Volume I. The second volume is given over to the second basic science of child psychiatry, that of *child psychopathology*. Included here are studies of etiology and nosology and an account of the more important syndromes. Volume III follows, and treats another great subdiscipline, the field of *therapeutics*. The final volume, Volume IV, covers the field of *prevention* and contains a series of studies on the impact of current cultural issues on children and child psychiatry.

It should be noted that the *Handbook* is calculatedly eclectic. It is written by the working child psychiatrist as well as by the researcher and by other mental health professionals; a variety of views and opinions are therefore presented. Differences will be found among theories of development, techniques of assessment, modes of psychopathology, and approaches to treatment. No one will agree with them all—the editors certainly do not. Nonetheless they are all serious positions that demand respect if not accord. Such is the state of the art.

Grants from the Commonwealth Fund, the Maurice Falk Medical Fund, and the Grove Foundation supported the development of these volumes, and the funds are gratefully acknowledged.

Early on, Ginger Bausch lent the use of the offices of the American Academy of Child Psychiatry in Washington as a mailing address and a site to store *Handbook* materials, and Jeanne DeJarnette took on the coordination of the *Handbook* as an after-hours job. She acted as guardian angel, financial manager and factotum, kept track of documents, typed correspondence, maintained files, saw that people were informed about what was happening, and, all in all, made the enterprise work. Three years after it began, the central effort shifted from her capable hands to the secretarial staff of the Department of Child Psychiatry at the Children's Hospital National Medical Center. The Chairman of the Department was at that time Jerry Wiener, who gave a full measure of support to the demanding effort that the host of accumulated documents required. Later, Dr. James Egan took over the chairmanship and continued the pattern of unstinting support. Within the department, Mrs. Shirley Wells, ably backed up by Mrs. Penny Nolton, carried the brunt of the responsibilities, and it was she who brought the work to its final form. The sheer time involved was prodigious.

While this was going on in Washington, parallel efforts were being exerted in Pittsburgh by Dr. Cohen and his staff; in Ann Arbor by Dr. Harrison and his people; in Seattle and then in Davis, California, by Dr. Berlin and his associates; in Irvine by Dr. Call and his associates; and in San Antonio by Dr. Larry Stone, his wife Marnette, and others who worked with him. Indeed, when one ponders the amount of university assistance offered to the many authors, as well as the intensive and extensive efforts made by their staffs, it is no small contribution that the *Handbook* received from the academic world in its largest sense. The work entailed a truly massive effort, and it is impossible to list the names of the many, many people who helped it come to fruition.

For the publisher, the *Handbook* was shepherded through its labyrinthine way by the tireless efforts of Herb Reich, Behavioral Science Editor of Basic Books. This involved visits back and forth between Washington, D.C., and New York, endless attention to detail, and a sort of total immersion in the fullness of the effort needed to turn the mass of documents into a printable manuscript. Among the highly skilled staff at Basic Books who labored long hours over the thousands of pages that comprised the manuscript were Pamela Dailey and Debra Manette. They copy edited the text, cleaned up bibliographies, queried areas of uncertainty, and saw to it that scholarly rigor and clarity of expression prevailed throughout. Maureen Bischoff as project director coordinated the publication work, and all played vital roles in the final outcome.

One final point remains. The original manuscript grew to such excessive proportions that it became necessary to cut out, cut down, and shorten materials. This distressing process was initiated by the publisher and then carried by the several editors, who trimmed and tightened until a shorter, more compact work emerged. In the course of editing, a number of papers were eliminated and several others were shortened. It caused both publisher and editors considerable pain to perform this task, yet it was vital to the actual production of the work. Both the editors and the publisher hope that the outcome will justify the surgery.

JOSEPH D. NOSHPITZ
Washington, D.C.
February 15, 1979

SECTION I

Normal Development

Justin D. Call / *Editor*

The preparation of Volume I of the *Basic Handbook of Child Psychiatry* would not have been possible without the support of the Department of Psychiatry and Human Behavior of the University of California, Irvine, and the suggestions and many hours of help provided by Mrs. Bea Noble, Administrative Assistant to Dr. Justin D. Call.

JUSTIN D. CALL

1 / Introduction

Justin D. Call

Development is the outcome of an interaction between genetically programmed patterns of biological growth, that is, maturation and environmental experience. Here, experience refers to everything from intracellular environment to the adolescent's experience in the sociopolitical environment. This section of the handbook will focus on the unfolding of development in the normal individual between the time of conception and entrance of the adolescent into the adult world as a full-fledged participant. This represents a period of some two decades, and during this time span many bodily, mental, and social processes are integrated to form the psychobiological unity which comprises the functioning personality. The emerging human being is complex. There is no stage of his development that can be described adequately in only one or two dimensions, nor even as the end product of interacting forces over time. The infant is as much a person as is the adult. As growth proceeds, the individual is not only what has emerged, he is a person with a history. Without this history, he is an enigma both to himself and to everyone about him. This section attempts to provide the student and teacher with a framework within which to view the multidimensional developmental processes which take place over time.

Definitions of Normal

The word "normal" deserves special comment, for it has at least four distinct definitions. A *statistical* norm is a statement about a group of individuals and sums up and averages out their differences. Such norms are often applied to individuals who might have little in common with the population from which the norm was originally derived. The age at which an infant may achieve object constancy, the period at which a child may achieve the capacity for cooperative play, the moment at which a child initiates two-word speech, the point at which a child can make use of abstract thought in problem solving, and the time of onset of the menarche can all be stated as statistical norms for a given group. At the same time, none of these statements adequately describes the developmental aspects of such achievements in an individual human being. A specific group must first be delimited, and only then can the amount of variability of the individuals within this group be measured statistically and used as a basis for judging the level of development in any one individual.

A second conception of normal is a social one. Each social group establishes its own standards, overt or covert. In this sense, normality is the degree of social acceptance or nonacceptance granted to a given adaptation or behavior. Incorporated in this determination are the values, attitudes, and expectations of society or of a special subgroup within the larger society. These standards may be utilized to define such behaviors as delinquency, such personality traits as introversion and extroversion, and such pillars of identity as sex roles. Even the definition of what constitutes a learning disability or a school maladjustment is founded upon these social concepts of norms. One of the roots of social prejudice toward particular individuals or subgroups is the overreliance upon the local conception of what constitutes normal behavior.

A third kind of normality consists of the identification of *individual-specific response patterns* over time, for example, the response of avoidance of hyperactivity to noise, light, or social stimuli. Such individual characteristics are seen first as organismic reactions and reflect the maturational unfolding of both *species-* and *individual-specific neurobiological predispositions*. The neurobiological substrate of personality is influenced by ongoing experience, i.e., during postnatal "fetal" development (up until about age two). The basic "constitutional complex"[17] is formed during this time. Individual-specific characteristics are often subsumed rather loosely under such terms as genetic inheritance, constitutional differences, temperament, unusual perceptual sensitivity, giftedness, vulnerability, and unusual ego or drive endowment or weakness. All of these characteristics are woven into the person's adaptive functioning and into the ego-syntonic aspects of his character structure. It is precisely these traits that over time provide the evolving personality with its own special stamp. This enduring pattern becomes the norm for that individual—it is specific, it is characteristic for him, it identifies him and, in this sense, it serves as his "norm." Overemphasis on this formulation of what is "normal" would reduce the importance of such conceptions as maladaptive or psychopathological behavior since all maladaptation and psychopathology take their origin in part from individual-specific response patterns.

For example, it is not uncommon in child psychiatric practice for a very energetic, active, curious, and provocative child with high cognitive abilities to be referred with the ready-made label of hyperactivity. Evaluation of such a child requires acknowledgment of his inherent, individual-specific response patterns, his adaptation to his environment, as well as his maladaptive behavior. Once inherent response patterns are defined for a given child, what constitutes a deviant pattern for him is more accurately determined.

A fourth definition of normal is deceptively simple—it is merely anyone without psychopathology. It is not easy to say exactly what acts, and under what circumstances certain behaviors, attitudes, and patterns of thinking constitute psychopathology. This can be defined as a fixation or narrowing of mental functioning which results not only in symptoms, but in a constriction of adaptive capacity. The adaptations of childhood often appear later on as the symptom patterns and character limitations of adulthood: for example, the child's withdrawal from family chaos is an adaptation which in adult life may show up as chronic depression with schizoid features. Thus, the psychodynamic processes concerned with the development of mental functions are central here. These, rather than the adaptations or symptoms resulting from such processes, become the appropriate focus for what constitutes normal. Definitions of normal or abnormal behavior can have far-reaching implications for the individual. They are no less important for the values, aims, and methods of socialization and social control imposed by society. In assessing both normal and psychopathological behavior, the clinician must be ever aware of this nonclinical environment.

All conceptions of what constitutes "normal" must be considered. Just as nosological problems now involve multidimensional schemes (the multiaxial system of DMH III), so too must normal functioning be viewed in its multiple aspects. A balanced view of the individual's functioning can be achieved by synthesizing all of the available data in the most comprehensive manner possible. The clinician encounters social complexities involving both usual and unusual modes of adaptation. To understand these, the full use of a developmental understanding of human functioning becomes indispensable.

Some of the chapters of this section of the handbook will keep theory at a low level of abstraction and stress observational work. Along with this, there will be cross-sectional and longitudinal studies of carefully defined, nondeviant populations. Other chapters will utilize theoretical propositions which were originally developed from studies of disturbed development such as broadly defined maladaptation.

Problems in the Path of Understanding the Developmental Process

Man has always been preoccupied with his origins. Only recently, however, have scientists become seriously concerned with the developmental process of the individual person. When students of psychology, psychiatry, and even psychoanalysis are introduced to concepts of normal development, considerable resistance is likely to be encountered. Despite the explosion of knowledge of early development, many parents are still amazed to discover even the gross details of the child's normal development. The basic Victorian attitudes are still prevalent: Children should be seen and not heard, they should speak only when spoken to, and they do not become full-fledged human beings until they have emerged from adolescence. What is the explanation for these attitudes? First, many adults emerge from childhood with a sense of having outgrown or triumphed over childish things. In order to embrace adulthood, they tend to cast off childhood experience with the claim that such modes of thought, feeling, and action no longer have a place in adult life (except during socially sanctioned, regressive states). Second, early infantile life is viewed retrospectively as a period of helplessness, while later life is viewed as a time of death. Only the present is safe. Third, the sheer complexity of the developmental process has been difficult to grasp. It is easier to view structure and function in terms of what is immediately manifest than to consider its evolution or its implications for the future. The tendency of humans to disregard or to falsify their cultural history is mirrored by the tendency of the individual to forget or falsify his own past. All of these resistances must be overcome if students of child psychiatry and child development are to address themselves effectively to the complex nature of the developmental processes.

Influence of Conflict and Choice on Conception and Child Care

In ancient times, the infant and young child were generally regarded as not yet full members of the group. They were still somewhat incomplete, still likely to die. The child was viewed as a miniature adult without a personal identity. Indeed, throughout many centuries, he was considered to be property. As such, a child could be punished and mistreated, even killed, without legal protection. He had no voice and no rights and was subject to the sometimes capricious whims of adults who did have power. They knew what was right and could disregard the rights of powerless members of society such as women and children. It is possible that these persistent attitudes of adults toward children are based upon the fact that until very recently there was no 100 percent effective and acceptable way of regulating when a woman became pregnant. Thus, if men and women were to enjoy sex, they were obligated to risk pregnancy. Under such circumstances, the potential for a conflict of interest between men and women and between adults and children is increased. A child born into such conflict is not likely to enjoy the thoughtful consideration of his needs by adults, let alone his rights.

One of the interesting paradoxes of the late 1970s is the fact that men and women may make more conscious choices regarding pregnancy and child care, and at the same time reduce the number of children in a given family. Along with this is the emerging possibility of exploring options and priorities which favor optimum opportunity for the development of children. It is perhaps not too much to hope that children born out of conscious and thoughtful parental decision will benefit from this. Also, the alternative occupational roles for women are associated with increased opportunities for choice regarding methods of delivery and infant care, such as family-centered pregnancy and breast versus bottle feeding. Re-

newed attention is thus being centered on the opportunities and methods for optimum development of all children and not only for those at risk and in need.

Even in the face of strong educational approaches, the curtain of repression on the events of early childhood is an ever-recurring phenomenon. The two most lasting contributions to the theory of childhood development are those of Darwin and Freud. The facts of human evolution and human psychological unfolding continue to stand even in the face of recurrent waves of forgetfulness.

The knowledge and understanding of human psychological growth is increasing by leaps and bounds, but nonetheless it is still fragmentary. Unfortunately, what has already been learned is only poorly assimilated into the work of child psychiatrists, mental health workers, and child care workers, let alone parents. The developmental perspective is in fact rarely included in the matrix of factors which contribute to adult self-understanding.

Child psychiatrists, child psychoanalysts, and other child mental health workers generally aspire to bridge the gap between their theory of normal and abnormal development and the practice of their specific child and family-centered discipline. But what data are available about normal development that can be helpful to the child mental health worker?

Sources of New Knowledge

Organization of the knowledge about normal child development has been complicated by an embarrassment of riches. New information concerning the "facts" of early development has been coming from many disciplines. For better or for worse, each has its own stated or unstated theoretical stance. This has made the field very exciting, but also makes it difficult to organize the data. It may be premature to attempt such organization and synthesis, especially in view of the accelerating rate at which new information is being produced. It might be helpful to take a look at the sources of data, the theory from which data is coming, and to examine at least one general theoretical framework systematically in relation to the others. A critique of psychoanalytic psychology as a developmental psychology will be used in this way. But first, let us summarize the methods, theory, and sources of data which provide new knowledge of mental life in early infancy. They include the following:

1. Evolutionary theory. The most recent edition of this theory to make its impact upon child development is the field of ethology with its emphasis upon naturalistic studies, critical periods, imprinting, and the like. This approach is exemplified in the work of Bowlby [4] and Tinbergen.[36] (See also chapter 6.)

2. Retrospective inference from the studies of older children and adults. Such studies come not only from psychoanalysis but also from each of the learning theories which focuses on one or another of the developmentally acquired functions.

3. Ongoing longitudinal studies utilizing direct observation of infants and children over time. These may extend over several generations or may be focused over the short term in the form of cross-sectional studies specifically directed at short-lived phenomena. Such studies may be organized along the lines of Piagetian cognitive theory[31] or other learning theories as well as psychoanalytic theory.

4. Experimental studies. These may include strictly controlled laboratory studies such as those which have utilized classical and operant conditioning (see chapter 5), in work done in both experimental and naturalistic settings to study the separation of the young from the mother,[23, 24] and increasingly sophisticated experiments utilizing the immature rat and which deal with the complex interactions between sensory experience, nutrition, and brain damage during the process of development.[37]

5. Use of the serious experiment in child psychiatry has been reviewed by Anthony.[1] This refers to planned clinical investigations of variables operating within a clinical setting. This environment is set up to resemble in some way the child's "landscape" and the child's "life space." The variables examined and altered within the context of clinical goals are those which have acquired an internal meaning for the child. The child is invited to respond seriously and thoughtfully to planned interventions. In this way, he provides new material regarding his own internal mental functioning, while at the same time offering data to test clinical hypotheses. The child thus becomes a participant in the experiment. Psychiatric treatment of infants and children may qualify as a serious experiment if the child's responses to ongoing intervention are utilized as the basis for new hypotheses and the generation of data to test them.

6. Experiments of nature. These include the study of blind children, such as those performed by Selma Fraiberg,[10] of deaf children, such as those performed by Hilde Schlesinger and Kathryn Meadow[34] and Galenson,[18] and of children with other handicaps present at birth or occurring subsequently.[6] Stella Chess's longitudinal studies[7] of multihandicapped rubella children have suggested a high level of plasticity in the developmental process. Alternative pathways to motor, social, and cognitive functioning in infants with different handicaps and multiple handicaps can be demonstrated. Chess believes that these findings contradict the idea that early experience according to the specific timetable of a maturational sequence is critical to later maturation. She believes there may be many alternative pathways to mental development and that the timing of environmental events may not be as critical as has been supposed.

7. Experiments of society. These include information coming from group upbringing,[22] cognitive stimulation,[29] multiple mothering,[40] psychohistorical studies of childhood and infancy,[2] and from cases of the father as primary caretaker.*

8. The natural, unplanned interventions and noninterventions of everyday life. These reflect the interactional style between the child and his caretakers such as the choice of parents to do something or do nothing about the endless list of concerns they have about their children in such issues as health, nutrition, accident prevention, toilet training, language development, attending day care or nursery school, and so on. Some parents tend to seek "professional advice" on the matters of child care and child raising. Others do not.

Child psychiatrists, child analysts, and other child mental health workers generally seek to bridge the gap between the theory of development, normal and abnormal, and the practice of their specific child and family-oriented disciplines.

But what is there in the canon of normal development which can be of help to the mental health worker? More important, which areas of knowledge are lacking or fragmentary and which are available to increase the therapeutic leverage of clinicians in their daily work? These questions are pursued systematically in the subsequent chapters of this section of the handbook.

Theory Building

Are the current theories of normal mental development good enough? Are they good enough to remain pertinent over long stages of development, and good enough to bridge the gap from theory to practice? These and related questions need to be explored.

In establishing any continuity of function or structure from infancy to later development, one faces an epigenetic series. That is, each earlier function or structure forms the basis of each sub-

---

* P. C. Rosenblatt and M. R. Cunningham, "Sex Differences in Cross-Cultural Perspective," in B. Lloyd and J. Archer, *Exploring Sex Differences*, pp. 71–94, Academic Press, New York, 1976.

sequent function or structure. In the course of this process, a transformation of function may occur so that the original function is no longer recognizable. The continuity of development can thus be established only if one looks at the processes which underlie change. To view such a sequence in an ontogenetic fashion, one must take into account not only the transformations of behavior and function, but also the layering and telescoping of developmentally analogous experiences. It is not easy to arrive at a synthesis of the various elements of the genetic construct. For example, a later function may be similar to an earlier one, but this resemblance, however, cannot be taken as an indication that it was in fact derived from this earlier similar function. To do so is to be deceived by appearances. For instance, a newborn infant makes swimming motions, holds its breath under water, and breathes when its head emerges from water. This looks like swimming, but is not the same as learning to swim later. Reading is a highly developed set of integrated perceptual and cognitive functions. A child may learn to read by many methods, combinations of methods, and sometimes with no systematic teaching at all. Reading may have a devouring quality during a hypomanic state, and may not be possible at all during a depression. Vision itself may become organized under the dominance of oral drive or may later become invaded by conflict derived from the oedipal situation. A child who does not read, one who reads well, or one who reads omnivorously may or may not have conflict at various levels of psychosexual development. Certain elements of reading including latent fantasies associated with it may be derived in part from the earliest processes of taking in, for example, the deciphering of the mother's face while nursing. Other fantasies may be derived from an identification with a parent who reads to a child on his lap. Taking in visually is analogous to the process of identification whereby earlier processes are endowed with the meanings derived from later processes and vice versa. This telescoping and layering of ontogenetic experience is not, under ordinary circumstances, easily discernible, but may become obvious only when a problem such as difficulty in reading is examined clinically.

What are the essentials of a good enough theory for developmental psychology?

1. Such a theory should include assumptions and propositions which bridge the continuity between man's biological experience and his evolutionary history.
2. Such a theory should place emphasis upon the developmental process and provide propositions to explain change throughout the life cycle.
3. Such a theory should be pertinent to many past and future biological and social changes.
4. Such a theory should account for high levels of variability both in the person and the group and variability which changes over time. This aspect of the theory will include the best synthesis of what constitutes normal functioning and will distinguish it from pathological deviations.
5. Such a theory should have predictive as well as heuristic power.

Current Status of Psychoanalytic Developmental Psychology

Psychoanalytic theory has very gradually become a general psychology. Today it contains propositions which account for normal as well as deviant modes of mental functioning within its framework. Within psychoanalysis there is a very special focus on the intrapsychic events of childhood. It seems safe to say that this was established when Freud shifted his attention to oedipally organized fantasy. Later, with Freud's "Three Essays on the Theory of Sexuality,"[16] a multidimensional ontogenetic framework for intrapsychic development was established. The effectiveness of this ontogenetic series in explaining normal sexual development, psychopathology (especially the sexual aberrations), and character was aided by ongoing clinical work.

This unique focus of psychoanalysis has gradually evolved into a metapsychological approach, the genetic point of view in psychoanalytic theory. It is important to emphasize that this genetic viewpoint was one which developed slowly and empirically by means of psychoanalytic reconstruction, i.e., through the psychoanalytic treatment of children and adults along with the efforts analysts have made to reconstruct the intrapsychic, ontogenetic, and developmental aspects of psychic life. The development of the genetic viewpoint in psychoanalytic theory has been reviewed in more detail elsewhere.[5]

It was not until later that psychoanalytic theory began to evolve as a general psychology. Eventually, it was able to account for variations in normal development and normal character, as well as for psychopathological development. These changes were heralded by the dawn of structural theory in 1923, the recognition of aggression as an instinctual drive,[15] and the assignment of central importance to identification in the formation of psychic structure.[13] In 1926, Freud[14] defined anxiety as a signal affect with both biological and early developmental roots. In 1937, Freud[12] postulated congenital variations in ego to explain the predisposition of individuals to the use of certain defense mechanisms. Since Freud's death in 1939, most, but not all, of the newer developments in psychoanalytic theory have been an extension of this ego psychology. Some of the major developments since that time are:

1. With the introduction of ego psychology and the emphasis on the structural point of view have come a systematic review of psychoanalytic theory in general and the emergence of psychoanalysis as a general psychology.[20, 33]
2. New methodology of direct infant and child observation and longitudinal study has been introduced in psychoanalytic research. This has brought with it a challenge to the genetic propositions of psychoanalysis, increased attention to the evolution of psychic reality during the earliest stages of development, and a slowly emerging psychoanalytic developmental psychology. Pioneers in this effort have been Spitz,[35] Winnicott,[38] Hartmann and Kris,[21] Greenacre,[19] Erikson,[9] Klein,[26] Benjamin,[3] Mahler,[30] Fraiberg,[11] and more recently, several of the contributors to this section.
3. There has been a reevaluation of some traditional psychoanalytic propositions such as anxiety, depression, superego development, theory of the neuroses, and problems involved in the development of psychic structure.
4. The widening scope of psychoanalysis has addressed itself to problems of the borderline personality and psychosis, as well as to normal phenomena.
5. A reconsideration of narcissism and object relationship has emerged.
6. There has been increased emphasis on the stages of separation and individuation during the second, third, and fourth year of life, and on their implications for later development.[30]
7. A whole new area was opened up by Winnicott's 1953 paper, "Transitional Objects and Transitional Phenomena."[39] If the first world of psychic life was the individual's experience in reality, and the second his experience with himself, his inner experience could be considered a third world. Winnicott's third world of transitional phenomena could be described as intermediate, one which the individual creates himself within the context of the holding environment. It partakes of inner subjective experience and outer reality, yet is bound exclusively to neither.

Perhaps the most encouraging development in psychoanalytic developmental theory has been this lively diversity of viewpoints, and, at times, outright conflict among investigators. Workers from many disciplines have renewed their interest in developmental studies, and with this has come increased attention to the reconstructive efforts of analysis. A subtle dynamism has resulted from the juxtaposition of these two multidimensional, ontogenetic sequences.

Several persistent problems, however, continue to be reflected in the application of psychoanalytic theory to developmental issues. They are:

1. Semantic issues. To what extent can the concepts and terminology derived from genetic reconstruction apply accurately to ongoing developmental issues? For instance, when psychoanalysts speak of infantile fantasy, are they referring to mental representations? Probably not, at least not in the sense that Piaget defines mental representations. But how are the processes of mental representation and infantile fantasy related? Are they similar or different?
2. Difficulties in arriving at what constitutes the undifferentiated ego-id matrix postulated by Hartman.[20]
3. Insufficient attention to the developmental aspects of aggression.
4. A persistent problem in ordering the developmental aspects of defense. Psychoanalysts are still quite vague about the primitive versus the more advanced forms of defense. Psychoanalytic experiences with borderline narcissistic and character problems as well as classical neuroses all show layering of various defenses without consistency in sequencing of defenses.
5. The articulation and integration of newer psychoanalytic viewpoints on separation-individuation[30] with those derived from a reconsideration of narcissism.[27, 25]
6. The elaboration of a psychoanalytic theory of affects. There is a need to sort out the developmental sequences involved in depression and the relationship of anxiety to depression in mental ontogenesis.
7. Those psychoanalytic propositions which involve the core of inner human experience. This is the same kind of problem which Freud was attempting to deal with when he defined the characteristics of libido.
8. The psychoanalytic view of language acquisition and development.
9. Integration of the oedipal and preoedipal phases of development.
10. Early phases of superego development.
11. Problems in the definition of object constancy.
12. Continued difficulties in the integration of the economic viewpoint, along with the associated question about whether or not to dispense with it.
13. The need for the development of a psychoanalytic theory of consciousness and attention. Freud had originally planned to do this; subsequently it was presented in general outline by Rapaport.[32]

It is evident that formidable gaps and difficulties exist in elaborating a truly comprehensive psychoanalytic developmental psychology. In the face of these, it would be all too easy to thrust aside major psychoanalytic contributions, or to claim that psychoanalytic theory is relevant for the psychopathology of adults and children, but has little usefulness in considering the developmental problems of infancy. Clearly, the existing gaps are being identified specifically and new questions are being generated actively around the problems of psychoanalytic developmental psychology. This would indicate that research endeavors appear on the horizon and that the heuristic use of psychoanalytic theory is as lively as ever.

Future Directions for Psychoanalytic Developmental Psychology

It is likely that psychoanalytic developmental psychology will continue to influence and be influenced by findings derived from the psychoanalytic treatment of adults and children. In addition, the emerging interest of analysts in ongoing studies of normal and deviant infants will have increasing influence on the evolution of psychoanalytic theory generally. The intensive case study method has been the wellspring of psychoanalysis from the beginning, and it will certainly continue to play a major role in the development of both psychoanalytic theory and psychoanalytic practice in the earliest period of life. To a unique degree, psychoanalysis has focused attention on the interplay of progressive and regressive forces and on the role of conflict in the developmental process. In all likelihood, this will offer new insights into the developmental process itself and into the evolution of gross motor functioning such as walking and other average expected normal functioning, such as hand use and semantic gestures.

The new field of developmental linguistics and language development has been of great interest to analysts. As they enter this field, they are likely to fill a gap currently present in the studies of early language development, for example, the problem of the relationship of affective development and the stages of separation and individuation to the evolution of language functions.

Psychoanalysis has much to offer toward a better understanding of the later phases of development, for example, of adults who take on the task of parenting. Up to the present, this area has received insufficient attention from analysts.

As long-term longitudinal studies become more refined, it is likely that the significance of early life events, especially the quality and direction of early object relations, will become clearer.

New Models for the Developmental Process

In addition to models emanating from psychoanalytic theory, future studies of normal development are likely to make use of new models based upon a better understanding of early psychopathological development. Newer models might also emerge from a deeper understanding of developmental biochemistry and of genetics. Embryological studies will provide additional conceptions of the developmental process. The role of evolution in the ontogenesis of human functioning and the mechanisms of evolutionary change as defined by modern biology will also provide possible new templates for the way humans grow. Ethological studies of the unfolding of behavioral sequences in animals will continue to be explored. Experiments of nature and of society will always be sources of new insights into human development. The very fact of various sorts of intervention will provide natural experiments to be observed. These will include changes in nutrition, education, adoption practice, the introduction of early treatment, group upbringing and alternatives to usual family life, and will provide newer information on how these variables operate during the developmental process.

The advent of planned pregnancies and child care as opposed to unintentional, accidental, or casual upbringing may provide new perspectives for the quality of life. Certainly, it should lead to a greater appreciation of the developmental process itself and will promote an even greater concern with ways of optimizing developmental experiences to enhance potentialities for human growth.

9

REFERENCES

1. ANTHONY, E. J., "The Use of the 'Serious' Experiment in Child Psychiatric Research," in Anthony, E. James (Ed.), *Explorations in Child Psychiatry*, pp. 383–414, Plenum Press, New York, 1975.

2. ARIÉS, P., *Centuries of Childhood: A Social History of Family Life*, Vintage Books, New York, 1962.

3. BENJAMIN, J. D., "Further Comments on Some Developmental Aspects of Anxiety," in Gaskill, H. S. (Ed.), *Counterpoint: Libidinal Object and Subject*, pp. 121–153, International Universities Press, New York, 1963.

4. BOWLBY, J., *Attachment and Loss*, vol. 2, *Separation*, Basic Books, New York, 1973.

5. CALL, J. D., "Some Issues and Problems in the Geography of Scholarship in Child Psychiatry," *Journal of the American Academy of Child Psychiatry, 15*:1, 139–160, 1976.

6. ———, "Psychosocial Problems of the Handicapped Child and His Family," Selected Workshop Papers 1970–1973, *Southwestern Region Deaf-Blind Center*, pp. 112–122, September 1974.

7. CHESS, S., KORN, S., and FERNANDEZ, P. B., *Psychiatric Disorders of Children with Congenital Rubella*, Brunner-Mazel, New York, 1971.

8. "Current Concepts of Object Relations Theory," Panel at the Fall Meetings of the American Psychoanalytic Association, New York, December 16, 1977.

9. ERIKSON, E. H., *Childhood and Society*, W. W. Norton, New York, 1963.

10. FRAIBERG, S., *Insights from the Blind: Developmental Studies of Blind Children*, Basic Books, New York, 1977.

11. ———, "Libidinal Object Constancy and Mental Representation," in Eissler, R. S., et al. (Eds.), *The Psychoanalytic Study of the Child*, vol. 24, pp. 9–47, International Universities Press, New York, 1969.

12. FREUD, S., "Analysis Terminable and Interminable," in *The Standard Edition of the Complete Psychological Works of Sigmund Freud* (hereafter: *The Standard Edition*), vol. 23, pp. 211–253, Hogarth Press, London, 1964.

13. ———, "The Ego and the Id," in *The Standard Edition*, vol. 19, pp. 3–66, Hogarth Press, London, 1961.

14. ———, "Inhibitions, Symptoms and Anxiety," in *The Standard Edition*, vol. 20, pp. 7–175, Hogarth Press, London, 1959.

15. ———, "Beyond the Pleasure Principle," in *The Standard Edition*, vol. 18, pp. 3–64, Hogarth Press, London, 1955.

16. ———, "Three Essays on the Theory of Sexuality," in *The Standard Edition*, vol. 7, pp. 125–245, Hogarth Press, London, 1953.

17. FRIES, M. E., and WOOLF, P. J., "The Influence of Constitutional Complex on Developmental Phases," in McDevitt, J. B., and Settlage, C. F. (Eds.), *Separation-Individuation: Essays in Honor of Margaret H. Mahler*, pp. 285–296, International Universities Press, New York, 1971.

18. GALENSON, E., et al., "Assessment of Development in the Deaf Child," Paper presented at the Twenty-fourth Annual Meeting of The American Academy of Child Psychiatry, October 22, 1977.

19. GREENACRE, P., "On Reconstruction," *Journal of the American Psychoanalytic Association, 23*:693–712, 1975.

20. HARTMANN, H., *Ego Psychology and the Problem of Adaptation*, International Universities Press, New York, 1958.

21. ———, and KRIS, E., "The Genetic Approach in Psychoanalysis," in Eissler, R. S., et al. *The Psychoanalytic Study of the Child*, vol. I, pp. 11–21, International Universities Press, New York, 1945.

22. KAFFMAN, M., "Characteristics of the Emotional Pathology of the Kibbutz," in Chess, S., and Thomas, A. (Eds.), *Annual Progress in Child Psychiatry and Child Development*, pp. 241–262, Brunner-Mazel, New York, 1973.

23. KAUFMAN, I. C., "Developmental Considerations of Anxiety and Depression: Psychobiological Studies in Monkeys," in Shapiro, T. (Ed.), *Psychoanalysis and Contemporary Science*, pp. 317–363, International Universities Press, New York, 1977.

24. ———, and STYNES, A. J., "Depression Can Be Induced in a Bonnet Macaque Infant," *Psychosomatic Medicine*, in press.

25. KERNBERG, O., *Borderline Conditions and Pathological Narcissism*, Aronson, New York, 1975.

26. KLEIN, M., "The Psycho-analytic Play Technique: Its History and Significance," in Klein, M., Heimann, P., and Money-Kyrle, R. E. (Eds.), *New Directions in Psychoanalysis*, pp. 3–22, Basic Books, New York, 1957.

27. KOHUT, H., *The Analysis of the Self*, International Universities Press, New York, 1971.

28. "Language and Psychoanalysis," Panel at the Fall Meetings of the American Psychoanalytic Association, New York, New York, December 16, 1977.

29. LEVENSTEIN, P., and SUNLEY, R., "An Affect of Stimulating Verbal Interaction Between Mothers and Children around Play Materials," *American Journal of Orthopsychiatry, 37*:334–335, 1967.

30. MAHLER, M., PINE, F., and BERGMAN, A., *The Psychological Birth of the Infant*, Basic Books, New York, 1975.

31. PIAGET, J., *The Origins of Intelligence in Children*, International Universities Press, New York, 1936.

32. RAPAPORT, D., *The Structure of Psychoanalytic Theory*, Psychological Issues, Monograph 6, International Universities Press, New York, 1960.

33. ———, *Organization and Pathology of Thought: Selected Sources*, Columbia University Press, New York, 1951.

34. SCHLESINGER, H., and MEADOW, K., *Sounds and Signs*, University of California Press, Berkeley, 1972.

35. SPITZ, R., *The First Year of Life*, International Universities Press, New York, 1965.

36. TINBERGEN, N., "Ethnology and Stress Diseases," *Science, 185*:20–27, 1974.

37. WALSH, R. N., and CUMMINS, R. A., "Neural Responses to Therapeutic Sensory Environments," in Walsh, R., and Greenough, W. T. (Eds.), *Environments as Therapy for Brain Dysfunction*, pp. 171–200, Plenum Press, New York, 1976.

38. WINNICOTT, D. W., *The Maturational Processes and the Facilitating Environment*, International Universities Press, New York, 1965.

39. ———, "Transitional Objects and Transitional Phenomena," *International Journal of Psycho-Analysis, 34*(Part 2):89–97.

40. YARROW, L. J., "Separation from Parents during Early Childhood," in Hoffman, M. L., and Hoffman, L. W. (Eds.), *Review of Child Development Research*, vol. 1, pp. 89–136, Russell Sage Foundation, New York, 1964.

2 / From Conception to Delivery

Julius B. Richmond and James M. Herzog

The order and connection of ideas is the same as the order and connection of things. (Spinoza, 1673)

Introduction

The notion that important clues to later development may be present before the birth of the baby and be related to prenatal development has now become widely accepted. The science of infant observation has reported that neonates differ in a variety of documentable ways, and the implication drawn is that either primary genetic endowment, intrauterine development, or both, is largely responsible for this fact. The early studies of Fries and Wolfe[10] on congenital activity types and the constitutional complex, Korner[22] on the significance of individual differences at birth for later development, and Weil[45] on "the basic core" represent some attempts to advocate and formulate this point of view.

The work of Richmond, Lipton, and Steinschneider[40] on individual differences continued this effort in the psychological realm, while Thomas and Chess,[48] among others, have explored the implications of these differences for psychological development.

This chapter will present an outline of the prenatal development of the human central nervous system in terms of embryology and behavioral capabilities. The underlying assumption is that the basic neurological apparatus that the neonate is born with is the fundamental structure or "basic core" with which he will meet, and to some extent influence, his environment.

The Embryology of Neurological Development

Unlike Hypocrates, who stated that "everything in the embryo is formed simultaneously," we now know that the central theme in prenatal development is the strict temporal ordering of all events.

Human development begins with fertilization of the human egg by the human sperm which follows sexual intercourse or artificial insemination. This process, which is in fact a fusion of the male and female gametes, probably occurs in the ampullary region or at least in the distal third of the fallopian tube. As a result of fertilization, the diploid number of chromosomes is restored, the sex of the zygote (the fused egg and sperm cell), is determined, and a series of mitotic divisions is initiated which are called cleavage divisions. When the fertilized zygote reaches the two-cell stage, it undergoes a series of mitotic divisions which leads to a large number of cells. With each cleavage division, the cells, called blastomeres, become smaller. As cleavage progresses and as the zygote passes down the fallopian tube, it attains a twelve- to sixteen-cell stage and is then called the morula. We know that although all of the cells of the morula appear similar, they are destined for disparate development. The inner cell mass of the morula gives rise to the tissues of the embryo proper, and the outer cell mass forming the trophoblast later develops into the placenta. The morula reaches the uterine cavity at approximately the third day after fertilization and it is here, as fluid from the uterine cavity passes into the intracellular spaces of the inner cell mass, that it is called a blastocyst and imbeds itself in the wall of the endometrium.

Over the next week, further cell divisions occur and the embryo implants itself securely in what is to be its home for the next eight and a half months. The central nervous system has yet to make its appearance. At the beginning of the third week of development, the embryo looks like a sphere. If it were to be sectioned, one could see that it consists of two cavities. These cavities are separated from one another by a double layer of cells. One of the cavities is called the yolk sac, and its roof is a layer of flattened cells called the endoderm. The other cavity is labeled the amniotic cavity, and its floor is composed of tall columnar cells called ectoderm. Both the ectoderm and the endoderm lie in direct apposition to one another. They are called the bilaminar membrane or disc.

Somewhere in the fifteenth or sixteenth day of development, a narrow groove can be seen on the ectoderm facing the amniotic cavity. This groove proceeds about midway across the surface and terminates in a pit. The groove and the pit are both surrounded by bulging areas on their sides. The name given to the groove is the primitive streak, and the pit and its surrounding ridge are called Hensen's node. It has been suggested that ectodermal cells from the ridges along the primitive streak invaginate downward, and then migrate laterally and caudally between the two cell layers forming an intermediate cell layer which is called the mesoderm. We now have a trilaminar membrane composed of three germinal cell types: the ectoderm, the mesoderm, and the endoderm. Each layer gives rise to specific tissues and organs. The brain and the central nervous system, whose progress we are following, are derived from the ectoderm.

The stage is now set for the rapid unfolding of development leading to the formation of the central nervous system. An oval thickening in the cephalic area of the ectoderm is the first sign of future nervous system tissue. There is a gradual elongation of this thickening which constitutes the neural plate. This plate itself expands toward the caudal end of the embryo. Thereafter, the edges of the neural plate elevate and form the neural folds. The depressed midregion between the two elevations is then called the neural groove. The neural folds approach each other in the midline and fuse and thus form a neural tube. There are temporary openings at both ends of this tube which are called neuropores. Eventually they close, creating a sealed tubular structure with a fluid-filled lumen. The narrow caudal portion of this tube gives rise to the spinal cord, and the broad cephalic portion with its several dilatations becomes the brain.

For orientation it is important to recall that these events, which occur between twenty-one and twenty-five days after fertilization, when the length of the embryo from crown to rump is between 2 and 3.5 millimeters, are going on at the same time as some other events in the non-neurological sphere. The auditory placode is just becoming an otocyst, the heart tubes are beginning to fuse and beat, and the aortic arch number one and the lung primordia first appear.

Within the next few days we see the appearance of three distinct bulges in the anterior part of the brain of the embryo. These constitute the primary brain vesicles from front to back, and they are labeled as the prosencephalon or forebrain, the mesencephalon or midbrain, and the rhombencephalon or hindbrain. Simultaneously, two flexures appear in the neural tube; the cervicle flexure at the rhombencephalon-spinal cord junction and the cephalic flexure at the mesencephalon region. Again, for orientation, we are now at about twenty-eight days and the embryo has increased in length to almost 8 millimeters. If one looks histologically at the cells in the developing brain, one sees that the primitive ependymal mantle and marginal layers are formed. The optic cup is beginning to make its appearance and some ganglia and nerves are also forming. Outside of the brain the otocyst has made its appearance, as has the septums and the branchial arches. We are at the forty-somite stage and the limbuds, the mesonephros, and other visceral primordia are beginning to appear.

The next step in the development of the brain is the division of the primary brain vesicles into secondary brain vesicles. The prosencephalon divides into two parts and its anterior portion is termed the telencephalon or endbrain. The telencephalon is characterized by two lateral outpocketings or bulges that are the primitive cerebral hemispheres. The posterior portion of the prosencephalon, which is called the diencephalon, can be identified by the bulging of the primitive optical vesicles. The mesencephalon does not change very radically at this stage of development, but the rhombencephalon also divides into two parts. Its anterior segment is named the metencephalon, while its posterior portion is called the myelencephalon. These five brain divisions occur at about the fifth week of development. By now the embryo is between 7 and 11 millimeters crown to rump. The posterior root ganglia and the choroid plexus have appeared. Again, outside of the central nervous system, at this stage of development the nasal pits can be discerned, the interatrial septa appears, and the lens primordiun is in evidence. It is a time when the tail is still prominent.

The brain as we know it at birth evolves from the five secondary brain vesicles. As it develops, two major changes are observed. First, the nervous tissue derived from the ectoderm experiences a massive increase in size and a complex transformation in morphology. Second, various changes in the shape of the neural tube lumen occur as it is twisted and compressed by the expanding tissue around it, until it assumes its final shape. It is destined to constitute the vesicles through which the cerebral spinal fluid flows and, by so doing, is able to provide nourishment and protection to the brain.

Because of the complexity of the development

of the brain after the end of the fifth week of development, a frequently utilized approach is to follow the separate fate of the five secondary brain vesicles as they proceed along the developmental path.

The myelencephalon, which is the lowest part of the brain stem and continues with the spinal cord, changes with the lateral movement of its walls. As a result, there is stretching of the roof plate and widening of the lumen of the central cavity. In this way, the fourth ventricle is formed and later the choroid plexus develops more fully to the point where cerebral spinal fluid can be manufactured. By the end of its development it has become the neonate's medulla oblongata.

The fourth ventricle of the myelencephalon continues into the next part of the brain stem, the metencephalon. Here, two important structures arise: The cerebellum develops from the tissue in the dorsal region, and important fiber tracts that act as a bridge between the cerebral cortex and the cerebellar cortex originate from the basal layer of cells. Because of this bridging function, this section is called the pons.

The mesencephalon, which is the most primitive and shortest of the brain segments, becomes very small and constricted as its central lumen enlarges and forms the cerebral aqueduct. This serves to connect the third ventricle below with the fourth ventricle above.

The cavity in the diencephalon becomes the third ventricle. Its shape changes from an initial oval lumen to a more compressed form as the thalamic, hypothalamic, and epithalamic nuclei develop within its walls.

The thalamus appears as a thickening in the caudal area of the diencephalon. Lower in the wall of the ventricle, the hypothalamus develops above the pituitary gland and the hypophysis, with which it has both anatomical and functional connections. Over time, the hemispheres envelop this region by fusing a segment of cerebral cortex to the diencephalon.

The telencephalon is situated atop the anterior end of the third ventricle. It is composed of two parts, a midportion and the bilateral outpocketings which are the cerebral hemispheres.

From the fifth week of development onward, the cerebral hemispheres expand in an upward direction, compressing the intraventricular foramen and thus diminishing its size. At first, the growth of the hemispheres is uneven. They grow forward, initially creating the frontal lobes. Then they grow laterally and upward to form the parietal lobes. The occipital and temporal lobes are last formed as the hemispheres grow both posteriorly and inferiorally. As a result of this tremendous expansion of the cortex, the brain stem is covered and literally buried by the cerebral hemispheres.

After reviewing the developmental progression of the five brain divisions it is important to note the development of the commissures, the bundles of nerve fibers that cross from one cerebral hemisphere to the other. The lamina terminalis, the tissue between the diencephalon roof plate and the optic chiasma, demarcates the cephalic end of the ventricular lumen. Here a bridge is formed for commissural fibers. It acts as a principal path for the important tracts which connect the two sides of the brain.

There are three major fiber bundles which arise and utilize the lamina terminalis. First is the anterior commissure, which connects the olfactory bulb and the temporal lobe of the cortex on one side with their counterparts in the opposite hemisphere. Second is the fornix, which runs along the inferior border of the hemispheres. Because the fornix connects the cortex of the hippocampus to each hemisphere, it is sometimes called the hippocampal commissure. The third tract, which makes its appearance latest in embryonic development, is called the corpus callosum. At first its fibers connect only the frontal lobes, but later grow to connect the parietal lobes too. The corpus callosum grows tremendously. It is pulled along as the neophallium grows forward, then backward, and arches over the third ventricle. The remaining lamina terminalis, lying between the corpus callosum and the fornix, is stretched into a thin membrane by the anterior movement of the corpus callosum. It forms the septum pellucidum between the lateral ventricles.

To review and summarize, we see that the major changes after the fifth week of development involve the appearance of three primary brain flexures and the cerebellar primordium. Simultaneously we see the segmentation of the sympathetic ganglionic masses and the nerve plexuses, and the appearance of the primordia of the meninges. In other parts of the embryo at this time, there is modeling of the inner and middle ears, the lower jaw is fused in the midline, the limbs are present, and primary ossification centers are initiated. The viscera appear well formed.

At seven weeks when the embryo is 25 millimeters or so in length, the cerebral hemispheres begin to enlarge, the optic nerve appears, and the infundibulum is in contact with Ratke's pouch. This is the time of the formation of the face and neck. The palate is fused in the midline and the tail is regressing. There are recognizable digits and a membraneous labyrinth. The skeletal muscles are assuming adult relationships and the kidneys begin secreting. The testes are distinguishable from the ovary, and adrenal medullary cells are invading the adrenal cortex.

At eight weeks, the cerebral cortex is still smooth-surfaced. The olfactory bulbs have evaginated, however, and one can see a distinct dura and pia-arachnoid.

By ten weeks, when the embryo is 40 to 45 millimeters long, the cerebral cortical plate is becoming thick. The cerebellum is fused in the midline and the spinal cord has a definitive structure.

In the next several weeks, as the embryo grows to a length of 120 to 130 millimeters, glial cells appear and lobules and fissures can be seen in the cerebellum.

In the nonneurological sphere by this time the face is well formed. As we shall see in more detail later on, there are muscular movements, body hair is developing, and the reproductive organs have definitive form.

By five months of development, when the embryo is in the range of 170 to 180 millimeters long, there are early fissures evident in the cerebral cortex and distinct histological layers are formed, the commissures are present, the spinal cord ends at the third lumbar vertebra and is myelinated.

By seven months of development, we are at perhaps 260 millimeters crown to rump length, the cerebral fissures have developed rapidly, and there are light sensitive photo-receptor cells in the retina. This process continues with further differentiation of neurones and myelination of tracts up until birth and beyond.

The central theme in the entire preceding section is the strict temporal ordering of events. It therefore follows that interferences in this morphological development will have critically different results depending upon the time at which they are introduced.

Of the many disorders which disturb the developmental processes as they have been outlined, the most frequent in incidence and the easiest to comprehend are those in which the neural folds fail to fuse dorsally to form a neural tube. There is then a secondary maldevelopment of skeletal structures that enclose the central nervous system. These disorders are known as dysraphic. The most extreme of these disorders is craniorachischistis totalis (the splitting of the entire skull and vertebral column). Milder and more restrictive degrees of dysraphism are the myelomeningocele and spina bifida occulta. The Arnold Chiari malformation is probably a dysraphic phenomenon too.

A secondary group of malformations that occur are the faciotelencephalic malformations which are thought to result from an early failure of developmental interaction between the prechordial mesoderm and the adjacent endoderm and ectoderm. There are often, as to be expected, gross defects of the eyes, nose, maxilla, and ethmoid bones. Arrhinencephaly is an example of this kind of malformation. Some of these disorders are associated with abnormalities of chromosomes, namely the thirteen to fifteen trisomy. In this condition, the absence of olfactory bulbs is combined with defective formation of inferior frontal and temporal cortex and in failure of normal development of ethmoid and nasal bones. There is some suggestion that Down's syndrome may also fall into this category.

It is presumed that in addition to the preceding disorder, there are also disorders of proliferation of cells, as perhaps in the case of von Recklinghausen's neurofibromatosis, tuberous sclerosis, and Sturge-Weber-Dimitri faciocerebral angiomatosis. It is also known that there are other migration disorders. Some of these have been labeled cortical dysgenesis. The pathonomonic features of the migration disorders are designated by special terminology. Noteworthy are cases of lissencephaly, in which the neonate has a smooth-surfaced cerebrum similar to that of the normal twelve-week embryo. This is thought to represent a failure of sulcation. States of micro- and macrogyria, where the gyral pattern is either too fine or coarse, also occur. Cases of schizencephalic (porencephalic) clefts, where there are symmetrically positioned deep indentions of the cortical surfaces at sites where large sectors of cerebral tissue are missing or underdeveloped, have also been observed. Kolpencephaly, which is a persistence of the large size and smooth configuration of the lateral ventricles, again pointing to the normal twelve-week embryo, has also been encountered by the fetal neuropathologist. In addition to these migrational and proliferative disorders, it is assumed that there are also organizational disorders which are undiagnosable by neuropathological and histological techniques.

Finally, it has been well-documented that there are acquired diseases of fetal life which can lead to brain malformation. These include: infection of the mother with rubella, or cytomegalic inclusion virus, congenital neurosyphillis, which is fortunately on the decline, and congenital toxoplasmosis.

The Development of Fetal Behavior

As our previous review of the embryology of the central nervous system in the fetus has revealed, there is a slow and complex process by which morphological structures accrue and develop. It is not unusual then for us to discover that there is also an increase in the complexity of behavior observable in the fetus which corresponds to the increasing complexity of the morphological substructure which subserves it.

Movement of the human fetus begins surprisingly early. A pregnant woman may well be aware of fetal movements by the seventeenth week, and spontaneous movements have been observed in surgically removed specimens and in abortuses estimated to be as little as eight weeks of gestational age.

In a comprehensive review of the subject, Barron[3] has concluded that early mammalian fetuses pass through three stages. He calls these the inactive, active, and reactive stages. In the inactive stage, there is no movement of any sort. Toward the end of this period, when the skeletal muscles become responsive to direct electrical stimulation, movement occurs. During this stage both afferent and efferent nerve fibers establish contact with the muscles they serve. There is, however, no central connection yet. Direct excitability of muscle first appears in the rat and the cat embryo at 11 days, and in the sheep embryo at thirty-two days.

The inactive stage is followed by a period which Barron calls the active stage. This period is characterized by more spontaneous muscular activity, but the point of origin of the stimulus within the central nervous system has yet to be documented. Sensory nerves have reached the alar lamina of the spinal cord; therefore, it may be that these apparently spontaneous movements actually represent reactivity of a primitive sort to external stimuli. However, definite reflex pathways have not as yet been established. It has been found in a variety of mammalian species that spontaneous movements are remarkably constant in pattern. They tend to be made up of slow ventral lateral bending of the neck and the thoracic trunk. Often this is accompanied by simultaneous rotation of the cephalic region. In the cat these can be seen by the twenty-fourth day, in the guinea pig by the twenty-eighth, and in the sheep by the thirty-fifth day of gestation.

Barron's third stage is termed the reactive stage. Here direct sensory stimulation evokes responses in the muscular system. There are reflexes of varying types. The variable involved is the degree to which internuncial neurones in the central nervous system have developed. Typical examples of the reactive stage are the movements of the forelimb and head observed by Windle[50] after tapping on the amnion of the fetus. These reflexes fatigue easily and disappear with either anesthesia or asphyxia. It appears that these early reflexes which involve head and neck movements utilize the spinal accessory and upper cervical spinal nerves as motor components. It is thought that either the trigeminal or the sensory elements of the second, third, and fourth cervical spinal nerves serve as sensory components. Hooker has thus related these activities to the development of the spinal nucleus and the tract of the trigeminal nerve.

The work of Hooker[15, 16] is a cornerstone of our knowledge of embryological behavior. In a comprehensive planned study which he conducted between 1936 and 1958, he observed the behavior of over 140 human embryos and fetuses. Using the tip of a fine hair as a tactile stimulus, he documented that the first reflex can be elicited between the middle of the seventh and the beginning of the eighth week of gestation in embryos 20 to 23 millimeters long. When he stimulated the mouth and alae nasi, the neck was flexed to the other side.

Later in development, at the eighth week, the flexion spread in the caudal direction to the upper part of the trunk. At eight and one-half to nine and one-half weeks, it extended to the whole trunk, while the excitable skin region gradually increased in size. Still later, the pelvis participated in the flexion, and there were occasional ipsolateral flexions, too. He further noted that when flexion of the trunk involved the shoulders, both arms were extended backward at the shoulder joint. When Hooker stimulated the oral region, extension, replacing flexion of the trunk and accompanied by inward rotation of both arms, gradually began to appear at about nine and one-half to ten and one-half weeks of embryological development. This response was even more clear-cut in the eleventh and twelfth weeks. At this point, the face moved away from the stimulus instead of merely being turned to the side. This response continued until the fourteenth week of embryological development.

Hooker further demonstrated that the earliest reflexes of the stimulation of the soles, that is a plantar flexion of the toes, occurred at ten and one-half weeks. This reflex was extinguished prior to the reflexes from the trigeminal region when there was oxygen deprivation. The local reflexes elicited by the stimulation of the trigeminus may well appear in a sequence similar to that in which food intake has phylogenetically developed. The mouth opening at nine and one-half weeks was followed by swallowing at ten and one-half weeks and preceded closing of the lips at twelve and one-half weeks. Hooker felt that this was an example of ontogeny recapitulating phylogeny. Some of this work has been confirmed by Carmichael.*

Hooker also stated that the area of the maxillary and mandibular trigeminal branches was excitable earlier in development than the region served by the ophthalmic branch of the seventh nerve. The first sensory field, he thought, was restricted to the lips and anal nasi. These first responses to stimulation of the oral region were not localized but they spread to all neural muscular mechanisms which were capable of functioning. He further demonstrated that two body areas could be stimulated to react simultaneously after it has become possible to elicit finger and toe reflexes by external stimulation of the palms and soles of the foot.

When he attempted to simultaneously stimulate the face and the hand in human embryos and fetuses of ten and one-half to thirteen weeks, and the hand and foot at thirteen to thirteen and one-half weeks, he could show distinct dominance of the proximal over the distal regions, that is, of the oral region over any others. Simultaneous stimulation of mouth and hand caused reactions only in the region around the mouth, and when he simultaneously stimulated both the hands and foot, he was principally able to elicit movement in the hand. Thus, the principle of cephalocaudal development is demonstrable at this stage in development too.

Hooker described the development of muscular activity and movement in the fetus as follows: (1) a muscle must attain sufficient morphological development to permit contraction in response to direct electrical stimulation, even before there are available neural mechanisms of activation; (2) motor nervous mechanisms become differentiated before corresponding sensory ones; (3) the reflex arc is completed by the differentiation of the sensory elements and ultimately by the appearance in the spinal cord of the internuncial neurones which connect sensory motor components; and (4)

reflexes which are based on proprioceptive sensation precede those which are based on extraceptive sensations.

After elucidating on these four steps, he concluded by suggesting that all evidence indicated that the motor side of the reflex differentiates prior to the differentiation of the sensory side. Moreover, he emphasized that functional development of motor neurones progress as is mentioned earlier, from cranial to caudal, in general agreement with the cephalocaudal sequence of differentiation which is found in all vertebrate embryos.

As Windle[50] points out, in mammalian fetuses the first stereotyped reflexes appear to gradually combine into increasingly complex reactive patterns until the complete and integrated behavior emerges. Barron feels that as development progresses, reflexes can be seen to become more discrete. This is so in regard to the area of the stimuli the restrictedness of the movement, and the segregation by muscle groups and degree of inhibition as well.

As gestational age advances, it may well be that centers appear in the brain that are able to coordinate the activity of heretofore uncoordinated spinal mechanisms. Thus, previously jerky movements now appear as smoother, more sustained ones, and somewhat more complex patterns of inhibition make their appearance.

Animal studies such as those of Kimel and Kavaler[20] on the functional maturation of the motor cortex of the guinea pig fetus have suggested that muscular responses to electrical stimulation can be elicited between the forty-first and forty-fifth days of development. This coincides with the time in which it is thought that cortical neuroblasts are differentiating in large numbers into still immature, but quite probably functional neurones.

Davis and Potter[7] have observed that complex patterns of movement related to visceral functions such as those concerned with respiration, defecation, and swallowing appear at surprisingly early stages of development. They observed a respiratory movement very similar to those seen at postnatal life beginning during the twelfth week of gestation and continuing intermittently throughout the remainder of intrauterine life. These do not occur over a prolonged period of time, but for only short periods, then spontaneously recur. It is, of course, well known that the fetus from very early on is able to swallow amniotic fluid. This has been demonstrated to occur with a thorotrast injection as early as the twelfth week.

Our knowledge of fetal behavior increases dra-

* Carmichael, L., "The Onset and Early Development of Behavior in P. H. Mussen (Ed.), *Carmichael's Manual of Child Psychology*, vol. 1, 3rd ed., pp. 447–563, John Wiley, New York, 1970.

matically when we look at fetuses who have attained the age of twenty-eight weeks or more. This is, of course, due to the fact that this is the age at which premature infants become viable. Gesell[11] published a summary of the behavior which he observed in premature infants. He thought that the behavior which he observed varies only slightly from that which would take place in utero. He supported his contention by saying that all infants of the same fetal age follow a rather similar pattern. In general, the week-old neonate exhibits a behavior picture remarkably like that of the mature fetal infants, and from previous studies in older premature infants he learned that the fundamental rates and patterns of development are disturbed very little by the displacements at birth. His summary of the behavior of fetuses—"in truth premature babies"—at various stages of development can be paraphrased as follows:

The fetus at 28 to 32 weeks has meager movements which are fleeting and poorly sustained. There is a lack of muscular tone. He evinces mild avoidance responses to bright light and sound. When in the prone position he turns his head to the side. Palmar stimulation elicits barely perceptible grasp. His breathing may be shallow and irregular. He can suck and does swallow, but lacks endurance in these modalities. It is hard to document a definite waking and sleeping pattern. His cry may be absent or very weak.

(Minkowski[30] described the weak cry of the premature infant 28 centimeters long in the sixth fetal month of development as the first audible sound of a human voice.) The fetus at this age also evinces inconstant tonic neck reflexes.

In contradistinction, Gesell[11] described the movement of the fetus of thirty-two to thirty-six weeks as sustained and positive, with muscle tone being fair in response to stimulation. The Moro reflex is present. There is strong but inadequate response to light and sound, and in the prone position the fetus both turns his head and elevates his rump. There are definite periods of being awake. When there is palmar stimulation there is a good grasp. The hunger cry is strong and good and there are fairly well-established tonic neck reflexes.

At thirty-six to forty weeks, Gesell's description of the fetus can be summarized as follows:

Now movements are active and sustained and muscle tone is good to excellent. There is brief erratic following of objects with eyes, and the Moro reflex is strong. When the fetus or neonate is in the prone position there are attempts to lift his head. There is active resistance to head rotation. He has definite periods of alertness and he cries well and lustily when hungry or disturbed. He appears pleased when he is caressed or held and he holds his hands as fists much of the time. His grasp is good. Tonic neck reflexes are more pronounced to one side, usually the right then to the left. He has a good, strong, sucking reflex.

Thus, we see that it is possible to document rather carefully the development of behavior which corresponds in complexity and execution to the morphological development of the central nervous system, just as in the development of other organs there is increasing complexity in the morphology and connection of the central nervous system tissue which underlies this behavior. This principle is also demonstrated and elucidated further if one studies electroencephalogram (EEG) tracings from in utero in premature infants.

It has been learned that it is not possible to differentiate between waking and sleeping states in fetuses before the eighth fetal month. There are great problems involved in sorting out noise from actual tracings when EEGs are conducted in utero from abdominal sites. It is hard to screen out artifacts produced by contractions of the uterus or abdominal muscles. However, Lindsley,[26] while recording fetal EKGs at the end of the seventh and eighth month of his wife's first pregnancy, noticed patterns of certain abdominal leads that he thought might well be EEG tracings. This was confirmed when he obtained comparable neonatal EEGs from the same infant. In the prenatal record most of the waves had a frequency of six to seven per second. There were also brief periods of faster activity. The neonatal tracing which was from the precentral motor region was almost identical.

Bernstine, Borkowski and Price[4] published reports of intrauterine EEGs and there were direct recordings from abortuses by Okamoto and Kirikae[34] and from premature infants (Hughes, Davis and Brennan[17]) in the same year. More recordings have followed, but probably mainly due to the circumstances of the recording, the information which can be derived from them is neither plentiful nor exceptionally rich. Most of the recordings are from fairly late in gestation and it is impossible to obtain exact localization.

In the case where abortuses have been examined or fetuses removed from the uterus prior to their removal from the amniotic sac, a high incidence of discontinuous irregular slow waves, 0.5 to 2 per second of low to moderate amplitude, upon which a considerable amount of low voltage faster activity, as high as 40 per second, have been reported. Of course, recordings from abortuses cannot be assumed to reflect normal physiological conditions. However, in general features there is some resemblance between these tracings and those from older viable premature infants. The principle significance of these recordings from abortuses is thought to lie in the demonstration of the human cortexes generating electrical potentials by at least the second month.

In later fetal development, a more detailed account of the evolution of the EEG is available. From extensive experience it is now clear that the EEGs of the premature infants surviving to a given age are like those of infants born at that age. One has to take into account, of course, that the earlier the birth of the premature infant, the more likely he is to be affected by anoxia. Even with this reservation, a number of generalizations about the prenatal development of the EEG can be derived from the work with premature infants. Features common to the period from five through seven months are discontinuity and occasional paroxysmal outbursts. (There may be sudden appearance of a series of potentials which differ in frequency and amplitude from the prevailing activity.) There is failure to react to stimulation and absence of interhemispheric (bilateral) synchrony. There is also no sleep-waking cycle. Rapid changes can be discerned during this time. In the fifth-month record, polymorphic rhythms may appear in bursts. These are chiefly found in the occipital areas between periods of prolonged electrical silence which may last from seconds to minutes. There is superimposed faster activity in the occipital, occipitotemporal, and central regions of the brain. Once again, these tracings lack organization and intrahemispheric or interhemispheric synchrony.

In the sixth month there may be a dimunition of disorganization and polymorphosis. There is often an increase in theta activity, and there is also an increase in the synchrony between the hemispheres.

Throughout the seventh month, there is a continual decrease in discontinuity. This is pronounced in the occipital or occipitotemporal areas. Localization, although increasing over the preceding months, is most peculiar to the seventh month EEG. Here slow waves mixed with theta waves prevalent in the preceding months predominate.

At the eight month there are major transitions. Of critical importance is the emergence of a sleep-waking cycle. This is barely distinguishable at the end of the seventh month. There are diffuse reactions to sensory stimuli which occur during sleep. Bilateral symmetry begins to emerge here too. It is initially found in the central areas and then spreads to the frontals. Activity is also con-

tinuous now in the waking state. It is less rhythmic than at seven months. There is some delta and a smaller amount of alpha and beta activity present. Theta frequencies become prevalent again, however. Another feature of the eighth-month record is the disappearance of occipital predominance. This causes the topographical pattern to appear more diffuse.

In the ninth month there is modification of the sleep sequence, but it is fair to say that from the eighth month through birth the record remains little changed. This seeming regression from regularity and localization to seemingly less mature patterns is not understood. It undoubtedly reflects the emergence of cortical functions, however, and has led to the hypothesis that the earlier more synchronous pattern is of subcortical origin.

Perhaps it is appropriate to conclude this section on fetal behavior by pointing out that ample evidence has been accumulated showing that the behavior of the fetus in utero can be affected by external events. Thus, Sontag and Wallace[46] demonstrated that the mobility of the fetus increases when the mother's abdominal wall is stimulated by vibration. Sontag[45] went further and suggested that apart from sound stimuli, the mother's fatigue and emotions affect fetal mobility. These researchers also investigated the influence of the pregnant mother's cigarette smoking on her unborn child's cardiac function. They reported an increase in the cardiac rate in mothers who smoked. Spelt[47] reported an experiment in which he was able to condition the human fetus in utero with an elaborate experimental method and equipment. It is not possible here to delineate syndromes of behavioral difficulties.

Deleterious Influences
on Prenatal Development

Late in the sixteenth century, the French surgeon Ambroise Pare[35] enumerated the theories proposed up to that time which bore upon prenatal disturbances and the emergence of abnormal children. These theories were: (1) the will and act of God; (2) overabundance or deficiency in the amount of the seed; (3) maternal impressions; (4) narrowness or malposition of the uterus; (5) physical injury to the mother; (6) inheritance of deformity or disease; and (7) the craft or subtlety of the devil and his agents. Even at this early stage in the history of medicine it was known that environment and heredity affect prenatal development.

This was demonstrated by Geoffrey St. Hilaire,[43] who worked in the 1820s, and is often called the father of era teratology. In 1908, when Franklin Mall[28] published his great classic monograph on the origin of human monsters, another major step forward occurred. As the science of genetics was evolving, the role of inherited factors became even clearer. We now know that there are two great classes of factors which are involved in the origins of developmental abnormalities. These are the genetic or intrinsic factors and the environmental or extrinsic factors. This discussion will deal principally with the extrinsic factors.

Although protected in the uterus and by his mother's body, the fetus is still quite vulnerable to his social surroundings and to a variety of factors which may come to affect him. He is affected by the nutrition of his mother, by the amount of rest she obtains, and by her general physical status. All of these factors are in some way or another related to the incidence of complications during pregnancy to prematurity, and to other assaults from the fetus before birth.

Knobloch et al.,[21] among others, felt that these biological factors which function before birth are the major contributors to the variation in developmental status manifested by infants at the time of their birth and later. Pasamanick[33] confirmed the results of an earlier study which compared black and white groups in Baltimore and showed that the incidence of prematurity was twice as great in the black group as in the upper portion of the white group—11 versus 5 percent. He further showed that white infants born to mothers of the lower socioeconomic group suffered an in-between risk of being born premature—8 percent. Even more striking differences were demonstrable in regard to other fairly serious complications of pregnancy. Only 5 percent of the white mothers from the upper socioeconomic groups suffered these complications, while 15 percent of the white mothers from lower socioeconomic strata suffered them. In contrast, 51 percent of the black mothers were thus afflicted with complications.

A comparable study* in New York in 1955 showed that the rate of premature births ranged from 7 percent in well-to-do white sections of the city to 13 percent in black slum areas.

---

* Wright, F. et al., "A Controlled Follow-Up Study of Small Prematures Born from 1952–1956," *American Journal of Clinical Diseases of Children, 124:*506, 1972.

In a complicated study in Aberdeen, Scotland, Baird and Scott[2] and Scott, Illsley, and Biles[44] found comparable data related to socioeconomic class in Scotland. They found that upper-class mothers had better diets as measured by calcium intake. It is possible that not only immediate socioeconomic class, but previous socioeconomic class is reflected in good child nutrition.

Cecil Mary Drillien[8] reported a higher correlation between prematurity and the economic class of the mother's father than between prematurity and the class of the child's own father. This data was interpreted by Masland[29] as indicating the possible influence of nutrition during the mother's childhood on the effects on the development of her own baby.

Baird and Scott[2] noted a significant positive relationship between the social class of the mother and not only her height, but the adequacy of her pelvic shape and size, all of which were determined during the growing years.

It has been shown that the dietary habits of laboratory animal mothers has a profound effect on the health of their fetuses. Although Winneck[51] and others have shown an effect between dietary intake and DNA synthesis in the developing brain of the fetus, the exact relationship between nutritional deprivation and fetal development is yet to be known. There is, however, good reason to believe that maternal malnutrition in the early stages of fetal growth is a decisive factor in the production of many congenital malformations.

Murphy[32] has shown that mothers whose diets during pregnancy were deficient in calcium, phosphorus, and vitamins B, C, and D, produced an unusually high frequency of malformed fetuses. The rate of stillbirths and premature births increased during the German occupation of the Netherlands in 1945, and decreased to normal when the food supply was increased after liberation.

Pasamanick and Knobloch[37] related the slight but significant seasonal variations in the birth of mentally deficient children, especially following very hot summers, to the effect of hot weather on the mother's appetite.

A study by Harrell, Woodyard, and Gates[13] showed a direct effect of poor nutrition during pregnancy on the intelligence of offspring. A significant superiority in test scores was shown for the children in Virginia whose mothers had received dietary supplements. In a 1950 review of the literature, Montagu[31] found extensive evidence of physical abnormalities and ill health in infants whose mothers had poor diets during pregnancy.

Other factors which are known to deleteriously

effect the fetus are acute maternal infections, such as rubella, chronic infections such as syphilis and toxoplasmosis, maternal sensitization as in erythroblastosis foetalis and other incompatibilities, and maternal dysfunctions such as hypertension and chronic diseases, such as diabetes.

Maternal age has definitely been correlated with adverse central nervous system outcomes. There is a pronounced relationship between the age of the mother at delivery and some deficiencies of the central nervous system. This is particularly true in regard to Down's syndrome and hydrocephaly. Paternal age has, as yet, only been correlated with achondroplasia. Increased parity also brings with it an increased risk of developmental deviations. There is, of course, a vast literature on the effects of radiation and drugs, both when prescribed for medical reasons and abused, on the development and status of the fetus and the newborn.

Of critical importance has been the emergence of syndromes involving alcohol and barbiturate addiction in the last several decades. Recently, aspirin has been added to the long list of drugs which appear to have a potentially deleterious effect on the fetus. It appears likely that as our knowledge of fetal development increases, more and more agents will be added to the above list, and the management of embryological development as undertaken by the obstetrician, the embryologist, and perhaps those in the field of child development, will become ever more complex.

Psychobiology of Expectant Parenthood

As the fetus develops within the mother's womb, certain parallel psychological changes are occurring in the expectant mother and father. Bibring et al.[5] assessed the psychological course of women attending the Prenatal Clinic at Beth Israel Hospital in Boston, and supplemented these observations from psychoanalytic practice. They attempted to define the psychobiology of the woman to her sexual partner, to herself, and to the child as shown by level, distribution, and vicissitudes of object libido and narcissistic libido.[9]

These investigators reported that pregnant women, prior to quickening, perceived the baby as a new object within the self, and thus experienced early pregnancy as a phase of enhanced narcissism. They indicated that the child will, as a result, always be perceived by the mother as a

part of herself, and, at the same time, an object of the outside world and a part of her sexual mate. The mother's relationship to her child will, as a result, be one of freely changeable fusion, varying in the degree and intensity of narcissistic and object libidinal strivings. All of the women in their study showed augmentation of earlier psychological conflict during pregnancy and a regressive shift in psychic life with the emergence of developmentally earlier patterns of behavior, attitudes, and wishes, with one exception—women of predominantly compulsive character structure showed a marked increase in their defensive patterns which precluded regression in the emergence of developmentally earlier psychological experience.

The Bibring et al. work underscored the notion that expectant parenthood was a time of important psychological upheaval which served to focus on the reworking of old conflicts, particularly the relationship between the mother and her own baby. They believe that this psychological work prepared the mother to undertake her role as an actual mother in a more adaptive way. Brazelton,[6] commenting on this study, stated that "psychological upheaval during pregnancy is like shock treatment; it clears the circuits and allows the mother-to-be to meet and to attach to her infant optimally."

Jessner, Weigert, and Foy[18] reported phase-specific psychological conflicts for each trimester of pregnancy which they believe needed to be mastered. They showed that these conflicts mirrored former life experiences in each of the women studied. Jessner and her collaborators suggested similar but less specific conflicts in the father, and indicated that such conflicts became manifest in the father's relationship to his work. Alan Gurwitt,[12] in a report on the analysis of a prospective father, suggested that the reworkings of conflict in the father are tied to physiological experiences of the mother-to-be.

Judith Kestenberg[19] reported studies on the progression toward femininity and motherhood in little girls and masculinity and fatherhood in boys. Her work is focused on the psychological regressions and reintegrations during pregnancy as related to the innergenital maternal phase of dedevelopment. By innergenital phase is meant the preoedipal development in boys and girls which provides the basis for child-nurturing attitudes and stems from urges to create and nurture a child in a dyadic relationship. Kestenberg has reported data from transcripts of analyses indicating that the prevailing regressions in pregnancy draw on earlier innergenital phases in which the pregenital regressions occurred. She feels that their orderly sequence during pregnancy does not duplicate the manner in which regression occurred in childhood. Rather, such regression seems to be directly linked to the sequence of physiological changes to which pregnant women react with special sensitivity. This, she feels, constitutes an aid in the transformation of earlier forms of child expectancy into the more appropriate young adult form. She states:

During the nidation in the first trimester, oral incorporative trends reflect the attachment of the fetus to the mother. With the formation of the placenta a true symbiotic state is established. During the time the pregnant woman carries the now securely attached fetus in the second trimester, anal retentive trends facilitate and aid the recognition of the fetus as a separate object, a host of the uterus. During the preparation for giving up the fetus in the third trimester, urethral letting go trends act as an aid for the anticipated conversion of the internal into an external object—the child. (p. 246)

Herzog[14] suggests that these forces are not only operative in women during pregnancy, but they also occur with predictable regularity in anticipatory fatherhood. He found Kestenberg's formulation of an innergenital maternal phase to be particularly useful in understanding not only the events of actual pregnancy, but in conceptualizing the psychobiological progression toward parenthood as it occurs in the development of both boys and girls.

This psychoembryology of parenthood, that is, the inner life of expectant mothers and fathers and the role that these inner events have on the parents' ability to greet, receive, and optimally parent their offspring, is part of and should be integrated into studies of fetal embryology.

This chapter has sought to review the embryological development of the central nervous system and current knowledge on behavioral capabilities during the development of the fetus. It also touches on the psychoembryology of parenthood. It notes that many environmental influences can exert a deleterious effect on development both morphologically and behaviorally. It is clear that Coleridge's observation that the first nine months of life in utero may well be the most interesting period in a human's life deserves some consideration.

REFERENCES

1. ADAMS, R., and SIDMAN, R., *Introduction to Neuropathology*, The Blakiston Division, McGraw-Hill, New York, 1968.

2. BAIRD, D., and SCOTT, E., "Intelligence and Child Bearing," *Eugen. Rev.*, 45:139–145, 1953.

3. BARRON, D. H., "The Functional Development of Some Mammalian Neuromuscular Mechanisms," *Biol. Rev.*, 16:1–33, 1941.

4. BERNSTINE, R., BORKOWSKI, W., and PRICE, A., "Prenatal Fetal Electroencephalography," *American Journal of Obstetrics and Gynecology*, 70:623–630, 1955.

5. BIBRING, G. L., et al., "A Study of the Psychological Processes in Pregnancy and the Earliest Mother-Child Relationship," in Eissler, R. S., et al. (Eds.), *The Psychoanalytic Study of the Child*, vol. 16, pp. 9–72, International Universities Press, New York, 1961.

6. BRAZELTON, T. B., "Parent-Infant Interaction," *Ciba Foundation Symposium, No. 33*, Elsevier, Amsterdam, 1975.

7. DAVIS, M., and POTTER, E., "Intrauterine Respiration of the Human Fetus," *Journal of the American Medical Association*, 131:1194–1201, 1946.

8. DRILLIEN, C. M., "Physical and Mental Handicaps in the Prematurely Born," *J. Obstet. Gynaecol. Brit. Empire*, 66:721–728, 1959.

9. FREUD, S., "On Narcissism: An Introduction," in *The Standard Edition of the Complete Works of Sigmund Freud*, vol. 14, pp. 73–81, Hogarth Press, London, 1953.

10. FRIES, M. E., and WOOLF, P. J., "Some Hypotheses on the Role of the Congenital Activity Type in Personality Development," in Eissler, R. S., et al. (Eds.), *The Psychoanalytic Study of the Child*, vol. 8, pp. 48–62, International Universities Press, New York, 1953.

11. GESELL, A., *The Embryology of Behavior*, Harper, New York, 1945.

12. GURWITT, A., "Aspects of Prospective Fatherhood," in Eissler, R. S., et al. (Eds.), *The Psychoanalytic Study of the Child*, vol. 31, pp. 000–000, Yale University Press, New Haven, 1976.

13. HARRELL, R., WOODYARD, E., and GATES, A., *The Effect of Mothers' Diets on the Intelligence of Offspring: A Study of the Influence of Vitamin Supplementation of the Diets of Pregnant and Lactating Women on the Intelligence of their Children*, Teachers College, New York, 1955.

14. HERZOG, J. M., "Patterns of Parenting," Paper presented at the Twenty-fourth Annual Meetings of the American Academy of Child Psychiatry, Houston, Texas, October 19–23, 1977.

15. HOOKER, D., *The Prenatal Origin of Behavior*, Porter Lectures, Series 18, University of Kansas Press, Lawrence, 1952.

16. ————, "Genetic Neurology," in Weiss, P. A. (Ed.), *Spinal Cord Regeneration*, p. 208, University of Chicago Press, Chicago, 1950.

17. HUGHES, J., DAVIS, B., and BRENNAN, M., "Electroencephalography of the Newborn Infant: Studies on Premature Infants," *Pediatrics*, 7:707–712, 1951.

18. JESSNER, L., WEIGERT, E., and FOYE, J. S., "The Development of Parental Attitudes during Pregnancy," in Anthony, E. J., and Benedek, T. (Eds.), *Parenthood: Its Psychology and Psychopathology*, pp. 209–245, Little, Brown, Boston, 1970.

19. KESTENBERG, J. S., "Regression and Reintegration in Pregnancy," Special Supplement on Female Psychology, *Journal of the American Psychoanalytic Association*, 24:213–251, 1976.

20. KIMEL, V. M., and KAVALER, F., "Biochemical and Physiological Differentiation during Morphogenesis; Functional Maturation of the Motor Cortex of the Fetal Guinea

Pig as Judged by the Appearance of Muscular Responses to Electrical Stimulation of the Cortex," *Journal of Comparative Neurology, 94:*257–265, 1951.

21. KNOBLOCH, H., et al., "Neuropsychiatric Sequelae of Prematurity: A Longitudinal Study," *Journal of the American Medical Association, 161:*581–585, 1956.

22. KORNER, A. F., "Some Hypotheses Regarding the Significance of Individual Differences at Birth for Later Development," in Eissler, R. S., et al. (Eds.), *The Psychoanalytic Study of the Child,* vol. 19, pp. 58–72, International Universities Press, New York, 1964.

23. LANGMAN, J., *Medical Embryology.* William & Wilkins, Baltimore, 1963.

24. LANGWORTHY, O. R., "Development of Behavior Patterns and Myelinization of the Nervous System in the Human Fetus and Infants," *Contr. Embryol., 139,* 1933.

25. LILIENFELD, A., and PASAMANICK, B., "The Association of Maternal and Fetal Factors with the Development of Mental Deficiency," *American Journal of Mental Deficiency, 60:*557–569, 1956.

26. LINDSLEY, D. B., "Heart and Brain Potentials of Human Fetuses in Utero, *American Journal of Psychology, 55:*412–416, 1942.

27. LIPTON, E. L., STEINSCHNEIDER, A., and RICHMOND, J. B., "The Autonomic Nervous System in Early Life," *New England Journal of Medicine, 273:*147–154, 201–208, 1965.

28. MALL, F., cited in R. J. Blattner, G. G. Robertson, and A. P. Williamson, "Principles of Teratology," in R. C. Cooke (Ed.), *The Biologic Basis of Pediatric Practice,* pp. 1401–1407, McGraw-Hill, New York, 1968.

29. MASLAND, R., SARASON, S., and GLADWIN, T., *Mental Subnormality,* Basic Books, New York, 1958.

30. MINKOWSKI, M., "Neurobiologische Studien am Menschlichen Fuetus, in E. Abderhalden (Ed.), *Handbuch der Biologisches Arbeits Methoden, 5:*511–618, 1928.

31. MONTAGU, M. F. A., "Constitutional and Prenatal Factors in Infant and Child Health," in Senn, M. J. (Ed.), *Symposium on the Healthy Personality,* pp. 148–175, Josiah Macy, Jr. Foundation, New York, 1950.

32. MURPHY, D. P., *Congenital Malformations: A Study of Parental Characteristics with Special Reference to the Reproductive Process,* 2nd ed., University of Pennsylvania Press, Philadelphia, 1947.

33. MURPHY, M., "Diagnostic Classifications, Intellectual Characteristics and Parental Occupations of 500 Severely Deficient Institutionalized Males," *American Journal of Mental Deficiency, 62:*905–907, 1958.

34. OKAMOTO, Y., and KIRIKAE, T., "Electroencephalographic Studies on Brain of Foetus," *Folia Psychiatrica et Neurologica Japonica, 5:*135–146, 1951.

35. PARE, A., cited in R. J. Blattner, G. G. Robertson, and A. P. Williamson, "Principles of Teratology." See reference 28.

36. PASAMANICK, B., "Influence of Sociocultural Factors in Mental Retardation, *American Journal of Mental Deficiency, 64:*316–320, 1959.

37. ———, and KNOBLOCH, H., "Epidemiological Studies on the Complications of Pregnancy and the Birth Process," in Caplan, G. (Ed.), *Prevention of Mental Disorders in Children,* Basic Books, New York, 1961.

38. PEIPER, A., *Cerebral Function in Infancy and Childhood,* Consultants Bureau, New York, 1963.

39. PENROSE, L. S., "Paternal Age and Mutation," *Lancet, 1:*312–313, 1955.

40. RICHMOND, J. B., and LIPTON, E. L., "Some Aspects of the Neurophysiology of the Newborn and their Implications for Child Development," in Jessner, L., and Pavenstedt, E. (Eds.), *Dynamic Psychopathology in Childhood,* pp. 78–105, Grune & Stratton, New York, 1959.

41. ———, and STEINSCHNEIDER, A., "Observations on Differences in Autonomic Nervous System Function between and within Individuals during Early Infancy," *Journal of Child Psychiatry, 1:*83–91, 1962.

42. ROGERS, M., LILIENFELD, A., and PASAMANICK, B., *Prenatal and Paranatal Factors in the Development of Childhood Behavior Disorders,* Johns Hopkins University Press, Baltimore, 1956.

43. ST. HILAIRE, G., cited in R. J. Blattner, G. G. Robertson, and A. P. Williamson, "Principles of Teratology." See reference 28.

44. SCOTT, E., ILLSLEY, R., and BILES, M., "A Psychological Investigation of Primigravidae: Some Aspects of Maternal Behavior," *J. Obstet. Gynec. Brit. Empire, 63:*494–501, 1956.

45. SONTAG, L. W., "The Significance of Fetal Environmental Differences," *American Journal of Obstetrics and Gynecology, 42:*996–1003, 1940.

46. ———, and WALLACE, R. F., "The Effect of Cigarette Smoking during Pregnancy upon the Fetal Heart Rate," *American Journal of Obstetrics and Gynecology, 29:*3–8, 1935.

47. SPELT, D. K., "Conditioned Responses in the Human Fetus in Utero," *Psychological Bulletin, 35:*712–713, 1948.

48. THOMAS, A., and CHESS, S., "Evaluation of Behavior Disorders into Adolescence," in Chess, S., and Thomas, A. (Eds.), *Annual Progress in Child Psychiatry,* pp. 489–497, Brunner-Mazel, New York, 1977.

49. WEIL, A. P., "The Basic Core," in Eissler, R. S., et al. (Eds.), *The Psychoanalytic Study of the Child,* vol. 25, pp. 442–460, International Universities Press, New York, 1970.

50. WINDLE, W. F., "Genesis of Somatic Motor Function in Mammalian Embryos: A Synthesizing Article," *Psychological Zoology, 17:*247–260, 1944.

51. WINNECK, M., "Effects of Early Nutrition on Growth of the Central Nervous System," in *The Infant at Risk,* pp. 29–37, Birth Defects Original Article Series, vol. 10, No. 2, The National Foundation March of Dimes, 1974.

---

3 / The Molecular Biology of Development

J. Gerald Young and Donald J. Cohen

Freud's recourse to "constitutional factors" when he had reached the limits of his technique echoes the judgment of clinicians over decades. Fundamental individual differences in biological makeup are critical determinants of personality and behavior. Nevertheless, the longer such differences were beyond the powers of isolated observation and measurement, the more they were excluded as central issues. Genetic components seemed inextricably interwoven with environmental influences, and each domain was left to its own experts and proponents, with a failure to accommodate both within clinical practice. Fortunately, tools are now available which enable preliminary specification of such inherently vague concepts as "constitution."

It requires a formidable conceptual leap to consider childhood development at a biochemical level, a jump from the gene to complex behavior. Along the way each area has been explored by developmentalists of differing interests with little experience outside their own discipline. This chapter outlines these overlapping areas and clarifies regions of exchange and mutual interest, with a focus on clinical neurochemistry. Clinical neurochemistry represents the assessment of the molecular end-result of events initiated at the level of the gene, traced through the synthesis of proteins, the interaction of proteins and other compounds within the cell, elaboration and regulation at the tissue and organ level, and the impact of environment.

This chapter is organized into sections describing fundamental disciplines within the developmental biology of behavior: human genetics, particularly biochemical genetics; clinical neurochemistry, emphasizing strategies of investigation of neurotransmitters; neuroendocrinology, specifically its interface with clinical neurochemistry; and the concepts of stress and trauma, clinically central phenomena which integrate the perspectives of preceding sections as well as intrapsychic, interpersonal, and social factors.

Human Genetics

The theme linking "constitution," "temperament," and "inborn endowment" is that of individual variation from the earliest stages of life. This variability stems from many origins, such as influences in utero and events during and immediately following birth, as well as "genetic" differences, to whatever degree they can be separated out for scrutiny. Such aspects of the personality as mood, tempo, cognitive style, and adaptability under stress are quite subtle, and until recently there was reluctance to apply genetic concepts and techniques to psychiatric research. Nevertheless,

there is now a solid foundation of methodology in psychiatric genetics.

Three levels of investigation within human genetics will be described, and one will be developed in more detail as the connector between questions of temperament and neurochemical research. *Population genetics* attempts to assess quantitatively the frequency and distribution of genes within a population, and makes extensive use of mathematical models. One laboratory approach to genetics is that of *cytogenetics*, which studies chromosomes and maps gene locations, utilizing increasingly sophisticated techniques, such as banding, autoradiography, and somatic cell hybrids. *Biochemical genetics* views the gene as a biochemical structure and investigates the sequence of events leading from gene transcription to molecular and structural changes within the cell; its domain includes the means of transmission of genetic information and the biochemical, metabolic errors which follow upon a breakdown in these molecular events. The gene exercises its function through the regulation of protein synthesis; because enzymes are proteins, the gene exerts regulatory control over the reaction rates of all metabolic events in the cell.[53]

Population genetics describes characteristics of individuals, determines gene frequencies in a large group of individuals, and follows them through generations or across populations. Clinical psychiatric syndromes whose boundaries are indefinite can usefully be examined in a larger context, and descriptive categories can be studied across diagnostic lines. In this way, although genetic investigation of behaviors or symptoms is difficult, a genetic component to more comprehensive behavior structures (for example, manic depressive disorder) can be hypothesized. Biochemical genetics makes dramatic contributions in metabolic diseases in which a genetic abnormality causes a clear alteration in the function of an enzyme and all symptoms are the clinical expression of the specific abnormality. Human behavior is so complex as to not make us optimistic that such single gene results will be obtained often in psychiatry. However, this concept can still be critically useful in studying questions of inheritance in psychiatry. It may be that an altered gene does not cause a full, typical syndrome, but may give a vulnerability which, given the required additional environmental events, may lead to phenotypic expression. Alternatively, this altered gene may be unrelated to the phenotype, other than in association with it through a *linkage* phenomenon. In this case, though it does not contribute to the pathology, it may serve as a marker for a genetic contribution. Many variations on these and other themes are possible. The frequency of variant genes is distributed along a continuum, and some may be so frequent that they no longer are thought of as mutants. Mutations may lead to dramatic, life-threatening effects or may influence the phenotype very little, and the viability of the organism not at all, leading to the common occurrence of the mutation remaining undetected. The same *phenotype* (appearance) may be derived from two or more *genotypes* (genetic makeup); or a genotype may be mimicked by the effects of the environment, producing a *phenocopy*.[8, 63]

CLINICAL GENETICS

A review of basic terms and concepts from clinical genetics will preface the biochemical description. A gene occupies a position on a chromosome described as its *locus*. Human cells contain 46 chromosomes, 22 pairs of *autosomal chromosomes* and one pair of *sex chromosomes* (XX in

females and XY in males). Those genes found at the same loci on each of a chromosome pair are termed *alleles*. When the genes at a given locus on both members of a chromosome pair are the same, the individual is said to be *homozygous* for that locus; when the genes at a specific locus differ, he is said to be *heterozygous*. One trait may be *dominant* over a second trait, said to be *recessive* to the first. An individual may be homozygous for the allele corresponding to a given dominant or recessive trait, or he may be heterozygous at that locus.

Three fundamental laws of inheritance were derived from Mendel's experiments. First, genes do not mix or blend but retain their identity through generations. Second, the two genes of a pair always segregate during the formation of a *gamete* (sperm or egg, always *haploid* or *monoploid*, containing one set of chromosomes as oppossed to the *diploid* somatic cells). Third, genes at different loci (nonalleles) segregate independently of one another. These laws are the basis of clinical genetic research methods, such as con-

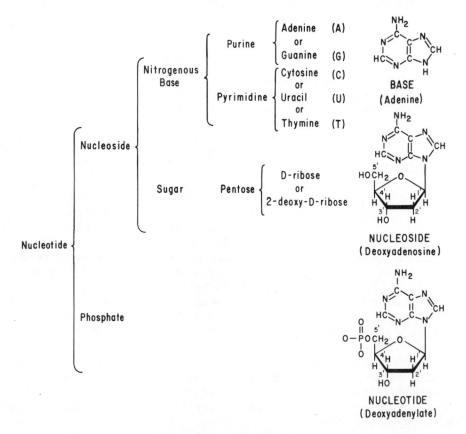

FIGURE 3–1
Outline of the composition of nucleosides and nucleotides and structures of a base, nucleoside, and nucleotide.

saguinity, twin, and adoption studies. Though the laws hold true, such factors as *polygenic inherit-ance* (multiple genes producing a cumulative phe-notypic effect), gene interactions, and environ-mental effects make clinical investigation strategies in psychiatric genetics complex and increasingly quantitative.[54]

BIOCHEMICAL GENETICS

The common ground of genetics and neuro-chemistry is the field of biochemical genetics. From this perspective molecules of specific interest to the child psychiatrist are viewed in terms of heredity, as concrete substances which can be utilized to distinguish and catalogue factors of individual difference. In simple terms, the events through which genetic information is translated into the molecular makeup of specific cellular con-stituents can be outlined as:

DNA ⟶ new DNA ⟶ RNA ⟶ protein (enzyme)

The Gene as a Molecule: Deoxyribonucleic acid (DNA) is the very large, elongated molecule of heredity formed through the combination of thou-sands of deoxyribonucleotides. *Nucleotides* are fundamental biological molecules involved in such critical processes as metabolic regulation, energy transformation, coenzyme function, and biological

syntheses. Chemically, a nucleotide is a phosphate ester of a nucleoside. A *nucleoside* is a compound consisting of a *sugar* (pentose) and a *nitrogenous base* (purine or pyrimidine) (figure 3–1). Thus, the nucleotide has three principal components: nitrogenous base, sugar, and phosphate.

The *pentose* of a ribonucleoside and a ribo-nucleotide (as in RNA) is ribose; the pentose of a deoxyribonucleoside and a deoxyribonucleotide (as in DNA) is deoxyribose. These two types of nucleosides (and nucleotides) each utilize four of five available bases in their formation, uracil being specific to ribonucleosides and thymine to deoxy-ribonucleosides. The nomenclature for nucleosides and nucleotides is given in figure 3–2.

The disposition of the three components in their formation of a nucleotide is critical, because the genetic function of a *nucleic acid* (DNA or RNA) is a product of its three-dimensional structure, or *conformation*, as well as the sequence of its com-ponents. DNA consists of an unchanging backbone of sugar and phosphate components: deoxyriboses connected by phosphodiester bridges. What is variable in the molecular structure of the gene (and therefore informative) is the sequence of bases. Figure 3–3 depicts a portion of a typical pentose backbone with linking phosphodiester bridges and varying bases.[62]

The classic work of Watson and Crick described the conformation of DNA and utilized this struc-

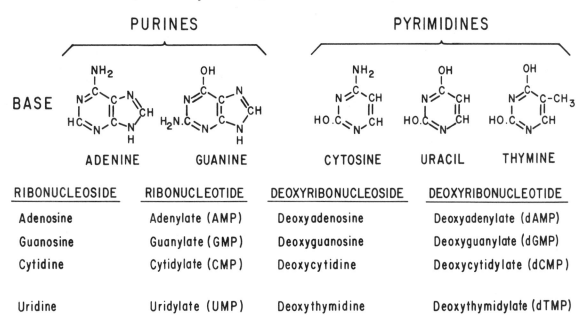

FIGURE 3–2

Structures of the purines and pyrimidines occurring in DNA and RNA and nomenclature of their respective nucleosides and nucleotides.

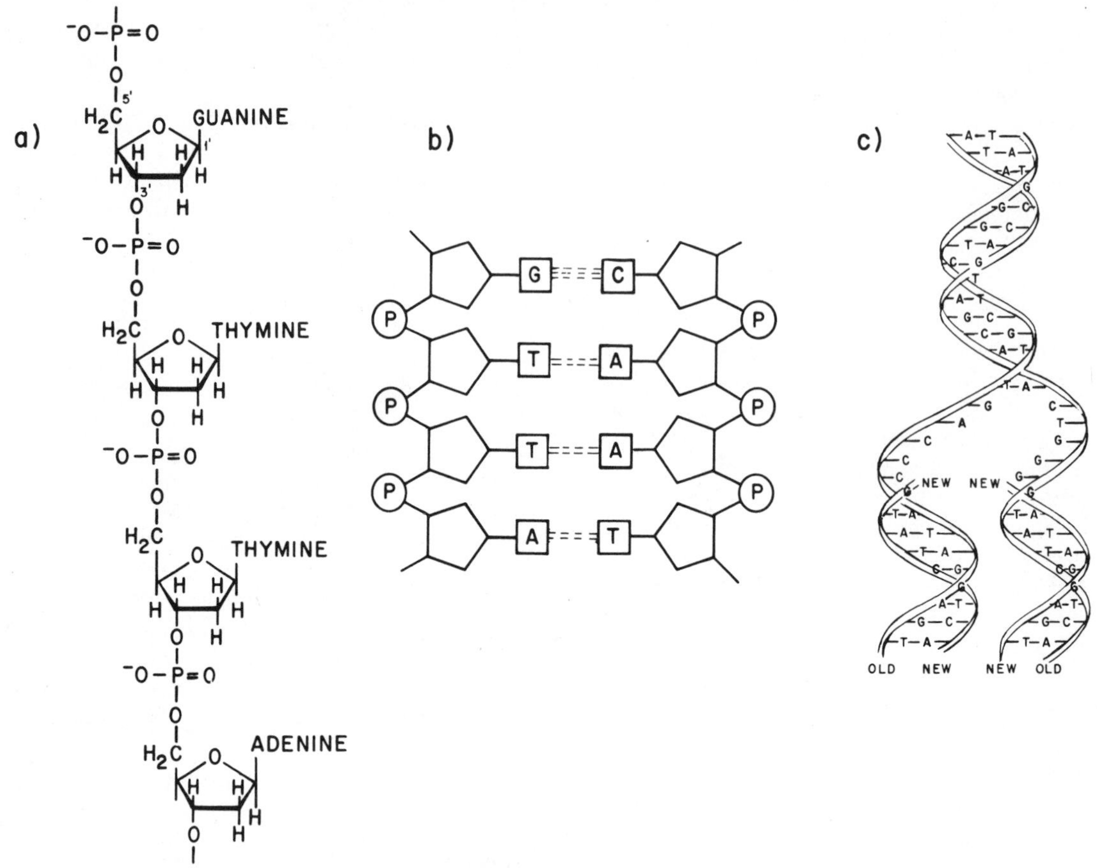

a)

b)

c)

FIGURE 3–3

(a) *Section of a DNA chain, showing chemical structure of the backbone, consisting of deoxyriboses and phosphodiester bridges.*

(b) *Section of two DNA chains, uncoiled, showing pairing of bases through hydrogen bonding. The allowed pairs in DNA are A–T (2 hydrogen bonds) and G–C (3 hydrogen bonds), on the basis of size (giving the best fit) and maximum number of hydrogen bonds (giving greatest stability).*

(c) *The double helix: Structural complementarity of the two DNA chains allows each to serve as template for another chain after they unwind. The base sequence of each new complementary strand is specified by the old, and the two new daughter molecules of DNA each consist of one new and one old DNA chain. Backbone of deoxyribose and phosphodiester bridges is represented by double lines.*

ture to suggest the mechanism of *replication* of DNA (genes). This clarified the molecular basis of the science of genetics. Analysis of x-ray diffraction photographs of DNA strands suggested that DNA is composed of two *helical polynucleotide chains* which coil about a comon central axis. The phosphate and deoxyribose units are situated on the outside of the helix, while the bases are stacked inside. The intervals between the repeating units are regular, and the two chains are held together by hydrogen bonding between base pairs, one base from each strand. The sequence of bases along a chain is not restricted, and this sequence provides the code underlying genetic transmission. However, the pairing of bases between the two chains is absolutely specific. Hydrogen-bonding and steric factors led Watson and Crick to the formulation that adenine must pair with thymine and guanine with cytosine. This specificity of bases within a double helix permits precise replication of genetic information. If each base has a complementary base in the other chain, then the chains themselves are complementary. When the hydrogen bonds of the double helix are broken, and the two chains unwind and separate, each chain acts as a *template* for another polynucleotide chain. The two strands duplicate themselves with exactly the same base sequence. Each new molecule is comprised of one new chain and one old chain (figure 3–3).

Many proteins take part in the complex events of DNA replication, but the principal enzymes are the *DNA polymerases*, which are template directed. DNA polymerases not only catalyze the formation of a phosphodiester bond for the addition of deoxyribonucleotides to a primer chain, but also check the base pairs and correct errors as nucleotides are added. *Nucleases* are enzymes which sever the phosphodiester bonds of polynucleotide chains, in some cases cutting internal bonds (*endonucleases*), while in others breaking off terminal nucleotides (*exonucleases*). A class of highly specific nucleases (*restriction enzymes*) make breaks only within certain sequences, and are the tools used to isolate polynucleotide fragments sufficiently small for determination of their nucleotide sequences.

The Genetic Code: Transcription and translation: The functional expression of genetic information contained in DNA occurs through synthesis of particular proteins characteristic of the cell. DNA, however, is not the direct template for protein synthesis. RNA is the intermediate link, first formed on the DNA template, then assuming the role of template for protein synthesis. The sequence of the replication, transcription, and translation of genetic information is as follows:

DNA $\longrightarrow$ new DNA $\longrightarrow$ RNA $\longrightarrow$ protein
(replication)   (transcription)   (translation)

DNA is located almost entirely in the nucleus, whereas RNA is found predominantly in the cytoplasm. Protein synthesis in the cytoplasm occurs at the *ribosomes*, consisting of RNA and protein. RNA structure is very similar to DNA, with the following differences: the pentose is ribose rather than deoxyribose; thymine is replaced by uracil as one of the four bases; and RNA molecules are essentially always single-stranded, although hairpin loops do lend a double-helix structure to portions of some RNA molecules, typically involving around 50 percent of the molecule.

Three types of RNA are found in cells, only one of which, *messenger RNA* (mRNA), acts as a template for protein synthesis. Amino acids in the cytoplasm are transported in an activated form to the ribosome by *transfer RNA* (tRNA), where mRNA, carrier of the transcribed genetic infor-

mation, determines the sequence of amino acids in the growing polypeptide chain. The major constituent of ribosomes is *ribosomal RNA* (rRNA), whose specific function is not yet clear. There is an mRNA molecule for each gene or related group of genes, and at least one tRNA for each of the twenty amino acids.

Synthesis of RNA (*transcription*) in the cell occurs through the action of *RNA polymerase* and is guided by a DNA template. Both start signals (*"promotor regions"*) and termination signals for transcription occur on the DNA template, and some modification of RNA molecules occurs following transcription ("maturation" or "processing"). The informative base sequence, derived from the DNA template, is maintained in newly synthesized RNA.

Once transcription has taken place, the next events concern the manner in which the information contained in the base sequence of DNA and mRNA is translated into the sequence of amino acids in a protein. The relation of the sequence of bases to the sequence of amino acids is known as the *genetic code*. The code is the same in all known organisms: An amino acid is specified by three bases, which are termed a *codon*. The genetic code consists of sixty-four codons, of which sixty-one code for a specific amino acid and three for termination of the chain (table 3–1). The code is described as *"degenerate,"* in that most amino acids are related to more than one codon; however, each triplet designates only a single amino acid. Degeneracy may be a built-in mechanism for minimizing the ill effects of mutations. Triplets that designate the same amino acid are described as *synonyms*, and they usually differ only in the last base of the triplet.

Transfer RNA acts as an adapter molecule in protein synthesis: an amino acid is plugged into it in order to be adapted to the language of nucleotide triplets. This amino acid attachment site is one of two critical attachment sites on tRNA; the other is operative once the tRNA has carried an activated amino acid to the ribosome. The template recognition site of tRNA consists of three bases known as the *anticodon*, which recognizes three sequential complementary bases on mRNA (the codon). These groups of three bases, each coding for one amino acid, do not overlap, and the sequence of bases is read from a single starting point without skipping any bases and with no bases acting as markers between codons.

The synthesis of proteins (*translation*) occurs on ribosomes and involves multiple large molecules. For example, just as there is at least one

TABLE 3-1

The genetic code, a dictionary of sixty-four codons; sixty-one code for specific amino acids, while three code for chain termination (End). AUG is part of the initiation signal and also codes for internal methionines. In most cases, degeneracy involves only the third base in the codon.

	U		C		A		G	
U	UUU	Phe	UCU	Ser	UAU	Tyr	UGU	Cys
	UUC	Phe	UCC	Ser	UAC	Tyr	UGC	Cys
	UUA	Leu	UCA	Ser	UAA	End	UGA	End
	UUG	Leu	UCG	Ser	UAG	End	UGG	Trp
C	CUU	Leu	CCU	Pro	CAU	His	CGU	Arg
	CUC	Leu	CCC	Pro	CAC	His	CGC	Arg
	CUA	Leu	CCA	Pro	CAA	Gln	CGA	Arg
	CUG	Leu	CCG	Pro	CAG	Gln	CGG	Arg
A	AUU	Ile	ACU	Thr	AAU	Asn	AGU	Ser
	AUC	Ile	ACC	Thr	AAC	Asn	AGC	Ser
	AUA	Ile	ACA	Thr	AAA	Lys	AGA	Arg
	AUG	Met	ACG	Thr	AAG	Lys	AGG	Arg
G	GUU	Val	GCU	Ala	GAU	Asp	GGU	Gly
	GUC	Val	GCC	Ala	GAC	Asp	GGC	Gly
	GUA	Val	GCA	Ala	GAA	Glu	GGA	Gly
	GUG	Val	GCG	Ala	GAG	Glu	GGG	Gly

particular tRNA for each amino acid, there is also at least one specific activating enzyme for each amino acid. The central event of translation is the formation of base pairs between a codon on mRNA and the anticodon on tRNA, accomplishing the transmission of the specific genetic information. The tRNA adapts this information to a single amino acid, which is added to the *polypeptide chain* being synthesized. The molecular events of protein synthesis have been investigated in detail and divided into four steps: activation of the amino acids, initiation of the polypeptide chain, elongation of the chain, and termination of the chain. However, for our purposes, the critical issue has been the demonstration of molecular specificity in the transmission of genetic (DNA) information to specific protein synthesis for a particular cell.[36]

Both DNA strands and polypeptide chains are linear, unbranched structures. The order of mutable sites along a genetic (DNA) map is the same as the amino acid order in the corresponding polypeptide chain (colinearity). *Mutations* of genes occur when the base sequence of DNA is altered. This can occur in several ways. The most frequent type of mutation is the *substitution* of one base pair for another. Other types of mutations are the *deletion* of one or more base pairs or the *insertion* of one or more base pairs. The various causes of mutations include spontaneous tautomerization of a base, defective DNA polymerases, the incorporation of base analogs (for example, 5-bromouracil), or reaction of various chemicals with the bases.

Rates of protein synthesis within the cell are carefully regulated for the economic use of precursor molecules and the production of differential quantities of individual enzymes and other specialized proteins. Regulation can occur at the level of transcription or translation. A chief means for achieving cellular efficiency in protein synthesis is enzyme induction. *Constitutive enzymes*, used in central reaction pathways fundamental to all cells, are formed at regular rates, leading to unchanging amounts of the enzyme. *Inducible enzymes* are present in the cell in very small quantities, but respond to the appearance of substrate by a rapid increase in concentration. Induced enzymes are, thus, made as needed.

The genetic regulatory events of primitive cells have been specified with some success, but gene regulation in more complex cells utilizes other

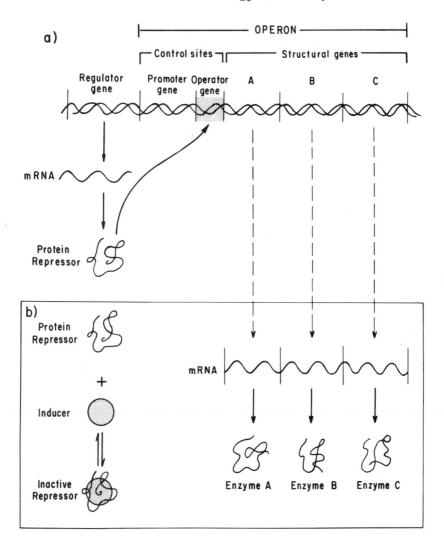

FIGURE 3–4

*The operon model. Schematic diagram of coordinate regulation in a simple cell.
(a) The regulatory gene codes for the synthesis of the repressor protein, which
binds to the operator gene, preventing transcription of the structural genes.
(b) When the inducer is present, it forms a complex with the repressor protein,
inactivating it so that it does not bind to the operator gene. Operator and promotor genes are then free to initiate transcription of the sructural genes. The
messenger RNA formed carries the code for synthesis of enzymes A, B, and C at
the ribosomes.*

mechanisms which are not yet fully understood. The *operon model* describes gene regulation in very simple cells (figure 3–4).

As the need for a particular enzyme in a cell wanes, *enzyme repression* occurs. In some instances all enzymes in a sequential pathway may be affected by regulation, known as *coordinate induction* or *coordinate repression*. The group of genes corresponding to the group of enzymes is known as the *operon*. The operon consists of an operator gene, a promotor gene, and their associated structural genes. *Structural genes* are those genes actually coding amino acid sequences for proteins. Apart from the operon is a *regulatory gene* which contains the code for the amino acid sequence of a *repressor* protein. The repressor binds to a specific locus on the DNA near the structural gene known as the *operator*; binding at this site prevents transcription of the structural genes. When an *inducer* (substrate) is not present, the repressor is active and binds at the operator; when the inducer appears, it combines with the repressor protein, forming a reversible complex which prevents binding at the operator. The *promotor gene* binds RNA polymerase indicating where transcription of the structural genes is to begin, and the operator gene is now free to initiate transcription. Cyclic AMP is also a general stimulant for the initiation of transcription at the operon, and cyclic AMP and inducers can act together as signal molecules for operons.[36]

The operon model may not be applicable to more complex cells where genes for sequential enzymes in a pathway are scattered throughout the chromosomes. The structural genes in these cells are only a small part of the total genome, since much of the total DNA has a regulatory function and even more DNA has an unknown function.

Many aspects of gene regulation are relevant to child psychiatry. For example, during differentiation and development some genes are transcribed, while others are repressed, often permanently. These events occur in patterns having a specific sequence and timing, and are additionally regulated by other molecules, such as glucocorticoids and thyroid hormones. The complexity of genetic regulation is dramatically stated when it is remembered that each cell of an organism contains the total genome for the organism. Thus, a cell from one tissue has the information required for forming cells of any other type of tissue in the organism, although the processes of differentiation restrict actual gene expression.

Clinical Neurochemistry

A wide array of biochemical strategies for investigating behavioral disorders and elucidating mechanisms of action of neuroleptic drugs are now available. The chemical compounds studied are products of genes: enzymes directly flowing from the processes of transcription and translation, or many other compounds whose synthesis and function are regulated by enzymes. All substances found in nervous tissue are of potential interest, but the neurotransmitters have been the basic elements in biological investigations of adult psychoses and affective disorders and of the developmental disturbances. These compounds can be viewed in terms of their immediate clinical application (for example, studies of drug and stress effects) and additionally in terms of heredity (for example, enzyme abnormality or individual differences in baseline levels of a compound).

NEUROTRANSMITTERS

The brain consists of numerous anatomically, biochemically, and functionally definable subsystems. Each subsystem consists of millions of neurons, billions of interconnections, and a vast number of glial supportive cells. In spite of chemical and morphological diversity, there is a remarkable regularity in chemical processes which occur at points of communication between neurons.

Nervous tissue is specialized for the rapid conduction of signals over long distances, at velocities up to 120 m/sec. Complex electrophysiological and biochemical changes lead to the release of a chemical substance (the *neurotransmitter*) which crosses a physical space (the *synaptic cleft*) and affects the signal function of another neuron. The neurotransmitter exerts one of two effects on the postsynaptic cell: *excitation* (by depolarizing the cell membrane) or *inhibition* (by hyperpolarizing the membrane). The final membrane state reflects the balance of up to several thousand synaptic inputs acting on this single neuron. Neuronal function may be assessed by measuring excitation, inhibition, or the concentrations of neurotransmitters.

Disease, drugs, or toxins can act on a neurotransmitter at any point along the metabolic sequence: synthesis of the transmitter; its storage, release, or action at the postsynaptic receptor; re-uptake by the presynaptic neuron; or its catabolism. The mechanism or action of a drug may be clarified by the use of isolated peripheral neural tissue, and such studies may, in turn, illuminate the basic functioning of the neuron. Such studies have yielded a basic model of neuronal function at the synapse, involving an increasing number of putative neurotransmitter substances, such as acetylcholine, norepinephrine, histamine, several amino acids, and other compounds. The use of this model for investigation of the central nervous system introduces a host of technical and conceptual problems—such as differing functions of a neurotransmitter within brain structures and interactions between different neurotransmitter systems. A description of the basic model will be followed by discussion of complications when extrapolating from peripheral nervous tissue to the human brain.[16]

CATECHOLAMINES

Two major classes of neurotransmitters studied in clinical psychiatry are the *catecholamines* and the *indoleamines*. The major indoleamine transmitter is serotonin. The term "catecholamine" designates three neurotransmitters which follow sequentially in the synthetic pathway illustrated in figure 3–5: dopamine, norepinephrine, and epinephrine.[2, 46, 56]

Dopamine was initially thought to be only a precursor in catecholamine synthesis, but is now recognized as a brain transmitter centrally involved in a variety of movement and severe behavior disorders. *Norepinephrine*, found in postganglionic sympathetic nerve endings, the adrenal medulla, and the spinal cord and brain, is released along with the enzyme which catalyzes its formation from dopamine, dopamine-β-hydroxylase (DBH). The third catecholamine, *epinephrine*, is found in the adrenal medulla, from which it is released into the blood to act on several other organs as a stress-related hormone.[37] Epinephrine recently has been identified in specific areas of the brain, where it is thought to function as a neurotransmitter.

NEURON AND SYNAPSE

A typical nerve cell consists of a *cell body*, straight or branched *axon*, and *dendritic tree*

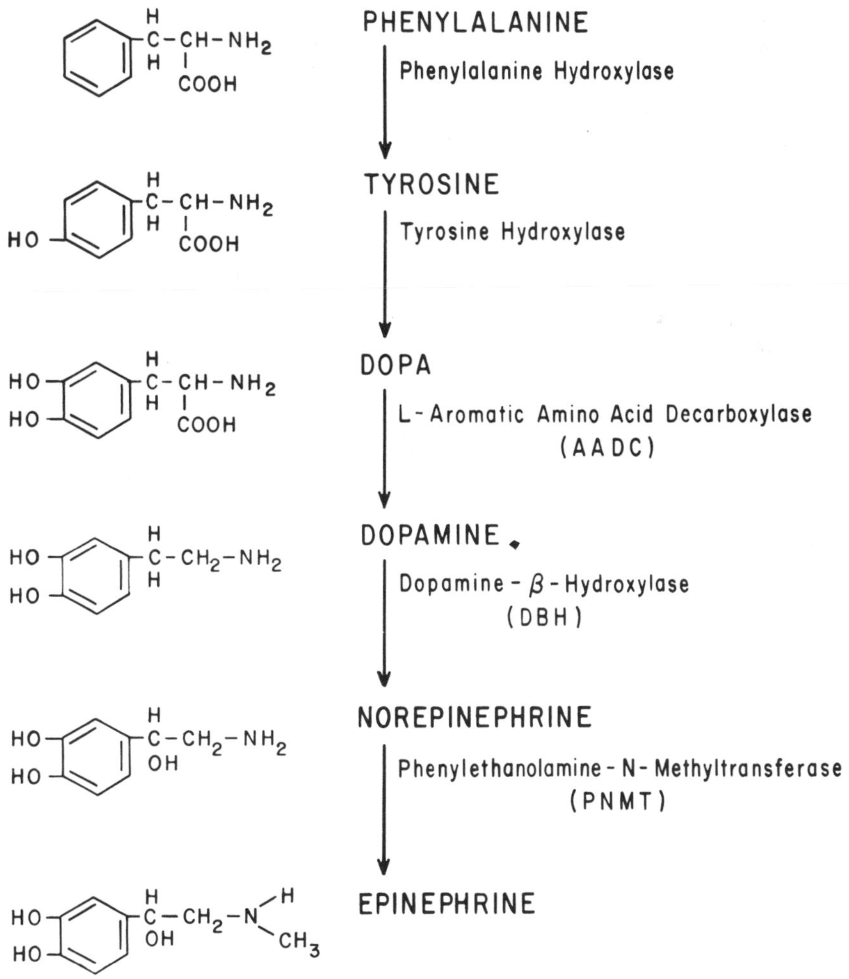

FIGURE 3–5
Synthetic pathway of catecholamines.

NOTE: Reprinted by permission of the publisher from "Neurochemistry and Child Psychiatry," by D. J. Cohen and J. G. Young, *Journal of the American Academy of Child Psychiatry*, 16:353–411, 1977.

which varies in size and complexity (figure 3–6). *Receptors* for transmitters released by other neurons are located primarily on the dendrites, as well as on the cell body and the small, proximal area of the axon, the hillock. Impulses generated by the neuron are conducted down the axon to its synaptic junction with another cell. *Axon terminals* have *varicosities* containing mitochondria and storage vesicles, but no ribosomes, so proteins cannot be synthesized. Enzymes such as tyrosine hydroxylase, necessary for the synthesis of the transmitter, are formed in the cell body and are transported down the axon to the varicosity, where the transmitter is synthesized and stored in *vesicles* or found free in the cytoplasm.

In noradrenergic neurons, a synthesizing enzyme is also stored in the vesicle with the norepinephrine and both are released following stimulation of the nerve. Transmitter release occurs through the process of *exocytosis*: a vesicle fuses with the cell membrane, an opening forms, and molecules move into the synaptic cleft. The unidentified mechanism which couples nerve impulse to secretion of the transmitter is of special interest with regard to drug action. When an impulse arrives at the nerve terminal, there is an influx of *calcium* into the terminal just prior to the release of the transmitter. Calcium might participate in the binding of synaptic vesicles to the presynaptic membrane.

The catecholamine metabolic pathway within

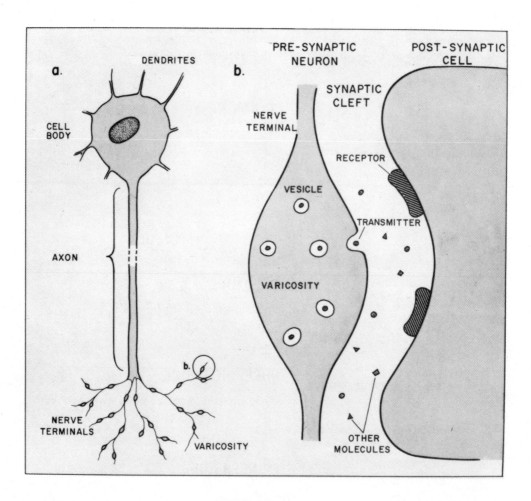

FIGURE 3–6

(a) Typical neuron with terminal varicosities at end of long axon. (b) Schematic representation of presynaptic varicosity, synaptic cleft, and postsynaptic cell.

NOTE: Modified from J. Axelrod, "Neurotransmitters," *Scientific American*, 230:58–71, 1974; reprinted by permission of the publisher from "Neurochemistry and Child Psychiatry," by D. J. Cohen and J. G. Young, *Journal of the American Academy of Child Psychiatry*, 16:353–411, 1977.

a varicosity of a noradrenergic neuron is depicted in figure 3–7. Norepinephrine is synthesized in the storage vesicle through the activity of the DBH present there. Protein and adenosine tri-phosphate (ATP) apparently bind the amines within the vesicle. The rate-limiting step of the synthesis is the point of action of tyrosine hydroxylase (TH), where a feedback mechanism of

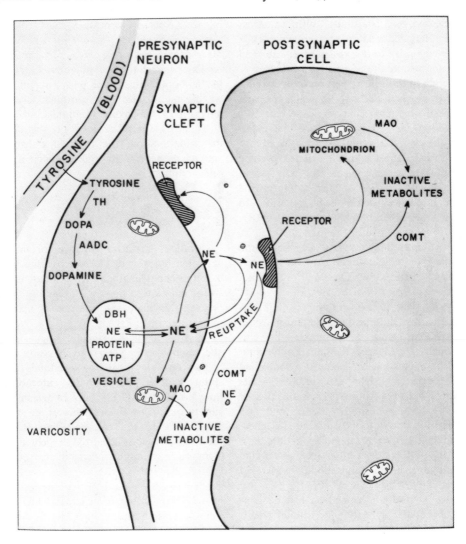

FIGURE 3–7

Norepinephrine synthesis, release, and inactivation in schematic pre- and post-synaptic cells.

TH = tyrosine hydroxylase
DOPA = dihydroxyphenylalanine
AADC = L-aromatic amino acid decarboxylase (DOPA decarboxylase)
DOPAMINE = dihydroxyphenylethylamine (DA)
DBH = dopamine-β-hydroxylase
NE = norepinephrine
ATP = adenosine triphosphate
MAO = monoamine oxidase
COMT = catechol-0-methyltransferase

NOTE: Modified from J. Axelrod, "Neurotransmitters," *Scientific American*, 230:58–71, 1974; reprinted by permission of the publisher from "Neurochemistry and Child Psychiatry," by D. J. Cohen and J. G. Young, *Journal of the American Academy of Child Psychiatry*, 16:353–411, 1977.

the transmitter substance on tyrosine hydroxylase inhibits its activity and reduces synthesis. Nerve stimulation lowers the level of transmitter in the varicosity, with a resultant decrease in inhibitory feedback.[16]

Once released, the transmitter diffuses across the synaptic cleft and acts on a *receptor* which is specifically responsive to this neurotransmitter and located on the membrane of the *postsynaptic cell*. The interaction of transmitter and receptor initiates sequential events specific to the cell type and function. Conformational changes in the receptors appear to allow ions to pass through the membrane, and the chemical signals are transduced into graded electrical signals by *ion currents*. In some neurotransmitter systems the receptor activates an enzyme, *adenylate cyclase*, which catalyzes the conversion of adenosine triphosphate (ATP) to cyclic adenosine monophosphate (cyclic AMP). *Cyclic AMP* is known as a "second messenger" because of an intracellular role analogous to the extracellular role of messenger compounds such as hormones (figure 3–8). The cyclic AMP activates *protein kinases* which function in ways specific to the type of cell. Although still hypothetical, the end result appears to be phosphorylation of proteins, such as membrane proteins (altering electrical properties) or nuclear histones (affecting the expression of genetically controlled metabolic properties). The cell returns to its initial state when (1) cyclic AMP is inactivated by another enzyme, *phosphodiesterase*; and (2) the mobile phosphate group utilized in phosphorylation is removed through the action of a phosphatase. *Xanthine derivatives* such as caffeine and theophylline inhibit phosphodiesterase and prolong the activity of cyclic AMP.

Functional control of the neuron can be considered at subcellular, synaptic, and cellular levels. Regulatory mechanisms at the *synapse*, generally known as *synaptic modulation*, utilize regulatory sites on the postsynaptic membrane. Nontransmitter molecules interact with regulatory sites, leading to conformational changes in adjacent receptor sites and modification of postsynaptic cell response. Substances which might contribute to synaptic modulation include other molecules released from the axon terminal, compounds originating in nearby glial cells, or hormones from distant tissues. For example, the amino acid glutamate nonspecifically depolarizes essentially all neurons and could act as a modulator of general neuronal excitability.

Exquisite regulation of neuronal function at the *cellular* level is achieved through a complex system of multiple self-modulatory influences. For example, in one neuronal control mechanism, *presynaptic receptor sites* become responsive to a critical concentration of transmitter in the synaptic cleft and the transmitter inhibits its own release. Another control system consists of a *"neuronal feedback loop"* in which increased firing of one neuron leads to an ultimate negative feedback mechanism via other consecutive neurons in the loop. A third type of self-regulation occurs when a neurotransmitter substance is released not only from the axon terminal, but also from anatomical *"specializations"* on the *dendrites* of the same neuron; the released transmitter then acts on its neuron of origin to elicit a process of self-inhibition.

METABOLISM AND RE-UPTAKE OF CATECHOLAMINES

Duration of transmitter-receptor interaction is regulated by processes of *inactivation* which must be rapid enough to achieve an adequately responsive fluctuation in signal information. Two general processes regulate the amount of catecholamine transmitter in the synaptic cleft: active re-uptake by the presynaptic neuron and other adjacent cells, and catabolism by specific enzymes.

Two enzymes *degrade catecholamines*: monoamine oxidase (MAO) and catechol-O-methyltransferase (COMT). *MAO* is present in a wide variety of tissues and oxidatively deaminates any monoamine to the corresponding aldehyde. Intraneuronally, it is localized largely in the outer membrane of mitochondria; it also occurs extraneuronally. Its activity in the accessible blood platelet has been the object of intensive study in recent years. Intraneuronal MAO metabolizes the transmitter and other amines free in the cytoplasm but does not affect vesicle-bound transmitter. It has a regulatory impact on catecholamine synthesis but its contribution to inactivation of the neurotransmitter in the synaptic cleft is apparently slight. *COMT* is also found in numerous tissues in man and methylates any catechol compound. Its function in the metabolism of catecholamines appears to be predominantly extraneuronal, where it plays an important role in transmitter inactivation.

Norepinephrine continues to be rapidly inactivated following the administration of compounds which specifically inhibit the activity of MAO and COMT. This inactivation is accomplished by *re-uptake* and binding by the *presynaptic neuron*, the dominant mechanism responsible for rapid

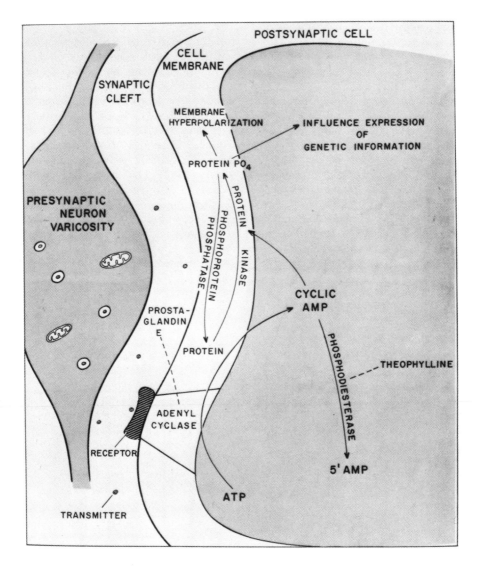

FIGURE 3–8

Schematic representation of proposed mechanism for receptor physiology at synapse.

NOTE: Modified from P. Greengard, D. A. McAfee, and J. W. Kebabian, "On the Mechanism of Action of Cyclic AMP and Its Role in Synaptic Transmission," in *Advances in Cyclic Nucleotide Research*, vol. 1, ed. P. Greengard and G. A. Robison (New York: Raven Press, 1972); reprinted by permission of the publisher from "Neurochemistry and Child Psychiatry," by D. J. Cohen and J. G. Young, *Journal of the American Academy of Child Psychiatry, 16*:353–411, 1977.

inactivation of the transmitter. Less importantly, extraneuronal cells may also take up transmitter with subsequent methylation by COMT.

In the catabolism of catecholamines by MAO and COMT, the intermediate products formed reflect the order in which the enzymes act. A general scheme for the lines of metabolism of a catecholamine (i.e., dopamine, norepinephrine, or epinephrine) is given in figure 3–9. Deamination by MAO leads to the formation of the corresponding aldehyde. This aldehyde is present only transiently and is rapidly metabolized by one of two reactions: oxidation to an acid by aldehyde dehydrogenase or reduction to an alcohol by aldehyde reductase. Figure 3–10 depicts the specific metabolic pathways for dopamine, norepinephrine, and epinephrine. For clarity, some transient intermediate aldehydes have been deleted, as well as clinically less significant portions of the pathways (for example, the catechol alcohol). The catecholamines and most of their metabolites are phenols, for which a common additional form of inactivation (not shown) is *conjugation* with glucuronic acid or sulfuric acid.

Norepinephrine and epinephrine metabolism leads to two major products, *VMA* and *MHPG*, depending upon whether oxidation (leading to VMA) or reduction (leading to MHPG) of the aldehyde predominates. The chief products of dopamine in the CNS are two acidic metabolites, *DOPAC* and *HVA*; HVA is the predominant metabolite in the cerebrospinal fluid and urine.[66] The principal pools of norepinephrine and epinephrine, their manner of inactivation, and their metabolic fate and products are described in table 3–2.[37]

INDOLEAMINES

Serotonin has been the subject of intensive research in relation to neurological and severe psychiatric disorders of childhood and has been implicated in a wide range of processes and disorders—temperature regulation, sensory perception, movement and seizure disorders, appetite, sleep, and mental retardation—but, in comparison with catecholamines, factors controlling the indoleamine synthetic pathways are less well defined (figure 3–11).[9] The rate-limiting step is the point of activity of tryptophan hydroxylase. Unlike the catecholamines, end-product inhibition is apparently insignificant. Factors that have been demonstrated to have an impact on serotonin synthesis are the level of neuronal activity, the availability of tryptophan in the diet, and the presence of

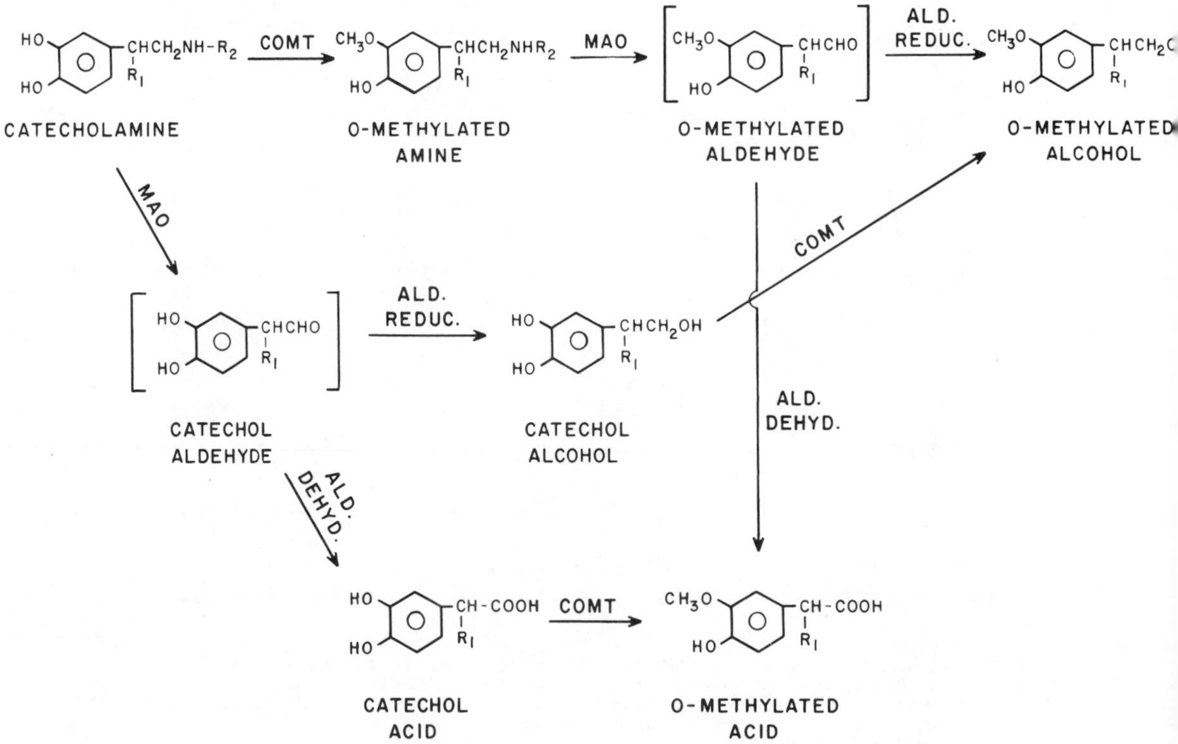

FIGURE 3–9

General pathway for metabolic degradation of catecholamines. R_1 and R_2 are side chain constituents which distinguish dopamine, norepinephrine, and epinephrine.
COMT = catechol-0-methyltransferase
MAO = monoamine oxidase
Ald. Reduc. = aldehyde reductase
Ald. Dehyd. = aldehyde dehydrogenase
Aldehyde intermediates, in brackets, exist only transiently.

NOTE: Reprinted by permission of the publisher from "Neurochemistry and Child Psychiatry," by D. J. Cohen and J. G. Young, *Journal of the American Academy of Child Psychiatry*, 16:353–411, 1977.

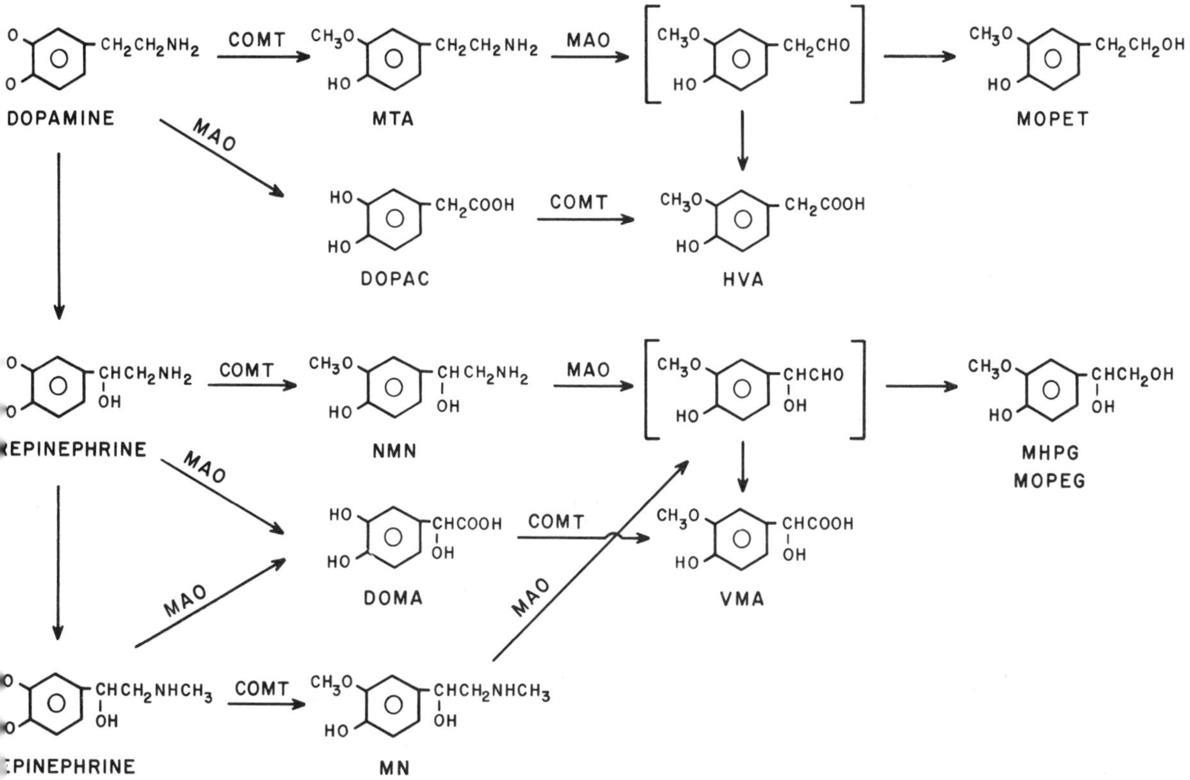

FIGURE 3–10

Specific pathways for metabolic degradation of dopamine, norepinephrine, and epinephrine, with minor steps and products omitted (see text). Aldehyde intermediates, in brackets, exists only transiently.
COMT = catechol-0-methyltransferase
MAO = monoamine oxidase
MTA = 3-methoxytyramine
DOPAC = 3,4-dihydroxyphenylacetic acid
NMN = normetanephrine
DOMA = 3,4-dihydroxymandelic acid
MN = metanephrine
HVA = homovanillic acid
VMA = vanillylmandelic acid
MOPET = 3-methoxy-4-hydroxy-phenylethanol (MHPE)
MHPG = 3-methoxy-4-hydroxy-phenylethyleneglycol (MOPEG)

NOTE: Reprinted by permission of the publisher from "Neurochemistry and Child Psychiatry," by D. J. Cohen and J. G. Young, *Journal of the American Academy of Child Psychiatry*, 16:353–411, 1977.

oxygen and pteridine. The major mechanism for the metabolism of serotonin is degradation by MAO with subsequent oxidation to 5-hydroxy-indoleacetic acid (*5-HIAA*). The neuronal *uptake* process for serotonin is similar to that for the catecholamines. Serotonin reaches a much higher concentration in the pineal gland than in any other tissue, and its levels there vary according to a diurnal rhythm.[3]

ACETYLCHOLINE

Acetylcholine (ACh) has been studied in the peripheral nervous system for decades, but its transmitter function in the CNS has been clarified in only a preliminary way. The structure of the ACh molecule is $CH_3COOCH_2CH_2N(CH_3)_3$; the methyl and carbonyl sides of the molecule have differing affinities for the two receptor types to be

TABLE 3–2

Inactivation and Fate of Norepinephrine and Epinephrine

Pool	Inactivation*	Metabolic Fate†	Excretory Products
NE released from the sympathetic nerve endings	1° Re-uptake 2° O-methylation	Excretion unchanged or conjugated; O-methylation followed in part by deamination	Free or conjugated NE and NMN; VMA
Circulating E (from adrenal medulla) or NE (from adrenergic synapses)	1° O-methylation 2° Uptake	Excretion unchanged or conjugated; O-methylation followed in part by deamination	Free and conjugated catecholamines and metanephrines; VMA
NE stored in nerve endings	Inactive in stored form	Intraneuronal deamination followed by O-methylation	VMA
CNS NE	Re-uptake O-methylation Deamination	O-methylation Deamination	MHPG VMA

* Termination of biologic effects
† Principal metabolic pathway
1° = Principal
2° = Subsidiary

NOTE: Modified from R. J. Levine and L. Landsberg, "Catecholamines and the Adrenal Medulla," in *Duncan's Diseases of Metabolism*, ed. P. K. Bondy and L. E. Rosenberg (Philadelphia: W. B. Saunders, 1974); reprinted by permission of the publisher from "Neurochemistry and Child Psychiatry," by D. J. Cohen and J. G. Young, *Journal of the American Academy of Child Psychiatry*, 16:353–411, 1977.

described. The final step in the synthesis of acetylcholine (ACh), the acetylation of choline with acetyl coenzyme A, is catalyzed by *choline acetyltransferase (CAT)*. When released at the synapse, ACh activity is terminated by a rapid hydrolysis facilitated by the enzyme *acetylcholinesterase (AChE)*. A variety of inhibitors of AChE are used in clinical medicine, all based on their prolongation of the availability of ACh at the receptor. The most familiar of these is physostigmine.

Acetylcholine receptors in the periphery have classically been described as either muscarinic, or nicotinic, because the effect of ACh can be mimicked by one or the other of these alkaloids, depending on the receptor site examined. In the *muscarinic* effect, ACh from the postganglionic parasympathetic cell (for example, the vagus nerve) acts on the autonomic effector cell (for example, smooth muscle of the intestine or heart) to produce an action which is slow in onset but relatively sustained. This muscarinic action at the receptor is blocked by atropine and other drugs. In the *nicotinic* effect, ACh is released from two types of presynaptic neurons: the motor nerves (acting on end-plates of skeletal muscles) and preganglionic autonomic fibers (acting on autonomic ganglion cells). The ACh initiates two dose-related effects on nicotinic receptors. At low concentrations, ACh rapidly stimulates the receptors; at higher concentrations, receptors are blocked. Curare and similar drugs block all activity at the nicotinic receptors.[32]

Like serotonin, ACh levels in the brain are partially controlled by the availability of its precursor, *choline*. Another rate-regulatory mechanism in the cholinergic neuron is feedback inhibition on CAT by the end product, ACh.

ENKEPHALINS AND ENDORPHINS

Opioid peptides are transmitters consisting of a series of amino acids. Two pentapeptide transmitters have been isolated from the brain, identical except for their terminal amino acid: *leucine-enkephalin* (consisting of the amino acids tyrosine-glycine-glycine-phenylalanine-leucine) and *methionine-enkephalin* (consisting of tyrosine-glycine-glycine-phenylalanine-methionine). Three longer opioid peptides, known as *endorphins*, have been isolated from the pituitary. Endorphins contain

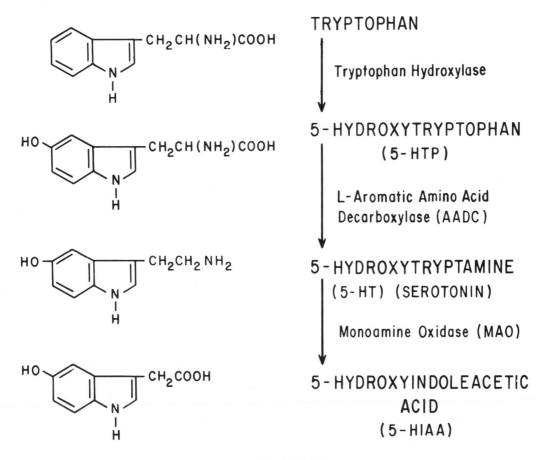

TRYPTOPHAN

Tryptophan Hydroxylase

5-HYDROXYTRYPTOPHAN
(5-HTP)

L-Aromatic Amino Acid
Decarboxylase (AADC)

5-HYDROXYTRYPTAMINE
(5-HT) (SEROTONIN)

Monoamine Oxidase (MAO)

5-HYDROXYINDOLEACETIC
ACID
(5-HIAA)

FIGURE 3–11
Synthesis and metabolism of serotonin.

NOTE: Reprinted by permission of the publisher from "Neurochemistry and Child Psychiatry," by D. J. Cohen and J. G. Young, *Journal of the American Academy of Child Psychiatry*, 16:353–411, 1977.

the methionine-enkephalin peptide as one segment. The enkephalins and endorphins are all contained as segments of a 91 amino acid pituitary peptide, *beta lipotropin*. This larger peptide appears to be the inactive prohormone from which the smaller, biologically active peptides are cleaved, under the control of still unknown mechanisms.[24]

Enkephalins and endorphins were discovered in the search for the endogenous substances which react with the specific brain receptors for opiates, such as morphine. Drugs with a spectrum of opiate effects bind to these receptors: opiate agonists with high addictive potential (morphine); opiate antagonists which block narcotic effects (naloxone); and drugs which have mixed, agonist and antagonist effects (nalorphine and pentazocine). The *opiate receptor* has two conformations, depending on the local concentration of sodium. In the presence of sodium, the receptor equilibrium tends toward the antagonist conformation and the

dissociation of morphine, leading to a sixty-fold reduction in its potency. Sodium reduces the agonist activity of drugs with mixed, morphinelike effects (the "sodium index"). The binding of antagonist drugs to the receptor is not affected by sodium.[61]

The mechanism of the neurotransmitter action of peptides is not fully understood. Enkephalins and endorphins may decrease neuronal activity by reducing sodium permeability at the ion channel in neuronal membranes. The agonist conformation of the opiate receptor appears to be linked with the inhibition of adenylate cyclase, the enzyme involved in the formation of cyclic AMP.

NEURONAL LOCALIZATION IN THE BRAIN

Neurons utilizing a specific transmitter are not uniformly distributed throughout the intact brain. Techniques such as fluorescence histochemistry

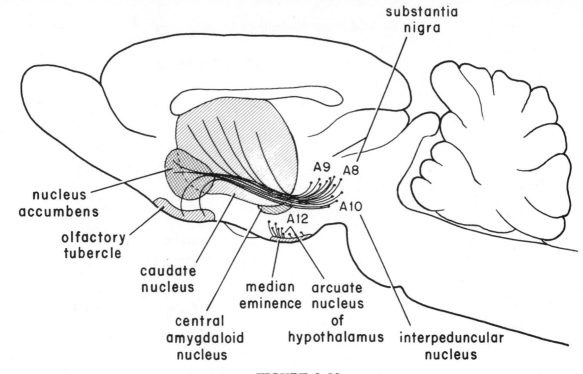

FIGURE 3–12

Schematic representation of major dopamine neural tracts in rat brain. Shaded areas indicate principal nerve termination regions. Nomenclature of cell groups as in Dahlström and Fuxe, 1965.

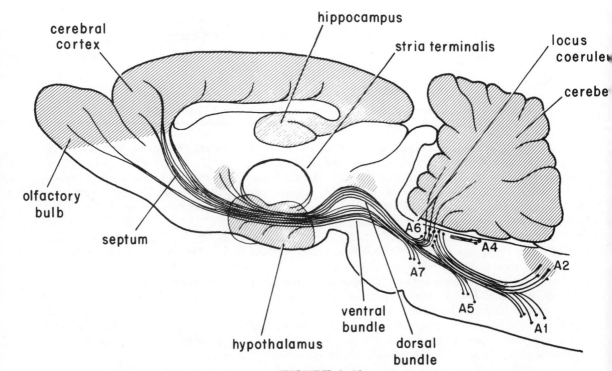

FIGURE 3–13

Schematic representation of major ascending norepinephrine neural tracts in rat brain. Shaded areas indicate principal nerve terminal regions. Nomenclature of cell groups as in Dahlström and Fuxe, 1965.

NOTE: Modified from U. Ungerstedt, "Sterotoxic Mapping of the Monoamine Pathways in the Rat Brain," *Acta Physiologica Scandinavica* (Suppl. 367), 1–29, 1971, and J. R. Cooper, F. E. Bloom, and R. H. Roth, *The Biochemical Basis of Neuropharmacology* (New York: Oxford University Press, 1974); reprinted by permission of the publisher from "Neurochemistry and Child Psychiatry," by D. J. Cohen and J. G. Young, *Journal of the American Academy of Child Psychiatry*, 16:353–411, 1977.

permit localization of discrete transmitter-specific neuronal populations. For example, when freeze-dried brain sections are exposed to formaldehyde vapors, condensation of formaldehyde with catecholamine molecules results in compounds which emit a green fluorescence; this produces the distinctive appearance of catecholamine-containing nerve terminals in the fluorescence micrograph.[17] Neurotransmitter mapping may suggest functional hypotheses. For example, a disease presumably involving a neuroanatomical locale might then logically be approached with drugs affecting a relevant specific transmitter system, an approach most vividly illustrated by the findings in Parkinson's disease of anatomical changes in the substantia nigra and biochemical depletion of dopamine in the caudate nucleus.

Dopaminergic Neurons: Figures 3–12, 3–13, and 3–14 schematically map the dopamine and norepinephrine tracts within the rat brain. Cell bodies of dopaminergic neurons lie rostrally and contribute axons to three dopamine systems. The

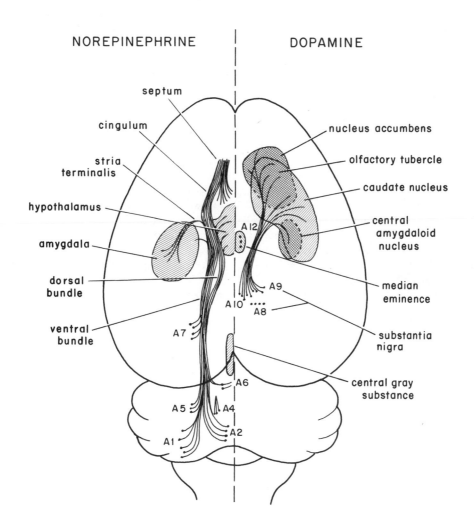

FIGURE 3–14

Schematic representation of horizontal projection of ascending dopamine and norepinephrine neural tracts in rat brain. Shaded areas indicate principal nerve terminal regions. Nomenclature of cell groups as in Dahlström and Fuxe.[17]

NOTE: Modified from U. Ungerstedt, "Sterotoxic Mapping of the Monoamine Pathways in the Rat Brain," *Acta Physiologica Scandinavica* (Suppl. 367), 1–29, 1971; reprinted by permission of the publisher from "Neurochemistry and Child Psychiatry," by D. J. Cohen and J. G. Young, *Journal of the American Academy of Child Psychiatry,* 16:353–411, 1977.

nigrostriatal system, active in motor control, projects from the substantia nigra (A8 and A9 in figures 3–12 and 3–14) to the caudate and amygdaloid nuclei. The *mesolimbic* projection, possibly involved in emotional responses, arises from the region dorsal to the interpeduncular nucleus (A10) and terminates in the nucleus accumbens and olfactory tubercle. Terminals in the cingulate cortex and parts of the frontal cortex have also been described. The *hypothalamic* dopamine system, concerned with hypothalamic-pituitary-endocrine regulation, lies completely within the hypothalamus; cell bodies are found in the arcuate nucleus and innervate the median eminence. Also, there may be dopaminergic projections to the spinal cord.[65]

Noradrenergic Neurons: The pons and medulla oblongata are the locus for cell bodies of the norepinephrine-containing (or noradrenergic) neurons. Cell bodies are found in compact groups, but the nerve terminals spread diffusely through many brain regions and the spinal cord. The first of two ascending noradrenergic tracts projects from the *locus coeruleus* (A6 in figures 3–13 and 3–14) via the *dorsal bundle* to the cerebral cortex, the cerebellar cortex, and the hippocampus. A *ventral noradrenergic bundle* from other cell groups innervates the lower brain stem and, via the medial forebrain bundle, the hypothalamus and limbic system.[65] Stimulation and lesions of the locus coeruleus have provided direct methods for assessing the impact of noradrenergic pathways on behavior and emotions. Two *descending tracts* are significant in the control of blood pressure. The widespread distribution of noradrenergic fibers is consistent with the prominent role this system plays in the modulation of emotional state and mood.

Serotonergic Neurons: Because the yellow fluorescence of serotonin-containing nerve terminals is weak and the serotonin pathways are diffuse, it has been difficult to identify all the areas innervated. Figure 3–15 depicts the major known tracts and terminal regions. Serotonergic cell bodies are found in the *nuclei* of the *raphe system*, a midline brain stem structure (figure 3–15, B5 to B9). *Ascending* projections reach multiple brain regions, including the hypothalamus, amygdala, forebrain, and cerebral cortex. Fibers also *descend* (from B1 to B3) to the lower brain stem and the spinal cord.[1, 6, 22] There may be another nonserotonergic system of indoleamine-containing neurons in the raphe nuclei. Inhibitory serotonergic neurons have been postulated to play a role in screening or sensory-gating mechanisms and the control of arousal. Their broad distribution would make them suitable for exerting a pervasive influence on CNS function (for example, in regulation of state).

Cholinergic Neurons: Acetylcholine has both muscarinic and nicotinic effects in the brain, as well as a novel inhibitory effect. However, it is unusual for a brain neuron to have a single characteristic response to ACh. Most cells appear to have either a receptor with an intermediate response or more than one type of ACh receptor.

Relatively pure, slow muscarinic excitation occurs only in the deeper neuronal layers of the forebrain. Mixed muscarinic excitation has been found in varying degrees elsewhere in the cortex, in other brain areas, and in the spinal cord. Also, presynaptic muscarinic receptors have been found in several brain areas. Rapid, nicotinic response is clearly observed only in the Renshaw cells of the spinal cord, innervated by recurrent collateral branches of motor neurons. Inhibitory muscarinic receptors, found in superficial cortical neurons, have a depressant action on single neuronal discharges.[34]

The most generally distributed effect of ACh throughout the brain is slow muscarinic excitation, which is unsuited to fast, discrete signal transmission. Stimulation of these ACh receptors leads to decreased potassium conductance at the membrane; neurons become more excitable and responsive and neurotransmission is enhanced. This process may have a slowly developing, arousing influence on CNS activity. For example, stimulation of the *reticular activating system (RAS)* activates the cerebral cortex and leads to the release of cortical ACh, a phenomenon which can be inhibited by muscarinic antagonists. This cortical ACh release has been suggested as a physiological basis for conscious awareness and, at local structural levels, as an aspect of conditioned learning and memory.

Enkephalin and Endorphin Neurons: Enkephalin nerve terminals and axons are concentrated in areas of the brain rich in receptors for opiates. The distribution of these drug receptors, determined by autoradiographic binding of isotopically labeled opiates, such as (^{3}H) naloxone, agrees with the clinical neuroanatomical description of pain perception. These areas include brain structures subserving *deep* (but not fine) *pain perception* (medial thalamic nuclei, substantia gelatinosa of the spinal cord and trigeminal nucleus) and *emotional responsivity* (amygdala). Anatomical

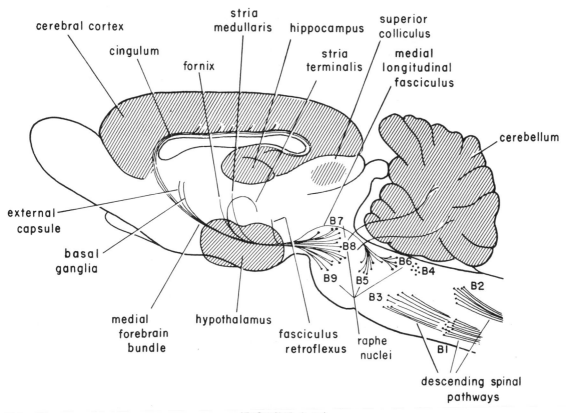

FIGURE 3–15

Schematic representation of major serotonin neural tracts in rat brain. Shaded areas indicate principal nerve terminal regions. Nomenclature of cell groups as in Dahlström and Fuxe.[17]

NOTE: Modified from G. R. Breese, "Chemical and Immunochemical Lesions by Specific Neurotoxic Substances and Antigera," in *Handbook of Psychopharmacology*, vol. 1, *Biochemical Principles and Techniques in Neuropharmacology*, ed. L. L. Iversen, S. D. Iversen, and S. H. Snyder (New York: Plenum Press, 1975) and K. Fuxe and G. Jonsson, "Further Mapping of Central 5-Hydroxytryptamine Neurons: Studies with the Neurotoxic Dihydroxytryptamines," in *Serotonin—New Vistas: Histochemistry and Pharmacology* (New York: Raven Press, 1974); reprinted by permission of the publisher from "Neurochemistry and Child Psychiatry," by D. J. Cohen and J. G. Young, *Journal of the American Academy of Child Psychiatry*, 16:353–411, 1977.

structures predicted by opiate side effects, such as decreased coughing, blood pressure, and gastric secretion (solitary nucleus of the brainstem) or nausea and vomiting (area postrema and the chemoreceptor trigger zone) are also regions endowed with opiate receptors.[61]

The endorphins are found in the pituitary, especially the posterior pituitary, where opiate receptors appear to be involved with hormone release.

In addition to the enkephalins, many other amino acid and peptide neurotransmitters and hormones have been identified, such as glycine and somatostatin. These compounds are broadly distributed in the brain, gastrointestinal tract, and other organs; their interrelations and physiological functions are only in the first stages of clarification.

DIET AND NEUROTRANSMITTERS

Many well-defined physical and behavioral syndromes are related to gross disturbances in diet, to the inability to appropriately utilize food, to unusual physiological reactions to normal dietary constituents, or to dietary deficiencies at crucial periods of development. Familiar examples are pellagra and pernicious anemia, malabsorption syndromes, favism and other inborn errors of metabolism, protein-calorie malnutrition (kwashiorkor), and true reactive hypoglycemia. Some conditions respond dramatically to dietary management or replacement—for example, injections of vitamin B_{12}, gluten-free diets, avoidance of the fava bean, control of carbohydrate intake. In addition, there are common-sense observations on the importance of reasonable diet for optimal performance in childhood, for example, that hungry children are less likely to concentrate in school. There is increasing popular interest in the relation between diet and behavior. Research on the impact of subtle dietary variations on long-term behavioral change is, however, methodologically difficult, and few, if any, studies have been done in childhood in which description of method, results, and controls have approached rigorous standards.

Investigations with animal models have demonstrated an "openness" of brain neurotransmitter metabolism to the influence of dietary precursor availability. Brain concentration of *serotonin* is partially controlled by the availability of dietary tryptophan. This regulatory system is dependent on an active transport system for the precursor into the brain, for which tryptophan must compete with other neutral amino acids. Tryptophan uptake into the brain is affected by the amount of ingested protein and its amino acid composition, as well as by alterations in concentrations of plasma amino acids which result from the release of insulin following ingestion of carbohydrates. Tyrosine and phenylalanine compete with tryptophan for the carrier system, and the brain uptake of tyrosine appears to affect the synthesis of catecholamines. *Acetylcholine* is more sensitive to diet than indoleamines and catecholamines. Augmenting dietary choline increases ACH synthesis and release at the synapse, altering postsynaptic dopaminergic function (for example, in the caudate, where the concentration of the catecholamine synthesizing enzyme, tyrosine hydroxylase, increases in response to choline administration).[69] The sensitivity of the cholinergic system to dietary manipulation is therapeutically useful in the treatment of tardive dyskinesia, a movement disorder associated with chronic use of neuroleptics. The amelioration of this syndrome with choline suggests an underlying imbalance between cholinergic and dopaminergic activity in the striatum (as in Parkinson's disease). In addition to precursors, the availability of dietary vitamins (which serve as cofactors in the synthesis of neurotransmitters) and inorganic ions has a clearly defined impact on CNS metabolism.

The role of neurotransmitters in the monitoring of fluctuations of metabolic state is evident in the hypothalamic control of satiety and hunger. Depletion or disruption of indoleamine and catecholamine pathways leads to profound disturbances in eating and in body weight. The availability of precursors and other compounds necessary for normal neuronal functioning may enter into complex feedback systems and affect organized behavior patterns (such as food-seeking). The anorectant effect of stimulants appears to depend on such mechanisms, and the significance of neurotransmitter metabolism for studies of disorders of eating and mood (such as anorexia nervosa and forms of obesity) is a promising new area of study.

Clinical Neurochemical Investigation

The relation of impaired neurotransmitter metabolism to specific clinical syndromes or symptom clusters is difficult to investigate. First, it is not likely that only one transmitter neuronal system would be involved in an illness. Presumably, in syndromes such as the childhood psychoses, many different kinds of cells are affected and a balance between neuronal systems is upset. Second, the types of specimens which can be obtained to test hypotheses about brain transmitters are severely limited. Since biopsy specimens can rarely be obtained from the living human brain, except for therapeutic and diagnostic neurosurgical procedures, researchers are restricted to the use of a variety of indirect techniques involving problematic assumptions. Six indirect clinical research methods will be described.

BLOOD

Plasma and Whole Blood: Catecholamines in plasma are derived from sympathetic nerve endings and the adrenal medulla, rather than the central nervous system. Because of the blood-brain barrier, unmetabolized catecholamines from the brain do not ordinarily reach the peripheral circulation. However, activation of central noradrenergic mechanisms, for example, by stimulation of the locus coeruleus, may increase plasma levels of catecholamines or metabolites (such as MHPG) through descending noradrenergic pathways to the spinal cord. *Norepinephrine* in the plasma represents the very small amount which escapes inactivation by re-uptake or metabolism (at peripheral adrenergic synapses) and which is not metabolized in such organs as the liver and lung. Plasma *epinephrine* is the direct product of adrenal chromaffin cells. Determination of plasma catecholamine concentrations has, until recent years, involved fluorometric assays with a sensitivity inadequate for the very small amounts present in plasma. Reliability and sensitivity have improved with less complicated radiometric enzymatic assays which have been used to define sympathetic nervous system function in response to physiological stimuli (for example, postural change, the cold pressor test, and exercise) and in various disease states (for example, hypertension).

About 90 percent of the *serotonin* in the body is in the gastrointestinal tract; another 8 or 9 percent is in the platelets. The remaining 1 or 2 percent is CNS serotonin. Serotonin, like the catecholamines, does not cross the blood-brain barrier. Nearly all of the whole blood serotonin is contained in the platelets, where it is concentrated by an active transport system located in the platelet membrane. Assays are available for whole blood serotonin, platelet serotonin, and whole blood 5-hydroxyindoles (5 HI). Of the latter usually 99 percent is serotonin and 1 percent is 5-HIAA, except in the presence of a carcinoid tumor. In sum, catecholamine and serotonin concentrations in blood specimens provide a measure of peripheral metabolism, and plasma norepinephrine indirectly reflects central nervous system noradrenergic activity.

The accessibility and convenience of using blood specimens has led to an intensive search for possible abnormalities in central enzyme systems which may be reflected in peripheral enzyme levels. Relevant enzymes in the major synthetic pathways are indicated in figures 3–5 and 3–11. The rate-limiting step for the catecholamine pathway is the hydroxylation of tyrosine to form DOPA by *tyrosine hydroxylase (TH)*, an intracellular enzyme which is soluble in the cytoplasm. Tyrosine hydroxylase is present in the adrenal medulla, adrenergic nervous tissue, and brain, but is not ordinarily present in the blood. *DBH*, another intracellular enzyme, is found in soluble and membrane-bound forms in storage vesicles of the nerve endings; it catalyzes the final step in the formation of norepinephrine and is released with norepinephrine into the synaptic cleft. DBH thus has access to the bloodstream, and it had been hoped that it might provide an index of sympathetic activity because of its proportional release with the transmitter from neuronal vesicles. Large differences in serum DBH activity are observed among individuals with equally competent sympathetic function, and genetic control is the predominant influence on serum DBH concentrations. Comparisons across diagnostic groups, therefore, must be very cautiously interpreted. However,

there are some interesting correlations between serum DBH levels and changes in physiological processes under autonomic control, such as blood pressure, which suggest the possible value of DBH determination as a marker of an individual's change of state.

Platelets: Blood platelets share several critical features with monoamine neurons and serve as a useful biochemical model in studies of serotonin, dopamine, and MAO. The *Shared characteristics* include an active transport system, located in the cell membrane, for active uptake of biogenic amines; distinctive intracellular vesicles for amine storage; the presence of metabolically relevant enzymes; and similarity in receptor function and response to drugs. Studies of platelet models are more convenient than work with less accessible and more complex central or peripheral neurons; yet, these two types of tissue may be fundamentally different in the expression of underlying disturbances in amine metabolism because of the different roles the amines play in brain transmission and blood coagulation. Extrapolations, thus, must be cautious, and even basic questions, such as the relation between platelet and brain MAO levels, are only at the first stage of resolution.[48]

URINE

The urine contains a variety of neurotransmitters and metabolites, derived from various sources (table 3–3). Clearly, free epinephrine and norepinephrine comprise only a small percentage of the total excretion, with VMA and MHPG predominating. Peripheral neuronal activity and the adrenal gland contribute minor metabolites in addition to VMA and MHPG. The central nervous system, in contrast, contributes little to the minor metabolites but preferentially metabolizes norepinephrine to MHPG and, less importantly, VMA.[39] MHPG diffuses into the peripheral circulation, as well as into the cerebrospinal fluid (CSF). The preferential metabolism of *brain NE* to *MHPG* is important for clinical research, because it means that MHPG, although measured in a peripheral fluid, nevertheless is largely the product of brain metabolism and reflects central noradrenergic activity. Measurement of MHPG in twenty-four-hour urine specimens provides the best available clinical method using urine for assessing brain norepinephrine metabolism and has been widely employed in clinical studies of depression and mania.[38] Urinary metabolites of dopamine, primarily HVA, are overwhelmingly the result of peripheral metabolism, and their

TABLE 3–3

Representative Excretion of Norepinephrine and Epinephrine and Their Metabolites in Humans

	μg./day*	% of Total Excretion	Source†
Epinephrine (free)	5	0.1	ADRENAL MEDULLA
NE (free)	30	0.4	SYMPATHETIC NERVE ENDINGS Adrenal medulla
Conjugated catecholamines	100	1.6	SYMPATHETIC NERVE ENDINGS Dietary catecholamines Adrenal medulla
MN (Total)	65	1.0	ADRENAL MEDULLA
NMN (Total)	100	1.6	SYMPATHETIC NERVE ENDINGS Adrenal medulla
VMA	4000	63.5	SYMPATHETIC NERVE ENDINGS (Storage pool) ADRENAL MEDULLA, BRAIN
MHPG	2000	31.8	BRAIN SYMPATHETIC NERVE ENDINGS (Storage pool) ADRENAL MEDULLA
TOTAL	6300	100	

* Average approximate figures from literature; not upper limits.
† Major sources in capitals.

NOTE: Modified from R. J. Levine and L. Landsberg, "Catecholamines and the Adrenal Medulla," in *Duncan's Diseases of Metabolism*, ed. P. K. Bandy and L. E. Rosenberg (Philadelphia: W. B. Saunders, 1974); reprinted by permission of the publisher from "Neurochemistry and Child Psychiatry," by D J. Cohen and J. G. Young, *Journal of the American Academy of Child Psychiatry*, 16:353–411, 1977.

measurement has contributed little to understanding CNS function.

CEREBROSPINAL FLUID

The brain is bathed by CSF which is constantly produced, circulated within the brain ventricles and spinal canal, and reabsorbed into the peripheral circulation. In addition to proteins and cells, the CSF contains a variety of compounds related to neural transmission. The neurotransmitters themselves are found in such low concentrations that their measurement has not been feasible until recently; the NE concentration in CSF, for example, is reported to be approximately 60 percent of the plasma NE concentration. However, the major metabolites of dopamine, serotonin, and norepinephrine (*HVA, 5-HIAA*, and *MHPG*, respectively) are relatively easily measured by fluorometric and mass spectrometric methods; the more sensitive, newer methods also permit the study of other metabolites, such as *DOPAC*. Endorphins can be assayed by radioimmunoassay and other techniques, but these studies are now only at the first stages.

HVA, 5-HIAA, and MHPG are produced as the result of brain metabolism and are transported into the CSF, from which they are actively removed. Measurement of metabolites has been used as an index of "turnover rate" for the parent amines within the brain—the rate at which the amine pool in the brain is replaced. "*Turnover rate*" reflects neuronal activity and is not the same as the actual synthesis rate of a neurotransmitter. In conditions such as Parkinson's, reduced brain synthesis of dopamine is reflected in reduced CSF concentrations of HVA. While measurement of CSF metabolites is the most direct method currently available for clinical study of brain biochemistry, there are many methodological and conceptual problems.

Interpretation of HVA and 5-HIAA concentrations in the CSF is hazardous for several reasons. First, the CSF is a dynamic system in which components are constantly removed and replenished. The acid metabolites of dopamine and serotonin are among these components, and their concentration at any one moment reflects the resultant of brain turnover, secretion into the CSF, and active removal. A specific value may not reliably indicate brain function during a day. Second, the concentrations of HVA and 5-HIAA in the CSF are so low that measurement error may obscure findings, especially using fluorometric methods. Third, the concentrations of the metabolites are not homogeneous throughout the course of the CSF; the metabolism of the spinal cord, for example, contributes substantially to the 5-HIAA and MHPG concentrations of the CSF obtained from the lumbar space. Fourth, concentration of the metabolites in the CSF does not reflect neurotransmitter function in all parts of the brain to an equal extent. Brain activity in areas adjacent to the ventricles (for example, the basal ganglia) may be more accurately represented than activity in areas more distant from the CSF (for example, the cerebral cortex). Fifth, to obtain CSF one must perform a lumbar puncture, an uncomfortable procedure which introduces new parameters such as anxiety and physical manipulation. If CSF metabolites relate to an individual's state as well as an enduring behavioral or pathological trait, the procedures involved in obtaining CSF may influence biochemical findings. And, sixth, the CSF metabolite pool probably reflects global brain function; alterations in biogenic amine metabolism in small areas of the brain, even those near the ventricles, may have profound effects on CNS physiology yet lead to inconsequential change in the concentration of a metabolite in the lumbar CSF.

Two of these methodological problems—moment-to-moment variability and low metabolic concentration—may, in part, be overcome by the use of probenecid loading. *Probenecid,* a benzoic acid derivative, blocks membrane transport in various organs. In clinical medicine, it is used to block active transport in the kidney in order to achieve higher levels of penicillin in the blood (by blocking penicillin transport into the urine) or to reduce blood uric acid in patients with gout (by blocking reabsorption of uric acid from urine). In the brain, probenecid reduces the active reabsorption of the metabolites of biogenic amines, HVA, 5-HIAA, and MHPG, from the CSF. When their egress is blocked over a period of time (usually eight to eighteen hours), the concentrations of the metabolites increase and progressively become more reliable indicators of turnover of the parent amines in the brain substance during a representative period.

The use of probenecid introduces its own methodological difficulties: It tends to produce stomach irritation and nausea, and the blockade produced by probenecid is not all or none, but progressive. Until a relatively high level of probenecid is reached, the concentrations of the metabolites are, in part, a function of the degree of blockade which has been achieved. This relationship must be considered in interpreting biogenic amine metabolite data. Differences between individuals (and populations) must also be considered. More cooperative patients may ingest, or retain, more of the prescribed probenecid than less compliant individuals, and there may be individual and group differences in gastrointestinal absorption and the effect of the medication in producing blockade. Thus, probenecid must be measured in the CSF and the metabolite concentration expressed in relation to the level of probenecid achieved.[15]

POST-MORTEM WHOLE BRAIN

Problems in the use of post-mortem brain specimens include obtaining the specimen, lack of historical information about the subject including concurrent diseases or drug usage, and rapid post-mortem decline in activity of the monoamines and related enzymes. These difficulties have been overcome with more success in neurological than psychiatric diseases, for example, in the demonstration of reduced dopamine in the basal ganglia of patients with Parkinson's disease. Studies of synthesizing enzymes and amines in the brains of schizophrenics have been suggestive but equivocal. Since amine concentrations vary widely between brain areas, studies must be performed on discrete regions suggested by theoretical models; this may be particularly important in mental illnesses. Post-mortem fluorescence histochemistry offers the possibility of demonstrating impaired function in specific monoamine systems.

ANIMAL MODELS

Use of an animal model allows direct access to brain neuronal systems and the possibility of precise anatomical, biochemical, and functional correlations. These studies can illuminate normal physiology but are limited by the unavailability of animal models for many psychiatric disorders. While the use of primates is generally desirable, the cost and practical problems in studying a sufficient number of animals has often led to the use of more distant species, generally the rat. The comparative ease with which rodent early life experiences can be manipulated and longitudinal studies of multiple generations can be undertaken make the animal model especially attractive for child psychiatric research.

Ideal animal models for human developmental disorders would satisfy the following criteria: (1) the syndrome produced in animals would share the cardinal, diagnostic criteria of the human syndrome; (2) the pathogenesis of the animal syndrome would bear a theoretical or actual similarity to the pathogenesis of the human disorder; (3) the animal syndrome would be produced in the developing organism, not only in the mature animal, and would follow a developmental course similar to that of the human counterpart; and (4) the response of the animal syndrome to intervention—for example, therapy with medication—would parallel the response seen clinically in children. Usually, animal models of human diseases represent abstractions and analogies, and fall short of the ideal. As abstractions, the models isolate one factor or set of factors for more refined analysis. As analogies, they are founded on the idea that syndromes that are alike in some ways (for example, major symptoms) may be alike in others (for example, underlying pathophysiology).

Relatively few animal models for child or adult psychiatric disorders have been proposed which convincingly satisfy the major criteria and have been the subject of metabolic investigation. Based on Harlow's observations of young monkeys reared without mothers, ethologists have described the profound and enduring impact of separation and the phenomena associated with reunion. These studies serve as animal models of separation distress and anaclitic depression, as well as, perhaps, more prolonged psychopathological syndromes.[5, 29] A variety of experimental methods have been advanced as models of the minimal brain dysfunction (MBD) syndrome. These include administration of lead compounds, viral infections of the central nervous system, and surgical lesions of the brain (especially the corpus callosum). One neurochemical model utilizes the permanent depletion of brain dopamine in infant rats by the intracisternal injection of 6-hydroxydopamine. Animals depleted of brain dopamine in this manner display disturbances in activity, habituation, and learning, and respond positively to stimulant medication (such as methylphenidate) in a manner analogous to certain neuropsychiatrically impaired children. While the animal's activity tends to normalize, behavioral and social deficits persist into adulthood, as has been observed in the human syndrome.[2, 58]

As a single strategy among many, animal models extend understanding of brain-behavior relations and permit pharmacological and behavioral manipulations which are not possible with humans. However, they are relevant and interpretable only in the context of other clinical investigations.

PHARMACOLOGICAL STUDIES

Drugs are used as chemical probes in dissecting neuronal function and neurotransmitter metabolism. By augmenting or inhibiting enzymatic and neurophysiological processes (for example, reuptake and release), medications may reveal the relative importance of various neurotransmitter systems, control mechanisms, and the potential for CNS compensatory changes. Of course, *in vitro* findings cannot be applied directly as the presumed CNS drug effect *in vivo*. Complications arise because a medication may have similar effects on more than one neurotransmitter system or differing effects on two or more different compounds. For example, tricyclic antidepressants block catecholamine uptake, alter acetylcholine metabolism, and inhibit MAO. Because drugs have many effects, clinical improvement with a medication does not unequivocally point to one specific underlying metabolic dysfunction. Eight major types of pharmacological intervention are relevant to understanding neurotransmitter function (table 3–4). These interventions augment, inhibit, or specifically block important steps and processes in normal neural activity and have behavioral consequences.

The modes of action of antipsychotic (neuroleptic) agents demonstrate some underlying physiological and pharmacological mechanisms.

Phenothiazines, larger and more complex molecules than dopamine, block the functioning of dopaminergic systems. On the basis of x-ray crystallography, the structure of the phenothiazines has been elucidated. *Structure-function correlations* demonstrate that specific alterations in side-chain configuration and constituents account for varying degrees of clinical effectiveness. When the side chain and adjacent portion can be superimposed over the dopamine or norepinephrine molecule, the phenothiazine effectively blocks the dopamine receptor.

The *conformation of the receptor* might vary and exert a controlling effect on the overall system.

TABLE 3–4

Neurotransmitter Pharmacology

Type of Action	Drug Effect on Transmitter Physiology	Examples of drugs
1. Inhibition of transmitter synthesis	Interferes with an enzymatic step in the synthesis of a transmitter by interacting with an enzyme or a cofactor	AMPT (inhibits tyrosine hydroxylase); disulfiram (inhibits DBH); fusaric acid (inhibits DBH); PCPA (inhibits tryptophan hydroxylase)
2. Depletion of stored transmitter	Interferes with uptake and storage mechanism of the intraneuronal amine storage vesicle	reserpine (long-lasting depletion of DA, NE, and 5-HT); tetrabenazine (short duration depletion)
3. False transmitter	"False transmitters" are stored in vesicles with the transmitter and are released with it, but do not efficiently interact with the receptor. They reduce the effect of the transmitter	octopamine; alpha-methyldopa; metaraminol
4. Enhanced transmitter release	Increases release of the neurotransmitter resulting in its increased availability for interaction with the receptor	Sympathomimetic amphetamine —tyramine, phenylethylamine; cholinomimetic carbachol
5. Inhibition of re-uptake of transmitter	Blocks re-uptake resulting in an increase in available transmitter	amphetamine (blocks DA and NE re-uptake); cocaine (blocks DA and NE re-uptake); tricyclic antidepressants (block NE and 5-HT re-uptake); benzotropine (blocks DA re-uptake)
6. Inhibition of transmitter metabolism	Interferes with inactivation by degradative enzymes and increases transmitter at the synapse	MAO inhibitors—parglyine, phenelzine, iproniazid; COMT inhibitors—pyrogallol, tropolones; AChE inhibitor—physostigmine
7. Receptor blocking	Interacts with the receptor but does not elicit the usual postsynaptic events. With fewer receptors available for the usual transmitter, there is a net decrease in transmitter-receptor interaction and a feedback mechanism may increase transmitter turnover	phenothiazines (block DA receptor); butyrophenones (block DA receptor); d-Tubocurarine, atropine, benzotropine (block ACh receptor)
8. Receptor stimulating	Stimulates the receptor like the usual transmitter, leading to an "increase" in transmitter-receptor interaction with decreased turnover of the transmitter	apomophine (DA receptor agonist); clonidine (NE receptor agonist); morphine (opiate receptor agonist)

NOTE: Reprinted by permission of the publisher from "Neurochemistry and Child Psychiatry," by D. J. Cohen and J. G. Young, *Journal of the American Academy of Child Psychiatry*, 16:353–411, 1977.

Changes in the number of active catecholamine molecules interacting with a pineal gland receptor site lead to the rapid development of receptor subsensitivity or supersensitivity. When a large number of active transmitter molecules are near the receptor sites, there appears to be a reduction in the coupling between postsynaptic receptor and adenylate cyclase on the cellular membrane, leading to a decrease in the formation of cyclic AMP (*subsensitive response*). In the reverse situation, when fewer than normal transmitter molecules are in the pineal receptor locale, there is an increase in receptor-adenylate cyclase coupling and a consequent increase in cyclic AMP formation (*supersensitive response*). Because these changes occur so soon it has been suggested that the responsible mechanism is a (reversible) alteration in either the conformation or availability of the receptor.

This provides a useful model for both denervation supersensitivity and drug tolerance (subsensitivity) phenomena.[4]

The antipsychotic activity of phenothiazines and butyrophenones is contrasted to their action at extrapyramidal system receptors in the striatum. It might be predicted that if two phenothiazines (for example, thioridazine and fluphenazine) are given at dosages eliciting comparable antipsychotic effects, they would cause a similar degree of extrapyramidal side effects. Considerable clinical experience, however, indicates that this is not the case, and that *antipsychotic and extrapyramidal effects* can be *dissociated*. From a neurochemical perspective, this evidence suggests that drugs do not have a similar effect on all dopamine receptors and that the dopamine blockade theory of neuroleptic drug action may be in error. However, this apparent discrepancy has been explained by studies of the antimuscarinic effects of various medications.

Anticholinergic agents, such as atropine, are antagonists at muscarinic receptor sites (as discussed earlier). These compounds have long been useful in the treatment of Parkinson's disease and, more recently, have been the principal drugs used to minimize the side effects of the neuroleptics. It appears that they compensate for a relative dopamine deficiency in the striatum and restore balance between dopamine and acetylcholine. On the basis of clinical findings, it was hypothesized that *phenothiazines with fewer extrapyramidal side effects had an anticholinergic potency*. This hypothesis has been supported by ranking antipsychotic agents by anticholinergic potency. Those with high potency (for example, thioridazine) have few extrapyramidal side effects because of their built-in anticholinergic activity; those with low potency (for example, fluphenazine and butyrophenones) have prominent side effects, presumably because they fail to balance their strong antidopaminergic effects.

Recent work has indicated that neuroleptics may have a presynaptic effect in addition to the dopamine blockade indicated in table 3–4. Although the butyrophenones are among the clinically most potent antipsychotic agents, their efficacy as blockers at the dopamine-sensitive adenylate cyclase in animals is not particularly high. One explanatory model for this phenomenon is that *haloperidol* and related compounds have a particularly strong *presynaptic effect*. Several types of presynaptic actions have been suggested, but one attractive theory is that haloperidol interferes with the mechanism which couples neuronal impulses to the neurosecretion of dopamine. This inhibition then leads to the observed compensatory increase in neuronal firing and dopamine turnover.

Pharmacological techniques have been used to characterize properties of the opioid peptides. In classic bioassays and studies of single neuron responses, enkephalins and endorphins behave like morphine and other agonists. Administered to laboratory animals, the three types of *endorphins* elicit replicable behavioral and physiological effects: (1) analgesia, tranquilization, hypothermia; (2) catatoniclike stupor, profound analgesia, hypothermia; and (3) irritability, hypersensitivity, and hyperthermia. These effects subside spontaneously, over a few hours, and can be terminated almost instantaneously with morphine antagonists such as naloxone.

The discovery of endorphins and enkephalins has led not only to better understanding of the action of opiates but to new hypotheses about the mechanism of action of other compounds which affect mood and sensory processing. For example, it has been suggested that a mechanism of the therapeutic effect of *lithium* in the treatment of mania may be its effect on the conformation of the opiate receptor. Because of homeostatic processes, it is difficult to alter the bodily concentration of sodium; however, lithium, perhaps in conjunction with sodium, may alter the opiate receptor to the conformation favoring the dissociation of endogenous agonists, thus leading to a lowering of euphoric mood. This idea receives support from observations that lithium tends to block the action of exogenous euphoriants such as heroin and stimulants.

Pharmacological research strategies have been applied to specific etiological and physiological hypotheses.

Administration of Methyl Donors: Some hallucinogens are methylated derivatives of either indoleamines or catecholamines. The *transmethylation hypothesis* for schizophrenia suggests that abnormal transmethylation of an endogenous amine may form a hallucinogen and lead to the cognitive and other disturbances found in schizophrenia. To test this hypothesis, methyl donors (for example, *methionine* and *betaine*) have been administered to schizophrenic patients and alterations in symptomatology concurrently assessed. The difficulty in distinguishing toxicity from a more specific exacerbation of schizophrenic symptomatology poses a problem when interpreting results.

An enzyme capable of forming the hallucinogen *dimethyltryptamine* (*DMT*) has been demonstrated in normal human plasma, red blood cells, and platelets. The enzyme activity in nondialyzed platelets of patients with schizophrenic and psychotic depressive illnesses is higher than the activity in normal volunteers, suggesting that a dialyzable inhibitor might be present in normal persons but reduced in the psychotic patients. When studied in monozygotic twins discordant for schizophrenia, it was found that the schizophrenic individuals had elevated enzyme levels as compared to their nonschizophrenic twins; interpretation must be tentative because of methodological difficulties, such as the possible effects of the illness and drugs and absence of more complete genetic studies.

Administration of Methyl Acceptors: If transmethylation does, in fact, contribute methylated derivatives which are significant in producing schizophrenic symptoms, then methyl acceptor substances might be useful in treatment. *Nicotinic acid* and *nicotinamide* have been tried empirically but have not been demonstrated to be useful therapeutically.

Administration of Amine Precursors: Precursors of amines have been given to normal subjects in an attempt to induce psychotic symptoms, and to schizophrenic patients in order to exacerbate or elicit symptoms. For example, large doses of *phenylalanine* were administered daily to chronic schizophrenic patients for one week with and without MAO inhibitors: No mental changes were evident. Investigations using parallel methods (for example, administration of *tryptophan*) to demonstrate an abnormality in central amine metabolism in psychotic children have not led to definitive behavioral correlations. Administration of tryptophan has been useful in neurological diseases. For example, patients with myoclonic epilepsy, a debilitating, multicausal syndrome, have lower levels of serotonin metabolites in their CSF and respond positively to large doses of the serotonin precursor, tryptophan, when combined with a compound (carbidopa) which blocks the utilization of tryptophan for peripheral serotonin synthesis.

Isotope Methods: The advantages of isotopically labeled compounds are their marked *sensitivity* and *specificity*. The technical difficulty in the separation of a compound from all other substances in the tissue is simplified to a separation of the desired (isotopically labeled) compound from the few interfering radioactive substances.

The use of labeled neurotransmitters for the estimation of turnover rates involves a variety of problems, especially the inability of the amine to penetrate the blood-brain barrier. In animals, labeled compounds can be administered by intracisternal or intraventricular injections. In man, isotopic precursors (for example, labeled tyrosine or DOPA) cross the blood-brain barrier and are utilized in the synthesis of (labeled) dopamine or norepinephrine in the brain.

Chemical Lesions: In an organ with peripheral sympathetic innervation, the neuronal function may be studied by surgical denervation. However, a more widespread denervation involving multiple organs may be desired or the innervation of a single organ may not be adequately specific and separate for surgical denervation. Immunological and chemical techniques have been devised which selectively destroy monoamine nerve terminals and produce a general chemical ablation of sympathetic pathways. The sympathetic nerve endings in the periphery efficiently take up 6-hydroxydopamine, which causes degeneration of adrenergic nerve endings and a functional "chemical sympathectomy." When given by intraventricular injection, 6-hydroxydopamine selectively and permanently destroys dopaminergic and noradrenergic neurons in the brain. Similarly, *5,6-dihydroxytryptamine* preferentially destroys serotonergic nerve endings, although with somewhat less specificity. A major potential use of chemical ablation is the production of animal models approximating specific behavioral deficits.[6, 14]

Neuroendocrinology

The endocrine system may be conceptualized as a principal output channel for brain activity, transducing CNS information into the modulation of metabolic state. Assessment of the changing status of the endocrine system provides another means for obtaining information concerning brain function. The process of transduction can be considered to occur at the level of the hypothalamic neurotransmitter regulation of the endocrine system.

The neuroendocrine system is characterized by complex regulatory feedback processes at staggered levels, and it produces substances with multiple physiological functions. For clarity, neuroendocrine regulation will be discussed in terms of distinct anatomical-functional levels, consisting of peripheral target-organ glands, pituiatry tropic hormones, hypothalamic hormones, and hypothalamic neurotransmitters.[43]

HYPOTHALAMIC-PITUITARY AXIS

The neuroendocrine system refers to those parts of the central nervous system which control or directly affect endocrine function. This section will be centered on the *hypothalamic-hypophyseal axis*, although there is also direct innervation from the CNS to the *adrenal medulla* and the *pineal gland*. The pituitary gland (hypophysis) may be divided into three parts: the *anterior pituitary* (adenohypophysis), the *posterior pituitary* (neurohypophysis), and the *pars intermedia* (vestigial in man), which may be considered as part of the neurohypophysis. The hormones (and respective target organs) associated with these divisions of the pituitary are given in table 3–6; abbreviations for pituitary and hypothalamic hormones are listed in table 3–5.[49]

The *hypothalamus* influences the posterior pituitary through neuronal connections running from the supraoptic and paraventricular nuclei to the neurohypophysis, where oxytocin and vasopressin are released from the nerve endings. A distinctly different mechanism releases tropic hormones from the adenohypophysis. Axons from particular hypothalamic neurons course to the median eminence or infudibulum, where the terminals are adjacent to capillary loops of the portal system. The blood-brain barrier is not present in the median eminence (which is part of the neurohypophyseal tissue), so that compounds released from the axonal nerve endings diffuse into the portal system, just as they diffuse into the general circulation from the posterior pituitary. The hypothalamic hormone is carried by the portal system to the anterior pituitary, either stimulating or inhibiting one or more pituitary hormones there.[27, 56, 57]

The nature and effects of pituitary and peripheral hormones are described in detail in standard endocrinology texts.[31] The following sections discuss the interface between neurotransmitters and endocrine function and describe two sets of hypothalamic and pituitary hormones (thyrotropin and prolactin) as models of neuroendocrine function and regulation at multiple levels.

HYPOTHALAMIC NEUROTRANSMITTERS

It has long been clear that many regions of the brain affect pituitary hormonal output, but specific linkages are only now being defined. Dopamine, norepinephrine, serotonin, acetylcholine, histamine, and opioid peptides are all neurotransmitters which have been identified in the hypothalamus, predominantly within nerve endings. In addition, a major dopaminergic system, the tuberoinfundibular tract, runs entirely within the hypothalamus from the arcuate nucleus through the median eminence to the portal plexus.[23, 40] Neurotransmitters represent a specific interface between brain function and endocrinology. The knowledge that emotions affect endocrine function has, thus, reached a state permitting experimental investigation. Reciprocally, the endocrine system is a source of additional strategies for the indirect clinical study of the brain. Alterations in brain function and metabolism, reflected in changes in the activity of specific brain transmitter systems, affect the secretion of pituitary hormones through their respective releasing and inhibiting factors. This

TABLE 3–5

Abbreviations for Pituitary Hormones and Hypothalamic Regulatory Factors

Pituitary Hormone	Hypothalamic Hormone
(LH) Luteinizing hormone	(LH-RF) Luteinizing hormone releasing factor
(FSH) Follicle-stimulating hormone	(FSH-RF) Follicle-stimulating hormone releasing factor
(ACTH) Corticotropin	(CRF) Corticotropin-releasing factor
Prolactin	(PIF) Prolactin release-inhibiting factor
	(PRF) Prolactin-releasing factor
(TSH) Thyrotropin	(TRF) Thyrotropin-releasing factor
(GH) Growth hormone	(GH-RF) Growth hormone releasing factor
	(GH-IF) Growth hormone release-inhibiting factor (somatostatin)
(MSH) Melanocyte-stimulating hormone	(MIF) Melanocyte-stimulating hormone release-inhibiting factor
	(MRF) Melanocyte-stimulating hormone releasing factor

TABLE 3–6

Hypothalamic Neurotransmitter	Hypothalamic Hormone	Pituitary Hormone	Target Organ
Anterior Pituitary			
DA+* NE+ 5-HT+	LH-RF FSH-RF	LH FSH	Gonads
ACH+ 5-HT+ DA— NE—	CRF	ACTH	Adrenal cortex
DA— 5-HT+	PIF PRF	Prolactin	Mammary glands
DA NE+ 5-HT—	TRF	TSH	Thyroid gland
DA+ NE+ 5-HT+	GH-RF GH-IF	Growth Hormone	Multiple tissues
Pars Intermedia			
	MSH-IF MSH-RF	MSH	Melanocytes
Posterior Pituitary			
Oxytocin	Oxytocin (Storage and secretion)		Mammary glands, Uterus
Vasopressin	Vasopressin (Storage and secretion)		Kidneys, vascular smooth muscle

* + (stimulation) or — (inhibition) with reference to release of pituitary hormone. Determination of neurotransmitters controlling hypothalamic hormones is still in a preliminary stage, and this table is very tentative. Abbreviations as in table 3–5.

provides novel methods of manipulation of input to the brain and measurement of compounds at various levels in the endocrine axis.

PITUITARY-THYROID AXIS

Thyrotropin (*thyroid-stimulating hormone,* or *TSH*) is a glycoprotein whose activity maintains the structure and function of the thyroid gland. Thyrotropin accelerates adenyl cyclase activity in target cells in the thyroid, causing increased formation of cyclic AMP in the cell. Uptake of iodine by the thyroid gland increases, as does release of thyroid hormone from the gland, resulting in higher blood levels of thyroxine (T_4). Thyrotropin may also affect some tissues outside the thyroid gland. The regulatory relation between the anterior pituitary and the thyroid gland typifies the feedback control system for pituitary hormones which act on specific target glands. *Thyrotropin-releasing factor (TRF)* is produced predominantly in the anterior areas of the hypothalamus and is released into the portal circulation in the median eminence, which carries it to the adenohypophysis. It is a tripeptide which stimulates not only TSH release, but also prolactin release from the pituitary. TSH may have an inhibitory feedback effect in the hypothalamus, acting to reduce the production of TRF (a "short" or "internal" feedback loop).

When isolated from the hypothalamus, the pituitary continues to secrete a basal level of TSH which maintains production of thyroid hormone, though at a lesser level. There is also some degree of feedback control of thyroid hormone on the anterior pituitary production of TSH when isolated from the hypothalamus (a "long" feedback loop). However, the general production and range of TSH levels from the pituitary is much increased through hypothalamic effects. Undefined cellular systems in the relevant hypothalamic centers detect the circulatory levels of thyroid hormone, and the synthesis or release of TRF is adjusted through another "long" feedback loop. It has been hypothesized that "ultrashort" feedback loops may also exist, with releasing-factor concentration affecting the synthesis and release of further releasing factor, or pituitary tropic hormone acting at the level of the anterior pituitary to inhibit further tropic hormone production.[42, 45]

Other peripheral hormones may affect production of a specific pituitary hormone; for example, large amounts of glucocorticoids may diminish TSH concentrations.

PROLACTIN

The regulation of prolactin secretion is typical for those three pituitary hormones which do not act on specific target organs (GH and MSH are others). The lack of feedback inhibition from a target-gland hormone seems to be compensated for by regulation through the secretion of a hypothalamic-inhibitory factor, in addition to the hypothalamic-releasing factor.

Prolactin is a polypeptide of 198 amino acids which shares some homologous segments, as well as some biological properties, with growth hormone and placental lactogen. Its principal roles in females are those involving development of the mammary gland and milk formation; its functions in the male, for example, in calcium metabolism and growth, are not well defined. Its activity is dependent on the presence of several other hormones: growth hormone, adrenal glucocorticoids, estrogens, and progestins.

Experimental lesions of the hypothalamus or pituitary stalk in animals leads to a decrease in pituitary output of hormones, with the exception of prolactin, which is increased. This reflects the dominance of the *prolactin-inhibiting factor (PIF)* in the hypothalamic control of prolactin secretion. It is not yet clear whether this low molecular weight compound is identical with a catecholamine transmitter, or is a peptide or other compound. A hypothalamic prolactin-releasing factor has been hypothesized and may be identical with TRF, which has been shown to have prolactin-releasing activity.

Dopamine (and possibly norepinephrine) is the neurotransmitter responsible for stimulating production of PIF, or may be the actual PIF itself. An increase in dopaminergic activity through administration of L-dopa or apomorphine (which stimulates the dopaminergic receptor) depresses prolactin secretion. Phenothiazines, which block the receptor, reduce PIF and therefore increase prolactin secretion.

Estrogens act at both the hypothalamic and pituitary levels to stimulate prolactin secretion; progesterone has a stimulatory effect through the hypothalamus, although very high progesterone levels become inhibitory.

Prolactin levels may be regulated in part by a short feedback loop of prolactin, enhancing elaboration of PIF in the hypothalamus.[40, 59]

NEUROENDOCRINE REGULATION

Hormone secretion is highly responsive to multiple levels of control, which overlap and balance one another. *Inhibitory feedback loops* are the primary mode of regulation, and are particularly characteristic of gonadal steroids, adrenocorticosteroids, and thyroid hormones. However, there are instances in which a *stimulatory feedback loop* occurs, so that the system rapidly reaches a high level of activity. Estrogen and LH can participate in this kind of increasing series, and some method of turning off the stimulatory feedback loop is required, in this case the negative feedback of LH on itself. Another control mechanism is *dual hypothalamic control*, i.e., the presence of both releasing and inhibiting factors, characteristic of prolactin, GH, and MSH.

Endocrine feedback loops may be grouped according to the compound and the locus of its feedback as follows (see also figure 3–16):

1. Long feedback loops
   a. Peripheral hormone on anterior pituitary
   b. Peripheral hormone on hypothalamus
2. Short feedback loop
   Pituitary hormone on hypothalamus
3. Ultrashort feedback loops
   a. Hypothalamic hormone on hypothalamus
   b. Anterior pituitary tropic hormone on anterior pituitary.

These multiple control circuits achieve a high degree of sensitivity in the maintenance of appropriate hormonal levels and a corresponding complexity for investigators studying a single aspect of the endocrine axis.[59]

The activity of a given pituitary hormonal axis does not represent a simple summation effect of all levels of feedback. For example, in the pituitary-thyroid axis the time frame of the effects increases at each level of the axis. TRH quickly

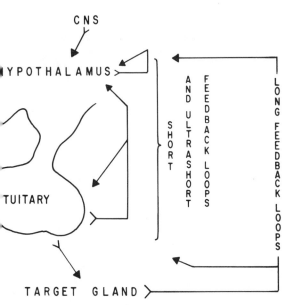

FIGURE 3–16
*Schematic diagram of neuroendocrine
feedback control loops.*

rat heart increases in rats subjected to hypophys-ectomy or thyroidectomy but returns to normal with thyroid replacement therapy.[35] Plasma NE is increased in myxoedematous patients and decreased in thyrotoxic patients, and spinal fluid HVA, the principal metabolite of dopamine in the brain, may be increased in hypothyroidism and decreased in hyperthyroidism.[10] A parallel *negative* association between *thyroxine* and *DBH* (a NE-synthesizing enzyme) has been shown in hyper- and hypothyroid patients, as well as euthyroid subjects.

This negative relationship between thyroid state and catecholamine activity has, in general, been hypothesized to hinge on (1) thyroxine effects on presynaptic transmitter synthesis or (2) alteration of receptor sensitivity by thyroxine, with consequent feedback regulation of transmitter turnover. More recently, the properties of iodothyronines as tyrosine analogues have been reviewed, and it has been hypothesized that such analogues might be transformed into adrenergic neurotransmitters.[19] Whatever the eventual explanation, it is clear that this is another instance in which endocrine effects are critical to clinical neurochemical investigation.

ACTIVATIONAL AND ORGANIZATIONAL EFFECTS

The direct effects of hormones on the brain may be classified as activational and organizational. *Activational effects* enhance the likelihood that a specific physiological or behavioral sequence will occur. The modulating hormone facilitates the initiation of the specific sequence, although, given an adequate stimulus, the sequence will begin regardless of the presence or absence of the hormone. For example, estrogens facilitate a variety of sexual and maternal behaviors, which can nevertheless occur without this permissive hormonal effect.

Organizational effects are developmental effects; they typically occur at a specific early developmental phase and exert organizational effects at levels from the molecule to behavior. These effects do not occur (or are less likely to occur) without the hormone and are retained long after the actual time of activity of the hormone.[41] For example, a normal level of thyroid activity in the first weeks of life is necessary for such critical CNS structural events as myelinization and synapse formation. Brain tissue has mitochondria with a functional site responsive to thyroid hormones during a critical early period, but this sensitivity is lost as the organism matures. Organizational hormone effects may represent irreversible

releases TSH, and its effects are short lived. TSH acts on the thyroid over a period of several hours, initially causing a preferential increase in T_3. Finally, the metabolic effects of T_4 have a duration of several days. The axis of activity is in this way structured so that anything which impacts abruptly on it will cause an effect which will be smoothed out over a longer period.[42]

Endocrine regulation also occurs through *peripheral mechanisms*. The metabolically active form of thyroid hormone, tri-iodothyronine (T_3), is derived from the prohormone thyroxine (T_4), under the control of various peripheral factors involving hormonal cellular receptor sites. Conversion of T_4 to T_3, and the ratio between these two, is altered in disease. Another type of peripheral regulation is exemplified by insulin's regulation of its receptor. These peripheral mechanisms are integrated with and affect diverse central mechanisms.

NEUROTRANSMITTERS AND HORMONES
AT THE SYNAPSE

A further interaction of neurotransmitters and the endocrine system can occur at the synaptic level. For example, a generally *inverse* relationship between *thyroid* hormone level and *catecholamine* concentration has been demonstrated in a variety of circumstances. Norepinephrine turnover in the genetic regulation, for example, the permanent induction or repression of an enzyme; activational hormone effects may involve reversible regulation of genetic expression.

Stimulation, Stress, and Trauma

Stimulation, stress, and trauma can be viewed as a continuum of disruptions in experience, reflecting a series of interrelated phenomena: the nature and intensity of the stimulus; the congenital endowment, previous experience, physiological status, and adaptive competence of the organism; the quality of the individual's initial response to the stimulus; and traces left in the wake of the experience. Problems in stress research occur because of the diverse phenomena entangled in "stress" and the consequent difficulties in definition and boundaries. Nevertheless, the stress paradigm can be used to unify and organize disparate domains of data.

STIMULATION AND ATTENTION

On the occurrence of a *stimulus*, animals and people exhibit an integrated *orienting response*, having behavioral, hormonal, and cardiovascular components. Behaviorally, the individual may attend to the external stimulation, categorize it, integrate it with previous experience, and organize a motor or mental response. Alternatively, the individual may raise his threshold for stimulation or resist sensory input in some other manner, for example, directing his attention elsewhere or inward. The way in which a stimulus event is received or searched for is a function of many determinants, including competing sensory and motor commitments, the danger of missing a stimulus or of responding when none is present, the level of consciousness, and the personal significance of the stimulus event. Concomitant with the activation, arousal, and mental effort involved in an attentional response are various psychological responses. These have been utilized as measures of physiological processing, providing clues to internal mechanisms which may be absent from conscious awareness or unavailable for direct study in nonverbal organisms.

When exposed to a dangerous situation or one previously associated with physical pain (for example, electric shock), people and animals exhibit a specific cardiovascular response to stimulation characterized as the "*defense reaction*." In this reaction, increased heart rate, increased skeletal blood flow, and increased skeletal muscle activity place the individual in a state of readiness for withdrawing from the noxious situation. Similarly, characteristic cardiovascular patterns occur in situations which are more subtly defined relative to the direction of attention. Measurement of peripheral vascular blood flow into skeletal muscle is possible by relatively simple physiological techniques. Threats, fear, difficult mental tasks, and imagined scenes lead to peripheral vascular dilatation and increased muscle blood flow. More refined analyses show that changes in peripheral blood flow reflect whether an individual is taking in or rejecting sensory input.

When an individual is required to maintain an *external focus of attention*, for example, to read a blurred word on a screen or to respond to a social engagement, cardiovascular responses include decreased peripheral blood flow, increased peripheral vascular resistance, and decreased digital pulse volume. In contrast, when children and adults are engaged in tasks which require an *internal direction of attention* and rejection of sensory input from the external world, such as when engaged in mental arithmetic or difficult memory tasks, their cardiovascular responses are distinctively different: decreased peripheral vascular resistance, increased peripheral blood flow, and increased heart rate.[13] The cardiovascular responses to *sensory intake* are similar to those observed with peripheral sympathetic nerve discharge; those observed with *sensory rejection* are similar to the cardiovascular response to epinephrine. Direct assessment of peripheral enzymes (such as dopamine-beta-hydroxylase) during such psychological states may be supportive of the role of catecholamines in the cardiovascular responses to attentional deployment.

There are numerous connections between the anatomy of attention and cardiovascular control, as would be predicted from the central role of the cardiovascular system in preparation for response to environmental circumstances. Blood pressure and other cardiovascular phenomena are largely controlled by two central adrenergic pathways with opposite effects: an excitatory pathway centered in the hypothalamus and an inhibitory pathway centered in bulbar nuclei. Regions of the brain subserving cardiovascular function overlap with areas regulating attention, for example, the amygdala, basal ganglia, and hippocampus. Hypothalamic mechanisms have been especially implicated in the "defense reaction."

Cardiovascular responses to attentional states are observable from the first days of infancy. Transient cardiac deceleration following a stimulus or during visual scanning is a reliable indicator of sensory intake in newborns and older children. More dramatic are elevations in heart rate and blood pressure at moments of behavioral upset, such as the newborn's crying or experience of pain.

Thus, there is a continuum of cardiovascular response, with distinct patterns associated with shifting psychological responses to sensory input. These patterns reflect inborn neuroanatomical mechanisms in which there is association between the regulation of attention and behavior, on one hand, and cardiovascular phenomena, on the other. The adaptive significance for psychological reactions is obvious in such instances as the "defense response," but not clear in such changes as the increased peripheral blood flow which accompanies mental arithmetic. Neuroanatomical overlap between attentional and cardiovascular regulation is mirrored in the neurotransmitter function of norepinephrine and serotonin in cardiovascular regulatory pathways and the modulation of mood and behavior.[67]

STRESS

An individual's response to sensory stimulation, as a model of adaptation, naturally merges with the psychiatric concept of "stress." One cause of the ambiguity in discussions of stress is the two-faced nature of the concept. From the outside, stress may be characterized according to the intensity and apparent noxiousness of the stimulus, or some other a priori or common-sense classification of the circumstances to which a person is exposed. From the inside, however, stress may be described in terms of the individual's actual adaptation and response. For the individual, stress is accompanied by the development of nonadaptive behavioral responses (persistent anxiety, nonapative avoidance or withdrawal, decrement in pleasure and satisfaction, specific symptoms, etc.), physical disability (specific illness or disease, failure to thrive, bodily symptoms), and transient or prolonged physiological signs (increased blood pressure or heart rate, palor or flushing, sweating, etc.). Most often, these aspects of the concept are complementary, with noxious environmental events highly correlated with maladaptive or disturbing patterns of response. There is great divergence in the interpretation and response to potentially stressful environmental events.[30] Thus, children in a family differ in the degree to which parental psychopathology shapes maladaptive patterns of behavior or symptomatology in their own lives; similarly, individuals exposed to the same catastrophic event (for example, a natural disaster) may differ markedly in the type of response to stress which they experience (physical, physiological, or psychological). Genetic endowment, personal history, cultural influences, and current metabolic functioning are among the many factors which have been investigated in relation to individual differences in response to external stress.[12] Several animal and human studies will exemplify these interrelating determinants.

Neurochemical Transduction of the Stress Experience: Experimentally imposed stress, such as electrical shock or overcrowding, induces specific changes in adrenal enzymes synthesizing catecholamines. For example, electrical stimulation of the hypothalamus of the cat, evoking sham rage, elevates adrenal gland tyrosine hydroxylase (TH) fourfold and phenylethylamine-N-methyltransferace (PNMT) twofold. This neurochemical response is not observed when the electrical stimulation merely produces alertness or movement but no attack behavior, nor is it elicited when the adrenal is denervated.[51] The stress of prolonged immobilization or exposure to cold leads to similar adrenal alterations. These and similar studies demonstrate that sustained neural activation of the adrenal gland leads to increases in enzymes synthesizing catecholamine neurotransmitters.

Psychosocial variables, such as *social stimulation* or *deprivation,* may have equally potent effects on adrenal enzyme activities in rodents. With social isolation, mice have a decrease in adrenal TH and PNMT but no significant change in adrenal NE and E or in peripheral MAO and COMT. In contrast, mice provided with social stimulation exhibit marked increases in adrenal TH, PNMT, and MAO activities, as well as in NE and E content. As with sham rage, neuronal mediation is necessary. Thus, both physical (immobilization, cold, and electrical stimulation of the brain) and social stimulation may alter catecholamine synthetic enzymes in the adrenal gland, as well as the concentration of the neurotransmitter itself.

Augmentation of catecholamines and adrenal cortical hormones following crying in human newborns has been the subject of preliminary investigation and seems to be a response to physiological upheaval. Observations of monkeys that experience disturbances in mother-infant bonding may be applicable to more subtle human behavioral phenomena. Separation of an infant monkey from its mother at age four months leads to a pattern of behavioral response similar to that described for human infants at a later age, with periods of rage and despair followed by equilibration. When infant monkeys are sacrificed six days after separation from their mothers, during the period of "protest," their adrenals show significant increase in tyrosine hydroxylase, DBH, PNMT, and choline acetylase. Concentrations of catecholamines are not changed. TH and choline acetylase activity in the cervical ganglia are also significantly increased, suggesting general activitation of the sympathetic nervous system during protest. In the central nervous system, hypothalamic serotonin concentration is increased while TH, DA, and NE are apparently unchanged. The augmentation of serotonin metabolism is consistent with observations in rodents and with elevation of serotonin following marked increases in sensory input.[7]

TRAUMA

The basis for the enduring influence of certain powerful or recurrent environmental occurrences in childhood has intrigued child psychiatrists since Freud's early formulations on trauma. As with the concept of stress, trauma, too, has two interlocking aspects: a focus on the event or series of events as traumatic in quality, on one hand, and recognition of the unique coping mechanisms and defenses of the individual which define whether a particular occurrence is experienced as traumatic, on the other. This balance between the perceived event and the perceiving organism has been characterized in many ways, including the nature of available defenses, ego strengths, ease of regression, symbolic significance of the occurrence, the role of the parents as supplements to the child's stimulus barrier, and the specific developmental phase in which the events are embedded.[21] As with stress, inborn vulnerabilities and invulnerabilities also have been suggested as relevant to the impact of potentially traumatic occurrences on developing children.[60]

Genetic Setting for Stress and Trauma: Genetic determinants of the physiological response to stress or potential trauma may be thought of in terms of baseline and response rates of function of specific enzymes. Genes and genetic mutations determine the baseline setting for enzyme activity, but these activities are readily influenced by environmental and physiological events. The induction of enzyme activity by diet or medication (for example, the effect of barbiturates on liver enzymes) is well known, as are the influences of environmental events, as described previously.

Enzymes involved in catecholamine metabolism in the brain may be affected by factors similar to those described for adrenal enzymes. Alterations in diet, social stimulation, drugs, and physical stress have all been associated with alterations in brain metabolism, suggesting the responsivity of genetically programmed metabolic processes in response to an individual's environmental provision. The baseline or "inborn" enzyme activities are also quite broadly varied within populations. This genetic basis of enzyme activity is one aspect of differences in temperament observed from the very first days of life.

In addition to the normal variance observed for enzymes involved in catecholamine metabolism, mutations and other genetic atypicalities influence enzyme function. The enzyme protein may be structurally altered, interfering with or facilitating its catalytic properties in a major or minor way. A structural change may not affect the catalytic properties of the enzyme but may render it more or less stable than initially, resulting in an increase or a decrease in its activity. Alternatively, changes in structural or regulatory genes can result in differences in the rate of synthesis of the enzyme. Enzyme activity may also be affected indirectly through gene mutations which alter the levels of an activator or inhibitor of the enzyme. Clearly, the multiplicity of influences on enzyme activity allows for numerous variations on these themes, and this multiplicity provides a basis for the complexity of the mature organism which is necessary for individual adaptation.

The variation in enzyme function is vividly evident in the study of isoenzymes. *Isoenzymes,* or *isozymes,* are multiple molecular forms of an enzyme, distinct and specific proteins which exhibit identical or similar functional activities. Isozymes may arise from several causes, such as multiple gene loci, multiple allelism at a single locus, or through secondary, posttranslational changes in the enzyme.[28] In short, there are many routes to differences in the activity of a specific enzyme in any individual, and the sum of these enzyme differences constitutes genetic individuality or individuality in the expression of potential, genetic endowment.

Clinical neurochemistry is in the earliest stages of investigating genetic differences in neurotransmitter-related enzymes and the possible relation between such differences and behavioral disturbances. These relations have been examined in inbred strains of mice, revealing systematic differences in catecholamine and indoleamine enzymes among the strains, as well as in certain aspects of behavior and physiology (for example, susceptibility to seizures, hyperactivity, or hypertension). The apparent reduction in platelet MAO activity in severely disturbed adults, particularly in adults with chronic schizophrenia, is the best known clinical parallel in psychiatry. This reduction in monoamine oxidase has been suggested as a critical biological marker of vulnerability. Individuals with this vulnerability who are exposed to personally "stressful" environmental or interpersonal circumstances are more likely to develop prolonged schizophrenia than those whose endowment is more fortunate.[48] Another fundamental enzyme in catecholamine metabolism has a greater variation than MAO. DBH differs by a range of over a hundredfold within the normal population, but the functional implication of this enormous variation is not yet apparent. Nor is it clearly understood whether alterations in enzyme activity, for example, in MAO and DBH, are significantly modified early in development by the type of experiences to which an individual is exposed, in addition to the documented genetic determination of baseline activity. The pivotal role of neurochemical mechanisms as transducers of experience make it quite difficult to clearly delineate the degree to which they cause, or are caused by, a person's life history, current adaptations, and tendencies toward specific actions or feelings.[20]

Neuroendocrine Response to Stress and Trauma: The intimate associations between endocrine and catecholamine mechanisms, described earlier, are reflected in alterations in endocrine status with stress and trauma. For example, an early study of parents of children suffering from acute leukemia demonstrated a sensitive relationship between the parent's urinary 17-hydroxycorticosteroids (17-OHCS) and his psychological coping. With effective integration of the experience associated with the child's illness, 17-hydroxycorticosteroids were lower; when psychological defenses failed, leading to high levels of arousal and emotional distress, the steroid levels were likely to increase. Over longer periods, adaptation to stressful situations (for example, military training) is reflected in gradual reduction in urinary 17-hydroxycorticosteroid levels. These observations have been extended to schizophrenic and depressed adults. In these studies, acute emotional distress (manifested by depression, anxiety, turmoil, or other symptom patterns) is associated with elevation of steroid levels and stabilization following emotional distress with decreasing levels.[44, 55]

More recently, attention has turned to understanding the *profile of endocrine response*, rather than one hormone's changing levels. In this new approach, various hypothalamic-releasing factors, pituitary hormones, and other hormones are seen as a finely tuned orchestration of response. Interacting with neurotransmitters and cyclic AMP (the second messenger system, operating within cells), the endocrine apparatus provides background and general modulation of the organism for specific adaptations occuring over longer periods of time than the milliseconds involved in neuronal transmission.

Another integrative approach is illustrated by studies of stimulation of the *locus coeruleus*, the major site of origin of noradrenergic neurons in the brain. Stimulation of the locus coeruleus, mobilizing central noradrenergic pathways, produces marked elevations of cerebrospinal fluid and peripheral MHPG, the norepinephrine metabolite. Behaviorally, electrical stimulation has been noted to alter the mood and appetite of the animal. Connections between the locus coeruleus and the experience of satiety have been observed. Animals with a locus coeruleus lesion lose their appreciation for the signals associated with hunger and fulfillment. These variegated responses to stimulation or alteration of one specific brain center suggest the range of control mechanisms which are involved in the central regulation of mood, appetite, endocrine response, and behavioral activation.[33, 50]

Comprehension of metabolic function is confounded when a single hormone is examined in isolation. Hormones are mutually interacting compounds, and considered in this way, give a more realistic picture of their balanced physiological impact. For example, glucocorticoids and thyroid hormones have interlocking effects in the CNS and on general metabolism, effects balanced in terms of time scale and systems affected.

OVERVIEW

In the molecular biology of development, multiple dimensions of physiological adaptation and response are conceptualized in a hierarchy of biological processes, reaching from the molecular basis of genetic transmission through the integrated functioning of the nervous system expressed in social and symbolic behavior.[68] In the model we have described, the starting point is the child's genome, the sum total of his genetic inheritance. This genome is far greater in potential than is ever expressed phenotypically. Those aspects of the genetic endowment which do become expressed are closely attuned to the environmental and physiological provisions to which the child is exposed.[11]

Based on their genomes and earliest experiences (in utero and during the first weeks of life), children display quite disparate temperaments. They differ in the constellation of processes which underlie their attention, vigor, response to calming, and other dimensions of behavioral functioning.[64] In interaction with their caregivers, their early, organized patterns of behavior are shaped into more complex behavioral processes, with neurochemical responses increasingly differentiated in relation to the child's reactions to his environment and the reactions of the environment to the child. Early experiences, including psychological responses of the environment, nutrition, infection, drugs, and physical trauma, may lead to enduring patterns of behavior which are encoded in central nervous system metabolism (enzyme induction or repression, neurotransmitter levels, alterations in inborn "wiring diagrams," etc.). For example, stimulation and an optimal amount of environmental stress may be reflected in increases in enzyme levels and alteration in hormonal orchestration which are most appropriate for development of the central nervous system, sensitizing it toward further development but not overwhelming or short-circuiting its unfolding.

Based on the match between the child's genetic endowment, the environment's early provisions, and other determinants of adaptation, the child develops patterns of perception and response. For example, persistent early adaptations, such as the habitual fear or anxiousness of a child who has a low threshold for disorganization with stimulation, may shape the child's later adaptation and his style of approach to other, emerging developmental tasks. Action tendencies may assume an autonomy or become relatively crystallized characteristics of a child's behavior, recurrently reinforced by the experiences he creates for himself or the responses he elicits in others.

Of particular interest to child psychiatrists are the means by which the environment facilitates or disrupts the normal unfolding of competence. Changes in the environment elicit organized patterns of attentiveness, arousal, activation, and mental effort. These adaptations involve coordinated behavioral and physiological changes, exemplified by alterations in cardiovascular functioning but observable in many areas of physiological functioning. Stress can be defined in two ways: emphasizing the nature of the objective changes in the child's environment or focusing on the nature of the child's response. From the internal perspective, the concept of stress signifies the degree and nature of the functional organization or disorganization produced by environmental or internal stimulation. What for one child may be optimal stimulation facilitating the unfolding of congenital potentiality may, for another child, even one with the identical genome, be a stress leading to disorganization of behavior and reduction of potential. Sensitive parents are aware of these differences. They protect the child, as far as possible, from overly stressful or traumatic experiences while providing adequate stimulation for development to proceed.[18]

The biological basis for these developmental phenomena embraces the integrated action of multiple systems: genetic replication and the regulation of enzyme synthesis; the synthesis and metabolism of neurotransmitters; the interaction between neurotransmitter systems; the modulating influence of hormones; and the constant, subtle alterations in physiological parameters with environmental provisions.[52] Contemporary biology presents us with an array of phenomena which are as dynamic, fluid, complex, and richly variegated as concepts of mind and culture have always predicted.

The brain, as the contemporary embodiment of social and personal history, has been the object of psychoanalytic scrutiny. Molecular and physiological studies, as described in this chapter, do not detract from the wonder experienced in analyzing a dream, tracing a symptom as a matrix of metaphors, or observing a child during his first years of life. The molecular biological approach provides new methods for investigating those phenomena which are most fundamental to child psychiatry—what the child brings to the world, what the world offers to the child, and how infants grow into healthy and not-so-healthy adults, the parents of the next generation.

ACKNOWLEDGMENTS

We appreciate the collaboration of Ms. Barbara Caparulo and Dr. Bennett Shaywitz, Yale University School of Medicine. Dr. Albert J. Solnit, Director of the Yale Child Study Center, has facilitated all aspects of the research. Textual excerpts and several figures are reproduced from an article by the authors in the *Journal of the American Academy of Child Psychiatry*,[15] with consent of the editor and publisher. The research was supported in part by Public Health Service research grant HD–03008, the William T. Grant

Foundation, NIH Children's Clinical Research Grant RR 00125, The Jean T. Schall Trust, National Research Service Award MH 05223, Mr. Leonard Berger, the Ford Foundation, and the Yale Mental Health Clinical Research Center grant #1 P50 MH-30929.

REFERENCES

1. AGHAJANIAN, G. K., HAIGLER, H. J., and BENNETT, J. L., "Amine Receptors In CNS. III. 5-Hydroxytryptamine in Brain," in Iverson, L. L., Iverson, S. D., and Snyder, S. H. (Eds.), *Handbook of Psychopharmacology*, vol. 6, *Basic Neuropharmacology: Biogenic Amine Receptors*, pp. 63–96, Plenum Press, New York, 1975.

2. ALPERT, J. E., et al., "Animal Models and Childhood Behavioral Disturbances: Dopamine Depletion in the Newborn Rat Pup," *Journal of the American Academy of Child Psychiatry*, 17:239–251, 1978.

3. AXELROD, J., "Neurotransmitters," *Scientific American*, 230:58–71, 1974.

4. ———, "The Pineal Gland: A Neurochemical Transducer," *Science*, 184:1341–1348, 1974.

5. BOWLBY, J., *Attachment and Loss: I. Attachment*, Hogarth Press, London, 1969.

6. BREESE, G. R., "Chemical and Immunochemical Lesions by Specific Neurotoxic Substances and Antisera," in Iversen, L. L., Iversen, S. D., and Snyder, S. H. (Eds.), *Handbook of Psychopharmacology*, vol. 1, *Biochemical Principles and Techniques in Neuropharmacology*, pp. 137–189, Plenum Press, New York, 1975.

7. ———, et al., "Induction of Adrenal Catecholamine Synthesizing Enzymes Following Mother-Infant Separation," *Nature* [*New Biology*], 246:94–96, 1973.

8. CAVALLI-SFORZA, L. L., and BODMER, W. F., *The Genetics of Human Populations*, W. H. Freeman, San Francisco, 1971.

9. CHASE, T. N., and MURPHY, D. L. "Serotonin and Central Nervous System Function," *Annual Review of Pharmacology*, 13:181–197, 1973.

10. CHRISTENSEN, N. J., "Plasma Noradrenaline and Adrenaline in Patients with Thyrotoxicosis and Myxoedema," *Clinical Science and Molecular Medicine*, 45:163–171, 1973.

11. COHEN, D. J., "Psychosomatic Models of Development," in Anthony, E. J. (Ed.), *Explorations in Child Psychiatry*, pp. 197–212, Plenum Press, New York, 1975.

12. ———, "Competence and Biology: Methodology in Studies of Infants, Twins, Psychosomatic Disease, and Psychosis," in Anthony, E. J., and Koupernik, C. (Eds.), *The Child in His Family: Children at Psychiatric Risk*, pp. 361–394, John Wiley, New York, 1974.

13. COHEN, D. J., and JOHNSON, W. T., "Cardiovascular Correlates of Attention in Normal and Psychiatrically Disturbed Children: Blood Pressure, Peripheral Blood Flow, and Peripheral Vascular Resistance," *Archives of General Psychiatry*, 34:561–567, 1977.

14. COHEN, D. J., and YOUNG, J. G., "Neurochemistry and Child Psychiatry," *Journal of the American Academy of Child Psychiatry*, 16:353–411, 1977.

15. COHEN, D. J., et al., "Dopamine and Serotonin Metabolism in Neuropsychiatrically Disturbed Children: CSF Homovanillic Acid and 5-Hydroxyindoleacetic Acid," *Archives of General Psychiatry*, 34:545–550, 1977.

16. COOPER, J. R., BLOOM, F. E., and ROTH, R. H., *The Biochemical Basis of Neuropharmacology*, Oxford University Press, New York, 1974.

17. DAHLSTRÖM, A., and FUXE, K., "Evidence for the Existence of Monoamine Neurons in the Central Nervous System," *Acta Physiologica Scandinavica* (Suppl. 247), 64:1–85, 1965.

18. DOHRENWEND, B. S., and DOHRENWEND, B. P., *Stressful Life Events: Their Nature and Effects*, John Wiley, New York, 1974.

19. DRATMAN, M. B., "On the Mechanism of Action of Thyroxin, an Amino Acid Analog of Tyrosine," *Journal of Theoretical Biology*, 46:255–270, 1974.

20. FREEDMAN, D. X. (Ed.), *Biology of the Major Psychoses: A Comparative Analysis*, Raven Press, New York, 1975.

21. FURST, S. S. (Ed.), *Psychic Trauma*, Basic Books, New York, 1967.

22. FUXE, K., and JONSSON, G., "Further Mapping of Central 5-Hydroxytryptamine Neurons: Studies with the Neurotoxic Dihydroxytryptamines," in Costa, E., Gessa, G. L., and Sandler, M. (Eds.), *Serotonin—New Vistas: Histochemistry and Pharmacology*, pp. 1–12, Raven Press, New York, 1974.

23. GANONG, W. F., "The Role of Catecholamines and Acetylcholine in the Regulation of Endocrine Function," *Life Sciences*, 15:1401–1414, 1974.

24. GOLDSTEIN, A., "Opioid Peptides (Endorphins) in Pituitary and Brain," *Science*, 193:1081–1086, 1976.

25. GREENGARD, P., "Possible Role for Cyclic Nucleotides and Phosphorylated Membrane Proteins in Postsynaptic Actions of Neurotransmitters," *Nature*, 260:101–108, 1976.

26. ———, McAFEE, D. A., and KEBABIAN, J. W., "On the Mechanism of Action of Cyclic AMP and Its Role in Synaptic Transmission," in Greengard, P., and Robison, G. A. (Eds.), *Advances in Cyclic Nucleotide Research*, vol. 1, pp. 337–355, Raven Press, New York, 1972.

27. GUILLEMIN, R., "Neuroendocrine Interrelations," in Bondy, P. K., and Rosenberg, L. E. (Eds.), *Duncan's Diseases of Metabolism*, pp. 951–960, W. B. Saunders Company, Philadelphia, 1974.

28. HARRIS, H., *The Principles of Human Biochemical Genetics*, North Holland Publishing Company, Amsterdam, 1975.

29. HINDE, R. A., and SPENCER-BOOTH, Y., "Individual Differences in the Responses of Rhesus Monkeys to a Period of Separation from Their Parents," *Journal of Child Psychology. Psychiatry and Allied Diseases*, 11:159–176, 1970.

30. JANIS, I. L., *Psychological Stress: Psychoanalytic and Behavioral Studies of Surgical Patients*, John Wiley, New York, 1958.

31. KNOBIL, E., and SAWYER, W. H. (Eds.), *The Handbook of Physiology, Section 7, Endocrinology*, vol. 4, Parts I and II: *The Pituitary Gland and Its Neuroendocrine Control*, Williams and Wilkins, Baltimore, 1974.

32. KOELLE, G. B., "Neurohumoral Transmission and the Autonomic Nervous System," in Goodman, L. S., and Gilman, A. (Eds.), *The Pharmacological Basis of Therapeutics*, pp. 404–444, Macmillan, New York, 1975.

33. KORF, J., AGHAJANIAN, G. K., and ROTH, R. H., "Stimulation and Destruction of the Locus Coeruleus: Opposite Effects on 3-Methoxy-4-hydroxy-phenylglycol Sulfate Levels in the Rat Cerebral Cortex," *European Journal of Pharmacology*, 21:305–310, 1973.

34. KRNJEVIĆ, K., "Acetylcholine Receptors in Vertebrate CNS," in Iversen, L. L., Iversen, S. D., and Snyder, S. H. (Eds.), *Handbook of Psychopharmocology*, vol. 6, *Basic Neuropharmocology: Biogenic Amine Receptors*, pp. 97–126, Plenum Press, New York, 1975.

35. LANDSBERG, L., and AXELROD, J., "Influence of Pituitary, Thyroid, and Adrenal Hormones on Norepinephrine Turnover and Metabolism in the Rat Heart," *Circulation Research*, 22:559–571, 1968.

36. LEHNINGER, A. L., *Biochemistry: The Molecular Basis of Cell Structure and Function*, Worth Publishers, New York, 1975.

37. LEVINE, R. J., and LANDSBERG, L., "Catecholamines and the Adrenal Medulla," in Bondy, P. K., and Rosenberg, L. E. (Eds.), *Duncan's Diseases of Metabolism*, pp. 1181–1224, W. B. Saunders, Philadelphia, 1974.

38. MAAS, J. W., "Biogenic Amines and Depression," *Archives of General Psychiatry, 32:*1357–1361, 1975.

39. ———, and LANDIS, D. H., "*In Vivo* Studies of the Metabolism of Norepinephrine in the Central Nervous System," *Journal of Pharmacology and Experimental Therapeutics, 163:*147–162, 1968.

40. MCCANN, S. M., FAWCETT, C. P., and KRULICH, L., "Hypothalamic Hypophysical Releasing and Inhibiting Hormones," in McCann, S. M. (Ed.), *Endocrine Physiology*, pp. 31–65, Butterworths, London, 1974.

41. MCEWEN, B. S., "Endocrine Effects on the Brain and Their Relationship to Behavior," in Siegel, G. J., et al. (Eds.), *Basic Neurochemistry*, pp. 737–764, Little, Brown, Boston, 1972.

42. MARTIN, J. B., "Regulation of the Pituitary-Thyroid Axis," in McCann, M. (Ed.), *Endocrine Physiology*, pp. 67–107, Butterworths, London, 1974.

43. ———, REICHLIN, S., and BROWN, G. M., *Clinical Neuroendocrinology*, F. A. Davis, Philadelphia, 1977.

44. MASON, J. W., "Psychologic Stress and Endocrine Function," in Sachar, E. J. (Ed.), *Topics in Psychoendocrinology*, pp. 1–18, Grune & Stratton, New York, 1975.

45. ———, "A Review of Psychoendocrine Research on the Pituitary-Thyroid System," *Psychosomatic Medicine, 30:*666–681, 1968.

46. MOLINOFF, P. B., and AXELROD, J., "Biochemistry of Catecholamines," *Annual Review of Biochemistry, 40:*465–500, 1971.

47. MOSKOWITZ, M. A., and WURTMAN, R. J., "Catecholamines and Neurologic Diseases," *New England Journal of Medicine*, Part I, *293:*274–280; Part II, *293:*332–338, 1975.

48. MURPHY, D. L., BELMAKER, R., and WYATT, R. J., "Monoamine Oxidase in Schizophrenia and Other Behavioral Disorders," *Journal of Psychiatric Research, 11:*221–247, 1974.

49. NEY, R. L., "The Anterior Pituitary Gland," in Bondy, P. K., and Rosenberg, L. E. (Eds.), *Duncan's Diseases of Metabolism*, pp. 961–1008, W. B. Saunders, Philadelphia, 1974.

50. REDMOND, D. E., et al., "Behavioral Effects of Stimulation of the Nucleus Locus Coeruleus in the Stump-Tailed Monkey *Macaca arctoides*," *Brain Research, 116:*502–510, 1976.

51. REIS, D. J., et al., "Changes in Adrenal Enzymes Synthesizing Catecholamines in Attack Behavior Evoked by Hypothalamic Stimulation in the Cat," *Nature, 229:*562–563, 1971.

52. REISER, M. F., "Changing Theoretical Concepts in Psychosomatic Medicine," in Reiser, M. F. (Ed.), *American Handbook of Psychiatry*, 2nd ed., vol. 4, pp. 477–500, Basic Books, New York, 1975.

53. ROSENBERG, L. E., "Inborn Errors of Metabolism," in Bondy, P. K., and Rosenberg, L. E. (Eds.), *Duncan's Diseases of Metabolism*, pp. 31–58, W. B. Saunders, Philadelphia, 1975.

54. ROSENTHAL, D., *Genetic Theory and Abnormal Behavior*, McGraw-Hill, New York, 1970.

55. SACHAR, E. J., "Neuroendocrine Abnormalities in Depressive Illness," in Sachar, E. J. (Ed.), *Topics in Psychoendocrinology*, pp. 135–156, Grune & Stratton, New York, 1975.

56. SCHALLY, A. V., ARIMURA, A., and KASTIN, A. J., "Hypothalamic Regulatory Hormones," *Science, 179:*341–350, 1973.

57. SCHALLY, A. V., KASTIN, A. J., and ARIMURA, A., "Hypothalamic Hormones: The Link Between Brain and Body," *American Scientist, 65:*712–719, 1977.

58. SHAYWITZ, B. A., YAGER, R. D., and KLOPPER, J. H., "Selective Brain Dopamine Depletion in Developing Rats," *Science, 191:*305–308, 1976.

59. SIEGEL, G. J., and EISENMAN, J. S., "Hypothalamic-Pituitary Regulation," in Siegel, G. J., et al. (Eds.), *Basic Neurochemistry*, pp. 445–467, Little, Brown, Boston, 1972.

60. SOLNIT, A. J., "The Meaning of Change in Child Development," in Anthony, E. J., and Koupernik, C. (Eds.), *The Child in His Family*, vol. 5, John Wiley, New York, forthcoming.

61. SNYDER, S. H., "Opiate Receptors in the Brain," *New England Journal of Medicine, 296:*266–271, 1977.

62. STRYER, L., *Biochemistry*, W. H. Freeman, San Francisco, 1975.

63. SUTTON, H. E., *An Introduction to Human Genetics*, Holt, Rinehart and Winston, New York, 1975.

64. THOMAS, A., CHESS, S., and BIRCH, H. G., *Temperament and Behavior Disorders in Children*, New York University Press, New York, 1968.

65. UNGERSTEDT, U., "Stereotoxic Mapping of the Monoamine Pathways in the Rat Brain," *Acta Physiologica Scandinavica* (Suppl. 367), 1–29, 1971.

66. USDIN, E., and SNYDER, S., *Frontiers in Catecholamine Research*, Pergamon Press, New York, 1973.

67. USDIN, E., KVETNANSKY, R., and KOPIN, I. J., (Eds.), *Catecholamines and Stress*, Pergamon Press, New York, 1976.

68. WEINER, H., *Psychobiology and Human Disease*, Elsevier, Amsterdam, 1977.

69. WURTMAN, R. J., and FERNSTROM, J. D., "Control of Brain Neurotransmitter Synthesis by Precursor Availability and Nutritional State," *Biochemical Pharmacology, 25:*1691–1696, 1976.

4 / Organizers of the Psyche and EEG Development:

Birth Through Adolescence

David R. Metcalf

The ontogenesis, preferably the *development* of the electroencephalogram (EEG), has been the object of investigation from the very inception of electroencephalography.[4] This has continued through the infancy of the field, [21, 40, 22] its clinical elaboration,[11, 19, 9] and into its current maturity with burgeoning application of the associated computer-methodologies. These recent advances have resulted in more refined, accurate, and detailed descriptions of the EEG in the form of visual displays[5,10] and as mathematical and statistical transforms.[10, 38, 6] Two areas peripheral to but involving electroencephalography have also provided rich data. These bear on EEG development as well as on the focal topic of this chapter, the relationship of the developing EEG to aspects of personality, behavior, and psychological functioning. These areas are: first, the application of the EEG derivative, the sensory-evoked response, to understanding information-processing aspects of brain function,[39] and second,[7] the recent discoveries regarding the physiology and psychophysiology of sleep and related brain and EEG functions.[8, 37, 1, 12]

Although Berger,[4] the father of electroencephalography, was interested in elucidating relationships between EEG and various aspects of psychological functioning (particularly personality typology), he soon abandoned this aim and concentrated his efforts on technological, methodological, and neurophysiological aspects of this new approach to brain function. Many others have since worked and published in this interfacing, bridging area; Knott[20] has done a great deal of work in this area and has also provided a number of useful critiques of some of the simplistic and overenthusiastic reports which appear from time to time.

The author's studies[30, 12, 46, 31] have sought to understand the connections between brain function (viewed through the EEG) and behavior. These studies focus on the changes which take place in the EEG at different age levels, and on the relationships of these changes to the sequential emergence of critical periods in development and of organizers of the psyche.

The aim of this chapter is to describe the development of the electroencephalogram during wakefulness and sleep, from birth through adolescence. This description will take cognizance of deviations, delays, and accelerations along this developmental line. It will also attempt to define the occurrence of development-specific normal variations within this progression. These variants are in themselves normal, but appear to mimic electroencephalographic abnormality as it might appear during adulthood.

In addition, the material will outline the development-specific timing and functioning of a number of organizers of the psyche.[42, 46, 26] As originally developed by Spitz, the concept of psychic organizers was, in itself, a biopsychological and psychobiological formulation. It arose out of biological principles and has proven to be an exceedingly heuristic concept for those interested in biopsychological and psychobiological factors in development.[42, 43, 46] For this reason, the author has chosen to connect the *development of organizers of the psyche* with development of the electroencephalogram. Thus, a parallel can be drawn between electroencephalographic (and by implication, brain) development on the one hand, and emotional and psychological development (seen through the binding concept of the development of psychic organizers) on the other. This makes it possible for these viewpoints to serve as bridges between "the psyche and the soma."[41]

The basic EEG data reported here are derived from volunteer families who were enrolled in a long-term, longitudinal study of human development.* This involved 180 children, 80 of whom were followed from birth through mid-adolescence. During the course of this program, subjects were studied repeatedly by a variety of means, including long bone x-rays, physical anthropmetry, psychological evaluations, physical evaluations, pediatric histories, and for a smaller number, repeated play interviews. Significant clinical pathology did not occur, and nutrition was excellent for all members at all times. Physical growth was within nor-

* Child Research Council, Department for the Study of Human Growth Council, University of Colorado Medical Center, Denver, Colorado.

mal limits and there were no brain disturbances in these subjects. The mothers of this group of subjects were also followed throughout pregnancy. At the clinical level these children represent a normal population. Electroencephalograms were done on each subject shortly after birth, then every three months during the first two years of life, every six months until age six years, and once a year (close to the birthday) from that time on.

As compared with the adult, a larger range of variability has long been recognized in the EEG of the normal infant and child. It is less well known that this variability includes shifting, multifocal "aberrations" in the EEGs of children below adolescence, such as random focal sharp waves, spikes, slow waves, or persistent focal slowing, etc. These findings are often misinterpreted as representing brain abnormality. The data in the author's group add the important clarification that there is a fairly high incidence of such EEG "aberrations" in this clinically normal population. Moreover, they occur without antecedent, concurrent, or subsequent clinical, central nervous system or electroencephalographic disturbances. These "aberrations" disappear during early adolescence.

The word "aberration" is used for these EEG findings in order to be nonjudgmental and nonpejorative. These "aberrations" are deviations from the expected straight-forward, deviation-free normality of the "ideal normal" adult EEG. Often, the normal deviations in the preadolescent EEG resemble epileptiform abnormality in the adult EEG.

Since these EEG findings were first published,[30, 29, 33] it has been amply documented that there are numerous "discontinuities," i.e., shifts in the rate of development during the childhood years which connect with physiological development as well as with psychological development.[13] It is this region which will be discussed.

Psychic organizers are sometimes spoken of as "critical periods in development." As the author has said previously,[26] "all experience subsequent to the operation of a new psychic organizer is differently organized than prior to that time in development; it is as if the very reality with which the individual deals is now altered." New stages in psychobiological development are heralded and ushered in by the presence of new psychic organizers.

The concept of psychic organizers requires that a particular criterion be met, namely, the presence of a specific affective behavior. This is considered to indicate the presence of the new organizer and, therefore, the inception of a new stage in development. An organizer of the psyche implies a unique aspect of *psychological* organization. For example, during the first three months of life (and later), maturational factors bring about many reorganizations and progressive integrations and reintegrations of neuromuscular behavior. However, these are not considered psychic organizers because an affective indicator such as smiling or specific anxiety is absent. The presence of such an affective signal or indicator indicates the existence of an intrapsychic change or a new intrapsychic process. Thus, at about age three months, the inception of a smiling response indicates a basic intrapsychic change. It marks the termination of the stage of nondifferentiation and the earliest beginnings of ego organization.

When new affective behaviors or new affective indicators appear, they betoken the concomitant evolution of organized shifts in the intrapsychic economy. These can be conceptualized as changes in the patterning of intrapsychic force fields—new centers and modes in patterning of dynamic balance and conflict organization. Such intrapsychic changes will of necessity be manifest at the behavioral level.

Our specific use of the terms "development" and "maturation" should be elucidated at this point. We have stated:

At all developmental levels, maturationally guided processes are turned into developmental processes as a result of the adaptations enforced by exchanges with the surround and the organism's response to them.

In this sense, postnatally, the concept "maturation" is a useful construct, even though *unrealizable*; *all is development*. For development is the result of a constant interaction between environment (or experience) and the innate; these interactions operate at all levels, whether molecular, cellular, or organismic.

Maturation, as a functional reality, is that aspect of development which provides potentialities on the one hand, and limitations on the other . . . development is not blind. It is responsive to the surround in terms of the *law of effect* . . .

Conversely, maturation is blind, for it is the product of phylogenesis over geological time span. Development, through the impact of experience, is the means through which maturationally given potentialities are realized. It is one of the *inducers* of organizers. Organizers are formed out of species-specific, innate potentialities and directions, interacting with the species-unique demands of the surround.[46] [pp. 431–432]

Generally, regular, age-correlated changes in the electroencephalogram have been treated as if they were somewhat akin to the major maturational aspects of physical growth, brain growth, etc. It is the author's contention that electroencephalographic changes are derivatives of changes in brain function and should therefore be regarded as developmental rather than maturational phenomena. Hence, one would expect that nodal points in development, the emergence of new psychic organizers, would be accompanied by significant shifts in electroencephalographic organization. Just as behavioral and emotional development do not proceed in a steady, monotonic fashion but tend rather to advance through a series of stepwise discontinuities,[13, 46] so should the developing electroencephalogram proceed in stepwise and somewhat discontinuous fashion with its own nodal points related to observed nodal points in psychobiological development.

As the child grows older, the initial simplicity disappears. There is an increasing complexity which accompanies psychobiological and psychological organization associated with increasing age. This renders the hoped-for correlations increasingly difficult to perceive. In the earliest months of life when development of all sorts proceeds most rapidly, psychological as well as electroencephalographic development are under strong maturational pressure (with maturation becoming less significant with increasing age). This makes it easier to observe electroencephalographic and behavioral correlations. With increasing age, the complexities introduced by developmental variability, variability of experiential factors, and so on render such correlations more difficult to observe.

One of the great human psychic organizers is the period of the Oedipus complex. Studies at this time illustrate the complexity and difficulty in demonstrating the relationships between electroencephalographic and behavioral development. However, so long as one does not oversimplify and search for simple linear relationships, the psychobiological focus of these investigations remain viable.

The focus here will be primarily on the development of the sleep electroencephalogram in the first few years of life and the awake and sleep electroencephalogram after age three years.

The First Three Months

Approximately the first three months of life is occupied by what Spitz has termed "a stage of nondifferentiation."[43] Both in timing and in content this approximates the undifferentiated stage of Hartmann, Kris, and Loewenstein,[18] and the autistic stage of Mahler.[24]

The sleep electroencephalogram shows regular changes from the time of intrauterine life (in prematures, from earliest viability) through the entire period of nondifferentiation. However, during this stage, these progressing changes are minimal, suggesting the impact of a major (but not exclusive) maturational factor. The ontogenic course of the awake and sleep EEG in prematurely born infants has been described by a number of investigators.[9, 34, 28, 47] All these studies have shown the close relationship between developing EEG morphology and gestational age in prematures, and in infants during the first two to three months of life. The opinion of most of these investigators is best exemplified by Dreyfus-Brisac, who maintains that the electroencephalogram during these early ages is primarily, if not exclusively, under maturational influence, with little or no experiential influence. The author has shown that during prematurity and early postmaturity, the developing electroencephalogram is under significant developmental impact. This is demonstrated by the gestationally earlier onset of nodal points in EEG development in prematures as compared with full-term infants, notably the timing of the onset of sleep spindles and of K-complexes. This work clearly demonstrates the impact of experience on an otherwise maturational event (the average time of onset of sleep spindles in the developing electroencephalogram).

The sleep EEG of premature infants of about thirty-two weeks shows three principle types of activity. These are: Large amounts of sleep time (up to 70 percent) are spent in Stage 1 rapid-eye movement (REM) sleep. This is associated with an activated, relatively low amplitude, polyrhythmic electroencephalogram associated with rapid eye movements, generalized physiological activation, activation of voluntary muscles of face and extremeties, and notable irregularities of heart rate and respiration. The remainder of the sleep EEG consists of poorly formed slow wave sleep and small amounts of intermediately organized awake EEG.

An outstanding feature of the EEG during prematurity consists of the *tracé alternant* record which is generally seen during quiet non-REM sleep. The *tracé alternant* EEG, although seen almost exclusively during prematurity, is also seen in mature infants during the first three weeks of life. However, it disappears earlier in prematures than in full-term infants of comparable gestational age, again indicating the impact of experience on the developing EEG. It is generally agreed that the *tracé alternant* EEG represents unmodulated cortical, neuroelectrical activity. With postnatal development, this gradually becomes more organized as dendrodendritic and axodendritic connections become established and active. These findings are consonant with well-known clinical observations concerning the impact of experience on early ego development.[42, 2, 24] During this early era, the intermittent sharp and slow bursts of a *tracé alternant* EEG gradually become filled in as these variations disappear within the background of the developing electroencephalogram. After forty gestational weeks, the intermittent and relatively discontinuous record seen during prematurity is no longer seen during early quiet sleep. However, it remains evident in very deep, quiet sleep. Persistence of clear *tracé alternant* recording or polysharp and slow bursts is uncommon around the time of expected term and thereafter. It raises the suspicion that a cortical-subcortical disturbance exists, reminiscent of cortical isolation from subcortical modulating structures. The remnants of this activity persist until age four to five weeks in full-term infants and are very rare after six weeks. In the first month or two of life, the developmental status of *tracé alternant* activity and its remnants can therefore be used as a diagnostic criterion of brain developmental status.

Benjamin[2] has noted an early behavioral change which may be a possible precursor of anxiety as an affect. At three to four weeks, the appearance of manifestations of *active* responses (most notably negative responses) coincide roughly with an EEG developmental landmark, the inception of EEG sleep spindles. He terms this a "critical period" in development. It is made possible by a step in brain maturation (indicated by the first presence of sleep spindles) and therefore has the status of a prototypic organizer. This period is a pre-ego state, mostly of somatic and maturational significance. But it is a precursor of the period of the first organizer where an *affective* sign, the smiling response, also participates.

Three Months—The First Organizer

The next important landmark in the developing electroencephalogram is the switchover from the "infantile" method of falling asleep (i.e., directly from the wake to the rapid-eye movement state) to the more "mature" method of falling asleep (whereby sleep proceeds electrographically from the awake record through Stage 1 non-REM to Stage 2, gradually to a deeper slow-wave sleep, and finally rising to REM sleep). This change from the infantile falling-asleep method to the more mature falling-asleep method coincides with the onset of the first psychic organizer at about three months, namely the onset of a reliable but automatic smiling response.[42, 46, 26, 12] Parenthetically, falling asleep directly into rapid-eye movement sleep, i.e., the normal infantile method, is one of the more clear electrographic, diagnostic indicators of classical narcolepsy. Prior to this switchover, it has been shown that there is an interesting behavioral-sleep physiological paradox in which concomitant with the EEG and physiology of Stage 1 REM sleep, infants can be seen to be drowsy-awake, crying, fussing, feeding, or smiling. After the age of three months, this disparity between electrographic indicators of sleep and behavioral sleep disappears, after which behavioral sleep is always associated with electrographic indicators of sleep. Metcalf and Spitz[27, 46, 31] suggest that both physiologically and psychologically, the psychic precursors and prototypes of dreaming, commence during this switchover period. Emde[13] has shown that before the time of this major switchover, infants tend to fall directly into quiet sleep and display much longer than "normal" episodes of quiet sleep under the impact of physical trauma; this experiential impact on the electroencephalogram and on sleep physiology is generally not seen after age three months.

The first organizer of the psyche, indicated by the social smile, appears to be under primary but not exclusive maturational control. The most potent stimulus for eliciting the smiling response is a slowly nodding human face.[45] Spitz has shown that a pattern or gestalt organization resembling the schematic feature of the face (eyes, nose, and mouth) are sufficient to trigger into action a maturationally formed potential organization, or potential schema resulting in the smiling response. At about three months, the infant has emerged from the state of nondifferentiation.[43] It is the beginning of the separation-individuation process of Mahler,[24] and therefore coincides with the differentiation of self from object, of psyche from soma, and the inception of separable psychic structures.[26]

This is a period when there is strong interaction between central nervous system (CNS) maturation, central nervous system development, and behavioral development. It is during this time that the infant begins to wait and to anticipate. Social smiling as such advances rapidly, and the beginnings of affective attachments exist and develop apace. This is a time when there is a confluence of numerous maturational CNS factors along with the beginning organization of memory traces and engrams. Together these lead to the development of rudimentary psychic structures.

Three to Six Months

Between age three months and six to seven months, the awake electroencephalogram develops slowly and regularly. There is a gradual appearance of low to medium amplitude activity in a dominant 3 to 5 cps frequency range with some early inchoate alpha rhythms being present. This is best discerned by a variety of computer-derived mathematical transforms of the EEG. The developing sleep electroencephalogram continues to show remarkable and highly visible evidences of its own progressive changes. Throughout the life cycle, the Stage 1 sleep EEG shows few changes in its qualitative features. However, during the first year of life, deep, quiet, slow-wave sleep changes are becoming progressively more differentiated. One important point of differentiation takes place at about age six months, with the first clear appearance of K-complexes. These are evidence of a new step in central nervous system information processing.[33] Prior to this, Stages 3 and 4 (deep, slow-wave sleep) become differentiated from the previously evident Stage 2 sleep. Stage 4, the deepest stage of high-voltage slow-wave sleep, is not well developed until twelve months or afterward, but its first emergence is discernible at about age six months. This is approximately the same time that K-complexes begin to be clearly seen.

Many later features of the mature electroencephalogram take definitive form at about age six months. During this time, sleep spindles become sharp, comblike, very well formed, and often show scalp-positive sharp components. The sharp sleep spindles can be mistaken for electroencephalographic abnormality, but those familiar with developmental vicissitudes of the EEG will not be misled. Hemispheric voltage asymmetry begins to develop at about age six months, but lateral EEG balance in normal subjects is not generally established before age three years. These findings will be detailed subsequently.

The Second Organizer— Eight-Month Anxiety

After age six months, variability in sleep spindles and K-complexes continues. Many deviations from expected ideal norms occur after age three years.

The period of the onset of the second psychic organizer is therefore a watershed in association with EEG development. Subsequent to this, all adult features of the electroencephalogram are manifest, whereas prior to this, their ontogenesis and development are all in stages of inception. The appearance of the second psychic organizer during normal development is indicated by the onset of anxiety at about age seven months. Originally, this was termed "8-months anxiety" by Spitz.[42] Benjamin [3, 2] and Tennes et al.[48] studied this in detail and were able to differentiate between stranger anxiety and separation anxiety. Stranger anxiety had its inception at about six to seven months, and separation anxiety began at about eight to nine months and reached its peak at twelve to sixteen months. Benjamin[2] also noted a possible prototype and precursor of stranger anxiety occurring at about age three weeks. The author has noted the EEG concomitants (sleep spindles) of this maturational change, which he would also suggest is a prototype of future somatopsychic and psychic organizers. It is likely that the eight- to ten-months anxiety noted by Spitz represents some combination of stranger and separation anxiety. Mahler[23] has shown that this early anxiety can be modified (intensified or reduced) by factors in the early mother-infant relationship. There is a great need for further work in this area, of defining and describing these early anxieties. A significant step in this direction has taken place with the publication of the monograph of Emde et al.[13]

The period of the second organizer begins with the infant's ability to differentiate mother from strangers, i.e., nonmother. From other observational stances, this has therefore been termed the onset of stranger anxiety or, as Benjamin called it, fear of the strange as such. Stranger anxiety appears to have important maturational roots whereas separation anxiety, occurring a little later, is under much more significant experiental impact. Thus, the period of the second organizer is a watershed for brain electrophysiological development; it is also the time when a major shift from soma to psyche in Spitz's terms[41] also takes place. The rapid changes in the electroencephalogram betoken a critical period in brain development. In terms of mammalian CNS maturational time tables, this appears to represent a human period, comparable to the period for critical dendritic development in kittens, outlined by Purpura.[36] This is the time which also coincides approximately with the inception of what Mahler[23] has termed "the psychological birth of the human infant." This period has been typified by Metcalf as follows:

The period guided by the second organizer commences with the infant's ability to differentiate Mother from strangers (i.e., from non-Mother) and proceeds through a period of rapid emotional growth during which thought processes become established, differentiation of self from others begins, and exchanges between infant and Mother take place and promote the infant's development. There is rapid development of many systems and functions, including sensory-motor development, early cognitive development, progressive differentiations of self from object, and progress along the separation-individuation line. During this time, from 7 to 14 or 16 months, psychic structure begins to differentiate and we can speak topographically of conscious, preconscious and unconscious. Patterned memory traces organize out of their primordial engrams, and boundaries begin to be created between ego and id, ego and reality, I and non-I, self and non-self. It is during the period of the second organizer that a number of differential developmental lines begin to emerge. During this time the importance of maturational factors begins to give way to biasing in favor of developmental factors, i.e., the experiential, in development. Toward the end of this period, fusion of aggressive and libidinal drives begins to occur. Thus, developing object relations at this time, emerging drive-fusion, and advances in the separation-individuation process, are all particularly vulnerable to derailment or distortion.[26]* [p. 150]

Parenthetically, starting at about age six months, there is another notable electrographic development visible during the dominance of the second organizer. It consists of the onset of electroencephalographic "drowsy hypersynchrony." This is the type of electroencephalogram seen during behavioral drowsiness and is composed of medium- to high-amplitude delta and theta activity. This occurs synchronously in all scalp regions during drowsiness. This type of EEG commences at about age six months or a little later, and lasts normally until age five or six years. It is always associated with behavioral drowsiness, although in a few children, it is seen during behavioral early sleep. It is also very similar to and perhaps identical with, the prearousal state following very deep Stage 4 sleep. In pathological situations (sleepwalking especially), arousal hypersynchronous activity following deep Stage 4 sleep is difficult to differentiate morphologically from drowsy hypersynchronous activity. It is the type of EEG associated with sleepwalking. Thus, sleepwalkers at age six or older seem to show a persistence of or regression to the arousal hypersynchronous electrographic activity of an earlier developmental period and also a failure of the muscular inhibition which normally occurs during sleep.

After eight to nine months, when the period of the second organizer is well established, electro-

* Reprinted by permission of the publisher.

graphic development appears to reach a plateau, to slow down and regularize. EEG sleep stages become well differentiated from each other and show the classical sleep stages that are seen thereafter throughout life. The percentage partitioning of sleep stages during the night begins to approach the normal pattern for the young child and young adult levels. Approximately 20 percent of sleep time is taken up by REM sleep, with the usual partitioning of other sleep and awake stages during the eight-hour night's sleep. The awake EEG now begins to show regular development and acceleration of development of alpha rhythms.

By approximately age three, lateral balance of the alpha rhythms begins to occur. In normal right-handed people, this means that the electroencephalogram over the right hemisphere is more regular, better sustained, and a little higher amplitude than the alpha EEG over the left hemisphere. The specialized and nonspecific lateralizing functions of the cerebral hemispheres have been studied with increasing intensity in recent years.[17] These investigations may clarify "brain-behavior" relationships at the level of psychic structure, within a psychoanalytic theoretical framework.[23] From the developmental viewpoint, this has been delineated in a study comparing the electroencephalogram of normal infants and those with sex chromosome anomalies.[32] The author has shown that lateral dominance of rhythmic activity in the EEG develops over an extended time period, and in normal children, it is often not complete until about age five. However, children with the 47 XXX and 47 XXY chromosome abnormality show early development of EEG lateralization. Indeed, 50 percent of these cases show established laterality by ages thirteen to eighteen months. This is consistent with a selective blocking of left-hemisphere EEG activity and is also consonant with the earlier development of verbal activity in girls as compared with boys.

The Third Organizer—
Semantic "No" Gesture

It is therefore not surprising that sleep EEG activity shows no further nodal points of organization. Cognitive organization begins to achieve primacy after the ages of twelve to fifteen months. The indicator of the onset of the *third organizer* is the acquisition at about sixteen months of semantic communication for the word or concept "no."[44] The indicator for the semantic "no" can be a headshake or the word "no" can represent the inception of concept formation. In a sense, this also requires a new integrative use of aggressive energy and therefore involves the operation of the defense mechanism "identification with the frustrator," i.e., mother's "no." "No" is the child's first abstract concept. It is a significant step beyond the prior demonstration and use of need-indicating or wish-indicating global words or gestures, such as "mama," "dada," etc. During the period of the third organizer, speech develops rapidly and not only furnishes the infant with new, more efficient and creative communication, but also stimulates cognitive development. Indeed, it depends upon independently originating cognitive developments; a normal circular cognitive developmental process. Object permanence and object constancy[25, 35] come into being during this period and become better established by age eighteen to twenty-four months.[15]

The Fourth Organizer— Verbal Reporting of Dreams

The first verbal reports of dreaming at eighteen to twenty-four months are preceded by approximately ten months, more or less, of predreaming.[27] A shift in intrapsychic balance, internal integration, integration of inside and outside, and movement in intrapsychic organization and activity, take place at eighteen to twenty-four months. From this time onward, particularly after the onset of the third organizer itself, landmarks in electroencephalographic development take place primarily in organization and gradual development of the awake EEG. This is particularly evident in growth of the alpha rhythms.

This general time period and developmental period has been characterized as follows:

The onset of dreaming, at about age 18 months, is a *fourth psychic organizer* during infancy. It is quite likely that some form of dreaming, which we have termed "predreams," occurs after about age 12 to 16 months, with more primitive "protodreams" taking place between six months and 12 months. The onset of dreaming, which is manifest by an increase in affective behaviors during sleep and on awakening at about age nine months (night terrors, sleep drunkeness, dream reports with first language), overlaps the period of the transitional object. Thus at this more complex period in development, evidence of dreaming or attachment to transitional objects are interchangeably indicators of the onset of this fourth organizer, namely, a shift from primary libidinal object-constancy to the secondary form, differentiation of primary and secondary process activity, organized mental activity awake and asleep, and the more full and differentiable developments of psychic structure with fulfillment now possible in the unconscious and in dreams. The period of the transitional object has been shown by Winnicott (1951)* to represent an important stage in memory development, affect development and structural differentiation. It probably represents an important, in between, developmental line particularly involved in the shift from poorly differentiated self to a further differentiation of self from Mother and from the outside. The infant's ability to replace Mother with a doll or fuzzy blanket also indicates intrapsychic development in progress. This development involves memory shifts, the beginnings of organized memories and or cognition, symbolization, and the construction of fantasies and wishes, all prerequisites for dreaming.[26]† [p. 151]

These overlapping periods for psychic organization take place during the transition from the narcissistic phallic state into the phallic oedipal state and then into the oedipal complex proper. Presently this gives way to latency. It is during latency that one sees some of the most interesting EEG "deviations" (see chapter 15) but without notable nodal points in EEG development.

These EEG deviations consist of perturbations in the previous, fairly regular aspects of EEG development. This regularity now becomes discontinuous, and various transitory EEG discharges show numerous escapes from control. It is during latency that one sees an upsurge in 6 and 14 per second positive spikes in the posterior temporal regions during light sleep, particularly in the right hemisphere, focal slowing again more in the right posterior hemisphere than the left, vertex spikes which appear to be distortions of combined vertex sleep spindles and K-complex activity, and disruptions of general rhythmicity. Details of these deviations have been described in detail elsewhere.[30] Thus, it appears that brain electrophysiological development shows significant nodal points during early development. These have to do with integration and interaction between maturational and developmental aspects of psyche and central nervous system. Periodically they give way to intermittent escape of cortical EEG from subcortical control. This takes the form of rhythmic and transient disturbances in the electroencephalogram, primarily during latency. The latency shifts

* D. W. Winnicott, "Transitional Objects and Transitional Phenomena," in D. W. Winnicott (Ed.), *Collected Papers*, pp. 229–242, Basic Books, New York, 1958.
† Reprinted by permission of the publisher.

in the EEG are heralded by the onset of the fourth and fifth organizers, namely dreaming and the transitional object. These announce the onset of entrance into maturity. The shift from an affective integrative focus in the developing infant to a more cognitively centered developmental focus is represented in these awake and sleep EEG deviations. It has been described from other viewpoints by Anna Freud[16] and by White[49] in his studies of cognitive development in children. One may speculate that the "escape" of EEG cortical transient discharges (spikes, etc.) takes place during the latency age period when there is a relative "failure" of CNS inhibitory functions in the course of shifting from an "affective focus" to a "cognitive focus."

Adolescence is preceded by a remarkable spurt in EEG development and by a virtual cessation of all EEG disturbances and deviations. The electroencephalogram is now dominated by high amplitude, regular alpha rhythms in the awake EEG. These are often sharp but never seriously deviant. Indeed, there is a remarkable absence of EEG disturbances, normal or pathological of any sort, during sleep. The EEG is now launched inexorably on its own adult-bound trajectory. By age seventeen years, the EEG begins to assume the normal, young adult form, with leftovers of the high-voltage, regular alpha rhythm of adolescence being seen on the average until about age twenty-two.

The great psychic organizers that have been so briefly outlined are associated not with specific EEG changes or with specific morphological or focal EEG alterations, but rather with new movements in EEG organization. These betoken changes in brain organization and changes in the nature of the bridging and the nature of the interfaces between psyche and soma, so well described by Spitz.[41]

The material has repeatedly shown the intimate interactions between aspects of central nervous system development on the one hand and behavioral development, emotional development, and the emerging psychic structure on the other. Search for specific, one-to-one or monotonic relationships between EEG development and some aspect of behavioral development is doomed to failure. But the search for parallels in integrative processes and in developmental trajectories is fruitful and bears continuing investigation.

REFERENCES

1. ANDERS, T. F., "An Overview of Recent Sleep and Dream Research," in Goldberger, L., and Rosen, V. H. (Eds.), *Psychoanalysis and Contemporary Science*, vol. 3, pp. 449–469, International Universities Press, New York, 1974.

2. BENJAMIN, J. D., "Further Comments on Some Developmental Aspects of Anxiety," in Gaskill, H. (Ed.), *Counterpoint: Libidinal Object and Subject*, pp. 121–153, International Universities Press, New York, 1963.

3. ———, "Some Developmental Observations Relating to the Theory of Anxiety, *Journal of the American Psychoanalytic Association*, 9:652–668, 1961.

4. BERGER, H., "Über das Elecktroenkephalogram des Menschen," *Archiv fuer Psychiatrie und Nervenkrankheiten*, 87:527–570, 1929.

5. BICKFORD, R. G., "Computational Aspects of Brain Function," *IEEE Transactions of Biomedical Engineering*, 6:164–167, 1959.

6. BURCH, N. R., et al., "Period Analysis of the Electroencephalogram: Maturation and Anoxia," in Prescott, J. W., Read, M. S., and Coursin, D. B. (Eds.), *Brain Function and Malnutrition: Neurophysiological Methods of Assessment*, pp. 141–159, John Wiley, New York, 1975.

7. CALLAWAY, E., *Brain Electrical Potentials and Individual Psychological Differences*, Grune & Stratton, New York, 1975.

8. DEMENT, W., and KLEITMAN, H., "Cyclic Variations in EEG During Sleep and Their Relation to Eye Movements, Body Motility and Dreaming," *Electroencephalography and Clinical Neurophysiology*, 9:673–690, 1957.

9. DREYFUS-BRISAC, C., "The Electroencephalogram of the Premature Infant and Full-term Newborn: Normal and Abnormal Development of Waking and Sleeping Patterns," in Kellaway, P., and Petersen, I. (Eds.), *Neurological and Electroencephalographic Correlative Studies in Infancy*, pp. 186–208, Grune & Stratton, New York, 1964.

10. DUMMERMUTH, G., and FLUEHLER, H., "Some Modern Aspects in Numerical Spectrum Analysis of Multichannel Electroencephalographic Data," *Medical and Biological Engineering*, 5:319–331, 1967.

11. ELLINGSON, R. J., "The Study of Brain Electrical Activity in Infants," in Lipsitt, L. P., and Spiker, C. C. (Eds.), *Advances in Child Development and Behavior*, vol. 3, pp. 54–98, Academic Press, New York, 1967.

12. EMDE, R. N., and METCALF, D. R., "An Electroencephalographic Study of Behavioral Rapid Eye Movement States in the Human Newborn," *Journal of Nervous and Mental Disease*, 150:376–386, 1970.

13. EMDE, R. N., GAENSBAUER, T. J., and HARMON, R. J., *Emotional Expression in Infancy: A Biobehavioral Study*, Psychological Issues, Monograph Series, vol. 10, no. 37, International Universities Press, New York, 1976.

14. ERIKSON, E. H., *Childhood and Society*, 2nd ed., W. W. Norton, New York, 1963.

15. FRAIBERG, S., "Libidinal Object Constancy and Mental Representation," in Eissler, R. S., et al. (Eds.), *The Psychoanalytic Study of the Child*, vol. 24, pp. 9–47, International Universities Press, New York, 1969.

16. FREUD, A., *Normality and Pathology in Childhood*, International Universities Press, New York, 1965.

17. GALIN, D., "Implications for Psychiatry of Left and Right Cerebral Specialization: A Neurophysiological Context for Unconscious Processes," *Archives of General Psychiatry*, 31:572–583, 1974.

18. HARTMANN, H., KRIS, E., and LOEWENSTEIN, R. M., "Comments on the Formation of Psychic Structure, in Eissler, R. S., et al. (Eds.), *The Psychoanalytic Study of the Child*, vol. 2, pp. 11–38, International Universities Press, New York, 1946.

19. KELLAWAY, P., and FOX, B. J., "Electroencephalo-

graphic Diagnosis of Cerebral Pathology in Infants During Sleep. I. Rationale, Technique, and Characteristics of Normal Sleep in Infants," *Journal of Pediatrics, 41:262–287,* 1952.

20. KNOTT, J. R., and GOTTLIEB, J. S., "Electroencephalographic Evaluation of Psychopathic Personality," *Archives of Neurology and Psychiatry, 52:*515–521, 1944.

21. LINDSLEY, D. B., "Electrical Potentials of the Human Brain in Children and Adults," *Journal of General Psychology, 21:*285–306, 1938.

22. LOOMIS, A. L., HARVEY, E. N., and HOBART, G. A., "Electrical Potentials of the Human Brain," *Journal of Experimental Psychology, 19:*249–279, 1936.

23. MCLAUGHLIN, J. T., "Primary and Secondary Process in the Context of Cerebral Hemispheric Specialization," *Psychoanalytic Quarterly, 47(2):*237–266, 1978.

24. MAHLER, M. S., *On Human Symbiosis and the Vicissitudes of Individuation,* vol. I, Infantile Psychosis, International Universities Press, New York, 1968.

25. ——, PINE, F., and BERGMAN, A., *The Psychological Birth of the Human Infant: Symbiosis and Individuation,* Basic Books, New York, 1975.

26. METCALF, D. R., "Organizers of the Psyche," in Wolman, B. B. (Ed.), *International Encyclopedia of Neurology, Psychiatry, Psychoanalysis, and Psychology,* vol. 8, pp. 148–152, Van Nostrand Reinhold, New York, 1977.

27. ——, "Sleep and Dreaming: Protodream and Predream," in Wolman, B. B. (Ed.), *International Encyclopedia of Neurology, Psychiatry, Psychoanalysis, and Psychology,* vol. 10, pp. 246–257, Van Nostrand Reinhold, New York, 1977.

28. ——, "Development of States in Infants," in Clemente, C. D., Purpura, D. P., and Mayer, R. E. (Eds.), *Sleep and the Maturing Nervous System,* pp. 216–219, Academic Press, New York, 1972.

29. ——, "Effect of Extrauterine Experience on Ontogenesis of EEG Sleep Spindles," *Psychosomatic Medicine, 31:*393–399, 1969.

30. ——, and JORDAN, K., "EEG Ontogenesis in Normal Children," in Smith, W. L. (Ed.), *Drugs, Development and Cerebral Function,* pp. 125–144, Charles C Thomas, Springfield, Ill., 1971.

31. ——, and SPITZ, R. A., "The Transitional Object: Critical Development Period and Organizer of the Psyche," in Grolnick, S. A., and Barkin, L. (Eds.), *Between Reality and Fantasy,* pp. 99–108, Aronson, New York, 1978.

32. ——, and WATSON, M., "A Prospective Study of Children with Sex Chromosome Anomalies: Electroencephalographic Findings, unpublished manuscript.

33. ——, MONDALE, J., and BUTLER, F., "Development of Spontaneous K-complexes," *Psychophysiology, 8:*340–347, 1971.

34. PARMALEE, A. H., et al., "Maturation of EEG Activity During Sleep in Infants," *Electroencephalography and Clinical Neurophysiology, 24:*319–329, 1969.

35. PINE, F., "Libidinal Object Constancy: A Theoretical Note," in Goldberger, L., and Rosen, V. H. (Eds.), *Psychoanalysis and Contemporary Science,* vol. 3, pp. 307–313, International Universities Press, New York, 1975.

36. PURPURA, D., "Morphological and Physiological Properties of Chronically Isolated Immature Cortex," *Experimental Neurology, 4:*366–401, 1961.

37. ROFFWARG, H., MUZIO, J., and DEMENT, W., "Ontogenetic Development of the Human Sleep-Dream Cycle," *Science, 152:*604–619, 1966.

38. SALTZBERG, B., and LUSTICK, L. S., "Signal Analysis: An Overview of Electroencephalographic Applications," in Prescott, J. W., Read, M. S., and Coursin, D. B. (Eds.), *Brain Function and Malnutrition: Neurophysiological Methods of Assessment,* pp. 129–140, John Wiley, New York, 1975.

39. SHUCARD, D. W., SHUCARD, J. L., and THOMAS, D. G., "Auditory Evoked Potentials as Probes of Hemispheric Differences in Cognitive Processing," *Science, 197:*1295–1298, 1977.

40. SMITH, J. R., "EEG During Infancy and Childhood," *Journal of General Psychology, 53:*431–469, 1938.

41. SPITZ, R. A., "Bridges: On Anticipation, Duration and Meaning," Annual address at the meeting of the American Psychoanalytic Association, Washington, D.C., May 1971 (reprinted *Journal of the American Psychoanalytic Association, 20(4):*721–735, 1972).

42. ——, *The First Year of Life: Normal and Deviant Object Relations,* International Universities Press, New York, 1965.

43. ——, *A Genetic Field Theory of Ego Formation, With Implications for Pathology,* Freud Anniversary Lecture Series, International Universities Press, New York, 1959.

44. ——, *No and Yes: On the Genesis of Human Communication,* International Universities Press, New York, 1957.

45. ——, and WOLF, K., *The Smiling Response: A Contribution to the Ontogenesis of Social Relations,* Genetic Psychology Monographs, no. 34, pp. 57–125, 1946.

46. ——, EMDE, R. N., and METCALF, D. R., "Further Prototypes of Ego Formation: A Working Paper from a Research Project on Early Development," in Eissler, R. S., et al. (Eds.), *The Psychoanalytic Study of the Child,* vol. 25. pp. 417–441, International Universities Press, 1970.

47. STERMAN, M. B., and HOPPENBROUWERS, T., "The Development of Sleep-Waking and Rest-Activity Patterns from Fetus to Adult in Man," in Sterman, M. B., McGinty, D. J., and Adinolfi, A. M. (Eds.), pp. 23–43, Academic Press, New York, 1971.

48. TENNES, K., EMDE, R. N., KISLEY, A., and METCALF, D. R., "The Stimulus Barrier in Early Infancy: An Exploration of Some Formulations of John Benjamin," in Holt, R., and Peterfreund, E. (Eds.), *Psychoanalysis and Contemporary Science,* vol. 1, pp. 206–236, International Universities Press, New York, 1972.

49. WHITE, B. L., *The First Three Years of Life,* Prentice-Hall, Englewood Cliffs, N.J., 1976.

50. WINNICOTT, D. W., "Transitional Objects and Transitional Phenomena: A Study of the First Not-Me Possession," *International Journal of Psycho-Analysis, 34:*89–97, 1953.

5 / The First Two Months: Recent Research in Developmental Psychobiology and the Changing View of the Newborn

Robert N. Emde* and Jean Robinson

Introduction

The nature of psychological interest in the human newborn has changed in recent years, a student could compare the literature of today with that of twenty years ago and conclude that two different species were under study. In the second edition of *Carmichael's Manual of Child Psychology*,[235] there were about 500 references for the review of the literature on the young infant. Sixteen years later, the corresponding chapter for the third edition contained four times the number of references.[164] Although the newborn cannot communicate with language, much more is known about his internal states and his capacities for behavioral regulation than was the case in the past. In those days, James [149] spoke of the newborn's "blooming, buzzing confusion," Watson[319] of the newborn's love, rage, and fear, and Freud[108] of the young infant's hallucinatory wish fulfillment in the absence of the breast.

Today massive amounts of new information are generated. The research enterprise has moved away from global theories toward formulations which use specific inferences at low levels of abstraction. Concepts must have operational referents in the observational field while the trend away from abstract theory is apt to make the clinician impatient. This chapter is intended to respond to that impatience in two ways. First, it will summarize research information which is likely to be clinically useful. Second, it will offer perspectives on research trends. While not in themselves theoretical syntheses, these will hopefully illuminate the ways in which such syntheses are emerging from new looks at the infant. In addition, it is hoped that the presentation will to some extent sensitize the clinician to more reliance on the kind of observation that is fueling the new research. Lastly, even a review of this length cannot pretend to be encyclopedic. This chapter, which focuses on

* Dr. Emde is supported by Career Scientist Award MH 26808 and NIMH Project Grant MH 28803.

the "normal," has not yet discussed the premature. Some areas have been selected which are believed to be important. It is hoped that the clinicians will find this chapter a useful guide to the research literature.

Some Research Trends

THE INFLUENCE OF APPROACHES FROM OUTSIDE PSYCHIATRY AND PSYCHOLOGY

In recent years, three major approaches have had a pervasive influence on how behavioral research is conducted in early infancy. These approaches have affected the questions that are asked, how they are asked, and how their answers are interpreted.

1. The first approach comes from the discipline of *ethology*. This discipline has been fundamental in generating a fresh look at the newborn. It has countered two previous flaws in research thinking: (1) an exclusive reliance on information derived from laboratory observations of highly selected phenomena, and (2) a reliance on information derived from retrospective verbal reconstructions from older, as well as selected, patient populations. Ethology proposes that the organism under study be observed first in its natural habitat. This enables the investigator to arrive at a full description of a behavioral repertoire and the context in which it appears. Only after this should experiments be introduced to investigate causal chains. In addition, all laboratory observations should be related to observations of behavior in the naturalistic setting.

2. A second approach derives from the *neurosciences* where major advances have occurred in the understanding of brain functioning. Its research influence might be stated as follows: Since the brain is the organ regulating behavior, all behavior should be related to knowledge of brain functioning; furthermore, any proposition about

behavioral regulation which is not compatible with what is known about neurophysiological regulation is not worthwhile.

3. A third approach comes from a *multidisciplinary* framework. This assumes that the most productive research often emerges from the simultaneous application of multiple techniques and vantage points and that all research findings must be subjected to multidisciplinary scrutiny. Indeed, most programmatic research on the newborn is now done by teams of researchers made up of individuals who differ in their training, professional identity, and skills.

As the reader might anticipate, these three approaches have resulted in some "fresh looks" at the newborn and some old biases have been uncovered. Some instructive examples merit discussion. They include biases about "passivity," about "undifferentiation," and about "drive reduction."

For a long time, researchers and clinicians had thought of the infant as relatively passive, an organism that reacts to stimuli and behaves primarily so as to reduce stimulation. Even though there was little to support this idea, the assumption dominated much of the literature of developmental psychology and psychoanalysis. From a multidisciplinary point of view, a different picture emerges. Embryology informs us that during embryogenesis, primordial motor cells migrate from the central canal earlier than do sensory cells. In addition, motor neurons send processes to muscle cells and establish transmission pathways before the sensory half of the reflex arc becomes functional. According to the neurophysiologist Robert Livingston,[201] these facts imply that the nervous system is built for *action prior to reaction*.

Another corrective influence comes from the perspective of Jean Piaget. In the last decade, his sensorimotor theory has proven to have enormous usefulness in generating hypotheses and organizing data concerning the early development of cognition and perception. At its core, this theory is one of action—mental functions emerge from motor actions on concrete objects.[330, 232] Still another challenge of the long-standing view about passivity has come from recent developmental research on humans and animals. The position that has emerged states that the newborn has definite stimulus needs, both for soothing and arousal. These needs result in active and complex encounters with a varied environment.* The newborn's active adaptations are prominent features of his earliest experiences.[232, 62]

A related bias holds that the newborn's behavior is "undifferentiated." Again, embryology gives perspective for looking backward from birth; it is evident that an enormous amount of differentiation has taken place during embryogenesis. In addition, when making detailed naturalistic observations of the newborn's behavioral repertoire, as in the ethological approach, one is impressed with the amount of organization and endogenous control present in the first postuterine days. The pioneering observations and studies of Peter Wolff[331, 327] showed that the newborn's behavioral repertoire includes a multiplicity of clearly circumscribed and highly organized behaviors which are related to internal state. These behaviors, sometimes described as "spontaneous" since they are largely under endogenous control, have since been studied by others.[239, 178, 86, 87]

A high degree of organization and endogenous control is even more apparent in the rhythmic features of newborn behavior. There are "microrhythms" involved in sucking, crying, and in certain stereotypic behaviors;[326] there are "macrorhythms" involved in sleep-wakefulness cycles and rest-activity cycles.*

Another limiting bias arose from the drive-reduction model. This model has assumed that an infant comes to learn about his world exclusively or primarily through the reduction of his drives. There is no need now to belabor the limitations of this view, so long dominant in behavioristic psychology and psychoanalysis. Excellent data reviews and statements of why this runs counter to modern biology have been offered by Bertalanffy.[36, 37] White[323] has addressed the limitations of this view from the aspect of psychoanalytic developmental psychology, and Miller, Galanter, and Pribam[210] from the point of view of neurophysiology and information theory. The earlier ideas and experiments of Hebb,[134] Heron et al.,[135] deriving from adults, and of Harlow[130, 131] deriving from monkeys must also be mentioned. What is generally not appreciated is that the newborn's behavioral organization is of sufficient complexity that it, too, provides dramatic examples of phenomena not explainable by the drive-reduction model. Such a model would assume, for example, that the newborn's wakefulness and interest in the external world are enhanced primarily through association with satisfaction from hunger or thirst. That this is not the case is shown by these observations, originally emphasized by Wolff[331, 328, 327] but which can readily be replicated by anyone. The first

---

* See references 160, 323, 124, 207, 311, 209, and 152.

* See references 171, 274, 300, 113, and 91.

is that a newborn will interrupt a feeding (at breast or bottle) in order to look at a novel and interesting stimulus; the second is that wakefulness can be prolonged by such a stimulus; and the third is that mild crying can be converted to a state of quiet alertness by the introduction of such a stimulus. These observations are clearly not compatible with the view that the newborn's wakefulness is based exclusively on drive reduction. Nor are they compatible with its corollary that there is a primary organismic tendency to reduce the level of stimulus input. Other observations indicate that whether or not he is fed, the newborn has an endogenous sleep-wakefulness rhythm; these are equally incompatible with the earlier view.[91]

In summary, today's researchers have a modified image of the newborn infant. He is seen as primarily active rather than passive, with a preformed organization worthy of study in its own right, and with rhythmically organized behaviors and internal states as a part of that organization. Any baseline for behavioral development cannot appropriately consider birth as a zero point. Nor is it correct to assume that behavioral development depends exclusively on its association with feeding. In other words, subsequent experience is not superimposed on a formless beginning. Rather, experience serves to modulate preexisting endogenous behaviors according to laws and operations yet to be discovered. It is no exaggeration to state that the newborn is active, stimulus-seeking, and creative in the ways he begins to construct his world.

SOME CURRENT TRENDS

The newborn infant is more active, organized, and stimulus-seeking than had been assumed, and this has in turn influenced another major research trend, namely, that of *studying the young infant as part of a developing interactional system.* For years, researchers were concerned primarily with the caretaker's role in nurturing and shaping the infant's behavior. Interaction was felt to be essentially unidirectional, going from mother to baby. Then, a small group of clinician-researchers, influenced in part by psychoanalytic theory and an increased understanding of genetics, pioneered in the study of early individual differences and infant contributions to development.* In addition, the ethological orientation led to a description of the newborn's repertoire of behaviors within his family.[327, 325, 250] As further knowledge accumulated

* See references, 31, 97, 98, 179, and 310.

concerning the young infant's complex organization, more research attention became devoted to interactional exchanges originating within the newborn.[25, 174] It is not surprising that such effects are major. For example, when one stops to think of it, the newborn's crying presents such a compelling call for caretaking that it would be expected to initiate a great deal of interaction, a notion which is supported by data from two systematic studies.[214, 26]

An emergent research trend which is increasingly prominent today is that of looking at both sides of a developing interactional system—infant and caretaker are viewed simultaneously. Each partner is regarded as having separate competencies which affect the other's behavior and as initiating and reinforcing that behavior. The system is characterized by ongoing mutual adaptation. Research dealing with developing interactional systems is quite difficult to conceptualize, and computerized statistical techniques for data analysis have only recently become available.[261, 262, 193] Again, clinician-researchers have been pioneers in this trend. Most prominent is the early work of Sander. Originally it arose out of his longitudinal study with Pavestedt,[275] and continued with his precise monitoring of long-term rhythms of infant and caretaker activities over the first two months.[276, 274, 273] Other current programs in this area are represented by the work of Stern,[302, 301] and Brazelton.[53] Although a strong interactional framework will be apparent throughout this chapter, specific data in this area will be reviewed when the concept of attachment is discussed.

A final research trend worth mentioning at the outset is that of *conceptualizing the newborn in terms of developing processes.* In the past, researchers have tended to reify concepts and make them static. For a while, this was fueled by the newfound enthusiasm for demonstrating that the newborn infant was indeed organized. Thus, concepts such as "conditioning," "habituation," "attention," and, more recently, "competence" were used to justify research programs to find out who could demonstrate a previously undiscovered capacity in the newborn. There was little concern for naturalistic relevance of such capacities, nor did it matter how many infants were required to find some who could reach the criterion of experimental results—it only mattered that the capacity could be demonstrated. This "gee whiz" kind of research is fast declining. There is less interest in conditioning in its own right, for example, and more interest in using learning paradigms to study developing processes of behavior.* It is now demanded that worthwhile research include relevance to the developing infant, to his naturalistic surroundings, and, ultimately, to his processes of brain functioning. It is in this spirit that an extended definition is offered of what constitutes the newborn period itself. This seems to make more sense in terms of developing processes whether they be behavioral, interactional, or neurophysiological.

A Comparison of the First Two Months with Afterward: Evidence for a Major Shift in Organization

Standard pediatric nomenclature defines the neonatal period as that from birth through twenty-eight postnatal days.[8, 59] In this chapter, it seems convenient to extend the view of the newborn to include the first two postnatal months. Recent psychobiological research leads to the conclusion that there is a qualitative difference between the very young infant of the first two months and the infant of three to four months. Developmental psychology has provided evidence for this in studies of learning, perception, emotionality, and psychophysiology. Neurology and neurophysiology are beginning to point toward underlying structures and mechanisms possibly accountable for such a difference.

Perhaps the most dramatic evidence for such a qualitative change in development has come from learning studies showing that the results are different before and after two months. This is striking because the field originally had been dedicated to demonstrating that the nature of learning does not change.[319] That such differences could nonetheless emerge is a tribute to the careful methodology and respect for the rules of evidence which has characterized recent work. Details will be presented later in this chapter, but it suffices to say that before two months, classical avoidance conditioning is very difficult and the effects of operant conditioning short-lived. After two months, this is not the case. Similarly, it is difficult if not impossible to establish habituation before two months whereas after that time, experimental habituation has been established in auditory and visual modali-

* The authors are grateful to M. Haith for stimulating a number of ideas in this section.

ties in a number of carefully controlled studies. Certainly learning through active adaptation and through reciprocal interaction takes place before two months. But after that time, its modes and mechanisms evidence a shift in organization. In terms of perception, more studies need to be done after the newborn period. However, substantial evidence already exists for a shift of perceptual organization during the second month. This is especially true for visual development, as will be reviewed. In addition, the literature on heart rate responsiveness demonstrates a difference. The stimulus conditions which are required for predictable decelerations during the first two months are not the same as those of the months afterward. In the social affective sphere, research has highlighted a change from the newborn's distress-quiescence organization to the dramatically different social smiling and prominent eye-to-eye contact which emerges after two months. This change seems to indicate a shift from endogenous to exogenous control, with the social smile inaugurating an expanding interest in the environment. The change is also concomitant with a decline of nonhunger fussiness which in turn heralds the infant's being able to use wakefulness in "new ways," as will be described.

Aside from wakefulness, there are marked changes in sleep states during this time. There is a doubling of the quiet-sleep active–rapid-eye-movement (REM) sleep ratio during the first three months. Electroencephalogram (EEG) and polygraph studies show a marked decline in the behaviorally undifferentiated REM states: Before two months, REM-state physiology can occur during nutritive sucking, fussing, crying, and drowsiness, whereas afterward, it is u.iusual.[88] There is a decrease in the large amount of behavioral activity seen during sleep. EEG sleep spindles have their onset during the second month, and an investigator can begin to stage quiet sleep according to EEG criteria after this time but not before. In terms of sleep distribution, there is a dramatic increase in the ability to sustain long periods of sleep with a shift to a diurnal pattern of nighttime sleep and "settling," or sleeping through the night, becoming characteristic in more infants after two months. Sleep onset shifts from the newborn mode (entry through active-REM) to the "adult" mode (entry through drowsiness and quiet sleep), although this change is not nearly as age-locked to two months as had been thought.[35, 172]

The notion of a major qualitative difference between the very young infant and the infant older than two months is supported by the neurosciences.

In fact, the notion of a behavioral discontinuity or of a qualitative shift in development becomes much less mysterious when one looks at how the brain develops. From the viewpoints of neurology, neurophysiology, and neuroanatomy, an overriding impression emerges—in early infancy, growth is less by steady accretion and more by irregular stepwise jumps. More attention is continually drawn to changes in quality than to changes in quantity.

In pediatric neurology there are a host of reflexes which are active within the first two months and decline thereafter. Among these are the Babkin reflex, the steppage reflex, the palmar grasp, the Moro, and the tonic neck reflex. Because they decline after two to three months without normally reappearing afterward, they are often referred to as the "transitory reflexes" of the newborn, and their decline is thought to reflect the postnatal maturation of forebrain inhibitory areas.[230, 222, 227] Another rapid maturational change involves the cortical visual evoked response. The latency of this response is presumed to reflect information processing in the visual system. Ellingson[82] documented that this interval shortens markedly between four and eight postnatal weeks. After eight weeks, changes are relatively small from infancy to adulthood.

On the tissue level of anatomy, Conel's classic works[70, 69] document the changes which occur in human cerebral cortex during the first postnatal months, but a precise knowledge of rates of change is lacking. The same could be said for other early rapid postnatal changes which have been documented: changes in (1) dendritic arborization, (2) increased vascularization of the brain, (3) myelinization, (4) glial proliferation, and (5) postnatal neurogenesis in limited areas.[6, 23] In their review of postnatal neural ontogeny, Bekoff and Fox[23] concluded that myelinization in the human infant does not occur uniformly but in pulses or waves, and furthermore, it can happen that one system of fibers may start this process and then slow down and be surpassed by another system in which the process began later. They illustrate this by reference to the auditory and visual systems. By eight fetal months, the acoustic pathway is myelinated to the level of the inferior colliculus, whereas the optic fibers do not undergo myelinization until after birth. In spite of this, optic projection fibers to the cortex become myelinated ahead of tracks from the cochlear nuclei.

It has been presumed that a "discontinuity" exists between the behavioral organization of the newborn and that of the post newborn infant. A possible animal model for investigating the associated underlying mechanisms is found in the cat (*felix domestica*). Kittens are widely available, susceptible to experimental manipulation, and also provide promise of advancing the understanding of the sleep-wakefulness shift in the developing human. Not unexpectedly, postnatal development in the kitten is more rapid than in the human, but similar events do occur. As in the human infant, overall amounts of the active form of sleep diminish with development, wakefulness and drowsiness increase,[67] and the quiet form of sleep also increases.[206] In further analogy to the human newborn, the very young kitten falls asleep into an active phase instead of a quiet one.[154]

It would appear that there is a major organismic shift in the early postnatal weeks of the kitten's development, and McGinty[206] has mustered experimental evidence to correlate this with what he refers to as "the encephalization of the neural control of sleep." His proposition is that the newborn's sleep in general, and most of the adult's active portion of sleep, is controlled by the brainstem. It is during postnatal development that these brainstem mechanisms come progressively under the control of higher level forebrain mechanisms, resulting in more quiet sleep, less active sleep, and other changes.

However, of all the research done in the neurophysiological bases of the postnewborn organizational shift, the most compelling is the precise experimental work done on the maturation of two brainstem reflexes in the kitten by Chase.[66, 65, 64, 63] He devised a preparation in which the moving kitten could be continually monitored for the EEG and for a number of physiological variables, and in which specific reflexes could then be stimulated and recorded with implanted electrodes. With this, Chase obtained a sequence of consistent results. With regard to a monosynaptic reflex (the masseteric) the kitten before two weeks had its highest amplitude of response in active sleep, a lower response in quiet sleep, and the lowest response in wakefulness. Such a pattern of results is exactly opposite to that which is found in the adult cat, where reflex amplitude is highest in wakefulness and lowest in active sleep. But even more remarkable is the fact that this maturation to the adult state-related pattern, with a complete reversal, was completed by six postnatal weeks! Similar findings with regard to a polysynaptic brainstem reflex (the digastric) were equally dramatic, with a shift at the same age. It seems likely that future experiments will yield neurophysiological explanations of this shift in the developing kitten. Such explanations may bear upon a shift in the organization of wakefulness as well as sleep. Chase and Sterman[67] have shown that there are negative correlations between the development of active sleep and of wakefulness in the cat; that is, as the former declines in amount, the latter increases. Others have speculated about the reciprocal role of the development of these two organismic states in the human.[257, 294]

The Usefulness of the Concept of State

An important characteristic of the newborn's behavioral organization is its high level of endogenous control. This is most apparent when one considers how much behavior can be accounted for by its correlation with internal state. Whether one looks at spontaneous activity or at caretaking behavior variables such as sensory thresholds and reflexes, the overriding importance of internal state is clear. The concept of state derives from systems theory[16] where a pattern of events is recognizable because it recurs. In the newborn, state refers to constellations of certain patterns of physiological variables and/or patterns of behavior which seem to repeat and which appear to be relatively stable.[243, 146] Thus, state is a "low-level" concept which is subject to ready operational definition, and it is useful to a wide range of researchers in the physiology and behavior of the newborn.* It is useful chiefly because it allows for prediction, but it has theoretical implications both for the organization and the sequencing of behavior. Perhaps the most eloquent statement of its usefulness as well as its limitations occurs in Wolff's monograph.[330] In the author's research, it has been found useful to think of the state concept as referring to these variables at a given point in development which can define readiness to act, on the one hand, and readiness to react on the other.

There are several descriptive systems for newborn behavioral states that can vary according to how global any investigator wants to be. All systems recognize two qualitatively distinct states during sleep: an active state with irregular respirations, rapid eye movements, and varying amounts of behavioral activity; and a quiet state with no eye movements, regular respirations, and behavior quiescence aside from intermittent startles. All systems also recognize two states of wakefulness, one usually called quiet wakefulness and the other, active wakefulness. A fifth state recognized in all systems is that of crying. These five states form the essence of the system used by Prechtl,[236] Theorell, Prechtl, and Vos,[308] and Brazelton.[54] Some researchers further subdivide the states to include states of drowsiness and other substates of sleep and wakefulness.[327, 87, 13] Recent studies have employed time-lapse movie recording[172] and video recording† of behavioral states; the video technique holds special promise for long-term recording which is both valid (assessed by polygraphic correlations) and reliable.

Table 5-1 illustrates the state-dependent nature of the newborn's response to stimulation. (State 1 in Prechtl's scheme is quiet sleep, 2 is active sleep, and 3 is awake-inactive.) Prechtl's 1974 paper[236] can be consulted for an index to original studies which form the basis for this table. Wolff's monograph on the newborn still offers one of the best sources for a description of the state-dependent nature of spontaneous behaviors.[327]

AMOUNT AND QUALITY OF STATES

Following Wolff's initial work,[328, 327] many have verified his finding that during the alert-active state the newborn is maximally capable of processing information and responding to his environment. It may be that the newborn's wakefulness and sleep states are under relatively fixed homeostatic control. If so, then any environmental influence to increase or decrease their amount at one point in time will be compensated for later on.[113] However, short-run influences on the amount of wakefulness may be important for caretaking. Visual fixation and visual pursuit are relatively mature behaviors in the newborn's wakeful repertoire. They are undoubtedly related to the later development of eye-to-eye contact which contributes so prominently to mother's sense of pleasure in her baby.[329, 255] Wolff[328] has shown that the duration of alert inactivity can be extended by an attractive visual stimulus. Korner and Thoman[181, 180] compared six common maternal soothing interventions. They found that putting the infant to the shoulder was not only the most effective in diminishing crying, but was also a potent elicitor of visual alertness. Nearly 80 percent of forty crying infants responded with visual alertness. Since this maneuver involved more vestibular-proprioceptive

---

* See references 327, 146, 178, 12, 54, 86 and 87.

† Sostek, A. M., Anders, T. F., and Sostek, A. J., "Diurnal Rhythms in 2- and 3-week-old Infants: Sleep-waking State Organization as a Function of Age and Stress," *Psychosomatic Medicine, 38(4)*:250–256, 1976.

TABLE 5–1

Response to Stimulation in Different States

	State 1	State 2	State 3
Proprioceptive reflexes			
Knee jerk	+++	±	++
Biceps jerk	+++	±	++
Lip jerk	+++	±	++
Ankle clonus	+++	−	−
Moro tap	+++	−	++
Moro head drop	+++	−	++
Exteroceptive skin reflexes			
Tactile			
Rooting	−	−	++
Palmar grasp	−	+	++
Plantar grasp	−	++	++
Lip protrusion	−	+++	++
Finger reflex	−	+	++
Toe reflex	−	++	++
Tibial reflex	±	++	++
Fibular reflex	±	++	++
Axillary reflex	±	++	++
Pressure			
Babkin	−	+	++
Palmomental	−	++	++
Nociceptive			
Babinski reflex	++	+++	+++
Abdominal reflex	++	+++	+++
Thigh	++	+++	+++
Pubic	++	+++	+++
Inguinal	+++	+++	+++
Auditory response			
Auditory orienting	±	++	+++
Visual response			
Visual pursuit	−	−	++
Vestibular response			
Vestibulo-ocular	−	++	+++

NOTE: Reprinted by permission of the publisher from "The Behavioural States of the Newborn Infant (A Review)," by H. F. R. Prechtl, *Brain Research*, 76:185–212, 1974.

stimulation than the other soothing interventions, it was held accountable for the differences. Subsequent speculation concerned the effectiveness of this stimulus modality in relation to its relative state of advanced development at birth.[174]

What about sleep? Although the newborn spends two-thirds of his early existence sleeping, this was of little interest in the past, for sleep was considered a "natural state of rest," and therefore static. But recent research has changed this attitude about sleep. It has become an exciting area for developmental research promising new and significant knowledge. To begin with, the newborn infant is not "at rest" but is behaviorally active

during sleep, and has a rather extensive repertoire of well-organized sleep behaviors. In fact, sleep activity is such that if one measures the output of such behaviors by means of a sensitive air-filled crib mattress, their amount can exceed that observed during noncrying wakefulness.[89]

But the baby's sleep is not *all* active. As has already been mentioned, there are at least two "types" of sleep, separable into "active" and "quiet" phases. A new era of modern sleep research began with the discovery by Aserinsky and Kleitman[15] that newborn infants had alternating sleep periods which corresponded to rest-activity cycles within sleep itself. The active form of sleep occurred with rapid eye movements (REM sleep), and the quiescent form occurred without rapid eye movements (NREM sleep). Although similar observations had been reported earlier (1929) in the Russian literature by Denisova and Figurin[74] the Aserinsky-Kleitman finding, subsequently generalized to adult humans and mammals, stimulated an enormous productivity in multidisciplinary behavioral-biological research.[63]

In what is now a classic paper, Roffwarg et al.[257] reviewed research findings relative to the ontogeny of these types of sleep. Far from being static, sleep evidences rapid developmental change. Roffwarg and associates estimated that the newborn spends 50 percent of his total sleep time in REM sleep as compared with 30 percent at the end of the first year and 20 percent in adolescence. But why such a high amount of REM sleep in early infancy? they wondered. They reviewed another body of research literature which suggested that the young organism was programmed not so much to shut out stimulation as to seek it because it was needed for neural growth. They then offered what has become known as the "ontogenetic hypothesis" for the biological functioning of REM sleep. This hypothesis states that early in ontogeny, REM sleep, with all of its behavioral and neurophysiological activation, serves to provide a source of endogenous afferentation needed for central nervous system growth. They reasoned that this afferentation was particularly important in the altricial human whose immaturity at birth precludes such activity during wakefulness.

More recently, attention has been directed to the development of NREM or quiet sleep. This form of sleep increases during infancy, and there is some suggestion that it is correlated with the postnatal maturation of forebrain inhibitory centers.[299, 206] Perhaps the most important fact about quiet sleep is that, in contrast to active-REM sleep, it evidences a great deal of *qualitative* developmental change during the first year. Parmelee et al.[229] have pointed out that active-REM sleep can be regarded as a more primitive state than quiet sleep. The changing postnatal physiology of quiet sleep, according to these investigators, may reflect basic maturational events in higher centers which bear a fundamental relation to developmental changes in wakefulness.

Such is the remarkable change in the current attitude toward the development of sleep which has taken place in the span of less than two decades. Sleep is the arena for both quantitative and qualitative changes which undoubtedly reflect basic developmental shifts in central nervous system organization and in total organismic functioning. Thus, even though wakefulness is the time when novelty is experienced, when one's world is expanded, and when one changes and is most changed, and even though wakefulness is the time in development when most learning takes place, it may be sleep which holds up a more accessible mirror to the rapid organismic changes of early development. It is no longer useful to regard sleep merely as the negative aspect of wakefulness. In fact, sleep development may provide a key to understanding the development of wakefulness itself, where major physiological changes over time are less evident. Excellent reviews of research in this area have been written by Anders and Hoffman,[11] Hutt et al.,[146] and by Parmelee and Stern.[228]

RHYTHMS OF STATES

Thus far, allusion has been made to the importance of studying the *organization* and the relative *amounts* of newborn states. As important as these are for determining momentary activity and reactivity, there is another aspect of states, namely, their *rhythmicity*, or sequencing, which is equally important for behavioral development. Kleitman[170] suggested that the recurring REM phase of sleep in the human was a manifestation of a more fundamental physiological rhythm, which he termed the basic rest-activity cycle (BRAC). In the adult, the cycle has a ninety-minute period, and in the newborn, the period is one-half that duration.[300] The BRAC is most prominent in sleep, manifesting itself in the alternation of REM and NREM phases. However, even in adults, recent research has borne out Kleitman's suggestion that the BRAC modulates daytime activity.[183, 221, 114] Sterman and his group,[298, 297, 300] Sterman, and Sterman and Hoppenbrouwers, have shown that the BRAC is evident during the last two trimesters

of fetal life. In the author's research, the BRAC was found to be present in the early hours after birth, following the two-hour postbirth wakeful period which is characteristic of the unmedicated infant. Figure 5-1 illustrates this rhythmicity. It is taken from a study of infants who were observed without intervention of any kind in the ten hours immediately after birth.[91]

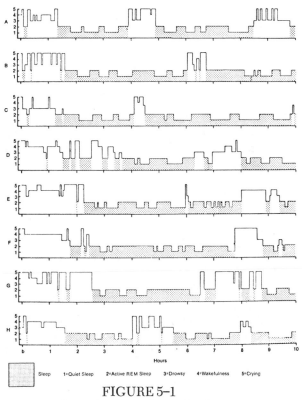

FIGURE 5-1
Behavioral cycles of sleep wakefulness and rest-activity.

Eight normal newborns observed for ten hours following birth. Graphs A through D from infants whose mothers received sedative medication; E through H from infants born to unmedicated mothers.

NOTE: Reprinted by permission of the publisher from R. N. Emde, J. Swedberg, and B. Suzuki, "Human Wakefullness and Biological Rhythms After Birth," *Archives of General Psychiatry*, 32:780-783, 1975. © 1975 by the American Medical Association.

Figure 5-1 also illustrates the presence of another endogenous rhythm, that of sleep and wakefulness. This cycle seems to have a periodicity of approximately three and one-half hours during the first postnatal days and, in a demand-fed infant, is usually synchronous with feeding. In some nurseries, the lack of synchrony of this rhythm with the strictly scheduled feedings may account for disruptions encountered in such feedings.[113] On the other hand, the influence of this particular sleep-wakefulness rhythm is probably short-lived.

The predominant sleep-wakefulness rhythm in the human is that of daytime wakefulness and night-time sleep. Sleeping through the night is a developmental arrival which pediatricians have long referred to as "settling." It occurs only after the newborn period, with one study finding 70 percent of infants settling by three months.[212] However, Sander and Julia[276] have shown that an early adaptation to a diurnal rhythm of sleep and wakefulness can be seen at ten postnatal days. The importance of Sander's research technology is considerable since his activity interaction monitor allows for continuous monitoring of both infant and caretaking interventions during the entire period being considered. The technique is relatively unobstrusive since infant and mother are free of electrodes. Recently, the monitor has been able to yield reliable assessments of sleep and wakeful states.[277]

Crying, although considered a state, is more important as an affect expression and thus will be taken up in that section.

The Extrauterine Adaptation Syndrome and Perinatal Variables Affecting Behavior

The picture portrayed thus far is of the newborn as an organized entity who is by no means a passive, *tabula rasa* in his initial encounters with the extrauterine environment. At birth, the newborn has a behavioral repertoire which is a result of long intrauterine development (this has been documented and discussed by Minkowski,[211] Hooker,[140] and Humphrey.[145] Organized behavioral responses begin as early as seven and one-half weeks in gestation, when it can be shown that tactile stimulation of the skin in the perioral area of the fetus produces an aversive response. Following this, many other organized responses can be demonstrated. As has been mentioned, the BRAC, a fundamental biological rhythm which modulates spontaneous activity, has its onset in the second trimester.[298] Still, all would agree there is a dramatic change in behavioral adaptation requirements occasioned by the process of birth. The situation is stated cogently by Hutt, Lenard, and Prechtl.[146]

The human infant thus already possesses at birth a wide behavioral repertoire of motor patterns and responses to stimulation, at least some of which have played an important role in the intrauterine environment. Nevertheless, the fetus lives relatively passively, in an environment with a constant temperature, regular oxygen supply and nutrition. Since it is suspended in amniotic fluid it is not fully exposed to the force of gravity and sensory stimulation is relatively weak. When, however, the infant is born around the fortieth week of gestation, the conditions in which he lives change dramatically. With physical separation from the mother, he is exposed to a climatically, physiologically, and nutritionally novel environment. This is a critical phase in the baby's development and carries great risks. He now has to work for food, regulate his own body temperature in a climatically inconstant environment, and breathe in order to secure oxygen. He is now fully exposed to gravity against which he must achieve at least rudimentary postural adjustments. Moreover, he is exposed to a whole range of novel sensory stimuli. [p. 130]

Not surprisingly, given even the best of circumstances, there is considerable evidence that responsiveness is apt to be more sluggish and variable during the first and second postnatal days than it might be later.[22] Variables such as length of labor, maternal medication, postconceptional age, and birthweight are known to be important influences on the regulatory capacities of the infant. Complications during pregnancy and delivery increase the risk of brain dysfunction and/or disturbing effects on the initial adaptive processes.[237, 22, 241, 146] The adaptation of physiological systems, including the proper regulation of autonomic function, electrolyte metabolism, oxygenation, fluid balance, etc., will underlie any behavioral stability. All the factors involved in the process of postnatal adaptation, sometimes referred to as "the postnatal adaptation syndrome," has become central in the new field of neonatology.[17, 167]

The effect of maternal medication on newborn behavior is worthy of special consideration in this review. Considering that such effects are pervasive, it is surprising that they were generally unappreciated until the 1960s. Routine amounts of sedative medication and narcotics, when given to a mother during delivery, have been found to decrease the amount of the baby's visual alertness for several days after birth.[295] Depressant effects on infant sucking and feeding have been documented by Kron et al.[185] and by Brazelton.[55] Others have reported that obstetric sedation has postnatal depressant effects on spontaneous REM behaviors,[86] on a variety of behaviors measured by the Brazelton Neonatal Assessment Scales,[141, 5] on the amount of wakefulness,[58, 91] and on the infant's later ability to habituate to stimulation.[43] Kraemer et al.[182] have cautioned that increased durations of labors may be confounded with maternal drug effects in some studies. Nonetheless, it would seem reasonable to assume that, until facts prove otherwise, any medication which has a sedative effect and which is given to a mother during labor may have a depressant effect on infant wakefulness and on infant behaviors in the first two or three postnatal days. Of considerable interest are the reports of effects on behavior beyond the first week.[43, 5] The fact that such effects may last so much longer than in adults is due to the infant's immature enzyme and excretory systems. Not surprisingly, infants born to mothers addicted to heroin have shown signs of major and prolonged central nervous system instability, including disruptions of sleep and increased amounts of activity even after clinical signs of withdrawal have abated.[281] The assessment and management of newborns addicted to narcotics has been reviewed by Finnegan et al.[104] and Kron et al.[186] Strauss et al.,[306] using the Brazelton Assessment Scale, found that in addition to usual clinical signs of withdrawal, newborns were less able to be maintained in an alert state and were less able to orient to visual and auditory stimuli.

Recent study has also investigated hospital procedures which may be alterable and which may place unnecessary stress on newborn behavior and adaptation. Circumcision is such a procedure. Emde et al.[92] found that routine circumcision using a ligature technique designed to effect an ischemic necrosis was followed by prolonged quiet (NREM) sleep. Such a dramatic response was interpreted in terms of an adaptive lowering of thresholds in the midst of continued painful stimulation, possibly an early example of "conservation-withdrawal" as proposed by Engel.[93] (As a "turning-off" response, such a change to quiet sleep would also be consistent with the capacity for state regulation involving a shutting-out of disturbing aspects of the environment, a capacity which is a central concept in Brazelton's assessment of newborn behavior.[54, 51] Subsequent studies of circumcision have also found significant effects on newborn state, although the prolonged quiet-sleep effect has not been directly replicated.[10, 46] Predominant effects of prolonged wakefulness and crying in later studies may be attributable to differing techniques of circumcision observed. Nonetheless, all three of these studies have shown that circumcision has significant disruptive effects on state, and the fact is that no current necessary medical indication for routine circumcision exists.[244, 8] Hence, it is puzzling to ponder why this procedure persists. Aside from any long-term effects on the infant, would not such state changes be less than salutary for early caretaking? As will be seen later, there is increasing interest in maximizing positive opportunities for early wakeful infant-parent interaction. Questions are therefore being asked about procedures which might interfere with early eye-to-eye contact, handling, and social experiences between mother and infant. Indeed, Richards et al.[251] speculate that some reported differences in maternal caretaking responses to male as opposed to female newborns may be a consequence of circumcision rather than gender.

Assessment of Neurological and Behavioral Integrity in the Newborn

As the reader might imagine, the assessment of the newborn's neurological and behavioral integrity is closely related to the concept of state. Such assessment has been especially important for clinicians who are concerned with identifying those infants with brain dysfunction or those infants who are at high risk for developing such dysfunction. Two groups of European neurologist-pediatricians, one in Paris and one in Groningen, have developed standardized neurological assessment procedures specific for use with the newborn. The Paris group[266] has developed a test which emphasizes evaluation of muscle tone, posture, and various automatic responses. The Groningen group[240, 237] has developed a test which emphasizes detailed evaluation of multiple reflexes and related responses. Both tests allow for assessment of neurological organization and have predictive validity with respect to the more extreme outcomes of gross brain dysfunction; however, the degree of prediction is disappointing with respect to mild pathology and within the normal range of individual differences. As can be inferred from table 5-1, Prechtl found that the use of behavioral state assessments greatly increased the reliability and validity of his neurologic tests. Along this same line, in a discussion of the newborn neurological examination, Parmelee and Michaelis[227] emphasized the value of general factors in assessing abnormality—factors such as behavioral state, activity, and threshold levels.

A useful test for the assessment of behavioral integrity in the newborn was developed by Frances Graham and her colleagues,[118, 121, 122] a test which was later modified by Rosenblith.[259, 258] As has been the case with assessments of neurological integrity, the behaviorally oriented tests have thus far shown more value in documenting current status in normals and traumatized newborns than they have in predicting later outcome. More recently, Brazelton[54] has introduced his "Neonatal Behavioral Assessment Scale" which has the purpose of documenting insofar as possible the wide range of behaviors available to the newborn. Ultimately, according to Brazelton, its purpose is not just to enhance the prediction of pathological outcome, but also to reveal precursors of later personality development. Observations of behavioral state are central, for Brazelton believes that an infant's state in a particular circumstance reflects his capacity for self-organization and his ability to control his responsivity to his environment. The test combines many features derived from the standard behavioral and neurological tests which have been noted with features derived from Brazelton's years of clinical experience as a practicing pediatrician. Thus far, the scale has been able to discriminate individual differences among normal infants and to discriminate high-risk infants (for example, prematures) from low-risk infants. Currently, the scale is in wide use by researchers, and a variety of long-term outcome studies are underway. Aside from its other uses, this test is well suited for demonstrating the behavioral competence and optimal responses of a particular infant to his mother. It is for this reason (enhancing a mother's getting to know her baby) that Brazelton recommends that the test be administered in the mother's presence if at all possible.[52]

Another area which is assuming increasing prominence is the multivariate assessment of newborn sleep states. Such assessments are underway in a number of clinical labs and involve the use of the polygraph along with various techniques of computer analysis.[13, 76, 228] Prechtl et al.[243] and Dreyfus-Brisac and Monod[77] have described abnormal sleep organization in a variety of abnormal infants, and Schulte[283, 282] has reported immature sleep patterns and bioelectrical activity in infants born to diabetic and toxemic mothers. A useful review of sleep and its disorders has been written by Anders and Weinstein.[12] Most investigators have developed assessment techniques to differentiate pathological states of central nervous system disorganization from normal functioning and also to assess prognosis, but as techniques are becoming more refined, there is increasing interest in understanding underlying neurophysiological and maturational processes and in delineating individual differences. There is also the hope that more will be understood about the processes underlying the newborn's behavioral regulation in general. In current research, there is increasing attention focused on the relative coherence among multiple indices of state as these are affected by maturation, pathology, and individual differences. A promising example of a new assessment technique of this nature is Anders' Infant Sleep Profile.[9]

Individual Differences in the Newborn and the Problems of Predicting Subsequent Behavior

The subject of individual differences has been of central concern to those interested in understanding the early roots of mental illness. It can be assumed that fundamental and stable individual differences in the newborn do exist. It then becomes tantalizing to think that if one could but isolate and describe such traits before the impact of enormous variations in experience, one could in turn isolate those factors which contribute to or buffer against pathogenesis. The traits that could be found could be considered inborn. Not having been "shaped" by parenting, one might discover how they might in themselves shape later parenting. After more than fifteen years of intensive research in this area, this hope remains, although the information generated is leading to new research approaches rather than to immediate clinical application.

In order to define individual differences, one must study a group of infants longitudinally and note the stability of differences among them over time. Unfortunately, a limiting feature of research findings to date is that "stability" has been short-term. In the case of the findings to be cited, individual differences have been observed from one interfeeding period to the next or, at the most, over a few days. As will be discussed later, individual differences over longer periods of time are difficult to document and are related to the general problems in predicting subsequent behavior from observations made during the newborn period.

SHORT-TERM INDIVIDUAL DIFFERENCES

Korner and her group[176, 177, 180] found individual differences in the amounts of crying, waking activity, and in the frequency of spontaneous and naturally elicited alertness. Barten, Birns, and Ronch[21] found individual differences in the capacity for visual pursuit. In addition, both groups documented individual differences in soothability.[60, 40, 180] Along this line, one of the few individual differences which could be considered a "trait" with evidence of stability beyond early infancy is "cuddlability." Schaffer and Emerson[280] in their eighteen-month longitudinal study found that some infants appear to enjoy being cuddled, or held close, while others resisted any physical contact which involved restriction.

In another study, Birns[38] found evidence of individual differences in newborn arousal responses following auditory, tactile, and pacifier stimulation when such stimulation was offered over four successive days. Particularly interesting in this study was the finding that threshold levels tended to be similar across sensory modalities, although Bell, Weller, and Waldrop[29] calculated that the highest product moment correlation between days in the Birns study was only 0.32, indicating a level of stability which is quite low. In their own research, Bell et al.[29] documented individual differences between two interfeeding periods in tactile response thresholds and in response to nipple removal during nonnutritive sucking. In addition, Korner[174] recently reported individual differences in newborn auditory response thresholds.

Stable individual differences in activity levels have not been convincingly demonstrated in the newborn in spite of the fact that a number of excellent clinician-researchers have offered compelling arguments for the enduring importance of this variable both for infant and caretaker.[97, 56, 310] Early reports indicated short-term stability on this characteristic.[27, 147, 165] However, Bell et al., in their detailed 1971 study,[29] were unable to find stable individual differences in a number of measures of activity across an eight-hour period in seventy-five newborn infants.

EFFECT OF INFANT DIFFERENCES ON CARETAKING RESPONSES

A current research trend focuses on infant effects on the developing caretaker-infant relationship. Prechtl's longitudinal study of eight infants born with "hyperexcitability syndrome"[238] offers a vivid, early example of such an effect. The infants in Prechtl's study had suffered a variety of perinatal complications and were quite irritable, with rapid and unpredictable state changes. Toward the end of the first postnatal year, seven of the eight mothers in the study expressed rejecting and/or overanxious attitudes about their infants even though none realized that their infants were showing signs of brain dysfunction. In a control group, consisting of ten normal infants and their mothers, Prechtl found only one mother who was upset in any similar way.

The study of newborn sex differences also illustrates a trend toward increasing interest in the effects of infant on caretaker. Korner[175, 174] has offered some evocative discussion of newborn sex

differences in which she points to a number of studies which have shown that mothers' treatment of newborn boys differs from their treatment of newborn girls. Moss and Robson[214] and Lewis[192] found that mothers of three-month-olds were more apt to respond with talking to girls and with holding of boys in certain situations. Thoman et al.[309] found evidence for similar differences in the first postnatal days; primiparous mothers talked to and smiled more at girls during feedings than at boys. Perhaps, Korner suggests, this may be due not just to parental reinforcement of cultural views about sex-appropriate behavior, but also to subtle sex differences in the newborns themselves. While noting that relatively few neonatal studies have found sex differences, she pieces together a pattern of findings which indicate that the female may have greater tactile sensitivity.[28, 325, 199] Korner advances the possibility that mother's greater use of proximal-tactile stimulation of their male infants may therefore be in response to the male's lesser cutaneous sensitivity. Korner also reviews evidence for neonatal sex differences with respect to the female's increased "oral sensitivity": This involves a greater responsiveness to taste,[216] an increase in spontaneous mouth behavior,[178] and an increased tongueing during feeding.[18] (See Call's 1971 findings as well, wherein girls were found capable of targeting more of their hand-face contacts to the snout area.[61]) Korner links these findings with similar evidence from later development, such as the greater thumb sucking in girls after one year,[139] and wonders if mothers also have an empathic sense of their girls' affinity for oral comforting. This might explain the finding that mothers give oral pacifiers to girls more than boys.[214]

In spite of this intriguing pattern of findings, one must be cautious about interpreting sex differences in the newborn. There are two other findings about early behavioral sex differences which may override: First, on almost every dimension, males show more variability than females (see discussion in Kagan[155]); and second, females are maturationally more advanced than males. Thus, the findings reviewed by Korner may be part of a general advanced maturational level in the central nervous system of females, evidencing itself in the sensory area. This possibility finds support in the finding of the shorter latency of response to photic stimulation in female newborns.[94]

Finally, a great deal has been learned from the last decade's research on the embryophysiology of sex differentiation—that "maleness" is in large part determined by the fetal androgenization of the "resting state" female brain, and that such androgenization has early behavioral correlates in laboratory animals.[153, 305, 304] In view of this, it would be surprising if future research did not find sexual differences in the human newborn's behavior. The question the clinician must decide is one of relevance: Will such subtle differences as are found have consequences for development in the naturalistic setting?

ISSUES IN PREDICTING BEHAVIOR
FROM THE NEWBORN PERIOD

In light of the discussion about the short-term nature of demonstrated individual differences, the reader will not be surprised to learn that predictions of childhood behavior from newborn assessments have not been dramatic.

Bell et al.[29] reviewed the four studies in the English scientific literature which investigated this area prior to their own work. These studies did not deal with "predictions" but, more modestly, with seeking continuities in behavior between the newborn and the young child. Three of the studies were done more than thirty years ago, and it may be instructive to discuss one of these to illustrate problems of work in this era from the vantage point of today's standards for methodology and reporting of data. The work of Fries and her colleagues[111, 110, 109, 112] is of major historical importance since its assertions about enduring congenital activity types have been widely quoted. Unfortunately, as Bell et al. point out, observations of the newborn and those at later stages were not made independently, and reporting does not include any clear description of samples, procedures, and reliability of observations. Others have since been unable to verify the enduring nature of individual differences on any global measures of activity and responsiveness to stimulation. Another problem of the Fries work is that selection of cases who were extreme with respect to activity level may have included some who suffered from neurological disorders, with hyperactivity or hypoactivity resulting from perinatal complications.[241] The study provided for totally independent assessments at the newborn and two-to-four-year age periods. It took account of a variety of behaviors and their relation to internal stable variables, and it also gave specification to both sample and observations. On the other hand, the primary purpose of the Prechtl and Dijkstra study was to describe probabilities of abnormal neurological outcome in a group of newborns at risk.[241] Hence, little can be inferred about individual differences or prediction of activity level traits in normal infants.

In their own study, Bell and his colleagues[29] first considered thirty-one promising measures of newborn behavior. Of these, they determined that only twelve showed sufficient stability with respect to individual differences between two feeding periods to be of use in longitudinal studies. These measures were then used with seventy-five normal infants, and several were indeed found to be related to measures of behavior during the preschool age. The relationships, however, were negative ones! In the words of the authors:

. . . respiration rate, tactile threshold and reaction to interruption of sucking in the newborn period were most effective in measuring overly intense behavior, in terms of frequency, speed, or amplitude. The later outcome at the preschool period was low intensity (low interest, participation, assertiveness, gregariousness, and communicativeness). In other words, there was a longitudinal inversion of intensity. [p. i]

There is data to suggest that this finding of an inversion in intensity may be more than a curiosity. This is indicated by Bell's recent review of three other longitudinal studies which used the reaction to interruption of sucking in the newborn.[24] Moss[213] reported follow-up information during the first three months, Birns et al.[39] reported data for the third to fourth month, and McGrade[205] observed the eight-month age period. Bell reviews data from each of these studies showing that when the newborn reacts to interruption of sucking in a slow, low-magnitude fashion, this seems to be associated in later infancy with the expression of pleasurable emotional responses. Bell had conducted a study of preschoolers that had produced similar findings. He had found that when he followed children who as newborns displayed low-magnitude reactions to interruption of sucking as preschoolers, they regularly exhibited an interest and active involvement in games. Bell reasoned that there might be a fundamental developmental shift in longitudinal relations taking place in early infancy. Based on data from the Moss study, Bell places the time of such a shift between the third week and the third month and urges further study of this phenomenon.

In view of what is known about modern genetics and its major importance for psychiatry,[260, 166] why should prediction of behavior from the newborn be so poor? One obvious possibility is that genetic determinancy may be most prominent for the extremes of behavior, such as are involved in schizophrenia and the manic-depressive psychoses, while the mid ranges of behavior may be more the product of interaction with the environment and therefore less predictable. Another possibility follows from this and has to do with the diversity of the interacting environment. How could one possibly know in advance about the multiplicity of events which could influence the young child's development? Such variations are in no way trivial. Not only are psychological structures and interactional modes highly likely to be influenced by early variations in experience, but recent research indicates that brain structures themselves can be altered. Animal experiments have shown that environmental stimulation can enhance postnatal myelinization, or the lack of it retard myelinization.[217] Similar influences are demonstrable on the dendritic connectivity system of the cortical neurons themselves.[6, 263, 264, 125] Thus, an early environmental influence could yield changes in fundamental brain structures which could cause a diversion in the epigenetic pathway involving a behavior under observation.

Another reason for poor prediction may have to do with the differences in biobehavioral organization between the newborn and the infant after two months. Bell has summarized evidence for an inversion of intensity between the third week and the third month in certain longitudinal variables. The changes that have been reviewed in this chapter highlight the fact that there is a shift in behavioral organization to a new level of functioning after two months. After this time, behavior cannot be accounted for by endogenous rhythms and internal state. After two months, there is a shift away from endogenous control. More of life is in wakefulness and less is in sleep and, as Dittrichova puts it, "wakefulness becomes used in a new way."[75] Another factor which complicates the predictive task is that new behaviors emerge after birth. The timetable of some of these, such as the social smile and fearfulness to strangers, appears to be under genetic control.[107] Nonetheless, these new behaviors must necessitate a reorganization of the already existant behavioral repertoire. In the midst of these shifts, "the laws of transformation" from one level of behavioral organization to the next are unknown. How, then, can one predict?

Finally, prediction from the newborn may have faltered because of an oversimplified notion about newborn individual differences. As has been noted, such differences are not stable in any simple way. Instead, an individual newborn may be better characterized as having a range of behaviors which do not remain constant in any dimension, but oscillate and vary over time. Perhaps the primary influence of genetic heritage is on the "rate, range and tempo"[284] of behaviors, new and old. Perhaps the synchronization of the rhythms of these behaviors with particular environments and with particular caretakers could be characterized by consistent adaptational modes. Perhaps these "adaptational constants," in this sense, would reveal more stable individual differences over the course of development. This viewpoint finds support in the work and conceptualization of Sander.[273] It is likely that better predictions will emerge from a better grasp of interactional modes, and that individual interactional differences will emerge where individual differences have not.

Perception

Research on the newborn's perception has profited both from recent advances in bioengineering computer technology and from a conceptual readiness to appreciate organized complexity. It seems difficult to realize that scarcely a decade ago, pediatric textbooks contained assertions that a newborn could not fixate a visual target or track a moving stimulus. Today, data exist to contradict these assertions, but even more important than this has been a change in research attitude—the newborn is seen less as a passive recipient of sensations, and more as an active organism who often controls and regulates his sensory input.

VISION

Both in comparison with other mammals and in comparison with other human systems, the human visual system is relatively advanced at birth.[127] Vision has also played a significant role in psychoanalytic concepts of early ego development and ethological concepts of imprinting. Perhaps for these reasons, this sensory system has received the lion's share of research effort. Since Fantz's evocative findings[101] suggesting that the human newborn looks preferentially at a facial pattern, research in pattern perception has been especially vigorous. Excellent reviews of this area have been written by Hershenson,[136] Bond,[42] and Haith.[127] This review can therefore be brief.

As Haith has reviewed, a number of studies have shown that the pupillary light reflex, although sluggish, is present in full-term and premature newborns. Some controversy exists concerning the newborn's accommodative ability. Haynes et al.[133] studied accommodation by dynamic retinoscopy and estimated that the lens appeared to be relatively fixed at a median accommodative distance of 19 centimeters and gradually became adaptable over the first four months of life. Hershenson[136] and Haith[127] have questioned Haynes's findings on the basis of the lack of attractiveness of the stimulus and the lack of control of state and eye-movement variability. Presumably their estimates would be less conservative. Based on the optokinetic response and on visual orienting,[71, 103, 117] it has been shown that the newborn can attain a focused retinal image for stimuli, and estimates of visual acuity of 20/150 to 20/800 have been made. Although maturation of the retina continues throughout childhood, the photopic and scotopic systems are differentiated and functional at birth. There is a good deal of converging evidence that the human newborn's visual cortex is also functional at birth. Embryologically, it is known that the first-order projection sites of geniculate fibers in primates are formed early.[142] Ellingson[81] has shown that the visual evoked response in the newborn is present at birth, even though that of monkeys and kittens develops somewhat after birth. The elegant single cell recording studies of Hubel and Wiesel in kittens[143] and of Wiesel and Hubel in newborn rhesus monkeys[324] have established active areas in the visual cortex with motion selectivity and binocular responsivity of single cells.

What can the human newborn perceive with this visual equipment? It has been establshed that he can discriminate brightness intensities.[137] In addition, he can apparently detect separable angles as small as 7.5 minutes.[71] Studies reviewed by Haith[127] document the ocuomotor capability in the infant as being sensitive to visual movement. A study by Dayton et al.[72] documents the visual tracking of a moving stimulus. Many studies have been done on the ability of young infants to discriminate color but, as reviewed by Haith,[127] controversy remains about interpretation because it has not been possible to ensure that intensity levels of different hues were equivalent for the infant.

Reviews by Bond[42] and Haith[127] agree that literature on early form perception contains a number of unresolved questions. After a decade of research, there is little reason to conclude that newborns have holistic perception of forms. Instead, there is reason to believe there is scanning of contours and angles. Haith[127] points out that our knowledge of scanning has progressed far beyond Fantz's demonstration in 1963 that newborns look at nonhomogeneous fields more than homogeneous fields. The work of Haith and his colleagues[33, 127, 128, 129] is especially instructive. These investigators have devised an infrared video technique for recording newborn eye movements and direction of looking in both light and dark conditions. Each eye movement can be given a precise time and location in relation to a variety of visual targets, such as simple lines, angles, or mother's face. Haith found that significant scanning of the face does not occur until around seven weeks of age when there is prominent scanning in the region around the eyes.[33] Such a finding corresponds to the naturalistic observations of the age of onset of eye-to-eye contact between mother and infant made by Robson.[255] As the reviews of Bond and Haith point out, preferential looking at faces before seven weeks is probably explanable in terms of its being a rich source of complexity.

Another set of findings from Haith's laboratory concerns the newborn. Using the infrared technique, Haith has evidence that the newborn engages in organized visual scanning in darkness and in a formless light field. In addition, he has extensive data on the newborn's fixation and scanning of edges and bars. Haith interprets his data to suggest that the newborn is active and seeks to optimize exposure to informative aspects of his visual world. In so doing, the neonate appears to operate according to the basic principle of keeping the firing rate of neurons in the visual cortex at a maximal level. Furthermore, two "eye-movement control routines" appear to implement this rule. The first is what Haith calls an "ambient scan routine" that appears responsible for finding portions of the visual field which can be scanned to increase firing. This is an endogenous system manifested by the organized eye movements that occur during darkness and during light when there is no visual pattern in the field. The second routine is an "inspection scan routine" that operates when the stimulus is detected and serves to maximize the visual cortex firing rate by such maneuvers as repeated edge crossing. In effect, Haith has proposed a model, based on the principle of maximal cortical firing, in which the newborn comes pre-programmed to operate with an endogenous activity pattern resulting in a searching; this then becomes inhibited by a scanning routine when an edge is found. It remains for future research to determine if the "rules" which Haith derives from the model will apply to all visual scanning before seven weeks.

The changes around the two-month age period in visual organization are of considerable interest. In addition to Haith's findings about the onset of face scanning and eye contact, others have found the onset of a responsiveness to internal aspects of displays[267] and a reversal of the early preference of a checkerboard over a bull's eye.[102] Kagan[156, 157] emphasizes that after two months, discrepancy begins to operate to control infant attention. That is, after this time, stimuli will attract the infant to the extent that there is a fitting of input into a familiar internal image or schema. Such schemas are built up through experience with systematic inputs. If a given input is either too familiar or too discrepant from any stored schema, it will be ignored. Before two months, on the other hand, discrepancy does not account for visual attending, and physical dimensions (contour, complexity, etc.) are more prominent, according to Kagan.

HEARING AND OTHER SENSES

Is there a corresponding set of age-related findings for pattern perception in hearing? Research in this area has been more difficult since it is often hard to specify appropriate stimulus and response dimensions. Nonetheless, there is some evidence for an organization at birth, one in which there is preadaptation to the human environment. Eisenberg,[80, 79] after reviewing methodological problems of studies in this field, gives data to support the contention that the newborn comes to the world especially responsive to sound frequencies in the range of human speech (approximately 500–900 Hertz). Others have made the same point by demonstrating that young infants respond to and even prefer speechlike sounds.[146, 78, 312] Certainly responsiveness to speech sounds, combined with the infant's tendency to look at faces, the rich source of vision and sound, place the young infant in a strategic position to acquire schemas which would be important for the later development of language.[248]

That it is normal for the infant to hear soon after birth has apparently never been in doubt. (Presumably this is because of the easily demonstrated startle response to loud sounds.) The newborn's blink response in combination with changes in bodily activity have been used as a screening test for deafness.[73, 252] More recently, research has been directed to the auditory-evoked response with computer-averaged EEG responses to repeated sounds. This has provided a more precise index of auditory sensitivity.* Unfortunately, experiments designed to define the newborn's ability to discriminate either intensity or location of sound have been problematic. There are major difficulties in the definition of stimulus dimension,

control of ambient noise, and control of internal state.[164] Experimental control of state is especially important since it is known that a sound may startle or soothe, or arouse or quiet, depending on initial state. The situation is compounded by the fact that auditory stimulation itself can change internal state. Repetitive sounds, for example, can have a soothing effect. Understandably, this has led to problems in research which require such repetition, as in the auditory-evoked response technique.

The fact that sound can be an effective soothing stimulus in the newborn[41] has led to other problems of interpretation. A flurry of excitement followed Salk's proposal[268] that the newborn becomes "imprinted" on its mother's heartbeat. Salk based his proposal on his findings that continued exposure to a recorded heartbeat resulted in diminished crying and a greater postnatal weight gain. Subsequent studies have confirmed the soothing effects of the repeated sounds but have failed to support the specific effect of the maternal heartbeat.[314, 50, 289]

A curious paradox exists with respect to research concerning the newborn's other senses. Clinicians and researchers alike have noted the obvious importance of the proximal sensory modalities involving touch, position sense, and equilibrium.[293, 176, 29] Yet, except for tactile thresholds, there have been few measures of stimulus dimensions and fewer attempts to understand processes of perception in these modalities. In view of the relative maturity of these systems at birth and in view of recent progress in the neurosciences, it seems a sure bet to predict that research in this area will thrive over the next decade. Already, two sets of findings stand out: (1) tactile threshold measures are among the very few which have some stability over time in individual infants,[29] and (2) vestibular stimulation is a potent determinant of alert wakefulness.[181] These findings require further research to understand the mechanisms and general principles underlying them. A number of investigators have documented the responsivity of the newborn to differences in smells, temperatures, and tastes. But little can be said beyond stating that the newborn infant does have discriminatory capacity in these modalities. The early work of Lipsitt and his colleagues[200, 95] on newborn olfaction is prototypic of such research. Again, programmatic research is required into the mechanisms underlying fundamental processes of behavior, both in the laboratory and the home. The recent experiments of Macfarlane,[204] indicating that six-day-old newborns can

* See references 116, 321, 4, 83, and 19.

use smell to differentiate between their own mother's breast pad and that of another mother, is most intriguing and requires replication.

Another area of research linked to issues of early perceptual organization has been that of heart-rate responsiveness to initial stimulation. Heart-rate deceleration has been thought of as related to processes of attention, stimulus intake, and integration, [187, 291] while heart-rate acceleration, on the other hand, has been thought of as related to processes of stimulus rejection. In a series of papers, Graham and her associates[119, 120, 148] reviewed evidence which suggested a shift between the newborn period and the period from six to eight weeks and after. Characteristically, a tone presented to an older infant evokes a deceleration in heart rate whereas before six weeks, the response is typically one of acceleration. Even in awake infants, there seemed to be few decelerative responses during the early period. There seemed to be a developmental shift, but was it an either/or phenomenon? Certainly, converging evidence did not support the notion that the newborn was incapable of paying attention to stimuli in the first six weeks of life. This made the either/or possibility unlikely. Graham and Jackson[120] pointed out that the use of intense stimuli with short rise times may have biased results in these kinds of experiments. In their view, it would be valuable to do experiments with more mature sensory modalities—with the vestibular system, for example, while controlling for state to make sure of using an awake infant. Subsequent studies have proven the wisdom of these remarks. A number of investigators have found cardiac deceleration in newborn responses to a low- to moderate-intensity stimulus with slower rise time; all have used awake infants. Kearsley[161] obtained these results with auditory stimuli, Lipsitt and Jacklin[197] with olfactory stimuli, and Sameroff et al.[272] with a patterned visual checkerboard stimulus. Pomerleau-Malcuit and Clifton[233] found cardiac deceleration in response to presentation of vestibular and tactile stimuli. The latter work, along with that of Kearsley, indicates the marked dependency of this response system on internal state. Findings of deceleration in both studies occurred in awake newborns, before feeding but not afterward.

Learning

Studies done in the early part of the century were enthusiastic in their demonstrations of learning in young children. (See Razran[245] for a review of work done in Russia and Watson and Watson[320] and Jones[151] for work done in the United States.) In 1931, Marquis wrote an article for the *Journal of Genetic Psychology* entitled "Can Conditioned Responses be Established in the Newborn Infant?" and answered in the affirmative.[208] A second era of learning studies began in the late 1950s with the demonstration of operant conditioning of smiling[48] and of vocalizations[247] in four-month-old infants. Since then, an impressive number of studies has been carried out with newborns. As increasing advances have been made in experimental design, it has become apparent that results have pointed to age-related differences in the processes underlying learning.

In 1967, Lipsitt reviewed the growing number of experimental studies in infant learning and raised important methodological issues concerning controls in earlier studies. He concluded that it is difficult to demonstrate aversive conditioning in the first three weeks, although the modification of appetitional responses, such as sucking, seemed more promising.[196] Soviet research with classical conditioning encountered similar findings. Kasatkin, in 1962, summarized the situation as follows: "With a few exceptions, conditioned reflexes are weak and unstable up till the fourth to fifth weeks of life. . . . A firm and well expressed conditioned reflex is sometimes formed in the fourth week and almost always in the second month." (Quoted in Kessen, Haith, and Salapatek[164] [p. 324].)

In a subsequent review, Kasatkin[159] states that stable conditioned responses with auditory stimuli will not occur before thirty-two days of age. Operant conditioning of newborn sucking, on the other hand, has been demonstrated in infants as young as four days old. Lipsitt and Kaye,[198] Kron et al.[185] and Sameroff[271] all achieved operant conditioning in the newborn although learned modifications were short-lived. In a still later review, Hulsebus[144] points to these and other studies which attempted operant conditioning of sucking, head turning, and visual attending in early infancy. For the most part, successful operant conditioning in the first months has involved sucking. Although subjects for head-turning experiments have been as young as four days old, most have been between two and five months. Operant conditioning of visual attending in the neonate has been unsuccessful, as has contingent reinforcement of social behavior in the infant under two months of age.

Among the most enlightening developmental studies of infantile learning have been those of Papoušek.[224, 223, 225] Using the head-turning response in an experimental design with aspects of both classical and operant conditioning, he has studied the rate at which infants can be conditioned from birth through six months of age. The bulk of his study has been carried out in a research unit in Prague where infants lived with their own mothers or with trained surrogate mothers, and subsequent findings came from a residential nursery in the United States. His findings were that conditioning under these circumstances is quite difficult to obtain during the first month of life, with a marked increase in conditionability occurring during the second and third months of life. He emphasizes that individual differences are great, but that the general validity of the finding is indicated by equivalent results obtained with a conditioned eye-blink technique.

Reconsidering Marquis's original question, Sameroff asks: "Can conditioned responses be established in the newborn infant?"[271] The answer to this question now becomes more complex and challenges the existing assumptions about learning in the newborn. From his data review, Sameroff concludes that classifical conditioning is difficult if not impossible to demonstrate before three weeks of age. Using Piagetian concepts, he reasons that there must be a differentiation of response systems during these early weeks, and only after this neonatal phase may such individual systems be coordinated with other sensory motor schemas, such as sucking or head turning. Sameroff also speculates that maturational factors may play a role in the transition from neonatal to later stages of learning. In a 1972 review, Sameroff explores further the dichotomous onset of classical and operant conditioning and relates it to the physiological patterns of orienting and attending.[270] He hypothesizes that classical conditioning cannot take place before the organism has the general capacity of orienting to a variety of stimuli. Operant conditioning, on the other hand, is theoretically possible earlier since the contingent stimulus may correspond to some aspect of the infant's environment to which he is preprogrammed to respond. Sameroff argues that there may be species-specific programming of associations between stimuli and responses that facilitate the learning of certain patterns at certain points in the development of a given organism. By contrast, a potential conditioned stimulus, such as a bell or a flickering light, has no necessary biological connection in the development of the organism and must wait upon individual experience before it becomes relevant.

Sameroff also assigns central importance to internal state in newborn learning studies. As the infant becomes increasingly capable of prolonged alert states, more energy can be directed to acquiring information from the outside world. This agrees with evidence (reviewed elsewhere) in support of the conclusion that a new stimulus facilitation system emerges at about two months.[89] Shifts in internal state organization, learning capacities, and exploration seem to occur together.

A similar group of age-related findings has emerged in the field of habituation research. Habituation refers to a response decrement which occurs under experimental conditions when a stimulus is presented repeatedly. It is distinguishable from other types of response decrement (such as fatigue of the receptor or response apparatus) by the fact that the response returns when a new stimulus is introduced which is similar to, but in some ways discrepant from, the original stimulus. In their excellent review of this subject, Jeffrey and Cohen[150] consider a number of studies which have used stimuli in auditory and visual modalities. They document the general failure to obtain clear evidence for habituation in infants under two months of age. Beyond two months, however, habituation has been demonstrated in a variety of modalities and with a number of responses. The authors point out that this represents a major developmental change in the phenomena under investigation. Possibly, habituation, like the initial heart-rate deceleration response (orienting) and operant conditioning, will be found as a possible response in the newborn under special and limited conditions. However, this would not eliminate the necessity to explain a developmental shift. Currently, there is not enough information to understand to what extent these developmental changes represent primary changes in *perceptual organization* or *response organization*. Furthermore, habituation, like classical and operant conditioning forms of behavior modification, must involve mechanisms for retention, and adequate knowledge about the development of memory in early infancy is seriously lacking.

In reviewing recent work on learning in early infancy, one cannot help but get the impression that the field is on the threshold of major discoveries concerning changing parameters of learning during this period. A great deal of learning occurs during the newborn period through adaptation and "entertainment" of endogenous rhythms and other activities and also as part of the intricate and ongoing processes involved in reciprocal interaction with caretakers. One needs to know more about how early learning takes place, about how it is retained, and about how it is integrated into the life of the organism after two months.

Perhaps further understanding will come from a synthesis of the knowledge from separate paradigms (operant conditioning, classical conditioning, habituation, and learning observed in a naturalistic setting). Such a synthesis will undoubtedly also rest on a greater understanding of developmental neurophysiology.

Affect Expressions

This section will review the two major expressions of affect which are prominent during the first two months. Crying offers a strong social signal for caretaking immediately after birth; smiling does not, but instead undergoes a process of development. It ultimately reaches full social significance with an unambiguous signal after two months.

CRYING

The newborn's cry provides a universal message; under most conditions, it calls for the caregiver to come and change something whether it be feeding, diapering, positioning, or removing a particular hurt.[296, 89] Studies by Wolff,[325] Bernal,[34] and Thoman et al.[309] have pointed out that when one compares them to primiparous mothers, there are differences in the way multiparous mothers respond to newborn crying. A greater amount of experience with babies appears to result in a more relaxed attitude about crying and in a more efficient feeding interaction.

A number of investigators have asked about whether there are specific cry patterns with acoustical properties which might correspond to more specific messages. Evidence from these studies is informative but mixed. In 1951, Lynip introduced the sound spectrograph in the study of infant cries, and many contributions have followed.* Wolff[325] and Wasz-Hockert et al.[318] have identified some types of cries by relating the circumstances which elicit the cry to the patterns produced on the sound spectrograph. Both have identified a "basic" or hunger cry and a pain cry. As Wolff describes it, the hunger cry is 250–400 cycles per second; a typical sequence begins with a cry followed by a brief silence, an expiratory whistle, another brief rest, and then a cry again. The pain cry is characterized by the sudden onset of a loud, long cry with extended breath holding and ex-

* See references 313, 318, 253, 287, 195, 325, 194, 219, 220, and 231.

piration afterward. Wolff also notes a "mad cry," which is a variation of the hunger cry except with turbulence due to excess air forced through the vocal cords. It would seem that Wolff's "mad cry" is difficult to distinguish from an intense cry under circumstances when mother knows that she has not been able to meet a specific need as soon as she would like and therefore interprets her infant's cry as "impatient" and/or "angry." This agrees with the viewpoint of Richards and Bernal.[250] Wasz-Hockert et al.[316] also identify a "pleasure cry" which seems to have an entirely different vocalization pattern from crying in the usual sense. Wolff points out that in the human infant—as opposed to lower species—crying does not result in stereotypical responses by mothers. Previous experience with what stops crying is of major importance. A similar conclusion results from Wasz-Hockert et al.[317] They found that "correct" identification of cries (as validated under spectrographic patterns) is dependent upon the listener's experiences as well as the typicality of the cry. Since there are a great many individual differences in infant cry patterns, most mothers will have to learn about specific cry patterns from their particular infants. Bernal reports that experience with what works seems to account for much of a mother's behavior in response to the cry.[34] Furthermore, it is a common observation that even experienced mothers can be wrong about identifying their infant's cries. There seems to be little efficiency in diagnosing the cause of infant distress from the cry sound alone.[218] Except for the pain cry, mothers do not seem to respond on the basis of sound patterns. Rather, the nature of past experience with individual infants and the context of current crying is paramount: Mothers recognize the significance of crying as a part of the general pattern of behavior, not as a single stimulus to elicit a specific response. There seems to be little promise to the original suggestion that a better understanding of typical spectrographic patterns of crying would lead to more appropriate and specific caretaking.[318]

To what extent can mothers recognize the cries of their newborn infants? Evidence has been either inconclusive or negative. Poitras et al.[234] noted that mothers had a lowered threshold for wakening from sleep after delivery, but they did not note a difference in response to different auditory stimuli, one being a taped baby's cry, the other a taped woman's voice. Greenberg et al.,[123] using mother's self-report, noted that rooming-in mothers seemed more able to abstract information from their infant's cry than those who had traditional hospital care and less contact with their infants. Valanne et al.[315] did a study to see if a mother can pick out her own infant on the basis of its cry in the nursery, with results that perhaps some could but most could not. Ostwald[218] points out that although the arousing function of the cry often seems essential for a maternal response, mothers can also "tune out" their infants' cries and thus ignore their distress. Thus, it is necessary to understand more about individual differences in distress signals and individual differences in caretaking responses and their interaction.

Even if only in passing, mention must be made of the diagnostic aspect of the newborn's cry. Karelitz and Fisichelli[158] found that for brain-damaged infants, more stimulation is required than in normal infants in order to evoke the same amount of crying; this finding needs further elaboration. Others, including Wasz-Hockert et al.[318] have described the shrill, piercing quality of the brain-damaged infant's cry and have discussed its usefulness in monitoring the course of illness. The special use of the sound spectrograph in the differential diagnosis of central nervous system dysfunction, on the other hand, has apparently not been as promising as first thought.

Increasingly, crying is being studied within the context of the developing mother-infant relationship. Sander and Julia[276] have included a measurement of crying in their continuous automatic monitoring system for infant-caretaker environments and have shown that a change in caretakers can result in an increase in crying. Others have shown that crying can be increased by inappropriate rocking of the infant[290] and by inappropriate feeding.[2] Rebelsky and Black[246] and Sander et al.[277] have reported a diurnal rhythmicity in crying and have noted that the major peaks are associated with feeding.

There is another aspect of crying which becomes prominent during the first two months and declines toward the end of the third month, one that seems relatively independent of mothering. This type of cry is not in response to pain or hunger. It is usually referred to as "fussiness." It causes bewilderment even to experienced mothers who often express uneasiness about the difficulty of soothing their infants, even though they may console themselves with the thought that the fussiness will be "outgrown." This form of crying has also been puzzling to researchers. A number of careful, descriptive studies have concentrated on extreme instances (often labelled "colic") which came to the attention of pediatricians.[303, 322, 57, 226] Two recent longitudinal studies of normal infants conducted by a research group[307, 89] noted the presence of such unexplained fussiness in all the infants studied. About one-fourth of the infants developed extreme fussiness, with some unofficially labelled as "colicky" by pediatricians. However, all had some amount of fussiness which appeared to have a typical developmental course, largely independent of variations in mothering. This course included fussiness with an average onset around three postnatal weeks and an average decline around three months. The time course corresponded with the predictions of John Benjamin,[30] although the investigators did not find evidence for an "active stimulus barrier" postulated by Benjamin to account for the decline. Instead of finding a new capacity to avoid stimulation, it was observed that the social smile—a new stimulus-facilitating system—emerged during the time of fussiness decline. As a result of this work, it was concluded that the period from one to three months seems to be one in which there is a psychological propensity for prolonged, nonhunger fussiness. Since no evidence was found that environmental factors, such as variations in mothering or changes in the surroundings, played a major role in its emergence, maintenance, or decline, it is speculated that it might have an adaptational advantage, perhaps an inborn "attachment behavior,"[45] with a function of ensuring survival by promoting closeness with the caretaker at times in early infancy not necessarily taken up with feeding.[89]

Thus far, crying has been discussed from the point of view of its social-message characteristics. Another viewpoint about crying concerns its importance as an internal state. Because of its particular pattern of activity and reactivity in most schemes of behavioral state, it is usually considered as a separate state category. Indeed, the way that any newborn affect expression is viewed seems closely related to the concept of state. The bright-eyed state of alert wakefulness, so central in feeding and social interaction, is sometimes interpreted as communicating contentment or pleasure. Stechler and Carpenter[296] point out that these two states—crying and alert wakefulness—can be thought of as representing extremes on a dimension of receptiveness to information: The infant is maximally receptive during alert wakefulness and minimally receptive during crying. The states of alert activity, drowsiness, and sleeping fall somewhere in between. These authors have proposed a theory which includes the postulate that there are innate links in the newborn between perception and the organized regulation of excitatory-affective states. According to Stechler and Carpenter, such regulation can take place either through change as a result of the social-message characteristics of these states, or as a result of a change in the states themselves. This, in turn, would affect the level of receptiveness to information.

The decline of crying after early infancy has posed the learning theorists a serious dilemma. Why should crying decline if mothers give it positive reinforcement? A related question is more practical. When one looks at individual cases, is there any evidence that those infants whose cries are responded to in early infancy do more crying in later infancy? Ainsworth and Bell[2] studied this problem longitudinally. They opposed the classic learning theory position to an ethological view which regarded crying as an inborn signal behavior for eliciting early caretaking. From the latter standpoint, crying would be phase-specific, and, if responded to appropriately, would not persist. The findings of the study were compatible with the ethological view. Those infants whose mothers responded to cries early in infancy had less crying in the later part of infancy. Rather than becoming "spoiled" and having increased crying as learning theory would predict, it was as if those infants whose cries received attention were free to develop other communicative behaviors. This study provides another indication of the inadequacy of the drive-reduction point of view and the need for alternative explanatory systems.

Another question about the development of the cry concerns its relationship to later language development. Lenneberg[190] and Ostwald[218] both emphasize that there is a marked difference between the crying of the first two months and the coo-babble types of vocalization which appear by three months. The three-month vocalizations occur at a more mature level of social functioning and are subject to a variety of social reinforcements.[285] In addition, Lenneberg[190] points out that the cooing sounds which appear toward the end of the second month are acoustically distinct from crying sounds. The duration of cooing is characteristically about one-half second. Energy is distributed over the frequency spectrum in a way that begins to remind one of vowel formants. In contrast to crying, cooing shows resonance modulation almost at once in addition to fundamental frequency modulation. Moreover, during cooing, some articulatory organs, such as the tongue, are moving, whereas in crying, they tend to be relatively still. Lenneberg et al.[191] have also drawn an analogy between the pleasurable cooing which has its onset at around

six to eight weeks and the onset of the social smile. Both seem to have the characteristics of a new response system which is elicited by a social stimulus. As a result of this evidence, it would seem unlikely that the newborn's crying later differentiates in any simple manner into a distress cry on the one hand and a pleasurable vocalization on the other. Instead, it seems more likely that a new response system emerges as part of a new level of organization.

SMILING

Unlike crying, smiling is not present immediately after birth as a full-fledged response system. Koehler[173] and Wolff[331] described newborn smiles occurring during sleep and drowsiness, and Wolff[329, 327] also described early smiles seen during wakefulness. As a result of several studies in their laboratory, the authors have found it convenient to think of two systems of smiling that arise in development before the predictable social smiling response, which begins at two months. One system of smiling arises as a correlate of an observed behavioral and physiological state pattern, and hence is referred to as endogenous. The other system of early smiling is stimulated from the outside and is spoken of as exogenous. Endogenous smiling has been found to be a consistent correlate of the REM state either in drowsiness or sleep.[86, 87, 88] These studies found no evidence that this smiling could be explained by what common folklore calls "gas." REM smiling was found to have a tendency to cluster and to be correlated with an expectable electrophysiological pattern within the REM state no matter where it occurred in the feeding cycle or the twenty-four-hour cycle. Thus, REM smiles appear to be one of a number of spontaneous behaviors occurring during the REM state. Mothers do not usually regard these smiles as indicative of pleasure or as related to anything they do. An endogenous frowning was also studied and, in addition to having a spontaneous base rate during REM periods, frowning increased beyond base rates during those REM periods before an infant awoke, cried, and was fed. Thus, during sleep, frowning appeared to exist both as a spontaneous REM state behavior and also as a potential indicator of hunger distress and/or impending awakening. In contrast to this, endogenous smiling carried with it no such additional indication. Other studies [90, 132] led to the tentative conclusion that endogenous smiling was mediated by brainstem structures. Prematures were found to have more

REM smiling than full terms and a microcephalic with anatomically verified severe impairment of both cerebral cortex and limbic system was found to have as much smiling as intact, normal full terms during the REM state. In the course of longitudinal observations, such smiling was seen to diminish during the third and fourth postnatal months. It was concluded that endogenous smiling is probably organized and mediated within the brainstem along with other REM spontaneous behaviors, and that increasing neurological inhibition probably related to maturation of cerebral cortex results in such diminution.

Unlike endogenous smiling, exogenous smiling is not present at birth. It begins in an irregular fashion during the first month and increases in specificity and importance thereafter. These studies[85] have shown that during the period when such smiling is irregular, up until two and one-half months, stimuli from visual kinesthetic, auditory, and tactile modalities will elicit it. Following this, there is a period during which brief smiling is not irregular, but is a frequent response to a wide variety of stimuli. Only after this, from two and one-half to three months, does the regular social smile occur. Smiling is best elicited by visual stimuli, especially those contained in the human face. During the next phase, at three months and after, early differentiated smiling occurs. At this point, social smiling becomes even more specific within the visual modality (more smiling in response to a three-dimensional stimulus, and, later, more smiling in response to mother's face). These data were interpreted in the following manner: In early infancy there is a brief period in development when there is a maturational "push" manifested by an emergency propensity to smile in reaction to a wide variety of moderately intense stimuli; the response soon becomes more specific; and after three months of age, nonspecific smiling does not survive, presumably because, unlike social smiling, it is not normally reinforced within the social context of the developing infant. Thus, maturation would seem to be the major determinant of the onset of smiling to multiple stimuli, while learning would account for its subsequent decline and inhibition. This speculative interpretation seems to gather some concrete support from observations of congenitally blind infants.[105] Although without vision from birth, these infants exhibit the same early phases of smiling to multiple stimuli followed by a specific smiling phase, but after this, there is a shaping to an auditory-tactile stimulus Gestalt rather than to a visual one.

Research on Attachment

Research on attachment illustrates many of the research trends which have been emphasized throughout this chapter. The attachment concept became prominent with Bowlby's classic paper[45] on the nature of the child's tie to its mother. Bowlby brought data and principles from ethology as an alternative to the prevalent drive-reductionistic view inherent in psychoanalytic and learning theories of early development. The infant did not develop a social bond solely because of the association of mother with satisfaction from hunger or relief from pain, but carried within him an inborn biological propensity for the development of social bonds independent of such needs. "Attachment" was chosen as a term to designate the emergent social relationships, with "attachment behaviors" operationally defined as those behaviors which function to maintain the proximity of another person. Attachment behaviors which have been designated in human infants are sucking, crying, smiling, clinging, following, calling, using the mother as a base from which to explore, and greeting and approach behaviors directed toward the mother after her return from a brief separation.[45, 3] In his 1969 discussion of the concept of attachment, Bowlby emphasizes that attachment behaviors are controlled by a dynamic feedback system existing between mother and child. Within this

> . . . the internal standards against which the consequences of behavior are appraised by both mother and child are such as strongly to favor the development of attachment: for proximity and affectionate interchange are appraised and felt as pleasurable by both whereas distance and expressions of rejection are appraised and felt as disagreeable or painful by both. For no other behavioral consequences, perhaps, are standards of appraisal in man more clear-cut from the start, or more environmentally stable. [44] [p. 242]

Most of the research generated by this line of thinking has centered on the development of the infant's specific attachment to a particular caretaker. Behaviors under scrutiny have been those typical of later infancy such as separation distress, stranger distress, and reunion behaviors. The newborn has been studied less, although the period from birth through six to eight weeks has been described as one in which there are indiscriminate attachment behaviors—the child gives signals without recognition of specific figures.[44, 1] Call documents anticipatory approach behaviors during newborn feedings.[62] Behaviors of early infancy have been viewed primarily as elicitors of maternal caretaking. In this context, Robson[255] added eye-to-eye contact to Bowlby's original list of important releasers of maternal caretaking and noted the special pleasure mothers take when their infants "see them." In their study of the developing maternal sense, Robson and Moss found that four to six weeks was a transitional period during which mothers became more confident in their caretaking and felt that their infants were "becoming human."[256] Mothers spoke of their infants' greater responsiveness, especially in smiling, laughing, eye contact, and "seeing." It was after this, by seven to nine weeks, that the mothers felt that their infants recognized them specifically by reacting differently to them as compared with other adults. Similar findings emerged from a longitudinal study by Emde, Gaensbauer, and Harmon.[89] During the first two months, any reported differential responsivity of infants could be accounted for by their mother's "tuning in"—for example, learning what soothes a particular infant best and when. The importance of infant smiling, vocalizing, and bright-eyed wakefulness in eliciting positive maternal feelings after two months has already been noted in the discussion of affect.

Since 1970, research generated by the attachment concept has progressed with some vigor along a line quite different from that emphasized by Bowlby. In that year, two groups of clinician-researchers, one at Case Western Reserve University[169] and the other at Stanford University,[20] pointed out that the field had been grievously ignoring *maternal* attachment during the newborn period. Barnett et al.[20] commented that whereas research supported the inference that the ages of six months to two years may be the most sensitive period for interactional deprivation in the infant, comparable research had not been done on the mother's side of the attachment dyad. On the basis of their clinical experience, they speculated that the immediate postpartum period was probably the most sensitive for the mother, and that early separation could cause major disruptions in the developing maternal attachment bond. Perhaps the usual hospital routine of separating mother and infant during the lying-in period is hazardous, and the more prolonged separation when a mother is separated from her premature even more so. As Klaus et al.[169] pointed out, the incidence of child abuse is increased markedly in prematures where early postnatal separation of mother and infant is such a prominent feature.[84, 288] A cross-cultural survey revealed that provisions in other countries are usually made for mothers and infants to be

together and have intimacy in the days after birth. Furthermore, in many species of mammals, even brief separations in the early postnatal hours can cause complete maternal rejection.[169]

Klaus et al.[169] systematically observed the first postnatal contact of mothers with their undressed infants and found an orderly pattern of maternal interactive behavior similar to what had been observed earlier by Rubin.[265] The pattern was described thus:

Commencing hesitantly with fingertip contact on the extremities, within 4 to 5 minutes she began caressing the trunk with her palm, simultaneously showing progressively heightened excitement, which continued for several minutes. Her activity then often diminished, sometimes to such a degree that she fell asleep with the infant at her side.[169] [p. 188]

Mothers expressed an intense interest in looking at their infants' open eyes, often verbalizing an eagerness for them to open them. Several mothers mentioned that they felt much closer once their infants looked at them.

A subsequent study by Klaus et al.[168] is worth describing in some detail because of its actual and potential impact on hospital nursery practices. A group of primiparous mothers and their infants were randomly assigned to one of two groups, a control group which experienced the usual hospital nursery routine and an extended-contact group which experienced sixteen additional hours of mother-infant togetherness. Control-group mothers saw their infants briefly after birth, had a brief contact for identification at six to twelve hours, and remained separate except for twenty- to thirty-minute visits for bottle feedings five times a day. In addition to this routine contact, the fourteen mothers in the extended-contact group were with their infants for one hour within the first three hours after birth and also for five hours on each afternoon of the three days following delivery (an added total of sixteen hours). At one month, mothers returned for an interview about their caretaking experiences and were observed during a physical examination of their infants and also during a bottle feeding. Statistically significant differences were found between extended-contact mothers and control mothers in all three areas of data collection: (1) extended-contact mothers indicated more concern about their infants on interview; (2) they were observed to have more physical proximity to them during the physical examination; (3) they fondled their infants more and also held them more in an *en face* position during observed feedings. Subsequent follow-up studies of these mother-infant groups revealed continued significant differences at one year[163] and at two years.[254] At one year, extended-contact mothers spent more time assisting the doctor during the physical examination and in soothing their own infants. At two years, such mothers asked more questions and gave fewer commands to their infants.

In the case of prematures, separation of mother and infant is especially pronounced and prolonged. Not only is the infant removed to an intensive-care nursery after birth, but the mother typically goes home alone. Separation may extend for weeks and even months. Leifer et al.[188] and Seashore et al.[286] found that mothers of full terms smiled at and held their infants close to their bodies more frequently than did mothers of prematures. Furthermore, mothers who had more contact with their prematures expressed more confidence in their caretaking abilities. These researchers speculated that the hormonal state of the mother at the time of her first contact with her infant and/or the time of her first assuming caretaking responsibilities could determine the quality of maternal attachment. The readiness for acceptance of mothering seemed highest soon after birth. They also concluded that periodic contacts with an infant during the necessary period of separation can facilitate maternal attachment. Kennell, Gordon, and Klaus[162] compared two groups of mothers with premature infants, those who were permitted contact with their infants during the first few days of life and those who only handled them at twenty days of age or later. In a predischarge observation, they found that the early-contact mothers spent more time in the *en face* position with their infants and cuddled them for longer intervals. In a follow-up study of premature infants, Fanaroff et al.[99] found that there was a high incidence of disorders of mothering in those mothers who visited their prematures infrequently while the babies were still in the hospital.

From another angle, interactive research has until recently focused too exclusively on the mother's side. In the 1950s and early 1960s, mother's importance in fostering the early one-to-one relationship in the growing child was presumed to be the foundation of basic trust[96] and was explored as such. The burden of this empathic, constant relationship was upon the mother, since she was seen as the active, controlling person and the member of the dyad who bore total responsibility for its functioning. With the increased understanding of the degree of organization and the wide range of behaviors available to the newborn, this view has changed. Infant contributions to the developing relationship are of major proportions. Systematic observation has again been helpful. For example, Moss and Robson[214] found that the infant initiated 50 percent or more of the interactions with its caretaker. Bell[24] has also drawn attention to evidence that an infant often contributes to the syndrome of child abuse—that is, a set of parents can have five children and one of them, by virtue of its shrill cry or aversive behavior, evokes battering when the others do not. Considerable research has been done describing the effects of congenital defects such as blindness[105] and deafness[106] on altering mother-infant interaction. Other infant variables influencing caregiving such as state, maturity, and sex have been reviewed by Korner.[175]

It has indeed been established that the young infant is not a *tabula rasa*—he is an active and complex being. However, by focusing on infant contributions to the developing interaction, one runs the risk of shifting the burden of responsibility heretofore laid upon the caretaker. It is possible to cling to the unidirectional model, but with a change in the direction of effect. Growing appreciation of this tendency has led to a new emphasis in which attachment is seen neither as a "trait" of one partner, nor as a static product, nor as an outcome of interaction. Increasingly, the study of interaction is dealing with process variables and with the study of conditional probabilities for certain sequences of events as opposed to single "rings" on an interaction chain.[261, 262] This approach may enhance the investigator's ability to make predictions. For example, given an infant's internal state, one may be able to predict the probability of particular caretaking behaviors with some certainty. However, different infants will have different rates, ranges, and tempos of these states that will in turn affect the outcome of interactions from individual to individual. In addition, as the research of Sander[273] has so aptly demonstrated, the differing experience and styles of mothers will contribute to any such interaction. Research has already shown an interesting interaction between maternal experience and infant state. Thoman et al.[309] studied the characteristics of feeding behaviors of primiparous and multiparous mothers during the newborn period and found that multiparous mothers were more efficient during feedings. They often stimulated their sleepy infants' mouths and lips with a nipple, whereas primiparous mothers held the nipple passively while giving verbal encouragement. In a similar study (Emde and Harmon, unpublished), it was found that when experienced mothers and nurses noted that their infants fell into an active REM sleep during feeding, they aroused the babies vigorously. As a result, they woke them up and continued the feeding or they let them sleep and discontinued feeding altogether. This stood in contrast to the behavior of inexperienced mothers and nurses. These caretakers often tended to misinterpret the behavioral activities seen during this form of sleep and regarded it as indicating wakefulness. They consequently continued a gentle feeding which often resulted in regurgitations in the infant and perplexity in the feeder. The research programs of Stern[301] and of Brazelton[53] have already yielded reports on the lawfulness of the visual interactive behavior between mother and infant. Their research concerns a study of such interactions primarily after the first two months. Before this time, more of the infant's behaviors seemed to be endogenous; this will require further study. In the words of Richards:

> The role of the infant in patterning the interactions with the mother and influencing her maternal attitudes has been stressed. It is argued that a central issue in the growth of the relationship between mother and child is the temporal phasing of each partner's behaviour. The infant's behaviour which is involved in the interactions has a number of levels of serial ordering. At least at the lower levels this ordering seems to be . . . endogenous . . . [p. 41]*

Through a microkinesic movie analysis, Condon and Sander,[68] found that as early as the first postnatal day, newborns moved in precise synchrony with the articulated structure of adult speech. Such sustained synchrony between infant body movements and adult speech sounds is highly organized and occurs within epochs of less than one second. A documentary movie of this phenomenon has been prepared by Hack and Klaus.[126] These findings imply that the human is born already prepared for a highly organized form of active participation in human social interaction. Condon and Sander point out that from the beginning, attachment must be viewed in terms of participation rather than in terms of two individuals sending discrete messages. Their view is also consistent with the Brazelton group, which is also using video recordings subjected to microkinesic analysis.[51] The group is studying infant-mother reciprocity in a face-to-face play situation. Reciprocity of behaving is fundamental to the human species and appears soon after birth. It reveals much about

* Richards, M. P. M., "Social Interaction in the First Weeks of Human Life," *Psychiatria, Neurologia, Neurochirugia, 74:*35–42, 1971.

early bonding. In the face-to-face paradigm of these investigators, by three weeks of age infants evidence behaviors which are different for objects than they are for human interactions. Furthermore, infants demonstrate an expectancy for interaction with their caretakers which includes an engagement in a rhythmic cycling of attention and nonattention. If caretakers violate expectancies for reciprocities—by not moving their faces, for example—infants alter their interactive rhythms and eventually "turn off." Fortunately, this occurs only under unusual circumstances and is nearly impossible for normal mothers to do for any length of time.

Conclusion

A decade ago, in a survey of learning studies, Gollin[115] commented on the tendency of researchers to use infants as a vehicle in order to illustrate the excellence of their theoretical modes. In so doing, they downplayed questions about developmental processes and individual differences. To offset this tendency, Gollin suggested that infancy researchers pay more attention to perspectives from comparative, physiological, and developmental approaches. This review of current trends of newborn behavioral research shows the wisdom of Gollin's suggestion. The comparative or ethological approach has stimulated research, bringing with it a new appreciation of the full behavioral repertoire of the newborn and the meaning of this behavior in an expanding social world. The neurosciences have stimulated research which has led to a greater understanding of the organization of the newborn's behavior along with its essential underpinnings in terms of processes of brain functioning. The developmental approach, itself enhanced by a multidisciplinary enthusiasm, has fostered research which has led to an appreciation of the newborn as active and as changing over time in the direction of increasing behavioral complexity. Many lines of evidence point to a major shift in the infant's organization around two months of age. Since this shift is evidenced in the home as well as in the laboratory, and in the brain as well as in behavior, it has been found useful to extend the usual pediatric concept of the newborn period to include the second postnatal month. Another research trend has produced an increased understanding of the young infant as an influential participant in an intricate and developing interactional system. Up to now, observed individual differences in newborn behavior have not been stable, possibly because of the developmental shift around two months and possibly because of the lack of attention to interactional factors. A final trend of the last decade's newborn research was also implied by Gollin's suggestion, namely, a trend away from reliance on theoretical models. As was pointed out in the introduction, the previous view of the newborn had largely been deductive. It was clouded by a variety of imaginative propositions derived from abstract theories. The research reviewed here has for the most part been inductive, and, to a large extent, atheoretical. Perhaps the next decade will see the emergence of more explanatory theoretical statements, and perhaps there will be new models based on the growing body of research data.

At this juncture, it seems worth recalling Benjamin's discussion dealing with the state of scientific knowledge in clinical psychiatry.[32] Benjamin entitled his essay "Knowledge, Conviction and Ignorance" to refer to the separate domains of "what we know, what we think we know, and what we know we don't know and wish we did." In this review, what would be considered knowledge has been small and largely at the descriptive level. What would be considered ignorance is large, especially when one considers the lack of explanations for what has been described. Most of what has been reviewed is in that area of uncertainty which Benjamin called "conviction." It is relevant to the conclusion that Benjamin distinguished between two types of convictions. "First-order convictions" are those which are scientifically sound and based on evidence which has not yet been put in systematic form for rigorous testing. Many empirically based clinical generalizations are of this sort. "Second-order convictions," on the other hand, are those which are scientifically unsound and are based primarily on inner wishes, needs, and fears. In addition, these often represent compliance with subcultural value systems.

It seems that today's scientific climate offers increasing safeguards against being falsely swayed by second-order convictions. Widespread advances in research methods, in the use of standard rules of evidence, and in the practice of multidisciplinary scrutiny have reduced the danger of the investigator falling in love with his own theories and being blinded by them. Abstract theories, derived from other sources, no longer seem particularly useful. This includes thinking of the young infant as having a global "stimulus barrier," or as undergoing a change from "physiological functioning" to "psychological functioning." Nonetheless, there is a risk that this scientific climate will be transient, particularly as the clinical need for new theoretical statements becomes pressing. A recent book written by an obstetrician asserts that the transition from intrauterine to extrauterine life is one of "violence" and agony for the infant and that those parents and professionals who do not recognize this are callous to such suffering.[189] The popularity of this work demonstrates that there is already a need in today's society for accepting second-order convictions. Whether or not the author's suggested alternative methods of facilitating the birth process are useful is a matter of scientific clinical testing. In spite of the fact that it contains no evidence for the assertions made beyond the author's own feeling states, the book has enjoyed enormous popularity.

It seems to be true that the newborn has provided a recurrent focus for second-order convictions from behavioral scientists and clinicians, and these convictions have then become popularized and misconstrued as knowledge. One might ask why. Several thoughts are suggested, not as answers or as "knowledge," but as speculative hypotheses. First, young infants cannot talk—they cannot tell how they feel, what their ideas are, or what their plans are. The realm of private experience, so important for the clinical understanding of older children and adults, is unavailable here. Second, the infant of the first two postnatal months is unique. In comparison with the amount of his behavior under endogenous control, so very little is under exogenous control. As a consequence, relatively less behavior is available to contradict the investigator if he is wrong in his convictions. Third, there is a special drawing power or "attractiveness" about the physical appearance of the young infant, a feature which Lorenz has referred to in his cross-species comparison as "babyness."[202] People become emotional about babies—perhaps such emotions color all perceptions and thinking. But this evokes still another question: Why is it that the experienced mothers do well in interpreting the behaviors of their infants, while researchers cloud interpretations with their own feelings (or as Spitz[292] termed it, "adultomorphize")? Certainly, mothers are no less emotional about their infants. The difference may have to do with the psychodynamics of perceived helplessness. Mothers are primed psychologically, biologically, and practically to recognize their newborn's helplessness and respond to it with appropriate interventions.

Researchers are not so primed. Instead, as adults, they may feel the helplessness in a situation where they cannot act to help. Such an atmosphere of abstinence, as in the clinical psychotherapy setting, may be fertile ground for fantasies of omnipotence and omniscience. These, in turn, may yield second-order convictions.

It is also noted with some concern that today there are new mothers (and fathers) who are not primed or practiced for taking care of babies. In spite of more planning for parenthood, young adults become parents without having trust in themselves for parenting. The extended family has declined, and with it, there has been a loss of the opportunity to learn from aunts and grandmothers and to care for infant brothers and sisters in the process of growing up. Instead, new parents typically learn about babies from school, college, and the popular "psychology" that deals with child rearing. Unfortunately, these are the accepted substitutes for the variety of apprenticeship experiences which used to be available. Thus, the obligation of professionals who contribute to this psychology is all the more important. They must avoid misleading the uncertain public with unscientific convictions.

Is there a process whereby one can recognize unscientific convictions? Can the professional avoid contributing to contemporary cultural myths? First, it may help to realize that there are two subtypes of such myths—the "adultomorphic myth" brought to attention by Spitz, and what might be called the "theoreticomorphic myth." The former ignores development and operates according to the formula "that baby is like me"; the latter ignores day-to-day reality and is based on the formula "that baby is like my theory." Second, it is suggested that the clinician, once he suspects that an assertion is mythological, might test it by asking several questions. Does this assertion make sense in terms of the day-to-day context of the baby's life? Does it make sense in terms of the way the brain works? Does it make sense in terms of what happens in the family? And lastly, does it make developmental sense? Answers to these questions may guide clinicians and researchers in the continuing quest for knowledge about the psychology of the newborn.

REFERENCES

1. AINSWORTH, M. D. S., *Infancy in Uganda: Infant Care and the Growth of Attachment*, Johns Hopkins University Press, Baltimore, 1967.

2. ——, and BELL, S., "Some Contemporary Patterns of Mother-Infant Interaction in the Feeding Situation," in Ambrose, A. (Ed.), *Stimulation in Early Infancy*, pp. 133–170, Academic Press, London, 1969.

3. ——, and STAYTON, D. J., "Infant-Mother Attachment and Social Development: 'Socialization' as a Product of Reciprocal Responsiveness to Signals," in Richards, M. P. M. (Ed.), *The Integration of a Child into a Social World*, pp. 99–135, Cambridge University Press, Cambridge, England, 1974.

4. AKIYAMA, Y., et al., "Acoustically Evoked Response in Prematures and Full-Term Newborn Infants," *Electroencephalography and Clinical Neurophysiology*, 26:371–380, 1969.

5. ALEKSANDROWICZ, M. K., and ALEKSANDROWICZ, D. R., "Obstetrical Pain-relieving Drugs as Predictors of Infant Behavior Variability," *Child Development, 45:* 935–945, 1974.

6. ALTMAN, J., "Postnatal Growth and Differentiation of the Mammalian Brain, with Implications for a Morphological Theory of Memory," in Schmitt, F., Quarton, G., and Melnechuk, T. (Eds.), *The Neurosciences*, pp. 723–743, Rockefeller University Press, New York, 1967.

7. American Academy of Pediatrics, *Standards and Recommendations for Hospital Care of Newborn Infants*, Evanston, Ill., 1972.

8. ——, *Hospital Care of Newborn Infants*, 5th ed., Committee on Fetus and Newborn, Evanston, Ill., 1971.

9. ANDERS, T., "The Infant Sleep Profile," *Neuropadiatrie, 5:*425–442, 1974.

10. ——, and CHALEMIAN, R., "The Effects of Circumcision on Sleep-Awake States in Human Neonates," *Psychosomatic Medicine, 36:*174–179, 1974.

11. ——, and HOFFMAN, E., "The Sleep Polygram: A Potentially Useful Tool for Clinical Assessment in Human Infants," *American Journal of Mental Deficiency, 77(5):*506–514, 1973.

12. ——, and WEINSTEIN, P., "Sleep and Its Disorders in Infants and Children: A Review," *Pediatrics, 50(2):* 312–324, 1972.

13. ——, EMDE, R., and PARMELEE, A. (Eds.), *A Manual of Standardized Terminology, Techniques and Criteria for Scoring States of Sleep and Wakefulness in Newborn Infants*, Brain Information Service, University of California at Los Angeles, NINDS Neurological Information Network, 1971.

14. ARIETI, S., *American Handbook of Child Psychiatry, Child and Adolescent Psychiatry, Sociocultural and Community Psychiatry*, vol. 2, 2nd ed., Basic Books, New York, 1974.

15. ASERINSKY, E., and KLEITMAN, N., "A Motility Cycle in Sleeping Infants as Manifested by Ocular and Gross Bodily Activity," *Journal of Applied Physiology, 8:* 11–18, 1955.

16. ASHBY, W. R., *An Introduction to Cybernetics*, Chapman and Hall, London, 1957.

17. AVERY, G. B., *Neonatology*, Lippincott, Philadelphia, 1957.

18. BALINT, M., "Individual Differences of Behavior in Early Infancy and an Objective Way of Recording Them," *Journal of Genetic Psychology, 73:*57–117, 1948.

19. BARNET, A. B., et al., "Auditory Evoked Potentials During Sleep in Normal Children from Ten Days to Three Years of Age," *Electroencephalography and Clinical Neurophysiology*, 39:29–41, 1975.

20. BARNETT, C., et al., "Neonatal Separation: Maternal Side of Interactional Deprivation," *Pediatrics, 46:*197–205, 1970.

21. BARTEN, S., BIRNS, B., and RONCH, J., "Individual Differences in the Visual Pursuit Behavior of Neonates," *Child Development, 42:*313–319, 1971.

22. BEINTEMA, D. J., *A Neurological Study of Newborn Infants,* Clinics in Developmental Medicine 28, Heinemann, London, 1968.

23. BEKOFF, M., and FOX, M., "Postnatal Neural Ontogeny: Environment-Dependent and/or Environment-Expectant," *Developmental Psychobiology, 5(4):*323–341, 1972.

24. BELL, R. Q., "A Congenital Contribution to Emotional Response in Early Infancy and the Preschool Period," in *Parent-Infant Interaction,* Ciba Foundation Symposium 33 (new series), pp. 201–212, Elsevier, New York, 1975.

25. ———, "Contributions of Human Infants to Caregiving and Social Interaction," in Lewis, M., and Rosenblum, L. A. (Eds.), *The Effect of the Infant on Its Caregiver,* vol. 1, pp. 1–19, John Wiley, New York, 1974.

26. ———, "Stimulus Control of Parent or Caretaker Behavior by Offspring," *Developmental Psychology, 4:* 61–72, 1971.

27. ———, "Relations between Behavior Manifestations in the Human Neonate," *Child Development, 31:*463–477, 1960.

28. ———, and COSTELLO, N., "Three Tests for Sex Differences in Tactile Sensitivity in the Newborn," *Biologia Neonatorum, 7:*335–347, 1964.

29. ———, WELLER, G. M., and WALDROP, M. F., *Newborn and Preschooler: Organization of Behavior and Relations between Periods,* Monographs of the Society for Research in Child Development, vol. 36, nos. 1 and 2, April–July 1971.

30. BENJAMIN, J., "Developmental Biology and Psychoanalysis," in Greenfield, N., and Lewis, W. (Eds.), *Psychoanalysis and Current Biological Thought,* pp. 57–80, University of Wisconsin Press, Madison, 1965.

31. ———, "Some Developmental Observations Relating to the Theory of Anxiety," *Journal of the American Psychoanalytic Association, 9:*652–668, 1961.

32. ———, "Knowledge, Conviction and Ignorance," *Journal of Medical Education, 36:*117–132, 1961.

33. BERGMAN, T., HAITH, M. J., and MANN, L., "Development of Eye Contact and Facial Scanning in Infants," Paper presented at the Society for Research in Child Development Convention, Minneapolis, Minn., April 1971.

34. BERNAL, J. F., "Crying in the First 10 Days of Life and Maternal Responses," *Developmental Medicine and Child Neurology, 14:*362–372, 1972.

35. BERNSTEIN, P., EMDE, R., and CAMPOS, J., "REM Sleep in 4-Month-Old Infants under Home and Laboratory Conditions," *Psychosomatic Medicine, 35(4):*322–329, 1973.

36. BERTALANFFY, L. VON, *General System Theory Foundations, Development, Applications,* Braziller, New York, 1968.

37. ———, *Organismic Psychology Theory,* Clark University Press with Barre Publishers, Barre, Mass., 1968.

38. BIRNS, B., "Individual Differences in Human Neonates' Responses to Stimulation," *Child Development, 36:*249–256, 1965.

39. ———, BARTEN, S., and BRIDGER, W. H., "Individual Differences in Temperamental Characteristics of Infants," *Transactions of the New York Academy of Science, 31:* 1071–1082, 1969.

40. ———, BLANK, M., and BRIDGER, W. H., "The Effectiveness of Various Soothing Techniques on Human Neonates," *Psychosomatic Medicine, 28:*316–322, 1966.

41. ———, et al., "Behavioral Inhibition in Neonates Produced by Auditory Stimuli," *Child Development, 36:* 639–645, 1965.

42. BOND, E. K., "Perception of Form by the Human Infant," *Psychological Bulletin, 77(4):*225–245, 1972.

43. BOWES, W. A., et al., *The Effects of Obstetrical Medication on Fetus and Infant,* Monographs of the Society for Research in Child Development, vol. 35, serial no. 137, 1970.

44. BOWLBY, J., *Attachment and Loss,* vol. 1, *Attachment,* Basic Books, New York, 1969.

45. ———, "The Nature of the Child to His Mother," *International Journal of Psycho-Analysis, 39:*350–373, 1958.

46. BRACKBILL, Y., "Continuous Stimulation and Arousal Level in Infancy: Effects of Stimulus Intensity and Stress," *Child Development, 47(2):*364–369, 1975.

47. ———, "Research and Clinical Work with Children," in Bauer, R. A. (Ed.), *Some Views on Soviet Psychology,* American Psychological Association, Washington, D.C., 1962.

48. ———, "Extinction of the Smiling Response in Infants as a Function of Reinforcement," *Child Development, 29:*115–124, 1958.

49. ———, et al., "Obstetric Meperidine Usage and Assessment of Neonatal Status," *Anesthesiology, 40:*117–120, 1974.

50. ———, et al., "Arousal Level in Neonates and Preschool Children under Continuous Auditory Stimulation," *Journal of Experimental Child Psychology, 4:*178–188, 1966.

51. BRAZELTON, T. B., "Anticipatory Guidance," *Pediatric Clinics of North America, 22(3):*533–544, 1975.

52. ———, Personal communication, 1975.

53. ———, et al., "The Origins of Reciprocity: The Early Mother-Infant Interaction," in Lewis, M., and Rosenblum, L. (Eds.), *The Effect of the Infant on Its Caregiver,* vol. 1, pp. 49–76, John Wiley, New York, 1974.

54. ———, *Neonatal Behavioral Assessment Scale,* Lippincott, Philadelphia, 1973.

55. ———, "Effect of Prenatal Drugs on the Behavior of the Neonate," *American Journal of Psychiatry, 126:* 1261–1266, 1970.

56. ———, *Infants and Mothers, Differences in Development,* Delacorte Press, New York, 1969.

57. ———, "Crying in Infancy," *Pediatrics, 29:*579–588, 1962.

58. ———, "Effect of Maternal Medication on the Neonate and His Behavior," *Journal of Pediatrics, 58:*513–518, 1961.

59. BRAZIE, J. V., and LUBCHENCO, L. O., "The Newborn Infant," in Kempe, C. H., Silver, H., and O'Brien, D. (Eds.), *Current Pediatric Diagnosis and Treatment,* pp. 40–89, Lange Medical Publications, Los Altos, Calif., 1973.

60. BRIDGER, W. H., and BIRNS, B., "Neonates' Behavioral and Autonomic Responses to Stress During Soothing," *Recent Advances in Biological Psychiatry, 5:* 1–6, 1963.

61. CALL, J., "Emotional-Social Factors," *Journal of Special Education, 4:*349–359, 1971.

62. ———, "Newborn Approach Behaviors and Early Ego Development," *International Journal of Psycho-Analysis, 45:*286–294, 1964.

63. CHASE, M., "Somatic Reflex Activity During Sleep and Wakefulness," in Petre-Quadens, O., and Schlag, J. (Eds.), *Basic Sleep Mechanisms,* pp. 249–267, Academic Press, New York, 1973.

64. ———, "Patterns of Reflex Excitability During the Ontogenesis of Sleep and Wakefulness," in Clemente, C. D., Purpura, D. P., and Mayer, F. E. (Eds.), *Sleep and the Maturing Nervous System,* pp. 253–285, Academic Press, New York, 1972.

65. ———, "Brain Stem Somatic Reflex Activity in Neonatal Kittens during Sleep and Wakefulness," *Physiology and Behavior, 7:*165–172, 1971.

66. ———, "The Digastric Reflex in the Kitten and Adult Cat: Paradoxical Amplitude Fluctuations During Sleep and Wakefulness," *Archives Italiennes de Biologie, 108:*403–422, 1970.

67. ———, and STERMAN, M. B., "Maturation of

Patterns of Sleep and Wakefulness in the Kitten," *Brain Research,* 5:319–329, 1967.

68. CONDON, W., and SANDER, L., "Neonate Movement Is Synchronized with Adult Speech: Interactional Participation and Language Acquisition," *Science, 183:*99–101, 1974.

69. CONEL, J. L., *The Postnatal Development of the Human Cerebral Cortex,* vol. 3, *The Cortex of the Three-Month Infant,* Harvard Unnversity Press, Cambridge, 1947.

70. ———, *The Postnatal Development of the Human Cerebral Cortex,* vol. 2, *The Cortex of the One-Month Infant,* Harvard University Press, Cambridge, 1941.

71. DAYTON, G. L., JR., et al., "Developmental Study of Coordinated Eye Movement in the Human Infant. I. Visual Acuity in the Newborn Human: A Study Based on Induced Optokinetic Systagmus Recorded by Electrography," *Archives of Ophthalmology,* 71:865–870, 1964.

72. ———, et al., "Developmental Study of Coordinated Eye Movements in the Human Infant: II. An Electrooculographic Study of the Fixation Reflex in the Newborn," *Archives of Ophthalmology,* 71:871–875, 1964.

73. DEMETRIADES, T., "The Cochlea-Palpebral Reflex in Infants, *Annals of Otology, Rhinology and Laryngology,* 32:894–903, 1923.

74. DENISSOFF, M., and FIGURIN, M., "The Question of the First Associated Appetitional Reflexes in Infants," *Voporsi Geneticheskoy Reflexologii i Pedologii Mladentchestva,* 1:81–88, 1929.

75. DITTRICHOVA, J., and LAPACKOVA, V., "Development of the Waking State in Young Infants," *Child Development,* 35:365–370, 1964.

76. DREYFUS-BRISAC, C., "Ontogenesis of Sleep in Human Prematures after 32 Weeks of Conceptional Age," *Developmental Psychobiology,* 3(2):91–121, 1970.

77. ———, and MONOD, N., "Sleep Behavior in Abnormal Infants," *Neuropadiatrie,* 3:354–366, 1970.

78. EIMAS, P. D., et al., "Speech Perception in Infants," *Science,* 171:303–306, 1971.

79. EISENBERG, R. B., "Auditory Behavior in the Human Neonate," *International Audiology,* 8:34–45, 1969.

80. ———, "Auditory Behavior in the Human Neonate: I. Methodologic Problems and the Logical Design of Research Procedures," *Journal of Auditory Research,* 5:159–177, 1965.

81. ELLINGSON, R. J., "Cerebral Electrical Responses to Auditory and Visual Stimuli in the Infant (Human and Subhuman Studies)," in Kellaway, P., and Petersen, I. (Eds.), *Neurologic and Electroencephalographic Correlative Studies in Infancy,* pp. 78–114, Grune & Stratton, New York, 1964.

82. ———, "Cortical Electrical Responses to Visual Stimulation in the Human Infant," *Electroencephalography and Clinical Neurophysiology,* 12:663–677, 1960.

83. ———, et al., "Variability of Auditory Evoked Potentials in Human Newborns," *Electroencephalography and Clinical Neurophysiology,* 36:155–162, 1974.

84. ELMER, E., and GREGG, G., "Developmental Characteristics of Abused Children," *Pediatrics,* 40:596–602, 1967.

85. EMDE, R. N., and HARMON, R. J., "Endogenous and Exogenous Smiling Systems in Early Infants," *Journal of the American Academy of Child Psychiatry, 11(2):*177–200, 1972.

86. ———, and KOENIG, K., "Neonatal Smiling and Rapid Eye Movement States," *Journal of the American Academy of Child Psychiatry,* 8:57–67, 1969.

87. ———, "Neonatal Smiling and Rapid Eye Movement States. II. Sleep-Cycle Study," *Journal of the American Academy of Child Psychiatry,* 8:637–656, 1969.

88. ———, and METCALF, D., "An Electroencephalographic Study of Behavioral Rapid Eye Movement States in the Human Newborn," *Journal of Nervous and Mental Disease,* 150:376–386, 1970.

89. ———, GAENSBAUER, T. G., and HARMON, R. J., *Emotional Expression in Infancy: A Biobehavioral Study,*

Psychological Issues, Monograph no. 37, vol. 10, International Universities Press, New York, 1976.

90. ———, McCARTNEY, R. D., and HARMON, R. J., "Neonatal Smiling in REM States. IV. Premature Study," *Child Development,* 42:1657–1661, 1971.

91. ———, SWEDBERG, J., and SUZUKI, B., "Human Wakefulness and Biological Rhythms after Birth," *Archives of General Psychiatry,* 32:780–783, 1975.

92. ———, et al., "Stress and Neonatal Sleep," *Psychosomatic Medicine,* 33(6):491–497, 1971.

93. ENGEL, G., "Anxiety and Depression-Withdrawal: The Primary Affects of Unpleasure," *International Journal of Psycho-Analysis,* 43:89–97, 1962.

94. ENGEL, R., CROWELL, D., and NISHIJIMA, S., "Visual and Auditory Response Latencies in Neonates," in B. N. D. Fernando, (Ed.), *In Honour of C. C. DeSilva,* Kularatne and Co., Ceylon, 1968.

95. ENGEN, T., LIPSITT, L. P., and KAYE, H., "Olfactory Response and Adaptation in the Human Neonate," *Journal of Comparative and Physiological Psychology,* 56:73–77, 1963.

96. ERIKSON, E. H., *Childhood and Society,* W. W. Norton, New York, 1950.

97. ESCALONA, S. K., *The Roots of Individuality: Normal Patterns of Development in Infancy,* Aldine, Chicago, 1968.

98. ———, and HIEDER, G., *Prediction and Outcome: A Study of Child Development,* Basic Books, New York, 1959.

99. FANAROFF, A., KENNELL, J., and KLAUS, M., "Follow-up of Low Birthweight Infants: Predictive Value of Maternal Visiting Patterns," *Pediatrics,* 49:287–290, 1972.

100. FANTZ, R. L., "Pattern Vision in Newborn Infants," *Science,* 140:296–297, 1963.

101. ———, "The Origin of Form Perception," *Scientific American,* 204:66–72, 1961.

102. ———, and NEVIS, S., "Pattern Preferences and Perceptual-Cognitive Development in Early Infancy," *Merrill-Palmer Quarterly,* 13:77–108, 1967.

103. ———, ORDY, J. M., and UDELF, M. S., "Maturation of Pattern Vision in Infants During the First Six Months," *Journal of Comparative and Physiological Psychology,* 55:907–917, 1962.

104. FINNEGAN, L., et al., "Neonatal Abstinence Syndrome: Assessment and Management," *Addictive Diseases: An International Journal,* 2(1):141–158, 1975.

105. FRAIBERG, S., "Intervention in Infancy: A Program for Blind Infants," *Journal of the American Academy of Child Psychiatry,* 10(3):381–405, 1971.

106. FREEDMAN, D., "On Hearing, Oral Language and Psychic Structure," in Holt, R., and Peterfreund, E. (Eds.), *Psychoanalysis and Contemporary Science,* vol. 1, pp. 57–69, Macmillan, New York, 1972.

107. ———, "Hereditary Control of Early Social Behavior," in Foss, B. M. (Ed.), *Determinants of Infant Behavior,* vol. 3, pp. 149–159, John Wiley, New York, 1965.

108. FREUD, S., "Formulations on the Two Principles of Mental Functioning," in *The Standard Edition of the Complete Psychological Works of Sigmund Freud,* vol. 12, pp. 218–226, Hogarth Press, London, 1958.

109. FRIES, M. E., "The Child's Ego Development and the Training of Adults in His Environment," in Eissler, R. S., et al. (Eds.), *The Psychoanalytic Study of the Child,* vol. 2, pp. 85–112, International Universities Press, New York, 1946.

110. ———, "Psychosomatic Relationship Between Mother and Infant," *Psychosomatic Medicine,* 6:159–162, 1944.

111. ———, "Mental Hygiene in Pregnancy, Delivery, and the Puerperium," *Mental Hygiene,* 25:221–236, 1941.

112. ———, and WOOLF, P. J., "Some Hypotheses on the Role of the Congenital Activity Type in Personality Development," in Eissler, R. S., et al. (Eds.), *The Psycho-*

analytic Study of the Child, vol. 8, pp. 48–62, International Universities Press, New York, 1953.

113. GAENSBAUER, T., and EMDE, R. N., "Wakefulness and Feeding in Human Newborns," *Archives of General Psychiatry, 28*:894–897, 1973.

114. GLOBUS, G., "Rapid Eye Movement Cycle in Real Time," *Archives of General Psychiatry, 15*:654–659, 1966.

115. GOLLIN, E. S., "Research Trends in Infant Learning," in Hellmuth, J. (Ed.), *Exceptional Infant*, vol. 1, *The Normal Infant*, pp. 241–266, Brunner-Mazel, New York, 1967.

116. GOODMAN, W. S., et al., "Audiometry in Newborn Children by Electroencephalography," *Laryngoscope, 74:* 1316–1328, 1964.

117. GORMAN, J. J., COGAN, D. G., and GELLIS, S. S., "An Apparatus for Grading the Visual Acuity of Infants on the Basis of Opticokinetic Nystagmus," *Pediatrics, 19:* 1088–1092, 1957.

118. GRAHAM, F. K., *Behavioral Differences Between Normal and Traumatized Newborns. I. The Test Procedures*, Psychological Monographs, no. 70, pp. 1–16, 1956.

119. ———, and CLIFTON, R. K., "Heart-Rate Change as a Component of the Orienting Response," *Psychological Bulletin, 65*:305–320, 1966.

120. ———, and JACKSON, J., "Arousal Systems and Infant Heart-Rate Responses," in Reese, H. W., and Lipsett, L. P. (Eds.), *Advances in Child Development and Behavior*, vol. 5, pp. 60–111, Academic Press, New York, 1970.

121. ———, MATARAZZO, R. G., and CALDWELL, B. M., *Behavioral Differences Between Normal and Traumatized Newborns*, Psychological Monographs, no. 70, pp. 17–23, 1956.

122. ———, et al., *Development Three Years after Perinatal Anoxia and Other Potentially Damaging Newborn Experiences*, Psychological Monographs, no. 76, pp. 1–53, 1962.

123. GREENBERG, M., ROSENBERG, I., and LIND, J., "First Mothers' Rooming-In with Their Newborns: Its Impact upon the Mother," *American Journal of Orthopsychiatry, 43(5)*:783–788, 1973.

124. GREENBERG, N. H., "Development Effects of Stimulation During Early Infancy: Some Conceptual and Methodological Considerations," *Annals of the New York Academy of Sciences, 118*:831–859, 1965.

125. GREENOUGH, E., "Environmental Effects on Brain Anatomy," Presentation at the Winter Conference on Brain Research, Vail, Colorado, January 1973.

126. HACK, M., and KLAUS, M., "The Amazing Newborn," Movie distributed by Ross Laboratories (Division of Abbott Laboratories), Columbus, Ohio, 1976.

127. HAITH, M., "Visual Competence in Early Infancy," in Held, R., Leibowitz, H., and Teuber, H. L. (Eds.), *Handbook of Sensory Physiology VIII*, Springer, New York, 1976.

128. ———, "Visual Scanning in Infants," Paper presented at the Regional Meeting of the Society for Research in Child Development, Clark University, 1968. Reprinted in Stone, L. J., Smith, H. T., and Murphy, L. B. (Eds.), *The Competent Infant: A Handbook of Readings*, pp. 320–323, Basic Books, New York, 1973.

129. ———, "Infra-Red Television Recording and Measurement of Ocular Behavior in the Human Infant," *American Psychologist, 24*:279–285, 1969.

130. HARLOW, H. F., "Mice, Monkeys, Men and Motives," *Psychological Review, 60(1)*:23–32, 1953.

131. ———, HARLOW, M. K., and MEYER, D. E., "Learning Motivated by a Manipulation Drive," *Journal of Experimental Psychology, 40*:228–234, 1950.

132. HARMON, R., and EMDE, R. N., "Spontaneous REM Behaviors in a Microcephalic Infant: A Clinical Anatomical Study," *Perceptual and Motor Skills, 34*:827–833, 1972.

133. HAYNES, H., WHITE, B. L., and HELD, R., "Visual Accommodation in Human Infants," *Science, 148*:528–530, 1965.

134. HEBB, D. O., *The Organization of Behavior*, John Wiley, New York, 1949.

135. HERON, W., BEXTON, W., and HEBB, D., "Cognitive Effects of a Decreased Variation to the Sensory Environment," *American Psychologist, 8:*366, 1953.

136. HERSHENSON, M., "Development of the Perception of Form," *Psychological Bulletin, 67*:326–336, 1967.

137. ———, "Visual Discrimination in the Human Newborn," *Journal of Comparative and Physiological Psychology, 58*:270–276, 1964.

138. ———, KESSEN, W., and MUNSINGER, H. "Occular Orientation in the Human Newborn Infant: A Close Look at Some Positive and Negative Results," in Walthen-Dund, W. (Ed.), *Models for the Perception of Speech and Visual Form*, pp. 282–290, MIT Press, Cambridge, Mass., 1967.

139. HONZIK, M. P., and McKEE, J. P., "The Sex Difference in Thumb-Sucking," *Journal of Pediatrics, 61*: 726–732, 1962.

140. HOOKER, D., *The Prenatal Origin of Behavior*, University of Kansas Press, Lawrence, 1952.

141. HOROWITZ, F., ALEKSANDROWICZ, M., and ASHTON, J., "American and Uruguayan Infants: Reliabilities, Maternal Drug Histories and Population Differences," Paper presented at Society for Research in Child Development, Philadelphia, March 1973.

142. HUBEL, D. H., and WIESEL, T. N., "Receptive Fields and Functional Architecture of Monkey Striate Cortex," *Journal of Physiology, 195*:215–243, 1968.

143. ———, "Receptive Fields of Cells in Striate Cortex of Very Young Visually Inexperienced Kittens," *Journal of Neurophysiology, 26*:994–1002, 1963.

144. HULSEBUS, R. C., "Operant Conditioning of Infant Behavior," in Reese, H. W. (Ed.), *Advances in Child Development and Behavior*, vol. 8, pp. 112–153, Academic Press, New York, 1973.

145. HUMPHREY, T., "Postnatal Repetition of Human Prenatal Activity Sequences with Some Suggestions of Their Neuroanatomical Basis," in Robinson, E. J. (Ed.), *Brain and Early Behavior*, pp. 43–71, Academic Press, New York, 1969.

146. HUTT, S. J., LENARD, H. G., and PRECHTL, H. F. R., "Psychophysiological Studies in Newborn Infants," in Lipsitt, L. P., and Reese, H. W. (Eds.), *Advances in Child Development and Behavior*, vol. 4, pp. 127–172, Academic Press, New York, 1969.

147. IRWIN, O. C., *The Amount and Nature of Activities of Newborn Infants*, Genetic Psychology Monographs, no. 8, pp. 1–92, 1930.

148. JACKSON, J. C., KANTOWITZ, S., and GRAHAM, F., "Can Newborns Show Orienting?" *Child Development, 42*:107–120, 1971.

149. JAMES, W., *Principles of Psychology*, Henry Holt, New York, 1890.

150. JEFFREY, W. E., and COHEN, L. B., "Habituation in the Human Infant," in Reese, H. W. (Ed.), *Advances in Child Development and Behavior*, vol. 6, pp. 63–97, Academic Press, New York, 1971.

151. JONES, M. C., "The Development of Early Behavior Patterns in Young Children," *Journal of Genetic Psychology, 33*:537–585, 1926.

152. JONES, N. B. (Ed.), *Ethological Studies of Child Behaviour*, Cambridge University Press, Cambridge, England, 1972.

153. JOST, A., "A New Look at the Mechanisms Controlling Sex Differentiation in Mammals," *Johns Hopkins Medical Journal, 130*:38–53, 1972.

154. JOUVET-MOUNIER, D., ASTIC, L., and LACOTE, D., "Ontogenesis of the States of Sleep in the Rat, Cat and Guinea Pig During the First Postnatal Month," *Developmental Psychobiology, 2(4)*:216–239, 1970.

155. KAGAN, J., *Change and Continuity in Infancy*, John Wiley, New York, 1971.

156. ———, "Attention and Psychological Change in the Young Child," *Science, 170*:826–832, 1970.

157. ———, "The Distribution of Attention in Infancy," in Hamburg, D. H. (Ed.), *Perception and Its Disorders*, pp. 214–237, Williams & Wilkins, Baltimore, 1970.

158. KARELITZ, S., and FISICHELLI, V. R., "The Cry Thresholds of Normal Infants and Those with Brain Damage," *Journal of Pediatrics*, 61:679–685, 1962.

159. KASATKIN, N. I., "The Origin and Development of Conditioned Reflexes in Early Childhood," in Cole, M., and Maltzman, I. (Eds.), *Handbook of Contemporary Soviet Psychology*, pp. 71–85, Basic Books, New York, 1968.

160. KAUFMAN, I. C., "Symposium on 'Psychoanalysis and Ethology,' III. Some Theoretical Implications from Animal Behaviour Studies for the Psychoanalytic Concepts of Instinct, Energy, and Drive," *International Journal of Psycho-Analysis*, 41:318–326, 1960.

161. KEARSLEY, R. B., "The Newborn's Response to Auditory Stimulation: A Demonstration of Orienting and Defensive Behavior," *Child Development*, 44:582–590, 1973.

162. KENNELL, J. H., GORDON, D., and KLAUS, M., "The Effect of Early Mother-Infant Separation on Later Maternal Performance," *Pediatric Research*, 4:473–474, 1970.

163. ———, et al., "Maternal Behavior One Year After Early and Extended Postpartum Contact," *Developmental Medicine and Child Neurology*, 16:172–179, 1974.

164. KESSEN, W., HAITH, M. M., and SALAPATEK, P., "Human Infancy: A Bibliography and Guide," in Mussen, P. H. (Ed.), *Carmichael's Manual of Child Psychology*, vol. 1, 3rd ed., pp. 287–445, John Wiley, New York, 1970.

165. ———, WILLIAMS, E., and WILLIAMS, J. P., "Selection and Test of Response Measures in the Study of the Human Newborn," *Child Development*, 32:7–24, 1961.

166. KETY, S., "From Rationalization to Reason," *American Journal of Psychiatry*, 131(9):957–963, 1974.

167. KLAUS, M. H., and FANAROFF, A. A. (Eds.), *Care of the High Risk Neonate*, W. B. Saunders, Philadelphia, 1973.

168. ———, et al., "Maternal Attachment: Importance of the First Postpartum Days," *New England Journal of Medicine*, 286:460–463, 1972.

169. ———, et al., "Human Maternal Behavior at the First Contact with Her Young," *Pediatrics*, 46(2):187–192, 1970.

170. KLEITMAN, N., *Sleep and Wakefulness*, University of Chicago Press, Chicago, 1963.

171. ———, and ENGELMANN, T. G., "Sleep Characteristics of Infants," *Journal of Applied Physiology*, 6:269–282, 1953.

172. KLIGMAN, D., SMYRL, R., and EMDE, R. N., "A 'Non-Intrusive' Home Study of Infant Sleep," *Psychosomatic Medicine*, 37(5):448–453, 1975.

173. KOEHLER, O., "The Smile as an Innate Facial Expression," *Zeitschrift fuer Menschliche Vererbungs und Konstitutionslehre*, 32:390–398, 1954.

174. KORNER, A., "The Effect of the Infant's State, Level of Arousal, Sex and Ontogenetic Stage on the Caregiver," in Lewis, M., and Rosenblum, L. A. (Eds.), *The Effect of the Infant on Its Caregiver*, vol. 1, pp. 105–121, John Wiley, New York, 1974.

175. ———, "Sex Differences in Newborns with Special Reference to Differences in the Organization of Oral Behavior," *Journal of Child Psychology and Psychiatry*, 14:19–29, 1973.

176. ———, "Individual Differences at Birth: Implications for Early Experience and Later Development," *American Journal of Orthopsychiatry*, 41:608–619, 1971.

177. ———, "Visual Alertness in Neonates: Individual Differences and Their Correlates," *Perceptual and Motor Skills*, 31:67–78, 1970.

178. ———, "Neonatal Startles, Smiles, Erections and Reflex Sucks as Related to State, Sex and Individuality," *Child Development*, 40:1039–1053, 1969.

179. ———, "Some Hypotheses Regarding the Significance of Individual Differences at Birth for Later Development," in Eissler, R. S., et al. (Eds.), *The Psychoanalytic Study of the Child*, vol. 19, pp. 59–72, International Universities Press, New York, 1964.

180. ———, and THOMAN, E., "The Relative Efficacy of Contact and Vestibular Proprioceptive Stimulation in Soothing Neonates," *Child Development*, 43:443–453, 1972.

181. ———, "Visual Alertness in Neonates as Evoked by Maternal Care," *Journal of Experimental Child Psychology*, 10:67–78, 1970.

182. KRAEMER, C. H., KORNER, A., and THOMAN, E., "Methodological Considerations in Evaluating the Influence of Drugs Used During Labor and Delivery on the Behavior of the Newborn," *Developmental Psychology*, 6:128–134, 1972.

183. KRIPKE, D. F., "An Ultradian Biologic Rhythm Associated with Perceptual Deprivation and REM Sleep," *Psychosomatic Medicine*, 34:221–234, 1972.

184. KRON, R. E., "The Effect of Arousal and of Learning upon Sucking Behavior in the Newborn," in Wortis, J. (Ed.), *Recent Advances in Biological Psychiatry*, vol. 10, pp. 302–313, Plenum Press, New York, 1968.

185. ———, STEIN, M., and GODDARD, K. R., "Newborn Sucking Behavior Affected by Obstetric Sedation," *Pediatrics*, 37:1012–1016, 1966.

186. KRON, R., et al., "The Assessment of Behavioral Change in Infants Undergoing Narcotic Withdrawal: Comparative Data from Clinical and Objective Methods," *Addictive Disease: An International Journal*, 2(2):257–275, 1975.

187. LACEY, J., and LACEY, B., "The Relationship of Resting Autonomic Activity to Motor Impulsivity," in *The Brain and Human Behavior*, vol. 36, pp. 144–209, Proceedings of the Association for Research in Nervous and Mental Disease, Hafner, Darien, Conn., 1966.

188. LEIFER, A., et al., "Effects of Mother-Infant Separation on Maternal Attachment Behavior," *Child Development*, 43:1203–1218, 1972.

189. LEBOYER, F., *Birth Without Violence*, Knopf, New York, 1975.

190. LENNEBERG, E. H., *Biological Foundations of Language*, John Wiley, New York, 1967.

191. ———, REBELSKY, F. G., and NICHOLS, I. A., "The Vocalizations of Infants Born to Deaf and to Hearing Parents," *Human Development*, 8:23–37, 1965.

192. LEWIS, M., "State as an Infant-Environment Interaction: An Analysis of Mother-Infant Interaction as a Function of Sex," *Merrill-Palmer Quarterly*, 18(2):95–121, 1972.

193. ———, and LEE-PAINTER, S., "An Interactional Approach to the Mother-Infant Dyad," in *The Effect of the Infant on Its Caregiver*, pp. 21–48, John Wiley, New York, 1974.

194. LIEBERMAN, P., et al., "Newborn Infant Cry and Nonhuman Primate Vocalization," *Journal of Speech and Hearing Research*, 14:718–727, 1971.

195. LIND, J., et al., "Vocal Response to Painful Stimuli in Newborn and Young Infants," *Annales Paediatriae Fenniae*, 12:55–63, 1966.

196. LIPSITT, L. P., "Learning in the Human Infant," in Stevenson, H. W., Rheingold, H. L., and Hess, E. (Eds.), *Early Behavior: Comparative and Developmental Approaches*, pp. 225–247, John Wiley, New York, 1967.

197. ———, and JACKLIN, C., "Cardiac Deceleration and Its Stability in Human Newborns," *Developmental Psychology*, 5:535, 1971.

198. ———, and KAYE, H., "Change in Neonatal Response to Optimizing and Nonoptimizing Sucking Stimulation," *Psychonomic Science*, 2:221–222, 1965.

199. ———, and LEVY, N., "Electrotactual Threshold in the Neonate," *Child Development*, 30:547–554, 1959.

200. ———, ENGEN, T., and KAYE, H., "Developmental Changes in the Olfactory Threshold of the Neonate," *Child Development*, 34:371–376, 1963.

201. LIVINGSTON, R. B., "Brain Circuitry Relating to

Complex Behavior," in Ouarton, G. C., Melnechuk, T., and Schmitt, F. O. (Eds.), *The Neurosciences*, pp. 568–576, Rockefeller University Press, New York, 1967.

202. LORENZ, K., "Über die Bildung des Instinktbegriffes," *Naturwissenschaften*, 25:289–300, 307–318, 324–331, 1937.

203. LYNIP, A., *The Use of Magnetic Devices in the Collection and Analysis of the Preverbal Utterances of an Infant*, Genetic Psychology Monographs, no. 44, pp. 221–262, 1951.

204. MACFARLANE, A., "Olfaction in the Development of Social Preferences in the Human Neonate," in *Parent-Infant Interaction*, pp. 103–117, A Ciba Foundation Symposium 33 (new series), Elsevier, New York, 1975.

205. MCGRADE, B. J., "Newborn Activity and Emotional Response at Eight Months," *Child Development*, 39:1247–1252, 1968.

206. MCGINTY, D. J., "Encephalization and the Neural Control of Sleep," in Sterman, M. B., McGinty, D. J., and Adinolfi, A. M. (Eds.), *Brain Development and Behavior*, pp. 335–355, Academic Press, New York, 1971.

207. MARLER, P., and HAMILTON, W. J., *Mechanisms of Animal Behavior*, John Wiley, New York, 1966.

208. MARQUIS, D. P., "Can Conditioned Responses be Established in the Newborn Infant?" *Journal of Genetic Psychology*, 39:479–492, 1931.

209. MASON, W. A., "Motivational Factors in Psychosocial Development," in Arnold, W. J., and Page, M. M. (Eds.), *Nebraska Symposium on Motivation*, pp. 35–67, University of Nebraska Press, Lincoln, 1971.

210. MILLER, G. A., GALANTER, E., and PRIBRAM, K., *Plans and the Structure of Behavior*, Henry Holt, New York, 1960.

211. MINKOWSKI, M., "Neurobiologische Studien am menschlichen Foetus," in *Handbuch der biologischen Arbeitsmethoden*, pp. 511–618, Abt. V, Teil 5B, Heft 5, Ser. 253, 1928.

212. MOORE, T., and UCKO, L., "Night Waking in Early Infancy: Part I," *Archives of Diseases in Childhood, 32:*333, 1957.

213. MOSS, H. A., "Sex, Age, and State as Determinants of Mother-Infant Interaction," *Merrill-Palmer Quarterly*, 13:19–36, 1967.

214. ———, and ROBSON, K., "The Role of Protest Behavior in the Development of Mother-Infant Attachment," Paper presented at the Meeting of the American Psychological Association, San Francisco, 1968.

215. NEWSON, J., and NEWSON, E., "Cultural Aspects of Child-rearing in the English-Speaking World," in Richards, M. P. M. (Ed.), *The Integration of a Child into a Social World*, pp. 53–82, Cambridge University Press, Cambridge, England, 1974.

216. NISBETT, R. E., and GURWITZ, S. B., "Weight, Sex and the Eating Behavior of Human Newborns," *Journal of Comparative and Physiological Psychology*, 73:245–253, 1970.

217. O'BRIEN, J. S., "Lipids and Myelination," in *Developmental Neurology*, pp. 262–286, Charles C Thomas, Springfield, Ill., 1970.

218. OSTWALD, P. F., "The Sounds of Infancy," *Developmental Medicine and Child Neurology*, 14(3):350–361, 1972.

219. ———, FREEDMAN, D. G., and KURTZ, J. H., "Vocalization of Infant Twins," *Folia Phoniatrica*, 14:37–50, 1962.

220. OSTWALD, P. F., PHIBBS, R., and FOX, S., "Diagnostic Use of the Infant Cry," *Biologia Neonatorum*, 13:68–82, 1968.

221. OTHMER, E., HAYDEN, M., and SEGELBAUM, R., "Encephalic Cycles During Sleep and Wakefulness in Humans: A 24-Hour Pattern," *Science, 164:*447–449, 1969.

222. PAINE, R. S., "The Contribution of Developmental Neurology to Child Psychiatry," *Journal of the American Academy of Child Psychiatry*, 4(3):353–386, 1965.

223. PAPOUŠEK, H., "Experimental Studies of Appeti-

tional Behavior in Human Newborns and Infants," in Stevensen, H. W., Hess, E. H., and Rheingold, H. L. (Eds.), *Early Behavior*, pp. 249–277, John Wiley, New York, 1967.

224. ———, "Conditioned Head Rotation Reflexes in The First Months of Life," *Acta Pediatrica*, 50:565–576, 1961.

225. ———, and BERNSTEIN, P., "The Functions of Conditioning Stimulation in Human Neonates and Infants," in Ambrose, A. (Ed.), *Stimulation in Early Infancy*, pp. 229–252, Academic Press, New York, 1969.

226. PARADISE, J., "Maternal and Other Factors in the Etiology of Infantile Colic," *Journal of the American Medical Association, 197:*191–199, 1966.

227. PARMELEE, A., and MICHAELIS, R., "Neurological Examination of the Newborn," in Hellmuth, J. (Ed.), *The Exceptional Infant: Studies in Abnormalities*, vol. 2, pp. 3–23, Brunner-Mazel, New York, 1971.

228. ———, and STERN, E., "Development of States in Infants," in Clemente, C. D., Purpura, D. P., and Mayer, F. E. (Eds.), *Sleep and the Maturing Nervous System*, pp. 199–228, Academic Press, New York, 1972.

229. ———, et al., "Sleep States in Premature Infants," *Developmental Medicine and Child Neurology, 9(1):*70–77, 1967.

230. PEIPER, A., "Cerebral Function in Infancy and Childhood," in Wortis, J. (Ed.), *The International Behavioral Sciences*, pp. 1–683, Consultants Bureau, New York, 1963.

231. PELTZMAN, P., GREENBERG, M., and MEYER, J., "Cries of a Trisomy 13–15 Infant," *Developmental Medicine and Child Neurology*, 12:472–477, 1970.

232. PIAGET, J., *The Origins of Intelligence in Children*, 2nd ed., International Universities Press, New York, 1952.

233. POMERLEAU-MALCUIT, A., and CLIFTON, R. K., "Neonatal Heart-Rate Response to Tactile, Auditory and Vestibular Stimulation in Different States," *Child Development*, 44:485–496, 1973.

234. POITRAS, R., et al., "Auditory Discrimination during REM and Non-REM Sleep in Women Before and After Delivery," *Canada Psychiatric Association Journal*, 18:519–526, 1973.

235. PRATT, K. C., "The Neonate," in Carmichael, L. (Ed.), *Carmichael's Manual of Child Psychology*, 2nd ed., pp. 215–291, John Wiley, New York, 1954.

236. PRECHTL, H. F., "The Behavioural States of The Newborn Infant (A Review)," *Brain Research*, 76:185–212, 1974.

237. ———, "Prognostic Value of Neurological Signs in The Newborn Infant," *Proceedings of the Royal Society of Medicine, 58:*3–4, 1965.

238. ———, "The Mother-Child Interaction in Babies with Minimal Brain Damage," in Foss, B. M. (Ed.), *Determinants of Infant Behavior*, vol. 2, pp. 53–59, John Wiley, New York, 1963.

239. ———, "The Directed Head-Turning Response and Allied Movements of the Human Body," *Behavior*, 13:212–242, 1958.

240. ———, and BEINTEMA, D., *The Neurological Examination of the Full-Term Newborn Infant*, Little Club Clinics in Developmental Medicine No. 12, Heinemann, London, 1964.

241. ———, and DIJKSTRA, J., "Neurological Diagnosis of Cerebral Injury in the Newborn," in Ten Berge, B. X. (Ed.), *Proceedings of the Symposium on Prenatal Care*, pp. 222–231, Noordhoff, Groningen, The Netherlands, 1960.

242. ———, WEINMANN, H., and AKIYAMA, Y., "Organization of Physiological Parameters in Normal and Abnormal Infants," *Neuropadiatrie, 1:*101–129, 1969.

243. ———, et al., "Polygraphic Studies of the Full-Term Newborn: I. Technical Aspects and Qualitative Analysis," in Bax, M. C., and MacKeith, R. C. (Eds.), *Studies in Infancy*, pp. 1–25, Heinemann, London, 1968.

244. PRESTON, E., "Whither the Foreskin? A Considera-

tion of Routine Neonatal Circumcision," *Journal of the American Medical Association*, 213:1853–1858, 1970.

245. RAZRAN, G. H. S., "Conditioned Responses in Children: A Behavioral and Quantitative Critical Review of Experimental Studies," *Archives of Psychology, 148:*73–109, 1933.

246. REBELSKY, F., and BLACK, R., "Crying in Infancy," *Journal of Genetic Psychology, 121:*49–57, 1972.

247. RHEINGOLD, H. L., GEWIRTZ, J. L., and ROSS, H. W., "Social Conditioning of Vocalizations in the Infant," *Journal of Comparative and Physiological Psychology, 52:*68–73, 1959.

248. RICHARDS, M. P. M. (Ed.), *The Intergration of a Child into a Social World*, Cambridge University Press, Cambridge, England, 1974.

249. ———, "First Steps in Becoming Social," in Richards, M. P. M. (Ed.), *The Integration of a Child into a Social World*, pp. 83–97, Cambridge University Press, Cambridge, England, 1974.

250. ———, and BERNAL, J. F., "An Observational Study of Mother-Infant Interaction," in Blurton-Jones, N. (Ed.), *Ethological Studies of Child Behavior*, pp. 175–197, Cambridge University Press, Cambridge, England, 1972.

251. ———, and BRACKBILL, Y., "Early Behavioral Differences: Gender or Circumcision?" *Developmental Psychobiology, 9(1):*89–95, 1976.

252. RICHMOND, J., GROSSMAN, H., and LUSTMAN, S., "A Hearing Test for Newborn Infants," *Pediatrics, 11:*634–638, 1953.

253. RINGEL, R., and KLUPPEL, D., "Neonatal Crying: A Normative Study," *Folia Phoniatrica, 16:*1–9, 1964.

254. RINGLER, N., et al., "Mother to Child Speech at Two Years—Effects of Early Postnatal Contact," *Journal of Pediatrics, 86:*141–144, 1975.

255. ROBSON, K. S., "The Role of Eye-to-Eye Contact in Maternal-Infant Attachment," *Journal of Child Psychology and Psychiatry, 8:*13–25, 1967.

256. ———, and MOSS, H. A., "Patterns and Determinants of Maternal Attachment" *Journal of Pediatrics, 77:*976–985, 1970.

257. ROFFWARG, H. P., MUZIO, J. N., and DEMENT, W. C., "Ontogenetic Development of the Human Sleep-Dream Cycle," *Science, 152:*604–619, 1966.

258. ROSENBLITH, J. F., "Prognostic Value of Neonatal Assessment," *Child Development, 37:*623–631, 1966.

259. ———, "The Modified Graham Behavior Test for Neonates," *Biology of the Neonate, 3:*174–192, 1961.

260. ROSENTHAL, D., *Genetic Theory and Abnormal Behavior*, McGraw-Hill, New York, 1970.

261. ROSENTHAL, M. K., "Attachment and Mother-Infant Interaction: Some Research Impasses and a Suggested Change in Orientation," *Journal of Child Psychology and Psychiatry, 14:*201–207, 1973.

262. ———, "The Study of Infant-Environment Interaction: Some Comments on Trends and Methodologies," *Journal of Child Psychology and Psychiatry, 14:*301–317, 1973.

263. ROSENZWEIG, M., "Effects of Experiments on Rat Brains: A Model for Aspects of Human Development and for Memory Storage?" Paper presented to the Winter Conference on Brain Research, Vail, Colorado, January 1973.

264. ———, et al., "Modifying Brain Chemistry and Anatomy by Enrichment or Impoverishment of Experience," in Newton, G., and Levine, S. (Eds.), *Early Experience and Behavior*, pp. 258–298, Charles C Thomas, Springfield, Ill., 1968.

265. RUBIN, R., "Maternity Care in Our Society," *Nursing Outlook, 11:*519–521, 1963.

266. SAINT-ANNE DARGASSIES, S., "Neurological Examination of the Neonate," *Proceedings of the Royal Society of Medicine, 58:*5, 1965.

267. SALAPATEK, P., "The Visual Investigation of Geometric Patterns by the One- and Two-Month Old Infant," Paper presented at Meetings of the American

Association for the Advancement of Science, Boston, 1969.

268. SALK, L., "Mother's Heartbeat as an Imprinting Stimulus," *Transactions of the New York Academy of Science, 24:*753–763, 1962.

269. SAMEROFF, A. J., "Psychological Needs of the Mother in Early Mother-Infant Interactions," in Klaus, M. H., and Fanaroff, A. A. (Eds.), *Care of the High Risk Neonate*, pp. 1023–1045, W. B. Saunders, Philadelphia, 1973.

270. ———, "Learning and Adaptation in Infancy: A Comparison of Models," in Reese, H. W. (Ed.), *Advances in Child Development and Behavior*, vol. 7, pp. 169–214, Academic Press, New York, 1972.

271. ———, "Can Conditioned Responses Be Established in the Newborn Infant: 1971?" *Developmental Psychology, 5:*1–12, 1971.

272. ———, CASHMORE, T. F., and DYKES, A. C., "Heart Rate Deceleration during Visual Fixation in Human Newborns," *Developmental Psychology, 8(1):*117–119, 1973.

273. SANDER, L., "Infant and Caretaking Environment: Investigation and Conceptualization of Adaptive Behavior in a System of Increasing Complexity," in Anthony, E. J. (Ed.), *Explorations in Child Psychiatry*, pp. 129–166, Plenum Press, New York, 1975.

274. ———, "Regulation and Organization in the Early Infant-Caretaker System," in Robinson, R. J. (Ed.), *Brain and Early Behavior*, pp. 311–332, Academic Press, New York, 1969.

275. ———, "Issues in Early Mother-Child Interaction," *Journal of the American Academy of Child Psychiatry, 1:*141–166, 1962.

276. ———, and JULIA, H., "Continuous Interactional Monitoring in the Neonate," *Psychosomatic Medicine, 28:*822–835, 1966.

277. ———, et al., "An Investigation of Change in the Infant-Caretaker System over the First Week of Life," Paper presented at Biennial Meeting of the Society for Research in Child Development, Denver, Colorado, April 1975.

278. ———, et al., "Continuous 24-Hour Interactional Monitoring on Infants Reared in Two Caretaking Environments," *Psychosomatic Medicine, 34:*270–282, 1972.

279. ———, et al., "Early Mother-Infant Interaction and 24-Hour Patterns of Activity and Sleep," *Journal of the American Academy of Child Psychiatry, 9:*103–123, 1970.

280. SCHAFFER, H. R., and EMERSON, P. E., "Patterns of Responses to Physical Contact in Early Human Development," *Journal of Child Psychology and Psychiatry, 5:*1–13, 1964.

281. SCHULMAN, C. A., "Alterations of Sleep Cycles in Heroin-Addicted and 'Suspect' Newborns," *Neuropadiatrie, 1(1):*89–100, 1969.

282. SCHULTE, F., HINZE, G., and SCHREMPF, G., "Maternal Toxemia, Fetal Malnutrition and Bioelectric Brain Activity of the Newborn," *Neuropadiatrie, 2:*439–460, 1971.

283. ———, et al., "Brain and Behavioral Maturation in Newborn Infants of Diabetic Mothers, II. Sleep Cycles," *Neuropadiatrie, 1:*36–43, 1969.

284. SCHUR, M., *The Id and the Regulatory Principles of Mental Functioning*, International Universities Press, New York, 1966.

285. SCHWARTZ, A., ROSENBERG, D., and BRACKBILL, Y., "Analysis of the Components of Social Reinforcement of Infant Vocalization," *Psychonomic Science, 20(6):*323–325, 1970.

286. SEASHORE, M. J., et al., "The Effects of Denial of Early Mother-Infant Interaction on Maternal Self-Confidence," *Journal of Personality and Social Psychology, 26:*369–378, 1973.

287. SEDLOCKOVA, P. E., "Analyse acoustique de la voix de nouveau-né," *Folia Phoniatrica, 16:*44–58, 1964.

288. SHAHEEN, E., et al., "Failure to Thrive—A Retrospective Profile," *Clinical Pediatrics, 7:*255–261, 1968.

289. SMITH, C. R., and STEINSCHNEIDER, A., "Differential Effects of Prenatal Rhythmic Stimulation on Neonatal Arousal States," *Child Development, 46:*574–578, 1975.

290. SMITHERMAN, C., "The Vocal Behavior of Infants as Related to the Nursing Procedure of Rocking," *Nursing Research, 18:*256–258, 1968.

291. SOKOLOV, E. N., *Perception and the Conditioned Reflex,* Pergamon, London, 1963.

292. SPITZ, R., *The First Year of Life—Normal and Deviant Object Relations,* International Universities Press, New York, 1965.

293. ———, "Diacritic and Coenesthetic Organizations," *Psychoanalytic Review, 32(2):*146–162, 1945.

294. ———, EMDE, R. N., and METCALF, D. R., "Further Prototypes of Ego Formation: A Working Paper from a Research Project on Early Development," in Eissler, R. S., et al. (Eds.), *The Psychoanalytic Study of the Child,* vol. 5, pp. 417–441, International Universities Press, New York, 1970.

295. STECHLER, G., "Newborn Attention as Affected by Medication During Labor," *Science, 144:*315–317, 1964.

296. ———, and CARPENTER, G., "A Viewpoint on Early Affective Development," in Hellmuth, J. (Ed.), *The Exceptional Infant,* vol. 1, *The Normal Infant,* pp. 163–189, Special Child Publications, Seattle, 1967.

297. STERMAN, M. B., "The Basic Rest-Activity Cycle and Sleep: Developmental Considerations in Man and Cats," in Clemente, C. D., Purpura, D. P., and Mayer, F. E. (Eds.), *Sleep and the Maturing Nervous System,* pp. 175–197, Academic Press, New York, 1972.

298. ———, "Relationship of Intrauterine Fetal Activity to Maternal Sleep Stage," *Experimental Neurology, 19(4):*98–106, 1967.

299. ———, and CLEMENTE, C. D., "Forebrain Inhibitory Mechanisms: Sleep Patterns Induced by Basal Forebrain Stimulation in the Behaving Cat," *Experimental Neurology, 6:*103–117, 1962.

300. ———, and HOPPENBROUWERS, T., "The Development of Sleep-Waking and Rest-Activity Patterns from Fetus to Adult in Man," in Sterman, M. B., McGinty, D. J., and Adinolfi, A. (Eds.), *Brain Development and Behavior,* pp. 203–227, Academic Press, New York, 1971.

301. STERN, D., "Mother and Infant at Play: The Dyadic Interaction Involving Facial, Vocal and Gaze Behaviors," in Lewis, M., and Rosenblum, L. (Eds.), *The Effect of the Infant on Its Caretaker,* pp. 187–213, John Wiley, New York, 1974.

302. ———, "A Micro-Analysis of Mother-Infant Interaction: Behavior Regulating Social Contact Between a Mother and Her 3½ Month-Old Twins," *Journal of the American Academy of Child Psychiatry, 10:*501–517, 1971.

303. STEWART, A., et al., "Excessive Infant Crying (Colic) in Relation to Parent Behavior," *American Journal of Psychiatry, 110(9):*687–694, 1954.

304. STOLLER, R. J., "Overview: The Impact of New Advances in Sex Research on Psychoanalytic Theory," *American Journal of Psychiatry, 130(3):*241–251, 1973.

305. ———, "The 'Bedrock' of Masculinity and Bisexuality," *Archives of General Psychiatry, 26:*207–212, 1972.

306. STRAUSS, M., et al., "Behavior of Narcotics-Addicted Newborns," *Child Development, 46(4):*887–893, 1975.

307. TENNES, K., et al., "The Stimulus Barrier in Early Infancy: An Exploration of some Formulations of John Benjamin," in Holt, R. R., and Peterfreund, E. (Eds.), *Psychoanalysis and Contemporary Science,* vol. 1, pp. 206–234, Macmillan, New York, 1972.

308. THEORELL, K., PRECHTL, H. F. R., and VOS, J. E., "A Polygraphic Study of Normal and Abnormal Newborn Infants," *Neuropädiatrie, 5(3):*279–317, 1974.

309. THOMAN, E. B., LEIDERMAN, P. H., and OLSON, J. P., "Neonate-Mother Interaction During Breast-Feeding," *Developmental Psychology, 6:*110–118, 1972.

310. THOMAS, A., et al., *Behavioral Individuality in Early Childhood,* New York University Press, New York, 1963.

311. THOMPSON, W., and GRUSEC, J., "Studies of Early Experience," in Mussen, P. H. (Ed.), *Carmichael's Manual of Child Psychology,* 3rd ed., vol. 1, pp. 565–654, John Wiley, New York, 1970.

312. TREHUB, S. E., and RABINOWICZ, M. S., "Audiolinguistic Sensitivity in Early Infancy," *Developmental Psychology, 6:*74–77, 1972.

313. TRUBY, H. M., "Some Aspects of Acoustic and Cineradiographic Analysis of Newborn Infant and Adult Phonation and Associated Vocal-Tract Activity," *Journal of the Acoustical Society of America, 32:*1518, 1960.

314. TULLOCH, J. D., et al., "Normal Heartbeat Sound and the Behavior of Newborn Infants: A Replication Study," *Psychosomatic Medicine, 26:*661–670, 1964.

315. VALANNE, E. H., et al., "The Ability of Human Mothers to Identify the Hunger Cry Signals of Their Own Newborn Infants During the Lying-In Period," *Experientia, 23:*768–769, 1967.

316. WASZ-HOCKERT, O., et al., *The Infant Cry: A Spectrographic and Auditory Analysis,* Clinics in Developmental Medicine, no. 29, Heinemann, London, 1968.

317. ———, et al., "Effect of Training on Ability to Identify Preverbal Vocalizations," *Developmental Medicine and Child Neurology, 6:*393–396, 1964.

318. ———, et al., "Analysis of Some Types of Vocalization in the Newborn and in Early Infancy," *Annales Paediatriae Fenniae, 9:*1–10, 1963.

319. WATSON, J. B., *Behaviorism,* 1st ed., University of Chicago Press, Chicago, 1930.

320. ———, and WATSON, R. R., "Studies in Infant Psychology," *Scientific Monthly, 13:*493–515, 1921.

321. WEITZMAN, E., FISHBEIN, W., and GRAZIANI, L., "Auditory Evoked Responses Obtained from the Scalp Electroencephalogram of the Full-Term Human Neonate During Sleep," *Pediatrics, 35:*458–462, 1965.

322. WESSEL, M., et al., "Paroxysmal Fussing in Infancy, Sometimes Called Colic," *Pediatrics, 14:*421–434, 1954.

323. WHITE, R. W., *Ego and Reality in Psychoanalytic Theory,* Psychological Issues, Monograph no. 11, International Universities Press, New York, 1963.

324. WIESEL, T. N., and HUBEL, D. H., "Ordered Arrangement of Orientation Columns in Monkeys Lacking Visual Experience," *Journal of Comparative Neurology, 158:*307–318, 1974.

325. WOLFF, P. H., "The Natural History of Crying and Other Vocalizations in Early Infancy," Foss, B. M. (Ed.), *Determinants of Infant Behavior,* vol. 4, pp. 81–109, Methuen, London, 1969.

326. ———, "Cognitive Considerations for a Psychoanalytic Theory of Language Acquisition," in Holt, R. R. (Ed.), *Motives and Thought: Psychoanalytic Essays in Honor of David Rapaport,* Psychological Issues, Monograph no. 18/19, pp. 299–343, International Universities Press, New York, 1967.

327. ———, *The Causes, Controls, and Organization of Behavior in the Neonate,* Psychological Issues, Monograph no. 17, International Universities Press, New York, 1966.

328. ———, "The Development of Attention in Young Infants," *Annals of the New York Academy of Science, 118:*815–830, 1965.

329. ———, "Observations on the Early Development of Smiling," in Foss, B. M. (Ed.), *Determinants of Infant Behavior,* vol. 2, pp. 113–167, John Wiley, New York, 1963.

330. ———, *The Developmental Psychologies of Jean Piaget and Psychoanalysis,* Psychological Issues, Monograph no. 5, International Universities Press, New York, 1960.

331. ———, "Observations on Newborn Infants," *Psychosomatic Medicine, 21:*110–118, 1959.

6 / Development of the Human Infant from Two to Six Months

Kenneth S. Robson

Introduction

During the thirty years since the end of World War II, the study of human infancy has steadily advanced. Clinical observations, basic research efforts, and their theoretical foundations have witnessed a remarkable expansion. Different bodies of knowledge have converged. And the curiosity about infants seems to have overcome the awe and reluctance with which clinicians and adults have tended to approach them. Empathy, one of the most powerful clinical tools, may be a liability in the exploration of infancy. To become empathic with helplessness and the affect states of the first years of life is a difficult if not unwelcome task. However, it is a task with promising rewards. To begin to master the archaeological maps of human infancy opens up the potential for a more complete understanding and modification of the more disabling forms of human suffering with which clinicians are regularly faced.

The aim of this chapter is to review some aspects of development during the second through sixth months of life. Specifically, its purposes are to examine psychomotor, perceptual-cognitive, and interpersonal processes in relation to four major vantage points—psychoanalytic object-relations theory, ethology, the cognitive theories of Jean Piaget, and the perspectives of learning theory. Wherever possible, direct observations of infants and their caretakers will be cited. This will take issue with the starling in *Mary Poppins*:

> *"There never was a human being that remembered after the age of one. . . ."*

With effort one may remember that era which all have traversed and recorded each in his own way.

A review of this sort cannot be comprehensive; it is also subject to the author's biases. The reader is encouraged to reach his own conclusions by referring to the basic texts and references included in the reference list. A scholarly review and comprehensive collection of classical papers is now available as a single volume.[34]

Theoretical Positions

There is, at present, no single model of infant behavior that successfully integrates all the observational data. Familiarity with several theoretical schools—their similarities and differences—seems useful, albeit confusing at times. Some of these positions will be reviewed as the background against which infant behaviors can be studied.

PSYCHOANALYTIC OBJECT-RELATIONS THEORY

Classical psychoanalysis focused its attention primarily upon intrapsychic phenomena. Within this tradition, there has been increasing interest in studying the nature of interpersonal processes, and it is upon these that object-relations theorists have concentrated. Guntrip[13] has written an excellent synopsis of the subject. He reviews the contributions of Freud, Klein, Fairbairn, Winnicott, and others—all of whom were practicing analysts. Two prominent figures can be added—Spitz[31] and Mahler.[22] Their work has involved direct observations of mothers and infants in a nonclinical situation.

Early psychoanalytic views of the human infant described an unintegrated organism dominated by powerful instinctual forces—aggression, primitive sensuality, and hunger. The child's attachments to his parents and the development of his ego (including the subjective awareness of self) were viewed as *secondary* phenomena. They evolved from the caretakers' management of the child's drives and appetites. It was assumed that the search for love emerges from the discharge of visceral tensions. This view portrays the infant as shaped by what his parents do without his simultaneously influencing them.

Within object-relations theory, *primacy* is given to *social motivations*. These are present in the infant at birth in varying degrees. Instinctual drives are viewed as person-related and as located within a fragile but already intact ego. (The question of "symbiosis" as a normal phenomenon and its relation to ego intactness will be discussed later in this chapter.) Fairbairn (see Guntrip[13]) describes the infant as "object-seeking." Winnicott[38, 39] derived his exquisite sensitivity from his experience as both pediatrician and psychoanalyst. Throughout his career he paid increasing attention to the critical nature of experiences of "ego-relatedness." There are casual sequences of play that often occur between mother and infant after a feeding or during a diaper change. These become more significant for subsequent development than are the feeding or diapering themselves. In an effort to enter and understand the silent but crucial emergence of the self, both Spitz[31] and Mahler[22] scrutinized the social life of babies and their caretakers. Object-relations theory also deals with the more academic approaches to developmental theory and research such as the discipline of ethology.

ETHOLOGY

Systematic studies of animal behavior have now been carried on *in situ*. These have produced helpful concepts and methodologies for research in human infancy. Comprehensive surveys of this field include those of Hess,[16] Hinde,[17] and Eibl-Eibesfeldt.[9] Tinbergen's monograph[35] on social behavior is especially pertinent.

The interest in instinctual patterns of behavior has allied ethology with classical psychoanalysis. At the same time, there are common bonds with object-relations theory. Ethologic investigations depend upon observable behavioral sequences. These behaviors are seen within an evolutionary context, and survival value for the species is therefore a major criterion for retention of a given behavioral pattern within the animal's repertoire of actions. The motivation for these behaviors was viewed in a similar manner both by Freud and by the great Austrian ethologist Konrad Lorenz.[21] Both conceived of a "hydraulic system within which a reservoir of instinctual energy accumulates to the point of overflow and, thus, discharge of

the particular behavior in question." More recent ethologic approaches to motivation[17] emphasize the complex interplay between internal factors (i.e., hormones and neurophysiologic mechanisms) and external releasing or terminating stimuli. Such stimuli play a critical role in regulating social behavior between members of the same species. Ethology, like object-relations theory, pays keen attention to interactive processes and the forces that control them.

More specific human ethologic studies are now appearing in the literature. John Bowlby is the outstanding advocate of this position, and his work[5, 6] provides a major link between object-relations theory and ethology. Bowlby is a psychoanalyst who has carefully studied the problems of attachment and loss. His contributions are substantial and are summarized in his two-volume texts. Attachment is viewed as developing out of the interaction between a series of innate infant behaviors—crying, sucking, smiling, clinging, and following—and the responses they release. The origins of this bond are vested in its survival value, thus emphasizing the *relational aims* of instinctual behaviors. Within this model, there is ample room for infant and caretaker to shape one another's behavior. The *direction of effects*, (see chapter 5), or who influences whom, can be more precisely studied using the ethological approach.

Attachment of mother and infant to one another seems to be the critical task of the first six months of life. The sequences of behavior that mediate the attachment process appear to leave indelible stamps upon the developing infant's subsequent adjustment both to himself and to others around him. Further light has been shed on these sequences by the observations and theory of Jean Piaget.

THE COGNITIVE/DEVELOPMENTAL THEORIES
OF JEAN PIAGET

Jean Piaget has devoted his life to charting the microstructure and function of cognitive processes in infants and children. His studies, now a discipline in their own right, have been thoughtfully summarized by others.[40, 10, 3] But the early papers, reviewing the behaviors of his own children, make Piaget one of the classical scholars of infancy.

Piagetian theory pays scant attention to affective phenomena. It nonetheless shares common elements with both object-relations theory and ethology. Development is seen as *intrinsically motivated* and *interactive* from birth onward. The basic behavioral unit—a *schema*—is an innate reflexive behavior such as sucking, clinging, grasping, and looking. Within ethology, these same basic behavioral units are called *fixed action patterns*. These schemata are self-motivating. Their activation and refinement, which serve to incorporate increasingly complex aspects of the self (particularly the body) and the externally perceived world, provide their own reward. This emphasis upon the motive power of mastery, on "the infant's delight in being a cause," is central to Piaget's theories. Although not indebted to Piaget, both Hendrick[15] and Robert White[37] have explored the clinical significance of effectiveness as a crucial fuel for growth and well-being.

According to Piaget, the infant's expectancies in relation to events are always salient. A baby's ability to shape his world in a predictable manner seems central to a comfortable sense of self.[25, 26] These response expectancies, the infant's feel for what is coming next, are particularly important to Piaget's concept of *object conservation*—the capacity to perceive the outside world as stable and expectable through internal representations of it that are not influenced by the vagaries of perception or the object's actual presence. The infant's ability to conceive of his mother (i.e., primary caretakers) in this way represents a crucial developmental achievement. The clinical significance of this Piagetian achievement has been thoughtfully studied by both Fraiberg[11] and Bell.[4] The knowledge of infant memory may soon extend adult remembrance of things past.

LEARNING THEORY

Before turning to the development of behavior from two to six months, one can note the contributions of learning theory to infant observation. Piaget stresses repetitive behavioral sequences as the means by which babies learn about their world and themselves. Learning theorists such as Gewirtz[12] study the *contingencies* that determine these sequences. Attachment is viewed as a learned phenomenon. Bonding to the mother depends upon the degree to which her behaviors are contingent upon the baby's signals (crying, smiling, etc.). Once more, response chains, expectancies, and the factors controlling them seem central to the understanding of the infant's earliest relationships.

Against the backdrop of these theoretical points of view, some aspects of normative development from two through six months of life can now be explored. The reader should keep in mind that the division of this period of human infancy into *stages* is in certain respects arbitrary and is not to be taken literally.

Developmental Observations

BIRTH TO TWO MONTHS

Emde (chapter 5) characterizes much of behavior during these early weeks as *endogenous* both in origin and aim. In some respects, the infant can be seen as a closed system whose signals have only limited interpersonal significance. In a similar vein, Mahler[22] labels this period of life the Normal Autistic Phase. She sees the task of this phase as the ". . . achievement of homeostatic equilibrium of the organism within the new extramural environment by predominantly somatopsychic, physiological mechanisms." In this regard, it is of interest that the infant mortality rate during the first year of life approaches the death rate during the seventh decade. Two-thirds of these infant deaths occur within the first twenty-eight days of life.[23] From an evolutionary point of view this may be adaptive for the species. The death of an infant who fails to adapt at a time when he relates minimally to his caretakers spares both parties the effects of disrupted human bonds.

The dominance of reflexive behaviors in this opening period of life is apparent even to the casual observer. These reflexes, such as the startle, grasp, and Moro, seem to have little value in facilitating attachment. Piaget[10] has labeled the first month of life the reflexive stage. Significantly, Piaget stresses that some reflexes like sucking and looking *need objects* with which to sustain their functioning (his allusion to "objects" is not to be confused with the psychoanalytic use of the term, i.e., people). In the earliest days, the infant is unaware of what target he seeks with mouth or eyes and he is seen by Piaget to exist in a state of ". . . utter and complete egocentrism." In the second month of life, according to Piaget, these reflexes begin to interact with and to objectify the environment.

Bowlby[5, 6] emphasizes the role that sucking, looking, crying, smiling, and following play in the development of attachment of the infant to his caretakers. He takes a teleological position and sees the infant's more or less automatic behaviors as tending to drive the bonding process. Sucking at the mother's breast or smiling *at* her elicit crucial *affects* and *behaviors* that purchase parenting.

Nevertheless, the nature and quality of life during the first two months suggest a form of psychic and physiological insulation from the world around. It is as if nature is taking no chances. Clinicians know that certain infants, children, and seriously disturbed adults either fail to leave this stage or retreat back to it and exist in a kind of psychological death in life. For the most part, however, the newborn is propelled forward into the world around him both by inner and outer forces.

What of the caretakers? How do they experience this earliest portion of their offspring's life? In a study of maternal attachment[27] a group of fifty-four primiparous mothers reported little sense of relatedness to their babies in the first four to six weeks of life. One subject noted that ". . . at times I felt that she was completely unconnected to me in any way, flesh or otherwise, [and] that she was just a little thing that had come into my life and brought all this trouble. . . ." Another mother observed that during the first month or two ". . . I don't think there is an interaction . . . they are like in a little cage surrounded by glass and you are acting all around them but there is *no real interaction*." As will be seen, there is a shift in this perception toward the middle of the second month of life.

One must question the roots and nature of mother love and subject it to scrutiny. The human infant, at least in Western culture, seems poorly designed to elicit sustained feelings of fondness. Marshall Klaus and his colleagues[18, 19, 20] studied the earliest contact between mother and infant, and they have documented an orderly and predictable pattern of exploration of the newborn during first contact with his mother. There appears to be particular interest in establishing face-to-face contact in the eye area as a form of social relating. Klaus believes that he has also discovered a "maternal sensitive period," such as exists in subhuman species, where disruption of these initial contacts may impair bond formation. While the evidence for this critical period is still limited, it appears certain that maternal needs to establish *relatedness* in general, and through face-to-face interaction in particular, are important anlagen of subsequent parenthood. A few comments regarding face-to-face social interaction are in order before moving into the next stage of infancy.

The visual system occupies a key position in human social interchange. This system, relative to other perceptual modes, is highly developed at birth and provides a major channel through which the outside world is taken in. Indeed, what the infant cannot hold with his hands, he holds with his eyes.[26] Mutual gazing, or eye contact, is a powerful releaser of the infant's *social* smile. And language development, too, seems functionally related to reciprocal gazing. Mothers and babies vocalize to one another mainly during gaze interchanges.* Condon and Sander[8] discovered a fascinating synchrony between adult speech and neonatal movement—a kind of reflexive choreography in which the baby dances to the adult's voice. Finally, aberrations in language development, smiling, and gaze behavior accompany all of the major behavior disorders of infancy. During the early months of life, as the infant enters the social world, the viscissitudes of the gaze system provide an index to his development and his experiences in the presence of his mother.

TWO TO FOUR MONTHS

Mahler[22] describes the era from two to four/six months of life as the stage of "normal symbiosis." In the autistic phase, the infant was quite unaware of his mother (a position that some current perceptual studies call into question; see, for example, Carpenter et al.[7]), but in the symbiotic phase an awareness exists. According to Mahler, "the essential feature of symbiosis is hallucinatory or delusional somatophsychic *omnipotent* fusion with the representation of the mother . . . [with] . . . the delusion of a common boundary between two physically separate individuals." Mahler and her colleagues found that symbiosis was *optimal* when the mother naturally permitted the young infant to face her, promoting eye contact, talking, and singing to him.

Mahler's concept of symbiosis has had a significant impact on developmental theory and clinical model building. The term is borrowed from biology and, unfortunately, takes on several different meanings both to Mahler and to her readers. Observational data that support her view are sparse. For present purposes, it is critical to know whether the experience of psychic fusion with the parent represents a *normal developmental phase* or, as the author believes, is *always pathological*. The "self" may be experienced from the beginning of life. It is suggested that there is more evidence to support the idea of an ego intact at birth (see chapter 5). The fantasy of fusion with the mother would then be the result of hereditary/constitutional vulnerabilities and/or certain "invasive" patterns of mothering that may flood the fragile ego with unmanageable tension.[25] One need not posit fusion or symbiosis to recognize the shift

---

* These are some unpublished observations of H. A. Moss and K. S. Robson.

into the interpersonal world that is so striking during this phase of infancy.

The cognitive advances that characterize this period are also notable. Piaget[10] focuses on the acquired adaptations—the shaping of reflex by experience—from the second to fourth months. Now ". . . things out there [are seen as] distinct from one's actions." Coordinations such as hand-mouth and, more important he believes, eye-hand, lead to "objectification of the universe . . . and . . . will eventually extricate the child from the stifling egocentrism of early infancy." Piaget stresses that at this time these infant behaviors lack *intentionality* and conscious goal-directedness. In keeping with Piaget's observations, learning now begins to take place whereas, in earlier weeks, this seems not to be the case (see chapter 5).

At this stage of life, learning and cognition both prosper most clearly through the visual mode. Indeed, Piaget stresses that ". . . vision will grow in importance as a vehicle for forming liasons with reality. . . ." This observation is especially apparent if one examines the infant's liasons with interpersonal reality. As noted by Emde (chapter 5), true eye contact, early vocalizations, and social smiling emerge toward the end of the second month and become key elements in the repertoire of *response-linked behaviors* so crucial for the development of attachment.

In one study, mothers reported little sense of relatedness to their babies until the latter part of the second month.[27] At this time, the majority of these mothers felt an increasing sense of pleasure in and affection for their babies. The infant's "*responses*" (a concept implying reciprocity) were emphasized as a source of acknowledgment of the mother's presence. Smiling, being looked at, visual fixations, and following led the list of behaviors mentioned. It appears that an infant's ability to engage in dyadic social exchange is an essential aspect of developing parental attachment. During this stage, these infant behaviors tend to be *indiscriminate*, and the human craving ". . . not for universal love but to be loved alone"[2] is satisfied with love in general. By the end of the fourth month, however, parental attachment appears to be well consolidated. Similarly, those who study infant attachment note the beginnings of a discriminated bonding to the primary caretakers.[6]

From the infant's vantage point, the development of this attachment is necessary for survival. Hence, the interactive processes through which it is achieved are of great interest to the understanding of early object relations. Classical psycho-analytic theory suggested that biological "need-fulfilling" was the fuel that fired infant love. More recent observational studies such as Schaffer and Emerson's[30] conclude that the "need-fulfilling" and attachment systems are separate. A mother's face as a "feast for the eyes" may be more significant in facilitating attachment than her breast as a source of relief from hunger. Harlow's experiments with infant monkeys demonstrated the prepotency of "contact comfort" over nourishment.[14] It appears that the emerging attachment of infant to mother is mediated by perceptual-cognitive processes and their affective accompaniments, rather than by the satiation of instinctual needs. The intensification of this bond and its contributions to the earliest stages of separation phenomena take place in the fifth and sixth months of life.

FOUR TO SIX MONTHS

In the course of his development, it is not enough that an infant become attached to one or more primary caretakers. For optimal maturation and development, this tie must be focal and discriminated. Without this specificity, the inner sense of "wholeness" never emerges fully, and relationships with others may be both shallow and indiscriminate. Psychic emptiness is both observed and felt. Furthermore, without attachment, by definition, detachment cannot adequately occur. In the preceding section, it was noted that selective smiling, looking, and vocalizing are evident in the fourth month. This selectivity heightens in the fifth and sixth months, and its facilitation is of considerable interest.

According to Mahler, these months represent the end stages of "normal symbiosis." They herald the onset of a period of "differentiation" that occupies the second half of the first year of life. She emphasizes that "safe anchorage" with the mother provides the impetus for the earliest moves toward automony.[22] To be safely anchored is to be *specifically* anchored to one's primary caretakers. In what ways does this occur? To answer this question, the cognitive abilities of the infant and his capacity to use them for learning must be kept in mind.

The period from four to eight months covers the third stage of Piaget's sensorimotor period (birth to two years). As a whole, the accomplishments of this stage constitute the first definite steps toward *intentionality*.[10] In earlier months, the infant was interested in his own body per se—he sucked for the sake of sucking. Now he shows an interest in the environmental consequences of his acts and he invents "procedures" to make interesting sights last. These new reactions are seen as the forerunners of *contemplative recognition*. It is in this latter state, of course, that maximal learning takes place.

Infants of five and six months exhibit notable contemplation both of objects and people, especially the objects that special people introduce them to.[28] It is commonplace to see a baby of this age enthusiastically exploring his mother's face and all its surroundings—hair, jewelry, glasses, etc. Similarly, the faces of strangers may be soberly scrutinized. In this regard, it should be kept in mind that throughout the first year of life, the visually perceived part of the mother is the *face*. Comparisons appear to be made. And in order for this to occur, a familiar and secure perception of her face must exist. Infant studies suggest the manner in which that special face is taken in.

The timing, intensity, and quality of mother-infant interaction provides some clues to the development of an inner object—a stable maternal "template." As noted earlier, both mother and infant build up *expectancies* vis-à-vis one another's *responses*. The behavior of each member of the dyad influences the other. Observe, for example, the activities of a mother whose five-month-old infant fails to smile at her glance or greeting. In recent years the nature of this interactional behavior has been studied with increasing intensity.* Richards[24] suggests that the central problem in understanding mother-infant interaction is "the timing and phase relationships of the two participants' behavior." The *reliability* and *modulation* of sequences of interaction, the smooth patterning with which they begin, evolve, and cease, tell much about the dyad. The ensuing "anchoring" process facilitates a stable inner representation of the mother. Conversely, it is far too easy to find interactions characterized by disjointed and unmodulated styles of relating. These appear disruptive to the maintenance of equilibrium, and in these instances the mother becomes the first feared object in the infant's world. Learning theory stresses the role of *contingencies of responses* in the acquisition of knowledge.[12] It is suggested that the degree of contingency in the interaction with infants helps to convey the "fit" or "nonfit" of the pair at any one point in time.

The concept of "direction of effects," or who does what to whom, has helped to objectify studies of infancy.[4] Clinical observations tend to be judgmental. In past years, the parents, and the mother in particular, have born the brunt of responsibility for problems of development. Increasing evidence suggests that this simplistic notion should be tempered with the knowledge that infants markedly influence parental behavior. How they join, interact with, and begin to leave their objects of attachment should be studied more humbly (and accurately) with these findings in mind.

Mahler[22] observes that toward the sixth month, one starts to see signs of separation, differentiation, and beginning individuation in the infant. Tentative experimentation in these directions are evidenced by intense manipulation of the mother's face and "feeding" of the mother. The baby strains his body *away* from her in order to have a better look at her and the world beyond. Peek-a-boo may begin—a universal game of loss and restitution in the service of growth. And as the infant begins to move into the second half of the first year of his life, the constancy of the inner representations of mother lends him freedom.[11, 4] Winnicott, always a sensitive observer, came to believe that social interchange in general, and play in particular, occupied crucial positions in the matrix of life. How mother and infant came to be with and without one another could be learned from the nature of their play. This was a better indicator than the quality of biological drives and their release. He put it this way:

> Psychoanalysts who have rightly emphasized the significance of instinctual experience . . . have failed to state with comparable clearness or conviction the tremendous intensity of these nonclimactic experiences that are called playing. We now see that it is not instinctual satisfaction that makes a baby begin to be, to feel that life is real, to find life worth living . . . here is a part of the ego that is not a body-ego . . . but that is founded on body experiences [that] belong to object-relating of a non-orgiastic kind, or to what can be called ego-relatedness. . . .[38] (p. 368)

The advent of speech, upright posture and locomotion, and certain gestures more similar to those of the adult world often leave both infant and mother with only fleeting memories of the first six months of life. These early stages become a kind of silent area. During this time, the adequacy of development is perhaps best indicated by the sense of differentiation in the child and by the depths and quality of relatedness of which he is capable. These capacities represent some of the most fundamental achievements of humankind.

* See references 32, 31, 29, 25, and 1.

SECTION I / Normal Development

REFERENCES

1. Ainsworth, M. D. S., Bell, S. M., and Stayton, D. J., "Infant-mother Attachment and Social Development: Socialization as a Reciprocal Response to Signals," in Richards, M. P. M. (Ed.), *The Integration of a Child into a Social World*, Cambridge University Press, Cambridge, England, 1974.

2. Auden, W. H., "September 1, 1939," in Williams, O. (Ed.), *The Pocket Book of Modern Verse*, Pocket Books, New York, 1954.

3. Baldwin, A. L., *Theories of Child Development*, John Wiley, New York, 1967.

4. Bell, S. M., "The Development of the Concept of Object as Related to Infant-Mother Attachment," *Child Development, 41:*291, 1970.

5. Bowlby, J., *Attachment and Loss*, vol. 2, *Separation—Anxiety and Anger*, Basic Books, New York, 1973.

6. ———, *Attachment and Loss*, vol. 1, *Attachment*, Basic Books, New York, 1969.

7. Carpenter, G. C., et al., "Differential Visual Behaviors to Human and Humanoid Stimuli in Early Infancy," *Merrill-Palmer Quarterly, 16:*91, 1970.

8. Condon, W. S., and Sander, L. W., "Neonate Movement Is Synchronized with Human Speech: Interactional Participation and Language Acquisition," *Science, 183:*99–101, 1974.

9. Eibl-Eibesfeldt, I., *Ethology*, Holt, Rinehart and Winston, New York, 1970.

10. Flavell, J. H., *The Developmental Psychology of Jean Piaget*, Van Nostrand, Princeton, N.J., 1963.

11. Fraiberg, S., "Libidinal Object Constancy and Mental Representation," in Eissler, R. S., et al. (Eds.), *The Psychoanalytic Study of the Child*, vol. 24, pp. 9–47, International Universities Press, New York, 1969.

12. Gewirtz, J. L., "A Learning Analysis of the Effects of Normal Stimulation, Privation and Deprivation on the Acquisition of Social Motivation and Attachment," in Foss, B. M. (Ed.), *Determinants of Infant Behavior*, John Wiley, New York, 1961.

13. Guntrip, H. J. S., *Psychoanalytic Theory, Therapy and the Self*, Basic Books, New York, 1971.

14. Harlow, H. F., "The Nature of Love," *American Psychologist, 13:*673, 1958.

15. Hendrick, I., "Discussion of the 'Instinct to Master,'" *Psychoanalytic Quarterly, 12:*561–565, 1943.

16. Hess, E. H., *Ethology*, Holt, Rinehart and Winston, New York, 1970.

17. Hinde, R. A., *Animal Behavior*, McGraw-Hill, New York, 1966.

18. Klaus, M. H., and Kennell, J. H., "Mothers Separated from Their Newborn Infants," *Pediatric Clinics of North America, 17:*1015–1037, 1970.

19. Klaus, M. H., et al., "Maternal Attachment, Importance of the First Postpartum Days," *New England Journal of Medicine, 286:*460–463, 1972.

20. Klaus, M. H., et al., "Human Maternal Behavior at the First Contact with Her Young," *Pediatrics, 46:*187–192, 1970.

21. Lorenz, K., *On Aggression*, Harcourt, Brace, and World, New York, 1966.

22. Mahler, M. S., Pine, F., and Bergman, A., *The Psychological Birth of the Human Infant*, Basic Books, New York, 1975.

23. Nelson, W. E., *Textbook of Pediatrics*, 10th ed., Vaughan, V. C., and McKay, J. M. (Eds.), W. B. Saunders, Philadelphia, 1975.

24. Richards, M. P. M., "Social Interaction in the First Weeks of Human Life," *Psychiatria, Neurologia, Neurochirurgia, 74:*35–42, 1971.

25. Robson, K. S., "Development of Object Relations during The First Year of Life," *Seminars in Psychiatry, 4:*301–314, 1972.

26. ———, "The Role of Eye-to-Eye Contact in Maternal-Infant Attachment," *Journal of Child Psychology and Psychiatry, 8:*13–25, 1967.

27. ———, and Moss, H. A., "Patterns and Determinants of Maternal Attachment," *Journal of Pediatrics, 77:*976–985, 1970.

28. Rubinstein, J., "Maternal Attentiveness and Subsequent Exploratory Behavior in The Infant," *Child Development, 38:*1089, 1967.

29. Sander, L., "Issues in Early Mother/Child Interaction," *Journal of the American Academy of Child Psychiatry, 1:*141–166, 1962.

30. Schaffer, H. R., and Emerson, P. E., *The Development of Social Attachments in Infancy*, Social Research in Child Development, Monograph no. 29, 1964.

31. Spitz, R. A., *The First Year of Life*, International Universities Press, New York, 1965.

32. Stern, D. N., "Mother and Infant at Play: The Dyadic Interaction Involving Facial, Vocal and Gaze Behaviors," in Lewis, M., and Rosenblum, L. (Eds.), *The Origins of Behavior*, vol. 1, John Wiley, New York, 1973.

33. ———, "A Microanalysis of Mother-Infant Interaction," *Journal of the American Academy of Child Psychiatry, 10:*501–517, 1971.

34. Stone, L. J., Smith, H. T., and Murphy, L. B. (Eds.), *The Competent Infant*, Basic Books, New York, 1973.

35. Tinbergen, N., *Social Behavior in Animals*, John Wiley, New York, 1953.

36. Travers, P. L., *Mary Poppins*, Harcourt, Brace, and World, New York, 1934.

37. White, R. W., *Ego and Reality in Psychoanalytic Theory*, Psychological Issues, Monograph no. 11, 1963.

38. Winnicott, D. W., "The Location of Cultural Experience," *International Journal of Psychoanalysis, 48:*368, 1966.

39. ———, "The Capacity to Be Alone," in Winnicott, D. W., *The Maturational Process and the Facilitating Environment*, International Universities Press, New York, 1965.

40. Wolff, P. H., *The Developmental Psychologies of Jean Piaget and Psychoanalysis*, Psychological Issues, Monograph no. 5, 1960.

7 / Development from Six to Twelve Months

Sally Provence

Summary of Physical Development

CHANGES IN PHYSICAL GROWTH

A reasonably reliable pediatrician's rule of thumb is that a full-term normal infant will generally double his birth weight by age five months and triple it by the first year. In length, he starts at an average 50 cm (20 in.) at birth, and grows 25 to 30 cm (10 to 12 in.) in the first year.

Subcutaneous tissue increases conspicuously in the early months of life, and reaches its peak at about nine months. Head circumference is 34 to 35 cm at birth, about 44 cm at six months, and increases to 46 cm by the first year. At birth, the circumference of the head is larger than the chest, but by one year they are about equal. The anterior fontanel usually diminishes in size after six months, and it may become effectively closed at any time from nine to eighteen months. Between about five to six months and one year, most infants have six to eight deciduous teeth.

The above are averages or modal values,[5] and thus do not reflect the range and variability of what is accepted as normal growth. Body proportions change gradually, too, as the extremities lengthen and the head comprises relatively less of the total stature.

Physical growth charts have long been an integral part of the health records of infants and children and are helpful in many ways. They have many uses and have been widely recognized as helping to heighten the awareness of health professionals. Moreover, in adverse psychological and psychosocial situations, disturbances in physical growth occur commonly in children and can be readily monitored.

SENSORY AND MOTOR DEVELOPMENT

At about six months of age, the infant's motor development has proceeded so that he has gained control over the muscles that support his head and move his arms. His head is held erect and steady, he can roll over from back to front and back again, and can keep his trunk erect when supported in a chair. About this time, he can support much of his weight if placed in a standing position and can "bounce" on his legs. Between six and nine months, he at first crawls on his belly and then creeps on all fours with reciprocal and coordinated movements of upper and lower extremities. At nine months, most infants are able to pull themselves into a standing position and soon begin to cruise around the crib by holding the rail or around the furniture with a side-stepping gait. Walking forward with two hands held and then walking without assistance are accomplished by many infants by twelve months, and by many others soon thereafter.

Concomitant with gross motor development are progressions in eye-hand coordination and manipulative skills. At about six months, an infant can reach out to grasp a toy, using each arm independently and employing a whole-hand or mitten-like form of grasping. He can easily get his thumb to his mouth and can touch all of the parts of his body at will. He has the ability to hold on tightly to something he wants. Between six months and a year, there is an impressive increase in the precision of finger skills. The grasp matures from whole-hand to finger-grasping, and from the ulnar to the radial side of the hand. At about eight to nine months, the child employs a radial digital grasp for picking up objects such as a small block, and by twelve months, he can grasp even tiny objects between index finger and thumb in a pincer grasp of almost adult precision. During the second half of the first year, motor skills emerge, as well as their coordination and integration. This is evident in the child's ability to fully exploit toys in the midline, to transfer them from one hand to the other, to manipulate two at the same time, and to combine them in a variety of ways. Intrinsic maturational progress is a necessary but not sufficient condition for adequate development of the motor system. Motor phenomena are coordinated with development in other areas. They are dependent not only on the integrity of the apparatus but on the quantity and quality of the infant's experience with his environment, especially with those who nurture him. It is useful for the clinician, now and later, to try to look both at the progressive acquisition of motor skills and at the use to which the child puts these skills. Motility both expresses and becomes the servant of the rapidly expanding mental life of the infant. An examination of the ways in which this happens has many clinical applications. Motility is one of the autonomous functions of the ego, and as such, it is widely acknowledged to be an essential aspect of the infant's mastery of self and environment. It is also an expressive function—fluctuations in and patterns of motor activity are often reliable indicators of feeling states.

The functions of the sensory systems also show increasing differentiation and selectivity. During the six- to twelve- month period, this is easiest to discern in behavior which reflects the development of the visual system. There are some indicators that tell of progress both in sensory function and in intelligence. These include such observations as the infant's growing ability to distinguish between familiar and unfamiliar persons, the capacity to pay attention and be selectively interested in very tiny objects in addition to larger ones, and the readiness to recognize not only sharp contrasts in the appearance of things but much smaller differences.

Acoustic attention also shows refinement, and several indications of hearing and attention are noted during this period. These include the infant's monitoring of his own vocalizations, his ability to be involved in mutual imitation of sounds with varying inflections and vowel-consonant combinations, his ability to localize the source of sounds in his environment, and selective responsivity to music. Again, the child's ability to enjoy tactile and kinesthetic sensations is reflected in his increasing experiences in self-touching and his reactions to being touched. Experiences of touching and being touched (including self-touching) have important effects. It is believed that they play a special role in the perception and differentiation of body boundaries and the dawning awareness of the body self.

Psychosocial Development

The six-month-old child is already quite experienced in relationships with others. He has not only been smiling responsively for a long time, but has also become active in initiating social contact by smiling and vocalizing. He reacts in ways that indicate his clear distinction of the mothering person from others. Increasingly, he communicates his needs, desires, displeasure, and attitudes with full expectation of a response from the human environment. His behavior suggests that there is considerable awareness of a distinction between himself and the other, enough so that he perceives that there is someone outside of himself whom he can influence by his increasingly voluntary, selective, and focused behaviors.

During the last half of the first year, the specificity and intensity of the attachment to the maternal figure increase. Surely, this is a continuation of the period of attachment to the need-satisfying object which had begun earlier, but now the relationship grows deeper and more complex. The infant is so much under the influence of his needs that he will accept care from almost any reasonably skillful and benevolent person. However, there is no doubt about the greater strength of his tie to the mother. This is evidenced by his strong reactions of pleasure in social interaction with her, and by his responses to her protective and comforting functions. The relationship to the primary object was characterized earlier by a clear predominance of positive emotions in the infant. This is believed to reflect a predominance of the attitudes that accompany libidinal drive development. This too becomes more mixed and complex as the second half of the first year proceeds. One may readily observe the infant's cognitive discrimination of strange places and persons.

Equally striking, however, are his anxious apprehensiveness in reaction to the appearance of the stranger and his distress when separated from the mother. It is believed that the infant's anxiety at this time is triggered by concern that the stranger's presence means disappearance of the mother, for he is now developing some awareness not only of his positive feelings toward her, but of his negative feelings as well. Since not all experiences can (or should) be fully gratifying, he sees her correctly not only as the one who gives him pleasure and protection, but also as the source of frustration. Spitz[7] and Benjamin[1] in particular have drawn attention to an important element in theory. They suggest that the child's growing awareness, discrimination, and intensification of the relationship to the mother reflect not only cognitive elements, but the effect of differentiation and maturation of aggressive as well as libidinal drive development.

Another infant of between the age of eight to twelve months may be an object of attention and interest to a baby. In general, however, peer relations at this age are an unimportant part of the infant's life. From six to nine months or so, being in the presence of another baby may excite pleasurable interest and laughter as well as touching, pushing, licking, and poking, much as the infant might respond to an interesting animated toy. Toward the end of the first year, there is more awareness of the connection between one's own action and the response to the other infant. For example, deliberate repetition of certain actions suggests that a baby begins to be aware that a certain kind of touching might produce a cry in the other or a particular social approach might produce an inviting response from the other. However, except for the more complex relations of twins, there is little dependence upon or seeking the company of another infant during this period.

Growing sensory and cognitive capacities—the ability to sit erect, to view the world from a new perspective, to creep about, and to walk—bring the infant into more varied, frequent, and self-initiated contact with parents and siblings. This makes him both more interesting to his siblings and more intrusive into their play. There is also a rapid development of interest and ability to imitate that continues and becomes more elaborate as time passes. Mutual imitation of sounds, facial expressions, gestures, and other movements are a frequent part of the social interaction between infants and others at this age. Such games as peek-a-boo, pat-a-cake, and other forms of social play are common examples.

These are impressive developmental characteristics that the well-nurtured infant will display in the last half of the first year. In particular, there is his ability to be increasingly active not only motorically, but also in the manipulation of toys, in attentiveness to his environment, and in personal contacts. He both initiates more contacts with another person and actively avoids or rejects them. In so doing, he uses the various skills that he has developed. He may make a contact with another person by smiling, by using his voice, or by looking. He may extend a toy, sometimes giving it to the other person, sometimes pulling it back in a playful manner. If he is in the arms of the adult, he may gently pat the face, or finger the nose or mouth, or not so gently pull hair or push the person away. He can pull hard on a toy, insisting on his right to have it. He can express his refusal by shaking his head no, actively avoid something he fears or dislikes, or actively attack it. These are most vividly observed in his relationships with people, but they extend to many of his interactions with the remainder of his environment as well.

Between six and twelve months, a child who is healthy and well nurtured has developed an attitude in which basic trust predominates. As Erikson[2] emphasizes, this involves reliance on the benevolence and continuity of the outer providers, and stands in contrast to basic mistrust and feelings of frustration and deprivation. The balance between these opposite attitudes colors his relationships with others, his style of action and reaction, his interests, and, to some extent, his needs.

Communication Skills

Although by definition this period belongs to the preverbal phase of life, the beginnings of speech development are clearly discernible and follow a predictable sequence. Prior to six months, the infant's major vocalizations were merely responsive to the stimulation of others or were primarily expressive of his major feeling states. By this time, however, he has acquired the ability to use his vocalizations to express interest and attention toward the outside world. Indeed, he often seeks to initiate contact with other persons, especially those closest to him. Between six and twelve months, vowel and consonant sounds become combined into clear syllables. First he vocalizes *dada* and *mama* and *papa* sounds in a nonspecific way. At about the same time he uses vocal signals to express peremptory demands or to renew social contact. By about nine or ten months, the *dada* and *mama* or other similar combinations come to stand for the important adults, and by the age of twelve months most infants use one or two specific words besides the names of the parents. These first words are most often closely related to the child's central needs or demands: *up, go, more,* and so on. Along with the development of the first words, the number and variety of vocalizations increase.

Nonverbal communication is also a very rich and vital part of the communication system. It is anchored in the mutuality of the early relationship between mother and infant, and in the well-nurtured child of six months, it has become astonishingly complex. The infant has, for example, learned to look at the face and gestures of the adult and to listen to the tone of voice. These give him the cognitive and affective cues that guide his actions, for they are associated with his expectations as well as with his feeling states. A certain way of being held or lifted or a certain way of being restrained are all important communications. They allow him to make some kind of postural adjustment, impel him to action, or help him to regulate or delay such action. Some of this nonverbal communication is mediated through the near receptors and some of it via the distance receptors. Both those cues that come from physical contact and those that the child is able to see or hear from across the room are registered and responded to in increasingly specific ways. Affective communication is difficult to describe in terms of concrete variables, but it is not difficult to recognize when one sees a parent and infant in tune with one another, or a parent and infant in disharmony.

Self-concept

During the six- to twelve-month period, there is only a small amount of relevant observational material available to allow any inference about the self-concept. The infant's behavior at six months includes the progression from the period of looking at and fingering his own hands and playing with them, to sucking his thumb, playing with his feet, and reaching to touch all parts of his own body. From about six months on, he can partially comfort himself when in distress by sucking his thumb or giving himself a pacifier. He stimulates his own body by touching or grasping, by rocking, or, at times, by genital play for pleasure or self-comfort. By around nine months, he recognizes his name when it is used, and by the end of the first year he can identify parts of himself—for example, his foot, his eye, and so on—in social play with the adult. All of these behaviors, it is believed, are concomitant with advances in the structuralization of the psychic life.

Reference has been made to the beginning distinction between self and other, between inside and outside. In regard to separation-individuation, this period is concomitant with Mahler's hatching (five to nine months) and the beginning of the practicing (nine to fourteen months) subphases.[4] Many of the baby's actions appear to indicate he has some awareness of himself and some sense of being able to change things or make things happen. For example, his attention to changes produced by manipulation of objects or by his

peremptory demand for services are cases in point. To the extent that he has been well nurtured, his happy expectation that good things will happen most of the time at least conveys an impression of a person quite satisfied with himself and other people. When he is in physical or psychological distress, he expresses this with the expectation that his parents will restore him to comfort or good humor.

Cognitive Abilities

According to Piaget,[6] one way of describing the cognitive abilities of the infant age six to twelve months is in terms of his progress in sensorimotor intelligence. During this six- to twelve-month time, the infant increasingly acts upon persons and things in his environment. He approaches, grasps, and manipulates objects. He shows definite indications of an awareness that objects continue to exist even though they are out of sight. At the beginning of this period, he can uncover a toy that has been concealed in his presence, but is unable to find it if it has been moved from one hiding place to another. By twelve months, he has made further progress in the development of grasping the concept of object permanence, and now he begins to be able to remove an obstacle or make a detour in search of an object that has been hidden.

Gesell and Amatruda[3] defined a group of responses on the Gesell Test as adaptive. They view these as convenient categories for reflecting the child's capacity to initiate new experiences and to profit from past experiences. Many of these reactions are indicators of intellectual development. The infant's ability to play with two toys simultaneously, for example, is a capacity acquired somewhere around nine months. It is evidently a step forward in the ability to manipulate. Moreover, it reveals that the child is now able to encompass and coordinate his interest in two items at once rather than being limited to dealing with one at a time. From this point on, in ever more complex ways, the capacity to cope with multiple stimuli partially reflects his cognitive abilities. Around the same nine- to ten-month interval, his increased visual and digital inspection and exploration of toys is accompanied by a heightened attention to small details. Together, these bear witness to his growing discrimination and the variety of interests. In play, he shows distinct preferences for some toys over others, and there is no doubt that his recognition of differences in the toys forms the basis of his preference. Presumably, this also indicates that at that moment, the toys have some psychological meaning for him which makes them more attractive, desirable, or satisfying. Increasingly, too, he sees relationships between objects and recognizes ways in which they go together. An infant of twelve months, for example, can perceive the similarity between a round block and the place where it fits into a formboard. Furthermore, he has a strong enough memory for a vanished object, and enough initiative and motivation to make a detour around a solid screen to find the object hidden there. He is now entering the period when the early indicators of semiotic mental operations are visible. His cognitive progress is also revealed, as has been noted earlier, in his discrimination and beginning use of names of persons and of actions. The same holds true for his object relationships: His recognition of specific others and of the meaning of their behavior always contains cognitive elements.

Affective Life

Between the ages of six and twelve months, the forms of expression providing clues to the infant's affective life become increasingly differentiated and accessible to observation. Studies of affective development are notoriously difficult to carry out, and there is much in this area still to be learned. The developmental aspects of anxiety described by Benjamin[1] are perhaps the most clearly delineated. Prior to six months, the infant has shown discrimination and often reaction to a strange setting. Between six and twelve months, however, he is likely to react to strange persons and to separation from the emotionally important adults with evident anxiety.

Anxiety is an affect experienced by the ego, and there is no doubt that its appearance is both a possible and a predictable development. In some well-nurtured infants, it may appear as a transient phenomenon, but in those who are more sensitive, it will be strongly expressed and persistent. While distressing to the child and often to his parents, its presence is, in fact, a part of healthy personality development. If the anxiety of this period is excessively prolonged and/or difficult to alleviate, it then falls into the category of a symptom which requires attention. By the same token, the absence of some degree of anxiety suggests a defect or disturbance in the specificity and depth of object relationships, often of an ominous nature.

Other aspects of the child's affective life are more difficult to trace. Nonetheless, in an infant of six to twelve months, one is able to recognize indicators of an increasing number and variety of emotions. Compared with the six-month-old, the greater differentiation and affective versatility of the twelve-month-old are clearly discernible. Pleasurable reactions vary all the way from low-keyed satisfaction to joyous excitement. By the end of the first year, observers see (among others) behavior and expressions that they are willing to interpret as joy, sadness, anxiety, distaste, perplexity, anger, and reproach. Emotions are labile, and at times one is not quite certain whether an infant is going to laugh or to burst into tears, whether a situation is going to delight or frighten him. It can be assumed that the developments of the first year have made it possible for the one-year-old child to feel a wide variety of emotions in distinctive ways. It can also be assumed that when the environment has been geared to an infant's individuality and to his developmental needs, he views his world with a predominance of pleasure, trust, and positive interest. At the same time feelings of frustration, anxiety, perplexity, and rage are by no means unknown to him. The richness of the emotional life of the six- to twelve-month-old in a reasonably adequate environment stands in sharp contrast with the infant who has been deprived, psychologically traumatized, or has endured painful bodily experiences beyond the capacity of his parents to relieve.

REFERENCES

1. BENJAMIN, J. D., "Further Comments on Some Developmental Aspects of Anxiety," in Gaskill, H. S. (Ed.), *Counterpoint: Libidinal Object and Subject*, pp. 121–153, International Universities Press, New York, 1963.
2. ERIKSON, E. H., *Identity and the Lifecycle*, Psychological Issues, vol. 1, Monograph no. 1, International Universities Press, New York, 1954.
3. GESELL, A., and AMATRUDA, C. S., *Developmental Diagnosis*, Paul B. Hoeber, New York, 1941.
4. MAHLER, M., PINE, F., and BERGMAN, A., *The Psychological Birth of the Human Infant*, Basic Books, New York, 1975.
5. NELSON, W. E., VAUGHAN, V. C. III, and McKAY, R. J., *Textbook of Pediatrics*, 9th ed., W. B. Saunders, Philadelphia, 1969.
6. PIAGET, J., *The Origins of Intelligence in Children*, International Universities Press, New York, 1952.
7. SPITZ, R. A., "Anxiety in Infancy: A Study of Its Manifestations in the First Year of Life," *International Journal of Psychoanalysis, 31*:138–143, 1950.

8 / A Theoretical Overview of Preoedipal Development During the First Four Years of Life

Herman Roiphe

Introduction

Almost from the outset, psychoanalysis has uniquely been a developmental psychology. Freud's early investigations of the mind culminated in a radical set of inferences about the sexual drive organization of behavior.[6] The sequential oral, anal, and phallic zonal influences along with the concomitant mental representations in phase-specific zonal fantasies established the essential outline of the psychoanalytic developmental schema.

In the 1920s, there were wide-ranging revisions in Freud's metapsychological thinking.[2, 3, 4] These resulted in a significant shift in emphasis to ego psychology and to the role of object relations as major determinants of development. These new trends in psychoanalytic thought have been perhaps most comprehensively synthesized in Mahler's generative conceptualization of object relations development, which she has termed the separation-individuation phase.[15, 16, 17, 18] Mahler's clinical and observational data were examined largely from the viewpoint of their relevance for the separation-individuation process rather than in regard to Freud's theory of psychosexual development. The task of integrating these two major theoretical frameworks remains to be accomplished.

At six to eight to ten months every infant has the developmental task of psychologically mastering the recognition of its own separateness. That is, it must face the dawning awareness that the mental representation of the maternal object is external to the sense of self. This personal birth of man is no less awesome a passage than the earlier physical birth, for it establishes a major disequilibrium which results in a whole new organization, not only of object relatedness but of the sexual and aggressive drives as well. Some two to four years later this disequilibrium normally attains some measure of resolution. The outcome is evident in the structuralization of the ego that is involved in the attainment of relative object constancy. Failure to resolve the disequi-

librium inherent in the separation-individuation process may well result in the broad range of narcissistic disorders, at the core of which is the ever-present threat that the sense of self may be utterly annihilated and the object world may cease to exist. The mounting tension from ungratified need states then threatens existence.

The differentiation process has a radical and thoroughgoing impact on every aspect of the infant's functioning. It may well turn out that the ego as a coherent organization finally emerges out of this cataclysmic process. It would seem that there is a new quality of experience that emerges which, if it is not as organized a quality as consciousness, nevertheless has many of its attributes. Certainly those primal polarities of experience, the me and not me, the self and the object, the inside and the outside, the animate and the inanimate, seem rapidly to be consolidated at this time, and probably as a consequence of this process.[22] It may be that in certain respects the differentiation process is an inborn capacity. However, it is equally clear that the interactional parameters—that is a certain core of good-enough mothering—is the overwhelming determinant of this fateful process.

The anxiety function consequent upon the differentiation process undergoes a qualitative transformation. Earlier it is essentially a somatic process, probably best understood as a form of organismic distress (Mahler's term); it expresses itself as a rapidly mounting general body tension arising from unfulfilled need states. Following on the differentiation process and, in most instances, coincident with it, stranger anxiety emerges. With the appearance of the stranger reaction, the anxiety function undergoes a desomatization process and now operates as true signal anxiety.[25, 26] The anxiety which the infant experiences is no longer confined to the context of mounting need states. Instead, the recognition that the stranger is not the external maternal object confronts the child with something new; now that he is a more individuated being, he encounters the anticipated danger of his own helplessness in the face of need states without the mother. Spitz expressed it this way:

> Like the smiling response of three months, the eight-month [stranger] anxiety marks a distinct stage in the psychic organization. In the case of the smiling response, the sign-Gestalt of the face is experienced as the homologue of the human partner. In the case of the eight-month anxiety, the percept of the strange face is confronted with the memory of the mother's face. It is found to be different and will therefore be rejected. We assume that this capacity of cathectic displacement on reliably stored memory traces in the eight-month-old child reflects the fact that he has now established a true object relation and that the mother has become his libidinal object.[27] [p. 156]

Spitz's discussion is highly condensed. It seems clear that he had not yet succeeded in integrating Mahler's generative concept of the separation-individuation process into his own thinking, but nevertheless, he was following a closely parallel course. It would appear that Spitz correctly underscores the two major stages in the organization of the infant's narcissism—the smiling response and the stranger reaction. The smiling response is characterized in his somewhat elliptical statement that the sign-Gestalt of the face is experienced as the homologue of the human partner. This seems to suggest that out of the repeated pattern of need arousal, satiation, and sleep, there develops a significant coalescence of primitive cognition, memory, and expectancy, so that the nurturing environment, essentially the mother, is introjected into the internal milieu of the infant. This signals that major accretion in infantile narcissism which has been termed the symbiotic stage. The mother's face evokes primitive memories of need arousal and satiation which trigger the smiling response.

By contrast, if the nurturing environment has been rich enough, the differentiation process which emerges represents a major breach in the primary infantile narcissism. It is like an amoeba which feeds and grows and splits into two. Spitz observed that the capacity of cathectic displacement on reliably stored memory traces reflects the fact that the eight-month-old child has now established a true object relation and the mother has become his libidinal object. This suggested to Spitz that the object schema is now experienced as external to the self, and no longer subject to the omnipotent control that prevailed during the symbiotic stage. Moreover, his consideration of the relatively complex and integrated functions of cognition, memory, and anticipation of danger would seem to point to a coherent ego structure.

One of the signal achievements of the nascent ego's integrative capacity in the face of the significant assault on the infant's primary narcissism and the major disequilibrium and strain implicit in the differentiation process is the emergence of the transitional object and transitional phenomena.[31, 29, 21] The child's first possession is related both backward in time to autoerotic phenomena, fist and thumb sucking, and also forward in time to the doll. It is related both to the internal object (the subjective, magically introjected breast) and the external object (the mother's objective breast), but is distinct from each. In other words, the breast, that is, the nurturing environment, is created by the infant over and over again out of its capacity for love—out of need. A subjective phenomenon develops in the baby which we call the mother's breast. The mother places the actual breast just there, where and when the infant is ready to create it.

From birth onward the human being is concerned with the problem of the relationship between what is subjectively conceived and what is objectively perceived, and in the solution of this relationship, there is no health for an individual who has not been started-off well enough by the mother. Winnicott introduced the terms *transitional object* and *transitional phenomena* as a designation for the intermediate area of experience between the thumb and the doll, between primary creativeness and objective perception based on reality testing. This early stage in development is made possible by the mother's special capacity for adapting to the needs of her infant, thus allowing the infant the illusion that what he creates really exists. This intermediate area of experience, unchallenged as to its belonging to either internal or external shared reality, constitutes a significant part of the infant's experience, and throughout life it is retained as a central support for the individual's concept of the external object world, in the intense experiences that belong to religion, mythology, belief systems, and the arts.

Any functional consideration of the transitional object, however, confronts observers with a set of startling paradoxes. For example, the integrity of the differentiation process and the sense of separateness are supported and facilitated through the transitional object's function of blurring the same. It serves, in part, to support reality testing but is based on an illusion supported by the mother's collusion, in that she agrees never to challenge her infant by asking the question "Did you create it (i.e., the nurturing environment), or was it always there?" The transitional object is inanimate and external to the self, and yet, through the interposition of projective mechanisms, it is invested with the qualities of the object. In the process it becomes animated and thus can serve as a comfort for the infant. This latter argument serves to underscore the important mirroring function of the transitional object. Through its externalization of the object, the differentiation process results in a major depletion in the infant's primary narcissism. This, in turn—at least potentially—makes for a feeling of deadness at the core of the self schema, a feeling that follows from the implicit loss of the symbiotic object. For the infant, the projective cathexis of the external, inanimate transitional object serves to restore the narcissistic balance. Finally, the external inanimate object comes to stand for the live, real, good-enough object. As a result, this transitional process is the earliest and most regular context for the emergence of the symbolic process.

Thus far the discussion has primarily addressed the effect of the differentiation process on the infant's developing object relatedness and on the emergent ego organization. However, the differentiation process also involves the differentiation of the new psychological drive organization as well, so that the infant directs hostile, aggressive impulses toward the very same external object whom he at the same time loves out of need. In fact, the major breach in the primary narcissism as well as the implicit loss as the object becomes external to the self seems to evoke, at least potentially, an upsurge in aggression directed toward the external object. This is the regular and normal context for the emergence of the infant's primary ambivalence to the external object world. This state of affairs is very much complicated by the fact that the tendency of the aggressive drive at this point in development is, at least potentially, to destroy, to annihilate the very object who is loved out of need. This is of course a very unstable state and from this point on, the whole thrust of development must be to contain this disruptive force while preserving the basic attachment to the object world.

In those instances where the mother-child interaction has been satisfying enough, the object-directed aggression which is mobilized as a consequence of the differentiation process seems for the most part to remain a potentiality rather than an actuality. It may be that the extraordinary turn toward activity in the perceptual, cognitive, and motor spheres serves to channel the aggression in a nonhostile fashion. However, it is much more likely that the major explanation for the relative moratorium in the actualization of object-directed aggression, which normally lasts for a variable period of from three to six months, lies in the normal child's ready capacity for a rapid but transient dedifferentiation which tends to blur the sharp sense of separateness; the transitional process is but one of the channels for this dedifferentiation mechanism. This normal regression serves to spare the still unstable object schema from the potential annihilation which is the aim of the object-directed aggression at this stage of development. The adaptive value of this normal moratorium in the actualization of object-directed aggression is that it allows some consolidation in the object schematization which serves to make it relatively more secure against the normal vicissitudes of aggression.

In those instances where the mother-child interaction has been less than good enough, as for example, maternal depression or serious bodily illness, there seems to result a greater than normal instability in the body-self and object schemata. Moreover perhaps an even larger than normal quantum of hostile aggression emerges consequent to the differentiation of the infant. In such developmental situations there seems to be an impaired capacity for transient dedifferentiation. As a consequence, there are a number of possible alternative developmental resolutions of this highly unstable state. These may range from the highly pathological symbiotic psychosis,[17] in which the heightened aggression serves to shut out and virtually destroy any connection to the outside object world, to psychosomatic illness, in which the hostile aggression is bound in body reactions,[19] to addictivelike oral fixations and the less compromising, precocious anal zonal arousal.

Some time during the period from thirteen to sixteen months, there seems to be a significant consolidation in the body-self and object schemata along with a growing stability and integrity of ego structures. At this stage, the potential primary ambivalence which was mobilized consequent to the differentiation process now is actualized, and one may regularly observe a marked and frequently sudden upsurge in sharp, hostile attacks on the mother. As a rule this appears in the face of frustration, anticipated loss, or the emotional unavailability of the mother. While the mother in the flesh is relatively safe from the direct attack of the infant as a consequence of its relative physical weakness, the integrity of the child's body-self and object schemata as well as the coherence of the ego is in considerable danger of destruction because of the unbridled force of the aggressive drive.

The major developmental task proper to this period must be to establish some channel to take up and serve to discharge the aggressive drive and yet spare the fundamental structures of self and object. The dedifferentiation mechanism which served this function very well during the earlier moratorium stage no longer seems as readily available since, in the interim, there has been a significant consolidation in ego structures and in the self and object schemata. As a consequence, there is a sharply increased resistance to regression. It would seem that the optimal developmental strategy is to develop discreet channels that take up and discharge sexual and aggressive drives, and ultimately to develop ego structures which serve to transform the very nature and aims of these drives. The optimal developmental strategy is to split the ambivalence until reliable ego structures are consolidated which transform the basic nature and aims of the drives. There can then be a synthesis of the hostile aggressive self and the loving self as well as a complementary integration of the bad, hated object and the good, loved object.

In this general dynamic context and significantly unstable state, we regularly see, in rapid sequence, the emergence of the anal, urinary, and early genital zonal arousal.[20] By the second year, there is an awareness of the object concept as external to the self concept and a gradual consolidation of distinct and separate self and object schemata. It seems that in the course of this process, the two parallel zonal vectors, anal and early sexual, become increasingly important. By virtue of its functional characteristics, fullness and loss, the anal zone is ideally suited to channel feeling and experience having to do with the mother of separation (Mahler's term). Consequently, it becomes, at least in part, a natural means for the expression of aggression directed toward the object. From this same viewpoint, the early genital zone would become the channel for the more purely libidinal attachment to the object; through the manipulation of his own genitals, the child now actively produces warm, good feelings in his own body which earlier he had experienced only passively through maternal care. It should then be clear that, normally, this early genital phase has to do with the consolidation of the primary structures of self and object and appears to be entirely free of any oedipal resonance. The current thinking about genital sexuality has become firmly embedded in the whole oedipal fantasy constellation, to such a degree, that many colleagues find it difficult to consider a genital sexuality that is involved with the more primal existential issue of the you and the me. The anal and the early genital zones are thus two major highways on the child's tortuous journey toward a basic connection to the real object world and the gradual organization and internalization of the inner self and object schemata. These two zones serve as body nuclei around which coherent islands of mental, ideal schemata of the good and bad object world gradually consolidate.

Anal Zone

Early in the first year, the infant tends to have his stool during feeding or shortly thereafter. As a rule, there is no attention to or behavioral reflections of the bowel movement. Toward the end of the first year and certainly early in the second, there commonly is a tendency for a general body rigidity to be present along with some straining; not infrequently, there is an associated brief stilling of other body activity and a withdrawal of attention from the outside as the child turns his attention to the inner body sensations of the bowel movement. It is not uncommon with fourteen- to fifteen-month-old children to note a new fascination with the toilet. They seem particularly intrigued by the flush, with the highly exciting and absorbing observation of the controlled disappearance of the stool, toilet paper, or toy.

This shift in the child's relationship to his own bowel movement seems to follow and to be organized by the normal, and at this age, typical emergence of a separation conflict with all that this implies about the inner consolidation of self and object schemata.[19] At this stage, the bowel movement is ideally situated to express the double-faced developing inner concept: something which is part of self, can be felt inside, has a movement and yet is not alive; has a climactic expulsive pattern, a texture, a smell, and very importantly, a relationship to the nourishing object; and yet when expelled is neither self nor object. Its movement and consistency are subject to the vicissitudes of health and sickness and loving and hating feelings toward the object. Ultimate control of the toilet process awaits some partial resolution of the conflicts around self-dissolution and object loss. The whole sequence of attention to the bowel movement and the new relationship to it follows from and is a reflection of the new developing self and object relationship. In this sense, it is quite independent of any demand from the parents, either explicit or implicit, for control of these functions.

Perhaps the most dramatic reflection of the anal channeling of object-loss and self-dissolution concerns is the growing anxiety manifested by the child when an effort is made to change a soiled diaper. This is frequently fiercely resisted with the new word *no*. It is commonplace for children during the second year to show a marked reluctance to having their soiled diapers changed for a variable period of time after a movement. It would seem that this period of time is required to detach from the stool its emotional significance of self and object.

Bowel patterning of general activity is readily observable in the emergence of endlessly repeated play or action sequences that seem to externalize sensations or feeling states which are mobilized around the bowel movement.[8] Children will climb into small, enclosed spaces, frequently out of sight of the mother, and there they will have their movement. A fascination with garbage often goes hand-in-hand with a fastidious interest in small pieces of lint or refuse. This is frequently accompanied with the new word *dirty*. There is commonly a renewed bout of peek-a-boo games, repeated sequences of stuffing small objects into containers and then emptying them, and passing objects through holes.

An interesting advance in the process of symbolization is implicit in the child's investment of the bowel movement with self-object significance. Whereas in the earlier transitional process, an external, inanimate object comes to take on this emotionally laden meaning through the mechanism of projection, now the stool, a part of the internal milieu of the child, has this accretion of meaning. For example, during this stage, when there is a strong separation-individuation thrust, it is quite common for the child to regularly have bowel movements during the day, when he is clearly aware of the loss, and to have a movement at night while asleep, without any consciousness of its passage only on those occasions when the mother has left him with a baby-sitter. While there continues to be something of the same level of concretization of the symbol, stool-self-object, as was the case with the earlier transitional object, there is now a considerable advance in that there is a significant internalization of the process.

The projective symbolization of the transitional stage is not as much superceded as it is overlaid by the more internalized process characteristic of the anal stage. In each case, the phase-specific symbolic process results from a structuralization of the ego as a consequence of the underlying dynamic context[8] and retains its integrity through-

out life. Throughout life, each level of symbolization is called into play whenever the same general psychological context holds sway. For example, the transitional-projective symbolization is probably central to the creative process, as delineated in the Pygmalion myth: It is characterized by a fluidity in the object concept. The object is at once both external to the self and part of the internal milieu, a condition which normally holds in the transitional process. This serves to blur the sharp sense of separateness that is established in the differentiation stage. It would seem that this provides the broad developmental context for Kris's concept of regression in the service of the ego in his discussion of the creative process.[14]

The specific sexual and aggressive drive organization lends the anal zonal arousal its particular coloring and content. As indicated in the foregoing discussion, the anal zone, by virtue of its functional characteristics of fullness and loss, lends itself as a channel for feelings and experiences having to do with the mother of separation. It consequently serves as a major channel, at least relatively, for the taking up, the expression of, and ultimately for the transformation of, the very nature and aim of the aggressive drive. The investment of the anal zone and its stool product with some quantum of the primitive oral-symbiotic libido as well as the major channeling of hostile aggression is then the normal drive distribution characteristic of the anal phase. The tension between the two drive cathexes probably accounts for the new level of bowel withholding, straining, and shift in attention which is usual at this stage. The oral-symbiotic libido with its introjective mode tends to incorporate the stool-object as an accretion to the internal, narcissistic milieu, whereas the tendency of the hostile aggression is to shatter and deanimate the stool-object. The investment of the stool product with sexual and aggressive drives accounts for the normal erotization of aggression which is ubiquitously observable in the emergence of some level of sadistic teasing during this stage.

There is, of course, a continuum of developmental contexts, deviant from the optimal, in which there are alternate, variable distributions of drive cathexes. One extreme form is childhood autism in which there is no significant investment in an object schema, and, consequently, at this period, no investment of the anal zone and its stool product. The more typical and far less deviant variants are characterized by the constipations, relatively fixed or more transient, and the noninfectious diarrheas which are frequently observable at this time. The constipations seem to develop in situations where there is a relative increase in hostile aggression consequent to greater than usual concerns with object loss. This mobilizes a compensatory augmentation of the libidinal cathexis of the stool-object. The diarrheas result from rapid, transient increments in hostile aggression where there are no complementary shifts in libidinal cathexes. The drive distribution implicit in the constipations seems to establish the condition for the characterological or perverse organization of sadomasochistic object relatedness.

Toilet training which is usual during the second or third year normally involves some resolution of the phase-specific separation conflicts in that the child actively holds onto or leaves the stool-object. With the achievement of toilet control and, perhaps of even greater importance, with the partial resolution of the phase-specific separation conflicts, ego structures are precipitated which have the capacity to transform the nature and aim of the aggressive drive—it no longer has the immediate tendency to globally annihilate the self and object schemata. This would seem to be the developmental precondition for the integration of the bad, hated object and the good, loved object which is characteristic of object constancy. The failure or impairment of this ego capacity to transform the nature of the aggressive drive seems to be the nuclear precondition for the major narcissistic disorders of adult life.

Early Genital Phase

In the preceding discussion, attention was drawn to the characteristic consolidation in the body-self and object schemata which took place during the early months of the second year. One result of this was the actualization of the primary ambivalence toward the object. The optimal developmental strategy is to split the ambivalence, utilizing the anal and genital zones to channel the aggressive and sexual currents differentially. The early genital zonal arousal ordinarily takes place at about the same time. It follows shortly after the anal zonal arousal and serves as a channel for the more purely libidinal attachment to the object. The child, by manipulating his own genitals, now actively produces warm, good feelings in his own body which earlier he only passively experienced through maternal nurturing care. It must be emphasized that this early genital phase has to do with the further consolidation of the self and ob-

ject schemata and is entirely free of any oedipal resonance.[20]

In the beginning, the general outline of early genital sexual development is the same for both boys and girls. In the first months of the second year, there is normally a sharp upsurge of genital manipulation as a consequence of the now-specific endogenous responsiveness of the genital zone. In time, this takes on a more recognizably masturbatory pattern. During the early genital phase, the general erotization of the body surface already becomes increasingly centered in a genital sensitivity; the mild, pleasurable tickling of the neck, chest, or abdomen may lead to genital masturbation.[22] From the beginning, along with genital arousal, there are signs of autonomic excitement as indicated by rapid respiration and flushing. This genital handling seems from the outlet to be object-directed; at such moments the child will often engage the mother visually as he smiles with pleasure. As the masturbatory pattern becomes better organized, the child seems more withdrawn as he handles himself. His gaze turns inward and he appears to be engaged in fantasies of closeness to the maternal object. This latter inference seems particularly commanding as the child is not uncommonly observed to use either bottle or transitional object with which to masturbate.[22]

An important and almost ubiquitous concomitant of the early genital zonal arousal is the emergence of a distinct pattern of curiosity about the anatomical difference between the sexes. Under the impact of his own endogenous genital sensations, the child will show a decided visual and tactile curiosity about his own genitals as well as those of his parents, other children, animals, and dolls. It is at just this point that one is able to discern significant and fateful divergences in male-female development organized around the reactions to the observation of the anatomical difference between the sexes.[9] It is true that from birth on there are distinct differences in parental handling of boy and girl infants which must have a differential impact on the cognitive experience of each sex. However, our research would tend to establish the primacy of the libidinalization of the genital zone in the second year, with the emergence of a sharp sexual curiosity and a reaction to the anatomical difference between the sexes, in the organization, elaboration, and content of the presently divergent lines of male-female development.[9]

Although little boys undoubtedly perceive the difference between male and female, they generally react with a profound and unusually thoroughgoing denial of the difference. This is undoubtedly supported by the fact that they can constantly reassure themselves by reference to their own bodies through visual and tactile means. The only sign of the underlying strain covered over by this denial is that in contrast to their sisters, boys tend to show gross motoric hyperactivity, along with a relative delay or inhibition in both symbolic fantasy play and body-image integration. In the thirty-five little boys whose development was observed during their second year of life, we intensively followed only two who developed a significant castration reaction. In both cases, follow-up study indicated that these castration reactions had decided pathological implications for further development.[11, 23] The general impression, gained by the author and as yet unsupported by systematic follow-up, is that from the third year on, this profound denial in the boys begins to break down and castration reactions begin more commonly to impact on their development.

By contrast, all thirty-five little girls in the study developed distinctly recognizable castration reactions which ranged from mild, transient patterns to severe, far-reaching, and relatively fixed reactions. The relatively mild castration reactions seemed to characterize those children who had had good-enough mothering. The more severe reactions developed in those children whose earlier experience had resulted in an unstable object schematization. This occurred, for example, where there had been an accompanying maternal depression, an absent parent, or in general not good-enough mothering. Another precursor of the more severe reaction was an uncertain and fluctuating outline of the body as a consequence of birth defect, severe bodily illness, or surgical intervention. Initially, on observing the anatomic difference between the sexes, these toddlers seemed to show a shocklike reaction; they exhibited a fixed staring frequently punctuated by uneasy laughter. This was usually followed by repeated references to the experience, or by an urgency to recreate the experience in actuality over and over again as if there were a need to reinforce the perceptual outline of what they had seen. During this initial shocklike response, the children seemed unable to mobilize any coherent reactions to contain the disruptive force of the experience; afterward, however, a pronounced denial seemed to appear quite regularly. The child became increasingly interested in the anal area and function, in the umbilicus, and in the nipple. She commonly showed a renewed fascination with the examination of eyes, ears, nose, and mouth as well as repeated comparison

of these features with those of her parents. This, of course, has the defensive advantage of shifting attention away from the area of difference to areas or functions which are after all the same in both sexes. In some of the more verbal children, this denial served to organize new speech patterns such as "I have a pair of shoes just like Johnny has."[24]

A significant set of reactions seems to reflect an ongoing intensification of object-loss concerns evoked by the child's observation of the anatomic difference between the sexes. This is reflected in the emergence of sleep disturbances, sometimes of rather intense proportions. Not uncommonly, the children show a sharp upsurge of anxiety about being left by mother; indeed, there is an increased anxious anticipation of being left with a resultant shadowing of the mother. There is often a marked intensification in the use of the transitional object with the implied restitutive effort to blur the sharp sense of separateness. Concomitantly, there is a renewed surge of peek-a-boo games.

Up to this point, the major thrust of development has been toward the differentiation of the self from the object and the consolidation of the self- and object representations. At this juncture, the specific anxieties of the two contiguous phases, object loss and castration, are indissoluble. Janus-like, we do not encounter one without significant resonance on the other plane. The later castration anxiety of the phallic-oedipal phase is genetically linked to that of the early genital phase, and by virtue of this has a direct developmental connection to the anxiety of object loss. In "Inhibition, Symptom and Anxiety", Freud discussed the analogic relation between the anxieties of object loss and castration.[3] Here the attempt has been made to demonstrate that this relationship is more than a formal one. It is developmentally prototypic and exists in actuality. Nevertheless, the castration anxiety of the phallic-oedipal phase, powerful and organized as it may be, normally no longer has the more global resonance of threatened object loss and self-annihilation as it does in the early genital phase. In the intervening period, the self- and object representations have become further solidified so that the constancy of the representation is to a large extent insured.

The awareness of the genital difference, with its underlying resonance of threatened object loss, produces the additional burden of disappointment and anger toward the mother. This, of course, very much increases the child's organizational problem. The anal and early genital zonal arousal opened important body channels for the differential discharge of the aggressive and libidinal currents. In effect, although it created body channels for the splitting of the normal primary ambivalence, this very arousal serves to intensify the ambivalence. As a consequence of the preoedial castration reactions, the milder castration reactions are seen exclusively in those girls. This group makes up over 50 percent of the girls in the study population where there has been good-enough mothering. Along with this there is only a moderate increment in aggression. As development goes on, this seems to facilitate a turning away from the mother as the primary object and leads to an increasing erotization of the relation to the father. This in turn is reflected in a new coyness and coquettishness toward him. This, of course, seems to establish the early developmental precondition for the later normal and positive Oedipus complex of the girl in which the father is the primary object.

In the study population, a severe preoedipal castration reaction developed in 25 percent of the girls, and two boys developed castration reaction during the second year. In such instances, a profound intensification of the ambivalence occurs with a consequent weakening of the developing object schematization. This commonly results in the mobilization of the pathological, fixed defensive splitting of the maternal image with the projection of the hated, bad object. This is reflected in an explosive expansion of object-loss anxiety and a recrudescence of the fear of the stranger. The stranger becomes the feared external, projected personification of the child's potentially destructive rage toward the mother. Ideally, these would be an expansion of independence supported by an increasingly reliable and coherent mental schema of the maternal object. Instead, these children demonstrate a heightened hostile dependence on the actual mother. They literally cling to her, and show sullen mistrust of other adults and children. This, of course, does not augur well for the age-appropriate thrust toward individuation.[10, 24] Moreover, in the later phallic-oedipal phase, this intense, hostile dependence on the mother would seem to foster the relative preponderance of a negative oedipal position.[9]

This sequence makes for a major interference in the normal consolidation of the object schematization. Simultaneously, there is a decided weakening in the normal integration of a coherent schematization of the body-self. This is reflected in a spreading castration hypochondria in which the child reacts to minor cuts and bruises with panic. Not uncommonly, he will anxiously point to imaginary hurts of body or limb. Frequently, the toddler will anxiously avoid or refuse to play with broken toys or crayons. In this general context, there is often the emergence of shifting phobiclike responses to dogs, horses, birds, sounds, and shadows. Perhaps one of the most dramatic reflections of the castration reactions of this period is the emergence of sharply organized penis-envy syndromes in the little girls. They will frequently be observed to hold sticks or toys in the genital area, and the more verbal children will insist that they are part of the body or that they have a penis. Constipation reactions are quite common at this time and have the underlying dynamic significance of holding on to the stool-penis.[10, 24] These tenacious penis-envy reactions do not follow from any inherent grandeur or superiority of the male organ but rather from the observation of phallic incompleteness at a time in life when the genitals have assumed a distinct narcissistic importance in the general body schema as a consequence of the early genital arousal. The little girl's observation that she does not have a penis has the immediate and global significance of threatened object loss and body dissolution.

In many of these children, an infantile fetish emerges as the heightened aggressivization of the child's functioning frequently interferes with the basic attachment to the transitional object. It can be shown that this is a true fetish which has a clear dynamic and genetic continuity with the fetishistic perversions of later life in that it serves to bolster and supplement the body schema, particularly the genital outline of the body. This reparative construct is precipitated and split off as a result of the undermining of the sense of body integrity which follows from the severe preoedipal castration reactions consequent upon the observation of the anatomical difference between the sexes. In the little girl, the fetish object serves to support the illusion of phallic completeness; in the little boy, it serves to deny the absence of a penis on the mother. Moreover, in his case, it also bolsters the genital outline of his body. An inevitable confusion is engendered by the presence of two competing genital schemata—the tactile, visual, sensorimotor schema of his own body and that which arises through the primary identification with the visual percept of his mother's genitals.[23, 21, 13, 12] It may even be that the infantile fetish and fetishistic phenomena are much more common than has generally been realized. Perhaps in all but the most severe preoedipal castration reactions, the young child's reliance on the fetish as a supplement to the body schema is ultimately diffused through its extension into play, fantasy, character formations, and other less concrete defensive forms. It may be that the fetish goes on to become an obligate prop to later sexual functioning only in those children who develop unusually severe preoedipal castration reactions as a consequence of major instability in the basic self and object schemata or if the children experience some further major castration insults during the phallic-oedipal phase.

The intense hostile aggression in these children arises as a result of the early disturbance in the mother-child relationship, with considerable increments of aggression as a consequence of the severe, preoedipal castration reactions. Ordinarily, the anal and early genital zones serve as body channels for the normal, temporary splitting of the primary ambivalence in the service of facilitating further consolidation of the self and object schemata. In these children, however, this splitting results in an intensification of hostile aggression and hence in persistent ambivalence toward the object. This basically unstable state of affairs serves to mobilize a relatively fixed and pathological defensive splitting of good and bad object representations, which interferes with the development of object constancy in a fundamental way. This then would establish the basic condition for the broad class of narcissistic disorders in contrast to normal development, or the neurotic disorders, both of which are based on that signal human achievement of self and object constancy.

The intense ambivalence in these children not only has the effect of weakening the developing self and object schemata, but seems also to mobilize a variety of pathological defenses, all of which are central to the narcissistic disorders. There is the basic, relatively fixed defensive splitting of the good and bad object representations. In addition, there is a ubiquitous, intense sadomasochistic erotization of aggression indicated by pronounced teasing and a tendency to masturbate when frustrated or angered. Another defense which is almost universally mobilized is bound in body reactions. This is the basic mechanism involved in psychosomatic disorders and hypochondriacal states.[19, 22] The adaptive value of even these highly compromising defenses is that they serve to blunt the heightened aggressive force which, while operating within the psychological sphere, threatens to absolutely destroy even the rudiments of the self and object world which are literally crucial for human existence.

The normal resolution of the basic instability consequent upon the differentiation process, with its mobilization of a primary ambivalence to the maternal object, is realized in the consolidation of a relative constancy of self and object schemata and a parallel coherence and integrity of ego structures which normally is characteristic of the third year of life. This involves the integration of the good, loved object and the bad, hated object into a relatively stable and unified object representation. This presupposes that circular process by which the object schematization both facilitates and is facilitated by a true transformation of the nature and aim of the sexual and aggressive drives.

Up through the symbiotic stage there is no true differentiation of sexual and aggressive drives. With the differentiation process, the child has to deal with the two discreet drives, sexual and aggressive. The nature of the sexual drive is to incorporate the object in unconscious fantasy as an accretion to the internal milieu of the child. The tendency of aggression, on the other hand, is to destroy the object in unconscious fantasy. The differentiation of the ego allows it to maintain all this on a mental representational plane, that is, in fantasy, rather than in actuality, which involves a shattering and annihilation of self and object structures and the ego as a coherent entity. When the relative stability of the ego and the constancy of the central self and object schemata are insured, the object may be loved without threatening its separateness from the self, and the object may be hated without the immediate danger of the global shattering of the ego and the inner representations of self and object.

REFERENCES

1. FREUD, S., "New Introductory Lectures on Psychoanalysis, Femininity," in *The Standard Edition of the Complete Psychological Works of Sigmund Freud* (hereafter: *The Standard Edition*), vol. 22, pp. 112–135, Hogarth Press, London, 1964.

2. ———, "The Ego and the Id," in *The Standard Edition*, vol. 18, pp. 3–66, Hogarth Press, London, 1961.

3. ———, "Inhibition, Symptom and Anxiety," in *The Standard Edition*, vol. 20, pp. 77–175, Hogarth Press, London, 1959.

4. ———, "Group Psychology and the Analysis of the Ego," in *The Standard Edition*, vol. 18, pp. 67–143, Hogarth Press, London, 1955.

5. ———, "Totem and Taboo," in *The Standard Edition*, vol. 13, pp. 1–162, Hogarth Press, London, 1955.

6. ———, "Three Essays on the Theory of Sexuality," in *The Standard Edition*, vol. 7, pp. 125–243, Hogarth Press, London, 1953.

7. ———, "The Interpretation of Dreams," in *The Standard Edition*, vol. 4, pp. 1–627, Hogarth Press, London, 1953.

8. GALENSON, E., "A Consideration of the Nature of

Thought in Childhood Play," in McDevitt, J. B., and Settlage, C. F. (Eds.), *Separation-Individuation*, pp. 41–59, International Universities Press, New York, 1971.

9. ———, and Roiphe, H., "Some Suggested Revisions Concerning Early Female Development," *Journal of the American Psychoanalytic Association*, 24:29–57, 1976.

10. ———, "The Impact of Early Sexual Discovery on Mood, Defensive Organization, and Symbolization," in Eissler, R. S., et al. (Eds.), *The Psychoanalytic Study of the Child*, vol. 26, pp. 195–216, Yale University Press, New Haven, Conn., 1971.

11. ———, et al., "Disturbances and Sexual Identity Beginning at Eighteen Months of Age," *International Review of Psychoanalysis*, 2:389–397, 1975.

12. Greenacre, P., "The Transitional Object and the Fetish," in Greenacre, P., *Emotional Growth*, vol. 1, pp. 335–352, International Universities Press, New York, 1971.

13. ———, "The Fetish and the Transitional Object," in Eissler, R. S., et al. (Eds.), *The Psychoanalytic Study of the Child*, vol. 24, pp. 144–164, International Universities Press, New York, 1969.

14. Kris, E., "On Preconscious Mental Processes," in Kris, E., *Psychoanalytic Exploration in Art*, pp. 303–318, International Universities Press, New York, 1952.

15. Mahler, M. S., *On Human Symbiosis and the Vicissitudes of Individuation*, vol. 1, *Infantile Psychosis*, International Universities Press, New York, 1968.

16. ———, "Thoughts About Development and Individuation," in Eissler, R. S., et al. (Eds.), *The Psychoanalytic Study of the Child*, vol. 18, pp. 307–324, International Universities Press, New York, 1963.

17. ———, and Goshiner, B. J., "On Symbiotic Child Psychosis: Genetic, Dynamic and Restitutive Aspects," in Eissler, R. S., et al. (Eds.), *The Psychoanalytic Study of the Child*, vol. 10, pp. 195–212, International Universities Press, New York, 1955.

18. ———, Pine, F., and Bergman, A., *The Psychological Birth of the Human Infant: Symbiosis and Individuation*, Basic Books, New York, 1975.

19. Roiphe, H., "Some Thoughts on Childhood Psychosis, Self and Objects," in Eissler, R. S., et al. (Eds.), *The Psychoanalytic Study of the Child*, vol. 28, pp. 131–144, Yale University Press, New Haven, Conn., 1973.

20. ———, "On an Early Genital Phase: With an Addendum on Genesis," in Eissler, R. S., et al. (Eds.), *The Psychoanalytic Study of the Child*, vol. 23, pp. 348–365, International Universities Press, New York, 1968.

21. ———, and Galenson, E., "Some Observations on Transitional Object and Infantile Fetish," *Psychoanalytic Quarterly*, 44:206–231, 1975.

22. ———, "Object Loss and Early Sexual Development," *Psychoanalytic Quarterly*, 42:73–90, 1973.

23. ———, "The Infantile Fetish," in Eissler, R. S., et al. (Eds.), *The Psychoanalytic Study of the Child*, vol. 28, pp. 147–166, Yale University Press, New Haven, Conn., 1973.

24. ———, "Early Genital Activity and the Castration Complex," *Psychoanalytic Quarterly*, 41:334–347, 1972.

25. Schur, M., "The Ego and the Id in Anxiety," in Eissler, R. S., et al. (Eds.), *The Psychoanalytic Study of the Child*, vol. 13, pp. 190–220, International Universities Press, New York, 1958.

26. ———, "Comments on the Metapsychology of Somatization," in Eissler, R. S., et al. (Eds.), *The Psychoanalytic Study of the Child*, vol. 10, pp. 119–164, International Universities Press, New York, 1955.

27. Spitz, R., *The First Year of Life*, International Universities Press, New York, 1965.

28. Winnicott, D. W., "The Use of an Object," *International Journal of Psycho-Analysis*, 50:711–716, 1969.

29. ———, *The Family and Individual Development*, Basic Books, New York, 1965.

30. ———, *The Maturational Process and the Facilitating Environment*, International Universities Press, New York, 1965.

31. ———, "Transitional Objects and Transitional Phenomena: A Study of the First Not-Me Possession," *International Journal of Psycho-Analysis*, 34:89–97, 1953.

9 / Development from One to Two Years: Language Acquisition

Robert Miller

Introduction

Language is the prime example of a rule-directed organization of the ego. It thus offers a special opportunity for tracing early differentiation in ego structure and later ego development. Since it comprises a hierarchy of structures and functions, language takes expression on many levels. This characteristic is amply demonstrated by the variety of definitions which have been suggested for it. These include: language as a system of voluntarily produced symbols;[75] language as a means of communication;[34] language as knowledge of a system of rules;[33] mnemic-language as knowledge of proper usage of a system of rules;[77] language as a specialized and conventialized extension of cooperative activity;[17] language as a mnemonic-representational organization within the ego;[72] and language as a system which mediates between the universe of meaning and the universe of sound.[25] Some of these definitions focus on syntactic aspects of language, some on semantic aspects, and some on pragmatic aspects. Each level of organization (for example, syntactic, semantic, and pragmatic) must be acquired. It is very probable that each has independent beginnings which are then integrated into the more general linguistic system.

General Issues

Several key issues dominate the problem of language acquisition.

1. Children follow principles in the production of language from the utterance of the first word, and probably even before that. "Baby talk" is not simply abbreviated or garbled versions of adult language, but a hierarchal organization, however primitive, which is governed by its own (i.e., nonadult) rules. Infants, like adults, are largely unaware of their knowledge of linguistic rules.

2. The process of language acquisition, although highly variable from child to child in terms of age of onset, extent of vocalization, etc., demonstrates a number of universal characteristics— that is, attitudes toward linguistic rules that are shared by most children. For example, nearly all children approach language with the assumption that word order is systematized rather than arbitrary. The precise system depends upon the language in question. The sequence "the rubber red large ball" is grammatically acceptable in Japanese, but not in English. Such language-particular facts are what children must relate to their universal assumption that word order occurs in a regularized manner. In other words, children are alert to differences in the surface form of sentences and use these to form hypotheses about the underlying logic in the language.

3. Knowledge of the rules governing the proper *use* of language is as central to linguistic competence as is knowledge of syntactic and semantic rules.

4. The relationship between cognitive structures and linguistic structures appears to be a shifting one. In the early stages of language acquisition, cognitive structures precede linguistic structures. The child seems to know what he means to say before he knows how to say it. "The first sentences express the construction of reality which is the terminal achievement of sensorimotor intelligence."[13] [p. 200] At later stages, by five years of age, linguistic structures seem to precede cognitive structures—for example, logical implicators such as "because" and "unless" can be used with grammatical corrections long before the cognitive operations they imply become part of the child's repertoire.

5. This shift may reflect a basic biphasic nature of language acquisition. In the first phase, language originates as a set of rules abstracted from the affectively laden context of jointly regulated activity between mother and child. In the second phase, language acquisition "uncouples" from this affective context and proceeds rapidly (and apparently autonomously) to structural completion by way of a variety of cognitive processes, such as disambiguation, clearing up of semantic novelties, learning from verbal context, and use of specific strategies—for example, paying attention to word order, avoiding exceptions, etc. There is some evidence suggesting that the focal point around which this shift occurs is the attainment of object constancy. Thus, the process of language acquisition can be viewed as a complex interplay between communicative structures and psychic structures. The establishment of preverbal communication between infant and caretaker (as in, for example, the hunger-cry-feed paradigm) encourages differentiation and distancing of self from others. This shift in psychic structure in turn provides the context (separation) and motivation (wish for cleanliness) for the acquisition of language per se, which supports a sense of closeness in two ways— first by being an internalized aspect of the caretaking person, and second by being a route of communicative contact. In turn, acquisition of linguistic structures enhances further psychic differentiation and structuralization.

6. Language as a system of communication differs from nonhuman systems of communication in the following ways:

Language demonstrates *duality of patterning.* Briefly, this refers to a double level of organization in which the basic elements of meaning in the structure of language (morphemes) are composed of smaller sound elements, the distinctive phonetic elements (phonemes), which, though meaningless in themselves, serve to signal differences in meaning. Thus both "cat" and "bat" are morphemes, while the initial "c" and "b" are phonemes. (Words consist of one or more morphemes. For example, the word "sleeping" consists of two morphemes, "sleep" and "ing.") Duality of patterning makes possible the combining of a small and limited set of phonemes into an almost unlimited lexicon.

Also, language demonstrates *productivity*—that is, the capacity to construct an infinite number of new and understandable sentences out of a limited set of existing elements and to do this independently of the organismic state.

Lastly, language demonstrates *displacement*— that is, the capacity to refer to that which is not present in space or time, that which is not perceived, or that which is not true.

7. As a system of symbols, language differs

from nonhuman systems in that the symbols are arbitrary, conventional, and rule-governed.

8. Any comprehensive theory of language acquisition will have to account for a wide variety of observed phenomena. These include the fact that the structure of language is acquired with tremendous rapidity (it is essentially complete by age four or five) without the presence of any consistently complete model, without the undertaking of any specific didactic effort, and often in the face of incorrect models. Furthermore, a child's early syntax is highly structured and regularized, but it is not organized according to the rules of adult grammar. While there is no single line of progression for acquiring different kinds of syntactic structures, the complexity of these structures does follow a regular progression, as does the complexity of verbally expressed semantic notions.

Other observations show that language cannot be acquired simply from watching television, that children talk to inanimate objects and to themselves, that children have different styles of language acquisition (some imitate, some don't; some vocalize a great deal, others little), and that girls generally acquire language faster than boys.

9. In considering the general question of language acquisition, the distinctions between communication, language and speech need to be specified. Although there can occur much overlap between them phenomenologically, they refer to three essentially distinct concepts.

   a. Communication refers to transfer of information.
   b. Speech refers to behavior—specifically the behavior of producing meaningful sounds.
   c. Language refers to knowledge—specifically knowledge of the rules underlying orderly speech production and comprehension.

Processes Involved
in Language Acquisition

BIOLOGICAL DETERMINANTS

Lenneberg[57] has been the foremost proponent of biological determinants of language acquisition. He argues that it is the unique biologically determined structuralization of the human brain that leads to the development of the child's knowledge of how language works. Specific structural attributes of the human brain include lateralization of function (for example, language in the left

hemisphere, spatial orientation in the right hemisphere), and a prolonged maturation process. The specificity of brain structure for human language is demonstrated by nanocephalic dwarfs, who have normal neuronal size and density but a diffuse reduction in number to about 50 percent, leaving them with a number of brain cells found in many lower animals; yet these individuals speak and comprehend language on at least the level of a five-year-old.

Lenneberg also points out that deaf children at age two manage their environment without difficulty. Since language is a very complex behavior, it follows that hearing children must take the step of learning language only because it is "natural" (that is, biologically determined) to do so. There is no evidence, he maintains, that language emerges as a response to experienced need, as a product of purposive striving toward facilitated verbal communication, or because its utility is discovered.

Along these same lines Condon and Sander[27] have reported a remarkable observation. When American infants, from twelve to forty-eight hours of age, were presented with tapes of American, English, and Chinese words, isolated vowel sounds, and tapping sounds, they were observed to move in precise synchrony with, and only with, the articulatory structure of adult speech. Thus, the neonate appears to participate immediately in communication and is not an isolate. Long before the infant engages in speech, he may have laid down the structure of his culture's language system, including syntactic hierarchies; patterns of pitch, stress, and rhythm; and paralinguistic nuances.

Using physiologic parameters (for example, heart rate), Eimas[32] has shown that infants at one month of age and perhaps earlier are able to discriminate segmental speech units. The basis for discrimination is the set of distinctive phonetic features, as it is in adults. For example, the "b" and "c" of "ba" and "ca" can be distinguished, but not the two "b's" of "baby," which are only acoustically different. That is, infants have knowledge of the phonetic feature code despite very limited exposure to speech, little or no ability to articulate these sounds, and no differential reinforcement for this behavior. It would appear that infants enter the world ready to process all (or most) phonetic features including those not in their native tongue.

Certain aspects of infant speech production, as well as speech reception, appear to have biological determinants. Wolff[89] has shown on the sound spectograph that the early cries of infants are differentiated and correspond to certain inner states, for example, the "basic" cry, cry of pain, cry of anger, cry of frustration, cry of gastrointestinal discomfort, and the "faking" cry. (For a more detailed discussion of infant crying, see chapter 5, herein by Emde and Robinson.) Furthermore, it is well kown that infants, even deaf infants, utter all, or most, known phonemes, even those not present in their linguistic surroundings, during the first half of the first year.

SOCIAL FACTORS

Social and environmental factors which may influence language acquisition can be divided into two main categories: characteristics of the patterns of verb interaction in which the child engages, and characteristics of the nonlinguistic environment. Regarding the first category, parents do not seem to correct errors of syntax but rather respond to the truth or falsity of the child's utterance. (On the other hand, parents do correct semantic and phonological errors,[71] such as the word "cat" being used to refer to a dog, or the utterance "poon" being used for the word spoon.) Nor does the grammatical correctness or incorrectness of a child's utterance appear to affect the ability of parents to comprehend the utterance.[16]

Furthermore, there is no evidence that adult expansions of children's utterances aid in language acquisition.[15] Parents regularly gloss and expand upon the incomplete and imperfect utterances of their children. For instance, if a child should say "car fast," the parent might respond with an appropriate expansion, such as, "The car is going fast." It has long been thought possible that expansions of this sort might play a major role in the child's acquisition of language. Cazden,[23] however, carried out a study testing for the effect on young children's speech of deliberately interpolated expansions, and she could demonstrate no significant effect whatever. Nonetheless, because Cazden did not use expansions which provided only morphemes of a complexity within the child's current capabilities, the possibility that expansions might be effective cannot be completely ruled out.

In fact, Frank and Seegmiller,[38] have shown that mothers regularize and simplify their speech to children, using a level of complexity that is about two to three years in advance of the child's, and that mothers are unaware of this process. There is also some evidence suggesting that when mothers provide a great deal of verbal feed-back, children use language predominantly to refer to objects or events in the environment, but when verbal responses from mothers are minimal, language is used more to express needs and feelings.[63] Furthermore, mothers use a very high proportion of questions in their speech to children, perhaps as a means of drawing children into dialogue.[73]

Regarding the second category, Kagan[53] has demonstrated that when mothers talk to their four-month-old infants, college-educated mothers (as opposed to high-school-educated mothers) provide more "distinctive vocalization"—that is, when talking to their infants, these mothers less often provide simultaneous tactile or kinesthetic stimulation. College-educated mothers as a group have children whose language develops faster, but a causal relationship with "distinctive vocalization" has not been demonstrated.

Mothers who are permitted to be with their newborn infants round the clock as opposed to the regular nursery routine, have been found on follow up two years later to ask more questions of their infants, to use more adjectives, to use longer utterances, and to use fewer commands. Thus, language acquisition may be differentially shaped by events in the newborn period.[70]

Bernstein[7] has suggested that nonlinguistic factors in child rearing and schooling control the development of the use of language in context-bound or context-free ways, such that working-class English children demonstrate the former and middle-class children the latter. He has also demonstrated differential use of language between five-year-old girls and boys of the working class (the girls show greater complexity of noun phrase) and relates this to the different role-set for the girls. He suggests that the range of roles a child learns may effect his/her ability to use language.

IMITATION AND RULE FORMATION

Imitation has been strongly implicated in various theories of language acquisition. Piaget[65] especially has presented arguments that the development of representation in general is an outgrowth of imitation. In support of the role of imitation, it can be shown that between the ages of two to six years, linguistic imitation is in advance of comprehension which, in turn, is in advance of production. On the other hand, it is known that while some mothers attempt to elicit imitation, others do not. Some children imitate a great deal, others hardly at all, and some lexical items seem to be imitated before comprehension, but others only after comprehension.

Intonation patterns do, indeed, seem to be imitated very early. In Chinese, pitch contrasts are mastered by age twenty-eight months. Mastery of segmented forms (phonemes, words), however, seems to be governed by rule formation rather than imitation. First grammars are structured and rule-governed, but are not simple reductions of adult grammars. Children, for example, persist in using nonadult forms such as "feets," "it broked," "all gone sticky," "more page," and "where I can put them," in spite of concerted parental efforts to have them imitate the correct forms. In Russian, children produce typical rule-governed word orders in the face of an adult model which has highly variable word order. Furthermore, when asked to imitate a sentence such as "Where can I put them," a child seems to filter it through his own rule system and produce "Where I can put them." This suggests that small children are constrained in the number of operations they can perform in generating a sentence, and that they are unable to imitate structures that they are not already capable of producing spontaneously.[80] Nevertheless, recent evidence suggests that in some instances, especially under the age of three, new words and new grammatical forms are used spontaneously only after they have first been used imitatively.[73]

Even in the realm of phonetics, where imitation seems fundamental, there is evidence that other processes are at work. For example, distinctive features are observed entering a child's language systematically. Thus, when the contrast "p" and "b" occurs, other voiced/voiceless contrasts (for example, "t" and "d," "s" and "z") occur at the same time.

CONDITIONED RESPONSES

Stimulus-response models of language have been popular. The model of grammar most frequently proposed is the left-to-right probabilistic model in which the occurrence of each word is held to be determined by the immediately preceding word or group of words. Such a model, however, does not explain a word string such as "Colorless green ideas sleep furiously," which though bizarre and without transitional probabilities between words can be recognized as a grammatical sentence. Nor does it account for a sentence such as "Rapid righting with his uninjured hand saved from loss the contents of the capsized canoe," in which comprehension of an early word depends on occurrence of much later words. And finally, it cannot explain a sentence that has two possible meanings, for example, "They are visiting firemen."

COMPREHENSION

Semantic features seem to play an important part in the evolution of grammatical classes and in the order of acquisition of grammatical markers. For example, the suffix "ing," the article "a," and the modifier "some" are all formal class markers in adult grammar, but children seem to select these forms on a semantic basis, "ing" meaning action, "a" meaning a contoured object, and "some" meaning material. The suffix "er" can be used to form the conversion "big" to "bigger" long before the conversion "farm" to "farmer," presumably because of the greater shift of meaning in the latter. For the same reason, the past tense is learned prior to the conditional, though formally they are of the same complexity. The suffix "s" for pluralization appears with the word "many." Gender, one of the least semantically based markers, is also one of the last to be learned.

MOTIVATION

Aspects of motivation will be considered in later sections.

Models of Language Acquisition

Two contrasting kinds of theories have been proposed to explain the shift from prelinguistic babbling to the first use of sound for making reference and describing relationships—those that suggest an innate predisposition on the part of the human infant to acquire language, and those that suggest that linguistic knowledge, like all knowledge, is derived from experience. None of the proposed models fully accounts for all the known aspects of language acquisition.

CHOMSKY

Chomsky's theory[26] of generative grammar, while constructed to describe adult linguistic competencies, turned out to have important implications for child language acquisition. His theory of language is based on the fundamental assumption that language is knowledge—knowledge specifically of grammatical structure. The assumption stems from the fact that sentences are, by and large, novel events, and this necessitates the formation of something psychologically equivalent to a system of rules on the basis of which linguistic intuitions can be made, such as intuitions of: (1) grammatical (The dog looks terrifying vs. The dog looks lamb); (2) grammatical relations (John is easy to please vs. John is eager to please); (3) sentence relations (The President makes decisions vs. Decisions are made by the President); and (4) ambiguity (Visiting relatives can be a nuisance).

Chomsky's initial formulation consisted of a phrase-structure grammar, in which a sentence (intuitively defined) could be broken down into or formed from its constituent elements (intuitively defined), such as verb phrase or noun phrase. These rules of formation, however, did not explain the relationship between certain sentences in which surface elements had been rearranged, such as, "The boy hit the ball," and "What did the boy hit?" Thus, phrase-structure rules, which generated deep structures (for example, the underlying, fundamental sentence structure, usually of simple, declarative, affirmative form) were supplemented by rules of transformation, which converted deep structure into surface structure.

Chomsky postulated that this knowledge of grammatical structure was innate on the grounds that every child rapidly develops a complete grammatical competence despite incomplete and even incorrect samples, without specific instruction, and prior to full intellectual development. The work of Lenneberg,[57] indicating a set of biological peculiarities that accounts for the presence of language in man and only man, gave strong support to this view.

For all its brilliant insights, Chomsky's model is open to a number of criticisms. One is that his theories, derived as they are from ideal adult sentences, do not fit the characteristics of child language. In fact utterances made by infants often seem governed more by semantic relationships than grammatical ones—a child might say "boom bell" when a bell rings but "bed boom" when he falls from a bed.[79] Infants also have the cognitive and physiologic capacity to make two-word syntactic combinations significantly earlier than they actually do so.[9]

A completely different line of criticism comes from the functionalist position that the uses of language are central to the understanding of how it is acquired.[17, 68] In this tradition, language is regarded in relation to behavior generally, rather than as a formal set of rules, and meaning is regarded in terms of effectiveness in achieving the speaker's intention, rather than in terms of good grammatical form, or truth, or falsity. In short,

linguistic competence is equated with communicative competence rather than syntactic competence. The contrast between these two approaches is made clear by comparing Bruner's claim that "communication, then, must be learned and must depend upon a reciprocal code that precedes language proper" (p. 8)[18] with Chomsky's claim that "language acquisition is based on the child's discovery of what from a formal point of view is a deep and abstract theory . . . many of the concepts and principles of which are only remotely related to experience (p. 58).[26]

SPEECH ACTS

One particular formulation of communicative competence which has lent itself to the study of language acquisition is speech act theory, which takes the speech act rather than the sentence as the basic or minimal unit of linguistic communication.[78] Speech acts are acts such as making statements, giving commands, making promises, predicating, and referring, etc. According to speech act theory, the essential part of the meaning of any sentence is its potential for conveying the intent of the speaker to the hearer. For example, the intent of the utterance "Can you pass the salt?" does not correspond to its interrogative grammatical form. In other words, linguistic competence is a matter of knowing how to perform speech acts.

Speech acts can be further characterized by their several elements. These include the "locutionary element," roughly corresponding to the conceptual content or (verbal) proposition of the utterance and the part of the utterance consisting of referring or predicating, and the "illocutionary element," which indicates how the utterance is to be taken (indicated in a variety of ways, for example, by word order, stress, verb mood, etc.).

Developmentally, speech acts evolve out of the neonate's early cries which, within the first week or two, can be differentiated in respect to various inner states—for example, pain, hunger, or gastrointestinal distress. The communicative nature of these cries is essentially created by the caretaker's consistent response to them as if they were communications rather than simple undirectional expressions of inner state. During the next six to eight months, vocalizations become progressively more differentiated. In this stage, they have the same physical characteristics in all languages studied, and are associated with the same general affective states, such as pleasure, recognition, etc.[28] In addition, throughout the child's first year, there is growing differentiation of his responses to the intonational features of adult speech, for example, rising versus falling contours, friendly versus unfriendly voices, male versus female voices, statement versus question intonation.[62]

Around nine to ten months of age, along with the first production of recognizable words, comes the first production of adultlike prosodic features (for example, intonation, pitch, intensity, duration, pause, contour, etc.). These vocalizations, for example, prosodic patterns, are relatively stable and discrete and suggest increasingly specific interpretations, such as "thank you" or "all gone," greeting, answering, questioning, etc. Hence they function as "primitive" elocutionary elements, indicating how the utterance is to be taken. In these early stages, they are not used consistently; they are frequently used without a word-form, either alone or with gesture; and a specific pattern will not be used with word-forms associated with other patterns. In the course of the next year (approximately, the second year of life), "primitive" illocutionary elements stabilize their functioning. They are paired consistently with intent; they are used predominantly in association with word-forms; and they can be transferred to new word-forms. Their presence implies only a contrastive system to convey different intents, not an underlying syntactic structure.

The propositional component of the adult speech act is derived from the differentiation of preverbal cognitive schema and their subsequent association with words. Thus, identifiable cognitive notions, such as disappearance, recurrence, and "upness" come to be specified by words such as "gone," "again," and "up." Such single word utterances do *not* partake of grammar since they indicate the presence only of cognitive categories, not linguistic categories. (A linguistic category is a collection of words that forms a class in so far as these words relate to other classes of words. Thus, the words (cognitive categories) "Mommy," "Daddy" and "Baby" form a certain class and mean the same thing in relation to other classes of words). As with "primitive" illocutionary elements, single word utterances undergo an evolution, becoming increasingly context free (for example, horses will be named in the city as well as the country) and semantically stable (for example, the phenomena of under-inclusion and over-inclusion of the appropriate referent—such as calling all four-legged animals dogs—diminishes.)

Even the first two- and three-word strings do not represent grammar because they are not dependent on the relationships of grammatical classes of words to each other. An utterance such as "more milk" does not necessarily demonstrate an underlying rule system.[10] The combination depends on context and the meaning of *individual* words rather than rule governed order of classes of words.

Thus, two developmental lines are proposed, one from cry to prosody to illocutionary force, and the other from preverbal cognitive schema to word to proposition. Just as individual words imply a cognitive category before they indicate a linguistic category, prosodic features imply an affective intent before they indicate a linguistic intention or attitude. Ultimately, relatively stable forms of words are used in conjunction with relatively stable forms of prosody to form primitive speech acts, for example the word "book" with rising terminal pitch to indicate a request for the book.

Development of primitive speech acts has been related to infant play by Bruner.[18] He suggests that since effectiveness in achieving the speaker's intention will depend on learning to use the conventions and rules of a particular subculture, the initial learning of language will be heavily influenced by the context of mutual interaction undertaken by mother and infant, and a knowledge of the requirements and structure of such interaction will be prerequisite to effective intentionality. Bruner suggests that the ritualized, reciprocal mother-child interchanges in play provide the context for drawing the child's attention to communication itself, to the structure of the acts in which communication takes place, and to the (maternal) utterances that accompany these acts.

The claim of speech act theory is that the use of "primitive" speech acts is necessary (but not sufficient) for the acquisition of syntax. Words (as cognitive categories) and prosody are inputs to syntax in that most of the conceptual notions and illocutionary elements which are expressed in combined form in early syntax have already been expressed separately as word and prosody in primitive speech acts.[29] For example, the concepts and attitudes contained in the grammatical utterance "me want book" occur in the primitive speech act of the word "book," uttered with rising contour to indicate request.

What speech act theory does *not* account for on the route to syntax is the acquisition of grammatical categories. Dore proposes an hypothesis in which he supplements the development of speech acts with inborn, biologically determined capacities to refer and to predicate. Bruner, however, has advanced the intriguing idea that the universal agent—object structure of language is isomorphic with the structure of action. The regulation of joint activity between infant and mother gives rise to a conceptual framework. The child then gains his knowledge of syntax by virtue of its correspondence with this framework. (See also section, "Transition from One Word to Syntax.")

The speech act approach to language acquisition, though incompletely worked out, has several points to recommend it: (a) it accounts for the well-known impression that in the acquisition process some children use language predominantly to refer (the "namers") while other use language predominantly to express (the "vocalizers"); (b) it provides a context for Vygotsky's[86] view that true language is the result of the confluence of two independent lines of development, pre-verbal thought and pre-intellectual speech; (c) it focuses on the distinction between referential meaning, relational or combinatorial meaning, and intentional meaning; (d) it provides a means of investigating communicative and syntactic competencies at the same time; and (e) it takes only observed phenomena for analysis, not inferred deep structure.

PIAGET

Piaget,[65] like the speech act theorists and sociolinguists, views language acquisition as a dependent process, but dependent on development of the symbolic function as opposed to the communicative function. The symbolic function (as manifested in different modes of representation—linguistic, graphic, mental imagery, imaginary play, and deferred imitation) arises out of the progressive separation of signifier from signified. It awaits the development of specific cognitive functions, namely: object constancy and the related categories of space, time, and causality; separation of action from object; and distinguishing internalized actions from physical and causal attributes of objects on which the action was exercised.

Before the symbolic function is attained, speaking a word constitutes only one of many motor attributes by which the child comes to know the object. These first utterances resemble personal symbols (for example, the use of a broom handle as if it were a baby's bottle) in their mobility of content, which is based on the infant lifting a dynamic property of an object out of the total context, assimilating it to a sound, and then generalizing it to events with similar dynamic properties. Thus, in one case "aplu" indicated, in sequence: departure, throwing away, falling, out

of reach, reciprocal giving and taking, and finally, starting over again.

Language ceases to be merely an accompaniment of action in progress only when it can be used to reconstruct or evoke past action, which requires the capacity to differentiate signifier from signified. As this capacity develops, deferred imitation begins and soon constitutes the main transition between the sensorimotor and the symbolic function.

Sinclair,[79] a Piagetian psycholinguist, proposes specific acquired cognitive precursors for the innate universals postulated by Chomsky. Thus, the invariant meaning of the base structure through various transformations derives from object permanence, the recursive nature of sentences derives from embedding one action schema into another, and concatenation of words derives from temporal and spatial ordering.

In another interesting experiment, Sinclair[80] attempted to demonstrate that the nearly universal grammatical order of subject-verb-object develops from prior cognitive strategies—i.e., is not innate. By asking children of various ages to interpret three-word combinations of the nature noun-verb-noun, noun-noun-verb, and verb-noun-noun, she showed that, according to age, children chose different strategies of interpretation. First, the noun nearest the verb was taken as agent, then it was taken as recipient, and finally proximity to the verb lost interpretive importance. The relative order of the two nouns became differentiating, the first being agent and the second recipient. Thus, she claims the linguistic universal to be constructed, not innate.

VYGOTSKY

Historically, Vygotsky[86] developed his theory of language acquisition in response to Piaget's. For Piaget, earliest speech was egocentric, a passive running accompaniment of activity, unintended for others, and essentially without function. It slowly atrophied, to be replaced by social speech. For Vygotsky, earliest speech was social and communicative, with global functions that later became differentiated. He believed egocentric speech originated through differentiation from social speech. He tried to demonstrate this by showing that the production of egocentric speech dropped radically when there was no possibility of being understood—for example, in a room full of deaf children. Vygotsky also believed that egocentric speech acquired the important function of being an instrument of thought in ordering reality and in planning solutions to problems. He tried to demonstrate this by showing that when a child's efforts at problem solving were interfered with, his production of egocentric speech almost doubled.

Thus, he viewed egocentric speech as a crucial transitional form having the function of inner speech but remaining similar to social speech in its expression. As egocentric speech, initially identical in structure with social speech, is transformed into inner speech, it becomes progressively less coherent, less complete, and less frequent (more internalized).

PSYCHOANALYTIC MODELS

No adequate model for language acquisition has yet been formulated within the psychoanalytic framework. In fact, "the only explicit psychoanalytic statement about language learning is that mechanical associations are formed between auditory traces of words and the sensory traces of things by the laws of frequency, contiguity, and effect,"[88] implying a direct correspondence between objective event, the event as registered in memory, and the recalled event. This, of course, is in contrast to the general psychology of psychoanalysis, which stresses the activity of the organism as a crucial factor in organizing experience. Wolff argues that in order to give an adequate description of the human capacity for representation and language, a priori organizing structures independent of antecedent experience must be postulated. He suggests Erikson's concept of organ mode[33] as analogue of Piaget's sensorimotor schema which could replace the trace conception of memory and still be compatable with instinct theory.

Another main theme of psychoanalysis has been that the acquisition of language, through its external manifestation as speech, derives from the need for closeness in the face of the ongoing separation individuation process by being an internalization of the caretaking person, and by being an avenue of communicative contact. The original experiences of gratification provided by the mother are replaced, as psychological separation increases, with the sounds made by the mother. In this identification, the child becomes able to replace actively by way of sound the original passive gratification. Hence, the earliest relationships between child and mother should have a decisive influence on the child's acquisition of and ability to use language. This is the so-called "inner core" of language described by Greenson.[44] In deaf infants who have been aided for sound in the first eighteen months of life, it has been observed that progress in acquiring oral language was more closely associated with the affective aspects of the mother-child relationship than with the specifics of the mother's language or language use.[45] This finding supports the psychoanalytic notion that language represents an internalization of the caretaker in the face of object loss.

Little is stated about the acquisition of grammatical structures in the psychoanalytic literature. Balkanyi[2] has tried to relate linguistic rules (syntactic, semantic, and pragmatic) to the role of the superego as guardian of conventions. Yet it seems clear that first grammatical structures are developmentally pregenital. The following formulation attempts to relate first grammar to object relations and superego precursors.

In Mahler's scheme of separation-individuation,[51] cathexis of the mental representation of the mother leads to object constancy. The establishment of object constancy is important for language acquisition in three respects: (1) it provides the basis for language constancy, i.e., the permanence of structure of the basic linguistic unit, the morpheme; (2) it indicates a separation of signifier from signified, an important component of the symbolic process; and (3) it provides the groundwork for words to become signals of signals (i.e., words as signals for concepts) and thus to release mentation from the immediacy of the perceptually present, either inner or outer.

Cathexis of the mental representation of the "self" however, lags somewhat behind that of the "other." As Jacobson[49] describes it, "the distinction between objects can probably proceed more rapidly and consistently than the distinction between self and object, because perception of the external world is easier than self-perception" (p. 60). In other words, to cathect his own mental representation, a child has to separate the mental representation of the self from his actual, concrete self, whereas this is not true for a mental representation of the mother. With growing cathexis of self-representation, an important condition is progressively approximated—two symbols (mental representations) standing in relationship to each other. This can be viewed as the affective phase of language acquisition in which rules governing the use and structure of language are abstracted from the affectively laden context of jointly regulated activity between mother and child. Its emergence hinges upon the establishment and maintenance of object constancy and "self-constancy." In the subsequent cognitive phase of language acquisition, rule formation "uncouples" from its prior affective context and proceeds rapidly (and apparently autonomously) to structured completion. It gets there by way of a variety of cognitive processes, such as disambiguation, clearing up of semantic novelties, learning from verbal context, paying attention to word order, avoiding exceptions, etc.[17]

The preceding formulation is congruent with several other analytic propositions concerning language acquisition, including the roles attributed to the self-observing attitude of superego precursors,[87] to the third ego organizer of Spitz in which the ego directs aggression upon itself,[82] and to the process of identification with the aggressor.[40] Together, these formulations provide an explanation for the long delay between the appearance of first words and the appearance of first word strings. They are given further substance by both systematic and anecdotal clinical findings. For example, Steingart and Freedman,[83] in advancing the general hypothesis of a relationship between stages of syntactic competence and stages of object relations, have shown that as paranoia increases in adults, use of the other as subject-of-sentence increases, as does use of conditional sentences, while as schizophrenic disorganization increases, use of self as subject-of-sentence increases as does the occurrence of fragmented sentences. Fraiberg and Adelson[37] have described the grammatical usage of the pronoun "I" in a blind child only after she could use a symbolic substitute for herself in her imaginary play. Wyatt[90] has conducted a study which demonstrated a pattern between language disturbance and unresolved separation anxiety, and Kaiser[54] has several case reports to the same effect. Bergman[6] has described the parallel development of language and object relations in the treatment of an autistic child.

Descriptions of First Language

PREVERBAL ROOTS

Some of the advances in the *production* and *reception* of sound in the prelinguistic era cluster around levels of ego organization and object relations in an interesting way. The appearance of the smiling response (indication for Spitz's first ego organizer[82]) is associated with the beginning of vocal response to mother's voice, increased attention to mother's face (specifically to the detailed interior features) while she speaks, and the first production of sound to express pleasure. These behaviors would seem to indicate a cathexis of the vocal-auditory apparatus.

The period of stranger anxiety (evidence of Spitz's second ego organizer) is associated with the beginning shift to production of only native phonemes and with the production of specific (familiar) intonation patterns, suggesting a kind of "stronger response" to nonnative aspects of the child's own utterances. During this period, decreased babbling, decreased vocal play between mother and infant, and the first imitations of mother's mouth movements also occur.

Subsequently, a burst in babbling takes place around the time the first transitional object appears. By the very nature of the vocal-auditory apparatus, with its built-in feedback system, babbling, and ultimately speech, becomes the transitional object par excellence, the link between me and not-me, inside and outside, that can be used by the infant in an illusory way to bring his mother closer or to project himself into the environment.

Spitz's third ego organizer is manifested by the appearance of the word "no," marking a shift from immediate drive discharge through action to delay of discharge via communication. Use of the word "no" represents the first semantic event. Intrapsychically, it indicates a restructuring of the ego on the basis of an identification with the aggressor (parent) as "frustrater" as well as "watcher." Shift of aggressive cathexis at this time also leads to the capacity for abstraction, according to Spitz.

As for preverbal aspects of *dialogue*, Bateson[4] has observed alterations in noncry vocalization between mother and two-month-old infants that match the constraints of adult conversational dialogue (for example, initiation and termination, alternation, pacing, etc.). In addition, Jaffe, Stern, and Perry[50] have described regularities in the gross temporal pattern of four-month-old infant-mother gaze behavior which are identical to those found during adult conversation. Such regularities may represent a universal formal property of dyadic communication which is detectable long before the onset of speech.

In addition, recent work by Brazelton et al.[12] and Stern and Beebe[84] based on frame by frame analysis of videotaped interactions between infants and mothers has demonstrated the presence of an elaborate "microlevel" interaction between them by as early as three weeks. The "interaction is a mutually regulated system in which both partners modify their actions in response to the feedback provided by their partner" (p. 147).[12] Because the mother-infant interaction brings affective synchrony and occurs in a cyclical rhythm, Brazelton believes that it is an important mechanism for homeostasis. He also suggests that the quality of the interaction can enhance the infant's capacity for attending to his mother's important cues.

Trevarthan,[85] also using videotape techniques, has demonstrated that within eight weeks of life, infants develop behaviors indicating that they perceive objects and people differently. The acts of infants responding to people include "prespeech," distinctive movements of lips and tongue indicating a rudimentary form of speaking, with or without sound. "Prespeech" is often accompanied by "handwaving," movements that are developmentally related to the gestures of adult speech. "We are now sure that, not withstanding the importance of cultural development in the formation of language, both of speech and of gestures, the foundation for interpersonal communication between humans is 'there' at birth and is remarkably useful by eight weeks" (p. 66). From the discovery of "embryonic" speaking in the social animation of infants, Trevarthan concludes that language is embedded in innate context of nonverbal communication. The long delay in the onset of speech does not depend on the formation of cognitive structures as Piaget holds, but rather indicates a need for development of communication without words before words can be used to signify.

Concerning aspects of *linguistic environment*, infants whose mothers respond to crying, cry less in the second half of the first year and use more of a variety of ways to communicate than do infants whose mothers ignore crying.[5] Infant vocalizations increase if responded to vocally by mother, but gaze aversion results if she does not respond.[11, 69] As early as two months, infants in orphanages show diminished vocalization, impoverishment of intonations, and later inability to direct vocalizations at people.[66] Infants of mothers who use speech a great deal develop a large naming vocabulary.[63]

As for the *influence of gender*, it is generally agreed that girls acquire language faster than boys. While this may have biological determinants, various interactional patterns may be at work, for example, mothers are more likely to respond to girls in the first year of life by talking to them, to boys by touching them;[73] fathers treat girls more gently and with more talking than they do boys;[85] boy infants tend to initiate dialogue more than girls;[85] girls are more likely to become affectively aroused by an interesting event and more likely than boys to vocalize as an accompaniment.[53]

TRANSITION FROM BABBLING TO FIRST WORDS

Between babbling and first words there exist developmentally important transitional structures called phonetically consistant forms (PCF's).[30] Structurally, these are readily isolable units bounded by pauses (unlike babbling), which exhibit phonetic elements more stable than babbling but less stable than words, for example, "ubeebu" or "upeeba" or "upeebu." Functionally, four categories can be identified: affect expressions, indicating expressions, appeals, and grouping expressions (reflecting and fusion between subjective stage and aspects of the environment). PCF's are theoretically important because linguistic reference may result from the confluence of the different function categories, possibly in association with development of the pointing gesture.[20]

THE ONE-WORD STAGE

Controversy about the one-word, or holophrase, stage abounds, and many formulations have been offered, such as; (1) the holophrase is a name for a concept; (2) it is an elliptical sentence; (3) it is a part of speech; and (4) it is a primitive speech act.

The main controversy concerns the sentential or nonsentential nature of the holophrase, since this has important implications for nativist versus empiricist viewpoints. The fact that children seem to comprehend syntactic relations before they produce them, that they use contrastive intonations with the same word, and that there are possible cognitive limitations on actual sentence production in speech (for example, memory span), have all been used to support the notion of innate grammaticality of holophrases,[60] or the idea that syntax resides in the non-verbal events (such as affect and gesture) associated with an utterance.[43, 47] On the other hand, there is evidence that what children comprehend in the one-word stage are not syntactic relations, but stressed lexical items; that intonation patterns are contrastive for intent rather than for semanticity; and that children are capable of producing two-word utterances that are not syntactic (by virtue of either absence of constraints on word order, use of multiple prosodic envelopes, or use of a word form lacking a referent) long before they produce two grammatically related words.[10] These latter observations suggest that syntax must be learned as a linguistic means of coding developmentally prior sensorimotor concepts. This view is given support by the fact that virtually every appropriate study shows that first syntax consists of a basic set of two-term relations (such as agent-action) expressing the construction of reality which is the end achievement of sensorimotor intelligence.[13]

TRANSITION FROM ONE WORD TO SYNTAX

Between the one-word stage and the first two-word combination in a single prosodic envelope in which the relation between the words determines meaning (at least in part)—i.e., between holophrase and first syntax—transitional presyntactic devices occur.[31] These are utterances that consist of more than one item, so they are not single words, but do not meet the criteria for syntax. Examples would be "car car," or "te bottle." These devices appear to serve a bridging function. They allow for a transition from single-word utterances to syntax without requiring the child to deal with the conceptual content. They reflect, as do PCF's the partially independent development of sound and meaning. The hypothetical structural unit for relating meaning to phonetic output without requiring specifically syntactic knowledge is termed the syntagma.)

One of the complicating features of this period is that the first word combinations to appear, such as "Mommy sock" or "more milk," are not grammatical. They rather represent a capacity to juxtapose two cognitive categories in one utterance. While this is a psychological requirement for the appearance of sentences, it provides no evidence that the child has the capacity to employ linguistic categories or rules. The nature of the relationship between the two words is derived either from the context of the utterance—so that "Mommy sock" may be used by the child when his mother is dressing him or when he notices a sock belonging to his mother—or the constant meaning of one of the words, such as "more."

How children go about forming grammatical categories remains one of the mysteries of language acquisition. Innate structures, inductive reasoning, and an isomorphism between the structure of action and the structure of language are some of the hypotheses which have been put forward. There is virtually no observational data upon which to base a compelling argument. (See also Speech Acts, p. 132.)

WORD ORDER

Use of correct, adult word order by the child, when present, can be taken as a discriminating response giving evidence that a child intends certain semantic relations, even though it might not necessarily signal semantic differences (for example, the utterance "Christy room" indicated place when "room" was the stressed word but possession when "Christy" was the stressed word). Children do not seem obligated to use adult word orders, or any particular word order, to express semantic intent, however. In German, first word orders are much freer than in the adult model, and in Russian, children impose rigid word orders when none exist in the adult model, with the same child sometimes shifting between different self-imposed word orders. Examples from Finland show that some children use free word order, as in the adult model, and others impose their own rules for ordering. In English and Swedish, correspondence with adult word orders is high. In general, the ordering of words seems independent of the order in which events take place.

All children probably pay attention to word order, but they seem to draw different conclusions about it, perhaps based partly on permissible orders in the adult model, partly on the frequency with which parents use certain orders to describe events, and partly on unknown variables of learning.

For the child, the importance of word order probably lies in its being a means of increasing communicative accuracy, rather than as a means of ordering semantic relations.

FIRST GRAMMARS

Whether children grammatically mark their early semantic intentions depends on the complexity of the marking system. For example, a child bilingual for Hungarian and Serbo-Croatian will say the equivalent of "doll drawer" in Serbo-Croatian and "doll into drawer" in Hungarian, reflecting the additional complexity of appropriate case endings in Serbo-Croatian.

Early characterizations of first grammars were descriptive and not semantically based. In "pivot grammars," a small group of high-frequency "pivot" words appears in restricted combinations with a large number of other "open" words. For example, the forms "more car," "more juice," and "more tickle" occur, but not the forms "more more" or "car more."

Another early characterization of infant grammar was "telegraphic speech," designed to describe the strings of contentives (for example, large open word classes such as nouns and verbs) which occur in the absence of functors (small closed word classes such as prepositions and articles), for example, a word string such as "want see cow."

More recent characterizations of grammar have been based on a "rich" interpretation, using the nonverbal context of the utterance to demonstrate that the child was expressing one of a limited set of intended semantic relations. The main examples of "rich" interpretations are Schlesinger's realization rules,[76] Fillmore's case grammar,[36] and Bloom's transformational grammar.[10]

Schlesinger posits semantically based "realization rules" which order preverbal, universal, and cognitively determined concepts into a verbal relationship, generally of correct adult form (though errors occur, such as "apple eat"). First language learning is learning of realization rules for a given community. By directly transforming semantic intent to surface structures, the realization rules not only bypass the level of grammatical deep structure but map semantic relationships (for example, agent or object) onto surface word order without using grammatical classes such as subject, object, etc.

In Fillmore's case grammar, semantic relations are represented in deep structure by labeling the noun or verb with a particular case. Thus, in the sentences "John opened the door" and "The door was opened by John," "John" remains the agent (agentive case) despite shifting position and change from grammatical subject to object. Examples of semantic relationships and their cases include agentive (animate instigator of action), instrumental (inanimate force or object causally involved in the state or action named by the verb), locative (spatial orientation of state or action named by verb), and dative (animate being affected by state or action named by verb). As in Schlesinger's model, semantic intent bypasses grammatical deep structure, but unlike Schlesinger, surface structure is assigned by transformational rules determining grammatical class.

In Bloom's grammar, extrapolated from Chomsky's analysis of adult grammar, grammatical structure is assigned in the base and has formal configurational properties which distinguish semantic roles. This model, unlike the models of Schlesinger and Fillmore, must support the implication of a whole reorganization of knowledge from the sensorimotor to the linguistic level. Additionally, it contains a major flaw, in that it postulates earlier grammatical forms as being more complex than later ones. For example, "mommy sock" has the same derivational base structure as "mommy put on the sock" but it has one more transformational operation, namely a reduction transformation deleting the verb. Nevertheless, Bloom's theory claims validity by being the most widely applicable of all present theories of first grammar (in that it is able to account for question formation, for the division of sentences into constituent parts, and for the distinction between main verb and copular sentences).

Language and Psychic Differentiation

This section will briefly discuss the influence of language on psychic differentiation once early object relationships and early grammar have been established.

THE EGO

Freud originally conceptualized the ego as a coherent organization of mental processes and indicated that "the character of the ego is a precipitate of abandoned object cathexes, and that it contains the history of those object-choices.[11] The relationship between language acquisition, the separation/individuation process, object loss and the capacity to recreate experience has already been discussed in the sections on "preverbal roots of first language," and "psychoanalytic model of language acquisition." Suffice it to add here that the consistent observations that weaning is followed by a spurt in language development and that brief separations from the parents do the same indicate the importance of object loss and internalization for the acquisition of language.

More recently, the elaboration of the concept of autonomous ego functions within ego psychology has led to another line of thought. Edelheit[31] contends that the ego is a vocal-auditory apparatus whose structure and function are determined principally by speech and hearing. His view is derived from a correlation he makes between certain design features of the vocal-auditory system and certain characteristics of the ego. For example, discreteness, i.e., the sharp differentiation of the specific sound categories (phonemes), constitutes a stimulus barrier and helps establish ego autonomy from the environment, while duality of patterning contributes to ego autonomy from the drives. Edelheit further cites studies showing that delayed speech feedback produces panic and confusion in psychotic children, arguing that the psychotic child remains in a primitive (developmentally normal) state of obligatory dependence on his own speech to maintain a sense of self and ego intactness.

While Edelheit's proposal provides important conceptual bridges between language structure and ego structure, it almost completely excludes object relations. From the discussion in previous sections it seems most likely that the acquisition of language emerges out of an interaction between developing object relations (in particular, object constancy) and autonomous ego functions (in particular, cognitive).

The acquisition of linguistic structures influences the functioning and further differentiation of specific ego capacities.

Perception. It is well established that spoken words reinforce typical conditioning processes. Thus, in an experiment in which an infant learns he will find candy under a red box and not under a blue box, he will do so more readily if a verbal cue is given. According to Luria,[59] speech associations influence perception to the extent of bringing about a readjustment of the relevant strengths of stimuli. Thus, when children name objects, they are organizing their acts of perception. Piaget, on the other hand, views linguistic structures as being verbal representations of pre-existing cognitive structures. A possible resolution between the opposing views is suggested by the observation that the naming effect may occur only after the achievement of object permanence.[71]

The Executive Function: Until the infant is twelve to fifteen months old, speech simply facilitates impulse discharge, tending to set off whatever response is "pre-potent" at the moment— for example, once a child begins an activity, instructions to stop may merely increase his activity. At fifteen months of age, verbal instructions given by *others* become specifically directive, but *self*-given verbal instructions continue predominantly to set off non-specific "pre-potent" activities up to the age of four to four and one-half years. Only then do children begin to follow given instructions more effectively if they accompany this action with appropriate vocalizations. That is, only then do they begin responding to the semantic aspect of their own utterences. (This may be related to the finding that sound rather than meaning is the basis for generalization of conditioned responses in the pre-school age group.) As the directive role passes increasingly from the perceptual-motor to the semantic aspect of speech, speech in its external, concrete form becomes superfluous.[58]

Thus, two related shifts take place: direction of behavior passes from perceptual-motor to semantic aspects of speech, and also from external to internal speech.

Memory. The influence of language on memory can be demonstrated by an experiment in which a figure such as 0–0, which might be seen either as eyeglasses or dumbbells, is presented to subjects labeled either as "eyeglasses" or "dumbbell." Subjects tended to reproduce the ambiguous figures to conform better with whichever verbal label was presented to them.[22]

Motility. Greenacre[42] has reported that in patients prone to acting-out, speech was inhibited relatively more than motor discharge during infancy. There is some evidence indicating that hyperactive children have delayed language acquisition.[18]

Thought. There are two major theoretical positions regarding the intellectual functioning of children as it relates to language. One position is based on a "concept-matching" scheme, in which the child learns to match the word he hears with the objects and relations he has long since understood on a nonverbal level. This approach seems essentially valid for a wide range of lexical items and such semantic relations as possession ("Mommy cup"), disappearance ("all gone car"), recurrence ("more milk") and the like.[63]

The other position is based on the idea of "concept-formation," in which the child learns a word and then searches for its referent.[14] This view, which has been most fully developed by the Russian theorists, claims that the child's learning of words is central to his concept development. The word at first directs the processes of attention, abstraction and synthesis of elements and plays the role of means in forming a concept, and later becomes its symbol. There is some evidence to suggest that the "concept-formation" view is valid when the child is confronted by linguistic terms for which there is no perceptually available referent (such as the word "why.")[8]

Thought can be conceptualized as operating along a spectrum ranging from primary process activity (absence of negation, timelessness, pars pro toto) to secondary process activity. Verbalization is, in turn, that function which provides thinking with the basic secondary process mechanisms.[2] (Verbalization here refers to a mental process, not to the verbal production of words). First, verbalization entails naming, and thus negation enters the mental economy (since naming implies A but *not* B). Second, grammar does not permit the simultaneity of the primary process, but only sequence. And third, the word limits freely displaceable energy of the unconscious through its power to ensure meaning, using the bound energy to maintain the separation of signifier and signified. In addition, it is through the process of verbalization that unconscious "thing-presentations" are linked with corresponding "word-presentations," and that the quality of the content of the mind thereby changes from unconscious to preconscious and conscious.[64]

Language as a full instrument of thought awaits the organization of experience into hierarchies isomorphic with its own syntactic structure, for example, causation being isomorphic with the predicate-object relationship. "The outward form only of language is constant; its inner meaning, its psychic value or intensity varies freely with attention, selective interest, also with the mind's general development" (p. 14).[75] Thus, while all known languages are equally complex, the level of cognitive complexity associated with each can vary. Once the isomorphism is established so that linguistic structures can be applied to experience coded in congruent form, it becomes possible to gain surplus meaning from experience by pursuing the implications of linguistic rules.[9]

The theory of linguistic relativity, which states that differences in language structure determine differences in thinking processes, is not supported by Piaget's findings concerning nonverbal cognitive structures, Chomsky's proposition of linguistic universals, and the findings in various psychological and anthropological studies that, while certain descriptive words may not be present in a lexicon, that fact does not exclude the presence of the corresponding concept or perceptual discrimination. "Weak" forms of the theory, currently widely held, merely assert that certain aspects of language can predispose people to think or act one way or another.[81]

Symbolism. Symbols link multitudinous sensory phenomena from the external world to bodily functions, feelings, and parts, and relate these to experiences and objects of gratification or frustration. The genetic origin of this capacity lies in the early differentiation stages of self from other, during which bodily world and outer world establish specific symbolic relationships to each other, so that each can be used to represent the other. Jones's initial formulation[51] made symbolism exclusively defensive, the result of conflict and repression. More recent views[74] suggest that symbolization is a general capacity of the mind, underlying the maintenance of a sense of reality as much as the maintenance of a neurosis, and it may be used by either primary or secondary processes. The difference in the two uses is not fundamentally energic, but object-related—for example, whether gratification is sought from the inner world immediately but transiently, or from

external objects, necessitating delay and communication.

Words arise just as other symbols do, for example, by displacement of affect, but they have special attributes in that the word is conventional, it remains distinguishable from its referent, and the symbolic connections of the word remain conscious. With these attributes, the word forms part of the secondary process and remains directed toward the outside world, communication, and object relations. When used by the primary process, as in dreams or schizophrenia, words lose their differentiating characteristics and are treated like other symbols—they become interchangeable, they become equivalent to their referents, and they acquire unconscious meanings. It seems likely that all disturbances in the capacity for object relations are reflected in impairment of the capacity to use words intelligibly.

Bruner[18] has postulated three different systems for representing information about the world—enactive, iconic, and symbolic—stressing the increasing level of abstractness in each. What may be more to the point, however, is that each system has its own intrinsic organizational properties. The three systems may act in concert through reciprocal feedback to maintain good ego functioning or the boundaries between the systems may serve to foster defensive functioning, to isolate experience, or to impair cognitive functioning.

THE SUPEREGO

The self-observing reflective attitude of superego precursors, originating in identifications with the frustrating parents (i.e., aggressors) enables man to create symbolic language.[87] Reciprocally, at a later stage of development, the auditory sphere, as modified in the direction of a capacity for language, becomes the nucleus of the mature superego by way of its importance in establishing permanent introjections.[48]

Second language learning may either bolster superego repression of infantile conflicts or weaken it to allow previously prohibited impulses to be discharged. For example, Buxbaum[19] describes an analysis in English with a native German woman during which her intense incestuous wishes associated with the recurrent symbol of a sausage were released from repression only when she translated "sausage" into "Blutwurst." A new language provided the ego with an additional defense in accordance with Fenichel's[35] observation, "A person's relation to language is often predominantly governed by super-ego rules." She also mentions two boys with strong foreign accents taken over from their fathers in hostile identifications. These accents disappeared completely once they were able to express their hostility openly.

Verbal expression (speech) thus serves both a discharge function in which tension is released and in which affects become an external reality as well as an internal reality, and a binding function in which the discharge of affect is attenuated.

Inhibition and Expression
of Drives and Affects

Induction of Drives and Affects

Vocalizations initially implement release of affects and tension. Ultimately, according to Freud,[41] the association of vocal activity with word representations creates motor surrogates of action, and speech acquires a signal function and implements reality testing.[55] "The association of affects and drive processes with verbal signs is the first and most important step in the direction of the mastery of the drives."[40] Affects, unlike other unconscious contents of the mind, can reach consciousness directly, i.e., without being associated with word representations. It is through the process of verbalization, in which affects are identified and "put into" words, that they become subject to modulation and delay. Balkanyi[3] suggests that verbalization is indeed that function which provides thinking with basic secondary process mechanisms. The interposition of words delays discharge of affects by distilling them into semantic meaning.

Observations relating to an experiment of nature, congenital deafness, suggest that sound and/or language may play a role in the induction of affects. The deaf adult often shows relatively shallow affect, as well as an undependable sense of object. These characteristics could be due either to deprivation of sound and language experience, or to disturbed mothering, or to both. In reporting the absence of retarded depression (i.e., internalized rage) in deaf adults, Altshuler[1] attributes this finding to distortions in object relationship imposed by the communication barrier. In contrast, in evaluating five deaf preoedipal girls, Freedman and his associates[39] found object relations to vary individually, according with quality of mothering—that is, to be independent of the communication barrier as such. At present, the relationship between language and affect induction remains unclear.

REFERENCES

1. ALTSHULER, K., "Personality Traits and Depressive Symptoms in the Deaf, in J. Wortis (Ed.), *Recent Advances in Biological Psychiatry*, vol. 6, pp. 63–73, 1963.

2. BALKANYI, C., "Language, Verbalization and Superego: Some Thoughts on the Development of the Sense of Rules," *International Journal of Psychoanalysis, 49:* 712, 1968.

3. ———, "On Verbalization," *International Journal of Psychoanalysis, 44:*64–74, 1964.

4. BATESON, M., "Mother-Infant Exchanges: The Epigenesis of Conversational Interaction," in D. Aaronson and R. Rieber (Eds.), *Developmental Psycholinguistics and Communication Disorders*, Annals of New York Academy of Sciences, vol. 263, 1975.

5. BELL, S. M. and AINSWORTH, M. ,"Infant Crying and Maternal Responsiveness," *Child Development, 43:*1171–1190, 1972.

6. BERGMAN, A., "I and You: The Separation-Individuation Process in the Treatment of a Symbiotic Child," in McDevitt, J., and Settlage, C. (Eds.), *Separation-Individuation*, pp. 325–355, International Universities Press, New York, 1971.

7. BERNSTEIN, B., "A Socio-linguistic Approach to Socialization," in Gumperz, J. J., and Hymes, D. (Eds.), *Directions in Socio-linguistics*, pp. 67–93, Holt, Rinehart and Winston, New York, 1972.

8. BLANK, M. and ALLEN, D., "Understanding 'Why'," in M. Lewis (Ed.),*Origins of Intelligence: Infancy and Early Childhood*, Plenum, New York, 1976.

9. BLOOM, L., "One Word at a Time: The Use of Single Word Utterances Before Syntax," Mouton, The Hague, 1973.

10. ———, *Language Development, Form and Function in Emerging Grammars*, MIT Press, Cambridge, 1970.

11. BRACKBILL, Y., "Use of Social Reinforcement in Conditioning Smiling," in Y. Brackbill and G. G. Thompson (Eds.), *Behavior in Infancy and Early Childhood*, Free Press, New York, 1967.

12. BRAZELTON, T. et al., "Early Mother Infant Reciprocity," in *Parent-Infant Interaction, Ciba Foundation Symposium*, No. 3, Elsevier, North Holland, 1975.

13. Brown, R., *A First Language: The Early Stages*, Harvard University Press, Cambridge, 1973.

14. ———, *Words and Things*, Free Press, New York, 1958.

15. ———, Cazden, C., and Bellugi, U., "The Child's Grammar from I to III," in J. Hill (Ed.), *Minnesota Symposium on Child Psychology*, vol. II, University of Minnesota Press, Minneapolis, 1969.

16. BROWN, R. and HANLON, C., "Derivational Complexity and Order of Acquisition in Child Speech," in J. Hayes (Ed.), *Cognition and the Development of Language*, John Wiley, New York, 1970.

17. BRUNER, J., OLIVER, R., and GREENFIELD, P., "Ontogenesis of Speech Acts," *Journal of Child Language, 1(1):3–28*, 1975.

18. ———, *Studies in Cognitive Growth*, John Wiley, New York, 1966.

19. BUXBAUM, E., "The Role of a Second Language in the Formation of Ego and Super-Ego," *Psychoanalytic Quarterly, 18(3):279*, 1949.

20. CALL, J., "Developmental and Executive Aspects of the Pointing Gesture and the Sound 'ush' in a Fourteen-Month Old Infant," in S. Ghosh (Ed.), *Biology of Language*, Academic Press, New York, in press.

21. CAMPBELL, R. and WALES, R., "Study of Language Acquisition" in J. Lyons (Ed.), *New Horizons in Linguistics*, Pelican, Middlesex, 1970.

22. CARMICHAEL, L., HOGAN, H., and WALTER, A., "An Experimental Study of the Effect of Language on the Reproduction of Visually Perceived Form," *Journal of Experimental Psychology, 15:73–86*, 1932.

23. CAZDEN, C., "Acquisition of Noun and Verb Inflections," *Child Development, 39:433–448*, 1968.

24. ———, "Environmental Assistance to the Child's Acquisition of Grammar," doctoral dissertation, Harvard, 1965.

25. CHAFE, W., *Meaning and the Structure of Language*, University of Chicago Press, Chicago, 1970.

26. CHOMSKY, N., *Language and Mind*, Harcourt, Brace, Jovanovich, New York, 1968.

27. CONDON, W., and SANDER, L., "Synchrony Demonstrated between Movements of the Neonate and Adult Speech," *Child Development, 45:456–462*, 1974.

28. CRYSTAL, D., "Prosodic Systems and Language Acquisition," in P. Leon (Ed.), *Prosodic Feature Analysis*, Didier, Montreal, 1970.

29. DORE, J., "Development of Speech Acts," doctoral dissertation, City University of New York, 1973.

30. ———, et al., "Transitional Phenomena in Early Language Acquisition," *Journal of Child Language*, in press.

31. EDELHEIT, H., "Speech and Psychic Structure, the Vocal-Auditory Organization of the Ego," *Journal of the American Psychoanalytic Association, 17:381–412*, 1969.

32. EIMAS, P., "Infants, Phonetic Features and Speech Perception," Paper presented at Symposium on Developmental Psycholinguistics, American Association for Advancement of Science, January 1975.

33. ERIKSON, E. H., *Childhood and Society*, rev. ed., W. W. Norton, New York, 1963.

34. EVELOFF, H., "Some Cognitive and Affective Aspects of Early Language Development," *Child Development, 42(6):1895–1907*, 1971.

35. FENICHEL, O., *Psychoanalytic Theory of Neurosis*, W. W. Norton, New York, 1945.

36. FILLMORE, C., "The Case for Case," in Bach, E., and Harms, R. (Eds.), *Universals in Linguistic Theory*, pp. 1–87, Holt, Rinehart and Winston, New York, 1968.

37. FRAIBERG, S., and ADELSON, E., "Self Representation in Language and Play: Observations of Blind Children," *Psychoanalytic Quarterly, 42:539–562*, 1973.

38. FRANK, S., and SEEGMILLER, M., "Children's Language Environment in a Free Play Situation," Paper presented to Society for Research in Child Development meetings, Philadelphia, 1973.

39. FREEDMAN, D., CANNADY, C. and ROBINSON, J., "Speech and Psychic Structure," *Journal of the American Psychoanalytic Association, 19:765–779*, 1971.

40. FREUD, A., The Ego and the Mechanisms of Defense, Peller, L. (trans.) in Freud's contribution to *Psychoanalytic Study of the Child*, vol. 21, pp. 448–467, 1936.

41. FREUD, S., "Project for a Scientific Psychology," in Bonaparte, M., et al. (Eds.), *Origins of Psycho-Analysis: Letters to Wilhelm Fliess, Drafts and Notes (1887–1902)*, pp. 347–445, Basic Books, New York, 1954.

42. GREENACRE, P., *Trauma, Growth, and Personality*, W. W. Norton, New York, 1952.

43. GREENFIELD, P., SMITH, J., and LAUFER, B., *Communication and the Beginning of Language*, Academic Press, New York, 1973.

44. GREENSON, R., "The Mother Tongue and the Mothers," *International Journal of Psychoanalysis, 31:1–6*, 1950.

45. GREENSTEIN, B., et al., "Mother-Infant Communications and Language Acquisition in Deaf Infants," Final Report, Grant No. OEG-0-72-5339, Office of Education, 1974.

46. HOROWITZ, M. J., "Modes of Representation of Thought," *Journal of the American Psychoanalytic Association, 20(4):793*, 1972.

47. INGRAM, D., "Transitivity in Child Language," *Language, 47:888–910*, 1971.

48. ISAKOWER, O., "On the Exceptional Position of the Auditory Sphere," *International Journal of Psychoanalysis, 20:340–348*, 1939.

49. JACOBSON, E., *The Self and the Object World*, International Universities Press, New York, 1964.

50. JAFFE, J., STERN, D., and PERRY, J., "Conversational Coupling of Gaze Behavior in Pre-linguistic Human Development," *Journal of Psycholinguistic Research, 2:321–329*, 1973.

51. JONES, E., "The Theory of Symbolism," in Jones, E., *Papers on Psychoanalysis*, 5th ed., Bailliere, Tindall and Cox, 1948.

52. KAGAN, J., "Change and Continuity in Infancy," John Wiley, New York, 1971.

53. ———, "On Cultural Deprivation," in Glass, D. C. (Ed.), *Environmental Influences*, Rockefeller University Press and Russell Sage Foundation, New York, 1968.

54. KAISER, S., "Disturbance of Ego Functions of Speech and Abstract Thinking," *Journal of the American Psychoanalytic Association, 10:50–73*, 1962.

55. KLEIN, G., "On Hearing One's Own Voice," in Schur, M. (Ed.), *Drives, Affects and Behavior*, vol. 2, *Essays in Memory of Marie Bonaparte*, pp. 87–117, International Universities Press, New York, 1965.

56. LENNEBERG, E., "On Explaining Language," *Science, 164(3880):65–88*, 1969.

57. ———, "A Biological Perspective of Language," in Lenneberg, E. (Ed.), *New Directions in the Study of Language*, MIT Press, Cambridge, 1966.

58. LURIA, A., "The Directive Function of Speech," in R. Oldfield and J. Marshall (Eds.), *Language*, Penguin, Middlesex, 1968.

59. ———, *The Role of Speech in the Regulation of Normal and Abnormal Behavior*, Liveright, New York, 1961.

60. MCNEILL, D., *Acquisition of Language*, Harper & Row, New York, 1970.

61. MAHLER, M., PINE, F., and BERGMAN, A., *The Psychological Birth of the Human Infant*, Basic Books, New York, 1975.

62. MENYUK, P., "Bases of Language Acquisition: Some Questions," *Journal of Autism and Childhood Schizophrenia, 4(4):325*, 1974.

63. NELSON, K., *Structure and Strategy in Learning to Talk*, Monograph of the Society for Research in Child Development, vol. 38, Nos. 1 & 2, 1973.

64. PELLER, L., "Freud's Contribution to Language Theory," in Eissler, R. S., et al. (Eds.), *The Psychoanalytic Study of the Child*, vol. 21, pp. 448–467, International Universities Press, New York, 1966.

65. PIAGET, J., *Play, Dreams and Imitation in Childhood*, W. W. Norton, New York, 1962.

66. PROVINCE, S. and LIPTON, R., *Infants in Institutions*, International Universities Press, New York, 1962.

67. RAINER, J. D., "Some Observations on Affect Induction and Ego Development in the Deaf," *International Review of Psychoanalysis*, vol. 3, part 1, p. 122, 1976.

68. REES, N. S., "Noncommunicative Functions of Language in Children," *Journal of Speech and Hearing Disorders, 38(1)*:98–110, 1973.

69. RHEINGOLD, H., GEWIRTZ, J., and ROSS, H., "Social Conditioning of Vocalizations in the Infant," *Journal of Comparative Physiological Psychology, 52*:68–73, 1959.

70. RINGLER, N., et al., "Mother to Child Speech at Two Years: Effects of Early Postnatal Contact," *Journal of Pediatrics, 86(1)*:141–144, 1975.

71. ROBERTS, G. and BLACK, K., "The Effect of Naming and Object Permanence on Toy Preferences," *Child Development, 43(3)*:858, 1972.

72. ROSEN, V., Paper presented at the Symposium on Language and the Development of the Ego, Annual Meeting of the American Psychoanalytic Association, Detroit, May, 1967. (Reported by Edelheit, H., in *Journal of the American Psychoanalytic Association, 16*:113–122, 1968.

73. RYAN, J., "Acquisition or Grammar," in R. Lewin (Ed.), *Child Alive*, Temple Smith, London, 1975.

74. RYCROFT, C., "Symbolism and its Relationship to the Primary and Secondary Processes," *International Journal of Psychoanalysis, 37*:137–146, 1956.

75. SAPIR, E., *Language: An Introduction to the Study of Speech*, Harcourt, Brace and World, New York, 1921.

76. SCHLESINGER, I., "Production of Utterances and Language Acquisition," in Slobin, D. (Ed.), *Ontogenesis of Grammar*, Academic Press, New York, 1971.

77. SEARLE, J., "Chomsky's Revolution in Linguistics," *New York Review of Books*, June 29, 1972.

78. ———, *Speech Acts: An Essay in the Philosophy of Language*, Cambridge University Press, Cambridge, England, 1969.

79. SINCLAIR, H., "Sensorimotor Action Patterns as a Condition for the Acquisition of Syntax," in Huxley, R., and Ingram, E. (Eds.), *Language Acquisition: Models and Methods*, pp. 121–135, Academic Press, London, 1971.

80. ———, and BRONKMART, F., "S.V.O.—A Linguistic Universal?" *Journal of Experimental Child Psychology, 14*:329–348, 1972.

81. SLOBIN, D., *Psycholinguistics*, Scott Foresman, Glenview, 1971.

82 SPITZ, R., *No and Yes: On the Genesis of Human Communication*, International Universities Press, New York, 1957.

83. STEINGART, I., and FREEDMAN, N., "A Language Construction Approach for the Examination of Self/Object Representation in Varying Clinical States," in Holt, R., and Peterfreund, E. (Eds.), *Psychoanalysis and Contemporary Science*, vol. 1, pp. 132–178, Macmillan, New York, 1972.

84. STERN, R.. and BEEBE, B., "Early Coping Operations in Interpersonal Situations and their Possible Internal Representation." Paper presented at Conference on Communicative Structures and Psychic Structures, January 15, 1976, SUNY, Downstate Medical Center, New York, 1976.

85. TREVARTHAN, C., "Early Attempts at Speech" in R. Lewis (Ed.), *Child Alive*, Temple Smith, London, 1975.

86. VYGOTSKY, L. S., *Thought and Language*, MIT Press, Cambridge, 1962.

87. WAELDER, R., *Basic Theory of Psychoanalysis*, Schocken, New York, 1960.

88. WOLFF, P., "Cognitive Considerations for a Psychoanalytic Theory of Language Acquisition," in Holt, R. (Ed.), *Motives and Thought: Psychoanalytic Essays in Honor of David Rappaport*, pp. 300–343, International Universities Press, New York, 1967.

89. WOLFF, P. H., "The Natural History of Crying and Other Vocalizations in Early Infancy," in Foss, B. (Ed.), *Determinants of Infant Behavior*, vol. 4, pp. 81–109, Methuen, London, 1969.

90. WYATT, G., *Language, Learning, and Communication Disorders in Children*, Free Press, New York, 1969.

10 / Development from One to Two Years: Object Relations and Psychosexual Development

Eleanor Galenson

Introduction

The second year of life has been described by Mahler[40] as that era whose rich and almost boundless capacities for development are equaled only by those of the adolescent period. Yet these enormous potentialities in every area of growth depend for their optimal unfolding upon what Mahler has called the continuing "libidinal availability" of the mother, that is, her optimal participation in her child's development.

It was Freud[12] who orginally indicated that the child's first love is experienced toward the mother in her feeding relationship with him. Freud considered this to be the prototype of all later love relations. In 1938, Freud added that the mother's role was unique and without parallel—it established for a whole lifetime not only the first but the strongest love relationship.[8] A complete view of development during the second year of life must, therefore, take cognizance of this phenomenon. It would include theoretical and behavioral material which pertains to changing aspects of the child, but it must also encompass the mother's changing attitudes to her child. Mother's feelings will alter as the child progresses from pretoddlerhood through the era of "unbounded delight" in

144

the newly attained free walking and exploration, and then into the relative sobriety of the end of the second year. In keeping with this, aspects of the child's development pertinent to the second year will be correlated with material relating to maternal attitudes.

Behavioral Derivatives Relating to Psychosexual Development

ORAL ZONE BEHAVIOR

Freud's theory of psychosexual development has provided a set of constructs for organizing many of the behavioral phenomena of the first five years of life. According to these constructs, the first year is characterized by the fact that the predominant source of pleasure consists of a variety of oral activities, while beginning with the second year, anal activities begin to provide a new and major source of gratification. There is, however, considerable overlapping in the emergence of all three erotogenic zones as prime pleasure areas, since pleasurable oral activities continue throughout the second year and, to some degree, persist throughout life. Ordinarily, however, they are neither as intense nor as pervasive as they are during the height of the oral period in the first year.

In recent years there has been an increasing interest, particularly among middle-class mothers, to continue breast feeding into the second and even the third year of life. Furthermore, many babies in our culture continue to use bottles for sucking pleasure as well as for taking in food well into the second year. They begin to be able to support the bottle by themselves from seven to eight months on if allowed to do so, or even earlier. During the second year, the evening bottle seems to begin to serve as a bridge between daytime contact with the mother and the nighttime and naptime separation of sleep, a function which Spock[65] and Winnicott[68] regard as a transitional object. It is a common experience that weaning from the bottle becomes more difficult for the infant if it is postponed beyond the end of the first year. Mahler and LaPerriere[49] have suggested that this is probably due to the fact that during the second year the nursing bottle, particularly in its nighttime form, is used increasingly as a substitute for the mother. It is part of the infant's struggle against the regressive pull backward toward an earlier, more symbiotic relationship with the mother, since

such a regression endangers the infant's newly gained and still fragile independence from the mother.

Sucking for pleasure, however, is usually not confined to the bottle. It includes such other objects as pacifiers, diapers, blankets, soft toys, or the infant's own thumb. This nonnutritive sucking tends to occur whenever the infant finds himself overtaxed. Under conditions of frustration or fatigue, it serves as a respite and a period of temporary regression. While sucking, the infant's state of alertness is decreased. This indicates that there has been a temporary withdrawal from immediate contact with the external world. As Freud described long ago, many infants finger an ear lobe, or a smooth blanket binding, twirl a lock of hair, or stroke the upper lip as they suck, activities which are probably remnants of an earlier interaction with the mother during which the baby stroked the mother's skin or maintained some other form of tactile contact with her. These behaviors which accompany sucking may be analagous to the genital play which Freud[12] described in infants from eleven to fourteen months.

Biting is another form of oral behavior which persists into the second year. In contrast to the unintentional biting of the first year, however, it becomes focused and directed at the mother accompanied by unmistakable signs of anger, and it occurs largely in response to specific frustration. If the mother's response is a strongly disapproving one, the infant may shift his biting to his peers, or to inanimate objects, and in some instances he may even bite his own hands. As in many other areas of development, the mother's attitude determines the eventual fate of the child's particular expression of both love and hate. If the mother's reaction is neither excessively erotic nor excessively angry, the biting soon subsides.

Other oral activities during the second year include the continued use of the mouth for exploring the world at large. Although eating has become a much more autonomous function than it was during the first year, it remains a source of pleasure nonetheless. The twelve-month-old finger-feeds himself delightedly, and the fourteen-month-old enjoys his increasingly grown-up fare as he handles a spoon with great enthusiasm, even if clumsily. Yet the pleasure of eating is still vulnerable to invasion and disruption. Such experiences as prolonged periods of separation from the mother, the presence of too many strangers, or a pronounced shift in the mother's attentiveness to her infant or in her basic mood state may interfere with oral pleasures. When this happens meals no longer provide an opportunity for pleasurable taking-in. Eating disturbances of this period range from simply holding food in the mouth or refusing to accept it, to more extreme forms as gagging, spitting, or even vomiting.

ORAL DERIVATIVE BEHAVIOR

According to Freud's theory of psychosexual development, the drive impulse is expressed at the erotogenic zones directly. In addition, the particular zone currently in ascendancy exerts an organizing influence over every other aspect of behavior. It is this far-reaching organizing effect which lends such significance to the psychosexual theory of development.

In Erikson's conceptualization[6] of the organizing effects of the erotogenic zones, he emphasized the particular mode of operation of each zone, defining it according to its specific structural or organizational properties. He then went on to describe many forms of play behavior in which the structural aspects of the play resemble those of a particular erotogenic zone. Galenson[13] applied Erikson's concept of instinctual mode organization to a wide variety of play behaviors of infants, and she found that much of infant play is still dominated by the type of functioning which characterizes the oral zone during the first months of the second year. Children of this age delight in putting fingers and sticks into apertures, and enjoy feeding adults, peers, animals, and dolls. It is through this extension that the associated emotional stress is normally alleviated and resolved. In effect, the tensions and uncertainties connected with the erotogenic zones are in this way extended to less significant "others" and to the inanimate world.

ANAL ZONE BEHAVIOR

Freud[12] conceptualized the sequence of the emergence of the erotogenic zones as a biologically predestined, regularly occurring maturational process. Greenacre[25] has proposed a modification, suggesting that all three erotogenic zones are active to some degree from the first months of life, with peaks of relative ascendancy of each zone and with the possibility that any zone may be prematurely activated.

Freud's theoretical premise of the biological determinism of psychosexual development has been difficult to validate, particularly in view of the paucity of data relevant to the anal and phallic phases of development. For example,

Mahler[45, 44] noted that she was able to catch only glimpses of anal phase-related behavior in her direct observational research, although there was ample evidence of the emotional ambivalence and negativism which are characteristic of object relations during the anal phase. Kestenberg[34] has approached this issue through her study of body rhythms, noting that there are certain rhythmic patterns during the second year which she has designated as governed primarily by anal zone functioning.

In more recent years, however, research has provided considerable behavioral evidence for the onset and development of anal phase organization.[19] In this study, certain criteria and behaviors have proven useful in defining both anal zone and anal derivative behavior. These behavioral manifestations at the anal zone itself include:

1. Changes in bowel patterning, including diurnal variations, diarrhea and/or constipation and stool retention;
2. Behavioral changes during or directly preceding defecation, including squatting, flushing, straining, grunting, pulling at the soiled diaper, abrupt interruption of other activities, the "inward gaze" of concentration on inner sensations, hiding in corners or in separate rooms, sitting on the toilet or toidy, attempting to take off pants, etc.;
3. Behavioral changes directly following defecation, including signaling for or resisting diaper changes, playing with, smearing, or attempting to eat stool;
4. Affective concomitants of defecation, including excitement, pleasure, and fearfulness;
5. Anal area self-exploration.

According to the criteria mentioned above, and based upon the study of seventy infants (thirty-five boys, thirty-five girls), anal awareness has emerged as early as the sixth month (in two girls) and as late as the nineteenth month (in one boy). In most of the children there was a clustering about the twelfth to the fourteenth month. The emergence of this awareness appeared to be independent of efforts at toilet training, but was related to the progression of the separation-individuation process. This will be amplified in the section describing behavioral landmarks of separation-individuation progression.

ANAL DERIVATIVE BEHAVIOR

This includes not only action, gestures, and words, but also behavioral evidence of internal affective states. Freud[12] described such phenomena as aggressiveness, ambivalence, and fear of anal loss as integral aspects of anal phase development. Behavioral evidence of the psychological devices for coping with these affective states are also included here. Among them are actions such as attempts to investigate the anal area in others including parents, peers, animals, and dolls, by touching the buttocks, following parents to the bathroom, and peering into the toilet, etc. In play behavior as a psychological coping device, the form, structure, or other attributes, such as an olfactory quality, are similar to those of either the anal area or the stool itself. At the same time, these play sequences may represent other psychological constellations as well.[67]

Examples suggesting the many and varied forms which such play may take include: interest in toilets, particularly in flushing them; interest in garbage cans, incinerators, and garbage trucks; "collecting" and piling inanimate objects; games involving banging, throwing, scattering, pushing, and smearing; interest in emptying and filling hollow or "container" types of toys and kitchen utensils; noise-making games; and doll play involving toileting and diapering dolls.

Hostile aggression as an affective state may take many forms, including a mild degree of generally increased motor activity, general negativism, focused angry behavior such as biting, hitting, scratching, or pushing people, and the diffuse discharge of anger in tantrums and provocativeness. The fear of anal loss may be expressed as fears of the toilet flush, garbage trucks, loud noises, and water draining from the bathtub.

Psychological devices for coping with the child's inner aggressive wishes and fears of anal loss are manifested in such activities as hoarding objects (for example, small toys and coins), insistence upon having toys arranged in a particular order, and excessive neatness and orderliness. Symbolic behavior includes both gestural and verbal reference to the anal area or its products, and to aspects of the toilet apparatus.

ANAL DERIVATIVE BEHAVIOR:
RESEARCH FINDINGS[19]

Anal derivative behavior makes its appearance only after direct anal zone awareness has already emerged. Curiosity about the anal area of other people and in the toilet itself appears first. This is soon followed by the many forms of derivative play behavior already mentioned. Some of the affective states specifically connected with anal phase development begin to be evident as soon as anal awareness emerges, and as the months go by, these become more intense and fears of anal loss appear. These developments usually reach a peak toward the middle of the second year. Psychological coping devices reflected in excessive hoarding and orderliness begin to proliferate as the affective anal attitudes intensify.

The time of onset of gesturing and verbal labeling in relationship to the anal zone, its products, and its function is extremely variable. In general, this depends upon the level of general symbolic development that has been reached.

It is interesting that both Mahler's data[44] and the subsequent research findings of Galenson et al.[19] point to the coincidental occurrence of several developmental events during the first half of the second year. Early signs of directed aggression appear along with other anal phase derivative behavior such as growing possessiveness and acquisitiveness. This development coincides with the replacement of vocalization and gesture by verbal communication. The significance of this confluence of developmental events has yet to be evaluated.

Toilet training: It is common knowledge that even very young infants can be "trained" to produce a stool if they are regularly placed on a toileting device whenever defecation is imminent. It is evident, then, that the anal sphincter is capable of functioning well before the end of the time when anal zone functioning and anal products have attained psychological significance. In most children, such significance begins to be evident only at about fourteen months. Under the special circumstances mentioned above, however, this may appear months earlier. In any case, once the anal function and the stool itself have begun to have psychological significance, toilet training mobilizes important affective responses. Since there are two opposite innervations involved in the operation of the anal sphincter, one for retention and the other for elimination,[27] mastery of this function also serves as a model for learning control.

In summary, the increasing interest in anal function and products which usually develop during the first half of the second year lends an affective significance to toilet training experiences. This emotional development is enhanced and complicated, as the stool takes on even more complex psychological meaning during the following era of genital awareness.

URINARY ZONE BEHAVIOR

Infants are aware of and take pleasure in the urinary function and its product. This has received far less attention than development associated with the anal zone. Yet phenomena connected with the early urinary experience have been described in relation to many psychopathological findings in children as well as adults. (See for example the considerable literature concerning enuresis, as well as Greenacre's description[23, 21] of the childhood roots of the affect of awe and the development and function of tears.)

The research of Galenson et al.[19] has provided data in this area. Behavioral evidence for the onset of urinary organization has been categorized according to certain criteria of behavioral manifestations at the urinary zone including:

1. Changes in patterns of urination, including diurnal variations and urinary retention;
2. Behavioral changes directly preceding or during urination, including selective attention to wet diapers (in contrast to fecally soiled diapers), pulling at the wet diaper, squatting, watching one's own urinary stream, and urinating selectively (in reference to timing, location, and initiation and inhibition of the urinary stream), directing the stream (in boys), and the "inward gaze" of concentration during urination;
3. Behavioral changes directly following urination, including signaling for a diaper change, hiding, and interest in urinary puddles;
4. Affective concomitants of urination, including excitement, shame, embarrassment, and anxiety in relation to urination;
5. Urinary area self-exploration.

The study of thirty-five boys and thirty-five girls has shown that in most infants behavioral manifestations of urinary awareness begin sometime between the eleventh and fourteenth month and continue from that time onward. Onset of urinary awareness usually, but not invariably, follows the onset of anal zone awareness. This appears to be independent of the initiation of toilet training, but is related to the progress of the separation-individuation process, as will be described in a later section.

URINARY DERIVATIVE BEHAVIOR

The following categories have served to classify urinary derivative behavior.

1. Actions such as attempts to investigate the urinary area in others, including adults, peers, children, and animals;
2. Play behavior where the form, structure, or other attributes of the play are similar to those of the urinary area and function itself, such as play with toilet water, faucets, hoses, water cans, bottles and nipples, pouring and squirting liquids with the mouth or hands, and toileting and diapering dolls;
3. Affective reflections which usually occur in connection with events other than urination itself, including embarrassment, blushing, excitement, and anxiety;

4. Symbolic reference to the urinary area or function, including gesturing and labeling and interest in other symbolic "urinary" forms, such as water hydrants, umbrellas, and writing implements.

In respect to urinary derivative behavior, the findings show that it appears shortly after the onset of awareness of the urinary zone and its function; this has been noted in all seventy children in the study. Almost all have shown intense curiosity about both parents' urinary areas and functions, and most of the small subjects succeeded in being admitted to the bathroom during their parents' toileting. Then, with the onset of their awareness of the sexual anatomical difference, the toddlers' interest in and curiosity about their own urinary function as well as that of others become enmeshed with the emerging genital curiosity and concerns about the genital area. This will be discussed presently.

Toilet Training for Urination: This is often not achieved during the course of the second year. However, the urinary area and its functioning acquire increasing psychological meaning as this year progresses. This lends considerable affective significance to parental attempts at urinary toilet training. These efforts may then become the focus of conflict between mother and child.

THE GENITAL ZONE

The concept of an early genital phase,[57] occurring during the latter half of the second year, has already been described. It is seen as a developmental precipitate of the process of separation-individuation and of sphincter control. This phase appears to have critical importance for the developing sense of self and objects and for every area of emerging ego function.

Although the concept of an early genital phase is not as yet generally accepted, some of the behavioral phenomena which have been offered by Roiphe[57] and Galenson and Roiphe[14] as evidence for the existence of such a phase have been described by others as well. Genital self-stimulation in normal children has been reported by Spitz and Wolf[64] and Kleeman.[41, 40, 39, 38] Genital behavior in children in institutions or under other unusual circumstances has also been reported by Spitz and Wolf,[64] Spitz,[63] Provence and Lipton,[56] and A. Freud and Burlingham.[7]

Kleeman's review[38] of five girls described a developmental line beginning with random fingering of the genitals usually beginning during the first year and proceeding thereafter toward masturbation. However, since the genital play of the first sixteen months does not appear to be either directed or volitional, Kleeman does not consider it to be true masturbation as yet. The change to true masturbation is, in his view, a gradual, discontinuous, poorly defined, and variable process, varying for different children.

A number of studies concur, however, that an increase of genital sensation and awareness as well as a qualitative change in genital behavior appear sometime between fifteen and twenty-four months.* This heightened genital sensitivity serves as a source of focused pleasure which is far more intense than that derived from the previous form of genital self-stimulation. Kleeman has pointed out that the increase in genital sensation coincides with the increase in anal and urinary sensations, as well as in the capacity for sphincter control. He regards the genital self-stimulation of this latter half of the second year as a behavioral indicator of a variety of factors: the progressive self-image differentiation, the quality of maternal care,[63] maturational processes, and environmental events such as the birth of a new sibling and exposure to the view of the genitals of the opposite sex. During the course of the second year, Kleeman has also reported the beginning of body and genital pride, as well as exhibitionism and castration anxiety, but he has found no evidence of orgastic capacity.

The pattern of development of genital self-stimulation in girls differs from that in boys, according to Kleeman as well as Galenson and Roiphe.[14] Kleeman found that girls begin genital self-stimulation later than boys and that this behavior is less vigorous, less focused, less frequent, and less intentional than in boys during the first year and the early months of the second year. The girl seems to have a less distinct awareness of her labia, clitoris, vagina, and urinary meatus than the boy has of his penis, scrotum, testicles, and urinary meatus. Kleeman attributes this difference between the genital behavior of boys and girls to the greater visual and tactile accessibility of the boy's genitals, to the fact that the penis, a urinary as well as a genital organ, has been subject to erections from birth, to the greater stimulation of the penis and scrotum by the general motility of the child, and to the differential reaction of parents to children of each sex. It has been noted, for example, that mothers have much greater difficulty in naming their little girl's genitals than those of their boy infants.

The research findings of Roiphe,[57] Roiphe and Galenson,[60, 62] and Galenson and Roiphe,[15, 14] have been based upon the study of a population of thirty-five boys and thirty-five girls of a middle-class white group.

They reported that sometime between fifteen and nineteen months of age, genital behavior (which differs from the earlier genital exploratory play) along with genital derivative behavior emerge for the first time. This occurs in a regular and predictable sequence, but only after the emergence of both anal and urinary awareness. The earlier genital play pattern of the boys in the research group differed from the girls in that the boys generally began genital exploration sometime between seven to ten months of age, while the girls began several months later. Furthermore, the early genital play of the boys was, as described by Kleeman,[37] less focused, more intermittent, and less intentional than the genital play of girls.

The criteria used to define genital awareness are behavioral manifestations at the genital zone itself and include:

1. Touching the genital area either manually or by indirect means, such as rocking, thigh pressure, etc.;
2. Affective concomitants, including evidence of erotic arousal, such as pleasure and autonomic excitation (rapid respiration, flushing, perspiration, physical tension, and penile erections in boys;
3. Affectionate behavior directed toward others accompanying genital manipulation;
4. Use of inanimate objects for genital self-stimulation.

Every infant in the research sample of seventy developed a new quality of genital behavior during the latter part of the second year, usually sometime between sixteen and nineteen months of age.[15] Genital manipulation became more focused and was a more absorbing activity, with the infants clearly deriving pleasure and experiencing varying degrees of erotic arousal. In the girls, the masturbation which usually occurred initially during bathing and diapering consisted of manual repetitive rubbing, pinching, and squeezing of the labia, mons, and clitoral area. Although the finger was introduced into the vagina by several infant girls, this could not be clearly evaluated as a masturbatory activity because of the small size of the entire genital area. Nonmanual masturbation was carried out at the outset of this period mainly through straddling parents' bodies, furniture, or toys, or through perineal rocking. In boys, the masturbation was largely manual.

During the first week or so after the onset of the new type of genital self-stimulation, both boys

*See refernces 37, 57, 62, 60, 15, and 14.

and girls look at the mother and touch her affectionately and tenderly during their self-stimulation. However, this is soon replaced by the inner-directed gaze and general withdrawal of attention which accompanies all later forms of self-stimulation. The research team regard this new type of genital manipulation as true masturbation, the inner-directed gaze and withdrawal probably indicating the presence of a rudimentary form of masturbatory fantasy.[15]

Many of the children, particularly the girls in this sample, used inanimate objects for their genital self-stimulation. These objects included nursing bottles, transitional-object blankets, stuffed toy animals, and dolls, particularly soft ones. Since these inanimate objects had earlier been used in interaction with the mother, they probably offer concrete support to the masturbatory fantasy.

Parental reaction to the child's masturbation plays an important role in determining its future fate. All children understand and tend to comply with parental attitudes, whether conscious or unconscious, whether expressed through verbal or nonverbal routes. However, from this time on, the parents' attitudes combine with the reality of anatomical sexual differences to lead to a distinctly different line of genital development in the two sexes. Differences are found between boys and girls in both the forms of genital derivative behavior as well as genital zone behavior. All the girls in the sample reacted in a special way to their awareness of the sexual anatomical differences. They displayed some form of preoedipal castration reactions which were modified both by the nature of their earlier experiences and by their mothers' attitudes toward femininity.

In the course of the study, it was found that during the early weeks following the discovery of the sexual anatomical difference, both boys and girls behaved in similar fashion.[15] They continued the genital zone behavior described above, and developed considerable pride and pleasure in their bodies. All but two boys in the research sample then continued to masturbate manually and at the same level of intensity and frequency. Within a few weeks of the discovery of the sexual differences, however, all thirty-five girls in the study showed definite changes in their masturbatory patterns as well as many other reactions. These reactions ranged from mild and transient affairs to profound disruptions which involved almost every area of functioning. It is suggested that they are best understood as preoedipal castration reactions.

In most of the girls, the pattern of masturbation changed as well. Manual masturbation was often replaced by indirect masturbation using rocking horses, parents' legs, or thigh pressure, while some girls abandoned masturbation altogether. In others, masturbation was displaced to such other areas as the umbilicus or anus, while still other girls continued to masturbate manually but without pleasure.[58]

GENITAL DERIVATIVE BEHAVIOR

It is in this area that the differences in the lines of development in the boys and girls were most striking. The criteria for genital derivative behavior were as follows:

1. Curiosity regarding the genital areas of adults, peers, animals and dolls, or marked inhibition of this curiosity after its initial expression;
2. Masturbatory-like behavior at other areas such as umbilicus, anus, hair, etc.;
3. Play behavior where the form, structure, or other attributes are similar to those of the genital area and its function—i.e. play with cars, trucks, planes and other phallic-like toys in boys, doll play in girls (and some boys), and collecting phallic-shaped objects;
4. Affective reflections—such as exhibitionism in boys, and flirting, cuddling, and "body-pride" in girls;
5. Symbolic reference to the genital area, including gestures and labeling.

Castration reactions in these girls included oral regression, anal regression with anal exploration and masturbation, and the reemergence of only recently allayed fears of object loss and anal loss.[14] Affective changes ranged from a temporary loss of zestfulness and enthusiasm to more profound reactions of sadness, with the establishment of what appeared to be the forerunner of a basic depressive mood.[44, 16] Distortions of the symbolic function in several girls during these preoedipal castration reactions were also noted. One of the striking findings in this research[16] as well as in Kleeman's series[37] is that parents label the girl's genitals for her later and far less accurately than they do for the boy. Indeed, the entire female ano-genital-urinary area is often given only one name. Under the impact of the early castration reaction, many of the girls lost the use of even these global labels and developed a temporary distortion in the use of other previously acquired male-female differential labeling.[16, 17]

However, there was also another variety of adaptation noted in the wake of the discovery of genital difference. This consisted of a spurt in the utilization of a variety of defensive and other ego capacities. Among the most striking of these new psychological mechanisms was the extensive use of displacement, externalization, and symbolic elaboration. Masturbation, as well as genital curiosity, were displaced to such areas as umbilicus, anus, hair, feet, etc. Most of the girls became much more intensely attached to dolls or other inanimate objects. In effect, these inanimate objects seemed now to serve as "infantile fetishes" supporting the sense of wavering genital schematization in the face of the girl's castration reaction.[60, 61, 16, 14] Indeed, for many of the little girls after they discovered the genital differences, these inanimate objects became involved in remarkable symbolic elaboration. Their fantasy life, including their doll play, became much more extensive and complex and they began to insist on using crayons, pens, and pencils in early attempts at graphic representation. This elaboration of the symbolic function[53, 17] will be described in greater detail in chapter 11, which is devoted to developing ego functioning.

In contrast to the girls, intense preoedipal castration reactions were observed to occur far less frequently in the boys, although when they did occur these were profound.[20] However, the boys generally showed an increase in their overall motor activity and from this time on they became ever more involved in the use of various mobile toys, such as trucks, planes, and bicycles.

Effect of Preoedipal Castration Reactions upon Object Relations

The developmental landmarks indicative of the progress of object relationships will be discussed in a later section. Here the material will summarize the specific influence of the preoedipal castration reactions described previously* on developing object ties.

As part of their growing separation from the mother,[1] both boys and girls develop a special relationship with the father toward the end of the first year. However, in the research group, following their discovery of and reaction to the sexual anatomical difference, most of the girls became increasingly angry at the mother and began to approach the father in a new erotic way. In some cases, the earlier relationship with the mother had been of poor quality, or the birth of a sibling, particularly a boy, had occurred during the latter

* See references 57, 62, 60, 59, 16, 15, and 14.

part of the second year. Under these circumstances, the hostile dependency upon the mother increased, and the erotic shift to the father did not occur. It had been postulated that the milder form of castration reaction facilitates the girl's turn to the father as her new love object. This goes along with a loosening of her attachment to the mother and leads toward the oedipal attachment that will soon follow. On the other hand, the more profound form of preoedipal castration reaction interferes with this shift in love object and binds the girl to her mother in an ever more ambivalent relationship.

Gender Identity

There had been little research in this area for many years. Recently, however, there have appeared the studies of Money and Ehrhardt[54] in regard to genetically and hormonally deviant individuals, Stoller's clinical studies[66] of transsexuals, and Kleeman's studies[40, 41, 39, 38] of normal infants. Money and Ehrhardt studied (1) those genetically male individuals where the complete absence of gonadal hormone during their prenatal period had produced female-appearing external genitalia at birth in some; (2) those genetically male individuals in whom insufficient prenatal androgens had resulted in anomalous external genitalia which were neither definitely male nor female at birth; and (3) genetically female children who had been hormonally androgenized during the prenatal period, and were reared as girls. From their study of these three groups, Money and Ehrhardt concluded that the primary determinant of feminine gender identity is neither prenatal gonadal hormones nor genetic endowment; it is instead the sex designation of the rearing environment. In several of the infants studied, sex reassignment had been attempted after the second year of life because of the surgical impossibility of providing these genetically male infants with adequate male genitalia. In each case, a serious degree of psychological disturbance ensued. Money and Ehrhardt feel that in contrast with lower species, it is primarily postnatal factors which account for much, if not most of human gender identity.

Stoller's work[66] with transsexuals has shown the decisive influence of early parental rearing upon "core gender identity," a term which Stoller has found useful. This small group of patients have mothers who share a particular psychosexual constellation. Under the impact of the mother's femininizing attitude toward her young son, these children reach a critical point in their sexual identity toward the end of the second year. However, Stoller feels that under normal circumstances, in addition to the psychological factors, there are endocrinological and neurological influences which also contribute to the establishment of the sense of sexual identity.

In a recent overview of the current status of gender identity, Kleeman[38,37] came to the conclusion that femininity arises in the first year of life. This stands in contrast to the hypothesis that femininity appears only after the phallic phase, as Freud[12, 11, 10] had originally maintained. Kleeman pointed out that Freud continued to claim that femaleness came into being only after puberty and stressed the parallel development of boys and girls. Later, however, Freud[10, 9] traced out a different course of development for males and females. Freud's later view involved both the girl's strong and enduring preoedipal attachment to her mother and the differing chronological sequences for the castration complex and the oedipal constellation in boys and girls. Throughout, Kleeman notes, Freud continued to maintain that masochism was truly feminine. Kleeman has also reviewed various amendments or challenges to Freud's position, including those of Horney,[29, 28] Jones,[32, 31, 30] Greenacre,[26, 24] and Kestenberg.[36, 35]

Drawing upon his own data from direct infant observation, Kleeman has acknowledged the influence of innate differences, but feels that learning via the parents plays a more crucial role in determining early gender identity. Kleeman believes this becomes set before penis envy, castration anxiety, and the oedipus complex exert their influences. Kleeman does not agree with Freud that penis envy initiates feminine gender identity; he stresses instead the cognitive aspects of gender identity, particularly the role of language development, as described in Kohlberg's studies[42] of self-labeling.

Kleeman recognizes the many areas of agreement between his research data and those of Galenson and Roiphe, including the commonly observed preoedipal castration reactions, as well as penis envy during the latter part of the second year. But he does not view these as primary organizers in the developing sense of femininity.

Galenson and Roiphe[14] agree with Kleeman that genital experiences begin very early, that they arise in connection with maternal caretaking and feeding, and that they are profoundly modified by parental attitudes. (See, for example, Murphy[55]

in regard to different maternal feeding patterns of boys and girls.) Like Kleeman, they also describe the differing patterns of early genital play in the two sexes.

However, Galenson and Roiphe have described the emergence of a qualitatively new type of genital manipulation sometime between fifteen and eighteen months of age. In their view, this zonal activity, along with its influence on the rest of behavior, constitutes an early genital phase. They believe that this phasic organization is profoundly different for the two sexes and leads to basically divergent subsequent psychosexual development, object relations, and ego development in boys and girls.

There have been relatively few reports concerning the concomitant period of early genital awareness in boys, except for individual case descriptions. Kleeman[41,40] described the genital play which appeared in an eight-month-old boy, when he first "discovered" his penis and then his scrotum two and one-half months later. A more specific focus on both areas did not appear until the second half of his second year, an age range which corresponds with that described in the individual cases reported by Roiphe and Galenson[60] and Galenson et al.[20]

Kleeman's material confirmed Bell's findings[2, 3] that there is meaningful knowledge of the scrotal sac and the testicles during infancy, but he found this occurred later than the comparable awareness of the penis. However, Kleeman's small subject did not exhibit the confusion of testes with stool, as described by Bell.

Landmarks of Developing Self and Object Representation: The Separation-Individuation Process

It is by now generally accepted that the normal psychological development of the child is a multi-determined process, with a confluence of constitutional, maturational, and environmental factors. Earlier, considerable progress had been made in identifying the milestones in such areas as motor and cognitive development. More recently, there have been significant achievements in identifying the landmarks of both Mahler's separation-individuation process of object-relations development and psychosexual development. However, the emergence of these sequences has often been described in terms of separate and distinct trends;

their integration and correlation has posed a most difficult task. Furthermore, psychoanalysts have been increasingly interested in the pathological vicissitudes of the narcissistic line of development. The works of Kernberg[33] and Kohut[43] have been particularly outstanding in this regard. Yet their work has been insufficiently integrated either with Freud's own work or with the contributions of Mahler and her colleagues. Although this chapter will certainly not resolve these several dilemmas, one can approach such a synthesis if each individual line of early development can be successfully delineated.

MAHLER'S SEPARATION-INDIVIDUATION
PROCESS

Mahler's conceptualization has been the second major theory which has attempted to organize and codify the array of observational material derived from early development. In essence, she has described a process whereby the child achieves a state of psychological separateness or "psychological birth" from the mother, along with a sense of his individual identity. In the course of her work, the clinical and observational data were examined largely from the viewpoint of their relevance to the separation-individuation process, rather than to Freud's theory of psychosexual development. The task of coordinating and integrating these two major theoretical frameworks remains to be accomplished.

Truly communicative speech does not develop until the latter part of the second year, and often not even then. As a result, behavioral landmarks are not only useful, they are essential. They are, in fact, the only available evidence that certain psychological processes are taking place, or have been accomplished. Many of the landmarks to be discussed have been described in the publications by Mahler and her coworkers. Although different theoretical issues have been raised in each publication, those which have provided the specific clinical and observational data most useful for identifying the landmarks of separation-individuation include Mahler,[46, 45, 44] Mahler and Furer,[47] Mahler and Gosliner,[48] and Mahler and La-Perriere.[51]

CHRONOLOGY OF THE SEPARATION-
INDIVIDUATION PROCESS

Mahler has emphasized repeatedly that the various subphases of the separation-individuation process overlap and that the beginning and end points of each subphase vary considerably from child to child. She has stated emphatically and reiterated many times that the child's emotional dependence upon the mother during this period is a critical and universal factor. This makes the mother's emotional availability to the child during each of these phases indispensable for the optimal development of the child's potentialities.

Subphase I—Differentiation: This phase begins at about five or six months of age and continues for the next four to five months as a gradual "hatching" process. In behavioral terms, it is characterized by the child's decreasing bodily dependence upon the mother. Creeping, climbing, and standing up replace the passive means of transportation of the first five or six months, and the use of the distant visual modality for scanning the environment begins to replace the earlier reliance on tactile and kinesthetic contact. These new motor and perceptual capacities are gradually integrated with increasingly effective hand, eye, and mouth coordination. This total sensorimotor apparatus is utilized in the service of increasing alertness. A new psychological attitude emerges whereby the child turns attention toward the outside world as the source of both pleasure and stimulation. Without the impetus of this psychological change, the apparatus itself fails to continue its optimal development.

At this time, the most important aspect of the outside world for the young infant is the mother. It is her face and body which the baby now begins to investigate with his hands as well as with his vision. Thus, peek-a-boo games which were first initiated by the mother are now initiated by the infant. But parallel to and pari passu with the infant's dawning awareness of his mother's face and body is his exploration of his own hands and feet and their movements—behavior which indicates a beginning psychological awareness of his own body and its potentialities.

Mahler's Subphase II—the Practicing Period: Overlapping the differentiation subphase, the practicing period begins sometime after ten months of age and continues until about fifteen months. It is a time of tentative experimentation in psychological separation and individuation.

Mahler prefers not to use the term "separation anxiety" in relation to the physical act of separation. Instead she confines it to the intrapsychic differentiation of self from the symbiotic object which appears in the course of the normal separation-individuation process. This intrapsychic separation may, and often does, take place in the actual physical presence of the mother, and requires her emotional availability. From Mahler's point of view, "separation anxiety" is not an observable behavioral sequence in response to physical separation from the mother, as Bowlby[5] or Benjamin[4] have described it. There is, rather, a gradually developing, intrapsychic signal anxiety which emerges in a more discrete form in the third year, toward the close of the normal separation-individuation process. Mahler regards the earlier behavior in the face of physical separation as "separation reactions" rather than as "separation anxiety." These reactions reach peak intensity at twelve months of age and include such varied affective states as anger and sadness. The inner psychological danger to which infants react at this state is that of helplessness and longing, and its consequent anxiety. As Mahler sees it, true separation anxiety appears only at the stage when the mother has already become an intrapsychic reality to the child, and when the child's memory of her presence is available for bringing relief from pain and displeasure.

Toward the end of the first year, the child's tentative and active experimentation at separation-individuation is signaled by many activities; in each of these he actively repeats behavior which formerly had been initiated by his mother. The main focus of his interest, however, has now shifted. It has turned from his mother and her activities to his own body and its capacities. These have undergone enormous proliferation within the previous few months. There is an ever increasing practice with his motor skills as he advances from crawling, through walking with support to broad-based toddling. More than that, as the larger environment of his expanding reality is explored, he displays a remarkable imperviousness to falls and hurt of all kinds, and to frustration. The general mood is characteristically an elated one, with a seeming sense of magical omnipotence. When fatigue sets in, momentary contact with the mother seems to provide the resources for renewed exploration, the "emotional refueling" which is a necessary ingredient for satisfactory progression of the ongoing separation-individuation process. Mahler has further characterized the practicing subphase by reality testing par excellence and a spurt in all areas of autonomous functioning.

Behavioral evidence for the increasing stability of the mental representation of mother includes the capacity to keep in touch with her at a distance, using visual and auditory contact. The mother is now subjected to both visual and tactile exploration; the child reciprocally compares her face and body with his own equivalent features.

Moreover, both aggressive and affectionate impulses which were formerly diffusely discharged now become directed against her. Such maternal interactions as feeding and being put to bed had included the presence of certain inanimate objects possessing special qualities of texture or smell. These had presently become very familiar to the child, and indeed had begun to play the role of Winnicott's "transitional objects."[68] In effect, these are important representatives of the amalgamated maternal and infant experiences, the "me" and "not me." They may be taken along on the infant's forays and are required for support at times of separation such as bed time or visits away from home. The use of these objects, the extensive peek-a-boo games initiated by the child, and the sleep problems so characteristic of this period attest to his ongoing efforts at consolidation of the still unstable maternal representation. At the same time, the child is coping with the old threat of object loss and the new awareness of anal and urinary loss. There is also a great deal of behavior which gives evidence of the consolidating self-image. Self-feeding, although still relatively unskillful, becomes even more mandatory. Furthermore, the infant explores his own face and body attentively; he begins to examine and respond to his own mirror image, and awareness appears of both anal and urinary functioning. Moreover, there is a wave of negativism as he demands control over his own body by refusing to lie down for dressing or diapering.

It is, of course, of great significance that evidence of increasing self-object differentiation, or "psychological birth,"[52] is correlated with the emergence of such early symbolic forms as imitation, gesture, interest in pictorial representation, beginning verbal expression, and semisymbolic play with toys in which concrete representation is still evident. It appears that the achievement of a certain minimum degree of self-object differentiation is necessary for the development of symbolic functioning, an area which will be discussed later.

Mahler's Period of Rapprochment: Beginning at about eighteen months of age, and extending to twenty-four months or beyond, this period is characterized by two distinct but complimentary and intertwined lines of development. As the child individuates psychologically through his motor, perceptual, and cognitive activities, he achieves an increasingly independent status. At the same time, there is a clearer intrapsychic differentiation of himself, a sense of separateness from his primary love object, his mother. This growing sense of separation is achieved in parallel with many important accomplishments. There is improvement in the child's fine and gross motor skills, his affects become more modulated, and he begins to utilize his symbolic capacity for the expression of affect and of ideas through gesture and beginning language.

Behavioral evidence of the increasing self-object differentiation includes: naming body parts, actions, and objects; communication through language; increasingly elaborate semisymbolic play; and the new awareness of genital anatomy and sexual anatomical differences. However, this clearer definition of self and object is not without its resultant danger for the child, for as time goes on he finds it more and more difficult to maintain his sense of omnipotent control over his mother. Mahler has described a "rapproachment crisis"

which follows the toddler's realization and acceptance of the abrogation of his omnipotence as a time when the toddler returns to his older clinging and increasingly negativistic behavior. The intrapsychic experience of loss, which is signaled by the increased clinging, is compounded if toilet training is initiated, or if there is the birth of a new sibling.

Mahler has described the wide variation in maternal reactions to the child's increasing activity and independence. These range from "mourning reactions" to an optimum state of emotional availability and playful participation. Maternal libidinal availability facilitates an optimal unfolding of the child's potentialities. In every case, these maternal reactions are crucial determinants of the child's future development.

REFERENCES

1. ABELIN, E. L., "The Role of the Father in Separation-Individuation Process," in McDevitt, J. B., and Settlage, C. F. (Eds.), *Separation-Individuation: Essays in Honor of Margaret S. Mahler*, pp. 229–253, International Universities Press, New York, 1971.

2. BELL, A., "Bowel Training Difficulties in Boys: Pre-Phallic and Phallic Considerations," *Journal of the American Academy of Child Psychiatry*, 3:577–590, 1964.

3. ———, "Some Observations on the Role of the Scrotal Sac and Testicles," *Journal of the American Psychoanalytic Association*, 9:261–286, 1961.

4. BENJAMIN, J. D., "Further Comments on Some Developmental Aspects of Anxiety," in Gaskill, H. S. (Ed.), *Counterpoint: Libidinal Object and Subject*, pp. 121–153, International Universities Press, New York, 1963.

5. BOWLBY, J., "The Nature of the Child's Tie to the Mother," *International Journal of Psycho-Analysis*, 39:350–373, 1958.

6. ERIKSON, E. H., *Childhood and Society*, Norton, New York, 1963.

7. FREUD, A., and BURLINGHAM, D., "Infants without Families, Reports on the Hampstead Nurseries," *The Writings of Anna Freud*, vol. 3, pp. 543–564, International Universities Press, New York, 1973.

8. FREUD, S., "Outline of Psychoanalysis," in *The Standard Edition of the Complete Psychological Works of Sigmund Freud* (hereafter: *The Standard Edition*), vol. 23, p. 188, Hogarth Press, London, 1940.

9. ———, "Female Sexuality," in *The Standard Edition*, vol. 21, pp. 223–243, Hogarth Press, London, 1931.

10. ———, "Some Psychical Consequences of the Anatomical Distinction between the Sexes," in *The Standard Edition*, vol. 19, pp. 243–258, Hogarth Press, London, 1925.

11. ———, "The Infantile Genital Organization," in *The Standard Edition*, vol. 19, pp. 140–145, Hogarth Press, London, 1923.

12. ———, "Three Essays on the Theory of Sexuality," in *The Standard Edition*, vol. 7, pp. 125–243, Hogarth Press, London, 1953.

13. GALENSON, E., "A Consideration of the Nature of Thought in Childhood Play," in McDevitt, J. B., and Settlage, C. F. (Eds.), *Separation-Individuation, Essays in Honor of Margaret S. Mahler*, pp. 41–49, International Universities Press, New York, 1971.

14. ———, and ROIPHE, H., "Some Suggested Revisions Concerning Early Female Development," *Journal of the American Psychoanalytic Association*, 24(5):29–57, 1976.

15. ———, "The Emergence of Genital Awareness During the Second Year of Life," in Friedman, R. C. (Ed.), *Sex Differences in Behavior*, pp. 223–231, John Wiley, New York, 1974.

16. ———, "The Impact of Early Sexual Discovery on Mood, Defensive Organization and Symbolization," in Eissler, R. S., et al. (Eds.), *The Psychoanalytic Study of the Child*, vol. 26, pp. 195–216, International Universities Press, New York, 1971.

17. ———, MILLER, R., and ROIPHE, H., "The Choice of Symbols," *Journal of the Academy of Child Psychiatry*, 15(1):83–96, 1976.

18. ———, "The Capacity for Symbolic Expression: An Ego Function," Paper presented at Sarah Lawrence Symposium on play, 1975.

19. ———, et al., "Behavioral Landmarks of Psychosexual Development," unpublished manuscript, 1975.

20. ———, et al., "Disturbance in Sexual Identity Beginning at 18 Months of Age," *International Journal of Psycho-Analysis*, 2(4):389–399, 1975.

21. GREENACRE, P., "On the Developmental Function of Tears," in Eissler, R. S., et al. (Eds.), *The Psychoanalytic Study of the Child*, vol. 20, pp. 209–219, International Universities Press, New York, 1965.

22. ———, "Considerations Regarding the Parent-Infant Relationship," *International Journal of Psycho-Analysis*, 41:571–584, 1960.

23. ———, "Experiences of Awe in Childhood," in Eissler, R. S., et al. (Eds.), *The Psychoanalytic Study of the Child*, vol. 11, pp. 9–30, International Universities Press, New York, 1958.

24. ———, "Early Physical Determinants in the Development of the Sense of Identity," in Greenacre, P., *Emotional Growth*, vol. 1, pp. 113–127, International Universities Press, New York, 1971.

25. ———, "Certain Relationships Between Fetishism and the Faulty Development of the Body Image," in Eissler, R. S., et al. (Eds.), *The Psychoanalytic Study of the Child*, vol. 8, pp. 79–98, International Universities Press, New York, 1953.

26. ———, "Special Problems of Early Female Sexual

Development," in Eissler, R. S., et al. (Eds.), *The Psychoanalytic Study of the Child*, vol. 5, pp. 122–138, International Universities Press, New York, 1950.

27. HARTMAN, H., and KRIS, E., "Comments on the Formation of Psychic Structure," in Eissler, R. S., et al. (Eds.), *The Psychoanalytic Study of the Child*, vol. 2, pp. 11–38, International Universities Press, New York, 1946.

28. HORNEY, K., "The Denial of the Vagina," *International Journal of Psycho-Analysis, 14:57–70*, 1933.

29. ———, "The Flight from Womanhood," *International Journal of Psycho-Analysis, 7:324–339*, 1926.

30. JONES, E., "Vicissitudes of Female Sexuality," *International Journal of Psycho-Analysis, 16:263–273*, 1935.

31. ———, "The Phallic Phase," *International Journal of Psycho-Analysis, 14:1–33*, 1933.

32. ———, "The Early Development of Female Sexuality," *International Journal of Psycho-Analysis, 8:459–472*, 1927.

33. KERNBERG, O., *Borderline Conditions and Pathological Narcissism*, Aronson, New York, 1975.

34. KESTENBERG, J., "Rhythm and Organization in Obsessive-Compulsive Development," *International Journal of Psycho-Analysis, 47:151–159*, 1966.

35. ———, "Outside and Inside, Male and Female," *Journal of the American Psychoanalytic Association, 16: 456–520*, 1958.

36. ———, "Vicissitudes of Female Sexuality," *Journal of the American Psychoanalytic Association, 4:453–476*, 1956.

37. KLEEMAN, J., "Freud's Views on Early Female Sexuality in the Light of Direct Child Observation," *Journal of the American Psychoanalytic Association, 24(5): 29–57*, 1976.

38. ———, "Genital Self-Stimulation in Infant and Toddler Girls," in Marcus, I., and Francis, J. (Eds.), *Masturbation from Infancy to Senescence*, pp. 77–106, International Universities Press, New York, 1975.

39. ———, "The Establishment of Core Gender Identity in Normal Girls," *Archives of Sexual Behavior, 1: 103–129*, 1971.

40. ———, Genital Self-Discovery During a Boy's Second Year," in Eissler, R. S., et al. (Eds.), *The Psychoanalytic Study of the Child*, vol. 21, pp. 358–392, International Universities Press, New York, 1966.

41. ———, "A Boy Discovers His Penis," in Eissler, R. S., et al. (Eds.), *The Psychoanalytic Study of the Child*, vol. 20, pp. 239–266, International Universities Press, New York, 1965.

42. KOHLBERG, L. A., "A Cognitive-Developmental Analysis of Children's Sex-Role Concepts and Attitudes," in Maccoby, E. (Ed.), *The Development of Sex Differences*, Stanford University Press, Stanford, Calif., 1966.

43. KOHUT, H., *The Analysis of the Self*, International Universities Press, New York, 1971.

44. MAHLER, M. S., *On Human Symbiosis and the Vicissitudes of Individuation*, vol. 1, *Infantile Psychosis*, International Universites Press, New York, 1968.

45. ———, "Thoughts About Development and Individuation," in Eissler, R. S., et al. (Eds.), *The Psychoanalytic Study of the Child*, vol. 18, pp. 307–324, International Universities Press, 1963.

46. ———, "Autism and Symbiosis: Two Extreme Disturbances of Identity," *International Journal of Psycho-Analysis, 39:77–83*, 1958.

47. ———, and FURER, M., "Certain Aspects of the Separation- Individuation Phase," *Psychoanalytic Quarterly, 34:1–14*, 1963.

48. ———, and GOSLINER, B. J., "On Symbiotic Child Psychosis: Genetic, Dynamic and Restitutive Aspects," in Eissler, R. S., et al. (Eds.), *The Psychoanalytic Study of the Child*, vol. 10, pp. 195–212, International Universities Press, New York, 1955.

49. ———, and LAPERRIERE, K., "Development of 'Defense' from Biological and Symbiotic Precursors: Adaptive and Maladaptive Aspects," in Wallerstein, R. S., "Development and Metapsychology of the Defense Organization of the Ego," *Journal of the American Psychoanalytic Association, 15:130–149*, 1967.

50. ———, "Notes on the Development of Basic Moods: The Depressive Affect," in Loewenstein, R. M., et al. (Eds.), *Psychoanalysis—A General Psychology: Essays in Honor of Heinz Hartmann*, pp. 152–168, International Universities Press, New York, 1966.

51. ———, "Mother-Child Interaction During Separation-Individuation," *Psychoanalytic Quarterly, 34:483–498*, 1965.

52. ———, et al., *The Psychological Birth of the Human Infant*, Basic Books, New York, 1975.

53. MILLER, R., GALENSON, E., and ROIPHE, H., "The Language of Behavior," unpublished manuscript, 1975.

54. MONEY, J., and EHRHARDT, A. A., *Man and Woman, Boy and Girl*, Johns Hopkins University Press, Baltimore, 1972.

55. MURPHY, L., *The Widening World of Childhood*, Basic Books, New York, 1962.

56. PROVENCE, S., and LIPTON, R., *Infants in Institutions*, International Universities Press, New York, 1962.

57. ROIPHE, H., "On an Early Genital Phase," in Eissler, R. S., et al. (Eds.), *The Psychoanalytic Study of the Child*, vol. 23, pp. 348–365, International Universities Press, New York, 1968.

58. ———, and GALENSON, E., "Some Observations on Transitional Object and Infantile Fetish," *Psychoanalytic Quarterly, 44:206–231*, 1975.

59. ———, "A Narcissistic Disorder in the Process of Development," unpublished manuscript, 1974.

60. ———, "Object Loss and Early Sexual Development," *Psychoanalytic Quarterly, 42:73–90*, 1973.

61. ———, "The Infantile Fetish," in Eissler, R. S., et al. (Eds.), *The Psychoanalytic Study of the Child*, vol. 28, pp. 147–166, International Universities Press, New York, 1973.

62. ———, "Early Genital Activity and the Castration Complex," *Psychoanalytic Quarterly, 41:334–347*, 1972.

63. SPITZ, R. A., "Autoerotism Re-examined," in Eissler, R. S., et al. (Eds.), *The Psychoanalytic Study of the Child*, vol. 17, pp. 283–315, International Universities Press, New York, 1962.

64. ———, and WOLF, K. M., "Autoerotism: Some Emperical Findings and Hypotheses on Three of Its Manifestations in the First Year of Life," in Eissler, R. S., et al. (Eds.), *The Psychoanalytic Study of the Child*, vols. 3/4, pp. 85–120, International Universities Press, New York, 1949.

65. SPOCK, B., "The Striving for Autonomy and Regressive Object Relationships," in Eissler, R. S., et al. (Eds.), *The Psychoanalytic Study of the Child*, vol. 18, pp. 361–364, International Universities Press, New York, 1963.

66. STOLLER, R. J., *Sex and Gender*, Science House, New York, 1968.

67. WAELDER, R., "The Psychoanalytic Theory of Play," *Psychoanalytic Quarterly, 2:208–224*, 1933.

68. WINNICOTT, D. W., "Transitional Objects and Transitional Phenomena," *International Journal of Psycho-Analysis, 34:89–97*, 1953.

11 / Development from One to Two Years: Ego Development

Jan Drucker

Introduction

Although physical growth during the first year is undoubtedly more dramatic, the second year of life may well be the single most crucial twelve-month span in the child's overall development. The psychological events and achievements of this period are of paramount significance for later functioning in all major areas. During this year the first dominant psychosexual phase is gradually replaced by the next; the most treacherous waters of the separation-individuation process are traversed; and the symbolic capacity, organizer of all subsequent ego functioning, is acquired. In this chapter, we will be examining some of the fruits of the recent emphasis on the early years of life, and particularly the systematic study of cognitive development in infancy and early childhood.

In considering ego functioning, it is important to make a distinction between maturation—the biologically programmed unfolding of the capacities of the ego apparatuses over time—and development—the process by which these apparatuses, through interaction with the environment, come to function smoothly in the service of the needs of the organism and the demands of external reality. It is often possible, through careful observation, to follow the varying patterns of development of different ego functions in an individual child. One can then see the complicated interactions among maturational spurts, environmental responses, changes in behavioral patterns, and overall psychological growth. Frequently, a new skill, for example, walking, ushers in a new era in the development of object relations, or makes possible new adaptive solutions to ongoing intrapsychic conflicts. Each advance in cognitive, motor, and perceptual functioning is a new achievement and must be considered in relation to its availability to, and its effect on, the ongoing development of drives and object relations. The division of this discussion of the second year of life into drive, object relations, and ego development sections is a somewhat arbitrary one; this is especially true in terms of new ways in which the child perceives and organizes its experiential world.

The average twelve-month-old baby can crawl, babble, feed itself with its fingers, pick up and manipulate objects in a playful and exploratory fashion, make complicated perceptual discriminations, recognize and express focused affection and annoyance towards its parents and other familiar people, and coordinate certain information about how the world works in order to create spectacles and gain gratification. By twenty-four months, however, the toddler will be walking and running, speaking in a competent communicative fashion, using fine motor movements in a well-coordinated way in order to scribble with crayons, make toys work and build block towers, and will recognize pictorial representations and play pretend games. Moreover, the toddler will solve a variety of cognitive problems which require drawing on concepts of space, causality, and the permanence of objects, and involve the manipulation of mental representations of objects and their properties. The following discussion will review some aspects of the growth and behavioral indices of thought in the toddler, with special emphasis on the acquisition of the symbolic function and its manifestations in language development.

The Growth of Thought
in the Toddler

In recent years, psychologists have focused increasingly on the first few years of life. As a result, much work has addressed itself to the question of what infants can do at birth and how their various capacities develop postnatally. Since the early 1960s, many studies have demonstrated that neonates are creatures of far more complexity than previously thought, that their perceptual behavior involves active processing of sensory information rather than passive receptivity, and that early in the first year the infant's behavior is already influenced by mental structures developed in interaction with the environment. In the cognitive domain, it is clear that much of later development is predicated on and influenced by the child's mental functioning in the earliest months of life. At the same time, there has been considerable disagreement about when an infant can be said to "think"—that is, to move beyond sensory registration and motor activity to the coordination of interiorized schemata in hypothesis-testing activity. The works of Kagan,[23] Bruner,[5] Bower,[4] and others have contributed empirical data and theoretical constructs to this debate. Psychoanalysts, whose theories have long included concepts of infantile mental activity, are also working to coordinate their postulates with the recent evidence and methodologies for examining infant thought.[42, 12, 29]

Most investigators agree that the latter part of the first year and the entire second year of life seem to be important periods for the development of thought. The acquisition of representational capacities during the second year is believed by many to be the nodal point of the process. White[40] has recently stated emphatically that he believes the period from eight to eighteen months to be not only important but critical in many areas of development, especially those related to later intellectual functioning. Whether or not one takes such an extreme position, it is evident that investigation within this age group of the transformations that take place in thinking should be given high priority.

The Piagetian View

The most systematic and comprehensive discussion of cognitive development in this age range is that of the Swiss psychologist Jean Piaget. Piaget brings to the consideration of early cognitive development the background of a biologist and philosopher, coming to his interest in the development of intelligence through studies of epistemology. His theory of cognition is based on the premise that the child goes through an invariant sequence of stages in the development of rational scientific and logical thought. Adaptation to the environment and the organization of experience along with it are the two processes Piaget thinks are common to all human beings. Our mental apparatus must develop in such a way as to facilitate these processes. To do this, Piaget says, we are always engaged in both *assimilation*—the incorporation of new information and experience in terms of preexisting mental schemata—and

accommodation—the modification of those schemata to conform to the nature of new experiential data. A balance between these two processes, a kind of homeostasis, is as essential to mental functioning as it is to biological systems.

Piaget's observations of his own children from infancy on led him to formulate the child's major ways of organizing experience at different periods of life: the *sensorimotor* period, from birth to eighteen or twenty-four months; the *preoperational* period, from two to six years; the *concrete operations* period, from seven to eleven years; and the *formal operations* period, beginning in early adolescence. Piagetian theory rests upon several basic tenets: that every child passes through each stage and substage in the same sequence, though not on any given timetable; that strategies or schemata for interacting with the environment and knowing its properties are developed; that there is a gradual progression from one period to another, with each new operation being acquired by building on the already existing ones; and that the process of development is one in which increasing differentiation and complexity is matched by increasing integration and coordination of various schemata.

The sensorimotor period, which is of most relevance here, is characterized by a close linkage between active experience and its mental representation. The development which takes place during this period involves a shift from reflexive behavior to the beginnings of intentionality and voluntary organization and control of behavior, and eventually to the establishment of mental representations and the ability to manipulate and coordinate them in a planful way. As a result, the child can evoke memory images of absent objects and predict properties of objects in the external world. The culmination of this process is the acquisition of the ability to create, manipulate, and comprehend symbolic conveyers of meaning —words, gestures, and pictorial representations. A brief overview of the six substages of sensorimotor development will establish a framework within which to consider this major achievement of the second year of life.

Stage 1: Birth to one month. During this period the baby is primarily involved in reflexive behavior. However, in the course of the infant's need to exercise his innate capacities for activities such as sucking and looking, learning takes place, mostly on the basis of simple adaptive accommodation. For example, the head is turned to reach the nipple.

Stage 2: One to four months. Accidental pleasurable occurrences lead the baby to repeat behavior which seems to have produced the pleasure. Primary circular reactions, the first schemata, are thus established.

Stage 3: Four to ten months. This stage is characterized by the beginnings of intentionality: that is, deliberate attempts to modify behavior in accordance with external phenomena (secondary circular reactions). At this point, some capacity for anticipation and some knowledge of the existence of objects when they are out of sight have been achieved.

Stage 4: Ten to twelve months. The baby is now able to apply old schemata to new situations—an important change in the flexibility of mental functioning, and a highly adaptive one. Intentionality is well developed and schemata are invoked in order to create a particular effect or solve a particular problem. Several schemata or secondary circular reactions may be combined in a given activity.

Stage 5: Twelve to eighteen months. This stage is characterized by active experimentation with the properties of objects. Objects have existence even when out of sight and effects have causes other than the baby itself (tertiary circular reactions).

Stage 6: Eighteen to twenty-four months. This stage includes what Piaget deems the beginnings of true thought—the point at which mental activity can replace bodily movement in figuring out the solution to the problem of, say, opening a matchbox by the child visualizing the box as analogous to her mouth and trying out a way of using her finger to open the box by first inserting it in her mouth. The ability to conceptualize external reality in this way, a capacity which corresponds to Freud's definition of thought as trial action, is clearly a crucial developmental achievement.

Much of Piaget's writing[27, 28] focuses on three major sets of knowledge the child must acquire during the sensorimotor period: knowledge about the permanence of objects (even in situations where the child has no sensory evidence of them), knowledge about the cause-effect relationships which govern the surrounding world, and knowledge of spatial relationships involving first one's own body and then "objective space" and its properties. In each of these domains, stage 6 functioning involves the manipulation of mental representations of things and actions, anticipation of events and consequences of actions, and the ability to evoke the image of an absent object or agent, rather than simply to recognize it once it appears. These capabilities, as will be described, are important components of the ability to use an aspect of tangible experience, whether word, pictorial image, or gesture, to represent another, often intangible, aspect of experience—that is, the process of symbolization.

Once representational intelligence has been achieved, the child enters the preoperational stage in which aspects of experience are classified and categorized according to basic properties such as size and shape and number. Experience with such activities eventually leads to the acquisition of rules about the physical and other properties of matter, time, number, etc., which are the concrete operations of the latency-age child. According to Piaget, most classifying activities develop only in the third year and later, and most operationalized studies of children's cognitive capacities have been carried out on subjects age three and over. However, in one recent study[25] where twelve- to twenty-four-month-old subjects were asked to create groups of objects out of a total set, the two-year-olds were often able to group the objects. They did so on the basis of function—what could be done with them—rather than shape or color or size, which are categories favored by preschoolers. This experiment supports Piaget's view that rudimentary cognitive functioning precedes the development of language. (This relationship of thought and language is further developed in the discussion of language development in chapter 9.) This study also demonstrates some of the complexity of mental functioning already attained by the toddler, and points to the need for further imaginative studies of the cognitive capacities of this age group.

Whether or not one takes a whole Piagetian view of the growth of thought, there is general agreement that symbolization is central to the child's cognitive functioning. Some brief comments on the nature of "intelligence" and approaches to its assessment during the second year will be followed by a more comprehensive discussion of symbolization.

Measuring and Evaluating Cognitive Development

Psychologists have long depended on standardized tests to investigate cognitive development. However, if it is to be useful for research, a test item must relate closely to the construct being measured. Thus, tests designed to measure "intelligence" or "mental development" are useful only to the extent that their content deals with basic components of these aspects of mental functioning in some reliable way. Unfortunately concepts such as "intelligence" are broad and are used differently by various investigators. It is therefore crucial to specify what one means by the term, and what aspects a given test is tapping. This is basic to any communication and discussion of the measurement of cognitive functioning.

Numerous tests of infant development have been widely used for a number of years. These include the Bayley and Cattell scales, and other rating instruments which are based on giving the child items such as puzzles, objects to name, and problems to solve; the Griffiths, Gesell, and other scales which can be rated by means of observation and parent interview; and the Merrill-Palmer, Stanford-Binet, and others which are modeled on standardized intelligence tests for older children but are scaled downward for toddlers. All of these approaches evaluate the child's performance and assign it an intelligence, or developmental quotient; one which reflects the presumed normal distribution of intelligence in the population at large and indicates the child's relative level of current functioning. They are essentially quantitative measures.

This kind of approach to the assessment of cognitive development has come under increasing scrutiny and questioning in recent years. The concept of "intelligence" has been challenged in regard to both its definition and its utility, and there have been debates as to the possibility of inborn limitations on cognitive potential. Equally important, however, has been the attempt to define the strengths and limitations of both the concept of intelligence and the testing procedures. These have been approached through empirical studies of the reliability, long-range predictions, and accuracy of various measures. Such studies have not shown encouraging results. Bayley's own follow-up study[37] indicated that while some items from her scale correlated well with later IQ scores—for example, the level of vocabulary attained by the end of the toddler period—the overall developmental quotients assigned the babies were poor predictors. Lewis[24] has reviewed a number of studies also showing that quantitative scales in infancy are poor predictors of later intelligence test scores.

Such studies lead to caution in the use of tests to make predictions; at the same time, they do not invalidate the use of infant tests for other purposes. For the clinical or research assessment of development at any given time, these tests are not only valid but extremely important objective instruments and should be used in comparing a child to his peer group and analyzing both quantitative and qualitative aspects of his development. However, the studies of their limitations have led to increasing attention to the use of alternative, more qualitatively structured instruments for infant and toddler assessment. Some of these, such as the developmental lines approach of Anna Freud[13] or the recent work at the Child Development Center in New York City[11] emphasize descriptive and clinical assessments in terms of lines of normative psychological development. Rather than yielding a score, these provide a profile of the child's current functioning in a variety of areas of psychological significance.

Another important group of investigations has derived from Piaget's model of intellectual growth, and several scales of sensorimotor development have been devised which are based on his concepts and observations. These lend themselves to replication and standardization.[19, 7, 33] Like Piaget's, these approaches are qualitative in nature —they posit an invariant sequence in the development of problem solving in a number of areas (for example, object permanence, means-ends relationships, imitation, etc.) over time. They describe levels in this progression, but not specific ages at which they are expected to take place. Again, the end point of such an evaluation is not an IQ score but an assessment of the sensorimotor stages at which a child is operating at a given point. Such approaches are more closely related to the conceptualizations of the theory they derive from; they describe the quality or "style" of the child's development, and they are therefore increasingly favored by researchers. Their clinical use, for example, with normal preverbal children, psychotic children, and deaf children, is beginning to be explored. Furthermore, initial studies that have been carried out on the correlations between early performance on such scales and later performance on standard intelligence tests indicate a higher level of predictability than was achieved by the older tests.[34]

At its best, all psychological testing involves the use of a standardized procedure as the basis for informed clinical judgments. This is especially true with toddler testing since the age and behavior of the child often make the most rigorous testing procedures impossible to carry out. The difficulties compound at certain points in the second year. The negativism of toddlers, their fears of being separated from their mothers or of strange places and people, and their push for autonomy and resistance to demands act cumulatively to make the administration of seemingly simple items a complex art. To engage the toddler's attention and enthusiasm, to avoid confrontations, and to elicit the highest level of performance without being able to engage cooperation through any explanation of the process requires experience. It also implies an attitude which regards the tests as aids in establishing a clinical judgment rather than as ends in themselves. Thus, the new emphasis is on testing procedures which elicit toddlers' strategies and thought processes rather than simply measuring their performance levels; this is well suited to the vicissitudes of toddler testing in general.

Out of the current concern about the nature, validity, and utility of intelligence testing, infant scales have come under close scrutiny. Currently, a variety of attempts to find more meaningful and heuristic testing procedures are beginning to come to fruition. Above all, emphasis has been placed on the importance of specifying both the conceptual definitions and limitations of the area of psychological functioning being tapped. This allows for the continued use of a major component of the psychologist's armamentarium for study of the development of thought in infants and toddlers.

The Development of Representational Thought

As was discussed earlier, most developmental psychologists point to the acquisition of the capacity for representation, or symbolization, as the major accomplishment of the second year of life. It radically alters the nature of the child's thought processes, makes communication of abstract ideas possible, and distinguishes human preschoolers from all other species of animals. (Recent work with primates has sought to establish whether or not they can be taught a symbolic communication system. This has engendered considerable debate, but the question remains open at this point.) It is clear that the first task is to understand what takes place during the acquisition of the symbolic function. This will provide considerable insight into the development of cognition generally, and perhaps into its interrelation with other aspects of personality functioning. For these reasons, increasing interest, both theoretical and methodological, has been directed toward the phenomenon of symbolization in its early stages. The following discussion will review some of the

issues of definition and some of the nonverbal precursors of symbolization during the second year. More detailed consideration will be given to these and other issues in discussing the development of language—the most dramatic and perhaps the most far-reaching achievement of the second year.

ISSUES OF DEFINITION

On the most general level, symbolization involves substitution, having one thing "stand for" another, using one aspect of experience to represent another. The underlying process involves the "endowing" of an object with a meaning which it does not intrinsically possess.[9] Thus, a word used to stand for a concrete object, a set of lines used to stand for the shape of countries on a map, a set of actions used to stand for putting a baby to sleep—all of these symbolic activities involve the embodiment of meaning in a new medium, separate from, though related to, its original context. More specific definitions of symbolization rest on the theoretical point of view from which the phenomenon is approached.

For most cognitive theorists,[27, 39] an essential aspect of symbolization is the subject's conscious awareness of the process as well as awareness of some aspects of the link between the symbol and that which it represents. On the other hand, psychoanalytic writers, beginning with Freud, reserve the term symbolization for unconscious mental activity, where that which the symbol represents, as well as many of the intermediary links, have been repressed; the symbol operates in the domain of conscious thought, while its referent remains unconscious. This can be seen most clearly in dream symbolism, but also in certain symptom formation, in aspects of children's play, and in artistic activity. From the point of view of understanding the underlying thought processes involved, the emphasis on the distinction between conscious and unconscious symbolization is an important one. However, it does not mitigate against the possibility that the two processes are highly interrelated and probably interdependent. More than that, they may each stem equally from an underlying capacity of the mind to make linkages and to shift meanings from one domain of experience to another. Such a capacity may best be conceptualized as an ego function, and recent work has been directed increasingly toward such a formulation.[30, 14]

Similar definitional issues arise in relation to how to view the involvement of communication in symbolization. Some writers, for example, Werner and Kaplan[39] and Gardner,[16] build a paradigm for symbolic activity which includes the sender and the receiver of a symbolic "message." At times the "receiver" may be the self of the sender. Other approaches see the communication of meaning as a frequent concomitant of but not intrinsic to symbolization. Much investigative work also remains to be done in exploring how symbolization actually develops in the child over time, and especially how the development of different symbolic activities—for example, play, language, and drawing—interrelate in a given child. Finally, the effects of perceptual handicaps and other special developmental situations—for example, deafness, psychopathology, and retardation—on the development of symbolization remain to be explored. Despite the fledgling state of the field, the work on symbolization has already generated many interesting ideas and observations, some of which will be discussed in relation to the exploration of precursors, symbolic play, and, especially, language.

PRECURSOR PHENOMENA OF SYMBOLIZATION

One of the most interesting questions about symbolization is also one of the most difficult to investigate empirically: What are the origins and precursors of the ability to symbolize? In relation to the acquisition of first words, much work has been done, and Piaget has described in some detail the beginning symbolic play activities of his young children. But in examining the antecedents of such functioning, one must look to the nonverbal and less clearly organized behavior of the period before representational thinking becomes possible. Here one enters the realm of gestures, preverbal vocalizations of need states, and a type of early play referred to as "transitional phenomena."

Transitional phenomena were first described by Winnicott in 1953 and have since been examined increasingly in a variety of populations.[41] The concept refers to those objects, and sometimes tunes, routines, or other behaviors, which infants latch onto and use consistently for self-comforting. Linus's security blanket is the most famous example of a transitional object, though for other children dolls, teddy bears, sheets, pillows, or even bottles may serve the same purpose. What appears takes place in a child who is just becoming able to distinguish the nature of the external world. He now endows an aspect of this world with qualities both of the mother (especially those relating to her soothing functions) and of the self. He then develops an attachment to this object which stands for both "mother" and "me." Behaviorally, it can be seen that toddlers use such special objects, particularly at moments of stress, to buttress their still shaky ability to tolerate physical and psychological separateness. Thus, these blankets and other phenomena are most often called for at bedtime, at the point of actual separation, and when a physical or emotional wound has threatened the child's sense of intactness and safety.

Winnicott and many others believe that the endowing of the transitional object with meaning is the first "truly creative" act of the baby. Certainly, although the use of transitional objects appears to rest on their involvement in blurring the distinction between self and object, some degree of self-object differentiation is essential before any such endowing activity can take place.[9] Thus, the establishment of a transitional object heralds more than the libidinal attachment to the mother as a specific object and the beginning need for assistance in dealing with the potential loss of the object. It also marks a beginning capacity to relate to external objects, at least to some extent, in terms of their own properties, and it serves as well to establish a vehicle for the conveyance of meaning. This activity, or others like it (for not all healthy children establish well-defined transitional object patterns), appears to be an essential precursor to the later ability to play symbolically. Winnicott suggested, and other work has supported the idea, that from transitional phenomena stems a gradually proliferating set of play activities directed toward a variety of objects outside the self. To the extent that the child is able to endow such objects with meaning, symbolic play will develop. Many writers also feel that the creativity involved in transitional object behavior is a precursor to later artistic activity as well.

THE DEVELOPMENT OF PLAY

Play is a natural medium of expression for children, and a phenomenon with which everyone is familiar. Yet among psychologists there have been as many approaches to its study as there are schools of thought about development. In any case, it remains an area of great interest due to the light it sheds on very many aspects of the child's intrapsychic functioning. The psychoanalytic approach to play grows out of Freud's formulation of the repetition compulsion—the organism's need to repeat, in tolerable degrees, an experience which had formerly been overwhelming. The first observation of this was of an eighteen-month-old child who repeatedly threw away and retrieved a bobbin and string. Freud perceived that in this way, the child actively played out the separation from his mother which he had experienced passively and with much sadness. In a rich 1933 exposition,[35] Waelder set forth the psychoanalytic theory of play and pointed out that it has multiple determinants and multiple functions. Since then, various psychoanalytic writers have explored the cathartic value of play, its use in child psychotherapy, its organization by psychosexual phases, etc.[26, 10]

Other developmentalists have looked at play as reflective of the child's developing social awareness and role taking, and as elucidating the nature of cognitive development. The early sensorimotor play of the infant with its own body, gradually extending to reciprocal exploration of the mother's body, and eventually interest in and exploration of the inanimate world, has been described. From the point of view of whom the baby plays with, the progression seems to be from solitary play to simple reciprocal games with special people, to simple reciprocal play—for example, rolling a ball, hiding, and finding—with other toddlers. By the age of two, this becomes what psychologists call parallel play—two children playing side by side at the same game but without real interaction. Children become interested in and capable of true cooperative play only gradually during the preschool years. During such activity, more than one child is necessary and coordination of different peoples' activities takes place. Of course, all of these frames of reference are illustrative of the multiplicity of functions of toddler play.[9]

In the current context, the approaches of Piaget and Werner and Kaplan are most relevant. They have considered the play of toddlers from the viewpoint of emerging symbolization—the progression from concrete, or sensorimotor manipulation of objects, to what Waelder so succinctly described as "the weaving of unreality about a real object."[35] Piaget's description[27] of the evolution of his little daughter's game of going to sleep has become a classic illustration of this process. Early in the second year she invented the game of lying down on her own bed and closing her eyes, then opening them and laughing. This gradually evolved into her lying down on her pillow on a couch, then simply putting her head down on a hard object, nowhere near her own bed, but understanding that she was, in a totally separate context, "pretending" to go to sleep. It can be seen that the use of a vehicle (here a pretend action to convey a separate meaning) previously described as the essence of symbolization, has been achieved.

Play, then, flowers in the second year of life because the attainment of symbolic capacities makes possible a new type of interaction. This occurs not only with other people but with inanimate objects as well. Once the child can repeat and work through situations in play, the possibilities for new coping mechanisms and defensive activities expand dramatically. The turning of passive experience into action through imaginative play is the result of the development of symbolic play during the toddler era. Later, it will serve as one of the mainstays of the preschooler's ability to deal adaptively with the stress of the oedipal period.

REFERENCES

1. BAYLEY, N., *Mental Growth during the First Three Years: A Developmental Study of 61 Children by Repeated Tests*, Genetic Psychology Monographs, vol. 14, no. 1, 1933.

2. BEE, H., *The Developing Child*, Harper & Row, New York, 1975.

3. BELL, S. M., "The Development of the Concept of Object as Related to Infant-Mother Attachment," *Child Development*, 41:291–311, 1970.

4. BOWER, T. G. R., "The Visual World of Infants," *Scientific American*, 251(6):80–92, 1966.

5. BRUNER, J., *Processes of Cognitive Growth: Infancy*, Clark University Press, Worcester, Mass., 1968.

6. CHURCH, J., *Three Babies: Biographies of Cognitive Development*, Random House, New York, 1968.

7. CORMAN, H. H., and ESCALONA, S. K., "Stages of Sensorimotor Development: A Replication Study," *Merrill-Palmer Quarterly*, 15:351–362, 1969.

8. DRUCKER, J., "The Affective Context and Psycho-dynamics of First Symbolization," in Smith, N., and Franklin, M. B. (Eds.), *Symbolic Functioning in Childhood*, Erlebaum, Hillsdale, N.J., forthcoming.

9. ———, "Toddler Play: Some Comments on its Functions in the Developmental Process," in Spence, D. P. (Ed.), *Psychoanalysis and Contemporary Science*, vol. 4, pp. 479–527, International Universities Press, New York, 1975.

10. ERIKSON, E. H., *Childhood and Society*, W. W. Norton, New York, 1950.

11. FLAPAN, D., and NEUBAUER, P., *Assessment of Early Child Development*, Aronson, New York, 1975.

12. FRAIBERG, S., "Libidinal Object Constancy and Object Permanence," in Eissler, R. S., et al. (Eds.), *The Psychoanalytic Study of the Child*, vol. 24, pp. 9–47, International Universities Press, New York, 1969.

13. FREUD, A., *Normality and Pathology in Childhood*, International Universities Press, New York, 1965.

14. GALENSON, E., "The Capacity for Symbolic Ex-

pression: An Ego Function," in Franklin, M. B., and Drucker, J. (Eds.), *Perspectives on Play*, forthcoming.

15. ———, MILLER, R., and ROIPHE, H., "The Choice of Symbols," *Journal of the American Academy of Child Psychiatry, 15(1):83–96, 1976.*

16. GARDNER, H., *The Arts in Human Development*, John Wiley, New York, 1973.

17. GESELL, A., *The Mental Growth of the Pre-School Child*, Macmillan, New York, 1925.

18. GINSBURG, H., and OPPER, S., *Piaget's Theory of Intellectual Development*, Prentice-Hall, Englewood Cliffs, N.J., 1969.

19. GOUIN-DÉCARIE, T., *Intelligence and Affectivity in Early Childhood*, International Universities Press, New York, 1966.

20. GRIFFITHS, R., *The Abilities of Babies*, McGraw-Hill, New York, 1954.

21. HERRON, R. E., and SUTTON-SMITH, B., *Child's Play*, John Wiley, New York, 1971.

22. HONZIK, M. P., "The Constancy of Mental Test Performance during the Preschool Period," *Journal of Genetic Psychology, 52:285–302, 1938.*

23. KAGAN, J., "Do Infants Think?" *Scientific American, 226(3):74–82, 1972.*

24. LEWIS, M., *Infant Intelligence Tests: Their Use and Misuse*, Educational Testing Service, Research Bulletin RB–73–10, 1973.

25. NELSON, K., "Some Evidence for the Cognitive Primacy of Categorization and its Functional Basis," *Merrill-Palmer Quarterly, 19:21–40, 1973.*

26. PELLER, L., "Libidinal Phases, Ego Development and Play," in Eissler, R. S., et al. (Eds.), *The Psychoanalytic Study of the Child*, vol. 9, pp. 178–198, International Universities Press, New York, 1954.

27. PIAGET, J., *Play, Dreams and Imitation in Childhood*, W. W. Norton, New York, 1962.

28. ———, *The Origins of Intelligence in Children*, International Universities Press, New York, 1954.

29. PINE, F., "Libidinal Object Constancy: A Theoretical Note," in Goldberger, L. (Ed.), *Psychoanalysis and Contemporary Science*, vol. 3, pp. 307–313, International Universities Press, New York, 1974.

30. SARNOFF, C., "Symbols and Symptoms," *Psychoanalytic Quarterly, 39:550–562, 1970.*

31. Society for Research in Child Development, *Cognitive Development in Children*, University of Chicago Press, Chicago, 1970.

32. SUTTON-SMITH, B., *Child Psychology*, Appleton-Century-Crofts, New York, 1973.

33. UZGIRIS, I. C., and HUNT, J. MC. V., *Assessment in Infancy*, University of Illinois Press, Urbana, 1975.

34. WACHS, T. D., "Relation of Infant's Performance on Piaget Scales between Twelve and Twenty-four Months and Stanford-Binet Performance at Thirty-one Months," *Child Development, 46:4, 1975.*

35. WAELDER, R., "The Psychoanalytic Theory of Play," *Psychoanalytic Quarterly, 2:208–224, 1933.*

36. WATSON, R. I., and LINDGREN, H. C., *Psychology of the Child*, 3rd ed., John Wiley, New York, 1973.

37. WERNER, E. E., and BAYLEY, N., "The Reliability of Bayley's Revised Scale of Mental and Motor Development during the First Year of Life," *Child Development, 37:39–50, 1966.*

38. WERNER, H., *Comparative Psychology of Mental Processes*, Follet, Chicago, 1948.

39. ———, and KAPLAN, B., *Symbol Formation*, John Wiley, New York, 1963.

40. WHITE, B., *The First Three Years of Life*, Prentice-Hall, Englewood Cliffs, N.J., 1975.

41. WINNICOTT, D. W., "Transitional Object and Transitional Phenomena," *International Journal of Psychoanalysis, 34:89–97, 1953.*

42. WOLFF, P. H., *The Developmental Psychologies of Jean Piaget and Psychoanalysis*, Psychological Issues, Monograph no. 5, vol. 2, no. 1, 1960.

12 / Development from One to Two Years: Normal Coping Mechanisms

Catherine B. Shapiro

Introduction

"Normal pathology" may sound like a contradiction in terms, but it is an apt way to describe the manifestations of developmental stress as they occur during the second year of life. This is a period of great developmental flux, similar to the oedipal stage or, for that matter, adolescence, in being tumultuous. It is a time of rapid growth and quickly shifting affect and is characterized by the toddler's valiant struggle to harness his or her primitive impulses in line with the newly per-

ceived demands of family and society. Of central importance are issues of autonomy, holding on and letting go, as well as the friction and negativism which are inevitable outgrowths of the socialization process and concomitant setting of limits by parents.

As is detailed throughout this chapter, many developmental thrusts are taking place simultaneously during the second year. The waning of the oral phase and the emergence of the anal zone as a psychic organizer, as well as the vicissitudes of the separation-individuation process, bring new experiences of anxiety about loss and new ambivalence toward significant objects. A new capacity for the focused expression of both affection and anger,[2] but also a new tendency toward clinging, whining, and temper tantrums, are hallmarks of toddlerhood. Despite all of his or her new achievements, the toddler's ego functioning is far from the mature organization and defensive strength it will later achieve. Behind the bravado of his or her posture, the toddler is unsteady and insecure, with a ready tendency to wobble; and following on the heels of the exuberant elation with which he or she meets the world comes the period Mahler[10] has characterized as the psychologically most vulnerable in the child's life.

The confluence of rapid developmental shifts, each bringing with it new pleasures but also new strains and anxieties, at a point when the child's ego is relatively incapable of organized defensive maneuvers, leads inevitably to considerable distress. Still largely preverbal, the toddler must resort to behavioral communications. Tantrums and panics reflect the experience of being overwhelmed by affect; behavioral regressions express not only a need for earlier, more predictable forms of gratification, but also the sense that too much has been taken on and still more will be expected of the child; somatic distress reflects the still close relationship between soma and psyche and the toddler's limited arsenal of coping mechanisms. A temporary retreat, under such circumstances, enables the toddler to marshall his or her forces for the next foray into early childhood.

In this context, it becomes apparent that behavior patterns and discomfort, which at other ages and stages would be considered symptomatic of pathological development, must often be viewed in toddlers as normal manifestations of stress, most of which indicate the appropriateness of the ongoing development and bring the toddler relief, as well as serving as an impetus to further ego development and mastery. Moreover, limited regressions are a necessary aspect of psychological development at all ages. As Anna Freud[6] discussed so elegantly, it is normal for the child, and a better guarantee for his or her mental health, that he revert occasionally to more infantile modes of behavior, providing the regression is limited in time and scope. In the following pages, a number of common disturbances of the toddler period are described; some involve temporary regressions of both ego and drive organization, while others seem more clearly discharge phenomena, and still others, such as the early phobias, reflect new ego capacities put to the service of protecting important objects and the self.

Disturbances in Oral Behavior

During the second year, aggression toward the maternal object is frequently expressed around oral issues. Shifting rejections of certain foods and preferences for others, even on a daily basis, are common, as are transient refusals of all solid food. Quite often it is milk, symbol of the "good mother," which is singled out for rejection. Typical is the toddler who will drink water and juices and even chocolate milk from a cup but insists on his or her cherished bottle for milk. The finicky and variable appetite of some toddlers can bring despair to their mothers who, in part responding to the aggression being expressed, often engage in pitched battles over quality and quantity of food intake and table manners.

The mother of Gwenie, a petite twelve-month old, spent many hours frantically trying to invent new taste treats to entice her daughter to eat more. Though Gwenie was healthy, her food intake had fallen off markedly just at the time she began crawling freely. At the same time, Gwenie weaned herself from the breast. Her mother experienced these developments as rejections of her mothering and began to focus much of her attention on what Gwenie ate. Gwenie, in turn, teased her mother by rejecting one preferred food after another, finally deigning to eat the ninth or tenth type she was offered.

Later in the second year, toddlers who are dealing with anal phase concerns may regress to intensified orality briefly or may manifest aspects of their new behavioral organization in the old familiar manner of the oral phase. Thus messing and smearing of food or, inversely, fastidiousness and expressions of disgust at particular types of food, are often seen.

Disturbances in Anal and Urinary Functioning

Once anal and urinary awareness has been established, issues of object loss and body part loss, as well as others centering on autonomy and control, are played out in relation to anal and urinary zonal behavior. Transient stool and urine retention, as well as selective soiling once toilet training has begun, are frequently encountered.

Jessica, a hearty, gregarious seventeen-month-old, withheld her urine for many hours and would urinate only standing up in the bathtub, in her mother's presence. This behavior, which persisted for several weeks, followed closely Jessica's awareness of sexual differences, the birth of her baby brother, and her mother's first attempts at toilet training.

fears of injury, dislike of broken toys, crayons, and crackers, and concern for missing pieces of puzzles and the like become quite common.

Fears, Anxieties and Early Phobias

In the early phases of life, when the child is not only preverbal but in a relatively undifferentiated state, unpleasure is presumably experienced globally. These primordial anxiety experiences are retained as archaic fears of being engulfed, starving, being cold, wet, or in pain. Once some degree of self-object differentiation has taken place, the child attributes relief and gratification to the mother's ministrations and comes to fear abandonment by her in a specific way. Transient fears of strangers, of separation situations, of going to sleep, and of anger toward the mother contribute to the establishment of a specific attachment and are ubiquitous experiences of normal toddlerhood.

Teddy was a sturdy, handsome toddler whose delight in exploring his world was a pleasure to his whole family. At about thirteen months, Teddy began to cling to his mother at moments of parting and to mildly resist being put to sleep. He did not seem excessively anxious about separation and greeted his familiar baby-sitter cheerfully. However, on nights when his parents went out for the evening, Teddy regularly awakened several times during the night.

Sometime during the second year, most children begin to have bad dreams, or even nightmares. Such early projections of anger are also seen in the typical fears at this age of animals, strangers, loud noises, trucks, and other machines. Later in the year, cognitive development and, particularly, the capacity for symbolization make possible, through the mechanism of displacement, the formation of early organized phobic responses.

Jan, a two-year-old girl described by Sarnoff,[12] developed a fear of plants, particularly seaweed, following a separation from her mother at the seashore. The projection of her hostile aggressive impulses onto the seaweed protected the maternal object from the full brunt of her rage and limited her fear to a specific set of objects, preserving the libidinal object relationship.

Once genital arousal and awareness of the anatomical difference has been established, early castration anxiety may arise as fear of body part loss is added to basic concerns about object loss.[11, 7] In the second half of the second year,

Somatization Reactions

Pediatricians are familiar with the prevalence of mild gastrointestinal and upper respiratory illnesses during the second year of life. A major factor in this increased incidence may well be the effect of psychological stress. Gastrointestinal upsets, colds, ear infections, and skin rashes may be somatic manifestations of tension, anxiety and/or body-bound aggression. In extreme cases, exczema, asthma, or colitis may result, but, in the normal child, such illnesses are mild and have no sequelae. Especially prevalent are intestinal problems, such as diarrhea and constipation, which reflect the centrality of the anal zone, as well as the immature ego's continued body channeling of affect and conflict.

Impressionistic data from the Albert Einstein College of Medicine Research Nursery suggests that many episodes of minor illness during the second year follow brief separations from the parents.

Disturbances Related to the Expression of Aggression

As discussed previously, with the achievement of self-object differentiation, the focused expression of aggression toward the object becomes possible, manifested first through the oral mode in biting and spitting, and later, under the impact of the anal phase, in teasing, hitting, messing, withholding, throwing, destructiveness, stubbornness, willfullness, disobedience and general naughtiness. Despite the toddler's new degree of psychic organization, it is still necessary from time to time for more immediate, unmodulated discharge to be sought, often in the form of temper tantrums. Parents frequently find themselves responding to the primitivity of the toddler's expression of rage with their own lowered frustration tolerance, and an intense contest of wills may ensue.

Transient Regressions in Relation to Ego Attainments

While any ego function is potentially subject to temporary regression under stress, those of the toddler are especially unstable because they are so newly acquired. Anger, anxiety, separation from the mother, illness, and fatigue can all precipitate varying degrees of ego regression. Speech, motor behavior, symbolic capacities, judgment, and reality testing can all be invaded at one time or another.

Murray, a well-coordinated boy of fifteen months, went through a period of clumsiness and tripping whenever his mother left the room. This behavior had a secondary determinant in the attention and affection Murray received from those around him following each small spill, support which appeared to help him tolerate his mother's brief absence.

Though there is much general discussion in the literature of early development,* few devote much space to the "normal pathology" of the period.

In the preceding pages, however, we have seen that a number of temporary disruptions of the toddler's functioning are an expectable aspect of normal development in the second year of life.

* See references 1, 3, 4, 5, 8, 13, 14, and 15 for some of the best discussions.

REFERENCES

1. ARNSTEIN, H. S., *The Roots of Love*, Bobbs-Merrill, Indianapolis, 1975.
2. AUSUBEL, C., "Negativism as a Phase of Ego Development," *American Journal of Orthopsychiatry, 20:* 796–805, 1950.
3. BEE, H., *The Developing Child*, Harper & Row, New York, 1975.
4. CHURCH, J., *Understanding Your Child from Birth to Three*, Random House, New York, 1973.
5. FRAIBERG, S. H., *The Magic Years*, Charles Scribner's Sons, New York, 1959.
6. FREUD, A., *Normality and Pathology in Childhood: Assessments of Development*, International Universities Press, New York, 1965.
7. GALENSON, E., and ROIPHE, H., "The Impact of Early Sexual Discovery on Mood, Defensive Organization, and Symbolization," in Eissler, R. S., et al. (Eds.), *The Psychoanalytic Study of the Child*, vol. 23, pp. 348–365, International Universities Press, New York, 1971.
8. ISAACS, S. S., *Troubles of Children and Parents*, Vanguard Press, New York, 1948.

9. MAHLER, M. S., *On Human Symbiosis and the Vicissitudes of Individuation*, International Universities Press, New York, 1968.
10. ———, PINE, F., and BERGMAN, A., *The Psychological Birth of the Human Infant*, Basic Books, New York, 1975.
11. ROIPHE, H., "On an Early Genital Phase: With an Addendum on Genesis," in Eissler, R. S., et al. (Eds.), *The Psychoanalytic Study of the Child*, vol. 26, pp. 195–216, International Universities Press, New York, 1968.
12. SARNOFF, C., "Symbols and Symptoms: Phytophobia in a Two-Year-Old Girl," *Psychoanalytic Quarterly, 39:* 550–562, 1970.
13. STONE, L. J., and CHURCH, J., *Childhood and Adolescence*, Random House, New York, 1973.
14. SUTTON-SMITH, B., *Child Psychology*, Appleton-Century-Crofts, New York, 1973.
15. WATSON, R. I., and LINDGREN, H. C., *Psychology of the Child*, John Wiley, New York, 1973.

---

13 / Development from Two and One-half to Four Years

Christoph M. Heinicke

Introduction

As in all development, this period in the child's life typically integrates previous achievements and at the same time it is characterized by new forms of growth which predict future achievements. The writings of the two foremost theorists in the field who shall be used most extensively here agree that the course of growth is not unidirectional. Thus, according to Piaget, the move to representational intelligence constantly draws on its sensorimotor past and foreshadows its symbolic future. The core of Anna Freud's framework of assessment of the normal child is to ask: "To what extent do the progressive forces of the child predominate over those representing regression?"

To organize certain experiential sequences typical for this age, the material will focus on the three that seem central and which, in turn, seem nodal to closely related experiences. The first of these is the growth of intelligence as conceptualized by Piaget and Bruner and his colleagues.[12] The related issues of linguistic and conversational competence will be discussed in this context. Second, the discussion will turn to the increasing elaboration of the awareness of sexual differences and how these are related to developing concepts of self and of parental interrelationships. Third, attention will be directed to the ability of the child to maintain a predominantly positive representation of the absent love object (object constancy) and the child's psychological move from the initial home base to the new involvements as exemplified by entrance into nursery school.

Before turning to these major developmental issues, certain milestones of the motor and intellectual development in the age interval two and one-half to four years that are assessed by the Gesell Developmental Schedules and the Stanford-Binet IQ will be summarized.

Milestones of the Motor and Intellectual Development of the Child in the Interval from Two and One-half to Four Years of Age

The research of Gesell et al.[22] and subsequent summaries of that research[31] indicate certain milestones of motor development for the two-and-one-half- to four-year-old age interval. Thus, standing now requires little effort and the child is as likely to run as to walk. The movements are smoother and include more accurate acceleration, deceleration, and turning of corners. The four-year-old can stand on one foot for two seconds, and can go on a 6 cm walking board with minimal stepping off. By age four, a definite throwing stance has developed. Even though the finger control is still limited, boys are favored in the growth of this skill. Both boys and girls are, however, very much involved in the motor conquest of space. This is consistent with their questioning, their language growth, their growing sexual curiosity, and their

general intrusiveness. The ability to build a tower of nine cubes further represents the growth of their fine motor skills and their general expansiveness.

The large muscles are still better developed than those involved in fine motor control, but by four years, the child holds a pencil in near-adult fashion, can make clear vertical and circular lines, trace a diamond, and draw beginning "pictures." A further indication of the development of fine muscle coordination is the ability to fold a paper diagonally and to trace a path between two parallel lines.

Several other skills characterize the psychomotor growth seen by four years of age and have important implications for the issue of individuation and self-reliance. At this point, the children can not only feed themselves while spilling relatively little, but they can serve themselves and others by such acts as successfully pouring from a pitcher. Considerable competence at dressing and cleaning themselves has also been acquired, and the putting on of shoes and buttoning of clothes is no longer that difficult.

It is, however, the burst of speed and control of the tricycle, as seen, for example, as the child rides away from his mother, that seems best to represent the growing independence resulting from the new-found motor coordination. The same thrust toward individuality is manifested in the act of climbing to the top of the jungle gym and swinging.

Between two and one-half and four years of age, milestones of the child's intellectual development can be obtained by following the various Stanford-Binet IQ tasks. Among the other advances, there is a change from simple naming to the use of more abstract concepts. This is illustrated by contrasting the tasks typically posed to the two-and-one-half-year-old of identifying parts of the body and naming objects, with the kind of request directed to the four-year-old to formulate opposite analogies. In regard to the latter, the child is asked to complete: "Brother is a boy; sister is a . . ." These changes in the demands to conceptualize are in turn related to changes in the complexity and structure of the child's language, which will be discussed shortly.

The test items at age four compared to age three also reflect the increasing capacity for memory. Naming the objects missing from a series of previously seen items is very much different from simply identifying one animal picture which has been temporarily removed from vision. But this identification in turn seems to require greater capacity for memory than asking the child of two-and-one-half to repeat two digits like 4 and 7.

The increase in the capacity for fine visual-motor coordination is again suggested by the following sequence of test requests: building a tower of four or more blocks at two years of age, stringing beads and building a block bridge at age three, and sorting buttons at age three and one-half.

With these sketches of certain milestones of psychomotor and intellectual development, we will now discuss the latter in terms of the quality of the thought process and the nature of linguistic competence.

From Sensorimotor Intelligence to Representative Thought

During this period of his life, the child increasingly demonstrates the power of being able to signify or represent something external to himself in thought and to do this relatively independently of the actions involved with that external object.[33, 17, 13] Piaget and Inhelder stress five behavior patterns as indices of what they call the semiotic function or, rather, the internal representative evocation of an object or event which is not pressent. They are: (1) deferred imitation such as spanking a doll in the manner in which the child has seen the parent spank someone; (2) symbolic play in the sense of washing dishes in the doll corner; (3) drawing a graphic image that is clearly based on the memory of something —a house, for example; (4) other evidence for a mental image for which there is no clue in the immediate sensorimotor environment; and (5) verbal evocation in the sense that a child says "meow" after a cat has disappeared.[32]

Prior to this representation of the object (person or thing) in thought, there is, of course, the development of object permanence itself around the eighteen- to twenty-month period. Two systematic research projects have suggested that person permanence—for example, the permanence of the mother representation—is likely to precede inanimate object permanence.[4, 18] Bell has shown that those children having the more harmonious relationship with their mothers are most likely to develop this person permanence before the inanimate object permanence.[4] This point will be explored later in the discussion of emotional object constancy. Here it suffices to say that the possibility of the representation of the mother image might also occur prior to the representation of the inanimate object. The doll play of children in the second year of life, as well as observation of their behavior, permits inference of the signifier of "mother" quite apart from certain sensorimotor action sequences.[24, 34]

There are tremendous advantages to freeing the process of knowing and mastery from immediate action sequences. Thus, the child is now able to represent an angry mother doll, or a baby doll that is being fed, and then to explore their interaction once removed. This becomes especially evident in the explosion of play that occurs toward the end of the third year and during the fourth year. As is so often true in development, the specific characteristics of representational thought present at this time can be further defined through contrast with what is to follow. Thus, as will be delineated in other chapters, the preoperational thought of this period stands in contrast to the increasing capacity for dealing with the intellectual operations involved in the problem of conservation, in seriation, in classification, in number manipulation, and in the knowledge of space, time, and speed. Piaget and Inhelder[33] as well as Flavell[17] frequently use the child's ability to deal with the conservation of mass to illustrate this basic difference between preoperational and operational thought. Thus, the two-and-one-half- to four-year-old typically believes that, when equal quantities of water are poured into two containers, one taller and narrower than the other, the quantities are no longer equal. In effect, the child can represent and in a sense signify and retain the mental image. To some extent, however, he is still tied to the perceptual image and has difficulty in dealing with more than one property of the experience at a time.

The continuing adherence at this age to the perceptual, the limitation in dealing with more than one dimension of a stimulus situation at a time, and how indeed this changes after the age of four, are beautifully illustrated in studies by Bruner and Kenney.[12] Nine clear plastic beakers, which varied three degrees in height and three degrees in diameter, were placed on a three-by-three matrix essentially identical to the tic-tac-toe arrangement. One is dealing then with the dimension of the initial matrix and the simultaneous changes in both the height and diameter of the plastic beakers. The findings are clear. The children of the age group considered here, namely two and one-half to four, could in each instance accurately replace one single beaker when it was removed. If two were removed, 30 percent were already likely to reverse the positions and 55 percent of the children of this age group failed to replace the beakers correctly when a full diagonal involving three beakers was removed. The children were also asked to reproduce the total matrix after it had been scrambled, and, finally, to transpose the matrix when the smallest beaker was put in the opposite corner of the matrix. The latter is the most challenging task in terms of understanding the concept involved. These children neither reproduce nor transpose to any but the most limited extent, and the task of transposition was successfully handled only by the seven-year-old child. It can be seen, then, that these older children were able to free their concept of the immediate perceptually influenced boundary of the matrix and at the same time deal with more than one dimension. At this point one may ask: Could not the thrust of the so-called phallic development and the move to the more complex matrix of the oedipal situation be derived from more than one source? Could it not be a function of both developing sexuality and object relations, on the one hand, and a reflection of the child's changing cognitive capacities on the other?

It is true that the growth of language is initiated well before the period from two and one-half to four years; however, an accelerated growth of the complexity of language usage does characterize this interval. This chapter cannot do justice to the field of developmental psycholinguistics. Certain relevant statements, however, can be made. Brown[10] has focused on the development of sentence structure and has been able to demonstrate how the mean length of utterance defined in terms of the number of morphemes used by the child grows dramatically during roughly this interval. He shows that the order of acquisition of these grammatical usages is the same for each child, but the rate of acquisition differs. He suggests that this rate of acquisition is likely to be influenced both by family-child interaction variables and by general intelligence.

A study of three-year-old Dutch preschoolers by van der Geest et al.[21] lends some support to Brown's hypothesis. A Syntactic Complexity Score was developed by these researchers and its various subcomponents factor-analyzed. Factor 1 was considered a general planning factor; it described the mental activities needed to bring the various parts of the sentence together. For example, it considered the planning of the constituents which are inherently connected with the verb, after this verb has been chosen. Factor scores derived from Factor 1 correlated significantly with IQ ($0.59**$) and also with such quantitative indices as the number of different words used ($0.92**$), mean word length of sentence ($0.96**$), and the mean length of the five longest sentences ($0.93**$).

It turned out that the middle-class preschool children did not differ significantly from two lower-class groups at age three; by four years of age, however, the middle-class children had developed at a faster rate on this planning component (Factor 1) than did the other two lower-class groups. This suggested the possibility that environment could influence the rate of linguistic development.

Another feature of language in this age interval is captured by the distinction between private, egocentric, and social speech. Initially, Piaget had viewed egocentric speech as characterizing this phase; subsequently, this has been reappraised.[32] Private speech is not meant for others, whereas social speech is intended to and effectively does communicate information which aids adaptation. Egocentric speech refers to socially intended language which in fact fails to communicate. This occurs because of the speaker's inability to estimate the cognitive perspective of his listener. It follows that the greater the semantic capacity of a given child as compared to other children of the same age, the less likely it is that that child is going to exhibit egocentric speech. It would be expected that at this age, conversational competence is likely to be correlated with the general cluster of adaptation-competence (see chapter 9 for a discussion of this cluster). Clarke-Stewart's study[15] of seventeen-month-old children supports this hypothesis. Language assessments dealing mostly with naming objects and tests of comprehension correlated 0.81 with a general competence factor. It is certainly true that the enhancement of communicative competence is likely to enhance general adaptation and vice versa; however, it is very likely that in certain contexts, communication in an egocentric or private context is also going to have adaptive functions. Conversations with a favorite teddy bear, for example, may be extremely helpful in dealing with the stress of separating from the parent.

Communication by the child, especially where it is private and egocentric, must also be seen in the context of the potential listener. What is communicated may not be in the form of adult-defined information giving or consonant with an adult-defined view of reality, but nevertheless, it represents important information capable of being understood by another child or adult. When there is an impending separation of mother and daughter, the child's verbalized concern about who will take care of her teddy when she is gone and whether teddy will behave himself will be readily understood by many children and adults. One may hypothesize that the parent's ability to "understand" these communications would, in general, further conversational skills. Carried to an extreme, it could lead to symbiotic communication. Similarly, it has been noted that children find partners to play who are able to "listen to" and "understand" certain emotionally laden, not clearly verbalized, and yet quite coherent types of communication. It is well known that the attractiveness to the child of a contact with a therapist lies in part in the sense that these less clearly verbalized communications are being listened to, and understood. One is left then with the general impression that by four years of age, extensive and complex communication exists even though it is not always structured in adult readable terms.

The preceding material has stressed certain aspects of the cognitive development of the child at this age, and the ensuing portions of the chapter will emphasize the affective and social aspects of the child's development. If one places the distinction within psychoanalytic theory as outlined in the Anna Freud developmental profile, these sections will deal primarily with drive development; however, certain aspects of ego development will also be discussed as well as the combination of the two as conceptualized by Anna Freud in the notion of the developmental line.

Psychosexual Development: the Growing Awareness of Self and Entry into the Phallic Phase

According to psychoanalytic theory, it is in this age interval that the child proceeds beyond the anal to the phallic level of libidinal or psychosexual development. From the observation of young children, it can indeed be readily documented how the child's dominating bodily interest moves from the anal to the phallic zone; nor is it difficult to trace the many behavioral derivatives of this focus as one moves from two to four years of age. For the boy, in particular, it is assumed (and again observations tend to confirm) that certain sensations in his phallus do accompany various thrusting and masturbatory activities. In these instances, the pleasure and excitement seem obvious. Nor is it that difficult to infer excitement in the little girl when an enthusiastic youngster is lying on top of her. The manner in which little girls rub their genital areas against the knees of adults, especially adult males, and the manner in which they sit on the laps of such adults, seems not only an affectionate seeking for body contact but appears to be specifically accompanied by sensuous feelings.

A great variety of self-initiated play can also be related to the growing emphasis on the phallus. Girls as well as boys build the kinds of towers that Erikson[16] first described in his classic work on play configuration. It is suggested that systematic observation of this age group will confirm the presence of important differences in the doll play of boys and girls. Observations contrasting the doll play of three-to-four- and four-to-five-year-old boys and girls in relation to a standardized doll house and doll family[24] did reveal important sex and age differences.[37] It terms of age differences, the four-to-five-year-old more clearly differentiated where children and adults slept. It was perhaps of greatest interest that when the less that four-year-old played out the child entering the parental bedroom, some kind of aggressive or explosive sequence followed. By contrast, for the child older than four, it was more frequent to have the child doll enter but then withdraw.

Turning to the sex differences found in play, the following themes occurred more often among the boys: car collisions, moving or pushing cars, and tower building.[36] In their extensive review of the research on sex differences, Maccoby and Jacklin[28] also found that males are more aggressive, that the evidence for this is substantial, and that the difference is found as early as two or two and one-half years of age. Using a variety of evidence, they agree that the male's greater aggression has a biological component.

During this age period, it is also true that there is likely to be rapid regression from this early phallic emphasis to play of a more anal derivative sort, such as water play at the doll play-sink. More important, both sexes are typically found to experiment with behavior more classically associated with the other sex. Thus, the little girl riding a broom leaves little to the imagination. Similarly, little boys often "experiment" by dressing in a long skirt and "trying on" lipstick. It must be stressed that interpretations of these behaviors must be done in the context of the total assessment of the child. Thus, the building of a house or enclosure may have relatively little to do with the child's sensations of bodily enclosures but may relate instead to the wish to have a stable home or to the struggle to control certain internal impulses in an enclosure.

As previous chapters have shown, the awareness of sexual and bodily differences is by no means a new phenomena at this age. In individual cases, it is possible that nursery school may be the first occasion that children have seen each other in the nude. On the other hand, the reaction to and further adaptation to this awareness takes on the special characteristics of this phase of development. Thus, the boy experiences a new quality of sensation and power in connection with his erect penis. Given the overwhelming nature of these sensations, at least at certain times, he does indeed become concerned about the potential loss of his precious organ. This is clearly accentuated by viewing the female genitals, as well as by the not infrequent teasing which takes the form of the penis being grabbed at by other children, and, particularly by the girls.

In recent years, the role of the little girl's envy of the boy's penis in current and future psychopathology has undergone considerable reexamination. At this age, the evidence for such envy can be readily inferred from the direct observation of children. The impression gathered is that the little girl does envy the boy his special organ. This is particularly the case in the sense that she feels, and perhaps justly, that it brings him much closer to the valued affection of the mother. The boy's envy of the girl's future procreative powers is less readily observed, but the male adult's envy of the pregnant woman has been documented from clinical material.[40] Clinical material also indicates the powerful impact on children younger than four years old of a birth of a sibling. The frequency with which that happens suggests that an excellent field for the study of envy would be the short-term, longitudinal study of the child's immediate reactions to the mother's pregnancy and to the birth of the sibling.

Many other inferences have been made about the fate of psychosexual development.[14] A number of these hypotheses may indeed prove very useful clinically. All too often, however, they may make much clinical sense in terms of the treatment of patients but are indeed difficult to document from observations made during this age interval. One such example is the formulation that the little girl gives up her desire for the phallus and initially wishes to incorporate that of the father. It is hard to demonstrate this. This is not to say, of course, that the little girl does not turn her sexual seductiveness to her father or other male adults. This will be discussed in subsequent chapters.

What is readily observed is the beginning of a role enactment highly suggestive of either actual observations of adult intercourse or fantasies about it. Time and again one can observe what is essentially a mutual attack when both sexes are playing both the active and the passive as well as the sadistic and masochistic roles. Contrary to the relatively sophisticated play sequences of the child older than four years, these initial encounters often look more like wrestling matches than the elaboration of something like doctor-and-nurse play. In one corner of the nursery school, one can observe the boys setting up various towers and then shooting cars off a chute into these towers until all are knocked over, while in another corner, three girls dressed in bathing suits are trying out the new rock-and-roll movements that they have seen on television or in real life. The next minute, however, one of the same little boys may be seen prancing in an elegant dress with handbag, accompanied by his best friend dressed in similar garb, giggling immensely and wanting everyone to see him. In still another area, a little girl has built a rocket with a baby bottle as the capsule and a little ballet doll dress to indicate the rocket's exhaust.

Such experimentation and the subsequent growth of an increasingly complex sense of sexual identity is likely to continue throughout childhood and adolescence. However, by the time the child is two and one-half to four years old, the basic structure of the gender identity has already developed. Stoller[38] has defined gender identity as that part of the identity concerned with masculinity and femininity. In line with the theory of bisexuality, gender identity is conceptualized as the intricate balance of masculinity and femininity in each child. Initially, it is based on the assignment made to a given sex on the basis of anatomical distinctions. Stoller[39] argues for the hypothesis that gender identity is in many different ways learned and shaped by the reinforcements and expectations of the environment. Thus, the study of transsexuals, and, especially, of male transsexuals, reveals a set of parental circumstances and expectations which lead to identity formation. This emergent is not simply a product of the resolution of conflict, but specifically a response to these parental expectations. In the extreme "experiment" of the transsexual male, there is consistent sex typing by the mother who wishes a feminized male coupled with the inability of a passive, distant father to interfere in this "casting." These act together from the earliest times to prevent the development of a clear sense of masculine identity. In contrast to the development of various forms of sexual perversion in this form of transsexual, nonconflictual learning plays a much greater role. It is important to note that gender identity is not just the resultant of the influence of biologically determined factors or the resolution of conflict as typified by the oedipal conflict and problems of castration anxiety. It is rather a function of parental "shaping" and modeling, and of the child's experimenting with and learning about sexual stereotypes. These in turn are not necessarily represented by the parents but are to be found in a wide variety of sociocultural situations.

In relation to all this development, play increasingly becomes a mode of mastery and/or preparation for more task-oriented activities. This often indeed reaches the level of peer-group activity, especially when particular events in the environment have crystallized generally felt concerns. The fantasy of a child being injured, or of another one being sick or dying, readily forms a focus for group play; potentially, group or individual discussion may then follow. Observations of preschool children have led to the distinction between fairly time-limited play on the one hand (related to a certain event impacting a group, such as a child breaking an arm), and ongoing group play on the other (which addresses specific unresolved intrapsychic and family issues in the children's lives which remain unresolved over a period of time).[26] Thus, three four-year-old children developed a variety of games in which the common theme was their taking turns rejecting each other. The further evidence of their ardent need to reject the male observer and yet to become quite seductive with him at times suggested that in each case, this behavior was an effort to deal with feelings of being rejected by their father. While not necessarily effective in the sense of resolution, clearly one of the functions of play is an effort at adaptation. It is a way for the child to try to control and affect events that he is unable to dominate and execute in other contexts.[41]

The example just cited also illustrates the effort made through play to move toward greater psychological autonomy. As long as a sense of paternal deprivation continued to capture their conscious and preconscious experience, these children would be emotionally less available to form mutually gratifying relationships with male adults. Much typical group play does change over time, and, in that sense, a normal resolution takes place. Some of it, such as mutual feeding, cleaning, and reading to, clearly are functions to assist the child in the transition from being cared for by the parents to taking care of himself. This issue is discussed further in the next section.

What must be stressed again (and will be elaborated subsequently) is the fact that the new phallic development, the new levels of group play, and the new exploration of various meanings will periodically still give way to the pull of regressive yearnings. These may take the form of a return to water play, or simply standing around, and, ultimately, sucking a thumb, or holding a blanket, or, most preferably, climbing onto a lap.

The Development of Object Constancy: The Psychological Move from Home to Nursery School

Within the framework of Anna Freud's concept of developmental lines, there is a sequence of special interest that describes the growth from dependency to emotional self-reliance and adult object relationships. It is here that one finds the stage of object constancy defined as the level of development which enables a positive inner image of the object to be maintained irrespective of either satisfactions or dissatisfactions.[20] Can the child maintain a predominantly benign inner image of the parent even though anger is also being experienced in relation to that maternal or paternal representation? Not surprisingly, the most vivid test of this development is likely to occur in situations of the child's separation from the main caretaker, be that mother or father or some other adult.

Heinicke and Westheimer[24] have prepared a summary of findings on the effects of children being separated completely from their parents for relatively brief periods of time. In chapter 12 of their volume, they note that effects of separation change as a function of the age at which the object loss occurs. Children separated into a residential nursery between the ages of one and three show profound distress and maladaptive modes of coping. A similar quality of distress is seen in the responses of the child between three and six years of age, but the older child adapts better to the separation, and for him the usual dramatic reaction observed with the younger child at the point of reunion is rarely in evidence. That is, by three years of age, emotional object constancy has typically been achieved.

Heinicke and Westheimer[24] then put the findings on the separated one- to three-year-old into the context of the discussion of emerging object constancy. They were thus able to report not only the emergence of intense anger and longing toward the missing mother and father, but a typical mode of coping with this anger, a pattern which indicated clearly that the separated children could not sustain a benign representation of the absent parent in the face of such anger. They failed to make any emotional contact with the visiting parent for whom they might have been crying for that same day, and they seemed unable even to recognize the visiting parent. These reactions were accompanied by intense hostility expressed toward doll representations of the parents in the nursery and also toward certain caretakers. All these, taken together, indicate the primitive character of the defensive measures that had to be resorted to in an effort to isolate the benign parental representation from the angry affects being experienced. Further evidence of this interpretation was seen in the reunion. The children responded with the same kind of hostile nonrecognition and suppression of all affect seen during the separation. Indeed, it was only after restoration of the affectionate relationship and the expression of residual angry affects that the development of the mother-child relationship as well as certain important ego functions could once again be restored.

Using a less traumatic form of separation, namely movement away from the mother from one room to another and for much shorter periods of time, Mahler, Pine, and Bergman[30] have considered the ability to make such a move within the context of their study of separation-individuation. In particular, the earlier phases of differentiation, practicing, and rapprochement are followed by the fourth subphase, the consolidation of individuality and the beginning of emotional object constancy. Through the use of detailed examples they not only show that the separation from the mother can typically be achieved around the end of the third year of life, but also emphasize the great variation in this ability that still occurs at this point. They relate these variations not only to the child's previous development but particularly to the previous and current experiences in the mother-child relationship. Thus, one little girl whose mother had been optimally available (and perhaps even too much so), separated relatively easily at about the age of twenty-six months. She could become involved in play initiated by another adult and was then able to return to her mother with relative ease. The authors concluded that the inner image of the mother is likely to be positively and unambivalently cathected. They gave other examples, at this particular age, where they felt this was not yet the case.

For several decades, the preferred age for starting the young child in nursery school has been about the age of three. This further reflects the ability of a child at that age to separate relatively easily from the primary caretaking adult for at least half a day. While most children can deal with this psychological move from home to nursery school, systematic study reveals that there are considerable variations even within a fairly homogeneous sample. These variations during this moment of entry, as well as the developments in the year to follow, are likely to reflect quite accurately both the child's growth in the past and his future developmental status as assessed in the period before adolescence.

Daily observations of the process of entry into nursery school reveal a step-by-step sequence which can be described as follows (one may concentrate first on that instance where the movement is a progressive one). During approximately the first week, after some initial longing and fretting for the caretaker (be it parent or other adult), one typically sees an increasingly affectionate and trusting involvement with the adults in the nursery school. Through this developing new relationship, the teacher can interest the child in certain tasks and toys. These may involve making a collage, playing with play dough, or getting the child interested in the doll corner. Again, quite typically, from these early involvements in tasks the child moves increasingly toward relationships with peers. In terms of its titer of basic trust, the relationship with the teacher does not diminish but becomes less dominant from the standpoint of the sheer quantity of interaction. Similarly, the involvement in tasks, if anything, increases in parallel with the progressive move toward what Anna Freud[20] called the peer partnerships. This involves a shift from isolated play, to parallel play, and to a mutual exchange between peers. At first the other child was simply not there, or is used as an object, but now his point of view begins to be taken into account, and there is thus the beginning of mutual need satisfaction. By four years of age, one characteristically sees the beginnings of what could be called continuing friendships.

One can construct a developmental profile when considering this period as a whole.[20] Heinicke et al.[26] used dimensions based on this profile, made certain additions, and developed a set of ratings. These evaluated both the child and the parent-child relationship in terms that sought to capture the character of development at the end of the period being discussed. One question that was examined carefully was "To what extent has the child been able to demonstrate object constancy?" Or, stated differently, "How well has he been able to maintain a predominantly positive relationship to his basic caretakers while at the same time forming new, and relatively unambivalent, relationships to the caretakers in the nursery school?" Another major consideration has already been suggested: "To what extent does the child have genuine peer relationships and what is their quality? Can one see these as partnerships, is the child playing in parallel, or is he isolated even from the larger peer group?"

Two areas of drive development were found to be particularly sensitive to variations occurring at this age. The one follows closely Anna Freud's developmental line describing the movement toward autonomous sphincter control. Experience shows that wetting during the daytime and especially at night is not infrequent even in the fairly well-developed child. Soiling is a less likely event in the age span of three to four years, yet even this occurs in many otherwise well-developed children. There seems little doubt, however, that used within the total context of judging development, sphincter mastery is a sensitive index.

One that is perhaps even more sensitive, both in representing past and anticipating future development, is what Heinicke et al.[26] called the child's capacity to modulate aggression. The question was posed: "Were the aggressive affects or their derivatives either excessively expressed or repressed? Has the ability to modulate the inevitable aggressive affects led to effective assertiveness?" Other indices need to be included. Here one must stress again that, at this age, the multiple aspect assessment suggested by Anna Freud seems to be especially essential. This is true even though the details of such assessment may need further elaboration. At this point, development is still so fluid that a wide net of variables is needed to capture the main thrust. Ultimately, one would also certainly want to include a more systematic evaluation of the child's self-esteem. Just as the specified indices of the child's functioning tend

to intercorrelate,[26] it might be anticipated that more direct indices of self-esteem would similarly be correlated with at least some of the indicated dimensions. Studies by Kagan and Moss,[27] Schaefer and Bayley,[36] and Baumrind[1] similarly show the general intercorrelation of various indices of child development in this age interval. This does not warrant dealing with only one such index, but it does support such concepts as the general adaptive level of the child or, as others have preferred, the general level of competence seen in the child.

The developmental status of the four-year-old cannot be accurately assessed, however, without simultaneously evaluating the nature of his psychologically significant environment. There are clusters of child development variables that would describe the general level of adaptation or competence at a given point in time. If one focuses on these, a review of the research literature suggests that high levels of functioning in the child are associated with a limited number of clusters of parent-child interaction ratings. These typically include the responsiveness and efficiency of the parent in meeting the child's needs, the parent's affection for the child, the parent's ability to communicate with the child, the parent's ability to provide appropriate stimulation which will enhance the learning of the child, and the parent's ability to enhance the child's move toward autonomy and new experiences as well as new relationships.* Furthermore, a review of the research relating child and parent-child variables at various ages shows that from six months of age onward, similar clusters of parent-child interaction and associated child development variables can be isolated.† It is of course important to examine the cross-sectional correlations such as those for the age interval under discussion (two and one-half to four). But it is of equal importance to study the influence of earlier measures on later assessment of the same or different sets of variables in terms of some such devices as cross-lag correlation.[15]

On the one hand, one cannot ignore the complexity and specificity of individual variations, nor can anyone suggest that there is one best way to bring up a child. On the other hand, this research, as well as the other writings reviewed by Heinicke et al.,[26] does suggest that certain fundamental variations in the child's adaptation appear early, and that they are heavily influenced by certain persisting patterns of family interaction.

Two extensive illustrations of these essential

---

* See reference 26 for definitions of these ratings.
† See references 26, 7, 8, and 46.

points are given in a paper by Heinicke et al.[25] The adaptation of two three-year-olds to nursery school is discussed in considerable detail, particularly the nature of the expectations with which these two girls entered nursery school. It is linked to the nature of the previous and ongoing relationships that they had had with their families and the new and supplemental relationships that they could form in the nursery setting. To summarize certain aspects of the contrasts in their development:

Paula had internalized and continued to experience a caretaking situation that led to the expectation that she would be cared for again. There is no doubt, however, that the initial supplemental affectionate relationship to Sarah, a student teacher, greatly enhanced Paula's eventual commitment to the new relationships and tasks of the nursery.

By contrast, Jean had in the past experienced, and once more reexperienced during entrance into nursery school, that people make an initial engagement but then depart. All her commitments including those to the task reflected the expectation that abandonment would follow. Characteristically, she would flee the situation first. It was particularly through the reassurance that she would not be abandoned and could be loved for herself, as opposed to being someone else, that her teacher, Esther, could in important ways enhance her development.

Both the nature of the regressions that developed and the manner in which the conflict derivatives were or were not altered, highlights once more the contrast in the two girls and allows us to make more general inferences about the balance of progressive and regressive trends. When experiencing the stress of separation from her parents, Paula sucked her thumb but retreated mainly to a person and specifically to Sarah's warm lap, only to emerge again into activity. By contrast, Jean turned for comfort to her body and to certain pieces of clothing. At one point, the regression in her ego functioning went to the point of experiencing extreme helplessness.

Similarly, whereas Paula could gradually master her anxiety of making too big a mess or being attacked by a boy, Jean continued to be preoccupied with making messes and lying on the floor like a baby. More generally, many factors combined to make Paula's functioning less subject to conflict interference.[25] [pp. 195–196]

In further research, Heinicke and his colleagues[26] demonstrated that various social work interventions in family functioning were able to change the above-mentioned cluster of parent-child interaction variables. The change in any given function, broadly speaking, might be progressive or regressive in nature. However, it turned out that any such function was correlated with the subsequent changes in many indices of the child's functioning. This does not indicate that the child's growth at this point of development is simply a reflection of parent-child developments, but it does underline that even at this developmental level, child functioning is still tremendously intertwined with family functioning.

These findings on the three-year-old permit examination of the question of when the developing structure of the child is still accessible to change. The general assumption has been that by the age of three, much structuralization has occurred. It was indeed true that in the sample studied by Heinicke et al.[26] With mostly single-parent, low-income families, fairly extensive and intensive work had to be done with the family to produce the kinds of changes in that family that would be reflected in the child. No direct work was done with the child, but each one was attending an individualized day-care preschool.

Even more important, there were certain families (about 10 percent) who needed but could not utilize the social work help that was offered. It was their children who in turn showed the most dramatic declines. One such child had clearly learned to expect that he could not rely on the psychological availability of his mother. Only under certain specific circumstances could he attract her attention, and those circumstances were also not clearly defined. Being "sweet" did seem to do the trick. In identification with his mother when he was frustrated (and this occurred easily), his anger took the form of an all-demanding temper tantrum. At such times, he expected to be physically controlled and beaten by the mother's boyfriend.

The warm and steady, but nevertheless firm, availability of a nursery school teacher did much to challenge these various expectations and did lead to some alterations in his behavior. Unfortunately, this teacher left, and the mother continued to be unable to make use of even the most sensitive help. Together, these led eventually to a behavioral pattern in kindergarten where destructive violence and delinquency were clearly foreshadowed. In this way this boy seemed to confirm once more the conclusion strongly supported by the research of Kagan and Moss.[27] In brief, they found that the child's status at about the third to sixth year reflects not only past influences and developments but anticipates quite accurately his subsequent preadolescent status.

These findings in turn raise important questions as to the type of mental representations that can be evoked at a particular age. It would seem that it is not typically possible, until the end of the third year, for the child to maintain the benign mental representation of his mother while he is also angry with her (as in the separation situation).

It also seems highly likely, however, that in the first two years of life, certain pervasive though less specific expectations are already evoked. Some examples would be the general expectation that someone will meet the child's needs and the expectation that the caretaking person will assist the child in achieving impulse control. Much more research will have to be done to determine whether such expectations can in fact be inferred at even earlier ages. It seems clear that by two and one-half to four years of age, these and other expectations form an essential part of the developing structure of the child.

REFERENCES

1. BAUMRIND, D., *Child Care Practices Anteceding Three Patterns of Preschool Behavior*, Genetic Psychology Monographs, vol. 75, pp. 43–89, 1967.
2. BALDWIN, A. L., KALHORN, J., and BREESE, F. H., *Patterns of Parent Behavior*, Psychological Monographs, vol. 58, no. 3, pp. 1–75, 1945.
3. BELL, R. Q., "Stimulus Control of Parent or Caretaker Behavior by Offspring," *Developmental Psychology*, 4:63–72, 1971.
4. BELL, S., "The Development of a Concept of Object as Related to Infant-Mother Attachment," *Child Development, 41*:291–311, 1970.
5. ———, and AINSWORTH, M., "Infant Crying and Maternal Responsiveness," *Child Development, 43*:1171–1190, 1972.
6. BRAUNWALD, S., "Forms of Children's Speech: Private, Social and Egocentric," unpublished manuscript, 1976.
7. BRODY, S., and AXELRAD, S., *Anxiety and Ego Formation in Infancy*, International Universities Press, New York, 1970.
8. ———, and MORROW, M., "Continuity and Conflict in Maternal Behavior, unpublished manuscript, 1974.
9. BRONFENBRENNER, U., "Is Early Intervention Effective: A Report on Longitudinal Evaluations of Preschool Programs," DHEW publication #(OHD) 14–25, 1974.
10. BROWN, R., *A First Language: The Early Stages*, Harvard University Press, Cambridge, 1973.
11. ———, and BELLUGI, U., "Three Processes in the Child's Acquisition of Syntax," *Harvard Education Review, 34*:133–151, 1964.
12. BRUNER, J., and KENNEY, H., "On Multiple Ordering," in Bruner, J., et al., *Studies in Cognitive Growth*, pp. 30–67, John Wiley, New York, 1966.
13. BRUNER, J., et al., *Studies in Cognitive Growth*, John Wiley, New York, 1966.
14. BRUNSWICK, R., "The Preoedipal Phase of the Libido Development," in Fleiss, R. (Ed.), *The Psychoanalytic Reader*, pp. 231–253, International Universities Press, New York, 1969.
15. CLARK-STEWART, A., *Interactions between Mothers and Their Young Children: Characteristics and Consequences*, Monographs of the Society for Research in Child Development, Serial no. 153, vol. 38, nos. 6–7, 1973.
16. ERIKSON, E. H., *Childhood and Society*, W. W. Norton, New York, 1963.
17. FLAVELL, J., *The Developmental Psychology of Jean Piaget*, Van Nostrand, New York, 1963.
18. FRAIBERG, S., "Libidinal Object Constancy and Mental Representation, in Eissler, R. S., et al. (Eds.), *The Psychoanalytic Study of the Child*, vol. 24, pp. 9–47, International Universities Press, New York, 1969.
19. FREEBERG, N. E., and PAYNE, D. T., "Parental Influence on Cognitive Development in Early Childhood: A Review," *Child Development, 38*:65–87, 1967.

20. FREUD, A., *Normality and Pathology in Childhood*, International Universities Press, New York, 1965.
21. GEEST, A. VAN DER, et al., *The Child's Communicative Competence*, Mouton, The Hague, 1973.
22. GESELL, A., et al., *The First Five Years of Life: A Guide to the Study of the Preschool Child*, Harper, New York, 1940.
23. HEINICKE, C. M., "Change in Child and Parent: A Social Work Approach to Family Intervention," *American Journal of Orthopsychiatry, 45(2)*:296–297, 1975.
24. ———, and WESTHEIMER, I., *Brief Separation*, International Universities Press, New York, 1965.
25. HEINICKE, C. M., et al., "Parent-Child Relations, Adaptation to Nursery School, and the Child's Task Orientation: A Contrast in the Development of Two Girls," in Westman, J. C. (Ed.), *Individual Differences in Children*, pp. 159–197, John Wiley, New York, 1973.
26. ———, "Change in Parent and Child: Relationship Opportunities in Day Care and the Child's Task Orientation," Final Report, Office of Child Development, grant #48, 1977.
27. KAGAN, J., and MOSS, H. A., *Birth to Maturity*, John Wiley, New York, 1962.
28. MACCOBY, E. E., and JACKLIN, C. N., *The Psychology of Sex Differences*, Stanford University Press, Stanford, Calif., 1974.
29. MAHLER, M., "Thoughts about Development and Individuation," in Eissler, R. S., et al. (Eds.), *The Psychoanalytic Study of the Child*, vol. 18, pp. 307–325, International Universities Press, New York, 1963.
30. ———, PINE, F., and BERGMAN, A., *The Psychological Birth of the Human Infant*, Basic Books, New York, 1975.
31. MUSSEN, P. H., CONGER, J. J., and KAGAN, J., *Child Development and Personality*, 2nd ed., Harper & Row, New York, 1963.
32. PIAGET, J., "Comments," in Vygotsky, L., *Thought and Language*, MIT Press, Cambridge, 1962.
33. ———, and INHELDER, B., *The Psychology of the Child*, Basic Books, New York, 1969.
34. ROBERTSON, J., and ROBERTSON, J., "Young Children in Brief Separation: Jane, Aged Seventeen Months, in Foster Care for Ten Days," New York University Film Library, 1969.
35. SEARS, R. R., MACCOBY, E. E., and LEVIN, H., *Patterns of Child Rearing*, Row & Peterson, Evanston, Ill., 1957.
36. SCHAEFER, E. S., and BAYLEY, N., *Maternal Behavior, Child Behavior, and Their Intercorrelations from Infancy through Adolescence*, Monographs of the Society for Research in Child Development, vol. 28, no. 3, 1963.
37. STIER, S., "Sex and Age Differences in the Doll Play of Preschool Children," unpublished honor's thesis, Stanford University, 1960.
38. STOLLER, R. J., "Healthy Parental Influences on the

Earliest Development of Masculinity in Baby Boys," *Psychoanalytic Forum, 5:*232–262, 1975.
39. ———, "The Male Transsexual as Experiment," *International Journal of Psychoanalysis, 54:*215–225, 1973.
40. VAN LEEUWEN, K., "Pregnancy Envy in the Male," *International Journal of Psychoanalysis, 47:*319–324, 1966.
41. WEISLER, A., and MCCALL, R., "Explorations and Play: Resume and Redirection," *American Psychologist, 31:*492–508, 1976.
42. WHITE, B. C., and WATTS, J. C., *Experience and Environment,* Prentice-Hall, Englewood Cliffs, N.J., 1973.
43. WRIGHT, H. F., "Observational Child Study," in

Mussen, P. H. (Ed.), *Handbook of Research Methods in Child Development,* pp. 71–139, John Wiley, New York, 1960.
44. YARROW, L. J., "The Development of Focused Relationships during Infancy," in Helmuth, J. (Ed.), *The Exceptional Infant,* Special Child Publications, Seattle, 1967.
45. ———, "Research in Dimensions of Early Maternal Care," *Merrill-Palmer Quarterly, 9:*101–114, 1963.
46. ———, RUBENSTEIN, J. L., and PEDERSON, F. A., *Infant and Environment,* Hemisphere, Washington, D.C., 1975.

14 / Psychosexual Development: Three to Five Years

Albert J. Solnit

Introduction

By the time most healthy children begin their fourth year, they have a considerable capacity for directing their body, using their mother tongue, and being socially aware. As a rule, this is sufficient to enable them to be away from their home and parents for the periods of time associated with nursery school and formal education in prekindergarten settings. In this chapter, the focus will be on the normal development and socializing capacities of such children as they move from an egocentric to a sociocentric orientation.[2, 8, 10] At this time, the child begins to have a sense of himself in relationship to others as well as a sense of others in relationship to himself.[6]

Regression in Normal Development

During his toddler period, the preschool child has mastered erect posture, locomotor skills, and the beginning of symbolization for understanding and communication. However, he is still dependent and has a haunting sense of how it was to be helpless and totally dependent on his parents for survival, comfort, relief, and pleasure. This awareness is painful on two counts: It hurts to give up the gratifications of such total care; and at the

same time it is terrifying to think of returning to the chaotic infantile state, giving up the orderliness and satisfaction of mastery that one has gained through growth. This conflict is felt most keenly during periods of regression associated with illness or injury, with exhaustion, or with overstimulation. Regressive reactions are common, and they are evoked when developmental tolerances are exceeded either by environmental demands or by the child's own physical and emotional needs or intense reactions. In the case of some children, a precocious "little adult" stance might be assumed in the face of stress.

The Role of Parents

It is during this period of development that speech, language, mobility, running, climbing, and the achievement of refined grasp skills become available. These competencies are associated with the child's development of pride in his body, and they gradually come into the service of socialization and promote interaction with other children. Of course, these developmental tasks cannot be mastered without the support, guidance, and powerful expectation of parents. To be sure, such achievement can be accomplished with the stimulating and regulating expectation of only one parent. Nonetheless, all other things being equal, there is little doubt that having both mother and father available is optimal.

From recent work, it is clear from children's behavior patterns that they differentiate mother and father at an early age.[9, 7] It is both understandable and desirable that the child should regard father as a different person than mother, as someone who can be approached for differing kinds of care and play. Although they may overlap in some measure, there are then distinct forms of maternal and paternal care. At the same time, each parent responds to the child according to what he or she views as appropriate and satisfying, and thus expresses the uniqueness of his or her own personality and set of attitudes.

Children three to six years of age gradually learn that parents, siblings, and their homes have a relative permanence and are a persistent reality that they can count on.

Socially, as Piaget has demonstrated, children ages three to six move from playing alone, to playing in parallel, to playing together, i.e., they move from egocentric to sociocentric play and other social and school activities.[10] Similarly, physical and cognitive styles begin to emerge. For some children, it is their preferred style to use trial and error in practicing a new skill in order to achieve mastery. A few children will not try a new task until they are ready to master it the first time. These are examples of differing styles of learning and of behaving, components of personality functioning that shape the uniqueness of each individual child and adult.

It is also during this period that the child moves from a dyadic, preoedipal interactional relationship with mother or father to a triadic relationship with both. In association with the transition from preoedipal to oedipal attitudes and relationships, the child has available the capacity to know himself as different than his parents. He is now able to feel himself less under the domination of appetitive impulses for immediate gratification or tension reduction. He has new physical skills, and his capability of using mental activity for remembering and simple problem solving have reached a level at which he can tolerate and accept short separations from his mother and father when he is three or four years old. By six years of age, he is ready for a half or full day of school in a kindergarten or first-grade setting without the actual physical presence of his parents. However, their psychological presence may be noted by how children identify in part with their parents as they play with other children, play with toys, and become a member of a group led by one teacher.

The Work of Separation-Individuation

At the same time, the younger child cannot easily make the distinction between a feeling, wish, or strong impulse and the act that would express such mental activities. Thus, the toddler or preschool child who feels angry at the mother for not giving him what he wants may feel the angry wish as equivalent of the act of sending the parent away, or of destroying her. During the day, the sight of the parent will be reassuring enough for the child; at night, however, in the dark, with the parent in another room, there may be the return of the anxiety that this favorite person has been destroyed by the angry wish. Often, only the physical presence of the beloved person will bring reassurance since the magic power of the thought, wish, or impulse seems to threaten again when that person is absent.[1]

Also, during this period the child utilizes separation from the parental figures as another form of "practicing" experience, one that promotes a sense of self and an awareness of time. Coping with separation experiences stimulates the utilization of memory and the exercise and elaboration of fantasies for comfort, relief, and anticipation. If it is done gradually and if the child's emotional and cognitive capacities are progressively maturing, separating from the parents can also promote the differentiation of self from important others.

Imitation and Identification

Starting during the second year of life, as part of their attachment to their parents, children feel close to them through imitating them. Mirroring and imitation are at one and the same time processes of psychological resonance and of self-definition. They are also a source of what later becomes the capacity for empathy. As imitation yields to the more subtle and internalized process of identification, the child is able to carry the psychological presence of the parent with him in his behavior as well as in his mental attitudes. The composite of these components of identifications is also associated with the development of the psychic or mental representation of the person or love object in the child's psychological functioning. The love object representation, then, is not only a subtle, internalized product of the bonding between child and parent, but it also represents a reassuring, shaping influence in the child's daily life and in his future development. Identifications with the parents and the internalizations that are libidinally invested (cathected) as love-object representations are forceful as well as reassuring, stimulating, and influential.

The Development of Genital Awareness and Masturbation

Emotionally and cognitively, the child is now able to note genital characteristics and differences in more precise detail and to begin to understand and to cope with what he perceives.

An awareness of sexual differences has gradually been dawning, but now these perceptions become far more stimulating and threatening. This takes place as children compare themselves to others and are aroused or frightened by the differences. It also occurs concretely when boys feel puzzled, anxious, and gratified by the sensual experiences evoked by the erection and detumescence of the penis in association with autoerotic experiences, and when girls are puzzled and disappointed that they cannot visualize or touch an outside organ.

By their own manual or thigh pressure, however, girls do feel and can bring about sensual excitation and pleasurable erotic suffusion that eventually reaches a climactic intensity. It is then followed by a soothing and gratifying tension reduction. Since the vagina is not visible, the little girl has some difficulty in localizing the area of sensitivity and pleasure. It is only when she discovers the concentrated sensitivity available in clitoral stimulation that there is more of a focus. However, the discovery of clitoral sensation also tends to be unfocused, spreading as a sensual suffusion throughout the body in association with differing feeling- and thought-states.

Early Oedipal Object Relations

Under ordinary circumstances, at this point the children are deeply attached to both parents. With the advent of this developmental epoch, however, intense exclusive longings for the mother begin. Inevitably, a threatening competition with the beloved father ensues. For little boys, the already established identification with the father moves forward, which in turn leads to a deferred romantic attachment to the mother. For the little girl, her ongoing identification with the mother leads to a romantic attachment to the father. This, however, gradually becomes deferred as the strong attachment to the mother continues and the threat of competition is avoided.

In the transition from dyadic to triadic relationships, gender and sexual differences are always influential in shaping individual development. All human beings are bisexual,[5, 4, 3] and the bisexuality plays a continuing role in the configuration and resolution of normative developmental crises. Ordinarily, the boy is predominantly male and masculine, and his biological equipment and psychological development enhance each other. The girl is predominantly female and feminine, again demonstrating the convergence of biological, psychological, social, and cultural components of normative human development.

The three- to five-year-old boy not only becomes strongly attached to his mother and has the ambitions to have an exclusive relationship with her in competition with the father. He also is strongly attached to his father, often seeks an exclusive relationship with him, and feels in competition with the mother for the father. Using his parents as models and driven by his sexual and aggressive drives, the little boy normatively wants to hold on to his mother, but to change from being her baby to being her boyfriend and husband, a positive oedipal relationship. However, out of fear of his father's disapproval and out of his wish to retain the affectionate closeness with his father, the little boy at times identifies with the mother and has the longing for replacing the mother in his father's affection. This is termed a negative oedipal relationship.

Normatively, in behavior, longings, and imagination, the little boy explores both positive and negative oedipal longings. Under the felt threat of losing the love of his father and fearing a castrating retaliative reaction by the father (castration anxiety) in response to his rivalrous ambitions, he gives up his wishes to replace the father. In this connection, autoerotic behavior focused on the erect penis and the associated longings evokes the desire for closeness with the pleasure-providing mother, often expressed in masturbatory fantasies; just as the detumescence of the penis after a period of erection is often associated with fear of castration—it might become smaller and smaller and disappear, as punishment for the wishes associated with the erection to have the mother exclusively and to replace the father. Thus, the little boy gradually accepts the deferment of his wishes for the mother toward whom biologically, psychologically, and culturally he feels the strongest pull. At the same time, by deferring his ambitions, he safeguards an affectionate relationship with his father. His identification with his father, at ages three to five, serves as a guide to his own growing-up. The parent whom he most resembles biologically provides the encouragement and direction to his future development. This includes the addition of the new inner voice of conscience, the superego, established as part of the new identification with the parents, especially the father, as the castration threats perceived in association with the positive oedipal ambitions are deferred. One could say the little boy intuitively moves toward being like father rather than persisting in an ambition that biologically and psychologically requires postponement.

It is the child's bisexuality, which is especially prominent during the early oedipal phase, that enables him to identify with both parents, to acquire a maternal as well as paternal psychological capacity, and to be able to emphathize with boys and girls.

In the three- to five-year-old girl, there is also a strong persistent attachment and identification with the mother. As the little girl becomes aware of sexual differences, she perceives herself as lacking both the breasts of the mother and the visible penis and testicles of the boy and father. Feeling as though she is lacking in valued bodily equipment, the little girl experiences the lack of clear boundaries and of a sharp focus of erotic intensification in the genital area as confirmation that there is deficiency in her physical make-up. Ambiguity about organs and feelings in the genital-perineal area may be experienced by the little girl as deficiency and frustration or as a promise of better, more clear-cut things to come. The expectations of the parents and the prevalent sociocultural attitudes and values expressed toward girls and boys in a particular society and in a particular period of history can have a formative influence. Just as the little girl perceives herself as different, she may feel cheated and/or envious in comparison to little boys because their genital area has a visible, well-defined penis and testicles. Although those reactions may be minimized by the parents and sociocultural attitudes, there is a visible difference to be accounted for. Also, the stress of having to wait for an improvement of definition of sensuality and for a completion of the promise of the suffusion of feeling in periods of vaginal-clitoral stimulation produced by thigh pressure or manual stimulation may be a vulnerability as well as a challenge. In coping with these ambiguities and promises, the little girl often feels disappointed and resentful toward the all-powerful mother who seems to have failed her. She may turn toward the father for a better promise and in pursuit of completion. Her bisexuality enables her to identify with her father at the same time as her powerful identification with her mother presses the little girl toward a longing for what the father can give her that he has given to the mother—his penis, a baby, a sense of completion and of being specially cherished.

Thus, the little girl tries to retain a positive relationship with the mother while also seeking to compete with her for what the father can give her. The little girl explores, as did the little boy, the positive oedipal longings of wanting the father for herself while she identifies with her mother and wishes for the breasts and body her father will cherish. At other times, she rallies to an intimacy with mother and excludes the father from their closeness, while putting aside the feelings of deficiency or envy that have been evoked by sexual differences, i.e., she displays a negative oedipal configuration in her love relationships.

The fear of the mother's rivalrous disapproval and the threat of losing the mother's nurturance leads the little girl to defer her ambitions to have an exclusive relationship with the father. This postponement is also associated with the wish for a phallus-baby, the restitution of what may be missing. Similarly, wanting to have the father's love and admiration for her femininity, to be specially cherished, the little girl gives up the ambitions of the negative oedipal longings. Deferring these ambitions is often sensed by the little girl as a promise that in the future she will grow up to be like mother, with large breasts and with a husband like daddy who will give her a baby. Thus, through an acceptance of herself as she is and through a firm identification with her mother, she can wait while retaining the father's affection and tenderness toward her.

Although this outline of the Oedipus complex and its wide range of exploratory patterns clearly is rooted in the bisexual make-up of boys and girls, there is a tendency to overlook how little boys and girls cope with the differences between themselves as children and the older, stronger adults with whom they compare themselves. Much more research is needed to illuminate this universal developmental task of comparing and identifying with adults who are so much larger than and different from young children. The difference in size may be as challenging as the sexual differences.

To a significant extent, we assume that children can work out the curiosity, anxiety, and excitement evoked by sexual differences more comfortably with their siblings than they can with the important adults in their lives. The size of the gigantic adult not only fosters the comforting and fearful aspects of the child's attribution of omniscience and omnipotence to the adult, it also arouses envy and awe in both boys and girls. With peers and siblings whose size, strength, and tolerances are more proportionate to those of the young child, the relationships, explorations, and limits are more comfortably established and practiced. Sibling relationships, important in their own right as a community of interests, are also a safe staging area for working out, once removed, one's feelings about the all-important parents. Playing house, doctor and nurse, and many other variations of oedipal longings and ambitions are more "natural" and tolerable than a direct approach to the large person who is the delight of one's romantic yearnings. Practicing and playing in the minor leagues is more comfortable and safe than making a direct bid for the major leagues.

It is beyond the scope of this presentation to go into more detail about sibling experiences. Suffice it to say, the sibling relationship can be a vital, mediating influence on the oedipal relationships and their resolution. This may be particularly true in connection with modifying toward a more gentle voice the influence of the superego, the heir to the oedipal complex.

Early Superego Development

The superego is the child's internalized, directing inner voice of conscience and moral values. Derivative of the parents' influence and value preferences as well as those of sociocultural expectations and prohibitions, the superego is a new addition to the child's psychic structures and functions.

At the normal preschool level of cognitive and emotional development, the child is motivated by the wish to gain the approval and love of his parents and nursery school teachers. By the same token, he will learn to avoid behavior that earns their disapproval and leads to the withholding of their affection. When these later patterns are internalized, they become the basis for superego development. They thus determine the child's capacity to have a useful conscience available during the school-age years.

All of this takes place over time. There is much trial and error and testing-out of the boundaries of behavior. The child may not be as bold or sure of himself as his parents desire, or he may be too bold and aggressive to suit them. He has many fantasies and is often considered funny by adults, yet he is perceived as lying and not telling (in some instances not knowing) the truth. If the voice of conscience is gentle and friendly, it becomes an aid to the child's increasing autonomy in planning and making decisions which involve harmonious or conflicted aspects of doing what society or the family views as right or wrong, or as good or bad behavior. If the conscience is severe and cruel, the child may be self-punishing for thoughts and wishes, let alone behavior. Guilt may be the burden for acting whenever conflict is involved, regardless of the child's behavior, if the superego is harsh and punitive.

Self, Differentiation and Socialization

Of overriding importance in these developmental experiences and changes is the child's perception of his or her own body. The child gradually acquires a sense of self from the mosaic of mental activity and imagery associated with the body-mind-self functions that have phase-specific configurations such as those outlined in this chapter in regard to the Oedipus complex and its vicissitudes.

As the child separates from the parents and individuates,[8] play with peers becomes increasingly satisfying. The child's progressively advancing sense of self along with the sense of other children as different individuals leads to group socialization, i.e., to sociocentric play.[10] During this period of development, the child's capacity to feel alone in the presence of others also enlarges the basis on which the capacity for empathy can develop.[11] This enables the child to feel the comfort of private thoughts and feelings and to understand how others feel in social situations. Throughout this period, children turn to toys and other inanimate objects as instruments of play and as a means of expression. This is a natural and essential way of gaining pleasure and discharging tension. At the same time, children practice differentiation of self from parents. While these differentiating and individuating developments proceed, the children retain and indeed are dependent on the core closeness and warmth that they and their parents established in the first years of life. Thus, there persists an echo of the era when the child had been relatively helpless and dependent. As separation and individuation proceed, this helpless infant presently becomes the colorful, energetic, ambitious, partly autonomous toddler and preschool child. Along with Mahler, it is useful to assume that as the child progresses into each new epoch of his growth and unfolding, each previous phase of development is reviewed anew.[8]

Developmental and Family Dynamics

In the course of this developmental epoch, as the child differentiates himself and becomes more independent, the imitative behavior gradually changes. The child's past identifications with the attitudes of the parents become more subtle. Just as children's sexual and aggressive drives in combination with their marked dependency and helplessness are the roots of their loving and ambivalent feelings toward the primary love objects (parents), so the parents resonate with mixed feelings about the independence and assertiveness of their little boy or girl. These children can be winning and seductive; they can also invite the parents' regressive and aggressive behavior toward them. When the child-parent relationship is healthy, it is characterized by a predominance of positive affectionate libidinal ties. However, transient, angry, resentful, and even envious feelings also contribute significantly to the repertoire of affects that appear. These are experienced, repressed, sublimated, and integrated into what can be viewed as the individual's temperament, personality, and character structure; they become part of what he will bring into any social context. The context in which these develop is that of relationships to parents and other important persons.

During this period, the child's later autonomy is being crucially shaped. This takes place in connection with the social expectations and pressures that are associated with the vital functions of eating, sleeping, toileting, playing, and fitting into the family. Each family has its own unique sociocultural traditions with a highly individual structure. In transmission, these traditions are subject to specific organizing influences. For example, the achievement of using utensils to eat by oneself, of asserting self-control in regard to defecation and urination, and of mastering various kinds of play take place in a particular cultural context of expectations and provide the child with a sense of self-esteem and confidence about future tasks. At the same time, the healthy child and the ordinary devoted parents are engaged in a process of mutual adaptation. Despite transient episodes of anxiety and sadness, they are able to find a great deal of satisfaction in the course of their continuing interaction. As a result, the child becomes more active, independent, and increasingly unique as a personality.

The growing child enjoys emulating his parents. On their part, they are usually pleased by this and foster it, while it allows the child to continue to wrap himself in part with the mantle of omnipotence and omniscience which he attributes to his parents. In a simpler sense, such identifications are guides to behavior and have an organizing impact on the child that is satisfying and comforting. Conversely, the parents enjoy seeing miniatures of themselves even with a certain amount of caricature, especially when the attributions are positive and compare favorably with the traits and behavior of other children.

The preschool period is one of great learning, and play is the most universal medium for such learning—in effect, it is the child's "work." Curiosity and interest in learning are at a high pitch, and the senses at a high level of responsiveness. Gradually, the magical quality and power of feelings, thoughts, and mental activities become concretely and reassuringly different from acts and consequences.[10] This is accompanied by an interest in moving from an earlier exploration of the body to exploring the world of things. Words are discovered and played with, often regressively. This goes on as the oral- and anal-erotic impulses are regressively experienced in derivative, partly sublimated form. There is much pleasure for children (and often for the parents) from the way children name, rhyme, and echo words for their sounds and their effects. In the rich soil of such mental and emotional "exercises" and in a social context, cognition flourishes, especially if it is encouraged, appreciated, and guided by responsive parents and teachers. Of course, it also plays a part in the way children of this age play together in neighborhoods, nursery schools, and day-care centers.

REFERENCES

1. FRAIBERG, S., "Libidinal Object Constancy and Mental Representation," in Eissler, R. S., et al. (Eds.), *The Psychoanalytic Study of the Child*, vol. 24, pp. 9–47, International Universities Press, New York, 1969.
2. FREUD, A., *Normality and Pathology in Childhood*, International Universities Press, New York, 1965.
3. FREUD, S., "The Dissolution of the Oedipus Complex, in *The Standard Edition of the Complete Psychological Works of Sigmund Freud* (hereafter: *The Standard Edition*), vol. 19, pp. 173–179, Hogarth Press, London, 1961.
4. ———, "A Special Type of Choice of Object Made by Men," in *The Standard Edition*, vol. 11, pp. 163–175, Hogarth Press, London, 1957.
5. FREUD, S., "Three Essays," in *The Standard Edition*, vol. 7, pp. 125–245, Hogarth Press, London, 1953.
6. KAPLAN, L., *Oneness and Separateness: From Infant to Individual*, Simon and Schuster, New York, 1978.
7. LAMB, M., *The Role of the Father in Child Development*, John Wiley, New York, 1976.
8. MAHLER, M., PINE, F., and BERGMAN, A., *The Psychological Birth of the Human Infant*, Basic Books, New York, 1975.
9. NEUBAUER, P. B., "The One-Parent Child and His Oedipal Development," in Eissler, R. S., et al. (Eds.), *The Psychoanalytic Study of the Child*, vol. 15, pp. 286–304, International Universities Press, New York, 1960.
10. PIAGET, J., and INHELDER, B., *The Psychology of the Child*, Basic Books, New York, 1969.
11. WINNICOTT, D. W., "The Capacity to Be Alone," *International Journal of Psycho-Analysis*, 39:416–420, 1958.
12. ———, "Transitional Objects and Transitional Phenomena," *International Journal of Psycho-Analysis*, 34:89–98, 1953.
13. ———, and STEVENSON, O., "The First Treasured Possession: A Study of the Part Played by Specially Loved Objects and Toys in the Lives of Certain Children," in Eissler, R. S., et al. (Eds.), *The Psychoanalytic Study of the Child*, vol. 9, pp. 199–217, International Universities Press, New York, 1954.

15 / Psychosexual Development: Five to Ten Years

Albert J. Solnit, Justin D. Call, and Carl B. Feinstein

It is a misconception to consider the sexual drives quiescent during latency. There is ample clinical data that between five and ten years of age, sexuality manifests itself in a polymorphous perverse manner in both boys and girls. What is brought into latency are sexual wishes directed toward parenting figures within the positive (heterosexual) and negative (homosexual) oedipal constellations.

The Oedipal Constellation

Briefly, in a family with both mother and father present, for the male child the positive oedipal situation proceeds from its roots in preoedipal development as follows:

1. As the mother nurtures the child during the pre-oedipal phase, his predominantly anaclitic relationship toward her presently develops into a positive libidinal interest. The father and other caring figures are also involved in gratifying experiences with the child, and, to the extent that they do so, they share this bond.
2. As the boy's psychosexual development proceeds

from anal to phallic dominance, incestuous wishes toward the mother develop.
3. The father is then seen as a superior rival for mother's love.
4. During moments of sexual excitement, especially in the course of masturbation, the child elaborates many oedipal fantasies. As rivalry with the father increases, the child dreams of taking away father's genital and making it his own. But this evokes fantasies of revenge, and he fears castration (damage to the penis) from father.
5. This conflict persists for months. Ultimately it is resolved through the child's identification with the father, i.e., the child takes in those aspects of the father which signify the father as the superior rival for mother's love. In fantasy, the boy thereby gains mother's love vicariously.
6. Incestuous wishes toward the mother are repressed and the superego is established. This comes about through the child's identification with both parents. Freud[6] referred to the superego or ego ideal as the heir to the Oedipus complex.

In the case of the girl, the positive oedipal situation develops as follows:

1. As with the boy, the libidinal attachment to the mother is established during the period of infantile dependency. The mother thus becomes the

prime libidinal object, although the father may share in this.

2. During the anal-urethral stage of psychosexual development the girl discovers the pleasurable sensations in her clitoral area. (See chapter 10.)

3. She becomes interested in the father's phallus and with this she begins to feel rivalry with the mother for the father.

4. In fantasy, the little girl sees herself as the father's preferred love object and displaces the mother as father's lover and as the woman of the house. The wish for a baby with the father replaces her wish for a penis.

5. Since the girl is still dependent upon the mother for love and care, her rivalry with the mother for the father is associated with threatened loss of love from the mother and abandonment by her. Loss of love and threat of abandonment are, for the girl, the equivalent of castration anxiety to the boy.

6. The method of resolution for the girl is the same as for the boy, namely, identification. In this case, however, it is with the mother. The child thereby gains father's love vicariously. Incestuous wishes are repressed and the superego is established.

For both the boy and the girl, the oedipal situation is considerably more complex than the algebraic sequence just described. With any given child, the outcome is related to other factors such as: (1) the fact that ambivalence reigns in all object relations; (2) the fact that preoedipal conflicts are telescoped into the oedipal conflict; (3) the fact that the capacity for object constancy varies in each child; (4) the fact that earlier sources of anxiety (separation) determine the intensity of castration anxiety; and (5) the fact that the child is also drawn toward a homosexual object choice and experiences the parent of the opposite sex as a rival.

Ultimately, the superego is an amalgam of identifications with both parents. It consolidates into two general categories of mental functioning: the conscience which serves as the prohibiting and punitive agency, and the ego ideal, which offers an idealized model of what ought to be.

The following is Freud's last description of the formation of the superego.[5]

. . . a portion of the external world has at least partially been given up as an object, and instead by means of identification is taken into the ego, i.e., it has become an integral part of the internal world. This new mental agency continues to carry on the function which has hitherto been performed by the corresponding people in the external world . . . [p. 205]

Thus, before the establishment of the superego proper, those objects which regulate the child's behavior exist in the external world. After the superego forms, they come to occupy a place in the child's internal world.

According to Sandler,[14] the formation of the superego results from both identifications and introjections. Introjection is a term used in many different ways by various authors. Sandler states: "Introjection is the vesting of certain object representations with a special status so that these are felt to have all the authority and power of the real parents." Thus, it is not the mere identification with the object which is the hallmark of the superego; rather it involves the loading of these identifications with authority. In fact, prior to this phase, many representations of and identifications with these parents had already formed. Now, however, the child not only identifies with the parents, but he has inside himself the power of their authority. In effect, the child is not so much saying, "I shall be like my parents," as he is asserting, "I shall be as my parents would want me to be if they were here."

Identification continues on through childhood and into later life. The forcefulness and authority by which identifications come to function as an internal lighthouse for moral precepts, i.e., the formation of the superego by introjection, is determined by the resolution of the oedipal phase.

Satisfying the ego ideal is a method of regulating self-esteem. It leads to the same feeling of mental comfort and well-being as that experienced by the very small child when the all-powerful parent shows approval and pleasure with his performance. If that feeling of approval and support can be obtained by allegiance to external authority or to a group, or by chemical means such as ingesting a drug, the internal commandments of the superego can be readily overridden. Thus, the love which is so important to the ego can be obtained in varying ways. It can come from within, by meeting the standards of the ego ideal, or from without, by following a powerful leader, by losing oneself in some intense group participation, or by sedating the superego.

Another outcome for the positive oedipal situation is the boy's concept of himself as masculine and the girl's concept of herself as feminine. It is now well known that parents' oedipal strivings are rekindled in specific ways with each of their children. This occurs during both the child's oedipal phase and again during adolescence.

The nature of oedipal strivings inevitably calls into play a set of critical responses on the part of the parents. For example, the boy may beg to see his mother's vagina; or the little girl may be relentless in her pursuit of taking a shower with the father. Parents can be seduced into such sexual encounters with their children. Or, because of their conflicts and inhibitions, they may respond in an overly rejecting or even punitive fashion.

The shape and character of the child's gender identity are heavily influenced by parental responses to the child. A great deal is said about the importance of the child's identifications with the same-sex parent for establishing appropriate gender identity, and this is easily recognized and understood. However, insufficient attention is given to the way in which identification with the opposite sex parent influences the child's gender identity. By early latency, children have already developed a clear-cut notion of what is masculine and feminine. Because of their immaturity, children from five to ten must keep gender dichotomies rigidly enforced. A "liberated mother" may become exasperated with the fact that her little girl wants to grow her hair long or wear certain kinds of feminine clothing or stay home and take care of the kitchen. The little boy may well insist on seeing his father along stereotyped, masculine, aggressive lines. In single-parent families with the mother as the head of the household, a little boy's masculinity depends not only on his identifications with what he knows or fantasizes about his missing or sometimes-present father, but also upon what kind of boy or man he believes his mother would admire and love. Children from single-parent families overidealize the missing parent and do not have the opportunity for comparing such idealization with reality.

Thus, the oedipal constellation plays a major role in organizing the child's psychosexual development and subsequent ego and superego formation. In evaluating its influence, however, many factors must be taken into account. The outcome is not always predictable on the basis of what might be expected in the positive oedipal situation. Preoedipal factors have a critical influence on the way that the child experiences the oedipal situation. While oedipal struggles are repressed, various themes in the oedipal constellation continue to be worked over unconsciously. The adult outcome of conflicts within the oedipal constellation is codetermined with ongoing experience and maturational change. This is particularly true during adolescence. At that point, group formation and identification with peers outside of the family occurs, prior libidinal object ties are loosened, and a new love object is chosen.

With the resolution of the oedipal conflict, there are associated transformations that reflect biological and psychological maturational changes. Like other developmental phases, latency is activated by experiences that transform maturational potential into developmental changes and increased psychological resources.

During latency, physical and psychological changes are more gradual, less eruptive, and more synchronous. Thus, to some extent, the term latency conveys the meaning of balance and equilibrium of forces in psychic life and of greater harmony between agencies of the mind. The spurt in ego development and the useful functioning of the superego at seven or eight provides an opportunity for an orchestration of instinctual drive demands, executive ego functions, and superego guidance. This balance frees the child from the dominance of his inner volcanic drives; at the same time, it enables him to use cognition and social relations in a satisfying and esteem-promoting manner.

Early Latency

Berta Bornstein[3] has divided the child's psychosexual development during latency into two periods. These consist of early latency, from age five and one-half to eight, and late latency, from age eight to ten. Maturation continues during early latency, and the child struggles with the emergence of incestuous wishes during periods of sexual excitement. Under such circumstances, the curtain of repression becomes semitransparent. In defending against such wishes, the superego is alternately harsh and ineffective. As heir to the Oedipus complex, the superego is new, untested, untried, and often ineffective. An additional defensive maneuver that occurs during early latency is a regressive move of the sexual life to a pre-oedipal position. Anal and oral themes emerge, replacing the oedipal ones. The ego of the early-latency child is usually not sufficiently consolidated to provide for that stability of structure which affords complete mastery over the task of learning in school. The subject matter and social structure at school are easily instinctualized and can become conflictual. The early-latency child continues to be vulnerable to regression and to the overharsh, punitive superego. At this point, some of the guilt feelings are managed by projection, i.e., the child tends to blame others for things which he does himself. Through provocative misbehavior, he also attempts to evoke punishment from authority figures in order to deal with his guilt feelings.

Late Latency

The situation in late latency, eight to ten years of age, is quite different. At this point, the superego is more firmly established. The ego is stronger, and sexual excitement and masturbatory activity are under greater control.

In late latency, the drives are more in the service of the ego and of adaptation. Inner and outer worlds are more evenly opposed. Identifications are more subtle, complex, and far reaching; i.e., the imitative aspect slips away and the child now has a style that may be similar to, reminiscent of, or an echo of how a parent figure speaks or views the world, but one which is now an inextricably interwoven part of the child's individual personality. Thus, identifications are much more internalized and embedded in the unique personality of the child. One can begin to see early features of the character plating, the character formation, as it starts a long process of crystallization. It is still fluid, but early configurations are now discernible. "He is a sullen fellow." "She is a determined person." "He is too cautious." "She is so curious," etc.

As Berta Bornstein put it in 1951:

For the sake of adults, the child behaves as though he were living by the rules of the secondary process. However, listening to children 5 to 8 years old, when they are engaged in conversations with each other, convinces us that conscious production does not necessarily mean constant utilization of the secondary process. Their conscious thought processes (on the surface similar to ours) can during the latency period still easily dip into the primary process. Any newly-acquired accomplishment can easily be undone by regressive processes and the child senses that this would occur were he to attempt to express whatever comes into his mind. Therefore, the child [in this period of development] must fight free association more than the adult.[3] [p. 279]

A particularly strong anticathexis is needed to safeguard the recently achieved intactness of ego functioning. For example, in the clinical situation, free association is possible only after children have gradually developed the capacity for introspection. This hardly ever occurs before prepuberty, when the superego approaches a state of consolidation.

Through his identifications with a peer group, the late-latency child has gained additional strengths in the ego and has moved away from the incestuous object attachments. His new environment in school is more firmly consolidated. Teachers often become the authorities, the love

and the hate objects which once were the parents' roles in the life of the child. The child is physically more capable. The electroencephalogram is more stable.[11] The late-latency child is a good learner, he has become an objective scientist whose defenses are well organized, often along obsessional lines. That phase of science characterized by quantification and strict adherence to methodology typifies the approach of the late-latency child to the outside world. Such a child becomes an investigator of the world. He, like Linnaeus, organizes categories of experience, quantifies them, and finds compartments for each experience and observation. He has reached the epitome of operational logic.

Now the pleasure principle is protected by the reality principle. With this, the child has the ability to postpone drive discharge, to use thought as a trial action, and to arrange for gratification at a time and in a way that is more likely to be associated with acceptance and social approval.

There is a newly acquired maturational capacity to understand time, especially in being able to wait until tomorrow or next week. Most children in early latency can read time (clock or watch)[1] and begin to use the calendar with comprehension of a week or a month.[13]

Thus, with a greater ease in inhibiting, transforming, and controlling drive tension, action can be postponed, and thinking and memory can be exercised. There is an increasing use of secondary process modes of thinking and discharge, while less recourse to primary process modalities is permitted.

As always, the emotional, psychological, and biological factors in development are intrinsically interwoven. However, in latency, with more balance and integration, this equilibrium is reflected and reinforced by the more even, gradual physical growth, the completion of myelinization of the central nervous system, the increasing autonomy of perceptual distinctions and coordinated functions, the distance from the drive demands, the availability of an inner guiding sense of right and wrong, and the more realistic evaluation of the parents.

In regard to the latter, during the preoedipal and oedipal periods of development, a mantel of omnipotence and omniscience had been thrown over the parents. This begins to be critically observed by the child in the postoedipal period. This mantel was an assertion by the younger children that they felt secure because their parents were assumed to be omnipotent and omniscient. In effect, these fantasies of their parents' power give assurance that parents can protect and care for them, and can serve as guardians of safety and security (auxiliary ego functions). This is especially important in helping the child control his feelings and behavior when he feels as though he or the environment might become uncontrollable. For example, their presence helps with angry feelings associated with wishes to kill those who thwart him and the fear of playing with fire or at the top of stairs.

In the postoedipal period, new controls and balances are available. Now cognitive and emotional immaturities no longer interfere, and children can be more understanding of the realities. For the first time, parents' inconsistencies and frailties can be registered and understanding begins to dawn. In some precocious children, this is the moment when the gradual, desirable disillusionment about parents is set in motion.

Such disillusionment may be excessive in intensity and in speed of unfolding. On the other hand, if the seven- or eight-year-old child is still working out poorly resolved oedipal conflicts, or if some trauma or deprivation has disrupted the transition from a little boy or girl becoming a big boy or girl, it may be inhibited. During these developmental changes, the sexual differences are most significant. This is true not only in terms of which parent is the more or the less difficult to relate to in respect to gradual disillusionment, but also because developmentally, during this period, the little girls are usually significantly ahead of the boys.

The process of disillusionment and its relationship to the oedipal conflict is classically expressed by an accomplished writer, Gosse:

My mother always deferred to my father and in his absence spoke of him to me as if he were all wise. I confused him in some sense with God; at all events I believed that my father knew everything and saw everything. One morning in my 6th year, my mother and I were alone in the morning room, when my father came in and announced some fact to us. I was standing on the rug, gazing at him, and when he made this statement, I remember turning quickly in embarrassment and looking into the fire. The shock to me was as that of a thunderbolt for what my father said was not true—Here was the appalling discovery, never before suspected, that my father was not as God and did not know everything. The shock was not caused by any suspicion that he was not telling the truth, as it appeared to him, but by the awful proof that he was not, as I had supposed, omniscient. . . .

"The theory that my father was omniscient or infallible was now dead and buried. He probably knew very little; in this case, he had not known a fact of such importance that if you did not know that, it could hardly matter what you knew.[8] [pp. 33–34, 36]

During late latency, the child's overt interest in heterosexual objects is lessened by reaction formation. A late-latency boy does not easily identify himself as interested in girls, and a late-latency girl does not easily acknowledge her interest in boys. Both genders are prejudiced toward each other. Masturbatory activity has diminished, although not receded. The child's interest in sexual matters is now polymorphous and objectified as a science in its descriptive phases. The late-latency child is proud of his knowledge of sexual matters, anatomy, geography, and related subjects and is the master of time, place, and circumstance.

A third phase of latency (nine to eleven years of age) has been described by Williams.[16] During this era, further consolidation of ego and superego take place and the events of puberty and adolescence are anticipated.

Shapiro and Perry[15] have reviewed psychoanalytic studies of latency together with numerous developmental studies. These include studies of the central nervous system, of perception, of learning, of Piaget's cognitive development,[12] Kohlberg's description of moral development during this time,[10] and of language development during latency. As a result, they have postulated that latency, age seven plus or minus one, is in part a reflection of a higher level of organization of mental processes. Hence, they advance this as a factor to explain why ego functions become stronger, moral judgment is refined, and defenses established against drives and primary process thinking. Shapiro and Perry do not contradict the psychoanalytic concept of latency as a time when oedipal strivings are repressed. They cite Freud's[7] original support of this idea and conclude that developmental studies of the brain show an impressive confluence of data indicating that higher brain functions become dominant in the regulation of mental life at about age seven plus or minus one.

Sex Differences

In the early postoedipal latency period, the girl senses her ultimate development as a female, one destined to become an adult woman, with more conviction and cognitive awareness. Similarly, the boy is evermore aware that he is male and will become an adult man. There is a drift toward boys playing with boys and girls with girls. To a significant extent, it may be a historically culture-bound folk wisdom that views schooling, playing, and socializing as desirably less complicated during this period if boys and girls are encouraged to segregate themselves. This one-sided perspective* may intuitively reflect the fact that girls are developmentally ahead of boys, and that they explore and experience issues of sexual curiosity, erotic fantasies, and masturbatory behavior in more sublimated forms. Thus, friendships with those who are alike at this age may be more comfortable and less stimulating. Moreover, they are less likely to uncover the painful oedipal longings and incestuous conflicts that have so recently been set aside and transformed into socially acceptable derivatives (for example, having a crush on the kindergarten teacher).

These socially acceptable derivatives include the skills and capacities for organized games, athletics, and social events. The use of rules, logically related to a large extent, becomes a comfort in playing games and in socializing with peers and adults. In this context, physical, emotional, and intellectual capacities are strengthened both in their functioning and in their synchronization. This is achieved by mastering socially agreed-upon rules, for example, traditions and customs, that bring focus to the continuum of winning-losing, right-wrong, and socially acceptable-unacceptable behaviors. Motor action and intellectual activity are in a new balance, and the rules of the game promote social interaction and acceptability. At the same time, they strengthen the barrier against regressive behavior. Thus, in early latency, there is often a "passionate" commitment to inflexible rules.

From another angle, Phyllis Greenacre[9] has put it succinctly: "A generally expanding environment dilutes the genital urgency."

With the first basic resolution[2] of the oedipal complex and the beginning of latency, there is a structuralization of the mental apparatus into three functional components, the id, the ego, and the superego. Anna Freud[4] has also formulated it as three lines of development which can be viewed as sensitive indicators in assessing the state of the child's mental health, developmental progress, and developmental psychopathology. Of course, each of the three lines influences and is interwoven with the other two. Thus there are:

---

* The advantages of grouping boys and girls together, rather than segregating them, could also be a cultural pattern which, under present circumstances, is much preferred.

the biological or innate resources that provide the constitutional raw material out of which id and ego are differentiated; the social-environmental demands, conditions and shaping influences which foster, stunt, impair, or modify health, growth and development; and the interactions between internal and external forces which make up the unique experience of each child.

Progress along any one of these avenues of development may lag behind or accelerate ahead of the others. Following the intense, at times rapid crystallizing and explosive interactions of the oedipal period, in early latency, there is the expectation in healthy boys and girls of slow forward movement on all lines, i.e., a somewhat slower and more balanced kind of growth. What constitutes the uniqueness of each individual, the innumerable variations in human character and personality, the mosaic of developmental successes, lags, and failures, can be seen reliably during latency in various states of health and psychopathology. During normal developmental crises such as the oedipal period, the child passes through intense, rapidly changing states, and it is much more difficult to interpret the observations necessary for such an inventory.

It should be apparent that continued integration of findings from the study of psychosexual, psychosocial, cognitive, and biologically derived studies of latency-age children will continue to throw more light upon this fascinating period of development. From an observational standpoint, it is full of shifting stress and subtle change; but viewed in retrospect, it is often idealized by adults. While the term *latency* may suggest a period of quiescence, what seems to be taking place is a quiet revolutionary change in the organization of all aspects of mental life.

Conclusion

Latency is the second of three opportunities for the reorganization of mental life. The first occurs at age two when modes of thought are channeled by language, i.e., two- and three-word speech. The third occurs in adolescence. A better grasp on any one of these nodal points for the reorganization of mental life provides additional insights into the other two.

REFERENCES

1. AMES, L. B., "The Development of the Sense of Time in the Young Child," *Journal of General Psychology,* 68:97–125, 1946.
2. BLOS, P., *On Adolescence*, Free Press, Glencoe, Ill., 1962.
3. BORNSTEIN, B., "On Latency," in Eissler, R. S., et al. (Eds.), *The Psychoanalytic Study of the Child*, vol. 6, pp. 279–285, International Universities Press, New York, 1951.
4. FREUD, A., "A Psychoanalytic View of Developmental Psychopathology, *Journal of the Philadelphia Association of Psychoanalysis, 1:7–17,* 1974.
5. FREUD, S., "Outline of Psychoanalysis," in *The Standard Edition of the Complete Psychological Works of Sigmund Freud* (hereafter: *The Standard Edition*), vol. 23, p. 205, Hogarth Press, London, 1961.
6. ———, "The Ego and the Id," in *The Standard Edition*, vol. 19, pp. 3–66, Hogarth Press, London, 1961.
7. ———, "Three Essays on the Theory of Sexuality," in *The Standard Edition*, vol. 7, pp. 125–243, Hogarth Press, London, 1953.
8. GOSSE, E., *Father and Son: A Study of Two Temperments*, Heinemann, London, 1909.
9. GREENACRE, P., "Anatomical Structure and Superego Development," *American Journal of Orthopsychiatry, 18:* 636–648, 1948.

10. KOHLBERG, L., "Development of Moral Character and Moral Ideology," in Hoffman, M. L., and Hoffman, L. W. (Eds.), *Review of Child Development Research*, pp. 383–432, Russell Sage Foundation, New York, 1964.
11. METCALF, D. R., and JORDAN, K., "EEG Ontogenesis in Normal Children," in Smith, W. L. (Ed.), *Drugs, Development, and Cerebral Function*, pp. 125–144, Charles C Thomas, Springfield, Ill., 1971.
12. PIAGET, J., *The Psychology of Intelligence*, Routledge & Kegan Paul, London, 1950.
13. POLLACK, M., and GOLDFARB, W., "Patterns of Orientation in Children in Residential Treatment for Severe Behavior Disorders," *American Journal of Orthopsychiatry, 27:*538–552, 1957.
14. SANDLER, J., "On the Concept of Superego," in Eissler, R. S., et al. (Eds.), *The Psychoanalytic Study of the Child*, vol. 15, pp. 128–161, International Universities Press, New York, 1960.
15. SHAPIRO, T., and PERRY, R., "Latency Revisited: The Age 7 Plus or Minus 1," in Eissler, R. S., et al. (Eds.), *The Psychoanalytic Study of the Child*, vol. 31, pp. 79–105, Yale University Press, New Haven, Conn., 1976.
16. WILLIAMS, M., "Problems of Technique During Latency," in Eissler, R. S., et al. (Eds.), *The Psychoanalytic Study of the Child*, vol. 27, pp. 598–620, Yale University Press, New Haven, Conn., 1972.

16 / Psychosocial Development: Eight to Ten Years

Gloria Johnson Powell

Introduction

The school-age period embraces the years from six to twelve. This period is aptly named, for during this time, next to family influence, school-related experiences are the most powerful vectors that bear on the social, emotional, and intellectual development of the child. The specific years from eight to ten are most often referred to as "middle childhood" and, indeed, they mark the transitional period between preschool and adolescence. The child usually settles into a developmental quietude —a time that most parents describe as that "delightful period of childhood," a time often referred to as latency, however.

Although the time span has been referred to as "quiet" and "delightful," it is a period when a tremendous amount of development takes place and numerous problems arise that need to be handled. The major psychologic landmark during these two to three years is the development of friendships. As a rule, the ties that count the most are those made with children of the same sex. The child begins to free himself from his primary emotional dependence on his parents and moves into a world of peers. Within this new context, a child begins to establish an identity separate from his parents' and to assume a pattern of maleness or femaleness. In order to accomplish this task successfully, he must learn to give love and to develop social rules and group morality. He must acquire ways of coping and controlling the physical world as well, and this involves many competencies ranging from the refinement of small muscle skills to achievement of proficiency in language. To help master the external world, he begins to use "scientific" observation in his approach to new situations. Indeed, in many ways, the child now begins to show in minature something of what he is going to be like when he is an adult.

Physical Development

National surveys indicate that children of this age period tend to enjoy relatively good health. For the past three decades, there has been a decided decrease in mortality rates for heart disease, tuberculosis, pneumonia, influenza, and appendicitis. Accidents are the leading cause of death, but most accidents take place in the home and may be largely preventable.

One of the major trends of physical growth in middle childhood is a gradual decrease in the elaboration of fatty tissue along with an increase in bone and muscle development. The building up of muscle is generally more rapid in boys, while girls continue to retain thicker layers of fat. This fatty tissue is so distributed that the girls usually have rounder, smoother, and softer contours and may frequently keep their babyish appearance. Although the average girl may be as much as three-quarters of an inch shorter at the age of six, by ten years of age she has caught up with and often surpasses the average boy. In respect to weight, however, at age six, girls are close to two pounds lighter than boys and do not catch up in this respect until age eleven. Table 16–1 shows height (in inches) and weight (in pounds) for boys and girls between eight and ten at the 50th percentile.

By the tenth birthday, control of the large muscles has become nearly perfect and control over the small muscles is much improved. The changes in the child's locomotor skills, his agility, his coordination, and his physical strength are significant. In terms of their interests, there are marked differences between the sexes which are reflected in the following profiles of the eight-, nine-, and ten-year-old.[2]

THE EIGHT-YEAR-OLD

By the child's eighth birthday, he is aware of his own posture and remembers to sit upright. However, he is constantly on the go—running, jumping, chasing, and scuffling. Most are ready for more organized sports. The child can skate, jump rope, and swim, and is open to learning new tricks.

There is an increase of speed, smoothness, and even gracefulness with a noted improvement in approach and grasp. When writing, the child can space words and sentences with a more uniformed slant and alignment, although his ideas may still exceed his ability to write. The child of eight begins to draw pictures more in perspective and is more aware of body proportions in the drawing of human figures.

Although the eight-year-old may still have some food dislikes, he begins to develop a good appetite and will venture to try new foods. Some eight-year-olds may be able to cut their meat with a knife. In general, eight-year-olds handle the table implements fairly well, although some boys still hold the fork and spoon pronately, which results in a pushing rather than a scooping manipulation.

The eight-year-old is often described as a "wonderful sleeper." The bedtime hour tends to be later and the total hours of sleep have dropped to an average of ten hours. Nightmares are rarer and toileting needs are more infrequent.

Dressing and care of clothes are done with more ease and speed. Shoe laces are easily handled and are kept tied.

In general, the eight-year-old is much less fatigable than he was at seven. Improved school attendance reflects the improvement in health. There are fewer communicable diseases and a more rapid recovery from colds and the like.

THE NINE-YEAR-OLD

At age nine, individual skills stand out in bold relief. Typically, the nine-year-old is more skillful and likes to display his skills. The eyes and hands are now well differentiated and the hands can be used quite independently. The fingers also are more differentiated and the child is reported to be either good or poor with his hands. His timing is under better control, and he participates well in competitive sports.

The child of nine tends to be a keen observer. An open-eyed stare can be maintained for several seconds without blinking. Nine-year-olds can write

TABLE 16–1

Age (Years)	Height		Weight	
	Girl	Boy	Girl	Boy
8	50½	51¼	58	60
8½	51½	52½	61	63
9	52¼	53¼	63¾	66
9½	53½	54¼	67	69
10	54½	55¼	70¼	74¾
10½	55¾	56	74½	72

SOURCE: Milwaukee Health Department.

for a prolonged time and add more details to their drawings.

In eating, nine-year-olds may still prefer plain foods, but they are more positive in their food likes. Although many can cut well with a knife, a few may still need help or tend to saw.

Sleeping habits continue to be good. A few children may awaken screaming from a deep sleep, but are usually quieted easily. The elimination functions continue to be under the child's control. The child may get up at night to urinate, but such trips are infrequent. Reminders to go to the bathroom are unnecessary, for the child now possesses both an inner and outer control.

Dressing is done completely independently and so is bathing. On the whole, the nine-year-old is very independent and very healthy. Children at this age can throw off colds rather quickly. However, a few children show marked fatigue and need to be protected from doing too much.

THE TEN-YEAR-OLD

Most ten-year-old children enjoy very good or excellent health. Many of the somatic complaints that might have been common earlier (for example, stomachaches, sick headaches, dizziness, and leg pains) are ceasing, or have disappeared entirely. Girls at the tenth birthday appear to be about even with the boys in size and in sexual maturity. But, unlike the boys, the majority of girls will show the first slight, but unmistakable, signs of approaching puberty. The body forms undergo a slight rounding, especially in the hip region. There is often a slight projection of the nipples. The waist becomes more accented and the arms become rounder. With very slim girls, who may not show the other body contours, there is a filling out in the face area with a more oval shape. The majority of girls are just beginning to start their rapid height growth and in a number of girls, some light, downy pubic hair makes its appearance. Very few girls begin to menstruate before eleven years.

Although boys and girls are of comparable height, the boys' growth is slower. The boys often do not appear to have changed much in physique, but closer inspection reveals some subtle changes. There is a slight rounding of the body contour, especially around the chin, neck, and in the chest area. However, only in a very small number of boys will there be any signs of sexual maturing.

At the age of ten, the appetite is on the increase and there is expression for favorite foods and favorite meals. The time of sleeping is now re- duced from ten to about eight or nine hours, with boys sleeping longer than girls.

In visual behavior, the fixating mechanism is in control, but the focusing system is still loose. It will take another year for this sharp precision mechanism to develop. Binocular vision is better than the monocular which becomes more perfect later on.

Emotional Development

Between eight and ten years of age, the child loses his primary emotional dependence upon and identification with his parents. A more realistic picture of the parents develops. At this time, the child begins to have his own opinions and begins to make some of his own decisions. The time of blind obedience to authority is gone, and there are likely to be many secrets.

As the dependence upon his parents decreases, the dependence upon the peer group becomes greater. In fact, for some children, the opinion of the playmates may be valued more than that of parents or teachers. The primary interest is in the peer group and for the most part, that peer group is of the same sex.

If the child has received enough love earlier in his life, he is now ready to give affection to peers especially, but to parents as well, and even to his siblings. If he has not received such love in the past, he may be handicapped in developing a satisfactory relationship with his peers.

THE EIGHT-YEAR-OLD

The eight-year-old child has been described as less sensitive, less within himself, and less apt to withdraw. His interests, however, are short-lived, and the child shifts rapidly from one thing to another. The child of eight is often very impatient, especially with himself. Because of his inability to sustain his own interests, ceaseless demands are made of the mother and there is an evident desire for her complete attention.

Some eight-year-olds may still be afraid of fighting, of failing, of criticism, or of snakes, and there may still be a lingering fear of the dark. Others may attack any feared experience directly and repeat it compulsively in order to resolve the fear. Instead of having outright fears, still others may be great worriers.

On the whole, if an eight-year-old dreams, the

dreams are of daily happenings and pleasant things. Frightening dreams can usually be traced to some immediate influence from television, the movies, or reading.

The eight-year-old is increasingly aware of himself as a person. He is becoming an individual, a member of a social world. At this age, the child is more conscious of the self as it differs from other people, and is interested in evaluating his own performance and relationship with others. In short, the eight-year-old has the capacity to operate as a distinct self within the give-and-take of a relationship with other people.

This is a time when the relationship between mother and child is both complicated and subtle. It is still very important to the eight-year-old to know what his mother thinks and feels about him, as well as what she does for him. He is not naively docile and compliant, however, and even the mother's complete attention may not be enough to maintain a smooth relationship.

The child can lose himself in his very real ability to dramatize. Through dramatization, he can try on new roles and identities and sort out how he would or ought to feel under certain circumstances. The dramatic play illustrates two of his major characteristics—the capacity for expansiveness and the capacity to evaluate. His thinking is less animistic than it was, and he is more aware of the forces of nature.

Individual differences at this age are great and sex differences are becoming significant. Boys and girls share many interests, but they are also becoming vividly aware of the distinctions which separate them. There is almost universal interest in babies and groping questions about birth, procreation, and marriage.

Parents of eight-year-olds report very few tensional outlets. Thumb sucking, especially in boys, may reoccur, but tends to take place while the child is reading, watching television, or sleeping. This is often the last age at which thumb sucking occurs.

THE NINE-YEAR-OLD

Nine is an age when strong feeling tones prevail. The emotional reactions are fluid and variable and quick mood swings may be observed from one extreme to another. For example, an existing state of marked shyness may make a complete turnabout with an act of complete boldness. Sometimes it happens this way:

It was Daniel's birthday and as a special treat, dinner was planned at his favorite pizza restaurant to be followed by a surprise birthday cake. During dinner, Daniel sat close to his father and smiled shyly at the waitress and waiters who came to wish him happy birthday. He went along demurely and with some seeming reluctance when one of the waiters took him to see the large pizza ovens, and let him help put the garnishes on his own pizza. Earlier, he had stated that this was something he would like to do. With encouragement he put on a few handfuls of grated cheese, but could not be persuaded to do more.

Later, on the way home, he expressed a wish to have some ice cream at the local ice cream parlor. When the family entered, there was a large crowd waiting to be served. Before anyone could stop him, Daniel was out of the car and in the parlor. He was standing at the door passing out the numbers and instructing people to line up to the left. He greeted everyone who entered with a number for his turn, chatted amicably with several adults, and could be heard telling riddles to one gentleman, much to the amusement of the entire crowd.

Another polarity is evident in the child's fluctuation between a "don't care" attitude and an extreme sensitivity to criticism along with a desire to please.

On the whole, however, parents of most nine-year-olds describe them as responsible, more independent, more dependable, congenial, and trustworthy. The key to understanding such a child's progress toward maturity is his self-motivation. The development of self-organization is occurring and significant reorientation takes place. The child can initiate activities, he is persistent, and he is less dependent on environmental support. His interest in perfecting skills is evident in the willingness to repeat a performance over and over again.

Added to the self-motivation now is a new capacity for self-appraisal. The child shows considerable ability for social and self-criticism. The new forms of self-dependence may in turn modify his relations to his family and to the outside world. The changes in the nine-year-old may be so subtle that his parents are not aware of them. The nine-year-old is no longer a mere child; he is midway between kindergarten and his teens. New emotional patterns are emerging and may be reflected in his complaining and moodiness. The child is developing a sense of individual states which needs to be understood by the significant adults in his life. Although he likes his home and is loyal to his parents (with a special pride in his father), he also feels the need to detach himself from his family and be on his own. There may be resentment at being treated like a younger child, but too much responsibility cannot be foisted upon him too soon.

Most nine-year-olds have few fears. Some,

however, are still resolving the residuum of earlier fears, such as fears of storms, the sight of blood, or swimming with the face underwater. At this age, such fears may have a specific neurotic content and consequently pursue a prolonged and intense course. The nine-year-old may be a great worrier, readily upset by mistakes or apprehensive about crossing the street at a traffic light. Reassurance and praise are helpful in resolving these worries.

Horrid dreams are commonly reported, but are often explained in terms of what has happened during the day. When they wake up, these children usually know they have been dreaming and are quickly calmed. Most nine-year-olds try to protect themselves from stimuli that might produce bad dreams. The pleasant dreams, however, are more difficult to remember and come in the early mornings.

Although most nine-year-olds are self-reliant in their actions and thoughts, some lack confidence, underrate themselves, and are anxious and apprehensive about their work. Such children need much reassurance and praise. They should be given tasks in which success lies well within their capabilities in order to help establish more self-confidence and feelings of competency.

There are varied forms of new awareness of the reproductive aspects of sex. Most nine-year-old girls have some knowledge of menstruation and most boys and girls have some understanding of the father's role in procreation. The girls are nearer to the age of puberty than the boys, and this fact accounts for the wide range of individual differences so apparent at this age. The nine-year-old is truly marked with individuality in his gestures, moods, speech, and humor. This individuality reasserts and reorganizes itself into the lineaments of a distinct person.

THE TEN-YEAR-OLD

The changes from age nine to age ten may be imperceptible. They come so gradually that it is only by comparing the child as he is at one point in time to his status at a later point that the changes can be noted. On the other hand, the changes may come suddenly and there may be a real division between nine and ten. The ten-year-old is in a new cycle of growth and is approaching adolescense. Parents of ten-year-old children describe them as nice, happy, casual, unselfconscious, straightforward, sincere, relaxed, companionable, poised, friendly, frank, and open.

By this age, fears are at a low ebb. However, there may be many worries. There are lessons and homework to worry about and getting to school on time. The contented, nice little ten-year-old may suddenly explode into anger, but the anger is short-lived. Earlier, the boys may have cried just as much or more than the girls; now, however, the girls have a greater tendency to tears. The ten-year-old also may have sudden bursts of affection with physical expressions of warmth, such as hugging and kissing.

In general, however, the ten-year-old is casually sure of himself and content within himself. He has a wide range of interests, but can concentrate on one interest at a time, moving from one to the next with the same sustained interest. There is a tendency to take stock of assets and faults, with reading, spelling, or some specific sport being the greatest assets.

Many children at age ten have started to think of the future in terms of career and marriage. Such choices are strongly influenced by the parents, their socioeconomic status, and their cultural heritage. The ten-year-old also has decided wishes for himself, both general and specific.

This is the last epoch for some time to come when the child will enter into a family excursion with full enjoyment. Later, peer-group activities take on major importance. Both boys and girls get along well with their mother and admire her. Fathers are also important and may sometimes surpass mother. Girls, especially, show strong feelings for their fathers and may be devastated when father scolds them. Companionship with father is greatly enjoyed, and for their part, most fathers enjoy their relationship with the ten-year-old. Premonitory rumblings of future discord may sometimes overcast the ten-year-old girl's relationship with her mother. There may also be sibling conflict, especially for those siblings between age six to age nine. However, much of this squabbling may be culturally induced. There is, for instance, much less sibling discord in Mexican-American families, where children are taught to share and protect one another.

On the whole, however, the ten-year-old is happy in himself, in his parents, and in his home.

Social Development

Socialization includes all the changes in the child's abilities, attitudes, personality characteristics, and beliefs which help him adapt to society. The school experience, peer groups, sex roles, and the development of morality are all crucial to the growth of socialization at ages eight, nine, and ten. Although socioeconomic status, cultural and ethnic background, and even geographic location may each influence the development of the socialization process, there are some experiences that are common to most American children.

One of the tasks of middle childhood is learning how to belong. The child's peer group provides an opportunity for the child to develop the capacity to live with his fellow men. The later ability to work together with other adults peaceably, and with a common purpose, will depend greatly on how well the individual was able to learn to do this in his peer-group activities as a child.

There is social pressure for boys to learn to act like men, and girls to act like women. During this age period, one typically sees boys playing mostly with boys, and girls with girls. The child becomes increasingly aware of the behavior that his culture defines as acceptable and desirable for his or her sex. This process is called sex typing and is partially a cultural process and partially a physiological process. The personality traits traditionally associated with being male or female apparently result from the combined influence of all the agents of socialization defined by the culture.

In addition to learning how to belong and learning to identify with peers of the same sex, part of the social development of the child also includes learning how to use language, to exchange ideas, and to influence people. Language is important to the child not only in his conceptual life, but also in his group relationships. Language is used to explore the ideas of others and to influence others with one's own ideas.

A fourth task in the development of social skills is the learning of social rules and morality. Play is now characterized by more organized games involving many people and many rules. Through such group activities, children learn about the rights of others and the rules of social living. The games are characterized by numerous regulations, the adherence to which is necessary for group acceptance. The concepts of fairness and unfairness become important, socially desirable aspects of the conscience.

During this age period, the child is a moral hedonist and a conformer to rules. That is, the child interprets good as that which is pleasant, and evil as that which has undesirable consequences. He will do someone good if he will gain something good in return. The morality of conventional role conformity reflects the increasing importance of peers and of social relations to the child.

And finally, a major task in the process of social development is to take the first decisive step into community living through the school. The schools are major disseminators of culture. It is in school that children learn the skills and knowledge for effective interaction with the complex world, the world beyond the circle of home and family. Within this context, he develops the social skills and public personality that will be retained throughout life.

THE EIGHT-YEAR-OLD

Special friends begin to play a part in the life of the child at age eight. School becomes important because friends are there. The relationship between friends may be very close and demanding, very similar to the mother-child relation. Eight-year-olds argue, dispute, and get angry with each other. Alliances are fragile, and tend to be shifting. It is best for parents not to take sides, for the bad guys or gals today may be the best chums tomorrow.

In spite of the minor verbal disagreements, the trend is toward longer periods of relatively peaceful play with others. In fact, at this age, the child abhors playing alone. He has developed a sense of interplay and desires active relationships. For this reason, he enjoys school and dislikes staying at home. There is more interaction between home and school and the child likes to bring to school things from home which relate to his school projects or to his personal experiences. At school, the teacher is treated less like a parent and more like a member of the peer group. The child is oriented chiefly toward his own group, room, or teacher, and enjoys school work that involves total group inclusion such as a spelling bee.

In the ethical sense, the eight-year-old wants to be good. The awareness of two opposing forces, good and bad, has become clearer. In fact, he may consider them to be absolutes, and cannot yet think in terms of something being relatively good or bad. However, the child is more capable of orderly thought and of thinking situations through. He becomes more responsible for what he does and is willing to take the consequences. The eight-year-old can now begin to see contexts, implications, and to see himself more clearly as a person among persons.

THE NINE-YEAR-OLD

The tendency to have special friends that was starting to form at age eight is even stronger at age nine. The nine-year-old chooses a member of his own sex for a special friend, and together they criticize peers of the opposite sex.

In his play and chosen activities, the nine-year-old is extremely busy. He particularly enjoys group play and may seek out formal clubs such as Cub Scouts or Brownies. There may be certain absorbing interests such as football or doll playing at which he or she will persist most of the day.

At age nine, the child wants to be independent of his teacher. Strong friendships are being formed and there may be a definite shift toward twosomes; nonetheless the identification with the classroom group is still powerful. Boys and girls continue to play separately, and exclude the opposite sex from play groups.

In the ethical sense, by age nine the child has acquired a credo of fairness. Acceptance of blame comes more easily when it is due. The rudiments of a conscience are developing and the child thinks in terms of right and wrong. The awareness of the errors of omission, as well as of commission begins to emerge, and the need to confess is strong. The words "honest" and "truth" are now part of the child's vocabulary. A sense of ethical standards and the means to live up to them is emerging rapidly. The nine-year-old's major traits are realism, reasonableness, and self-motivation. The child has become a fair-minded, responsible individual and is trending toward the teens.

THE TEN-YEAR-OLD

The delight in friendships with peers continues during the tenth year and play is still paramount. Boys and girls still separate in their choices of activities. Both boys and girls share an interest in horseback riding, although girls often show a far greater desire for this activity and for some girls this becomes a passion. Clubs of all kinds are forever forming, dissolving, and reforming, and organized activities take high priority. The child now has the skill and stamina to enjoy the fruits of a variety of pleasure-oriented competencies.

Although the ten-year-old is fond of friends, his friendships may be rather fluid. Girls have a tendency to get angry with one another and not to speak or play with one another for several days. Girls also tend to like smaller and more intimate groups; they may choose one "best friend" for an extended time, and the name of this friend can be a secret carefully guarded from other girls—who would feel hurt if they were not the chosen one. The boys tend to be more inclusive and less incisive in their day-to-day friendships. The reciprocal adjustments between friends play a powerful role in enhancing personality development and social competencies. The ten-year-old also likes school and his school-group association is motivated by camaraderie rather than competition.

The ten-year-old has a strict moral code with a strong sense of justice. At this age, however, he is more concerned about what is wrong rather than what is right. Although the parents are still the major source of law, the child may not restrict himself to just what his parents have taught. There is a beginning capacity to think things through, and the child has enough of a conscience to know when a decision is a bad one. Withal, the conscience is in a state of relative immaturity, and is still actively growing. The ten-year-old recognizes the growing-up process and from time to time may demonstrate more mature interests along with less mature activities.

Intellectual Development

A very significant landmark during this period is the emergence of a scientific approach to learning and thinking. The child may no longer believe everything he is told. The why and wherefore of things are extremely important. Concepts of the world and people expand rapidly, and the development of reasoning is clearly evident. The ability to use visual symbols for reading and writing and abstract thinking becomes a prominent feature of this intellectual repertoire, and the use of language begins to dominate his conceptual life.

Along with and as important as the development of rational thought and language, the child acquires a sense of duty and accomplishment and learns the value of application. His future attitudes toward study and learning depend to a very large extent on whether or not he can make the adjustment to school life during the first three or four grades. Successful adjustment in school involves several factors, not the least of which are the social and emotional readiness on the part of the child and an accepting, flexible atmosphere in the school. Indeed, the child must be intellectually, physically, emotionally, and socially ready for the tasks demanded by the school curriculum. If a child cannot employ his capacity when he is ready, boredom is all too likely to ensue with the consequent development of poor study habits. On the other hand, if a child is pressured to learn before he is ready or at a level that is beyond his capabilities, failure, defensiveness, and loss of motivation may ensue. The resulting hopelessness and feeling of incompetence may have a most adverse effect on personality development, and occasionally it will lead to serious behavioral problems.

About 3 percent of school-age children are mentally subnormal and require special classes or schools. About 10 to 25 percent are slow learners for a variety of reasons. Such children encounter educational difficulties and need an adequate assessment to determine the cause of the learning problems. About 20 to 25 percent of school children are bright and above average, and about 30 percent are gifted. The remaining 40 to 50 percent are in the average range of intelligence. A significant number of children are under-achievers because of emotional problems. These children often benefit from special guidance.

The period from approximately age seven to eleven is described by Piaget as the "concrete operational stage." The child approaches this period by way of the sensorimotor period (birth to two years), preconceptual thought (two to four years), and intuitive thinking (four to seven years). Toward the end of the latter period, the child's thinking is egocentric, perception-dominated, and intuitive, with contradictions and errors of logic. Upon the advent of the period of concrete thought, many of these cognitive qualities disappear and are replaced by more logical thinking.

The beginning of such concrete operational thinking is a major turning point in development. The child begins to understand operations in terms of actions which integrate with other actions to form general reversible systems. Indeed, the main change is that the child's thinking becomes reversible, which is to say that he recognizes the possibility of returning to the starting point of the operation in question. With the advent of reversibility, there is a permanent equilibrium between assimilation and accommodation. Consequently, intelligent adaptation can be made to more complex aspects of reality, and range and depth of understanding are increased.

The development of concrete operational thinking brings with it the ability to coordinate successive changes in time and space. The child is no longer dominated by the configurations which he perceives at a given moment. In addition, the child is freed from the tendency to focus only on one aspect of a situation or on his own viewpoint. Two variables can be considered at the same time with the realization that a change in one can be compensated for by a change in the other.

Operational thinking also includes the attainment of conservation, seriation, and classification. Once conservation is achieved, length is maintained through changes of shape, or numbers remain invariant despite changes in spatial configuration. In addition, numbers are understood as forming a series. The child can place a series of graded sticks in order, and if they are out of order, he can reposition them in their appropriate places. Similarly, the child now has the schemata of thinking that enable him to classify objects when two variables are involved and to arrange them in an ordered sequence. For example, he can correctly sort objects that vary both in form and in color by the use of a single criteria—for example, form. Given the view of a model mountain range and asked how it would look if he were opposite his present position, or to the left of it or to the right, the child can now reproduce it correctly. The difficulties with problems of time and space that were characteristic of previous stages are no longer in evidence.

Concrete operations are limited by both the form of the operation and the content with which they deal. The operations are confined to organizing immediately given data and do not include working with hypothetical formulations. With regard to content, the schema of serializing can be applied more readily to lengths than to widths. At this level, the child does not yet formulate hypotheses and organize his observations. This approach will emerge during the abstract operational stage. However, the practical application of Piaget's conceptualizations can be observed especially well in the children's school performance.

THE EIGHT-YEAR-OLD

The eight-year-old child is more capable of managing his thoughts and of thinking things through. He can manage transitions fairly smoothly, and he likes to change from one thing to another. Reading is usually a source of pleasure, and those who are just beginning to read well now enjoy reading spontaneously. The child can now tackle new words through context or by phonetics. He is more skillful, and only occasionally makes the typical errors of the six- or seven-year-old. His speed is more uniform and he can stop and talk about the story, and then pick it up again. Many read well enough now to prefer silent reading. Some eight-year-old children may not spend as much time reading by themselves as they did at age seven and prefer to be read to.

At age eight, writing is less laborious and there is more uniformity in slant and alignment as well as in spacing of words and sentences. However, his reach of his ideas may exceed his ability to express them, and he may not be able to write out a story to full length. He is also becoming a good observer. All in all, the eight-year-old enjoys school and enters the classroom with enthusiasm.

THE NINE-YEAR-OLD

The nine-year-old child makes up his mind rapidly and definitely, and his decisions are made easily, almost automatically. He now manages his own independence and can think and reason for himself. Characteristically, he has acquired the capacity to set his mind to a task and see it through. This new-found independence is reflected in his school work.

Most nine-year-olds enjoy school and are intent upon improving their skills. At the same time, teachers report that fourth grade is a more difficult grade to teach than third grade. The nine-year-old is afraid of failing and is also ashamed of having failed. Because of these emotional tensions, it is very important to be sure that the nine-year-old can handle the more demanding tasks of school. He is happier in a group which will allow him to operate at his optimal level rather than at his minimal level. The change from third to fourth grade is a crucial one. Many children who have been developing on the slower side may now show a real spurt in achievement. Others with some degree of reading or arithmetic disability may begin to feel overwhelmed by the demands of fourth grade. Failure may then all too readily ensue if immediate intervention is not forthcoming.

The nine-year-old is capable of a measure of critical evaluation of his own abilities; he has determined and can describe his preferred method of working. In reading, he may prefer to read silently and may dislike reading before the group. He can sound out any word, but usually he is not too concerned if he does not know the meaning unless it is important to the story.

He is able to write for a prolonged period and, indeed, writing may now be put to more practical uses such as keeping a diary or ordering things by mail. In general, girls' penmanship is smaller, neater, and performed with less pressure than boys' penmanship; boys still tend to write with heavy strokes. Arithmetic is perhaps the most talked of subject in fourth grade; it is either strongly liked or strongly disliked.

By and large, nine-year-olds can work independently both of other children and of the teacher. The child is intrigued by tasks, and often has more interest in problem solving than his school work may demand. Individual differences are very marked at this age and individual skills are highly noticeable.

THE TEN-YEAR-OLD

The ten-year-old child has inner sources of motivation and potential for action. This is particularly evident in his control of time and space. These concepts are still rather static and specific, but nonetheless, they stand the child in good stead. He relates to time in terms of the clock and the calendar—i.e., hours, minutes, and seconds, or days, or time of the year. Although he does not have much of a feeling for the larger passage of time, he may grasp its variations, that is, sometimes there is not enough time, or, again, too much. The ten-year-old achieves the same success in his conquest of immediate space as in his conquest of immediate time. Space is rather specific—it is where things are, or outer space is a place where nothing is. Space for the ten-year-old is the void between two different things. All and all, the ten-year-old's thinking includes the very specific "here and now" as well as a wider concept of generality.

School life is very important to the ten-year-old. He likes his teacher, he likes to learn, and he needs to be kept interested and motivated. Albeit not teacher-centered, the teacher is still very important to him.

The ten-year-old likes to read and reads to himself with great absorption. He likes to listen to stories, but better yet, he likes to tell his own, usually about something he has seen or read. It has been observed that talking can be one of his favorite activities, and indeed, in some instances the talking may be continuous.

Although studies are generally taken in stride, there are usually specific preferences. The child loves to take dictation, and to memorize. In fact, he can master long poems and recite them with good expression. He does have difficulty, however, in combining or connecting two facts. This is especially evident in arithmetic. Even when two tasks are pictured out for him, the child may not see the relationship. For that reason, more time should be spent on memorizing and less on abstraction in thinking. The cataloging and memorization of material will stand the child in good stead later when he is ready for abstract operations.

In general, such a child prefers oral work, or visual work through pictorial material. This is an excellent age for educational television, for the youngster sees and listens well, and loves to discuss what he has seen and heard. In educational planning for ten-year-olds, it should also be noted that the interest span may be short. Consequently, a ten-year-old may need a certain amount of liberty to move around the room. There should be sufficient time spent exercising out of doors or in a gym, and brief breaks given from the routine of the classroom.

Conclusion

The child from age eight to age ten is at the center of middle childhood. During this period, certain psychologic landmarks should be achieved if the child is to be prepared for the tasks of entry into adolescence. Such landmarks include the following:[1]

1. The acquisition of special friends of the same sex;
2. Avoidance of the opposite sex;
3. Membership in a group of friends;
4. Knowledge of the rules of the games and an ability to follow or enforce them;
5. The ability to read and the enjoyment of reading;
6. A scientific approach to a new situation;
7. Knowledge of right and wrong;
8. The ability to tell the truth.

There are certain aspects of the growth process which are common to most children of this age period, but which may cause parents some concern. These include self-assertive or aggressive behavior, moodiness, temper, and secretiveness.[1] These are an indication of the child's strivings for independence, and of his entry into the process of resolving the former dependency on parents and attempting to enter the wider world beyond the home. Such development may be fraught with some anxieties and inconsistencies. The parents' role is to be supportive and understanding and to provide a great deal of praise when independent tasks are accomplished.

REFERENCES

1. CALL, JUSTIN D., "Psychologic and Behavioral Development of Children," in Kelley, V. C. (Ed.), *Brenneman's Practice of Pediatrics*, vol. 1, pp. 1–14, Harper & Row, New York, 1977.
2. CRATTY, B. J., *Perceptual and Motor Development in Infants and Children*, Macmillan, New York, 1970.
3. GESELL, A., *The Child from Ten to Sixteen*, Harper and Brothers, New York, 1944.
4. ———, *The Child From Five to Ten*, Harper and Brothers, New York, 1942.
5. GINSBERG, H., and OPPER, S., *Piaget's Theory of Intellectual Development*, Prentice-Hall, Englewood Cliffs, N.J., 1969.
6. JERSILD, A. T., *Child Psychology*, 6th ed., Prentice-Hall, Englewood Cliffs, N.J., 1968.

17 / Development from Ten to Thirteen Years

Herbert J. Goldings

Introduction

The child's development during the prepubertal period, age ten to thirteen, is marked by restless and uneasy transition: a temporarily increased exposure to conflicts and problems of the prelatency years; a renewed reliance upon prelatency defenses; and a foreshadowing of the developmental tasks and challenges of adolescence. Both the regressive and progressive sides of this transition are pursued with fear and timidity at one moment, with enthusiasm and zest at another. The personal climate and landscape within this child changes rapidly and with alarming inconsistency. He is, at times, a stranger to himself as new needs and interests articulate with rapid changes in bodily growth, physical appearance, and hormonal function. He is often an exasperation to adults around him as the ever-enlarging body suddenly becomes the instrument of the long-ago tears, rages, and tantrums of the preschool child and yet, moments later, a vehicle of deep intimacy, of nearly adult sensitivity to the rights and feelings of others. There are times of ruthless disregard for all but the most self-centered projects and wishes, contrasting with some sustained periods of self-examination and self-criticism and of serious reflection on the human condition and the state of the universe. Only among his peers does this enigmatic, demanding, turbulent person find a surer and more solid footing. And even here, the steady state may be short-lived because the universe of ten- to thirteen-year-olds is populated with other creatures who are as volatile and everchanging as he, and who may be for him, psychologically and physically, "here one minute, gone the next."

Small wonder, then, that the earliest object ties, pregenital affections to the mother in particular, become reactivated, renewed, and reexperienced with conflict. The so recently achieved solid latency accomplishments consisting of solutions to the oedipal conflict, formation of ego-ideal identifications, refinement of superego structures, and ego achievements (in school, learning, and defensive structure) may be—one or all of them—temporarily resigned before being resumed and further elaborated.

The social context of the prepubertal period is itself more precarious and unsettled than it was even half a generation ago. With the propensity for "adolescence" itself to move to an earlier chronological point both in its biological onset and its social authorization, all of the developmental stages prior to adolescence become somewhat compressed, and the period of prepuberty, which is caught between the firm and solid structure of the latency period on the one side and the insistent urgencies of adolescence proper on the other, is subjected to special stresses of compression and torsion. These forces serve to accentuate and intensify the instabilities already intrinsic to this transitional period and to augment both the child's regressive thrusts and his progressive sallies.

Prepuberty as a Distinct Developmental Epoch

"Prepuberty" is a misleading term. To a limited extent, it accurately describes the chronological position of the ten- to thirteen-year-old child, but it calls forth an erroneous image of a period of suspension or expectancy as if a "waiting state" before something big and really important is to happen. The term "postlatency," although less frequently used, is similarly misleading. Disagreements as to the conceptualization of the period from ages ten to thirteen have resulted in two polar viewpoints. For Deutsch,[4] prepuberty (in girls, at least) is viewed as a "last stage of latency" in which there is a final thrust toward reality adaptation. For Blos,[3] however, prepuberty is the earliest phase of adolescence characterized by a quantitative increase in instinctual drive, a reactivation of all earlier modes of drive gratification, as well as "the onset if not the roots" of all adolescent disturbances. It is now increasingly apparent that the child in the ten to thirteen developmental period is neither merely tidying-up the unfinished work of the latency period nor simply preparing himself for the real business of adolescence proper. He is doing both of these things but, in addition, and most significantly, he is engaged in a developmental effort continuous with each of these periods but having a distinct and definable biology, psychology, and phenomenology of its own.[5] Failure of the child to accomplish the work intrinsic to this period, whether through biological accident, adverse psychological or social influence, or misdirected therapeutic zeal (for example, "to help get the child into adolescence"), carries with it the same hazards and deleterious consequences which accompany truncated, arrested, or accelerated development in other growth periods.

Physical Growth and Development from Ages Ten to Thirteen

The advanced development of girls as compared with boys reaches a dramatic point during this period. Girls, who from birth (and even before) are more advanced developmentally than boys, have consolidated a full two-year lead by age thirteen and hence show a physiological maturation significantly and consistently in advance of the boys who are their chronological peers. Despite the earlier occurrence of puberty during this past century (menarche for British girls is now occurring shortly before age thirteen compared to age fifteen some forty years ago) and regardless of variations due to social class, climate, and nutritional factors, the two-year difference between boys and girls remains a biological constant and is one of the physiological realities within which any consideration of the psychology of this period must be placed.[13, 15]

A second biological fact pertains to the variability of the rate of accomplishment of the pubertal changes with the result that at any one point in time some girls age eleven, twelve, and thirteen will have completed their entire adolescent physiological development, whereas others will not even have begun to mature. The same is true of boys age thirteen, fourteen, and fifteen. While the *onset* and *rate* of these changes is variable, the sequence of bodily changes is relatively fixed for girls and for boys. For girls, the budding of breasts and skeletal growth spurts begin around nine or ten years of age. During the ensuing years, there is generally the appearance of pubic hair and a fiftyfold increase in estrogen secretion. Accompanying these endocrinological events is a remolding of the bony pelvis, and an enlargement of uterus and vagina as well as labia and clitoris. The spurt in skeletal growth reaches its peak shortly after the twelfth year. Axillary hair and menarche occur around age thirteen, and following this latter event the rate of skeletal growth declines rapidly. Although the menarche indicates mature uterine development, it does not generally indicate full reproductive capacity. Irregular and anovulatory menstrual cycles may occur for an additional twelve to eighteen months.

For the boy, the growth events may be less obvious and dramatic during the ten to thirteen period since the major spurt in skeletal growth occurs at age fifteen years and the apex of the strength spurt is at sixteen years. From ages ten to eleven, there is a slight increase in the size of the penis and testes and the appearance of downy pubic hair. This is followed by increased prostatic activity and excretion of urinary gonadotropins, with attendant enlargement of the nipples and areolae. At the age of fourteen there is growth of the genitals with testicular enlargement proportionately greater than that of the penis. (Seminal ejaculation generally occurs one year after the maximal penis growth, and the breaking of the voice occurs quite late in adolescence.) Testicular enlargement is the greatest bodily change during the prepubertal period and includes change in size (from a weight of 4 grams at age nine to seventeen grams at age fourteen and 20 grams at age seventeen), in scrotal coloring, and in pain sensitivity.[1, 5]

The velocity of growth in both boys and girls doubles for a year or more, thereby achieving a rate of growth equivalent to that experienced by the child at age two. While hormonal functions, particularly pituitary gonadotropins, govern the course of this complex process, the onset of prepubertal and pubertal changes is controlled by the brain (hypothalamus) and not by the pituitary gland itself. Brain maturation, not hypothalamic maturation, is essential for the onset of puberty.

While the impact of earlier or later maturation is always a highly personal matter for the individual child, some general observations in this area deepen our appreciation of the psychology of this period. There is a consistent *group* difference in which physically advanced and physically larger children show an improved intellectual performance (on IQ tests), social adaptation, and psychological health over the group of slower maturers and smaller sized children. For boys, in fact, at least part of the height-IQ correlation demonstrated between early and late maturers persists in adult form when both groups have finished growing and show no differences in height. The boys' world at ages ten to thirteen (and in midadolescence too) places a premium on bodily prowess as a social and personal tool—both socially and psychologically, physical capabilities may resonate in the child with the issues of his endowments (or deficiencies) from earlier life. When these early anxieties receive a physical confirmation in the tempo of growth, important psychological dislocations can be precipitated or fixed.

Early maturation presents other problems to the child—for example, a longer period of delay in the gratification of sexual needs, and in social and occupational "authentication" as a grownup—but overall these would appear to be of lesser importance, although often an issue of much importance to any individual child.

The prepubertal child's behavioral and psychological response to these physiological events is a complex mixture of physiological sensation, social impact, and his own fantasy life. Some of the sensations which accompany these physiological changes are often vaguely conveyed to us by children and may be vaguely experienced by them.

Some inner somatic, visceral, and genital sensations are poorly localized and incompletely apprehended.[10] Other sensations are more clearly defined and variously invested. Erections in boys, for example, often experienced as painful and unwelcome in the four to seven-year-old, now become constantly pleasurable, excitingly, and purposefully produced by masturbation in the ten to thirteen-year-old. The child is vitally aware of the changes occurring in children around him. He may express his mixed longing and apprehension in condensed and poignant ways. One eleven-and-one-half-year-old boy of slightly small stature complained to his parents that he had not yet had his "growth squirt." An eleven-year-old girl returned from summer camp determined that she would not marry because the kind of boy she liked was strong and muscular and might "beat me up and make me bleed."

Psychosocial Development

Psychosocial development may be viewed at this time as the resultant of the growth forces outlined earlier, ego capacities emerging and accessible at this time, and the recasting of the two main classes of object relations which are so vital to the child—parents and peers.

The drive pressure increases diffusely during this period. The aggressive thrust of latency is no longer fully present, nor is the prelatency or adolescent erotic life fully emergent. New and vague but strong sensations are felt, and a full array of earlier defenses are called into action to deal with them. For boys in this age group in particular, there is a resurgence of anal humor openly and in more private boy groups. This behavior blends imperceptibly with old castration anxieties renewed by having to deal with newly developing girls—peeping, joking, exploring, derogating, envying, and eschewing these new body-creatures so startlingly similar to the boys' mothers. Physical prowess and refined physical skill in individual and group competition become accentuated. In public games of organized sport, team spirit and allegiance to training—rather than to strictly individual virtuosity—is paramount, and private games such as those resting on the length and strength of the urinary stream serve to bring these timely concerns out into the open. The relationship to the father (and to adult men teachers) becomes less troubled and supportive of ego-ideal identifications, which began in early latency and now are even more vital in order to resolve the bisexual dilemma in the unconscious and fantasy life of preadolescent boys.

Shifts in cognitive abilities and the acquisition of new cognitive skills are already taking place in both boys and girls. The basic learning tools of the latency period have long since been acquired and consolidated. School as a setting in which to achieve, to relate to adults other than parents, and to sublimate, has been mastered. Both boys and girls are now much more capable of "abstract" rather than concrete intellectual operations, of propositional thinking, of "how" rather than "why," and children now address their curiosity less exclusively to the "inside" and more to the "outside" (outside the body, outside of the family, outside the child) activities. Concomitant with these changes, however, the active academic output, particularly of boys, declines—the so-called "seventh-grade slump." This is not due to any flagging of mental ability, but probably to the fact that now the usual school tasks can neither bind the energy as they could for the latency age child nor provide the gratifications and excitement which they did in early latency (and will again as puberty becomes more solidly advanced). Girls are, by and large, better students at this time. Their sublimations are more serviceable, their social contacts are more of a piece with the academic situation. This makes them all the more the objects of dread, ridicule, and envy by the boys whom they derogate at this age.

The girl's development during this time is beset with two hazards: first, the regressive attachment to the mother of preoedipal years with whom she has become allied in her final oedipal identifications; and second, renewed difficulties in dealing with old and current bisexual aspirations.[2] More intense chum-peer relations evolve between girls at this time, and often the adolescent girl just a few years senior becomes the object of an intense —even slavish—identification and anaclitic cathexis. This latter is sometimes so intense as to remove the prepuberty girl from some of the active, age-appropriate growth experiences of the prepuberty period itself.

The dramatic and momentous physical changes occurring in girls at this time evoke a full range of behaviors designed to preserve the bisexual potential and to postpone an inevitable affirmation of her final femininity. The early breast changes are often dealt with first by denial, or shame, or efforts at concealment. Ambivalence was strikingly illustrated by an eleven-and-one-half-year-old girl who insisted that her mother get her a bra (for which there was only the most minimal need) and which she then undertook to wear continuously day and night. The next week she spent her own money to buy weightlifting equipment.

Often the denial of breast development reflects a concern about forestalling the menarche which has by now been intimately and infinitely discussed by parents (well-meaning, eager, or anxious), by schools (which now aim their "health and hygiene" course at about the fifth-grade level), and, most significantly, with the peer group. A careful tally may be kept as to who has and who has not had her period, what it was like, how you can tell. Emphasis on the future role of the menstrual period in terms of fertility is far overshadowed by the thoughts and fantasies of hurt, damage, and mess—the early pregenital themes again.

Among the newer activities of mastery and sublimation in current vogue is the fad for having ears pierced. Formerly only practiced by a few subcultures in our society and perhaps an occasional enterprising individual, ear piercing has become a widespread preadolescent activity for ten to twelve-year-olds in most social classes (and for some younger girls also). The affect, and fantasy, related by the girls leaves little doubt as to its unconscious counterphobic function: "The doctor has a special sharp needle for it. . . . Sometimes a nurse can do it but not often. . . . One real prick, one tiny drop of blood and it's over. . . . You can be beautiful forever. But you've got to keep the thing in [ear stud] or you'll heal over and close up." One ten-and-one-half-year-old girl was convinced that you had to keep the "thing" in for *nine months*.[6]

In boys, the regressive forces previously discussed place violence, aggression, and motoric uncontrol in close proximity to regressive anality. This makes a potential for the exercise of sadistic gratifications more palpable and accessible. When ego-ideal identifications are unstable, contaminated with real-life sadisms or with the especially virulent and compelling fantasy fare of modern televised violence (whether fictional or newscast), serious disruptions of social control and inner-affective balance can ensue. As indicated throughout this section, there exists a broad range of countermeasures within the child which are variably effective.

Ego Ideal and Superego Development in Prepuberty

The ego ideal undergoes especially important development during the prepubertal period. Most prominent in both boys and girls is the elaboration of the "concrete ego ideal" usually in the form of a chum, an older adolescent, or a nonparent adult who is seen by the child as embodying specific achievements, characteristics, goals, attributes, and skills which the child himself would wish to achieve. Along with this facet of the ego ideal there is a more abstract ego ideal, a narcissistic, idealized structure whose distance from the real self and from all which the real self might actually expect to achieve is not the ultimate developmental concern of the prepubertal child but of the adolescent and adult. The persistence of the prepubertal ego ideal as the sole or major ego-ideal structure, unmodified by developmental experiences, carries with it serious character pathologies recognized and described by Hendrick[8] and by Jacobson.[9]

As might be expected from the generally reciprocal relationship between superego and ego ideal, further elaboration of the superego, beyond its state in late latency, is not especially prominent during the period of prepubertal development, and the differences between the superego structure of girls as compared to boys, noted in earlier latency development, tend to persist. This structure undergoes further revision and refinement at a more advanced stage of adolescence.

Creativity, Fantasy, and Play in Prepuberty

A lessening of creativity and a muting of fantasy life are sometimes cited as features of the prepubertal child. It would be more accurate to describe the situation as one where fantasy is more structured in its expression and more formal in its representation as a result of expanded and more specialized development of ego capacities. Children's drawings at this age, for example, are more representational, formalized, make use of perspective, and show a greater skill in the control of the media than is the case with the younger child. The drawings can still retain originality, however, and they are capable of being vehicles for affective and fantasy expression. Many children at this age love handwork—carpentry, weaving, macrame, model building—done individually or in a group setting. The final product is more intricate and sophisticated than that of the younger child, but there is the same pleasure in exhibiting it to others, both peers and adults.

It is in children's play and reading activity that one can sometimes get the freshest view of the affective changes and preoccupations which are alive for the prepubertal child. In jump-rope games, for example, the skills acquired by early- and middle–latency-age girls are practiced with rhymes and chants which enunciate the incipiently heterosexual alongside with the anogenital confusions which beset the prelatency child. A typical rhyme of early latency is:

> Standing on the corner
> Chewing bubblegum
> Along came a boy
> And asked for some.
> No you little boy
> No you dirty bum
> You can't have any
> Of my bubblegum.

For the girl age ten and older, the following rhyme is more representative:

> Johnny gave me apples
> Johnny gave me pears
> Johnny gave me fifty cents
> And kissed me on the stairs.
> I'd rather wash the dishes
> I'd rather scrub the floor
> I'd rather kiss the dirty boy
> Behind the kitchen door.[7]

Here again we see in condensed form the fusion and progression from oral to anal and finally heterosexual emphases as the girl's prepuberty advances. An especially clear view of the internal panorama of development for boys of this age period is afforded by a close look at the content of the kinds of rhymes to which they may devote themselves during this time. The following set of verses, popular with boys in this age group, is an example cited by Opie as the use of parody and impropriety through which "children get their own back on the great ones." Taking Mrs. Hemans's classic of literature, ten- to thirteen-year-old boys may modify it as follows:

> The boy stood on the burning deck,
> His legs were covered with blisters;
> His father was in the public house,
> With beer all down his whiskers.

> The boy stood on the burning deck,
> His legs were covered with blisters;
> And when his pants began to burn
> He had to borrow his sister's.

> The boy stood on the burning deck,
> Picking his nose like mad;
> He rolled them into little balls
> And flicked them at his dad.

> The boy stood on the burning deck
> Melting with the heat;
> His big blue eyes were full of tears
> And his shoes were full of feet.

> The boy stood on the burning deck,
> Selling peas at a penny a peck;
> No, by heck!

> The boy stood on the burning deck
> Playing a game of cricket;
> The ball rolled up his trouser leg
> And hit the middle wicket.[12] [p. 93]

The full range of psychosexual and interpersonal preoccupation from an oral through the anal, and culminating in the genital, are conveyed in this rhyme (and many others). Allusions to the bisexual conflict (sister's pants) and to the growth changes (the shoes full of feet) are also mentioned here.

For girls at this age, the love of horses can be a passion which burns brightly on the fuel of powerful instinctual forces. The child frequently entertains the unconscious hope that the bisexual yearning will be made real and gratified by the experience (or fantasy) of mounting, galloping, directing, and controlling this powerful force beneath her, and by caring for, combing, cleaning, caressing, and loving it as well. Animal stories in general and horse stories in particular have a compelling interest and a deeply moving appeal for the prepubertal girl. Unlike the animal stories of the younger child where anthropomorphism gives the power of human speech and thought to even the lowliest arthropod, the stories for older children can convey the full range of sentiments of love, rage, fear, cruelty, loyalty, revenge, joy, and bitter disappointment through sensate clues more eloquent than the mere spoken word—and more resonant with the child's inner life at this stage of development. For boys tales of heroic adventure, physical prowess, and bodily and spiritual excellence have perennial appeal alongside with rhymes, jokes, and fantasies where smut and anality are blended in an intoxicating brew.

The body of the prepubertal child is not only a vehicle of his superb growth and evolution during this time but also the receptacle of a myriad of symptoms and complaints due both to the stresses of growing up and, at times, to frank neurotic symptom formation. Headache, stomachache, and insomnia are not uncommon. The attentive parent or physician will also hear deep feelings of sadness and an enunciated sense of lack of self-worth and personal badness (related more often to roughness of the psychosocial terrain than to primary superego forces); desolation at the loss of a favorite friend, or a school, or a neighborhood; and even the enunciation of a terrible and inconsolable loneliness which the child knew all along could exist but can only now put into words.

A number of forces impinging on the prepubertal child (and, in some instances, on all children) are so new that data are not yet available to assess their impact on development: the relative availability of drugs (alcohol, marijuana, barbiturates, and amphetamines) to the prepubertal child; the presence of serious and long-standing social disruptions, particularly in urban schools; the blurring of traditional family structures and the proliferation of alternative family styles; and efforts to redistribute parenting functions as well as other "traditional" male and female social roles and opportunities. Our present knowledge of child development would permit us to make some predictions of the effects of many of these forces, and when actual data regarding these influences become available, we will then be able to test further the adequacy of some of our formulations regarding the psychological development of the prepubertal child.

REFERENCES

1. BELL, A. I., "Some Observations on the Role of the Scrotal Sac and Testicles," *Journal of the American Psychoanalytic Association, 9*:261–266, 1961.
2. BLOS, P., "The Child Analyst Looks at the Young Adolescent," *Daedalus, 100(4)*:961–978, 1971.
3. ——, *The Young Adolescent*, Free Press, New York, 1970.
4. DEUTSCH, H., *The Psychology of Women*, vol. 1, *Girlhood*, Research Books, London, 1947.
5. GALENSON, E., "Prepuberty and Child Analysis: Report of Panel," *Journal of the American Psychoanalytic Association, 12*:600–609, 1964.
6. GOLDINGS, H. J., "Ear-Piercing and Development," unpublished manuscript, 1975.
7. ——, "Jump-rope Rhymes and the Rhythm of Latency Development in Girls," in Eissler, R. S., et al. (Eds.), *The Psychoanalytic Study of the Child*, vol. 29, pp. 431–450, Yale University Press, New Haven, 1974.
8. HENDRICK, I., "Narcissism and the Prepuberty Ego Ideal," *Journal of the American Psychoanalytic Association, 12*:522–528, 1964.
9. JACOBSON, E., *The Self and the Object World*, International Universities Press, New York, 1964.
10. KESTENBERG, J. S., *Children and Parents: Psychoanalytic Studies in Development*, Aronson, New York, 1975.
11. MUSSEN, P. H., and JONES, M. C., "Self-concepting Motivations and Interpersonal Attitudes of Late- and Early-Maturing Boys," *Child Development, 28*:243–256, 1957.
12. OPIE, P., and OPIE, I., *The Lore and Language of Schoolchildren*, Oxford University Press, London, 1959.
13. TANNER, J. M., "Sequence, Tempo, and Individual Variation in Growth and Development of Boys and Girls Aged Twelve to Sixteen," *Daedalus, 100(4)*:907–930, 1971.
14. ——, "Galtonian Eugenics and the Study of Growth," *The Eugenics Review, 58*:122–135, 1966.
15. ——, *Growth at Adolescence*, 2nd ed., Blackwell Scientific Publications, Oxford, 1962.

18 / Development from Thirteen to Sixteen Years

Carl P. Malmquist

Physical Development

GENERAL PRINCIPLES

In weighing the relative significance for development of psychological and physical factors, questions about priorities can be somewhat academic. However, neglect of their dual presence and of their interactions is not. If one starts by considering the definite bodily changes that occur at the commencement of puberty and then proceeds to a review of its psychological aspects, this does not imply that one is more significant than the other. It would be quite amiss if one did not emphasize these enormous physical changes which take place in the period between thirteen to sixteen years of age. Only during the fetal and infantile periods do bodily changes occur at a faster rate. On the other hand, when puberty begins, the accompanying psychological changes are enormous. Any comparison with infancy growth rates becomes meaningful only if one relies simply on straight growth measurements. It must also be noted that changes in physical growth did not just begin at age thirteen; this is especially true for girls.

By way of a summary, some of the salient facts about physical development for the adolescent in this age range are the following:

1. Enormous variation occurs among individuals, and this is true for several biological variables.
2. Albeit not precisely, the *sequence* of unfolding events in males and females seems to hold from individual to individual.
3. An overlapping of different bodily changes tends to occur, with one aspect beginning before other changes are completed.
4. The age range for the beginning and end of certain bodily changes varies widely—indeed, an early maturer may have completed a certain phase of development before someone of the same chronological age has even begun it.
5. In terms of her rate of growth, the adolescent female in Britain or North America peaks about two years before her male counterpart—on the average, this is about twelve years for girls and fourteen years for boys with a standard deviation of 0.9 years. While different studies vary somewhat in terms of absolute averages, the two-year differential seems to be maintained.
6. The initiation of puberty occurs in response to maturational changes which begin in the central nervous system. More specifically, the hypothalamus must attain sufficient physiological maturity for puberty to begin. It, rather than the pituitary gland, is the prime mover of this process. The mechanism seems to be this: From infancy on, traces of sex hormones circulate in the blood. These function as inhibitors of the prepubertal hypothalamus.[7] When the hypothalamic cells have matured sufficiently, a sensitization mechanism is set on a cellular level for the commencement of puberty. At that time, the hypothalamic cells become less sensitive to circulating sex hormones; they secrete "gonadotrophin releasers" which can now spring into action. Their site of action is the pituitary, which in turn releases gonadotrophins, along with other activating hormones such as TSH (thyroid stimulating hormone), ACTH (adrenocortictrophic hormone), and growth hormone. The feedback circuit has then been established.
7. At puberty, the rate of growth accelerates to a peak—the adolescent growth spurt. For a period of a year or more, the velocity of growth approximately doubles. This is a rate not experienced since age two. Those adolescents who peak early also reach a relatively higher level than those who peak later.[21] It appears that this growth spurt is partly under the control of different hormones than was the growth which occurred during the preceding period.[19]

Various authors often use the terms "puberty" and "adolescence" interchangeably, as well as differently. A workable set of definitions is therefore desirable. "Puberty" refers to the external and visible changes that take the form of the secondary sexual characteristics. These are induced by sex hormones and serve reproductive activity. They are distinguished from the primary sexual characteristics which are determined by the form of the reproductive organs as such. "Nubility" means that full reproductive capacity has been attained. "Pubescence" fuses these two concepts and includes the onset of secondary sexual changes and reproductive viability. "Adolescence" is a broader term which often includes all of the above changes, but it encompasses the sociocultural changes and interactions as well.

PHYSICAL CHANGES

Height: In an impressionistic sense, the most striking changes in the adolescent are the widening hips in the girl and the height and increased shoulder breadth in the boy. During the growth spurt period of approximately one year, 2.75–4.75 inches are likely to be added to the height of a boy and slightly less than this for a girl (about two years earlier). As noted, all skeletal and muscular dimensions take part in this growth pattern, but not necessarily proportionately. Head, hands, and feet achieve adult size first, followed by arm and leg lengths. The shoulder girth and trunk length are last, but this is what actually contributes the most to the adolescent growth spurt. An old saying is that ungainly hands and feet give rise to trousers which are too short and then jackets which are too small.[17]

Body Composition and Demands on the Body: Along with increasing height, there is an alteration of muscle and body fat. While boys develop relatively more muscle, they simultaneously lose more fat than girls. The basal metabolism rate (BMR) declines, which means that energy turnover is less. However, boys retain a higher rate than girls, reflecting their greater muscle mass which consumes more oxygen. In addition, girls lack the rise in red. blood cells and hemoglobin brought about by testosterone.[23] Nutritional demands increase for both, depending on the growth, body size, and the individual's activity level.

Organ Changes: Although the heart, lungs, and other internal organs increase in size, the size of the brain changes relatively little during the period of thirteen to sixteen years. At six months of age, the brain is already nearly 50 percent of its adult weight, and by ten years of age, it is 95 percent. In contrast to this, only 50 percent of body weight has been attained by age ten. Because of the complexity of such research, detailed knowledge is lacking of specific changes which occur in the brain compared to other organs. Nor is size alone the crucial variable since endless connections between millions of dendrites occur, and these require little space. Their number and quality can, however, have endless repercussions on learning, cognitive functioning, and behavior.

Along with neurochemical changes, which will not be discussed here, changes in electroencephalogram (EEG) patterns emerge. By age fourteen, a mature alpha rhythm is established. These waves have a frequency of 8–13, and average 10 per second. Regularity, regional differentiation, and stability continue to develop through adolescence. During states of mild physiological stresses, greater fluctuations are present than in normal adults. In the frontal and temporal areas, beta frequencies (fast waves with frequencies of 18–30 per second) come to replace theta activity (intermediate waves of 4–7 per second) as adolescence proceeds. During the remainder of this era, the EEG still displays a few more temporal theta waves; these are less regular than in adults and more susceptible to activation.[8]

Changes of Strength: Until puberty, boys and girls are similar in strength except for the hands and forearms, as might have been predicted. Taken together, the new developments give rise to a marked increase in strength (as determined by measures of arm pull and thrust) which is much greater in boys than in girls. Once into adolescence, the strength of boys is also related to their having larger hearts and lungs (relative to body size), a higher systolic blood pressure, a lower resting heart rate, a greater capacity for carrying oxygen in the blood, and a greater power for neutralizing chemical products of muscle exercise such as lactic acid.[20] These changes account not only for changes in boys' physical dimensions, but for their increased ability to perform in athletics and accompanying interests. This is true quite apart from the massive cultural indoctrination and exposure to athletic participation which usually occurs.

Reproductive Changes

The changes in reproductive capacity can best be conceptualized by following the respective maturation of reproductive organs and their accompaniments on two levels. This can first be studied for both genders in general, and then for each respectively. The primary sexual characteristics for boys are testes, epididymus, seminal vesicles, prostate gland, penis, and urethra. There are only two for girls: the uterus and the ovaries. The secondary sexual characteristics are those not directly involved in reproduction. Boys show an increase in size of genitals, the appearance of pubic, axillary, and facial hair, deepening of the voice, and bone and muscle growth. The secondary sexual characteristics in girls are breast growth, pelvic and hip changes, the appearance of pubic and axillary hair, and the onset of menses.

By age thirteen, some changes have commenced in boys. Figure 18-1 illustrates the wide variation in age, the changes in these organs, and the characteristics encompassed.

While the changes begin in boys during the prepubertal period, they continue during the entire thirteen to sixteen age period. Increase in the growth rate of the testes may be noted first, closely followed by the appearance of pubic hair. These are actually outward manifestations of processes which began at about age ten with an increase in the size of the seminal tubes and the recognizable development of "Sertoli cells" and spermatogosina.

Growth in height begins about a year after the first testicular acceleration, along with penis growth and the development of the seminal vesicles, prostate, and bulbo-urethra glands. While the exact time of the first ejaculation is situationally determined, it can only occur in a state of biological readiness; this is arrived at about a year after the acceleration of penile growth. Nocturnal emissions usually begin a year or two after the onset of puberty, and despite increased sex education, some boys may still exhibit anxiety about these experiences. Such anxiety is not so much associated with a lack of knowledge per se, as in the past, but with the significance this event has in terms of their ovarall sense of adequacy as maturing males. Factors such as guilt about associated dreams, concerns about loss of control, fear of discovery, and the like, may all color boys' responses.

Axillary and facial hair appears about two years after pubic hair growth, and for some, the remaining body hair continues to develop there-

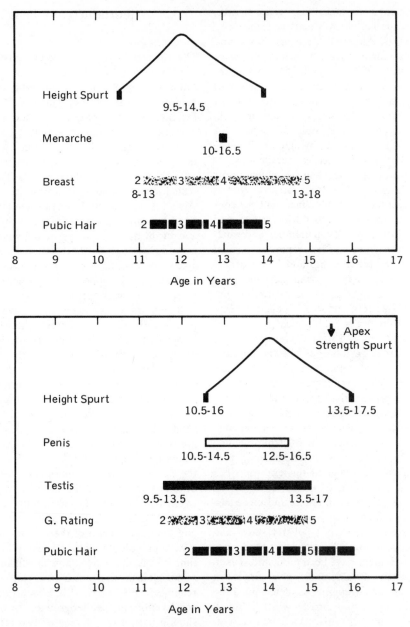

FIGURE 18–1

Sequence of Events (beginning and end) for Changes in Adolescents

NOTE: Reprinted by permission of the publisher from "Variations in the Pattern of Pubertal Changes in Boys" by W. A. Marshall and J. M. Tanner, *Archives of the Diseases of Childhood*, 45:13, 1970.

after. The final amount and distribution are determined by heredity. "Breaking" of the voice occurs late, and the change in pitch is thought to be influenced by the lengthening of the vocal cords associated with higher testosterone levels. Skin changes in the form of acne and roughening become a source of distress to both sexes. These are actually commoner in boys than in girls since these skin changes are connected with androgenic

activity. Glands in the axilla, genital, and anal regions develop rapidly in adolescence and are manifested by changing body odors. By mid-adolescence, about 20 to 33 percent of boys show some breast enlargement as well.

As can be seen from figure 18-1, the development of the "breast bud" in girls is one of the first signs of puberty. However, in the Tanner data cited, one-third had pubic hair before breast buds.

Note the range: In some girls the onset was at age eight, while in others this did not occur until age thirteen. At the same time, the uterus and vagina are developing along with the labia and clitoris. Menarche is a later phenomenon and takes place after the peak of the growth spurt has occurred. Menstruation should not be construed as equivalent to fertility since anovulatory cycles can occur for the first twelve to eighteen months; for any given individual there is a period of variability. Again, the range of variation is impressive; some girls begin to menstruate at ten and others not until sixteen and one-half years. This means that some girls are menstruating during the elementary school years, but others not until senior high school. In European populations, a regular trend has been noted over several generations—since 1850 the onset of menstruation has arrived four months earlier each decade.[18] Attempts have been made to explain this by an evolutionary hypotheses, but in fact, it may reflect nothing more than improved health and medical care, along with improved diet.

Anxiety Associated with Physical Development

BOYS

One of the most important points to emphasize for adolescents is the factor of variability in development. It is not only the age range over which changes occur, but the rate change for any individual once the sequence begins. Adolescents can react to the alterations within themselves with a good deal of self-awareness as well as self-monitoring and self-appraisal. Part of the problem with such unpredictable growth is the need to conform to a peer group which accompanies all the variations in development. These factors also contribute to problems with self-concept, sex role, and gender identity. An adolescent who develops at either extreme of these ranges is exposed to special types of problems. A late-maturing boy has a handicap with respect to athletic competition, and he has even more of a problem with respect to interaction with girls who are, to begin with, relatively more advanced sexually and socially. While the disadvantage for the early maturer lies in his having to compete with older boys too soon, the disadvantage for a later maturer is that secondary psychological difficulties are more likely to develop earlier. Data from past studies indicate that

boys in the lower 20 percent on skeletal age were affected, tense, and eager.[14] This led them to seek attention as well as to become more restless and talkative. It is even more unfortunate that these handicaps persist. A longitudinal follow-up of late maturing boys when they were age thirty-three indicated that at that point they had less self-control and were seen as less responsible and more dependent individuals than other adults.[13] Another study has shown them as more likely to display guilt, inferiority, and depressive tendencies with generalized anxiety.[22] If these observations are confirmed, there are preventive mental health implications which need application in dealing with these late-maturing youths.

GIRLS

Although menstruation was once seen as a source of great anxiety and adjustment difficulties for girls, this is probably much less so at present. When adolescent girls are anxious, guilty, and ashamed about their development, it is more likely to be the product of a carryover of distorted ideas and conflicts about sexuality from their younger years. Over half of a group of 475 girls reported their reaction to menstruation as being one of indifference.[16] Variations in mood, as related to different hormonal levels, become a reality. There are interesting data indicating greater anxiety and feelings of inadequacy premenstrually as compared to the period of ovulation.[2]

The psychological impact of late maturing for girls is more difficult to assess than for boys, and its consequences do not seem as predictable. One study ascribes this to early adolescent girls evaluating themselves and others more in terms of the statistical average as a desirable trait rather than any advantages of early physical maturity in itself.[11] However, there are social advantages for early maturers in the thirteen to sixteen age group in terms of attention from older boys and social leadership. This is congruent with the fact that for girls in this age group, their self-image tends to be correlated with their outward appearance.[7] Girls who mature earlier appear to marry earlier (which is not necessarily an advantage).[5]

Psychological Development

SOURCES OF INSTABILITY

By the time age thirteen arrives, many shifts have occurred in internal psychological development. An increasing degree of socialization on a peer level has taken place, along with the accompanying influences on identification. In addition, there has been a constant reappraisal of the external world. Once into this age period, an increase in drive activities is witnessed on many fronts which lacks the quality of mutuality customarily witnessed in the younger child. The manifestations are seen in many undifferentiated activities relating to aggressive display and to a variety of sexualized activities. These reflect an expansion of the different kinds of feelings and urges which are present and which, at times, make the young adolescent appear quite egocentric and inconsiderate.

The degree of aggressiveness displayed varies widely among adolescents. It takes myriad forms, such as being sadistic, cruel, exploitative, or inquisitive. Impulsive and unpredictable behavior in turn activates exaggerated defensive efforts in a striving to maintain better control. The need to externalize conflicts or to see oneself as under attack from without (rather than from within) leads to a sensed camaraderie among adolescents and feelings of unity against the world. This is the handmaiden of patriotism as well as idealism in general, and these young people often seek common causes to join such as helping the oppressed or downtrodden.

OBJECT RELATIONS

During early adolescence, the intensity and exclusivity of earlier attachments begins to give way. At a time of increase in urges and physiological readiness for erratic and aggressive action, closeness to family members can be quite threatening. While an expanded peer life and increased social activities facilitate this distancing, the need for an internalized autonomy from early objects is not easily resolved. Some indicators of the severity of the struggle are such behaviors as insolence, the disparagement of the parents, and a devaluation of past connections. In some people this struggle for internal emancipation goes on for many years —into the third and fourth decades of life—and it is not unusual for the issues to be displaced onto battles with cultural institutions or value systems. Vacillations, conversions to, and abandonments of causes are well-known phenomena that occur with enormous zeal and fall within the context of reaction formations.

This lessening of earlier attachments is a necessary developmental step if the identity and the ego ideal of an individual adolescent are to take on their own uniqueness. When deficiencies exist in this area, they show up in the form of adolescents who appear to be copies of the parental models. If this is the case, they exhibit the typical developmental impairment of an individual who has not been able to expand beyond the earlier types of identification with parental figures. The restructuring of ideals leads to the quest for new heroes—a Daedalus in search of alternative routes for moral development.

Each adolescent thus has to pursue his own line of development with respect to his ego-ideal system. Among the factors which can complicate this quest are parental figures who are confused about their own value systems and who have themselves repressed these conflicts. This problem is not necessarily confined to parents; it is a message that can be transmitted by anyone with whom the adolescent comes into any kind of meaningful relationship. "Crushes" as eroticized relationships with some older and obviously inappropriate object can be with either sex. They can consume a great deal of time and energy and have a one-sided quality which is not based on mutuality. However, an adult who is the target of this adoration is in a position to exploit the object-hungry adolescent. The possibilities are almost endless. In one situation, there are a male and female high school teacher, each in their midtwenties, who spend their free time at high-school student parties smoking marijuana and buying it for the adolescents. They share their oral intake; the male teacher becoming romanticized by the fifteen-year-old girls, and the female teacher becoming a source of many erotic fantasies for the boys. Another example is that of a single male athletic coach in his twenties who takes the adolescent girls on his team on long and extended trips with sexual overtones. A third example is a counselor who employs a pretense of utilizing adolescent discussion groups regarding sex and drugs as a format for eroticized body contacts which gratify his own voyeuristic needs. Of course, long ago it was noted that parental superego deficits permitted the acting-out of repressed parental impulses through children.[12] This illustrates how ubiquitous the deficits may be and how readily they may play a role in the behavior of any adult in a position of authority with teenagers.

Part of the need for separation arises from the need for sexual attachments to occur outside the family. As the ego seeks to redirect sexual strivings outside of the family, a complicating factor is the need not to lose the capacity for tender affectivity in connection with sexuality. This delicate developmental shift in object relations can become impaired to different degrees with a resultant split in object ties.

While masturbation may have existed earlier than the onset of puberty, a new meaning is attached to this activity when ejaculation becomes possible. As noted, sex education in schools does not get to the deeper sources of anxiety, such as the threat of loss of control associated with nocturnal emissions in boys. Self-condemnation results in struggles over these threats to self-control —to give in means that one is weak or incompetent—and this challenge to self-esteem exists apart from education dicta that masturbation does not produce physical harm. It is also naive to believe that simple educational measures can alleviate guilt over acts where fantasies may involve forbidden and guilt-laden themes. In both boys and girls, guilt can develop over homosexual or thinly disguised incestuous desires.

FANTASIES AND DEPERSONALIZATION

Fantasies or daydreams can assume a preeminence in the thirteen to sixteen age period. This is not solely from their wish-fulfilling aspects (analogous to dreams), but also with respect to the themes of power related to narcissistic strivings. Fantasies permit a private indulgence in all the conglomerate of wishes which emerge in the adolescent along with a distancing from external objects and their demands. The fantasies that accompany masturbation achieve this as well as the Walter Mitty fantasies of grandiose power. However, if used in a realistic manner, the fantasies can also be employed in the service of bridging the gap to external objects.

Depersonalization tendencies occur in a manner parallel to the increase in the fantasy life of the adolescent. These changes of state are a response to heightened anxiety, and they are experienced by the youths as feelings of estrangement from their own bodies and/or a distantiation from their surroundings. While daydreams are ego-syntonic, depersonalized states are not. Hence, if the depersonalization goes to the extent of feeling "flat" or "like I'm dead," the sense of reality becomes impaired beyond the usual developmental fluctuations. If such states are experienced as more than transient occurrences, they merit assessment of their psychopathological implications.

INDIVIDUATION

Many of the factors which give the adolescent his own distinctive style are related to the type of synthesis achieved in the course of these years. In an overall sense, adolescence is viewed as the second major period for individuation.[4] The first was during the period of infancy when by twenty-six to thirty-six months, the goal of attaining object constancy was reached.[15] If a stable sense of individual autonomy is to be achieved by adolescence, it requires an acceptance of the fact that emotional dependence on others is going to be present, that it is relative, and that it will vary in different contexts. Although many discussions emphasize "gaining independence," the focus is too often on physical separation. In contrast, the main task is that of gaining emotional independence from the inordinate degree of control which internalized objects continue to exert on the adolescent. If antecedent conflicts from earlier childhood over dependency, ambivalence, and control have not been resolved by adolescence, a variety of defenses and character traits emerge to handle the anxiety that arises over the need to individuate. Some of these defenses take the form of displacements, substitutions, or repetitions with others in the environment, or they may show up in the form of ego disturbances such as acting-out, negativism, learning disabilities, exaggerated moodiness, or episodic acts of violence. Achieving individuation is a hallmark of both ego maturation and ego strength.

SELF-CONCEPT, COGNITIVE ABILITIES, AND SELF-ESTEEM

Self-concept is a complicated topic about which opinions differ and theoretical explanations diverge. Some stress external achievements or failures as the most significant events on the formation of adolescent self-concept; others stress the defective regulation of self-esteem associated with superego development as the most crucial variable. It would be presumptuous to take either extreme position on this point. Different personality theorists will assign different weightings as well to the factor of individual variation in life history. A sociological orientation emphasizes the alienation arising in adolescents who may perceive themselves as outsiders. For example, those reared in a minority group, the impoverished, those who bear the impact of broken families, whose geographic location is unusual, or who, for any reason, suffer from the sense of not being able to cope might develop a defective self-concept. The impact of family disorganization and attendance at overcrowded schools with discouraged teachers may together reinforce the cycle of an existing inadequate self-concept and continuing low self-evaluation. Although they feel alienated from the value system of a majority of society, many of these adolescents have nonetheless assimilated enough of the majority's goals to put them into a state of conflict. The result is an enhancement of their readiness to rage against authority figures, and from this they can move gradually toward a commitment to a negative ideal. In a sense, they make a trade: They reject socially acceptable ways in order to gain self-esteem.[10]

In contrast to these views on the self-concept of the adolescent are those which regard the crucial component to be the capacity for critical self-appraisal. This is a process which goes on recurrently in the adolescent. How the ego deals with affects such an anxiety, depression, guilt, shame, disgust, and rage is related to this process of self-evaluation. According to one formulation, self-esteem is regulated by the introjected standards, codes, and ideals instilled in the child long before he reaches age thirteen. What makes these guides to self-appraisal so potent is their relatively blind transmission and assimilation—what parents and society have dictated has been taken in wholesale. Hence, once into adolescence, deviation from these norms can lead to a good deal of conflict and harsh self-criticism. Simultaneously, the thirteen-to sixteen-year-old is conducting a vital and detailed reexamination of these dicta, and as part of his normal growth, he raises many challenges about what has been transmitted to him as norms. An inner questioning about transmitted "facts" and values is going on, and there is now a reaching-out, a readiness for empathy with diverse types of possibilities to which the adolescent has been exposed in some manner. This challenge to the superego of childhood is an essential aspect of adolescent development.

Beginning at about age twelve, cognitive abilities move to the level of formal operations. In brief, the adolescent's thinking can begin to transcend the immediate here and now of earlier concrete operations. This permits much more complex types of reasoning and allows different possibilities to be entertained. Hypotheses about what might occur, and what are the alternatives, raise possibilities about contrary outcomes. At age thirteen, this is almost nonexistent, but it emerges with increasing richness over the next few years.[9] The egocentrism present in early adolescence is diminished by age fifteen or sixteen when formal operational thinking becomes firmly established. These cognitive developments permit the youth to achieve a clearer differentiation of his own preoccupations from those of others.

In terms of affectivity, the adolescent acquires a progressively greater ability to empathize with the emotions of others. In the earlier phases, the egocentrism contributes to strikingly narcissistic preoccupations. With advances in development, the formulation of alternative hypotheses begins to occur in which questions are raised about what was previously accepted as obviously valid and truthful. This allows for a playing-out of different ideas, and it takes the form of verbal teasing and manipulation such as puns, double meanings, and plays on words. By the time he arrives at age sixteen, the adolescent is thus much more able to grasp the character of political ideologies, as well as to perceive the duplicities present in political discourse. This capacity is almost nonexistent at age thirteen.[1]

Conclusion

In summary, the self-concept of the adolescent is related to many variables. Vectors impinge from outside the self which relate to experiences with others, especially peers, that may confirm or challenge certain ideas that adolescents have about themselves. In turn, these may act either to enhance or to threaten the entire structure of their self-esteem. Variables that arise from within the self include the entire superego and ego-ideal systems, cognitive abilities, intellectual competence, body image, athletic talents, physical appearance, and resolution of identity conflicts. What needs emphasis is that at any given historical time, the self-esteem of an adolescent is heavily dependent on society's prescription of what a youth is supposed to be. Dealing with the external and internal referents of sex-typed identifications is a very important aspect of maintaining emotional balance, for it involves regulating self-esteem and avoiding those anxious and depressive types of responses which carry with them the potential for enduring neurotic conflict. In recent years, empirical research has begun to question the assumption of many personality theories that identification with one's sex role and with the parent of the same sex is the best insurer of healthy psychological development. At best this may be warranted only for males. A high degree of sex-role socialization in girls has been found to be negatively related to such qualities as autonomy, self-esteem and later adjustment.[3] For the adolescent girl and her family, such disturbing data raises questions of a preventive nature. However, if identifications with the same sex are discouraged in the young adolescent, subsequent problems of a different type and of even greater seriousness may well appear.

REFERENCES

1. ADELSON, J., "The Political Imagination of the Young Adolescent," *Daedalus, 100:*1013*ff.*, 1971.
2. BARDWICK, J., *Psychology of Women: A Study of Bio-Cultural Conflicts*, Harper & Row, New York, 1971.
3. BARUCH, G. K., and BARNETT, R. C., "Implications and Applications of Recent Research on Feminine Development," *Psychiatry, 38:*318*ff.*, 1975.
4. BLOS, P., "The Second Individuation Process of Adolescence," in Eissler, R. S., et al. (Eds.), *The Psychoanalytic Study of the Child*, vol. 22, pp. 162*ff.*, International Universities Press, New York, 1967.
5. BUCK, C., and STAVRAKY, K., "The Relationship Between Age of Menarche and Age at Marriage Among Childbearing Women," *Human Biology, 39:*93*ff.*, 1967.
6. DOUVAN, E., and ADELSON, J., *The Adolescent Experience*, John Wiley, New York, 1966.
7. DONOVAN, B. T., and VAN DER WERFF TEN BOSCH, J. J., *Physiology of Puberty*, Arnold, London, 1965.
8. EICHORN, D. H., "Physiological Development," in Mussen, P. H. (Ed.), *Carmichael's Manual of Child Psychology*, 3rd ed., vol. 1, pp. 248*ff.*, John Wiley, New York, 1970.
9. ELKIND, D., "Egocentrism in Adolescence," *Child Development, 38:*1025*ff.*, 1967.
10. ERIKSON, E. H., *Identity and the Life Cycle*, Psychological Issues, Monograph no. 1, pp. 129*ff.*, 1959.
11. FAUST, M. S., "Developmental Maturity as a Determinant in Prestige of Adolescent Girls," *Child Development, 31:*173*ff.*, 1960.
12. JOHNSON, A. M., "Sanctions for Superego Lacunae of Adolescents," in Eissler, K. R. (Ed.), *Searchlights on Delinquency*, pp. 225–245, International Universities Press, New York, 1949.

13. JONES, M. C., "The Later Careers of Boys Who Were Early or Late Maturing," *Child Development, 28:*113*ff.*, 1957.
14. ———, and BAYLEY, N., "Physical Maturing Among Boys as Related to Behavior," *Journal of Educational Psychology, 41:*129*ff.*, 1950.
15. McDEVITT, J. B., "Separation, Individuation and Object Constancy," *Journal of the American Psychoanalytic Association, 23:*713*ff.*, 1975.
16. MUSSEN, P. H., CONGOR, J. J., and KAGAN, J., *Child Development and Personality*, 4th ed., Harper & Row, New York, 1974.
17. TANNER, J. M., "Sequence, Tempo, and Individual Variation in the Growth and Development of Boys and Girls Aged Twelve to Sixteen," *Daedelus, 100:*911*ff.*, 1971.
18. ———, "Physical Growth," in Mussen, P. H. (Ed.), *Carmichael's Manual of Child Psychology*, 3rd ed. vol. 1, pp. 77–155, John Wiley, New York, 1970.
19. ———, "Puberty," in McCaren, A. (Ed.), *Advances in Reproductive Physiology*, vol. 2, Logos, London, 1967.
20. ———, *Growth at Adolescence*, 2nd ed., Blackwell Scientific Publications, Oxford, England, 1962.
21. ———, WHITEHOUSE, R., and TAKAISHI, M., "Standards from Birth to Maturity for Height, Weight, Height Velocity, and Weight Velocity: British Children 1965," *Archives of Diseases of Childhood, 41:*454*ff.*, 1966.
22. WEATHERLEY, D., "Self-Perceived Rate of Physical Maturation and Personality in Late Adolescence," *Child Development, 35:*1197*ff.*, 1964.
23. YOUNG, H. B., "Aging and Adolescence," *Developmental Medicine and Child Neurology, 5:*451*ff.*, 1963.

19 / Adolescent Development: Sixteen to Nineteen Years

Anne C. Petersen and Daniel Offer

Overview

This review of adolescent development will focus on the physiological, cognitive, and psychosocial development of individuals during the years sixteen to nineteen. There will be a brief discussion of the importance of parents at this stage, and the review will conclude with a summary of a psy-chiatric study of adolescent boys along with mention of areas needing further research.

The content will be restricted to normal or modal adolescence rather than to its deviations. This does not, however, yield only one model, for as the study of adolescent boys demonstrates, there are alternative routes through normal adolescence. In addition, it is important to note that most of current knowledge is based on middle- or upper middle-class children who are primarily white and male.

As a background for this review of adolescent development, let us consider some sociocultural issues. As Baumrind[7] and others have pointed out, in the Western world adolescence lasts much longer than it does in other societies. Crosscultural studies[104, 143] demonstrate that the length of the adolescent period ranges from a few days to many years. Young people in Mexico, Thailand, or Jordan may assume adult responsibilities by age thirteen or even earlier; a longer adolescence is a luxury of affluent societies. In those societies where it does exist, especially into the post–high-school years of sixteen to nineteen, adolescence takes on much of the character of the society that creates it. As Bronfenbrenner[21] has noted, American society has not made clear to the adolescent the relationship between his past, present, and future, a sense of continuity which is central to the development of identity.[45] Thus, many of the conflicts and issues discussed in this review are enhanced, exacerbated, or perhaps even created by this society.

During the years sixteen to nineteen within the American context, boys and girls are expected to make the transition to adulthood. It is anticipated that they will separate from their families and begin to form their own identities and that they will establish a pattern of interpersonal relationships and educational and occupational goals. Even those young people who continue to live at home while they work or go to school are struggling nonetheless with the search for a separate identity. This process of separation from family is a major one, influencing the development of identity in a profound way and recapitulating the separation-individuation phase of early childhood.[15, 97]

The material that illustrates some of the transitional phenomena will be presented in a sequence that passes from physiological and cognitive development to psychosocial issues during the years sixteen to nineteen.

Physiological Development

NORMAL GROWTH

For the majority of adolescents, by age sixteen adult physical maturity has been attained. This is especially true for girls. The most comprehensive recent study of physical development has been conducted by Tanner and his associates in England.[101, 102] Except where noted, the following results are based on their work.

Boys: For the male, on the average, growth in height is completed by age sixteen, although some boys continue to grow until age seventeen and one-half. Indeed, there are boys who do not begin their adolescent growth spurt until as late as sixteen. The average age at attainment of full skeletal maturation, indicated by closure of the bone epiphyses, is seventeen years. During this entire interval from sixteen to nineteen years there is a progressive growth in strength.

Penis growth generally ends at age fifteen, although with some boys growth may continue until age sixteen and one-half. The testes usually have completed their growth by age sixteen; again, with some individuals it may take until age eighteen. Pubic hair development has generally attained adult form by age sixteen, but there are boys who do not achieve the adult distribution of pubic hair until age eighteen. Axillary hair develops about two years later than pubic hair; for both males and females, the greatest amount of axillary hair is not achieved until the third decade of life.[33] Facial hair shows growth similar to axillary hair in terms of the ages at which an adult distribution is attained. Hair on the chest is frequently the last secondary sex characteristic to be attained in males; in some instances an adult distribution may not be developed until the late twenties. In general, however, most sixteen-year-olds look like men in terms of their secondary sex development and other physical characteristics.

Girls: Girls develop about two years earlier than boys.[101] Therefore, by age sixteen, physically almost all girls appear to be adult females.[117] While the average age at menarche in the United States is twelve years, it may occur as late as sixteen and one-half within the framework of normal adolescence. Menarche generally occurs shortly after the peak growth in height.[47] The uterus experiences a growth spurt between ages ten and seventeen but continues to grow after that time.[33]

SEX DIFFERENCES IN HEIGHT

It is commonly believed that the sex differences in mature height (achieved during or just prior to the period from sixteen to nineteen years) are due to the magnitude of adolescent growth. In fact, these differences may owe far more to the timing of maturation.[13, 137] The factors influencing growth in adolescence are not yet completely understood, but it has been hypothesized that adult males are taller than adult females because of the influence of testosterone during puberty. Bock et al.[17] found no differences, and subsequent studies with different samples have found small differences, at most, between males and females in the amount of growth occurring during adolescence. The various parameters involved in total growth in height were assumed by Bock and co-workers to have two components: one representing the continuous growth from infancy to adulthood, presumably due to growth hormone, and the other due to the adolescent growth spurt, presumably related to the sex hormones. Estrogen may also contribute to the adolescent growth spurt.[125] This hypothesis would support the statistical estimation of these two components of growth.

HORMONES

Sex hormone levels increase throughout adolescence and correlate very closely with the stages of pubertal development.* For most hormones, adult levels are attained by age sixteen. Serum and urinary follicle stimulating hormone (FSH) and luteinizing hormone (LH) also increase throughout adolescence; luteinizing hormone is frequently elevated above adult values in the period from seventeen to eighteen years.[14] Regular fluctuations in the values of luteinizing hormone, characteristic of adult functioning, begin in late adolescence.[76] During the ages sixteen to seventeen there appears to be a large increase in average testosterone levels.[92] Both blood pressure and hemoglobin levels appear to attain adult values by age seventeen.[146]

PHYSICAL HEALTH

A study of adolescents was carried out in Harlem by Brunswick and Josephson.[24] They found that youths sixteen and seventeen years old experienced a marked increase in the number of health problems from the level they had shown earlier in adolescence. The nature of these difficulties included vision, respiratory distress, headaches, emotional problems, and skin troubles. Anemia increased among girls. The sixteen- and seventeen-year-olds also showed increased evidence of hard drug use. While this specific group of adolescents may differ from others, the increase in health problems in late adolescence is nonetheless striking.

* See references 144, 65, 14, 30, and 64.

PHYSICAL MATURATION AND PSYCHOSOCIAL CHARACTERISTICS

Few studies have integrated physical growth in adolescence with other aspects of development. The primary exception to this neglect is the set of longitudinal growth studies of this century, at Berkeley, Fels Institute, Denver, and Harvard, which have attempted to follow all components of development to maturity. We now discuss the results of these more general longitudinal studies as they apply to the years sixteen to nineteen.

It is evident that the new physical manifestations of approaching adulthood, which generally occur in earlier adolescence, will require numerous complex psychological adjustments. In particular, those physical aspects of maturation appear to influence one's view of oneself in relation to others. Indeed, during adolescence, for any given individual, the stage of physical development appears to bear important social stimulus value. In this connection, one problem that is likely to appear during the sixteen- to nineteen-year span is that of late maturation. Studies have found that adults rate late maturers less physically attractive, less well groomed, and more unrealistic, on the one hand, while higher in sociability, social initiative, and eagerness, on the other.[77, 27, 106] Peers tend to rate late maturers as more attention-seeking, restless, bossy, less grown-up, and less good-looking. Late maturers report themselves to have negative self-concepts, feelings of inadequacy, strong feelings of rejection and domination, prolonged dependency needs, and a rebellious attitude toward parents. Late maturers also tend to perform less well than early maturers on tests of mental ability. Many have noted that overconcern by parents may exacerbate the late maturer's problems.

It is important to evaluate these studies of late versus early maturing in terms of the age at which these comparisons were made. The vast majority of adolescents attain their adult size by age eighteen; hence, the differences between early and late maturers that appear earlier begin to disappear after this age. We may therefore expect that many of the relationships between maturation and psychosocial factors would also tend to wash out by this age. Peskin[116] followed up some individuals who were studied when they were adolescents and classified them according to their time of physical maturation. He found that adults who had been late maturers tended to display more exploratory behavior, less social submission, and have more intellectual curiosity. Apparently, then, some effects do persist, although they express themselves differently from the ones that appeared earlier.

The work just cited considers physical development only as it influences social interaction and then psychological development. However, psychoanalytic and cognitive development theories link physical maturation directly to psychological and cognitive development, respectively. Kestenberg[81, 82, 83] describes the mechanisms by which the increasing hormone levels at puberty may influence the various psychological states characteristic of different phases of adolescence. She proposes that in postpubescence the progressive differentiation of physical and psychological traits parallels the sorting-out of sex-specific hormonal constellations. This is followed by a consolidation of adult sex-specific attitudes and mechanisms of hormone production and metabolism.

In our discussion of Piaget's theory of cognitive development, we shall mention his hypothesis regarding the necessity of neural maturation for formal operational thought at adolescence.

Cognitive Development

FORMAL OPERATIONAL THOUGHT

The work of Piaget[120, 122] has had a profound impact on our understanding of the development of cognition. With Inhelder,[74] he gave more systematic attention to the development of logical thought in adolescence. Piaget claimed that formal operations, the logical thought characteristic of adolescence, begins at about ages eleven to twelve and is fully developed by ages sixteen to seventeen. If this were the case, formal thought would usually be fully developed by the age period of interest here, sixteen to nineteen years. But recent research suggests that formal operations actually develop later and are, in fact, never attained by many adults. We will discuss this research and its implications later. First, it is important to elaborate Piaget's theory.

Piaget posits three essential factors for development in general and for the formation of mental functions in particular: (1) the maturation of the nervous system; (2) experience in interaction with physical reality; and (3) the influence of the social environment. He especially links the appearance of formal thought at adolescence to the maturation of the brain which occurs during puberty, a point to which we shall return later. But, while Piaget acknowledges the importance of maturation in the development of thought, his equilibration-equilibrium model places major emphasis on dynamic interaction with the physical and social environment.

Piaget maintains that learning takes place by way of assimilation of and accommodation to the environment. New experiences are first assimilated, then the existing cognitive structure changes to incorporate or accommodate the new experience. Once a balance between assimilation and accommodation has been achieved, a state of equilibrium is said to exist. Piaget posits that each stage culminates with a state of equilibrium. But soon new stimuli upset the balance and the process, called equilibration, continues.

Formal Thought: Upon attainment of the level of formal thought (the final stage of cognitive development) Maier[98] has characterized Piaget's view of the mature individual by the following characteristics:

1. The social world becomes an organic unit with laws and regulations and roles and social functions.
2. Egocentricity has been dissolved by a consciously cultivated sense of moral solidarity.
3. Personality development from now on depends upon an exchange of ideas by social intercommunication in place of simple mutual initiation.
4. A sense of equality supercedes submission to adult authority.

These four characteristics make it apparent that while Piaget's theory focuses on cognitive development, it overlaps into and has implications for other aspects of development. Indeed, Piaget views human development as a total system, and there are strong parallels between his theory and that of Erikson's (to be discussed later).

Formal thought involves reasoning based on verbal propositions. An individual with formal thought capabilities can make hypothetical deductions and entertain the idea of relativity. Particularly when formal thought is new to the individual, it is especially appealing to form bizarre or grandiose theories. Such thought may be creative, but without a strong grounding in reality and experience.

With the initiation of formal thought, the direction of the thought processes changes. There is a reversal of direction between reality and possibility. In concrete inferences, one starts with empirical data and uses it to derive a rudimentary type of theory. In contrast, formal thought begins with a hypothesis, a theoretical synthesis of what is possible, and then proceeds to what is empirically real.[74]

With formal operations, the adolescent can combine propositions and isolate variables in order to test hypotheses. Furthermore, the operations can be performed using symbols rather than the concrete objects or events characteristic of earlier stages. Piaget has grouped these propositional operations under two systems, a combinatorial system and a transformational system each with four possibilities. These two systems, cross-classified, form the basis for the total formal operational system which includes sixteen (four times four) propositional operations.

It was earlier mentioned that recent research suggests that formal operations are not necessarily attained in adolescence. Dulit[35] studied three groups of adolescents: age fourteen, ages sixteen to seventeen, and a group of gifted sixteen- to seventeen-year-olds; in addition, he studied a group of average adults. He found that only about 10 percent of the younger group and 35 percent of the older average group had attained a capacity for formal operations. About 60 percent of the gifted group functioned at the fully formal level and only about 25 to 33 percent of the adults could successfully perform the experiments measuring formal operations. In all groups, males were two to four times as likely to function at the formal level as were females. Hobbs,[72] Elkind,[41, 42] Tomlinson-Keasey,[139] and Graves[62] report similar results though the percentages of individuals attaining formal operations appear to be dependent upon the particular experiments performed, some being more difficult than others. Indeed, Bynum, Thomas, and Weitz[25] found evidence for only eight of the total sixteen propositional operations in formal thought.

Piaget links the capacity for formal operations to the maturation of the brain at puberty. Does the failure of many adolescents, and even adults, to demonstrate formal operational thinking imply that their brains are immature? A more likely explanation is that brain maturation is a necessary but not sufficient condition for this attainment. Once the brain is mature, it needs practice and experience with these functions. Indeed, training studies[130] demonstrate that it is possible to teach formal operations to adolescents who have not yet acquired them. (Piaget,[119] questions whether such training produces real competence or mere performance capability.) Furthermore, as Elkind[38] points out, unlike earlier stages of cognitive functioning, the ability to operate at this level is not necessary for most adult roles in our society; their importance must therefore be kept in perspective.

INTELLIGENCE AND COGNITIVE ABILITIES

A more conventional, though not identical, aspect of cognitive development is intelligence as measured by IQ.[32] Early cross-sectional studies had suggested that it is during this period from sixteen to nineteen years that intelligence generally reaches its peak. As many[127] have noted, however, this result appears to be an artifact of the cross-sectional methods used; in these studies, each younger generation tested was increasingly better educated. More recent studies have found that as long as the individual is active in intellectual pursuits, intelligence continues to increase throughout most of the life cycle.[37, 128] This is especially true in terms of verbal ability.

An alternative approach to the study of intellectual functioning is that of investigating independent abilities—for example, verbal ability, spatial ability, and mechanical ability. One interesting result of these studies relevant to adolescence is that for some of these abilities, the sex differences appear only at adolescence. Sex differences in verbal, mathematical, and spatial ability are not generally manifest until about ages eleven to twelve.[95] The differences become more extreme by late adolescence and into adulthood. The origins of the emergence of these differences at adolescence are not currently known. Various possibilities that have been suggested include the sex hormones,[22, 118] differential rates of brain maturation,[141, 142] and differential socialization pressures.[115] (See also Wittig and Petersen for comprehensive reviews of current hypotheses for the development of sex-related differences in cognitive functioning.[145])

Psychosocial Development

The remainder of this review of adolescent development from the years sixteen through nineteen will use the theoretical framework developed by Erikson in *Identity: Youth and Crisis*.[45] The authors agree with Gallatin[56] that Erikson's theory is the most comprehensive, and his perspective that life consists of a sequence of normative crises best fits the results obtained in investigations of adolescence. Before focusing on adolescence, Erikson's theory of the entire life cycle will be briefly reviewed.

ERIKSON'S THEORY OF LIFE-CYCLE CRISES

Erikson divides the life cycle into eight normative crises, each corresponding to a particular stage of development. The first crisis, in infancy, is trust versus mistrust. In early childhood, the normative crisis involves autonomy versus shame and doubt. The next is initiative versus guilt. Among school-age children, the primary crisis is that of industry versus inferiority, and in adolescence, identity versus confusion. Among young adults the primary crisis is that of intimacy versus isolation; in middle age, generativity versus stagnation; and finally, in old age, integrity versus despair.

According to this theory, each stage involves some resolution of the crisis. It is not so much a clear choice between one alternative and the other; instead, under normal circumstances, a balance is established in which the growth-related alternative predominates. If crises are not mastered at the appropriate stage, they persist as problems into subsequent stages. In addition, at each stage the particular crisis is related to the crises at all other stages. Thus, psychosocial development during the years sixteen to nineteen will be related to aspects of identity development during the other seven stages.

THE ADOLESCENT STAGE OF THE LIFE CYCLE

The primary task of adolescence is the development of an identity. Erikson considers this fifth stage in the human life cycle as a critical period in that it determines much of the development occurring thereafter. Needless to say, the events at this time are partially determined by development occurring in previous stages. But it is a pivotal time of life. As noted, this is an epoch when the individual begins to look like an adult. Until adolescence, however, the child cannot function as an adult. It is only then that the individual has the opportunity to assimilate what has been learned in previous stages and to prepare for what is to come. By the end of adolescence, the individual's identity should be emerging as a functional entity.

TEMPORAL PERSPECTIVE VERSUS TIME DIFFUSION

The first aspect of adolescent development to be considered is that related to the crisis of infancy, trust versus mistrust. The adolescent version of this crisis is temporal perspective versus time diffusion. During adolescence the individual must coordinate past with future. Piaget has laid the groundwork for understanding the development of the concept of time. More recent research verifies that a sense of time does not emerge until late adolescence, at about fifteen or sixteen years of age.[50] It is not until late adolescence that the individual is able to differentiate time itself from the measurement of time, and to understand that the latter is an artificial convention. LeBlanc[91] found that compared to all other age groups, college students were the most time- and future-oriented. Douvan and Adelson[34] found sex differences in this characteristic; boys appeared to be more future-oriented and girls were less realistic in integrating their future possibilities with their current potential. Other researchers[84, 105] found differences among social classes such that the higher the class, the greater the ability to delay gratification for future success.

SELF-CERTAINTY VERSUS SELF-CONSCIOUSNESS

Erikson relates self-certainty versus self-consciousness to the early childhood crisis of autonomy versus shame and doubt. Under this aspect of adolescence, a particular phase of the development of the ego, called egocentrism, will be discussed. In addition, attention will be directed to affective development during late adolescence as well as self-image and body-image.

Egocentrism: Cognitive development is one of the processes which Erikson[45] includes under ego development. He points out the importance of formal operational thought to the development of a sense of identity. These cognitive processes are used to test all hypothetical propositions in order to make a series of ever-narrowing selections of personal, occupational, sexual, and ideological commitments.

A particular aspect of ego development which links cognitive development with the affective aspects is egocentrism. This concept generally refers to a lack of differentiation in some area of subject-object interaction.[119] This lack of differentiation may appear at any stage of development, but takes a unique form at each stage.

With the advent of formal operational thought, the adolescent can conceptualize his own thoughts, as well as the thoughts of others. Adolescent egocentrism emerges because of a failure to differentiate one's own preoccupations from the contents of other people's minds. Thus adolescents overgeneralize; they assume that their concerns are shared by others, and that others are preoccupied with their appearance and behavior.[40] As a consequence, the adolescent anticipates and continues to react to an imaginary audience.

This is complemented by another mental construction, the overdifferentiation of feelings. Feelings are thought to be unique. Elkind labels this personal uniqueness and immortality a "personal fable."[40] Adolescent diaries characteristically represent personal fables recorded for posterity.

Both aspects of adolescent egocentrism are more typical of early than of late adolescence. They tend to disappear with the establishment of formal operations in thought and intimacy in relationships. But formal operations may not appear until later, if at all, and intimacy is more characteristic of early adulthood.

The overgeneralizing aspect of adolescent egocentrism is generally resolved with experience. After repeated interactions with others, the adolescent comes to realize differences in concerns; in addition, the older adolescent is frequently less self-conscious about appearance and behavior and is more self-assured.

Belief in personal uniqueness is modified by intimacy.[46] Once the adolescent is aware of the real, as opposed to the imaginary audience, he can establish true, less self-interested relationships. In these relationships the older adolescent, or more likely the young adult, discovers that others share his own feelings.

Affective Development: What feelings concern adolescents? Masterson[103] compared psychiatrically ill adolescents with a matched normal control group. He found that neither anxiety nor depression differentiated the two groups; both affects appeared to be common.

Similarly, among a group of normal boys at age sixteen, Offer[109] found anxiety to be the most prevalent and the most severe symptom. This would flare up before a performance, such as a sports event, an exam, a class talk, or a concert. These boys worried about the adequacy of their abilities and about how they were evaluated by others. In terms of behavior, however, this anxiety was facilitative rather than inhibitory; in most instances it was resolved by appropriate action.

Depression also occurred frequently with Offer's adolescent boys, although it was less severe than the anxiety. It appeared most frequently in response to an event such as the death of a loved one, sickness, some failure or disappointment in oneself, or from feelings of rejection. Among this group, depression usually lasted longer than did anxiety, with the duration dependent upon the gravity of the event. In time, the event was set aside, but not totally dismissed.

Self-image: Rosenberg[124] has made it clear that adolescent self-image is a relative concept, greatly influenced by the extent of dissonance in the social environment. He points out that according to theories of self-esteem or self-concept, certain groups of people should have lower self-esteem than other groups. But this does not always follow. For example, some have claimed that children from poorer families have lower self-esteem than children from wealthier families. A poor child who goes to school with wealthier children may well develop a poor self-image. However, the same child might have a positive self-image in a school where everyone was poor. In brief, students in dissonant environments suffer more than students in consonant environments. Similarly, individuals tend to consider their competence in comparison to others in the immediate environment and not in terms of some absolute value. Thus, very bright students, in a highly competitive school, will consider themselves less competent than they would in a less competitive setting.

In a related study, Simmons and Rosenberg[132] concluded that adolescence is most difficult for white females. When compared to white males, and to black youth of both sexes, white girls are found to suffer from a poorer self-image, greater self-consciousness, lower self-esteem, and a higher level of instability. They are less satisfied with their sex role, less future-oriented in terms of education and occupation, and less pleased with their physical appearance.

In contrast to the Rosenberg research, Hauser[69] found that among a group of working-class boys, the black teenagers maintained stable self-images throughout adolescence but were characterized by identity foreclosure; the white boys produced integrative self-images and displayed progressive identity formation. A major difference between these two groups was the greater likelihood of the continuing presence of a father for the white boys as compared to the black boys.

Carlson[26] studied stability and change in adolescent self-image. She found that by the last year of high school, the girls had changed dramatically in self-image, while the boys maintained a stable personal orientation. In sixth grade, for example, girls were primarily characterized by a personal orientation, that is, one in which the individual is able to evaluate his own abilities individually rather than by comparison to other individuals. By the last year of high school, however, the girls had become far more dependent upon the opinions of others for their self-image; they were more socially oriented.

In another study of continuity in self-concept, Engel[44] found continuous development rather than a radical change; the changes which did occur were in a positive direction. Offer and Howard[110] also found that older adolescents of both sexes tended to have a better self-image than did younger adolescents.

The different results for sex and role differences may be related to the methods used. Both Carlson and Hauser were studying qualitative changes while the other studies measured quantitative change.

Body Image: By late adolescence, a good sense of body image has usually been achieved. This aspect of self-image is generally problematic for young adolescents, but by age sixteen, and surely by age nineteen, most boys and girls have adjusted to their adult bodies. However, this does not mean that they accept their bodies. Studies of body satisfaction[51, 136] find that most late adolescents would like to improve their appearance, to become more like the societal ideal for their gender. Furthermore, boys are more satisfied with their bodies than are girls.[36]

ROLE EXPERIMENTATION VERSUS ROLE FIXATION

This aspect of the adolescent identity crisis relates to the earlier crisis during the third stage of life centering around initiative versus guilt. The adolescent who finds himself confronted with too many possibilities, or restricted to too few possibilities, may experience a kind of role fixation or, in Erikson's terms, a negative identity.

The introduction of new roles is a part of adolescence. During this time young people begin to see themselves as sexual beings and develop intimate relationships with the opposite sex. They begin to consider life plans and think about future job possibilities. They also begin to develop values and ideals which are made manifest in religious and political views. Those adolescents who fail to experiment with the role opportunities before them at this time may be characterized by identity foreclosure or role fixation; at the same time it must be remembered that some adolescents face real limitations in role opportunities. Those overwhelmed by too many role opportunities may find it impossible to make a choice. They become profoundly confused and uncertain. In sheer self-defense, they may ignore, refuse, or oppose all the opportunities. Thus, identity diffusion can give way to negative identity formation.

APPRENTICESHIP VERSUS WORK PARALYSIS

This aspect of identity in the development of adolescents is related to the work of latency. This is Erikson's fourth stage of life in which the central issue of the crisis is industry versus inferiority. The selection of a work role is one of the major tasks of adolescence. Some degree of work paralysis is normal, but failure to develop an adequate identity in terms of a work role leads to further conflict.

Education. For all adolescents up to age sixteen, school is the major focus of work activities. It continues to play this role for the many adolescents who continue on to college. Numerous authors have criticized the role that schools have played in adolescent development. Hall,[67] Friedenberg,[54] and Silberman,[131] have all complained about the inadequacy of our schools in fostering development of appropriate role identifications. Surveys of youth, on the other hand, suggest that the teenagers are less dissatisfied than are the adults.[93]

Other critics, such as Coleman,[28] have placed the blame upon the anti-intellectual atmosphere of the American educational system. Coleman's results show the extent to which boys and girls value physical appearance and athletic ability over academic competence. While Coleman holds the children themselves responsible, Friesen[55] and Boyle[19] suggest that it is the characteristics of the schools that influence the values and attitudes of the students. Borow[18] and many others demonstrate the importance of socioeconomic variables in determining educational and occupational motives and roles. In addition, Douvan and Adelson[34] relate high achievement motivation to upward mobility, a future orientation, a positive self-image, more experimentation activities, and better sexual adjustment.

Occupation: At the end of high school many adolescents must go to work; the rest must at least begin to select future occupational roles. Most experts in this area have suggested that adolescence is *the* critical period for this decision. Nelson[107] found that not until the late high-school years did young people know much about jobs and know their own occupational inclinations. The recent trend is toward beginning career education early in the school years; this may alter these findings in the future.

In some studies, occupational role demonstrates

clear sex differences. Douvan and Adelson[34] concluded that girls had fuzzier and more tentative perceptions of what the future would bring than did boys. Girls were also less ambitious than boys. Gribbons and Lohnes[63] found that for boys, salary and prestige were the most important occupational considerations, whereas for girls, personal contact and social service took precedence. Most researchers consider these results realistic on the part of an adolescent girl; for in many cases her future is somewhat more vague and tentative. Socialization pressures teach girls that their adult role is that of a wife and mother, occupations for which they cannot prepare through formal education. Horner,[73] Komarovsky,[88] and others have found evidence for strong pressures on girls to suppress their intellectual talents for supposed social gains. Bardwick[6] suggested that girls cannot develop themselves in terms of occupational roles until the crisis of intimacy is resolved in early adulthood. Bernard[12] suggests that the women's liberation movement is beginning to relieve the socialization pressures on girls; she expects that we will begin to see the results with the next generation. Indeed, in a recent study of adolescent girls, Konopka[89] found that most girls were planning to combine careers with motherhood.

SEXUAL POLARIZATION VERSUS BISEXUAL CONFUSION

Gender Identity: This aspect of the adolescent search for identity relates to the young adult crisis of intimacy versus isolation. It is assumed that the vast majority of adults will find their most intimate relationship with a person of the opposite sex. Erikson suggests that, in anticipation of later heterosexual intimacy, early adolescents engage in attempts to define what it means to be male and female. As a result, a kind of sexual polarization occurs among them. In Erikson's view a firm delineation of sexually differential roles in adulthood is vital both to individual identity development as well as to the integrity of society.

Whether or not Erikson is correct, we are currently experiencing a decreasing emphasis on masculinity and femininity. There is an increasing merging of sex roles and the related psychological attributes which constitute gender identity. The end point of this trend has been termed psychological androgyny, a gender identity combining masculine and feminine attributes.[10, 70] Whether this represents diffusion of sexual identity or a new resolution of sexual identity issues cannot

yet be determined. Preliminary evidence suggests that for some people, in some situations, an androgynous identity is adaptive.[9] Whether or not it serves the best ends of society as a whole is unknown.

While the presence of anatomical differences between the sexes is obvious, the existence of differences in personality traits or in abilities is quite controversial. In their comprehensive review of research on sex differences, Maccoby and Jacklin[95] dispelled many myths in this area. They concluded that the only sex-related differences for which there is strong evidence are in the areas of verbal, spatial, and mathematical abilities, and in aggression. There are many other areas where the current evidence is inconclusive. The origins of these sex differences are even more controversial, with explanations ranging from societal and cultural to biological. It seems most likely that these differences are in fact overdetermined and are influenced by all these factors.

Whatever the underlying realities, sexual stereotypes are in fact widely held and seem to have broad implications. The now-classic study of Broverman et al.[22] showed that men were viewed as having the more positive human qualities, while women were described as relatively less competent, less independent, less objective, and less logical. The self-descriptions were similar to the appropriate stereotypic male and female descriptions produced by the subjects in the study. Other researchers[11, 43, 60, 96] report comparable findings. These stereotypes appear to be similarly shared by males and females of all classes. While the attitudes appear to develop throughout childhood, they become crystallized in adolescence. This may well be related to the greater cognitive ability to differentiate at this age, as well as to the increasing concern with sexual functioning.

Sexual Behavior: Sexual behavior is a problem for most adolescents.[108, 129] Our society imposes sanctions against sexual activity until marriage or near marriage. As a result, for a period of years the adolescent is all too aware of sexual desires and needs for which there is no approved means of satisfaction. Offer[108] found that the anxiety and taboos regarding sex grew less troublesome during the normal course of adolescence. Older subjects were less fearful of sex and more likely to agree that sex gives them pleasure. Many researchers have found that among college students, intercourse is considered permissible if the couple is in love, though the double standard appears to persist.

Late adolescence has been characterized as the

time of heterosociality as opposed to the homo-sociality of early adolescence.[133] Same-sex relationships remain stable but at this point, teenagers are able to begin forming attachments to individuals of the opposite sex. Feinstein and Ardon[48] considered the dating stage from fourteen to seventeen years to be a period of practicing. There tended to be no strong commitment between individuals and the focus was on experiencing the acts themselves. The next stage was characterized by more serious dating with a greater focus on interpersonal relationships.

In a study of sexual relationships during this age period, Simon, Berger, and Gagnon[134] found no evidence of a sexual revolution in their sample. Traditional factors, such as parents and religion, restrained the likelihood of early coitus, while on the other hand, more frequent dating and related factors appeared to facilitate or enhance the likelihood of early coitus. Overall, however, the statistics on frequency of sexual intercourse appeared quite similar to those obtained by Kinsey twenty years earlier. Offer[108] obtained similar results with his study of adolescent boys. He also found no evidence for a change in attitude toward sex. The only observable change in his sample was that boys became more open about sex as they grew older.

In a detailed discussion of all stages of sexual development, Offer and Simon[113] discussed the particular aspects of sexual development in late adolescence. Masturbation persists with males, heavy petting is typical of most individuals at this age, and both the majority of working-class males along with a slightly lower proportion of middle-class males have experienced coitus during this stage. The initial coital acts are considered experimental and the sexual act appears to be more ego-oriented rather than libido-oriented. Though there is no evidence of a sexual revolution, there does appear to be a recent change in partners for the early sexual experiences of males. There is a decrease in the double standard such that the sexual partners of the males are more likely to be of the same class, and the females are also more likely to engage in sexual intercourse. As a result, the prevalence of coitus among males appears to have decreased somewhat, while among females it has increased slightly. By the end of this stage —by eighteen or nineteen—coitus is more accepted and expected and premarital intercourse becomes normative.

More recent data, however, is beginning to show increasing sexual activity among teenagers.[29] Self-reports of coital experiences as well as the incidence of pregnancy show dramatic increases among college and high-school youths.[3, 4]

LEADERSHIP AND FOLLOWING VERSUS AUTHORITY CONFUSION

This characteristic of late adolescence relates to the seventh life crisis of generativity versus stagnation which takes place in the middle years. The adolescent's role experimentation helps him to become socially involved. The society of the family gradually gives way to the larger society. The adolescent both generalizes and refines the values learned in the home in the course of applying them to the larger society. Participation in society will likely require abilities both to lead and to follow.

With this expanding world, the adolescent may become aware of many competing and sometimes contradicting demands for allegiance. Authority confusion may result, a confusion which is resolved only when the adolescent formulates his own value system. This resolution is strongly linked to the adolescent aspect of ideological commitment versus confusion of values related to the eighth life crisis.

Parental Relationships: A key factor in most aspects of identity formation is the relationship of the adolescent to his parents. A clear understanding of, and experience with, authority, as leader and as follower, is first learned in the family. Parents are, therefore, especially critical to this aspect of development.

Adolescence is marked by a particular change in the parent-child relationship.[5, 94] As the adolescent becomes more adult, the parent is more likely to identify with the offspring. Parents who enjoyed their own adolescence will treat it as an enjoyable period for their children, while parents who experienced great difficulties in adolescence are more likely to expect, and perhaps create, difficulties for their children. Parents may create a double bind for the adolescent by admonishing against particular behaviors at the same time that they clearly expect them, frequently because they themselves engaged in such behaviors as adolescents. Generally, the adolescent will both live up to this expectation and also experience the guilt, thus replicating the parental pattern.

In a society like ours which places so high a value on youthfulness, parents may also envy their adolescent children. This envy is frequently sexually laden; the parent may envy the increasing sexual attractiveness of the developing adolescent. As Anthony[5] has noted, many parents of adolescents are themselves enmeshed in a similar life crisis, the "midlife crisis," which includes menopause for women and fears of decreasing sexual potency for men.

Sexual problems exist as well on the adolescent's side of this relationship. Anna Freud[53] interpreted the youthful rebellion at adolescence as a function of the resurgence of infantile sexuality. For the youth, powerful new sexual urges and capabilities make the former emotional attachment to parents a dangerous presence. The emerging sexuality in the former child may confuse parents as well. The once-asexual cuddling may now be accompanied by sexual feelings, and lead to embarrassment or acting-out on the part of the parent.

In late adolescence, the concept of separation-individuation[97, 15] is especially appropriate for understanding the intrapsychic aspects of the adolescent-parent relationship. Not until the end of adolescence do self and object representations acquire stability and firm boundaries.[15] A necessary aspect of this process is disengagement of the self from parental egos. Equally critical is the reorganization of the superego. This process is more or less tumultuous, depending on how defective or intact is the early ego organization. And related to this, with additional influences specific to adolescence, is the parent's support or lack of support for the work of individuation and separation.

Despite all the potential problems with adolescent-parent relationships, most current research has refuted the notion of a strong youth culture distinct from and at odds with the generation of the parents. Haan, Smith, and Block,[66] Offer and Offer,[111] as well as others,[49, 78] find a continuity of values and ideals extending across generations. It is when relationships with parents are weak or conflicted that peers appear to become more important. In one study of delinquents, family interaction patterns were found to be neither primarily restrictive nor permissive as has been commonly believed.[135] Instead, the families of these delinquents were characterized by inconsistent interaction patterns. This inconsistency included disagreement between the parents, marked variation in the behavior and relationships over different time periods, or both.

IDEOLOGICAL COMMITMENT VERSUS
CONFUSION OF VALUES

The final aspect of adolescent development is related to the last life crisis, integrity versus despair. As we have noted, this conflict is closely related to the issues around authority. Ideological commitment involves a sense of unity in one's values and a compatibility between personal and societal values. Erikson suggests that the elaboration of an ideology or personal philosophy permits the adolescent or young adult to resolve *all* the partial conflicts of the adolescent identity crisis. It is the integrating process of the adolescent stage.

Values: Any discussion of values must note the relevance of the sociocultural framework. American values have undergone a series of shifts over the last twenty years[61] that make it especially difficult for the adolescent to develop individual values.

Values or ideologies have been defined many ways. For the most part, they can generally be categorized as either political or religious. The results of several studies showed that neither religion[8] nor politics[75, 90] are of central concern to adolescents. This has led some researchers to conclude that these values are acquired before adolescence.[71] Alternatively, these values may actually be acquired later; moreover, current values may be more global than the usual considerations of religion or politics.

The work on moral development has demonstrated a different quality of moral thought in children and adolescents, a difference based primarily on cognitive development.[121, 85, 87, 123] This difference in moral development has also been observed specifically in religious views.[39]

Kohlberg[85, 86] proposes six stages of moral development that fall in three broader categories: preconventional, conventional and postconventional. Postconventional morality may first develop in adolescence. The first postconventional stage, stage 5, has two substages; stage 5a involves a social contract orientation, and stage 5b develops this into an orientation to internal decisions of conscience, but without clear rationale or universal principles. Stage 6 involves an orientation toward ethical principles appealing to logical comprehensiveness, universality, and consistency; it is abstract and ethical in nature.

Adelson and colleagues[1, 2, 58, 59] have done the major work with political ideology in adolescence. Paralleling Kohlberg's findings, the Adelson group found a distinct shift from a primitive and categorical stance characteristic of children to a more humanitarian and idealistic orientation during adolesence. The principles of a social contract had emerged by late adolescence with government given recognition as a necessary presence to balance the various forces in society. These results have held for American, British, and German youth across the spectrums of class, sex, and ethnic differences. In addition, Gallatin[57] as well as Tapp and Levine[138] found evidence that these changes were in fact ideological, that is, they were a basic set of principles held by the individual and which cut across any particular context such as politics, crime, law, poverty, and so forth.

Values and Identity: There does seem to be some evidence that the formulation of a system of personal values is a concomitant of an integrated identity. This is one of Erikson's postulates.[45] Marcia[99, 100] found that in a group of males, those who had experienced an identity crisis and resolved it by developing such a personal value system (the Achievements) were the best adjusted. The adjustment ratings of the other three groups declined as follows: those who were in the process of finding their values (the Moratoriums), those who adopted parental values without a crisis (the Foreclosures), and, finally, those who engaged neither in struggle nor resolution (the Diffusions).

Though Keniston's alienated Harvard freshmen did not appear to be mentally healthy,[80] his later study[79] of young Vietnam war protesters showed that these youth appeared to have strong ideological commitment together with integrated identities. Others[49, 140] have also found that student activists attained better grades, were more open minded, and reported themselves on better terms with their parents. In his comprehensive review of youth movements, Braungart[20] agrees that activist youth appear to be mentally healthy.

As Gallatin[56] notes, however, one must be extremely cautious in interpreting these results. The samples have consisted primarily of students from elite universities. In addition, Haan, Smith and Block[66] found a group of Berkeley radicals to be a very mixed lot as measured by Kohlberg's Scale of Moral Values. Some of these students were at a "premoral" level, with moral values based on expediency. These researchers concluded that there are many different reasons why students become involved in activist efforts. In addition, they caution against equating political idealism with participation in a cause.

Keniston[79] observes that several characteristics appear to be critical in catalyzing moral development. The adolescent needs to be in a stage of disengagement from the adult society, needs to go through an experience of confrontation with alternate moral viewpoints, and needs to "discover" corruption. His conclusions are based on the existing evidence, but they serve as well to integrate the various results that have been found.

Three Developmental Routes Through Normal Male Adolescence

Because most studies focus on particular aspects of development, it is difficult to piece together profiles of how adolescents do in fact look during this phase. The longitudinal growth studies done earlier this century did attempt to measure various aspects of physical, cognitive, and psychosocial development and have proven to be extremely important to the understanding of normal development. On the other hand, these studies were, by definition, limited by their methodologies and generally involved samples of limited size.

An example of a longitudinal psychiatric approach to this phase of growth is Daniel and Judith Offer's 1975 study of adolescent boys.[111] In addition to clinical interviews, the Offers used surveys, psychological testing, and questionnaires to obtain information from the boys as well as from their parents and teachers.

Psychoanalytic and psychiatric theoreticians have described one specific route as best typifying adolescent development, a route in which adolescent turmoil was a necessary component.[16, 52, 31] In their study of normal adolescent males, the Offers found three alternative routes through adolescence. They found that about 23 percent of their group developed continuously through adolescence and 35 percent showed developmental spurts alternating with periods of conflict and turmoil. The third group, about 21 percent of the total group, experienced the kind of adolescent turmoil described by previous psychoanalytic research. Each developmental style characteristic for these young men was exhibited continuously throughout the period from fourteen to twenty-two years. The remaining 21 percent of these youth could not be classified; clinically, they most resembled the first two groups.

The sample in this study consisted of middle-class, Midwestern, adolescent males. They were selected from high schools in two suburban communities. While most of the boys in this study were white, 7 percent belonged to various minority groups, the same percentage as minority group populations in the suburbs studied. These young men were first seen at fourteen, when they were freshmen in high school, and were last seen when they were twenty-two years of age. This review will focus on the period of transition from high school to college or work situations.

Using the Offer Self-Image Questionnaire[110] a

normal sample was selected from all the freshmen in two suburban high schools. This questionnaire consists of ten scales developed to measure adolescent functioning in significant areas. The aim was to find a modal population and to eliminate the extremes of psychopathology, deviancy, and superior adjustment. Hence, those students were selected whose responses fell within one standard deviation from the mean in at least nine out of ten scales. To corroborate the selection, information concerning the subjects was also solicited from teachers and parents. There were only three cases where strong disagreement existed between the teachers' ratings and the test data; these subjects were not included in the study. No parent disagreed with the research findings.

Once the subjects had been selected, the perspective on normality shifted. The investigation now focused on differing patterns of meaning for each individual set of responses. The normality as transactional system[112] approach was utilized for describing the population under study. Within this approach, change or processes are the crucial variant of normality.

The primary source of data for this study was the semistructured psychiatric or clinical interview. Other procedures were utilized as well so that the bias of the experimenter or interviewer would be minimized.[126] Thus, in addition to the psychiatric interviews of the subject, interviews of parents, ratings by teachers, and psychological testing of the subject were also carried out. The staff collecting the data did not share their findings until the project was completed. This was done in order to increase the validity of the conclusions.

The sample followed through high school included seventy-three young men. Sixty-one of these subjects were followed for four years after high school; ten of the individuals' families had moved away from Chicago and could not be located, and two of the original subjects refused to participate. Of the sixty-one who were studied after high school, 74 percent went on to college, 13 percent joined the armed forces, and 13 percent went to work.

An examination of the clinical as well as the statistical groupings of the subjects led to a differentiation of their psychological growth patterns. Even within these groups chosen for qualities of homogeneity, factor and typal analyses revealed that there were five discernible subgroups. Because two of the pairs of these five subgroups were very similar, statistically as well as clinically, they were collapsed into three clinically meaningful subgroups. Each followed a different route through adolescence. There was extensive clinical material on the subjects. This demonstrated both the psychological similarity of the subjects within each of the subgroups and their differences from members of other subgroups.

A complex interaction of variables, such as child-rearing practices, genetic backgrounds, experiential factors, cultural and social surroundings, and the psychological defenses and coping mechanisms of the individual makes up the route pattern. No single item included in the analyses would produce the three routes. Together the routes provide a means of conceptualizing the period of adolescence for a large group of young men.

The three groups are called the Continuous Growth, Surgent Growth, and Tumultuous Growth groupings. The ensuing material will present each of these in greater detail.

CONTINUOUS GROWTH

The subjects described within the continuous growth grouping progressed steadily throughout adolescence and young manhood. There was a quality of smoothness of purpose and self-assurance in their progression toward a meaningful and fulfilling adult life. These subjects were favored both by circumstances and prior development. Their genetic and environmental backgrounds were excellent. Furthermore, their family's history had not involved extremely stressful and upsetting events. Their childhoods had been unmarked by death or serious illnesses of a parent or sibling. The nuclear family remained a stable unit throughout their childhood and adolescence.

These subjects had mastered previous developmental stages without serious setbacks. They had learned to cope with internal and external stimuli through an adaptive combination of reason and emotional expression. They accepted the general cultural and societal norms and felt comfortable within this context. They had a capacity to integrate experiences and use them as a stimulus for growth.

The parents were able to encourage their children's independence; indeed, the parents themselves grew and changed with their children. Throughout the eight years of the study there was basic mutual respect, trust, and affection between the generations. The ability to allow the son's independence in many areas was undoubtedly facilitated by the son's behavior patterns. Since the young men were not behaving in a manner clearly divergent from that of the parents, the parents could continue to be provided with need gratifications through their sons. The sense of gratification was reciprocal; the sons gained both from the parents' good feelings toward them and from the parental willingness to allow them to create their own individual lives outside of the household. The value systems of the subjects in this group dovetailed with those of the parents. In many ways the young men were functioning as continuations of the parents, living not so much lives the parents had wished for but not attained, but rather lives that were similar to those of the parents.

In their interpersonal relationships the subjects showed a capacity for good object relationships. They had close male friends in whom they could confide. Their relationships with the opposite sex became increasingly important as they reached the post–high-school years. Intimacy in the Eriksonian sense was being developed, and it was a goal toward which these subjects continued to strive.

The youngsters tended to act in accordance with their consciences. They manifested little evidence of superego problems, developed meaningful ego ideals, and often identified with persons whom they knew and admired within the larger family or school communities. They were able to describe feelings of shame and guilt, and to explain not only how the experiences provoking these responses had affected them, but how they brought closure to the uncomfortable situations as well. A subsequent similar experience was frequently described by these young men, but this time they were prepared to handle it better, putting the earlier upsetting experience into a past-time frame of immaturity conquered.

The young men's fantasy lives were relatively active, and they were almost always able to translate their fantasies into reality and action. They could dream about being the best in the class academically, sexually, or athletically, though their actions would be guided by a pragmatic and realistic appraisal of their own abilities and of external circumstances. Thus, they were prevented from meeting with repeated disappointments.

The subjects were usually able to cope with external trauma through an adaptive action orientation. When difficulties arose, they used the defenses of denial and isolation to protect their egos from being bombarded with affect. They could postpone immediate gratification and work in a sustained manner for a future goal. Their delay mechanisms worked well and involved temporary suppression (rather than repression) of affect. In general, they were successful in responding to their aggressive and sexual impulses without being overwhelmed or without acting-out in a self-destructive manner. Nor did they experience prolonged periods of anxiety or depression, two of the most frequent affects described by the entire subject population, including this subgroup.

Members of this group shared many of the qualities attributed to ideal mental health. No one subject would portray all of these qualities, and there would usually be some difficulties in one or another area. What was most distinctive about members of the continuous growth group was their overall contentment with themselves and their place in life. When compared to the other two groupings, this group was composed of relatively happy human beings. There was a quality of order to their lives which could be interrupted but which would not yield to states of symptomatology or chaotic behavior.

None of the subjects in this group had received psychotherapy or were thought to need it. The significance of this data lies in the fact that they are then least likely to be studied in any way by members of the helping professions.

SURGENT GROWTH

Adaptively, the surgent growth group functioned as well as the first group. However, differences in ego structure, in background, and in family environment sufficed to place them in a different subgroup. Characteristically, the pattern of growth of the surgent growth group was a sequence of developmental spurts. These subjects differed from the continuous growth group in the amount of emotional conflict experienced and in their patterns of resolving conflicts. There was more concentrated energy directed toward mastering developmental tasks than was obvious for members of the continuous growth group. At times these subjects would be adjusting very well, integrating their experiences and moving ahead, while at other times they seemed to be stuck at an almost premature closure and unable to advance. A cycle of progression and regression is more typical of this group than the continuous growth group. They tended to use anger and projection, defenses which represent more psychopathology than the defenses used by the first group.

There were major differences between the surgent growth subjects and those in the continuous growth group. For the surgent youngsters, their genetic and/or environmental backgrounds were not as free of problems and traumata, and the nuclear families were more likely to have been affected by separation, death, or severe illnesses.

Although subjects in this category were able to cope successfully with their "average expectable environment,"[68] they were unable to deal with unanticipated sources of anxiety. At a time of crisis such as the death of a close relative, affects which were usually flexible and available would become stringently controlled. This, together with the fact that they were not as action-oriented as the first group, made them slightly more prone to depression. The depression would accompany or openly follow the highly controlled behavior. On other occasions, when their defense mechanisms faltered, they experienced moderate anxiety and a short period of turmoil resulted. When disappointed in themselves or others, there was a tendency to use projection and anger.

These subjects were not as confident as were the young men in the continuous growth group; their self-esteem wavered. They relied upon positive reinforcement from the opinions of important others such as parents and/or peers. When this was not forthcoming, they would often become discouraged about themselves and their abilities. As a group, they were able to form meaningful interpersonal relationships similar to those of individuals in the continuous growth group. A greater degree of effort had to be expended, however, to maintain these relationships.

For these subjects, relationships with parents were marked by conflicts of opinions and values. There were areas of disagreement between father and mother concerning basic issues such as the importance of discipline, academic attainments, or religious beliefs. In several cases, each parent came from a different background. The mothers of some of these subjects had difficulty in letting their children grow and in separating from them.

The subjects might work toward their vocational goals sporadically, or with a lack of enthusiasm, but over the long-range they would be able to keep their behavior in line with their general goals.

Some members of this group were afraid of emerging sexual feelings and impulses. For most, meaningful relationships with the opposite sex began relatively late. A small subgroup started experimenting with sexuality early in high school, possibly on a counterphobic basis. These early sexual relationships were not lasting, although they could be helpful in overcoming anxiety concerning sexuality.

The overall adjustment of these subjects was often just as adaptive and successful as that of the first group. But the group as a whole was less introspective than either the first or the third group. The adjustment was achieved with less self-examination, with suppression of emotionality, and with a more inhibited surge toward development.

TUMULTUOUS GROWTH

The third group, the tumultuous growth group, is similar to the adolescents so often described in psychiatric, psychoanalytic, and social science literature. These are the students who go through adolescence with much internal turmoil which manifests itself in the form of overt behavioral problems in school and in the home. These adolescents display self-doubts and braggadocio, escalating conflicts with their parents, debilitating inhibitions, and, often enough, inconsistent responses to their social and academic environments.

This tumultuous group experienced growing up from fourteen to twenty-two as a period of discord, a transitional phase for which their defenses needed mobilizing, and for which their ego-adaptations had to be strengthened.

They came from backgrounds that were less stable than those of the other two groups. Some of the parents had overt marital conflicts, and others, a history of mental illness in the family. In brief, both the genetic and environmental backgrounds of the tumultuous growth group subjects were decidedly different from those of the other two groups. A social class difference was present as well. The overall study population was primarily middle class, but this tumultuous group contained many subjects who belonged to the lower class. For them, functioning in a middle- and upper middle-class environment might have been a source of additional stress.

The tumultuous growth group experienced more major traumatic events. The difficulties in their life situations seemed to be greater than the satisfactions. A relatively high percentage of this group had overt clinical problems and had received psychotherapy. Their defenses were not adequate for handling emotionally trying situations.

Separation was painful to the parents, and it became a source of continuing conflict for the subjects. The parent-son relationships characterizing this group were similar to those of many of the neurotic adolescents seen in outpatient psychotherapy. Further, parent-son communication of a system of values was poorly defined or contradictory.

Strong family bonds, however, were as marked within the tumultuous growth route subjects as they were within each of the other route patterns. The revealed differences technique was used for evaluating strength and openness of family communication. This method clearly differentiated the families of the modal sample along the three developmental routes. Best understanding between the generations was observed among the continuous growth group, the poorest in the tumultuous growth group, with the surgent group in between.[114]

The ability of this group to test and act in keeping with reality was relatively good. This stands in contrast to the typical findings in patient populations. When contrasted to other non-patients, a prevalent attitude was disappointment in others and in themselves. Action was accompanied by more anxiety and depression in this group than in the other two groups. Emotional turmoil was part of their separation-individuation process. Without the tumult, growth toward independence and meaningful interpersonal relatonship was in doubt. Wide mood swings indicated a search for who they were as separate individuals and concern about whether their activities were worthwhile. The members of this group often expressed feelings of mistrust toward the adult world. Affect was readily available and created experiences that were both intensely pleasurable and equally painful. Changes in self-concept could precipitate moderately severe anxiety reactions. These subjects were considerably more dependent on peer culture than were their age-mates in the other groups. This may have been the case because they received fewer gratifications from relationships within the family. When they experienced a personal loss, such as the ending of a relationship with a good friend, their depression was deeper, though only very rarely associated with suicidal feelings and impulses.

The tumultuous growth subjects began dating at a younger age than had their peers. In early adolescence, a relationship with a female was characterized by dependency, with the female standing as a substitute for a mothering figure. In late adolescence, for some, their heterosexual relationships matured and they were able to appreciate the personal characteristics of their female friends.

Many subjects in the tumultuous growth group were highly sensitive and introspective. They were usually aware of their emotional needs. Academi-

cally, they were less interested in science, engineering, law, and medicine, and preferred instead the arts, the humanities, or the social and psychological sciences. However, business and engineering careers remained the most usual choices for this group as well as for the first two groups.

On the whole, these subjects did not do as well academically as did members of the first two groups. It is possible, however, that in the long run they will do just as well. As with other variables, academic success differentiated the groups, but honor students and average students or workers could be found within each of the groups. The academic or work failures were more likely to be found in the tumultuous group; they would find repeatedly that the tasks upon which they had embarked were incompatible with their needs or abilities.

This group of adolescents experienced more psychological pain than did the others. Nonetheless, in terms of their overall functioning within their respective environmental settings, they were still well adjusted. They were less happy with themselves and more critical of their social environment, but they did attain success academically or vocationally.

The Offers' longitudinal study[111] demonstrates a continuity between the generations as well as a continuity of coping styles from childhood into adulthood. From the ages of twelve to twenty-two, changes in appearance and changes in the ability to make judgments were far more prevalent than were changes in levels of functioning, changes in defenses, or changes in emotional equilibrium. At the same time, this study demonstrates that there is a variety of developmental pathways through adolescence, each of which is normal.

Conclusion

It is evident, that, during the years sixteen to nineteen, the adolescent completes many aspects of development toward maturity, but continues to work on others. By age nineteen, young people are physically mature and are most likely to have attained their peak level of cognitive development (although their fund of knowledge can increase continuously). Psychosocial development, on the other hand, will have come a long way, but is by no means complete. The major psychosocial task of adolescence is the formation of an identity; however, some aspects of identity continue to develop throughout life. There are also aspects of psychosocial development which appear to be dependent upon and therefore limited by cognitive development.

Using Erikson's framework, one may summarize the development of identity by age nineteen. Most youth of this age have achieved temporal perspective; in fact, they appear to have a heightened awareness of time. Self-certainty is a more difficult task to master, and many individuals maintain some degree of self-consciousness throughout life. Egocentrism, however, is less prevalent by age nineteen.

At this age many youth are still actively experimenting with roles. Limits on future opportunities require other young people to take on roles without much experimentation. By age nineteen most youth are at least beginning to consider occupational choices. The majority have begun to develop intimate relationships.

The last two conflicts of the adolescent crisis involve the dimensions of leadership and followership versus authority confusion, and ideological commitment versus confusion of values. These are less likely to be resolved by age nineteen. Most college-age youths struggle actively with these issues; relatively few actually resolve them much before the end of college.

In the Offers' study, about one-fourth of their modal sample progressed continuously and developed values similar to those of their parents. A second group developed by growth spurts alternating with periodic turmoil. The third group negotiated the years from fourteen to twenty-two with a kind of turmoil (a state of affairs that is frequently generalized to all adolescents). For them, the developmental tasks leading to an identity were difficult.

There is good evidence that parental influence is especially important to adolescent development. Well-adjusted parents can facilitate development in this period, while conflicted parents may exacerbate difficulties.

What is true of parents is equally applicable to society. History suggests that when society itself is in turmoil, adolescents have greater difficulty making the transition to adulthood. It is important to differentiate which manifestations are related to adolescence and which are specific for a particular society at a particular point in time.

Most youths of nineteen are capable of living independently and making their own decisions. One might question their judgment, but as young adults, they must begin to experience their own successes and failures. To the extent that adulthood was present, the turmoil of adolescence had now subsided—not into calm, but into a more controlled, reasoned approach to the many problems presented by life.

Further Research Needs

The field is still a long way from totally understanding this period of life. A major contribution could be made by studies taking a more integrated approach to this stage. Each discipline has its own theories and methodologies which tell a great deal about particular aspects of the problem. But it is frequently difficult to integrate these results in a way that permits a comprehensive understanding either of the stage as such or of any individual traversing it.

This chapter has discussed adolescent development in three broad areas: physiological, cognitive, and psychosocial. The systematic research which could integrate these spheres is, however, lacking. None of the existing theories of development accomplishes this in a comprehensive way, although psychoanalytic theory comes closest. It is hypothesized that there are relationships among physiological, cognitive, and psychosocial development, and specific speculations have been alluded to in the text. Major questions remain, however, as to the particular relationships. For example, is physiological maturation necessary for cognitive and psychosocial development? Both Piaget and Erikson claim that it is, but systematic evidence is lacking. On the other hand, physiological maturation is clearly not sufficient for cognitive and psychosocial maturation; here other factors become important. Cognitive maturation has been shown to be necessary for some aspects of psychosocial development, such as time perspective and moral values. Again, however, this is probably not a sufficient condition, and other factors can enhance or inhibit potentials. Articulating the precise interrelationships among these various aspects of development would appear to be an important research priority to better understand adolescence, as well as other stages of life.

It seems particularly important to integrate clinical observations with developmental research. Only by understanding normal development can one understand its deviations. For example, by comparing factors involved in normal development with those in delinquency or psychopathology one can learn how problems develop and hence be better able to plan effective interventions. Similarly, the study of psychopathology or delinquency will point to problem areas and will greatly enhance the understanding of significant aspects of normal development. For example, it would tell a great deal about normal development to know why schizophrenia does not appear earlier than adolescence. In addition, the study of treatment course also tells a great deal about human development and its influences.

The authors therefore stress the importance of a systems theory approach to clinical research focusing on the relevant problems of adolescent development. Clinicians and researchers working together can greatly enhance each other's efforts.

Finally, as was noted at the beginning of this review, the authors' understanding of normal adolescence is based primarily on white, middle-class males. Very few studies have included blacks or other minority groups. And while there have been more studies of females in the past few years, there are very few on populations younger than college-age. Probably because most research is done with college populations, or in college communities, lower-class groups are seldom included. Studies with these populations of adolescents may greatly alter the understanding of this stage of life.

REFERENCES

1. ADELSON, J., and O'NEIL, R. P., "Growth of Political Ideas in Adolescence: The Sense of Community," *Journal of Personality and Social Psychology, 4:*295–306, 1966.
2. ———, GREEN, B., and O'NEIL, R. P., "Growth of the Idea of Law in Adolescence," *Developmental Psychology, 1:*327–332, 1969.
3. Alan Guttmacher Institute, *Special Report: House Committee on Population*, New York, 1978.
4. ———, *11 Million Teenagers*, New York, 1976.
5. ANTHONY, J., "The Reactions of Adults to Adolescents and Their Behavior," in Kaplan, G., and Lebovici, S. (Eds.), *Adolescence: Psychosocial Perspectives*, pp. 54–78, Basic Books, New York, 1969.
6. BARDWICK, J., *The Psychology of Women*, Harper & Row, New York, 1971.
7. BAUMRIND, D., "Early Socialization and Adolescent Competence," in Dragastin, S. E., and Elder, G. H., Jr. (Eds.), *Adolescence in the Life Cycle*, pp. 117–143, Halsted, New York, 1975.
8. BEALER, R. C., and WILLITS, R. K., "The Religious Interests of American High School Youth," *Religious Education, 42:*435–444, 1967.
9. BEM, S. L., "Sex-Role Adaptability: One Consequence of Psychological Androgyny," *Journal of Personality and Social Psychology, 31:*634–643, 1975.
10. ———, "The Measurement of Psychological Androgyny," *Journal of Consulting and Clinical Psychology, 42:*158–162, 1974.
11. BENNETT, E. M., and COHEN, L. R., *Men and Women: Personality Patterns and Conquests*, Genetic Psychology Monographs, vol. 50, pp. 122–123, 1959.
12. BERNARD, J., "Adolescence and Socialization for Motherhood," in Dragastin, S. E., and Elder, G. H., Jr. (Eds.), *Adolescence in the Life Cycle*, pp. 117–146, Halsted, New York, 1975.
13. BLIZZARD, R. M., et al., "The Interrelationship of Steroids, Growth Hormone, and Other Hormones in Pubertal Growth," in Grumbach, M. M., Grave, G. D., and Mayer, F. E. (Eds.), *Control of the Onset of Puberty*, pp. 342–359, John Wiley, New York, 1974.
14. ———, et al., "Recent Developments in the Study of Gonadotropin Secretions in Adolescents," in Heald, F. P., and Hung, W. (Eds.), *Adolescent Endocrinology*, pp. 1–24, Appleton-Century-Crofts, New York, 1970.
15. BLOS, P., "The Second Individuation Process of Adolescence," in Eissler, R. S., et al. (Eds.), *The Psychoanalytic Study of the Child*, vol. 22, pp. 162–186, International Universities Press, New York, 1967.
16. ———, *On Adolescence*, Free Press, Glencoe, Ill., 1961.

17. BOEK, R. D., et al., "A Parameterization for Human Growth Curves," *Human Biology, 45:*63–80, 1973.
18. BOROW, H., "Development of Occupational Motives and Roles," in Hoffman, L. W., and Hoffman, M. C. (Eds.), *Review of Child Development Research*, vol. 2, pp. 373–422, Russell Sage Foundation, New York, 1966.
19. BOYLE, R. P., "The Effect of High School on Students' Aspirations," *American Journal of Sociology, 71:*628–639, 1966.
20. BRAUNGART, R. G., "Youth and Social Movements," in Dragastin, S. E., and Elder, G. H., Jr. (Eds.), *Adolescence in the Life Cycle*, Halsted, New York, 1975.
21. BRONFENBRENNER, U., *Two Worlds of Childhood: U.S. and U.S.S.R.*, Russell Sage Foundation, New York, 1970.
22. BROVERMAN, I. K., et al., "Sex-Role Stereotypes, A Current Appraisal," *Journal of Social Issues, 28:*59–78, 1972.
23. BROVERMAN, D. M., et al., "The Automatization of Cognitive Style and Perceptual Development," *Child Development, 34:*1343–1359, 1946.
24. BRUNSWICK, A., and JOSEPHSON, E., "Adolescent Health in Harlem," Supplement, *American Journal of Public Health*, 1972.
25. BYNUM, T. W., THOMAS, J. A., and WEITZ, L. J., "Truth Functional Logic in Formal Operational Thinking: Inhelder and Piaget's Evidence," *Developmental Psychology, 7:*129–132, 1972.
26. CARLSON, R., "Stability and Change in the Adolescent Self-Image," *Child Development, 36:*659–666, 1965.
27. CLAUSEN, J. A., "The Social Meaning of Differential Physical and Sexual Maturation," in Dragastin, S. E., and Elder, G. H., Jr. (Eds.), *Adolescence in the Life Cycle*, pp. 25–48, Halsted, New York, 1975.
28. COLEMAN, J., *The Adolescent Society*, Free Press, New York, 1971.
29. CVETKOVICH, G., and GROTE, B., "Adolescent Development and Teenage Fertility," Paper presented at the Planned Parenthood Regional Conference on Adolescence, Boise, Idaho, 1977.
30. DALZELL, D. P., and ELATTAR, T. M. A., "Gas Chromatographic Determination of Urinary Excretion of Testosterone, Epitestosterone and Androstenedione in Preadolescent and Adolescent Children," *Journal of Clinical Endocrinology and Metabolism, 36:*1237–1243, 1973.
31. DEUTSCH, H., *Selected Problems of Adolescence*, International Universities Press, New York, 1967.
32. DEVRIES, R., "Relationships Among Piagetian,

I.Q., and Achievement Assessments," *Child Development,* 45:746–756, 1974.

33. DONOVAN, B. T., and VAN DER WERFF TEN BOSCH, J. J., *Physiology of Puberty,* Williams and Wilkins, Baltimore, 1965.

34. DOUVAN, E., and ADELSON, J., *The Adolescent Experience,* John Wiley, New York, 1966.

35. DULIT, E., "Adolescent Thinking à la Piaget: The Formal Stage," *Journal of Youth and Adolescence, 4:* 281–301, 1972.

36. DWYER, J., and MAYER, J., "Psychological Effects of Variations in Physical Appearance During Adolescence," *Adolescence, 3:*363–360, 1968–1969.

37. EICHORN, D., "The Institute of Human Development Studies, Berkeley and Oakland," in Jarvik, L. F., Eisdorfer, C., and Blum, J. E. (Eds.), *Intellectual Functioning in Adults,* Springer, New York, 1973.

38. ELKIND, D., "Recent Research on Cognitive Development in Adolescence," in Dragastin, S. E., and Elder, G. H., Jr. (Eds.), *Adolescence in the Life Cycle,* pp. 49–62, Halsted, New York, 1975.

39. ——, "The Development of Religious Understanding in Children and Adolescents," in Strommen, M. P. (Ed.), *Research on Religious Development,* pp. 655–685, Hawthorn, New York, 1971.

40. ——, "Egocentrism in Adolescence," *Child Development, 38:*1025–1034, 1967.

41. ——, "Quantity Conceptions in College Students," *Journal of Social Psychology, 57:*459–465, 1962.

42. ——, "Quantity Conceptions in Junior and Senior High School Students," *Child Development, 32:* 551–560, 1961.

43. ELMAN, J. B., PRESS, A., and ROSENKRANTZ, P., "Sex-Roles and Self-Concepts: Real and Ideal," Paper presented at the meeting of the American Psychological Association, Miami, 1970.

44. ENGEL, M., "The Stability of Self-Concept in Adolescence," *Journal of Abnormal and Social Psychology, 58:*211–215, 1959.

45. ERIKSON, E. H., *Identity: Youth and Crisis,* W. W. Norton, New York, 1968.

46. ——, *Identity and the Life Cycle,* Psychological Issues, Monograph no. 1, pp. 1–171, 1959.

47. FAUST, M. S., *Somatic Development of Adolescent Girls,* Monographs of the Society of Research in Child Development, Serial no. 169, 1977.

48. FEINSTEIN, S. C., and ARDON, M. S., "Trends in Dating Patterns and Adolescent Development," *Journal of Youth and Adolescence, 2:*157–166, 1973.

49. FLACKS, R., "The Liberated Generation: An Exploration of the Roots of Student Protest," *Journal of Social Issues, 23:*52–73, 1967.

50. FRAISSE, P., *The Psychology of Time,* Harper & Row, New York, 1963.

51. FRAZIER, A., and LISONBEE, L., "Adolescent Concerns with the Physique," *School Review, 58:*397–405, 1950.

52. FREUD, A., "Adolescence," in Eissler, R. S., et al. (Eds.), *The Psychoanalytic Study of the Child,* vol. 16, pp. 225–278, International Universities Press, New York, 1958.

53. ——, *The Ego and the Mechanisms of Defense,* International Universities Press, New York, 1936.

54. FRIEDENBERG, E. Z., *The Vanishing Adolescent,* Beacon Press, Boston, 1960.

55. FRIESEN, D., "Academic-Athletic Popularity Syndrome in the Canadian High School," *Adolescence, 3:* 39–52, 1968.

56. GALLATIN, J., *Adolescence and Individuality: A Conceptual Approach to Adolescent Psychology,* Harper & Row, New York, 1975.

57. ——, *The Development of Political Thinking in Urban Adolescents,* Final Report, Office of Education Grant 0–554, National Institutes of Education, Washington, D.C., 1972.

58. ——, and ADELSON, J., "Legal Guarantees of Individual Freedom: A Cross-National Study of the Development of Political Thought," *Journal of Social Issues, 27:*93–108, 1971.

59. ——, "Individual Rights and the Public Good: A Cross-National Study of Adolescence," *Comparative Political Studies, 3:*226–242, 1970.

60. GARAI, J. E., and SCHEINFELD, A., *Sex Differences in Mental and Behavioral Traits,* Genetic Psychology Monographs, vol. 77, pp. 169–299, 1968.

61. GETZELS, J., "On the Transformation of Values: A Decade after Port Huron, *School Review, 80:*550–519, 1972.

62. GRAVES, A. C., "Attainment of Mass, Weight and Volume in Minimally Educated Adults," *Developmental Psychology, 7:*223, 1972.

63. GRIBBONS, W. D., and LOHNES, P. R., "Shifts in Adolescents' Vocational Values," *Personnel and Guidance Journal, 44:*248–252, 1965.

64. GRUMBACH, M. D., GRAVE, G. D., and MAYER, F. E. (Eds.), *Control of the Onset of Puberty,* John Wiley, New York, 1974.

65. GUPTA, D., ATTANASIO, A., and RAAF, S., "Plasma Estrogen and Androgen Concentrations in Children During Adolescence," *Journal of Clinical Endocrinology and Metabolism, 40:*636–643, 1975.

66. HAAN, H., SMITH, M. B., and BLOCK, J., "Moral Reasoning of Young Adults: Political-Social Behavior, Family Background, and Personality Correlates," *Journal of Personality and Social Psychology, 10:*183–201, 1968.

67. HALL, G. S., *Adolescence: Its Psychology and Its Relations to Physiology, Anthropology, Sociology, Sex, Crime, Religion and Education,* Appleton, New York, 1904.

68. HARTMANN, E., *Ego Psychology and the Problem of Adaptation,* International Universities Press, New York, 1958.

69. HAUSER, S. T., "Black and White Identity Development: Aspects and Perspectives," *Journal of Youth and Adolescence, 1:*113–130, 1972.

70. HEFNER, R., REBECCA, M., and OLESHANSKY, B., "The Development of Sex-Role Transcendence," *Human Development, 18:*143–158, 1975.

71. HESS, R. D., and TORNEY, J., *The Development of Political Attitudes in Children,* Aldine, New York, 1967.

72. HOBBS, E. D., "Adolescent's Concepts of Physical Quantity," *Developmental Psychology, 9:*431ff., 1973.

73. HORNER, M., *Differences in Achievement Motivation and Performance in Competitive and Non-Competitive Situations,* Unpublished Ph.D. dissertation, University of Michigan, 1968.

74. INHELDER, B., and PIAGET, J., *The Growth of Logical Thinking from Childhood to Adolescence,* Basic Books, New York, 1958.

75. JENNINGS, M. K., and NIEMI, R. G., "The Transmission of Political Values from Parent to Child," *American Political Science Review 62:*169–184, 1968.

76. JOHANSON, A., "Fluctuations of Gonadotropin Levels in Children," *Journal of Clinical Endocrinology and Metabolism, 39:*154–159, 1974.

77. JONES, M. C., and BAYLEY, N., "Physical Maturing Among Boys as Related to Behavior," *Journal of Educational Psychology, 41:*129–148, 1950.

78. KANDEL, D., and LESSER, G., *Youth in Two Worlds,* Jossey-Bass, San Francisco, 1972.

79. KENISTON, K., "Student Activism, Moral Development, and Mortality," *American Journal of Orthopsychiatry, 40:*577–592, 1970.

80. ——, *The Uncommitted: Alienated Youth in American Society,* Harcourt Brace Jovanovich, New York, 1965.

81. KESTENBERG, J., "Phases of Adolescence with Suggestions for a Correlation of Psychic and Hormonal Organizations. Part III: Puberty Growth, Differentiation,

and Consolidation," *Journal of the American Academy of Child Psychiatry, 7:*108–151, 1968.

82. ———, "Phases of Adolescence with Suggestions for a Correlation of Psychic and Hormonal Organizations. Part I: Antecedents of Adolescent Organizations in Childhood," *Journal of the American Academy of Child Psychiatry, 6:*426–463, 1967.

83. ———, "Phases of Adolescence with Suggestions for a Correlation of Psychic and Hormonal Organizations. Part II: Prepuberty, Diffusion, and Reintegration," *Journal of the American Academy of Child Psychiatry, 6:*577–614, 1967.

84. KLINEBERG, S. L., "Changes in Outlook on the Future between Childhood and Adolescence," *Journal of Personality and Social Psychology, 7:*185–193, 1967.

85. KOHLBERG, L., "Development of Moral Character and Moral Ideology," in Hoffman, M. C., and Hoffman, L. W. (Eds.), *Review of Child Development Research*, vol. 1, pp. 383–432, Russell Sage Foundation, New York, 1964.

86. ———, and GILLIGAN, C., "The Adolescent as a Philosopher: The Discovery of the Self in a Postconventional World," *Daedalus, 100:*1051–1086, 1971.

87. ———, and KRAMER, R., "Continuities and Discontinuities in Childhood and Adult Moral Development," *Human Development, 12:*93–120, 1969.

88. KOMAROVSKY, M., "Functonal Analysis of Sex Roles," *American Sociological Review, 4:*508–516, 1950.

89. KONOPKA, G., *Young Girls: A Portrait of Adolescence*, Prentice-Hall, Englewood Cliffs, N.J., 1976.

90. LANGSTON, K. P., and JENNINGS, M. K., "Political Socialization and the High School Civics Curriculum in the United States," *American Political Science Review, 52:*852–867, 1968.

91. LeBLANC, A. F., "Time Orientation and Time Estimation: A Function of Age," *Journal of Genetic Psychology, 115:*187–194, 1969.

92. LEE, P. A., JAFFE, R. B., and MIDGLEY, A. R., JR., "Serum Gonadotropin, Testosterone and Prolactin Concentrations Throughout Puberty in Boys: A Longitudinal Study," *Journal of Clinical Endocrinology and Metabolism, 39:*664–672, 1974.

93. LEIDY, T. R., and STARRY, A. R., "The American Adolescent—A Bewildering Amalgam," *National Education Association Journal, 56:*8–12, 1967.

94. LIDZ, T., "The Adolescent and His Family," in Kaplan G., and Lebovici, S. (Eds.), *Adolescence: Psychosocial Perspectives*, pp. 105–112, Basic Books, New York, 1969.

95. MACCOBY, E., and JACKLIN, C. N., *The Psychology of Sex Differences*, Stanford University Press, Stanford, Calif., 1974.

96. McKEE, J. P., and SHERRIFFS, A. C., "Men's and Women's Beliefs, Ideals, and Self-Concepts," *American Journal of Sociology, 64:*356–363, 1959.

97. MAHLER, M., "On Human Symbiosis and the Vicissitudes of Individuation," *Journal of the American Psychoanalytic Association, 15:*740–763, 1967.

98. MAIER, H. W., *Three Theories of Development*, Harper & Row, New York, 1965.

99. MARCIA, J. E., "Development and Validation of Ego-Identity Status," *Journal of Personality and Social Psychology, 3:*551–558, 1966.

100. ———, and FRIEDMAN, M. L., "Ego Identity in College Women," *Journal of Personality, 38:*249–263, 1970.

101. MARSHALL, W. A., and TANNER, J. M., "Variations in Pattern of Pubertal Changes in Boys," *Archives of Disease in Childhood, 75:*13–23, 1970.

102. ———, "Variations in Pattern of Pubertal Changes in Girls," *Archives of Disease in Childhood, 44:*291–303, 1969.

103. MASTERSON, J. F., JR., *The Psychiatric Dilemma of Adolescence*, Little, Brown, Boston, 1967.

104. MEAD, M., "Adolescence in Primitive and in Modern Society," in Maccoby, E. E., Newcomb, J. M., and Hartley, E. (Eds.), *Readings in Social Psychology*, pp. 6–14, Holt, New York, 1947.

105. MISCHEL, W., and METZNER, R., "Preference for Delayed Reward as a Function of Age, Intelligence, and Length of Delay Interval," *Journal of Abnormal and Social Psychology, 64:*425–431, 1962.

106. MUSSEN, P. H., and JONES, M. C., "Self-Conceptions, Motivations, and Interpersonal Attitudes of Late- and Early-Maturing Boys," *Child Development, 28:*243–256, 1957.

107. NELSON, R. C., "Knowledge and Interests Concerning Sixteen Occupations among Elementary and Secondary School Students," *Educational Psychology Measurement, 23:*741–754, 1963.

108. OFFER, D., "Attitudes Toward Sexuality in a Group of 1500 Middle-Class Teenagers," *Journal of Youth and Adolescence, 1:*81–90, 1972.

109. ———, *The Psychological World of the Teenager*, Basic Books, New York, 1969.

110. ———, and HOWARD, K. I., "An Empirical Analysis of the Offer Self-Image Questionnaire for Adolescents," *Archives of General Psychiatry, 27:*529–537, 1972.

111. ———, and OFFER, J. B., *From Teenage to Young Manhood: A Psychological Study*, Basic Books, New York, 1975.

112. ———, and SABSHIN, M., *Normality: Theoretical and Clinical Concepts of Mental Health*, rev. ed., Basic Books, New York, 1974.

113. ———, and SIMON, W., "Stages of Sexual Development," in Freedman, A. M., Kaplan, H. I., and Sadock, B. J. (Eds.), *Comprehensive Textbook of Psychiatry*, 2nd ed., pp. 1392–1400, Williams and Wilkins, Baltimore, 1975.

114. ———, MAROHN, R. C., and OSTROV, E., *Psychiatric Studies of Juvenile Delinquents*, Basic Books, New York, 1978.

115. PARLEE, M. B., "Comment on Roles of Activation and Inhibition in Sex Differences in Cognitive Abilities," *Psychological Review, 79:*180–184, 1972.

116. PESKIN, H., "Pubertal Onset and Ego Functioning," *Journal of Abnormal Psychology, 72:*1–15, 1967.

117. PETERSEN, A. C., "Female Pubertal Development," in Sugar, M. (Ed.), *Female Adolescent Development*, Brunner-Mazel, New York, in press.

118. ———, "Physical Androgyny and Cognitive Functioning in Adolescents," *Developmental Psychology, 12:*524–533, 1976.

119. PIAGET, J., "Intellectual Evolution from Adolescence to Adulthood," *Human Development, 15:*1–12, 1972.

120. ———, *The Language and Thought of the Child*, trans. M. Gabain, Meridian Books, New York, 1957.

121. ———, *The Moral Judgment of the Child*, trans. M. Gabain, Free Press, Glencoe, Ill., 1948.

122. ———, *The Psychology of Intelligence*, trans. M. Piercy and D. E. Berlyne, Harcourt, Brace, New York, 1947.

123. REST, J., "Developmental Psychology as a Guide to Value Education: A Review of 'Kohlbergian' Programs," *Review of Educational Research, 44:*241–259, 1974.

124. ROSENBERG, M., *Society and the Adolescent Self-Image*, Princeton University Press, Princeton, 1965.

125. ROSENFIELD, R., "Discussion," in Grumbach, M. M., Grave, G. D., and Mayer, F. E. (Eds.), *Control of the Onset of Puberty*, p. 360, John Wiley, New York, 1974.

126. ROSENTHAL, R., *Experimenter Effects in Behavioral Research*, Appleton-Century-Crofts, New York, 1966.

127. SCHAIE, K. W., "Translations in Gerontology—from Lab to Life," *American Psychologist, 29:*802–807, 1974.

128. ———, and STROTHER, C. R., "Cognitive and Personality Variables in College Graduates of Advanced

Age," in Talland, C. A. (Ed.), *Human Aging and Behavior*, pp. 281–308, Academic Press, New York, 1968.

129. SHIPMAN, G., "The Psychodynamics of Sex Education," *Family Coordinator, 17:*3–12, 1968.

130. SIEGLER, R. S., LIEBERT, D. E., and LIEBERT, R. M., "Inhelder and Piaget's Pendulum Problem: Teaching Preadolescents to Act as Scientists," *Developmental Psychology, 9:*97–101, 1973.

131. SILBERMAN, C., *Crisis in the Classroom*, Random House, New York, 1970.

132. SIMMONS, R. G., and ROSENBERG, F., "Sex, Sex Roles, and Self-Image," *Journal of Youth and Adolescence, 4:*225–258, 1975.

133. SIMON, W., and GAGNON, J. H., "On Psychosexual Development," in Goslin, D. A. (Ed.), *Handbook of Socialization Theory and Research*, pp. 733–752, Rand McNally, Chicago, 1969.

134. ——, BERGER, A. C., and GAGNON, J. H., "Beyond Anxiety and Fantasy: The Coital Experiences of College Youth," *Journal of Youth and Adolescence, 1:*203–225, 1972.

135. SINGER, M., "Delinquency and Family Disciplinary Configurations," *Archives of General Psychiatry, 31:*795–798, 1974.

136. STOLZ, H. R., and STOLZ, L. M., *Somatic Development in Adolescent Boys*, Macmillan, New York, 1951.

137. TANNER, J. M., "Growth and Endocrinology of the Adolescent," in Gardner, L. I. (Ed.), *Endocrine and Genetic Diseases of Childhood*, pp. 19–60, W. B. Saunders, Philadelphia, 1969.

138. TAPP, J. L., and LEVINE, F. J., "Compliance from Kindergarten to College: A Speculative Note," *Journal of Youth and Adolescence, 1:*233–250, 1972.

139. TOMLINSON-KEASEY, C., "Formal Operations in Females from Eleven to Fifty-Four Years of Age," *Developmental Psychology, 6:*364ff., 1972.

140. TRENT, J. W., and CRAISE, J. L., "Commitment and Conformity in the American College," *Journal of Social Issues, 2:*34–51, 1967.

141. WABER, D. P., "Sex Differences in Mental Abilities, Hemispheric Lateralization, and Rate of Physical Growth at Adolescence," *Developmental Psychology, 13:*29–38, 1977.

142. ——, "Sex Differences in Cognition: A Function of Maturational Rate," *Science, 192:*572–574, 1976.

143. WHITING, J. W. M., KLUCKHOHN, R., and ANTHONY, H., "The Function of Male Initation Ceremonies of Puberty," in Maccoby, E. E., Newcomb, T. M., and Hartley, E. L. (Eds.), *Readings in Social Psychology*, pp. 359–370, Holt, New York, 1958.

144. WINTER, J. S. P., and FAIMAN, C., "Pituitary-Gonadal Relations in Female Children and Adolescents," *Pediatric Research, 7:*948–953, 1973.

145. WITTIG, M. A., and PETERSEN, A. C., *Sex-Related Differences in Cognitive Functioning: Developmental Issues*, Academic Press, New York, 1979.

146. YOUNG, H. B., "The Physiology of Adolescence," in Howells, J. G. (Ed.), *Modern Perspectives in Adolescent Psychiatry*, pp. 3–27, Brunner-Mazel, New York, 1971.

20 / Sources of Anxiety and Intrapsychic Change During Adolescence

Justin D. Call

One of the perplexing aspects of behavior during adolescence is its inconsistency from day to day. This is due not only to the rapidity of change in physical, cognitive, and social growth, but to differences in the urgency of drive discharge with its associated affects and moods. As in earlier phases of life, the drives stem from biological forces and follow a more or less genetically determined timetable of maturational unfolding. However, within this general biological framework, day-to-day and hour-to-hour changes in attitudes and moods along with affects of depression and anxiety are set in motion. These are then organized by events and persons in the outside world and by perceived dangers. Each adolescent responds to these external events in his own way; this depends upon the meaning of such events to the individual. This meaning is, in turn, determined by earlier identifications, values, social learning, ego strength, ego defenses, and superego development. The strength of drives in relation to the strength of the ego and superego determines whether anxiety occurs. Conflict and compromise are shown by transient symptoms, moods, behavioral change, and attempts at work, play, and sublimation. Signicant internal conflict occurs between and within the several psychic structures. Symptoms, rigidity of character, and failures in adaptation are all a measure of the degree and kind of this conflict. The nature of intrapsychic conflict can be revealed by a study of character traits, transient symptoms, dreams, masturbation fantasies, and sublimations.

EXAMPLE

At age seventeen, Gloria was an excellent student. However, her social life did not go beyond that which she had had as a younger child. At home, she did her chores, kept her room neat, and maintained her religious observances. When menses appeared at thirteen and one-half, her mother became depressed and could not speak to her about growing up. The physical education teacher told her about menstruation, ovulation, intercourse, and pregnancy, but not about erotic feelings, contraception, or boys. Gloria developed an elaborate fantasy about being a child in another family where parents were more freely open in their expression of feelings and personal concerns. She developed a crush on a woman teacher in high school, and she attended school functions but did not date boys at all. On the surface, her behavior and performance were untroubled. She fantasied attachments to older men in positions of authority and power. Later, her honeymoon was an anxious nightmare, and she soon discovered she was frigid and could not conceive. She began having affairs with married, older men who were essentially unavailable for a continuing relationship.

Comment: In survey studies, interviews, and questionnaires, Gloria would have shown up as a healthy, well-adjusted teenager. It was only as she entered adult life that the psychological difficulties during adolescent development revealed themselves in retrospect. Developing a crush on a woman teacher is often considered a normal event. For Gloria, this was a search for a mothering figure and an attempt to flee from heterosexual relationships. It was only after many years, and within the context of ongoing treatment, that Gloria's disturbed development during adolescence could be revealed.

Menstruation usually occurs at the point of maximum acceleration of skeletal growth in girls. The time of occurrence of nocturnal emissions has not been systematically studied in boys. Such changes are of extraordinary importance. Symptoms, attitudes, and dream contents show traces of these somatic events. Once they are underway, nothing is quite the same again.

EXAMPLE

"Woman of Heart and Mind" by Joni Mitchell:

I am a woman of heart and mind with time on her
   hands, no child to raise
You come to me like a little boy and I give you my
   scorn and my praise
You think I am like your mother or another lover or
   your sister or the queen of your dreams
Or just another silly girl when love makes a fool of
   me.*

Comment: A girl can become a woman of heart and mind only after the onset of menses. Following menarche, her first love object is likely to be a boy whom she can mother as if he were her baby whom she raises with scorn and praise. Formerly, this was called puppy love. Such early loves are often confusing, leaving the lovers feeling like fools, bemused by immature affection and unconsumated womanhood.

EXAMPLE

Byron was the father of two children. In his thirties, while puzzling out his rather compartmentalized sexual life, he revealed his first wet dream at the age of fourteen. "I got excited while being attacked by a furry beast, half human and half like a lion with a shaggy mane. When I awakened, I discovered my p.j.'s all sticky. My brother said I'd had a wet dream."

Comment: During adolescence, this boy was not considered by anyone to be in need of psychiatric care. This dream marked the onset of his nocturnal emissions. The analysis of this dream showed that the emerging mature sexuality of adolescence was associated with preoedipal fixations involving both mother and father.

As a rule, adolescence is a period of blooming health and widening adaptive capacity. However, the study of exceptional adolescents, those who become openly troubled, provides important clues to the intrapsychic life of all youngsters of this age. This is because pathological responses are almost always an exaggeration of healthy ones.

EXAMPLE

At age sixteen, Joannie was hospitalized because of a thirty-pound weight loss. This was due to self-imposed starvation during the previous months. Her high school counselor disclosed that Joannie and her three closest girl friends were very calorie conscious and competitive with each other for best figure, clothes, boys, etc. One of Joannie's friends said sagely that "Joannie was the most attractive but she carried things too far." It was evident that she was frightened of her emerging sexuality and her attractiveness, and this together with her poorly developed self-concept, led her to the excessive dieting (carrying things too far).

The most authentic information on the intrapsychic life of nonpatient adolescents is drawn from the psychoanalytic treatment of young adults. Such individuals can look back upon their apparently untroubled adolescence from a safe distance and, in the controlled regression of analysis, can describe what it was like.

A man in his forties recalled that during adolescence he told his male companions many tall tales about heterosexual exploits. Only in retrospect was it possible for him to acknowledge that such stories were a cover for underlying homosexual wishes which were directed toward the very boys who were the recipients of his tall tales.

Parents tend to dramatize their own unresolved earlier oedipal themes with their adolescent children. For example, a father brought his teenage daughter to a family health clinic to be placed on birth control pills. While there, it suddenly occurred to him that he should have a test for venereal disease just to be sure about his wife. It turned out that he had had sex with no one besides her for many years, not in fact since his own adolescence, when he himself was frightened of getting a venereal disease from girls his daughter's age.

External bodily change during puberty is easily recognized and measured. Underlying growth in the organs of reproduction, in the brain, the heart, bones, joints, connective tissue, liver, and kidney is only vaguely conceptualized by the teenager. Physiological and biochemical changes in hormones, metabolism, muscle strength, and gonadal functioning can only be imagined. Changes in the processes of thought, and in the response to psychological and physical stress all accompany bodily change during puberty. These include problem solving, conceptualization, and the capacity for abstract thinking. As the child experiences these external and internal changes, including the strength of the sexual and aggressive drives, the entire internal physiological and psychological milieu undergoes change. However, such change is not experienced consciously and is, therefore, not under voluntary control. Changes in moods, feelings, and behavior during adolescence must be interpreted in the light of more profound internal transformations. Since external bodily appearance and change can be seen and measured, what takes place internally tends to be displaced on to the surface structure of the body.

As the child enters the expanding world of adolescence and becomes involved in the youth culture to some degree, old as well as some new sources of anxiety emerge. What are some of the basic sources of stress during adolescence? In the female, anticipation of menstruation is often accompanied by such anxiety along with changes in attitude toward oneself and others. In addition, phobia, hypochondriasis, changes in appetite, and other somatic preoccupations are often present. At the most obvious level, the girl is concerned about the change and character of her body. At a deeper level, she is concerned about the implications of these changes in her relationship to members of both sexes. The anticipation of bloody show with menstruation is often regarded as an indication of some internal violence or susceptibility to violence. This may occur even in the presence of adequate explanations for menstruation. There may be both wishes for and fears of pregnancy. Once puberty begins, some girls expect that they should blossom immediately into full womanhood. The secondary sexual characteristics during puberty come unpredictably; the rate of change is very variable. More important, the changes of puberty are not something which the child can control (except, of course, when a child discovers that starvation can produce drastic bodily change). Some children employ starvation as an attempt to delay and reverse puberty. In their vacillation between childhood and adulthood, others are caught up in the cycle of anorexia and obesity. During early adolescence, both progressive and regressive psychological changes can be observed. These are accompanied by internal changes in psychic structure which affect both the capacity for adaptive functioning in the external world and the reorganization of one's internal world, i.e., a change in ego functioning. As the child's superego, derived from earlier stages of childhood, is tested against the values and attitudes of the wider social culture and the peer group, superego functioning also undergoes changes. In the male, the onset of puberty is often associated with feelings of competition with other boys and feelings of inferiority.

The young adolescent boy is usually pleased and happy with the increased strength and height which puberty confers upon him. A renewed interest in masturbation and/or its equivalents is ushered in with the emergence of such secondary sexual characteristics as nocturnal emissions and spontaneous erections. The boy too may undergo as much regressive as progressive psychological change. When regressions occur, they often proceed to pregenital points of fixation in the oral and anal spheres. These regressive moves are often initiated by renewed intensity of castration and mutilation anxiety, or by separation fears, sometimes accompanied by feelings of helplessness and confusion. In dealing with the increased strength of aggressive and sexual drives, the old, well-established modes of superego control no longer suffice. The superego had been constructed largely by means of identifications at an earlier period of childhood; now it is challenged by the changing social scene and peer group. Many boys are frightened of the damage they can do to girls, as well as by the damage they fear from them. While the boy is proud of the increased size of his penis, he is also often concerned about the events occurring in the girl's body, about menstruation, and about impregnation.

Mental Life During Adolescence

Whether conscious or unconscious, or whether set in motion by external or internal change, anxiety prepares the way for many new developments. Among these are:

1. Bodily change, i.e., the stimulus giving rise to anxiety is turned upon the bodily self. Illness may result.
2. Defense. The unconscious mechanisms of defense have been elaborated at an earlier period of development. During adolescence these are further elaborated and defined, particularly those which are compatible with basic underlying character structure. The conflict between the drives giving rise to anxiety and the unconscious defenses elaborated by the ego may produce symptoms which are essentially compromise formation.
3. Action in the external world. This may be adaptive, as for example, any kind of activity which increases enlightenment about the external world and offers a better opportunity for choice of action; or maladaptive, as during acting out of conflicts, repetition of old conflicts within the new social scene of adolescence, and regression with the repetition of old conflicts.
4. Delay of action, delay of defensive maneuvers in the ego, and delay of bodily response as found in more sublimated forms of thought which include fantasy, play, creative expression (in music, poetry, writing, sculpting, weaving, painting, pottery making), and the elaboration of transitional phenomena. The dreams of adolescents can be understood as representing the unconscious aspects of all of the preceding four alternatives.

During adolescence there is a constant effort on the part of the child to alleviate anxiety. Within that context there is a reworking of both preoedipal and oedipal themes. This involves a restructuring of ego and superego structures and the intensive realignment and redefinition of ego ideal. The adolescent is faced with old struggles and conflicts along with beckonings toward the future as he anticipates new roles in later adolescence and adult life. Most important, however, the adolescent is constantly engaged in attempts at reworking and firming up his sense of self in the midst of ongoing change. Erikson[1] has put this succinctly, stating that the identity of adolescence results from a consolidation of all previous identifications.

REFERENCES

1. ERIKSON, E. H., *Identity, Youth and Crisis*, W. W. Norton, New York, 1968.

SECTION II

Varieties of Development

Joseph D. Noshpitz and Irving N. Berlin, Editors

PART A
Sociocultural Factors

21 / The American Indian Child

Carolyn L. Attneave

Nature of American Indian Children: Who Are They?

No one expects to see in this or any other handbook a chapter on the European child. It is obvious even to someone who hasn't traveled that a Swedish child, an Italian child, a Polish child, an Irish child, would each embody different genetic and cultural traits. It would be expected that any child from Europe, from any of the countries mentioned, or from a dozen others, would each express his problems both idiosyncratically and as an outgrowth of a different social matrix and historical context. At a highly abstract level, these might be traits that unite the group in contrast to the Oriental or perhaps the African child. Yet each of these, too, would be expected to be more heterogenous and more individual than such titles would suggest.

Nevertheless, it seems that the uninitiated general public expects that the people of North America, a continent twice the size of Europe, can be summarized and subsumed under a single rubric. Even if they concede that American Indian and Eskimo children may be different, within each group the children are expected to be alike.

Perhaps the most important single piece of information needed to understand these children is that they are heterogenous in culture and physical type. In linguistic terms, this can be illustrated by taking the single state of Washington and identifying the languages spoken there before commerce with Europe was established. It turns out that within the boundaries of that state, more specific languages—not dialects—were spoken than one would encounter traveling from Leningrad to Paris, or Oslo to Athens. And this is one small portion of the territory inhabited by American Indians.

Having reminded oneself of these facts, when an American Indian child is presented for diagnosis, therapy, or preventive intervention, it is incumbent upon the professional to find out *who* he is. What tribe or tribes are his family? Where have they lived? What languages are spoken in the home? Are there extended family or others of the tribe nearby, or are they living far from home, kin, or friends?

Number of American Indian Children: Their Distribution Throughout the United States

The ubiquity of the American Indian is the second important and disillusioning factor of which the professional needs to become aware. The popular myth is that Indians live in remote places—foreign and exotic environments known as reservations. And in fact, some do. However, visiting a reservation is apt to be disappointing, since it turns out to be a rural area, with farms, small towns, rural slums, and outdoor recreation facilities. Its people look pretty much like any other people of the state or region. A few will have dark hair, bronze skin, and, very rarely, will be wearing something more distinctive than blue jeans or other storebought clothes appropriate to the time and place. Feathers, elaborate jewelry, and other identifying garb are dress-up clothing for Indians, used only for special occasions. Utilitarian dress is the same for everyone in that region.

Only half the present American Indian population lives within the arbitrarily established boundaries of the reservations. The other half are scattered throughout the United States in such a fashion that no state has fewer than 3,000 to 5,000 Indians. The seventeen western states have many, many more. Most of these off-reservation Indians have migrated to the cities for employment, either at the behest of the Bureau of Indian Affairs (BIA) and its "relocation" programs, or after military experience during and between wars.

Perhaps because of the heterogeneity mentioned earlier, perhaps for other reasons, most cities do not have Indian ghettos comparable to Chicano barrios or Black neighborhoods. There will be many pockets of friends, neighbors, and relatives from back on the reservation living fairly close to one another. But these pockets seldom make an enclave large enough to form Indian neighborhoods or communities.

IDENTITY: HOW IS AN INDIAN RECOGNIZED?

If there are Indian children scattered all over, how does one recognize them? To find out if a patient is an Indian one need only ask. Almost always the Indian people will proudly identify themselves. If the information is not routinely elicited on intake and application forms, or in the referral, it probably should be.

One reason for ambiguity about status and identity is lack of good census data. The 1970 census, relying on many returns by mail, allowed self-identification. The resulting count of nearly 1 million Indians surprised nearly everyone but the Indians themselves. The Indians know that this is still an undercounting, since mails do not reach everyone, and the novelty of the census makes it still a matter of suspicion to many of their folk. If plans for 1980 are implemented, it is estimated that the total will be closer to 2 million—with half under the age of eighteen.

WHERE ARE THE 1 MILLION CHILDREN?

Indians occupy all classes of American life. At present, however, the largest number are found disproportionately in the lower socioeconomic levels. The profile of their distribution reminds students of demography of an emigrant population (an ironic finding when one considers that these represent the original peoples of the land).

POPULATION GROUPS OF INTEREST TO CLINICIANS: THE SCHOOLS

Until the 1940s the education available for most Indian youth was a government-created boarding school. The turn of the century experiment at Carlisle established the fact that American Indian boys could learn as well as white youth. The idealist, ever hopeful of a quick and bloodless solution to "the Indian problem," built boarding schools and literally rounded up the children and shipped them far from their pagan tribal and parental influences to make them into "Americans" in a few short years.

In these large (1,000 to 3,000 children) and smaller (300 to 500 children) schools, academic instruction in the basics of reading, writing, and arithmetic usually was limited to half a day, while vocational training occupied the rest of the time. For girls this was housekeeping, practical nursing, and for a few who would supply government offices, clerical skills. For boys the emphasis was on manual labor, mainly of the agricultural type, since it was the general consensus that the individual farmer was the backbone of the nation.

Since the 1940s two trends have broken up this tight monopoly on education. First has been the dispersion of the population, as already mentioned. Second, the persistence of the various Indian cultures has become a recognized, and, to a certain extent, an accepted fact. As Indian voices are heard, more schools are being opened close to the large reservations. These are both boarding schools and dormitories where students can attend urban public high schools. Through several funds established by Congress, local public schools receive compensation for Indian pupils, and have opened up enrollments to reservation as well as to off-reservation pupils. Tribes, especially the Navajo and some in the Northwest, have begun operating their own schools either by contract with the BIA or, in a few instances, through tribal school districts and school boards. An outstanding example is Rough Rock School, with classes from kindergarten through community college. It is an all-Navajo-operated school, where English is a second language introduced late in the curriculum, and where respected medicine men dominate the school board.

SCHOOL PROBLEMS: THE DROPOUT

A major concern in both the boarding school and the day or public school has been the tendency of most Indians to leave school at adolescence. The highest attrition is in grades seven, eight, and nine.

This trend seems particularly accentuated by the growing awareness of inequalities that seem apparent at every interface between Indian and non-Indian. Although equality is given lip service, the dominant culture is not able to recognize differences in value and custom. There are real contrasts in the traditions and expectations of both cultures.

For instance, at puberty almost all tribes had initiation ceremonies which marked the youngsters as men and women, able to take up responsible roles in the group. Many adults, particularly grandparents, clearly remember this pattern. The contemporary complex technical economy makes it impossible for fourteen-year-olds to assume either the old roles of hunter and defending warrior or the new roles of wage earner and head of household. Comparable changes have occurred for girls and women.

When the elders scorn the teenagers as worthless, it confirms the young people's own sense of uselessness. This lends a feeling of desperation to these dropped-out youth. Where there have been interested mental health staff able to make an impact, the successful programs have an approach that combines therapy with an increase in competency and skills. These programs are few, and, for most youth, unavailable.

The result is restlessness along with active tendencies to drink, fight, and get into trouble. This creates a high proportion of socially rejected Indian young people. Many come into the hands of the juvenile court. At this juncture the BIA-operated boarding schools become available to the Indian youth as an alternative to other correctional institutionalization.

BIA SCHOOLS AS ALTERNATIVES

These BIA schools are also available for children whose homes disintegrate, or for whom adequate care and supervision cannot be provided in the expected and mainstream-approved manner.

This tends to fill these institutions with children who often have major social and emotional problems. However, the BIA educators have not changed their own image to incorporate a residential treatment model.

Mental health consultation to these BIA schools is increasingly requested. However, there is grave resistance to suggestions that the schools modify their own structures and processes; they expect the mental health staff to "adjust" the youngsters. In the 1960s[19, 18] and again in the 1970s[6, 15] several major research and "model" programs were mounted. These demonstrated that changes in attitude, the availability of humanistic role models, and other relatively inexpensive shifts in staffing and practice could dramatically improve the retention, the achievement levels, and the mental health of both pupils and staff. However, the slowness of bureaucratic change frustrates psychiatrists unfamiliar with the complexities of twenty-four hour residential care. There is a general level of distrust by BIA staff of psychiatric advice when it implies system or adult change. All this defeats piecemeal attempts to improve conditions. Examples of effects and of the frustrations experienced are frequent in the records of the Indian Health Service (IHS) and in the experience of other consultants.[2] The situation has become so critical that the American Psychiatric Association published an editorial statement prepared by its Task Force on Indian Affairs entitled "A Hazard to Mental Health: Indian Boarding Schools."[3]

INDIAN HEALTH ACT

This type of public protest, together with Congressional hearings on the needs of Indian children,[23] has begun to build pressure for new solutions to these problems. Some funding has become available for implementation of changes (Indian Health Act). Child psychiatrists in the western states can expect increasing opportunities for involvement in this process.

Impact of Cultural Differences

The media reinforce negative stereotypes of American Indians, as well as many of the problems experienced by Indian children themselves. These derive in part from films, from television westerns, and from the vestigial animosities that remain between the conqueror and the defeated.

Dissonance between the present realities and the glamorized ideal image of a noble savage creates problems both for the non-Indian and the Indian populations. In the twentieth century, some new and different identities and relationships have come into being.

THE MIRROR OF HISTORY

Over the past several hundred years, attempts to "solve the Indian problem" have included outright genocide. This has been true as recently as the present grandparent generation. When various actions of the non-Indian majority are perceived as having similar intent, this evokes panic in the Indians, along with massive defensive reactions. This is evident in such highly publicized events as the 1960s take over of the Interior Building, and in the escalation of tensions at the "Second Battle of Wounded Knee." It is hard to exaggerate the intensity and apparent contradictory emotional reaction on the part of many Indian people at great distances from the scene of such confrontations.

Non-Indian populations also find their fears of savage attack and revenge evoked by economic competition, and by assertions of demands for civil rights and for treaty compliance. History reveals an ongoing oscillation between determined efforts to stamp out traditional Indian identity and culture and a condescending "Lady Bountiful" effort to do what is best for a "beaten and dying race."

It is not difficult to discern the cumulative impact of several generations of these inconsistencies. Policies may be overtly or passively aggressive, but in either case, the aim is to preserve the Indian in museums as exotic examples of a culture otherwise obliterated, reshaped, and/or bleached into nonexistence. The effects vary from fragmentation of cultural patterns to distrust of self and one's own perceptions. Often, reaction formations and overidentification with the projections of the major culture complicate the ordinary problems of child rearing. As a result, normal developmental crises can turn into episodes on which pivot the issues of the life and death of the self.

Familial Reactions

These dissonances are reflected in different ways by Indian families, according to their tribal and personal histories. Each tribe has its own unique blend of traditional culture and adaptations to the twentieth century. Any therapist or consultant aiming at preventive intervention must therefore accept the necessity of becoming as informed as possible about the culture and the in-depth history of these children and their families. The full range of personality types and developmental stages are represented in the American Indian population. What they look like, however, will be characterized by a history that does not always permit the usual interpretations.

LOSS OF PARENTING ROLE MODELS

One example, given by experienced therapists working with quite different tribal populations,[5, 1] is the loss of parental role models. This is the product of several generations having only boarding-school experience during the years eight to fourteen. In the case of Alaska native families the separation in the parental generation is even more complex—as late as the 1960s[20, 2, 7] long hospitalization of adults was common as a treatment for tuberculosis.

When parenting roles have not been part of life experience for several generations, the adults rely on their instincts, on partially understood books and magazines, and even on television soap operas for guidance. This can lead to apparently bizarre and disturbed behavior on the part of parents, and to consequent confusion and defensive reactions in children. The professional called in to help must have patience. Supportive guidance and long-term but not necessarily intensive relationships are often required. A search for community groups and extended family members with more intact life histories often provides more useful resources than therapy or PET classes.

OEDIPUS REINVENTED

The novelty of conventionally expressed oedipal conflict is a somewhat related phenomenon. A family characteristic that may surprise the mainstream culture-bound therapist is the confusion and surprise that often accompany behavior characteristic of the "normal oedipal stage of development." It would appear that in most if not all tribal groups, traditional child rearing was a shared undertaking in which many adults participated. Uncles, aunts, and grandparents had traditional roles which diffused oedipal tensions so that this phase of development expressed itself mildly and often passed unnoticed. Certainly it seldom assumed crisis proportions.

Relocation of family units due to military assignments or economic migration has placed a great many Indians in a more isolated nuclear family setting for the first time in collective memory. This creates a hothouse effect, intensifying the emotions of both parent and child, who lack conventional experience in expressing or controlling them.

The persistent apprehensiveness and mystification of adults in the face of the complexities of unresolved oedipal and Electra feelings are compounded of surprise mixed with a sense of modesty. The reaction often includes attitudes derived from the puritanical, victorian ethic transmitted by missionaries and government schools.

The therapist treating these situations is frequently caught off guard since he cannot assume conventional behavior, or attitudes, or experience. If the caseload has included families with more intact traditions, these will stand in marked contrast to the earthiness, ritualized teasing, and frank discussions of sex which other Indian clientele bring with them to the consulting room.

A WARMING AND A BONUS

When the unmistakable signs of oedipal conflict appear, traditional methods of treatment may work quite well. The real point of this discussion, however, is to alert the therapist not to jump to awkward conclusions when they do not. There is still much to be understood about development in other cultures. One thing they can teach those fortunate enough to work with them is the enormous variety of developmental possibility. Freudian theory was based on data from an urbanized population, far along in the transitions that many Indian familes are only beginning to make. Many of these families are resisting such transition and innovating new models that blend different experiences, along with a different set of values and perceptions.

There are now a number of therapists who have emerged from the Indian population, or who have had long and intense experience with the Indian people. They often find that when they work with Indian children and families, they no longer think in the conventional terms of their formal training. Among these therapists are several whose practice has contained a mixture of populations. It is this group in particular who find that some of the new insights gained from intimacy with another culture are helpful; these aid materially in understanding the problems of the mainstream patients who have seemed untreatable, or baffling. This bonus is far more rewarding than tortuously pressing all persons, Indian or otherwise, to fit the procrustean bed of a single theory.

Cultural Patterning of Behavior

Apparently deviant behavior may be an expression of cultural traits. These need to be evaluated carefully before deciding whether or how to change them.

For instance, among the Crow tribe it is still not customary for a mother-in-law to speak directly to a son-in-law. This holds true even though the household contains three generations. Among Navajo and other tribes one does not mention a person who is dead. This can be carried so far by Northwest coastal tribes that words sounding like the name of a recently deceased family member are banned from the language. For instance, a red-headed duck must be called a yellow-legged swimmer if Mr. Redhead dies.

One trait is especially common and is widespread among many tribes. Eye contact while talking is seen as rude, assaultive, or sexually threatening. Children are taught not to stare at anyone. To non-Indians, they appear shifty-eyed or evasive.[14]

When taboos of this nature are common in the local culture, they are usually easily identified by the alert and interested professional. Acquaintance with nonpatient members of the tribe is almost essential. Unless there is some overriding reason for violating it, something that is apparent to everyone, it is essential for a therapist to demonstrate a sincere interest in custom and a willingness to observe it. These are recognized by Indian communities as well as by the patients as signs of a real desire to help rather than to convert, and to relieve rather than to make over the persons exhibiting distress.

ESTABLISHING A THERAPEUTIC RELATIONSHIP

The preliminaries of establishing a relationship often include an entry period. During this interval, the family and child are likely to be cautious, apparently passive, and withholding of emotional or social interaction. It is as important not to diagnose this behavior quickly as schizophrenic withdrawal, as it is not to miss the deep depression, or even the psychotic stress that it may mask. In reflecting on the extremes of passivity he observed while visiting the Sioux in the 1920s and

1930s, Erik Erikson now feels that this outward passivity was probably the only socially tolerable defense available during these periods of extreme cross-cultural stress.[12, 13]

CROSS-CULTURAL STRESS

Even in today's society which is more open to pluralism, many sources of cross-cultural stress persist. There are numerous complementary behaviors valued and reinforced, often unconsciously, in a typical school setting and within a model Indian home. In considering these, it is relatively easy to see the origins of this stress.

Age-specific Reactions

THE YOUNG CHILD

A careful scanning of the columns of table 21–1 shows that where young children are involved, there is less clash between cultures over differences in orientation. For instance, animal characters abound in all children's literature, so that treating animals as people is a fairly common preschool and elementary school characteristic. Most elementary school teachers expect to try to socialize children into less selfish behaviors than they exhibit at home. As a result, their talk of sharing, like their talk of being responsible for self, seems to reinforce the home standards.

This partial congruence probably accounts for the relatively easy entrance of most Indian children into preschool and elementary school life. Referrals to the child psychiatrist from this age group resemble those of mainstream youngsters. For the most part, these are cases of mental retardation, genetic defects, and problems stemming from serious illness, injury, or deprivation.

With the advent of the civil rights movement, considerable discussion and excitement directed the attention of test constructors and assessment-oriented psychologists to the problems of cross-cultural testing. The evidence now seems to be clear that the distribtuion of abilities, including intelligence, is the same in Indian and non-Indian populations. What is important in identifying the abilities (and deficits) of the American Indian child is that the content and context of the assessment be congruent with the life experiences and cultural orientation of the child under study. The

TABLE 21–1

Contrasting Values and Attitudes

Indian Home	White School and Home
Tribal loyalty	School, town, team loyalties
Respect for elders	Premium on youth and young adulthood
Reticence	Openness, verbosity
Humility	Competitiveness
Giving and sharing	Thriftiness, property acquisitiveness
Economy based on group sharing with extended family and wide range of relatives	Economy based on individual self-support
Roots permit exploration without breaking ties to people and places	New frontiers have high value while old ties may be felt as shackles
Attribution of human characteristics to animals and nature	Scientific objectivity
Strong spiritual beliefs; pantheism-monotheism, including unity of whole world	Rationalistic attitudes, particularistic personal beliefs, usually monotheistic
Individual responsible to group	Individual responsible for self
Group decisions by consensus; internal conflict resolved or action not taken	Group decisions by majority, internal conflict continues and may provide new decision
Appeals to tradition as final authority supported by spiritual beliefs	Appeals to power as final authority, supported by pragmatism, efficiency, and sometimes abstract ideals
Inborn characteristics unchangeable, growth in unfolding if innate trends	Malleability and changeability of human beings, especially children as they grow
Parents and elders provide opportunities for learning, discovery of capacities	Parents, teachers, peers shape outcome

best examples of this type of test adaptation are probably to be found in the growing literature influenced by Piaget.[24, 8]

THE ELEMENTARY SCHOOL AND THE INDIAN PUPIL

Most of the formal contact between child psychiatrists and Indian youth in separate groups may be via the contracts for consultation with the BIA and IHS. At the same time, nearly every clinic or mental health center will be utilizing child psychiatrists in consultation with urban elementary schools as well.

Some reporting and advice-giving literature is available for teachers, counselors, and special consultants in locations with an expectable high proportion of Indian children.[25] However, in most instances, the majority of American Indian children are invisible participants in the public school classrooms.

They remain invisible until either their low achievement or the expression of their social adjustment problems in the form of dramatic acting-out thrusts them into the limelight. These are two common negative stereotypes of Indian children; together they form quite a contrast. On the one hand, the children are seen as shy, uncommunicative, noncompetitive slow learners, who are inattentive, untrustworthy, and unpunctual. Those that do not fit this pattern are often described as rude, aggressive, destructive; moreover, they are said to be incorrigible thieves. Frequently these children are assigned to classes for brain-damaged children, either because of apparent hyperactivity or erratic learning patterns.

ASSESSMENT OF THE STATUS OF A CHILD IN FOSTER CARE

There is one task that child psychiatrists may be called upon to perform for American Indian and Alaska native children of preschool and primary school age which calls for a particularly careful examination. This involves the evaluation of children in custody cases. It had formerly been assumed that, if a child were removed from home and educated in the all-white atmosphere of a boarding school, the pagan and unwholesome impact of being Indian would be eliminated. Similar energy had been directed toward placing Indian children in non-Indian foster and adoptive homes. In the past ten years, the Indian tribal organizations have made formal protests over this with increasing intensity.[11, 10] It is now commonplace

to receive requests from families for concrete support because they wish to retain their children or to have them returned.

With all the good intentions in the world, however, to decide what is best for the child, or even to go "beyond the best interest of the child" and to attempt to determine what will do the least harm, is not easy. A large percentage of such children who are made frankly aware of their Indian heritage are apparently happily placed in infancy or young childhood. Nonetheless, at adolescence, they have serious difficulty establishing identity. Every Indian community has tales to tell of such adolescents and young adults who come searching for relatives, seeking affinity. A double rejection comes about. Their perceptions are of necessity filtered through fantasies and stereotypes developed in a non-Indian world, and they have had none of the cultural and socializing experience that permits them to fit into the Indian community. The results are traumatic, both to the community and to the individual youth.[22]

Where proposals for foster care and adoptive placement arise in cross-cultural situations, issues are present that may not occur in conventional settings. This is especially true where the family structure varies considerably from middle-class white norms. Hence, the child psychiatrist who is called upon as expert witness needs to take greater than usual care to examine the available options. It is possible that continued support to the child and the foster family as well as to tribal members may make possible many more healthy resolutions of such cases than would appear likely according to the present statistics.

There are no pat solutions for these cases. When he is asked to evaluate and to testify about whether a child should be returned, placed with his tribal family, or remain in a state-approved non-Indian home, the child psychiatrist may well find himself in considerable sympathy with Solomon's plight. Perhaps the wisest course is a conservative one— and an acknowledgment of the limitations of any discipline in answering all the questions that can be raised. Along with this however, an openness to new, potentially preventive arrangements, and a willingness to see cases beyond the point of court decision are also in order.

ADOLESCENT PROBLEMS

As the child emerges from latency into the identity crises of adolescence, the clash in attitude and orientation becomes extremely stressful. Where previous historical attempts at forced assimilation and acculturation have been partially successful, they have also increased the dissonance between ideal self-image and actual self-perception. In general this broad theme probably accounts for the sudden boiling over of adolescent problems so widely reported in the literature. Truancy, delinquency, drug, and alcohol abuse, suicide attempts, and early teenage child bearing are among the most common problems.

There is some evidence that in some tribes, traditional expectations for machismo and risk taking exacerbate the behavioral disturbances of this kind of adolescent and young adult.

Interestingly enough in the 1970s, the number of girls referred for these antisocial acting-out behaviors seems to equal or exceed the number of boys.[9, 4] This stands in marked contrast to the epidemiologic evidence from other populations.

THE LONG-RANGE IMPACT OF THESE PROBLEMS

The long-range impact of the high percentage of adolescent disturbances can make for a gloomy prognosis. This casts a shadow on the future stability of this small but significant minority population. The usual experience parallels that in other groups. A large proportion of those adolescents who survive the life-threatening consequences of their behavior become unstable adults with poor parenting potential. It is probable that they will later be prone to child neglect and abuse. This creates a self-perpetuating cycle of more children in distress than can possibly receive adequate treatment and preventive help.

Coping Behaviors

Not all Indian youths disintegrate under this stress, however. An increasing number are completing school, entering college, or going into the skilled trades or professions. These survivors, who cope successfully with these cross-cultural stresses and strains, have developed a wide range of coping behaviors.

FANTASIES

Some of these include fantasies not unlike those of children in more conventional cultures. The myths, legends, and moral tales of the Indian tradition fulfill the same functions as the fairy tales and fables familiar to children of Anglo-European background.

Instead of Peer Gynt or Robin Hood, the Indian child knows Coyote or Raven. Instead of King Arthur, Charlemagne, and Roland, they may use Spider Woman or Degadawimda and Hiawatha. Instead of Jonathan and David there are the Twins. In place of a boogeyman there is the Hoo Hoo, the Congan, the Whipperman, or Sasquach. Instead of St. Nicholas there may be kachinas.

There are more sophisticated projections also. There is a double-headed creature whom it is dangerous to see. However, to get to know one with proper preparation gives great strength. This may be interpreted as the prototype of man's dual nature. It is also a metaphor for the struggle to blend two very different cultures. The reality of witches, sorcery, and of shamanistic healing are also omnipresent.

To point out the fantasies as kindred of those more familiar to the non-Indian therapist does not mean that they are one to one isometric projections. Louise Jilek-Aall has provided an insightful discussion of her work with women and girls of the Northwest coastal tribes.[16, 17] In the course of this, she has given a number of case examples of the clues to the conflicts experienced by her patients which derive from references to their tribal mythology and traditions. Her presentations call clearly for therapists working with Indian families to take the time to familiarize themselves with that tribe's culture and its own expressions of values, meanings, and means for the resolutions of conflict within and between persons. To know that such a body of shared fantasy exists is a first step. To learn, however partially, the characteristics of what has been transmitted to the children is an obligation for any child psychiatrist engaged in a cross-cultural practice.

MAINSTREAM FANTASIES

At the same time that he discovers these traditional forms of fantasy and is alert to their expression, the therapist must also remember that today's Indian children are in contact with television, comic books, radio, and movies. They are not unaware of Disneyland, cowboy and Indian motifs, rock lyrics, or Batman. All these are also part of the repertory of fantasy and metaphor for the children and adolescents of any cultural background. It may be confusing to have an Indian child in play therapy utilize the stockade and the cavalry as superego elements to control the id impulses represented by savage Indians. This may not be as confusing to the patient. After all, Indian men have always been warriors and are as overrepresented in the ranks of United States veterans as they are in United States prisons. In point of fact, many of the real-life fabled screen cowboys were and are Indians—whether it be Tom Mix and Hoot Gibson or the rodeo stars of today. The challenge for the therapist as well as the Indian child is to resolve these fantasies in an integrated and constructive fashion.

Social Structures Needed

The richness of available fantasy material, and its closeness to the surface, give the empathetic and insightful therapist an opportunity to function with few barriers and fulfill the roles of observer, interpreter, guide, and friendly adult. Nonverbal communication is a mode of the culutre, as is metaphoric discussion. To turn a pencil into a story-telling stick[22] is congruent with the child psychiatrist's role. To consider the medicine man a colleague may be a new but fruitful concept. To take on the responsibility of social engineer and redesign society so as to make it more comfortable and more adequate for these children is, however, beyond what can normally be expected of therapists. Perhaps the only solid contribution that can be made in that direction is to be adequate in helping those Indian youngsters that do come to the clinic. Then *they* may be able to collaborate with the other minorities and with the majority to solve this problem.

REFERENCES

1. ATTNEAVE, C. L., Coordinator of Community Guidance Services, Shawnee, Oklahoma 1960–1968, Presently at the Psychology Department, University of Washington, Personal observation.

2. ———, and BEISER, M., *Service Networks and Patterns of Utilization. Mental Health Programs, Indian Health Service*, Partial fulfillment of IHS Contract No. IHS HSM 110–73–342, 1975.

3. BEISER, M., "Editorial: A Hazard to Mental Health: Indian Boarding Schools," *American Journal of Psychiatry 131*:305–306, 1974.

4. ———, and ATTNEAVE, C. L., Unpublished report of in-progress work on staff patterns of services performed, by Indian Health Service Mental Health and Social Services staff based on case data for 1974.

5. BERGMAN, R., Chief of Indian Health Service Mental Health Programs 1968–1975, Presently at the Department of Psychiatry, University of Washington, Personal communication.

6. ———, and GOLDSTEIN, G. S., "The Model Dorm: Changing Indian Boarding Schools," Paper prepared for the A.P.A. 126th Annual Meeting, Honolulu, Hawaii, May 7–11, 1973.

7. BLOOM, J., "Psychiatric Problems and Cultural Transition," *Arctic 25*, 1972.

8. BULLIS, D., "Cognitive Development of American Indian Children, A Study of Thinking in Physical and Social Realms," Ph.D. dissertation, Harvard University, 1976.

9. ———, "Mental Health Services with Specific References to Indian Children and Adolescents in the State of Maine: 1971–1973." Harvard University, 1973.

10. Center for Social Research and Development, *Indian Child Welfare: A State-of-the-Field Study*, Denver, Center for Social Research and Development, Study supported by U.S. Department of Health, Education, and Welfare, Grant no. HEW–100–75–0177, 1976.

11. Center for Social Research and Development, *Legal and Jurisdictional Problems in the Delivery of SRS Child Welfare Services on Indian Reservations*, Denver, Center for Social Research and Development, Study supported by U.S. Department of Health, Education, and Welfare, Social and Rehabilitation Service, Grant No. 08–P–57784/8–01, 1975.

12. ERICKSON, E. H., *Childhood and Society*, Norton, New York, 1950.

13. ———, Address to the Annual Training Meeting of Indian Health Service Mental Health and Social Service Staffs, Albuquerque, New Mexico, 1974.

14. GOLDSTEIN, G. S., "Behavior Modification: Some Cultural Factors," *Psychological Record, 24*:89–91, 1974.

15. ———, "The Model Dormitory," *Psychiatric Annals*: 85–92, 1974.

16. JILEK-AALL, L., "Identification of Specific Psychosocial Stresses in British Columbia Indian Patients," Paper presented at the Second Transcultural Workshop on Native Peoples Mental Health, under the auspices of the Canadian Psychiatric Association, Manitou College, Quebec, September 1976.

17. ———, "Psychosocial Aspects of Drinking Among Coast Salish Indians," *Canadian Psychiatric Association Journal 19*:357–361, 1974.

18. KRUSH, T. P., et al., "Some Thoughts on the Formation of Personality Disorder: Study of an Indian Boarding School Population," *American Journal of Psychiatry 122*: 868–876, 1966.

19. ———, and BJORK, J. W., "Mental Health Factors in an Indian Boarding School," *Mental Hygiene, 49*:94–103, 1965.

20. RICHARDS, W., Unpublished paper, 1974.

21. ———, Chief of Indian Health Service Mental Health Programs, and Mendhlsohn, Barry, Personal communication.

22. SHORE, J. H., "Whose Property Is the Child Now?" Keynote address at the Annual Meeting of the Morrison Center, October 21, 1976.

23. U.S. Congress, Senate, Committee on Interior and Insular Affairs, Subcommittee on Indian Affairs, "Problems the American Indian Families Face in Raising Their Children and How These Problems Are Affected by Federal Action or Inaction," 93rd Congress, 2d Sess., 1974.

24. VOYAT, G., "A Study of Cognitive Development on the Pine Ridge Reservation," Study supported by the U.S. Department of Health, Education, and Welfare, Public Health Service under contract no. HSM80–69–430, 1969.

25. YOUNGMAN, G., and SADONGEI, M., "Counseling the American Indian Child," *Elementary School Guidance and Counseling, 8*:273–277, 1974.

The child psychiatrist wishing more information on the American Indian child will also find discussion of the issues in the report to the Joint Commission on the Mental Health of Children.

ABLON, J., ROSENTHAL, A. H., and MILLER, D. H., "An Overview of the Mental Health Problems of Indian Children," Report prepared for Social Psychiatry Research

Associates under contract to Joint Commission on Mental Health for Children.

Interested professionals may wish to consult the American Indian Mental Health Bibliography Project, mail stop GN–05, University of Washington, Seattle, WA 98195, for specific references on specific topics or tribal backgrounds.

22 / The Black Child

Jeanne Spurlock and Leonard E. Lawrence

The title, "The Black Child," suggests that black Americans form a homogeneous grouping and/or that their children are wholly different from other children. This is scarcely true, although their history is certainly unique and different from that of other American children. Taken in aggregate, there are similarities and differences among black children as there are similarities and differences between them and the young of other racial groups. One must ask: What makes for differences and for similarities? Evidently, environmental factors are of pronounced importance, nor are intrapsychic factors to be underestimated. An obvious difference, and one of major proportions, however, is the factor of racial identity. This is related to the attitude of society at large, to the responses of the surrounding community, to the views of the parents and immediate family, as well as to the feelings of the individual child himself.

The Black American Child

Born into Slavery

The African parents of the first American children born into slavery came from a group of distinctive cultures with many positive features. Until recently, the positive influences of the African background and culture had been addressed in only a limited fashion. Herskovits[13] has dispelled a number of myths about the savagery of the African culture and other misconceptions that had been untilized in order to characterize blacks in negative terms.

Examining the culture of West Africa, Senegal, and the Congo it has been shown how they manifest a degree of complexity that on this ground alone places them high in the ranks of the nonliterate, nonmachine societies over the world, and makes them comparable in many respects to Europe of the Middle Ages. Some of the traits of those West African civilizations are: well-organized, intricate economic systems, which in many areas include the use of money to facilitate exchange; political systems which, though founded on the local group, were adequate to administer widespread kingdoms; a complex social organization, regularized through devices such as the sanction of the ancestral cult in its kinship aspects, and including societies of all kinds, secret and nonsecret, performing functions of insurance, police, and other character; involved systems of religious belief and practice, which comprise philosophically conceived world views and sustained cult rituals; and a high development of the arts, whether in folk literature, the graphic and plastic forms, or music and the dance. (pp. 296–297)

More recently, Haley[12] has added many new dimensions to the understanding and interpretation of African culture. The forced transportation of masses of black Africans to the American shore resulted in an abrupt disruption of an existing cultural equilibrium. It is evident that, thereafter, this traumatic event would weigh heavily upon the developmental experience of black children.

A cursory look at the history of slavery in the United States clearly presents black children as devoid of a childhood. They often experienced only an abortive relationship with their biological parents, and were frequently deprived of knowledge of their fathers.

In his autobiography, Frederick Douglass[9] provided vivid but painful illustrations of this experience.

The reader must not expect me to say much of my family. Genealogical trees did not flourish among slaves. A person of some consequence in civilized society, sometimes designated as father, was literally unknown to slave law and to slave practice . . . My own recollections of my own mother are of a few hasty visits made in the night on foot, after the daily tasks were over, and when she was under the necessity of returning in time to respond to the driver's call to the field in the early morning. Of my father I know nothing. Slavery had no recognition of fathers, as none of families . . .

Living thus with my grandmother, whose kindness and love stood in place of my mother's, it was some time before I knew myself to be a slave . . . that my grandmother herself and all the little children around her belonged to a mysterious personage . . . "Old Master." Thus early did clouds and shadows begin to fall upon my path . . .

I learned that this old master, whose name seemed ever to be mentioned with fear and shuddering, only allowed the little children to live with grandmother for a limited time, and that as soon as they were big enough they were promptly taken away to live with the said old master. (pp. 28–29)

Douglass writes that he was probably seven years of age when he was taken to the plantation home of "old master," some twelve miles from his grandmother's dwelling, to begin his existence formally as a slave.

Comer and Pouissant[5] describe the deprivations of childhood under the system of slavery. Children "were put to work at very early ages picking cotton in the fields. As house slaves, they cared for members of the mistress' family, including the children . . ." Often a black child was assigned as a servant and companion to the child of the master of the plantation, and he would be used by the white children "to test objects of curiosity or go first into strange places. Slave children attended to every minor need of the white children." Such were the black child's early experiences of slavery; experiences that instructed him, directly and indirectly, of his inferior status.

Some Psychological Sequelae of the Slavery Experience

Pinderhughes[24] writes that "severe alterations in the personalities, family and group structure, and culture of black people were made forcibly by whites in the slave and segregation systems." On the basis of long-term psychoanalytic studies of intrapsychic phenomena in some black patients, Hunter and Babcock[16] reported findings that the culture of the dominant white population continues to have a profound influence on the intrapsychic structure of black Americans. They view

derivates of the slave system, the residual "slave psychology," as impediments to normal development and maturation. These include experiences of separation anxiety and parental loss which mar the establishment of basic trust. Such stresses serve to seed the development of depressive disorders and poor interpersonal relationships. They must be considered as important factors in understanding the personality development of the black child of today.

However, historical accounts of scores of black Americans who were exposed to the slave system and its derivates suggest that there were many who hurdled the culturally determined barriers successfully, and who achieved healthy maturity, even though at considerable cost. Billingsley[1] illustrates this in his account of several generations of the Martin Luther King family. He identifies varied sources of stability and achievement, reflections of the "resiliency of the human spirit, and the survival and adaptative capacities of Negro family life in America." Billingsley also refers to the support systems outside the immediate family—the school and church, along with the role models provided by the teacher or minister. These are assets that have contributed to the development of black children throughout American history. The values of these support systems are also addressed by Davis and Coleman[8]:

The extended family, with its loyalties and mutual obligations, particularly to care for any children in the family it can take in, provides a net through which such children are not allowed to fall into a mire of neglect. The awareness of such safeguards must be communicated very early to the child through observation of the passing around and embracing of siblings, cousins, nephews and nieces in the family. (p. 6)

It is a historical fact that plantation masters, overseers, and their male kin were the fathers of many slave children; this was evident in the vast physical differences among these youngsters. The resultant life experiences and their psychological repercussions have been varied. Haley[12] writes of the shame and anger experienced by the grandson of the African Kunte Kinte, as well as his longing to establish a father–son relationship with his father, who was also his master. The child was flooded with confusion, and continued to be troubled about this until he was a young adult. On the other hand, Haley describes a young black woman as seeming "to harbor no distress whatever about her color . . . [She] volunteered to George that her pappy was the white overseer on a big

South Carolina rice and indigo plantation . . . where she had been born and reared . . ." (p. 403). During the period of slavery, some mulatto children were freed and sent to the North. Obviously, this "benefit" was not devoid of separation anxiety and the experience of parental loss. The advantages and disadvantages of white physical characteristics have not been constant; they appear to reflect, in part, attitudinal changes in the broader community. Malcolm X, of fairer complexion than his siblings, discussed this in his autobiography.[21]

My father was also belligerent toward all of the children, except me. The older ones he would beat almost savagely if they broke any of his rules—and he had so many rules it was hard to know them all. Nearly all my whippings came from my mother. I've thought a lot about why. I actually believe that as anti-white as my father was, he was subconsciously so afflicted with the white man's brainwashing of Negroes that he inclined to favor the light ones, and I was his lightest child. Most Negro parents in those days would almost instinctively treat any lighter children better than they did the darker ones. It came directly from the slavery tradition that the "mulatto," because he was visibly nearer to white, was therefore "better." (p. 4)

In a study of black children in the rural South, Johnson[17] determined that

social values associated with color have extremely serious consequences . . . It often happens that darker children in families feel that their parents give preference to the children of lighter complexion. Even such

inadvertent and casual comparisons as "better hair," "nicer complexion," "prettier skin," "nicer shade" affect the more sensitive young people and contribute to their feelings of inferiority . . . By far the most frequent instances of color sensitivity, however, occur outside the home as the child attempts to make adjustment to new groups. (p. 267)

Similar incidents have been experienced by myriads of black children in other geographical sections throughout the country. However, during the 1960s the label of inferiority was ripped from the characteristic of blackness and replaced with the concept that "black is beautiful." An adolescent patient (treated by one of the authors) viewed her light skin as a liability. She resented being mistaken as white by her black classmates, and was bitter about the exclusions that resulted. Acceptance based on skin color, or hair texture, has sharply diminished since the sixties.

Family Patterns

As previously implied, black American families stem from various backgrounds. They share a wide range of characteristics and are found throughout the socioeconomic lattice. However, as will be elaborated, the majority are concentrated within

TABLE 22–1

Family Structure of the Black Americans

Types of Family	Household Head		Other Household Members		
	Husband & Wife	Single Parent	Children	Other Relatives	Non-Relatives
Nuclear Families					
1. Incipient Nuclear	X				
2. Simple Nuclear	X		X		
3. Attenuated Nuclear		X	X		
Extended Families					
4. Incipient Extended	X			X	
5. Simple Extended	X		X	X	
6. Attenuated Extended		X	X	X	
Augmented Families					
7. Incipient Augmented	X				X
8. Incipient Extended Augmented	X			X	X
9. Nuclear Augmented	X		X		X
10. Nuclear Extended Augmented	X		X	X	X
11. Attenuated Augmented		X	X		X
12. Attenuated Extended Augmented		X	X	X	X

NOTE: Reprinted with permission of the publisher from A. Billingsley, *Black Families in White America*, p. 17, Prentice-Hall, Englewood Cliffs, N.J., 1968.

the lower ranges of the socioeconomic structure. Some black families are intact and stable; some are unstable but nevertheless intact; and others live at a level of near total disruption. Some single-parent households, often aided by members of the extended family, do provide an atmosphere of stability; in others, the instability is beyond repair. In the experience of the authors, many black families are not unlike other American families; similar values and aspirations can be identified in their life style and outlook.

The contemporary black American family, as described by Billingsley[1] may be nuclear, extended or augmented. The several types of families identified in each general group are depicted in table 22–1. Billingsley presents data that refute the widely held concept that the structure of the family determines the functioning of its members. Two-parent families are not necessarily stable, nor are single-parent families necessarily disorganized and unstable.

The Impact of Poverty

The economic class structure into which the black child is born also accounts for a difference observed in children, both black and white, who are financially better off. Hill et al.[14] note that three-fifths of black children are born to poor families, both to single- and to two-parent family units. With its characteristic features of inadequate housing, nutrition, and medical care, poverty has a pronounced effect on child development. Limited and/or poor pre- and postnatal care and undernourishment take their toll, resulting in defective physical and psychological development. Pasamanick and Knoblock[20] address this in presentations of the concept of the continuum of reproductive casualty.

Davis[7] cites poverty as a sizable factor that decreases the effectiveness of many black mothers in providing the necessary ingredients for healthy mothering. The impact of poverty is equally damaging to the support figures, namely the father and members of the extended family.

Number and Distribution

Table 22–2, an excerpt from a U.S. Bureau of Census report, reflects the sizable decrease in the birth rate of black children, and the sharp increase in the adolescent population during the 1970–1976 period. These figures parallel the changes that have taken place in the population as a whole, i.e., a decline in the birth rate. However, it should be noted that the previous birth rate in the black population had been proportionately higher than in the white population. This accounts for the fact that in the 1970–1976 period, there was a higher percentage (8.8 percent) of black adolescents as compared to their white peers.

Distribution is reflected in the following random sample of demographic data, selected from a study of Cannon and Locke.[3]

In 1970 58% of the black American population as opposed to 28% of the white population lived in the Central city . . . most of this black urban growth was in the inner city . . . a special Census Bureau report released in 1973 states that married white men between 25 and 54 years of age living in large metropolitan areas earned an average annual salary of $10,853 compared to $6,040 for black men of the same age and marital status living in identical areas. . . . in 1974, 31% of black persons as compared to 9% of white persons were living in poverty . . . 35% of all black families had a female head as compared to 11% of white families.

TABLE 22–2

(Numbers in thousands)

Age	Population		Percent distribution		Population Change	
	July 1976	April 1970	July 1976	April 1970	1970 to 1976	% 1970–76
Under 5	2,317	2,434	9.3	10.7	−117	−4.8
5–13	4,801	5,009	19.3	22.1	−208	−4.1
14–17	2,360	2,073	9.5	9.1	+287	+13.8

SOURCE: U.S. Bureau of the Census, 1977.

Impact of Blackness at
Different Levels of Development

When black parents are economically insecure, the child in utero may be particularly likely to encounter potential hazards. The end result is a child born "at risk." The high incidence of hypertension and toxemia in pregnant black women puts in jeopardy the lives of both mother and infant. The extreme youthfulness of a great many black mothers, their malnutrition, and their inadequate prenatal care often result in premature births and babies of low birth weight. Sickle cell disease is known to be the major genetic disorder in blacks; it is a life-threatening condition and is to be differentiated from sickle cell trait. In many black communities, even the newborn is a victim of the widespread presence of substance abuse. Withdrawal symptoms are frequently observed in the infant born to a mother addicted to hard drugs or barbiturates.

In another communication, Spurlock[29] referred to the influence of the parents' cultural experiences on the development of their child. Attention was called to Davis's observation[7] that there is a decrease in a mother's capacity to provide emotional security for her child if she is hampered by an inability to obtain the necessary physical, economic, and emotional support for herself in the mothering role. Davis noted:

The chances for successful negotiations of infantile stages of personal development are significantly decreased for the child of any family at the lowest end of the socio-economic scale, but there will be a larger proportion of dark-skinned children emerging from infancy with specific vulnerabilities to later damaging experience since their families occupy a disproportionately large segment of the population at that end of the scale.

Much has been written about the roots of these "specific vulnerabilities." Single parenting, multiple mothering, absent fathers, and successive father figures have often been identified as the seeds of pathology. However, as previously cited,[1, 8] the support provided by members of the extended family (both biological and "adoptive") often dilutes the impact of the pathological features of the environment.

The early spoken language of the majority of Afro-American children has often been described as primitive. There is no question that their language differs from that which is described as "standard English" in that there is, for example: (1) a pattern of dropping final consonants; (2) the omission of the verb "is" in the present tense; and (3) the use of the singular noun for plural objects. However, as Houston[15] suggests, this form is not necessarily deficient in that it is not the total of the child's "linguistic performance nor in any way representative of their linguistic competence." She refutes the assumptions that this language does not provide the child with an adequate basis for abstract thinking. According to Houston, the child's lack of abstract terminology has been considered as evidence for such assumptions.

This is probably the most usual basis for the notion that disadvantaged children cannot think properly, since deductions about the thought processes of the children seem to be based primarily or entirely on evidence from language. Unfortunately, this tends to render the conclusions invalid for the following reasons.
. . . the direction of dependence between language and cognition is still undetermined. However, it is no longer considered possible to extrapolate cognitive patterns directly from specific linguistic patterns . . . if a language or form of language is found to lack a unitary term for a certain phenomenon, this does not indicate . . . its speakers are unaware of the phenomenon or that they cannot deal with it when it occurs. (pp. 243–244)

By the time the black child has reached the early oedipal period of development, he has an awareness of racial differences. Prior to the civil rights movement of the 1960s, most of the mental health professional literature that dealt with the matter of a child's awareness of color tended to focus on the negative responses to blackness. Clark[4] wrote of a common fantasy of black children—to pretend they are white. It was his opinion that the self-concept of black children seemed to be directly related to skin color itself. Goodman's[10] study on race awareness in young children revealed different children to have different levels of awareness. She concluded the "color casts a shadow, faint or strong, over the lives of all these children. It gets on the nerves of many. There is trouble brewing, and they have a sense of it." Coles[6] wrote of a six-year-old black girl who had been enrolled in a previously segregated school and who responded to taunts of white peers and parents with anorexia and a repetitive question: "Is it only my skin?"

Spurlock[29] observed socioeconomic issues to be a determining factor in the black child's self-concept. Black children from stable families appeared to feel more comfortable about their color than did those from unstable backgrounds. For many in the latter group, their assertions that "black is beautiful" were observed to be a reaction formation. It has been suggested that the frequent appearance of black people in the media has provided black youngsters with influential models, which have enhanced their self-concept. However, in view of the failures to implement civil rights legislation and the continuing restrictive practices on the part of national and local organizational bodies, the extent and the quality of this influence is under debate. Powell[25] reports significant findings from her study of the self-concept of several groups of junior high school students. She made use of the Tennessee Self-Concept Scale, which was standardized by administration to a broad sample of black and white persons from a wide range of ages and geographical locations. She noted that there were regional as well as ethnic differences which could not be attributed solely to the stability of the family and/or the parents' occupational and educational levels.

The most significant finding was that the black students in the Southern city scored significantly higher on the total positive score, indicating more certainty about the self than the white students in the same city.
In the Northern city, the black students did less well than the white students on the total positive score, but the difference is not statistically significant. The Northern black students also achieved a higher variability score compared with the whites . . . This indicates that the Northern black students have greater inconsistency in their self-picture or that their self-concept is less integrated.
. . . In comparing Southern blacks to Northern blacks, it would seem that, although both groups are subject to racism . . . the capacity for the Southern black students to overcome, as it were, is facilitated by a strong cohesive black community which has some power base in terms not only of numbers but also of achievements.
The low scores of white students . . . would seem to be a general reflection of the alienation which white youth are experiencing . . . (p. 314)

Spurlock[28] has noted that for many black children, especially those at the lowest rung of the socioeconomic ladder, the approach to adolescence is accompanied by feelings of intense alienation from society. In part this arises from their poor educational experiences, which have prompted them to drop out of school. (In many instances, the educational system has been viewed as pushing them out.) They have observed their parents' futile attempts to combat many problematic situations generated both by poverty and racism; presently this acts to further the alienation these adolescents experience. For the black teenager, "the streets" are frequently the only source of any of life's good things. These youngsters readily assimilate the patterns of interaction that they see about them within the environment. Whether it be through alcohol or drug abuse, through the kind of sexual activity which so often results in teenage pregnancy, or perhaps through overt criminal behavior, the black teenagers are generally in search of some sense of well-being. Unfortunately, this is not usually recognized. The adolescent is labelled as delinquent and is then more likely to be added to the rolls of a correctional system than to those of a mental health facility.

Thus, the all-too-common outcome is entanglement in a life of antisocial behavior. For these adolescents, it would seem that this antiauthoritarian rejection of society, combined with the aggressive antisocial activity, serves to maintain some measure of insulation around their vulnerable self-esteem. This process has been vividly described by Malcolm X[21] and by Claude Brown[2] in their respective autobiographies.

For other black children, the period of adolescence is less stormy. They may continue to cope with the burdens of racism by excessive use of denial and/or continuous expenditure of energy; some find ways and means to remain invisible. Others are known to direct their energies toward developing some talent, or excelling in an area of learned skill and competence. For scores of black youth, their coping efforts have yielded extraordinary achievements. Clark[4] has noted that their academic achievement often reflects compensatory behavior related to racism. However, the importance of the attitudes and expectations of teachers should not be underestimated. This is evident in the Rosenthal and Jacobson[27] study. These investigators determined that the teacher's attitudes and expectations have a pronounced influence on the child's learning. When teachers expected children to do poorly, even when their abilities were documented (but incorrectly stated to the teachers), the children did indeed underachieve. Thus a self-fulfilling prophecy was observed.

Familial Reaction

As discussed under "Family Patterns," black American families are as varied as those in the population generally. By the same token, their reactions to their racial identity and to the pressures related to racist practices are fully as varied. For many, the reaction to suppression provokes a tendency to identify with the aggressor. The sequelae of racism are multiple and are reflected in unemployment, underemployment, poor housing, limited health, and inadequate social services. For most black people, the price of survival is high. It is seen in the high incidence of somatic disorders, depression and other psychiatric illnesses, child and wife abuse, and homicide. For many who live in poverty, their orientation is to the here and now, and the passive-dependent stance is paramount.

For others, however, the aggression takes the form of goal-directed assertiveness; their goal is upward mobility. There is often extensive assistance provided by members of the extended family (not always biological kin) and other support persons in the community. The effects of upward mobility on child-rearing practices are not without consequences that may lead to impaired functioning. For example, the practices of strictness and vigorous push for conformity (often to standards and models that are not an integral part of the immediate community) may lead to the child's compliance out of fear. However, the accompanying underlying resentment often results in passive-aggressive behavior that thwarts the child's overall progress.

Obviously the middle- and upper-class families are subject to less suppression, and their economic stability lends to and reinforces security. In some families, the elders can successfully deny the phenomenon of racism; in others, the elders have been active participants in civil rights struggles over the years. The children growing up in these families can be dependent for a longer period of time; they can pursue college and postgraduate education relatively free of the concerns that daily confront the offspring of families in the lower economic group. Under stress, however, the children from these more fortunate families, too, may suddenly become overwhelmed by their own guilt at being better off than so many of their peers and/or by anger stemming from their awareness of widespread oppression of black people.

Cultural Reactions

The reactions of the broader culture have also been varied. The negative reactions continued after the end of formal slavery and ranged from overt brutality to gross indifference. In another form, the forced separation of families was maintained by the welfare system. It is only very recently that an unemployed father could legitimately remain at home without depriving his wife and children of welfare assistance. The attitudes that led to the passing of Jim Crow laws in the South during the period of Reconstruction appear not unlike those that have prompted the designing of restrictive covenants in housing in the North. Redlining by mortgage companies and the gerrymandering of school districts and voting precincts are other examples.

On the other hand, there have been the reactions of the abolitionists who actively "battled" for the emancipation of the slaves, and a multitude of members of the majority group who have continued to work in the arenas of civil rights struggles throughout post-Civil War history. However, there have been many swings in the responses of the majority group; by and large most of the population has continued to resist equal opportunities for black people. This has been reflected in the difficulties of civil rights legislation and the vigorous activities directed toward repealing these laws. It is visible as well in some of the reactions against active endeavors to achieve school integration.

Characteristic Forms of Emotional Disturbance

THE EXPRESSION OF THE DISTURBANCE AT DIFFERENT MOMENTS OF DEVELOPMENT

Davis and Coleman[8] discussed the difficulties of ego development in ghetto living.

. . . We expect and often find a mottled ego, with patches of constriction and defect, but we also expect and often find the emergence of resilient strengths which serve to establish effective areas of autonomous function in relation to vital task requirements. We have a tendency to overgeneralize our concept of ego development to conform to our middle class standards and ideologies. In ghetto families, there are often special problems in ego development, such as that of establishing an ego ideal, internalizing an apparently hostile outer world, and securing a firm base of trusted object relations. (p. 1)

A number of studies have shown that many black children born into poverty have experienced retarded development. It has been alleged that the understimulation that these children receive is related to characteristics of the black family or features that accompany poverty. This is currently under active debate. Rainwater,[26] Ladner,[19] and Meers,[22] among others, have called attention to the experiences of overstimulation and the negative sequelae. Overstimulation stems from multiple sources, ranging from overcrowding and noise pollution to scenes of violence. Meers[22] writes of the "apparent resilience" of ghetto children, their ability to adapt "without readily observable, external evidence of neurotic symptomatology" (p. 210). He posits "intellectual and academic retardation as a possible 'symptom choice.'" The authors, too, have observed that many children are misdiagnosed as primarily mentally retarded; some diagnosticians have missed or failed to consider the depressive features in which the intellectual slowness is rooted. The bulk of referrals of the school-age child to psychiatric facilities are for learning difficulties and behavioral disorders. A history of poor prenatal care along with undernourishment and poor or limited medical care for the child have often been viewed as begetters of minimal brain dysfunction. Pica, too, is said to be common in this population. However, it is most unlikely that these problems are related to racial identity per se.

Psychiatric referrals of preadolescents are most often for help with behavioral problems. These range from aggressive defiance at home, and/or disruptive, destructive, aggressive behavior, to overt acts of delinquency. The formal diagnosis attached to such children has usually been phrased as Adjustment Reaction, or some version of Personality Disorder. Unfortunately, many of these children are given diagnostic labels without the benefit of a complete diagnostic evaluation. The clinician must constantly be aware that, in these children, many of these overt behaviors actually reflect significant levels of depression. A careful history will frequently elicit psychosomatic symptomatology as well as an account of more neurotic components. The fact that this syndrome of depression in black children is so frequently overlooked is perhaps the most distressing aspect of the problem. Without intervention, feelings of hopelessness and helplessness, to some degree secondary to intrapsychic factors, may portend much greater future difficulties for such a child.

Proportionately, more black adolescent males are adjudicated delinquent than are their white peers. Does this indeed indicate some cultural and/or familial predisposition toward antisocial or criminal behavior? Or do these delinquent behaviors quite frequently represent the only way in which these young people may legitimately call attention to their inner psychic pain? And do these behaviors truly represent the adolescent's cry for help? Certainly, for the white middle-class population, when adolescent delinquent behavior has occurred the first stop is likely to be the psychiatrist's office. It is much more difficult for the black adolescent to find his way into this site of intervention.

Long-range Effects

Unless vigorous efforts are directed to therapeutic interventions and to programs which focus on prevention, the long-range effects point to continuation of similar mental health problems in the next generation. The correctional system is known to rehabilitate relatively few; the pattern of shepherding a high percentage of black youth with behavioral disturbances into this system rather than toward mental health service programs destines them for total destruction. Pierce[23] posits that black adolescents will continue to experience a "confusion of cues," related to acceptance by the majority culture. During the next decade, the implication is that mixed messages will continue. This will considerably increase the number of dissatisfied adolescents who will experience a variety of symptoms, stemming from their life situations.

The increase in severe depression, suicidal ideation, and actual suicide in young black women is already of intense concern to their families and clinicians alike. There also appears to be an increase in homosexual tendencies in both men and women. For young women, the unavailability of male relationships has been identified as one of the determinants. As previously indicated, the early entry of black males into the correctional system is an important factor here. Recent cultural shifts must also be considered as possible causative agents. Of no little import is the indicated preference of some black males, who serve as important models of identification, for non-black mates.

Forms of Coping Behavior

Again, it is necessary to address the fact that there are decided differences among black children; differences which are often commonly related to socioeconomic levels. In the lower socio-economic group, many children of deprived families tend to have a restricted fantasy life. When asked about their wishes they will often list material needs; frequently they identify an object that could be of considerable help to their parent(s). However, it should be emphasized that television plays an integral role in the fantasy life of these children and serves to expand this dimension of their lives. Many boys are known to see themselves in fantasy as highly paid athletes or entertainers. Others think about themselves in negative terms, identifying with the demeaning roles played by some highly paid black performers. In the opinion of the authors, the fantasy life of black children from economically secure families is essentially no different from those of their same class structure peers in majority-group families. The fantasies are less related to survival, and are linked instead with ideas of creativity and fulfillment. Most black boys have been exposed to the practice of "playing the dozens."* The authors regard this as a vestige of the pattern of continuing self-deprecation; however, it also has defensive meanings. The characteristic of creativity is usually overlooked by "outside" observers. Grier and Cobbs[11] suggest it is "more than chance that the

* As defined by Grier and Cobbs, "a degrading, humiliating custom of mutual vilification . . . the rhyming of obscenities describing the speaker and, most often, the mother of the victim in some gross sexual act" (p. 3).

introduction of the black boy to manhood is made via insult, and that manhood is proven by an ability to stand by while those he holds dearest are vilified."

Skills and Sublimations

The skills these youngsters acquire are varied, and cover a fairly wide range, from natural competencies in the area of intellectual abilities, to achievements in sports, music, and other arts. Over the years, the manual skills (carpentry, masonary, tailoring, etc.), once so prevalent among black Americans, have been disappearing in the face of increasing economic barriers. For the youngsters growing up in poverty, action-oriented skills are probably most typical. Many children in the heart of Harlem or the ghetto of any urban community have used improvised equipment of the streets or littered vacant lots to develop their athletic skills. In terms of rapid and broad recognition and money, musical abilities have yielded more success than talents in the other arts. Clark[4] remarks that, in certain circumstances, racial oppression has served as an added goal to achieve excellence in various intellectual pursuits. In addition to these, humor and church activities have served as effective channels for sublimation.

REFERENCES

1. BILLINGSLEY, A., Black Families in White America, Prentice-Hall, Englewood Cliffs, N.J., 1968.
2. BROWN, C., Man Child in the Promised Land, Signet Books, New York, 1965.
3. CANNON, M. S., and LOCKE, B. Z., "Being Black is Detrimental to One's Mental Health," Presented at the W.E.B. DuBois Conference on the Health of Black Populations, 1976.
4. CLARK, K. B., "The Negro Child and Race Prejudice," in Clark, Kenneth B, Prejudice and Your Child, pp. 37–65, Beacon Press, Boston, 1963.
5. COMER, J. P., and POUSSAINT, A. F., Black Child Care, Simon and Schuster, New York, 1975.
6. COLES, R., Children of Crisis, Little, Brown & Co., Boston, 1967.
7. DAVIS, E. B., "The American Negro: Family Membership to Personal and Social Identity," Journal of the National Medical Association, 60:92–99, 1968.
8. ——, and COLEMAN, J., "Interactions Between Community Psychiatry and Psychoanalysis in the Understanding of Ego Development," Presented at the Annual Meeting of the American Psychoanalytic Association, May 1974.
9. DOUGLASS, F., Life and Times of Frederick Douglass, Collier-Macmillan Ltd., London, 1962.
10. GOODMAN, M. E., Race Awareness in Young Children, Collier Books, New York, 1964.

11. GRIER, W. H., and COBBS, P. M., "Black Survival," in Grier, W. H., and Cobbs, P. M., The Jesus Bag, pp. 1–22, McGraw-Hill, New York, 1971.
12. HALEY, A., Roots, Doubleday, Garden City, New York, 1976.
13. HERSKOVITS, M. J., The Myth of the Negro Past, Beacon Press, Boston, 1958.
14. HILL, R., et al., Black Families in the 1974–75 Depression, Washington, D.C., National Urban League Research, 1975.
15. HOUSTON, S. H., "A Re-examination of Some Assumptions About the Language of the Disadvantaged Child," in Chess, Stella, and Thomas, Alexander (Eds.), Progress in Child Psychiatry and Child Development, pp. 233–250, Brunner-Mazel, New York, 1971.
16. HUNTER, D. C., and BABCOCK, D. G., "Some Aspects of the Intrapsychic Structure of Certain Negroes as Viewed in the Intercultural Dynamic," in Eissler, R. S., et al. (Eds.), The Psychoanalytic Study of the Child, vol. 4, pp. 124–169, International Universities Press, New York, 1967.
17. JOHNSON, C. S., Growing Up in the Black Belt, Schocken Books, New York, 1941.
18. Joint Commission on Mental Health of Children, Digest of Crisis in Child Mental Health, Challenge for the 1970s, 1969.

19. LADNER, J. A. *Tomorrow's Tomorrow: The Black Woman*, Doubleday, New York, 1972.

20. KNOBLOCK, H., and PASAMANICK, B., "Mental Subnormality," *New England Journal of Medicine*, 266: 1092–1097, 1962.

21. MALCOLM X, *The Autobiography of Malcolm X*, Grove Press, New York, 1966.

22. MEERS, D. R., "Contributions of a Ghetto Culture to Symptom Formation," in Eissler, R. S., et al. (Eds.), *The Psychoanalytic Study of the Child*, vol. 25, pp. 209–230, International Universities Press, New York, 1970.

23. PIERCE, C. M., "Problems of the Negro Adolescent in the Next Decade," in Brody, E. (Ed.), *Minority Group Adolescents in the United States*, pp. 17–47, Williams and Wilkins, Baltimore, 1968.

24. PINDERHUGHES, C. A., "Pathogenic Social Structure: A Prime Target for Preventive Psychiatric Intervention,

*Journal of the National Medical Association, 58:*424–435, 1966.

25. POWELL, G. J., "Self-Concept in White and Black Children," Willie, C. V., Kramer, B. M., and Brown, B. S. (Eds.), *Racism and Mental Health*, University of Pittsburgh Press, Pittsburgh, 1973.

26. RAINWATER, L., *Behind Ghetto Walls*, Aldine Publications Co., Chicago, 1970.

27. ROSENTHAL, R., and JACOBSON, L., *Pygmalion in the Classroom*, Holt, Rinehart, and Winston, New York, 1968.

28. SPURLOCK, J., "Problems of Identification in Young Black Children—Static or Changing?" *Journal of the National Medical Association*, 61:504–507, 1969.

29. SPURLOCK, J., "Some Consequences of Racism for Children," in Willie, C. V., Kramer, B. M., and Brown, B. S. (Eds.), *Racism and Mental Health*, pp. 147–181, University of Pittsburgh Press, Pittsburgh, 1973.

23 / The Chicano Child and His Family

Alberto C. Serrano and Fortunato G. Castillo

Introduction

Clinicians emphasize that biological and psychological growth cannot be well understood outside the sociocultural context in which development takes place. This is particularly true when dealing with minority groups. The Mexican-Americans number over five million, almost 80 percent of whom reside in the states of Arizona, California, Colorado, New Mexico, and Texas.[20] They thus reflect a broad range of experiences across the Southwest. The remaining 20 percent are to be found in smaller communities, usually in isolated pockets—notably in Illinois, Michigan, New York, and other states.[21] All in all, they comprise a complex minority that shares with other groups the problems of poverty and the slow struggle to obtain an equitable share of the resources and opportunities available to the "Anglo" majority. Although the Mexican-American, the Puerto Rican, and other Spanish-speaking minorities in the United States share a Hispanic cultural background, there are important differences between them that can be identified.

In Puerto Rico, the indigenous Indians were virtually eradicated by the Spaniards, who replaced them with Negro slaves. In Mexico, Indian populations fared somewhat better; they had achieved a high degree of civilization and were

subjugated by the Spaniards, but not altogether eliminated. Thus the Mexican-American carries with him an ethnic and cultural background which is at once a blend of the Indian and the Spaniard.[14]

More than 350 years ago, Spanish-speaking peoples colonized the Southwest of the United States and exercised the dominant political and military power. Two centuries later, the Anglo-American colonizers entered the region and soon expanded the size of the area under their control. They defined the "differentness" of language, history, culture, religion, and customs of the indigenous inhabitants as a reflection of "inferiority" in cultural, economic, and intellectual terms.[14] The rights of these people became increasingly less important, and a state of poverty, lack of education, and inadequate health care was perpetuated. This persisted with little change for more than a century. The Mexican-American was stereotyped as lazy, fun loving, modest, docile, unable to lead, intellectually slow, primitive in the handling of aggression, and prone to use alcohol and drugs. Many other cliches that reinforced this status of inferiority were accepted as axioms.[14] If a Mexican-American was ambitious and wished to become "Americanized" and accepted by the "dominant" culture, it often became necessary for him to downplay his background. During the 1960s, the Mexican-American youth acquired a new pride in their background and their identity.[13]

The word *Chicano* (from *Mejicano* "Mexican") became a symbol. The term was used initially in a political sense; it was soon to play a role in the generational differences between the older people, who preferred to consider themselves "Mexican-American," as opposed to the younger "Chicanos" who accused their elders of being *tios Tomases* ("Uncle Toms").

Differences in Child-rearing Patterns Between Anglo and Mexican-American Families

THE INFANT—NURTURANCE, TRUST, AND DEPENDENCY

In the Mexican and the Mexican-American household, there is more exclusive handling of the infant by women. Thus the mother, the grandmother, women relatives, friends, and helpers seem to provide more cuddling and kissing of the infant than would be true with Anglo parents.

Feeding is more likely to be on demand, and the frequency of breast feeding is greater among the Mexican-Americans and the Mexicans. Another important factor at this stage is the terms of endearment that are directed to the infant. The Mexican-American mother and father refer to their children as being "pretty and beautiful." While the Anglo-Saxon parents may use terms of endearment, they also stress the "goodness" of the child. Thus the Mexican-American mother would be more likely to show off her nice-looking child, and the Anglo-Saxon mother her good child. The Mexican-American parents would buy pieces of jewelry for their baby girls in their first year, and it is not unusual to see Mexican-American girls with pierced ears from very early on. Another issue which is of paramount importance as it settles patterns for a lifetime in both groups is the fact that the needs of children in terms of cuddling are automatically, in general, acknowledged by the Mexican-American mother. In this respect, in middle-class Mexican families, help is engaged specifically to pick up the child and cuddle and comfort him when he cries. A Mexican mother is less likely to worry about cleanliness as long as the child is contented. In addition to being fed on demand, a Mexican child would be allowed to use pacifiers with much more spontaneity than would happen in an Anglo-Saxon home.

Both breast and bottle feeding are likely to continue longer in the Mexican-American families than in the Anglo-Saxon ones, and weaning occurs more gradually. It is true that the more educated and affluent a Mexican-American family becomes, the more Anglo-Saxon patterns are adopted. Nonetheless, the concept of set dates to do certain things is less prevalent. It is noteworthy that the Anglo parents who belong to counterculture groups are more likely to resort to the less scheduled patterns of infant feeding that is typical of the Mexican-Americans.

Particularly in the lower socioeconomic groups, the Mexican mother feels no embarrassment about breast feeding infants in public. The concept of baby-sitting is very strange to these mothers; either they stay at home when their children are growing up, or, if they do have to go out, they take their children with them, wrapped in their big *rebozos*. This intense involvement of the mother with her young child, her concern about the emotional and physical needs of her infant, and her sense of dedication toward giving him pleasure in feeding together give women extraordinary power in Mexican culture. Indeed, in contrast to Anglo-Saxon Protestantism, in Mexican religious practices the Madonna, the mother of Jesus, is more likely to be the object of worship than either Jesus himself or the "Father."

The imprint of the oral stage on the child's personality lasts the lifetime through. Among other factors, it can be discerned in such adult attitudes as the following:

The Mexican-American is affectionate, and uses terms of endearment very readily as an adult; he talks not only with his voice but readily embraces people he likes and is spontaneous in the exchange of physical affection.

The Mexican-American thinks that the Anglo-Saxon is stuffy and unfriendly. The Anglo-Saxon perceives the Mexican-American as mushy and overfriendly.

The Anglo-Saxon cannot understand why, if the Mexican-American is poor, he "wastes" his money on great amounts of food for friends and relatives. The Mexican-American, on the other hand, cannot understand why if the Anglo-Saxon has money, he only gives his guests what is perceived as too little to eat.

THE TODDLER AND THE FIRST THREE YEARS—AUTONOMY, INDIVIDUATION, AND REGULATION

As the Mexican and the Chicano child enter their second year, it is not unusual for them to be displaced by a new baby. The maternal grandmother often takes over the primary care of the child. This tends to coincide with the beginning of the separation individuation phase. Because the culture emphasizes compliance, loyalty, and dependency, efforts at autonomous behavior are not encouraged. This stands in contrast to the Anglo culture in which individual assertiveness and openness are more frequently reinforced.

In terms of toilet training the differences continue. It is not that important for the Mexican whether a toddler is wet or dry, and toilet-training schedules are not so strictly applied. Indeed, from the point of view of the Mexican-American mother, if the child is content and happy he will gradually toilet train himself. A traditional pattern popular in Mexico was to start "training" the baby soon after six months; this was managed by the mother anticipating his reflexes. Young Chicano mothers often disagree with their own mothers over this question, but may feel inadequate if their child is not successfully trained by eighteen months of age. Typically, the issue will not attain guilt-provoking intensity. From the Anglo-Saxon's point of view, on the other hand, punctuality, a sense of duty, serious effort, and trying hard are all very important.

Unless he is of the aspiring middle-class, the Mexican-American will be more likely to spend his money on a big stereo set with plenty of music and a large refrigerator and stove than in having two or three toilets in his home. On the other hand, in Anglo-Saxon homes the cleanliness of the toilets and their number are signs of prestige.

The permissiveness of the Mexican-American mother about toilet training overlaps with her non-scheduled feeding. Parallel with this, the Anglo-Saxon mother's scheduled feeding ties in with her strictness about toilet training. Psychoanalytical research has demonstrated how personality traits in the adult such as punctuality, responsibility, parsimony, pedantry, cleanliness, and sense of duty can be traced, among other factors, to the manner in which one is toilet trained. The well-scheduled, clean, neat person may not realize that the standards to which he adheres are perceived by people from other backgrounds as a form of cold demandingness.

Even in common parlance there are differences between the Mexican-Americans and the Anglos in their perception of time. The Mexican-American says, *"El reloj anda"*—"The watch runs." A Mexican-American would say to a friend "I will be ready in a little moment—a little second," (*"Estare listo en un momentito—un segundito"*). A little moment and a little second can be from half a minute to half an hour. To anyone who knows the cultural background this would be self-evident.

There is a great deal of emotional fervor in Mexican-American politics. The setting up of organizations, neatly administered, appropriately designed, and able to channel the emotional fervor effectively is not as prevalent.

This brings to the fore another issue, that of internalized controls. The Mexican-Americans are predominantly Catholic in the continental European sense. For them, the church may be perceived as an external voice indicating what is right and wrong. One can go to it and confess one's sins, do some form of penance, and achieve forgiveness.

In the Protestant and Irish Catholic framework, one's own conscience is the judge. Ordinarily there is no access to external means for the handling of guilt. Near religious sanctuaries, Mexican peasants can be seen walking on their knees on prickly cactus leaves toward the sanctuary. They are punishing themselves physically in order to be forgiven. In the Anglo counterpart that guilt is not so easily disposed of. Again, misunderstandings arise very easily. The Anglo regards the Mexican-American as a slave to primitive religious practices, and the Mexican-American would find it difficult to understand the lingering, internalized guilt of the Anglos.

THE PRESCHOOL CHILD—SEXUALITY AND INITIATIVE

The next stage, in turn, is the phallic oedipal. The child is concerned with sexual differences and death, and becomes responsive to his own sexuality and that of his parents. He is also likely to be intrusively curious about the world around him.

The Mexican-American mother who has been feeding on demand, and who was permissive in toilet training, remains a very powerful figure for the child. The father has to protest too much in order to be taken into account. This might be one of the factors which would explain the machismo of the Mexican man. He tends to compensate with a display of strength in order not to be overwhelmed by the feeling of the power of the woman (mother). The Anglo father, on the other hand, more often shares in the duties of the mother, assisting in the feeding and toilet training of the children, and does not have to call attention to himself so dramatically. Given the spontaneity of physical exchange in the Mexican-Americans and the apparent permissiveness of internalized controls, both incest and gross hysteria could be more prevalent. The Anglo, on the other hand, may find it more difficult to acknowledge his sexual feelings in the family consciously; his feelings may therefore be internalized in the form of neuroses.

On the surface, the Mexican-American mother may be very obliging, particularly in paying explicit obeisance to the man of the house. Yet, the mere fact that she is the exclusive feeder gives her great power, which makes her so secure that she can afford to protest, albeit unconsciously, by going to the other extreme, i.e., "I am a martyr to my family." In the Anglo stereotype, the woman may not be so martyrlike; she may complain openly and have the man help in the home (which the Mexican-American man would ordinarily find unacceptable). All in all, she is less inhibited and can verbalize her demands. She may appear bossy, but she is less insidiously controlling than the Mexican-American woman with her suffering.

The role of the father in the Mexican family is one that can be invested with power and fear. The relationship of the boys to the mother is very close; the father on the other hand is distant, and typically less involved. The distance prevents the give-and-take of an ordinary relationship in which the boys could accept him as a man. Thus, the Mexican father can either become a big powerful male, overtly dominating his children and inspiring fear in them (this can be a defense against the overall importance of the mother, his own mother included); or he can choose to be inadequate, fail to assume an independent role, and become dependent on the mother-surrogate of drink or welfare. The mother "bears her cross" not only in terms of her identification with the overtly submissive role of her own mother, but also because eventually she comes to realize that hers is the real power. She manipulates with food, guilt, and seductiveness. The typical Mexican-American family presents a very dominant father and a submissive mother who share a mutual acceptance of the doctrine of male superiority. Their child-rearing practices include indulgent affection and harsh punishment.[14]

In the Anglo stereotype, the father often participates more in the upbringing of the children and may be more readily available as a person in his own right, not a legend or a myth, but an approachable human being. Of course, alienation from the father occurs in Anglo as well as in Mexican families.

The boys and girls in the Mexican family experience the oedipal conflicts more overtly, whereas in the Anglo children these are more likely to be internalized and expressed in neurotic symptoms or depression. In their later years the Mexican daughters appear to be more easily subject to overt seduction from the father than their Anglo counterparts. This appears particularly true since from the earliest years the easy exchange of physical expressions of affection is part of the culture.

In terms of his upbringing, the Mexican-American male is more likely to find it difficult to adhere to the monogamous mold of marriage. In his view, an embrace, a kiss, a sexual relationship should be enjoyed rather than rebuffed, and the concept of faithfulness in matrimony is less pressing. Mexican-American males can thus have extramarital affairs without too much guilt, and without feeling that they are betraying the trust of their spouses. These patterns now can be found in both groups, and yet the difference remains. Thus, Protestant Mexican-Americans can be as rigidly restricting and disciplined as their Anglo counterparts, in contrast to the more fluid and more spontaneous Mexican Catholics.

There is mutual mistrust in terms of these attitudes toward sexuality. The Mexican-American suspects that the Anglo is a repressed hypocrite who is frightened of expressing his true feelings. The Anglo may accuse the Mexican-American of being primitive and a libertine. Again, in terms of the manner in which they relate, the Mexican-American mistrusts and fears the apparent self-control of the Anglo-Saxon stereotype, whereas the Anglo despises the lack of discipline and the effusiveness of the Mexican-American. They say that Mexicans cannot be sincere because their feelings are so much on the surface.

The Significance of the Extended Family for the Mexican-American

As in other Spanish-speaking groups, the Mexican-American shows a strong attachment to his extended family. The family members, in turn, function as a natural resource and a support system for all types of emotional and material help. Frequently there are numerous siblings, and, during their early years, it is not unusual for some of the children to be reared by grandparents and/or other relatives. This is even more frequent in the case of broken homes. The clinician should know that for the Mexican-American adult to remain in frequent contact with his mother is expected behavior; by the same token, evidence of distance and aloofness may represent some form of alienation and even of psychopathology. It is more typical for advice to be sought through family members, godparents (*padrinos*) or a close friend (*compadre*), than by means of professional help. A return to his old neighborhood (*barrio*) or a visit to relatives in "old Mexico" may also be associated with seeking assistance. Thus for the Mexican-American, dependency on the extended family represents adaptive behavior. The mental health clinician should be aware of the family as a healing resource. Despite its obvious regressive potential, the family more often than not will help the individual in distress to reduce his anxiety and find solutions. Furthermore, enlisting the family in active collaboration during the diagnostic and treatment process will often facilitate effective therapeutic participation.

The Significance of Folk Medicine

A number of syndromes that have often puzzled traditional medicine are clearly understood and accepted by the Mexican-American. He will often seek help from a *curandero* (folk healer) for such ailments as *maldeojo* (the evil eye), *susto* (fright), *empacho* (surfeit), *embrujo* (witchcraft), *mal puesto* (hex), or *caida de mollera* (fallen fontanel), which are conditions frequently seen in children. They can be treated with certain curative rites; these may include a diagnostic interview (often involving the family) followed by nonintrusive procedures such as the laying on of hands, the use of herbs, and prayers.[3] While the number of *curanderos* and *curanderas* appears to be diminishing and their age is increasing, they are still easily accessible in the Southwest. These practitioners are inexpensive, they are knowledgeable of the culture of the barrio, and they respect the old family traditions.[11] They have credibility. The younger Chicano depreciates the value of folk beliefs and often finds himself in conflict with the older generation. The latter typically hold *curanderismo* in high regard even though they may also use modern medical care. At times they employ both modalities simultaneously.

Some Remarks on the Significance of Bilingualism

For the majority of traditional Mexican-Americans, Spanish is the language of the home and family. Children often get their first formal exposure to the English language when they go to school. For most, Spanish will remain the expressive language with which they will deal with intimacy and spontaneity. English will be used as the instrumental language in school and in interactions with Anglo institutions. Few Mexican-Americans are totally bilingual in terms of understanding, speaking, reading, and writing both Spanish and English. Unfortunately, until the recent development of bilingual education in schools, it was almost impossible for a Mexican-American to develop bilingual proficiency. Up until recently, Chicano children were discouraged from and even forbidden to speak Spanish in schools and correctional institutions. This pattern is now rapidly changing. At the same time, second- and third-generation Mexican-Americans who are growing up in metropolitan areas appear more comfortable using English in most instances. This is so even when they understand the Spanish spoken by their elders. Indeed, in their everyday communication, they will frequently mix words from both along with neologisms. A barrio "Chicano" language has thus emerged.

LANGUAGE DEVELOPMENT IN THE CHICANO CHILD

Early studies have argued that bilingualism may interfere with cognition,[4] and others have implied that Mexican-American children are deficient in the linguistic skills that underlie verbal mediation.[17] Recent studies by Palmer[15] and Feldman[5] suggest that bilingual skill may be associated with advanced cognitive processes. The fact that these children learn dual language codes may give them a certain advantage.

Mexican-American children tend to speak Spanish first in the home; later, English becomes the language of school. It is not yet clear what impact this switching has upon personality and cognitive development.[18] Early studies measured language dominance, fluency, or preference. Since they were confined to such isolated factors, they were inevitably inadequate. Recent studies of multivariate measurements of language skills appear more promising;[6] they are as yet far from clarifying these questions.

Intelligence, Academic Performance and the Chicano Child

Mexican-Americans, along with other Spanish-speaking groups, blacks, and other culturally disadvantaged minorities, perform consistently below average in IQ scores. Chicano children have a high dropout rate from elementary to secondary schools and are underrepresented in skilled occupations and professions. At the same time, they are also overrepresented in manual and unskilled jobs. This has been often blamed on their inherently low IQ.

As early as 1937, Mitchell reported[12] that intelligence tests administered to these children in English were not valid. The same author observed that bilingual (Spanish–English) children did significantly better when tested in Spanish. Other authors, however, continued to use the lower IQ scores as a reflection of genetic inferiority.[8] More recent studies[9] suggest that the bilingualism may not be as significant in school performance as are sociocultural variables such as poverty, restriction of experience, and differences in value systems. Mercer is critical of IQ tests which are seen as Anglocentric[10] and "tend to measure the extent to which an individual's background is similar to that of the model cultural configuration of American society." The same author defines the following five sociocultural characteristics as the most significant in influencing IQ scores:

1. Living in a household in which the head of household has a white-collar job;
2. Living in a family with five or fewer members;
3. Having a head of household with a skilled or higher occupation;
4. Living in a family in which the head of household was reared in an urban environment;
5. Living in a family in which the head of household was reared in the United States.

Currently there is less reliance on intelligence testing. It is generally accepted that intelligence is associated with cognition and language development. Psycholinguistics, however, has not adequately investigated cognitive processes in the bilingual; in particular, the many questions about whether bilingualism inhibits or facilitates cognitive development still await answers. Other pertinent observations include the fact that among the children who attend school, Mexican-Americans are frequently older than their classmates, there is a higher frequency of failing grades, and a higher dropout rate. They also obtain lower scores on tests of academic achievement and intelligence. Poor motivation on the part of parents and children[22] is still frequently used as a simplistic explanation. Other factors such as poor housing, inadequate teaching materials, poorly trained teachers, and improper attention to the specific cultural and language differences of the Mexican-American child should be considered.

Interesting but not surprising findings[7] suggest that the Mexican-American "achiever" displays less hostility toward authority figures, more willingness to conform, and better work habits. The same study shows that underachieving boys and achieving girls have dominating mothers, whereas the reverse is true among achieving boys and underachieving girls. The authors suggest that the boys may perceive maternal domination as an infringement on their autonomy and react to it negatively. Daughters may perceive similar behavior as "affectional concern." Anderson and Johnson[1] suggest that one of the most significant findings to emerge is that despite parental encouragement and high academic expectations, Mexican-American children have relatively less personal confidence in their ability to perform academically. Inadequate nutrition, poor health care, inferior housing, and low enforcement of school attendance are only some of the factors influencing poor academic performance. A bilingual and culturally sensitive faculty, along with appropriate curricula, new textbooks, and innovative teaching methods, is needed. Positive self-esteem and the development of "pride in heritage" are said to enhance learning. Culturally relevant teaching methods such as suggested by the work of Castaneda's group[2] offer a measure of promise.

Social Stress and the Chicano

The higher degree of stress, discrimination, and poverty as compared with the majority group seem to be associated with maladaptive, self-destructive, and escapist behavior. Mexican-Americans tend, however, to underutilize mental health services. The Chicano is typically defensive about being considered "crazy" or "retarded." This is often based on the experience of relating to culturally insensitive Anglo professionals who may misinterpret traditional beliefs as psychopathology.[14] As discussed earlier, the extended family is very significant and often "protects" deviant behaviors and acts as a buffer between the "sick" member and society.

On the other hand, police departments in major southwestern cities report that there is a higher incidence of arrests associated with delinquent behavior, in the abuse of drugs and alcohol by the Chicano population. One should be cautious in examining this data because it may reflect prejudice. At the same time, juvenile departments and reform schools in the Southwest report higher proportions of Chicanos (and other minority groups) in their populations. No specific patterns could be assigned to the Chicano juvenile offender, however, that is different from other Spanish-speaking or black minorities.

Conclusion

The child psychiatrist should be able to recognize the significance of language, customs, and culture in the assessment and treatment of emotional, behavioral, and learning problems in the Mexican-American child and his family. While knowledge of Spanish is useful, strong familiarity and deep respect for cultural differences are most essential. With them, the clinician will possess the necessary credibility that will help him understand behaviors in the Mexican-American child with a higher degree of objectivity.

REFERENCES

1. ANDERSON, J., and JOHNSON, W., "Stability and Change Among Three Generations of Mexican-Americans: Factors Affecting Achievement," *American Educational Research Journal*, 8(2):285–307, 1971.

2. CASTANEDA, A., RAMIREZ, M., and HEROLD, L., "Culturally Democratic Learning Environments: A Cognitive Styles Approach," Prepared for the Multi-Lingual Assessment Project, Riverside Component, Copies available from Systems and Evaluations in Education, P.O. Box 1567, Riverside, Calif. 92502, 1972.

3. CRESON, D., McKINLEY, C., and EVANS, R., "Folk Medicine in Mexican American Subculture," *Diseases of the Nervous System*, 30(4):264–266, 1969.

4. FABREGA, H., JR., SWARTZ, J. D., and WALLACE, C., "Ethnic Differences In Psychopathology. II Specific Differences with Emphasis on the Mexican American Group," *Psychiatric Research*, 6(3):221–235, 1968.

5. FELDMAN, C., and SHEN, M., "Some Language-related Cognitive Advantages of Bi-lingual Five-year-olds," *Journal of Genetic Psychology*, 118(2):235–244, 1971.

6. FISHMAN, J., and COOPER, R., "Alternative Measures of Bilingualism." *Journal of Verbal Learning and Verbal Behavior*, 8(2):276–282, 1969.

7. GILL, L., and SPILKA, B., "Some Nonintellectual Correlates of Academic Achievement Among Mexican-American Secondary School Students," *Journal of Educational Psychology*, 53(3):144–149, 1962.

8. JENSEN, A., "Learning Abilities in Mexican-American and Anglo-American Children." *California Journal of Educational Research*, 12(4):147–159, 1961.

9. KILLIAN, L. R., "WISC, Illinois Test of Psycholinguistic Abilities, and Bender Visual-Motor Gestalt Test performance of Spanish-American Kindergarten and First-grade School Children," *Journal of Consulting and Clinical Psychology*, 57(1):38–43, 1971.

10. MERCER, J. R., "Pluralistic Diagnosis in the Evaluation of Black and Chicano Children: A Procedure for Taking Sociocultural Variables into Account in Clinical Assessment," Paper read at the Meetings of the American Psychological Association, Washington, D.C., September 3–7, 1971.

11. MEYER, G., "Folk Medicine in the Southwest," *Texas Medicine*, 71(2):96–100, 1975.

12. MITCHELL, A. J., "The Effect of Bilingualism in the Measurement of Intelligence," *Elementary School Journal*, 38(1):29–37, 1937.

13. MOORE, J., and CUELLAR, A., *Los Mexicanos de los Estados Unidos y el Movimiento Chicano*, Fondo de Cultura Economica, Mexico 12 DF, pp. 276–289, 1972.

14. PADILLA, A., and RUIZ, R., *Latino Mental Health: A Review of Literature*, DHEW Publication No. (HSM) 73–9143, U.S. Government Printing Office, 1973.

15. PALMER, M., "Effects of Categorization, Degree of Bilingualism, and Language upon Recall of Select Monolinguals and Bilinguals." *Journal of Educational Psychology*, 63(2):160–164, 1971.

16. PENALOSA, F., "Recent Changes Among the Chicanos," *Sociology and Social Research*, 55(1):47–52, 1970.

17. RAPIER, J., "Effects of Verbal Mediation upon the Learning of Mexican-American Children," *California Journal of Educational Research*, 18(1):40–48, 1971.

18. RIEGEL, K., RAMSEY, R., and RIEGEL, R. M., "A Comparison of the First and Second Languages of American and Spanish Students," *Journal of Verbal Learning and Verbal Behavior*, 6(4):536–544, 1967.

19. SERRANO, A., and GIBSON, G., "Mental Health Services to the Mexican-American Community in San Antonio, Texas," *American Journal of Public Health*, 63(12):1055–1057, 1973.

20. U.S. Bureau of the Census, "Selected Charatceristics of Persons and Families of Mexican, Puerto Rican, and Other Spanish Origin: March 1971," *Current Population Reports*, Series P–20, No. 224, Washington, D.C., U.S. Government Printing Office, 1971.

21. U.S. Bureau of the Census, "Persons of Spanish Origin in the United States: November 1969," *Current Population Reports*, Series P–20, No. 213, Washington, D.C., U.S. Government Printing Office, 1971.

22. YARBROUGH, C., "Age-grade Status of Texas Children of Latin-American Descent," *Journal of Educational Research*, 40(1):14–27, 1946.

24 / The Puerto Rican Child

Ruth L. LaVietes

Nature of the Characteristics that Define the Child

The personality development and life course of the Puerto Rican child and adolescent are affected by several sociological variables which, taken together, constitute his unique environmental experience.

MIGRATION

Puerto Ricans are United States citizens and, as such, can enter and leave the mainland freely. Large numbers of the poorest urban and rural Puerto Ricans came in the 1950s and 60s in search of better economic opportunities. While most of the migration was toward the United States, the ease and relative low cost of plane fare resulted in a pattern of immigration which differed from other groups in this country. Many Puerto Ricans return to their homeland in response to economic fluctuations, either permanently or for visits of varying periods. With family members in both countries ready to receive travelers in either direction, emigration represents less of a commitment to a new life pattern with its attendant adaptations than was true for other immigrant groups. Fathers come without their families, mothers and children come leaving the father behind, and children may be sent to live with relatives in either country for a variety of reasons. Actually and symbolically, Puerto Rico with its tropical climate, slower pace, and extended kinship remains an idealized homeland to which return is always possible. These migration patterns may result in family fragmentation, delay in acquiring English, slow acculturation, educational handicap due to changing schools, and limited community organization and leadership.

POVERTY

While poverty and its attendant risks for families and children are not unique to Puerto Ricans, there are several features of slum life in this group which make it particularly burdensome. Puerto Ricans in New York City have the lowest income level, lowest educational level, largest families, and highest birth rate of any identified ethnic or racial group, including nonwhites and other Hispanics.[2, 3] One-third live below the poverty level.[10] As there are few residential areas for newer migrants to occupy in the cities to which they come, they tend to cluster in crowded neighborhoods where Puerto Rican neighbors and stores give them some sense of community and continuity. Crowded living conditions are aggravated by their clinging to these neighborhoods (*barrios*), harboring visiting friends and relatives from Puerto Rico, and fear of allowing children outside in dangerous streets. Children are subjected to limited space for play, lack of privacy, bed-sharing, and a high degree of body contact and sexual stimulation.

TRADITIONAL AND CULTURAL FAMILY FACTORS

The Hispanic cultural tradition of family life is based on an authoritarian father, passive martyr-like mother, docile, respectful children, and an extended kinship system. While these values are changing even in Puerto Rico, sufficient remnants remain in the transplanted Puerto Rican family to cause difficulty in adapting to the cultural norms of the United States. Husbands expect to be able to play a machismo role; this involves competency, fearlessness, virility, and freedom to pursue their interests outside of the family. When the Puerto Rican male comes to the United States, he suffers a loss of self-esteem because of lack of skills, language handicap, and dependence on the welfare subsidy which comes through his wife and children. The greater equality of the female in the United States threatens his masculine identity. Wives become resentful of their husband's authority, especially as welfare makes them less dependent financially. Family structure and cohesiveness disintegrate with changing roles. Yet practices of child-rearing seek to continue the old values. Sons, while expected to respect their fathers and idealize their mothers, are required to prove themselves aggressively and sexually outside the home. Daughters are raised to be house-bound, passive, and virginal until their early marriage. Identification difficulties are aggravated by the contrary expectations of the culture of the United States. Male physical aggressiveness and early sexuality, and female lack of ambition and independence, are rejected in school and in the community outside the barrio. Extended family relations are attenuated by distance from relatives, the emphasis on the nuclear family in the U.S., and the breakdown of many Puerto Rican marriages. With inconsistency of roles and disorganization of family structure, there is increased drinking, gambling, and promiscuity among men which further fragments families. The fact that Puerto Ricans, especially males, have the highest rate of mental illness of any group[3] may be the result of their inability to adapt to the changing economic and cultural expectations.

LANGUAGE

The delay in acquisition of English, resulting in major adaptive disability, has been greater in Puerto Ricans than in previous immigrant groups. Factors responsible include isolation in a Puerto Rican neighborhood, clinging to a symbol of attachment to their homeland, emphasizing their Hispanic origin to separate them from the Negroes, and a reluctance to add another burden to the many they already have. Women who have been in the United States for many years may speak almost no English, relying on husband and children to translate on the few occasions they leave the barrio. Spanish is spoken at home so that children born in this country enter school with a language handicap. Negotiations with social institutions such as schools, hospitals, and welfare departments are difficult and often avoided. When children learn English better than parents, the family heirarchy is adversely affected. Limited competence in English is the major disability of Puerto Rican children in school. From the earliest grades they fall progressively behind and drop out earlier. Puerto Ricans have the lowest level of educational attainment of any identified ethnic group in New York City.[2]

COLOR

Puerto Ricans derive racially from a mixture of native Indian, Negro slave, and Spanish conqueror. There is a wide range of skin color, hair texture, and facial features which has class significance. Racial prejudice, while present in Puerto Rico, is less pronounced than in the United States, and the Puerto Rican immigrant finds himself engaged in distinctions here which he did not have to face previously. About one-fourth of Puerto Ricans appear black. These individuals meet with prejudice in American society as well as within their own community and families, where lighter skin and Caucasian features are more highly valued. The clinging to the Spanish language may be the Puerto Rican's attempt to separate himself from the Negro. It is said that the darker the Puerto Rican's skin, the more Spanish he speaks, and that Puerto Rican drug addicts are frequently the darkest-skinned members of their families.

RELIGION AND SPIRITUALISM

While most Puerto Ricans are nominally Catholic, the religion has little impact on their lives, being used mainly for sacraments and for the opportunity to send children to parochial schools, which are seen as having educational and protective advantages over public schools. A number of Puerto Ricans have joined Protestant, evangelical Pentecostal "storefront" churches. Unlike the Catholic priests, the ministers are Puerto Rican and offer the newcomer a social as well as a religious structure. Requirements are austere—daily devotion, prohibition of smoking, drinking, dancing, and parties, and separation of the sexes in worship. Emphasis is put on sinfulness and the ardor of confession and regeneration. Aberrations of behavior and exaggerated claims may play a part in the ceremonies. While such sects reach out to families in time of need and act as a community support system, the asceticism which is imposed on the children of Pentecostal families often has a negative effect, particularly on adolescents.

While few Puerto Ricans admit to a belief in spiritualism, it is commonly practiced. Many small *botanicas* in the barrio sell herbs, oils, and candles for use in influencing the spirits. Spiritualism is a form of folk healing for somatic as well as psychiatric disorders. Seances are held, utilizing the burning or ingesting of exotic substances, calling forth the dead, speaking with the voices of others, and invoking spells and counterspells. Personality development and psychopathology are influenced by children's exposure to experiences which involve danger, magical thinking, and extrasensory perception.

PERSONALITY CHARACTERISTICS

While there is little clear evidence for a national character, typical personality traits of Puerto Ricans have been described. Emotions are readily expressed—both positive ones, such as pleasure, love, and tenderness, and negative ones, such as anger, jealousy, and fear. Affects have a motor component with overt gestures of affection—touching, standing close, caressing—and of rage—destruction of objects, attacking others. Quick changes are possible. Even adults seem to have temper tantrums. Puerto Ricans are voluble and gregarious. Even in the cold climate of northeastern United States, they stay outdoors as much as possible—on windowsills, entrances to apartment houses, and on the sidewalks. There can be an air of easy-going gaiety, motion, noise, and amiability on a Puerto Rican block, as well as the possibility of volatile outbursts.

The Distribution of Puerto Rican Children in the Culture

According to the 1970 census,[10] there are about 1.4 million Puerto Ricans living in the United States. Most of them, 800,000, are in New York City, but there are sizable concentrations in Chicago, Philadelphia, Los Angeles, and in the bigger cities of New Jersey, Connecticut, and Massachusetts. Only a few live in nonurban areas. The population distribution is skewed toward younger persons, both because this is a migrant group and there is a high birth rate. About 45 percent are under the age of eighteen and 13 percent under the age of five.

Different Levels of Development

Puerto Rican infants are born into a household restricted in space and crowded with children and adults. They are welcome to the father as a sign of his masculinity and to the mother as a source of closeness, although she may feel already burdened by too many children. Boys are preferred and favored. High levels of body contact and affection are available. For the first three years, mothers are indulgent and permissive. They do not encourage independence, preferring to feed and dress the child to save time. Toys are bought for their popular or visual qualities, rather than as educational devices. Sometimes household items are the only toys available. Pacifiers are offered freely, even past the age of two. Spanish is either the primary language at home or it may be mixed with simple English. The Puerto Rican mother takes more interest in her child's physical health and motor development than she does in his intellectual, verbal, or independent achievements. She is too busy to spend much time talking to the child or interacting with him individually. Verbalizations are affective in nature, not task-directed. After the age of three, there is less indulgence. The child is expected to obey and not to disturb others by disorder, noise, or excessive activity. Considerable motor inhibition is required and disobedience is punished physically. Nursery schools are underutilized by the Puerto Rican population and only 25 percent of Puerto Rican children attend kindergarten. Social experiences are exclusively intrafamilial as the mother is busy and does not appreciate the value of the playground and peer group. Since there are few pressures concerning routines of eating, sleeping, and dressing, the child does not develop a sense of time requirements. Dependency on the mother is encouraged—the child's rewards are in terms of parental approval, not mastery. Puerto Rican parents do not associate early childhood behavior with later success in life.

Adaptation to school is difficult for the Puerto Rican child. His past social and developmental experiences have not prepared him cognitively or emotionally for an American school. Language is a major factor. Even if he speaks English, he is not as fluent as his peers and often has a Spanish accent. He is dependent and passive, needing more direction and structure than may be available in a large class. He has had no social experiences to aid him in interactions with a variety of children. He is neither time-oriented nor task-oriented. He has little investment in working for future goals. He responds more to people than tasks.[5] His functional IQ is lower than average even when tested in Spanish and on "culture-free" tests,[2, 7] although there is evidence that it approaches average when he is given a great deal of encouragement and warmth.[9] When not supported, he can be distractible or passively resistant. Early failure in school grows worse with the passing years. By third grade, 10 percent of Puerto Ricans are reading at grade level; by eighth grade, two-thirds are three years behind.[2] Inadequate performance leads to feelings of helplessness, dependence, and inferiority. At home, sleep problems are common, reflecting school anxiety surfacing the night before. Half of Puerto Rican children between five and nine have difficulty in going to bed, nightmares, fears of going to sleep, and sleepwalking. Conflicts with parents over new rules which they must now obey (bedtime, doing homework, getting up on time) lead to disciplinary issues in the family.[8] In later latency, boys especially are more resistant to remaining confined at home although their parents are still concerned about dangerous neighborhoods, bad companions, and traffic in the streets. The need to establish masculine superiority, fostered by tradition and feelings of inferiority in school, leads them to value action on the street—sports, fighting, and acts of daring. Docility at home may be counterbalanced by aggression in school and in the neighborhood. Identification with the male is complicated by the father's appearing simultaneously powerful in the family yet inadequate in the society. While girls face the same problems as boys, there is more compliance during latency, possibly because there is less inconsistency in expectations and a clearer role model in the mother.

Adolescence is a period of variable vulnerability for Puerto Rican youngsters. The high dropout rate (less than half finish high school)[10] indicates the low value school has come to have for them by adolescence. Few are ambitious vocationally, neither aspiring to leave the neighborhood nor to improve their standard of living. As the school issue is "resolved" by a reduced investment in it on the part of the child and the family, there is a decrease in conflict. By adolescence the family gives the boy considerable freedom and his mother, especially, is indulgent. If he remains out of trouble, she is satisfied and will reward him with money to buy the apparel and gear he craves. He in turn does not attempt to separate from the family as he feels accepted and unpressured. There is license to have sexual experience without guilt. Adolescent gangs are formed for social purposes or competition for status. Greater self-acceptance occurs as the street peer group becomes the frame of reference rather than society as a whole. Planning for the future, postponement of pleasure, "success" in life, all appear less important than living in the present. Girls have more difficulty with adolescence. They are still kept close to home. Efforts to separate from the family are blocked by expectations of the girls' continued dependence on the family and the real requirements that they help with younger siblings or household chores. Fathers often are overconcerned about their daughters' growing sexuality, an attitude engendered not only by tradition but by unresolved oedipal remnants. Girls are faced with the inconsistency of remaining virtuous without much hope of a satisfying marriage. Some adoles-cent girls adapt to family requirements and remain dependent, coming directly home from school each day, attending church with their mothers, and restricting their activities to home and family. Increasing numbers, however, are breaking with tradition and following the patterns of the larger culture to which they are exposed in school, on TV, etc. This brings them into conflict with fathers, while mothers may covertly aid them to greater freedom. Adolescent girls have fewer aspirations than boys—only occasional girls aim even to enter the clerical fields.

Familial Reactions

The Puerto Rican family in the United States finds itself in a depreciated position as a result of its low socioeconomic status, language handicap, segregation, and color. Most choose to remain here because of economic advantages but suffer self-depreciation and increased stress. Adults react by avoidance of the mainstream of the culture, high levels of somatic and psychiatric illness, and by marital disorganization. Parents find their child-rearing practices dissonant with American culture. Dependent, present-oriented, person-oriented, nonverbal children are not equipped for the cognitive demands of the school. Teachers' encouragement of assertiveness, curiosity, and exploration runs counter to tradition. Puerto Rican parents would prefer the schools to be more authoritarian and to teach the children respect. Children's school problems are often blamed on the school's laxity in enforcing discipline. There is concern that girls be protected from sexual opportunities. Egalitarian attitudes toward girls' roles and activities and the freedom given American youth is rejected. The strong influence of the peer group upon children is alien to the Puerto Rican concept that support systems derive from family and kin. Beset by multiple problems, Puerto Rican mothers, who are often managing their families without the father, tend to become resigned to uncontrollable factors, a posture which makes them appear passive to the main culture.

Cultural Reactions

To most urban Americans, any migrant group which crowds the city, increases welfare costs and crime, competes for employment, and burdens the school system is unwelcome. The special negative reaction to the Puerto Rican group focuses upon its slow pattern of assimilation. In the northeastern part of the United States the Puerto Ricans are the largest migrant group within recent memory, and they have been the slowest to adopt the language, desegregate living areas, rise in the socioeconomic scale, and blend into the mainstream. They have presented special problems in their high representation on the welfare roles and in crime statistics. Efforts by the school system to be effective with Puerto Rican youngsters have exceeded those made for previous groups and have been less successful. These factors create resentment and condescension, but its virulence is tempered by the visible "personality" of the Puerto Rican, which is perceived by the majority group as easy-going, pleasure-loving, and friendly. The Puerto Ricans are also seen positively as family-oriented, in that mothers remain at home and are devoted to child rearing while many fathers, even when out of the home, continue an interest in their children. Puerto Ricans have been much less militant than, for instance, the blacks in seeking special services or political power and while this may be to their disadvantage, it makes them less resented by the cultural majority.

Characteristic Forms
of Emotional Disturbance

EXPRESSION OF DISTURBANCE AT DIFFERENT MOMENTS IN DEVELOPMENT

Few preschool children are brought to the attention of clinicians. As with all children from poverty groups, only a severe disturbance is seen by parents as significant. Mental retardation is judged to be high among Puerto Rican children by the fact that their admission rate to state schools for the retarded is more than double their representation in the population.[3] While the incidence of psychosis reported in Puerto Rican adults is high, there is no comparable trend with children. In surveys of Puerto Rican children, 50 percent of mothers complain of hyperactivity,[8] a symptom engendered by large families confined to small apartments with few opportunities for children to play outside. The mother often interprets the level of activity as a sign of disobedience.

As the child separates from the home to go to school, problems appear. Most children have had no previous social experience and have been encouraged to dependency by child-rearing practices. In response to cognitive and emotional impediments to mastery in the school, young latency-age children may react with increased demands for attention, restlessness, and aggression. Others become passive, withdrawn, and preoccupied with daydreams. It is the former group that, presenting as a behavior problem and learning problem by the third or fourth grade, is referred by the school for clinical attention. These children tend to come from families marked by single parents, somatic or psychiatric illness, delinquency, or alcoholism. One child in five has signs of minimal cerebral dysfunction. Although the vast majority of Puerto Rican children have difficulties in adapting to the school system, those who develop psychiatric disorders are the ones with complicating cerebral or familial factors. In a study of elementary school-age Puerto Rican children, not referred by the school, mothers report negative moods, poor social relations, hyperactivity, and disciplinary problems at home, usually in combination, in over 50 percent of the cases. The symptom of self-inflicted injuries and suicidal threats was also reported by parents in 16 percent of children.[8] Parental requirements for compliance and dependency from early childhood may be connected with such distorted expressions of aggression.

In preadolescence, behavioral problems of uncontrollable aggressive behavior in school, delinquency in the neighborhood, and, less often, resistance to authority at home, are the chief complaints. These behaviors usually started in the early grades of school but concern by school and family heightened as the child approached adolescence. Often the child had been referred once or twice previously with the parent evincing too little interest to maintain efforts at intervention. Whereas diagnoses of reactive disorder had been given earlier, greater fixation is apparent in time, with the development of personality disorders and neuroses. Psychosomatic disorders, especially asthma, are seen commonly in Puerto Rican children (and parents). Difficulties in resolving dependency and aggressive conflicts are apparent, but intervention on a psychiatric level is opposed by families and children who find a nonsomatic interpretation of the illness largely unacceptable.

Clinical problems in adolescent boys are focused primarily in the areas of delinquency and drug abuse. The antisocial behavior is the culmination of a series of life experiences born basically of poverty and peer influence and aggravated by the disorganizing result of migration, the alienating effects of language impoverishment, and racial prejudice. Adolescent girls in the clinical Puerto Rican population commonly develop hysterical conversions or act impulsively. Suicidal gestures and attempts, sometimes fatal, are not infrequently seen. In an effort to resolve the conflict between her own needs for individuality, freedom, and sexuality and the cultural traditions of overprotection and chastity, the adolescent girl may become rebellious and act-out, often by running away (sometimes to Puerto Rico), or may develop neurotic derivatives. Dramatic gestures and somatic symptoms are meaningful signals to Puerto Rican parents who might otherwise ignore signs of discontent in their daughters. Hysterical manifestations are encouraged by overuse of repression, suppression of self-assertiveness, emotionality, and a style of expression encouraged by spiritualistic experiences.

LONG-RANGE EFFECTS OF THE DISTURBANCE(S)

There is no clear information on the long-range effects of disturbances of Puerto Rican children and adolescents beyond general sociological and psychiatric demographic data. Even this data is complicated by the fact that Puerto Rican children in the United States today were born here and have parents born in Puerto Rico. Data on adult Puerto Ricans are primarily based on Puerto Rican-born adults with a more traditional background, not a comparable group. There is more evidence to substantiate the long-range effects of the "culture of poverty"[6] which the Puerto Ricans share than the effects of their uniquely Puerto Rican qualities.

Forms of Coping Behavior

In discussing the issues of coping behavior it should be noted that intragroup similarities along socioeconomic lines are greater than along ethnic lines. Persons who have had the opportunity to study both middle- and lower-class Puerto Ricans report that the former are closer in their psychological styles and capacities to Americans of their own class than to their lower-class compatriots.[1]

FANTASIES

There is a paucity of fantasy and a limitation of its range in the Puerto Rican child and adolescent. Wish-fulfilling fantasies are for material posses-

sions such as food, money, and a large house, or for magical powers to overcome the real dangers, for example, criminals, of their world. Fantasies serve the goal of survival rather than imaginative fulfillment, delay of action or creativity. Fantasy is neither a bridge toward the achievement of a better life nor a rehearsal for an alternative role. Curiosity about or concern for events in the larger world is minimal. One common fantasy is of return to Puerto Rico, the motherland which is idealized in contrast with the grim reality of the urban ghetto.

SKILLS AND SUBLIMATIONS

Action rather than contemplation is the ego-syntonic mode of the Puerto Rican. In keeping with expressive emotionality is a dramatic life-style with intense episodes of love, despair, jealousy, and rage demonstrated openly and without much concern for the long-range result. The moment is pervasively important. Pleasure is found in the enjoyment and display of the performing arts—music, dance, drama, and singing—although talents are seldom pursued to the point of skill and professionalism. Fashionable clothes are valued by both sexes. Humor, joking, and kidding are characteristic of social interaction. There is less sexual repression, especially in males; both sexes have culturally determined outlets for hostility. The spontaneous expression of feeling is valued and expected. These tendencies, along with low levels of aspiration, tend to decrease the use of sublimation. Males are greatly interested in competitive sports both as spectators and, even through adulthood, as participants. Many adult women are intensely involved in church activities but it does not appear that their U.S.-born daughters will emulate them. The Puerto Rican, unlike other immigrant groups, has not consistently utilized militant tactics or the political process to gain power. Although constituting a sizable part of the population in some cities, especially New York, Puerto Ricans are not yet organized to maximize their impact.

SPECIAL DEFENSE PATTERNS

The paradoxical pattern of child rearing among Puerto Ricans influences the defense structure. Authoritarian attitudes demand docility and conformity in children. Yet emotional behavior is traditional and outbursts of it are demonstrated within family and community. Self-control is neither valued nor taught. Inadequate impulse control in some individuals can lead to antisocial activities. In others there are hysterical phenomena, somatization, and regression to primitive ego states such as the attaqué. Individuals may combine opposing trends by shifting the arena of their behavior. Adolescent boys can be compliant at home and delinquent on the street. Action is used as a defense against anxiety as in identification with the aggressor. Self-esteem is bolstered by acts of danger and daring in the machismo tradition. The ego has a low tolerance for tension, discharging it with a burst of action which is often harmless, but may be dangerous, as in the high incidence of crimes of passion. There are not infrequent incidents of older Puerto Rican adolescents hanging themselves in jail while awaiting trial on minor charges.

The ego-ideal is not well developed. Living in the present, with few concerns for the future and little sense of responsibility for shaping their lives, Puerto Rican youngsters tend to externalize sources of discontent, blaming reverses on bad luck, fate, the neighborhood, bad friends, etc.[1] Likewise they seek solutions in material goods and new possessions. There is a denial of time and of future expectations although the unreality of this attitude impinges upon them constantly in their ghetto life and role models. Humor is a widely used Puerto Rican defense against fear, despair, or resignation. Puerto Ricans have an ability to laugh at themselves and see the funny aspect of their situation even when it is dire.[1] This may explain the resiliency which they often demonstrate.

UNUSUAL COMPETENCIES

The greater self-acceptance of the Puerto Rican, usually male, child and adolescent, born of his fatalism, tolerant superego, and limited ego-ideal leads to certain freedoms which are absent in the larger culture. There is a capacity for the short-term enjoyment of bodily and social pleasures in the midst of a marginal material existence. A low aspiration level balances the discrepancy between their standard of living and others. Fatalism cushions failure. Family ties and acceptance and the option of returning to the beautiful homeland aid in the development of a pleasure-seeking style of life which seems to survive the rigors of growing up impoverished in an alien culture.

Needed Social Structures

Since the major disabilities of Puerto Rican children stem from poverty, economic interventions such as increased employment opportunities and improved housing are primary needs. The special requirement of Puerto Rican youth is aid in acculturation into American institutions and practices while encouraging the maintenance of ethnic individuality.

The public schools have wrestled with this problem for twenty years. Efforts have included development of special curricula, adaptation of teaching techniques to the Puerto Rican child's style, recruitment of Spanish-speaking teachers and aides, exchanges of teachers with Puerto Rico, smaller classes, involvement of parents in the school organization, reduction of the culture conflict between the school and the home, special vocational and guidance programs, and the introduction of Puerto Rican role models. None of these methods has been effective, possibly because they have not been followed consistently or with enough financial support. Current efforts are focused upon bilingual education. Children who are expected to progress more satisfactorily in Spanish are taught mathematics, science, and social studies in Spanish while they are becoming competent in English. It is hoped that the use of this system will preserve cultural identity, increase proficiency in Spanish, and enhance pride by official sanction of the language. A danger is that ethnic separatism will increase.

Puerto Ricans have lagged in the development of organizations and leadership to enhance their political role. Their politicalization can be a means of heightening the power to obtain increased and relevant services, and bolstering ethnic pride. As major consumers of welfare, educational, police, and health programs, they can seek the right to influence these governmental services.

Cultural activities which will strengthen Puerto Rican participation in communications and the arts would be influential in overcoming their isolation and in developing their cultural contributions. Spanish programs on public television have begun but there is a dearth of Puerto Rican newspapers, magazines, theatre, and performing arts.

Mental health services for Puerto Ricans should include the primary preventive goal of counteracting cultural stress by such methods as community education, bilingual manpower training, consumer participation in development of services, and consultation to other institutions providing services (for example, welfare, schools, and developing alternative patterns of health care delivery, such as neighborhood walk-in clincs). Early screening and intervention in preschool years could modify the child-rearing practices which contribute to social and educational maladaptation. Collaboration with influential persons in the community, for example, political leaders, spiritualists, can augment clinical impact.

Many measures to aid Puerto Rican youth should be directed at the social institutions that affect their parents. This is a necessary approach to a population which is at high risk from early childhood for the development of disabilities.

REFERENCES

1. BENITEZ, J., Personal communication, 1975.
2. CORDASCO, F., and BUCCHIONI, E., *The Puerto Rican Community and its Children on the Mainland*, Scarecrow Press, Metuchen, N.J., 1972.
3. FITZPATRICK, J., and GOULD, R., "Mental Health Needs of Spanish-Speaking Children in the New York City Area," Paper prepared for Task Force IV, The Joint Commission on Mental Health of Children, 1968.
4. GLAZER, N., and MOYNIHAN, D., *Beyond the Melting Pot*, M.I.T. Press, Cambridge, Mass., 1963.
5. HERTZIG, M., et al., "Class and Ethnic Differences in the Responsiveness of Pre-School Children to Cognitive Demands," Monograph of the Society for Research in Child Development, University of Chicago Press, Chicago, 1968.
6. LEWIS, O., *La Vida*, Random House, New York, 1966.

7. PADILLA, A., and ARANDA, P., "Latino Mental Health, Bibliography and Abstracts," Department of Health, Education and Welfare Publication No. HSM 73–9144, 1974.
8. THOMAS, A., et al., "Cross-Cultural Study of Behavior in Children with Special Vulnerabilities to Stress," in Ricks, D., et al. (Eds.), *Life History Research in Psychopathology*, vol. 3, pp. 59–62, 66–67, Minneapolis, 1974.
9. THOMAS, A., et al., "Examiner Effect in I.Q. Testing of Puerto Rican Working-Class Children," *American Journal of Orthopsychiatry, 41(5):* 1971.
10. U.S. Bureau of the Census, Census of Population, Final Report PC (2)-IE, *Puerto Ricans in the United States*, U.S. Government Printing Office, Washington, D.C., 1970.

25 / The Catholic Child

Joseph Reidy

Introduction

"We grew up different," Garry Wills wrote of his Catholic childhood. A generation ago the environment of most Catholic children in America differed in many ways from that of other children; the Catholic rearing favored the development of a certain personality type and influenced to some degree the symptoms of emotional disorders. In terms of basic pathology, the illnesses of troubled Catholic children did not differ from those of other children with difficulties. Nor were these young Catholics particularly religous or holy; indeed, their symptoms were usually a distortion of genuine religion. Recently many changes have taken place in the Catholic Church, and Catholic children for the most part no longer grow up "different." To understand what has come to pass, it is important to look at the Catholic teaching and practices before the renewal in the church, at what Catholics were required to believe and how they were expected to live. This will shed light not only on the present religious environment, but also on the vestiges of the past that remain in some children and families who come to the psychiatrist today.

Numbers and Distribution

Approximately 23 percent of Americans are members of the Roman Catholic Church, and almost one-fourth of all children and adolescents in this country are Catholic.[6, 7] They are most numerous in the large metropolitan areas. Nearly twenty million Catholics are in seventeen large metropolitan areas, each with a Catholic population of over one-half million. The greatest numbers of Catholics are found in the cities of New England, the Middle Atlantic and the North Central states, and in the state of California. In the South—

except for the cities of Baltimore, Miami, New Orleans, San Antonio, and Washington—and in the Western and the Plains states, the number of Catholics are well below the national average.

The Effect of the Environment at Different Levels of Development

The Catholic writer Michael Novak wrote that "to be a Catholic is in a thousand subtle ways to be different from others." For many reasons Catholics had been cut off from the mainstream of American culture and intellectual life, and being a Catholic did make a difference. The "Catholic" manner of child rearing had its effects at all levels of development. The church gave parents a philosophy of child rearing and charged them with the responsibility for the salvation of the child's soul. Parental authority was absolute (the only exception was that a parent could not command a child to do a sinful act), and it was an authority which was a reflection of the strong authority structure of the church itself. Many parents had little tolerance for the child's expression of ambivalent feelings toward them or for the adolescent's rebellion and search for independence. They were taught and were required to teach their children a very clearly defined morality, which some have called a "sin-oriented" morality. Every sexual act outside of marriage, even every willful thought about forbidden sexual acts, was sinful; a doctrine with major implications for the young. Often enough it affected the outcome of the childhood and adolescent conflicts about sexuality, particularly about masturbation, in an adverse way. There were a multitude of sins besides the sexual ones; it was a sin if you missed Sunday mass, if you took communion when you had broken your fast even by swallowing a few drops of water, if you ate meat on Friday, if you were angry without just cause, if you were envious, vain, and on and on.

The parents' task of child rearing was supplemented by or often taken over by the parochial school. Garry Wills wrote that when the American bishops decided in 1884 to require that every Catholic child receive a Catholic education the result was that "Catholicism would be in large measure child-centered, its piety of a feminine sort."[8] Pastors told parents they were obligated under pain of sin to send their children to Catholic schools, and in the schools the child was expected

to accept without question what the sisters taught him. As one Catholic said about his childhood: "Anything a nun said to me had to be right, more right than anything my parents said."

Forms of Disturbance

A Catholic child with neurotic tendencies could use his faith as a ready-made vehicle for the expression of his conflicts. The religious requirement for total submission to a powerful authority expressed through a centuries-old ritual with strong appeal to the emotions lent itself to such uses. Often enough the ritual became transformed into little more than magic and superstition. The religious training fitted in well with the kind of personality structure that relied on external sanctions and rigorous discipline. Many of those responsible for religious formation were suspicious of original ideas, suppressed dissent, demanded complete orthodoxy, and encouraged passivity and denial of some reality. This training often produced children who had immature consciences, who were inhibited, and who were afraid of their impulses. Many of these children never came to the attention of psychiatrists because they blended with their environment and gained acceptance and approval for their way of life.

A distinctively Catholic phenomenon is scrupulosity. This condition is marked by constantly recurring doubts about whether or not one has sinned and by endless repetition of prayers and other religious acts in order to undo the possible sins. This behavior can indicate a measure of psychopathology which can vary from a mild adjustment reaction to a severe compulsive neurosis. In some cases the symptoms become part of a psychosis. Non-Catholics, too, have suffered from this condition, but as a rule it has been a malady of Catholics. The Catholic spiritual writers have been familiar with this condition for several centuries.[5]

Coping Mechanisms

The child often handled his impulses by inhibiting their expression, for he was taught that only under certain conditions was the satisfaction of these impulses without sin. Children were thought to be capable of committing serious sin when they reached the "age of reason," which was considered to be the age of seven. The child who sinned must confess his sins to the priest, and he must have genuine sorrow for his sin (contrition), must do penance for his sin, and resolve never to sin again. This helped some children, but others found confession a frightening ordeal. Some could never be certain they were truly sorry or that their resolutions were sincere and in time gave up going to confession and thought of themselves as unrepentant sinners. Children were also taught to ward off temptations by prayers and other religious acts.

The exposure to this religious environment did not harm the healthy children, and the external structure and support helped many children in their struggle to master their impulses. There were, however, some children who did not fit in with their environment, who became neurotic, or showed severe behavior disorders. These difficulties indicated that the child had a weak will, lacked faith, or was not cooperating with God's grace. Those children were exhorted to pay more attention to their religious duties and devotions. Children who rebelled against an overly strict home or school regimen, who were trying to master their conflicts over dependency, and who in other ways were showing signs of normal emotional growth were thought to be disobedient and disrespectful.

Parents were not encouraged to seek psychiatric advice and treatment. The clergy distrusted psychiatrists, particularly ones who favored psychoanalysis, and they considered the theories dangerous to the belief of the faithful. Some of the common misconceptions about psychiatry were given total credence: that it reduced all human emotional life to narrow sexual (i.e., genital) sources, that it encouraged patients to be completely uninhibited, that it denied freedom of the will, and that it fostered an irresponsible moral attitude. If psychiatric help was recommended, the family was directed to a Catholic psychiatrist, for it was assumed only he would be able to understand the child's problems and safeguard his faith. Another reason not to send a child to the psychiatrist was the notion (still current) that childhood is a time of simple innocence, untroubled by emotional conflict or mental illness. Yet it was a time when this same unspoiled, essentially good child was capable of committing serious sins.

It was customary for the person troubled by scrupulosity to go to confession. Most priests thought scrupulosity was a spiritual disorder; accordingly they provided spiritual advice which often made the condition worse. In any case, psychiatric help was rarely advised. The result was that the mild cases cleared up; often enough the persons with severe illness remained emotionally crippled much of their lives.

These are but a few of the important features of Catholic life and of the religious training a Catholic child received before the recent religious renewal.* It must also be said that religion did not play a very important part in the everyday lives of many Catholic children. Then, as now, they were exposed to it, considered themselves to be Catholic rather than non-Catholic, but it went no deeper. Certainly it caused no serious emotional conflicts. There were other Catholic children who were able to integrate the spirituality and morality they were taught into a healthy personality.

The Catholic Child Today

In 1962 Pope John XXIII convened the Vatican Council II to bring the church into keeping with the times. For many years the prevailing theological view of human nature was one closed to the contributions of the behavioral sciences. The council turned to the knowledge gained by these sciences, and its documents reflect the contributions of psychology, sociology, and anthropology to the understanding of man's religious needs.[1] Once the step had been taken to "open the windows and let in the fresh air," in the words of the Pope, it freed the forces which led to change and there was virtually no aspect of Catholic life and belief that escaped questioning.

The Catholic Child Today Is
Less Different

Today's religious climate is less likely to produce the disorders that were noted earlier. Catholics have a less fearful view of their religion, and they are less dependent on the church to give them

* Those interested in learning more about the Catholic environment before the time of the Vatican Council II are referred to the works of Garry Wills,[8] Daniel Callahan,[2] and Michael Novak.[4] A recent work providing an excellent review of the changes in the Church is *American Catholicism* by George Devine.[3]

commandments and prohibtions for every aspect of their lives. Emotional maturity and close interpersonal relationships are now considered important, and greater emphasis is placed on the necessity for an informed and mature conscience. There is less stress on authority and unquestioning conformity, so it is no longer asserted that the church has the answers for every human problem, or even for every religious and moral problem. Catholics are less isolated from the world, more open to those who hold other views. Now the church is often characterized as a "pilgrim" church, searching for answers, working out God's plan for salvation in the world instead of fleeing from the world and its evils. All of these influences make the Catholic child appear less different today.

In times past candidates for the priesthood and members of religious orders were secluded in seminaries and convents. They were almost out of touch with other students, indeed, with the world in general. After they finished their training they went out to serve people, but they were not prepared for dealing with their emotional problems. The education of priests and nuns has changed; they are no longer isolated and, in their training, the study of the social and behavioral sciences takes an important place.

Some Forms of Disturbance Today

To most Catholics the changes came as a shock; and some are still critical or openly opposed to the changes. One effect of this opposition is an increase in conflict between parents and children. This is a likely sequence when the children opt for the "new" church while their parents cling to the "old." Organized religion has seemed irrelevent to many youths who feel a pressure to reject its authority as they reject parental authority. Moreover, in today's secular culture the things of the spirit often have far less appeal for youth than they might have had a generation ago. It may well be that the sexual experience of the Catholic adolescent now is closer to the norm for all adolescents than it was. However, it is often difficult to judge the effects of the contradictory messages Catholic children receive. The official teaching on many matters, especially sexual ones, is that nothing has changed. The Pope and the bishops repeat the centuries-old doctrines on contraception, premarital sex, masturbation, and divorce. At the same time many theologians and priests give people advice which is contrary to some of these teachings.

Catholic children who have emotional illnesses will continue to have, in many instances, a symptomatology with religious coloring. Even a religion that has been freed from magic and superstition deals with unknowns which often perplex and frighten adults, let alone children. There are still scrupulous children but they are likely to be more sick than many of the scrupulous children of earlier years because the religious climate is not so favorable to the development of these symptoms.

Effects on the Environment

There has been a sharp decline in the number of youths who have decided to become priests and nuns. This phenomenon dismays many older Catholics, but it may not necessarily be a great misfortune for the religion. Rather, it seems that the priesthood and religious life are no longer the refuge they once were for certain maladjusted persons. The decreasing numbers of priests and teaching sisters, together with the increasing costs of maintaining school systems, have forced the church to close many schools. In recent years the enrollment in Catholic schools has declined 25 percent. No longer are Catholics told they have a moral obligation to send their children to Catholic schools. The parishes provide religious education for children who go to public schools, but the attendance is often low, particularly among the adolescents.

Parental Attitudes

Some parents are unwilling or unable to raise their children differently from the way they were raised. There are now many angry parents who feel their authority has been seriously compromised by the changes. These parents feel betrayed by a clergy which has abandoned the old-fashioned discipline for the methods of "psychology," and they view the decline in vocations to the priesthood and religious life as still more evidence of the disastrous effect of the new religious climate on the young. These parents may cling to the older views about emotional problems. It must be said that many parents, perhaps the majority, welcome the changes and find the clergy to be more understanding of the stresses and problems they encounter with their children.

Other parents expect the psychiatrist to fill the void, to give them all the rules of child rearing and to supply moral guidance for their children. Often the younger children are led to expect this of the psychiatrist, and this becomes a source of resistance to effective treatment. Adolescents may see the psychiatrist as being in accord with their overbearing parents (in the same way their parents looked upon the priest when they were adolescents).

Other Significant Issues

Not everything has changed. Although many theologians have modified their views on the sinfulness of contraception and masturbation, there is no evidence of change on matters such as abortion. Catholics have emerged from their "ghetto" to know and to work with non-Catholics on many religious and civic issues, but this ecumenism has not changed their belief in the fundamental mysteries of the faith. In any large group of Catholics it might be difficult to find agreement on many substantial issues of the creed or the moral code, but they continue to believe in the divinity of Christ, the resurrection, the virgin birth, and the real presence of Christ in the Eucharist, to name but a few of the articles of faith. In general, they no longer accept the literal explanations of many of the mysteries just as they no longer accept the literal interpretation of many of the events in the Bible.

For many Catholics the renewal has resulted in a deepening of their faith. Not only has the religion been freed from superstition, prejudice, and authoritarianism, but it has become a religion expressive of concern for their fellow beings. More than rules and rituals it has become a very personal encounter with spiritual concerns and with God. In recent years many Catholics have joined the Pentacostal movement, which has long been a part of some Protestant groups. This movement does not rely on the traditional hierarchical structure for its leadership, nor does it confine its worship to the sacraments and the official liturgy of the church. In addition, it stresses the direct communication of the individual with God. The prayer meetings of the Pentacostals are marked by outpourings of emotion not found in the official rites. On the one hand, it may be a freedom from the formalized and sometimes grim fashion in which Catholics had been accustomed to worship. On the other hand, its freedom of expression may attract some persons who have emotional difficulties, or who need emotional catharsis.

The psychiatrist and the priest deal with many of the same things: life and death, guilt and atonement, sexuality, love and hate. Today the church does not hold these are solely religious and moral matters. The result is that many more Catholic children who are emotionally ill come to psychiatrists. Parents are better educated and can judge for themselves in these matters, or if they seek help from the priest they will find him aware of emotional problems and ready to recommend psychiatric care when it seems necessary.

REFERENCES

1. ABBOTT, WALTER M. (Ed.), *The Documents of Vatican II*, America Press/Association Press/Guild Press, New York, 1966.
2. CALLAHAN, DANIEL, *The New Church*, Charles Scribner's Sons, New York, 1966.
3. DEVINE, GEORGE, *American Catholicism*, Prentice-Hall, Englewood Cliffs, New Jersey, 1975.
4. NOVAK, MICHAEL, *All the Catholic People*, Herder and Herder, New York, 1971.

5. REIDY, JOSEPH, "A Case of Religious Scrupulosity," *Journal of Pastoral Counseling*, 5(2):32–50, 1970.
6. The Official Catholic Directory, "General Summary," pp. 1–14, P. J. Kennedy & Sons, New York, 1975.
7. U.S. Catholic Schools, National Catholic Educational Association, Washington, D.C., 1973–1974.
8. WILLS, GARRY, *Bare Ruined Choirs*, Doubleday, Garden City, New York, 1975.

26 / The Jewish Child

Joseph D. Noshpitz

A topic of endless interest to various Jewish youth groups and discussion seminars has been the issue: What is a Jew? The religious authorities have defined it clearly. It is that person whose mother is a Jew, or who has been converted to the Jewish faith according to a designated code (entitled *Halacha*, which translates loosely as *The Pathway*). However, it is evidently more than a matter of faith; any number of children born to mixed marriages in America consider themselves Jewish, and many Jews born to Jewish mothers are non-religious, anticlerical, or atheists; the matter is not simple.

For purposes of this discussion, any child raised to regard himself in some sense as part of the continuity of Jewish history will be considered Jewish. One must hasten to add that this definition is confined to the American scene; the issues of Israeli Judaism are a world apart.

Depending on how one estimates, in 1975 there were between 6.1 and 6.4 million Jews in America.[10] Given the national average for the number of children per family (Reform and Conservative American Jews do not usually have large families, Orthodox Jews do), there were then in 1975, some 2.4 million children who could fall under this rubric.

The cultural and familial factors in Judaism have two major determinants—the transmitted identity and cultural values carried within the people, and the social attitudes that characterize the populace among which Jews live. For, except in Israel, Jews are an eternal minority. They have held this status since approximately A.D. 70, and the 1,900 years that have transpired since that date have exerted profound formative influences both on the bearers of this designation and on those in whose lands they have dwelt. In effect, they have always been strangers. Sometimes they would be welcome guests, invited in, valued, and even offered special advantages. Often enough, while not exactly welcome, if they came, they would be accepted, or at least tolerated. More often still, they would be endured despite a standing, low-grade, popular general distaste. And now and then they would be totally rejected, persecuted, and driven out. In recent times, about once each

generation, in one place or another, they would be hunted down and killed en masse, explicitly for being Jews. The worst such episode was the destruction of six million Jews in Europe by the Nazis in the late 1930s and early 40s; this overshadowed the mere tens of thousands killed by the Russian pogroms around the turn of the century. It was, however, probably not much worse than the unbelievable Chmielniki massacres of a few generations ago.* The history goes on back to medieval days and beyond, and the chronic nagging sense of vulnerability, of the potential for persecution, is a very real part of Jewish consciousness. Sooner or later it is taught to every Jewish child.

From the point of view of the culture itself, Judaism includes a formal religion, a sense of historical origin and ultimate historical destiny, a conception of the self as a people bearing certain universal values, a number of "traditional" in-group languages, and a set of personal and social attitudes which extend from family structure, through various dimensions of group cohesion, to choice of occupation. There is, in addition, a rather unique kind of conscience formation. Finally, there are a number of tendencies toward particular patterns of social expression that have at least a measure of statistical validity. Thus, as he grows up, among the values a given Jewish child is likely to encounter is a very powerful and pressing sense of family and community togetherness. Since his external cultural adjustment has been freighted with tension, and even with downright menace, the Jew in the West has had perforce to turn to his in-group for security and comfort; the family and all its extensions, the neighbor set, and the overall sense of communal oneness with other Jews everywhere have been powerful forces in his life. These, coupled with the dictates of the religion, have made the giving of charity and the support of the brother in need an explicit and pressing aspect of Jewish adaptation. They have

---

* Starting in 1648 over one hundred thousand Jews were killed in Poland, along with numerous Catholics, Poles, and Germans. Many were slowly tortured to death; many were executed in multiple hangings. The most bestial atrocities were daily events, and the entire sequence persisted for a decade.

also led to a style of child rearing which strongly emphasized dependency as contrasted to autonomy, and attachment rather than independence. In the early development of the Jewish child, much emphasis is placed on holding and comforting the baby, and, in particular, on his protection. The world tends to be seen as a dangerous place where bad men can come and take you away, and the message is: Stay close to your mother and siblings. The usual image is one of oral nurturance; in fact, this is probably less true than the holding/comforting aspect of early rearing behavior. This may have much to do with the later preference for psychopathological forms which involve disturbed interpersonal relations more than they do substance abuse.

Many Jewish children would hear more than one language in their environments as they developed. Yiddish and Ladino* were the historical residues of the travels of Jewish populations in northern and southern Europe and about the Mediterranean basin; these languages often functioned as in-group speech forms where the outgroup language was laden with hostility and overt danger. These in-group languages then took on special warmth and intensity; as a result one often hears that Yiddish, for example, is untranslatable. In modern America such language usage is disappearing although, curiously enough, the pungency and intensity of many individual words persist, and even find their way into English (*shlemiel, meshugge, nebbisch, maven, kibitz, verschluggene,* etc.). In addition, the religion mandated a good knowledge of Hebrew, and, for the more learned, at least some command of Aramaic. The growing child was more likely to hear the Hebrew (as part of formal prayers, as blessings at meals, and/or at Sabbath observances, or at least as part of major ceremonies).

The culture demanded literacy. The religion is in itself peculiarly geared to complex cognitive forms; thus, there is a text of revealed truth, the Old Testament, a six-section (each a sizable volume) set of rabbinical commentaries on the text of the Testament, and a huge, sixty-three subsection legalistic exploration of the six-section commentary (the Talmud). More to the point, for much of Jewish history, any Jewish male worth his salt was expected to have some exposure to this Talmud, and enormous prestige attended any student who became genuinely learned in its

contents. In modern America, the practice of studying Talmud has largely dropped out (although it has by no means disappeared), but the basic value orientations that derived from this singular cultural presence continue to play a major formative role in the shaping of Jewish character. In any case, the emphasis on the verbal is extraordinarily powerful in Jewish child rearing; children are praised and valued for precocity of speech and of early mastery of reading, and their disciplinary management tends to involve a great deal of verbalization (which may vary from continuous nagging through endless moralizing, to much appeal to the child's better nature and dramatic verbal demonstration of the effects of his ill behavior on the emotional state of his caretaker).

Toilet training probably still bears the imprint of many biblical injunctions about ritual washing, the state of ritual uncleanliness (for example, the menstruating women may not be touched—anywhere—because doing so renders a man ritually unclean and in need of purification, etc), and the need of hygiene, sphinctric continence, and modesty in order to be a good person. Oedipal themes are in turn dominated by extremely powerful incest taboos (in eastern Europe a Jewish man could not choose a woman as a potential bride if she had the same first name as his mother). Indeed, morality could not help but be of special importance to a people whose concern with meeting the demands of a grudging surrounding world determined the external forms of behavior; and whose long tradition of biblical and talmudic principle impressed itself on the inner value set. Hence, from early in development, the superego tended to sit heavily on the Jewish child and to make unusual demands. The bible has lengthy passages forbidding revelation of the nakedness of close kin; and modesty, along with the derivative attitudes of continence, faithfulness, etc., are major cultural virtues. Like other traditions, these are melting away rapidly in the American ambience, but the echoes linger on.

The injunctions against violence are no less formidable; these were profoundly reinforced by the futility of a small scattered people taking up cudgels against the huge populace among whom it lived. Hence the instructions about complying with authority and not allowing oneself to enter into physical confrontations had both adaptive and ethical reinforcement.

This was complicated by a historical tradition filled with warrior heroes (Samson, David, etc.) and great rebels (the Maccabees, Bar Kochba). The endless thread of tragedy through most of

* A Spanish tongue written in Hebrew characters utilized by Jews who fled Spain in 1492 and who settled in the Mediterranean.

these narratives did little to quench their drawing power on the fantasy of children; they were therefore relegated to a glorious past and a mystical, often a messianic, future, but carefully forbidden for the present. Instead the emphasis was placed on succeeding, and surviving through wisdom, intelligence, learning, or any of the other versions of brain power. This included business acumen; great respect was accorded to the accumulation of wealth. After all, money brought with it not only comfort but a measure of safety. In this connection, all sorts of models would be employed to instill in the minds of the children ideals appropriate to this adaptive style. Great rabbis would be mentioned, Solomon's wisdom extolled, renowned scholars spoken of with reverence. In recent times, there would be the invocation of such Jewish figures as Einstein or Freud. In socialist homes, the fact that Marx was in part Jewish might be mentioned. Material success would also be spoken to with great awe, and the notion of being a wealthy man, of "not having to worry," would be held up as a vivid goal, something to be striven for if one but could. But again, the accent would fall on shrewdness, quickness of mind, being smart. That, rather than courage or drive, or correctness, or even luck, would be identified as the basic trait to be cultivated.

Thus, the two major ideals, to be a great scholar or a great businessman, were dominant themes in the cultural input to ego ideal formation for the Jewish child. At the same time, an antithetic value would be interwoven with these, a view that distilled much of the bitterness of the historical residues of Jewish history. A people who had been a chronic underdog and a frequent scapegoat had much reason to be concerned with fairness, and the protection of the weak. At the same time, the People of the Book had a weighty tradition of religious and legalistic involvement with divine law. This generated enormous inner tensions associated with the concepts of justice, with protection of rights, with the actual implementation in practice of legal and ethical principles. So, from early on, the Jewish child heard about issues of social justice, about the unfairness visited on members of the group, about exclusion and rejection and deprivation because one was Jewish, of the issues of rightness and righteousness and the implications for everyone—and concern with such sociopolitical matters was a vital thread in the pattern of the intimate family mesh that enfolded the child.

Latency was dominated by learning. In the poorer families this pattern might be brief and the child harnessed quickly to the needs of the family business; wherever possible, however, and particularly where a child showed some talent or an unusual interest in learning, the family would make immense efforts to encourage and support him on his academic path. In Europe, the community would often help out as well; a poor student would regularly be invited to the home of the well-to-do for his evening meal. This custom has largely dropped out in America, but it seems safe to say that the accent on learning, both religious and secular, as a primary virtue and an end in itself, has not. The Jewish family and the Jewish community continue to treasure and to take pride in the cognitive prowess of their children.

The advent of puberty brings with it ceremonies that continue this theme. The original puberty rite was assigned exclusively to males; it was called Bar Mitzvah [he who bears, or is responsible for, acts of virtue] and involved reading (more precisely, chanting) portions of the Old Testament aloud in public in the original Hebrew and employing an ancient stylized form of musical expression while doing so. The great thing was always to do it without error, either in the words or music. Often enough, the thirteen-year-old Bar Mitzvah would also make a speech. The accent of this speech might fall on the movement into puberty (Today I am a man), or on the entrance into the corpus of Judaism. Thanks were extended to parents and teachers. And high hopes expressed for the future. Parental pride and satisfaction would be a meaningful presence felt by everyone; and gifts would be showered on the youth by family and friends. (Often enough the promise of gifts would be the one reward that might have kept a reluctant nonstudent working at the drudgery of learning the unfamiliar and difficult Hebrew passage.)

The experience of this ceremony is no trivial one. It is a very public affair, it involves ordeal and the performance of a difficult feat, it is a test of intellectual prowess and poise, and the average youth experiences a great deal of stress as he faces this social exposure. (The author had a patient whose fantasy a week before this ceremony consisted of seeing himself crucified before the congregation.) In recent years there has been a strong movement toward providing an equivalent ceremony for girls; it is called Bat Mitzvah, and the girls perform a similar reading and might then make an appropriate speech.

For both genders then, this is a step in their movement into adolescence. Insofar as it is Jewish, the adolescence of these youngsters is characterized by a reencounter with the full mass of super-ego structures from early life, and the inevitable mixtures of compliance and defiance which this developmental stage entails. It is a time when many of these youngsters experiment with changes in the form of their religiosity. The Orthodox youth shifts from mere observance to joining the ranks of the mystics; or he goes in the opposite direction and becomes secular; contrariwise, the child of the reform family may turn Orthodox. Or the identity conflict may drive a youth into conversion; he abandons Judaism for a kind of secularism or atheism, or he goes through a formal ceremony and embraces some variety of Christianity. Because of its complex nature, Judaism can allow for identity shifts in realms other than religion. Thus, a particular youth might turn to Zionism and become actively engaged in one of the "movements" associated with the return of the Jews to Israel. Or, he may disaffiliate himself from this concept and become a critic of Zionism and a defender of the Palestinian Arabs. In every instance, there is likely to be some organization of youngsters to whom he can turn, whose ranks he can join, and in whose group experience he can participate.

In any case, adolescence brings with it the need for career choice. The previous legacy of valuation on erudition and on scholarly pursuits along with the strong emphasis on financial success tend to emerge at this stage as an interest in a professional career. Indeed, a disproportionately large percentage of Jews apply to professional schools and eventually join the ranks of their respective disciplines.[6, 2, 1, 8] In recent years, this has led to direct competition with other minority groups who are currently seeking to employ this route as they emerge from poverty and discrimination, and some painful confrontations have occurred.

Thus far, little has been said about the personality traits that are most characteristic of Jews. In terms of their patterns of defense, the strongest emphasis is likely to fall on the mechanisms of intellectualization and reaction formation. A great many Jews are volatile people, hysteroid in character makeup, with a trace of their Levantine and Mediterranean heritage still evident in their personality styles. This is balanced by a certain inclination toward the philosophical or, at any rate, the abstract. There is a very marked bent toward socially sanctioned forms of exhibitionism; and voyeurism, at least in the form of an unusual degree of curiosity, is rather common. A strong tendency toward scrupulosity is not unusual, however, and compulsive tendencies abound. One of

the major patterns is likely to be humor, and indeed, this, plus the exhibitionistic tendencies, have produced a remarkably large percentage of Jewish comedians. Indeed, there are many Jews in one aspect of show business or another, to the point that it is sometimes regarded as a largely Jewish profession. This is an exaggeration, but the numbers of Jewish youth who throng to the various paths into this arena are far out of keeping with their percentage in the population. Evidently, the early steps toward such a choice of career must be taken during adolescence—or earlier.

It is relatively easy to identify one of the major fantasies of this ethnic group since it has chosen this particular era to incarnate itself in action. Insofar as people are Jews, they seem inextricably involved with the dream of a return to Zion. This may be relegated to a future time when the world is a better place and all can be one with love and in peace; it may have a messianic cast and be viewed as something to be brought about by divine means when the Great Trumpet sounds. For many older Orthodox Jews, it is the place they want their bodies sent to for burial; for the young, it may take the form of ardent adventure-going in the here and now along with a sense of personal mission to go rebuild the Land of Israel. One way or another, however, over time, it has proven itself a persistent drive that is deeply locked into Jewish yearning.

Another powerful image is that of being a member of the Chosen People. The obvious question of "chosen for what?" has no straightforward answer; but the sense of specialness does not depart from the Jew. Nor does it seem possible for the people among whom he lives quite to give up on some cognate feeling (although in their case, the "special" quality may not be a good one; indeed, the quality of being a Jew might be viewed as something especially bad. In many contexts, the very word "Jew" has pejorative overtones, and the phrase "to jew someone down" is an expression of sharp practice).

For the individual Jewish youth, however, it seems safe to say that there is a touch of grandiosity here, a sense of narcissistic difference of a rewarding kind. For the religious youth there is the sure comfort of a unique link to God; the secular youth, in some obscure sense, is likely to conceive of himself as a value bearer. More than that, there is often a pervasive feeling of having to be an example, intellectual, ethical, moral, or creative. Typically, there is no coherent form to the fantasy, no specific role the youngster feels called on to play. Nonetheless, some sticky quality of this sort is likely to adhere to him as part of his Judaism; something more is expected of him as a Jew than is required of the gentiles about him.

There is much to suggest that a derivative idea is very common among Jews and that is the rescue fantasy. Somehow, quite a large number of Jews see themselves as obliged to or destined to, or merely desiring to rescue people. This leads them into mental health, into social work, teaching, medicine, law, political activism of all sorts, and into myriads of organizations and associations whose aim is to bring succor and help to some group somewhere. The young Jewish child used to be urged to eat because over in other parts of the world there were children who were hungry. Officially he was supposed to be glad of his good luck and take advantage of it, but the element was also there that by his partaking of food he would somehow atone for or ease their distress. The Jewish adult is endlessly enmeshed in a network of donations and charitable activities of all sorts. It is not hard to imagine how such a fantasy of the self as rescuer might have developed; the mere fact of their own recurrent experience of helplessness and enormous need for rescue throughout their history would have marked this people profoundly. But the roots are far more complex, and involve as well the messianic fantasy, the Chosen People idea, and the self-concept as value bearer.

Another form of this fantasy is the sense of self as bearer of the sins of the world. Within this framework the Jew is the Chosen One to expiate and atone for the sins of mankind; he suffers so that all men can be spared. The term *scapegoat* comes from the Old Testament and refers to a Jewish religious practice. In popular parlance the term has often been invoked to describe the way the Jews have been used by the people about them; it is not surprising that some Jews see themselves as the scapegoat of all humanity, not merely in the sense of helpless victims, but as actually put on earth somehow to lighten the burdens of everyone.

Characteristic Forms of
Psychopathology

Jews often speak of themselves as a neurotic people. Given the strong verbal flavor present as part of their child-rearing practices, their tendency to act out in violent ways is relatively diminished, and the Jewish mugger is an unusual figure on police rolls (although by no means unknown). The strong emphasis on closeness and dependency during early childhood seems to protect the Jew from later vulnerability to addiction; Jewish alcoholics are relatively rare. Again, however, this is only relative; they certainly do exist. On the other hand, this pattern of rearing inevitably exposes the child to all the derivatives of separation anxiety; there are many neurotic Jews with psychophysiologic reactions; lots of Jewish children are eneuretic; and phobias are common (including school phobia). The powerful incest taboo in so close a household predisposes the child to all manner of neuroses. Anxiety reactions, acute and chronic, are by no means unusual; and many Jewish youngsters suffer from obsessive compulsive symptoms and such hysterical symptoms as stomachaches and globus.

More common still are the narcissistic disorders and character problems. The centuries-long efforts to survive in the face of adverse social environments have tended to create a state of turning to the self in the sense of seeking narcissistic comfort in the face of an unrewarding reality. Within the context of family and in-group, a quality of narcissistic demandingness for attention, for a central role in everyone's concern, tends to be present in many Jewish children. They are taught survival techniques from early on, they are hovered over and worried over and not allowed out of mother's sight lest catastrophe befall, they know that outside the home one might need to learn how to become invisible, to pass through life without drawing attention to the self, that the only place they can afford to let loose is at home—and the result is a kind of nudging toward narcissism which a great many children heed. They are likely to be infantile, demanding, and to cry readily to get their own way. As they move toward oedipal development, their showing-off, their curiosity, and their precocious knowledgeableness (when present) will often excite considerable admiration and positive reward, and further intensify the tendency toward a narcissistic adaptation. This will sometimes be remedied by the hurly burly of latency interaction, and a more realistic sense of self and other ensue. Often enough, however, a strong narcissistic element persists into later personality growth. This not infrequently lends a grandiose color to adolescence when alternating surges of neurotic depression, grandiosity, asceticism, and idealism are likely to make for especially complex experiences during this phase.

The particular patterns of superego development

characteristic of Jewish rearing inevitably carry within them the seeds of their own forms of psychopathology. A healthy superego makes for a well-disciplined, socially adapted personality; excessive superego demands, however, evoke a variety of troublesome results. In particular, they weight the ego with neurotic self-criticism and pessimism that can amount to a depressive tendency. Or the child can employ defenses that will screen out the painful inner voice that constantly dins criticisms in his ears. And to keep it screened out, he develops a series of wily, deceiving, manipulative tendencies that are forever concerned with evading, corrupting, or subtly defying existing authority structures, internal and external. This means of coping can be reinforced if external reality is particularly hostile; then the profoundly adaptive use of dishonesty and deception strengthens such behavioral patterns. The argument has indeed been advanced that there is a genetic factor operating here, that over many generations of persecution, the process of natural selection eliminated those families who were not adept at survival tactics of this sort. In any case, evading a powerful superego is not so easily accomplished, and this form of ego structure is probably a good deal less common than the more neurotic pattern described previously.

Toward the end of adolescence the definitive identity decisions are made that will carry the youth into young adulthood and define marital choice. It is at this point that the question of Jewish identity often faces its most severe tests. For many American Jews, there is a relative absence of external threat. They have fairly free access to educational, business, and political opportunities. They can live in most settings that they can afford, join most organizations as they choose, study or teach where they would, and live lives unhampered by obvious threats or limitations that arise because they are Jews. Thus, the external dimension of pressure toward a particular form of adaptation is effectively absent. For many young Jews this has led to strong expression of the internal dimensions of their sense of Jewish identity: They join Jewish community centers, become members of Zionist organizations, participate in various Israel-connected activities, and attend services at the local synagogue or temple. For others, however, where the need for rebellion is more profound, or where the sense of Jewish identity more attenuated, it is a time for drifting away from Judaism. The old symbols lack all meaning, the usages of the past seem superstitious and old-fashioned, the entire historical tradition seems disconnected from the present, and in any case, irrelevant, and the existence of the state of Israel seems at once trivial, unrealistic, and unjust to the Palestinian Arabs. In any case, life as an unattached American seems preferable to what is experienced as the confining hobbles of limiting Judiac nationalism (or religion). The characteristic reaction is to marry outside the faith, with the express understanding or with passive acquiescence to the fact that the children are brought up as Christians. Although this tendency appears to be increasing, the large bulk of the Jewish parents still hold fast to the uses of their traditions and so continue to rear their children.

Appendix

In recent years, the only U.S. census study that asked for the religion of the respondents took place in 1957.[6, 5] Albeit twenty years old, the findings are suggestive. Within the overall American population the Jews demonstrated a number of highly defined demographic traits. They were less fertile than Catholics or Protestants[3] with fewer children. Their median age was older. At the time they were almost exclusively (96–17) city dwellers, and were heavily concentrated in the Northeast of the country (they comprised 8.5 percent of the population in that region compared to less than 1 percent in the Southwest). They evidently valued education, both for itself and for the social advancement it offered. Thus, the average number of years in school completed by Jews was 12.3 years as contrasted to 11.3 years by Protestants and 10.4 years by Roman Catholics. Seventeen percent of Jews completed four years of college, while this was true of 7.7 and 6 percent for Protestants and Roman Catholics, respectively. These observations held for both men and women.[6, 5, 8]

In terms of work, with their longer average education, Jews tended to enter the labor force later by a considerable margin than did the members of the other groups; with more professionals and self-employed in their ranks, they also retired much later. Jewish women were likely to be in the labor force in their young adulthood, but the least likely of all the groups to continue this pattern into middle adulthood. This tendency was especially marked where there were children below six at home (11.8 percent of Jewish women with children below six were in the labor force whereas

18.2 percent of white Protestant women were so designated). At work, three-fourths of Jewish males worked in white-collar positions, while just over one-third of the males of the other denominations did so; for men, the proportion in the professions came to twice as many Jews as non-Jews, and the proportion in the categories of managers, officials, and proprietors came to almost three times the corresponding figures in the other two religions. There was a high emphasis on self-employment (one out of eight among the managerial class of the two Christian groups). All this was associated with observable differences in income level, i.e., 8.7 percent of Jewish males reported incomes of over $10,000 per year vs. 5 percent of white urban Protestants and 3.9 percent of urban Catholics.

If one leaves the overall population characteristics to look at the internal configurations of this ethnic group, it appears that there are three main currents in American Judaism. These are designated respectively as the Orthodox, Conservative, and Reform. The members of these groups vary in a number of important ways. Thus, Reform Jews adhere most closely to patterns that might be identified as "typically American." They eat the same food as other Americans, conduct their religious services in English (and do so in a "temple" rather than a "synagogue"), share in such practices as having a Christmas tree each year, regard Saturday as a time for work or shopping, and maintain a self-concept of being members of one religious persuasion among the variety of the American mix. The Orthodox, on the other hand, tend to differ most radically from the overall American model. They confine their food intake to the ritually permitted, traditionally prepared kosher menu (many an Orthodox parent will visit but will not eat in the home of their Reform or Conservative son or daughter); conduct all religious observances in the synagogue, and strictly in Hebrew (with any explantory statements likely to be made in Yiddish); observe no practices other than those dictated by the traditional Jewish writings; regard Saturday as holy and neither work, write, nor shop on that day; and feel themselves to be a chosen people who have a unique compact with God, who carry forward an ancient tradition which they must preserve at all costs in its every detail, who carry a certain responsibility for the world on their shoulders, and who will be given their long-due recognition with the coming of the messiah. The Conservatives fall somewhere in between, seeking, on the one hand, to preserve much of the traditional, but finding ways, on the other, to adapt more flexibly to the American mode of life. Their food is likely to be "kosher style." Prayers are in mixed English and Hebrew (no Yiddish is likely to be used). They are not messianic or committed to live or die according to religious tradition; but they do feel themselves to be different, special, chosen for something (just what is often not very clear), and bearing special burdens as a people.

Intermarriage is not common, but is increasing. Thus, a generation ago the rate of marriage with non-Jews was something in the order of 7 percent; currently it is more like 14 percent and probably growing.[9]

REFERENCES

1. Bureau of the Census, "Characteristics of the Population by Ethnic Origin, March, 1972 and 1971," *Current Population Reports: Population Characteristics*, Series P, *20(249)*:21–22, 1973.

2. Bureau of the Census, "Characteristics of the Population by Ethnic Origin, November 1969," *Current Population Reports: Population Characteristics*, Series P, *20(221)*: 8, 1971.

3. Bureau of the Census, "Women by Number of Children Ever Born," 1970 Census of Population, PC(2)–3A, pp. 41–44, 1970.

4. Bureau of the Census, "National Origin and Language," 1970 Census of the Population, PC(2)–1A, pp. 86–87, 1970.

5. Bureau of the Census, "Religion Reported by the Civilian Population of the United States: March 1957," Current Population Reports, Population Characteristics, Series P, *20(79)*:1–8, 1958.

6. Bureau of the Census, "Tabulations of Data on The Social and Exonomic Characteristics of Major Religious Groups," March 1957.

7. Glick, P. C., "Intermarriage and Fertility Patterns Among Persons in Major Religious Groups," *Eugenics Quarterly, 7(1)*:31–38, 1969.

8. Goldstein, S., "Socioeconomic Differentials Among Religious Groups in the United States," *American Journal of Sociology, 74(6)*:612–631, 1969.

9. Lazerwitz, B., *Jewish-Christian Marriages and Conversions: Structural Pluralism or Assimilation*, (in press).

10. Weitzman, M., Personal communication.

27 / The WASP Child

Paul L. Adams

What WASPness Is

The subcultural differences that determine the variety of childhood called "WASP" (white Anglo-Saxon Protestant child) are, first, religious—Christian Protestantism; second, an ethnic difference, namely, whiteness; and third, a broadly linguistic and cultural distinctiveness that has wide-ranging historic and ethnic implications—namely, Anglo-Saxonism. Pervading this cluster of differentiating traits is economic class, a fourth force producing patterns that may or may not be congruent with the basic three-part constellation.

PROTESTANTISM

The key elements of the Protestant ethos are (1) individualism, (2) lay control as opposed to clerical control, (3) emphasis on personal salvation and awareness of self, and (4) an appeal to the Bible or individual conscience as a higher authority than ecclesiastical pronouncements.[4] In the more than 250 sects and denominations of Protestantism there is an intermingling of these key items in a richly varying combination, and, once combined, they form a set of assumptions and apperceptions that underlies the WASP child's view of existence.

All Protestants are not alike. They vary on theological, regional, and class lines. They range from the zealous snake handler[29] to a relatively dispassionate, tolerant secularism and humanism that is barely "religious" for want of a belief system. The rural Free-Will Baptist in Georgia definitely is set apart from the New England town-dwelling Unitarian or Congregationalist. As a general rule, the Protestant sects are made up of lower-class people, while the denominations—such as Methodist or Presbyterian—include more people of middle- and working-class membership. The ecclesiastical groups, such as Anglican or Episcopalian, seldom include lower- and working-class persons.[41] As Protestants undertook to bring about an organic merger of religious bodies, they jokingly asserted that what they ultimately sought to accomplish would be a united church endowed with "Episcopalian money and Baptist fervor."

Some of the major sequelae and concomitants of Protestantism, from the child's developmental perspective, are the sense of having a cherished family heritage, of not being rootless, of being individually accountable and responsible, of being willing to change and to take risks. Familism thereby joins forces with individualism, and out of the much valued mother-child symbiosis (conjuring up the madonna and Holy Child) there grows up—from birth onward—a sense of belonging and of rootedness. Later, to this sense of being caught up in a vital network of loving care there is added the sociocultural imperative of being one's own person—of hatching out of the bonds of incestuous family feeling and differentiating out of the undifferentiated familiar "ego mass." Only the child who has been loved and warmly nurtured, Protestants say, can come to love his fellow man beyond kinship and tribal boundaries, and only the person who in infancy has been bathed in nurturant communion can in later life develop a keenly individualized conscience and personality, an articulate awareness of self.

Psychologism and privatism sometimes are found among Protestants. Psychologism occurs whenever the attitude is propounded that the inner world takes precedence over the outer world of overt actions. "Our forefathers, chained in prisons dark, were still in heart and conscience free." Psychologism attends the Protestant ethos like an alter ego. Privatism, a pattern that holds one uninvolved until oneself or one's immediate world are touched, or encroached on, also lurks wherever the spirit of Protestantism reigns.

WHITE RACISM

Since this is a society where racism is engrained in the attitudes and institutional life of the populace, the WASP child must always be seen and understood with respect to his whiteness. Racism harms the white child, too, but rather less than it does the black one. Racism is acquired attitudinally by the five- or six-year-old who attends a segregated neighborhood school as well as by the child who, over parental racist objection, is sent by bus to a more integrated school. To the degree that whiteness means an advantaged position the white child is set up to think and act racism. Therefore, feelings of racial superiority appear to come naturally to many WASP children.

Protestantism greatly supported the era of black slavery in the U.S. by providing biblical sanctions for the subjugation of the blacks, presumably the "offspring of Ham" who were cursed by the god of the Judeo-Christians to be "bearers of water, and servants of unrelenting toil." After slavery, Protestantism helped to equate racial segregation with God and sexuality with Satan[50] and, although slavery had been legally ended, a system of prejudice and exploitation took over, retaining the blacks in a position of inferiority and subjugation and, predictably, giving the whites feelings of augmented worth and moral purity. Anglo-Saxon culture, all along, had tended to be more racist than Latin and Slavic cultures, prohibiting intermarriage[1] of Anglo-Saxons with "people of color," thereby maintaining the biologic base of racism.

ANGLO-SAXONISM

Other Anglo-Saxon traits enter into the personal development of the WASP child. These are populism-agrarianism, limited government, arrogant colonialism, and ethnocentrism. Populism-agrarianism tends to value rural living, and although it does not press toward fuller economic equality, it does devalue northeastern capitalists and industrialists, along with their commercialism, environmental pollution, and "wage slavery." The U.S. is now urbanized and industrialized, yet there are several indications that, among WASPs, agrarianism is alive still—the nationwide appeal of populists such as George Wallace, of groups such as the Scout and Campfire constituencies, and the current upsurge of ecology, environmental protection, and "greening of America."

Limited government, in contradistinction to tyrannical government without checks and balances, is an Anglo-Saxon trait that has linked itself closely to Protestantism and a limited equalitarianism. The ideologic stance is that one person is as good as another in the sight of God, perhaps, but certainly that in the eye of law no person should be given undue advantage over his fellows. Trial by jury is authentically an Anglo-Saxonism. Not only fair play, but also individual liberties for all races, creeds, and noncreeds seem to flow from the Anglo-Saxon premium placed on individual political liberties and rights.[7] Anglo-Saxons would join, for they certainly preceded, the popular folk singer who said, "I think the Bill of Rights is a gas."[19]

Arrogance and ethnocentrism, fused with a colonialist attitude, have contributed important ingredients to Anglo-Saxon culture.[47] In its least pleasant forms this is seen in racism, taboos against interbreeding and commensalism, and a feeling that it is the Britisher's manifest destiny to show the world proper manners.[48] The gist of the belief is that as underdeveloped peoples catch up, they will become more Anglo-Saxon, that is, more human, with what Edith Sitwell[49] called the Britisher's "peculiar and satisfactory knowledge of infallibility." Strong pro-British loyalties pervade North Americans, young and old, 200 years after the U.S. declared it would take an independent course.[3] This Anglophilia is most conspicuous among WASPs in particular, and in high school and college teachers of English.[28]

ECONOMIC CLASS AND WASPNESS

Economic differences have a telling influence on WASP children's development. Class affects the biologic survival of children in all groups and thereby influences not only the cultural and intrapsychic worlds but also the bodily existence and growth of every child. Class is, supremely, the sociocultural stratification that affects the biologic stock of large populations.[38]

Class is a reality that is learned unawares to a great extent, and its deepest injuries often lie hidden.[8] It is learned effectively, however, during the formative years of childhood, for, by the time of adolescence, lower-, working-, and middle-class youths have distinct life-styles and world views. They differ in their career plans and possibilities,[34] education test scores,[14] sexuality,[12] gestures, patterns of clothing, speech, and every other economically influenced trait.[54]

White racism, Protestantism, and Anglo-Saxonism all vary according to class. Hence, the WASP child is enculturated into his WASPness according to his family's class positioning. Protestant *sects* (such as Holiness and Church of God in the Rock) are mainly lower- and working-class, and *denominations* or *ecclesiastical* Protestant groups tend to be more affluent.[41] Working-class WASPs are often alleged to have greater racial prejudice than middle-class WASPs, but this has been disputed and perhaps disproven[6] when one compares working-class WASPs to workers from other ethnic groups. Similarly, populism, fair play, and respect for political differences all vary with class. Family styles or household life-styles differ according to class, in ways that sociologists have explored deeply.[13, 33, 55] Some of these findings are important for child psychiatry and will be summarized briefly here.

The middle-class WASP household stresses the growth and actualization of the individual, with personal development efforts deploying large time blocks and energy investment by both children and parents. Often "equalitarian," the family may through a front of equality mask the parents' childism[40] and the husband's patriarchal longings.[2] The family lives apart from relatives, by and large, but the kinfolk are important mostly at vacations and in times of family turmoil. Middle-class WASPs travel considerably and, while owning their dwelling places, move their place of residence frequently. Still, from sheer numbers alone, the mobility of poor and working-class people outstrips that shown by the middle class. The religion of the middle class is carried rather lightly, for it is a liberal religion, held and transmitted mainly by WASP middle-class mothers. Occasionally, upwardly mobile middle-class WASPs will belong to fundamentalist sects or to evangelical denominations, but this is rather like a vestige of "old-time religion" carried upward with them, or it attests to a more recent conversion experience by one of the parents. Valuing individual advancement and esteeming individualism to the extent of privatism, middle-class WASPs revere formal education. They are vigorous purchasers of services, ranging from those services supplied by barbers and diaper laundries to motels, restaurants, and child psychiatrists. Richard Sennett[46] characterized these families as having a family style of great intensity, for they believe that their family life is but a microcosm of all that is productive and valuable in the entire world at large.

Blue-collar WASPs are considerably more numerous than the middle class, for the U.S. remains a country with a working-class majority.[32] Working-class WASPs spend less money for services of all kinds and devote more time and motion to "do it yourself" projects. Compared to middle-class WASPs they show lower income and economic life chances, more familism at the expense of individualism, more employment of the mother as the family's only servant, more viewing education as an economic enhancement for the whole family, and an attitude that having a single home is good because it means escape from the restrictions imposed by bosslike landlords.[21] Working-class sons follow in their father's footsteps vocationally, educationally, and sexually. Males are accorded higher aspirations than females, educationally and vocationally, although progressively larger numbers of working-class women work both

in and out of the household. Sexual roles are sharply defined and workers' family lives are parent-centered, adult-directed, and father-controlled.

Class differences are telling. Lower-class WASPs resemble lower-class blacks or Chicanos, etc., more than they resemble whites, Anglo-Saxons, or Protestants as ideal types. Their family style is female-centered and directed. Adult males, when present, are likely to be marginal, part-time, and disvalued by the mother and maternal grandmother. Family pride and identity are carried by the mother who, with many of the values of a working-class woman, may make great sacrifices in order to get education for the "financial betterment" of her children. Not matriarchal because she stands alone, *faute de mieux* she rears her children under the shadow of considerable want and privation, in an action-oriented world. Little involved in social forms of every description, the lower-class WASP's religion typically shows diminished, sporadic, and intermittent features. The child psychiatrist needs to be especially attentive to the family history when studying lower-class WASPs, for a pervasive coloration results if the family during one or two generations earlier were working class or even "genteel poor." An understanding of individuals and families interplaying against an intimate subculture, over several years and generations, is more fruitful for psychiatric work than any facile stereotyping by class, gender, race, or religion.

Number and Distribution of WASP Children

In 1975 there were at least 71.67 million members reported by Protestant churches in the United States.[27] Assuming that these were largely adults, since Protestants as a group do not accept people into membership "before the age of accountability"—thirteen or more years of age—one could make a rough guess that over one-half the children in the U.S. are in a Protestant milieu and that two or three of every five children might be estimated to be WASPs in the nation at large. Rural areas, both farm and nonfarm, are found to be predominantly Protestant. The southern U.S. is a largely Protestant region and contains the Bible Belt of fundamentalism, hence, save in portions of southern states such as Louisiana, will be highly WASP in composition.

Developmental Impact of WASPness

The WASP values, like all other values, are implanted by precept and example as early as the neonatal maintenance and feeding. In their most vital aspect they are learned implicitly and assumptively, not overtly and verbally. However, Jules Henry[23] found nursing mothers to be verbalizing sturdy capitalist-Protestant virtues such as "Waste not, want not" while bottle feeding their newborn babies. A special mystique surrounds WASP mothering and the bond between infant and mother. That bond is reinforced further by the fact that among affluent WASPs a familiar awareness spanning many generations is present. The WASP infant learns, if circumstances are ideal-typical, that he is immersed in a sea of caring, loving interdependence.

Then, if the child is not held in bondage to symbiotic infantile patterns, he grows with the imprint of a model of altruistic optimism that serves him well for savoring all the face-to-face relationships to be experienced throughout life. Such a child has a zesty self-confidence and feeling of self-worth that can be observed readily in the toddler, nursery school, and elementary school eras. He feels he has hatched as a good egg and grown according to a good plan. If the ideal infantile-maternal relationship does not occur, as may happen in WASP households of both the lower class and upper middle class, the child will be more defensive, less secure, and less trusting of others.[52] If full dependence during infancy is not relished and acknowledged, there lurks a fear of domination that shadows the growing child's existence.[58] Or, if the WASP child does not progress beyond infancy, she or he will retain a mother-fixated immaturity that southern writers have described often and clearly.[35]

The anal and phallic oedipal phases create expected crises for WASP children. The familism of the WASP household has some drawbacks, for familial and tribal pride have frequently been made the basis of arrogance and provincialism, as manifested early, for example, in school children who derogate others who lack strong family roots. In preadolescence the WASP most frequently finds a WASP from a similar family for the beloved chum and, if so, development proceeds in a salutary way, validating worth and forestalling loneliness. Only in adolescence may the WASP youth undertake his first rebellious reinspection of the family pride package on which he was enculturated, and this undertaking gives pungency to the WASP adolescent's search for an identity of his own.

WASP parents show ambivalence about their child's freedom. On the one hand, they know that it is not what they enforce on the child but only what the child discovers directly and experientially that will serve to develop a conscience of his own. Hence, the parents are torn between their wish to have individuality unfold and, at the same time, their wish to civilize by extracting obedience. The child is caught in this ambivalence, concluding that he must be both a conformist and a reformer, or even if radical "respectable."[20] He must be a dutiful steward, industrious and rather joyless, as he learns to stand alone.

The child learns the subtleties of when and where and in what measure he can assert himself, and often the WASP child is pleasantly surprised that he is "allowed" considerable autonomy by parents and sibs, and encouraged to experiment and risk. At the same time at latency age the child may become so compulsively duty-bound that naturalness and spontaneity are in short supply. The Anglo-Saxon and Protestant threads interweave to strengthen the child's growing sense of autonomy and accountability. On the Protestant side the universal priesthood of believers is actualized, and every person stands accountable for his *own* decisions, commitments, and choices, without intermediary or interceder. The immediate encounter with "the indwelling Christ" is deeply felt and personal. Private prayer and devotional exercises are stressed. "As a man thinketh in his heart so is he."

Closely akin to these religious values are political values on liberty for the person, equality for any and all beliefs, and a sense of civic responsibility and duty.[30] All these seem to flower in the patriotic sentiments of WASPs at latency age.[43] Robert MacIver[36] described his WASP childhood as a time of being ever sensitive to the Great Taskmaster's all-seeing eye. Harry Emerson Fosdick[11] noted how his father had left word for him to cut the grass "if he feels like it" and after a few paces uttered the addendum, "Tell Harry he had better feel like it." Children are to do their thing if that coincides often enough with the godliness of adults and their life of stewardship. The latency period is enshrined in Protestantism. If Protestants hold life serious, and the purpose of Christian living is to set one's conscience aright, then it is an easy transition to the view that wasting time is sinful and earning money is a God-given warrant of virtue. Albert Schweitzer[45] learned as a Protestant child that carefree, lucky people must feel called to diminish the pain of others. Nearly any kind of work or duty comes to be thought better than fun and play. Another corollary is the opinion that the poor must have brought their misfortune on themselves. From puritanism to capitalism is not a giant step, as Max Weber[56] explained and Herbert Hoover[25] exemplified. By adulthood the WASP has been enculturated into an industriousness and seriousness that make for a good citizen, and parent, if "times are good." But if racism, economic collapse, and civil disorder characterize the times, the obverse side, the shadow of all WASP virtues, comes to the fore with intense bigotry, authoritarianism, exploitation, and violence—the dark side of whiteness, Protestantism, and Anglo-Saxon culture. "Violence has a very human face,"[5] and the WASP face is very human, regarding violence.

FAMILIAL REACTIONS TO WASPNESS

The WASP child derives support from the very fact that people of his cultural type are hegemonic, although in a community where differences are allowed, if not always praised. His family does not have the shame or defensiveness that are so often elicited from minorities in majority-ruled democratic societies. As pluralism comes to supplant the majority-minority system, WASPness, because of its premiums on individual diversity and the primacy of the individual's conscience, may be expected to give WASP families a sense of merit without imparting the arrogance historically associated with WASP dominance of national life.

CULTURAL REACTIONS TO WASPNESS

A prevailing form of radical or liberal chic during the past two decades has tended to ridicule WASP attributes, even those of children, while vaunting the features of almost all other ethnic groups.[37] That situation is in stark contrast to an earlier worshipful definition of "American" in a strictly WASPish model. The ideology of Americanization and the melting pot was one which stacked the cards in favor of WASP ways.[17] Culture change has already occurred in the power, status, and advantage formerly associated in the U.S. with whiteness, Anglo-Saxonism, and Protestantism. It would seem likely that these changes will advance apace as various non-WASP ethnic groups intensify their rhetoric and their effective instrumentalities for obtaining greater equality in the United States. The WASP establishment is dead[44] but its successor will, in all probability, retain certain of the external and some of the inner features of the WASP way of life which stamped the ethos of American life throughout most of the first bicentennium of the nation's existence.

CHARACTERISTICALLY WASP EMOTIONAL DISTURBANCES

Earlier psychodynamic theories postulated built-in, phylogenetically programmed conflicts and complexes: Freudians saw the Oedipus complex as instinctive and universal, Jung saw collective unconscious archetypes as part and parcel of the mental life of all children throughout the human species. Only the Adlerians and the post-Freudians turned their attention to experiential and social variables, thereby paving the way for the study of psychopathologic states that vary across cultures and subcultures, and are thus relative to the specific and intimate culture of the child's experiencing. Sullivan, Horney, Fromm, and Clara Thompson were leaders in this tendency to see child development, whether healthy or pathologic, from a social standpoint. Hence, the matter of emotional vulnerabilities within particular ethnic, religious, or racial subgroups of children is an issue that is alive only for the holder of a post-Freudian, sociopsychiatric perspective. Logically, we can see the import of WASP distinctiveness but regretfully we lack an adequate amount of clearcut empirical work to elucidate our logical expectations. The field of psychohistory as it pertains to the history of childhood represents an important endeavor in studying white Anglo-Saxon Protestant childrearing* as well as other cultural groups. Likewise, the older social anthropology concerned with "culture and personality studies"[24] and the sociology of childhood,[9] taken along with transcultural studies of familiar and exotic, culture-specific syndromes,[31] make for immense steps forward in a multi-discipline field that is still embryonic.

The following discussion is selective and speculative out of necessity, and truncated, but the reader is referred, for details, to the foregoing text and to other selections of this handbook containing descriptions of the different psychopathologic syndromes, particularly of character malformations. The orienting values of WASPness focus on the individual person—his values, identity, integrity, relations with others—that is, on the realm of neuroses and character problems.[26] In table 27–1, an effort is made to summarize the ways in which positively valued WASP traits can, by extension to rigidity or absurdity, become symptoms.

* See references 53, 10, 15, 22, and 51.

TABLE 27–1

WASP "Virtues" and Their Related "Symptoms" at Various Ages

Stage	Virtue Propounded	Symptom Picture
Oral	Do not spoil child	Neglect, inadequate "mothering"
Oral	Trust in others	Overdependence
Anal	Self-control	Overinhibition, phlegm, fears & shame
Anal	Independence, responsibility, accountability	Compulsion, scruple, overwork, officiousness
Anal, Oedipal	Be your own person	Oppositionism
Oedipal	Self-starting energy	Narcissism of the "self-made"
Latency	Self-awareness	Introversive isolation, quiet, self-criticism
Latency	Self-assertion	Tension discharge disorder
Latency	Fair play	Sentimentalism
Preadolescence, adolescence	Group belonging	Pseudo-mutuality, over-conformism
Preadolescence, adolescence	Self-reliance	Mistrustfulness
Adolescence	Identity	Ethnocentrism, intolerance

The long-range effects of the character structures of WASPness will include, provided that no more serious patterns than neuroses and character disorders develop, the neuroses and character problems of adult life,[42] with the potentiality of decompensating under grave stress to a psychotic disorder.[18] Probably the most frequent consequence of WASPness driven to absurdity is just short of symptom-formation. As has been formulated by Jung, Otto Rank, Erich Fromm, and others, it is the problem of an unfulfilled, "unlived life."[57] In some ways, it is an outcome that might be less happy than neurosis, and certainly less interesting.[16] The Protestant enthronement of Logos and devaluation of Eros create a corrective that may be called for in mass bureaucratic society, but it makes for an imbalance, a lack of wholeness, that, since it is unconscious, goes along unrecognized.[39] The Jungians—and Jung came out of a Protestant heritage—have stressed the "shadow" which is unconscious, unaccepted, and projected, filled with insufficiently developed functions (thinking, feeling, sensation, intuition) and subliminal perceptions. The WASP shadow of candor is sanctimoniousness; of compassion, inverted self-pity; of humility, inferiority; of loyalty, obstinacy; of considerateness, hypocrisy; of generosity, a grand mixture of inimitable fecklessness with corrupt calculation. WASP living is well endowed with shadow, compensations and reaction formations.

Coping Devices Among WASP Children

WASP culture does provide children with certain kinds of defenses, notably reaction formations and a sublimating love of hard work. The Protestant ethic has some residual utility for coping in the contemporary world. From a favorable perspective it can be said to enhance life, but from an unfavorable or detracting perspective it must be said to induce a rather grim seriousness of outlook.

Being white, Anglo-Saxon, and Protestant is not always an agonizing ordeal for the WASP child. Some of his attributes may be considered as special competences: a hustling industriousness, a feeling of stewardship, a strong sense of self (in self-identity, self-worth, self-control, self-assurance, self-study, self-help, self-enlargement or improvement, and even in self-transcendence), willingness to take the rap if failure devolves after "giving it an old-school try," a willingness to experiment, to make and to take changes, to take risks. The learning of the WASP child is frequently unhampered and joyous as a result of the WASP ethos already outlined (although it may be a recurrent anguish of inferiority). In general, the WASP image has had good press agents[47] and has, in fact, often oversold the product behind the image. Likewise, for WASPs to prosper in a pluralistic society there need be provided no "special arrangements" or "affirmative action"—unless these cultural traits come to be considered special: political democracy, guarantees of individual rights and liberties, trial by one's peers, respect for "different drummers," and a nation concerned for human welfare, even for the welfare of little children.

REFERENCES

1. ADAMS, P. L., "Counseling with Interracial Couples and Their Children in the South," in Stuart, Irving R., and Abt, Lawrence Edwin (Eds.), *Interracial Marriage: Expectations and Realities*, Grossman Publishers, New York, 1973, pp. 63–80. See also Kovel, Joel, *White Racism: A Psychohistory*, Pantheon, New York, 1970.
2. AGEL, J., *The Radical Therapist*, Ballantine Books, New York, 1971.
3. ALSOP, S., *Stay of Execution: A Sort of Memoir*, J. B. Lippincott, Philadelphia, 1973.
4. BOWIE, W. R., and GINIGER, K. S., (Eds.), *What Is Protestantism?*, Franklin Watts, New York, 1965.
5. BRONOWSKI, J., *The Face of Violence*, World Publishing Co., Cleveland, 1967.
6. CAMPBELL, A., *White Attitudes Toward Black People*, University of Michigan Institute for Social Research, Ann Arbor, 1971. See also reference 32.
7. CLAIBORNE, R., "My Turn: A WASP Stings Back," *Newsweek*, 84:21, 1974.
8. COBB, J., and SENNETT, R., *The Hidden Injuries of Class*, Knopf, New York, 1972.
9. DE MAUSE, L., et al., "The Evolution of Childhood: Symposium Article," *History of Childhood Quarterly*, 1(4):503, 1974. See also Bremner, R. H., *Children and Youth in America*, Harvard University Press, Cambridge, 1970.
10. DE MAUSE, L. (Ed.), *The History of Childhood*, Harper Torchbooks, New York, 1975.
11. FOSDICK, H. E., *The Living of These Days: An Autobiography*, Harper Chapel Books, New York, 1956.
12. GAGNON, J. H., and SIMON, W., *Sexual Conduct: The Social Sources of Human Sexuality*, Aldine, Chicago, 1973.
13. GANS, H. J., *Urban Villagers: Group and Class in the Life of Italian-Americans*, Free Press, New York, 1962.
14. GOODMAN, P., *Growing Up Absurd: Problems of Youth in the Organized Society*, Vintage Books, New York, 1960.
15. GORDON, M. (Ed.), *The American Family in Social-Historical Perspective*, St. Martin's Press, New York, 1974.
16. GREENBERG, S. I., *Neurosis Is a Painful Style of Living*, New American Library, New York, 1971.
17. GREENLEAF, B. K., *America Fever: The Story of American Immigration*, Four Winds Press, New York, 1970.
18. GROEN, J., "Psychosomatic Disturbances as a Form of Substituted Behavior," *Journal of Psychosomatic Research*, 2(2):85, 1957.
19. GUTHRIE, A., cited in *Look Magazine*, 33:64, 1969.
20. HAHN, J. A., "The Respectable Radical," Master's Thesis, Roosevelt College, 1971. See also Alinsky, S. D., *Rules for Radicals: A Pragmatic Primer for Realistic Radicals*, Vintage Books, New York, 1972.
21. HANDEL, G., and RAINWATER, L., "The Working Classes—Old and New," in Lopata, H. Z., *Marriages & Families*, p. 353, Van Nostrand Company, New York, 1973.
22. HANDLIN, O., and HANDLIN, M. F., *Facing Life: Youth & the Family in American History*, Little, Brown and Co., Boston, 1971.
23. HENRY, J., "The Problem of Invariance in the Field of Personality and Culture," in Hsu, F. L. K., (Ed.), *Aspects of Culture and Personality*, p. 139, Abelard-Schuman, New York, 1954.
24. HONIGMANN, J. J., *Culture and Personality*, Greenwood Press, Westport, Conn., 1973.
25. HOOVER, H., *On Growing Up: Letters to American Boys & Girls*, William Morrow & Co., New York, 1962.
26. HORNEY, K., *The Neurotic Personality of Our Time*, Norton, New York, 1937. Also Fromm, Erich, *Man for Himself: An Inquiry into the Psychology of Ethics*, Rinehart, New York, 1947.
27. JACQUET, C. H., JR. (Ed.), *Yearbook of American and Canadian Churches: 1975*, Abingdon Press, Nashville, 1975.
28. JONES, H. M., *The Theory of American Literature*, Cornell Paperbacks, Ithaca, 1966.
29. LABARRE, W., *They Shall Take Up Serpents: Psychology of the Southern Snake-Handling Cult*, Schocken Books, New York, 1969.
30. LASSWELL, H. D., "Democratic Character," in *Political Writings of Harold D. Lasswell*, p. 463, Free Press, Glencoe, Ill., 1951.
31. LEHMANN, H. E., "Unusual Psychiatric Disorders and Atypical Psychoses," in Freedman, A. M., Kaplan, H. I., and Sadock, B. J., *Comprehensive Textbook of Psychiatry II*, p. 1724, Williams & Wilkins Co., Baltimore, 1975.
32. LEVISON, A., *The Working Class Majority*, Coward, McCann & Geoghegan, New York, 1974.
33. LEWIS, O., "The Culture of Poverty," *Scientific American*, 225(4):19, 1966.
34. LIEBOW, E., *Tally's Corner: A Study of Negro Streetcorner Men*, Little, Brown and Co., Boston, 1967.
35. LOOFF, D. H., *Appalachia's Children: The Challenge of Mental Health*, The University Press of Kentucky, Lexington, 1971. See also the plays of Tennessee Williams and the novels and stories of Carson McCullers and Flannery O'Connor.
36. MACIVER, R. M., *As a Tale That Is Told: The Autobiography of R. M. MacIver*, University of Chicago Press, Chicago, 1968.
37. NOVAK, M., "The World of the WASP," *Christian Century*, 90:334, 1973. See also reference 7.
38. PASAMANICK, B., and KNOBLOCH, H., "Complications of Pregnancy and Neuropsychiatric Disorder," *Journal of Obstetrics and Gynaecology of the British Empire*, 66:753, 1959.
39. PHILLIPS, D. B., HOWES, E. B., and NIXON, L. M. (Eds.), *The Choice Is Always Ours: An Anthology on the Religious Way*, Harper and Brothers, New York, 1960.
40. PIERCE, C. M., and ALLEN, G. B., "Childism," *Psychiatric Annals*, 5:15, 1975.
41. POPE, L., *Millhands and Preachers*, Yale University Press, New Haven, 1942.
42. REICH, W., *Character Analysis*, 3rd ed., Farrar, Straus and Giroux, New York, 1971.
43. RENSHON, S. A., *Psychological Needs and Political Behavior*, The Free Press, New York, 1974.
44. SCHRAG, P., *The Decline of the WASP*, Harpers, 240:85, 1970.
45. SCHWEITZER, A., *Memoirs of Childhood and Youth*, Macmillan, New York, 1955.
46. SENNETT, R., *The Uses of Disorder: Personal Identity and City Life*, Knopf, New York, 1970.
47. SIMON, E., *The Anglo-Saxon Manner: The English Contribution to Civilization*, Cassell, London, 1972.

48. See reference 47; also Frazier, E. Franklin, *Race and Culture Contacts in the Modern World*, Knopf, New York, 1957.

49. Sitwell, E., *English Eccentrics*, Vanguard, New York, 1957.

50. Smith, L. E., *Killers of the Dream*, Norton & Company, New York, 1949.

51. Smith, S. R., "Religion and the Conception of Youth in Seventeenth-Century England," *History of Childhood Quarterly*, 2:493, 1975.

52. Stone, M. H., and Kestenbaum, C. J., "Maternal Deprivation in Children of the Wealthy: A Paradox in Socioeconomic vs. Psychological Class," *History of Childhood Quarterly: The Journal of Psychohistory*, 2:79, 1974.

53. Strickland, C., "A Transcendentalist Father: The Child-Rearing Practices of Bronson Alcott," *History of Childhood Quarterly*, 1:4, 1973.

54. Terkel, S., *Hard Times: An Oral History of the Great Depression*, Avon Books, New York, 1971. See also

Tumin, M. M., *Social Stratification*, Prentice Hall, Englewood Cliffs, N.J., 1967; Shuy, R. W. (Ed.), *Urban Language Series*, Center for Applied Linguistics, Washington, D.C., 1969.

55. Valentine, C. A., *Culture and Poverty: Critique and Counter-Proposals*, University of Chicago Press, Chicago, 1968.

56. Weber, M., *The Protestant Ethic and the Spirit of Capitalism*, Allen & Unwin, London, 1930. (Original 1904- 1905.)

57. Wilson, C., *New Pathways in Psychology: Maslow & the Post-Freudian Revolution*, Taplinger, New York, 1972.

58. Winnicott, D. W., "From Dependence Towards Independence in the Development of the Individual," in Winnicott, D. W., *The Maturation Processes and the Facilitating Environment*, International Universities Press, pp. 83–92, New York, 1965.

---

28 / The Catastrophically Uprooted Child:
Southeast Asian Refugee Children

Jean E. Carlin

Refugee children from Southeast Asia are different from other children who come to the attention of mental health professionals. The differences lie in their cultural backgrounds, their languages, and their reasons for being refugees (whether they are orphans, unaccompanied children under the age of sixteen, or children of refugee families). They may have come from Vietnam, Cambodia (Khmer Republic), or Laos. They are different also because in fleeing their war-torn country, they escaped the same war which divided the people in the country to which they have come. Most such refugee children left their homes with little or no planning or preparation. Many arrived in the United States possessing only the clothes on their backs; all else was lost. Many of these refugee children escaped during and after the sudden change of governments of Saigon and Phnom Phen at the end of April 1975. On the day of Saigon's fall, April 29, 1975, some people from the ever-increasing crowds were being lifted by helicopters from rooftops or were escaping in small boats or navy military ships from the Saigon harbor and from the numerous rivers of the Delta. The departures took place amid fires, shooting, sirens, and mortar shells. People were screaming, running, pushing, and shoving; all trying to get

away in order to survive. These people believed they would not be permitted to live in the new regime because they were high-ranking military officers or government officials or employees of the Americans, etc. Together with their immediate and extended families they were fleeing to somewhere, anywhere, as long as it was away from Vietnam or Cambodia.

The ships and the planes were unprepared for this sudden mass exodus, and many refugees boarded ships without adequate supplies of food. In addition, the navy ships had no shelter—only the open deck. Here, a mass of what later swelled to 3,000 people huddled together. There was room only to sit or stand, but no space to lie down for many days. Some people died en route.

Those who survived the escape eventually arrived in the Philippines or Guam where they were assigned to refugee camps for several weeks of confusion, waiting, hoping, and processing. At this juncture they were safe and fed, but still very frightened. Many families had been separated, and these now began the long and often fruitless process of searching for relatives and friends among the other escapees. Some did locate relatives, others did not.

Next these refugees were sent on to one of the

four refugee camps in the continental United States—in Florida, Arkansas, Pennsylvania, and California. More waiting in tents or quonset huts followed, with more processing and locating of sponsors, etc. This waiting amid cold and confusion was first met with euphoria and enthusiasm at having entered the United States. As the reality of being penniless, homeless, and "imprisoned" in a camp guarded with armed American soldiers began to be perceived, many of the refugees became afraid, depressed, or angry. In the new surroundings, some of these brave, courageous, and proud people became humbled, deferential, and fearful. Others, however, began to learn the English language and customs. Since the donated American clothes were often much too large for the small Southeast Asians, they began to sew to remake these garments. Some even unraveled sweaters and reknit them to smaller sizes. They began to scan newspapers for jobs.

The number of the uprooted refugee children is difficult to estimate. On the babylift, 2,043 young children came to the United States. There were 440 to 500 more unaccompanied minor children aged two to sixteen years. Eventually, for many of these children, some relative (however distant) was located, and they were reunited then with some remnant of family. The remaining unaccompanied minors were between the ages of twelve and seventeen. Approximately 70 percent of them were boys. They were placed in foster homes. Another sizable group of refugee children came with their refugee parents. All told, 130,000 refugees of all ages came to America (there were 135,000 who left Indochina—130,000 was the U.S. quota and 5,000 went to other countries). Since many families have several children, it is probable that at least 50,000 to 60,000 of these were refugee children (45 percent of the refugees were under seventeen years of age). Therefore, together these groups included over 60,000 Southeast Asian refugee children under the age of seventeen years now living in the U.S. Of all the male refugees, 44.3 percent were under age seventeen years; of the female refugees, 48.1 percent were in that age group.

The refugee children were scattered throughout the fifty states, Guam, and Canada. However, the largest concentrations of refugee families and hence refugee children settled in California, Texas, and Florida.

Many illnesses exist in Southeast Asia which are nearly unknown in the United States, but which needed recognition in these refugees. The most immediate health problems were dengue fever, cholera, plague, tuberculosis, diptheria, malaria, hepatitis, and skin diseases plus various kinds of intestinal parasites. Often, one or more illnesses plus several parasites were present in one person. During the first several months, the malnutrition and vitamin deficiencies were corrected, and the acute contagious diseases which manifested themselves had been treated. However, there still remained the anemias, parasites, and skin problems plus recurrent bouts of malaria and some leprosy, along with tuberculosis which could become active at any time. Tuberculosis is still endemic in Southeast Asia; 30 to 40 percent of the population have active tuberculosis, and a very high percent of adults exhibit positive tuberculin skin tests (proving that they have or have had the disease). The three to twelve months following these traumatic escapes were filled with stress. Initially there was malnutrition. Then came the attempt to become settled in the United States, working long hours at one or two jobs, plus studying. With all this, it could be expected some of these persons would and did demonstrate reactivation of their tuberculosis. Even small children may have tuberculosis; some infants received BCG prophylactically at birth in Vietnam and would have positive skin tests requiring chest x-rays for their evaluation.

In understanding and anticipating future developments, the age of the child at the time of arrival in the United States as a refugee or as an orphan from Southeast Asia is extremely significant. Infants under a few months of age will have little or no memory of their experiences in Southeast Asia or of their precarious and usually difficult voyages to the United States. The adjustment of the very young refugee infant is primarily a function of the infant's physical condition and the mental status of the caretaking adults in the new environment. Even for young infants, the dangerous escapes without food and clothing predisposed them to malnutrition, weight loss, and multiple illnesses. If the infant was part of an orphan babylift and was placed into an American adoptive family, the infant will face the same problems as any adopted child, plus the unique problems of the cross-racial adoptee. These difficulties have been described elsewhere and are not unique to refugee adoptions. Again, delayed development and serious physical problems may be noted. Since there were no unaccompanied children under the age of two years, there are no very young refugees in this category.

The very young infants who arrived in the United States with their refugee families also will have little or no memory of their countries nor the trip across. Some were born en route during the several-week voyage by boat to the Philippines and Guam and then to the continental United States. The adjustment of these very young infants will be a function of each infant's physical condition and the mental health of its parents and extended family. As the refugee family faces and copes with the crises of daily living in a Western culture, the child will learn to cope as well. The chances are they will be much like the first- and second-generation Chinese, Japanese, Cuban, and other immigrants and refugees in the United States.

The older infants between six months and two years of age will have some memories of the past which can present unique problems. They will seem to adjust well and quickly at first, but these memories are preverbal and hence not abstract. They involve primary process thinking and feeling. Ultimately, they might prove to be the most difficult problem of all. Because of the terror experienced from the loud noises of the mortar shellings, the parents' panic, or their loss, the frantic screaming of people, the crying, and the fleeing will remain vivid and will defy verbalization. Some of the Korean orphan children adopted by American families have had such terrors. For the most part it comes out in dreams—dreams which have a nightmarish quality and cannot be put into words.

Since there is no way to identify and deal with these fears, they may persist indefinitely. One Korean child who was adopted at age one year and who is now thirteen years old has continued to have these indescribable night terrors, although in all other aspects of her life she has adjusted very well.

Normally, by twelve to fifteen months, children are beginning to speak in their own language. Rapid acquisition of language then continues for the next twelve to twenty-four months up to age three years. From three years on, language becomes more refined and diversified. But, whenever a sufficiently traumatic event occurs during the time of learning any new skill, that learning can be significantly disrupted or even stopped. The babylift children aged twelve to thirty-six months were the children at risk for disruptions in language skills. Just as these children had begun to learn that certain sounds have meanings, they were uprooted and transplanted into a culture which does not reinforce the same sounds under the same circumstances. The babylift children were placed with foster parents who did not speak Vietnamese. These children were too young to

conceptualize language in the abstract and to realize that their task was to learn a new language which would give them a certain mastery of the new environment. The change in reinforcement systems is equivalent to giving an experimental animal an insoluble problem. This can lead to the development of neurotic behavior including disruption of language learning, and, conceivably, cessation of speech.

Yet another complication arose because children past the age of infancy were often assigned incorrect ages (at least by Western standards for calculating age). This could mean that these children would eventually be compared with incorrect norms for growth and development, and could be placed in the wrong grades in school.

For most Southeast Asian children, age is calculated roughly from conception. Thus, most village children are considered to be one year of age at birth, and they gain one year at every New Year's or Tet. If a child were born just before New Year's Day, he would be two years old immediately! Some of the children had no birth certificates. To facilitate their leaving the country, birth certificates often were forged with some arbitrary ages written in which might be older or younger than the calendar ages. At one refugee camp a tall young boy was introduced to the author as "twelve years old." When the author asked, "Is he *really* twelve years old?" his parents responded that this is what his birth certificate says. The author persisted. Finally, they admitted that the boy was really fifteen years old, but they had had the birth certificates forged to keep him out of the army longer. When asked "Is he fifteen years old by Vietnamese counting or by American counting?" they said: "By Vietnamese counting." It was suggested that by American counting, he was actually fourteen years old, and they agreed! This can be important in school placement, in athletic competition, and social situations.

The refugee child over the age of two years and up until nine or ten has many memories of the country from which he came and of the long trip which ended in the United States. Many families did not intend to come to the United States— they were simply fleeing to stay alive. They did not know where they were going. Hence, the children did not know what was happening either. These young children remember their languages, foods, culture, and customs. They remember the war, and they have some concepts about the Viet Cong (V.C.) in Vietnam, Cambodia, and Laos. Although they usually do not understand that V.C. are communist and that the war was a political and philosophical struggle, they well remember hiding from the V.C., running from the V.C., being taught to "hate" the V.C., and not always knowing why they must hate. To be sure, some have had the experience of watching parents or relatives killed by the V.C. and they hate for personal reasons. Others have had no experience and just know they are supposed to hate the Viet Cong.

One two-and-a-half-year-old Vietnamese boy had been in transit two months and in California for several weeks. One day he said in Vietnamese: "Mother, I don't hear any shooting." Another time he said, "Why did we leave our home . . . was it because of the V.C.?" And eight months later he hid behind the sofa and announced, laughing, "The V.C. won't let me come out!" His parents were startled that he remembered so much for so long. Evidently he had been thinking what had happened and finally asked about it. This youngster was fortunate in having parents who understood his language and who had been through it all with him. They could provide him a certain stability. They could answer his questions. They could understand his working through the problem in his play. At age three and a half, this same child heard a firecracker explode outside. He was very frightened and said, "Is it the V.C.?" The refugee children in adoptive or foster homes whose new parents cannot understand their language must face these haunting questions alone. Along with these burdens, they must grapple with many other questions regarding new customs and the whereabouts of their real parents. This can terrify each child until he has finally learned enough English to ask questions in English. But by that time, he has usually developed some fantasized cause-and-effect relations and may no longer ask the questions. These half-memories and distorted explanations can be the breeding ground for many later emotional problems which will be exceedingly difficult to untangle.

In learning a new language, in this case English, it is important to realize that the Southeast Asians have real language-learning abilities which may in part be genetic. During the 2,000 years of war or occupation, those persons who could most quickly learn the new languages were the ones who found good jobs and survived; it is their descendants who are now among the Southeast Asian refugees in the United States. For the same reason, namely, survival of the fittest, these refugees generally also have above-average intelligence. Perhaps in this instance intelligence is helped by the use of the abacus for learning mathematics. This makes the

learning of mathematics concrete, touchable, and visualizable instead of an abstract subject. In any case, the Southeast Asian people tend to excel in mathematics as well.

However, English is written with Latin Letters, and Cambodian, Thai, and Laotian are script languages (Chinese, Japanese, and Korean are written in characters); learning English therefore requires learning a new alphabet as well. For the Vietnamese learner of English, the alphabet is essentially the same since Vietnamese is written with Latin letters. If the Cambodian or Laotian learner reads French, he already knows the Latin letters and this should facilitate learning. One might predict that the Vietnamese refugees and other refugees who know the Latin letters from French should learn English more quickly and easily than will those Cambodians, Thais, and Laotians who do not read French because they have entirely different tasks.

The refugee children will learn English in the same sequence as the young child who learns English as his primary language. That is, the first words which will be learned will be nouns and proper names. Next will come action verbs. Third, adjectives will be learned. Then abverbs will follow. Next in turn, simple sentences will be formed which are agrammatical and asyntactical such as: "Huong no like shirt blue." In Vietnamese, the adjective generally follows the noun. Last to occur are the personal pronouns beginning with *I* and *you* and later followed by *my* and *yours*. Since Vietnamese contains no personal pronouns as such for he, she, him and her, his and hers, these personal pronouns continue to be used inappropriately long after learning English.

The refugee child between nine years and fifteen or eighteen years of age will also have some intricate adjustment problems. Children and adolescents in this group face the usual identity problems of early and later adolescence, but in addition they must work through an identity conflict about being Asians in America. Some of the children and adolescents who have been seen and worked with in this age group were unaccompanied refugee children. Their conflicts about being Vietnamese-Americans were manifested by intermittent resistance to the authority and rules of Americans. This included limit testing which went somewhat beyond the expected level for that age. The limit testing involved ignoring rules that had been previously stated and understood, refusing to stop some activities when told to stop, and instigating fights with peers, both Vietnamese and American. One twelve-year-old boy stated that he didn't have to follow the rules because the rules are for American children and he is Vietnamese. He fought both physically and verbally to prove his identity as a Vietnamese. He had been taught to hate Americans whom he felt had deserted his country and therefore caused his people to lose the war, and now he had to be dependent upon Americans. He was fighting to avoid "becoming" or "turning into" the American he was supposed to hate. He did not know how to deal with this ambivalence except by fighting.

These children have some unlearning and new learning to do in several areas of the new culture. Some of these were street children who had learned in Southeast Asia that for a child of five years old and older, survival depended upon rapid movement from one place to another without being caught or found, being resourceful in appropriating food and money, and learning to cheat or trick people when necessary. It was essential to save face frequently and to be able to fight to defend oneself or one's possessions. The children who came from educated and intact families were protected from these needs to survive on their own and were taught honesty and courtesy. The less fortunate children, however, learned their survival skills very well. It was not surprising that they began to apply the same solutions to problems in America. However, now their fighting or cheating or stealing did not lead to success—instead it resulted in trouble, and they did not understand why. They needed to learn other ways to reach their goals—ways which would be tolerated by the new society.

A basic dynamic issue in Southeast Asian cultures is fear of losing face. Individual behavior is molded by the culture through eliciting shame for significant deviations. This is in contrast to Western-Judeo-Christian cultures which mold individual behavior by eliciting feelings of guilt. The differences between control by guilt and control by shame are described elsewhere; these differences will be sources of confusion to Southeast Asian refugee children and the adults in their families. In its attempts to teach, control, and understand these refugees, it also poses problems to the majority culture of the United States. Many strange situations arise which cannot be comprehended within the framework of either culture without appreciating the relative differences in amounts of shame versus guilt control present in the other.

The social structures needed to respond to these uprooted Southeast Asian children in an optimum way must include:

1. Economic support systems available for the first twelve to eighteen months for the families; new occupational skills, vocational counseling, and job opportunities for the adults, and educational opportunities to learn to improve English. These economic systems are necessary so that the children perceive some sense of stability in their families and can dare to proceed to deal with their own adjustments from a secure base.
2. Educational support systems to aid these children in learning English and other subjects which are taught in English. These should include experiences in sports, art, music, and mathematics which are not primarily verbal and which allow these children to succeed or excel immediately, thus aiding and supporting their self-concepts. Many of these children were doing very well in school in Southeast Asia, and they are distressed at not being at the top of their class here immediately. Many will top their classes within one to two years, especially in mathematics, abstract reasoning, and foreign language studies. Educational opportunities to share their cultural experiences with American children aid the refugee children in forming their self-concepts and in maintaining their identity as Asian Americans. It has enriched and benefited the American children as well. Different can be interesting and valuable.
3. Educational programs on T.V. and radio, articles in newspapers and magazines, and books on the interesting aspects of other cultures and the American subcultures can all help. These emphasize customs, values, foods, philosophies, ways of rearing children, language structures and implications for thinking and behavior, etc. These educational interventions into the American media and reading diet add to the American culture, and reduce provincialism and discrimination; they benefit the refugees by hastening their acceptance and giving them a sense of pride at being able to contribute in a special way to the majority society.

Perhaps the best way to illustrate some of the characteristics of the catastrophically uprooted Southeast Asian refugee children will be by case histories. Therefore, two case histories plus some brief observations of other children are presented. All names of the children and staff have been changed to preserve confidentially.

Case History of Van

The patient was an unaccompanied Vietnamese male refugee child between the ages of eleven and thirteen years. He claimed to be thirteen years old, but he also gave his date of birth as December 1963 or 1962 which would mean he would be twelve or thirteen years old December 1975.

Chief complaint: The patient had no chief complaint. He was referred because he was considered unmanageable and hence not placeable by some of the people at the Unaccompanied Children's Center at the refugee camp. The H.E.W. authorities who were responsible for these children thereupon requested a psychiatric evaluation and recommendations for this child's future.

History of present illness was obtained from the child himself, and from the physicians and attendants at the refugee camp. Van presented a management problem at the Unaccompanied Children's Center because he was constantly testing the limits and was frequently involved in fights with other children and personnel. He often instigated these fights and attempted to control other children by verbal orders as well as by physical force. Because of this disruptive and unmanageable behavior he was seen by the child psychiatrist who was assigned to the children's unit. Foster home placement was being sought for all of these children, and Van was accordingly seen by the social workers from the County Welfare Department. The child psychiatrist's report and the opinions of the County Welfare Department were diametrically opposed as regards both this child's diagnosis and prognosis for adjustment. Numerous people in the military, both at the camp, in Washington, D.C., as well as Congressmen and Red Cross personnel became involved in the controversy over what to do with Van. In an attempt to resolve this problem, HEW authorized outside consultation.

The following letters by Van translated from Vietnamese were included in the background information provided.

Camp, August 25, 1975

I overcame hardship and arrived in California. I am very tired of life and wanted to die. Who will build for me a grave after I die? Who will bury my body? Who will say "I love you"? I need not live because life is not beautiful. I love girls best. When I am going to die only my parents, family, and fatherland are above all. I would like chicken and hamburgers to be served at the ceremony conducted in remembrance of the day on which I died. This will help my soul come to heaven soon. I always remember our friends and my family. [Note: Dying and suicidal thoughts plus dying as a Vietnamese and becoming an American who eats chicken and hamburgers. See later belief in rebirth.]
Died on 25 August 1975.
I had a photo of me taken before I died for use as a souvenir.

Van

Camp, August 26, 1976

Impressions of a Lonely Boy

There is not any fun to live a camp with a special name "orphan." The only thing which satisfies me is the fights with people who have a different nation with me. I wonder why I endure under such suffering like that. But I have to live—to revenge! To revenge the people who have a different race and blood with me.

A suffering boy, I let my life run the way it does. I don't know when I will be able to leave this Camp where I have many memories. Beside the name "Camp," we call it "a community prison" which was run under the organization of a terrible group. They revenge me with many means. But my fate is already arranged. Although many things happen to me, I'm always a clear boy as my parents name me, never become a turbid boy. Live, I have to live, live and see my parents the last time. The sadness, sometimes, made me not well thinking, and the terrible group named me "a crazy boy" in Camp and in a trailer with terrible memories. My friends, they are like me, why they don't have to hear this ugly name, they are luckier than me. But when I think deeply, I like this crazy name, it is like a name of a hero in a small country, everyone knows it. I am proud of it.

Some nights, I lie beside my friends, I think back about my past, present, and future, I cry myself. My tears of 12 years shed off my eyes in 1975. I don't know why I don't hate them, but they dislike me. Even they are well educated than me, they have a good position in the free country, they still don't think carefully if they hate me. Why, why they hate me. They told me to write my impressions about them. They hate me, but I do not hate them. They are pitiable, they might have mental illness or different diseases. Now I feel my mind is empty. I do not love or hate anyone. I hope that I can leave this military training school, the American soldiers. I only wish to have a sponsor to take me out and go back to school, have a new life and see my friends. That's all. I do not ask for anything. My heart is empty. I write this impression to show the people around me that I am a crazy boy, Van.

Van was transferred to the University of California, Irvine Child Psychiatry Unit, so that he could be in a closed environment under twenty-four hour observation by psychiatrists and nursing staff experienced and skilled in observing and dealing with disturbed children. On admission to the ward, Van was greeted by the other children who made rapid gestures of friendship. Van responded to this quickly and appropriately; an hour later, however, he requested that he be allowed to leave the hospital. He explained that all the children here were "crazy" and that he was "not a crazy boy."

Van told his doctor the following story: Many years ago his father had escaped from the Communists in Hanoi and had fled to the northern part of South Vietnam. There he became a lieutenant in the Vietnamese Marine Corps. The family lived in a city in the northern part of

South Vietnam. It was there that Van was born. He claimed the date of his birth was December 1962, however, his records at the camp say December 1963. Van's father was injured while in service and was unable to remain in the military. He bought a boat and worked as a fisherman until, somehow, his boat was sunk. He managed to buy another boat. It was in this boat that the family had hoped to escape, but it was presumably stolen by a Vietnamese marine. At the beginning of April 1975, the Viet Cong and North Vietnamese managed to capture the northern two-thirds of South Vietnam. Van and his family, which consisted of his mother and father and six siblings, fled to the south and finally ended in Vung Tau, a seaport town about twenty-five miles outside of Saigon. They had hoped to escape from there but the Viet Cong advanced rapidly and took Vung Tau. At this point the family's hope for escape was markedly decreased. Thousands of other refugees were also living in Vung Tau. He was able to play outside because he was a small child and the V.C. did not bother him. In fact, he followed the V.C. around and made friends with them and they gave him a pair of shoes. After two days the V.C.* saw a boat beginning to leave the shore and they sent Van out to tell that boatload of people to come back. Van said he would do it and he would be right back. Instead he ran and jumped into the boat and told them to keep going.

That is one version of the story. There is no way to verify any of Van's story, so the facts may not be correct. In any case, he escaped in this boat. After several days without food, he was able to get to a large American ship. It was during those several days that Van first realized that he had left his family behind and might not see them again. He became frightened and rationalized that he would go and see the American ship and then go back to the land to rejoin his family. However, when he arrived at the American ship he was told he would not be permitted to go back to Vietnam. A lieutenant commander from the Vietnamese Navy told Van to get on the American ship and stay with the commander's family, which Van did. He had known many people who had gone to America and had come back with amazing stories about a big and beautiful country, and he thought it would be interesting to see America. He was taken to Guam and was at the refugee camp there for a time. In Guam, he met a family

with whom he has since corresponded; they are said to be interested in having Van as a foster child. Sometimes Van says he wants to go back to Guam. At other times he says he wants to go to Hawaii where he thinks perhaps he might be able to locate his parents some day if they ever escape. From Guam, Van was sent to the stateside camp, and ultimately, to the Unaccompanied Children's Center there. During this time he had become alternately very angry and very sad—angry because he had been taught that many things about Americans were bad, and sad because he realized he might never see his family again. He didn't know if they were alive or dead, if they were starving or well, and the reality of what he had done began to be clear to him.

Van had numerous conflicts, ideological as well as psychological. One ideological conflict had several aspects—he had a positive interest in America and what it has to offer him, as well as a prior negative experience in Vietnam where he had been told that Americans sometimes are bad. Another conflict involved the Viet Cong—his father had fled the Communists in North Vietnam and was injured fighting them in South Vietnam. Van had also lost an older brother, whom he never knew, who had been killed by the Viet Cong. The whole family fled to Vung Tau and planned to escape the country to flee from the Viet Cong. At the same time, the two days of personal experience with the Viet Cong had been pleasant. They were good to him, they said they were his friends, and they gave him shoes. Thus, again and again, what he had been told and what he had experienced did not fit.

A third area of conflict for Van involved an important dimension of his own identity. He was very insistent upon remaining a Vietnamese child, but he desired an American education so that he could become the captain of a ship and maybe some day return to Vietnam. At the same time he did not want to become "an American," whom he has been taught to hate or fear. This conflict took unusual forms for its expression. For example, in some of his writings, he talked about dying as a Vietnamese; since the rest of his behavior did not suggest that he was suicidal, this could be interpreted in various ways. For example, he might need to die as a Vietnamese in order to become an American.* Another version of this conflict was observed in some of the play boats that Van made out of clay while on the Child Psychiatry

---

* The V.C. soldiers might have been fifteen to seventeen years old—not much older than Van, so it is not so strange that they would send Van to halt the boat.

* This interpretation was provided by Dr. Carlos Velez from the Department of Anthropology at the University of Southern California.

Ward. In one of these boats, he placed the body of a person lying in the bottom of a ship. He stated that the person was dead, and that this person was himself. (See figure 28-1.) A third example was Van's occasional reluctance to follow the rules on the Child Psychiatry Ward. He believed that being sent to his room or being sent to sit on a chair were rules for American children; since he was not an American child, he could therefore claim immunity from these rules. It is possible that to a Vietnamese, being sent to his room or being made to sit in a chair is in fact a loss of face. Thus the conventional methods for time out resulted in a considerable threat. Within this framework, Van would rather fight than lose face.

My LIFE WANDERS IN THIS SMALL SHIP

VIET NAM'S FLAG 3 STRIPES

HE SAID THAT HE WILL ACCEPT HIS FATE AS A BOAT DOES — HE IS THIS BOAT.

FIGURE 28–1

It was evident that such areas of conflict would require time, patience, and possibly some therapeutic intervention in order to be resolved. Only this would enable Van to deal with them, and to live comfortably. He would need help in understanding the war in Vietnam and America's involvement in it, if indeed this ever could be explained satisfactorily. Van was very angry toward Americans because he felt that in the last year, the Americans did not give support to Vietnam in terms of money and weapons; and it was for this reason that Vietnam lost the war to the Viet Cong. He knew that in 1968, at the time of the Tet Offensive, the Americans provided large amounts of money and ammunition for Vietnam, and that the Vietnamese were therefore able to defend their country successfully and to win against the V.C. at that time. Van was very proud of this accomplishment. But, he stated, in 1971, American aid was reduced, and in 1972 it was essentially stopped. When asked if he knew why this happened, Van said "Yes, President Ford [historically he is in error] wanted to give money to Vietnam but the American people wouldn't let him." When he was asked where President Ford would get the money to give to Vietnam, he seemed unable to answer this. When we discussed taxes, Van understood what was meant. Still, he was left with a profound sense of residual anger about this lack of support and it was to this that he attributed the loss of his country.

There was no signs of serious psychiatric disturbance in this child such as psychosis or suicidal depression. It is difficult to know what would be "normal" behavior for a child or an adult who had been through years of war and a frightening escape from a country such as Vietnam. Therefore, Van's reaction to these traumatic experiences cannot be evaluated in terms of any established norms. All things considered, however, it seemed that his adjustment and reactions to his experiences were well within normal limits. He showed a normal amount of fear and concern for his parents' current safety. He showed a large need for love and dependency, typical of a child between the ages of eleven and thirteen. At the same time, he made serious attempts to appear and, in fact, to be, independent of adults; this is also typical of boys his age. Van's ability to distort the truth, to manipulate others and to test the limits did not seem seriously disturbing to anyone on the ward. These abilities may have assured his survival in the very recent past, and were therefore adaptive. His own writings suggest that while at the refugee camp he was trying to play the part of a "fool" because people thought that he was a fool. Therefore, in order to have some identity and to gain a bit of extra attention from the few adults responsible for so many children, Van adopted a role. This certainly gained him significant amounts of attention, although most of it was negative. When other means for getting attention were available, Van knew how to utilize them appropriately.

CONCLUSIONS

For the above reasons, the discharge diagnosis was:

Situational adjustment of reaction of childhood in an unaccompanied Vietnamese refugee child manifested by (1) conflicts in identity, (2) sadness, (3) anger and aggressiveness as ways of warding off sadness, and (4) limit testing typical of age.

RECOMMENDATIONS FOR VAN

1. Foster home placement:
   a. if possible, with the family in Guam who wants him and to whom he wants to go;
   b. preferably where there are no young children;
   c. preferably where there is a warm, loving mother and a firm, loving father, where clear limits are set, and where discipline is consistent.
2. Inform the foster parents of the comments and recommendations in this evaluation.
3. Provide follow-up on Van's medical problems.

Subsequently, Van moved to Guam. The only available follow-up is through letters which indicate that he is adjusting satisfactorily.

Case History of Loc

Loc is a nine-year-old Vietnamese refugee child who was admitted to the University of California, Irvine Child Psychiatry Unit, in October 1975.

This child was at camp and was taken away from his parents because other people observed his mother beating him severely. The mother admitted in writing that she beats this child because he is a "naughty boy." She claimed that if he returned to her, she would continue to beat him. Therefore, for the child's protection, he was placed in the Unaccompanied Children's Center at the camp and thus came under the authority of HEW.

In a delegation of authority paper, Loc's mother wrote,

". . . my child Loc—I cannot educate him and he does not want to come back with me. However, I like him to live with me. I desert him to ARC to educate him—and I hereby do not have any liability against his acts in the future."

The child did not speak English. Therefore, the information had to be obtained from the child, Loc, through an interpreter, and from continuous twenty-four-hour-a-day observations by the trained child psychiatry staff. The author utilized a limited command of Vietnamese plus much nonverbal communication.

Chief complaints: Patient has no complaints currently—he claims he is here because he had been a "bad boy," and that he was put here so that the staff could decide what was wrong.

Past history: Loc is a Vietnamese refugee child who escaped from Vietnam on April 29, 1975 (the day Saigon fell). He escaped on a boat to an American ship bound for the Philippines, finally reaching the refugee camp in the United States.

The patient claimed his mother beat him severely and occasionally hit the other children. The father usually just watched. The mother hit the father sometimes also.

Loc is a very alert and active child who has good coordination and appropriate affect. He can be delightful and charming, but he can also be very stubborn and resistive. He had trouble following rules on the ward, partly because he could not understand English; even when the rule is explained to him in Vietnamese, however, he often tests the limits. While some of this is normal behavior for an eight- or nine-year-old, Loc's resistance is often much more than normal.

Loc does not want to return to his natural parents. He prefers the hospital or English-speaking American foster parents to his own family. He has consistently held this position while at the hospital. He showed no evidence of loss, sadness, or grieving when separated from his parents. On the contrary, he seems happy and free here. Under questioning Loc explained that he would not miss his parents or siblings in the future because he didn't live with them for the past two years in Vietnam—his mother had put him into boarding school and only visited him once.

The patient is a well-developed thin Vietnamese male of approximately eight or nine years (born 1966). He looks sad but is in no acute physical distress. His physical examination was normal except for evidence of old injuries.

Loc was admitted to the hospital October 1975.

He made good progress. From a rebellious, angry child who spoke no English, he became a cheerful, active, eager learner who could communicate very effectively in English.

During his hospital stay Loc learned English well enough to express anything he needed to ask or tell. He is now able to recognize his emotions and to acknowledge them in English. Predictably, this has decreased his outbursts of overt anger and frustration. He is also becoming aware of and concerned about other people's needs and feelings. He has developed the concepts of "his" and "others" in respect to material possessions. He accepts overt affection and enjoys it. He began to ask why other children already had been placed in foster homes or in residential care ranches but he had not yet been placed. He realized that he has been hospitalized longer than the other children and wondered about this too.

During the five and a half months of hospitalization in the Child Psychiatry Ward, Loc made rapid progress in learning English. He was nine years old and realized that there are other languages besides his in the world; he correctly perceived that the task he must undertake was to learn equivalent English sounds for his Vietnamese words. (If he had been a younger child, between three and six years old, he might not have comprehended the required task, and it would have been more difficult and confusing.)

Loc began learning English in the same way and with the same sequencing that a small child uses in learning its first language. That is, he began by learning names of people and things and places.

Next he began seeking out and learning action verbs, such as running, walking, sleeping, lying down, sitting down, etc.

Adjectives came next with colors and numbers being the first modifiers of objects. He learned from everyone. He placed the adjectives *after* the noun objects, i.e., *shirt blue, bear yellow*. In Vietnamese this would be the correct order. At first Loc was permitted to use any word order as long as it communicated. Very gradually the task was made more difficult. One day he was told, "Loc, Vietnam—*shirt blue*; America—*blue shirt*. He laughed and tried it. Then he tried "Vietnam—*bear yellow*; America—*yellow bear*. He went around the room reversing adjectives. Suddenly another unresolved issue found a method of solution—how to tell Loc that he must reverse the order of his name.

Cambodian and Vietnamese names begin with family name first, the middle name (often a sex marker such as *Van* for boys and *Thi* or *Tuyet* for girls), and then the person's given name last. He was told, "Loc, Vietnam—Nguyen Van Loc; America—Loc Van Nguyen." He said, "How come?" He was told, in Vietnamese, "Americans crazy." He laughed, and thereafter he reversed his name.

Personal pronouns presented a very special problem because in Vietnamese there are no personal pronouns (except *I*) in the sense in which we know them in English. There are other ways to indicate who is speaking, but personal pronouns like *he, she, him, her, his, hers, me, my, mine, your, yours* do not exist in equivalent forms. Therefore, Loc did not know what to do with these words. He said, "The book is in your room." When questioned he repeated this and ran to his room to get the book. *Your room* was what Loc thought the room was named, because people told him, "Go to your room." Solving this was a difficult task. Everyone on the staff began watching Loc's speech for personal pronouns and showing him how to say them correctly. One day he held a picture of himself and someone else. He pointed to the picture and said, "Me." He was assured, "Yes, that is you." He repeated, "Me." Again this was confirmed; then he got his scrapbook and again pointed to the picture. At last, he was told, "Yes, it is yours. You say 'Mine.' " He said "Me?" He was corrected, "No, 'mine.' " He said, "Why?" Again the only answer is, "I don't know. Crazy." He laughed. His personal pronoun usage improved but it is not perfect yet.

Loc learned English so rapidly because he is bright and he had a great need to know it so he could communicate his needs and thoughts. Finally, all of his communication was in English, but he still enjoys reading a Vietnamese-English New Testament.

After many months of uncertainty as to Loc's status, the court finally decided to retain its custody and place him in a foster home.

Now that he is able to express himself well, he said, "Doctor, when I first came to the hospital, I was upset." "Yes, you were very upset. Do you remember why?" He said, "Yes, I couldn't speak English, the other children thought I didn't know anything." He discussed how hard this had been for him. This same phenomenon of terrible temper outbursts not responding to reassurance has been reported in two Vietnamese girls in the American culture—one a seven-year-old street child adopted by an American doctor, and one adopted by one of the authors of the book *They Came to Stay*.[6] Each child improved greatly as soon as enough

English was learned to be able to express fears, needs, and past upsetting experiences (from one to several months). The tremendous anger, fear, and frustration which result from finally knowing how to express needs, thoughts, and ideas in one language and then suddenly switching cultures where no one understands that language is almost impossible to imagine. Emotional outbursts were the only way these children could express this frustration, anger, and fear.

Refugees from Cuba and Hungary

Among the unaccompanied Cuban refugee children, there were many who had communications problems. This was not just because of limitations in English; there was also blocking in speaking Spanish. Some children experienced it so acutely that they were nearly mute, even though they were twelve to sixteen years old at the time they came to the United States.[4] Some of these children have also had sexual identity problems and problems in their marriages.*

* Personal correspondence with Maria Poinsett from HEW, who has remained in contact with many Cuban refugees who came to the U.S.A. as unaccompanied children.

Other quieter refugee children, both boys and girls, can be expected to have some of these same conflicts and areas of frustration. These problems might manifest themselves later in other forms such as depression, withdrawal, daydreaming, night terrors, or antisocial behavior such as stealing, lying, or even violence. Recognizing these areas of conflict and frustrations as possible in every child should help in understanding each child's needs and might prevent more serious problems.

Even twenty or more years after fleeing their homelands, many of the Hungarian refugees continue to need and rely on the support system of the Hungarian refugee community. It meets their social as well as political and cultural needs. This might indicate the need for the newly emerging Vietnamese, Cambodian, and Laotian associations to be encouraged, strengthened, and funded as the best mental health agencies for the refugees.

In closing, it is important to stress that although the Southeast Asian refugee children have come from cultures very much different from the American culture, most of them will adapt well and can make a contribution to American society in the years to come. They can join the ranks of the Asian-Americans, and take their places and play their parts in the history of their newly adopted country.

REFERENCES

1. CALL, J. D., "Helping Infants Cope With Change," *Early Child Development and Care,* 3:229–247, 1974.
2. CARLIN, J. E., "The Southeast Asian Refugee Child: In Situ," Paper presented at the American Psychiatric Association, May 1976.
3. GOLDSTEIN, J., FREUD, A., and SOLNIT, A., *Beyond the Best Interests of the Child,* Collier, Macmillan, London, 1973.
4. GOLLNITZ, R., "What Type of Children Were Especially Vulnerable to Harmful Influences of War and Postwar Periods?" *Monatsschrift fuer Kinderheilkunder,* 103:91–92, February 1955.
5. LIFTON, B. J., *Vietnam Orphan Airlift.*
6. MARGOLIES, M., and GRUBER, R., *They Came to Stay,* Coward, McCann and Geoghegan, New York, 1975.
7. RATHBURN, C., DI VIRGILIO, L., and WALDFOGEL, S.,

"The Restitutive Process in Children Following Radical Separation from Family and Culture," *American Journal of Orthopsychiatry,* 28:408–415, 1958.
8. RATHBURN, C., et al., "Later Adjustment of Children Following Radical Separation from Family and Culture," *American Journal of Orthopsychiatry,* 35:604–609, 1965.
9. VAROCAS, H. A., "Children of Purgatory: Reflections on the Concentration Camp Survival Syndrome," *Corrective Psychiatry and Journal of Social Therapy,* 16:51–58, 1970.
10. VILLENGER, W., "After-effects of War on Children and Adolescents," *Monatsschrift fuer Kinderheilkunde,* 103:65–72, February 1955.
11. WRIGHT, H. L., "A Clinical Study of Children Who Refuse to Talk in School," *Journal of American Academy of Child Psychiatry,* 7:603–617, 1968.

29 / The Street Child

Virginia Nichols Wilking

I could tell you,
If I wanted to,
What makes me
What I am.

But I don't
Really want to—
And you don't
Give a damn.

Langston Hughes
"Impasse"[10]

The Street Child and
the World Around Him

THE PHILOSOPHICAL PURSUIT OF THE
STREET CHILD

To pursue the idea of the absolute street child
is to seek a will o' the wisp. His name may be
legion, but the legion exists only in the mind's eye.
There these children are seen as street-wise Arabs
of the urban desert in a company which includes
Fagin's gang, the lost of the Children's Crusade,
the small displaced pirates who look to Peter Pan
for protection in outer developmental space,
Hansel and Gretel in a fairy-tale forest and
Horatio Alger's newsboys of nineteenth-century
New York.[9]

Conceptually, the street child has suffered final
loss, where loss is defined as deprivation, and
where its mechanisms range among neglect, displacement, and abandonment.[4]

The street child stands as a model for the damage done to all emotionally deprived children.
Living on certain city streets and roaming the
adjoining blocks and avenues, he is often heard
of, but seldom seen; somehow he is always somewhere else. By definition he is hard to know; he
is not to be found at home, not in school, not
even in family court or in the precinct station
house, and very seldom in the child psychiatry
clinic. Those seen most often fit the stereotype
least well, and those who fit it best are seen least.

The Number of Street Children—

Their Distribution in the Culture

It has been pointed out that the street child represents a state of mind and a state of affairs; they
are relatively few in actual numbers. Wherever
they are, they serve as an individual deprivation
index; statistically, however, they are but poorly
represented.

To be sure, the available statistics do reflect
the state of the nation, and give at least some
information. In general, the number of such children will be highest where poverty is greatest; the
extent of poverty in turn correlates with the crime
rate, and welfare rate, and inversely, with the
reading level.

The Joint Commission on the Mental Health of
Children reported in "Crisis in Child Mental
Health"[5] that 25 percent of the children of the
United States live in poverty. Rainwater[30] points
out that in the cities, 64 percent of the children
live in poverty while only 38 percent of these or
other urban poor have fathers in the home.
Malone[20] indicates that only 10 to 20 percent of
the one-fourth of the families in the lowest socioeconomic group produce the severely handicapped
children. Out of this 10 to 20 percent come the
families who beget a street child. This 10 to 20
percent are at the far end of the poverty scale;
they are the most severely handicapped by the
nature of their environment and by the style of
their adaptation to it. In effect, these families and
their children have taken a crippling fall off the
wrong side of the bell-shaped curve.

Other statistics in "Crisis in Child Mental
Health" put the level of emotional disturbance at
10 to 20 percent of all children under the age of
eighteen years. (The available resources are estimated as having the capability of serving only 7
percent.) In fact, in an area like Harlem, 85 percent of children show reading level retardation.
Overall, 6 percent of all the families in the one-
fourth of the nation which is ill-clad and ill-fed
consume 55 percent of psychiatric, casework, and

protective services,[34] and 60 percent of the children live in families on welfare.[3] These are the same families most likely to produce the children who slide out of the home and onto the streets.

Why any given child who lives in a poor family in a poverty-stricken area is damaged to this point, or reacts in this way, is not clear. It may be a function of the extent of poverty (always severe in the families of these children); it may be an expression of the specific dynamics determining the nature of relationships and the extent of social disorganization.[28] Minuchin[24] describes these families as characterized by the most severe instability and the greatest degree of disorganization. Indeed, from the child's point of view there may be no characteristics of family life; care is cursory and unpredictable, and relationships so inconsistent as to be nonexistent.

Different Levels of Development

In children suffering different kinds of deprivation, interference with development occurs sporadically with what seems to be inborn inconsistency.

Sometimes the interference can be observed in action and reaction. Sometimes the child's response is positive and adaptive, sometimes it is sadly maladaptive. Marans and Lourie[22] describe the consequences of the use of culturally determined patterns of child rearing which, they feel, are passed on from generation to generation. Here the patterns of action are reflections of what family members have learned to expect. The consequences, seen in the child's patterns of action, are not what the adult wants; this, however, does not alter the adult's ongoing child-rearing practices.

In tracing the patterns of action these authors indicate some of the possible deviations in development at the different stages. In brief, the child who grows up against a background of poverty is deprived of appropriate feeling responses and so fails to react appropriately.

Rainwater[30] depicts some of the obstacles in their developmental path by noting how oblivious certain mothers are to their children's illnesses, and how slow to restrict them when it is indicated. The mothers' inability to respond is related to their concern with the child's potentiality for trouble, and their fear of and inability to admit to the possibility of any more trouble. Their disregard adds to the child's difficulties in developing

self-esteem. The necessary components that make for pleasure in self are lacking.

As Pelion is piled on Ossa, development begins to lag. Even by four years of age, a child can be two years behind in certain areas. Among the children studied in the Therapeutic Nursery of the North Point Project, Pavendstedt[28] describes the "prevalent tendencies." These cut across the usual developmental milestones to characterize these children from two and a half to six years of age in the following ways:

1. language so distorted that the sense was missing
2. pervasive use of denial
3. hyperalert audiovisual responses side by side with heedlessness
4. dependence on adult intervention
5. confusion in relationships by complex patterns of adaptation
6. literalness and inflexibility
7. absence of separation anxiety along with absence of trust
8. limitations in the capacity for gratification—little pleasure in self
9. pseudo-autonomy
10. lack of predictable sequences
11. precocity—capacities greater than age expectancy
12. self-depreciation and anticipation of failure
13. discharge of tension through physical activity

There was an initial sense that these children were "all right," but as the study continued, the spurious quality to the hyperalertness and the unsatisfactory quality of the overly quick reactions began to outweigh this first impression. The complaints of "I don't do it good" and the automatic smiles began to sadden the observers. The various kinds of failure in learning were seen as developmental failures, with the most serious failure of all being the failure to learn how to learn. This type of handicap expresses a serious defect in all spheres—emotional, social, and cognitive.[23]

Kellam and Schiff[15] and C. P. Deutsch[7] describe the maladaptation of the child in the first-grade classroom. The former describes the restless, aggressive behavior of the nonlearner. As scored by teachers at the beginning and end of the school year, his failure to learn eventually made him literally sick. The latter noted a falling off in cognitive function as adaptation was needed to allow for the appearance of learning based on prior experience.

The development of language was inhibited by its rudimentary use (Lerner[18] noted that the adult language developed in ghetto populations is highly descriptive, but is not based on formulation, or on the use of symbols). The integrative process in this and other spheres seems particularly at risk.

In their detailed discussion on the analysis of a Negro adult, Hunter and Babcock[13] review the development of intrapsychic structure as observed from within the culture of being poor and being black. They emphasize the importance of gratification of needs as part of an object relationship, the importance of dependency needs as a condition of being loved and loving, and the presence of the biological drives. Given certain defects in the intrapsychic structure of the adults involved, their discussion underlines once more the relationships and the responses which are at risk for infants born into certain households in the purlieus of poverty.

In spite of the likelihood of disaster, the law which states that "if something can go wrong, it will" is not always true. In the most disorganized and least stable families some of the children develop better than they "should." Psychiatrists are still better able to see the factors which make something go wrong than to identify the strengths which prevent such an outcome.

The most ubiquitous finding associated with developmental deviation seems to be reading retardation. The most serious failure, however, is the inability to integrate fragmented learning. That integrative process is essential to the "ease of aquisition" which serves as a necessary precursor to further learning.[7]

PRESCHOOL YEARS

In the preschool years, the children who may later fall out of the family cannot be recognized, even by their pseudo-precocity or spurious air of independence. All that can be recognized is the potential for trouble, measured as much by quantity as by quality. Occasionally a mother blames a four-year-old for being unable to go to the store, help get his supper, etc.

It is not so much a question of whether the mothering figure is alcoholic, psychotic, addicted, angry, depressed, or flattened by circumstance, nor even so much a question of how alcoholic, psychotic, or otherwise disturbed she may be. The really important question is, if help is made available, can the significant family member accept it? Vigorous intervention is essential. The interference with developmental process is early, and the intervention must be early. The sooner the child is recognized as a patient in his own right and the sooner the mother's needs are recognized, the better. In these tender years, the child is physically with the mother much of the time, and often poorly differentiated from her (although

often enough, the relationship may have already been interrupted by a hospital admission, his or hers).

No real connection can be made between the infants seen for failure to thrive and children later seen just off the street. In the infant, the end point of severe emotional deprivation is marasmus and death; short of the end point (for the toddler) are autistic behavior, failures in the early development of language, and the spectrum of other limiting responses (such as those already described). The three-year-old seen in one of the Harlem clinics who turned and put his pacifier in his mother's mouth to quiet her may or may not have outwitted the depriving system.

These young children are sometimes handed from one member of the family to another, rescued from one or another, and moved from one street to another (of the street but not yet on it). The nice godmothers who rescue them from the worst kind of deprivation are sometimes part of a fatal process of disengagement from their own families.

SCHOOL YEARS

When they finally do appear in clinics, these children are readily recognized. They arrive reluctantly, after several missed appointments, wary at first and then taking charge, and all the while maintaining little contact with any accompanying family member (usually the mother). As a rule, they are usually somewhat carelessly dressed, and reckless about using their smiles (although otherwise heedless of their physical appearance). The cognomen street child indicates a state of affairs and, indeed, an extremity in these affairs. The children are characterized by the damage they have suffered.

However, at the beginning of his regular schooling, the findings in the slightly older child are still nonspecific. The patterns of interaction are set but not always accepted; in their attempts to establish themselves in the eyes of their families, however, the children run the gamut of behaviors unacceptable to anyone. At this point, their charm may still be real and not indicate lack of discrimination, and their depression seems transient.

The histories their mothers give may emphasize their children's badness or minimize their behavior. It is clear that the children are sometimes at home, sometimes not. If not at home, they may "have been seen," they may "have went to my girlfriend's" or "he was on the avenue." They are only on the street part of the time but their absence from home reflects their isolation and the character of their involvement with their family. "Is he cared for?" "No."

The child explores the room first and, indirectly, the staff member. He may then move out of the room, into the hall, and on to the elevator. He may next be seen two years later, or, particularly in early adolescence, he may visit often at his own initiative, touching base, testing, and continuing to attempt a modicum of mastery. The first referral may have come from the school, the second from the Bureau of Child Welfare, and the third contact indirectly through the Family Court or the inpatient service of another city hospital.

The Harlem Child Psychiatry Clinic contacts are cross-sectional rather than longitudinal as described by Malone.[21] The attempts to follow up these children may have been quite vigorous, but when actual follow-up does occur, it is often in spite of the staff's efforts. As the hospital is in the center of the local street children's space, they may be seen passing; they usually speak, and may even make a point of a greeting.

Approximately one or two such children between seven and fifteen years of age may be seen in a year. The ratio is approximately one girl to every five boys and the overall picture is of continuing defeat; the course is downhill.

G. A. was referred to Child Psychiatry Clinic at six years of age. He was sent by the Developmental Psychiatry Clinic team who had seen his sister E. A. (admitted to Pediatrics at eighteen months for failure to thrive and now in the Therapeutic Nursery with another sibling). G. was referred because of hyperactivity. Multiple appointments were made to meet with G. but he was not seen for over a year. At seven years he was found to have a borderline IQ, to be depressed, and to show considerable impairment of fine visual motor function. He seemed forthright and open, and displayed a lively imagination. His mother, an ex-addict, had eluded psychiatric rehabilitation, was intellectually limited, saw G. as "the man of the house," and at the same time was slightly protective of him. He, in turn, worried about her. Recommendations were for special class or day program with consideration of individual psychotherapy. No outcome data is known, and recent appointments have been failed.

At the suggestion of the school, eight-year-old I. W. had been referred to Child Psychiatry Clinic by his father. The school complained that he refused to listen. He lived with his father, the building super, and two siblings. His mother, an addict, had died of tetanus when I. was four years old. The father is in a methadone program; he kept the children together. I. was stealing all over the block and known by name in the local precinct; nonetheless, father denied that any problems existed. I. had a full scale IQ score of 90, and was anxious and confused. His bravado was uneasy and he had some preoccupation with death. He had been coming and going from school and was on half-day attendance after stealing the principal's keys and threatening to burn down the school. He responded quickly to placement in a day program, but continues at risk.

ADOLESCENT YEARS

By puberty the superficiality of manner is disturbing, openness has often been replaced by suspiciousness, and matter-of-factness has given way to a certain grandiosity. There are some gaps in reality testing, and the child's insistence that his flat world is round does not hold up. As the sense of defeat comes home to the child, hostility and depression begin to appear. In quite a normal fashion, these children lose their beauty in puberty but their new awkwardness further isolates them. The signs of stunting of emotional growth are troubling both to child and staff. The incessant search for pleasure and easy gratification is time-consuming; school attendance falls off to the point of no return as the child, whatever his original capacity, falls further and further behind his peers.

To some degree disengaged from home, but always hopeful of sudden recognition there, these children remain on the periphery of almost everything; they continue to be and remain committed to existence in a highly physical environment. In their lives, the skilled use of physical senses is emphasized. The ability to elaborate on basic feelings and the capacity to appreciate nuances of feeling atrophy from disuse just as do their cognitive skills. Antisocial behavior ensues; it includes drinking, lying, and stealing. Experimentation with drugs may also occur, but those most seriously involved do not reach the child psychiatry clinics.

W. T. was first seen at ten years of age. At the time he was an open and somewhat engaging child living with an elderly aunt. Solid in status, his IQ was limited. His slow withdrawal from an unsatisfactory home to which he contributed little resulted in the imposition of fewer and fewer controls. By thirteen years, he was avoiding school and reality. He wanted to be a pimp, have three girls who would take care of him, and a big car. He was actively stealing and spent more and more time on the street; he is unlikely to succeed in that highly competitive world. He has been placed, pending return to those streets and that world.

At thirteen and fourteen years of age, the girls usually appear. Their role at home seems to bind them to the house until puberty. They attend school at erratic intervals; some go out and fight, others seek out friends and do not go. Their need to control, and their tendency to materialize suddenly, is quite like that of the boys. The few that are seen, however, show less tendency to act out against the clinic in their passage through it. The boys, more hostile and more aggressive, more aggrieved at not having "something," are demanding and infantile. Name calling and thumb sucking accompany their stealing, along with physical threats against clinic staff and forays into staff rooms and desks.

W. C. was referred by her mother at age ten. She had been living alone with mother for the first time. At the time, she had just been brought back after stowing away with a friend on a Pan American plane. W. was rather anxious, restless, and incapable of sustained contact. She truanted from school, had few friends, and was depressed, somewhat isolated, and available for trouble. W. had started leaving the house at four years of age and was frequently away for one to two days at a time. Her mother had the same difficulty in maintaining contact but had been able to work successfully. Through her grandmother W. was recently involved with an older woman selling stolen goods. She has not passed through the clinic lately.

Family Reactions

A FAMILY CYCLE: NOBODY KNOWS THE
TROUBLE I'VE SEEN

In their attempts to help the children past the old, familiar obstacles, at best, the families overly interfere; at worst, they see themselves as the obstacle. Malone[20] points out they see the children as an extension of the self, and Marans and Lourie[22] emphasize that, perhaps as a part of their parents, the children learn all too well. They develop survival techniques and there is a damaging consolidation of skills that appears prematurely. The family is usually incomplete, with its membership changing and unstable; when it does meet the child's dependency needs it is often in its own fashion. Inevitably, the interaction is tinged by the pervasive qualities of the parental character. The parents' perception is quite correct, of course—children are a trouble. But with their excessive burdens, these family members are necessarily self-protective. They see little leeway, and take very direct action to reduce the likelihood of trouble as well as to lessen their own concern. In so doing, however, they water down the relationship until it has little body and is unable to bear the weight of any feeling. Rainwater[30] is clear as to the whys of these families. As people,

they are not so very different from other people, but they have had too hard a time and the overall mood can be one of carelessness about the children.

If the trouble is not avoided, then the consequence is rage, and this may come to be directed at the child. The children can be provocative, and the timing of their demands can be disastrous; the end result is child abuse.[6]

Malone[20] describes the search for contact in these children and views their restlessness in this light. Similarly, their dependence and their demands for help are forms of response to their mother's behavior and her ways of doing for them. If they are in opposition, they maintain closeness in that way and don't move toward separation. If they become too anxious at inconsistent care on the part of the disorganized mother, they do for themselves, and again lose out. The passive responses and imitativeness are substitutes for assertiveness. The children do what the mothers want but, as Minuchin et al.[25] indicate, the cues given to the child by the parent as to preferred behavior are unclear.

Fathers are transient and often only passing through. These jobless black men are self-depreciatory in much the same way as their children. The absence of paternal feelings of self-worth carries with it inherent conflicts; these are transmitted to the sons as surely as are the feelings of special concern about the daughters. In the absence of a permanent relationship with a man, mothers turn to sons; the resulting confusion of roles (with role reversal as a major issue) sets cycles in motion. If the family relationships reflect oedipal strivings, the street child will not appear, for the family's neurotic traits will have a unifying effect. As stated and restated, the street child represents damage and deficit at a more primitive, preoedipal level.

Thus there is a special degree of poverty, a special degree of social disorganization, a special child-rearing process and, possibly, something special in the child; families say, in explanation, as rationalization, or even in all truth: "He has always been different, I don't know what's the matter with him." The idea of difference may lie entirely in the family's point of view, but it merits consideration.

Drawing on the background of his experience in the depression years in New Jersey, Plant[29] wrote of the impact of the world on the child. He was interested in individuality and in difference, and postulated that the child's "envelope" acted as a psychic membrane whose permeability was quite specific. The constitutional givens for this determined the nature of the child's responsivity and sensitivity.

Lourie[19] examined the evidence for a constitutional psychopathic state which he felt had to be reconsidered in the light of newer and more sophisticated research on the metabolism of the brain, enzyme systems, and hormones. In discussions among the child psychiatrists of the 1950s,[14] the importance of the family and infant experience was stressed while the idea of genetic inadequacy determining behavior to some point was circled uneasily, albeit with a sophisticated look at the possible role of organic factors.

Ten years later Lourie[22] pointed out that adaptation must be considered in relation to the inborn variables of reactivity or sensitivity and drive endowment.

Cultural Reactions

SOCIETY SEES TROUBLE

Reactions to the idea of the street child have been discussed in terms of their value in assuaging the adult's sense of loss. From the opposite point of view, the street child is beyond the pale and can be shut out and away. In a manner similar to that of a family, society recognizes the potential for trouble in this kind of child and is, indeed, oversensitive. These children, however, are really victims, and are themselves fearful.

For the schools, the trouble lies in their real failure to teach the children how to learn; the child's trouble is in not knowing how.

For the family courts, the trouble is what to do if you catch one. In the new framework of juvenile justice, these children will not come to the courts' attention nor will they be taken care of, a right to be pondered.

For the social agency, its problem is that it is quite aware it doesn't have any effective means for helping; it lacks the right facility. The families, usually part of the inner nucleus of hard-core families, are hard to bring to the point of decision. The greater safety lies in indecision and avoidance; children who might have had a chance for success in a residential setting continue to fail closer to home.

For the family, all the children may be seen as a trouble, especially as the toddlers change into school children. The children remain too freely on the street and around the block; ultimately, they

bring too many people to the house, people like the teacher, protective care worker, social worker, law guardian, et al.

For the child psychiatry clinic, trouble in the form of school failure is a frequently encountered clinical problem, occurring in conjunction with other troubles.

T. H. was referred to the Child Psychiatry Clinic at nine years of age because of learning problems. He was described as appearing almost angelic, albeit slightly disheveled and unkempt. He was seen briefly in individual psychotherapy, drawing thick messy pictures in fingerpaints without much form; after a year he dropped out of therapy. By this time, he was known to have a full scale IQ of 60 with great unevenness in his subscores; he was also depressed. His mother was accepting of T., but was ineffectual and sometimes argumentative. She described T. as an active, chubby toddler who was much loved. His real use of language had been delayed until three years of age, when he had been toilet trained. The need for placement away from home was acknowledged when T. was fourteen years old. In the interim, he and his mother had worked with the clinic in fits and starts. With the on-going threat of a more complete separation from home, T. continued to truant from school and spent the majority of his time on the street. Mother remained a bystander. There was little time spent in contact with the clinic. He would come for meals with one of the special classes, become increasingly restless, angry and agitated, and finally be escorted from the floor. His mother continued to deny real problems. As his outbursts became more and more severe, the plan for residential placement was eventually changed to one for hospitalization. He was admitted but continued to visit the clinic, simultaneously threatening the staff and sucking his thumb. He continues to elope and is now waiting for admission to a closed ward for violent adolescents.

Characteristic Forms
of Emotional Disturbance

HOW DISTURBED AND WHAT WILL HAPPEN

For the forseeable future the prognosis for the street child is one of inept struggles and failure; only in the unforseeable future is there any possibility of reprieve.

The "prevalent tendencies" noted by Mattick[23] and Malone[20, 21] describe the young children, two and a half to six years old, in Dr. Pavenstedt's North Point Project; the picture they paint is catastrophic. The point is made that not all the poor look like this, that these are the most vulnerable children of all because their families are farthest down on the socioeconomic scale. But these are the ways in which the children who drift to the streets begin. Undue demands are made by the family, demands the child is unable to meet. This complicates adequate coping behavior. Presently adaptation to the family demands becomes ego alien, a situation which poses a terrible developmental dilemma for any child at any age. Eventually it is handled by increased isolation and absence from home.

There is no diagnosis available in DSM-II which adequately represents these children. The picture is not unlike that seen in the institutionalized child; except for the degree of desperation it is somewhat like the child with affect hunger; it could be considered quite a bit like the borderline child; or it might be explainable in terms of a subtle kind of minimal brain dysfunction and/or genetic inadequacy to which the child then reacts. A symposium on the psychopathic child[14] considered these several possibilities, and offers much food for thought.

Not unexpectedly, Rexford[31] does best in representing these children. In describing the basic isolation they experience, and considering the associated maturational defects, she underscores their primary problems. These children are alone and lack the strengths to succeed at the task they are given. They must be regarded as belonging to the most severely damaged group of deprived children. They have suffered massive interference in the establishment of object relationships. They have little ability to exert controls, and possess very limited capacity to tolerate anxiety. Their reality testing is suspect; the gaps between what they can do and what they are asked to do are too wide to allow them to maintain a sense of reality. In the face of this picture, even rescue fantasies fail.

Forms of Coping Behavior

ALL THAT REMAINS OF COPING BEHAVIOR AMOUNTS TO: "I'M STILL HERE"

During the early years of childhood, the street child is still in the process of formation. Those who are badly battered emotionally have not yet been separated from the less badly injured, nor have the biological drives and special patterns of defensive reaction as yet emerged.

By the school years, the children who have had too painful a time at home begin to move down

the stairs to the street. Isolation and avoidance decrease the number of painful contacts, and the child progressively lowers his standards, asking less and less. There is more and more reliance on instant gratification which occurs outside the framework of individual relationships. With increased freedom from family demands, there is a further breakdown in controls. Except for glancing contacts, a similar distance is maintained from all authority figures. Since few dependency needs are met, anxiety and rage continue to accumulate, and both are discharged through hyperactivity and violent outbursts. Pleasure and pain are reacted to in primitive fashion, and there is little elaboration of coping behavior.

In early adolescence there may be a partial attempt at resocialization with some involvement in the peer group; the restless relationships with adults, however, largely serve short-term goals.

The child or adolescent is driven by his needs and his anxiety, and frustrated by being unable to find what he couldn't accept; at times, the pace becomes so frantic that he acts out in order to provoke limits. Sometimes he decompensates in the process.

The coping mechanisms are no more satisfactory than the general situation. These are children who cannot manage, who have been given no reason to manage, and who, indeed, do not.

Malone[20] describes the preschool child as not looking, not hearing, and not knowing, which, in the end, is safest.

Simple or elaborated fantasies are found in all children but communicated poorly. Elaborate fantasies may occur in those with good cognitive function. Cultural and individual impoverishment is obvious in the limitations of content.

The boys fall back on grafitti, the girls on the constant body movements of the latest dance steps. Girls rock more than boys and rock more in adolescence than during the latency period. Their goals are unrealistic in view of their inability to tolerate interference, and they substitute "I'm goin' to—" for "I am." "I'm goin' to do this—or that" offers escape rather than a defense. It is somewhat ritualized, "I'm goin' to have money, I'm goin' to go, I'm goin' to beat 'em up—" The sadness lies in the gap between fact and penny-dreadful fiction, but it is better and less painful if the fiction is maintained as such. As a result, reality testing is always at risk in the severely damaged.

The street provides some contrast; it suggests that things could be worse. There are people to be avoided and scenes to be forgotten. "I was there, I think I saw it—" "I saw the ambulance but I'm still here!"

> Looks like between 'em they done tried to make me
> Stop laughin', stop lovin', stop livin'
>   But I don't care!
>   I'm still here.
>
> Langston Hughes
"Still Here"[11]

POSSIBILITY OF A DIFFERENT RESPONSE TO THEIR SITUATION

The rescue of the street child involves a good deal of fantasy. Unless the present thesis is wrong (as hopefully it is with each case), they are limited by what they are until they can be given at least a trial of enough security and enough structure to allow for slow change over a long time. Given their antecedents, they seldom stay still long enough in informal foster homes, in the clinics, or in most programs for change to take place. At the point at which they are seen, a period of waiting is instituted in order to be sure. Eventually, however, a recommendation for placement away from home is usually made. If they are really taking to the streets to an unrealistic degree, there is little doubt that they should be offered another setting, in keeping with their age and stage. Experience suggests that the family, if in fact it really exists in any actual sense, cannot be rehabilitated at this stage. At least this cannot be accomplished in time to save the child from further damage or to alleviate the present danger. In spite of, or because of, their pseudo-precocity, these children are natural victims, and they are all too available for exploitation.

Any decision to recommend placing a child away from home is always a painful one. However weak the ties for these isolated children, they are all they have. Casting them loose looses or loses the child; his weightlessness is a further problem and there is no real solution. The field does not have a long term follow-up and one cannot be sure of what the alternative would have been had one left bad enough alone.

Social Structures Needed

WHAT SHOULD REALLY BE DONE

Intervention should start very very early and should continue, using the very effective means of prevention available.

Birch and Gussow[3] point out that one can break into the cycles of failure, but that this must involve combined approaches. Educational programs alone are not useful in the face of substandard nutrition. Pavenstedt[28] emphasizes that cognitive development is only a part of the whole and that one needs to support overall development and maturation. Berlin and Berlin[1] suggest immediate ways in which to begin using current programs and current structures in order to serve children further. Siegel, McBane, and Eisenberg[32] point out the need for remediation in the first years of schooling. Volunteer help is available in some communities but is not used early enough.

The first chapter and the first page of the report of the Joint Commission on the Mental Health of Children[5] suggests that poverty be eradicated along with the conditions which cause it. This is essential primary prevention. Undoubtedly, secondary prevention is better than tertiary prevention, and money is a great preventative at that level. The need is to go back to the beginning of the child (if not of society); there must be money for prenatal care, visiting nurses, community-based social agencies, high-risk infant centers to make up the seven maids with seven mops needed to serve families with young children.

Unfortunately there is no substitute for money. It staffs schools, cuts down the number of students in classrooms, establishes learning clinics, and provides for remediation, adult education, high school equivalency courses, block associations, and all the paraphernalia of self-help. Money will even provide the leeway necessary to allow relationships to develop and deepen in adults still capable of those relationships (even though it will not guarantee the quality of these relationships). However, funding for child psychiatry clinics, therapeutic nurseries, summer job corps programs, group homes, respite programs, et al., is essential. (It is sad to have to hope for the achievement of secondary prevention; but there is little hope for the more primary eradication of poverty.) Compromise planning could integrate present resources, and streamline those which are beside the point, while one continues to insist that children have some of what they need. For the street child, his social and emotional illness is such that one can only strive to prevent it.

> Sometimes when I'm lonely,
> Don't know why,
> Keep thinkin' I won't be lonely
> By and by
>
> Langston Hughes
"Hope"[12]

REFERENCES

1. BERLIN, I. N., and BERLIN, R., "Parents as the Developmental Advocates of Children," in Berlin, I. N. (Ed.), *Advocacy for Child Mental Health*, pp. 41–43, Brunner-Mazel, New York, 1975.

2. BERNARD, V. W., "Some Principles of Dynamic Psychiatry in Relation to Poverty," *American Journal of Psychiatry, 122(3):*254, 1965.

3. BIRCH, H. G., and GUSSOW, J. D., *Disadvantaged Children, Health, Nutrition and School Failure*, Harcourt, Brace and World, New York, 1970.

4. *The Concise Oxford Dictionary of Current English*, The Clarendon Press, Oxford, England, 1964.

5. "Crisis in Child Mental Health: Challenge for the 1970s," Report of The Joint Commission on Mental Health of Children, Harper & Row, New York, 1969.

6. DAVIS, E. B., and COLEMAN, J. V., "Interactions Between Community Psychiatry and Psychoanalysis in the Understanding of Ego Development," Paper presented at the Annual Meeting of the American Psychoanalytic Association, Denver, Colorado, May 3, 1974.

7. DEUTSCH, C. P., "Learning in the Disadvantaged," in Deutsch, M. (Ed.), *The Disadvantaged Child*, p. 147, Basic Books, New York, 1967.

8. DEUTSCH, M., et al., *The Disadvantaged Child*, Basic Books, New York, 1967.

9. FRY, A. R., "The Children's Migration," American Heritage, Dec. 1974, American Heritage Publishing Co., New York.

10. HUGHES, L., "Impasse," in Hughes, Langston, *The Panther and the Lash*, p. 85, Knopf, New York, 1967. Reprinted by permission.

11. ———, "Still Here," in Hughes, Langston, *The Panther and the Lash*, p. 32, Knopf, New York, 1967. Reprinted by permission.

12. ———, "Hope," in Hughes, Langston, *Shakespeare in Harlem*, p. 16, Knopf, New York, 1947. Reprinted by permission.

13. HUNTER, D. M., and BABCOCK, C. G., "Some Aspects of the Intrapsychic Structure of Certain American Negroes As Viewed in the Intercultural Dynamic," *Psychoanalytic Study of Society*, 4:128, 1970.

14. KARPMAN, B. (Ed.), "Symposia on Child and Juvenile Delinquency," Paper presented at the American Orthopsychiatric Association, Psychodynamics Monograph Series, Station L, Washington, D.C., 1959.

15. KELLAM, S. C., and SCHIFF, S. K., "Adaptation and Mental Illness in the First Grade Classrooms of an Urban Community," in *Psychiatric Research Report*, no. 21, p. 89, American Psychiatric Association, Washington, D.C., 1967.

16. LANGFORD, W. A., Personal communication.

17. LAWRENCE, M. M., *Young Inner City Families: The Development of Ego Structure Under Stress*, Behavioral Publications, New York, 1974.

18. LERNER, B., *Therapy in the Ghetto, Political Impotenic and Personal Disintegration*, John Hopkins Press, Baltimore, 1973.

19. LOURIE, R., "The Pediatric-Psychiatric Viewpoint" in Karpman, B. (Ed.), "Symposia on Child and Juvenile Delinquency," p. 67, Paper presented at the American Orthopsychiatric Association, Psychodynamics Monograph Series, Station L, Washington D.C., 1959.

20. MALONE, C. A., "Observations on the Effects of Social Deprivation on the Development of Young Children from Disorganized Slum Families," in Belsasso, G. (Ed.), *Psychiatric Care of the Underprivileged*, vol. 8, pp. 23, 21, 24, 38, 39, International Psychiatry Clinics, Little, Brown and Co., Boston, 1971.

21. ———, "Developmental Deviations Considered in The Light of Environmental Forces," in Pavenstedt, E. (Ed.), *The Drifters*, vol. 4, pp. 125–161, International Psychiatry Clinics, Little, Brown and Co., Boston, 1967.

22. MARANS, A. E., and LOURIE, R., "Hypothesis Regarding the Effects of Child-Rearing Patterns on the Disadvantaged Child," in Hellmuth, J., *Disadvantaged Child*, vol. 1, pp. 19–22, 35, Brunner-Mazel, New York, 1967.

23. MATTICK, J., "Description of the Children," in Pavenstedt, E. (Eds.), *The Drifters*, vol. 4, pp. 55, 69, International Psychiatry Clinics, Little, Brown and Co., Boston, 1967.

24. MINUCHIN, S., "Psychoanalytic Therapies and the Low Socioeconomic Population," in Marmor, J. (Ed.), *Modern Psychoanalysis*, p. 537, Basic Books, New York, 1968.

25. MINUCHIN, S., et al., *Families of the Slums*, Basic Books, New York, 1967.

26. *New York Times*, Editorial on urban disintegration, July 14, 1976.

27. PAVENSTEDT, E. (Ed.), *The Drifters*, vol. 4, International Psychiatry Clinics, Little, Brown and Co., Boston, 1967.

28. ———, "Introduction" in Pavenstedt E., (Ed.), *The Drifters*, vol. 4, p. 5, International Psychiatry Clinics, Little, Brown and Co., Boston, 1967.

29. PLANT, J. S., *The Envelope, A Study of the Impact of the World upon the Child*, Commonwealth Fund, New York, 1950.

30. RAINWATER, L., *Behind Ghetto Walls: Black Family Life in a Federal Slum*, Aldine Altherton, Chicago, 1970.

31. REXFORD, E., "Antisocial Young Children and Their Families," in Jessner, L., and Pavenstedt, E. (Eds.), *Dynamic Psychopathology in Childhood*, p. 192, Grune & Stratton, New York, 1959.

32. SIGEL, J. E., McBANE, B., and EISENBERG, L., "Cognitive Competence and Level of Symbolization Among Five Year Old Children," in Hellmuth, J. (Ed.), *Disadvantaged Child*, vol. 2, p. 426, Brunner-Mazel, New York, 1967.

33. WHITEMAN, M., BROWN, B. R., and DEUTSCH, M., "Some Effects of Social Class and Race on Children's Language and Intellectual Abilities," in Deutsch, M. (Ed.), *The Disadvantaged Child*, p. 323, Basic Books, New York, 1967.

34. ZILBACH, J., "Crisis in Chronic Problem Families in Belsasso G. (Ed.), *Psychiatric Care of the Underprivileged*, vol. 8, p. 88, Little Brown and Co., Boston, 1971.

30 / The Child in the Military Community

Jon A. Shaw

The Military Community

The military community includes approximately 2,100,000 children having a median age of 5.3 years. Ninety percent of this population is under 13 years of age.[3] The relatively large number of young children indicates the usefulness of attempting to gain a more comprehensive understanding of the influence of the military community on their development.

The assessment of behavior in childhood and adolescence is traditionally determined relative to a normal expectable sequence of regularly occurring developmental phases.[10] These phases in development reflect the intrinsic changes associated with biological and psychological growth as they emerge in interaction with the extrinsic influences of the sociocultural milieu. The children in the military community experience the same general developmental and maturational processes as other children in the United States, but they also experience a social and facilitating environment which is unique.

The military community prior to World War II represented a relatively closed social system. Its members experienced a shared network of values, accepted behavior patterns, and social cohesiveness often having the characteristics of "village life."[15] These attributes were common to a widely scattered, literally worldwide distribution of military posts. This system is gradually changing. A number of factors have contributed to the increasing "civilianization" of the military. The growing complexities of group management demanded unique technical skills to operate a highly organized bureaucracy. This, in turn, has resulted in the influx of a large number of noncareerists and careerists from diverse ethnic and academic backgrounds.[15] In spite of its increasing heterogeneity, however, certain aspects of the military way of life persist. They are realized in their purest form in the large number of troop training centers and garrisons relatively isolated from the civilian community, and located predominantly throughout the southern states and overseas.[14]

The family living on a military installation resides in a highly structured and observant community. There are clearly delineated patterns of conduct expected not only of the soldiers but of their dependents as well. It is a patriarchal society which exhibits limited tolerance for individual variation from the expected norms of behavior. The soldier-husband has only limited choices as to where his family will live and where his children will go to school. The behavior of family members is thought to reflect the competence of the soldier-father-husband to manage his own affairs. Demands are made upon the wife to be active in various social groups and to participate in numerous organizational functions. The trappings of the military hierarchy are everywhere evident and are intrinsic to the observed codes and to the formally practiced behavior. Rank permeates the social environment no less than the work environment; it is expressed in such factors as the location and quality of housing, social clubs, and recreational facilities. There is both a formal and an informal caste system which separates officers and their families from enlisted men and their families.

The military is more or less aware of its unique responsibility for the relative cultural isolation and specific stresses it imposes on its families and their children. It attempts to provide a total environment, to "take care of its own."[14] Every imaginable facility is offered to provide for the needs of its members. These include schools, recreational facilities, teenage clubs, youth groups, officers' and noncommissioned officers' social clubs, etc. The military community offers its members economic stability, consistent role definition, total medical care, and a general community atmosphere which has the characteristics of an extended family. One of the obvious advantages to children in a community with available medical care is that all mothers have had access to medical services which, if utilized, render excellent and systematic care during the prenatal period and throughout all the developmental stages after birth. The quality of military life is to extend to its members a feeling of camaraderie and a sense of belongingness. The shared loyalties and experiences confer on its members an unusual sense of interdependence and fidelity and the feeling of sharing a common commitment and life style.

Clearly, these advantages mitigate the intensity of many of the social stresses prevalent in other social groups. At the same time, they bring about other stresses of specific character which are inherent in the military way of life. These, in turn, necessarily influence the processes of child development. Among these critical pressures are frequent family moves, intermittent life experiences in strange and foreign cultures, father absence, and early military retirement. In this connection, it is well to remember that individual personality is never determined by the group as a whole, nor does any individual representative of a designated population bear all the characteristics imputed to that group. Culture determines only what an individual learns as a member of a group—not what he learns as a private individual or as a member of a particular family.[17]

Geographic Mobility and Transcultural Experience

The child within the military family is a member of a community which expects geographic mobility. Darnauer[8] noted that military adolescents sixteen to eighteen years of age had experienced an average of 5.8 family moves. The child's reaction to the family move is determined by his level of psychosocial development, his personality structure as it has been shaped by his life experiences, the inherent adaptive capacities of his family, and the vicissitudes of the specific social processes as they impress upon him. He is pressed for responsiveness, yet his alternatives are limited. At certain stages of development, children may be unusually vulnerable because the move, as such, exacerbates stage-appropriate conflicts.[23] Among the vulnerable groups are the early school children who are just in the process of resolving separation conflicts and adjusting their repertoire of behavioral patterns to peer group activities and to new authority figures, or young adolescents struggling to separate and emancipate themselves from the infantile ties to their parents. If the nature of the move forces these youths to become more dependent for a time on the directive and nurturing qualities of the parents, they may experience in-

creasing difficulty as they try to achieve a successful resolution of these conflicts. Stubblefield[25] has stressed the need to consider the child's peer relationships when evaluating the impact of the family move. One study of military adolescents indicated that they were ambivalent about geographic mobility.[8] They stressed its opportunities for travel and encountering broader cultural experiences, as well as its advantages in enhancing their tolerance for individual differences. Yet, they also described its disadvantages in terms of interruptions of friendships, school shifts, and the massive readjustments that had to be made after each move. As one young man indicated, "Somewhere I lost the continuity of my personality—the me in Alabama, the me in California, the me in Texas, the me in Hawaii—I never integrated them in my mind."

Recent studies have failed to reveal a significant relationship between emotional and behavioral problems in military children and geographical mobility.[8, 23, 11, 22] The factor of geographic mobility appears to be less important than parental attitudes toward moving and the army way of life.[11, 22, 19] Shaw[23] compared a number of military children referred to a child psychiatry clinic in Germany with a control group and found no difference between the two groups as to frequency of moves. Nor did the parents of the referred children regard the child's move to Germany as being an important factor in his emotional problems. The family move certainly represents a discontinuity within the sociocultural milieu which necessarily challenges the adaptive capacity of the family and of its individual members. However, it is not intrinsically pathogenic. The shared value system of military society, the expectation of anticipated moves, and the ready acceptance of these moves by many families mitigates the crisis potential of geographic mobility. When a military family moves, it does not experience the same degree of disruption that is so typical in civilian life. Most military installations are similar; the life style changes little from one to the other. The father frequently moves to the same job he had at his previous assignment, the family resides in the same type of housing, and the family members meet people who share their values and norms. Military children often exhibit a considerable readiness to accept newly arriving children. Instead of maintaining exclusive cliques, they tend to provide the newcomers with opportunities to fit into the various peer groups. Such groups are, on the whole, open because of the frequent translocation of its members.

But mobility is only one source of coping stress. Not only must the child adapt to frequent moves, but he frequently has to adjust to a new culture. In 1967 it was estimated that there were over 130,000 school-age children being educated via the U.S. Dependent Schools in the European area alone.[5] The great preponderance of these children belonged to the military community. It is known that living in a foreign country can produce the phenomenon of "culture shock." The impact of this experience on children is variable and not well known. It may have a profound impact on adolescents who are in the process of separating themselves psychologically from the infantile objects, resulting in a regressive shift to more dependent behavior. In the wake of a move, these youngsters may find themselves confronting an external social system that is not always well defined or congruous with their own upbringing. The patterns of moral norms, standards of conduct, and shared values may appear divergent and ill-defined in the new country. Collectively, all this may heap undue stress on superego mechanisms and the already precarious defenses of the adolescent. In one country prostitution may be both legal and commonplace, and in another the phenomenon of a boy and girl holding hands in public may be abrasive to the sensitivities of the members of the host nation. The ready availability of drugs and other temptations are frequently difficult attractions for the adolescent to resist. This is especially true when the jurisdictional system to which he is responsible may, itself, be ill-defined as it represents an amalgam between laws of the host country and the military's own regulations prescribing conduct for dependents.

One of the peculiar experiences of children living in a strange culture is that their mothers not infrequently turn over their child caretaking activities to servants or housekeepers who often become objects of intense attachment to the child. The unique child caretaking practices of the host country may have a determining influence on the child's personality development. In one case, a young girl's intense attachment to a housekeeper became a painful experience when all the special nuances of loving caretaking activities which had been her lot were redirected to a newborn male child which, in this southeastern Asian country, was the normal practice. The narcissistic injury associated with this experience contributed to this girl's impaired sense of self-worth and autonomy in subsequent years.

Transient Father Absence

In addition to the stress of frequent geographic mobility and translocation to other cultures, these children periodically experience a sustained period of father absence. Pedersen[21] found that by the age of fifteen, 85 percent of the children referred to an army psychiatric clinic had experienced long-term separation from their fathers. Crumley[7] described this recurrent and continuing cycle of father departure, interim absence, and subsequent reunion in the military as a gross developmental interference with the needs and rights of children. The specific reaction of the child to father absence is determined by the child's gender, developmental stage, the length of father absence, the capacity of the mother to expand her parental role, the availability of surrogate models, and the prior quality of the father-child relationship.*

The nature of father absence, particularly if it is in a combat area where his life is subject to risk and danger, imposes a unique stress on children. The child's ambivalence about father's leaving becomes even more painfully conflicting. Father's life being placed in jeopardy exacerbates the boy's internal conflicts and weaves into the oedipal tapestry, in an all too realistic fashion, the threats of real dangers.

Baker et al.[12] studied military boys from five to eight years of age whose fathers were assigned to an unaccompanied tour in a noncombat area for at least one year. These investigators noted that 68 percent of the mothers reported that "their children seemed quite upset and unhappy right after father left." Some of the boys became more difficult to manage and were generally less well-behaved. Increased masculine striving and poorer peer adjustment were observed, but there was little evidence that father-absent boys were more feminine or less aggressive. In some families, the absence of father enhanced the son's movement toward an increasing sense of responsibility and self-direction, and he became generally more helpful around the house.

In a follow-up study, Baker et al.[2] evaluated the effects of the father's reintegration into the family six months after his return and its impact upon the boys (who were now from seven to ten years in age). Generally, the children were reported to have responded to father's return by improvement in eating and sleeping habits, and by more effective involvement in school with

* See references 4, 26, 2, 1, 18, and 13.

resulting better grades. Some problems of readjustment were noted for the mothers. Mother was not always willing to give up her hard-won capacities and sense of competence in managing family affairs. The adjustments made in the father's absence now had to be undone, the new alignments reworked, and roles redefined. The return of the father may exacerbate the son's oedipal strivings. The idealization of the absent father now had to be tested against the reality of his presence. The return of father brought fewer difficulties for sons who had had a good relationship with the father prior to his absence.

It is increasingly evident that the impact of father absence is not simply a response to father's unavailability as such. It is determined as much by elements that are present before and after separation from father as it is by father absence itself. This is evident in a comparison of the Norwegian and Genoan sailor studies.[18, 13] In the former study, boys of eight to nine and a half years of age who experienced absence of their sailor-fathers exhibited immaturity, strivings toward father-identification, impaired masculine identification, poorer peer adjustment, and evidence of compensatory masculinity. This was in contrast to boys of the same age of Genoan sailor-fathers who were found no different from a control group with regard to peer adjustment and masculine identification. This difference was thought to reflect the unique influence and the varying cultural and social expectations as they determined the expansion of mother's role in husband's absence.

A recurrent finding is that family atmosphere and climate are more important than the number of parents in the home.[13] Father absence appears to be less salient among relevant family factors than are the ambience and tone of the home and the quality of supervision. It may be that the culture's tolerance and the mother's reaction to the father's absence are the determining variables that mediate the effects of this experience for the child. Pedersen's[21] study of military families suggests that psychologically healthy mothers may be able to counteract the effects of father absence. The emotionally disturbed and nondisturbed adolescent boys in this study experienced relatively long periods of father absence. However, the mothers of the disturbed group exhibited significantly more psychopathology than did the mothers of the nondisturbed group. It was only in the disturbed group of boys that father absence was related to level of maladjustment. It would appear that the transient nature of father absence in the military and the expectation of his return mitigate the deleterious effects of this event on personality development. Clearly, this is not comparable to other studies where father absence resulted from parental dissension, divorce, illness, or death. Nevertheless, father absence, in all its complicated dimensions, is a significant psychological stress for the developing child and has to be considered in evaluating the individual military child and his adjustment.

Military Retirement

One of the career attractions of the military life is early retirement. Yet, even this advantage is not attained without some possible deleterious effects on the children. It is estimated that by 1980 there will be over a million retired servicemen.[12] Many of these men are in their forties and suddenly have to find a second career—often starting from the bottom up. Where they have adolescent children, this poses special problems. Just as the adolescent is struggling to resolve his identity conflicts, he may encounter a father who is experiencing uncertainty in his own social, economic, and occupational identity. The loss of status and functional attachment to the military community can induce emotional turmoil in the whole family. One sixteen-year-old boy seen for psychiatric evaluation described the sense of depression and sadness he felt when his father retired because he was no longer a colonel's son. He had had an ascribed status in the child community of the military, and now he would have to acquire status and popularity in a civilian peer group entirely on the basis of his own achievement.

Cultural Reaction to the Military Child

The larger American culture regards the military child with considerable ambivalence. The label "Army Brat" which is so frequently used to characterize these children renders an explicit value judgment. "Brat" is defined by *Webster's New World Dictionary*[27] as an "impudent, unruly child." Cultural stereotypes of the military child appear to reflect opinions about national military policy. These attitudes vary as well with the degree of contact with military youth. It seems safe to say that outside military circles the view of military youth is generally unflattering. The military community has served, on occasion, as the object upon which the larger society has projected its unacceptable impulses. Because of the antimilitary sentiment directed toward their fathers, the children are often recipients of similar prejudice or stereotyping. One author noted that "service personnel encourage children to put their greatest trust in the military organization itself rather than the host country, the United States or their own sense of identity."[28] He further suggests that "service children, certainly a special group, are particularly susceptible to xenophobia and express this attitude by wanting to storm either the walls of the Soviet Embassy or engage in other destructive acts. . . . that they either come to hate the United States and everything it stands for or become superpatriots," yet he offers no substantiating evidence for these proposals.[28] Often the military child is envied because of his access to low-cost Post Exchange merchandise, and various recreational opportunities denied his civilian peers. An unpopular war in Vietnam resulted in many children being conflicted between their loyalties to their fathers and the military community on the one hand, and their own pacifist wishes amidst the derision of various parts of the civilian community. One preadolescent boy lost his father in Vietnam. He struggled to idealize his father as a hero fallen in the defense of his country, but was told by his peers that his father was "stupid" and a "killer" for fighting in Vietnam.

Characteristics of the Military Child

Given the unique stresses of the social milieu intrinsic to military life, what is the effect on these children? In spite of the general cultural expectation that military children are "brats," there is evidence that, as a group, they are less lawless than their civilian counterparts.[16, 9] A study in Wiesbaden, Germany, of 2,766 military children ten to seventeen years of age revealed an incidence rate of delinquency of 1.5 percent—significantly lower than the 4.1 percent reported for the United States population in 1962.[16] The author explains the lower rate of juvenile delinquency in this way: He believes that the military milieu with its authoritarian structure inhibits acting-out behavior as a means of expressing

childhood maladjustment. The result is an increase in neurotic and withdrawn childhood adjustment patterns. Frenkel et al.[9] compared illicit drug use between military and civilian students. They studied junior and senior high school populations near a large military post in southern United States, and found there was significantly greater drug use among adolescents from civilian families than from military families.

There have been studies of intelligence and academic achievement as well. Comparisons of these attributes between military children and their civilian counterparts tend to favor the former.[8, 16] The higher median IQ among military children is not surprising. The military is, in the nature of things, a select community in which mental retardate fathers are ruled out by preenlistment screening. They continue to be periodically reevaluated. It has been noted that approximately 50 percent of those eligible for the draft in 1962 were rejected for service because of either intellectual or emotional defects.[16] In choosing candidates for military service, an increasing emphasis on education and specialized training has resulted in a selective group of fathers. The United States Army's European area Dependent School system used the Iowa Achievement Test in 1963 to test more than 40,000 American children. The average overall academic achievement was above the 75th percentile, compared to the cultural norm at the 50th percentile.[16] While there have been reports that geographic mobility favors academic achievement, recent studies of military children indicate that when age and intelligence are held constant, travel has little or no effect on academic performance.[24, 20]

There has been some address to the question of whether there is more or less emotional disturbance in military children, and if there is any difference in the quality of their disturbance. No clear answer has been forthcoming. Kenny[16] found the incidence of emotional disorder to be less in military children, and noted that there were relatively more withdrawal reactions than acting out disorders. The nature of the longterm effects of being a military child on second-generation adaptation is also uncertain. The known differences in the rate of delinquency, the level of intellectual and academic achievement, and the character of emotional adjustment appear to favor military children. Presumably, this is explained by the fact that the military is a select community.

Every child has placed before him, however implicitly, the image of the hero—the culturally idealized model of identification whom he is to emulate and to model. The traditional hero in the military appears to represent a version of the John Wayne motif, action-oriented, decisive, adhering to the absolutarian values of duty, honor, and country, i.e., General George Patton. Such a model provides a somewhat unreal and exaggerated concept of masculinity difficult for the young male child to achieve. More recently, the contemporary soldier-father in the present technocratic army is valued more frequently for being a middle-management team player loyal to the military and his country. Such a concept of the hero is more in keeping with that of a General George C. Marshall or General Dwight D. Eisenhower.

One study has partially substantiated the impact of father's rank upon the adolescent's selection of friends.[8] However, 80 percent of the adolescents questioned denied that friend selection was influenced by their father's position—a conviction that was shared by a comparable percentage of parent sets. Those who noted the influence of rank on adolescent friend selection indicated that the rank structure determined both what recreational facilities were frequented and where family dwellings were located, and thus influenced peer relatedness. It would seem that the particular status of father's position and his place in the rank order has an influence on the internalized self-esteem of the child. There is a tendency of the children of noncommissioned officers to perceive themselves as second-class citizens in a subcultural system, which, however discreetly, recognizes their fathers as such.

It is interesting that in one study only a small percentage of adolescent children indicated they would like to follow in the parents' "military way of life."[8] There are suggestions that the frequency of mobility and the constant interruptions of friendships may result in an impaired capacity for intimacy. In addition to the mobility, the fostering of dependency on a patriarchal society may inhibit the development of autonomous capacities for self-direction and individuation. This will only be known, however, when the studies are carried through.

Adaptation to the Military Community

It would appear that the military child's reactions to stress can best be understood within the context of crisis theory. From this viewpoint, they represent an "emotionally hazardous situation temporarily upsetting, not always in an unpleasant sense, yet constantly requiring reorganization and mobilization of the individual's personality resources."[6] In this context, it is an experience which implies neither good nor ill. Some individuals arrive at a higher level of adaptation with effective coping and problem-solving patterns of behavior. Others may achieve a less adaptive equilibrium characterized by unusual sensitivity or separation conflicts, feelings of helplessness, and anxiety. These defensive reactions may well provide an increased susceptibility to additional emotional disturbances. It would appear that where the military mother and father have identified positively with the military community and are sensitive and understanding of the unique stresses imposed upon their children, a number of these stresses can be significantly mitigated.* Yet, a note of caution must be added. The existing group studies have minimized the pathogenic effects of geographic mobility and father absence. Instead they have stressed the multiple determinants that shape the child's mode of adaptation to these events. Nonetheless, it is well to remember the insensitivity of the methods of measurement employed in these studies. Often it is only with intensive psychotherapy or psychoanalysis that the powerful but subtle effects of these early experiences on the child's personality formation are revealed.

* See references 23, 11, 22, 19, and 21.

REFERENCES

1. BAKER, S. L., et al., "Impact of Father Absence: Problems of Family Reintegration Following Prolonged Father Absence," Paper presented to the American Orthopsychiatric Association meeting, Chicago, March 1968.

2. BAKER, S. L., et al. "Impact of Father Absence on Personality Factors of Boys: An Evaluation of the Military Family's Adjustment," Paper presented to the American Orthopsychiatric Association meeting, Washington, D.C., March 1967.

3. BENNETT, W. M., et al., *Army Families*, Published Group Research Project, Carlisle Barracks, U.S. Army War College, June 1, 1974.

4. BILLER, H. B., "Father Absence and the Personality Development of the Male Child," *Developmental Psychology*, 2(2):181–201, 1970.

5. BOWER, E. M., "American Children and Families in Overseas Communities," *American Journal of Orthopsychiatry*, 37:787–796, 1967.

6. CAPLAN, C., "Opportunities for School Psychologists

in the Primary Prevention of Mental Disorders in Children," *Protection and Promotion of Mental Health in Schools*, Mental Health Monograph 5, Public Health Service, Publication No. 1226, 1965.

7. CRUMLEY, F. E., and BLUMENTHAL, R. S. "Children's Reactions to Temporary Loss of the Father," *American Journal of Psychiatry, 130(7):*778–782, 1973.

8. DARNAUER, P. F., "The Adolescent Experience in Career Army Families," in McCubbin, H., Dahl, B., and Hunter, E. (Eds.), *Families in the Military System*, pp. 42–66, Sage Publications, Beverly Hills, 1976.

9. FRENKEL, S. I., ROBINSON, J. A., and FIMAN, B. G., "Drug Use: Demography and Attitudes in a Junior and Senior High School Population," *Journal of Drug Education, 4(2):*179–185, 1974.

10. FREUD, A., *Normality and Pathology in Childhood*, International Universities Press, Inc., New York, 1965.

11. GABOWER, G., "Behavior Problems of Children in Navy Officers' Families," *Social Casework, 41:*177–184, 1960.

12. GIFFEN, M. B., and McNEIL, J. S., "Effect of Military Retirement on Dependents," *Archives of General Psychiatry, 17:*717–722, 1967.

13. HERZOG, E., and SUID, W. C., *Boys in Fatherless Families*, Washington, D.C., U.S. Department of Health, Education and Welfare, Office of Child Development, Childrens Bureau, DHEW Publication No. (OCD) 72–33, 1971.

14. JANOWITZ, M., *The Professional Soldier*, The Free Press, Glencoe, Ill., 1960.

15. JANOWITZ, M., *Sociology and the Military Establishment*, The Russell Sage Foundation, New York, 1959.

16. KENNY, J. A., "The Child in the Military Community," *Journal of the American Academy of Child Psychiatry, 6:*51–63, 1967.

17. KLUCKHOHN, C., and MURRAY, H. A., "Personality Formation: The Determinants," in Kluckhohn, C., and

Murray, H. A. (Eds.), *Personality in Nature, Society and Culture*, Knopf, New York, 1948.

18. LYNN, D. S., "The Effects of Father Absence on Norwegian Boys and Girls," *J Abn Soc Psychol, 59:*258–262, 1959

19. McKAIN, J., "Relocation in the Military: Alienation and Family Problems, *Journal of Marriage and the Family, 35:*205–209, 1973.

20. PARTIN, G., "A Survey of the Effect of Mobility on Dependent Military Children," Ph.D. dissertation, American University, Washington, D.C., 1967.

21. PEDERSEN, F. A., "Relationships Between Father Absence and Emotional Disturbance in Male Military Dependents," *Merrill-Palmer Quarterly, 12(4):*321–331, 1966.

22. PEDERSEN, F. A., and SULLIVAN, E. J., "Relationship Among Geographic Mobility, Parental Attitudes and Emotional Disturbances in Children," *American Journal of Orthopsychiatry, 34:*575–580, 1964.

23. SHAW, J., and PANGMAN, J., "Geographic Mobility and the Military Child," *Military Medicine, 140(6):*413–416, 1975.

24. STRICKLAND, R. C., "Mobility and Achievement of Selected Dependent Junior High School Pupils in Germany," Ph.D. dissertation, Miami University, Miami, 1970.

25. STUBBLEFIELD, R. L., "Children's Emotional Problems Aggravated by Family Moves," *American Journal of Orthopsychiatry, 25:*120–126, 1955.

26. TRUNNEL, T., "The Absent Father's Children's Emotional Disturbances," *Archives of General Psychiatry, 19:*180–188, 1968.

27. *Webster's New World Dictionary*, The World Publishing Company, New York, 1957.

28. WERKMAN, S., "Hazards of Rearing Children in Foreign Countries," *American Journal of Psychiatry, 128(8):*106–110, 1972.

31 / The Child Raised Overseas

Sidney Werkman

The 230,000 American children who grow up overseas experience a unique group of psychological stresses that differentiates them from children who spend all of their lives in the United States. These stresses must be considered in the context of the positive growth potentials of living away from the United States—the vivid experiences and educationally and culturally enriching encounters that can add so much to the flexibility, autonomy, and maturity of character structure. The particular outcome of a childhood overseas will depend on the balance of a number of pivotal factors in the total environment of a child, factors that often can be identified and utilized by the

clinician when making a dynamic diagnostic assessment.

Within the myriads of individual variations to be found, certain natural groupings of children who share interests and attitudes can be identified. The largest group consists of 150,000 military dependents who live on or close to military bases. These children attend Overseas Dependents Schools of the Department of Defense which are patterned closely on the public school systems in the United States. They and their families share a common social and value orientation derived from the military service of the father. Approximately 70,000 children, the sons and daughters of parents in U.S. government service, international business, or academic work, are educated in 150 schools sponsored by the Office of Overseas Schools of the Department of State. In addition, a smaller number of American children attend private or missionary schools. Each group has individual characteristics, but two qualities that define them specifically are length of stay overseas and the area of the world in which they live. Some children may live in one city during their entire childhood and return to the United States only to go to college or seek out a career. Others, depending upon the nature of their parents' work, may move every several years from one hemisphere of the world to another. Each of these variables must be considered when examining the clinical psychiatric problems of a child raised overseas.

Mental Health Challenges

In addition to the universal concerns centering on psychosexual differentiation, family relationships, and socialization, children reared overseas confront a unique group of psychological and developmental challenges. Frequent travel and geographical mobility make it necessary for them to adapt to a variety of friends, neighborhoods, and schools, as well as to changing social and recreational activities. Because the typical child overseas is always in a transient status, he does not have an opportunity to set down deep roots in any community. Instead, he must become adept at developing short-term friendships and adapting to differing international athletic and recreational preferences. He must adjust to the language and culture of the country in which he lives and, ultimately, be able to readjust to the culture of the United States.

The fathers of many overseas children are carefully selected members of their business and government organizations, and are often called upon to be away from home for considerable periods of time on special assignments. A greater child-rearing burden is therefore thrust on mothers who are themselves experiencing the same need for cultural adaptation as their children. All families live without the support of relatives and close friends, necessarily left behind in the United States.

On the other hand, many such living situations allow for the employment of servants and nurse-maids in the household, an unusual circumstance for most families who live in the United States. The introduction of a new and significant member to a household may enrich or distort the nuclear family in fundamental ways; usually there have been no precedents for this in the ordinary life of those families while they lived in the United States. Thus, family relationships overseas are often significantly different from what they would have been in the United States.

Emotional and Behavior Disorders

In adults, geograpic mobility has been shown to be related to an increased incidence of alcoholsm, family disorganization, and a variety of psychiatric disorders. These relationships, though fairly well substantiated, are by no means simple, causal connections. Instead, they are interwoven with numerous socioeconomic, national, ethnic, career, and political variables. In summarizing conclusions derived from studies of geographic mobility, Kantor[6] placed great emphasis on the complexity of the problems inherent in the study of the psychiatric epidemiology of adulthood. Since the epidemiology of childhood psychiatric disorders is both more complex and less well researched than that of adulthood, any conclusions derived from the study of the effect of geographical mobility on character development must at best be tentative. The statistical data and clinical conclusions now available are of great clinical importance; it is therefore worthwhile to study them in order to build a firmer base for such knowledge in the future.

Because of the special stresses of overseas life for children—geographic mobility, transient living situations, confrontations with constant cultural novelty, altered family relationships arising from father absence or the presence of servants, separation from relatives, and the final stress of returning to a United States youth culture in which they had not grown up—it might be thought that these children would have a high incidence of psychiatric disorders. Clinical intuition would certainly support such an assumption. However, as accurate epidemiological data on prevalence and incidence of psychiatric disorders in children have not been gathered either for the United States or overseas population, it is not possible to make statistically valid comparisons of the two groups. The fact that overseas children and their families constitute a highly selected socioeconomic and motivational group adds to the complexity of the issues; it suggests caution in any attempt to make valid inferences about their mental health in comparison to that of people who live out their lives in the United States. The few studies that have attempted to assess the mental health of geographically mobile children have concluded that those children either did not demonstrate a higher incidence of adjustment difficulties than more sedentary children[7, 2] or that those differences that were found were of a minor nature, and could be explained by characteristics other than geographical mobility.[5] No studies have been reported as yet on the specific variables of overseas mobility, although research in this area is currently underway.

A number of clinical studies attest to the seeming significance of geographical mobility in the development of childhood adjustment problems,[8, 9, 4] and several authors[1, 11] identify the overseas living situation and its lack of mental health support systems as critical elements in the emergence of psychiatric problems.

Because of the many variables that can foster or impair the mental health of a child, at this time it is just not possible to assign any causative role in the production of emotional disorders to geographical mobility or to living overseas. However, clinical theory and practice strongly support the view that the child raised overseas is particularly vulnerable to certain behavior problems and intrapsychic conflicts, many of which may not become clinically evident until a number of years after the child has returned to the United States.

Unusual Developmental Pressures

Overseas life may complicate each psychosexual stage of childhood. The infant preoccupied with the development of a sense of trust needs a quiet, familiar environment and a consistent mothering figure: Moves, a strange culture, and father absences may leave a mother with little available energy to devote to her baby. The toddler needs freedom to exercise his exploratory urges and natural physical energy. Life in a hotel or under the care of a restrictive host country caretaker may inhibit the expression of curiosity and physical activity. The three- to six-year-old makes intense investments in his parents and is greatly preoccupied with sexuality: The absence of a parent or the imposition of idiosyncratic sexual views may distort these crucial aspects of character development. The latency child needs a long

period in one place to consolidate friendships and to develop his educational interests. Moves, disruptions, and changes of school frustrate the child's need for time to work on his social and cognitive skills. Adolescents need opportunities for work experiences, increasing independence, and privacy: Few jobs are available to teenagers overseas and they are under constant surveillance by the small, close-knit American communities that exist in most foreign cities.

Fears and sleep disturbances are frequent in young children anywhere. The child overseas must confront and master some special sources of anxiety. The occasional threat of epidemic illness or political uprising, the uncertainties of parents communicated to children, and the exotic fears instilled by caretakers can make it difficult for a child to feel safe during the day, and even less serene at night. A case example will illustrate the problem of the development of fears.

Carol was a ten-year-old girl whose presenting problems were an unusual fearfulness and depression. She had spent the first nine years of her life living outside the United States with her parents, who were on official business. The first child of a young and vivacious couple with high ambitions, she was placed in the care of a twenty-one-year-old nursemaid, a foreign national. Carol did well in many ways, but sucked her thumb constantly. The nursemaid encouraged this, saying it was a good thing for the child since it gave her comfort. Most children in this Middle Eastern country were encouraged in this practice. Carol's mother was in a quandary. Carol was her first child. The nursemaid was far more experienced in caring for children than she, and the mother was out of the house a good deal. As a result, Carol continued thumb sucking and other infantile behavioral patterns until she was ten years old.

When Carol was nine her parents, secure in their trust of the nursemaid who had been with them a long time, went away on a three-week trip, leaving Carol and her brother in the woman's charge. The parents returned from their trip to find their daughter and her younger brother extremely frightened. Carol, particularly, wanted her parents to stay with her constantly, refused to go out and visit other people's houses, and for the entire year following her parents' trip, continued to be extremely uncomfortable about being alone. She complained in a cryptic way that "Alkisti locked the door." The parents questioned the nursemaid about the matter, but she said she didn't know anything about it. Nor would Carol ever explain it any further. Not until the end of their tour did the parents learn, by a complicated coincidence, what had happened while they were away.

The nursemaid's boyfriend had moved into the house during this period. The nursemaid had previously been an open, warm person. During this time, however, she locked the children's bedroom doors when they went to sleep. She then furtively spirited her boyfriend in and out of the house. She swore both children to secrecy about these events under the pain of terrible punishment and loss of love. Carol was frightened, excited, perplexed, and, in a word, panicked by the experience.

Many aspects of child development practices in general and of basic trust, sexuality, and conflicting loyalties in particular, are present in this vignette of a child whose presenting psychiatric problems were inhibitions and depression. While presenting symptoms vary in such cases, the underlying issues stem from a common theme.

Overseas life places a strain on the marital relationship. The husband typically becomes heavily involved in a demanding and often highly visible career as a representative of the United States; his wife is often left without the support of relatives or close friends in an alien culture in which she has little to do and little opportunity to pursue a career outside of her home. Such strains may result in depression, drinking problems, or other incapacitating symptoms that powerfully affect a mother's ability to be nurturing to her children. In such situations children often show the results of this travail in the form of school difficulties or overt psychological symptoms.

For many children the most difficult hurdle is not the adaptation to living overseas, but the return to live in the United States. As one youngster put it, "I felt out of everything when I came back. I didn't know about music or what to wear or how to get in with the cliques in schools." Another said, "I had lots of friends and played on the school soccer team overseas. When I got back to the United States nobody noticed me and nobody was going to go out of his way to be nice to me in that big school. My marks slipped and I was miserable for two years."

Some children develop a kind of love affair with a foreign way of life, a nostalgia for a stage in life or an experience, often of a romantic nature, that may result in depression, pain, and grieving on return to the United States. Children who develop this syndrome have idealized every aspect of life overseas and repressed the ordinary, boring, or anxiety-provoking components. They dismiss everything in the United States as uninteresting, worthless, or harmful. When children with this problem return to the United States, they are unwilling to integrate themselves into a new school, to master the pleasures of American sports, or to accept the challenges of making friends. They hold on desperately to a fantasy that is particularly fulfilling precisely because it never again needs to be tested against reality. The dynamics of such children bear considerable resemblance to the cases conceptualized by Fleming[3] as "parent loss."

Treatment Considerations

The whole spectrum of clinical child psychiatric disorders is seen in children who live overseas and among those who return to the United States, though local circumstances or cultural influences may result in idiosyncratic manifestations or the exaggeration of certain symptoms. For example, night fears may be conceptualized as a response to a frightening jinn in Iran, the Boodie Mala in Afghanistan, or Babo Natale in Italy, depending upon the cultural background of a caretaker. Children who live in politically volatile countries are particularly susceptible to anxiety about kidnapping.

Sexual practices that are aberrant in the United States take place with greater frequency in some foreign countries. Unfortunately, parents do not learn about these practices until they leave their children in the care of other people. The following case illustrates these issues.

A five-year-old boy was referred for psychiatric evaluation because of regressed behavior and the use of idiosyncratic, highly symbolic language. Until the age of three he had developed well, living in Asia with his parents, who were part of a military mission. His parents found a male caretaker for him, thinking that the sex of the caretaker would make no difference and that a male companion would be helpful for this boy, whose father was away a great deal. At a certain point John became secretive and withdrawn from his parents. The family left when John was five, taking what they thought was a pleasant leave from the male caretaker.

John became increasingly withdrawn. He began to use odd, symbolic words in his speech. When he started school, it was apparent to his teacher that he was a markedly disturbed, frightened, and inhibited boy. On clinical investigation, it developed that John and his caretaker slept in the same room and had become involved in regular masturbatory and fellatio experiences. The young child had been sworn to secrecy and was told that he would be punished if he gave away the secret. His symptoms developed only when he was separated from his caretaker and began to reality test for himself the meaning of his idiosyncratic introduction to overt sexuality. (Though this case may seem grotesque, the author has dealt with others in which caretaker and child were actually surprised in direct sexual activities. These are not fantasies on the part of the child. Rather, they are experiences that occurred because naked impulse could be expressed directly and without the usual limits present in most households in the United States.)

Many variations in the development of sexuality and sexual identity occur overseas. Though often adaptive for a particular country, these practices may result in serious character deformation when a child returns to the United States.

For example, caretakers in a number of countries play openly with the penises of male children and compare penis sizes among their charges. On the other hand, American girls may find it trying and humiliating to grow up in certain Muslim countries in which males are highly favored. The prejudice of masculine superiority common in the United States occurs in more virulent form in countries whose religious and social values result in the degradation of women.

It is therefore particularly helpful for the clinician who is treating a child from overseas to have a detailed knowledge of the area or country in which the child has lived, and a familiarity with the cultural and psychosocial environment in which the child has developed.

Prevention

The actual work of treatment embodies the principles and techniques fundamental to all dynamic child psychotherapy. It is in the area of prevention that clinicians can be of most help to the child who grows up overseas, for certain issues can be anticipated and many adjustment problems can be avoided or alleviated.

As separation and loss experiences are central to overseas life, great attention should be paid to preparation, discussion, working through, and acceptance of necessary change. Children should be offered all possible supports in the form of continuity of cherished objects, caretakers, and family members. The unique hazards of psychosocial development overseas should be considered by all parents and mental health workers. Special attention is necessary to insure that such a child has the opportunity to work through the adaptational challenges of each psychosexual stage in the healthiest possible way. The particular changes in family relationship consequent upon a move overseas must be considered by parents, so that a child will have the opportunity to develop intimacy and a sense of identification and constancy with his mother and father. Many issues which are taken for granted in the United States need to be worked out with conscious ingenuity and effort abroad.

Adolescents need particular attention because they are moving from a family-centered to a society-centered orientation. In order for them to proceed healthily through psychosexual stage challenges, a community must attempt to provide recreational facilities, work opportunities, teen clubs, reasonable access to privacy, and a group of values and standards that the adolescent can transfer to the United States when he returns home.[10]

Finally, it is important to recognize that one deals here with a community of hundreds of thousands of children who have substantially no psychiatric or community mental health facilities specifically responsive to their needs. Mental health facilities need to be developed to work directly with those children who have clinical psychiatric disorders when they are overseas, and to help in the exceedingly difficult transition when overseas children return to the United States. Such a network of facilities would include preparation for families moving overseas, the provision of adequate health and mental health care in foreign countries, and specific attention to the children who return to the United States yearly.

REFERENCES

1. BOWER, E. M., "American Children and Families in Overseas Communities," *American Journal of Orthopsychiatry, 37:*787–796, 1967.

2. DOWNIE, N. M., "A Comparison Between Children Who Have Moved from School to School With Those Who Have Been in Continuous Residence on Various Factors of Adjustment," *Journal of Educational Psychology, 44:*50–53, 1965.

3. FLEMING, J., "Early Object Deprivation and Transference Phenemona: The Working Alliance," *The Psychoanalytic Quarterly, 41:*23–49, 1972.

4. GABOWER, G., "Behavior Problems of Children in Navy Officers' Families," *Social Casework, 41:*177–184, 1960.

5. KANTOR, M. B., "Some Consequences of Residential and Social Mobility for the Adjustment of Children," in Kantor, M. B., *Mobility and Mental Health*, pp. 86–122, Charles C Thomas, Springfield, Ill., 1965.

6. ——, *Mobility and Mental Health*, Charles C Thomas, Springfield, Ill., 1965.

7. PEDERSON, F. A., and SULLIVAN, E. J., "Relationships Among Geographic Mobility, Parental Attitudes, and Emotional Disturbances in Children," *American Journal of Orthopsychiatry, 34:*575–80, 1964.

8. STUBBLEFIELD, R. L., "Children's Emotional Problems Aggravated by Family Moves," *American Journal of Orthopsychiatry, 25:*120–126, 1955.

9. SWITZER, R. E., et al., "The Effect of Family Moves on Children," *Mental Hygiene, 45:*528–536, 1961.

10. WERKMAN, S. L., "Over Here and Back There: American Adolescents Overseas," *The Foreign Service Journal, 52:*13–16, 1975.

11. ——, "Hazards of Rearing Children in Foreign Countries," *American Journal of Psychiatry, 128:*992–997, 1972.

32 / Children of the Rich

Burton N. Wixen

The Child of Extremely Wealthy Parents

There are several fairly distinct variations on normal child development seen among the children of the rich. The existence of such a set of subgroups and its clinical significance has only recently been clearly delineated.[15, 11] There have been studies based on collections of variables that *included* wealth. C. W. Wahl has written about "the rich, the famous and the influential."[13] Hollingshead and Redlich have studied the nature of mental illness among different classes of the population.[5] However, their definition of upper class included variables other than wealth, such as level of educational attainment.

There is something fairly unique and characteristic about a particular group of the very wealthy. It has been my observation that certain features deserve to be investigated apart from the other variables with which they are so often grouped. The very wealthy child does not necessarily belong to a family of great fame or extreme social power. The level of education is often not particularly high. They are set apart solely by possessing—or belonging to a family that possesses—immense amounts of money. Several distinct syndromes will be described among the very affluent. The term "CORs" (an acronym for *c*hildren *o*f the *r*ich) is intended to separate a particular group of alienated wealthy persons—mostly those with "old money"—from those more actively involved in internal and external conflict concerning their position. They also must be separated from a fortunate group of fairly well adjusted individuals—the "successful rich."

There are no firm criteria setting this group aside from the merely "very wealthy." They have financial assets that certainly place them in a fraction of the top 1 percent of the population. They have so much wealth that they never need be concerned about earning a living. Their life styles almost invariably include huge estates, many servants, and attendance at private schools. Very often there is no great value placed on higher education, though college attendance may be encouraged as a family tradition or for social purposes.

The CORs tend to be narrowly distributed throughout the American society. They cluster around several very affluent communities or large land holdings far removed from population centers. They tend to cling closely together in what have been described as "golden ghettos." This clinging together may be due simply to a feeling of greater comfort with people of similar backgrounds. Sometimes it appears to be an almost phobic avoidance of those who must be more concerned with earning a living. Perhaps there is a feeling of shame associated with the loss of middle-class values. The net effect is a tendency toward great isolation.

Where the residences are not greatly separated, they are tightly clustered within what appears at times to be an almost armored compound. Vacation spots and private schools tend to be highly exclusive and thus add to the ghettolike isolation of this group. The isolation contributes to the relative lack of knowledge that psychiatry has about their unique kinds of problems.

One reason for this lack of knowledge certainly stems from the small numbers of such people. However, since there is often considerable personal suffering involved it would seem that their wealth would make access to psychotherapy fairly easy. It is a highly subjective impression that considering the degree of pathology that may be present, and the ease in obtaining care, they have actually been underrepresented in the average therapist's caseload.

One reason that severely disturbed CORs may never see a child therapist is that the great wealth can be used to shelter them so well that the impairment is extremely well hidden. A simple schizophrenic may be so well cared for by servants, nurses, and other caretakers that the aberration may be dismissed as a degree of eccentricity. Only with exposure to a peer group, as was sometimes seen during periods of military conscription, were the florid manifestations of mental illness dramatically revealed.

The Impact of Wealth on Development

There are several more or less unique features that great wealth visits on the circumstances of child rearing. These features in turn have definite effects on development. Of course, all of the innumerable variables that may impinge on a developing child may influence the CORs. Only those factors fairly unique to the wealthy will be stressed here.

The wealthy child is usually cared for to a great extent by servants. The role of the parents in the day-to-day child-rearing process is often proportionately decreased. The rearing by servants cannot be likened to the role of an extended family seen in other cultures and classes. The servants are not relatives—even in the unofficial sense often encountered in the extended family. They are always clearly in the position of employees. Great devotion and love may develop, but there is usually a significant difference from family care.

Typically, a family or extended family shares the social and cultural values of the children. The servants are invariably from lower socioeconomic classes. Furthermore, it is not part of their role assignment to impart values to their wards. They do not share common family traditions or heritage. They are employed solely to care for the children. Inevitably there is some transmitting of values—table manners by nannies, a love of books by talented tutors—but no systematic transmitting of family concerns and roles.

The values that are transmitted by servants are often a source of confusion to the developing COR. A middle-class concern for earning a living makes no sense at all to a child whose trust fund will supply the highest standard of living for a lifetime. Where such influences are not simply dismissed by the COR, a deep sense of shame may be detected.

Another obvious problem that may be produced by the excessive delegation of child rearing to servants involves the considerable envy that they often feel. This envy, when sensed, may also further enhance deep feelings of shame in the child, or may produce a state of alienation. It is not unusual to observe that while all the child's material needs are fastidiously cared for, the staff of servants retains a hostile aloofness. When this situation is not corrected or mitigated by family influence, a wide variety of emotional illness and ego defects may develop.

Familial Reactions

Another facet of this problem involves the relative absence of close contact with the family. Of course, there are exceptions. But when the family depends heavily upon servants for child rearing, the young person is deprived of enough exposure to the significant members of the family for certain important events to take place. Notably, there is a failure in the transmitting of family traditions, values, and role expectations.

A further complicating factor is the unfortunate fact that the parents have suffered a similar deficiency. They too were raised by servants and enjoyed relatively little contact with family. Thus, even if they were aware of the needs of their children, they may be literally inadequate to the fulfilling of those needs. One often encounters second and third generations with similar defects.

While a wide variety of problems may result from these circumstances, two are encountered with special frequency. There is a serious gap in the child's conception of his place in the world. He is lacking the necessary internal images that would normally be drawn upon to produce a secure sense of identity.

A second consequence of the CORs' state of emotional deprivation involves a tendency to develop inadequate ego structures that can contain anxiety. Very often one encounters an appallingly low degree of frustration tolerance. As with serious degrees of mental illness, this state of affairs may be masked by an environment that is uniquely structured to serve the child. There is thus a situation in which inadequate ego controls are not apparent because there is little frustration in reality. Rage reactions are sometimes encountered when circumstances force the COR outside the sheltered environment.

Cultural Factors

A final circumstance influencing development is the frequent absence of exposure to a peer group. Where the messages from the servants are confusing, and those from the family are absent or inadequate, exposure to a group of other children might be expected to fill in some of the vacuum. Unfortunately, the CORs tend to be deprived of that saving factor. They are often geographically isolated from other children. Where there is exposure to a group, it is often to a group of similarly impaired children.

By the time they may encounter a more varied group at a private school or college, much damage has already been done. And if the group is truly more heterogeneous, certain characteristic reactions are seen. The few CORs in the mix will isolate themselves from the others, forming an elite club. This protects them from whatever feelings of shame they may experience concerning the absence of more traditional middle-class values, and from the hostile envy they experience from the less affluent members of the group. The possible healing effects of peer-group exposure are thus lost.

Excessive exposure to servants, inadequate exposure to parents (or exposure to similarly damaged parents), and the absence of a healthy peer experience are the three most damaging effects that great wealth may have on children.

Dysgradia

The influences previously described can produce a wide variety of damaging effects. One set of characteristics has been encountered with enough consistency to appear to represent a distinct syndrome. A search of the literature has failed to indicate a description of these particular features, and the term *dysgradia* was coined by the author to describe it.[15]

There are several distinguishing features.

1. The complete syndrome is encountered most often among the very wealthy—particularly families in which there has been great wealth for several generations.
2. There is a remarkably low degree of frustration tolerance that is often virtually impossible to recognize because the life style produces so little frustration.
3. A state of boredom pervades the individual's affect. There is an appearance of aimlessness and restlessness. At first it appears to be depression. But the dynamics of depression are not found. The listlessness is not simply a withdrawal of interests from the environment. There is a defect in the capacity for forming interests. Perhaps the term *anomie* comes closest to describing the individual's sad countenance. However, anomie implies some anxiety, and that is usually absent.
4. The individuals tend to isolate themselves from the rest of society, and to associate only with those of similar backgrounds and those who serve them.
5. The sources of gratification are extremely constricted. Work achievement and family closeness are not thought of as sources of great satisfaction. Pleasures center around the immediate fruits of wealth. What appear to outsiders to be frivolous and extravagant purchases and travels are engaged in compulsively.

This list of characteristics is not intended to represent an indictment of the indolent rich. It describes a particular syndrome of unhappy, suffering individuals characterized by a particular developmental defect.

The Ego Defect:
A Theoretical Discussion

In the usual course of development each individual progresses along numerous lines of development. These lines vary tremendously, but are fairly consistent within each individual's particular cultural background. The lines may be thought of as a series of *role concepts* appropriate to each individual's age and stage of development. Each role concept involves thought content and imagery that serves as some basis for important ego functions. These role concepts are essential for implementing action and deriving gratification.

Before each role concept forms, it is preceded by a *role preimage*. The preimage is a rudimentary early version of the various roles toward which the individual is developing. The preimages are corrected as the individual comes closer to the point where he will assume the new role.

An example will help clarify these constructs. One line of development concerns education. A preschool child has various images of himself as a "student" long before he is ready for school. These are dependent on expectations within the family that the child be receptive to learning necessary motor and language skills.

As school approaches the child develops imagery of what it will be like. He will ride a bus every day to some big building where a lady will lead certain activities. This early imagery may be quite inaccurate, but it serves to bind the anxiety concerning a potentially frightening future event. The imagery is constantly corrected by family and peers as the anticipated events approach. The formation of these role preimages, their correction, the stepping into the actual role conception, and the formation of the next role preimage is a constant process throughout life.

Underlying the idea of the development of these role concepts are two formulations basic to the whole theory of ego-psychology: Freud's description of the ego as the precipitate of identifications with abandoned objects,[2] and Hartmann's development[3] of the concept of autonomous ego structures. The former concept enables us to describe the process by which the roles of the significant members of the environment are internalized and become a part of the ego. The latter concept is necessary to appreciate the importance of role preimages and role concepts. These are conflict-free structures necessary for the organization of a stable psychic apparatus able to maintain self-esteem and equipped to cope with the environment in an adaptive manner.

These processes of internalization proceed along numerous different lines. It would be impossible to delineate all of the overlapping lines of one's development. Social and sexual development, education and preparation for various work roles are some of the most encompassing and important lines of development. At some point between childhood and adulthood a crystalization of these internalized role conceptions contributes to an important and complex ego structure: Erikson's concept of *identity*.[1]

Piaget, in discussing ego structures, indicates that they require stimulation as nutriment for their maintenance.[7] Rapaport goes further and raises the question of whether ego structures can even develop without stimulus-nutriment.[8] He concludes they cannot. Thus, in considering the development of role preimages leading to ego structures encompassing internalized conceptions of roles, one must conclude that these structures cannot develop without adequate stimulus-nutriment.

The environment of the particular group of CORs under discussion could hardly be better designed to produce inadequate stimulus-nutriment for many crucial ego structures encompassing the formation of roles.

Ego Lacunae and Narcissistic Problems

When confusing information concerning role development is provided by servants, and when the family is too aloof from the developing child or does not itself possess adequate role concepts, the child will not be able to internalize useful and necessary images and concepts required for role development. A major source for the development of one's self-esteem involves the satisfactory achievement of goals related to internalized role conceptions. Where these role concepts have failed to develop, there will surely be difficulties in maintaining self-esteem. These early concepts of roles precede and define action—hence the paralysis and boredom. Without motivation for goal-oriented actions to maintain self-esteem, one can understand the sad, empty, goalless life style and the desperate need for "action" and material pursuits.

The term dysgradia is intended to describe the situation in which the ego is lacking the structures that would contain the needed hierarchy of role preimages and role concepts. In defining it, it is necessary to clarify its relationship to, and difference from, related concepts.

Of course the developing young person is exposed to various samplings of role possibilities in spite of the great isolation of his life. He has some exposure to a hierarchy of roles through his exposure to servants, teachers, family, television, and literature. What is lacking, unfortunately, is the necessary stimulus-nutriment from the environment to establish these fragments as autonomous ego structures. Rapaport refers to this situation as the absence of the *proximal guarantees* of autonomy.[8]

The absence of these ego structures should be differentiated from Hartmann's concept of intra-systemic conflicts within the ego.[4] In dysgradia an absence of structures is hypothesized rather than a state of conflict within these structures.

Spiegel has focused on the problems of role development in the framework of conflict within the family.[10] In passing, he refers to a state of "cognitive discrepancy" in which "one or both persons involved in the role system may not know or have sufficient familiarity with the required roles." The stress here is on conflict, although a deficiency is alluded to.

The closest parallel to this concept of defective ego development may be found in several studies on the superego. Johnson and Szurek have described observations of superego lacunae.[6] They recognize a state in which a significant person in the environment sanctions a child's failure to internalize particular superego contents. The author has described situations in which the superego regresses to an earlier state of development in which it is much more closely dependent on the immediate stimuli of the environment.[15] This may be seen as a condition in which superego contents are not autonomously internalized, but remain dependent for their functioning on constant stimulus-nutriment from the environment.

These views of the imperfectly formed superego closely approach the concept of the ego in dysgradia. Perhaps the term "ego lacunae" aptly describes this defect in internalized role concepts.

Grinker agreed with the concept of dysgradia, but felt that the patients he observed did have adequate exposure to role models.* Their inability to form healthy identifications was due to severe ego damage resulting from problems in the mother-child symbiosis and in Mahler's separation-individuation phases.† He described his patients as severe narcissistic characters.

Robert Coles has also focused on the problem of narcissistic distortions among the rich.‡ He observed a very common feeling of "entitlement" that at times could take on an excessively narcissistic quality. The condition described as "narcissistic entitlement" is a pathological state in which there is a major distortion of reality.§

We thus come to a state of affairs in which the ego lacks autonomous structures primarily concerned with role concepts and essential for formulating and executing action and maintaining self-esteem. This deficiency may be related to defects in the environmental situations that fail to offer adequate exposure to objects for identification or that offer objects for identification that themselves suffer from a distorted view of reality. Serious problems in early stages of development may produce a condition that becomes indistinguishable from the narcissistic character disorders.

Coping Behavior

The fantasies of CORs clearly reveal the deficiencies that are being discussed. If one asks a typical middle-class child of seven or eight what he wants to be when he grows up, one will usually receive an answer involving some conceptualization of education, fields of endeavor (often suggesting some degree of identification with parents), and ideas about advancement along that field of endeavor.

A child suffering from dysgradia will have difficulty in producing material relating to careers and earning a living. He would more likely produce material related to travel and references to the life style of his parents. One would certainly find an exaggerated view of his own importance, and that of his family.[11]

* R. R. Grinker, Jr. "The Poor Rich: The Children of the Super-Rich," *American Journal of Psychiatry*, *135*:914–915, 1978.
† M. Mahler, F. Pine, and A. Bergman. *The Psychological Birth of the Human Infant*, New York: Basic Books, 1975.
‡ R. Coles, *Privileged Ones*, Boston: Little, Brown, 1977.
§ Coles, *Privileged Ones*, p. 399.

There is relatively little data available to contrast the fantasy life of CORs with that more commonly encountered with the middle class. Their parents, as reflected in the deference they receive, are seen as virtually omnipotent long after the childhood fantasies of parental omnipotence should begin to fade. There is an impression that sexual taboos are less deeply entrenched and that actual and fantasied seduction by servants is more prominent in the sexual content. The importance and excitement of courtship, marriage, and parenthood are often diminished.

On the positive side of the ledger, the CORs are often quite comfortable in positions that would produce awe and anxiety in those from different backgrounds. Positions of great power are often handled with great ease. Association with the "elite" of the world may also be handled comfortably. This social skill may merge into apparent or actual sociopathy.[11]

A Second Syndrome: Neuroses of Mobility

The family of very wealthy children are often completely unaware that there is any problem at all. After all, they have often experienced a similar upbringing. And very often, they are so aloof from the chores of child rearing, and so dependent on servants themselves, that they have very little concern with what problems there might be.

One situation in which major family concerns are encountered is not infrequently seen. That is the case in which one or several members of the family have amassed great wealth in a fairly brief period of the family history. Most CORs are the beneficiaries of "old money." But where there has been a rapid upward movement in social class, there may be serious conflicts between the older and younger members of the family.

The older members of the family, those who amassed the fortune, were likely raised with traditional middle-class values. They were working hard and building their new life style during certain crucial years in their children's development. Their children are often caught in a very difficult identity crisis. They were exposed to some of the excitement of the dramatic events of the family's rapid ascent. They have some conception of the great value to be placed on hard work and creative business activities. At the same time the rapid changes have introduced exposure to servants and to CORs of several generations standing, and diminished contact with family. The consequences may be quite destructive.

A state of confusion, compounded of partially integrated middle-class values that are no longer relevant to the actual realities of the new life style may produce violent clashes between the generations. The older generation says, "I worked hard and did so much for the family, what are you going to do?" And the younger generation replies, "You can't expect me to follow in your footsteps —that's virtually impossible to duplicate. And why should I kill myself? We have the means to live the 'good life,' so why shouldn't we?" The conflicts often become heated.

Sometimes the young people "drop out." They may turn away radically in directions that appear diametrically opposed to all of the new values of the family. Van den Haag[12] and the author[15] have suggested that these "drop outs" may actually be returning to some vestiges of idealism that were once part of the family tradition. With surprising frequency the "antiestablishment" values of some of these young people may be seen to represent a return to a less materialistic, more idealistic period in the history of the family.

The author has called these problems *neuroses of mobility*.[15] They are encountered most often in the first generation that follows the acquisition of great wealth. These young people may be described as a "transitional generation," in that they are experiencing considerable turmoil and conflict. They are transitional in that they will either make a successful adaptation to the new family circumstances and become members of the group of "succesful rich," or they will produce children who will suffer from dysgradia.

The typical events occurring in those suffering from neuroses of mobility are (1) considerable overt conflict between the generations—often centering around issues of roles and values; (2) considerable internal confusion concerning these issues and a tendency toward difficulties in establishing a coherent sense of identity; and (3) a tendency to violent breaks with the new family life style— often betraying, however, a return to old family values. This active conflict situation is in marked contrast to the situation encountered among the CORs.

This group sometimes is seen in the ludicrous position of the "nouveau riche" caricature. They are in a state of transition and looking for some sense of identity. They possess great wealth but are not accepted by the CORs with "old money."

One sometimes observes a frantic (and expensive) search for status and acceptance involving a gaudy display of wealth. In some communities whole business enterprises are structured to cater to this group.

The Successful Rich

When rapid changes in socioeconomic status occur one may develop a neurosis of mobility. When the family loses its old middle-class values and is left with a vacuum in terms of meaningful life goals, the condition of dysgradia may develop. There is a fortunate group that successfully makes the transition from middle class to upper class. These are the successful rich.

When the immediate concerns of earning a living and social advancement are no longer of relevance to the family's life style, something must be found to replace them. The successful rich have made this transition and have incorporated as part of the family's new system of values certain meaningful role concepts. There are new goals that can be pursued and achieved as sources of pride and self-esteem.

The most common situations encountered involve philanthropy, political interests, and creative "big business." The activities of the Rockefellers and Kennedys immediately come to mind. In a much less conspicuous way there are groups of very wealthy young adults who have banded together to help each other lend meaning to their lives. They have taken up social and philanthropic causes with enthusiastic enterprise.[9, 14]

Social Response: Prevention

As more and more families are able to achieve giant advances in their economic status, it may be anticipated that these problems will be encountered more frequently. Those who are called upon to render assistance during the process of the rapid transition are in the most advantageous position to help in terms of primary prevention. Counseling families concerning the effect of the rapid changes on their developing children may dramatically alter the future of an entire family. Homely advice concerning an understanding of children's needs for relevant values under changing socioeconomic circumstances and the need for enough family closeness to insure a maintenance of adequate identifications may prevent the development of a series of bored, aimless, unhappy generations.

REFERENCES

1. ERICKSON, E. H., *Childhood and Society*, Norton, New York, 1950.

2. FREUD, S., "The Ego and the Id," in *The Standard Edition of the Complete Psychological Works of Sigmund Freud*, vol. 19, pp. 16–23, The Hogarth Press, London, 1961.

3. HARTMANN, H., *Ego Psychology and the Problem of Adaptation*, Rapaport, D. (Trans.), International Universities Press, New York, 1958.

4. ———, "Comments on the Psychoanalytic Theory of the Ego, in Eissler, R. S., et al. (Eds.), *The Psychoanalytic Study of the Child*, vol. 5, pp. 83–90, International Universities Press, New York, 1950.

5. HOLLINGSHEAD, A. B., and REDLICH, F. C., *Social Class and Mental Illness*, John Wiley, New York, 1958.

6. JOHNSON, A., and SZUREK, S. A., "The Genesis of Anti-Social Acting Out in Children and Adults," *Psychoanalytic Quarterly, 21:*323–343, 1952.

7. PIAGET, J., *The Origins of Intelligence in Children*, 2nd ed., International Universities Press, New York, 1952.

8. RAPAPORT, D., "The Theory of Ego Autonomy: A Generalization," *Bulletin of the Menninger Clinic, 22:*13–35, 1958.

9. SLATTERY, M., "Rich Is Beautiful," *The CoEvolution Quarterly, 4:*94–103, 1974.

10. SPIEGEL, J., "The Resolution of Role Conflict Within the Family," *Psychiatry, 20:*1–16, 1957.

11. STONE, M. H., "Treating the Wealthy and Their Children," *International Journal of Child Psychotherapy*, pp. 16–18, 1972.

12. VAN DEN HAAG, E., *The Jewish Mystique*, Stein and Day, New York, 1969.

13. WAHL, C. W., "Psychoanalysis of the Rich, the Famous and the Influential," *Contemporary Psychoanalysis, 10:*71–85, 1974.

14. WILLIAMS, R. M., "Young Foundation Puts Old Wealth in New Bottles," *The Washington Post*, Sunday, July 13, 1975.

15. WIXEN, B. N., *Children of the Rich*, Crown Publishers, New York, 1973.

16. ———, "Object-Specific Superego Responses," *Journal of the American Psychoanalytic Association, 18:* 831–840, 1970.

PART B
Varieties of Advantage

33 / The Intellectually Superior Child

Leah Levinger

General Characteristics

The syndrome of the intellectually superior child presents within itself a greater variety than almost any other syndrome imaginable. Yet, certain specific characteristics are observable and can be described.

Testing seven-year-old Michael with the standard scale of the Wechsler Intelligence Scale for Children, he was within 3 from the top most difficult questions in a particular subtest scale. The results of the test are as follows:

1. He surpasses most children his age and somewhat older children in a standard task.
2. He does particularly brilliantly on dealing with generalizations and abstractions—measured here by the Similarities Subtest. He was asked, "How are 49 and 121 alike?" This he could not solve, but did not seem downhearted. The next morning, he was waiting at my office door, almost unable to contain himself: "Dr. Levinger, I have it!"
3. He is able to endure working with a task until he solves it, needing, for his own sake, to reach a sense of closure, carrying curiosity about the task long after the adult expectancy has been removed. "I thought it over as I walked home and all the time I was watching TV and eating dinner."
4. "I tried all kinds of things with the numbers." He combines tenacity with the ability to flexibly try different approaches.
5. "49 and 121 are both squares!" By now he was dancing up and down with excitement, showing the true delight in an insight.
6. "I knew that there must be a name for what

happened with both numbers, but I couldn't figure out what it was." He recognizes the concept of classification. This may have reflected some incidental learning from having had the whole series of questions. Knowledge of a particular word was beyond a second grader's ken. But he recognizes that concepts can be named.
8. "I asked my father what was the word for both of these." He shows awareness that there will be a solution which may be obtained from another source if one cannot do it oneself.
9. "Was it fair to ask a grownup?" While most seven-year-olds are still unable to recognize the meaning of "cheating" and "plagiarism," Michael sees the concept of fairness in regard to intellectual endeavor.

A Qualitative Difference

A genuinely gifted child is qualitatively different intellectually rather than sheerly quantitatively. Analyzing his special characteristics, what is revealed is not the "how many," but the way he works. He does more tasks successfully than do other children his own age. Also, he does them differently than do other people of almost any age. Essentially, whether he does a task correctly or incorrectly is of less importance than the exploratory way he goes about doing it. As James Joyce said, "With a genius, his errors are portals to discovery." A capable fifteen-year-old who had had good training in mathematics might have been able, also, to see that 49 and 121 are squares, but

328

the way he would solve it would not include Michael's manner. Michael may essentially have more in common with the two-year-old who asked me. "What is the difference between twenty miles and twenty hours? What is a twenty?"

Define by Child, Not Test

It is a fallacy to define a gifted child by high scores on a standardized school achievement test, or by a high IQ, or by some particularly advanced piece of work in an academic or artistic area. There will be overlap between such measures and the nature of the intellectual endowment of an individual child in many instances, but scores and work produced miss the essential meaning of giftedness. Such definitions seem neat and usable. If one wishes to estimate the number of intellectually gifted in the population, defining giftedness as possessing an IQ of above 130, one finds 2.2 percent are present. This sounds plausible. But, since tests are normed with the concept of the immutable Normal Distribution Curve, the findings are an artifact of the test. Terman's and Cox's studies of genius, despite certain major contributions which they made, partake of this fallacy.[1, 16, 15]

Increasingly it is recognized that the test-defined child may be primarily a good test passer.[2, 16] The test through which the so-called geniuses were selected, the Stanford-Binet, has strong cultural biases.[5, 8, 13] More recent standard tests, also, emphasize convergent thinking, demanding a single focused answer. Intelligence also requires, at its highest level, divergent thinking, which will be open-ended and leading to a variety of possibilities. Efforts the past decade have been made to devise new tests, allowing for divergent thinking, rather than recognizing how, in the truly gifted person, there is a balance between the two. Getzels and Jackson[2] treat standardized tests as strawmen in their eagerness to demonstrate that other kinds of children are more talented than those with high IQ. In my experience, while a high score on the Wechsler or SAT does not guarantee that special extra quality of intellectual giftedness, it gives some indication of its presence.

The Rorschach has been insufficiently used as an experimental instrument in this area. As a clinician, I have found, similar to the findings of Roe,[11] that the richest, most creative Rorschach records also contain a high degree of analtyic and synthesizing ability and precise thinking.

Adult Achievement

A traditional way to establish what one means by gifted children is to work backwards from adulthood. Some criteria were established by adult success in particular fields of who is a gifted adult, and then their early childhoods are studied by whatever reminiscent hearsay material is available. Such studies, which hark far back in the history of psychology, are fascinating, but of only limited value. Criterion for adult success is based on the definitions given by the current culture. It cannot be judged on intellectual powers alone. As Terman's[15] studies showed, only a portion of gifted children fulfill their promise in later life. Conversely, the childhood of a number of recognized "great thinkers" has, at least by anecdotal account, failed to reveal conspicuous ability at an early age.

Cultural Bias

Judgments of superiority, based upon standardized testing or upon achievement, whether in school days or adulthood, are closely linked to sociological and ethnic backgrounds. No tests are culture free.[5, 13] At this particular time in our history, we cannot arrive at any but the crudest estimates of how much untapped intellectual ability might be present, trapped in the inner cities, in Appalachia, on Indian reservations, and so on. One can only speculate on the possibility of "some mute inglorious Milton." In some later period, we may be ready to abandon the belief in the Normal Distribtuion Curve and recognize that we can foster the development of far more gifted children than we do at present.

Early Manifestations

The early presence of intellectual superiority can be found in the observation of infants and toddlers. Precocity in evincing a particular skill is only one element. Such children will also have the qualities of alertness, reactivity, and ability to delay action. They set particular tasks for themselves even before they have language, and show a high degree of tenacity in coping with these tasks. A sixteen-month-old-child was trying to build pyramids of wooden figures, made to stand on each other's shoulders. This, itself, was difficult for a toddler, with his inevitably limited motor coordination and sense of balance. And this child compounded the difficulty by placing the bottom figures not on the floor, but on a narrow ledge where they could barely balance.

There is a vivid description in Stone and Church[14] of a preschool child called Stuart. He is an exceptionally gifted boy who, through his precocious use of language, is able to express many of the feelings that other children might experience. He shows, long before age five, capacity to deal with abstract concepts of time and space and relative size. He tries to get at the meaning and substance of emotional feelings and where they differ from physical feelings. He shows precocious concern for relations among people. His questions have depth and intensity. There is a kind of gleaming delight in discovery and sheer fun with words and ideas that fit the general syndrome of the gifted.

Young gifted children are very much aware of their own skills and also of some of their limitations. This serves as an asset in being able to break a task down into components, as when a six-year-old, copying the Bender designs, said of design A, "The circle will be cinchy to draw, but the diamond part is hard." Awareness of limitations may be an obstacle to attempting new things.

In the development of the young gifted child, too much weight is often put upon his language development. Precocity in language may not, itself, be a true reflection of high-level thinking. It may reflect cultural pressures and adult stimulation. This is particularly true in oldest children and only children. In contrast, quite a few gifted children do not need to go through the step-by-step development of single words, phrases, and then sentences. They wait until they are ready to speak in full complex sentences.

Emotional and Social Development

The Terman[15] studies refuted the old stereotype of the warped genius. They found that on the whole these children were better equipped physically than the average. They were far more likely to be popular and leaders than to be ostracized.

However, a degree of unevenness, which is inevitable in the development of all children, is likely to be present in greater degree for the gifted child. Children like Michael repeatedly revealed no limit to how quickly they can progress in the area of dealing with abstractions. But gradual maturation must be gone through in neuromuscular development and in social understanding. Despite Michael's precocious grasp of the concept of "fairness," in day-to-day personal relations he was still only a seven-year-old. There is less acceleration in social maturity than in the intellectual areas.

The bright child often is considered a leader and is highly popular because of the excellent ideas he has about games and his superior grasp of humor. In an imaginative fictional account, which is sound clinically,[7] the intellectually precocious hero has "a joke-exchange corner" in the classroom.

Yet, the intellectually gifted may have a number of social difficulties. He may be "teacher's pet." His enthusiasm for ideas, coupled with adult adulation for his precocity, may result, even by kindergarten, in his not knowing how to talk to others, but only how to lecture. He may be unable to listen and may mercilessly interrupt others. His sheer tempo may make him obnoxious and ultimately scapegoated.

Very young gifted children may be penalized by their unawareness of how unique they are. I observed Debbie, age three to six, in nursery school trying to be a traffic cop while the others were riding their tricycles helter-skelter around. She had printed on one side of a piece of cardboard "Stop" and on the other side "Go," and held the sign to direct traffic. Soon she was in a tearful rage as the other three-year-olds, all nonreaders, lightly misinterpreted her signals. Or, Helen Keller, in the first exhilaration of mastering communication through writing the letters on people's palms, tried to communicate to her favorite dog by writing on his paw. She, like Debbie, lacked the maturity to recognize a difference between herself and others.

There may even be a need to retain a naiveté in certain areas as a child advances in others. Norbert Wiener[17] still believed in Santa Claus at age seven. Clinging to the fantasy long after most children have discarded it is explicable. In his strenuous intellectual world, with so much unknown, he had far greater need than the average child for the security of the familiar myth. As one who had suffered affective deprivation, valued for his intellect rather than loved for himself, he had a special need to maintain the fantasy of the nurturant, all-giving Santa Claus.

Within the Family

Intellectually gifted children are particularly fortunate when, like the Bronte sisters, they share a companionship of siblings of their own intellectual caliber. They can then be allies against the world. But, when such a child is a deviant in his family, this may be even more painful than when he must deal with his peers. He feels a tremendous sense of disloyalty when he finds himself surpassing a sibling. If the sibling is preferred by the parents or is older, there may be a particular reaction formation against his jealousy. He becomes protective of such a sib and needs to deny his own superiority. Even more devastating is the experience of discovering oneself considerably brighter than one's parents that may come in later childhood or adolescence. Sometimes such a recognition is never obtained at a conscious level, but remains a severe blight on the person's total growth. He cannot let himself be more than his parent.

Emotional Disturbance

Since, as yet, we have little real knowledge of how many unrecognized gifted children are present in the population, we cannot give an accurate estimate of whether a disproportionate number is burdened by emotional problems.

Clinics and schools are aware that intellectually gifted children who are also emotionally disturbed cover the whole gamut of psychiatric disorders. Foremost as a symptom is the unevenness in development, already discussed, as a built-in quality for gifted children. This is particularly evident in the emotionally disturbed. There will be marked developmental extremes, lags in such areas as toilet training, self-help, general orientation, with precocious development in other areas.

A large number of gifted children who are considered emotionally disturbed show the same choice of defense structure common in the intellectually superior adult. They tend toward intellectualization and the obsessional devices of rumination, doing-undoing, extreme orderliness, suppressed hostility, isolation of affect, and so on. Thus, one finds among such children a large number of obsessional neurotics, obsessive-compulsives, stutterers, and (although this itself is a rare entity in childhood) paranoids, and preparanoids. One finds a stutterer expressing his ambivalence about

speech: In his imagination, he is secretely finishing the adult's sentences, but is unable to speak aloud clearly. Children with paranoid traits, like their adult counterparts, utilize their intelligence to deal with complex delusional systems and simultaneously simulate adaptive behavior. The experience of being overvalued as the wunderkind contributes to the formation of grandiose ideation.

Mahler[9] describes a syndrome of *Enfants Terribles* as children with provocative cleverness and exaggerated need for self-agrandizement. Many of the impulse disorders and various kinds of manipulative delinquents would show some quite similar patterns.

The Underachiever

Much has been written about this syndrome and here it will be dealt with only in passing.[6] While the general meaning is that there is a severe gap between the child's intellectual capacities and his actual achievements in school, this is often subject to grave misidentification. A large number of children are erroneously considered as "underachievers." They are actually misidentified as being gifted when they are really only fairly capable. Here they are falling below their parents' ambitions, but not necessarily misusing their capacities. Recently we have recognized that some highly gifted children cannot adequately cope with schoolwork because of perceptual difficulties. Such children can be identified through careful history taking and diagnostic testing, and then helped so they can overcome their perceptual handicaps.

The Wunderkind Fallacy

Genuinely gifted children, who have been overvalued for their intellectual powers and undervalued as people, show difficulties academically as they continue to operate too exclusively by the Pleasure Principle through childhood and adolescence. Any work that requires plodding, or has been imposed by the adult establishment, needs to be resisted. Such children want the immediate gratification of tasks which they already enjoy and already have mastered. They equate giftedness with speed. Needing to ponder or try different approaches is a threat to the wunderkind image. The very foundation of their self-recognition is shattered by having to work slowly or accept repetitive drill. School situations which demand good form and neat expression compound the anger and resistance of the intellectually superior.

Adult Attitudes

Gifted children evoke within adults extreme expectations and overidentification. This applies to parents, teachers, and, all too often, therapists.

Even the most capable and gifted adults have inevitably some gap between their achievement and the earliest aspirations which partook of infantile grandiosity. They reencounter the earlier self embodied in the gifted child and cannot do otherwise than encourage him to live out their own thwarted needs.

The adult may attempt systematically to train such a child (Wiener;[17] Sidis, in Hauck and Freehill, chap. 8[6]). Such training can be highly destructive of the total child development.

Adults find it difficult to accept the concept of unevenness. They become unduly angry if a gifted child indulges in ordinary misbehavior, lashing out as if he is being "deliberately bad." Adults may give a child special privileges or advantages as rewards for his rapid growth of skills and then become particularly disillusioned, in the basic sense betrayed, when the child logically concludes that if certain rules don't apply to him, no rules do.

Role of the Therapist

The therapist is not immune to the same countertransference and overidentification problems that beset other adults. Overidentifying with his own unfulfilled wunderkind self, he may side with the child against the parents. Delighted with the child's insights so brilliantly articulated, he may underestimate the pathology and encourage the skills and intellectualization.

The intellectually superior child evokes marked ambivalence in the adults around him. Adult expectancies in all areas may far outstrip what the child can actually attain. Disillusion and disappointment follow. On a less conscious level, there may be considerable jealousy of a child with a promise of an even brighter future than the adult has achieved. Or, for an adult of constricted or limited intellectual ability himself, the gifted child presents a real threat. The spectrum of adult attitudes toward the superior child is brilliantly depicted in *The Child Buyer*.[7] Hersey described a simple but gentle and nurturing teacher; a principal accepting a child as a gifted peer and colleague; a guidance counselor resenting the boy's brilliance and out to develop a bill of particulars concerning his pathology; a state legislator gleefully noting he is "too fat"; a mother wistfully encouraging and a father resenting.

Real and Pseudo-Enrichment

Schools have been able to alter and enlarge their programs to foster healthy development of intellectually superior children.[2, 6, 16] Allowing far greater scope for arts, athletics, and social development has been vital. Especially useful has been the development of emphasis upon divergent thinking and creative work in all areas of learning. Such programs which do exist, however hampered by poor funding, are at odds with many more programs of pseudo-enrichment in rapid advance and special progress classes. Emphasis in these latter is highly quantitative. The earlier the child learns his letters, reads, does mental arithmetic, the better it is. Work is pitched in a highly stereotyped fashion, competitive, with emphasis upon fact gathering and "show-off" skills. Such children are being trained not for intellectual development, but to become successful test passers.

Aiding the Disadvantaged Child

The aforementioned approach of sterile acceleration is particularly liable to be utilized in an attempt to expand the opportunity of the so-called disadvantaged child. These methods, which are themselves stultifying for the development of middle-class children from the dominant culture, may be particularly damaging for disadvantaged children. These children are vulnerable because within their culture they have already felt great pressures toward convergent thinking as rapid mastery to aid them in climbing the social ladder. They cannot afford playfulness and speculation which characterize the middle-class child.

Beyond the specific educational methods employed, there is the additional problem of the social transition required when the child from one culture is transplanted either part- or full-time into another. Hauck and Freehill[6] describe an Appalachian boy from an isolated farm making a transition to a boarding school. He reveals alienation from both family and school culture. Similar transition difficulties, often without the supportive elements that led this boy to a partial solution, occur for the ghetto children on scholarships in white middle-class schools. There may be no way to avoid bitterness and feelings of alienation in helping make social change at this period of history. But some of the destructive aspects, masked by liberal optimism, may be mitigated if far more careful selection is employed for the children who are to be burdened with this experience and, if along with the educational scholarships, such ancillary supports as therapy are offered.

Our Future

The 1960s may remain in our history as the "drop-out generation." Drop-outs had a wide range of intellectual abilities, including many of the most highly superior. It is beyond the scope of this chapter to deal with the multiplicity of causes for this phenomenon. Within the psychological area, the demands of parents, schools, and, all too often, therapists for the child to achieve at all costs and the emphasis upon product and always more product indubitably played a serious role. Adolescents who throughout childhood had been made to feel like unworthy stewards of their own ability had no recourse except to drop out. To avoid further waste and alienation, a drastic change in our approach in assessment of what constitutes intellectual worth is required. Children must be given freedom to grow on their own terms, to make mistakes, and, above all, to take delight in their own intellectual powers and know that their intellect belongs foremost to themselves.

REFERENCES

1. Cox, C., "The Early Mental Traits of Three Hundred Geniuses," *Genetic Studies of Genius*, vol. 2, Stanford University Press, Stanford, Calif., 1953.

2. Getzels, J. W., and Jackson, P. W., *Creativity and Intelligence; Explorations With Gifted Students*, John Wiley, New York, 1962.

3. Goodenough, F. L., *Exceptional Children*, Appleton-Century-Crofts, New York, 1956.

4. Gowan, J. C., and Torrance, E. P. (Eds.), *Educating the Ablest: A Book of Readings*, F. E. Peacock, Itasca, Ill., 1971.

5. Halpern, F., *Survival: Black & White*, Pergamon Press, New York, 1973.

6. Hauck, B. B., and Freehill, M. F., *The Gifted—Case Studies*, William C. Brown, Dubuque, Iowa, 1972.

7. Hersey, J., *The Child Buyer*, Knopf, New York, 1950.

8. Levine, M., *Psychological Testing of Children*, in Hoffman, L. W., and Hoffman, M. L. (Eds.), *Review of Child Development Research*, pp. 257–310, Russell Sage Foundation, New York, 1966.

9. Mahler, M., "Les 'Enfants Terribles,'" in Eissler, K. R., *Searchlights on Delinquency*, pp. 77–89, International Universities Press, New York, 1949.

10. Mead, M., "The Gifted Child in the American Culture of Today," *Journal of Teacher Education*, 5:3, September 1954.

11. Roe, A., *The Making of a Scientist*, Dodd, Mead and Co., New York, 1953.

12. Siegel, M. G., "Psychological Testing," in Wiedman, G. W., *Personality Development and Deviation*, pp. 456–486, International Universities Press, New York, 1975.

13. Silverstein, B., and Krate, R., *Children of the Dark Ghetto*, Praeger Publishers, New York, 1975.

14. Stone, L. J., and Church, J., *Childhood and Adolescence*, Random House, New York, 1958.

15. Terman, L., and Oden, M., "The Gifted Group at Mid-Life," *Genetic Studies of Genius*, Stanford University Press, Stanford, Calif., 1959.

16. Torrance, E. P., *Gifted Children in the Classroom*, Macmillan, New York, 1965.

17. Wiener, N., *Ex-Prodigy: My Childhood and Youth*, Simon and Schuster, New York, 1953.

34 / The Child with Exceptional Talent

Leah Levinger

Exceptionally talented children fall into two categories. Many reveal characteristics of generally high intelligence, accompanied by a particular talent in some specific field. These are the children whom Terman has described.[10] Another kind of child does not minifest particularly high intelligence outside of the area of a special talent. It is the latter who will be discussed in this paper.

It is futile to search for an agreed-upon definition. In our product-minded culture, there is a criterion of success rather than recognition of the process of discovery. Artistic circles have quite different criteria from academic and scientific ones, while the general public may prize entertainment ability or athletic powers. A distinction occurs between the values of the adult world and of the child's peer culture. Some third-grade children, asked which of their classmates possessed a skill they most admired, chose a boy who, in his teacher's eyes, was thoroughly ordinary. His peers extolled his ability to turn his eyelids inside out.

Talent Alone or Part of General Ability?

There is endless debate on whether exceptional talent is always a specific manifestation of high general intelligence which has become focused in one area, or whether the talent itself may be something that can exist without needing high general intelligence. For example, three-year-old Vicky already could play good chess. Since chess requires powers of long-range planning, complex visual imagery, mastery of intricate, highly artificial rules, etc., it would seem that chess requires high general intelligence. Three-year-old Carla is able to jump rope, a skill rarely found in children below age five. As jump-rope requires timing, spatial, and balancing judgments, is this also an example of high intelligence manifested physically? Or, could an average or dull child happen to be endowed with a particular physical skill? Far more exhaustive study of highly skilled children in a variety of areas is needed. In the meantime, one must frankly admit that the value system biases any method of trying to identify and recognize the presence of talent.

The presence of a talent without accompanying high general ability or a variety of high skills allows for several not necessarily mutually exclusive explanations. There may be a neurological or physiological substrate, perhaps of genetic origin, to account for elevation in this area. This has been suggested in regard to musical talent. There is the possibility that the potential for similar advanced development in other areas was within the child, but was lost at an early age because of the precocious narrowing of his energies to a particular field. The narrowing itself might occur because of the adults' social rewards, or the fulfillment of the child's dynamic needs through this expression, or a combination of these elements.

Taking a mystic view of the "inborn quality" prevents recognition of the role played in the development of talent by training or by the less tangible elements of home and social atmosphere. Many well-documented examples reveal how systematic training, granted the child has a capacity to utilize it, greatly inflates a basic gift. The role of the highly musical family atmosphere, coupled with demands for extreme application in practicing, are particularly well known in the case of the child Mozart. Similarly, Norbert Wiener[13] described the double stimulation of systematic training to produce a scientist and the highly ideational home atmosphere. Yet, there are many other instances where the child seems self-taught and self-impelled, as Milton described it, so "that one talent that is death to hide" spontaneously emerged.

So-called Abstract Talents

Certain talents appear either singly or in a cluster, having in common the quality of early aptitude for abstract thinking. These include mathematics, science, and chess. Wertheimer's description of how young Gauss spontaneously and seemingly effortlessly produced a new way of thinking exemplifies the beauty and power that certain young children may reveal.[12] A kindergarten teacher, introducing the concept of measurement, had the children use the width of their hands to measure the floor. The schoolroom floor was divided into large linoleum squares. Rodney, age four and a half, announced, "You just have to see how many hands wide one square is and then count all the other squares across the floor."

Music has, at times, been considered a part of the world of abstractions, although it contains additional elements requiring keen auditory acuity and emotional responsiveness. But, it does have the quality of a self-contained world of logic, similar to mathematics, science, and chess.

The literature[3] and observations with young children reveal the same instantaneous independent solutions in the field of music as in the field of mathematical thinking. I have observed an eighteen-month-old child toddle up to the piano, start, as young children do, hitting notes with his whole hand or arm in a random fashion, then go on to strike individual notes, stopping to listen, and continuing until he was spontaneously playing chords.

Maturational Limitations

These self-contained worlds of abstract endeavor seem the most likely ones in which a young child excels. They are all relatively independent of the step-by-step maturation which occurs either emotionally or neurologically. Skill in the visual arts, for example, never seems to be revealed with the full intensity of mastery that the musical prodigy possesses. However talented in drawing a very young child may be, he still needs to go through the developmental process of coordinating eye and hand and brain activities. Only at the end of childhood or in early adolescence do we have anything comparable to the four- or five-year-old flowering in music. The same occurs for the range of athletic skills. Certain phenomena, such as a three-year-old jumping rope, occasionally are found. But most children follow a fairly definite step-by-step development in their large as well as their small motor skills. This timetable can only be partially altered by systematic training. Observations of circus children, child ballet dancers, particularly in Russia where early training of a highly rigorous, systematic sort is available, might

furnish better understanding of what proportion is maturational and what is training.

One of the talents which is late in becoming unequivocally manifest is literary production. Here, as in art, one is handicapped by value judgments and biases about what is creative work. It is true many little children have an imaginative feel for language and play with it in a highly esthetic manner. They have awareness of the onomatopoeic qualities of the sound of language and aptitudes for new fresh metaphors.[1] Certain children show very precocious understanding of precise shadings of meaning. A child of four, being told that a traffic jam meant "lots of cars," countered, "Do you mean lots of cars in one place?" Creative use of language is common in many children, so one thinks of it, like making faces or rolling down a hill, as part of the endless energy and exuberance of childhood. But children do not stand out in literary skill as in other fields. Even in adolescence, many children appear to have the potential for writing lyric poetry, but it does not compare with adult poetry, as child or adolescent musical creations can hold their own with adults'. Only in late adolescence does a Chatterton or a Rimbeau appear with unmistakable literary talent. This may be a harder phenomenon to explain in terms of maturational stages than the artistic or athletic. Along with sensitivity to language, there needs to be the maturity to experience a range of emotions and awareness of such emotions, so that writing can contain meaningful content. Emotional development can neither be hurried nor made responsive to training. A child needs to go through a stage of living in a relatively pragmatic and self-absorbed world before he is ready for the imaginative risks of the stretching of the boundaries of empathy which are the emotional components of productive literary expression.

Talent in Human Relations

Most tenuous in its manifestations and hardest to evaluate is a special talent in human relations. (Incidentally, we would consider this equally hard to evaluate in the adult world as, for example, who is to decide what makes a gifted therapist?) Certain children seem to have high-frequency antennae, especially adept at picking up nuances of others' feelings. They may be especially sympathetic and able to sense the moods an adult tries to conceal. One must attempt always to discriminate between such children, who seem really to be part of our population (although how many one cannot ascertain) and other children who have spuriously precocious social awareness. The latter would include the "unliving doll" of a highly adaptive pseudo-related child; the manipulative, seductive child; and, finally, certain schizophrenic children who seem to have a direct line from their own unconscious to the unconscious of others and what, at times, uncannily appears to be "ESP" abilities.

Theories of Compensation and Disturbance

Far, far back in human history, and in modern times as well, there has been the popular conception of special talent playing a compensatory role for someone who was in some other way handicapped. The more extreme examples have been legends of "the mad genius." Merging of special talents with handicaps or stigmata that separate the person from the mainstream of humankind often lends an additional quality of the uncanny to the talent itself. The lame god, Vulcan, was a smith, dealing with the magic of metal in primitive society. The priestess of an oracle or the shaman is another case in point. Folklore and today's popular view should not be immediately dismissed. We have a large proportion of highly talented children free of any external stigmata or grave inner disturbance, yet there is a large group where the role of compensation is noteworthy.

Minimally Brain Damaged

With growing recognition of minimally brain damaged, dyslexic, or aphasic children, we are becoming increasingly aware of the special skills in other areas children with these syndromes develop.

Peter, age eight, was totally illiterate when placed in a residential treatment institution. He showed the minimally brain-damaged syndrome of hyperactivity and drivenness, as well as grave perceptual confusion, such as reversals and rotations on the Bender and on other standardized psychological tests.[8] He spoke glibly, but with many mispronunciations. He became notorious in the institution for exceptional mechanical talent, particularly in picking locks. The choice of lock picking seemed overdetermined by a background of a delinquent, deteriorated family structure, and also a need to fulfill an affective hunger by constantly stealing objects. The talent itself was real, requiring great skill in listening and manipulation of the locks, as well as tenacity and patience.

Wilfred, at nine, was also unable to read beyond the alphabet. He had the language difficulty of a borderline aphasic in expression and in comprehension. His spontaneous depictions of objects, such as trees, cats, men in armor, landscapes, etc., were highly advanced for nine, resembling, rather, the handiwork of a gifted adolescent. His pencil seemed to flow as if he were merely copying a figure clearly envisioned. Wilfred was able to maintain his status with other children by his drawing skills, which compensated in their eyes for the retarded academic performance and for the halting speech and verbal confusions. A history of his precocious drawing extends back to age two. At an age where most children are barely able to draw a circle, he was drawing recognizable objects. When unable to obtain the word he desired with which to ask for something, he would run for crayon and paper and sketch what he had in mind with sufficient clarity that the adult could respond appropriately.

The Idiot Savant

Such children as Wilfred and Peter, with highly developed compensatory skills for severe handicaps, are only one step from the classic Idiot Savant. While this syndrome is one of the most familiar in classic psychological literature (it involves a person functioning generally on an extremely infantile or "imbecile" or "idiot" level, but with one talent far surpassing the average person's), the basis for this is still in debate. Goodenough[5] makes a strong case for specialization and intensive practice of a particular skill when no other avenues are open for expression. But, while raising cogent questions about the construct of general intelligence, she takes too uncritically the concept of "imbecile." The fact that a person is unable to dress himself, or be continent, or has limitations in speech, or mutism, may not necessarily be evidence for intellectual defect, but rather for the presence of severe autism. With autism as an explanation, many of the classic cases of the so-called Idiot Savant may be far more intelligible.

Regarding the so-called talent itself, it is a highly complex and ambiguous task to disentangle and discriminate what is an expression of talent and what is deviant pathology. The limitations of a culture must be kept in mind. Another possibility is that a particularly brilliant new solution is beyond the ken of the professionally trained person to grasp, as the child is himself far more brilliant and gifted in that field. Trying to differentiate true creativity from signs of schizophrenic thinking remains one of the most difficult tasks for the clinician.

Saul was seen at age six years one month. He was reading, writing, and printing at a very advanced level. He could do quick mental calculations, knowing what date in a month a particular day would fall on. He could describe, street by street, alternate routes to travel from his home to an airport. All of these skills deal with impersonal areas of existence and treat symbols or words as having an important independent life of their own. To paraphrase the Gospel, "In the beginning was the Word, and the Word was never made Flesh."

A standard psychological battery was given to Saul.[8] This revealed the predominance of the word for Saul and his alienation from the world of objects and what we tend to call "reality." Asked to draw a house, he proudly printed "House." He did similar labeling rather than depicting for almost all his drawings. Finally, when cajoled into copying some geometric forms—which, incidentally, he did appropriately and skillfully for his age, despite his extreme haste—he had to first write the word "Copy" as if to make the task intelligible to himself. Drawings of people, labeled "Person," contained isolated features, eyes, nose, mouth, lacking the outline of the face and possibly breasts and genitals, with no bodily framework.

Saul's uncanny ability to visualize and reason in terms of time and space did not mean that he could do well on the standard psychological test. First, his extreme negativism played a role so he would only respond to a few of the tasks. Beyond this, however, even when engaged, he showed severe lacunae in his fund of general knowledge, particularly in any areas that impinged upon interpersonal relations. Thus, the IQ on the WISC was in the low 70s.

The physical picture Saul gave had the same extreme unevenness as his intellectual functioning. When he chews, he has difficulty keeping his mouth closed. He is just beginning to stand when he urinates. He does not seem to realize when he wets himself. He is quite agile in both small and large muscle behavior, but his sheer lack of attention to what he is doing makes for many blunders. The world is controlled through his verbalistic manipulations and the symbol has become more real than what it might symbolize.

The etiology includes other factors beyond the scope of this chapter. Evident at once was a parental need to produce a "genius." When I interviewed Saul's mother for a history, we were at cross-purposes. Asked "What was Saul like when he was little?" she eagerly responded, "You mean you want to know how early he started to read?" Practically any question somehow got deflected to boasting of his special talent. Saul's mother insisted that he was able to write and spell and read prior to talking, which may be a correct appraisal of this highly withdrawn negativistic child. He is reported not to have started speaking, except occasional phrases, until after age three, but earlier than that had mastered writing. This was not adult-imposed, but rather stemmed from the long hours when he was left alone. He had to keep himself busy, with TV turned on and crayon and paper available, while the adults were out working. When he started speaking, he would often spell a word, as "g-i-v-e" rather than pronouncing the word "give."

Within the total complex pathology of Saul's family, besides the extreme need to have a child genius as compensation for their own sorely blocked lives, another element stands out. This was an exceptionally disorganized family, with the most basic aspects of living, in the way of time, cleanliness, places for objects where they could be found, etc., disregarded. Saul was forced to orient himself within this by becoming excessively rigid and organizing the world through ideation when no other means was open to him.

The Healthy Talented Child

As long as our value system is so ambiguous, we cannot reach a crude approximation of how many children within the population have exceptional talents. Also, as long as there are conflicts in the values about what talent is, and about what "infantilism" and "emotional disturbance" are, there will be no good way to discriminate between talented children with emotional disturbance and those with a relatively normal personality. It is my impression that the latter considerably outweigh the former. I also believe there are many more highly talented children in the general population than have been recognized because of the limitations of adult perception.

A talent need not lead to social isolation, but may, instead, lead to warm communication with many other people. The talented child may be much freer of being bracketed by an age group than are most children in this culture. A good chess player is a good chess player, whether age seven or forty-seven, and the two will play together as peers. The demand for "an appropriate peer group" so popular in psychological and educational circles makes little sense for a talented two-year-old violinist who may join a string quartet of adults. In other parts of their lives, the child and adults have different interests and needs, but it is the talent which may bind them together humanly. For many people this may be one of the closest human bonds that life will give them.

There is the danger that talented children will be exploited as performers in some way or other, but without concern to avoid child exploitation, we should not minimize the furthering of talent. Talent needs expression. Exuberance and a sense of delight in what he is doing impel the talented child whether or not the world of others is receptive. Vachel Lindsay wrote of "The bronco who would not be broken of dancing," and these children, with their persistence and courage, will not be broken no matter how hard a society may try to do it.

REFERENCES

1. Chukovsky, K., *From Two to Five*, University of California Press, Berkeley, 1971.
2. Cox, C., "The Early Mental Traits of Three Hundred Geniuses," *Genetic Studies of Genius*, vol. 2, Stanford University Press, Stanford, Calif., 1953.
3. Fisher, R. B., *Musical Prodigies*, Associated Press, New York, 1973.
4. Getzels, J. W., and Jackson, P. W., *Creativity and Intelligence; Explorations with Gifted Students*, John Wiley, New York, 1962.
5. Goodenough, F. L., *Exceptional Children*, Appleton-Century-Crofts, New York, 1956.
6. Hauck, B. B., and Freehill, M. F., *The Gifted—Case Studies*, William C. Brown, Dubuque, Iowa, 1972.
7. Malone, C. A., "Developmental Deviations Considered in the Light of Environmental Forces," in Paven-

stadt, E. (Ed.), *The Drifters*, pp. 152–153, Little, Brown & Co., Boston, 1967.
8. Siegel, M. G., "Psychological Testing," in Wiedman, G. W., *Personality Development and Deviation*, pp. 456–486, International Universities Press, New York, 1975.
9. Silverstein, B., and Krate, R., *Children of the Dark Ghetto*, Praeger Publishers, New York, 1975.
10. Terman, L. M., "Mental and Physical Traits of a Thousand Gifted Children," *Genetic Studies of Genius*, vol. 1, Stanford University Press, Stanford, Calif., 1925.
11. Torrance, E. P., *Gifted Children in the Classroom*, Macmillan, New York, 1965.
12. Wertheimber, M., *Productive Thinking*, Harper and Brothers, New York, 1959.
13. Wiener, N., *Ex-Prodigy: My Childhood and Youth*, Simon and Schuster, New York, 1953.

---

35 / Beautiful Children: Special Problems in Treatment

Michael H. Stone

Among the various advantages that may set children apart from their peers, only one is immediately visible: beauty. The others, talent, intellectual brilliance, parental wealth or fame, or aristocratic lineage, became known through more indirect routes and have a different impact on the development of the child. Many of these attributes are discussed separately in the Handbook (see chapter 33 on intellectually gifted children; chapter 41 on the child of a famous parent) or elsewhere.[5, 3, 4, 1]

In discussing the impact of beauty, there are special problems in childrearing and early development that either predispose to functional breakdown or affect the shape and outcome of psychiatric disorders, should these arise. This discussion will be confined largely to beauty in girls or young women, since males are not customarily thought of in this connection.

Envy

The unusually pretty girl may become singled out even in elementary school as an object of admiration and envy. Envy from her female peers or her sisters may be so intense that it cannot readily be contained by them, or comfortably dealt with by the child. In particular, if the girl happens to be at "high risk" for a major functional psychosis, her responses to such envy may be highly maladaptive. A young schizophrenic woman of considerable beauty, for example, spoke of how her younger sister's hatred of her good looks was so unbearable that as a youngster, she went around with tousled hair and sloppy clothes, saying to herself, "I'm ugly." For her, this served as a means of minimizing the effects of this rather terrifying advantage. Even in her late teens, this woman could not accept unflinchingly the fact of being beautiful. Another woman, suffering from a schizoaffective illness, had worked as a model ever since she was in second grade. Throughout her school years she was taunted by her female classmates with whatever epithets they could scrape up: "skinny," "stuck-up," "pussy-cat," etc., with the net effect that she never made any close friendships with her own sex. As she grew older her (accurate) observation that other women eschewed her company became integrated in a delusional way: that they avoided her because she was "ugly."

Exploitation

Beautiful children, even when quite young, are prone to exploitation in a variety of ways. Ambitious parents may push such children into the performing arts or modeling, in hopes of capitalizing (in money or glory) on the child's physical assets without much regard for the child's actual talents or interests. This tendency has given rise to the expression "Hollywood mother," used to describe a particularly intrusive brand of parenting, which often leads to a paradoxical crippling of whatever talent the child might have possessed. Out of repugnance at being manipulated, some of these children subsequently refuse to develop their own capacities. Others feel swamped by the parent, and veer far from their own natural bent in order to preserve a shaky sense of identity *distinct* from that parent.

Perhaps a more frequent consequence, however, is sexual exploitation, either overt or covert. It is the author's clinical impression that the presence of an unusually beautiful daughter awakens more than ordinarily powerful incestuous feelings in fathers at or even before the menarche. In the last eight years, fourteen women have been referred to this author for psychotherapy who had in their background either an overtly incestuous

relationship with the father, a sexual relationship with a previous male therapist—or both. In all but two or three instances, these have been stunningly attractive women. In two of the cases, the sexual molestation by the father had begun as early as age seven.

The presence of an extremely attractive daughter can be quite jarring to the balance of forces in a family, unless the parents' marriage is unusually satisfying. Otherwise a kind of hydraulic effect is mobilized in which even small disappointments with the wife (not only in the area of sex) promote intense interest in the daughter, whom the father readily comes to envision as a much better "wife" than his real wife. Temptation need not be consummated to have damaging effects. One young woman who was worked with in psychotherapy was the product of a chaotic home characterized by severe marital discord. Her two average-looking sisters, both very bright, were encouraged in their academic pursuits, and eventually completed graduate school. The patient, equally bright according to the usual tests, was nevertheless the "pretty one"—as her father called her. Throughout her adolescence, she became the object of his not so subtle flirtations. To compound matters, her own academic interests were impugned as irrelevant: "Don't bother your pretty head; you'll catch a rich man and live happily ever after!" The price she paid for her "advantage" was a damaged self-image (She thought of herself as "dumb"), wasted years in which her education was neglected, and a distorted view of men (as interested only in sex). She made a disastrous first marriage; several years of intensive therapy were required before her perceptions about men and about herself could be normalized. Although many beautiful girls are allowed to grow up without much attention to self-discipline, this woman had some inner resources. Later she was able to tackle graduate school as her sisters had.

Social Mobility

History is replete with examples of beautiful girls from humble backgrounds who grow up to win acceptance in the highest social strata. Beauty is a great leveler in this respect, since it is found at all social levels, but helps its possessor gravitate toward the top. This is part of the human condition, and has certain fairly obvious advantages. Beautiful girls soon learn of the ease with which they are accepted in all social activities: They become the cheerleader, the majorette, the girl who sells the kisses at the church bazaar (*ad maiorem Dei gloriam!*), and so forth. Theirs is the widest choice of eligible males, and there are many pranks and irregularities they can get away with that an unprepossessing girl cannot. With a few tears the pretty girl can get into the circus without a ticket, or get out of a "ticket" about to be imposed by the traffic cop. But there are also disadvantages.

Girls of unusual attractiveness, who are also vulnerable to emotional illness, may find themselves catapulted into a social milieu where they are out of their depth. Despite being readily accepted, they presently find that on some level they cannot compete, and they end up feeling acutely out of place. At times this may serve as the precipitant of emotional breakdown. This may have been the situation with several movie celebrities, whose careers ended tragically (schizophrenic breakdown, suicide) when the discrepancies between outward appearance and inner substance became too glaring. A twenty-one-year-old woman, for example, sought help for a severe depressive illness. She was the only child of a wealthy, socially prominent family. A striking beauty by early adolescence, she became a model at twelve. Scholastic achievement was discouraged. At nineteen she married a history professor. While his colleagues' wives were busy envying her because of her appearance, she was busy envying them and their husbands for their capacity to converse on many subjects—about which she was woefully uninformed. The old pride in her looks was eclipsed by despair at having "nothing to say." Material comfort did not shield her against depression. In this regard, money and beauty may be seen as advantages of quite different species, since time causes the one to increase, but the other to fade. This woman had been taught from childhood to "make the most" of her beauty; by her early twenties, however, she looked forward with apprehension to the day when besides having "nothing to say," she would no longer be attractive. When she first entered treatment she felt it inevitable that she would kill herself "the day I turn thirty."

Choice of Partners

A girl of great beauty discovers during adolescence that she can date any boy she wishes. While she may have been the victim of exploitation in some of the ways referred to earlier, she can become exploitative herself. If so inclined, she can discard one boyfriend for another, always realizing that yet another will be waiting. Whereas deep relationships require tolerance, empathy, and patience, her beauty may allow her to feel that such virtues are expendable. Exchanging partners seems easier than resolving an interpersonal problem. Beauty predisposes to becoming "spoiled" in such a manner that no lasting heterosexual partnership can be maintained; regardless of whom one is with, there is a hovering awareness that a potentially superior mate is near at hand. In clinical practice, the author has encountered several patients whose beauty hampered their developing a sense of limitations; specifically, the recognition of when they must stop searching and start settling for the man they already have.

Unhealthy Narcissism

Because great beauty can obviate the necessity to share, to accept less than the "best" or even to develop marketable skills, it can also predispose to pathological character traits related to the narcissistic path of development. Such traits would include vanity, frivolity, imperiousness, shallowness, arrogance, and selfishness. Happily, one also encounters women whose beauty enhanced poise, self-confidence, and a sense of obligation to those less fortunate than themselves, such that their character was ennobled rather than deformed. Several winners of the Miss America contest have displayed these qualities, and have used their charm to promote programs beneficial to the general public.

If the parents have been exploitative, or have neglected the development of talents and interests, a girl of unusual beauty may also come to exhibit another manifestation typical of narcissistic character disorders, namely, the simultaneous feeling of specialness and inner unworthiness. To be admired only for one's beauty may provoke guilt in some girls (because they didn't "earn" their advantage by hard work) or arouse rage in others (stemming from the assumption that "all" men are incapable of prizing them for any quality *except* their beauty). If their personalities have strong narcissistic traits indeed, girls who feel, rightly or wrongly, that they have no other assets besides beauty may become frantic at any minor threat to their appearance: A pimple or a misplaced hair may suffice to move them from haughtiness to despair.

Concluding Remarks

It has been noted how beauty, if found in combination with heightened vulnerability to emotional disorder, may act as a modifying influence in either direction. In certain borderline adolescents, social awkwardness or poor vocational skills may be so well compensated for by physical beauty that they ultimately make an excellent recovery, find suitable mates despite their handicaps, and blend in quite well with the society around them. But there are other young women whose beauty has been exploited in so continuous and damaging a fashion that they never manage to avail themselves of the many advantages their attractiveness might otherwise have conferred on them. If such women seek help in psychotherapy, great caution must be exercised on the part of male therapists not to be overawed by their beauty. Feelings of attraction in and of themselves need not be harmful to the course of treatment: In any case they are almost inevitable. What matters is one's command over such feelings. If this is lacking, treatment will founder, or worse still, progress toward actualized romantic involvement. Another countertransference problem that may arise is the prolongation of psychotherapy beyond the limits of

utility. In this situation, what is at work is not so much the patient's desire to retain a relationship with the therapist as it is the male therapist's fantasy of enjoying forever the adoration of a beautiful young woman.

Whereas in a grown woman, problems in the area of beauty, seductiveness, and the like are probably best treated by a male (who can help the patient realize not all men are exploitative, for example), it may be better if the adolescent girl is treated by a female. A competent and seasoned male therapist might undertake the psychotherapy of an adolescent girl, confident that he would not get bogged down in unresolvable erotic "countertransference." But the young girl may become overwhelmed with her own sexual feelings toward the male therapist. If, as is often the case, she is unable to verbalize these feelings, treatment will be stalemated.

In general, narcissistic character pathology is more difficult to resolve psychotherapeutically than are the predominantly infantile, depressive, or hysterical character disorders. Paradoxically, beautiful adolescent girls who harbor overvalued ideas (or even delusions) of ugliness may be much easier to treat than their highly narcissistic counterparts who, if they are emotionally disturbed, may not even recognize the need for help.

REFERENCES

1. GRINKER, R. R., JR., "Children of the Rich," Paper presented at the American Psychiatric Association, Toronto, May 2, 1977.
2. STONE, M. H., "Boundary Violations Between Therapist and Patient," *Psychiatric Annals,* 6:670–677, 1976.
3. ———, "Treating the Wealthy and Their Children," *International Journal of Child Psychotherapy, 1:*15–46, 1972.
4. ———, and KESTENBAUM, C., "Maternal Deprivation in Children of the Wealthy," *History of Childhood Quarterly,* 2:79–106, 1974.
5. WEINTRAUB, W., "The V.I.P. Syndrome: A Clinical Study in Hospital Psychiatry," *Journal of Nervous and Mental Disease, 138:*181–193, 1964.

PART C
Varieties of Family Structure

36 / The Adopted Child

Jeffrey S. Schwam and Maria Krocker Tuskan

Nature of the Characteristics that Define the Adopted Child

The adopted child is defined by the fact that one or more adults who are not his biological parents become recognized before the law as his parents. In a more general sense, there are families who take in children and raise them as their own without legal action; psychologically, at least, some of these cases would fall within the same category.

Nature of Adopted Children— Their Distribution in the Culture

In 1971, the population of the United States under the age of eighteen was 68,559,000.[6] Of these, it is estimated 2,400,000 (3.5 percent) were adopted.[20] In that same year, there were 3,559,970 live births[35] and 169,000 children adopted.[12]

Of these 169,000 adoptions, 82,800 (49 percent) were nonrelative adoptions, that is to say, they were not transferred between members of an extended family. Of these 82,800, 87 percent were born out of wedlock, 79 percent were placed by agencies, and 65 percent were less than three months old when placed. The median age at placement was 1.9 months. For public agency placements, the median age was 4.0 months; for voluntary agency placements, 1.7 months; and for independent placements, less than a month.[2]

Of the 169,000 children adopted, 22,000 were members of minority groups. Of these, 56 percent were adopted by nonrelatives, and 67 percent were black.[2]

Impact of Being Adopted at Different Levels of Development

The adopted child has three main areas of potential difficulty: (1) the reaction of his adoptive parents to his being adopted; (2) his own reaction to being adopted; and (3) the effect of his separation from his biological parents and placement prior to going to his adoptive home. This chapter deals with the child's reaction to being adopted.

Typically, a child will learn of his adoption at around age three. At this age, all children distort or deny material that impinges on their vulnerable areas.[40] Thus, if the child does not use denial, learning of his adoption will generate fantasies. Given this information, any child may wonder why he is not with his biological parents. Among the frequently experienced fantasies are the ideas that he was bad and thus given away, that the biological parents were bad and thus gave him away, or that the adoptive parents kidnapped him. At three, the child cannot understand that a person can part with a child for a sober, practical reason.

The fantasy that he was bad, and thus given away, may be used to reinforce feelings of inferiority or being damaged. Schechter describes a

342

girl who felt her mother gave her up for adoption because she wasn't a boy.[43]

If the child believes that his biological parents were bad, he may generalize this to other grown-ups. This may lead to difficulty in making attachments, and in extending trust. Since he was given away once, the child may reasonably fear being given away again.

The fantasy of having been kidnapped can lead to anger toward the adoptive parents along with a wish to return to the biological parents. This fantasy may be intensified by several factors. Like the child whose parents have died, the adopted child may deny the finality of the loss, and "the lost object was not decathected, it became invested with intensified cathexis."[51] During this period of development, many children fantasize themselves as stepchildren with idealization of the fantasied biological parents. As Sigmund Freud pointed out in the "Family Romance," when a child feels "he is not receiving the whole of his parents' love . . . his sense that his own affection is not being fully reciprocated then finds a vent in the idea . . . of being a stepchild or an adopted child" and "his parents are replaced by others of better birth."[18] The adopted child knows that another family really exists and for him this tendency is intensified. One of the tasks of this stage is the giving up of the family romance. This involves reconciling of the overvalued fantasied parent with the real parent. Since adopted children really have two sets of parents, they are capable of keeping the good and bad images split, with subsequent problems in superego and ego ideal formation.[43] Eiduson states:

Our children never really came to terms with the fact that they both love and hate the same person . . . inability to accept ambivalence within themselves or within others. Because they do not incorporate the parental prohibition, they therefore show a defect in superego formation . . . the Rorschach reports so frequently stated that there was an absence of definite identification with either parental figure.[15]

The above children tended to see the therapist as either all-giving or all bad. To avoid this problem, it has been suggested that telling the child about the fact of his adoption be delayed until latency.[43] However, the act of adoption is not usually a secret, and the child may learn about it from someone else with "serious emotional reverberations";[42] moreover, the attempt to keep the adoption hidden can keep the parents in a state of chronic tension.

If one decides to tell the child at age three, should he be told "a story about the nice daddy and mother who didn't have any children of their own and who looked and looked for the right one until they found a baby that just suited them; and then they took it home and loved it, ending with the statement that they had gotten him that way, too"?[31] There are some professionals who feel that this romanticized version inhibits a more realistic acceptance of the adoption, especially the negative feelings. They suggest a version in which the adoptive process is described as it actually happened. How frequently should the prelatency child be told? Possibly the child should be told a few times, and then the subject should not be brought up again unless he brings it up, thus allowing him the use of denial. But this does not end the process, as "telling is a gradual process of communication over time."[42] At each stage in the adopted child's development, his fantasies relating to his adoption will vary, and the type of assistance needed will vary.

During latency, the subject of adoption can be reintroduced. The child can now understand a more factual report of the adoption. This might include pointing out the adoption agency and the courthouse. For the child adopted at an older age who has had several placements, additional assistance may be desirable. This might include counseling, and compiling a book containing pictures and statements which review the places and people the child has known.[4, 14] In adolescence or adulthood, the adopted person could learn about his biological parents and even meet them.[48] In a report of fifty reunions, forty adult adoptees found the experience satisfying.[38]

In latency, if attachment to biological parents is strong, there may be a lack of resolution of the oedipal conflict, decrease in identifications with adoptive parents, and impairment in social relations as others are seen as all good or all bad.

Learning may be impeded during latency due to several factors. Adoptive parents are often middle class with above-average intelligence. The children offered for adoption, however, often have average intellectual abilities. Hence, some adopted children prove academically disappointing to their parents, and to themselves.[52] This will be accentuated in a middle-class school system which stresses verbal abilities and college acceptance. Also, the adoptive child may feel insecure about his new parents keeping him, and hesitate to express hostility directly. Learning difficulties may be utilized as a safer more indirect channel. The child can say "It's not my fault if I'm not bright."[40] Also the knowledge of being adopted weakens the child's confidence in the parents "as the ego questions its primary introjects," and his "whole basic method of accumulating knowledge and relying on objects is doubted" which "must affect all subsequent learning."[43] To the extent that learning is related to looking at new areas of knowledge, the adopted child may experience an inhibition of his intellectual curiosity due to the inhibition in looking at his adoption.

As part of adolescence, the rise in libidinal drives with incestuous fantasies leads to "searching for substitutes for the parent figures or ego ideals with whom he can identify."[7] With this one sees "attempts to develop a perception of self, to integrate identifications."[7] The adopted adolescent may seek to solve developmental conflicts by turning away from adoptive parents and toward biological parents. This becomes manifest when the youth makes concrete attempts to find the biological parents and to identify with them. Clothier states, "identification with our forebears . . . gives us our most fundamental security."[8] "I have seen a number of cases in which children in adolescence start roaming around almost aimlessly, though sometimes they are aware that they are seeking someone or something. They then seem to be seeking the fantasied 'good real parents.' "[43] Schechter describes a girl who "did not fall in love until she . . . met men of the same religious faith as her fantasied father . . ."[43] Simon sees "the fantasy of reunion . . . to be an effort to deal with the depression that follows fantasies around abandonment."[45] This searching may represent an attempt to master the vagueness of the past. Novey describes a man who, during the course of analysis, sought out his biological parents' gravesites.

There was present the need of establishing a very specific real knowledge of these matters . . . the need to recapture and digest in the present context some past experience . . . a sense of gratification that comes at having established, through the physical setting, a certain firmness and reality in connection with the situation which had had something of a dreamlike and even sometimes nightmarish quality.[36]

Identification with the fantasied parent can lead to difficulty: "at 17 she revelled in cheap clothes, cheap jewelry, and cheap manners. Her fierce wish was to be like her own natural mother . . ."[43] Sometimes the fantasy of the biological parent takes a negative form; this may represent efforts of the adopted child to explain why he was given away.[45] The criticism adoptive parents sometimes level at biological parents only reinforces this trend.

Children generally lack the capacity to accept death and to mourn adequately when a parent dies.[34, 50, 51] One might wonder if some of the behavior of the adopted adolescent relates to the initiation of mourning for his biological parents.

Family Reactions to the Adoption

Adoptive parents must deal with issues that are unique to the adoptive process.

They have frequently engaged in unsuccessful attempts to conceive. There have been consultations with physicians, all sorts of studies, and, often enough, less and less pleasure in sexual relations.[2] If the cause of infertility is known, one spouse may feel guilty and inadequate, the other cheated and angry. If it is not known, both may blame the wife. Even after adoption, the new child may be resented as evidence of their infertility, proof of their damaged state.[41] Shame about infertility may lead to difficulty in discussing the adoption with the child as well as telling him how babies are conceived.[49]

On the other hand, the adopted child may be seen as a means for becoming fertile. Some infertility may be psychogenic, the product of conflicts around femininity, motherhood, and the inability to conceive.[2, 26] Acceptance by the adoption agency may represent an authoritarian parent who says it's okay to be a parent.[9, 2] The presence of the child may allow the sexual union to become fun. Statistical studies have not shown that adoption increases fertility, but some question whether these studies are definitive.[33]

If a couple conceives after adoption, they tend to maintain a good relationship with the adopted child. However, if a couple with one biological child adopts, seeking a second child, then conceives, the adopted child is sometimes resented as an outsider who is no longer needed.

The agency has the power to withhold a child. This stimulates both resentment and fear toward the agency, reminiscent of childhood feelings of helplessness in dealing with the omnipotent parent.[41] When the agency is so perceived, the couple may hesitate to return later if problems arise.

Once prospective parents are told that they can adopt, they may experience guilt over taking the child away from its mother. As the child becomes older, and the adoptive parents' love grows as well, this guilt frequently returns and has to be dealt with again.

Adoptive parents receive the child without

having experienced pregnancy, delivery, and the postnatal period. These phases play an important role in the attachment between parents and child, as well as preparing the husband-wife dyad to become a husband-wife-child triad.

All new parents must give up the idealized child they wished for.[3] Only then can attachment fully occur. This mourning process may be even more difficult for adoptive parents whose infertility leads them to regard the child they are receiving as a damaged second choice. This is similar to the task of parents who bear a handicapped child.[41, 47]

As a child is growing up, all parents may worry about the meaning of certain behavior, the significance of some physical peculiarity, or the adequacy of the child's intelligence. Such concerns are often intensified in adoptive parents. This is due to their reactions to a first child, their fears of hereditary taint, and their tendencies to project onto the child their own forbidden impulses.

The adopted child frequently is the couple's first child. Parents tend to overprotect and to expect more from first children.

The adopted child often arrives clouded in mystery. The usual fantasy is that he was conceived out of wedlock by impulsive and sexually promiscuous parents. Any peculiarity the child displays may cause anxiety, with fears that the difference portends other things. Normal variations in development may be seen as signs of retardation. Normal aggressive outbursts, masturbation, or sexual play with other children may all provoke undue parental anxiety.

The explanations that all parents may advance to account for their child's behavior usually reflect their own unconscious wishes. Forbidden impulses may be projected onto the child. Fantasies of hereditary influences will facilitate the process —"It can't belong to me." This may be especially resorted to by rigid parents who tend to overuse repression. "When such a mother observes in a child evidences of id impulses, her own repression is threatened, hence she has to reject the child in that moment,"[15] as she would her own forbidden impulses. Thus, appropriate behavior may be reacted to with excessive concern, and lead to rejection of the child.

Adoptive parents may have difficulty setting limits. It may be harder for them to tolerate the child's anger; they fear that the child will not love them. They may feel a need to reassure both themselves and the child that the child is loved and wanted. The result is difficulty in expressing anger at the child.[15]

The adoptive parents must deal with telling the child that he is adopted. Repeated telling can interfere with parenting by making it difficult for the parents to think of the child as their own. An adoptive father states: "You must completely forget about the adoption if you want to live your life with your children . . ."[39] Deutsch states: "Love and the continuous contact can make the adopted child her own as it were, and the fact that it is not her blood can be forgotten . . . he becomes a part of her ego, just as precious and loved as if she had engendered him."[11]

Cultural Reactions

Society tends to condemn adoption. Williams feels that the adopted child is "rejected" by the superego "as the child was probably illegitimate," and "rejected by the id" as the child "is not related by blood" and "comes into conflict with family narcissism."[42] Peller notes the frequency of "snide remarks" adoptive parents "get from neighbors, friends, from parents of schoolmates."[39] Grandparents, on the other hand, are generally accepting of the adoption.[30]

Relatives and neighbors may oppose transracial adoption with some vehemence, but opposition generally dissipates after placement.[23] Where a white family adopts a black child, some workers in the adoption field wonder if the child will have difficulty taking pride in his black identity, wth the inevitable subsequent problems. Such children seem to do well throughout latency,[24] but further studies are needed to know if these fears will prove justified in adolescence or adulthood. Presently, it is agreed that efforts should be increased to recruit black adoptive parents for black children[25, 19, 13] and to assist such transracial situations by helping the child maintain contact with black persons and other interracial families.[1, 28]

Tendency to Develop Characteristic Forms of Emotional Disturbance

There is disagreement as to whether the adopted child is more prone to emotional disturbances, whether the adopted child is more prone to specific types of emotional disturbances, and whether the age of adoption affects the type and severity of emotional disturbance.

There have been attempts to answer these questions by questionnaires to adoptive parents, reviews by psychiatric facilities, and follow-up studies. How applicable these studies are to the general adopted population, however, continues to be debated. And how applicable these studies are to children with varying placement experiences is also not clear.

Reviews of adopted children referred for psychiatric assistance have noted certain tendencies. A study comparing 159 adopted children with controls found that the adopted children showed no difference in suicide rate, but that they displayed significantly more destructive acts and sexual acting-out.[44] Sixteen adopted parents showed presenting symptoms "as varied as is generally found in pediatric psychiatric practice." "Superego and ego ideal" problems were noted.[43] In a study of 14 adopted children, 11 were referred with behavior disturbances. Aggressive behavior was noted in 7, stealing as a primary symptom in 6, and a learning disturbance in 5 of the children.[22] In a study of 17 adopted children, there was a tendency to sexual acting-out, aggressiveness, rebelliousness, and school difficulties.[45] Twenty-five adopted children had significantly more behavior problems than a control group. The later the age of the adoption, the greater the frequency and severity of the behavior problems.[37] On the basis of interviews with the adoptive parents, a study of 91 children adopted after the age of five concluded that adoptions of older children are as successful as adoptions of infants.[29] Eighty adopted children did not differ from controls except that those placed after the age of six months were significantly more apt to steal and lie, and showed a tendency toward cruelty to animals and to destroy property.[27]

Compared to controls, 44 adopted adults referred for psychiatric treatment showed significantly more alcoholism and sexual acting-out, a nonsignificant tendency toward more suicide attempts, and no significant difference in aggressive acts.[44] In a study of 250 adopted adults, average age thirty-one, who were adopted before age seven in Norway, the adopted adults did not differ from the average population in hospitalization for psychosis, mental retardation, alcoholism, and criminal involvement.[5]

Tendency of Adopted Children to Develop Different Forms of Coping Behavior

FANTASIES

The child may explain being given away as due to his being bad, his biological parents being bad, or his adoptive parents kidnapping him. There is a tendency to idealize biological parents and deprecate adoptive parents, with later inclinations to see people as all good or all bad. Again, fears of being given away may cause the child hesitation in expressing anger to the adoptive parents.

The adopted adolescent may show increased interest in his biological parents. This occurs due to the normal turning away from one's parents, the seeking for roots on which to build an identity, fears of genetic defects, and attempts to master the vagueness of one's past. There may be attempts to discover information about the biological parents, identifications with them, or attempts to establish relationships with them or with others who are fantasied to be like them.

SKILLS AND SUBLIMATIONS

Due to increased parental attention, some adopted children might show the kind of higher achievement motivation found in firstborns.

SPECIAL DEFENSE PATTERNS

The adoption may be dealt with via isolation of affect and ego splitting. One part of the ego may accept the adoption, and the other part never really believes it. Anger at the biological parents may be displaced on to the adoptive parents or turned against the self with resultant feelings of depression or inferiority. In adolescence, there may be an attempt to identify with the lost biological parents as a way of getting them back.

Social Structures Needed for the Adopted Child

Though a hard goal to attain, society should attempt to prevent delay between birth and placement with adoptive parents. To maximize parental attachment, placement should occur in the first few weeks of the child's life; to best support the child's development, it should take place by the second month[32] (as long as prior mothering is adequate).

All unwed parents should begin individual counseling by the third month of pregnancy, in order to explore available alternatives. The involvement of grandparents may be appropriate. If the parents choose to place the child for adoption, individual or group counseling should be given to deal with the difficulties of pregnancy out of wedlock and to resolve the inevitable ambivalence concerning the adoption. If this is not done, the child will be exposed to delay in union with his adopted parents. Ideally, the obstetrician would be medically responsible for arranging proper counseling in the same manner he is now responsible for arranging proper laboratory tests and medication.

Counseling of would be adoptive parents should begin well before the actual adoption. Once the child is born, a specially trained pediatric assessor[16, 17, 46] should discuss the meaning of any physical differences or handicaps with the prospective adoptive parents. If the given couple chooses not to adopt, there are families who will readily adopt a handicapped child.[10]

After placement, if handicaps are discovered, should the option of revoking the adoption be available, and should adoptions ever be revocable?[21] To allay anxieties, the adoptive parents can be assisted by good pediatric liaison, the opportunity for continued counseling, and the availability of toddler parent groups to provide peer support around parenting.

It is not clear how much data about the biological parents should be told to the adoptive parents or child. It seems that more information is better than less. As the adopted child becomes older, he will develop the ability to make appropriate use of more complex and detailed types of information. At a certain age, in certain cases, reunion with biological parents might be useful. A confidential national administrative structure should be established to facilitate reunion of adopted adults with their biological parents if both request it.

REFERENCES

1. ANDERSON, D., *Children of Special Value*, St. Martin's Press, New York, 1971.

2. ANDREWS, R., "Adoption and the Resolution of Infertility," *Fertility and Sterility*, 21(1):73–76, 1970.

3. ASCH, S. S., "Postpartum Reactions," *American Journal of Psychiatry*, 131:870–874, 1974.

4. BASS, C., "Matchmaker: Older Child Adoption Failures," *Journal of the Child Welfare League of America*, 54:505–512, 1975.

5. BRATFOS, O., EITINGER, L., and TAU, T., "Mental Illness and Crime in Adopted Children and Adoptive Parents," *Acta Psychiatrica Scandinavica*, 44:376–384, 1968.

6. Bureau of the Census, Personal communication.

7. BUXBAUM, E., "Scientific Proceedings—Panel Reports—The Psychology of Adolescence," *Journal of the American Psychoanalytic Association*, 6:111–120, 1958.

8. CLOTHIER, F., "The Psychology of the Adopted Child," *Mental Hygiene*, 27:222–230, 1943.

9. COOPER, H., "Psychogenic Infertility and Adoption," *South African Medical Journal*, 45:719–722, 1971.

10. CRAWFORD, S., "Adoption," *Lancet*, 2:962, 1973.

11. DEUTSCH, H., *The Psychology of Women*, vol. 2, Grune & Stratton, New York, 1945.

12. DHEW Publication No. (SRS) 73–03259, NCSS Report E–10 (1971), Adoptions in 1971, U.S. Department of Health, Education, and Welfare, National Center for Social Statistics, Washington, D.C.

13. DUNNE, P., "Placing Children of Minority Groups for Adoption," *Children*, 5(2):43–48, 1958.

14. EDWARDS, M., and BOYD, F., "Adoption for Adolescents," *Journal of the Child Welfare League of America*, 54:298–300, 1975.

15. EIDUSON, B. T., and LIVERMORE, J. B., "Complications in Therapy with Adopted Children," *American Journal of Orthopsychiatry*, 23:795–802, 1953.

16. FORFAR, J. O., "Adoption," *Lancet*, 2:1153, 1973.

17. ———, "Child Adoption," *The Practioner*, 205:51–57, 1970.

18. FREUD, S., *The Standard Edition of the Complete Psychological Works of Sigmund Freud*, vol. 9, Hogarth Press, London, 1959.

19. GALLAGHER, U., "Adoption Resources for Black Children," *Children*, 18(2):49–53, 1971.

20. ———, Specialist on Adoptions in the Children's Bureau, U.S. Dept. of Health, Education, and Welfare, Personal communication.

21. GOLDSTEIN, J., FREUD, A., and SOLNIT, A., *Beyond the Best Interests of the Child*, The Free Press, New York, 1973.

22. GOODMAN, J., SILBERSTEIN, R., and MANDELL, W., "Adopted Children Brought to a Child Psychiatric Clinic," *Archives of General Psychiatry*, 9:451–456, 1963.

23. GROW, L., and SHAPIRO, D., *Transracial Adoption*, Research Center—Child Welfare League of America, New York, 1975.

24. ———, *Black Children—White Parents*, Research Center—Child Welfare League of America, New York, 1974.

25. HERZOG, E., SUDIA, C., and HARWOOD, J., "Finding Families for Black Children," *Children*, 18(4):146–149, 1971.

26. HUMPHREY, M., "The Adopted Child as a Fertility Charm," *Journal of Reproduction and Fertility*, 20:354–356, 1969.

27. ———, and OUNSTED, C., "Adoptive Families Referred for Psychiatric Advice," *British Journal of Psychiatry*, 109:599–608, 1963.

28. JONES, E., "On Transracial Adoption of Black Children," *The Journal of the Child Welfare League*, 51(3):159–165, 1972.

29. KADUSHIN, A. "A Follow-Up Study of Children Adopted When Older: Criteria of Success," *American Journal of Orthopsychiatry*, 37:530–539, 1967.

30. Kirk, H. D., *Shared Fate*, The Free Press, New York, 1964.

31. Knight, R. P., "Some Problems Involved in Selecting and Rearing Adopted Children," *Bulletin of the Menninger Clinic, 5(3)*:65–74, 1941.

32. Mahler, M., Pine, F., and Bergman, A., *The Psychological Birth of the Human Infant*, Basic Books, New York, 1975.

33. Mai, F. M., "Conception After Adoption: An Open Question," *Psychosomatic Medicine, 33*:509–514, 1971.

34. Miller, J., "Children's Reactions to a Parent's Death," *Journal of the American Psychoanalytic Association, 19*:697–719, 1971.

35. National Center for Health Statistics, Personal communications.

36. Novey, S., "Why Some Patients Conduct Actual Investigations of Their Biographies," *Journal of the American Psychoanalytic Association, 14*:376–387, 1966.

37. Offord, D., Aponte, M., and Cross, L., "Presenting Symptomology of Adopted Children," *Archives of General Psychiatry, 20*:110–116, 1969.

38. Pannor, R., Sorosky, A., and Baran, A., "The Effects of the Sealed Record in Adoption," *American Journal of Psychiatry, 133*:900–904, 1976.

39. Peller, L., "Further Comments on Adoption," *Bulletin of the Philadelphia Psychoanalytic Association, 13*:1–14, 1963.

40. ———, "About Telling the Child of His Adoption," *Bulletin of the Philadelphia Psychoanalytic Association, 12*:146–158, 1962.

41. Rothenberg, E., Goldey, H., and Sands, R., "The Vicissitudes of the Adoption Process," *American Journal of Psychiatry, 128*:590–595, 1971.

42. Schechter, M. D., "Psychoanalytic Theory as It Relates to Adoption," *Journal of the American Psychoanalytic Association, 51*:695–708, 1967.

43. ———, "Observations on Adopted Children," *Archives of General Psychiatry, 3*:45/21–56/32, 1960.

44. ———, et al., "Emotional Problems in the Adoptee," *Archives of General Psychiatry, 10*:109–118, 1964.

45. Simon, N., and Senturia, A., "Adoption and Psychiatric Illness," *American Journal of Psychiatry, 122*:858–868, 1966.

46. Smith, D. C., "Pediatric Consultation in Adoption Practice," *Pediatrics, 41(2)*:519–523, 1968.

47. Solnit, A., and Stark, M., "Mourning and the Birth of a Defective Child," in Eissler, R. S., et al. (Eds.), *The Psychoanalytic Study of the Child*, vol. 16, pp. 523–538, International Universities Press, New York, 1961.

48. Sorosky, A., Baran, A., and Pannor, R., "Identity Conflicts in Adoptees," *American Journal of Orthopsychiatry, 45(1)*:18–27, 1975.

49. Taylor, D., and Starr, P., "The Use of Clinical Services by Adoptive Parents," *Journal of the American Academy of Child Psychiatry, 11*:384–399, 1972.

50. Wolfenstein, M., "Loss, Rage, and Repetition," in Eissler, R. S., et al. (Eds.), *The Psychoanalytic Study of the Child*, vol. 24, pp. 432–460, International Universities Press, New York, 1969.

51. Wolfenstein, M., "How Is Mourning Possible?" in Eissler, R. S., et al. (Eds.), *The Psychoanalytic Study of the Child*, vol. 21, pp. 93–123, International Universities Press, New York, 1966.

52. Wolff, S., "The Fate of the Adopted Child," *Archives of Diseases in Childhood, 49*:165–170, 1974.

37 / The Foster Child

Wiley R. Smith, Jr.

Nature and Characteristics of the Foster Child

When the child's own family cannot care for him for brief or extended periods and when adoption is neither desirable nor possible, a child may be placed in foster, group, institutional, or family care. Prospective advantages of a foster family over group, institutional, or residential care include closer relationships with maternal and paternal figures, socialization of the child within a family and cultural group, and continued active participation in the community. On the other hand, even when foster children adapt well within the home and community of the foster family, they are often identified as alien, derived from a different family and community, and dissimilar from their foster family. Termination of foster status occurs when the child returns home, is adopted, or becomes self-dependent.

Referral to foster care may be precipitated by maternal dysfunction from any cause, chronically disorganized and chaotic family settings, and unmanageability of the child's behavioral symptoms within his own home or community. Placement of children occurs at all ages from early infancy to adolescence, with an average age around nine. Reasons for placement vary from one agency or community to another. One study[7] cites the following reasons for placement: mental illness of the mother, 23.6 percent; neglect and abuse of the child, 17.4 percent; the child's own presumably unmanageable behavior, 13.9 percent; abandonment or desertion of the child, 12.5 percent; unwillingness of the mother to assume or continue child care, 12 percent; physical illness of the mother, 9.5 percent; family dysfunction, 8.1 percent. Other studies give less weight to emotional illness

illness in parents and emphasize primarily neglect or abandonment. Within the past few years foster home placement has been used selectively in the care of retarded or emotionally disturbed children as an alternative to institutional care. The goals of such specialized foster care differ from traditional ones in being more oriented toward therapeutic change and less toward return home.

The foster child is not a single entity or group. The category encompasses many children whose transient reactions to their difficult life situations and placements may fall well within the range of normal developmental variations. It also includes many children with extremely severe developmental deviations indicative of irreversible damage to the child. This chapter addresses itself to the more serious manifestations of psychopathology in foster children. However, one must keep in mind that approximately half of the children in foster placement make relatively successful adjustments with limited professional support before, during, and after placement.

Number and Distribution of Foster Children

Figures from California[24] indicate that over a twenty-five-year period foster care placements have increased about 900 percent. There has been about 100 percent increase over an eight-year period. Since the number of resources for foster placement has not risen as rapidly,[25] a potential crisis appears likely in securing adequate facilities. A count has been made by living arrangements of the children served by public and voluntary child welfare agencies.[25] This gives one a picture of the use of services available for foster care. The data is distorted by failure of some public and voluntary agencies to report services. Further skewing is seen when one considers an unknown number of children informally placed with relatives or friends, and an undetermined number of adolescents self-placed away from home. Within the population under age twenty-one, approximately three million children were served annually by child welfare agencies in 1970, 1971, and 1972[25] (about four children out of every hundred). Of these, about 250,000 were in foster family care (less than one child per 100 children). Estimates from other sources (1974 and 1975) indicate the number of children in placement at about 350,000.

A review of studies from different areas of the United States[9, 12, 24] suggests that the racial distribution of children in placement follows socioeconomic lines rather than the racial composition of the total community. Ninety-four percent of children reported were served by public agencies[25] (further evidence that the majority of children in placement are derived from indigent or disadvantaged economic groups). One study[24] noted that only 16 percent of natural parents owned personal property, only 5 percent owned real estate, and only 2.3 percent contributed to the support of the child in placement. Sex distribution in these studies was about 45 percent girls and 55 percent boys. Closer scrutiny suggests a predominance of males below age twelve and equality or predominance of females over twelve, especially in the fifteen- to sixteen-year-old group.

Impact of Early Developmental Experiences

There are two major areas of potential psychological damage for the foster child. These involve the management of separation and loss, and the development of a stable identity. In order to comprehend the trauma created by placement and its importance at different developmental levels, it is essential to know something about the child's prior developmental experiences. Psychological tasks confronting the child in placement include: (1) coping with the anxiety about separation from family and habitual surroundings; (2) developing or maintaining object constancy; (3) adapting to new parent-authority figures and managing closeness with them; (4) defending against feelings of rejection-abandonment and lowered self-esteem; (5) coping with the awareness of personal helplessness in influencing one's life situation; and (6) development of a stable identity. Several factors which affect the nature and degree of developmental distortion include: (1) age at placement; (2) type, number, and duration of prior placements; and (3) the variety and flexibility of ego defenses.

Psychoanalytic theory proposes that through a series of successful early developmental experiences with a constant and consistent mothering figure, the child attains object constancy around age three. This stable internalized mental representation of the mother, a presence even in her absence, provides security, comfort, and a partial mechanism of internal regulation as the child moves through successive developmental stages and shows increasing degrees of independence. There is a quality of basic trust and expectation of support that derives from this experience; this facilitates transfer of these attitudes to other prospectively helpful adults as the child moves into the community and total culture. The outcome (resolution) of each encounter with developmental or traumatic stress is dependent not only upon biological givens (special favored abilities, drive strength, intelligence, etc.), but also upon the nature of adaptation to previous developmental challenges.

At the onset of early adolescence emotional disengagement from these internalized object ties as they are projected onto parents begins. In the young adolescent, tension develops as the regressive attraction toward retaining or reestablishing these ties comes into conflict with increased drive strengths, mastery satisfactions, and a push toward individuation. As the adolescent shows greater emotional distance and less dependence upon parents, close peer relationships and attachments to adults outside the family prevent a state of emotional limbo. Both the condition of objectless libido and regression to preoedipal figures are intolerable, anxiety-laden experiences for the adolescent. With less dependence on parents and a wider field of figures for identification, an enhanced individuality emerges, freeing the person to make the decisions and choices necessary for further development. A number of studies of untroubled adolescents[10, 14, 19] suggest that when continuing relationships with parents are mutually satisfying, when the adolescent is able to share feelings and thoughts relatively easily with peers, when mechanisms for sublimation of aggressive and sexual energy are available and utilized, when turmoil and identity crisis are limited, then mood fluctuation is manageable and of short duration. New experiences can then be rehearsed, planned in fantasy, and integrated with past experiences that have produced satisfaction.[11]

Keeping in mind the importance of these early stabilizing experiences, the developmental products of early understimulation, loss, and ineffective attachment to adult figures will be briefly reviewed. All of these are experiences to which many prospective foster children have been repeatedly subjected, leaving the child less able to cope with the specific anxieties created by placement.

In reviewing the concept "maternal deprivation,"

Rutter[17] notes that many kinds of mothering experiences involving absence, loss, and distortion of nurturance are lumped together. This indiscriminate blurring of specific traumata obscures visualization of the impact of each one on the child's development and increases the difficulty of finding and applying appropriate corrective measures. Both successful and unsuccessful coping responses to the acute distress of brief separation with young children are well described by Robertson and Robertson.[16] Children with poorly developed object constancy, an immature ego, and weak ego defenses are more likely to exhibit symptom formation. Additional factors greatly increasing the likelihood of acute and chronic disturbance are environmental strangeness, unfamiliar adults, different foods, altered demands and disciplines, and painful somatic experience (illness or bodily restrictions). One concludes that the earlier and more prolonged the placement and the greater the change of environment and loss of familiar persons, the more profound and more fixed is the damage to the child. Spitz and Wolf's[22] description of anaclitic depression gives one picture of this occurrence.

Early prolonged institutionalization may produce different consequences. Prolonged absence of adequate stimulation experienced by some institutionalized infants produces the syndrome of hospitalism as described by Spitz.[21] This condition is marked by social unresponsiveness and apparent retardation; it has been shown to be reversible[17] by early adequate social, tactile, and perceptual stimulation.

A different picture, "affectionless psychopathy"[17] seems to be caused by failure to form consistent attachments during the first two or three years of life. Citing a study by Pringle and colleagues, Rutter[17] noted that emotionally stable institutionalized children had remained with their mother until after one year of age. He notes in contrast a study by Goldfarb showing that children remaining in an institution until after three years of age lacked guilt, were unable to keep rules, and were unable to make lasting relationships. Rutter concludes that failure to form attachments early in childhood is likely to produce attention seeking, uninhibited indiscriminate friendliness, and a personality characterized by lack of guilt and inability to form lasting relationships. A study of Colvin[5] showed that children in a residential treatment setting who had experienced early care in institutions had very low impulse control, high dependence, and unrealistically high self-evaluation especially within the areas of greatest ego deficit.

Compared with children whose early development was in their own home or in foster homes, children institutionalized early in life showed an absence of important ego structures (in the others, the ego structures were present but defective). Other studies of children temporarily placed after residential treatment record much better adaptation to foster care by children coming from intact families. In summary, these comparisons emphasize the interrelationship between different kinds of early developmental experience and later capacities for adaptation and for forming relationships.

Using Erikson's descriptions of identity components[6] one can readily visualize some of the problems foster children encounter in the course of identity formation. Erikson speaks of persistent sameness in one's self, sharing of essential characteristics with others, a sense of individual identity (and ego boundary), a sense of historical past and potential future, and an ego function which maintains inner solidarity in interactions with others. In describing the processes of identity development, an interpersonal model of interaction is emphasized. Further clarifying this model, concepts of "self-regulation coupled with mutual recognition," the give and take of interactions, and a need for reciprocal stimulation (communication) are described. Transient, partial identifications with adult attributes (often overvalued and coinciding with unconscious infantile fantasies) become the building blocks of identity. Once formed, this supersedes any single identification and merges all significant identifications into a unique and coherent whole. The uncertainties of the foster child's contact with his natural parents, his confusion about name and residence, the lack of stable figures with which to identify, and his transient and unstable peer relationships all contribute to the sense of uncertainty about one's self. In many foster children, early object constancy, one of the elements which forms the basic core of identity formation, is tenuous. Discontinuities of experience with the mothering figure, early understimulation, and raw abuse distort the capacity to trust or to form close relationships.

In latency these experiences lead to confusion, poor impulse control, distant relationships with peers and adults, and overt attempts to manipulate others. Closeness and emotional accessibility tend to reactivate the traumatic memories of the past along with their attendant anxieties. For the child, superficially using people is far safer than intense closeness and rapport. The child derives little gratification or sense of mastery in the present and anticipates no more in the future. In adolescence, the inability to set or pursue goals may alternate with transient, superficial overidentifications with peers; little individualization occurs, few relationships are maintained, and few characteristic traits emerge which mark the child as uniquely individual. Beyond this diffusion of identity, many of these adolescents identify with negative attributes of peer groups or withdraw into a constricted, detached, friendless existence.

Family Reaction to the Child's Placement

Superficially, many parents appear pleased or relieved to have a child in foster placement. This is particularly true in the face of progressive depletion of family energies or increasingly disruptive behavior on the part of the child. Empathic listening to the parents, however, will reveal a very different picture of shame, guilt, helplessness, and feelings of inadequacy. Unsuccessful attempts to cope with these feelings produce at least four possible outcomes: (1) internalization of shame and anger followed by depression, self-depreciation, and ambivalence both about visiting the child in placement and about his return home; (2) projection and externalization of many of these feelings toward the child with resultant rejection, abandonment, or inconsistent contact with the child who is "blamed" for all difficulties; (3) ambivalence and competitiveness toward foster parents resulting in disruption and undermining of the placement; (4) erratic visitation or loss of contact with the child.

Long before placement, a sense of failure, inadequacy, and frustration has often handicapped parental functioning. At the time of placement, a number of factors tend to reinforce these feelings. Among these are the concrete realities of a (temporary) loss of custody, lessened participation in both major and mundane decisions about the child, and the presence of other parent figures with a stable home situation who appear more organized and adequate.

Following release from direct responsibility for the child or daily confrontations with him, the natural parents may appear more supportive and accepting toward him. To repress and deny guilt, anxiety, shame, feelings of inadequacy, and negative feelings toward the child, seductive promises or placating agreements are often made. Subsequently, feelings of failure in the parent are heightened and the child's disappointment and rage are aggravated when these agreements cannot be kept.

Even under ideal circumstances competitiveness between the natural and foster parent is likely to be present. The parent, apologetic, defensive, and often needing approval, feels criticized and depreciated; this is particularly true when the child is adjusting well and being nurtured both physically and emotionally by the foster parent. Conflicts arise between natural and foster parents about dress, habits, and many other daily experiences; these tensions are frequently highlighted by the child in order to manipulate both sets of parents. By vying for the child's favor, or criticizing and undercutting the foster parents to the agency, the natural parents may destroy a previously successful placement.

Visitation of parents with the child in placement reduces anxiety about loss-separation, facilitates a more realistic view of the parents by the child, mobilizes repressed feelings for working through, and maintains the child-parent relationship for a possible later return home. However, the natural parent often experiences profound conflict about visiting, even inventing excuses or rationalizations to make his absence more palatable to himself. Frequently, before, during, and after the visit, the child is upset. Expectations of depreciation or criticism from foster parents and a reexperiencing of the pain of separation from the child magnify the anxiety about visiting.

feelings prompt subtle or overt rejection, withdrawal of "gifts" and attention, and sudden stringent demands for conformity and performance. The new community becomes wary, suspicious, and barely tolerates the foster child. Expectations of his acting-out sexual or aggressive impulses lead to treatment of the child as a potential contaminant, liable to infect other children. When deviant behavior occurs, it may not be viewed tolerantly as a maladaptive developmental or situational response. The child's difficulties may be rationalized as a basic defect caused by bad heredity, illegitimacy, or poor environment. These reactions may cause termination of placement, expulsion from school, or labeling of the child as delinquent or mentally ill. Other attitudes, derived from "childism,"[15] an unconscious egoistic presumption of adult superiority over children, may be more intense and open toward foster than toward natural children. Ergo, the adult's pompous expectations of gratitude, submissiveness, and compliance from the child, aptly caricatured in several of Dickens's novels, may quickly initiate a relationship with the child which further increases his defensiveness and loss of self-esteem. In response the child may passively comply, further withdraw, or rebel. The solution is often consistent, active casework which empathically supports the adults interacting with foster children (foster parents, teachers, community workers, etc.). The worker will recognize the interference of these feelings and attitudes, interpret the child's reactions, and counsel the adults toward more constructive responses or solutions.

Cultural Reactions to Foster Children

Attitudes within the culture toward children in foster placement are derived from several sources. Initially, unconscious critical, pharisaic judgments toward parents of foster children and sympathetic overidentification with the child's plight evoke pity, sympathy, and rescue fantasies within adults. At first, the child may be placed in a special position characterized by overindulgence and lenient accepting permissiveness toward disturbing behavior. Subsequently, when undesirable behavior persists or when the child is unable to form close attachments, all this begins to change. Feelings of failure, frustration and a sense of being used come to the fore in foster parents, teachers, caseworkers, and other adults involved with the child. These

Symptom Formation at Different Developmental Levels of Children in Placement

Two aspects of symptom formation should be kept in mind. Initially, at the time of placement, many children show transient distress, marked by sleep disturbance, excessive eating, behavioral regression, and withdrawal. Preplacement evaluation and preparation, if successful, help in making these symptoms of brief duration. As the child remains in placement, persistence of difficulties or onset of new symptoms may signal passage into a new developmental phase, poor match between child and foster setting, heightened conflict with parents, or a current situational problem. Assessment of the child's level of maturity and knowledge of his past development are essential if one is to distinguish between residuals of early life experiences on the one hand, and response to a current situational difficulty (the symptoms indicating an unresolved reaction to placement) on the other.

Very young children under four to six months show little response to separation and placement if receiving adequate sensory stimulation. Older infants and toddlers may react to the change of environment and different mothering with irritability, crying, sleep and feeding difficulties, rocking or head banging, and delays in development. Preschool children may regress in sphincter control and speech patterning, and show apprehension both toward peers and adults; they occasionally become phobic. Whining, overemphasis on bodily complaints, and other attention-seeking behaviors may alternate with random aggressive and destructive actions or withdrawal. Play activities become constricted, unimaginative, and repetitive. They often portray danger and disaster in a compulsive, frantic fashion, monotonously reenacted without solution. Occasionally extreme regression occurs with a child showing psychotic symptoms.

School-age children manifest both learning and behavioral difficulties, and may show transient regression in sphincter control. They may steal, fight, and exhibit persistent inappropriate sexual activity. Destructive or sadistic behavior becomes more patterned, often being directed toward helpless animate targets (pets or smaller children). Often, dependent, clinging, "sticky" behavior in the child or emotional detachment and isolation from foster parents causes much greater interference with placement than many of the antisocial behaviors. At adolescence increased biologic drives, with the physical apparatus for acting upon them, and the conflicts around dependence/independence come to the fore. These produce behaviors which are often quite threatening to adults without outward manifestations of discomfort to the child. Accentuation of mood swings, intensification of the need for immediate gratification, and fluctuation between regressed-dependent behavior and overly independent actions are played out between the adolescent and caretaking adults. Shoplifting, major thefts, frequent fighting, and overt destructiveness of property appear as statements of anger or efforts to assert physical prowess. Sexual preoccupation may be turned inward with frequent masturbation or turned outward in the form of promiscuity in a search for closeness, contact, and comfort with others. Runaways are most common at this age, both as an angry response to adult demands and frustration of immediate gratification, or as a reaction to the threat of potential intimacy and excessive dependence upon adults. Rejection of adult demands or assistance may become absolute; paralysis in current functioning and future planning may occur.

Coping Behavior of Children in Placement

Internal rage and behavioral regression dominate many children's initial reactions to placement. The severity and duration of the specific symptomatic behavioral responses reflect the ego strengths and defense capabilities of the child. Interference with biologic processes, broad developmental arrest, or unmanageable impulsive behavior indicate a lack of stable object attachments and deficits in the development of stable defense patterns in early childhood.

As developments in object constancy and cognitive thinking proceed, greater sensitivity to separation and more clearly discernible defense patterns occur. Primitive or basic ego defenses (denial, projection, displacement, rationalization, and repression) dominate responses of the chronologically and emotionally immature child. At this age, the overwhelmingly painful affective components of loss must be avoided or quickly repressed. Weak ego defenses and limited capacity for internalization of conflict lead most frequently to action models of tension reduction. Helplessness and rage derived from the sense of abandonment are quickly repressed, denied, and displaced either to the self or projectively to the persons outside the family. The child controls the situation by "blaming" himself or others, and preserves an image or fantasy of the idealized parent by releasing the anger toward himself or other adults. Within this self-blame, explanations for "badness" are associated with current developmental problems, resulting in shame for failing to perform adequately or guilt for harboring unacceptable impulses of a rivalrous, aggressive, or sexual nature. Internalized anger may be projected with resultant fear of punishment or unconsciously acted-out self-punishment through injury and accidents. Emotional and physical withdrawal in the form of running away defensively expresses the child's anger and rejection of the placement. In effect, it makes a behavioral statement about fantasied self-sufficiency, and questions the commitment and sincerity of the adults. Many latency-age and preadolescent children running away from placement return quickly to their neighborhood or community, but often delay returning home for several days. Older adolescents make a more definitive statement in withdrawing further and being less liable to seek out help.

Mastery of increasingly complex aspects of the environment through activity are part of the self-esteem- and confidence-building activities of childhood. They are both reflections and avenues of discharge for drives toward autonomy and self-dependence. Play activities and manipulation of household objects are concrete reassurances of potency and serve as a launching point for attempting new challenges. As noted, transient anxiety and regression occur in children even with brief separations. Consider the already frightened and insecure child with little control over his life situation. Play becomes constricted, unimaginative, and monotonously repetitious as the child holds in threatening feelings and wards off stressful environmental stimulation. Paradoxically, at times the child may engage in a frenzy of unsatisfying activity or demandingly attempt to control and manipulate all of the adults around him in an effort to reassure himself of having some influence on his life. The latency-age child's constriction in play and activity may present in older children as boredom, apathy and indifference; it is sometimes mistakenly viewed as "coolness" in adolescents.

Many fantasies of children in placement are identical to those of other children, reflecting the usual responses to expected developmental events. Most children in placement have fantasies of the idealized parent who is loving, nurturant, powerful, and able to rescue the child and reunite the family. This fantasy is maintained in the face of obvious confrontations with reality. Despite disappointments and rejection, this theme is often stubbornly resistant to discussion and working through by professional helpers. When the child has successfully faced the loss, worked through the helplessness and anger of his situation, and had an opportunity to accept the parents more objectively, this fantasy disappears or is displaced in a much less intense fashion toward other adults.

A second prevalent kind of fantasy of children in placement is one of exceptional strength, ability, or capacity for independence. Such children view themselves as capable not only of self-care, but of taking care of their parents. In the fantasy, they see themselves as leaders, exceptionally cunning or shrewd, and completely capable of independent living. A third less frequently seen kind of fantasy is one in which the child views himself as special and highly desired by others because of exceptional physical attractiveness or unique musical or acting ability. These fantasies provide only limited relief from the underlying depreciated, rejected, helpless self-concept.

Social Structures Needed for Optimum Use of Foster Care

In order to evaluate, support, and maintain the child, parents, and foster parents in a successful way, casework, psychiatric, psychological, legal, medical, and other professional services are needed. Empathic and objective understanding of the limitations and strengths of each component of the foster care system is basic; this facilitates quicker establishment and achievement of goals for both child and parents. Reuniting the family and returning the child to a more organized and effectively functioning family are still considered primary goals. Traditionally, foster care has been deemed the optimum placement of the child away from home; however, comprehensive preplacement evaluation may lead to a different kind of disposition (institution, group home, or residential treatment), one better suited to the child's needs and more emotionally manageable by both child and parents.

Unfortunately, agencies which sponsor and support foster care are frequently approached with crisislike urgency for immediate placement of the child. With rare exceptions, the crisis is a moment of transient situational strain within a context of chronic difficulty. However poorly, the child and family have usually adapted in this way for years.[20] The only situations demanding precipitous placement are those involving immediate physical danger or severe emotional trauma. The foster agency careworker serves a vital role in responding appropriately to the anxiety of the referral source, in helping natural parents make and effect a decision for placement, in preparing the child for the transition, and in working with foster families toward understanding and accepting the child and his parents. Two publications, *Standards for Foster Family Service Systems*[23] and *Child Welfare League of America Standards for Foster Family Care Service*[2] succinctly describe the rationale, organization, management, and evaluation of foster family care services. They cover the use of community resources and the provision of services to the child, parent, and foster parent, and they outline the scope of services from intake to the termination of placement. As space does not permit description of these materials, the reader is urged to review both in order to comprehend more fully the basic components of an adequate foster care system.

In most publications, the essential role of the social worker is taken for granted. This is true not only in direct service and work with the child but also as an organizer, facilitator, and participant in a triadic alliance of caseworker/natural parent/foster parent. Each component of this triadic alliance has a measureable effect on the success of foster home placement. Within the first year of a child's placement, the stability, experience, caseload size (low), and frequency of worker contact with the child's family increases the chance of the child's return home.[18] Preliminary services to the family may include medical, vocational, and financial help. However, in addition to frequency and intensity of casework contact with parents, the frequency and consistency of parental visitation with the child can be correlated with the probability of the child's return home. Careful selection, sensitive preparation, and frequent support of foster parents[1] increase both the likelihood of their remaining foster parents and the continuance of placement, especially with the more difficult children.

Research into several areas of foster care systems has sought to improve the selection of foster parents,[4, 1] to achieve a better "fit" between foster parents and child,[4] and to review the effect of long-term placement upon children and on the likelihood of their returning home. Little current research is available concerning the placement of that group of children who show minimal symptoms, satisfactory adjustment, and little long-term distortion of development. How these children and their families adapt and what kinds of professional assistance have been useful are tantalizing questions. Another area of research, with pragmatic implications, would be the discovery of that data which would help make earlier definitive decisions for long-term stabilization of the child's situation. More predictable and well-defined criteria are needed: (1) to assess the degree and reversibility of damage to the child; (2) to evaluate the strengths, potential for change, and rate of change in the natural parents; (3) to help both the child and natural parent in making a decision for adoption when indicated; (4) to effect residential or other treatment when indicated earlier in the child's placement; (5) to achieve maximum long-term stabilization of the child in his environment. All efforts which minimize multiple placements, especially with younger children, will serve to lessen emotional damage and enhance the child's responsiveness to future treatment and placement.

Creative innovative thinking is needed to find, apply, and evaluate new models for foster care. Foster family homes have been used for several years for the treatment of emotionally disturbed and retarded children. It is clear, however, that programs are needed in which natural and foster parents share child-care responsibilities to a much greater degree. One such endeavor is a five-day care program.[3] A different application of homemaker services could be developed in which the workers could serve as in-the-home-therapists for child and parents. Parents and children would be "fostered" in their own home while role models for parenting and homemaking would concurrently be provided. Maintaining family intactness, providing immediate therapeutic intervention, and observing the child's interaction with the family are all potential benefits that would also help with long-term planning.

Federal and state funding supplementing local public and voluntary programs does provide more effective programs of foster care. However, poorly coordinated services for children, insufficient professional time, inexperienced workers, and an orientation to immediate crises rather than to the prevention of breakdown or rehabilitation of families[12] perpetuate the phenomenon of multiple chronic placements. The humanitarian and developmental importance of alleviating the child's suffering is paramount. However, publicizing the long-term benefits solely on a cost basis may involve the community more quickly. Compared to the cost of rearing a child with natural or adoptive parents, foster care is three times, boarding care is four times, institutional care is five and one-half times, and residential treatment is approximately seven to eight times more expensive.[7] A larger accounting of the costs of mental illness, criminality, and chronic public dependence provides an additional but hidden cost factor. Early intervention with the child and more active early help directed specifically toward mothers are central to any foster care program.

Careful, early, regular case review of all children in foster placement is an essential mechanism to prevent the child's drifting into chronic placement. Approaches to review include:[3] (1) administrative review within the agency; (2) independent review boards sponsored by and reporting to several agencies; (3) mandatory court review at regular intervals. To be effective, any review must provide clearcut recommendations within the context of long-term planning and functioning legal mechanisms to implement recommendations. Despite the large number of children placed by court decision (50 percent or better)[3, 24] attempts to free the child for adoption are made in only about 10 percent of the cases.[3, 9] Some 30 to 40 percent[3, 24] of children remain in foster care five years or more with little possibility of returning home. Without defined, effective legal means to protect the child's best interest, adequate numbers of experienced workers, and further changes in policies for adoptive placement, support, and follow-up, large numbers of children will continue experiencing the subtle decay of multiple placements across vital developmental periods.

REFERENCES

1. ALDRIDGE, M. J., and CAUTLEY, P. W., "The Importance of Worker Availability in the Functioning of New Foster Homes," *Child Welfare, 54(6):*444–453, 1975.

2. *Child Welfare League of America Standards for Foster Family Care Service*, Child Welfare League of America Inc., New York, 1959.

3. CLABURN, W. E., "Approaches to Case Review of Children in Foster Care," Unpublished manuscript, 1975. (Mr. Claburn is with the Bureau of Research Planning and Program Development State of New Jersey Department of Institutions and Agencies, Division of Youth and Family Services.)

4. COLVIN, R. W., *Toward the Development of a Foster Parent Attitude Test; Quantitative Approaches to Parent Selection*," Child Welfare League of America Inc., New York, 1962.

5. ———, "Defective Ego and Social Development as Functions of Prolonged Institutionalization of Children," *American Psychologist, 13:*327, 1958.

6. ERIKSON, E. H., *Identity and the Life Cycle*, Psychological Issues, vol. 1, University Press Inc., New York, 1959.

7. FANSHEL, D., and SHINN, E., *Dollars and Cents in the Foster Care of Children: A Look at Cost Factors*, Child Welfare League of America Inc., New York, 1972.

8. FESTINGER, T. B., "The New York Court Review of Children in Foster Care," *Child Welfare, 54(4):*211–245, 1975.

9. Foster Care Survey, Iowa Department of Social Services, Bureau of Family and Adult Services, Report 1005, 1973.

10. GRINKER, R. R., SR., GRINKER, R. R., JR., and TIMBERLAKE, J., "'Mentally Healthy' Young Males (Homoclites)," *Archives of General Psychiatry, 6:*405–453, 1962.

11. KING, S. H., "Coping Mechanisms in Adolescents," *Psychiatric Annals, 3:*36–37, 1971.

12. KOLB, T. N., GRACE, P. J., and FARREL, K., *Study of the Placement Needs and Facilities in Hamilton County* (Ohio), unpublished report, 1974.

13. LOEWE, B., and HANRAHAN, T. E., "Five Day Foster Care," *Child Welfare, 54(1):*7–18, 1975.

14. OFFER, D., *The Psychological World of the Teenager*, Basic Books, New York, 1969.

15. PIERCE, C. M., and ALLEN, G. B., "Childism," *Psychiatric Annals, 5(7):*266–270, 1975.

16. ROBERTSON, J., and ROBERTSON, J., "Young Children in Brief Separation—A Fresh Look," in Eissler, R. S., et al. (Eds.), *The Psychoanalytic Study of the Child*, vol. 26, pp. 310–311, Quadrangle Books, New York, 1971.

17. RUTTER, M., "Maternal Deprivation Considered," *Journal Psychosomatic Research, 16:*241–250, 1972.

18. SHAPIRO, D., "Agency Investment in Foster Care: A Followup," *Social Work, 18(6):*3–9, 1973.

19. SILBER, E., et al., "Adaptive Behavior in Competent Adolescents," *Archives of General Psychiatry, 5:*359–365, 1961.

20. SMITH, W. R., and MORRISON, G. C., "Family Tolerance for Chronic, Severe, Neurotic and Deviant Behavior in Children Referred for Child Psychiatry Emergency Consultation," in Morrison, G. C., *Emergencies in Child Psychiatry*, pp. 115–128, Charles C Thomas, Springfield, Ill., 1975.

21. SPITZ, R. A., "Hospitalism: An Inquiry into the Genesis of Psychiatric Conditions in Early Childhood," in Eissler, R. S., et al. (Eds.), *The Psychoanalytic Study of the Child*, vol. 1, pp. 53–74, International Universities Press, New York, 1945.

22. SPITZ, R. A., and WOLF, K., "Anaclitic Depression: An Inquiry into the Genesis of Psychiatric Conditions in Early Childhood," in Eissler, R. S., et al. (Eds.), *The Psychoanalytic Study of the Child*, vol. 11, pp. 313–342, International Universities Press, New York, 1946.

23. *Standards for Foster Family Systems with Guidelines for Implementation Specifically Related to Public Agencies*, American Public Welfare Association, Washington, D.C., 1975.

24. *State Social Welfare Board Report on Foster Care; Children Waiting*, State of California Health and Welfare Agency, Department of Social Welfare, Sacramento, California, 1972.

25. U.S. Department of Health Education and Welfare, DHEW Publication No. (SRS) 75–03258, NCSS Report E–9, 1975.

38 / The Fatherless Child

C. Janet Newman and Jeffrey S. Schwam

The fatherless child has lost his father through death, separation of the parents (either prior to the birth or later), or severe psychological distancing from the family.

Statistics and Distribution

In 1975, according to the U.S. Bureau of the Census,[67] there were 30,057,000 families in the United States with one or more children of their own under the age of eighteen. This represents 62,733,000 children under eighteen.

Of these 30,057,000 families, 4,405,000 families, or 15 percent, had a female head. Of the 62,733,000 children, 9,227,000, or 15 percent, lived in a family with a female head.

Of the 4,405,000 families with a female head, 2,972,000 families, or 67 percent, are white, and 1,382,000 families, or 31 percent, are black. This represents 5,774,000 white children and 3,354,000 black children.

Of these 4,405,000 families with a female head, there are various reasons given for the male's absence. The female head is single in 12 percent of the families, separated in 27 percent, widowed in 18 percent, divorced in 38 percent, and the spouse is absent for other reasons such as employment or institutionalization in 5 percent of the families.

The percentage of children in fatherless homes has increased since the 10 percent figure widely used in 1970.[7, 27] There has also been a rapidly growing realization of the psychological importance of the father in the child's earliest years* as well as in the significance of his family role in the wider social structure.[38, 47, 65]

During the child's first years, mother's presence is primary. This is demonstrated by the fact that if she is absent, the child's survival requires immediate human substitution. The father's absence is rarely made up for in this way, or with urgent haste. At the same time, major institutions and governments debate the costs of welfare and of

* See references 1, 7, 32, 40, 53, 63, and 69.

other assistance for the fatherless family.[11] Father is apparently expendable, even though his loss is emotionally and socially incalculable. It is difficult to discern the subtle meanings and hidden dimensions of fatherlessness in an infant, child, or adolescent. It is from these current new perspectives of the great importance of the father to the child that the following material will begin to consider some of the effects of his loss. The emphasis will fall on the father's complementarity as an object relating to a child's specific personality needs and ego development.

Impact of Father Absence at Different Levels of Development

LOSS IN THE FIRST YEAR

During the first year of life, the child's main developmental task is to form a need-gratifying symbiotic tie with a nurturing figure. This will form the basis for later confidence and trust.[6, 43] Generally, this nurturing figure is the child's mother. The mother can fulfill her role in this intense mother-infant mutuality only if she is given adequate support. She may receive the necessary emotional supplies from her husband, close relatives, or a friend. Should her major adult ties be suddenly disrupted, as in death or through separation from her husband, she will commonly go into mourning and largely withdraw from the child. If her depression is milder, however, she may tend to convert the child into a source of support. The child invariably picks up the slightest cues of tension or distress in his mother. In such cases, the message he receives is that mother has become unattentive to his needs.

The immediate effect on the infant will be shaped by his stage of ego development. Unless a substitute mother can quickly be found, the child may react to his loss of mothering through a special sequencing of affects such as protest, despair, and detachment.[10] In severe cases, apathy or anaclitic depression may result.[61] Impairment of the development of self and object differentiation, reality testing, frustration tolerance, and capacity for trust and confidence usually occur. Developmental retardation, psychosis, and psychophysiological disorders are common results of "psychotoxic" relationships in infancy.[60]

LOSS DURING AGES ONE THROUGH THREE

If the child has received adequate mothering in the first year, he will be moving through the stages of separation-individuation, and the formation of early sexual identity in the second and third years.[43] The interaction of father and child now becomes increasingly direct, especially during the "practicing" subphase.[1] The father's presence facilitates successful separation-individuation. ". . . the father's image comes toward the child . . . from outer space as it were . . . as something gloriously new and exciting, at just the time when the toddler is experiencing a feverish quest for expansion."[41] The father represents the real external world, and, in turn, introduces the child to this world. He helps both child and mother to a successful mastery of the tasks of this phase, for the mother herself often needs help at this stage.

For both boys and girls, mastery of physical skills, childhood games, rough and tumble activity, toleration of anxiety in slightly risky adventures, and the development of assertiveness are all assisted by the presence of a competent father. A mother, especially one without a husband, may tend to be more gentle, protective, and anxious. Shared discussions and responsibility as to what is safe or dangerous are less available to the single mother; for the child this may lead to a measure of apprehension and some inhibition of his activities.

The father's presence reinforces effective limit setting and the development of superego precursors. According to Marsella, et al., who studied maternal attitudes when fathers were present or absent on sea duty, mothers tend to be more lenient when father is absent.[44] The "away" father can exercise the authority that a "constantly at home" mother shirks, partly because she cannot bear the daily onslaught of an angry child. The single mother's rage against the demanding child may reach a point where she fearfully withdraws from disciplining, and the father's return is a relief both to mother and child. When two parents can share and back each other up, value judgments can be made with conviction. To the extent that the single mother turns to the child for com-

panionship and fears the loss of her child's affection, she may find discipline correspondingly more difficult.

In order to achieve success in mastering the developmental crisis of "autonomy versus shame," ideally the mother-father unity shares in the shame that arises from parental or children's difficulties. The two parents can help each other, and either or both can help the child over the failures of any one of the threesome. Self-esteem can be restored.

The opposing viewpoints and the varying emotional tones of mother and father can be both exhilarating and growth promoting.[25] The father's presence aids the child's earliest challenges to the mother. The child's eggs are not, as it were, all in one basket. Experiencing the two parents' differences can aid reality testing. A moderate parental argument over what is "reality" strengthens the child's relativistic yet consensual sense of reality. Delay of gratification and tolerance of frustration are helped when a second parent may in some way redress the grievances against the first, or empathically correct a misperception by his spouse. Language development is stimulated in those children who can overhear, and strain eagerly to comprehend, the intriguing big-world conversation of two adults. Single parents often talk down to the perceived level of their children's understanding, which usually underestimates and hinders the child's full cognitive development. Another problem is the single mother's tendency to use a child as a confidant and expose him to more complex emotional material than that child is ready for.

Next to be considered is the preoedipal sexual role development.

Some research studies of father-absent boys suggest that these children show a tendency to decreased aggressivity[8, 7, 40] and diminished male aggressivity in doll play.[4] The investigators conclude that the diminished aggressivity represents diminished masculinity. Current thinking views aggressivity and passivity as important to both sexes. It is difficult to know whether diminished aggressivity relates to sexual role. It could represent accumulated deficits which arise from the effects of father absence. This affects the development of confidence, trust, and the tasks of separation-individuation.

At present, the important role of the father in assisting sexual role development in both boys and girls is becoming more clearly defined. It is felt that sexual role development is a result of warm and encouraging paternal and maternal attitudes toward the sex of the child, and toward its earliest manifestations. Stoller has stressed the impact of maternal attitudes which foster primary identification as etiologic in initiating transexualism and the "malignant feminization of boys."[62] These conditions are more frequently engendered by an existing father's lack of involvement in fathering than by his total absence. In these cases, the father fails to serve as a wedge to promote separation-individuation of a pathological mother and her son. For the girl, paternal attitudes also assist separation-individuation from the mother, and provide love and approval of the girl's pleasure in being feminine.[1]

FATHER LOSS DURING THE OEDIPAL PHASE

The oedipal phase introduces children to new emotional and cognitive challenges, far beyond those of relating to each parent separately. They now begin to observe and relate to their parents' intense and sometimes secret mutuality, responding to each parent's sexual personality in the threatening and exhilarating light of the newly discovered exclusive marital or intimate relationship. The varied but fundamental character of this primal tie witnessed by each child stimulates in him new developments of perception, reality testing, fantasy life, sexual conceptualizations, and finally a great acceleration of sexual fantasies, appetites, competitions, fears, and humiliations. Resolution of the oedipal triangle requires mastery of the rivalry with the parent of the same sex. The child does this by renouncing his libidinal attachment to the opposite sex parent and by identifying with the parent of the same sex. This identification leads to a more mature and realistic superego and ego ideal. In general, the oedipal child's complicated feelings about his "parents together" (and his strong subsequent evocations or relivings of this period) powerfully affect the unfolding of his future affectionate, intimate, sexual, and marital relationships.

The child who experiences father loss in the oedipal period at the height of his new preoccupation with the marital or sexual relationship in its own right will first of all have lost the opportunity to slowly develop his understanding of the vital relationships between his biological parents, and parents generally. His own sex-determined reactions to each parent and his mastery of his intense emotions will be thrown off balance. He will be especially vulnerable in dealing with the reasons for the marriage's disruption. He will be keenly affected by his mother's immediate and long-range responses to her loss and to her ways of helping him with his.

In a classic "turning point" paper on parent loss and "oedipal deficiency," Neubauer reviewed the sparse psychoanalytic literature prior to 1960 on the subject of the one-parent family.[49] Father absence during the oedipal phase may interfere with a successful resolution of this phase. The loss of the father forces the child to create fantasies of a father and/or to seek male substitutes in the environment. This fantasied father tends to be overidealized and "endowed with magical powers either to gratify or to punish."[49]

Leonard[39] is one of the few analytic authors to write on fathers' relationships to daughters; he stresses that a nonparticipating father will later lead the girl to search for overidealized love objects or to regress to preoedipal narcissistic attitudes. For the girl, libidinal ties may remain bound to the fantasied absent father. Her realistic relationships with boys and young men may be interfered with as she seeks to satisfy her oedipal longings via various father substitutes.[49] The remaining parent, the mother, may be endowed by children of both sexes with hostile powers of destruction. The girl's oedipal aggression against her mother is often blocked; she is, after all, the only parent available. As a result, reaction formation may be resorted to: Instead of challenging mother, the daughter becomes excessively attached and compliant.[29]

For the boy, his libidinal ties may take a variable course; his tendency to cling to the image of the absent father leads him to hypercathect it, to idealize it, to endow it with fearful powers.[49] The boy may pull away from potential oedipal rivalry, adopting a dependent relationship to his mother and a lack of competitiveness and aggressiveness in relations with other males. Or he may pull away from the oedipal rivalry via an excessive renunciation of his libidinal ties to his mother. Thus, in order to find libidinal gratification, he may turn away from women to men. He may attempt to remain the oedipal victor, and to deal with his fears of retaliation by displaying excessive pseudo-aggression and competitiveness. Father absence may lead the mother to turn to her son as a husband substitute; this increases his tendency to seek out the distorted oedipal alternatives previously described. In contrast to this, the mother may be overly cautious in distancing herself from her son, thus reinforcing some boys' oedipal feelings of being shamefully incapable of satisfying mother due to problems of smallness. This may leave the boy with feelings of inadequacy and a sense of narcissistic injury.

For the boy, there is a distortion of the internalization of, as well as identification with, his father as he attempts to resolve the oedipal situation. This is due to what Neubauer calls the "absence of oedipal reality,"[49] the fantasied magnification of the father's powers, uncorrected by reality. The superego becomes either defective through lack of realistic identifications (which allows incestuous acting out); or punitive, leading to symptoms of behavioral and intellectual inhibition. Similarly, idealization of the absent father may lead to unrealistic ego ideal expectations.

FATHER LOSS IN THE LATENCY PHASE

During latency, the child gradually moves away from the close oedipal family circle. He develops outside interests and relationships with peers and adults other than his parents. Ego mechanisms of denial, repression, reaction-formation, and symbolization are strengthened. During this phase the child develops a more realistic appraisal of the world. He acquires the ability of "ethical individuation"[57] and learns to make his own judgments in regard to conflicting viewpoints. Gradually the normally idealized oedipal and preoedipal father images become reconciled with a more realistically viewed latency father. This leads to resolution of earlier splittings, more realistically based superego and ego ideal internalizations, and a more mature relationship with the father and other adults.[57]

The relationship to the external world thus becomes more appropriate. This process is facilitated by the concurrent and more sophisticated ability to symbolize via fantasy which occurs in latency. These latency fantasies provide a safety valve for modified and evolving oedipal fantasies; they assist the child in entering the culture's value system by participating in shared myths and stories and they serve compensatory functions by helping preserve self-esteem. The fantasies assume many varieties, among them: dreams of magnificent achievement, grandiose, compensatory sexual images, and creative ideas.

Father absences prior to latency may prevent resolution of the oedipal phase. During latency, the child's fantasy life may remain too highly charged with primary process material. In such instances, latency symbolization cannot function effectively as a discharge mechanism, and ego development and adaptation to reality are interfered with. There may be a major "absence of grief."[14] Father absence may deprive the child of the opportunity for realistic deidealization of his father; this may lead to ego splitting with superego and ego ideal deficits. The acquisition of new skills may be interfered with without a father to continue what he began during the practicing subphase of toddlerhood, and to reinforce mastery and a sense of industry.

During latency, father loss is not as overtly traumatic as it was during earlier periods. Denial and splitting occur frequently, as in the case of a ten-year-old boy who said: "I know father is dead, but what I can't understand is why he doesn't come home for supper."[20] The child may regress from reality orientation to a hypercathexis of parental introjects; he will then have difficulty in moving to the peer group.[57] Affective disturbance may be absent, only to occur later in adolescence. Sometimes humor and euphoria are used as defenses against the loss, but closer examination will reveal more ominous signs of intellectual and emotional difficulties.

FATHER LOSS IN ADOLESCENCE

Adolescence has been called "The Second Individuation Phase."[9] The adolescent's task is to solidify identity formation as well as to decathect parents and develop relationships with peers and adults outside the home. Adolescence has been compared to a process of mourning; the adolescent usually works through the major farewell to his parents and his home life with them.[70] This phase-specific, natural, mourninglike process is what makes for the final spurt of growth and maturation preparatory to entering adulthood. According to Wolfenstein[70] it is the prerequisite for mourning of the adult type.

The father's presence is an important facilitator of this new separation process. He helps the child have successful outside experiences through advice and support. He offers a realistic view of life and work outside of the home. As in the first separation-individuation phase, he serves as a wedge, intervening between some of the child's and mother's tendencies to hold on. His presence offers mother support for her emotional and financial needs. In the father-absent family, the mother may turn to the children for support. They may feel guilty about their phase-specific separation. When they want to go out in the evening or take their own vacation, they will often think of her needs. It is difficult for the single mother to offer the firm backdrop against which the adolescent can develop the strength for his emancipation, and for the formulation of his own identity.

The task of mourning the earlier loss of the father can be reactivated and worked through, especially after adolescence.[70] If denial has been too powerful, the ego will often be arrested,[2, 14, 16] and special psychoanalytic or therapeutic help will be necessary to activate mourning and growth.[17]

When the father dies during this period, the adolescent is deprived of his father's support as well as of his own initiatives toward independence. The separation is imposed from the outside, beyond the adolescent's psychic work and control. He may react with anger and feelings of being thwarted. Unready to separate so rapidly, he may plunge into a regression with greater dependency on the mothering, or he may seek a pseudo-adult stance in order to deny these dependent needs. This may look like maturity, but is frequently a revival of symbiotic and oedipal ties. The mother may have prevented the preschool or latency-age child from carrying out similar impulses, but she may more easily allow this to happen in the adolescent. The size and periodic maturity of the adolescent deceive her, especially since she struggles with grief which may also be denied for a prolonged period. Often one child becomes the chief supporter for mother, or the several children compete to be the mother's husband, so to speak. The girl may develop into mother's confidante, and the boy may keep a certain distance; he is at once anxious about the oedipal implications, yet enjoys the role of helping mother. Both children will often conceal their own needs for support. During the acute mourning period, such relationships between willing widows and their children are rationalized by the immediate stress of the loss. If they are not transient, however, they can lead to psychological fixation of the type described previously[2] above with prolonged clinging to the home. The lack of opportunity for the adolescent to decathect his father gradually, which is an important element of adult mourning, will be replaced by problems in subsequent mourning, fears of unexpected losses, fixations to early relationships to the mother, and a developmental slowing-up or standstill.[2, 4, 16]

FAMILIAL AND CULTURAL REACTIONS

As mentioned earlier, father loss can occur from different causes: death, divorce, absence in the case of the unmarried woman, or lack of the father's involvement in the family due to other interests or societal deprivation. Each of these causes tends to elicit a different response in the extended family and community.

Initially, widowhood and orphanhood elicit compassion. The extended family and friends gather around tearfully and protectively, sometimes participating in the family's needs in the period prior to death. At the funeral and ritual events accompanying death, they are usually present in full supportive force. Later, help and understanding are extended to the fatherless family. According to Deuteronomy, the living brother takes over his dead brother's family in the so-called levirate (fraternal) marriage, and marries his brother's widow, so as to maintain the children in the same Jewish family.[13] In today's society, such protectiveness takes more remote forms. It may be extended through care given by the extended family or by distant social institutions. Gentle concessions are intuitively made to the developmental needs of the children. Tearful children will be comforted, and those children who seem absorbed in enjoying a table game among the company of sad adults will for the moment be left to their own self-protective defenses.

With divorce, the response from family and friends tends to be less supportive. Preliminary marital battles may have led to increased social isolation of the family and divisions among relatives and friends. Rather than receiving support, the children may become involved in severe conflicts and custody battles. Parental feelings will also be sorrowfully affected as the children serve as forces binding the earlier "life-long commitment" of the parents. After the divorce is final, parents often depreciate each other in various ways. Father frequently becomes like grandparent, seen on weekends, overly indulgent and setting few limits. Oedipal children's attitudes will be affected by developmental considerations. Boys suffer from guilt, girls develop shame from not having had the endearing qualities to hold the family together. Hetherington[29] noted the seductive attitudes daughters of divorced mothers tend to show toward men, in contrast to the shy and distant behavior of the daughters of widows.

Never-married mothers include husbandless women whose primary relationships often remain with their own family. These multigenerational families may be called "extended" as a kind of euphemism. Frequently, however, the support systems are not adequate. Severe conflicts are frequent, with bitterness and shame about the "fatherless" child. Who shall be the major caretaking figure, mother, grandmother, or someone else? This can become a subject of prolonged debate, with anger directed both at the child and the absent father. Rarely, however, is the child placed for adoption. A strong drive to keep and to nurture the child whenever possible overcomes the ambivalence around his conception. An equally strong maternal wish is for someone to care for and to love mother, or for a baby to cuddle as a sort of "transitional object."[68] These intense emotions later form the substrate for the child's internalizations of his fantasized father. He fantasizes an omnipotent protective figure. Among poverty groups, some families appear to be "extended." Many generations live under one roof. But the depletion of each member, and the unemployment of many of the males, is not compatible with the conventional view of the so-called extended family. Usually it is regarded as a solid backlog of support from which a number of uncles, aunts, and grandparents can step forward to support the fatherless child. Too often, each individual in such a household leads an impoverished, isolated life. Children are passed from one apartment or room to another; they form a variety of inconsistent, close but angry, intimate but frustrating relationships with any of these members. The male in this household, already suffering from major social discriminations and unemployment, will usually be unable to contribute fatherhood activities to his own family, or to anyone else's. Differentiation between black and social class issues are vital.[65]

All of the varieties of single-parenting mothers previously described set their social life and friendships adrift. Since the husband's employment usually determines the social class level, the family headed by a woman may be one which has lost this compass setting in the social scene. She can and may recreate her own. If she does not, or cannot, she and her children will frequently move into a state of isolation and social neglect. This change in social class adds still another burden to the children's lives.

Still another factor that ensues from father loss or absence for children is experiencing and witnessing mother's new relationships with men. Sometimes this involves courtships and remarriage. The primal scene fantasies of children are stimulated by the often open courting behavior. While some children are negative about the new man, others beg him directly to be their new father. Hopes and fantasies are intensely stimulated by these new relationships. Sometimes men use seductive friendliness to the children as the pathway to achieving their mother's acceptance. Oftentimes, if the men leave, the children's hopes are dashed once more, they feel betrayed, and they trust less and less.

A great many single mothers must work, and must therefore share the upbringing of their children with other women. These may include housekeepers, relatives, and day-care centers. The child looks to these surrogate mothers for important assistance in his development. To some extent the mother takes the traditional paternal role, and the surrogate mother the mother's role. (Many a "liberated mother" depends on the services of other women for her so-called liberation.)

Children's relationships to each of these mothers, the working "real" and the "at-home" surrogate, may affect their object choices in the future. They may feel greater warmth from the often lower-class mother surrogate.

Another cluster of father-absent families comes about when fathers are lost to their families because of their involvement in other activities. These may include intense career devotion, or earning extra money for the household in a second job. Or the fathers may be in the throes of severe forms of psychopathology such as absenteeism-alcoholism. The social disruptions here vary greatly, either upward or downward, but such families are all suffering from fatherlessness. Extreme pressures on men to succeed at work may exceed their desire to succeed as fathers. Ideally, these are pressures which could be understood by mothers who feel a parallel need of equal intensity to excel as an ideal mother. Presently father often feels trapped in the rat race and mother feels equally trapped in a home with young children. The marital isolation of psychological fatherlessness and embittered motherhood often goes mutually unsupported; only if both parents share their feelings of entrapment with each other can these feelings be alleviated to any extent.

There is a powerful factor which runs through all of these developmental, familial, and cultural observations. This is the mother's loss of male love and/or support, regardless of the specific circumstances which bring this about. She must handle her singleness in relation to her own self-esteem and self-equilibrium; these, in turn, will affect her children's self-concepts in all areas. The health and integrity of single parenthood involves a division of energies, and appropriate sharing of the mother and father roles with other adults and with the children as well. Those who would ascribe expressive and passive modes to the female, and instrumental and active modes to the male, should make a study of single heads of families. Here are adults who are required to make both economic and emotional provision for the whole family. "Roles" have been doubled and supports have been reduced. The so-called conflicts of a marital couple ("who pays the bills," "who takes car shifts," "who initiates sexual love") become the singular intrapsychic conflicts of the single parent. Some of the problems of the isolated nuclear family become magnified in the "sub-nuclear" family. The resilience and strength of the remaining parent are vital for the healthy development of children. The fatherless child has lost two known parents, and must become reacquainted with one as fantasy and memory and with the other as a new reality.

Characteristic Forms
of Emotional Disturbance

First, some remarks are in order about using adult mourning patterns (as described by Freud[18]) as a yardstick for assessing the child's capacity to mourn after a loss. According to Freud, mourning involves a prolonged and painful process of recalling innumerable memories of the lost object. There is a temporary hypercathexis of the lost object, which facilitates eventual "bit by bit" detachment.

Reality testing has shown that the loved one no longer exists, and it proceeds to demand that all libido shall be withdrawn from its attachments to that object. The mood of mourning is a painful one. . . . This demand arouses understandable opposition. . . . This opposition can be so intense that a turning away from reality takes place. . . . Normally, respect for reality gains the day. [pp. 244–245]

As mourning approaches completion, decathexis takes place. There then follows a freeing up of energies for new relationships.

J. B. M. Miller[46] gave an excellent review of the psychoanalytic literature on children's reactions to parent's death. She concludes that:

With regard to the responses of children to the death of an important figure, a position has recently emerged which is supported by almost all major contributors to the study of this question. Exponents of the view hold that the process of mourning, involving as it does the tolerance of powerful painful affects and repeated demands for reality testing in opposition to strong wishes, requires the operation of ego functions to which the child does not yet have firmly established access. Mourning, according to this view, does not occur in children of preadolescent age.

She goes on to state that the response of children to the death of a loved one assumes a regular pattern. In many ways, it is strikingly similar to the pathological forms of mourning seen in adults who have not been able to complete a mourning process. Instead of the ultimate decathexis, as Freud described, children (and fixated adults) retain an excessive attachment to the lost object, in order to "avoid acceptance of the reality and emotional meaning of the death and to maintain in some internal form the relationship that has been ended in external reality."[46]

Thus, maintaining an internal image of the lost parent to whom one is excessively attached can be a pathologically fixated type of behavior. However, it is suggested that the internal fantasy can also represent a form of ego strength, a source of internal growth in the absence of the lost object. This internal representational image of the father can then dictate and stimulate the selection of the external objects appropriate to the child's developmental needs. The overriding consideration in determining whether a given childhood fantasy is healthy is whether it grows developmentally with the child. For example, an early adolescent had lost his father at age seven. He appeared not to miss father until suddenly, at age twelve, he said longingly, "Oh, I really *do* miss him *now*." The image of his father appeared to have grown as the boy had grown. It was as if new years had been added to father's age, and the son speculated as to whether or not his father would have grown a beard. (This was in the 1960s.) His selection of friends did include a father figure. Later on he could admit he had cried in earlier years, but only in bed at night, by himself.

Parents differ from all subsequent object relationships in that they are the unique and irreplaceable partners (the "average expectable objects") in early drive and ego development. In addition, despite the excellent substitutions that occur with many adoptions, stepparents, foster homes, etc., many children express a powerful conscious or unconscious quest to see and know the truth about their biological parents. The extraordinary power of this quest is beginning to be recognized, especially among specialists in adoption. Such children thrive on the truth, the ultimate "reality" of "knowing" about their absent biological parents. While an oedipal child often needs to idealize his lost father, later, in latency, he will enjoy a realistic, new account. This will include the flaws and weaknesses as well as the strengths, which will make the absent father closer to his own capacities and goals. In adolescence, his temporary needs for depreciation will be aided by a more accurate history of his father's life as well as by idealization. For this to happen the surviving parent and others close to the family must bring a developmental perspective to the children and share more detailed experiences and recollections, appropriate to the child's age, growth, and new-found capacities. This is a form of "assistance of mourning."

Another issue involves the forms of denial and ego arrest in disturbed adults which are traced by analysts to early childhood losses. Such reactions are widespread among adults in this culture (as Becker[5] describes in *Denial of Death*) and can also be observed as overt behavior in many children.[2, 14] Children in war zones, urban poverty areas, or in other cultures where death takes place directly in front of their eyes, will have a far greater and earlier familiarity with and understanding of death. This may make them bitter or brutal, and ready to treat life more casually. But under such conditions, many children have conveyed a great deal of sadness and creativity in despair, along with a weariness toward the adult defensiveness, guilt, and "protective" attitudes which avoid recognition of their pain. The concept that children cannot long tolerate pain is simply inaccurate.

One can only agree emphatically with many of the findings of the Furmans[22, 21] and the Klimans,[35] and the concepts of Mendelson.[45] Together they assert that direct, immediate and dynamic interviews with a child and his family who are in a state of loss usually produces a flow of emotion that was often previously suppressed. In particular, it tended to be hidden in front of bereaved siblings and parents, for fear of hurting them further. The Furmans have reported many analytic studies of parent loss as well as "therapy through the parent."[21] In the studies of multiple losses (families, homes, and communities) in the Buffalo Creek Disaster[50] entire families were eager to pour themselves out to the investigators. Previously, they had kept their crying to their own rooms at night away from other family members for fear of upsetting each other to an overwhelming degree.

The authors' own clinical experience has included work with an in-patient, day-patient, and out-patient population of child patients from ages three to twelve. They have observed that early forms of mourning, not readily recognizable, occur in very young children. It appears that the greatest block to recognizing such developmentally early forms of mourning and grief in children is not only the adult's avoidance of the imminent severe pain and rage. It is also an avoidance of the intense anxiety aroused in the adult through a revival of his *own* childhood fears and his own wishes for his parents to die, along with the accompanying panic and guilt. A counterpart to

the "Family Romance" could be called the "The Fantasy of the Death of One's Parent(s)," frequently entertained individually, or shared by siblings. They fantasize a total reversal of family conditions with children as heroes taking care of each other and outwitting the adults. Glorified roles of courage, self-sufficiency, admiration from outsiders, and an idyllic life express the wishes of children to manage better in their own society. The atrocious outcome of such a fantasy was poignantly illustrated in Golding's novel *Lord of the Flies*. The role of oedipal patricidal and matricidal impulses as well as the destructive rages of the preoedipal period all contribute to the deep disavowal by parents of mourning and grief in childhood. Many authors point out that when a parent is lost in early childhood the predominant emotion may be rage.[45] Piety, however, interferes with this recognition. Freud quoted, *"De mortibus nil nisi bonum"*[19] (About the dead, [say] nothing but good). Children as well as adults are blocked by this unconscious command, felt by all, not to speak badly of the dead. In some cases, there is a fear of retaliation by spirits from the dead. For a long period, mother and child can support each other in this prohibition, and in the maintenance of a false ideal image of unambivalent love for the dead father. For the son, father's vengence is greatly feared. The daughter is enraged at her "rejection." At this point, things cease to be developmental and the stress falls on the bereaved family's mutuality as a whole in defending against their feelings of rage at abandonment. This block against rage also prevents the necessary expression of sorrow.

The "bit by bit" process described by Freud[18] for the adult disengaging from a spouse, a parent, or a friend takes far longer for children. This is so partly because of the unique developmental functions of their parents, and partly because "developmental time" is slow and long, taking years and years. From birth to adulthood, a child's needs for his father change constantly. From the developmental point of view, it is not surprising that the loss of a parent at any childhood stage becomes essentially a new one to be worked through at each subsequent developmental stage. What is involved here is shock trauma, strain trauma, and cumulative trauma[54] at a profound level of developmental interference.[48]

Thus the maintenance of an internal image of the lost parent which changes in form at each developmental age may be viewed as a nucleus of health, something to be supported by the adult environment. As he grows up, a given child may be capable of allowing his own fantasy of the lost father to grow. Such a child may approach late adolescence with a readiness for developmental decathexis and "object removal"; according to Wolfenstein, this is a precursor to adult mourning.[70] The child's hypercathected image of father which had been retained for so long does not need to be viewed as pathological (as would be true in a case of adult mourning). Instead, it can be regarded as a powerful inner resource which has run its course more or less simultaneously with the rest of development.

It is suggested that adults' own denial of death extends to a denial of the impact of death on their children. This blocks their communication and understanding of children in this painful area. Freud demonstrated the enormous amnesia for infantile sexuality in adults. In just the same way, there exists in adults a great denial of the child's deep affects and prolonged (if at times invisible) developmental mourning work after the death of a parent.

Infants and toddlers may experience even brief separations as catastrophic; indeed, such events are conducive to the kind of intense crying and separation anxiety seen in adult reactions to death. It therefore seems paradoxical to insist that the young cannot understand death. Cognitively they do not, but for their age, affectively they feel the meaning of death as abandonment.

In a child's immediate reactions to death, it is hard to discern whether these are "depressive equivalents" that take the place of depression and grief,[66] or forerunners of pathology. If a father dies, or is lost, the lives of his children will be irreversibly altered. Developmental interferences and deviations are inevitable, but these may lead to adaptive and creative resolutions.

Chapter 3 of G. Kliman's book, *Psychological Emergencies of Childhood*[35] is entitled "Death in the Family." It offers an excellent review of retrospective and anterospective studies on childhood bereavement. Further, Ann Kliman reports on eighteen untreated nonclinical orphans, from under one year of age to age fourteen. She describes the eagerness of many bereaved subjects to talk about their feelings. Eighteen children from seven bereaved families were seen. Both free and structured components were employed in the interviews. After careful accounting for the immediate circumstances of the deaths, which included five fathers and three mothers, she reviewed the findings. The first and the outstandingly significant finding occurred in eight children; it involved the presence of tears for just a few minutes on the

first day. Three of the children were more tearful, and cried up to an hour; and according to the informant, the parent, five manifested no tearfulness at all. Other findings included an increase in symptoms, the major new ones being fearfulness, separation difficulties, difficulties falling asleep, and eating disturbances. (The others ranged from nightmares to teeth grinding, enuresis and special destructiveness.) Tearfulness was *not* among them. This opens up the possibility that crying itself has quite different meanings to children and adults and should be studied further.

Long-range Effects of Father Loss

In 1968, Herzog and Sudia reviewed fifty-nine studies of the effects of father loss. Their overall conclusion was that "existing data do not permit a decisive answer to questions about the effects on children of fatherlessness."[28] [p. 348] They did note several general tendencies. Juvenile delinquency seemed to be related to fatherlessness, but "this consensus is strongly qualified by suspiciousness of confounding factors." [p. 343] As far as importance of sex roles, "the most frequent conclusion is that lacking a resident male model, the boy is more likely to become feminized. He may show this by dependency and passivity, or he may show it by compensatory masculinity." [p. 346] The measures most often used to test this are masculinity-femininity scales which are constructed by trial-and-error selection of items that discriminate most effectively between males and females. This includes such items as activity and occupational preference. Herzog and Sudia raise questions as to the validity of the tests and as to whether "masculinity or femininity should be a criterion in judging well-being." It is not clear whether these factors relate to present or later success in fulfilling the tasks required in adolescence and adulthood.

In 1971, Biller[7] reviewed the literature in regard to the effects of father loss, and mentioned the results of several studies. Sears[58] found that in three- to five-year-old boys, the doll play of father-absent boys tends to be less aggressive and to manifest less sex role differentiation. Bach[4] found the doll play of six- to ten-year-old father-absent boys to be less aggressive than that of father-present boys. Santrock[55] found the doll play of father-absent black disadvantaged boys to show more dependent behavior, though no difference in aggressive behavior. Stolz et al.[64] studied four- to eight-year-old children who had been separated for the first two years of their lives from their fathers by war. It was shown that their fathers perceived them as sissies; and, according to the authors, objectively they were less aggressive and independent with peers. They were more often submissive, or they might react with immature hostility. This picture might have been a reaction to the stressful presence of the father in the home. Biller adds evidence that the effects of father absence on boys may persist long after the father's return. Carlsmith[12] studied high school males who experienced father absence before the age of five during World War II. He found that on College Board Aptitude Scores, they displayed a female pattern, i.e., verbal scores higher than math scores. Hetherington[8] reported that nine- to twelve-year-old father-absent boys showed less masculine projective sex role behavior. Moreover, they were rated by male recreation directors as more dependent on their peers, less aggressive, and engaging in fewer physical contact games than were father-present boys. In the same study, boys who lost their father after the age of four did not show differences in sex role measures. Biller[8] noted that boys who had lost their father before the fifth year had significantly less masculine sex role orientation than did those where the loss occurred during their fifth year. In contrast, in studying ten- to fifteen-year-olds, McCord, and Thurber[41] noted that social workers did not observe sexually inappropriate behavior in boys separated from their fathers before age six. Santrock[56] found that boys who became father absent before the age of two were more handicapped in several dimensions of personality development than were boys who became father absent at a later age. Boys who became father absent before age two were found to be less trusting, less industrious, and to have more feelings of inferiority than boys who became father absent between the ages of three to five. Santrock's study dealt with lower-class fifth grade boys.

As far as later development, Biller notes[7] (p. 66) that "Glueck and Glueck reported that more than two-fifths of delinquent boys were father absent as compared with less than one-fourth of a matched nondelinquent group."

Many retrospective studies of adult clinic populations (schizophrenics, depressives) have shown a high correlation with early parent loss. However, except for the Gluecks'[23] study, none has been specific for father loss, over and above the usual ratio of father loss to mother loss (2½:1).

Seligman et al.[59] studied eighty-six adolescents referred from the adolescent medical service in Cincinnati General Hospital for a psychiatric evaluation. Twenty-two percent of the sample had a history of father loss. This stands in marked contrast to the 9 percent of the adolescent medical clinic sample and 9 percent of the matched school sample with such a history. An intriguing developmental sidelight which requires further study is their observation that the ages at which the losses occurred in the adolescent referral group were concentrated between three to six and again between twelve and fifteen years. The curve flattened in latency for the type of psychiatric referrals in this study.

In a unique anterospective study, Gregory[26] followed 11,329 ninth grade children for three years. He found that father absence was related to delinquency in boys, but not in girls, a finding similar to the Gluecks'.

Forms of Coping Behavior

FANTASIES

Kinesthetically, infants experience that the disappearance of good food is caused by swallowing, and that such swallowing adds a pleasurable feeling to their bodies. Oral incorporation themes are common in fairy tales, such as the "Gingerbread Man" and "Hansel and Gretel." Later expressions of such fantasies occur in religion. The sacrament of communion allows Christians to receive the strength of Christ by absorbing, either actually or symbolically according to belief, the body of Christ. They eat wafers (the body) and drink wine (the blood) of Christ as the earthly representative of the father-God. For Jews, the annual ritual of Passover involves eating the unleavened bread, matzoh. According to tradition, this was baked in haste by enslaved and persecuted Jews fleeing from Egypt toward the Promised Land under the fatherly leadership of Moses. A child in psychotherapy dreamed of her dead father turning into a loaf of bread; as she started to eat it, however, it disappeared.

A clinical example of father loss by a baby girl is that of Barbara, who lost her father before she was born. Her mother, feeling strong and brave, had never mourned her husband's death until late in treatment. Instead, she had used her baby daughter as a replacement for her dead husband, perhaps in the sense of a transitional object. Barbara was a twelve-year-old psychotic child in a residential center at the time that an intensive study was undertaken of the reaction of all the fifteen children to the assassination of President Kennedy.[37] This included immediate interviews, specially constructed pictures added to the selected TAT cards, and subsequent psychiatric and psychological interviews three months later. Shocked upon hearing of the president's death, Barbara muttered something about a mother having a baby take a father's place. She spent the weekend in front of the television watching the news coverage of the event, weeping profusely for the first time. Also for the first time, she collected and showed to others pictures of her own father. More than that, she demonstrated a very specific and intelligent knowledge of the details of the president's death. This increased her self-confidence and self-esteem enormously and altogether proved to be a turning point in her progress. It was speculated that her early grandiose fantasy of being the omnipotent baby who could replace a dead father was directly related to her need for a great figure, such as a president, with whom to work out her mourning. This resulted in a significant therapeutic improvement. Her early and persistent denial, reinforced by the grandiose fantasy, had both been shared with mother; together, they had immobilized her psychological development. She was apparently able to use the second death of a "father" at a later cognitive and affective stage to break through this developmental block. This is analogous to the use of psychoanalysis as a new opportunity to mourn a previous loss.[17]

During the separation-individuation phase, fantasies often involve a physical memory of the father's activities with the child. Clive, a case presented by E. Furman,[21] was two years old when his father died. Presently he began to repeat in action many of the daily activities he had shared with his father. His mother found it hard to tolerate this behavior; she could not bear her growing recognition of his overt longing and sadness. This case demonstrates the way young children use physical activity to express thought and emotion. (This is in line with Piaget's stage of sensorimotor development.) Indeed, such reenactment is the toddler's principle means of remembering (hypercathecting) his father's loss. Clive is one of twenty-three children with parent loss studied in clinical depth by the Furmans.[21] His activity fantasy of early childhood superbly and movingly demonstrates a condensation of denial, identification, separation-individuation, acceptance in "doing it alone," and working through by repetition. It also demonstrates a mother's painful struggle with her child's longing and sadness.

During the oedipal period, fantasies swell to gigantic proportions: Jack the Giant Killer for oedipal boys, Beauty and the Beast, Cinderella, and the Ugly Duckling for oedipal girls. Fathers are typically idealized by both sexes, but boys idealize their omnipotent power and punitive strength (i.e., Kung Fu, Superman, and other such figures), while girls idealize today's equivalents of knights in shining armor or adore kindly men on TV who are fatherly and smile affectionately (Mister Rogers).

The latency-age child is unique in that he has a wider range of fantasy side by side with a great burgeoning of defensive structures. When Helene Deutsch[14] noted cases of absence of affective response to bereavement in both childhood and adulthood, she added that "the ego is rent asunder for those children who do not employ the usual defenses, and who mourn as an adult does." It is evident that the ego is "asunder" in many children, but in latency, it is manifested by a developmental ego splitting as well as by the formation of a partial repression barrier. This allows strong defenses to arch over an underlying freedom of private or peer-shared anguishes and fantasies. The latency child is thus enabled to betray little mourning to the world, while he cries in his pillow at night. The fantasized quest for discoveries, which often represent reunion with the lost parent, are common in such children. Literature is also a source of vicarious mourning; the children can have strong reactions when they read the hardships of David Copperfield, Oliver Twist, and their modern contemporaries. Stories of orphans are popular, and children identify intensely with the grief, rage, heartbreak, glorious heroism, and nobility of their losses. Two neighboring families had respectively lost a father and a mother in the same month. The children had formerly used an attic to play "doctor games" and "teacher games." Now they created an addition to their play, a brand-new game called the "orphanage game." They played out heroic themes of children coping without any adults at all.

One seven-year-old girl had lost her father the previous year. She would gaze out at night upon a star, and communicate her day's feelings to her father located there. Several years later she reflected that she had never had a belief in heaven. She knew her father to be beyond all reach (reality testing), yet he remained within the perceivable universe (her psychological needs and development). Choosing nighttime for these fantasied conversations was typical of latency behavior; this epoch generally assumes that the open activities of the day will pass the scrutiny of adults, and the night is for oneself and one's peers. Many defenses lie in between.

Another girl of ten, who had lost her father two years earlier, dreamed that she had accidentally spilled a newly discovered chemical on a dead body, which then amazingly came alive. Later, she tried it on her father's body, but the chemical failed to revitalize him. Upon awakening, she realized that her wish to restore life to her father had worked in the dream on an unrelated person (representing the magical wish), but could not work on her dead father, not even, as she added, "in a dream." (Probably a partial reality acceptance of his death prohibited magic working on the dead father appearing in the manifest level of the dream. In addition, the prohibition of the basic oedipal wish interfered.) Here again, the latency child's sense of reality and his investment in fantasy are well developed and parallel. Both are useful to future development so long as reality testing, the difference between reality and fantasy, is clear.

Adolescents tone down their fantasies and increase their adulation of current heroes. It is hard for adults to keep up with who these heroes are. *Sanford and Son*, a recent television series, portrays an idyllic and warmly bantering relationship between a black father and his son. This statistically rare and ached-for relationship tells poignantly the fantasized yearnings of many a black or white fatherless adolescent. The experience of the generation gap is often suppressed but ever-present for fatherless children; it is well expressed and resolved in this show. Such intergenerational tensions are often muted in fatherless families; it is hard to fight a single parent, both for the mother's and for the children's sake. Sooner or later, however, the break must be made, and it is often made with guilt, indecision, and delay.

In addition, adolescents today may appear to "tough out" a lost parent, divorced parents, a never-known father. The ideal is not to feel, yet their songs tell of loss and despair. They reach out for each other. They include not only the parent loss but the parent-alienated young. They share diffuse losses and griefs in groups, but very toughly, in syllables. They do not even know that they grieve the absence of a loving father, a strong man, against whom they could have tested themselves, and who, in turn, would have cared deeply about their struggles and victories.

SKILLS AND SUBLIMATIONS

Many children use gross identification with the lost object as a defense. In some cases this leads to severe psychopathology and an arrest at the developmental level reached at the time of the parent's death.[2, 16] In other cases, the more selective, positive identifications have proven helpful in the process of mourning, and have added new dimensions to the youth's personality and adaptation.[52] The loss of the parent necessitates the learning of new roles, and their redistribution within the family. Children develop new family skills: They often become adept at such things as cooking, gardening, or car repair, and at comforting each other and their mother. In a less conscious way, others identify with pleasing mannerisms and habits of the lost father. If a boy incorporates those parts of his father's personality which are compatible with his age level, or if he uses his father as an ego ideal in the future, the outcome will be adaptive. On the other hand, if he identifies totally with the male parent by introjection, he will become a "pseudo-adult," a precocious "little man." This leads to a by-passing of childhood and adolescent development; in the long run it will impoverish him. Girls identifying with their fathers may adopt a character trait such as humor, or a favorite sport, or hobby, or even the parent's profession. So long as they do not identify overly with father's masculinity, and do not block their development of heterosexual relationships, these identifications are fruitful.

Another result of loss may be the development of special empathy for other persons who have also sustained losses. Sometimes the motive is to associate with such fellow sufferers in order to share the fixation point, or to be the provider of help: "Misery loves company." Some relationships lead to choosing a helping profession as their vocation.

Taking recourse to artistic expression to help resolve the grief may lead to the development of talents and creative productions. Those who use detachment or distancing to avoid feelings of grief may develop new interests in mathematics, physical sciences, skills in manipulating the inanimate world, or interest in travel and exploration. Exploration is partly motivated by the quest for reunion.

SPECIAL DEFENSE PATTERNS

The most pervasive defense system especially right after the loss is denial. This is most commonly found during the early response to trauma, and is especially strong if the loss has been un-expected and sudden. When severe denial persists, it is often accompanied by ego arrest.[2] Latency children are capable of denial and acceptance side by side, or suppression of affect on the surface with rich underlying and unshared fantasies. It is only when denial recedes that mourning can take place, although some authors consider denial to be the first phase of mourning.[10]

Children who use denial excessively will tend to ward off all feelings with an overall restriction of ego development. Learning, socialization, and a wide range of functions may be inhibited. Others use school work as a site for the defensive isolation of affect, or for intellectualization; this is similar to the "busyness" or overwork of the adult.

Anger and rage are especially strong components in children's grief, and may lead to reaction formations, with the children becoming excessively "good" and helpful.

Fear of death may lead to phobic avoidance of all reminders of death. One child was startled, cried, and jumped up in the air when a hearse went by. She became unusually fearful of all illnesses and injuries, and was terrified at the sight of them. Counterphobic defenses may lead to the choice of medicine or nursing as a vocation.

Another manifestation of avoidance is an extreme hunger for distraction, through restless entertainment, reading about exotic and faraway places, or science fiction. Derealization and depersonalization may occur.

Teenage girls seeking affection and acceptance can fall prey to promiscuity. Boys may also pursue a loveless sex life as a means of escape, or to prove their manhood in a fatherless environment. Drugs may be used for blunting or obliterating the pain of mourning or for creating beatific states of consciousness which seem to transcend death or to provide heavenly reunions. Suicidal ideation or impulses in children often represent an attempt at reunion with the lost parent.

Girls who have single mothers as objects of identification often experience uncertainties and anxieties in their future relationships with men. Fear of repeating loss often leads to the defense of distancing and problems of commitment.[29]

Regression is another mechanism which defends against current pain. In young children such behavior as enuresis, thumb sucking, or temper tantrums may recur. Increased fearfulness and dependency often develop. Earlier forms of soothing narcissism may be resorted to, or, as the point of defensive regression, one may revert to a concept of the omnipotent or grandiose self which

overcomes suffering. Suffering itself may be erotized to form a masochistic personality type. Suffering may also be used toward the creation of genuine courage, or exaggerated into exhibitionistic heroics.

Many religions have visions of an afterlife, a paradise, where reunion will take place, and the believer strives ever to gain entry there. Leonard[39] reports that one girl studied theology to bring herself into closer communication with her dead father.

UNUSUAL COMPETENCIES

In "Scientists, Their Psychological World" Bernice Eiduson[15] states that:

> One striking finding stands out immediately: Nineteen of the 40 scientists (47.5 percent) did not know their fathers very well. Four fathers had died early in their children's lives or had left home because of divorce when their sons were very young. Fourteen others either worked away from home or were so absorbed in their work that they were for all practical purposes absent most of the time. Ten of these were immigrants who had come to this country from Europe and had started small businesses of their own in the 1920's and 1930's. In other words, almost half the scientists had very little personal contact with their fathers. This sizable figure takes on added significance when compared with my findings from a previous study of 40 persons in the fields of painting, writing, music, and the theater arts. This earlier study revealed similarly that half of these artists had lost their fathers early in childhood (in contrast to a control group of men who had gone into business fields). [p. 22]

Illingsworth[33] compiled a list of outstanding figures in history who had lost a mother or father (or both) before age ten. His total father loss list includes Nero, Confucius, Mohammed, Fra Lippi, Copernicus, Raphael, Ivan, Ben Jonson, Rubens, Richelieu, Murillo, Newton, Leibniz, Jonathan Swift, Abraham Cowley, David Hume, Rousseau, Pestalozzi, Thomas Telford, Danton, Sir William Jones Jenner, Fourier, John Rennie, Humboldt, De Quincey, Byron, Chang and Eng, Thackeray, Alexander Dumas, Edward Bulwer Lytton, Nathaniel Hawthorn, Wagner, Balfour, Nietzche, Tolstoy, Baden-Powell, Sibelius, Curie, Somerset Maugham, Eleanor Roosevelt, Anna Pavlova. Needless to say the mother loss list is equally impressive (including Mohammed, Dante, Michaelangelo, Voltaire, Robespierre, Wordsworth, Lincoln, Darwin, Charlotte Bronte, Mary Baker Eddy, Conrad, Steinmetz, Eichman). Five of these parent-loss historical figures were included in his chapter "Some Evil Men."[33] These five are Nero, Ivan the Terrible, Danton, Robespierre, and Eichman.

One might extrapolate backward from these outstanding figures and gain some further speculative insights into the skills and sublimations of lesser known people who had lost fathers in childhood (see "Skills and Sublimations, p. 368).

The prevalence of this phenomenon within the group of leaders and discoverers, scientists, educators, tyrants, and writers is quite astounding. In the light of this, one may better understand Darwin, who lost his mother early, and his urge to travel and discover, as well as his fear of publishing his results until twenty-three years after his return from the voyage of the *Beagle*. Greenacre[24] writes that "his sense of patricide in entertaining this idea [of evolution of the species] was so great . . . that he wrote to his friend . . . that in stating his views he felt as though he were confessing murder [of God]."

The memorialization of the dead leads to countless creative and constructive monuments and works; these must also be considered a creative expression of the work of mourning.[51] Freud said that the loss of a father is the single greatest loss a person can experience.[20] After his father died in 1896 he undertook his self-analysis and wrote the monumental "interpretation of Dreams."

Winnicott called such creative works the adult forms of "transitional phenomena" in the "intermediate area" between the self and external reality, which contains "artistic creativity and appreciation, religious feeling . . . philosophy and culture."[68] As in the infant, these adult phenomena occur developmentally between the earlier inability and the growing ability to recognize and accept a painful aspect of external reality. Many of the creative works memorializing the loss of a father belong in this transitional zone between the inner mind and external reality.

Social Structures Needed to Respond Optimally to Father Loss

One may begin with a recognition of those father-loss families in which the children were essentially well adjusted, and see what positive strengths made this possible. In a classic study, Hilgard et al.[31] compared the parent-loss cases, gleaned from four census tracts, to hospitalized parent-loss cases in the area. They further subdivided their groups into father-loss, mother-loss, well adjusted, and poorly adjusted children. In considering the successful father-loss families, the most critical factor they described was that the mother kept the home intact. Her children characterized her as strong, responsible, thoughtful, and hard-working, rather than warm and tender. They stressed her hard work and energy far more often than her affection. The authors saw the strong working mother as a protective factor who engendered strong egos in her children, both through her example and her expectations of them. Another vital factor was the strength of the family prior to the loss; in these cases, both parents had well-defined roles which provided the children with stability, and the capacity for "separation-tolerance." Clinical experience also emphasizes that the mother's ways of talking about her absent husband and her relationships with male relatives and other men will strongly color her children's feelings about fatherhood in particular and will affect her sons' identifications with men, and her daughters' attitudes toward men. The children's future choices of love partners will be deeply affected.

Parents must prepare their children to be more purposeful about becoming parents, and to be prepared for various eventualities. Help for this can come from family life education courses in the schools and community mental health programs. Girls need help to avoid becoming single heads of households if possible, through greater foresight in sexual relationships, understanding of love, and choice of husband. Should they ever become single heads of families (and even if they never do), they need anticipatory emotional strength, including vocational self-development and economic know-how. Networks of support and socialization must be available.

Boys too need intensive learning of the paternal role. Many fathers have great resistance against "entering the nursery"[69] or facing "the mother in every man,"[53] because they feel this threatens their masculinity. Many a young unmarried father, with help, has been able to enjoy becoming an active parent to his child and a concerned partner with its mother. The ability to reach mature decisions has been arrived at through such experiences. Fatherly closeness to the infant brings with it a different smell, a firmness of holding, and a kind of unanxious "detachment" which greatly soothes infantile anxieties. This establishes for both a strong father-child bond,[69] as masculine and rewarding as the world of work.

Fathers active with their children and poised in their work and mothers who have resolved home and work conflicts have strong, convincing voices in the community, and in legislative and budgetary decisions at all levels. They will be more aware of racial and social class factors which are among "the concurrent circumstances" of fatherless families.[36] Financial assistance is obviously necessary not merely to support a fatherless family but to help its productivity. Increased psychological awareness is vital.

Several possible psychological interventions in fatherless families will be given. Family physicians and parents should be aware of the "anniversary reaction syndrome."[30] Here, the age of the parent at death, or the child's age on bereavement, exert strong transgenerational effects. Thus, the "child, now a parent" may become physically or mentally ill on arriving at the age of his parent's death, or on having a child of the age of his own bereavement. The physician who anticipates such possibilities can help his patient recognize an anniversary grief reaction and prevent serious illness.

Other useful information is available in such books as *What to Tell Your Child.*[3]

Another example is the need for awareness by pediatricians and relatives of grief and depression in the mothers of infants. This places the infants at high risk for severe psychopathology. These adults should also realize that during the separation-individuation phase, a sector of black children suffer from father-loss to an unusual extent. Such knowledge must mobilize far reaching interventions.

One neglected area in great need of further study involves the strong effects of father absence on girls.[29, 39] The provision of Big Brothers for boys but not for girls illustrates this. The present review of literature is very meager in this area.

People working with father-loss children need greater understanding of the developmental stages of father-loss in children. Factors of maternal strength, greater insights in the role of fatherhood, and socioeconomic conditions relevant to the family all play their role. Instead of "society without the Father,"[47] a society of fathers and mothers must develop which can understand and concern itself with all its children.

REFERENCES

1. ABELIN, E., "The Role of the Father in the Separation-Individuation Process," in McDevitt, B., and Settlage, F. (Eds.), *Separation-Individuation Essays in Honor of Margaret S. Mahler*, pp. 229–252, International Universities Press, New York, 1971.

2. ALTSCHUL, S., "Denial and Ego Arrest," *Journal of the American Psychoanalytic Association*, 16(2):301–318, 1968.

3. ARNSTEIN, H., *What to Tell Your Child About Birth, Death. Illness, Divorce, and Other Family Crises*, Pocket Books, New York, 1964.

4. BACH, G. R., "Father Fantasies and Father-Typing in Father-Separated Children," in Martin, W., and Stendler, C., (Eds.), *Readings in Child Development*, pp. 368–379, Harcourt, Brace and World, New York, 1954.

5. BECKER, E., *Denial of Death*, The Free Press, New York, 1973.

6. BENEDEK, T., "Adaptation to Reality in Early Infancy," *Psychoanalytic Quarterly*, 7:200–214, 1938.

7. BILLER, H. B., *Father, Child and Sex Role*, D. C. Heath and Co., Lexington, Mass., 1971.

8. ———, "Father Absence, Maternal Encouragement, and Sex-Role Development in Kindergarten Age Boys," *Child Development*, 40:539–546, 1969.

9. BLOS, P. "The Second Individuation Phase of Adolescence," in Eissler, R. S., et al. (Eds.), *The Psychoanalytic Study of the Child*, vol. 22, pp. 162–187, International Universities Press, New York, 1967.

10. BOWLBY, J., "Grief and Mourning in Infancy and Early Childhood," in Eissler, R. S., et al. (Eds.), *The Psychoanalytic Study of the Child*, vol. 15, pp. 9–52, International Universities Press, New York, 1960.

11. BURLINGHAM, D., and FREUD, A., *Infants Without Families*, George Allen and Unwin, London, 1944. (Note especially chap. 5, "The Role of the Father in the Residential Nursery," pp. 84–97, esp. pp. 84–85.)

12. CARLSMITH, L., "Effect of Early Father-Absence on Scholastic Aptitude," *Harvard Educational Review*, 34:3–21, 1964.

13. Deuteronomy, *The Holy Bible*, 25:5–10.

14. DEUTSCH, H., "Absence of Grief," *Psychoanalytic Quarterly*, 6:12–22, 1937.

15. EIDUSON, B., *Scientists, Their Psychological World*, Basic Books, New York, 1962.

16. FLEMING, J., "Evaluation of a Research Project in Psychoanalysis," in Gaskill, H. S. (Ed.), *Counterpoint: Libidinal Object and Subject*, pp. 75–105, International Universities Press, 1963.

17. ———, and ALTSCHUL, S., "Activation of Mourning and Growth by Psychoanalysis," *International Journal of Psychoanalysis*, 44:419–431, 1963.

18. FREUD, S., "Mourning and Melancholia," in *The Standard Edition of the Complete Psychological Works of Sigmund Freud* (hereafter *The Standard Edition*), vol. 14, pp. 237–258, Hogarth Press, London, 1957.

19. ———, "Totem and Taboo," in *The Standard Edition*, vol. 13, pp. 1–161, Hogarth Press, London, 1955.

20. ———, "The Interpretation of Dreams, in *The Standard Edition*, vol. 4, p. 254, Hogarth Press, London, 1953.

21. FURMAN, E., *A Child's Parent Dies, Studies in Childhood Bereavement*, Yale University Press, New Haven, 1974.

22. FURMAN, R. A., "Death of a Six Year Old's Mother During His Analysis," *Psychoanalytic Study of the Child*, 19:377–397, 1969.

23. GLUECK, S., and GLUECK, E., *Unravelling Juvenile Delinquency*, New York Commonwealth Fund, New York, 1950.

24. GREENACRE, P., *The Quest for the Father*, Freud Anniversary Lecture Series, International Universities Press, New York, 1963.

25. ———, "The Childhood of the Artist," in Eissler, R. S., et al. (Eds.), *The Psychoanalytic Study of the Child*, vol. 12, pp. 47–72, International Universities Press, New York, 1957.

26. GREGORY, I., "Anterospective Data Following Childhood Loss of a Parent," *Archives of General Psychiatry, 13:99–120,* 1965.

27. HERZOG, E., and SUDIA, C. E., *Boys in Fatherless Families,* U.S. Department of Health, Education and Welfare, Office of Child Development, Children's Bureau, Washington, D.C., 1970.

28. ———, "Fatherless Homes, A Review of Research," in Chess, S., and Thomas, A. (Eds.), *Annual Progress in Child Psychiatry and Child Development,* pp. 341–351, Brunner-Mazel, New York, 1969.

29. HETHERINGTON, E. M., "Effects of Father Absence on Personality Development in Adolescent Daughters," *Developmental Psychology, 7(3):313–326,* 1972.

30. HILGARD, J., and NEWMAN, M., "Anniversaries in Mental Illness," *Psychiatry, 22:113–121,* 1959.

31. ———, and FISK, F., "Strength of the Adult Ego Following Childhood Bereavement," *Journal of Orthopsychiatry, 30:788–798,* 1960.

32. HOWELLS, J., "Fathering," in Howells, J., *Modern Perspectives in International Child Psychiatry,* pp. 125–156, Brunner-Mazel, New York, 1971. (Includes excellent cross-cultural studies and animal studies.)

33. ILLINGSWORTH, R. S., and C. M., *Lessons From Childhood,* E. and S. Livingstone, Edinburgh, 1969.

34. KING, C. E., "The Negro Maternal Family, A Product of an Economic and Culture System," *Social Forces, 24:100–104,* 1945.

35. KLIMAN, G., "Death in the Family," in Kliman, G., *Psychological Emergencies of Childhood,* Grune & Stratton, New York, 1968.

36. KOGELSCHATZ, J. L., ADAMS, P. L. and TUCKER, D. McK., "Family Styles of Fatherless Households," *American Journal of Child Psychiatry, 11(2):365–383,* 1972.

37. KRUG, O., and DEMBER, C. F., "The Diagnostic and Therapeutic Utilization of Children's Reactions to the President's Death," in Wolfenstein, M., and Kliman, G. (Eds.), *Children and the Death of a President,* pp. 80–98, Doubleday, Garden City, N.Y., 1965.

38. LASCH, C., "The Weak Modern Family," *The New York Review of Books, 22(19):37–42,* November 27, 1975.

39. LEONARD, M. R., "Fathers and Daughters," *International Journal of Psychoanalysis, 47:325–344,* 1966.

40. LYNN, B., *The Father: His Role in Child Development,* Brooks/Cole Publishing Company, Monterey, Calif., 1974.

41. McCORD, J., McCORD, W., and THURBER, E., "Some Effects of Paternal Absence on Male Children," *Journal of Abnormal and Social Psychology, 64:361–369,* 1962.

42. MAHLER, M. S., "Discussion of Greenacre's Problems of Overidealization of the Analyst and of Analysis," Unpublished manuscript. Abstract in *Psychoanalytic Quarterly, 36:637,* 1966. Quoted by Abelin, see reference 1.

43. ———, PINE, F., and BERGMAN, A., *The Psychological Birth of the Human Infant,* Basic Books, New York, 1975.

44. MARSELLA, A., DUBANOSKI, R., and MOHS, K., "The Effects of Father Presence and the Absence Upon Maternal Attitudes," *The Journal of Genetic Psychology, 125:257–263,* 1974.

45. MENDELSON, M., "Mourning in Children and Adolescents in Psychoanalysis," in Mendels, Joseph, *Concepts of Depression,* p. 115 and pp. 130–142, John Wiley, New York, 1974.

46. MILLER, J. B. M., "Children's Reactions to the Death of a Parent, A Review of the Psychoanalytic Literature," *Journal of the American Psychoanalytic Association, 19(4):697–719,* 1971.

47. MITSCHERLICH, A., *Society without the Father, A Contribution to Social Psychology,* Harcourt, Brace and World, New York, 1963.

48. NAGERA, H., "Children's Reactions to the Death of Important Objects: A Developmental Approach," in Eissler, R. S., et al. (Eds.), *The Psychoanalytic Study of the Child,* vol. 25, pp. 360–400, International Universities Press, New York, 1970.

49. NEUBAUER, P., "The One Parent Child and His Oedipal Development," in Eissler, R. S., et al. (Eds.), *The Psychoanalytic Study of the Child,* vol. 15, pp. 286–309, International Universities Press, New York, 1960.

50. NEWMAN, C. J., "Children of Disaster: Clinical Observations at Buffalo Creek," *The American Journal of Psychiatry, 133(3):306,* 1976.

51. POLLOCK, G. H., "On Mourning, Immortality and Utopia," *Journal of the American Psychoanalytic Association, 23(2):334–362,* 1975.

52. ———, "Mourning and Adaptation. *International Journal of Psychoanalysis, 42:341–361,* 1961.

53. ROSS, J. M., "The Development of Paternal Identity, A Critical Review of the Literature of Nurturance and Generativity in Boys and Men," *Journal of the American Psychoanalytic Association, 23(4):783–817,* 1975.

54. SANDLER, J., "Trauma, Strain and Development," in Furst, Sidney S. (Ed.), *Psychic Trauma,* pp. 154–174, Basic Books, New York, 1967.

55. SANTROCK, J. W., "Paternal Absence, Sex-Typing, and Identification," *Developmental Psychology, 2:264–272,* 1970.

56. ———, "Influence of Onset and Type of Paternal Absence on the First Four Eriksonian Developmental Crises," *Developmental Psychology, 3:273–274,* 1970.

57. SARNOFF, C., *Latency,* Jason, Aronson, Inc., New York, 1976.

58. SEARS, P. S., "Doll-play Aggression in Normal Young Children: Influence of Sex, Age, Sibling Status, Father's Absence," *Psychological Monographs, 65:6,* 1951.

59. SELIGMAN, R., et. al., "The Effect of Earlier Parental Loss in Adolescence," *Archives of General Psychiatry, 31:475,* 1974.

60. SPITZ, R. A., *The First Year of Life,* International Universities Press, New York, 1965.

61. ———, "Anaclitic Depression," in Eissler, R. S., et al. (Eds.), *The Psychoanalytic Study of the Child,* vol. 2, pp. 313–341, International Universities Press, New York, 1946.

62. STOLLER, R. J., "Psychoanalytic Treatment of Male Homosexuality," Panel on Homosexuality at the 1976 American Psychoanalytic Association Meeting in Baltimore, 1976.

63. ———, *Sex and Gender,* Aronson, New York, 1968.

64. STOLZ, L. M., et al., *Father Relationships of War Born Children,* Stanford University Press, Stanford, Calif., 1954.

65. TENHOUTEN, W. D., "The Black Family: Myth and Reality," *Psychiatry, 33:145–173,* 1970.

66. TOOLAN, J. M., "Depression in Children and Adolescents," *American Journal of Orthopsychiatry, 32: 404–415,* 1962.

67. United States Bureau of the Census, *Current Population Reports,* Series p–20, No. 291, "Household and Family Characteristics: March, 1975," U.S. Government Printing Office, Washington, D.C., 1976.

68. WINNICOTT, D. M., "Transitional Objects and Transitional Phenomena: A Study of the First Not-Me Possession," *International Journal of Psychoanalysis, 34:* 89–97, 1953.

69. WISDOM, J. O., "The Role of the Father in the Mind of the Parents, in Psychoanalytic Theory and in the Life of the Infant," *International Review of Psychoanalysis, 3:231–239,* 1976.

70. WOLFENSTEIN, M., "How Is Mourning Possible?," in Eissler, R. S., et al. (Eds.), *The Psychoanalytic Study of the Child,* vol. 21, pp. 93–123, International Universities Press, New York, 1966.

39 / The Motherless Child

Besse-Lee Allnutt

Historical Background

In the higher animal kingdom, absolute mortality is expected for a motherless infant. The lamb whose mother dies, the fawn whose mother is killed, has no chance for survival. Of them all, at birth, the human infant is the most helpless mammal and requires the longest period of dependency. Certainly it would follow that such an infant when motherless is at risk. The plight of the motherless child has troubled philosophers and physicians for centuries. As early as the thirteenth century, Emperor Federick II of Germany experimented with foundlings hoping to discover the "true mother tongue."[26] He reasoned that by instructing their nurses not to speak in the childrens' presence he would discover what language they spoke naturally. The foundlings all died before their first year. By the twentieth century the mortality rates for children in the great foundling homes, where aseptic physical needs were met but not emotional needs, ran at times as high as 100 percent.

While working with foundlings in the early 1940s, Rene Spitz[28] reported astounding developmental problems. His interest sparked by these findings, Spitz studied foundlings in a medically oriented setting attached to a convent as compared to a control group from a prison nursery where inmate mothers cared for their babies. His classic paper[29] describes the deterioration of foundlings reared by the nuns in sterile cubicles while the prisoners' children thrived. Separation of the prison mothers from their babies resulted in serious deterioration of development, with dramatic reversal when the mothers and children were reunited.

In 1951 under the auspices of the World Health Organization, John Bowlby of London presented studies of the orphaned and displaced children of World War II and the results of the maternal deprivation they suffered.[6] He concluded that the effects of deprivation varied with its degree: Partial deprivation brought anxiety and affect hunger, feelings of anger and revenge, with attendant guilt and depression; complete deprivation correlated all too well with far-reaching effects on character

development which could distort the ability to develop any relationship with others. In either case he postulated that the child's development was retarded and that some children would be damaged for life.[7]

Following the emphasis placed on the importance of emotional nurturing for the development of children, institutional care improved dramatically. Bowlby's work, however, suggested that maternal deprivation could produce a permanent effect on character development. This brewed a storm of protest.

Definition and Qualifying Factors

Discussion of the "motherless child" demands clarification of the terms used by the various investigators. As stated earlier, absolute motherlessness leads inexorably to death. Obviously then there are degrees of being "motherless": The child may be orphaned and in an institution; the child may be separated from the mother by illness, by divorce, by adoption, or by socioeconomic problems in the family; the separation may be temporary or permanent. The presence and quality of the surrogate mother (who may be the father) are obviously important but seldom described in the literature on the subject.

Other factors are frequently noted by authors. The age of the child at the time of the loss, and, occasionally, the presence or absence of siblings are considered. Of current practical and political importance on the American scene are the effect of maternal employment and the use of day-care centers for young children and infants. A topic of high interest at the present time is the correlation to the fatherless or familyless child.[12]

Incidence

According to the United States 1970 census,[30] 3.1 percent of all families in the United States are headed by a man alone, including those who are separated, widowed, divorced, and single. In the homes headed by a man alone are found 1,250,000 children under the age of eighteen.

Employment statistics indicate that there are 6,000,000 children of working mothers, about 80 percent of whom are in family day care (in other words, left with a neighbor or a relative). Preschool children placed in nursery schools or day-care centers number 1,280,000 (the actual breakdown is not known).

Cultural Reactions

According to cultural anthropology, much of the concern about the motherless child being raised in an institution is peculiar to western civilization. In a primitive society, there are no impersonal institutions; rather the orphan or the infant of a sick mother is cared for by the extended family or by some neighborhood group on a personal basis.[21] In some societies, infanticide is a commonplace. In effect, an unwanted child is eliminated with cultural approval—by burying a newborn with the dead mother, or by exposure of the female infant when the food supply is low and there is no way to care for her as she grows older. Margaret Mead speculates that the high mortality rate of the old foundling homes may have represented cultural acceptance of the fate of the unwanted child.

In primitive societies the infant is entirely dependent on breast milk. Infants cannot suffer maternal separation and survive. In fact, where the infant does not thrive on the breast for whatever reason, he will die.

The Israeli kibbutz is a special example of maternal separation occurring on a cultural basis. Here the child is reared in the company of agemates by a children's nurse. Both parents remain actively involved with the child albeit for limited hours. These usually occur in the evening, with the parents taking more of a social than a training role. Children of the kibbutz show none of the signs of separation described by Bowlby. They are, however, very peer conscious, a characteristic which continues into adulthood.[15]

Characteristic Emotional Reactions

The age of the child at the time of the loss of mother is implicated by all investigators as a very important variable. Under the age of six months,

Spitz described the infant as adjusting to a new caretaker with relative ease. Others feel that if infants are placed in institutions at that young age, they react in a global fashion by constant watching of their environment. In addition the vocalization of these young infants develops slowly and they tend to be quiet babies who cry little. The older infant and preschool child develop a relatively severe reaction. Typically, this begins with an intense emotional response such as loud or prolonged crying and active reaching-out to adults.

After a while, however, when the mother does not return, the child begins actively to reject adults and finally sinks into a state of apathy. The eventual result is withdrawal of interest from people coupled with a generalized lower activity level. Should he continue to remain in a depriving institution, the child's development progressively deteriorates into complete withdrawal, refusal of food, physical disability, weight loss, and increased susceptibility to infection. Among these children, toilet training is frequently retarded and enuresis is common. Specific findings include slow language development, a sharp drop on the infant scales of the WISC, and difficulties in spatial awareness, visual memory, and concept formation.[4]

Not all children respond with such a severe disturbance[23] although the reason for this is not known. One possible factor may be that the infant with the most intense response seems to be the one who has had the closest affectional tie to the mother prior to the separation.

Over the age of five the results of mother loss seem to be less devastating. This difference is related to the prior development of interpersonal relationships within a secure environment.

Long-range Effects

The major controversies about the effect of maternal deprivation center around the long-term outcome. Obviously, researchers cannot place human infants into strictly controlled long-term deprivation settings. In addition, the large number of variables involved probably result in the very different conclusions drawn by different investigators.

There are children who are placed in severely depriving institutions before the age of two years, and who remain there for several years. Such children are almost universally found to be seriously disturbed.[11] A follow-up of the original children reported by Spitz revealed that over one-third died before the age of two years. Among those he was able to follow to the age of four years, development was seriously retarded in the areas of self-help, toileting, and language. Many investigators believe that this kind of serious deterioration may be irreversible.

Long-term Effects

For other children, the nurturing environment is more supportive and, within weeks, the depression lifts and the child improves.[7] However, since the child lacks the ego capacity for completing the task of mourning, he is "at risk" for developing a depression in adulthood. In recent years it has been recognized that the loss of the father in childhood is even more common as a possible determinant for adult depression. A recent study by Seligman[26] indicates that many of the adolescents who are admitted to a general hospital medical ward have suffered parent loss as children. She speculates that the teenage medical illness may be the precursor of emotional illness later on.

Not all investigators agree that early parental loss is a decisive factor in the development of depression in adulthood; many factors play a role in such an outcome. Others feel that the original Bowlby material was overstated and that carefully controlled studies are indicated.[12]

Some of the British investigators[24] report evidence that, despite the immediate distress caused by the child's separation from his mother, the separation has little direct importance as a cause of long-term disorder. Even the short-term effects do not appear to result solely from maternal separation. Interactions with other family members are found to be very important and undoubtedly provide one element which can diminish the ill-effects of maternal separation. In homes where there is a discordant marriage with much tension, the child is adversely affected more than in broken homes where tension is low.

Other factors that influence the child's reaction are his own temperament and his age (with older children better able to cope than younger ones). There is some evidence that boys are more adversely affected than girls, particularly when the separation has resulted from family discord.

Delinquency

Back in the 1930s workers became concerned about children who seemed to have no feelings for others, who committed many delinquencies, and for whom the maternal relationship seemed to be grossly disturbed. Partly because of their lack of meaningful relationships, these children proved very difficult to treat. Sometimes these children were found to have had prolonged separations from their mothers, and Bowlby speculated that this might prove to be a foremost determinant of the delinquency. Other investigators felt that his conclusion was overstated. It is very possible that the delinquency may result from imperfections of the superego and that the maternal deprivation is merely one of the antecedents. Most current work implicates the role of the absent father in a broken home to be of as great significance as the separation from the mother.[19]

Results of Maternal Employment

In the past it was postulated that maternal employment, which can be considered partial separation, led to emotional and cognitive deprivation of the child. Studies do not substantiate this conclusion. Instead evidence indicates that the working mother makes deliberate attempts to compensate for her working: Thus her mothering may be of better quality. A working mother, however, does have a recognizable effect on her family, and her role in the family does change. Working may have a more positive or more negative influence on the mother depending on the gratification she gains from the job. It is self-evident that supervision of the children by a working mother tends to be less adequate.[16]

In this connection, the effect of maternal employment on the infant and the very young child has been particularly suspect. The effects of day care and of multiple mothering[14] on the child obviously depend on the quality of the program provided, the length of time spent there, and how the mother reacts with the child when she is not working.

At times, children placed in the Israeli kibbutz system or in day care in Russia are compared to American children placed in day care in infancy. In both Russia and Israel mothers are encouraged to spend much time with their infants and nursing is encouraged for at least the first several months. Only somewhat later (in the kibbutz by age six months and in Russia by age one year) does the mother resume employment. Thus it would not be valid to compare these two groups when considering the effects of partial separation resulting from maternal employment in the United States.

Studies of children of working mothers in Great Britain attempted to determine the effects on the child who was left in infancy. The children displayed increased dependence on the parents coupled with signs of insecurity. The mothers were not attached to their children, possibly because of lack of contact with the child, but also perhaps because these mothers were different from the beginning, with strong motivations to escape from the children. Furthermore, adequate substitution was hard to find for the youngest children so that instability of their nurturing arrangements was very common. Such studies indicate that the results of the mother's employment depend to a large degree on the nature of the substitute nurturing and the stability of the child care arrangement provided.

Coping Mechanisms

Young children who are separated from their mothers are described at first as actively reaching out to other adults in search of a substitute mother. If this substitute is not available, they withdraw, and progressive ego deficits ensue. However, as all investigators have stated, not all children are so affected. Some, by virtue of strong constitutions,[31] or because of substitute nurturing, or because they are older with internalized ego strengths at the time of the loss, are able to continue with their development. Longitudinal studies show that in the future, even these children may be at risk, should the stress be severe enough.

The child who was not given a substitute nurturing person may withdraw, and subsequently refuse to be involved in a relationship. Because of his rage, and because he has not had appropriate models for identification, he lies, steals, and has little concern for others. Therapists describe these children as exceedingly hard to reach, and one may conjecture that, for them, withdrawal may have a defensive quality.

An interesting skill is developed by some few of the most able motherless children whose growth has not been seriously altered by the separation. Writing ability is developed apparently serving as a way to abreact, perhaps to recreate the mother in fantasy in order to please her with gifts, and as an attempt to master the hurt. Using psychoanalytic concepts William Saffady[25] presents a detailed analysis of Thomas More, who lost his mother early in childhood. More was preoccupied with death all his life. In his writings, as if to deny his mother's death, he never accepted the finality of death.

Research Issues

In the quarter of a century since Bowlby's hypotheses were published, a vast array of research has dealt with many facets of the subject of maternal deprivation. In addition, the controversies sparked by his conclusions have led to several excellent reviews supporting divergent views. Major points focused on have included: the effects of the age of the child at the time of the mother loss, the severity and duration of the motherlessness, the effects of other variables such as the presence or absence of the father, and various long-term results of the mother loss.

Brilliant studies by Harlow[13] on the relationship of the infant monkey to its mother demonstrated that the development of the infant is defective when the maternal relationship is lacking. Others have graphically presented the depression of the pigtail infant monkey who is separated from its mother. Although the depression of the baby monkey begins to lift gradually in about a week, even a month later the infant does not act normally. In contrast to this, another species of monkey, normally with closer relationships to other adults, does not reveal the depth of depression when the infant is separated from the mother and the other adults take over.[18, 17]

Imprinting, the phenomenon by which newly hatched birds attach themselves to their parent, has been ably described by Lorenz[20] and others. Recent work reveals that in many species there appears to be a physiological basis for the bonding of the mother to the infant as well as the infant to the mother. When interfered with, the mother rejects the child. The implications of such research on the development of the neonate are far-reaching. Speculation would indicate that in the first weeks of life, the infant develops bonding and attachment to the mother through the mother-child nurturing relationship.[9] Without such stimulation, and if the physical needs alone are met, these important relationships cannot develop to their potential. One can speculate there may be a critical period past which stimulation does not help and subsequent permanent crippling of development may result.[3] Should such be the case, the importance of primary prevention is paramount. By discovering those infants in newborn nurseries who are not responding well, by case finding in well-baby clinics and pediatrician's offices and identifying those infants who lack the bonding to their mothers, within the first weeks of life referral can be made for infant stimulation. Incidentally, the age-old argument of which comes first, the mother deficiency or the child's inability to react, would make no difference in the need for referral. The same mechanism for stimulation could pertain whether the block occurs because of metabolic or physiological deficits within the neonate, or because of depression or lack of experience on the part of the mother.

Implications for the Social System

Obviously the effects of mother loss for the infant and young child are devastating. The child suffers emotional deprivation that permeates his physical status and may even threaten his viability. Long-range effects of parental bereavement—although debated as to the specificity of the mother loss—may lead to inadequate personality development, interfere with cognitive development, predispose to delinquent reactions later in childhood, be a factor in the development of depression or other major psychiatric illness[22] in adulthood, and affect the adequacy of raising the next generation.

For the social structure, the results are far-reaching. The efforts of society need to be directed toward preventing the effects of maternal deprivation at all levels. Young girls and boys require education about nurturing and stimulating infants and young children. Mothers should be encouraged to remain with their young children when possible. Nurses of the newborn, pediatricians, and family-practice physicians need to watch for signs of infant emotional malnourishment. Day-care centers for children require careful programing and adequate staffing to provide individual attention and stimulation.

Mental health services for a marriage at risk could decrease the tension and discord even though the marriage may dissolve. Such centers can provide counseling to families recently bereaved, with one focus being substitute mothering for the children.[15] Subsidization of families to maintain their integrity and to provide substitute mothering could prevent the fragmentation which often occurs with mother loss.[10]

In the years since the 1930s and 1940s we have learned much about the quality of nurturing a child requires. The goal of society should be to implement that knowledge so that all children receive the necessary nurturing they must have for growth and development.

REFERENCES

1. AINSWORTH, M. D., "The Effects of Maternal Deprivation: A Review of Findings and Controversy in the Context of Research Strategy," in *Deprivation of Maternal Care: A Reassessment of its Effects, Public Health Papers No. 14*, pp. 95–165, Geneva, WHO, 1962.

2. BECK, A. T., SETHI, B. B., and TUTHILL, R. W., "Childhood Bereavement and Adult Depression," *Archives of General Psychiatry, 9*:129–136, 1963.

3. BESDINE, M., "Nurturing and Ego Development," *Psychoanalytic Review, 60(1)*:19–43, 1973.

4. BENDER, L., "Psychopathic Behavior Disorders in Children," in Lindner, R. M., Seliger, R. V. (Eds.), *Handbook of Correctional Psychology*, p. 360, Philosophical Library, New York, 1947.

5. BETTELHEIM, B., *The Children of the Dream*, Macmillan, London, 1969.

6. BOWLBY, J., *Maternal Care and Mental Health*, Monograph Series 2, Geneva, WHO, 1952.

7. ———, et al., "The Effects of Mother Child Separation: A Follow-up Study," *British Journal of Medical Psychology, 29*:211, 1956.

8. BROWN, F., "Depression and Childhood Bereavement," *Journal of Mental Science, 107*:754–777, 1961.

9. COATES, B., ANDERSON, E. P., and HARTUP, W. W., "Interrelations in the Attachment Behavior of Human Infants," *Developmental Psychology, 6(2)*:218–230, 1972.

10. GEORGE, V., and WILDING, P., *Motherless Families*, Routledge and Kegan Paul, London, 1973.

11. GOLDFARB, W., "Infant Rearing and Problem Behavior," *American Journal of Orthopsychiatry, 13*:249–251, 1943.

12. GREGORY, I., "Studies of Parental Deprivation in Psychiatric Patients," *American Journal of Psychiatry, 115*:438–442, 1958.

13. HARLOW, H. S., "Loves in Infant Monkeys," *Scientific American, 200*:68–74, 1959.

14. HEARST, M. C., "Group Day Care of Infants: A Review of Selected Studies," M.S.W. Thesis, *Smith College Studies in Social Work*, vol. 44, no. (1), pp. 46–47, 1973.

15. HILGARD, J. R., NEWMAN, M. F., and FISK, F., "Strength of Adult Ego Following Childhood Bereave-

ment," *American Journal of Orthopsychiatry, 30:*788–798, 1960.

16. HOFFMAN, L. W., "Effects of Maternal Employment on the Child—A Review of the Research," *Developmental Psychology, 10(2):*204–228, 1974.

17. KAUFMAN, I. C., and ROSENBAUM, L. A., "The Effects of Separation from Mother on the Emotional Behavior of Infant Monkeys," *Annals of the New York Academy of Science, 159:*681–695, 1969.

18. ———, "The Reaction to Separation in Infant Monkeys: Analytic Depression and Conservation-Withdrawal," *Psychosomatic Medicine, 29:*648–675, 1967.

19. KOLLER, K. M., "Parental Deprivation, Family Background and Female Delinquency," *British Journal of Psychiatry, 118:*319–327, 1971.

20. LORENZ, K., *Studies in Animal and Human Behavior*, Methuan and Co., London, 1970.

21. MEAD, M., "A Cultural Anthropologist's Approach to Maternal Deprivation," in *Deprivation of Maternal Care: A Reassessment of Its Effects, Public Health Papers* No. 14, pp. 45–62, Geneva: WHO, 1962.

22. PITTS, S. N., et al., "Adult Psychiatric Illness Assessed for Childhood Parental Loss, and Psychiatric Illness in Family Members," *American Journal of Psychiatry*, June Supplement, *121:*I–X, 1965.

23. ROBERTSON, J., "Young Children in Brief Separation: A Fresh Look," in Eissler, R. S., et al. (Eds.), *The*

Psychoanalytic Study of the Child, vol. 26, pp. 315–364, Yale University Press, New Haven, 1971.

24. RUTTER, M., "Parent-Child Separation: Psychological Effects on the Children," *Journal of Child Psychology and Psychiatry, 12:*233–260, 1971.

25. SAFFADY, W., "The Effects of Childhood Bereavement and Parental Remarriage in 16th-Century England: The Case of Thomas More," *History of Childhood Quarterly, 1(2):*310–336, 1973.

26. SELIGMAN, R., et al., Effect of Earlier Parental Loss in Adolescence," *Archives of General Psychiatry, 31:*475–479, 1974.

27. SOLNIT, A., "A Study of Object Loss in Infancy," in Eissler, R. S., et al. (Eds.), International Universities Press, *The Psychoanalytic Study of the Child*, vol. 25, pp. 267–313, New York, 1969.

28. SPITZ, R. A., *The First Year of Life*, International Universities Press, New York, 1965.

29. SPITZ, R. A., "Hospitalism: An Inquiry into the Genesis of Psychiatric Conditions in Early Childhood," in Eissler, R. S., et al. (Eds.), *The Psychoanalytic Study of the Child, International Universities Press*, vol. 1, pp. 53–74, New York, 1945.

30. United States Census Summary, 1970.

31. YARROW, L. J., "Maternal Deprivation: Towards an Empirical and Conceptual Reevaluation," *Psychological Bulletin, 58(6):*459–490, 1961.

40 / Children and Divorce

Israel M. Dizenhuz

Introduction

The process of divorce can be divided into three phases: (1) an initial phase of family stress, (2) a second phase dominated by the adversary legal process, and (3) a third phase of post-divorce restabilization.

In the phase of family stress, communication between parents fails, parental alliances begin to crumble, and adversary modes of communication come into play. Yet, despite their difficulties with one another, parents will often collude to "protect" their children as they attempt to conceal their differences. A nodal point in this phase is initial separation or initial filing for divorce, an event which is a public statement of failure in resolving family problems.

Because of the parents' inability to resolve family problems, society has provided a legal process which emphasizes adversary procedures. This process dominates the second phase. While this adversary legal process goes on, family members

experience uncertainty, ambivalence, alienation, loneliness, and changing personal alliances and emotional supports. In this phase the critical event is the act of divorce itself. For the fragmented family, this judicial action sets the pattern of life for the ensuing post-divorce phase.

The end point of the third phase of post-divorce restabilization is not clearly defined. Restabilization has occurred when there is clarity about the nature of the relationship existing among all members of the fragmented family. In the child's domiciliary family definitive family roles and responsibilities should be arrived at. Such vital matters as housekeeping, finances, individual vocational and academic goals, and consistency in patterns of communication within the family and with outside support systems need to be clarified. There should be a restoration of confidence that the social, emotional, and personal needs of family members will be recognized and met by the family. In this phase the child of divorce can come to feel certainty and predictability in relation to the two families which contain his parents. Even though the noncustodial parent may be intermittently present during visitation and vacations, most frequently he is experienced by these children as an absent parent.

What Is Different in the Experience of the Child of Divorce

The loss of a parent through divorce is different from other forms of parent loss. In divorce, the court divides the family resources, separates parents from one another, and determines matters such as child custody, parental visitation, financial support, and other matters the parents themselves may have difficulty deciding. Custody and child-care issues are common sources of conflict between parents. The children usually feel themselves brought into this conflict, often unwillingly. The older the child, the more likely he is to be involved directly in this legal process. In many jurisdictions, during the divorce proceedings, a child twelve years of age and older is expected to participate in the selection of a custodial parent; often the child's opinion is asked for directly by the judge of a family court, or inferred from the evaluation of court-related mental health professionals.

Frequently, the differences between the parents are not diminished by divorce. Following the court decision, parents must continue to communicate with one another about their children. This enables family dynamics to endure despite the divorce, and these dynamics often find expression in the arrangements imposed by the court. The "ghost" of the original family dynamics continues in the court-regulated activities regarding custody, financial support, visitation, etc. Even though allegiances to their new families develop, the psychological needs of both parents continue to play out the same themes.

Feelings in one spouse about the other, often communicated through the children, may continue with undiminished intensity rather than fade away. These feelings can be both positive and negative, including the wish to remarry and the wish to punish the absent parent.

As with other forms of parent loss, children experience distortion in their thinking about the loss of the parent. With death, the lost parent is often idealized. In divorce, the adversary nature of the legal process may contribute to a polarization of feelings with custodial and absent parent idealized and vilified.

Children of Divorce: Their Number

Divorce is a frequent outcome of marriage. In 1972[1] the divorce rate in the United States was 4.0 per 1,000 population. In the ten years between 1962 and 1972 the rate of divorce increased 81 percent in the United States while the marriage rate rose only 27 percent. Three of four divorces occur in marriages with children, frequently while the children are young. One in six children in this country will have experienced the divorce of their parents. This trend has continued; currently divorce is rising in all areas of the country and in all social classes.

Statistics about divorce do not include those families stressed by discord where a parent may file for divorce and withdraw the petition before completion of the process. It is estimated that including these families would double the number of children affected.

Impact of Divorce at Different Levels of Development

In their study of normal preschool children in families of divorce, Wallerstein and Kelly[3] found that in the youngest age group (age two and a half to three and a quarter years), family disruption triggered regression, bewilderment, and neediness. Responses in these children were similar to those seen with the loss of a caretaking parent. Disturbance was strongest where parental discord continued post-divorce. Adaptation to divorce was positively related to consistent loving caretaking. The most enduring symptom was that of a pervasive neediness.

In their middle preschool group (three and three-quarter to four and three-quarter years), in addition to the regression, there was an increase in aggressive behavior coupled with a fear of aggression. In this age group, their view of the dependability and predictability of relationships was threatened and their sense of order regarding the world disrupted. Their play expressed self-blame and reduced self-esteem. Here, vulnerability to impairment in psychological development was greater than in the younger age group. In terms of pathology, these children displayed increased inhibition, constriction in play and in fantasy, diminished self-esteem, and continuing sadness and neediness.

The oldest preschool child (five to six years of age) showed a reaction common to all children which included anxiety, irritability, aggression, and separation problems. In this oldest preschool group it became possible for some children to experience family turbulence and divorce without breaking developmental stride. These children seemed able to find gratifications outside of the home and to place distance between themselves and their parents. With some children in this group, the divorce was followed by a developmental surge. On the other hand, vulnerable children in this group had particular difficulty in resolving oedipal conflicts. They found it difficult to communicate their feelings, and used denial and reversal of affect. Often they were depressed. Visitation with the absent parent tended to stimulate peaks of excitement. Because of their overuse of denial through prolonged oedipal fantasy and a turning away from reality tasks, girls were more vulnerable to poor outcome.

Again, in latency-age children,[2] there were few mechanisms available to help the seven- and eight-year-old child alleviate the pain of family stress. These children were depressed, immobilized by their suffering, and vulnerable to regression. A strong sense of loss was felt by younger boys in particular in regard to an absent father. Latency boys sometimes used anger as protection against regressive oedipal fantasies, particularly if they were the eldest sibling or only child.

In their post-divorce sample, Wallerstein and Kelly[3] found about half of their normal preschool children and one-quarter of the latency-age group to be significantly worsened psychologically at one year follow-up.

The frequent conscious response of adolescents to the process of divorce is to distance themselves; they withdraw from both the parents and the legal process. Currently, there is increasing interest in respecting the rights of the adolescent; the court may therefore assign him his own attorney, and attach considerable significance to his wishes in designating a custodial parent.

Often the legal process makes it difficult for the adolescent to feel allied with one parent without being disloyal to the other. This increases the problem of working through the psychological ties to both parents in preparation for adulthood, and this developmental task becomes correspondingly more difficult.

For some adolescents and young adults, the divorce of their parents means that now they must challenge all aspects of their remembered family life. Years later, they may be confronted with difficulties in their own marriages; at this point, the doubts raised by the divorce of their parents may cause them to doubt the authenticity of their own good experiences as a child growing up in their family of origin. Divorce is more common in people whose parents themselves experienced divorce.

At all levels of development, parents find it hard to talk to their offspring either about their own feelings or about the child's feelings concerning divorce. With the parents inarticulate, hesitant, and uncertain about their feelings, and with the children lacking any clear awareness of their own feelings, much remains unsaid. When feelings cannot be talked about, however, fantasies proliferate, especially among children and adolescents.

Family and Cultural Reactions
to Divorce

In western culture, the social supports provided to marriage by religion, medicine, state economic policy, and the extended family have been institutionalized, but divorce has not been so favored. Although diminishing, there is still social stigma and economic penalty attached to divorce and to the one-parent family. Yet, in making divorce available as a social remedy to an unsatisfactory marriage, even the adversary legal process is a cultural advance. In many jurisdictions, new forms of family deformation such as dissolution of marriage by mutual agreement through the state are being devised.

Additionally, as children attain legal representation in some courts, the negative impact on them of the adversary process is being softened.

Stresses occur in the deformation of families and in the reconstitution of new family groups. A child may be uncertain about how he can love two people who hate each other, and how to communicate with one parent about this without being disloyal to the other. In the process of family change children may be uncertain about who to call mother and father, how to address stepmother and stepfather, and how to deal with new relationships in reconstituted families. Their friends may be uncertain as to who to identify as the correct parents. At best, these children feel different; and the feeling is accentuated if parents have difficulty talking about their feelings regarding these family changes. As a result, children often hide the fact of divorce in their lives, or at least fail to volunteer it.

Divorce presents a public failure of family life. To a parent, any change recognized or arranged by a court may be experienced as a judgment on their parenting. The feelings generated in parents by the adversary proceedings may make it difficult for a man or woman to take into account the changing needs of a growing child in considering changes in custody, visitation, vacations, support, etc. This may be true even though a given change may be in the child's best interest.

Characteristic Forms of Emotional Disturbance

There is no known uniform pattern of emotional disturbance attributable to the process of divorce. During the phase of family stress, the period preceding the initial separation or filing for divorce, the associated emotional disturbances have not been well studied. The general responses the children make to this stress are influenced by their developmental phase, the patterns of communication with parents, and the support systems available to them outside of the family.

Some study has been devoted to children in the next phase of the adversary legal process, but much more is needed. And even less is known about characteristic forms of emotional disturbance in the phase of post-divorce restabilization.

Because of the continuing contact with both parents, divorce should be studied as a process extended in time rather than as a single event. The more general state of parent loss has been given more careful scrutiny.

For the child, parent absence bears with it long-range consequences. Loss of the father in the first five years of life is a frequent consequence of divorce. The impact of such father absence on boys leads to later difficulties with assertiveness, aggressive behavior, and other behaviors linked to masculine identity. It is also linked to the later movement of boys toward delinquency.

In responding to the emotional disturbances in their children, parents going through a divorce may be seriously handicapped. They are likely to be less sensitive to the needs of their children, and they will have obvious difficulty communicating with the other parent around matters of treatment planning for the child. A working parental alliance is required for effective treatment intervention; this is not easily obtained during any phase of divorce.

Common Coping Behaviors

In the initial phase of family stress, children cope by using suppression or minimization of those interactional cues which point to marital disharmony. This is usually reinforced by the parents, who are at once fearful that these disharmonies will harm their children, yet are unable to talk with them about these differences. When the continuing confrontation between parents can no longer be dealt with in this way, children often assume the role of peacemaker. The youngsters hope that if they can keep the peace, reduce parental discord, avoid confrontation and effect reconciliation, parental harmony can be restored. Fantasies of responsibility for parental confrontations may be stimulated on the part of children as they attempt to gain mastery of the parental discord. As a consequence of this role, following separation and divorce the children may be used as the bearers of communications between parents. Such children may continue to act out their role of peacemaker for a long time. They dream of reducing the deterioration in their family's relationships, and develop fantasies of parental reconciliation and reunion. Despite realities such as the remarriage of one or both parents, these fantasies of reunion may endure, often for many years.

In the phases of the adversary legal process and post-divorce restabilization, children may polarize their feelings about the parents, with one parent idealized and the other vilified. Forms of identification with the absent parent may occur; these may often be seen more readily in a child of the same sex as the absent parent. These identifications may be either negative or positive. Either one may be effective in keeping alive affects about the absent parent in the family. Such identifications may be reinforced by the entire family; thus a family pattern of hostility, isolation, and rejection of the absent parent can serve as a way of continuing the original family dynamics.

What Is Needed to Respond
to the Stress of Divorce

As the family experiences the stresses of deformation, a child needs the love of both parents, and a sense of their continuity in his care and development. Above all, he must feel their wish to participate in this despite their changing roles. At the same time, he must come to terms with the differences between mother and father, and strive to retain a sense of belonging in both families, and in both worlds. He needs to know that it is possible to be cared for, to be parented, both by the custodial and the absent parent. He needs the opportunity for continued appropriate learning of positive role models from each.

In the course of divorce. the adversary process fosters feelings which make all this very difficult. Parents need separation counseling in order to find ways of reducing the impact of the adversary relationship on their parenting function. New social inventions, such as mandated court counseling prior to divorce, new legal forms, such as dissolution of marriage rather than divorce, and new social forms supporting children of divorce and their families will help with this.

Child psychiatrists and mental health professionals need to learn more about the process of divorce and understand the decision-making process related to custody, visitation, financial support, and the impact of society's values on families. From his special vantage point, a child psychiatrist can contribute to the new social inventions required to meet the emotional and developmental needs of children and parents experiencing these stresses in their families.[4]

REFERENCES

1. Bureau of the Census, Statistical Abstract of the U.S., 1972, Washington, D.C., U.S. Department of Commerce, 1973.

2. KELLY, J. B., WALLERSTEIN, J. S., "The Effects of Parental Divorce, Experiences of the Child in Early Latency," *American Journal of Orthopsychiatry, 46(1):20–32*, 1976.

3. WALLERSTEIN, J. S., and KELLY, J. B., "The Effects of Parental Divorce Experiences of the Pre-School Child," *Journal of Child Psychiatry, 14(4):600–616*, 1975.

4. WESTMAN, J. C., et al., "Role of Child Psychiatry in Divorce," *Archives of General Psychiatry, 23:416–420*, 1970.

---

41 / The Child of a Famous Father or Mother

Michael H. Stone

The annals of psychiatry are replete with articles outlining the impact upon children of poverty, deprivation, neglect, and other untoward factors in early life. Much less thought has been given to problems arising out of special endownment and privilege. The hoped-for advantages in life may be classified in a relatively few categories. Of these, the most important are: wealth, fame, beauty, talent, aristocratic lineage, and high intelligence. This chapter will deal with fame; specifically, with the paradoxical disadvantages for certain children that stem from having famous parents. Since fame is often an outgrowth of talent, lineage, etc., and in many instances is accompanied (sooner or later) by wealth, more than one special "advantage" is regularly present in the households of the famous. Elsewhere the author has discussed the impact of parental wealth upon children.[5, 6] By its very definition, fame implies being known publicly, whereas wealth as such does not. Here, attention will be restricted solely to the psychological consequences of having one or both parents in the public eye for some outstanding achievement or attribute.

Generally speaking, there are no special external characteristics that would serve to identify such children. They are in fact few in number, and constitute a tiny minority of all children; they comprise that group whose parents are celebrities of the entertainment industry, prominent politicians, well-known authors, scientists, musicians, artists, and the like. Though obvious exceptions exist, the bulk of these families will be found in the large metropolitan centers.

Ordinarily, parental fame does not exert much influence upon a child until the latter is old enough to go to school. An exception would be the situation where the famous parent travels widely and often, accompanied by the family: Here the children may experience frequent disruptions in their contacts with adults and other children. A parallel situation arises when parental fame is related to high political or military office. This can necessitate frequent prolonged absences from the home throughout the child's formative years. In these instances, emotional difficulties may arise, not as a consequence of fame per se, but because of the modifications in life style that sometimes accompany it.

Once school age is reached, especially during the latency years (seven to eleven), there is a rapid expansion of the child's grasp of his community and of the world itself. As the child begins to make comparisons between the celebrity of *his* parent(s) and the relative obscurity of his classmates' parents, the full meaning of a parent's fame comes to be understood. The child will soon develop a sense of being special, different, and, in certain respects, better than his playmates. Various privileges and deferential behavior are conferred upon the child, often as part of an attempt to curry favor with his famous parent. How this becomes integrated into the growing sense of self will be discussed in the following pages.

Apart from a few unusual situations, reactions of the famous parent to his own children are not especially noteworthy. One of these exceptional configurations comes about in the rare instance where a child's burgeoning talent poses a threat to a famous but also highly competitive parent. A gifted but less neurotic parent may of course welcome a child's talent, even in the same field (especially in the case of music or acting), and allow the child to take advantage of the parent's position and contacts. Respect for confidentiality does not permit mention of recent examples that come to mind (a special problem in writing about the famous), but one can mention the historical example provided by Giovanni Cellini, a celebrated craftsman in his own day, and his eventually more famous son, Benvenuto.[4] Mozart's development, too, was fostered by a musician/composer father.

A famous person may have a child who is delinquent or who otherwise attracts public criticism; owing to the dependency of the parent upon a "good image," this poses special problems for such a family. The author has encountered two instances of a delinquent son being precipitously disowned by a famous father who felt his reputation in jeopardy because of his son's activities. When the media suddenly provides thousands of onlookers a glimpse into some family matter, there may be unusual difficulty in resolving it in a mature and effective manner.

Much more noticeable are the *cultural* reactions to a child with a famous parent. These will be particularly apparent when the child enters school. Usually the child will be the subject of envy by the teacher and classmates alike. This will tend to interfere with the teacher's objectivity, and may lead to attitudes that are either too lenient or too judgmental. Classmates may feel ill at ease in the presence of this "special" child, with whom it may then be difficult to form ordinary friendships. The child will wonder—and will not be sure—whether he is being accepted for himself, or on behalf of the famous parent. The parent becomes the "substance" of the child's shadow. Whereas great musicians and performers tend to be admired universally, other famous people—especially politicians—may be controversial figures. In the latter circumstance, the child may become the target of derision (namely, by playmates whose parents' politics are different). Regardless of his own qualities, the child will then become unduly vulnerable to rejection. Again, the parents may become involved in a scandal or a bitter and publicized divorce. In the very earliest years of school, children of a famous parent learn that they can cut corners and take liberties not permitted ordinary youngsters. Conversely, at times their performance will be judged in comparison with the parent's achievements, with this image constantly held in front of the child as something to live up to.

Offsetting some of these negative factors are the counterbalancing forces of affluence and social contacts, as well as the greater power of the famous to insulate their families against many adverse influences. As a result, it is by no means clear that children of famous parents are more at risk for developing emotional disturbances than are children in general. What is clear is this: When emotional problems arise, (1) they are invariably colored by the heightened tension between public image and private self, and (2) they require special sensitivities in handling.

Earlier, mention was made of frequent travel

and repeated absences as occasional byproducts of parental fame. If pronounced enough, such factors will have a deleterious influence on any child; if less pronounced, problems may arise only in constitutionally vulnerable children. Either factor may contribute to instability or shallowness of object relations. Prolonged absences of the father may foster the development of antisocial personality features, especially if the famous parent is himself unscrupulous, and abuses the privileges of his position.

Emotional problems related *directly* to the fame of a parent almost always arise from conflicts between aspects of the self-image: the "private" self versus the "public" self. Children of the famous begin to develop a public self-image in school. This will be an amalgam of part-images of themselves in relation to other children, and of part-images of themselves as sons or daughters of a publicly known adult. Acquaintances and strangers will have already formed a mental image of this famous adult, sometimes based upon information inaccessible to the child, more often based on rumor or highly distorted and one-sided sketches in the media. These influences accelerate and intensify the process by which children develop a sense of who they are and who their parents are. Disturbances are therefore prone to occur in the narcissistic aspect of normal development, i.e., that aspect of development relating to the formation of identity.

If disturbances in identity formation are great enough, they may give rise to rather typical personality aberrations. These are often included under the label narcissistic character disorder (if severe) or narcissistic personality (if less severe). Kernberg[2] has described in detail the features of these character deformations, which may include an inflated sense of the self, manipulativeness, shallowness in relations with others, an exaggerated need for admiration, and a heightened sensitivity to criticism. It would appear that in famous people generally, pathological forms of narcissism tend to be overrepresented. Their children are even more prone to character disturbances of this sort, if only because their accomplishments are usually meager in comparison with those of the parent. The parent's image has inevitably become assimilated into the child's own self-image, and conflict ensues. Perhaps every child aspires to greatness, but where greatness already resides in the family, this aspiration is all the more tantalizing. A child of meager endowment born to (or adopted into) such a family will often feel crushed

by the difference between his capacities and those of the parent(s).

It is a rare parent whose actual behavior toward his children measures up to his professed image of parenthood. These and other discrepancies between the "advertisement" and the "package" are readily grasped by the child, usually during the latency and prepubertal stages. This process proceeds by small increments of awareness over an extended period. Ordinarily, it is accompanied only by transitory discomfort, especially if the parents are neither grandiose nor hypercritical. A child may have major problems, however, in integrating conflicting perceptions of a famous parent. For example, in the media, the parent may have a widespread reputation for compassion and wisdom—but at home, the child knows he is hypercritical and aloof. This may lead to early profound disillusionment with the publicly lionized but privately despised parent. All adults may become suspect. Some children will erect almost insuperable barriers against the recognition of decency and genuineness even in the most wholesome people. The opposite but equally damaging situation is also encountered: A still idealized parent, whose fame is highly tainted (as a politician or screenstar with an unsavory reputation), may be torn down before the child's eyes by means of "bad press" in the media, or vicious gossip at school. Either way the child may feel shattered; the result is a cynicism that can be lasting, and that impairs all future relationships.

During late adolescence, crystalization of identity ordinarily takes place and, with it, the final definition of career choice. In children of the famous, this step is often beset by a number of impediments. The less well-adjusted may feel hopeless about measuring up to a parent whose fame rests realistically on extraordinary skills. So much energy may nevertheless have been invested along the way in competing with the unbeatable parent that other capabilities which the child truly posesses are neglected. The end result may be an embittered individual with few marketable skills, capable at best of basking in the glory of his parent's fame. This outcome seems to be endemic among the children of great statesmen. In Bach's family there were both examples and exceptions.[4] The exception was the youngest son, Johann Christoph. For a while, he enjoyed more fame than his father, and always had a cheerful disposition. The example: Wilhelm Friedemann, who, after some temporary success as a young adult, eventually plagiarized his father's works, was ostracized, and became alcoholic. In some instances, the task of disidentifying with the famous parent is relinquished altogether in favor of a vicarious life devoted to writing the memoirs of the parent.

Inevitably, the vignettes available to the mental health professional will emphasize the negative aspects of having a famous parent; as a psychiatrist, one's experience in this area is necessarily skewed. A first-hand account of life in the home of a famous couple, written from the child's point of view, has recently become available in the form of a book by Brooke Hayward,[1] daughter of Margaret Sullavan and Leland Hayward. In this poignant and compassionate memoir, the reader will be able to grasp more fully a number of points touched on here. The envy of their schoolmates, to cite one instance, led to the parents' removing their three children to private tutoring at home. All three then grew up in a curious kind of splendid isolation. All three children were severely affected by the divorce of a supposedly "ideal" couple, the divorce occurring when the author was about ten. Miss Hayward also depicts vividly the effects of living under the glare of publicity, and the various maneuvers, not always successful, used by the family to retain some shreds of privacy. The reader is also afforded a glimpse of the topsy-turvy world inhabited by some children of the famous, where fantasy and reality somehow become reversed. Most children fantasize a good deal about life as a Hollywood star, about dining with the great and near-great, about being whisked from one elegant party to another in chauffeured limousines, and the like. For Brooke Hayward, these were the elements of reality as she knew it. If, however, "reality" meant people who had to struggle for their livelihood, people who stood in line to gawk at movie stars coming out of splendid restaurants, people who were not pretty, whose surroundings were often bleak, and who had to do things for themselves—these were the elements of her fantasies. She had almost no contact with this "real" world, and could only guess at its true proportions; this persisted until her own world collapsed at the time of her adolescence.

In general, children of the famous appear to elaborate grandiose fantasies of a very intense nature, the more so if adverse circumstances and serious emotional difficulties interfere with the fulfillment of even a portion of these fantasies. The more fortunate of these children can have their "wildest dreams" gratified all too easily; as a result, unless their parents make special efforts not to spoil them, they may evolve a narcissistic character structure. This occurs as a response to overgratification rather than as a defense against early injury to the sense of self. However, grandiose fantasies are encountered in the latter situation as well. These are exemplified by the "secret life" of one young patient with whom the author worked (his father was a famous artist): He constantly imagined himself Julius Caesar or Napoleon. As he put it: ". . . those were the two strong forces in my life. In order to tolerate all the crap my folks threw at me—and at each other—I had to imagine I was some hero. . . . Like, I never had the kind of power Dad had, myself . . . so I had to get it from somewhere else; I had to get it from these fantasies." In late adolescence this patient had had a schizophrenic break in which he imagined himself to be Picasso, an artist of even greater acclaim than his father.

There are, of course, many advantages to having a famous parent. Among them are certain skills and an enhanced capacity for effective sublimatory channeling that may be fostered in the early home environment. Even in the absence of special musical, artistic, or intellectual gifts, children from this background ordinarily develop excellent social skills and (oftentimes) a pleasing outward personality. This stems from constant and early exposure to persons of unusual social effectiveness: great "personalities," great "charmers," and the like, who will be among the people within the parents' circle of friends and acquaintances.

Similarly, children from these homes may develop an unusual ability to maintain a "public," as well as a private, face. This is a response to the necessity of living in the public eye. Under ideal circumstances, poise and diplomatic finesse may be acquired to a degree that will equip the child for the kind of career where these qualities are necessary. In this respect, merely growing up around a famous parent give the child a "head start."

With respect to defense patterns, children of the famous are probably not distinguishable from other children, except along the lines already outlined in regard to (1) the narcissistic path of development, and (2) the acquisition of a social façade. However, it needs to be emphasized how vulnerable these children may be to a drastic lowering of self-esteem. This is especially likely to occur when the disparity between their potential (as they and others esitmate it) and the actual accomplishments of the parent seems unbridgeable. In succeeding generations there may even be a regression toward the mean, where talent is concerned, as there apparently is in intelligence.[7] (According to this view, famous parents would have very few children who became famous in their own right. If this were so, it would imply that most children with a famous parent would have to grapple with the reality of being less gifted than the parent.) While working in an inpatient setting, the author became acquainted with several young schizophrenic men. The presence of a famous father served only to intensify the sense of worthlessness and despair. Despite high intelligence, each was so hampered by his illness that he could not have handled any kind of demanding, let alone interesting, work. Many schizophrenic patients ultimately adjust tolerably well to "menial" employment, realizing in the end that this is far superior to no employment. But these young men found this adjustment too humiliating. Two were suicides; one is still languishing in an institution. It is the author's impression that all three could have made some prideful, if modest, adjustment, were it not for their constantly comparing themselves to a father of extraordinary accomplishments.

Unusual competencies do occur in children of the famous. Besides the social skills spoken of earlier, they may also include the acquisition of whatever occupational skill the parent possesses in abundance. If the famous parent is also a patient and gifted teacher, inborn talent in a child may become "licked into shape" at an early age. This can lead to a parent-child team, or even a whole family of celebrated individuals. A number of famous father-son combinations in painting and violin playing come readily to mind, as do several mother-daughter actress pairs. There are many circus families famous for some special stunt where the young have been carefully prepared by parents and even grandparents. In the more distant past one may mention the Cremonese violin-building families (the Stradivarii, the Guarnerii, the Amati), the ballet families (Antoine and Auguste Bournonville, Gaetano and Auguste Vestris, Filippo and Marie Taglioni), the acting families (the O'Neills, the Barrymores), families in science and belles-lettres (the Huxleys, the Freuds), as well as America's own illustrious Adams' family in public affairs.

There is a special advantage enjoyed by many children of the famous, which is not due to "competence." It consists of the opportunity to select a mate from an unusually large group of desirable individuals—eager to date or to marry someone from a prestigious family. There is of course no guarantee this advantage will always be used wisely.

Special Treatment Methods

Having sketched some of the problems to which these children are prone, as well as some unusual assets they may possess, attention should now turn to the special treatment methods and social structures that may be required if their differences are to be handled in the most effective way.

If, for example, a child is having school problems because of envious schoolmates, or because mediocre schoolwork is provoking severe impairment in self-esteem (through comparison with the famous parent), a special school may be necessary. The child may regain his composure only if placed in a school far away—where the parent is perhaps less well-known—so that the child has a better chance of feeling like, and becoming, a separate individual. Enrollment in a school where the student body is made up largely of other specially advantaged children may be helpful in minimizing the likelihood of intolerable envy or gossip. These alternatives may be suitable for the sensitive, shy child. For a child in whom one can see the sprouting of a narcissistic character, on the other hand, it may be necessary to go to great lengths to treat the child just like everyone else. Such a child might ultimately be better off in a conventional school, where every effort is made *not* to treat him as "special." In an "ordinary" school, a child who is not yet narcissistic may become so, in part because of the envy of his classmates. But if a child is (for whatever reason) *already* narcissistic, he may be induced to relinquish some of his narcissistic traits, under pressure from peers who come from more conventional backgrounds.

When psychotherapy is indicated because of emotional or behavioral problems, one should be aware of special needs in the children, and of certain recurring attitudes in the parents, that may impede progress. In this respect children of the famous constitute one variety of "VIP," other species of which include the wealthy, the socially prominent, and—relatives of physicians (especially, other psychiatrists). A number of suggestions for improved ways of dealing with patients in these categories are to be found in the articles of Main,[3] Weintraub,[8] and Stone.[5]

Antisocial tendencies in such children are particularly difficult to treat. The famous are at once used to getting their own way and highly sensitive to adverse publicity. They may wish to bury certain problems rather than confront them head-on, preferring a sick child and no scandal to a better integrated child and a damaged career. On several occasions the author has felt compelled to recommend a chronic-care institution with no frills to a famous parent whose hospitalized child was manipulating the treating staff outrageously—to his own detriment. But the parent could not countenance the idea of his child being treated in an environment that was not plush, and took matters into his own hands (to the child's greater detriment). In two instances, if a delinquent adolescent were ever to get better, the author has urged jail rather than the hospital. In view of the terrible consequences the family imagines it will suffer, this kind of recommendation requires considerable salesmanship. In one case, the advice was taken—with a good result; the other family declined, and their son continued his antisocial ways.

There are always some famous families with a disturbed child, where the parents refuse to permit anyone not on their level to be involved in the treatment. Even when other therapists are more readily available who would do a better job, they may insist that therapy be carried out by the director of a hospital, by the author of some psychiatric text, or by some other prestigious clinician. If the child is to receive any help at all, at times one may need to go along with demands of this kind. In other cases, it may actually be quite functional for a prestigious therapist to treat the child. These are cases where a less prestigious therapist might be too awed by the family to handle the child objectively. If a famous parent attempts to interfere with treatment, indicating he knows the therapist's job as well as his own, a psychiatrist of great reputation may be able to save the day, saying, "Look: you're well known; I'm well known. Now let's forget about fame, and get down to business!" A skilled therapist without this extra "clout" might have a much harder time cutting through these sorts of resistances. Here one is also touching on a potential countertransference problem in the therapist. If a therapist really does feel excessively awed by a famous parent, he should have the humility to refer the child on to someone more comfortable with the situation. It need hardly be said that extraordinary care must be taken in guarding against the temptation to speak of having treated some famous person's child—either to friends or to colleagues. The rules of confidentiality which are designed to safeguard all patients go double for the famous. Realistically, they are in a much more vulnerable position to be hurt by what could be revealed. Admittedly it may be a feather in one's cap to treat the famous, but it should be a feather worn on the *inside*.

REFERENCES

1. HAYWARD, BROOKE, *Haywire*, Knopf, New York, 1977.

2. KERNBERG, O. F., *Borderline Conditions and Pathological Narcissism*, Aronson, New York, 1975.

3. MAIN, T. F., "The Ailment," *British Journal of Medical Psychology, 30*:129–145, 1957.

4. STONE, M. H., "Middle-class Childhood Between 1500 and 1800," *Journal of the American Academy of Psychoanalysis, 4*:545–574, 1976.

5. ———, "Treating the Wealthy and Their Children," *International Journal of Child Psychotherapy, 1*:15–46, 1972.

6. ———, and KESTENBAUM, C. J., "Maternal Deprivation in the Children of the Wealthy," *History of Childhood Quarterly, 2*:79–106, 1974.

7. WALLER, J. H., "Achievement and Social Mobility: Relationships Among IQ Score, Education and Occupation in Two Generations," *Social Biology, 18*:252–259, 1971.

8. WEINTRAUB, W., "The 'V.I.P.' Syndrome: A Clinical Study in Hospital Psychiatry," *Journal of Nervous and Mental Disease, 138*:181–193, 1964.

42 / The Only Child

Fedor Hagenauer and Helen Tucker

Nature of the Characteristics of the Only Child

The influence of family constellation, birth order, and lack of siblings on child development has attracted considerable interest and produced a voluminous literature. It has also brought out numerous findings and opinions, some consistent, and many equivocal. The basic postulate has been that birth order or lack of siblings may produce certain types of experiences. These, in turn, mold character formation along specific lines and result in typical pathologic tendencies and vulnerabilities. A family situation of particular interest is that with only one child. It seems likely that this would have special impact on the child's development.

Most of the early literature regarded the state of being an only child as a decided disadvantage. Consider the oft quoted statement of G. Stanley Hall that being an only child is a disease in itself.[12] Of course, all firstborns have been "only children" for various lengths of time, but this is usually short-lived, and siblings presently followed.

Later literature continues in part along the same lines; only children are said repeatedly to manifest a (statistically significant) greater incidence of neurotic and psychotic disturbances.[9] However, another body of opinion holds that only children achieve greater prominence in the arts and academic fields; they are more often represented in *Who's Who* than are children of other ordinal positions.

A good illustration of the complexity of the problem is the comprehensive review of literature by Clark and Capparell.[6] They demonstrate how the findings of different authors represent only children as doing better, the same, or worse than other children along a number of dimensions.

There are, however, a number of specific variables which do affect the only child's development. They are as follows.

Familial and Cultural Reactions to the Only Child

Within the life cycle, parenthood is one of the crucial developmental phases. The birth of the first child is the critical event which establishes this status.[11]

In Erikson's psychosocial schema, the concern about establishing and guiding the next generation gives rise to the polarity of generativity versus stagnation.[7]

Certainly, just having children does not make a parent; despite producing children, there are some people who manifest a genuine retardation in respect to this phase. One of the determinants of this state of affairs is the often intense ambivalence attached to being a parent, an emotional set directed particularly toward a child of the same sex.[11] There are many historical examples of this conflict; cf. "For I will pass through the land of Egypt this night and will smite all the first born in the land of Egypt." [Genesis 27:22] Oedipus, too, was the first and the only child of his parents.

PARENTAL REACTIONS

Several important parental factors exert a powerful influence on the development of an only child. To some degree these also apply to firstborns. To enumerate: (1) the inexperience of the parents, (2) their greater inconsistency and restrictiveness, (3) greater parental ambivalence toward the child who has brought about the parenthood, (4) heightened narcissistic investment, (5) more intense parent-child interaction, and (6) the magnified effects of parental pathology on the child.[10]

It has been said that the first child brings up the parents. Because of her inexperience, the new mother's anxiety results in vacillation between overgratification and too little gratification. The parents tend to rely more on outside advice, and the frequently conflicting counsel they receive increase their puzzlement and helplessness. They may have unrealistic expectations of the child's maturational level. For instance, they frequently expect verbal precocity while at the same time continuing to infantilize the child in the area of self-help.

Physical illness can be a source of considerable anxiety and overprotectiveness; for the child, this can result in his becoming more than usually sensitive to physical ailments. He may presently develop a tendency to allow illness to interfere with his daily activities.[2]

In general, parents of first (and therefore also of only) children set less consistent limits, are more restrictive of overt behavior, and expect greater conformity to adult standards.[13] They are less patient, more easily irritated, and quicker to resort to physical punishment. On the other hand, such parents also tend to be overprotective, and everything that happens to the only child is, of necessity, magnified.

The first child brings with him the condition of parenthood and creates intense ambivalent feelings. The parents identify with him positively and, through him, they achieve a sense of immortality. However, undercurrents of hostility and resentment are also present. There is a loss of their former freedom, and they see themselves at the beginning of years of increasing responsibility for raising a child.[11] This resentment is often acted out in the form of the parents' returning quickly to their extrafamilial activities.

Due to their intense narcissistic investment, the only child's parents are considerably more sensitive to their offspring's successes or failures. Their image of themselves as good or bad parents rests solely and without reprieve on this one child. They may turn to him to achieve all of their frustrated ambitions; at times this leads them to expect the child to fill a variety of roles which are often in conflict one with the other. If the success is forthcoming, the rewards are considerable; but if not, then the parents' sense of failure and inadequacy may be intense. This is likely to be communicated to the child in concentrated form. There are no other children to whom they can turn for soothing the narcissistic defeat. Adler described how the only child is exposed to all the educational assaults of the environment in undiluted form.[1] He is rarely treated in the leisurely, relaxed way typical of more experienced parents. The reason why a family has only one child is certainly very significant,

but very little is known about this area beyond the usual responses connected with economic pressures, and, more recently, with problems of overpopulation.

Another significant factor in parents' reactions to their only child may be their feelings about having had no more children. These emotions may range from the satisfaction of making this deliberate choice, to a deep sense of inadequacy over subsequent failure to procreate. In any case these reactions are highly individual and depend on the parents' own unique personality constellation.

CULTURAL REACTIONS

In all known cultures the problems of parenthood and of the firstborn have been of the utmost importance. No matter what happens thereafter, the first parentage marks an irreversible transition. In most cultures parenthood is desired and required; this comes about for a variety of reasons —legal, social, as status symbol, and as proof of male potency and/or female fecundity.[11]

Many anthropologists have described in detail the complex and various rituals, customs, and taboos designed to institutionalize this critical event, define it, and make it smoother. Mortality and decline on the one side and immortality on the other (one lives in one's children), issues of power, possessions, and inheritance, the conflict of generations and many other conflicts are involved in becoming a parent. The first child was called "the opener of the womb." [Exodus, 13:12]

In terms of getting more emotional and material supplies, the only child has definite advantages. He, therefore, stirs up considerable envy and fascination in other, nonsingle, children. This could in part explain the defensive prejudice of seeing the only child as always "spoiled and selfish."

Impact of the Difference at Different Levels of Development

Inevitably, these are environmental factors which impinge upon the only child at each successive level of development. Along with these, his own uniqueness colors his manner of approach to each new developmental task as well as the final resolution he achieves. He retains an exclusive relationship with his original love objects, which allows him to feel generally more secure in their affection and solicitude than would other first-borns, and he early develops a strong sense of his self-importance.[10] Conversely, any disruption of this relationship evokes a deeper sense of isolation and rejection in the child. To varying degrees, this important general factor is operative during each successive phase of development; ultimately it affects the structure of the adult personality.

INFANCY

The new mother's heightened anxiety creates tension in the firstborn; it predisposes him to more frequent and intense subjective anxiety in the face of subsequent stress. However, her solicitude and the greater time she devotes to the baby lead to more prompt relief of physical distress. She is more inclined to answer his first cry, and to hold, comfort, and play with him. In this sense, his dependency needs are usually well gratified, and a future expectation of this sort of caretaking is set up. It will remain with the only child throughout his life. Thus, whenever he is faced with anxiety-provoking situations he is likely to seek the security and comfort of others.[17] His parents' solicitude in times of physical illness and their attempts to comfort him are likely to beget in the only child a characteristic oversensitivity to his own physical symptoms. This usually develops early in life. Later on, such a tendency may add a mildly hypochondriacal quality to his personality. In this respect, his experience is closer to that of the last child (which, of course, he is), than it is to other firstborns.

SEPARATION-INDIVIDUATION

There is little in the literature to suggest that the development of symbiosis or its resolution in the second and third years is necessarily any more distorted in the only child than in children with siblings. If great enough in degree, the mother's overinvolvement may deprive him of gradual, well-timed separation experiences. At times this can lead to intense separation anxiety, a reluctance to attempt new ventures, and the persistent feeling of being a child among adults.[10]

OEDIPAL PHASE

The only child is most vulnerable to disturbances which occur during the oedipal phase.[8] His already-intense emotional relationships to his parents deepen. He has no siblings on whom to dis-place his wishes for closeness and intimacy with his opposite-sex parent. Therefore he maintains the illusion of a possible oedipal victory much longer than usual. The intensity of his feelings and fantasies often evoke equally intense competitiveness in the same-sex parent, precipitating a triangular emotional struggle of long duration. It is often more manifest than is the case in families with additional children.[10] During this phase he has no opportunity to see himself as larger and more mature than smaller siblings and so continues to feel more childlike in relation to others. This can persist throughout life, as will his tendency to expect greater reciprocity of whatever positive and negative strivings he may express.

LATENCY

For the only child, entry into school is accompanied by the sudden acquisition of a large number of surrogate siblings. If he has had few previous experiences with peers, he will find it difficult to cope with the demands of the group and with his own rivalrous impulses. He is no longer unique. His exhibitionistic tendencies are less accepted by adults and by other children. This may lead to intensification of his attempts to remain the center of attention or, in the face of repeated narcissistic injuries, to a rigid defensive inhibition of exhibitionistic impulses. Depending on his level of success in accomplishing previous developmental tasks, he may be obnoxious or shy, or his personality may be only mildly skewed in either direction. At any rate, he shares with other firstborn children a tendency to be less popular with peers, and to turn to books and to a desire for academic success as means of compensation.[16] Only children, however, seem to be somewhat more self-confident and less fiercely competitive in this regard than do other firstborns.[19]

ADOLESCENCE

During the second separation-individuation phase, the only child, like other adolescents, is confronted with the tasks of reworking earlier oedipal and preoedipal strivings. He must disengage from his parents and form his own individual sense of identity and his own ideals. Two factors in particular may interfere with the final resolution of the oedipal struggle. These are the intensity of the only child's incestuous wishes along with the strong internal prohibitions against them, and his heightened narcissistic vulnerability due to previous rejections by peers. If those factors are strong enough, he may retreat from the peer group (so important in adolescent adaptation) into fantasy and ascetic preoccupations. His propensity for acting out his conflicts is probably less than that of other adolescents, and more likely to be confined to the family circle.[20]

Personality Characteristics and Defense Patterns of Only Children

CONFLICTS

Among the conflicts reported in in-depth studies of only children are sibling rivalry and enhanced exhibitionistic strivings. The rivalry is directed first toward unborn siblings. Since he has remained his parents' sole offspring, he feels that in this realm he has competed successfully.[2] Coupled with the parents' intensely focused attention, this later stimulates the child to exhibit and display any special talents which he possesses.[10] Lifelong wishes for dependency gratification and continued sole possession of a maternal figure are also important.

COMMON DEFENSES

These are defenses which commonly arise from, but are not pathognomonic for, the only child's conflicts and personality structure. These include sublimation, reaction formation, and specific inhibitions. The prohibition of more direct drive expression by the harsh superego results in greater pressure toward sublimation. This often takes the form of creative productivity and scholarly achievement.[14] It may reach ascetic proportions, and be used as a defense against loneliness, especially if, due to other factors, the child has been socially isolated. Reaction formation against dependency wishes may lead to a brittle reactive independence,[2] which can break down in times of stress. The youth may strive to overcompensate for the wish to possess mother's nurturing; this leads to the frequently observed character traits of generosity and supportiveness, and may verge on altruistic surrender.[2] It is one of the mechanisms underlying the entry of many only children into professions in which they can behave as parent surrogates.[21] Inhibitions against their intense exhibitionistic impulses may lead to difficulties in attempting new ventures, for now they fear the retaliation of a new set of surrogate siblings.[2]

PERSONALITY STRUCTURE

Like other firstborn children, the only child internalizes his parents' stricter, more punitive, more precocious prohibitions in the form of a harsh, aggressive superego.[14] This gives rise to the subjective experience of intense guilt over having remained without siblings.[2] The adult ideals and standards which he adopted early in life become incorporated into a strong ego-ideal; this attains a more perfectionistic quality than average and may lead to disturbances in self-esteem later in life. The ideals of the only child retain a more externalized quality than do those of other firstborns; he is always the little child striving to please the parental figures around him.[10] He may also continue to overvalue himself as his parents once did; then, when he is unable to achieve unattainable goals or get the total approval of parent surrogates, he becomes vulnerable to a deep sense of failure.

COPING MECHANISMS

Fantasy is so striking a coping mechanism in only children that it deserves special attention. Parental overprotection, lack of interaction with siblings and peers, and loneliness[10] contribute to excessive daydreaming and overstimulation of fantasy as a mode of coping. This may in part account for the fact that so many prominent writers were only children. One specific fantasy of the only child was studied in depth by Arlow. He analyzed eleven patients who were only children and found that all of them felt responsible somehow for no other children being in the family. They elaborated a fantasy that they had eliminated potential rivals before they were even born. Arlow speculates that at times the character trait of generosity may be a reaction formation to this fantasy.[2]

Due to the only child's intense and prolonged exposure to adult language patterns, an extreme form of verbal precocity is likely to appear. This may lead him to develop a somewhat intellectualized and pedantic ego quality along with a tendency to imbue words with a magical quality. At the same time, he remains less attuned to more subtle nonverbal emotional nuances.[5] These characteristics only represent trends in certain directions; they cannot be considered pathological unless they lead to neurotic symptom formation, personality trait disturbances, or more serious breakdowns of personality structure.

In general, most only children cope and adapt

rather well throughout life. The ego strengths of intelligence and verbal ability are particularly striking, along with generally higher achievement motivation. These capacities better their opportunities for higher education and for eminence in fields requiring scholarly and creative effort. The greater material and financial resources at their disposal aid them in this respect.[16]

Characteristic Forms of Mental Illness in Only Children

An enormous amount of literature has been devoted to the study of whether only children are more prone to develop mental illness than those in other ordinal positions. Many of the older studies reported a strong tendency for these children to become emotionally disturbed, but the methods used were impressionistic and descriptive.

Some of the most recent studies, using more sophisticated statistical analyses of the data, report only a slightly positive correlation of only-child status with manifest pathology. In 1967, Barry and Barry concluded that the incidence of schizophrenia among firstborn males is higher than among those in other birth order positions.[3] In the same year, in a small sample, Borge and Kayton found a striking incidence of obsessive-compulsive personality disorder in male only children. They also found the same tendency among only females, although it was not as significant. They explained their findings by suggesting that the only child's more intensive relationship to his parents fosters premature ego development, a factor of importance in the development of obsessive-compulsive symptomatology.[5]

Birtchnell studied the prevalence of psychosis, neurosis, alcoholism, and personality disorders in sibships of from two to ten. He found a slightly higher incidence of psychosis and alcoholism among firstborns in small families, while the reverse was true in large sibships. Although his study excluded only children, his results raise the question again as to whether only children, who are also firstborn, are more likely to develop manifest psychopathology.[4]

One of the methodologically better studies on the role of birth order in mental illness was carried out by Schooler. It shows minimal, if any, difference that is clearly connected with birth order.[18] These findings also support the hypothesis of Price and Hare. They point out that the trends toward an increase in the number of families started and a decrease in family size lead to statistical biases.[15] Thus, reported correlations between birth order and schizophrenia stem from these distortions. For these reasons, it is almost impossible to give any meaningful statistics about the distribution of only children among the mentally ill.

Social Structures Needed to Respond Optimally to the Only Child

Based on the foregoing observations and inferences concerning the only child's development and personality, certain general recommendations can be made. The goal is to enhance the emotional health of such children and to allow parents and social institutions to provide a growth-promoting environment. Early parent education in child development and on the role of ordinal position in personality formation will allay anxiety and induce realistic expectations of their child. The gradual introduction to and the progressive lengthening of separation experiences for the child will foster independence. Reassurance that being an only child does not necessarily lead to "spoiling," egocentricity, or psychopathology will enable the parents to relax and enjoy their offspring.

Since he does not have these built into his family life, early group and social experiences for the only child deserve special attention. Nursery school or part-time day-care enrollment when the child is three or four brings him into association with parental substitutes and surrogate siblings during a phase when rapid social development is possible. This experience will foster resolution of separation anxieties and problems with sharing. It will help him integrate exhibitionistic impulses (prevalent in all children during the preschool years), while allowing him to continue to enjoy some of the benefits and advantages of his special status. This will prepare him gradually to become a more comfortable contributor to his peer group.

REFERENCES

1. ADLER, A., *Understanding Human Nature*, Greenberg, New York, 1927.
2. ARLOW, J., "The Only Child," *Psychoanalytic Quarterly, 41(4):*507–536, 1972.
3. BARRY, H., and BARRY, H., JR., "Birth Order, Family Size, and Schizophrenia," *Archives of General Psychiatry, 17:*435–440, 1967.
4. BIRTCHNELL, J., "Birth Order and Mental Illness," *Social Psychiatry, 7(4):*167–179, 1972.
5. BORGE, G. F., and KAYTON, L., "Birth Order and the Obsessive-Compulsive Character," *Archives of General Psychiatry, 17:*751–754, 1967.
6. CLARK, R. A., and CAPPARELL, H. V., "The Psychiatry of the Adult Only Child," *American Journal of Psychotherapy, 8:*487–499, 1954.
7. ERIKSON, E., *Childhood and Society*, W. W. Norton, New York, 1950.
8. FENICHEL, O., *The Psychoanalytic Theory of Neuroses*, W. W. Norton, New York, 1945.
9. FENTON, H., "The Only Child," *Journal of Genetic Psychology, 35:*546–556, 1920.
10. FORER, L. K., *Birth Order and Life Roles*, Charles C Thomas, Springfield, Ill., 1969.
11. FORTES, N., "The Firstborn," *Journal of Child Psychology and Psychiatry and Allied Disciplines, 15(2):* 81–104, 1974.

12. HALL, G. S., et al., *Aspects of Child Life and Education*, Smith, T. L. (Ed.), Ginn & Co., Boston, 1907.
13. LASKO, J. K., "Parent Behavior Toward First and Second Children," *Genetic Psychology Monograph, 49:* 97–137, 1954.
14. PALMER, R. D., "Birth Order and Identification," *Journal of Consulting Psychology, 30:*129–135, 1965.
15. PRICE, J. S., and HARE, E. H., "Birth Order Studies: Some Sources of Bias," *British Journal of Psychiatry, 115:*633–646, 1969.
16. SCHACTER, S., "Birth Order, Eminence and Higher Education," *American Sociological Review, 26:*757–767, 1963.
17. ———, *The Psychology of Affiliation*, Stanford University Press, Stanford, Calif., 1959.
18. SCHOOLER, C., "Birth Order Effects: Not Here, Not Now!," *Psychological Bulletin, 78(3):*161–175, 1972.
19. SELLS, S. B., and ROFF, M., "Peer Acceptance and Rejection and Birth Order," *Psychology in the Schools, 1:*156–162, 1964.
20. SMITH, T. E., "Birth Order, Sibship Size, and Social Class as Antecedents of Adolescents' Acceptance of Parents' Authority," *Social Forces, 50:*223–231, 1971.
21. SUTTON-SMITH, B., ROBERTS, J. N., and ROSENBERG, B. G., "Sibling Associations and Role Involvement," *Merrill-Palmer Quarterly, 10:*25–37, 1964.

43 / The Twins

Maria Krocker Tuskan and George Colombel

To give birth not only to one but to two or more new beings is a rarity among humans, a phenomenon fraught with biological, sociocultural, and psychological implications.[5] There are two categories of twins, monozygotic or identical twins and dizygotic or fraternal twins. The former are the result of very early fission (before fourteen days) of a single fertilized ovum; they are therefore virtually genetically identical. The latter are the result of the near-simultaneous fertilization of two ova by two spermatozoa; genetically, they are as similar or as different as ordinary siblings.

Distribution and Statistics

According to the Vital Statistics Report for 1971, the total number of births in the U.S. was 3,555,970 of which 64,332 were multiple births. This yields a ratio of 18.1 live births in multiple deliveries per 1,000 total live births; in 1971 the multiple-birth ratio for white and Negro births were 17.3 and 22.8 respectively. These statistics underwent considerable change during the next five years, and in 1974 there were 3,159,958 registered live births of which 58,841 were multiple births; the ratio of multiple births was 18.6 which sorted into 18.0 for white and 22.1 for Negro births. In addition, the statistics available show an increase in the number of births among women aged 20 to 24, 25 to 29 and 30 to 34 years, with the largest increase for women aged 25 to 29. There was a marked decrease in births to women younger than 20 and to women over 35.[10] Wyshak and White hypothesized that the decline of multiple births was a function of the maternal age, and, possibly, of other factors.[15]

Those same authors restate that in 1975, the evidence, albeit indirect, suggests that the correlation between the decline of twin births, the maternal age, and other factors related to the lower fertility of older women holds true for dizygotic twinning only.[14] None of this is true of monozygotic twins, for which the rate is a steady 4 to 5 per 1,000 regardless of race, age, or parity.[13]

Cultural and Parental Reaction to Twins

The phenomenon of twins has left a mark on every culture in every period of history. To primitive man a twin birth was seen as due to the intervention of supernatural forces, positive and negative. Indeed, highly ambivalent attitudes toward twins are pervasive on many levels. In numerous societies, twins have been accorded special status, and are considered "heavensent" or "godlike." There is often a mystical aura surrounding the birth of twins, and many customs and rituals reflect their privileged standing. On the other hand, some tribes are extremely hostile toward them. Some kill the twins; in others, even the mother is put to death. Sometimes only one twin is killed, usually the secondborn, who is seen as not a real person. In other cases, the girl twin of an intersexed pair is killed because of the perceived greater threat of incest. Some tribes kill one child because the burden of two children would be too great.

Literature and folklore are replete with examples of this phenomenon, many of which reflect this ambivalence (i.e., the ambivalence of people toward the exalted or privileged status of twins versus their cursed or negative status). There is a fascination both with the similarity or identity as well as the difference or polarities. Often one twin is depicted as good and the other bad.

Recent studies indicate that parents do not see their parenting of twins as being different than their parenting of singletons. Whether this is true or not, there can be no doubt that having twins poses a special challenge for parents. Families of twins are victims of cultural cliches which emphasize the positive aspects and which tend to ignore the frequent problems; this tends to set up a potentially frustrating bind. Mother may not be able to express her special difficulties. In reality, twins are often an economic hardship. There is also the emotional burden of having to cope with the demands of two infants instead of one, a burden that is not merely quantitatively greater but qualitatively special as well. Mother must establish simultaneously two intense, early nurturing relationships.

The similarity of twins carries with it a tendency to emphasize their likenesses by treating them always as a pair, giving them alliterative names, always dressing them alike, etc. The opposite tendency is also present, the inclination to overemphasize any differences. This would be in accord with the apparent need to deny the twinship, particularly if it is an identical one. It has been shown that the parents of fraternal twins are less likely to be confused about the zygosity than parents of identical twins, who more frequently mistake their twins for fraternal.[4]

Impact of Twinship at Different Levels of Development

From the phase of intrauterine development onward, the twinship represents a handicap for the child. It continues to be so after the delivery and throughout adolescence. At birth the twins are likely to be smaller than average and frequently premature; and the small size and low birth weight with their concomitant deficiencies are not compensated for until adolescence. Congenital defects are more common among twins than among singletons; the death rate, prenatal and postnatal, is also higher among twins. In fact, one in six of all twin pregnancies ends in the death of one or both twins.[7] The twinship and the concomitant prematurity require special handling measures, such as the incubator. This is often accompanied by an impoverishment of human contact. The resulting differences in the behavior of the twins may in turn program the mother to interact with them differentially.[12] One of the initial stresses in the mothering of twins is the need to evaluate which of the two infants needs immediate attention and which infant can better tolerate the stress of waiting for food or physical contact and nurture. Under these circumstances, it is likely that nurturing is related to maternal guilt, feelings of helplessness, and above all, to a certain degree of lack of pleasurable and satisfying feedback for the mother.

To this biological or constitutional substratum is added the insidious impact of mother's reaction to the twins, both her delight and her concern; of the twins' reactions to their special condition; and the response of the broader environment to "this special pair of like individuals."[3]

In the early stages of development, twins react to the mother just as single children do. It is only at a later stage of development that they become aware of the mother's pleasure in both of them, and in the comparisons she makes of one with the other. In this way, they become conscious of each other, and of the mother's pleasure in them as a unit.[3]

As a pair they are made to feel different, unique; indeed the fact of their twinship is continually forced upon them in the form of comparisons.[3]

It is at the time of the development of object relations that twins begin to be different from singletons. The ensuing deficit in their capacity to relate will mark the twins' interactions with mother, with each other, and with their peers. Later in development, it may influence their choice of sexual objects—that is, the resulting problems and conflicts will take the form of constant vying for attention, copying each other, longing for each other, competing with each other, excluding others and turning to each other.[2] Their mutual clinging to one another does not open the road to individuation, and it obstructs the process of socialization. The constant presence of the other twin, especially that aspect of it referred to as the living mirror image, is an added obstacle to adequate ego development.[8]

Some studies have indicated that the mean IQ of identical twins was slightly below the mean for the general population. This is a general finding whether the twins are reared together or apart.[6]

Language development is impaired as well, as their turning to each other isolates them from the language model provided by the mother. They frequently develop a "secret language," termed cryptophasia, which further isolates them from the environment. This, coupled with the limitations in their capacity for conceptualization and learning, further contribute to their social isolation.[11] Twins show an overall poverty and reduction of vocabulary, and use more immature and primitive sentence constructions. Intelligence tests generally show a relatively lower verbal score. In a study of 200 four-year-old twins using the Illinois Test of Psycho-linguistic Ability, the children showed an average retardation of six months in language development compared to 100 singleton controls. This was found in both identical and fraternal twins, and occurred across all but one of the nine subtests. Their performance suggested an overall immaturity rather than any characteristic pattern of linguistic functioning. Impairment on language tests was greater than that shown on nonverbal measures. Middle-class twins were at a greater disadvantage compared to middle-class singletons than working-class twins compared to working-class singletons.[9] It is also reported that the speech of such youngsters may be immature, and that at some time before seven years, approximately 11 percent of twins have stuttered noticeably.[7]

Twins' craving for attention and their mutual competition for it have been described in detail. It is felt that "this desire for individual attention and praise will not be less, perhaps it will be even greater because they will receive it more rarely, but the second desire will be there as well, and of great importance for them: The desire to please à deux."[3] [p. 72] Their similar looks make them feel that nothing about them is personal or unique. "They have therefore every reason to feel misunderstood, lonely and angry, for they never can be sure that even their own mother is not taking one for the other."[3] [p. 72]

By the time of latency, the twins already represent a close unit, special and unique. Peers relate to them as parents do, and the twins try to please à deux while continually struggling to be perceived as individuals. In addition, they are aware of the impact their identical appearance may have upon other children, i.e., both the fascination and envy they arouse in these others, as well as the fear of the loss of identity which the existence of a double may signifiy for other children.[3]

In adolescence each young person's struggle for his own identity becomes intensified, and each twin's rivalry correspondingly heightened. At the same time, some adolescent twins relate to each other as adolescent singletons relate to their parents, i.e., with emotional indifference or passionate rejection as they respond to the need to disengage from the early object ties.[1]

In a study of a borderline adolescent twin, Maenchen found that the core object tie was to the opposite twin, and the representation of other objects contained that of the twin; indeed all later ties appeared to be pseudo-ties.[8] Other special cases of disturbed twins have been studied, i.e., borderline states and psychoses. Many of these suggest a tendency to fixate at a certain level of object relations and at a level of the development of the self characterized by mirroring and twinship phenomena. Homosexual twins have also been studied in an attempt to show a correlation between twinship and this type of sexual adjustment.

As noted, twin births involve initial hazards, there is evidence for delayed development, and there are particular pathological trends observed in special cases. Despite this there are no convincing studies to show that the incidence of any of these problems among adult twins is any higher than is true for the general population. In fact, the literature emphasizes the negative aspects of multiple births, and little has been written of the possible advantages for human development of being a twin.

Social Structures Needed for Twins

It is obvious that it is important for parents and other key figures to pay attention to any differences between twins. In effect, they must be responded to as individuals, and not just as a unit. However, their natural and very special closeness must also be respected, and twins derive a certain pleasure in being responded to *à deux*, even into adulthood. This is directly related to the degree of likeness.

More particularly, twins should have the opportunity to play with other siblings and other children. It is likely, for instance, that twins may be kept together in cribs, playpens, etc., longer than other children. In some cases this may result in impaired individuation or impeded emotional development. It seems likely that they should be sent to nursery school, kindergarten, etc., at the same age as other children. There has been considerable debate as to the advisability of putting them into the same versus into separate classes. Cogent arguments can be marshalled on both sides, and it would appear that each case must be dealt with separately. Such factors as parental style, educational needs, personalities of the twins, and attitudes of school personnel obviously play a part in reaching these decisions.

REFERENCES

1. BURLINGHAM, D., "A Study of Identical Twins," in Eissler, R. S., et al. (Eds.), *The Psychoanalytic Study of the Child*, vol. 18, pp. 400–410, International Universities Press, New York, 1963.
2. ———, "The Relationship of Twins to Each Other," in Eissler, R. S., et al. (Eds.), *The Psychoanalytic Study of the Child*, vol. 3/4, pp. 57–65, International Universities Press, New York, 1949.
3. ———, "Twins: Observations of Environmental Influences on Their Development," in Eissler, R. S., et al. (Eds.), *The Psychoanalytic Study of the Child*, vol. 2, pp. 61–73, International Universities Press, New York, 1946.
4. COHEN, D. J., et al., "Separating Identical from Fraternal Twins," *Archives of General Psychiatry*, 29:469ff., 1973.
5. GEDDA, L., *Twins in History and Science*, Charles C Thomas, Springfield, Ill., 1961.
6. JENSEN, A., "Identical Twins' Gap Laid to In-Utero Facts," *Pediatric News*, 4(7):37ff., 1975.
7. KOCK, H. L., *Twins and Twin Relations*, University of Chicago Press, Chicago, 1966.
8. MAENCHEN, A., "Object Cathexis in a Borderline Twin," in Eissler, R. S., et al. (Eds.), *The Psychoanalytic Study of the Child*, vol. 23, pp. 438–448, International Universities Press, New York, 1968.
9. MITTLER, P., "Biological and Social Aspects of Language Development in Twins," *Developmental Medicine and Child Neurology*, 12:756ff., 1970.
10. Monthly Vital Statistics Report, Final Natality Statistics, 1971, 1972, 1973, 1974, U.S. Department of Health, Education and Welfare, Public Health Service, Health Resources Administration, Washington, D.C.
11. NEWBAUER, P. B., "Twins," in Freedman, A. M., and Japlan, H. T. (Eds.), *Comprehensive Textbook of Psychiatry*, pp. 1493–1494, The Williams and Wilkens Co., Baltimore, 1967.
12. SIQUELAND, E. R., "Biological and Experimental Determinants of Exploration in Infancy," in Stone, Joseph, et al., *The Competent Infant*, pp. 822–823, Basic Books, New York, 1974.
13. *World Medical Journal*, Editorial, "Twin Studies," Copenhagen, Denmark, p. 165, 1975.
14. WYSHAK, G., "Some Observation on the Decline in the United States Dizygotic Twinning Rate," *Social Biology*, 22:171ff., 1975.
15. ———, and WHITE, C., "Genealogical Study of Human Twinning," *American Journal of Public Health*, 55:1592ff., 1965.

44 / Children of Different Ordinal Positions

George Edington and Bradford Wilson

Introduction

Most clinicians recognize the relevance of being a firstborn or only child. Unfortunately, the significance of other ordinal positions in child development continues to be ignored. Examining birth order (as it is often called) offers the clinician a wide field for observation, for theory building, and for research. One's birth order makes for enduring attitudes about one's place in the scheme of things. Just as the mother and father are the first woman and man that the child knows, siblings are the child's first experience of competition, cooperation, mutual dependence, and mutual defiance of authority. The child's rivalrous tendencies can be modified by his recognition of siblings as a source of affection and support.

A proliferation of research into ordinal position over the past decade has been confined mainly to comparisons of "firstborn" versus "later-born" populations. Results are often ambiguous since "firstborn" constitutes a homogeneous, easily defined group, whereas "later-born" may refer to anything from the younger member in a two-sibling family to any child in a series of eight. The reader is referred to Sutton-Smith and Rosenberg's superb review and evaluation of this formidable body of data.[11] They conclude that research findings on the younger of two brothers and the younger of two sisters are the most consistent. The few clinical studies in this area are represented by the pioneering work of Koch,[*] Toman,[13] and a handful of others.

The present authors have long collected data from clinical practice, comparing them with data from others in the field. We believe that most patients can be better understood if their ordinal position and its various ramifications are given appropriate weight within their clinical profile. Twinship is the only major sibling constellation not included in this study since its complexity and scope do not lend themselves to abbreviation.[†]

Koch[5] devised a simple code to designate children in two-sibling configurations. The first letter of the code indicates the sex of the sibling in question; the number indicates whether the child is first- or second-born; and the second letter indicates the sex of the other siblings. Thus:

F-1-F   Firstborn girl with a younger sister.
F-2-F   Second-born girl with an older sister.
F-1-M   Firstborn girl with a younger brother.
F-2-M   Second-born girl with an older brother.
M-1-F   Firstborn boy with a younger sister.
M-2-F   Second-born boy with an older sister.
M-1-M Firstborn boy with a younger brother.
M-2-M Second-born boy with an older brother.

Only children are commonly referred to as singletons. By extension, Koch's code can be used for other configurations. A firstborn may be designated as F-1 or M-1 without reference to other siblings. In larger constellations, however, the code would become unwieldly; the present authors have not attempted to use it for other than the above categories.

The dynamics of two-sib combinations are often sufficient to explain behavior within larger sibling constellations. Thus, let us consider a patient who is the younger of two boys born three years apart. This pair was followed eight years later by two other siblings. In such an instance, the major dynamic constellation is more likely to be that of "younger of two brothers" (M-2-M in Koch's terminology) rather than "second-born of four." The rule of thumb here is that an age-gap of six or more years demarcates a new sibship.

The observations noted here are based partly (although not entirely) on adult clinical populations, although most research on birth order comes from nonclinical groups (such as Koch's work with six-year-old school children). Our overall data constitutes an amalgam of observations drawn from a number of sources in addition to our own.

Firstborn: Only Child

Note that "firstborn *oldest*" and "firstborn *only*" child (or singleton) are distinct categories—but with much in common. The *only* child is often

---

[*] See references 4, 5, 6, 7, and 8.
[†] The interested reader is referred to Helen L. Koch, *Twins and Twin Relations*, University of Chicago Press, Chicago, 1966.

born of a mother who had difficulty conceiving, or could not afford more than one child, or did not want *any* children, but "got caught." The parents of these children are frequently older than those of most firstborns (often being aged thirty and beyond) at the time of the child's birth, so that the usual give-and-take between young parents and their children may well be lacking.

During an only child's formative years, sibling rivalry in the usual sense rarely exists unless the nurturant household includes cousins or other contemporaries. This child is, however, confronted with formidable competition in the persons of the parents. Each of them is experienced as a rival for the other parent's attention and affection. In such a situation the child feels outclassed and outweighed by giants. If by chance the child is left alone to be raised with one parent, there may be no competition at all. But the guilt engendered by an unconscious "triumph" over the absent parent (and undiluted by sharing with siblings) can become acute.

Only children have a difficult time learning how to compete and how to share. Characteristically, they remain diplomatically aloof from both modalities: partnerships present extraordinary problems for them, and in emotionally competitive situations they abdicate, covertly manipulate, or else show ill-concealed vindictiveness and overdomination. We find the adult singleton to be the most intensely jealous of all ordinal positions and the most prone to act it out.

Never having had to share parental praise with other siblings, such individuals are inclined toward narcissism and egocentricity. On the other hand, not having others with whom to share blame renders them both perfectionistic and highly vulnerable to criticism. Extremely orderly and tidy in their habits, their living and work areas are usually immaculate and well-organized, with chores done punctually and conscientiously. As Sutton-Smith and Rosenberg[11] observe, this group is chiefly responsible for the traditional view that "the early born are especially eminent."

Having only one child to center their concern upon—a single link with posterity—the parents of singletons are, quite often, unintentionally over-intrusive, and this is especially true of the long-awaited child of older parents. Arriving as many as ten or fifteen years late (possibly after one or more miscarriages), this particular singleton is most likely of all ordinal positions to be "killed with kindness"—i.e., parental smothering and intrusiveness.

Sutton-Smith and Rosenberg[11] observe that mothers seem to favor the only boys more than the only girls, and they describe the boys as more "feminine" and the girls more "masculine" than their peers, adding that this leads to "a greater tendency toward sex deviations consonant with these tendencies." They note that as adults the only girls are more aggressive and less anxious than the only boys. Unless raised to be pathologically dependent on one or both parents, these girls are apt to develop self-sufficiency at a very early age and to delight in acquiring new and varied skills throughout life.

Another special category of singleton is the youngest child who is separated from older siblings by ten years or more, and thus grows up, as it were, with several "parents." If the siblings are adolescent, they may abhor the newborn infant for giving public evidence of parental fornication.

These difficulties are further compounded when the child arrives as an unwelcome surprise to parents unprepared for late-in-life offspring. Such a child is apt to develop depressed and confused responses to the mixed messages arriving from the environment. He may develop a life-style dedicated to pleasing everyone and not being a burden or a disgrace. These children early learn to keep thoughts and feelings to themselves and to avoid taking sides. While presenting a friendly and socially outgoing facade, they are inwardly quite withdrawn.

Because all firstborns are privy to "adult" information, singletons are almost invariably more comfortable with adults or much older children than with peers. They also display an exaggerated sense of responsibility and a well-developed, premature self-sufficiency. At the same time, they may feel needlessly isolated and lonely. We believe that frequent overnight (or longer) visits between the only child and contemporaries can help to remedy the disadvantages of this ordinal position.

Firstborn: The Oldest Child

What was said about the singleton can also hold true for the oldest child.

A singleton's birth can result from parental efforts to "prove" sex-role adequacy, "cement" a failing marriage, etc. The oldest child, on the other hand, is most often born at a time when parental attraction and compatibility are at their height. Whatever problems bedevil inexperienced parents, their firstborn receives considerable and lifelong attention. His or her status as the family prince or princess entails assets which are legendary: primogeniture (real or implicit), parental support in every endeavor, inclusion in adult counsels, respect (often grudging) from sibs, and a continuing sense of intrinsic worthwhileness. In a poor family where "hand-me-downs" are worn, the oldest child gets the most new clothes. The larger the age gap between the oldest and the next-in-line, the more singleton characteristics will predominate.

The liabilities, however, are considerable, and poignant. Oldest children are the frightened pioneer offspring of novice and anxious parents. Proud of their role as strawbosses and parental message bearers, they pay a price in overseriousness. Dignified and sober, they are under a tacit injunction to "grow up"—"you're older, you ought to know better" is never said to the youngest child.

These children usually grow up feeling that others depend on them and they mustn't betray that trust. This is particularly true of a firstborn girl in a large family, who functions as surrogate mother for her younger sibs. In poor or motherless families she is likely to become the housewife, cook, and keeper-of-accounts as well. With or without siblings, she seems to grow up with a single motto—"it's all up to *me*"—and she devotes her life to setting the world straight, never doubting that she alone knows what ails it.

In large families (especially in poor neighborhoods) the oldest boy may assume the role of family protector, obliged to defend his siblings even against heavy odds. He grows up serious and filled with a sense of responsibility toward others.

Koch[7, 4] finds firstborns in general to be especially high in curiosity, planfulness, competitiveness, and most self-confident in academics. She notes,[8] surprisingly enough, that firstborn male children show the highest verbal skills of any ordinal position—even firstborn girls. This may be due, she hypothesizes, to the fact that "they are very active and get around more on their own," and that mothers show firstborn boys special devotion. The resulting extra verbal stimulation then leads to accelerated language development. In adulthood we find them relatively lacking in originality, and their creativity tends toward synthesizing the traditional. Konig[9] points out that firstborns are par excellence the defenders of tradition, laws, and the continuity of customs.

As regards this conforming tendency, Smith and Goodchilds[10] find that they rank relatively low on self-confidence and in creative problem solving,

where they function better when supported by membership in *groups*. Social anxiety and ambivalence seem to be lifelong characteristics of this ordinal position.

Above all, these firstborn oldest children need to have areas in which they are free to be a child. Otherwise they grow up robbed of a certain playfulness permitted to others. For them, life is all too apt to be "real and earnest" at the expense of the carefree romping of later-born children. As for their exaggerated strivings for primacy, Forer[2] suggests that they need to learn how to avoid biting off more than they can chew, and adds that this holds particularly true for oldest girls.

The Middle Child

Alfred Adler[1] first pointed to the middle child's difficulties, especially in a three-sibling family. With neither the status of the oldest child, nor the maternal deference of the youngest, he or she can feel left out. Not every middle child, however, fits this pattern, and it cannot be laid down as a general rule.

In a multi-sib family, *any* one of the children may feel left out and feel like a fifth wheel in an already completed family (such as the "traditional" father, mother, son, and daughter). Any child resulting from an unwanted pregnancy may be made to feel superfluous to family happiness. However, we discuss these phenomena under the rubric of the "middle child" because it is the middle child who most often responds in these ways to these stresses.

Siblings have a way of staking out territories with firm, tacitly agreed-upon boundaries. Thus one child may become "the musician," another "the athlete," and so forth; or, pejoratively, "the black sheep," "the dumbell," etc. While two or more siblings may share a talent or interest in common, characterological roles tend to be more exclusive—only *one* child gets dubbed "the trustworthy one," another "the scatterbrain," etc.

Such sobriquets tend to be polar and to cluster at either end of a sibling array. The middle child, often passed over, feels left out. For example, if the oldest child is the conformist and the youngest the rebel, the middle child, sizing up the liabilities inherent in both roles, can refuse to play the game altogether. And if this child reaches similar conclusions about other domestic interactions, he or she may end up feeling superfluous, devoid of any meaningful family role.

Caught in such a dilemma, the middle child often abandons the family arena and turns to peers for affirmation, preferring to "run with the pack" at school or in the larger world while being enigmatic and "out of it" at home. For these children what the "gang" thinks takes priority long before the usual preteen and adolescent phases when greater peer-group concerns normally develop.

Like the singleton, he or she early acquires self-sufficiency and independence from family ties, but with sophisticated peer-group skills which the former usually lack. A liability of this birth order, however, can be a lifelong feeling that the doors of intimate trust and confidentiality are pretty much closed; the middle child knows and understands many other people but feels truly known and/or understood by very few. In our opinion, much needless isolation and loneliness can be forestalled by helping the middle child to carve out a valid and significant niche within the family at as early an age as possible.

The Youngest Child

Considered the most pampered, this "baby-of-the-family" is heir to many hidden liabilities. While the firstborn oldest child must by definition suffer "replacement" by younger siblings who make successive claims for parental attention, the youngest child comes into a world where everybody else "was there first" and seems to have been *born* knowing how to tie shoelaces and a host of other prestigeous, praiseworthy skills. More often than not, older sibs show off their skills at the younger's expense, thus confirming the latter's fantasy that "the big people" never had to learn all the things at which this child feels so woefully inept.

As a result, youngest children see two options: either to become adept at getting other people to do things for them, at the expense of developing a number of independent skills, or to become a dedicated "do-it-yourselfer" who refuses to be taught by anyone and feels compelled to "invent the wheel." Hobbies, and even vocational skills, are often learned in secret, by privately experimenting and covertly reading textbooks.

Although often retaining carefree attitudes toward the more "serious" aspects of existence, the youngest child may nevertheless carry a perpetual sense of unimportance and "failure"; the world always seems to say "not *yet*; there is still *one*

more hurdle." Whereas the oldest child is usually acclaimed for everything from teething to being awarded a Ph.D., the youngest child's identical landmarks are apt to be "old hat" when his turn comes around.

Ambivalent about yearned-for acceptance, the youngest child may abandon projects in midstream, unconsciously fearing retaliation by the "big people" for daring to aspire to their rank, or by other "little people" for betraying their camaraderie as outcasts and no-accounts. Or "big people" may be courted in order to counterreject them—the youngest often abandons his membership in clubs, professional organizations, and other groups without warning or without apparent reason.

The youngest nevertheless has a lifelong yen to make a contribution, to be needed and listened to. Forer[2] finds that youngest children are particularly vulnerable to the loss of a parent in early childhood, and populations of hospitalized schizophrenics and alcoholics show a significant preponderance of this group.

Finally, an unfortunate but inescapable fact about the youngest child is that, of all ordinal positions, he is the most likely to have been sired by a man other than the mother's legitimate spouse. In such cases, the presence of guilt, resentment, overprotectiveness, or rejection, etc., on the part of one or both parents (not to mention siblings who are quick to respond to parental cues) exerts a profound influence upon the subsequent development of this child. In any event, the question needs to be asked: "Why was this child the *last*?" Just as the firstborn is usually a "love baby," the last born is often an "accident," or a last-ditch effort to preserve parental eroticism, or (in poor families) "another mouth to feed"; "the last straw," or whatever. Much of the proverbial "spoiling" of this child may represent a compassionate reaction formation to parental consternation.

In child rearing it is important for the youngest child that genuine accomplishments receive the same parental affirmation as those of elder siblings; otherwise adulthood is likely to remain a mirage —always beckoning and forever out of reach.

Older of Two Boys (M-1-M)

This particular firstborn is prone to acquire the role of "heavy" quite early in life as he assumes the multiple burdens of trail blazer, role model, and stand-in for paterfamilias—both for his sibling and his mother. He tends to shoulder all responsibilities conscientiously, stoically, and unquestioningly. Careful to maintain his "princely" status, he is perpetually alert to maintain his defenses and to avoid the unconventional. According to Forer,[2] he absorbs parental values at an early age and proceeds to apply them rigorously both to himself and to others. Afraid of parental disappointment or of ridicule by his brother (or worse, by his brother's cronies), his fears are confided only to his closest (and usually only) friend.

Toman[13] reports that the older of two boys gets along well with other males and makes friends with both males and females who themselves have older brothers. He delights in exerting self-control, planning ahead in practical matters, and keeping his house (financial and otherwise) in order. Toman adds that this boy deals with male authority by either identifying with it or subverting it via subtle invasion or erosion of the authority's prerogatives.

Koch[4] and Sutton-Smith and Rosenberg[11] describe his childhood behavior as anxiously rivalrous over the mother's attention, quarrelsome, teasing, insistent on his rights, and of all ordinal positions the slowest to recover after upsets. These characteristics tend to become modified after about age ten.

Forer[2] points out that he needs to develop more patience and playfulness. Care should be taken during his growing-up years not to saddle him with so much work and so little play as to make him the proverbial "dull boy." He is usually less serious or more playful if one or both of his parents were younger children, even more so if one or both of his parents were firstborn oldest or singletons.

Younger of Two Boys (M-2-M)

This child usually grows up blissfully unaware of the buffering role of his sober elder brother. More gregarious and extroverted than his sibling, he fails to see what all the fuss is about. To his thinking, most things work themselves out eventually, so let others do the worrying at which they seem to be so proficient.

The youngest child syndrome is ameliorated for the younger of two boys by the fact that he has a single sib and may receive a greater share of parental affirmation than the youngest in a larger family. The smaller the age gap, the more likely he is to be both playmate and pal to his elder brother—provided that one of them being dubbed "Mother's Boy" and the other one "Father's Boy" does not engender a special rivalry. If that does occur, the ensuing competitiveness between same-sex siblings is usually far more bitter than that between parentally polarized boy and girl sibs.

This boy, generally easygoing and with a sunny disposition, is least likely of all ordinals to generate incapacitating psychiatric syndromes. He is often fonder of his brother than his brother is of him, unaware that in his own upbringing his parents relaxed many anxieties and strictures which had adversely affected the psychic economy of his elder sib. The younger of two boys' chief asset is his firm belief that the world stands ready to offer advice and help whenever needed. He does have a distinct disadvantage in the form of a certain reluctance to maintain a minority opinion against great odds, or to enter uncharted territory.

According to Toman[13] he is a "capricious and willful" iconoclast who depends on (and feels lost without) icons to react *against*. Irregular in his goal orientation, he either concentrates intensely or else dawdles and procrastinates—half hoping, half expecting that a magic rescuer will (as usual) relieve him of any onerous tasks. Inclined to live in the moment, he spends lavishly, disregarding the future. Childhood toys are likely to be soon lost, broken, or discarded. He often responds well to opportunities, but is not inclined to create them. Much depends upon his moods, which are in turn a function of the amount of seconding which he receives from his environment. Others (even his elders) can easily evoke his empathy and understanding.

In Toman's view this boy gets along best with boys who have younger brothers, girls with younger siblings, and with singletons. Generally antiauthoritarian, he prefers as allies an elite group or at best a benign, paternalistic authority. During childhood he often presents attention-seeking behavior problems.

Sutton-Smith and Rosenberg[11] find that as a preadolescent he is apt to display "a surge of emotional dependence and submissiveness." Of all ordinal positions he is likely to be lowest in conformity and affiliation, and highest in "masculinity" and athleticism. Koch[4] describes him as having "more readiness to anger" than boys in other ordinal positions. When the age gap is small he plays "follow the leader" to his older brother in social situations. She notes, however, that with a wider age gap he shows more aggressiveness, curiosity, originality, enthusiasm and planfulness, and is apt to be socially expansive and bouyant.[5] Meanwhile, he recovers more readily than his brother from emotional upsets.

Forer[2] feels that this boy needs to develop more confidence and initiative, to strike a better balance between work and play activities, and to develop more verbal skills.

Older Boy with Younger Sister

(M-1-F)

When a firstborn child gets to be three years old or more, the birth of a younger sibling may take on increasingly traumatic aspects. In a way, the parents "can't win"—if the secondborn is of the same sex as the firstborn, the (mute) complaint is "Why? Wasn't *I* a good enough boy (or girl)? Why did they want a *second* one?" And if the later-born is of the opposite sex, the complaint becomes "Wasn't *my* sex good enough? Why did they have to invite *this* kind of creature into the family?"

In the case of the older boy with a younger sister, the loss of maternal attentiveness constitutes a serious hurdle, and if he is aged four or older (a time when he is involved in ambivalent struggles with his father), any pronounced *paternal* involvement with the newborn girl can be devastating. Most commonly the boy clings tenaciously to his prior status of crown prince—a role which the younger sister (if not the parents) usually accepts completely. The sister, however, may be treated with lofty disdain (as adults, these males can go through forty or fifty psychotherapy sessions before mentioning that they grew up with a younger sister).

Koch[8] characterizes this child as highly jealous but otherwise aggressive, self-confident, curious, and planful. Toman[13] finds him a pacifist and reluctant to take risks—usually not "one of the boys" (although his relations with males are cordial enough) and often on the lookout for good father figures; "He wants his peace and his fun. That's what life is for." In fights among other boys "he is for mediation and reason, even if it earns him the reputation of a coward." Sutton-Smith and Rosenberg remark that his "maleness is more in his posture than his competence."[11] Like the younger brother with an elder sister, he tends to ensconce himself in emotionally dis-

bursed relationships to male peers en masse, with no male confidants whatever. Relations with females are distantly cordial although marked by an almost compulsive and obligatory seductiveness. As adults, Wilson[14, 15] finds older boys with younger sisters to be conventional and all-around good guys, while close associates frequently observe that even after many years of acquaintanceship, they really don't know him very well.

When the age gap is smaller (three years or less) this boy is apt to be close and protective toward his younger sister, resulting in an over-toleration of mistreatment by female peers. Nevertheless, a certain emotional distance and detachment characterizes his relationships to most people. Overt intensity seems to frighten him, threatening to open up a Pandora's box of undealt-with hostility and/or ambivalence, and he rarely has any confidential friends of either sex.

Younger Boy with Older Sister

(M-2-F)

Owing to the absentee role of fathers in Western culture, this boy often feels that his behavior is constantly being monitored by his older sister and his mother. By the time his father returns home from work, he feels that the damage has been done. He has either been bossed or wheedled into so many tiny concessions and thwartings of self-assertion that he can no longer remember exactly what they were about and he is likely to wind up being a "rebel without a cause." He often finds himself feeling resentful, angry, and rebellious without quite knowing why. Emotional detachment and rather ineffectual nay-saying may persist well into adolescence when the companionship and support of male peers finally exerts a calming and steadying effect.

He can achieve a kind of détente with peers of both sexes, but feels that his personal freedom is left on the doorstep when he enters the family circle. Rarely able to articulate this deeply felt problem, he usually finds himself unable to appeal to his father for sorely needed male support and thus runs the risk of estrangement. Consequently the all-important father-son relationship is seldom openly confidential, but is marked by quiet, nonverbal rapport.

Koch[5] notes that in childhood the younger boy with an older sister tends to be withdrawn and depressive ("sissyish, hostile and not very friendly") and not a joiner of peer groups. She finds him passive; low in ambition and initiative. Sutton-Smith and Rosenberg[11] see him as exhibitionistic, selfish, uncooperative with peers, and given to teasing. At the same time they see his high self-esteem as possibly explaining his apparently scant need for peer affirmation. According to them, of all male ordinal positions, he ranks highest on measures of "femininity." Toman[13] finds him to be "low on insight," hypothesizing that, owing to the attentions of his women folk, he never had a need to develop it. Toman adds that this ordinal tends to marry a woman whose sole career "is the background management of his interests and welfare," adding that he is apt to be unpopular with male peers, "who resent his taking help and support for granted and leaving them to clean up after him." Most researchers find him highly quarrelsome at all ages, and the authors note that he is prone to violent temper tantrums during adolescence and early adulthood. This seems particularly true when the division of labor between mother and father is blurred—i.e., when the mother seems to cut a more vibrant professional figure in the world such that the father's prestige appears dim by comparison. Given a weak or incapacitated (but not physically absent) father, this boy can get into serious emotional difficulties. This ordinal prefers environments that are gregarious but not intimate. As an adult he will most often enter a field which is (so far as possible) closed to women.

The best way for parents to avoid the pitfalls of this ordinal position is to initiate clearcut agreements regarding his territorial rights. There must be a firm guarantee that in such areas the mother and sister will respect his boundaries. The father can help by making special "unsmothering" efforts toward a personal level of rigorously private confidentiality that under no circumstances should be shared with the mother or sister without the boy's prior permission. For the younger boy with an older sister, no greater crime exists than for one fellow to betray another's confidences.

Older Girl with Younger Brother

(F-1-M)

This girl, like the older girl with a younger sister, may act out an oedipal fantasy about being the mother in the family (i.e., her father's wife) and copes with her resentment toward her newborn rival by becoming his nursemaid, thus turning her jealousy into a compensatory "overprotective" maternalism.

From mediating between her younger brother and the outside world it is but a short step to being a go-between and peacemaker in other family relationships—for example, bickering parents or other relatives. Her first motto is "It's all up to *me*."

While she may disdain her male contemporaries, she is apt to be more secure in male company, regarding other girls with suspicion and distrust. As Toman[13] puts it, she tends to patronize males while still being nurturant and helpful toward their goals.

Accustomed from early childhood to taking charge of things, she often acts "bossy" toward males without realizing it, but is generally adept at smoothing ruffled feathers and making necessary conciliatory gestures. In situations involving competition with other females, she prefers to behave as though they do not exist—much to their chagrin.

Koch[7, 5] found that in childhood this girl is friendly with her teachers, socially expansive, and noted for leadership. The authors' clinical observation is that the older girl with a younger brother often seems to have brought herself up; she can astonish her parents with an organization and precision not learned by precept or example.

According to Sutton-Smith and Rosenberg[11] she ranked high on conformity and emotional dependency. As she grows older, Sutton-Smith, Roberts, and Rosenberg[12] assert that she is likely to become "the most submissive, most dependent, most anxious, but also the most competitive of the female groups studied."

It appears that when the age gap is three years or more, this ordinal maintains her ascendancy by polishing her verbal and intellectual skills. She does this in an effort to maintain her father's respect and interest. As was noted earlier, her brother then tends to stake out nonverbal territories, putting him at a serious disadvantage, both socially and personally. The authors consider adult older sisters with younger brothers to be the most predictable of ordinal positions, displaying most of the following characteristics:

1. She does not particularly like children. While not rejecting her own children, she is apt to be more maternal as a teacher, child psychologist, etc., to other people's children.
2. She is usually a career woman. However, she may regard her marriage and homemaking ac-

tivities as her "career." Her second motto is "I'm from Missouri, *show* me." She takes nothing on faith, and demands proof. In therapy, she is affable and acts promptly on insights but makes it almost a point of honor never to acknowledge the therapist's contribution to her life.

3. Her genuine love for her parents is tempered by a keen awareness of their shortcomings so that her attitude toward them can be one of almost loving contempt implemented more by filial obligation than by genuine concern.

4. In her personal life the older sister with younger brother shows an underlying disdain for emotionalism. She tends to become attached to men who are intellectual, professional, who "believe in" solving every problem *rationally*, but who are inept socially—almost as though she seeks a man who will not compete with her in poise and social expertise.

Collaborative childhood undertakings carried out in the company of male and female peers with minimal adult supervision can go a long way toward correcting the imbalances that have been outlined.

she tends to see herself as being closer to her father, and her sister as closer to the mother. Toman likewise sees her as being strongly attached to her father, in competition with her mother; as father's helpmate or second-in-command. Sutton-Smith et al.[11, 12] find her "the most independent of all girls at all ages."

Where a narrow (one- to three-year) age gap exists, she may treat the younger sister more like a twin and they may become inseparable—confidantes, the proverbial "sister act." If the age gap is four years or more, rivalry usually takes over and this girl then regards her sister as the recipient of numberless parental favors, as being "spoiled" and unfairly indulged. In this case she can be the most bitterly hostile toward her sibling of all ordinal positions.

As with other two-sib configurations, when the special advantages of each birth order are openly spelled out to the child and consistently adhered to, many of these problems are avoidable. In the meantime it is best if the caretaking duties of this elder sister are held to a realistic minimum.

Older Girl with One Younger Sister

(F-1-F)

This child is more likely than her male counterpart (older boy with younger brother) to be nursemaid for the younger sibling at an extremely early age, perhaps because the transition from playing mommy to a doll to that of parenting a younger sibling is easy to make. Unaware of the pitfalls in such a role, parents may place a heavy burden of responsibility on this elder daughter. Such a policy fails to take into account the fact that the two children are siblings, and most important, that this little mother is herself a child, and entitled to the prerogatives of a bona fide childhood. Relinquishing these prerogatives plays into the little girl's desire to be a woman like her mother and makes it difficult for her to come to terms with the resentment and anger that such a heavy sacrifice entails.

Toman[13] finds her responsible, competent, often bossy, highly competitive with other females, conscientious, and inclined toward self-righteousness. He observes that while she relates best to younger sisters of sisters, both boys and girls may feel intimidated by her—which she doesn't seem to mind at all. Koch[5] notes that her childhood playmates are largely female and that in family terms

Younger Girl with an Older Sister

(F-2-F)

Like the younger girl with older brother and the younger boy with older sister, this girl is relatively rare in adult clinical caseloads. An examination of her childhood personality profile may help to explain why she so rarely seeks (needs?) psychotherapy.

While Koch[4] finds the younger girl with an older sister quite dependent on adult attention (especially the mother's) and having difficulty making final decisions, she is also described as being less moody, less fearful of physical activities, and less vacillating than other children. Apparently the wider the sibling age gap the better her social adjustment and the more self-confident, cheerful, and less moody she is apt to be. Sutton-Smith et al.[11, 12] find her conforming and affiliative, high in emotional dependency, and low in competitiveness. At the same time, they find her the "most feminine and least masculine of the two child female sibling statuses." As with the younger of two boys, Koch[5] notes that with a narrow age gap, this ordinal girl tends to be a hanger-on in social groups chosen by her elder sister.

The relatively few younger girls with older

sisters whom the authors have encountered clinically are gregarious, energetic, confident, ebullient (bordering on silliness), and breathtakingly verbose. The social chatterbox and single swinger is most apt to be such an ordinal.

Her rarity among patient populations may be due either to a highly successful social repertoire which serves to assuage and distract her from deeper internal concerns, or to the sense of total erasure which could result from a too serious defeat at the hands of a competitively successful older sister.

A problem met with in all two-sister families is that one parent may have wanted a boy and demands that one of the girls either fulfill this role or else do eternal penance for having failed to do so.

Forer[2] feels that a younger girl with an older sister needs much reassurance as an adolescent and young adult, and that it is "important for her to develop her own interests and abilities rather than compete with the sister on the sister's terms."

Younger Sister with an Older Brother
(F-2-M)

In a study of thirty-five therapist caseloads, the oldest sister of three or more siblings is the least likely ordinal position to seek psychotherapeutic help.[15] But this ordinal girl was the *next* rarest. Clinical experience with her older brother has convinced the authors that this girl frequently suffers serious and subtle childhood damage, the nature of which her older brother (who scarcely acknowledges her existence) is unable to elucidate.[14, 15] Combining limited clinical findings with extraclinical sources, one may hypothesize that her development proceeds as follows.

Her feelings toward the older brother (and males in general) seem marked by a lifelong ambivalence. She oscillates between anguished yearnings for his love and support accompanied by a sense of resentment and despair at feeling patronized, rejected, or totally ignored by the family "prince." At the same time she feels that her parents compare her unfavorably with her brother. A wish to be her brother's devoted sychophant wars with an equally strong impulse to compete with and defeat her lofty competitor. Her adult romantic relations with men seem to be governed by an unconscious

paradox: "I want a strong, self-assertive, masculine man *who will do exactly as I tell him to.*"

Sexual experiments between siblings are by no means rare. However, they can be traumatic for the younger sister with an older brother. She feels "used" by the older brother rather than loved, affirmed, or physically and emotionally appreciated by him. He, meanwhile, represses, denies, or dismisses such contacts as being mutually inconsequential. When the age gap is small, however, this pair can also be genuinely close.

Kammeyer[3] and Sutton-Smith and Rosenberg[11] comment upon her "masculine" qualities, which are more pronounced than for girls in any other ordinal position; she is most often involved in entrepreneurial activities and in college is apt to be "overrepresented among physical education majors." Rather than being "masculine" in the traditional sense, she plays down her vulnerability so as to avoid possible vanquishment either by males or by more dominant females. Toman[13] says that she collaborates well with males in work situations, but that other females, without knowing why, do not trust her. He further confirms that with a wide sibling age gap she often feels that she runs a poor second to her brother and dreads anything resembling failure in the eyes of the world.

Koch[4, 5] adds that with the wider age gap, the juvenile young sister with an older brother shows decreased cheerfulness, self-confidence, finality of decision making, and speed of recovery from emotional upsets; she is also less friendly toward adults. She displays an increased tendancy to alibi, to be critical, to bid for adult attention, and to be readily upset by defeats. Otherwise Koch describes her as dynamic, highly observant, and tenacious, although with a "tendency to procrastinate."

Sutton-Smith et al.[11, 12] find her to be low on affiliation and conformity, more emotionally independent than other girls, and "least powerful vis-à-vis siblings . . . a surprisingly unmitigated record of the older male sibling's influence on the younger girl." Toman[13] notes that she doesn't seem to seek friendship with females and Koch[6] reports that at the six-year-old level this ordinal girl is apt to display "tomboyish" qualities. Moreover, compared to other girls she is apt to be more quarrelsome, tenacious, resourceful, selfish, competitive, and confident as well as enthusiastic, popular, and "high on leadership." Koch further points to her "greater expressed desire to become the opposite-sex sibling than any [other] group."

More than any ordinal position (with the single exception of the younger boy with an older sister), from birth onward this child needs a great deal of love and affirmation from her same-sex parent (or parental surrogates).

Postscript

While the ramifications of birth order are manifold, appreciating the significance of ordinal position provides information crucial to understanding a given child. Knowing parental (and even *grandparental*) ordinal positions can widen the scope of that understanding. An older sister may see her own daughter as the embodiment of her younger sister and "transfer" onto the child her resentment of that sister's presumed privileges. Singleton parents become upset when their own children squabble, while parents who come from large families consider sibling quarrels to be run-of-the-mill. Finally, an eldest brother may resent his own children because they, like his siblings, compete for his wife's ("mother's") love and attention. As we have pointed out, these matters are not cut-and-dried, but are complicated by many modifying factors. Considerably more clinical investigation is called for in this largely neglected area, since the surface has hardly been scratched.

REFERENCES

1. ADLER, A., *Understanding Human Nature*, Premier Books (Fawcett Publications), New York, 1959.
2. FORER, L. B., *Birth Order and Life Roles*, Charles C Thomas, Springfield, Ill., 1969.
3. KAMMEYER, K., "Birth Order and the Feminine Sex Role among College Women," *American Sociological Review, 31:*508–515, 1966.
4. KOCH, H. L., "Some Emotional Attitudes of the Young Child in Relation to Characteristics of His Sibling," *Child Development, 27:*393–426, 1956.
5. ———, "Childrens' Work Attitudes and Sibling Characteristics," *Child Development, 27:*289–310, 1956.
6. ———, *Some Personality Correlates of Sex, Sibling Position, and Sex of Sibling among Five- and Six-Year-Old Children*, Genetic Psychology Monographs, vol. 52, pp. 3–50, 1955.
7. ———, "The Relation of Certain Family Constellation Characteristics and the Attitudes of Children towards Adults," *Child Development, 26:*13–40, 1955.
8. ———, "The Relation of 'Primary Mental Abilities' in Five- and Six-Year-Olds to Sex of Child and Character-

istics of His Sibling," *Child Development, 25:*209–223, 1954.
9. KONIG, K., *Brothers and Sisters*, St. George Books, Blauvelt, N.Y., 1973.
10. SMITH, E. E., and GOODCHILDS, J. D., "Some Personality and Behavioral Factors Related to Birth Order," *Journal of Applied Psychology, 47:*300–303, 1963.
11. SUTTON-SMITH, B., and ROSENBERG, B. G., *The Sibling*, Holt, Rinehart and Winston, New York, 1970.
12. SUTTON-SMITH, B., ROBERTS, J. M., and ROSENBERG, B. G., "Sibling Association and Role Involvement," *Merrill-Palmer Quarterly, 10:*25–38, 1964.
13. TOMAN, W., *Family Constellation*, 2nd ed., Springer, New York, 1969.
14. WILSON, B., "A Clinical Portrait of M-1-F, the Elder Brother with One Younger Sibling, a Sister," unpublished manuscript, 1966.
15. ———, "The Personality of M-1-F as Seen in An Out-Patient Population: A Pilot Study," unpublished manuscript, 1968.

45 / The Commune-reared Child

Bernice T. Eiduson

Definition of the Commune-reared Child

Today's commune-reared child dwells in one of the living groups, or extended families, or communities that came into existence as an offshoot of the counterculture movement of the late 1960s or early 1970s. His parents saw this living group as an alternative to the two-parent nuclear family, a variant that might more successfully meet their personal needs and their ideological preferences. They regarded mainstream society as alienating and fragmented, and fled from it. In the living group they sought a life style that was:

1. humanistically oriented
2. directed at meeting individual needs for self-fulfillment and creativity
3. divested from a preoccupation with possessions
4. in tune with the "natural," ecologically centered environment

5. independent of technological advances, which were perceived as artificial and "superficial"
6. respectful toward individual differences
7. founded on trust in other than intellectual sources of knowledge

In making their decisions about adopting an alternative life style, the psychological and physical welfare of their children were not their primary concerns.[11] However, as the responsibilities for eating, sleeping, and caretaking loomed, the needs of their children came ever more into focus. Translations of ideological perspectives into living group realities came to mean that:

1. the child lives in a group which can vary in size from eight to more than one hundred
2. the child may or may not have biological parents as his primary caretakers [18]
3. other adults can serve as parent figures and caretakers with or without biological parents present
4. the child's "family" is made up of socially related as well as biologically related children and adults [14]
5. peers become very important both as age-mates and caretakers
6. the child may share his living quarters on a twenty-four-hour basis with other children, and this may include sharing toys, clothes, eating in a group, and sleeping in children's quarters [15]

There are no typical or representative living groups.[13] There is so much diversity among them in respect to size, structure, membership, available space, locale, and organization that children in various groups may have quite different experiences and exposures.[9] The most well-publicized variety is the back-to-the-land isolated commune, whose members share one roof and are committed to a rural existence. A more common arrangement, however, is the small nuclear family unit existing in a mini-community. This is comprised of like-minded people who have chosen to reside in a circumscribed area so that they can be proximal to friends who share interests in crafts, values, philosophy, and child-rearing preferences. Living groups embrace triads, sizable religious communities, and groups identified by the name of their charismatic leaders. The common assumption that commune children are inevitably reared in similar circumstances or with common child-rearing perspectives is therefore incorrect. Parents who hold similar ideological perspectives implement these in a variety of ways that reflect their personal interests, sophistication, and experience in parenting. Inevitably, the consensual arrangements, attitudes, and supports of their group enter into the child-rearing patterns as well. Variations in socialization practices are very extensive; often they are much influenced by how the parents were

themselves reared. Hence, the task of achieving enough consistency to make living in a group viable often takes an inordinate amount of time and effort. During the late 1960s, communes were known to dissolve on the basis of disagreements over child care.

Child-rearing Orientations of Communes

Nevertheless, there are certain child-rearing orientations which seem to influence the socialization patterns of parents[11] who adopt living group milieus as their family unit.

They desire intense mother-child relationships from birth through the first two or two-and-a-half years, with a clear break in this pattern in the direction of independence and self-reliance at two-and-a-half or three years. The latter comes at a time when the youngster has been weaned (breast feeding may extend until this time), and is mobile, and when the mother begins to think of herself and her own needs and wishes to return to previous activities.

This style of child-rearing fosters an intense attachment to a single caretaker; at the same time, there is an attempt to develop in the child a generalized sense of trust in other caretaking adults. This may be through the use of multiple parents as caretakers, or through specific caretakers assigned to twenty-four-hour nurseries. These become the living quarters for infants and children.[21]

Since early independence from mother often moves a child into "juvenile groups" as replacement, child-peer relationships become potent socializing agents. Peers are depended upon for support and decision, and age-mates are closely modeled.

In line with the philosophy that a child has individual rights, as do adults, the child is encouraged early in his life to engage in decision making. In some family groups, conscious politicization of children is pursued. When there is group decision making by parents, it is modeled by the children as an important mode for solving problems. When other factors (such as the Bible) determine the basis for decisions about life, the child also becomes aware of his status early.

The first commune groups who were swept up by the Vietnam war generally espoused non-violence. At present, a variety of practices is seen in regard to the handling of aggressive behaviors among children, and in parental disciplinary attitudes and practices. In line with the nonsexist attitudes of some commune parents, it is considered desirable for each child to be assertive (and particularly for girls, upon whom a "passive role has been foisted by stereotypic cultural attitudes"). Children are therefore generally allowed to work out relationships with peers without adult interference; in fact, direct interrelations are fostered. Only the demands of safety take precedence. In other more conservative creedal communal groups, use of physical punishment starts early when children are "willfull"; this is rationalized as "spanking with love." Twenty-four-hour group living situations for children also employ peer pressure as a disciplinary tool.

Parallel with this, there are differences among and within family styles in regard to the expression of sexual desires. In general, parents aim for more freedom in their children and earlier sophistication, which may come with exposure to nudity and sexualized activities. Yet many communes— both creedal and noncreedal—are straightlaced so far as children's activities go. Their yougsters' attitudes and behavior are not expected to correspond in any one-to-one way to that of adults. Children are expected to be able to distinguish what is appropriate behavior within the "family" and in the "outside world."

Achievement striving for money, status, and external success is played down, except for the desire to become competent and thus fulfill individual potential and creativity. Such rewards are identified with the goals of straight society and hence discredited. Sensory impressions, intuition, and the occult as opposed to the rational are regarded as appropriate data for the enhancement of creativity.

Demographic Characteristics
of Commune Children

DISTRIBUTION

At most, commune children possibly represent only 1 or 2 percent of the population of youngsters under eighteen. This estimate is very appropriate since no statistics are available on their household, many of which are invisible to the uninitiated eye.

However, their numerical size seems inversely

related to their significance on the social scene. The areas of culture that most quickly reflect the changing trends introduced by counterculture concepts and styles are the realms of art, movies, and fashion. However, child rearing among middle-class families seems significantly affected as well. Pilot studies were conducted in 1972–1973 on a group of nuclear two-parent families who were living in traditional styles. These parents were shown to share some of the child socialization values and attitudes that had been identified among living group parents.[8] Ideologies and beliefs seem to be better crystalized in commune families and are given sharper focus than they are in "straight" families; there they appear in more amorphous or ambiguous form. Yet the same elements appear in both commune and establishment households. Thus the socialization process and development outcomes in commune children may be harbingers; they may presage patterns of child rearing and developmental experiences of change in the more conventional culture. Because of their predictive potential, then, the fate of commune children is significant in disproportion to their number.

SOCIOECONOMIC STATUS

Commune children are almost exclusively a caucasian group, with parents born and reared in middle-class or stable working-class families. The group who were originally attracted to the communes were the offspring of executive, professional, teaching, or managerial families, with at least some college education. As in the case of most social movements, the original membership attracted followers who were more heterogeneous in background and identification, and who were more widely distributed in their demographic characteristics.[16] Socialization practices within communes, then, reflect the more widely ranging values that go with the social class statuses of the family origins of the parents.

Impact of Commune-rearing
on Development

There are studies currently underway which attempt to sift out fact from hearsay in regard to child growth in living groups.[6, 7] Spurred on by studies of kibbutz children,[24, 20] researchers hypothesized that children may reach personal independence at earlier ages, develop the values of sharing, mutual trust, and within-family loyalty that accompany extended families, acquire a heightened social sensitivity, and show a shift away from individually oriented achievement motivation in favor of group goals and perspectives.

However, the analogy of American commune children with Israeli kibbutz children or Chinese commune children, while compelling, may be of questionable validity. American living groups grew up outside the mainstream culture, and literally drew vitality from the "counter-" or "anti-system" ideology; Israeli or Chinese communes are integral and accepted parts of their major respective cultures; they have not met the disfavor or suspicion of the dominant culture, nor have they had to generate a whole response system to such rejection. To date, only 40 percent of living group members are "resocialized" into straight society as expressed by their return to work, urban residence, or suburban community involvements; yet they often maintain their counterculture ideologies and values, especially those that bear children.[7]

The commune child in the United States, therefore, has one foot in each world—his "within-family" world and the mainstream world. He has to interface with both, as his parents do, and has to develop the kind of discriminatory skills that make equilibrium and appropriate behaviors possible.

Attitudes and behaviors valued within the family foster strength in certain resources. At the same time they lead to a lessening of both development and cathexis in others. As a result, certain "trade-offs" take place.[8] Some aspects of development, as, for example, sensitivity to the needs of others, or group decision-making skills, are reinforced, perhaps at the expense of the development of competencies in other areas.

While parents have a great investment—and even effectiveness—in bridging the "two-world" gap, the child's experiences are complicated by within-family inconsistencies. The parent-child conflicts which normally arise in the two-parent family may multiply in the face of a large number of adult "parents." This can happen even when group roles are explicit and hierarchically structured. Despite the alternative's rationale for multiple caretaking for the young child, some clinicians report that too many disparate identificatory models confuse some commune children.

Similarly for ideological reasons, children tend to be treated as adults. Thus, in line with the view that children are full-fledged individuals, it follows that they have the right to know. It is common for the children to experience early exposure to all family experiences including open and uninhibited sexual behaviors. All communes do not practice nudity or free sexual relationships; some show severely repressive attitudes and behaviors. In those in which nudity and adult sexuality are open, the disappearance of the latency period has been reported.[2] However, implications for adolescent and adult development have not as yet been established, nor has the phenomenon itself been evaluated in terms of the remarkable changes in sexual mores in contemporary American culture.

This mode of child rearing is likely to foster the kinds of competencies that go with adaptation to unusual ecological environments. Independence is thrust on these children following weaning and mobility; whether dependency needs are adequately met within the family that fosters such early self-reliance remains to be seen.[10]

Concern has been expressed about the achievement needs of commune children. Their parents have themselves rejected and "turned-off" such "establishment" values as performance and success. These are conventionally defined in terms of upward mobility, money, power, etc. Will children adopt parental models in the realm of achievement? Perhaps living group children may feel less internalized pressure for individual performance, unless such motivation is relevant to their own interests and creative development.[9]

Familial Reactions to Differences in Commune Children

The majority of two-parent nuclear families expect their children's choices to reflect the values and ideals in which they have grown up. In contrast to this, most communal families want to raise children who can make independent choices. The desire to provide the child with the opportunity to be an individual in his own right, to be free from guilt-provoking, entangling, neurotic emotional alliances, to be insightful to his own needs and motivations, and to be able to act on them if he wants to—these are the aspirations of the noncreedal communal families. Many communes would take offense at the term aspirations —so strong is their desire to liberate individual growth from the bonds of unconscious wishes or fantasies. Invested as they are in validating their own life styles, commune parents want their children to do the same. They want this even for the child who rejects them and their ways. A mother from a laissez-faire rural group could describe how adolescents from their group began to reject their family as "dirty hippies," once they had begun to identify with teachers and classmates from a conservative, highly scheduled "little red school house."[7]

Creedal or religious communes are different, especially those who actively proselytize. Here the children are expected to participate in the religious life early, and to assume the commune's religious affiliation. In these cases, a child's struggle for independence must take him into areas other than those with which the creedal group is identified.

The within-family attitude toward the commune-reared child emerges in still another way; it leads to a specific philosophy which defines the parents' role in shaping the child's development. Interventionists regard themselves as playing a decisive if not determinative role in what happens to the child, much as nuclear parents do. The more rural, "hippie" communities tend to be noninterventionists. This perspective may reflect a belief system which asserts that a child's fate is determined by the stars, or by holy forces beyond human control. Parents therefore cannot interfere with what happens to him. Other noninterventionist parents feel they should not put "their trip" on the child; they try, therefore, in so far as it is possible, to shy from assuming parental prerogatives. Early self-reliance is encouraged, as is reliance on peers, so that the child is responsible for his own decisions.

Inevitably, communal parents are forced to make compromises or accommodations in their stances as they touch base with mainstream society at many points in their lives. It will be interesting to see how their children will come to regard their parents' own perspective about them, especially in the light of these necessary adaptations.

Cultural Reactions to Differences in Children

The reactions of the mainstream culture to commune children are obviously ambivalent. On the one hand, the original reactions to the counterculture have generalized to today's communities, so that families and children are still regarded as drop-outs, "hippies," "druggies," or, in sum, irresponsible adults who continue a prolonged adolescence.[12] Straight society and its agents, such as teachers and doctors, presume the commune children to be like their parents—rebellious, un-yielding to societal authority, slovenly, and disorganized in personality functioning. If they are physically dirty and unkempt, as are some rural children because water, when available, is not hot, parental neglect and absence of self-esteem are charged. The lack of concern about the child's use of four-letter words is "early depraved morality." Such rejecting attitudes have crystallized defensive reactions within the commune subculture. The members desire to isolate themselves geographically and psychologically, to keep themselves alert and suspicious of outsiders (especially the "over thirties"), and to seek ever closer adherence to their life-style rationale.

At the same time, increasing numbers of middle-aged, intelligent, and often professional adults have identified with the counterculture in some measure. They try to incorporate some of the values, attitudes and even practices of living groups in their own lives; this extends to the clothes they wear, their living style, their art and books, and their food.[23, 5] Their resonance with the communes has resulted in hastening the already rapid diffusion of counterculture values into "straight" society, thus rounding out the pluralism of family styles in America. The commune child is now a curiosity; if the tempo and direction of change remain steady, however, he may find himself in the forefront of traditional middle-class values and behaviors.

Characteristic Forms of Emotional Adjustment

Thus far little data exists about psychological disturbances in children who grow up in living groups. Some clinical cases have hinted at certain areas in which problems are likely to arise: ambiguity around identification, the tendency to enter into emotional relationships and to relate oneself extensively at the expense of intensity; pseudo-maturity in psychological development without genuine childhood experiences; and a defensive focus on self-reliance and self-assurance accompanied by a denial of dependency needs.

Isolated clinical case material has also reported that commune children utilize peers as substitutes for adult parents to assist in learning, decision making, and meeting dependency needs. They are trained to work at and resolve conflicts that arise in group living, and therefore seem insightful about their psychological needs, and are able to verbalize them.

There is the same dearth of data on coping behaviors as on problem areas. Informal evidence has pointed to the following capacities in living group children:

1. An ability to adapt to many different adults and different children early in life; so far as appearances, mores, and interests are concerned, the children generally maintain a pluralistic outlook.
2. They display a high degree of independence in certain areas (motoric, decision making), and a lack of independence in others (intellectual, social).
3. There is a resistance to routines and scheduling, and a passive-aggresive attitude toward systematic performance.
4. Superior discriminatory reality-testing behaviors are present so that languages and behaviors appropriate to a variety of social situations are able to be utilized.
5. There are strong social sensitivities to age-mates (and not to adults), and a responsiveness to their needs for comfort, solace, and attention.
6. Little interest (perhaps ability) is noted in delaying gratification, together with an enhanced enjoyment of "now" gratifications.
7. A sublimation of violence or aggressive behaviors into more sympathetic, cooperative and prosocial modes has been noted.
8. When adolescent turmoil arises, rebellion tends to be directed against the nontraditional qualities of the commune family.

Such competencies have been attributed to living group children who range widely in experience, age, and background. Few of those studied have actually been reared in communes all their lives; as a result, the contribution of commune life to cognitive and personality functioning cannot be definitely sorted out. As in nuclear family youngsters, there are a plethora of factors that contribute to the characteristics of the family environments: parenting personalities, birth data, constitutional and physiological data, and health and illness patterns. Commune families tend to view economic factors as important determinants, and they accordingly espouse home rather than hospital deliveries, underuse traditional medical institutions, and live as "voluntary poor." Ecological factors which determine the life of the commune family show great variability. They include size, composition of membership, distribution of sexes, role dispersion, and the accessibility and utilization of community facilities. Each of these variables must be understood in terms of its influence on child growth and development.

Finally, the study of children in communes is an area in which what one finds, and how one evaluates what one finds, are related to one's personal and professional biases. Are the behaviors observed in the commune growth-producing and adaptive, or do they deflect growth and diminish adjustment? Such development can actually be evaluated only in terms of adjustment. It is striking that to date, the kinds of anxieties, tensions, and pathogenic signs that point to pathology have not frequently been reported. One explanation may lie in the way "Establishment" or mainstream society has effected compromises in its own institutions in order to accommodate to the needs of these alternative modes.

Needed Social Structures

The changing values and attitudes of living group families in areas related to medicine, education, social welfare, and religion are already beginning to find response in existing institutions. These were never designed to accommodate to a subculture about which so much ambivalence exists. At the same time, those who maintain the existing structures have begun to appreciate that attitudes originally identified as counterculture are taking on a different hue. They are already characterizing their usual clientele, the mainstream parents, and children. Some examples of changing attitudes point to the needs of tomorrow's parents and children and suggest target areas for change in existing institutions.

Medicine:
1. Recognize that commune parents do not put a premium of cleanliness, and that "dirty" children are not necessarily neglected or poorly parented.
2. Birth is not viewed as an illness; therefore, hospitalization practices (with accompanying sterility, separation of mother and child from father and friends, and "medical" birth-room conditions) are counter to a receptive climate for the new baby and his family.
3. Use of non-M.D.'s to accommodate the needs of women, and to give pediatric and psychological counsel.
4. Incorporate, when advisable, "tried-and-true" folk medicine along with conventional medical practices.
5. Aim for more centralized services in order to individualize treatment.

Education:
1. Make available alternative forms of schools, classes, teaching styles, and curriculum.
2. Incorporate life experiences (outside the classroom) as part of the curriculum.
3. Increase utilization of males as teachers and aides, especially in private grades.
4. Encourage more systematic programming of parent participation in decision making about

school policy and programs, and in actual classroom involvement.

5. Accept more pluralistic dress, mores, preferences, and interests of children and parents.
6. Deemphasize grades, performance scores, and IQ tests in favor of individually oriented goals.
7. Develop and use nonsexist books and materials.

Economics and Consumer:
1. Establishment of nutritional needs of children, with appropriate labelling and advertising; discouraging the supply of nonnutritional packaged foods in public buildings (museums, schools, etc.).
2. Encouragement of simplistic, semirural life styles by making them economically feasible. This is accomplished through developing support systems oriented toward families who try to be self-sustaining and who are not productive members of a larger community; and providing training in agriculture, house building, etc., for families who are oriented toward self-help.
3. Creation of more flexible financial support arrangements which would allow parents who are ambivalent about accepting outside help to cycle in and out of the social agency and social welfare system as their personal conditions necessitate.

Community:
1. Give credence to a variety of religious institutions in addition to the three major religions so that children who differ ideologically (and may dress and look different) are not considered deviant.
2. Expose adults and children to family style differences so that the two-parent nuclear family is seen as only one possibility among many pluralistic forms.
3. Encourage architectural and financial interest in the design and construction of dwellings appropriate to the contemporary extended family.
4. Facilitate legal registration of babies born at home, and provide other legal services so that the personal property and rights of parents and children in commercial arrangements are protected, and equal to those in nuclear families.

If journalistic attention is a valid indication, then a remarkable tide of services in line with some of these values and attitudes is already gaining force. The extent to which revisions and compromises are effected in existing structures in society will be interesting to see—especially since these are very relevant to the developmental task facing the commune child.

REFERENCES

1. ALEXANDER, J., "Alternate Lifestyles: Relationships Between New Reality and Practice," *Clinical Social Work Journal*, 4:289, 1976.
2. BERGER, B., "Child Rearing Practices of the Communal Family," Progress report to the National Institute of Mental Health, Bethesda, Md., 1971.
3. BERGER, B., "Hippie Morality, More Old Than New," *Transaction*, 5(2):19–23, 1967.
4. CAVAN, S., "Hippies of the Redwood Forest," Scientific Analysis Corporation, Berkeley, Calif., 1971.
5. DELORA, J. S., and DELORA, J. R., "Intimate Life Styles: Marriage and its Alternatives," Goodyear Publishing Co., Pacific Palisades, Calif., 1972.
6. EIDUSON, B. T., "Child Development in Alternative Family Styles: Phase II," Progress Report to the National Institute of Mental Health, Bethesda, Md., 1975.
7. ———, "Child Development in Alternative Family Styles: Phase I," Progress Report to the Carnegie Corporation of New York, New York, 1975.
8. ———, "Looking at Children in Emergent Family Styles," *Children Today*, 3(4):2–6, 1974.
9. ———, and ALEXANDER, J., "The Role of Children in Alternative Family Styles," in Feshbach, N. D., and Feshbach, S. (Eds.), "Changing Status of Children," *Journal of Social Issues*, 34(2):149–167, 1978.
10. EIDUSON, B. T., and COHEN, J., "Changing Patterns of Child Rearing in Alternative Life Styles," in Davids, A. (Ed.), *Child Personality and Psychopathology: Current Topics*, pp. 25–68, John Wiley, New York, 1975.
11. ———, and ALEXANDER, J., "Alternatives in Child Rearing in the 1970's," *American Journal of Orthopsychiatry*, 43(5):720–731, 1973.
12. ESTALLACHILD, V., "Hippie Communes," in Delora, J. S., and Delora, J. R. (Eds.), *Intimate Life Styles: Marriage and its Alternatives*, pp. 332–337, Goodyear Publishing, Pacific Palisades, Calif., 1972.
13. FAIRFIELD, R., *Communes USA*, Maryland, Penguin, New York, 1972.
14. HAUGHEY, J. C., "The Commune—Child of the 1970's," in Delora, J. S., and Delora, J. R. (Eds.), *Intimate Life Styles: Marriage and its Alternatives*, pp. 328–331, Goodyear Publishing, Pacific Palisades, Calif., 1972.
15. HOURIET, R., *Getting Back Together*, Coward, McCann and Geoghegan, New York, 1969.
16. KANTER, R. M., *Commitment and Community: Utopias and Communes in Sociological Perspective*, Harvard University Press, Cambridge, Mass., 1972.
17. ———, "Getting It All Together: Some Group Issues in Communes," *American Journal of Orthopsychiatry*, 42:499–517, 1972.
18. KINKADE, K., *A Walden Two Experiment: The First 5 Years of Twin Oaks Community*, Morrow, New York, 1972.
19. MELVILLE, K., *Communes in the Counter Culture*, Morrow, New York, 1972.
20. RABIN, A. I., *Growing Up in the Kibbutz*, Springer, New York, 1965.
21. ROBERTS, R., *The New Communes: Coming Together in America*, Prentice-Hall, Englewood Cliffs, N.J., 1971.
22. SCHULTERBRANDT, J. G., and NICHOLS, E. J., "Ethical and Ideological Problems for Communal Living: A Caveat," *Family Coordinator*, 21:429–433, 1972.
23. SKOLNICK, A., and SKOLNICK, J., *Family in Transition: Rethinking Marriage, Sexuality, Child Rearing and Family Organization*, Little, Brown and Co., Boston, 1971.
24. SPIRO, M., *Children of the Kibbutz*, Harvard University Press, Cambridge, 1958.

PART D

The Child with Severe Handicaps

46 / The Blind Child

Harold Balikov and Carl B. Feinstein

Introduction—

the Nature of the Problem

The child blind from birth has very special problems and unique handicaps. In certain ways, the development of these children is therefore profoundly different. The psychiatrist working with the blind patient must understand the impact of blindness at various crucial stages of cognitive development and personality unfolding in order to make effective therapeutic or preventive interventions. In addition, by studying these differences, a great deal of insight may be gained into the role of vision in normal development.

Definition of Blindness—

Etiology, Incidence, and Prevalence

In the United States, legal blindness does not imply the inability to perceive light. It is defined as central visual acuity for a distance of 20/200 or less in the better eye with correction, or, if greater than 20/200, a field of vision no greater than 20 degrees in the widest diameter.[12, 14] In 1968–1969, the National Society for the Prevention of Blindness conducted a census of blind children. The estimated total school enrollment, elementary and secondary, of such children turned out to be 20,216.[15] It was striking that since the 1933–1934 census, the prevalence of blindness in children had increased by 85 percent. Much of this increase was due to the impact of retrolental fibroplasia (RLF).[12, 15] This still not fully understood condition was first reported in 1942 as a sequella of the neonatal treatment of premature infants. The upward trend in the incidence of this condition was reversed in the mid-1950s when research disclosed the role of oxygen in its etiology.[12] However, cases of RLF still occur, since in order to save a child's life, the risk of a severe vision impairment must sometimes be weighed against a need for high oxygen. The rubella epidemics of the mid-1960s resulted in another sharp increase in the incidence of blindness in children, frequently associated with multiple other handicapping conditions.[12, 15]

For more than three-quarters of these children, the age of onset of blindness is under one year of age.[12] Two-thirds are blind from birth, but many others in this group become blind (because of some prenatal influence) sometime during the first year. Of this group 18.9 percent are absolutely blind, 12.3 percent have some light perception, 29.7 percent have vision substantially less than 20/200, and 32.6 percent have vision at about the 20/200 level.

In the 1968–1969 survey, 50 percent of these children were blind on the basis of some prenatal factor (41 percent from a hereditary condition, and 8 percent for other congenital reasons).

413

Approximately 6 percent of blind children have a firmly documented history of excess of oxygen suffered from RLF in the postnatal period. Another 18 percent had RLF but the use of oxygen in the postnatal period had not been definitely established. Since that survey, it is likely that an increased number of rubella victims have entered the school-age population.

It should be borne in mind that, although this discussion is concerned with the child whose visual deficits are in the legally blind range, there is probably an equally large group of children with severe visual impairment who are not legally blind but whose special needs must also be met.[14]

Development of the Blind Child

In general, a child's concept of the world, both of objects and self, is dependent on integrated information obtained from all sensory modalities, including vision. When a child lacks vision, his development must follow a course that is distinctly different from that of the normal child. This provides the clinical researcher with a kind of laboratory situation that would not otherwise be available. There have now been many studies on children who have been blind from birth. Major reviews of the literature have been done by Fraiberg and Freedman[9] and, more recently, by S. Fraiberg.[7, 9] Other major contributors to this area have been D. Burlingham,[3, 4, 5] A. Sandler,[20] Elonen and Caine,[6] and Omwake and Solnit.[17] Through the work of these authors, interest has now come to focus on how the absence of vision affects ego development. Affective expression, human attachments, and object relationships, the use of the hand as a perceptual organ, locomotion, language acquisition, and the formation of permanent self and object representations are among the ego functions which have been studied extensively in the blind child. Other workers in the field, such as Lowenfeld, have concentrated on the many practical daily-life problems which must be surmounted by the blind child in the attainment of independent functioning.

AFFECTIVE EXPRESSION AND HUMAN ATTACHMENT

When a mother discovers that her child is blind, the initial reaction is often one of depression and grief.[8, 7, 9] Initially, many parents experience fear and repugnance as well as a sense of inadequacy to the task of loving, responding to, and caring for a blind child. Unfortunately, this preexisting depression sometimes interacts with some of the early consequences of blindness to produce a situation of parental withdrawal and childhood understimulation.

Expressive communication and rapport between infant and mother form an essential part of their developing relationship.[7, 9, 10, 19] Without vision, this vital interaction is derailed from the outset. In the blind infant/mother interaction, the fate of the social smile plays an important role in this derailment. The social smile is a crucial early component and indicator of developing attachment.[7, 9, 10, 19] In normal full-term infants, studies of the smiling reaction have established that nonelicited "endogenous" smiling begins at birth.[7, 10, 19] Progressing from this, smiling in response to acoustical stimuli appears in the course of the third week, some time before it develops in reaction to visual stimuli. The social smile in response to the particular visual gestalt of the face normally develops between the second and third month. The study of blind infants has revealed that all infants develop a social smile in response to mother's voice between the second and third month; however, this smile is much less pronounced and irregular than the normal social smile.[7, 9, 10] Thus, the social smile of the blind infants has only a weak, positive effect on early social interactions.

It is at this crucial period (between the second and third month) that the mutually responsive, visually imitative expressive social dialogue between mother and child comes into full flower.[7] At this point, the blind child's experience differentiates sharply from that of the sighted child. Not only is the blind child unable to respond to the visually mediated communications of the mother, but, in addition, eye contact is also lacking.[8, 7, 9] Failure of eye-to-eye contact conveys a sense of nonresponsiveness; its alienating effect on the mother (and other observers) is marked.[7] In addition, as demonstrated by the work of Fraiberg and her coresearchers, vision plays a dominant role in the development of facial emotional expressiveness.[7] At birth, blind children do not differ from sighted children in this regard; after only a few months, however, the discrepancy is dramatic. Blind children's faces appear blank except in response to basic needs and distress, or when they form their weak social smile. The mothers studied by Fraiberg's group were unable to tell whether their blind infants were interested in anything, be it a favorite toy or their efforts to speak to them. This factor alone causes many such mothers to turn away from their children during infancy.

There is another aspect to the behavior of the very young blind child which further reinforces the withdrawal of the parent or caretaking person. From very early on, blind infants and young children revert to and maintain a state of passive immobility. They do this for prolonged intervals. They cry less than other children and, superficially, they appear to be "very good babies."[5, 3, 7] Dorothy Burlingham's work,[3, 4, 5] however, suggests that this kind of quietness may, in fact, be a state of active alertness. It is designed to enable the child to maintain orientation and maximum receptivity to the environment through sound stimulation. Fraiberg[8, 9] described several blind infants who apparently maintained maximum contact with their environment by lying against a floor or carpeted surface. This behavior can be understood as a tactile orienting activity, but could very easily be interpreted by the mother as either passivity, withdrawal, or disinterest on the part of the child.

For a long time, it was assumed that, as a substitute for the visual perception of the mother, blind infants would early turn toward the sound of their mother's voice. Contrary to this expectation, in fact, this development does not take place until between nine and twelve months of age.[4, 7] Thus, in many ways the mother of the blind child is deprived of the whole interacting, reinforcing, "appealing and seducing" behavioral repertoire by which the normal infant keeps the mother engaged, involved, and attached to himself. This sets up a potentially pathological, self-reinforcing pattern in which the initially depressed mother is continually discouraged by the absence of a recognizable response from her infant, who appears, instead, to be content to be left alone. Paradoxically, therefore, these infants, so much in need of extra sensory and affective stimulation, receive less of this than the normal child.

USE OF THE HANDS AS A PERCEPTUAL ORGAN

The study of blind infants has clarified the fact that vision is a necessary sensory modality for establishing midline hand coordination and reaching for objects.[7] In sighted infants, this development occurs between three or four months of age; but it does not happen the same way in blind infants. Unfortunately, sound does not function as an alternative stimulus for reaching toward an object until between nine months and one year of age.[1, 7] As a result of these two phenomena, the blind infant's use of hands and touch as a modality of perception undergoes little development. Thus, there is another divergance between the blind and the normal child: The blind infant does not develop reaching-out behavior.[1, 7]

This failure to reach out has major ramifications for ego development. In the first two months of life, it is the mouth which is the principal exploring and orienting organ. Following this, the "partnership" of the hand with the mouth gradually shifts as, under the influence of the visual modality, the child turns outward toward the environment.[1, 8, 7] Thus, in this next developmental stage, the infant is described as "grasping with his eyes alone." Over the next few months, vision becomes a progressively more important stimulus for the child's reaching out and grasping objects. As part of this progression, the hands become independent of the mouth in their exploration and mastery of the world. However, for the blind child, the eyes cannot lead the hand and it is not until the end of the first year that sound becomes a stimulus for reaching out and orienting to the environment. Therefore, for the blind child, the whole turning outward in the use of the hand is blocked for most of the first year. As Sandler described it, the hand remains subservient to the passive oral aims and to the direct body gratifications characteristic of the earliest oral stage.[20] Instead of reaching out with the hand, the child's hand returns to the mouth and the child's focus shifts back to internal body stimulation. As development proceeds for the blind infant, objects which are grasped are then brought to the mouth for feeling and sucking, demonstrating the ongoing primacy of the mouth as a perceptual organ. According to Fraiberg, for those infants who do not receive special early intervention, the hand may not develop as an autonomous organ of perception until the last half of the second year.[1, 7] She reports several cases in which this derailment of the normal visual-tactile sensory system was still in effect in the latency age range. As a result, these blind children have "blind hands" as well; that is, hands which do not make sensitive discriminations and are incapable of braille reading.[7]

Fraiberg and her group also explored the blind child's hands as organs of affective expression.[8, 7] When attention was turned away from the "blank" faces of these children, it was discovered that when being held by their mothers, these infants "lovingly" fingered their parents' faces yet quickly rejected the tactile exploration of stranger's faces. The interests of the infants cannot be detected by looking at their faces, but they become apparent from the manner in which their hands pass over or explore and touch various objects. Fraiberg states that the parents' capacity to recognize and respond to this unusual route of expressivity is crucial to the development of reciprocal affective communication between parent and child.

LOCOMOTION

All longitudinal studies have shown blind children to display a marked delay in locomotion.[1, 8, 7] The normal age at which they walk independently is two years, but many do not attain independent motility until substantially later. A smaller percentage of the more deviant members of this group may not have attained meaningful independent locomotion even by middle childhood. The earlier stages of gross motor development toward motility proceed in the same way as with sighted children. These stages include the ability to turn from the supine to the prone position, to sit up, to pull to an upright position, and to attain a state of readiness for creeping and crawling. At this point, however, the normal progression halts, and the blind child fails to start crawling.

Fraiberg and her colleagues found that vision is a vital incentive toward motility. Creeping occurs when the infant sees something attractive, reaches out, and tries to get it. The blind child, on the other hand, unaware of the presence of objects, does not move toward them. Instead, when he is not being tactilely or auditorily stimulated, he remains in an immobile posture.

Parallel to this delayed development of locomotion, Dorothy Burlingham and Selma Fraiberg report deviant development in the discharge pathways for aggression.[3, 7] While there is no consensus on this issue, there appears to be either an inhibition of the expression of aggression which parallels the inhibition in locomotion, or a failure in the differentiation of aggressive drive expression from other drive elements. In support of this latter idea, hand behavior such as scratching, clawing, and pinching was observed by Fraiberg in deviant blind children in cases where it was not really a direct expression of aggression but more a corollary of oral incorporative drives.

LANGUAGE DEVELOPMENT

To date, there have been several studies of language development in neurologically intact blind children.[7, 16, 13] These demonstrate that, in many ways, up to the age of two, language development is within the norm for sighted children. At about the age of two to two and a half, however, the normal course of language development deviates, especially in respect to the proper use of pronouns. As this appears to reflect an underlying delay in concept formation, it will be discussed further under "Formation of Permanent Self and Object Representations."

There appear to be some distinctive characteristics to the language of blind children. In general, they tend to imitate the colloquial expressions of sighted people, even when this involves visual descriptive aspects which cannot have meaning for the users.[4, 3, 7, 14] There are also important differences in the way the blind child uses speech in social interactions.[4, 7, 14] An example of this is the tendency to ask questions and to maintain discussion primarily in order to keep in contact with and oriented toward the people in his vicinity. Thus, language is used as a means of reaching out to and keeping in contact with people. It must be kept in mind that even in a roomful of people, if there are no sounds, blind persons are substantially disoriented with regard to these others; indeed, this is a continuous source of anxiety and vulnerability. There is a tendency toward "concreteness" in speech observed in some blind individuals from birth onward. This appears to be related in some way to a delay in the development of the capacity for abstraction, which is, in turn, secondary to difficulties with the formation of mental representations of physical objects.

FORMATION OF PERMANENT SELF AND OBJECT REPRESENTATIONS

The development of self and object representations is greatly hampered in the blind child. These children have no way of knowing about the existence of material objects of any kind other than through the tactile or auditory modes. Furthermore, without vision, the blind child cannot be aware that objects are permanent or that they continue to exist after tactile and auditory contact have been lost. It appears that both these modes, the auditory and the tactile, must be operating synergistically to provide sufficient input to form integrated images of objects. As described, however, it is not until the end of the first year of life that the infant can use sound stimuli as an indication of the presence of an object or person. The tactile mode is itself subject to many vicissitudes in the course of its development. In addition, locomotion is markedly delayed in the blind child, thus depriving him even further of opportunities to utilize his tactile capacities to explore the physical environment. Indeed, unless parents and caretakers make special efforts to support this kind of exploration, the immobile, passive-appearing, apparently disinterested, and unreaching blind toddler will be markedly deprived of tactile stimuli.

In her intensively treated group of children, Fraiberg studied the milestones of attachment such as stranger and separation anxiety.[7] For this group, milestones approached the norm for sighted children. Thus, for example, when picked up by strangers at nine or ten months of age, they responded by stiffening, crying, and pushing away, and were calmed when they were held by their mothers and had a chance to explore the mother's face manually. However, even the most thoughtful and vigorous intervention could not prevent the developmental delay that first manifested itself in the inability to use pronouns properly, such as confusion of the pronouns "I" and "you." From the age of two to two and a half, blind children diverge from sighted children in that they do not develop representational play at the usual time; in this respect they remain years behind the sighted norm. It must be kept in mind that unless someone speaks to him, makes a noise, or touches him, the blind child never sees another person perform an independent action. Also, for the blind child, there is no mirror. In all these ways, there is a delay in forming any concept of people or animals doing things that do not impinge on him directly. This delay retards the development of permanent mental representations of objects in the separation of the self representation from the environmental ground. The children in Fraiberg's group developed the correct use of pronouns and gained representational play at the same time; these took place between the ages of three and five. It is likely that in many blind children this progression may take a good deal longer to occur.

DEPENDENCE/INDEPENDENCE

The development of gradually increasing independence and autonomy in functioning goes on throughout the preschool period and into latency. The blind child, however, encounters many obstacles which can be overcome only by thoughtful attention to detail and sufficient educational exposure.[5, 14] There are constant difficulties in traveling from one place to another, orienting to unfamiliar surroundings, finding objects, and other aspects of function which are routinely and automatically part of the self-care system of the sighted child. The most capable blind child given an optimum environment will be more dependent on parents or caretaking adults than the normal child need be. Routine self-care skills such as dressing, eating with utensils, toilet training, hygiene, etc., all present practical problems. Each of these, however, can be surmounted. Given these constant background difficulties, the blind child is bound to have a high sensitivity and vulnerability to fears of failure and abandonment. This can easily lead to difficulties both on the part of the caretaker and of the child in relinquishing dependent protection and achieving a maximum degree of self sufficiency. As Dorothy Burlingham described: "the phase of conflict between dependence and independence . . . has to be immeasurably longer with the blind. With them, it is less a stage of development than a continued testing of their own powers of accomplishment as well as of adult reaction to what they are doing."[14]

As the child approaches school age, many of these issues of autonomy and dependency/independence have to be faced in the school and larger world environment. Nursery school may be a first experience in socialization with peers away from the specific support system of the home. Experience has shown that given a properly understanding and supportive teacher, many blind children can be successfully integrated into a regular sighted nursery school situation.[14] At the age of five or six, when the time of choice for regular schooling is reached, decisions have to be made among a variety of educational possibilities. There are public or private residential schools for the blind, public or private schools for the sighted with special resources available for the blind, or education with the sighted with itinerant specialized service for the blind available during the course of the school day.[14] Because of the many special educational techniques required in the teaching of the blind, and, undoubtedly, because of societal attitudes toward the blind, there has been a strong tendency toward utilizing residential schools designed exclusively for blind children.[14] The first such schools in the United States were founded in 1829.

There has been little written about the effect of removal of blind children from the home to the residential school in early latency. However, it is recommended that careful attention be paid to the individual vulnerabilities and needs of the child, the local community resources, and the strengths and weakness of the family situation.

Given the tendency to be segregated into special school situations, integration into normal society is a constant issue with the blind child.[14] This is an important function of all educational institutions serving such children. No particular pattern of cognitive deficit has been identified for the blind child other than what results from associated congenital impairments.[2, 14] Specialized psychological and cognitive testing is available for these children.[2] The braille system of printing and reading enables the skilled practitioner to read, although at a substantially slower rate than the skilled sighted reader.[14] However, as previously noted, many blind children have difficulty in attaining skill in braille reading. Talking books are an important, rapidly expanding educational and cultural asset.[14] They have the advantage of being accessible to all the blind, including those who cannot use braille efficiently, and can thus greatly increase "reading" speed and availability of text.

Deprived of vision, the blind child may be expected to have increased difficulties in understanding the anatomic differences between the sexes. Societal attitudes and possible normal developmental vulnerabilities in the children combine to make the use of touch an unresolved, insufficiently studied topic in aiding blind children with these gender issues. For reasons which now seem dated and inappropriate, historically there was strict segregation according to sex in the residential schools for the blind.[14] However, it is now recognized that this constriction of experience works against the general principal that everything possible must be done to enrich the blind child's opportunities for encounter, and patterns of sex segregation seem to be falling away.

Psychopathology and Developmental Deviation of the Blind Child

As has been described, the deprivation of vision results in deviant and delayed development of important ego functions.

The delay in locomotion, the problems in affective communication, and the delays in self and object representation have been discussed. There are certain very frequent behavioral consequences of the skewed development of blind children which are often referred to as "blindisms."[6, 7] These are repetitive actions such as body swaying, head knocking, eye rubbing, head rotating, or repetitive hand motions. The hand motions often take the form of the hands being held at shoulder height with stereotyped waving movements of the fingers. Grasped objects are brought to the mouth. As noted, these children often strike a posture of prolonged, apparently blank, but probably alert, attentive immobility. Much of this behavior can be understood as indicating alternate routes for drive discharge when motility and reaching interactions with the environment are impeded and the child is forced back to internal body sensations for self-stimulation. The greater the deficit in self and object representations, the more detached and unrelated to people the child will be, and the more he will rely on such discharge patterns.

The blind child experiences the world as a constant source of unpredictable and unidentifiable surprises. He tries to construct reality on the basis of sound, but he often cannot clearly discern the source of the sound, the nature of the sound, or whether it indicates a potential source of harm. Since orientation to distance is greatly impaired, there is little awareness of proximity concepts or any clear notion of the extended world. The disappearance of sound becomes the equivalent of the total disappearance of the object with concomitant fears of disorientation in space.

There is, to be sure, a wide variation in the degree of expression of these behavioral and developmental deviations. In particular, there is a group of more severely disturbed blind children who have been studied. David Freedman and Selma Fraiberg worked with twenty-seven blind children between the ages of three and fourteen.[9] Of these, seven presented a clinical picture that closely resembled the syndrome of autism in the sighted. Fraiberg feels that this is a realistic, replicable sample of the incidence of a severe and classic blind deviant child syndrome.[7] These children demonstrate stereotyped hand behaviors, rocking, swaying, and mutism or echolalic speech. They may sit for hours sucking on an object and rocking, while appearing detached, vacant, and virtually unresponsive to any approach by another human being. The hands are little used to gain information from the environment; instead they are involved in a "morbid alliance with the mouth." Many of these children have virtually no independent motility. They do not seem to be able to distinguish between self and others, or to have any firm sense of things being "out there." There appears to be a profound absence of human attachment.

The etiology of this clinical picture, particularly in respect to the question of the presence or absence of brain damage, is still debated. The situation is complicated by the fact that in spheres other than the visual,[7, 12, 18] substantial percentages of blind children, particularly those with RLF or rubella syndromes, do have some measure of brain damage. As noted, however, Fraiberg's studies reveal clearly that even without brain damage, blind children display deviant patterns of development.[7]

The RLF blind babies have been the subject of several studies, specifically regarding the pathogenic nature of RLF.[6, 13, 16, 18] Over and above the damage produced by the high oxygen concentration itself, a large percentage of these children are the product of premature births and, therefore, likely candidates for other forms of brain damage. The work of Norris,[16] Spalding, Brody, and Keeler[13] compared the outcome of blind children with RLF children and children blind from other causes. They established that the clinical picture of deviant ego development is not associated with any specific etiology for blindness. The Norris study has particular importance because it involved 295 children. These children were tested several times during the first six and a half years of life on several different measures of performance. It was found that the RLF children could not be distinguished from other blind children. Keeler's study in Toronto included RLF children, children congenitally blind from other conditions, and children blinded postnatally (most were in their first and second year of blindness, and many had vision substantially better than that of RLF children). Keeler concluded that when other brain damage is absent, the primary factors leading to ego deviation were total or near-total blindness from birth, and a history of inadequate emotional stimulation in the early months of life.

From the previous discussion of development, it can be seen that many factors lead to the increased likelihood of blind children suffering from severe environmental stimulus deprivation. Not only is there the direct effect of blindness on the inability to perceive objects, but the depression of the mother and the major abnormality in preverbal affective communication between mother and infant plays a large role in depriving the infant of environmental stimuli. All these combine to create a situation in which some children have never really had a chance to establish adequate human contact.[7] Thus, although the clinical picture of the blind deviant child may bear many resemblances to autism in the sighted child, there are probably important differences between these syndromes. For example, it would be inaccurate to speak of "avoidance of contact" or "autistic defenses" in children who, because of their sensory disability and stimulus deprivation, have never attained the concept of object permanence.

Intervention and Treatment

Fraiberg's recent work has demonstrated that active early intervention can greatly alleviate the problems in development for the blind child.[1, 7] In the earliest months of life, the therapeutic team sought to deal with the mother's depression and to train her to understand why her child's facial expressions were not communicative. Parents were taught to look at the children's hands as important indicators of affect and interests. Given this opportunity to learn to read their child's communications, parents were able to overcome their misperception that their child's apparently passive, inactive attitude represented a rejection of them. Furthermore, the parents' recognition of the importance of the hand as a tactile sensory and expressive organ enabled them to become more effective and creative in providing the specific kinds of stimulation their children needed. The therapeutic team working with the parents devised specially structured combined auditory-tactile stimulus patterns designed to help the infants overcome the absence of vision and to enhance the use of the hands as organs of perception. This was accomplished by the ingenious use of sound and textured objects placed in the child's midline; the child could thus explore the interactions of his hands while holding objects there. The handling of perceptually and auditorally interesting objects by the children was encouraged in every possible way. When the developmental impasse in motility was impending, the team intervened to facilitate creeping by placing highly attractive objects near the child; first they were just within reach, then slightly farther away, and thus on and on, so that the child continued to reach for them. In this way he began to move forward. It was discovered that the attainment of motility had a dramatic effect on the further development of these infants. Given this kind of early intervention, the children in Fraiberg's study had motility milestones much closer to those of the normal sighted population than of the group of blind children as a whole.

Psychotherapeutic work with deviant blind children is based on the principle that the child must be seduced and encouraged in every way to reach out into the real world, into the world of people and objects.[3, 6, 7, 17] Considerable activity and commitment is involved on the part of the therapist, who must literally pull the child out of the withdrawn state. Physical contact, particularly in the encouragement of motility, is extremely important, as is the use of attractive tactile and auditory stimuli. Much of the therapeutic work involves encouraging the further development of speech. The efforts of the therapist must be supplemented by a therapeutic school setting. Although full normality may not be attained with the most severely disturbed, given this kind of intensive intervention, many children can make substantial progress.

REFERENCES

1. ADELSON, E., and FRAIBERG, S., "Gross Motor Development in Infants Blind From Birth," *Child Development*, 45:114–126, 1974.

2. BATEMAN, BARBARA, "Psychological Evaluation of Blind Children," in Wolf, J. M. (Ed.), *The Multiply Handicapped Child*, pp. 297–303, Charles C. Thomas, Springfield, Ill., 1973.

3. BURLINGHAM, D., "Some Problems of Ego Development in Blind Children," in Eissler, R. S., et al. (Eds.), *The Psychoanalytic Study of the Child*, vol. 20, pp. 194–208, International Universities Press, New York, 1965.

4. ———, "Hearing and Its Role in the Development of the Blind," in Eissler, R. S., et al. (Eds.), *The Psychoanalytic Study of the Child*, vol. 19, pp. 85–112, International Universities Press, New York, 1964.

5. ———, "Some Notes on the Development of the Blind," in Eissler, R. S., et al. (Eds.), *The Psychoanalytic Study of the Child*, vol. 16, pp. 121–145, International Universities Press, New York, 1961.

6. ELONEN, A. S., and CAIN, A. C., "Diagnostic Evaluation and Treatment of Deviant Blind Children," *American Journal of Orthopsychiatry*, 34:625–633, 1964.

7. FRAIBERG, S., *Insights from the Blind*, Basic Books, New York, 1977.

8. ———, "Parallel and Divergent Patterns in Blind and Sighted Infants," in Eissler, R. S., et al. (Eds.), *The Psychoanalytic Study of the Child*, vol. 23, pp. 264–300, International Universities Press, New York, 1968.

9. ———, and FREEDMAN, D. A., "Studies in the Ego Development of the Congenitally Blind Child," in Eissler, R. S., et al. (Eds.), *The Psychoanalytic Study of the Child*, vol. 19, pp. 113–169, International Universities Press, 1964.

10. FREEDMAN, D. G., "Smiling in Blind Infants and the Issue of Innate Vs. Acquired," *Journal of Child Psychology and Psychiatry*, 5:171–184, 1964.

11. GESELL, A., et al., *Vision, Its Development in the Infant and Child*, Heaber, New York, 1949.

12. HATFIELD, E. M., "Why Are They Blind?" *Sight-Saving Review*, 45(1):3–22, 1975.

13. KEELER, W. R., "Autistic Patterns and Defective Communication in Blind Children with Retrolental Fibroplasia," in Hoch, P. H., and Zubin, J. (Eds.), *Psychopathology of Communication*, pp. 64–83, Grune & Stratton, New York, 1958.

14. LOWENFIELD, B., *Our Blind Children; Growing and Learning With Them*, Charles C Thomas, Springfield, Ill., 1971.

15. "Manual on Use of the NSPB Standard Classification of Causes of Severe Vision Impairment and Blindness," National Society for the Prevention of Blindness, New York, 1966.

16. NORRIS, M., et al., *Blindness in Children*, University of Chicago Press, Chicago, 1957.

17. OMWAKE, E. G., and SOLNIT, A. J., "It Isn't Fair: The Treatment of a Blind Child," in Eissler, R. S., et al. (Eds.), *The Psychoanalytic Study of the Child*, vol. 16, pp. 352–404, 1961.

18. PARMALEE, A. H., et al., "The Mental Development of Children with Blindness Due to Retrolental Fibroplasia," *The AMA Journal of Children's Diseases*, 96:641–645, 1958.

19. ROBSON, J., "The Role of Eye-to-Eye Contact in Maternal-Infant Attachment," in Ghess, S., and Thomas, A. (Eds.), *Annual Progress in Child Psychiatry and Child Development*, pp. 92–108, Brunner-Mazel, New York, 1968.

20. SANDLER, A. M., "Aspects of Passivity and Ego Development in the Blind Infant," in Eissler, R. S., et al. (Eds.), *The Psychoanalytic Study of the Child*, vol. 18, pp. 343–360, International Universities Press, New York, 1963.

47 / The Deaf Child

Hilde S. Schlesinger

Deafness can be defined as hearing loss that is present from birth or early childhood and that renders an individual incapable of effecting meaningful and substantial auditory contact with the environment.[25]

Nature of Hearing and Hearing Loss

Hearing loss can vary widely. Normal human beings can respond to frequencies from 20 to 20,000 cycles per second. The speech range for most purposes is defined as extending from 250 to 4,000 cycles. Low-frequency vowels are found near the 500 cycle band and high-frequency consonants near the 3,000 cycle band, with the majority of sounds falling between 500 and 2,000. Hearing losses are determined by computing the decibel loss on the speech range. A decibel is a ratio expressing the intensity of sound; and the human ear has an intensity tolerance range from 1 to approximately 120 decibels. Conversational levels of intensity fall between 50 and 60 decibels, a whisper between 25 and 30, while traffic noise may reach an intensity of 25 to 85 decibels. Mild hearing loss usually refers to 15 to 30 decibels, moderate from 31 to 50, severe from 51 to 80, and profound from 81 to 100. Total hearing loss is rare. The actual auditory contact with the environment also depends on the hearing threshold outside the speech range at both higher and lower frequencies.

Hearing loss is more than a medical and audiological diagnosis; it is a cultural phenomenon in which social, emotional, linguistic, and intellectual patterns and problems are inextricably bound together.[29] Although deafness occurs throughout the age span of humans and is stressful at any time, the complexities of early prelingual deafness are the most intricate and the least well understood.

The Typical Deaf Child

The "typical" deaf child and adult have been studied by many investigators.[15, 23, 1, 21] Most agree about the presence of academic and linguistic retardation despite normal intellectual potential and a psychological uniqueness characterized primarily by emotional immaturity. There is, however, a growing trend to indicate that these characteristics are not a necessary consequence of early childhood deafness. Furth[12, 11] has demonstrated that the deaf are not as retarded cognitively—in terms of nonlinguistic symbols—as previously believed. Schlesinger and Meadow[30] postulate that varying auditory and environmental conditions can significantly affect the cognitive and emotional development of the deaf child.

Previously, the deaf child was studied without clear delineation of a number of important variables that markedly affect the character of the handicap. More recently, studies are forthcoming with specific attention to variables such as etiology, extent, shape, and onset of the hearing loss, hearing aid usage, parental hearing status, parental involvement, and school environment.

It may be that the most crucial variables promoting optimal adaptation are related to a successful resolution of the impact of the diagnostic crisis and to an opportunity for early parent-child communication.

The Diagnostic Crisis

Most parents of deaf children can hear and the diagnosis of deafness precipitates a crisis. The defect is usually unexpected and invisible. The infant is seen and identified as normal, and expectations for normal growth ensue. At varying times in the child's life suspicions about his hearing loss develop, usually in the parents and grandparents (86 percent) and much less frequently in the physician (7.5 percent).[9] Suspicion is accompanied by anxiety. Unfortunately, the type of defect, its uniqueness, infrequency, and invisibility frequently delay the diagnosis. The symptoms produced by deafness—delayed speech and lack of attentiveness—are ubiquitous and often mimic other childhood disorders such as retardation, developmental lag, and emotional disturbance.

During the process of suspecting, recognizing, and identifying the handicap, fear, anger, guilt, bewilderment, sorrow, and resentment are experienced by the most normal parents. Physicians in the past have often compounded the anxiety by denying the diagnosis, or by false reassurance.[19] The medical expert is hampered by ignorance about deafness, a repugnance to give "bad news," a frequent reluctance to deal with so-called irreversible defects, and a vast array of conflicting ideologies surrounding deafness in the young child.[30] Distress about the diagnosis or lack of authoritative support may lead to overly rigid adherence to therapeutic regimens, vacillations between overprotection and rejection, and/or self-sacrifice and martyrdom for the chld's sake. In the face of this condition, many parents desire to produce an impossible normalcy, intactness, and conformity; they yearn to eliminate the defect itself and any differences which it might cause. Such desires occasionally lead to a search for miracles or a temporary paralysis in parenting.

Deaf parents appear to expect the diagnosis and to accept it at a much earlier age. Deaf parents cope with the crisis easily and quickly, while their hearing counterparts prolong and intensify it.[20]

Early Language Interchange

The second crucial variable may be related to an opportunity to establish an early, largely meaningful, reciprocal, and enjoyable language interchange between parent and child. This can happen when the hearing loss occurred after language acquisition, when the residual hearing was extensive, when the curve of the hearing loss was propitious, and when early appropriate and consistent amplification was provided successfully. All of the above increase the auditory contact with the environment and thus enable the infant to acquire the basic linguistic tools at the usual time and through the usual auditory route.

Deaf children of deaf parents also establish successful communication early through the visual modality of sign language. Without this early linguistic interchange through either auditory-vocal or visual-motor modalities (or both, to their respective optimal level) the deaf child suffers a cumulative linguistic deficit which in turn affects most areas of his life. Such a view corroborates an impression that some of the characteristics of deaf children should be examined in terms of the basic clash between the child and the environment,[6] a clash which is affected by linguistic restraints during the early years.

The Child's Coping Experience

INFANCY

Little is known about the infancy of deaf children. They are said to be normal, but one wonders. Auditory attachment behavior is diminished and compensatory visual and tactile stimulation may not be established in the absence of a diagnosis.

TODDLER STAGE

As one proceeds to the next stage of development serving separation and individuation, symbolic and linguistic communication assume a more crucial role. According to the cognitive view of early development, most early learning consists of the reduction of ambiguity, the ordering of the "buzzing confusion" that surrounds the child. Language plays a critical role, which is still under investigation. The youngster is now expected to learn how to forego, delay, substitute, or prohibit satisfaction of his own urges. The outer controls designed to help the child are more and more accompanied by linguistic symbols and communication. How difficult is this for and with a deaf child? If a child does not react or turn to mother's voice, the repeated maternal attempts may become increasingly shrill and irritated. Or they may be replaced by harassed physical contact such as chin jerking and body poking. In brief, the communicative frustration will be high prior to any actual interchange. The interchange itself is difficult with an absence or paucity of linguistic symbols.

Communication between parent and child may diminish drastically or may be an incomprehensible verbal barrage. More frequently, however, it is limited to the labeling of objects, persons, or qualities in the here and now. The hearing parents of deaf children, frustrated by the linguistic retardation, frequently resort to the restrictive, imperative, positional linguistic codes said to be the "hallmark" of the lower social class mothers. It is easier to say no to the deaf child than to make him understand "not at this time, not in this way, not in this place." In many ways the deaf child tends to resemble the child of poverty, and these maternal linguistic codes may contribute to this outcome. These codes do not provide freedom from immediacy. Words are slower to substitute for acts, and without them, the children do not as easily distinguish between wishes, fantasy, and reality. Discipline must rely on timing and intensity without adequate cognitive structuring.

Hearing parents of deaf children put a marked premium on verbalization on the part of their deaf child; paradoxically, their anxious insistence frequently leads to an increase in negative mutism. Power struggles usually seen in the battle over toilet training occur in the battle over words.

What happens to deaf youngsters? What happens to their hearing parents? Deaf preschoolers are frequently described as immature, impulsive, and showing a lower level of autonomy even in areas where skills are available.[6] In comparing deaf and hearing children and their mothers, it was noted that as a group, the mothers of deaf children were less flexible, permissive, encouraging, and creative; they were more frequently didactic and intrusive. As a group, the deaf children were less buoyant, less compliant, showed less enjoyment of their mothers, and less pride in their achievements. Within this group of deaf children, however, some revealed evidence of a more successful and gratifying communication with their mothers. These understanding-understood children had a higher level of communicative competence and more closely resembled hearing children and their parents.[30]

THE SCHOOL-AGE CHILD

Deaf children typically start school at three years of age, if not before. Adults who are in frequent contact with deaf children embroider upon the theme of the "differentness" of the child. Teachers, parents, and mental health professionals have commented on a bipolar behavior pattern. On the one hand are the "goody two shoes," emphatically obedient and compliant, and on the other, the "Attila the Hun" types, powerful and excessively defiant youngsters.

The author has previously indicated that cognitive structuring is more difficult for the mother of a deaf child and thus the rules of the moral order are more difficult to clarify. This presents an interesting hypothesis: It has been found by Cheyne[7] that cognitive structuring is important if the child is to pinpoint the effects of punishment to a specific response rather than producing a generalized response inhibition. Does the decrease of cognitive structuring relate to the two extremes of obedience and rebellion among deaf children or to the living by the book of etiquette code in deaf adults?

If the world outside remains confusing for too long, the growing child must find ways to give it meaning. One way to do this is by emphatic obedience to parental dicta; the world will then make sense by authority. It can also be done by total defiance; meaning can then reside in the very act of opposition. But many parental dicta remain ambiguous and confusing and are falsely interpreted by the child.

Meaning can be less ambiguous in the world of objects. Meaning for the young deaf child may reside in joyful or obsessional manipulation of the physical environment where the interplay of thought and action can progress more satisfactorily than in the world of persons. Behaviorally, this more ready understanding may have some noxious consequences such as overinsistence on orderliness in terms of space, sequence, and tempo. It is interesting to note that there are a number of theoretically important parallels between the dysfunctional thought processes of the obsessional and some of the psychological uniqueness of the deaf.

Cognitively, there are more felicitous outcomes. This greater ease, this more effective learning through the establishment of logical connections in the physical world may explain the impressive body of evidence[12, 11] that indicates that the deaf are not retarded in certain tasks which may require symbolic thought but are not bound to linguistic symbols per se. It may also account for some of the parallels between the "disadvantaged" and the deaf child.[26, 14]

Finally, both parents and school may contribute to what can be described as decreased creativity and/or a constricted life area. Most children learn about the world in some optimal combination of self-initiated exploratory maneuvers and other initiated "teaching" maneuvers, both occurring in a sensorily varied environment. Optimal development may require an ability and opportunity to get feedback from self-initiated actions. Furthermore, parental contributions to creativity in children appear to be related not only to close parental relationships but also to reciprocal enjoyment and fantasy play.

Both parents and school tend to inhibit the self-initiated maneuvers of the deaf child. This is due to their anxious urgency to communicate, to "pour language" into him as if he were a receptacle. Many linguistic stimuli offered the deaf child are either too difficult or too easy. The result is environmental monotony, another diminisher of creativity.[16] Unceasing drill, both in terms of vocabulary items and grammar, is not very effective; it tends to reduce aspects of reciprocity and enjoyment and to increase vastly frustration and disturbed communication.

THE ADOLESCENT

From the description of the younger age groups, it is not surprising that a study of hearing-impaired adolescent girls demonstrates a personality pattern characterized by (1) pronounced underdevelopment in conceptual forms of mental activity; (2) emotional underdevelopment; (3) a substantial lag in understanding the dynamics of interpersonal relationships as well as the world about them; (4) a highly egocentric life perspective; (5) a markedly constricted life style; and (6) a rigid adherence to the book of etiquette code rather than to an inner sensibility as a standard for behaving and even for feeling.[15] Other observers[24, 3] corroborate the above generalizations.

Overall Psychological Profile

Throughout his development the deaf child has been found to exhibit characteristics of rigidity, egocentricity, absence of creativity, absence of inner controls, impulsiveness, suggestibility, and lack of empathy[17] along with his markedly decreased linguistic competence and performance. However, it must be noted again that, in general, factors leading to intellectual, social, and physical restrictions and limitations (whether due to the nature of the handicap, its management, or parental attitude) all tend to result in similar findings.[10]

Hearing loss per se is usually an invisible condition. However, the deaf child appears to learn early whether the differences which spring from his hearing loss—hearing aids, divergent vocal quality, and increased use of gestures or signs—are seen as good or bad by the overall society. It is difficult, if not impossible, to differentiate clearly between the impact of extrinsic devices and the impact of other hallmarks of deafness.

Nevertheless, the following may elucidate some of the "difference" rather than body image disturbances seen in the deaf child.

"Difference Disturbances." Identity awareness occurs early; excited three-year-olds have been observed to point with pleasure to others wearing hearing aids or using sign language. One youngster at twenty-six months was said to be glued to a television program using sign language with utter disregard for other programs (the author is not claiming the child understood the content). Although there is early awareness of this difference, its interpretation takes considerable time. Thus some youngsters will call deaf anyone who uses sign language, or will repeatedly ignore explanations that others are deaf and could not hear them. By age eight, most of the deaf youngsters understand what deafness means in terms of "ears not working," "not hearing," and occasionally "that ears are broken."

Youngsters whose parents scorn sign language will occasionally show motor inhibition of their hands. This different approach to body image can also be seen in a study of body representation via the Draw a Man test.[23] In general, the deaf child was shown to have characteristic perceptual distortions regarding himself. His body image included altered perception of various body parts in terms of hands, ears, lips, and others. His body image tended to vary on the basis of school, i.e., schools using sign language had more distinctive representations of hands and fingers, while those stressing only oral language had more distinctive representations of mouth and lips. Both deaf groups were perceptually aware of the ear at an earlier period than hearing children.

Self-concept. How does the deaf child learn who he is and how others see him? He feels early that his hearing parents want to force him into the normalcy which is not available to him. He feels early that the language that others learn easily is to him a laborious task, the result of which is terribly important to his parents.

A number of self-concept tests have been used

with deaf children. However, most of them use sentence completion forms which require some degree of linguistic competence and which made them unsuitable for profoundly deaf children. Nevertheless, one interesting finding emerged in several studies that tended to indicate that deaf children were significantly less accurate in their self-perceptions than were hearing children[8] (with the misjudgment erring toward superiority[5, 13]). Among the reasons for this self-judgment of superiority may be that the studies did not differentiate between pre- and post-linguistically deaf children,[17] nor did they take into account the excessive praise for minor accomplishments frequently provided in deaf schools, or the relative isolation of those children from cultural restraints and coercions.[2]

There is one pictorial self-concept assessment[18, 30] which differentiates clearly between different groups of deaf children. The most positive scores were obtained by deaf children of deaf parents residing in residential schools, whereas the deaf children of hearing parents in either residential or day schools had a significantly lower self-concept. This pattern varied with age. Deaf children of deaf parents come to school with early acceptance by parents, superiority in achievement, and a high degree of self-esteem. This decreases somewhat as they note that the "hearing world" sees them as peculiar, and that early achievement will not necessarily be sufficient in the hearing world. Deaf children of hearing parents may increase in self-esteem as they proceed through residential school. From their unique position of being deaf in a hearing family they have come into an environment where they see successful deaf adults and find that deafness is not always stigmatized. On the other hand, deaf children of hearing parents remaining in day schools may show a decreasing self-concept as they find more and more that their achievement is depressed, that their hearing peers surpass them, and that their parents still despair about their difference. These differential patterns of self-esteem also lead to different patterns of identity formation.

Identity. Most deaf children are in a unique position in regard to identity formation. Born to hearing parents into a "hearing world," they appear to travel on an inexorable path toward the "deaf world." During their early years, they are characteristically deprived of contact with successful deaf adults, a fact that may deeply influence self-concept. For, if the deaf child only sees deaf children, he may develop distorted expectations of what happens to deaf children grown up: Do they become like the hearing? Do they go into hiding? Do they disappear? Do they die?[30] Later, despite early taboos, deaf children achieve competence in the American Sign Language, the hallmark of the deaf community.

The identity road of the deaf adolescent takes many paths. Ideally, he will have the competencies and the desire to live in both the hearing and the deaf world; he may, however, be a stranger to both. Some adolescents will militantly enter the deaf world and exclude at least temporarily any contact with the hearing world. Others avoid the deaf world, refusing any association with deafness. They may pursue an isolated "as if" identification with the hearing world.[30]

Intervention Programs

The most successful intervention programs are those that facilitate an early diagnosis with a sensitive alleviation of the traumatic impact of the birth of a "defective" child. A successful resolution of the diagnostic crisis requires emotional support to parents with a realistic, nonrosy, but nonsomber picture of the effects of the handicap. This can be provided by literature, but more importantly through contact with adults of similar background.

The diagnostic crisis is frequently followed by a treatment crisis; for parents must carefully evaluate advice given by experts—experts in audiology, speech therapy, and deaf education. Frequently the advice is—or is seen as—overwhelming, conflicting, or incompatible; for experts continue to disagree on the role of hearing aids, auditory training, and sign language. The successful resolution of the treatment crisis tends to depend on certain characteristics of the helping professional, who frequently, but not necessarily, is the initial teacher of the deaf child.

Through empathy, a sensitive teacher can reduce the burden of overwhelming advice, and through respect for diverging opinions, he can reduce the conflict for parent and child. Furthermore, by carefully clarifying the myriad prescriptions and proscriptions while still leaving the choice to the parent, the teacher of young deaf children can sensitively enlarge the parental role rather than usurp it.

Prognosis With or Without Adequate Intervention

There have been a number of studies summarized by Meadow[17] which have indicated that deaf children of deaf parents have significantly better scores on reading and written language, with no statistical differences on tests of speech and lipreading skill. These findings also tend to correlate highly with a more optimal adjustment in terms of maturity, responsibility, independence, popularity, and adjustment to deafness.[30] This superiority of deaf children of deaf parents has been postulated to depend on the early onset of manual communication as well as the less conflicted acceptance of the deaf child by his deaf parents.

More recently, because of shifting educational philosophies, it has been possible to study deaf children with hearing parents who also utilize some form of manual communication and thereby also implicitly accept the deafness of the child more realistically.

Moores[22] has reported initial results of an ongoing study of preschool children. He found that the more successful children were found in programs that had five elements in common: a strong cognitive and academic orientation; a concomitant usage of manual and oral communication; structured and organized classroom activities; auditory activities included in ongoing classroom events; and parents who view the program as a combination of oral and manual activities and felt comfortable with the communicative mode.

Brasel and Quigley[4] found that deaf parents using manual communication, especially manual communication closely approximating English, had youngsters who consistently outscored youngsters "whose parents do not use any form of manual communication even when those parents expend large amounts of time, effort, and money in obtaining early, intensive and continuous oral training for their children and work intensively with them at home during the preschool years." [p. 135]

Finally, the author's own longitudinal studies of deaf children of hearing parents may shed some light on optimal intervention. The parents were informed that the early use of sign language in a nonconflicted setting and in conjunction with auditory and speech training would enhance and promote the acquisition of language and speech and would contribute to the social and emotional development of the deaf child. The parents then elected to use manual communication. They elected to use one of the newer forms more closely approximating English, and they chose to pay careful attention to the auditory and vocal components of their youngsters' language. The children in turn revealed that the milestones in sign language acquisition generally paralleled the milestones of spoken language acquisition. Knowledge of sign language at these early ages has not interfered with speech acquisition; on the contrary, the number of spoken words and lipreading facility increased with sign language acquisition. Finally, there was noted a decreased level of communicative frustration[30] and an increased level of gratification.[28]

In general it would appear that deaf children who are able to establish a meaningful and joyful communication with their parents through whatever modality are more likely to resolve the Eriksonian crises successfully.

REFERENCES

1. ALTSHULER, K. Z., "Personality Traits and Depressive Symptoms in the Deaf," in Wortis, J. (Ed.), *Recent Advances in Biological Psychiatry*, vol. 4, Plenum Press, New York, 1964.

2. BARKER, R. G., et al., "Adjustment to Physical Handicap and Illness: A Survey of the Social Psychology of Physique and Disability," *Social Science Research Council Bulletin*, 55:200, 1953.

3. BINDON, D. M., "Personality Characteristics of Rubella Deaf Children: Implications for Teaching the Deaf in General," *American Annals of the Deaf*, 102:264–270, 1957.

4. BRASEL, K. E., and QUIGLEY, S. P., *The Influence of Early Language and Communication Environments on the Development of Language in Deaf Children*, Institute for Research on Exceptional Children, University of Illinois, Urbana, 1975.

5. BRUNSCHWIG, L., "A Study of Some Personality Aspects of Deaf Children, Contributions to Education No. 687," Teachers College Press, Columbia University, New York, 1936, quoted in Barker, R. G., et al., "Adjustment to Physical Handicap and Illness: A Survey of the Social Psychology of Physique and Disability," *Social Science Research Council Bulletin*, 55:200, 1953.

6. CHESS, S., KORN, S. J., and FERNANDEZ, P. B., *Psychiatric Disorders of Children with Congenital Rubella*, Brunner-Mazel, New York, 1971.

7. CHEYNE, J. A., "Some Parameters of Punishment Affecting Resistance to Deviation and Generalization of a Prohibition," *Child Development*, 42(3):1256, 1971.

8. CRAIG, H. B., "A Sociometric Investigation of the Self-Concept of the Deaf Child," *American Annals of the Deaf*, 110:470, 1965.

9. FELLENDORF, G. W., and HARROW, I., "Parent Counseling, 1961–1968," *Volta Review*, 72(1):53, 1970.

10. FREEMAN, R. D., "Emotional Reactions of Handi-

capped Children," in Sapir, S. G., and Nitzburg, A. C. (Eds.), *Children with Learning Problems: Readings in a Developmental-Interaction Approach*, p. 280, Brunner-Mazel, New York, 1973.

11. FURTH, H. G., "A Review and Perspective on the Thinking of Deaf People," in Hellmuth, J. (Ed.), *Cognitive Studies*, Brunner-Mazel, New York, 1970.

12. ——, *Thinking Without Language: Psychological Implications of Deafness*, Free Press, New York, 1966.

13. GILLIES, J., "Variations in Drawings of 'A Person' and 'Myself' by Hearing-impaired and Normal Children," *British Journal of Educational Psychology, 38:*88, 1968.

14. HESS, R. D., and SHIPMAN, V. C., "Maternal Influences upon Early Learning: The Cognitive Environment of Urban Pre-School Children," in Hess, R., and Bear, R. (Eds.), *Early Education*, p. 103, Aldine, Chicago, 1968.

15. LEVINE, E. S., *Youth in a Soundless World: A Search for Personality*, New York University Press, New York, 1956.

16. MADDI, S. R., et al., "Effects of Monotony and Novelty on Imaginative Productions," *Journal of Personality, 30:*522, 1962.

17. MEADOW, K. P., "The Development of Deaf Children," in Hetherington, E. M., et al. (Eds.), *Review of Child Development Research*, vol. 5, University of Chicago Press, Chicago, 1975.

18. MEADOW, K. P., "Self-Image, Family Climate, and Deafness," *Social Forces, 47(4):*428–438, 1969.

19. ——, "Parental Responses to the Medical Ambiguities of Deafness," *Journal of Health and Social Behavior, 9:*301, 1968.

20. ——, "The Effect of Early Manual Communication and Family Climate on the Deaf Child's Develop-ment," Ph.D. dissertation, University of California, Berkeley, 1967.

21. MINDEL, E. D., and VERNON, M., *They Grow in Silence—The Deaf Child and His Family*, National Association of the Deaf, Silver Spring, Maryland, 1971.

22. MOORES, D. F., MCINTYRE, C. K., and WEISS, K. L., *Evaluation of Programs for Hearing Impaired Children: Report of 1971–1972*, Department of Health, Education and Welfare, U.S. Office of Education, Bureau of Education for the Handicapped, 1972.

23. MYKLEBUST, H. R., *The Psychology of Deafness: Sensory Deprivation, Learning, and Adjustment*, Grune & Stratton, New York, 1960.

24. NEYHUS, A. I., "The Social and Emotional Adjustment of Deaf Adults," *The Volta Review, 66:*319–325, 1964.

25. RAINER, J. D., ALTSHULER, K. Z., and KALLMAN, F. J. (Eds.), *Family and Mental Health Problems in a Deaf Population*, New York State Psychiatric Institute, Columbia University Press, New York, 1963.

26. RIESSMAN, F., *The Culturally Deprived Child*, Harper & Row, New York, 1962.

27. SCHLESINGER, H. S., *The Acquisition of Bimodal Language*, Academic Press, San Francisco, 1978.

28. ——, "Diagnostic Crisis and Its Participants," in Norris, A. G. (Ed.), *Deafness Annual*, vol. 2, Professional Rehabilitation Workers with the Adult Deaf, Silver Spring, Maryland, 1972.

29. ——, "Beyond the Range of Sound," *California Medicine, 110:*213, 1969.

30. ——, and MEADOW, K. P., *Sound and Sign: Childhood Deafness and Mental Health*, University of California Press, Berkeley, 1972.

---

48 / The Child Amputee

Marshall D. Schechter and F. Robert Holter

Introduction and Background

In childhood there are two types of amputation: congenital and acquired. Congenital amputations are usually genetic and consist of either the total absence of a limb or a part of a limb, or of a deep circular constriction about an arm or a leg without amputation. Variations and deficits in bodily structure are also seen as the result of the ingestion of various agents during pregnancy (for example, Thalidomide). The commonest reasons for acquired amputations are: (1) trauma; (2) vascular accident or disease; (3) infection; (4) tumor; and (5) burns. Trauma and burns occur frequently; indeed, accidents are the leading cause of death in childhood. According to Fishman,[2]

the number of child amputees in the United States is 25,000.

Literature on amputation in adults is far more extensive than what has been written about children. Considering the high incidence of accidents in children, this is unfortunate. Shands et al.[10] indicate that children with amputations make up an important segment of all crippled children with great rehabilitation potential.

Developmental Considerations

As is true of other disorders, children tend to react to amputation differently than do adults. Also, children with an acquired amputation react differently than children with a congenital absence of a body part. Kolb[6] considers failure to reorganize the body image, after a reasonable period of time, to constitute a psychopathological adaptation. Shands et al.[10] state that, in children, phantom limb sensations are temporary and painless. Simmel,[12] however, reports that phantoms exist for many years in well-adjusted amputees. She also states specifically that phantom limb sensations will occur in very young children if they have had sensory experience with the body part before it is lost. Siller[11] studied the reactions of fifty-two children with amputations and felt that greater psychological disturbance occurred in children who had had traumatic amputations than in those with congenital amputations. Rochlin[9] emphasizes that all body parts have powerful narcissistic importance and the loss of a body part can be adapted to only slowly and painfully.

In spite of the various views of the responses of children, it seems clear that developmental factors as well as the type and circumstances of the amputation are important in the child's response. Considering the differences between children's responses to experiences and those of adults, Anna Freud[3] cites the egocentricity of the infant, the immaturity of the child's libidinal development (which affects his perception of events and experiences), the weakness of the toddler's secondary process reasoning (as compared to the strength of his fantasies and impulses), and the differences in the sense of time at various age levels.

Solnit and Stark[13] point out that psychological preparation for the new child during pregnancy includes the wish for a perfect child and the fear of having a damaged child. The birth of a defective child constitutes a loss to the parents and triggers a process of mourning. In the case of the infant amputee, there is the added danger that in her interaction with her infant, the mother's response may interfere with the satisfactory development of a realistic psychological body image. In an extensive discussion of the developmental aspects of motor activity, Mittelmann[7] stressed the interrelatedness of motor organization and all other areas of human activity. Mittelmann suggests that the infant's self-image and his ability to differentiate between himself and objects around him are closely related to the development of motility. The main avenues of this are the mouth-hand, finger-to-finger, and eye-hand coordination.[4] The implications for ego development of infants with upper extremity amputations are clear. Kaplan[5] has traced the evolution of motor activities in relation to drive, ego, and superego de-

velopment, with specific attention to the importance of rhythmical repetitive play in latency. She found that such activities are intertwined with and contribute to the further development of the ego and superego. Pearson[8] stressed the importance of rough-and-tumble free play among peers in latency. Given the tendency of such children to find a scapegoat and the prejudicial attitudes and avoidance behavior shown toward handicapped persons, one should anticipate that the child amputee would experience increased difficulty in mastering the developmental tasks of latency and adolescence. Bergmann, in collaboration with Anna Freud,[1] emphasizes the differential reactions of children and staff in a children's hospital to the difference between having body parts *present* even if they do not work, and having them *missing*.

Case Examples

The clinical phenomena in children with amputations are conditioned by many factors. There is the age at which the amputation occurs, its effects at subsequent stages of psychosexual development, and the meanings of hospitalization and surgical procedures performed at various ages. In addition, the disruptions in object constancy and continuity play a role, along with the disruptions in educational and other age-appropriate performances. Finally, there are the attitudes of caretakers, whether parents, siblings, extended family, hospital and school personnel, all of whom reflect cultural and societal concerns. These attitudinal influences will be dealt with more specifically in the next section of this chapter.

Tom was three when brought to an orthopedic hospital for evaluation and future planning related to a phocomelia of his left leg. In all other respects physically, Tom was healthy, having accomplished his developmental milestones early. The orthopedist was certain that a prosthesis could be attached which would function well mechanically. However, the surgeon was concerned that the child's passivity and dependence on the mother might subsequently prevent Tom from making adequate use of an artificial limb. When seen for three evaluation interviews, Tom clung to his mother throughout. He became anxious only when his mother tried to put him down or when direct physical contact was attempted by the psychiatrist. He showed little interest in his surroundings, lying passively on his mother's lap. Historically, his parents described that Tom seemed somewhat more active during his first year of life. At the point at which walking would normally occur, however, he began increasingly to require the parents' help. Presently this extended to feeding and exploratory behaviors and was accompanied by a marked prolongation of separation anxiety. This passive-aggressive behavior was noted in his whining and complaining voice. When left alone, even momentarily, this rose to a pitch of demandingness. This affected the parents profoundly, the mother in particular, and they carried him wherever they went. At moments of distress, Tom could best be comforted by this kind of close contact and by feeding.

Tom represents a child with a congenital disorder whose disability emphasized the oral phase of psychosexual development. The passivity and, at times, passive-aggressive attitudes which he displayed are quite characteristic of children with congenital amputations who become fixated at this early level. This evolution is clearly supported by the character of the environmental handling. Often the stamp of the developmental stage during which the amputation occurs can be identified many years later by the individual's behavior and defense patterns.

Bill, age ten, was a most active and adventuresome child. He had an ebullient, effervescent personality and was beloved by adults and peers. His deeds often got him into trouble with his parents and teachers. Occasionally he would injure himself, sometimes mildly but at other times more severely. He had sustained three fractures of his extremities at varying times and twice was unconscious for brief periods. Bill visited a traveling circus and, despite warnings from the guards, jumped over the protective railing to throw meat which had fallen outside back into the cage of a tiger. While Bill pushed the meat through the bars, the tiger jumped up and ripped at his arm, tearing it from its socket. Bill was pulled to the bars and when he attempted to pull away, the tiger ripped at his other arm, also tearing it from its socket. After the wounds healed, Bill was prepared for bilateral upper limb prostheses. When interviewed, Bill was once again the bouncy and extroverted youngster everyone had described before the accident. However, for months Bill suffered from severe night terrors; moreover, until he mastered the use of the artificial limbs, he had innumerable facial and bodily tics. These disappeared as he established an amazing facility in the integration and utilization of the prostheses. During this interval, however, his academic performance dropped markedly. Delinquent behavior appeared and he began to isolate himself from his peers. At age fourteen, Bill felt people were looking at him as if he were "a monster." As he entered active adolescence, the formerly elevated mood and attendant productive behaviors were entirely squelched. He felt he had no real vocational or heterosexual future.

Bill is illustrative of the changes that occur around puberty. A magical expectation beforehand of all being well and the bionic replacement (cf. the television series, *Six Million Dollar Man*) making him as he was or even better fails with the reality testing of adolescence. This reality consideration was supported not only by his precise self-perception, but also by the responses from his peer group who progressed to athletic and heterosexual relationships in which he was not able to participate. Adolescence is the time during which body image considerations are given a tremendous impetus. Moreover, this period of psychosexual development also pushes the individual away from primary process mechanisms (such as magical thinking) to the much more reality-oriented and logical considerations of secondary process thinking.

During his junior year in high school, Seth was elected to the all-state basketball team. A triple letter athletic recipient, he also was in the upper quarter and president of his class. During a basketball game, Seth complained of pain in his lower abdomen and left leg. When examined by the team physician, he was found to have a palpable mass in his lower abdomen. This was diagnosed as a rhabdomyosarcoma and amputation of his left leg was performed, followed by intense radiation to that entire area. Seth was physically debilitated because of these procedures and became suicidal. He felt all his dreams were over since he had anticipated going to college on an athletic scholarship and perhaps becoming a professional athlete. The ward personnel were depressed not only because of the illness and surgery that had destroyed such a promising future, but also because they were aware of the dubious outcome despite the most vigorous treatments. Seth's depression in these circumstances were echoed rather than empathized with by the staff. They felt that in a similar situation, they would seriously consider taking their own lives.

Depression is the most pervasive emotional state among congenital and acquired amputees. This applies to children that have had amputation of limbs as well as those with any chronic disability. Denial is frequently present and may take the form of hyperkinetic behavior, delinquent or antisocial activities during adolescence, or a marked increase in passive-dependent attitudes.

Beth was fifteen when seen in an orthopedic hospital for possible amputation of her feet and preparation for bilateral lower limb and left upper arm prostheses to habilitate her congenital triple phocomelias. She had considerable anxiety about the surgical procedures and about her ability to use the artificial lower limbs, as she anticipated she would have little balance. The major concern about Beth was her vitriolic verbal attacks on everyone. Since she felt completely helpless, she used her speech as a means of warding off people and protecting herself.

Beth exemplified what many amputees feel, a sense of total bodily incompetence and helplessness. When they are threatened, and a fight-flight reaction would be considered normal, these children feel they can neither actively fight nor have the capacity for flight. In the usual anxiety dreams of childhood, just as the monster is threatening to catch him, the nonhandicapped child awakens before the monster seizes him. In the amputee, these same anxiety dreams occur with the difference being that here the child is often caught. This makes the night panic states much more intense (as was the case with Bill and Beth). Similarly, these children are much more phobic about fires, possible injury from cars, and from violent acts of God. Contrary to the popular belief that lightning only strikes once, amputees, especially those who suffer this after infancy, believe the same physical disability can indeed occur again.

Attitudes in Families, Cultures, and Society

Seeing an amputee evokes strong emotions within people irrespective of age. These feelings involve anxiety often mixed with revulsion. When a child is born with such a defect, the parents' response includes guilt over possibly having done something to create the handicap, questions about why it should happen to them (a potential punishment for some misdeed?), compensatory attitudes of overprotection against their disgust with the child's appearance, and depression as they think about the burdens ahead for themselves and for their child.

In discussing the developmental history of their four-year-old son with a congenital upper extremity amputation, one couple told of their certainty that it was caused by their actions prior to the child's birth. The mother had put off visiting her grandmother with various excuses, but in preparing for when she would go, she had purchased a statue of the Virgin. As she was cleaning house, she accidentally knocked the statue off the mantel and it broke at the right arm, below the elbow. The mother repaired the statue as best she could, but before she could arrange a visit, she was informed that her grandmother had died. Three months later their son was born with the amputation below the elbow of the right arm.

Adverse parental attitudes and concerns tend to isolate the child from forming satisfactory early object ties. Such a child may not get sufficient bodily stimulation because of the amputation and subsequent hospitalizations. Often, the parents do not hold or talk to the child as much as they would a nonhandicapped child; this can create a serious problem of inadequate sensory input for proper development of the central nervous system. This possibility, plus many of the multiple adversities experienced by these children, may relate to why so many amputees seem markedly immature.

There is a persistent attitude in many subcultures that if a catastrophe the magnitude of an amputation occurs, it must be a sign of God's wrath for a sin. A number of affected families experience harassment from neighbors, who tell them that they must have been bad to have created such a deformity in their child, and it was God's punishment for their misdeed that finally came to light in their child's disability.

When these children are incorporated into normal classrooms, there is a tendency for the teachers to be overly protective about interactions with the other children. The repeated hospitalizations lead to disruptions in their educational development. These, coupled with possible immaturity, will often lead teachers to treat the amputee as a retarded child, reducing even further the opportunities for adequate stimulation and normal intellectual and emotional growth.

Nonhandicapped children in contact with the amputee on a day-to-day basis tend to exclude him from their play activities. After all, in team competitive games, the amputee clearly is seen as a sure guarantor of defeat. Sequestration by the peer group makes many amputees despair of entering the mainstream; they often ask to be placed in classes with other handicapped children. It becomes strikingly clear that the amputee adopts a self-concept which is formed out of others' opinions about and responses to him. The poor internal sense of self, the construction of a deformed body image, and the defeated and denigrated feeling about himself generally find little relief through societal supports for striving toward an ideal self. Amputees are disaffected in their gender concepts since so much emphasis and value is placed on physical agility or beauty.

Coping and Adaptive Behaviors

The fantasies of the amputee give ample understanding of the dilemma they face. Reflecting the primary process notion of "an eye for an eye, a tooth for a tooth," the amputee, whether congenital or acquired, repeatedly assumes that the absence of a body part is related to some basic fault which has been punished. Since most children view their "crimes" as related to aggressive or sexual feelings, there is a presumption that the amputation occurred because of unacceptable imagined thoughts. Such a concept leads toward a masochistic personality substructure with a deflection of most active strivings. Interpersonal relationships include frequent sadistic outbursts, as was the case with Beth. Vocational choices most frequently exhibit the identification with the aggressor: During latency many children wish to become orthopedic surgeons, "doing unto others what was done unto them."

Their pervasive depression is not easily lifted, as their passivity aborts any drive toward accomplishment. They fear repeated failure. Despite the weightiness and constancy of this depression, suicide attempts are not usual in this group. It would appear that the punishment for their aggression has already taken place through the amputation itself. However, continued castration fears are exemplified in their day and night dreams. These are far more profound than in the non-handicapped since their intensity reflects fears of annihilation and abandonment. Energies for sublimation are not very available as they are attached to the amputation and to their fantasy life. Despite the regressive pulls indicated, progressive developments can occur with the establishment of special talents and abilities.

Management

The management of the child amputee involves not only the child but the world in which he lives. Factors which need to be considered are: (1) the type of the amputation; (2) the developmental period in which it occurs; (3) the circumstances under which it occurs; (4) the social circumstances of the child; and (5) resources for treatment and rehabilitation. Few conditions require as lengthy surveillance or involve as many types of skills. More than that, all the many efforts on behalf of the child need to be well coordinated.

From the discussions of the developmental considerations, coping mechanisms, and the case examples, it follows that in managing the child amputee one must: (1) deal with the initial circumstances; (2) foster as normal a pattern of development as is possible; (3) prevent maladaptive mechanisms; and (4) institute short-term, middle-range, and long-term rehabilitative measures.

When the amputation is congenital, the initial measures involve helping the parents work to achieve a realistic acceptance of their handicapped child. In view of the importance of the early establishment of an optimal mother-infant interaction, this is a crisis in which auxiliary ego support must be provided for the parents. This initial phase should be carried out with the obstetrician, pediatrician, orthopedist, and other health professionals. The child psychiatrist can be of inestimable help with the ward personnel to prevent isolation of the infant and to foster normal feeding, handling, and interactions.

In order to establish an engramic concept of a body image which will allow for the later acceptance of a functioning prosthesis, a substitute limb or weight should be applied to the affected limb at the earliest possible moment—even during infancy. Later as the child is ready for turning, crawling, or standing, a regular prosthesis should be attached. The parents should be helped to handle the child normally and to encourage the use of the stump, especially with the prosthesis in place.

The help needed by the parents of a child with an acquired amputation should be determined by the developmental stage of the child and the parents' emotional strengths and weaknesses. Beyond the issue of congenital versus acquired amputations, the type of amputation has important consequences. When the child has already lateralized, the traumatic loss of the dominant arm is of greater significance requiring major cathectic shifts and reorganization than if the amputated limb is the nondominant leg. The amputation will require a modification of body image and feelings of self-esteem. Work with the child should be centered around his fantasies of what caused the amputation; the discussion is aimed at bringing to consciousness that it was not a punishment for misdeeds. The child needs to be encouraged, by physiotherapists, parents, teachers, etc., to continue an active exchange with the environment and to develop skills—physical, cognitive, and emotional—which are commensurate with abilities. So many of these children, with their intact sensory systems and compensatory capacities for muscular development and balance, are inordinately sensitive to others' feelings. This can be utilized in a positive way to give more options for later vocational choices. Prevocational counseling, therefore, can be of help not only to open new vocational vistas but also to help modify educational systems for the disabled child. Schooling with nonhandicapped children would be best.

However, there are times when perhaps brief periods with other handicapped children might be in order.

Throughout the childhood of both congenital and acquired amputees, there is a constant need to counsel parents, siblings and the extended family as well as school personnel and peers in order to prevent these significant people from causing the child to resort to unrewarding defense mechanisms. When fixations or regressions become chronic, psychotherapy with the child and/or family is indicated. The child must be given complete explanations of all operative procedures or manipulations. One should listen both preoperatively and postoperatively for any misunderstandings from the child or parents, which should be corrected immediately. Long-term psychotherapeutic habilitative efforts include delving into the crises, fantasies, and internal and external conflict areas, each of which change and modify according to the developmental stage through which the amputee progresses. The child psychiatrist can be of major help in encouraging exploration and understanding of feelings leading to a more positive interpersonal and vocational adulthood.

REFERENCES

1. BERGMANN, T., and FREUD, A., *Children in the Hospital*, International Universities Press, New York, 1966.
2. FISHMAN, S., "Amputation," in Garrett, J. F., and Levine, E. S. (Eds.), *Psychological Practices with the Physically Disabled*, pp. 1–50, Columbia University Press, New York, 1962.
3. FREUD, A., "The Role of Bodily Illness in the Mental Life of the Child," in Eissler, R. S., et al. (Eds.), *The Psychoanalytic Study of the Child*, vol. 7, pp. 69–81, International Universities Press, New York, 1952.
4. HOFFER, W., "Development of the Body Ego," in Eissler, R. S., et al. (Eds.), *The Psychoanalytic Study of the Child*, vol. 5, pp. 18–23, International Universities Press, New York, 1950.
5. KAPLAN, E. B., "Reflections Regarding Psychomotor Activities During the Latency Period," in Eissler, R. S., et al. (Eds.), *The Psychoanalytic Study of the Child*, vol. 20, pp. 220–238, International Universities Press, New York, 1965.
6. KOLB, L. C., "Disturbances of the Body-image," in Arieti, S. (Ed.), *American Handbook of Psychiatry*, vol. 1, pp. 749–769, Basic Books, New York, 1959.
7. MITTELMANN, B., "Motility in Infants, Children and Adults: Patterning and Psychodynamics," in Eissler, R. S., et al. (Eds.), *The Psychoanalytic Study of the Child*, vol. 9, pp. 178–198, International Universities Press, New York, 1954.
8. PEARSON, G. H. J., "The Importance of Peer Relationship in the Latency Period," *Bulletin of the Philadelphia Association for Psychoanalysis*, Philadelphia, 16(3):109–121, 1966.
9. ROCHLIN, G., *Grief and Its Discontents*, Little, Brown & Co., Boston, 1965.
10. SHANDS, A. R., JR., et al., *Handbook of Orthopaedic Surgery*, 7th ed., C. V. Mosby Co., St. Louis, 1967.
11. SILLER, J., "Psychological Concomitants of Amputation in Children," *Child Development*, 31(1):109–120, 1960.
12. SIMMEL, M. L., "Developmental Aspects of the Body Scheme," *Child Development Monographs*, 37(1):83–95, 1966.
13. SOLNIT, A. J., and STARK, M. H., "Mourning and the Birth of a Defective Child," in Eissler, R. S., et al. (Eds.), *The Psychoanalytic Study of the Child*, vol. 16, pp. 523–537, International Universities Press, New York, 1961.

---

49 / The Chronically Ill Child

John E. Schowalter

Characteristics Which Define the Chronically Ill Child

The chronically ill or handicapped child is different from other children. He is afflicted by a condition with a protracted course which is always debilitating to some degree and which may or may not eventually cause death. To care for himself realistically, the patient must understand that he is different, but he must also be made aware of those opportunities which are still available to him. His ability to grasp the concept of being both different and not different from peers is a crucial factor in modulating a chronically ill child's adjustment.

Such a child's development is often slowed.

Moreover, since many chronic diseases show remissions and exacerbations, his recent developmental gains may periodically be lost. Such confounding of the normal developmental lines leads to immaturity not only in the physical and social spheres but in the academic realm as well. This is especially true for the child who must spend prolonged periods of time in the hospital or follow restrictive regimens as an outpatient.

The chronically ill child, especially the young patient, usually must rely much on medical staff persons and parents, and this may lead to distance from and discomfort with peers. These children are therefore frequently described as getting along best with adults. An additional problem is that other children often cover their own fears of physical abnormality by scapegoating the sick one.

Mourning is a characteristic of many chronically ill and handicapped children. The mourning is for normalcy lost, skills destroyed, and, in some cases, for anticipated physical failure and death.

Magnitude of the Problem

The prevalence of chronic illness depends on one's definition; in any case, it is substantial. Pless and Roghmann in their review of the literature suggest that 5 to 20 percent of children under age eighteen fall into this category (depending on how broad one's definition of physical disorders is).[4] If mental retardation, visual as well as hearing impairments, and speech, learning, and behavior disorders are included, an estimated 20 to 40 percent of children under age eighteen are affected.[5] It must be added that since advances in medical care allow children to survive who in the past would certainly have perished, the number of chronically ill and handicapped children is rising.

The most common physical disorders in persons under age eighteen are asthma (2 percent), epilepsy (1 percent), cardiac conditions (0.5 percent), cerebral palsy (0.5 percent), orthopedic illness (0.5 percent) and diabetes mellitus (0.1 percent).

Mattsson classified the chronic disorders common to childhood into five categories.[3]

1. Those due to chromosomal abnormalities (for example, Down's, Klinefelter's and Turner's syndromes).
2. Those resulting from hereditary traits (for example, diabetes mellitus, sickle cell anemia, hemophilia, cystic fibrosis, inborn errors of metabolism, and some congenital malformations).
3. Those due to harmful intrauterine factors (for example, rubella, congenital syphilis, toxoplasmosis, drugs, radiation, or other insult).
4. Those due to damage secondary to perinatal trauma and infection.
5. Those due to serious postnatal and childhood infections, injuries, neoplasms, and other factors.

There do not seem to be great cultural differences in the distribution of chronic illness. Although poorer prenatal care is more usual in the lower socioeconomic classes and may result in more perinatal problems, children from lower socioeconomic families are also less likely to receive the prolonged care which keeps some seriously ill children alive but chronically ill. Financial considerations are especially important in certain conditions; this includes chronic kidney disease requiring renal dialysis, cystic fibrosis, and deformities requiring much reconstructive surgery.

Impact at Different Levels of Development

Unlike the patient with acute illness, the chronically ill child must attempt to adjust not only to his debilitation and treatments, but to the real possibility that a change in his condition will be for the worse. Denial, guilt, and anger are experienced strongly by almost all these children.

The young child cannot understand causality; he often believes that the illness with its restrictions and treatments is punishment for being "bad." Since many young children believe that adults can do what they wish, they can't help but resent the fact that their parents and physicians do not cure the malady or disability. If a disorder is hereditary, the children are even more likely to resent their parents, and the parents to feel increased guilt. Blame of physicians is common. It often takes the form of a belief that if the physician had "chosen" a different diagnosis or if he would but declare the treatment successful, the child would magically be relieved of his disorder. Deprivation in terms of diet, inconvenience, physical restrictions, and uncomfortable treatments can lead the young, chronically ill child to become bitter and withdrawn.

The older child, especially the adolescent, may act on his frustrations. He can use his body to

433

express simultaneously an assertion of rebellious independence by not following the prescribed treatment, and a yearning for dependence by forcing physicians to hospitalize and care for him. This allows a vulnerable body not only to represent a shameful weakness but also to serve as a powerful vehicle of influence over family, friends, and physicians.

For adolescents, there is an accentuation of the common fear of losing control of bodily functioning and of shame for "not being like everyone else" (the illusion of "belonging" is of paramount importance for this age group).

Familial Reactions

Parents must first give up their image and expectations of their child as normal.[6] Old goals may have to be adjusted and new goals formed. This requires time, support, and the work of mourning; moreover, it must be accomplished at the very time the child needs extra attention and care.

Parents often try to deny the diagnosis or its meaning and may search for other opinions. Guilt and anger are ubiquitous. A useful channel for these feelings lies in joining groups to lobby for more research and for improved facilities for children with their own child's condition. Such groups are helpful in stressing not only the limitations of the disability but also the potentialities which remain.

While some parents reject their defective child, if an error is made in closeness, it is usually in the direction of overprotection. In one study of children whose parents restricted them because of heart disease, for example, only 20 percent actually had significant disease.[1] Consequently, in the population studied, the amount of restriction from cardiac nondisease in children was greater than the disability due to actual heart disease.

Siblings often experience guilt for the relief they feel for not being the one stricken. They may also resent the extra time and attention given the ill child and respond with symptoms of their own, or with behavioral difficulties.

Cultural Reactions

Care of the chronically ill child is affected by socioeconomic factors. Poor people, as always, are at a disadvantage. They are often suspicious of hospitals and lose continuity of care by obtaining their medical treatment through the emergency room or at clinics where the staff constantly changes. At home, there is a greater chance of single-parent families or families in which both parents must work. Physicians, most of whom do not come from lower socioeconomic or minority class backgrounds, often have trouble empathizing and communicating with the disadvantaged. In addition, black, Puerto Rican, Chicano, American Indian, and other minority patients carry into and receive from the medical system biases which pervade society as a whole.

Patients from dominant ethnic or from upper socioeconomic backgrounds are more likely to be cared for by the same physician or by a consistent group of specialists. They are also more likely to receive support services or special schooling when these are indicated. However, because of unrealistically great expectations, the problems of a chronically ill child in an upper socioeconomic class family may become a greater psychologic stress than in a home where the originally fantasized goals are less grand. McDermott et al. found that parents in lower socioeconomic families were less likely than their more affluent counterparts to refer retarded or organically impaired children to a university mental health clinic.[2] One possible reason postulated for this finding was that successful parents had higher demands and expectations for their children and expressed less toleration for and greater concern over the child's subaverage performance.

Characteristic Forms of Emotional Disturbance

DEVELOPMENTAL CHARACTERISTICS

Very young children with chronic illness or disability may not at first realize that they are different from their peers. In time, however, dysfunction, pain, and restriction often frustrate development by delaying goals or causing temporary or permanent loss of landmarks already achieved. The greatest psychological influence on these children's lives is usually how realistically they are treated by their parents.

Through the use of denial and reaction formation, some parents push their disabled children to strive for overcompensation. Some of these patients form pseudo-mature relationships with adults or develop remarkable skills in various hobbies or intellectual pursuits. The pressure, however, may become evident in symptoms of stress such as stuttering, tics, sleep disorders, and fearfulness.

More common than the overly pressured child is the one whose illness or handicap prompts parental overprotection. These children may not learn to socialize or may have separation problems, show bodily overconcerns, or suffer school underachievement. Since school is the first occasion when children are systematically compared with a group of peers, school avoidance at the time of kindergarten or first grade is quite common, especially in children who show physical stigmata or who are significantly infantilized. During latency, when an important developmental goal is to learn to socialize comfortably outside the family, overprotected children are vulnerable to becoming loners. During adolescence, with the predictable vast changes in the body, hypochondriasis may occur. Because of their frequent medical contacts, overprotected patients are especially sensitized to the importance of bodily complaints. For them, these represent both present and potential difficulties, and serve as a means of attracting attention and succor. It is during adolescence that the final transition to independence is expected. Hence, it is at this age that chronically ill patients are most likely to show serious adjustment reactions. Denial and maladaptive bravado, especially in diabetic adolescents, are relatively common problems, and suicidal behavior and psychosis are occasionally seen.

LONG-RANGE EFFECTS OF CHRONIC ILLNESS

In Mattsson's review of the literature, he emphasizes that psychologically, chronically ill children often adapt well to their handicap.[3] In addition to the parents' own response to the illness, other important variables for successful adjustment include the general quality of the parent-child relationship, the patient's developmental level, and his available coping techniques. An often useful experience for patients is the association with others who have already made a successful adjustment to the same malady.

Pless and Roghmann reviewed the English National Survey, The Isle of Wight Study, and The Rochester, New York, Child Health Survey, each

of which is an epidemiologic study of the psychologic and social consequences of chronic physical disorders in childhood.[4] All three surveys found more psychiatric problems in the chronically ill children than in the controls. The length of illness was more important than the severity, and sensory disorders were especially hard to adjust to. Poor school performance was more common than in controls and was probably influenced by absenteeism. The self-perception of being of diminished value and worth was also considered likely to have contributed to underachievement.

Coping Styles

FANTASIES

Fantasies are common in children who cannot be active, and a great many very successful adults recall planning their success during periods of involuntary recuperation. Common shorter-term fantasies are that all will be well "once I am out of the hospital and home" or "once I grow up."

Frightening fantasies also occur and usually impede coping. Masturbation and other sins of commission or omission are often dwelt on as causative. Tests and treatments may raise fears of attack, mutilation, or annihilation. Worry of the ravages of the malady are ubiquitous with serious illnesses, and the primal terror of an inability to breathe is frequently prominent among patients with asthma and cystic fibrosis.

SKILLS AND SUBLIMATIONS

The prolonged periods of hospitalization and rest required by some illnesses provide time for children to read or to cultivate hobbies. Often intense interest will develop around one subject, such as geography or a language; this comes to represent an escape from the confines of restrictive reality. An inordinate number of chronically ill children plan to and do become physicians, usually specializing in understanding the disorder from which they suffer. Occasionally, children will work to overcompensate physically for their handicap and through endless exercise and practice become superb athletes.

SPECIAL DEFENSE PATTERNS

SPECIAL DEFENSE PATTERNS

Defense mechanisms are used to attempt to make the disability more bearable. Denial and regression are seen in almost all children, especially early in the process. As time goes by, it becomes increasingly important for successful coping that the child become as realistic as possible in assessing his situation. The use of intellectualization (which involves discovering as much as possible about the disorder), is often a very useful defense mechanism and should be encouraged.

UNUSUAL COMPETENCIES

Patients who adjust well to their disability may do so through special competency in patience, in organizational ability, and/or in the compensatory cultivation of intact sensory and motoric skills.

Importance of Social Structures

Total support for these children within hospitals, rehabilitation centers, and schools is crucial, and child psychiatrists' help in educating professionals and the public that this is a population of children who are psychologically at risk is an important endeavor. Although the need for more and increasingly psychologically sophisticated facilities such as intensive-care units, hemodialysis wards, burn centers, and chronic care hospitals is great, the social institution of most importance by far is the family. Since most chronically ill children are cared for at home and since the primary models for how they see their disorder and themselves are their parents' perceptions, work with parents' and siblings' own reactions to the patient's disorder is most important in fostering a successful adjustment.

REFERENCES

1. BERGMAN, A. B., and STAMM, S. J., "The Morbidity of Cardiac Nondisease in Schoolchildren," *New England Journal of Medicine*, 264(18):1008–1013, 1967.
2. McDERMOTT, J. F., et al., "Social Class and Mental Illness in Children: The Diagnosis of Organicity and Mental Retardation," *Journal of the American Academy of Chi'd Psychiatry*, 4(2):309–320, 1967.
3. MATTSSON, A., "Long-term Physical Illness in Childhood: A Challenge to Psychosocial Adaptation," *Pediatrics*, 50(5):801–811, 1972.

4. PLESS, I. B., and ROGHMANN, K. J., "Chronic Illness and Its Consequences: Observations Based on Three Epidemiologic Surveys," *The Journal of Pediatrics*, 79(3):351–359, 1971.
5. STEWART, W. H., "The Unmet Needs of Children," *Pediatrics*, 39(1):157–160, 1967.
6. TISZA, V. B., "Management of the Parents of the Chronically Ill Child," *American Journal of Orthopsychiatry*, 32(1):53–59, 1962.

---

50 / The Asthmatic Child: The High Cost of Protection

Jules M. Kluger

Characteristics That Define the Asthmatic Child

In this chapter, the term *asthmatic child* will refer only to a child whose entire life style is affected by his asthma. Such a child shows severely restricted patterns even when he is not suffering asthma attacks. Children whose life style is relatively unrestricted between such attacks will simply be called "children who have asthma." The adjective "asthmatic" will be used to imply fostering or supporting the more restricted pattern. Hence, reference will be made to asthmatic families and asthmatic therapists, as well as asthmatic children.

The frequency and severity of asthmatic attacks plays a smaller role in determining whether a child *has* asthma or *is* asthmatic than does the environment in which the child develops. Invalidism is a tenable behavior only in an environment that invalidates people (deprives them of their worth or force). Prevention of an asthmatic outcome should be a primary consideration for anyone treating a child with asthma, just as the restoration of less disease-oriented patterns of behavior should be the goal of treatment with the asthmatic family and child.

Asthma: What's Different About It?

Asthma is a disease of acute intermittent respiratory distress. It differs from most severe handicaps in that reminders about "being asthmatic" come from other people rather than from one's own body. In periods between attacks of asthma, the only physical signs may be those of cortisone treatment or a slightly larger, more muscular thoracic cage. Reminders take the form of repeated warnings of what might cause an attack. They also occur when a therapist's first question is: "When did the asthma start?" rather than: "What seems to be the problem?"

Asthma has a low mortality rate (less than 1 percent) and a good long-term prognosis for cure.[5] Therapy should not be directed at helping the child accept his limitations. The goal should be that of maintaining autonomy, social growth, and self-responsibility, so that these are available to allow for healthy functioning during the long periods of physical well-being.

Number of Asthmatic Children—
Their Distribution in the Culture

The reported incidence of asthma varies from 1 to 5 percent of all children under fifteen years of age.[4, 1] There is general agreement that the incidence is higher in boys and suggestions that it is more common in urban areas and high-income families.[1] There are no statistics available to determine what percentage of children who have attacks of asthma become asthmatic children. One may speculate that the availability of sophisticated medical care is almost as important a determinant as the type of family in which the child lives: Given the same frequency and severity of attacks of asthma, it is the child who lives near a medical school or large teaching hospital who is likely to become asthmatic.

Impact of Asthma at
Different Levels of Development

In the course of normal development there is a gradual transfer of responsibilities from parent to child. This transfer is markedly delayed for the asthmatic child—especially in the area of responsibility for bodily functioning and health. In fact, asthmatic parents often hold on to the responsibilities of the intrauterine period. It is not unusual for the asthmatic parent to talk about staying awake all night listening "to be sure Linda was still breathing."

The assumption of responsibility for social well-being is also delayed. At best it is difficult for a parent to decide when a child is capable of crossing the street alone, ordering his own meal at a restaurant, or staying overnight at a friend's.

The child's abilities, the logical referent for such decisions, are hard to assess until after the decision is acted upon. Asthmatic parents tend to simplify the process by using the child's health as a referent for most decisions. ("Come right home after school. You never know when you might have an attack.")

As the disparity between the asthmatic child's responsibilities and that of his peers' grows, so does the impact of this difference. More damaging than the delayed timetable, however, is the arbitrary nature by which control and responsibility are accorded him. Without a visible response to his use of good judgment, the asthmatic child never develops a feeling for the "rightness" of anything he does on his own.

Familial Reactions

All families foster differences among members. By differential expectations and attitudes, each member learns what role he is expected to play in maintaining the family equilibrium. Asthma provides a socially acceptable reason for family patterns which would normally be difficult to justify. It is not surprising, therefore, that attempts to modify the disease-orientation of the asthmatic family meet with considerable resistance. The change from "We can never go out because someone has to stay home with Bobby" to "If it weren't for Bobby's asthma we'd have no excuse for staying home all the time" is a painful one. The asthmatic family prefers to see itself as being composed of helpless victims. They act as though their roles (invalid, helpless parent) were thrust upon them rather than created by them. Asthmatic families are forced to deal with circumstances over which they have little or no control—as are all families. Their difficulties, however, are created by their refusal to accept responsibility for those situations over which they do have control.

Two separate stages are necessary to restore a climate of intentional activity to an asthmatic family. In the first, family members are encouraged to express their feelings of anger, fear, and helplessness in a supportive blame-free atmosphere. Who or what is causing the asthma is not a topic for discussion; how the asthma makes them feel is. In the second stage, who or what is responsible for the decisions they make is critically examined. (How do they decide whether Bobby needs to come home right after school? What data do they need to make such a decision? Who should be involved in making the decision? Who bears the consequences of such a decision?) As the expression of feelings becomes more open and decision making more shared and conscious, the need to invalidate family members diminishes.

Cultural Reactions to the Asthmatic State

American culture makes allowances for disease that it does not make for responsibility or health. It is acceptable to stay home from school because you're wheezing, even though it is not contagious or aggravated by school. It is not acceptable to stay home because you're bored, angry with the teacher, or not learning anything. It is less guilt-provoking for many parents to send their child halfway across the country for the treatment of his asthma than to leave him with a baby-sitter so that they can go to a movie. It is not surprising that hospitalization of asthmatic children follows social upheavals more often than it does physiologic upsets.[2]

The causal view of disease so strongly endorsed by this culture plays a part in the creation of asthmatic children: Something causes asthma, someone *is* asthmatic. It creates the adversary climate for the disputes between parents, child, allergist, and psychotherapist about what is "really" causing the asthma. As the dynamic interplay between parent, child, doctor, and society is

simplified to a static concept of cause and effect, the need arises for static roles such as asthmatic child and asthmatogenic mother.

Characteristic Forms of Emotional Disturbance

Characteristic of the emotional disturbances seen in asthmatic children are a reliance on physiological mechanisms to mediate interpersonal transactions and an unrealistic reliance on others for security and protection.

It is difficult to observe acute respiratory distress dispassionately; it calls forth almost immediate responses from anyone present. While many life-threatening situations elicit a paradoxically calm, unhurried demeanor in medical personnel, the author has witnessed a type of contagious panic in himself and others working with children experiencing acute asthmatic attacks. This reaction is far out of proportion to the risk. In fact, until he has observed and experienced this feeling of panic, one has a great deal of difficulty in understanding the dynamics of the asthmatic child and family. In the face of such a rapidly effective mechanism, it is easier to understand the asthmatic child's impatience and disdain for the ordinary hit-or-miss interpersonal tools. The urgency with which the asthmatic family experiences even trivial problems also seems more familiar and understandable.

If one has asthma, it is also more difficult to resolve the conflict between autonomy and security. It can turn into the familiar trade-off of compliance for love, with the stakes raised from love to air. While the air is out there for all to breathe, it is hard not to feel that it is controlled by those in charge of medications, diets, and other restrictions. Parents and doctors also need to exercise unusual restraint not to use this increased leverage over a child, and to settle instead for the more common, but limited, threats and persuasions.

Effects of the Asthmatic State at Different Moments of Development

The most prominent expressions of emotional disturbance in asthmatic children occur during latency and adolescence. Both the task of social exploration that comes with latency and the heightened awareness of the body that is part of adolescence put major stress on particularly vulnerable areas of the asthmatic child's adjustment.

LATENCY

The matrix within which the asthmatic child develops discourages exploration. There is no expectation that he could make things happen. He has no secure base from which to set out or to which to return. His security seems to depend on the whims or grace of others. He has no reason to believe that what he discovers or takes will be as valid as what he is taught or given. At this stage of development, the asthmatic child often presents himself as inhibited and frightened, frequently with nightmares and phobias. School phobias are especially common as the initial complaint.

ADOLESCENCE

For the youngster who has never experienced comfort and certainty about the reliability and ownership of his own body, adolescence is a particularly frightening time of life. "Are my sex organs developing all right? Are they going to work like they're supposed to? Will my parents trust me to use them, or will I have to get their instructions and approval?" The asthmatic adolescent often resorts to either strikingly immature dress and manners as a denial of any adolescent strivings or potential, or to alternative pose of very pronounced and public sexual promiscuity. While the latter instance represents some attempt at growth, the manner in which the youngster carries on insures concern and control from others almost as effectively as does the wheezing.

Long-Range Effects

Countless interactions in which the focus is the asthma rather than the child have their cumulative effect. A number of asthmatic children seen in a hospital for chronic chest diseases were all convinced of one thing: The most distinctive and interesting thing about them was their asthma. A great deal of their energy went into maintaining their identity as asthmatic (as though anyone could miss the large letter "A" elaborately embroidered over their entire lives). Initially, the author was surprised at how much resistance to

change from hospital to home environment came from the children rather than the staff. When he suggested that daily temperatures were not needed for asymptomatic children, the response was: "But what if I'm sick and don't know it!" The answer: "That's what's known as health" encountered the child's major objection: How could he feel safe in a place where people might see health as one of his attributes?

A young boy in that hospital struggling against being carried up the stairs to school, told it all. It was an angry "I don't want to grow up! My mother won't recognize me." He had verbalized the unspoken fear of many asthmatic children. Recognition was used, not just in the visual sense, but in the diplomatic one as well (as refusing to recognize Red China, for instance). Growing up meant a change in size and appearance—a commonly expressed fear was that on returning home from the hospital the child would be left at the airport by his parents, who would be unable to identify him. Growing up also meant developing new skills and attributes and risking that they will be effective, or even recognized. If this risk is not taken, the long-range effect is a paucity of skills and attributes that makes any existence other than an asthmatic one an impossibility.

Fantasies of Asthmatic Children

Given the extreme feelings of helplessness engendered by respiratory distress, it is not surprising that asthmatic children resort to fantasties which attempt to restore feelings of control. It should also come as no surprise that compensatory fantasies are used by asthmatic parents, physicians, and psychotherapists as well. The parent, mentioned previously, who acted as though responsible for the child's breathing by staying awake all night listening, was acting out a common fantasy. The student who reads this chapter in the hopes of finding out everything about a child the author has never even seen demonstrates another; likewise the doctor's unfailing diet or the therapist's certainty that it's nothing but a repressed cry. The disagreements between allergist and psychotherapist often have the appearance of two shamans disputing over who is more effective at driving out (which) demons. Fantasies usually contain some elements of truth. They are helpful in coping with periods of chaos by providing an initial basis for organization—the field of medicine has effectively used the notion of the causative agent as a means of binding anxiety and initiating treatment planning. Fantasies become maladaptive when acted upon as though they are the entire literal truth. Certain fantasies of family, physician, and therapist are particularly malignant because they provide sustenance for the asthmatic child's basic defense: Somebody else has the responsibility for my health.

Skills and Sublimations

Children who have asthma have skills in assessing their current respiratory state that the rest of the world has had neither the need nor the opportunity to develop. Such children and their families can develop considerable expertise in the prevention and treatment of attacks. They have immediate access to most of the vital information needed to insure adequate treatment. Professionals can inform them of other facts that would complete their information (for example, "This drug is the same as the one you've been taking, but it also has something in it to loosen the phlegm." "Keeping Bobby at home a lot makes you feel more secure, but it doesn't prevent attacks and does make it hard for Bobby to learn to care for himself").

A large number of professionals with a history of asthma are working in the field. One can therefore assume that working toward the relief or cure of the condition is a common sublimation. Children with asthma frequently choose doctor or nurse when asked what they would like to be when they grow up. Certainly, the exposure of these children to adults who are functioning effectively despite a history of asthma is clearly beneficial This encounter can also be detrimental should the adult use his position to experience a control over someone else's lungs that he never felt over his own.

Special Defense Patterns

The asthmatic child's pattern is to defend against anxiety and feelings of powerlessness by assuming a dependent role in relationships and relinquishing responsibility to others. He avoids confronting the powerlessness of those upon whom he depends

by assuming blame (but not responsibility) when things go wrong: "My doctor's really good, it's just that I don't always follow his instructions."

Members of the asthmatic family defend against change and growth by viewing themselves as inextricably caught in a net of circumstances. They eagerly seek outside support to confirm that position. They tend to listen selectively for those things they can't do because of one family member's asthma. They rarely explore alternatives to their constricted life style and avoid any awareness of the choices they are making.

Asthmatic therapists use rationalization and intellectualization to defend against feelings of perplexity. If one needs to find a specific precipitant (allergic, infectious, or emotional) to feel comfortable about asthma, it is not difficult to do so. Asthmatic attacks are high-frequency events, and if the time period preceding one is defined flexibly enough, one can find whatever one looks for there.

Unusual Competencies

Asthmatic children are capable of noteworthy feats of interpersonal manipulation. Even when deprived of opportunities to use physiologic means (either through treatment or change in social setting), they rapidly learn the necessary social devices to achieve the same ends. Undoubtedly a factor in this rapid learning is their ability to assess rapidly the weakness, strength, and current emotional state of significant others—a skill developed through years of operating from the dependent position. While this type of behavior can be irritating and provocative, it is a source of considerable therapeutic potential. Asthmatic children can be powerful allies in family therapy—they are capable of moving mountains (without even wheezing!).

It is fascinating to watch the development of such potential from the guileless "I just want to, that's all" to the more elaborate "Daddy said I could the day before yesterday. You do it all the time. The doctor says it's OK, and besides, don't you want me to ever grow up?" The prognosis for change was poor for any child in the hospital who could not stare down a nurse and lie about his physical condition in order to go on an outing. In fact, it was those children who earned an early discharge because their behavior became so difficult to manage who achieved the most stable posthospital adjustments. It is unrealistic to expect a child to go directly from wheezing to straight-forward verbal communication. Worse than that, it is unproductive. For the asthmatic family, the strongest motivation for change comes from recognizing how hopelessly outmaneuvered they are by the affected child until they all agree on straightforward communications.

Social Structures Needed to Respond to the Asthmatic State in an Optimal Way

A better understanding of the type of social structure that sustains asthmatic children can be achieved by considering the protection racket. In that setup, protection is sold by capitalizing on the fear of what would happen without it. It differs from legitimate insurance policies because the person selling the protection also threatens the destruction which makes the protection necessary in the first place. The asthmatic social structure is one in which all parties are engaged in buying and selling protection. Protection can be bought against many things besides asthmatic attacks. One can be protected against accusations of being a negligent parent, an incompetent doctor, or an ineffective therapist. Before passing off the analogy to a protection racket as being unnecessarily sinister, consider that the number of deaths from asthma has risen since the advent of steroid therapy.[3]

The single most effective measure toward preventing a social development in which fear plays a leading role is clarification of individual power and responsibility (even the Mafia derives its power from millions of individuals who are afraid to exercise theirs). Power can be exercised most effectively when the limits of responsibility are clearly stated as well. "I'm your father, not your doctor"; "I'm going to a party after school; if they serve anything that is not on my diet, I won't eat it"; "I can prescribe medication for you, but you'll have to decide when you need it"; and "I can tell you what I see you doing as a family, and you can change it if you want to" are all statements that diminish the chances for the threats and fears that breed asthmatic children.

REFERENCES

1. BRODER, I., et al., "Epidemiology of Asthma and Allergic Rhinitis in a Total Community," *Journal of Allergy and Clinical Immunology, 53(3):137ff.,* 1974.
2. KLUGER, J. M., "Childhood Asthma and the Social Milieu," *Journal of the American Academy of Child Psychiatry, 8(2):358ff.,* 1969.
3. MUELLER, H. L., "The Dangers and Consequences of Steroid Therapy in Children," *New York State Journal of Medicine, 61:2745ff.,* 1961.

4. PESHKIN, M. M., "The Diagnosis of Asthma in Children: Past and Present," in Schneer, H. I., (Ed.), *The Asthmatic Child,* p. 4ff., Harper & Row, New York, 1963.
5. RACKEMANN, F. M., and EDWARDS, M. C., "Asthma in Children: A Follow-up Study of 688 Patients After an Interval of Twenty Years," *New England Journal of Medicine, 246(22):863ff.,* 1952.

51 / The Child with a Seizure Disorder

Norman R. Bernstein

Character of the Handicap

Epilepsy is a recurrent paroxysmal and transitory disturbance of the brain which develops suddenly and ceases spontaneously.[5] This sudden and violent discharge of neurons was described by Hughlings Jackson[12] and may produce an enormous variety of visible physical phenomena. Many causes are described and the disease is prominently related to congenital birth defects, mental retardation, and cerebral palsy.

Seizure types are classified in many ways, but for the purposes of this discussion, only a few categories in terms of seizure patterns can be listed:

1. *Generalized convulsions* constitute the most usual form of grand mal seizure with diffuse generalized contractions, often accompanied by urinary and fecal incontinence.
2. *Status epilepticus* refers to a series of grand mal seizures without a return of consciousness which may produce irreversible brain damage. It is sometimes fatal.
3. *Psychomotor attacks*, fits, periods of confusions or automatic behavior may occur.
4. *Myoclonic seizures*, infantile spasms, and myoclonic twitchings are not uncommon.
5. *Abdominal epilepsy* may occur, producing repeated severe attacks of abdominal pain.
6. *Focal seizures* occur when a particular locus in the brain consistently initiates the seizures with characteristic symptoms. They may involve adversive turning, visual impressions, or sudden paralyses.
7. *Petit mal* in its most characteristic form will manifest sudden loss of consciousness only. The majority will also show some concomitant blinking or jerking of the body.

Incidence

Between 0.2 and 0.3 percent of the whole population is affected. Bakwin[3] estimates that about 7 out of every 100,000 school children are recognized as epileptics, but that more cases are probably missed. He also reports that in well-to-do children without organic defects, seizure disorders do not seem to be related to lower intelligence. However, Hurley[17] strongly indicts the coexistence of poverty and poor prepartum nutrition, along with brain injuries and absent obstetric and pediatric care in the production of birth injuries and retardation. These would be associated with the seizure disorders in the children with less intelligence.

Development

The tradition of ascribing special meanings to seizures and special status to the epileptic goes back several thousand years. Arguments about epileptoid personality, the development of "morose egotism," dementia, and mental deterioration have run through the scientific and popular literature of the last hundred years. They appear in Tolstoy's and Kraepelin's writings and continue into some of the recent controversies over the relationship of temporal lobe disorders and violence.[10] The atmosphere of old prejudices still influences all aspects of this disease. An associated guilt, mystery, and secrecy, accompanying concerns about feeblemindedness, insanity, and gross dyscontrol hover over the patient, his family, and all those around him. Despite earlier assertions, today most workers in the field hold that slowed responses, perseveration, emotional rigidity, religiosity, hypochondriasis, and self-centeredness are not essential concomitants of the disease in adults. Indeed Ervin[10] states that the personality range of epileptics is the same as the rest of the population's, and that some of the characteristics listed in the past may not have been personality traits so much as they were actual symptoms of cerebral dysfunction. These remain hard to separate.

Ford[12] states that one-tenth of all epileptics show symptoms in the first three years of age, and half develop symptoms before age ten. Therefore, large numbers of children have the experience of growing up marked by this specially handicapping condition. Goldin[15] reiterates the general view that the disability of epilepsy in children is as much a psychosocial as a physical handicap. The young child with seizures is plunged into this hard and controversial milieu as soon as epilepsy is raised as a diagnostic possibility or when his behavior shows convulsive properties as in breath-holding spells. Many an infant has febrile convulsions associated with an infectious disease. His parents may thereupon receive either blanket reassurance or dire warnings about the outcome. The family may be told these are insignificant and will disappear when the fever subsides, or they may hear that this is one way epilepsy begins, triggered by a fever. In fact, either sequence may follow. Bakwin[3] notes that about half of all children with epilepsy have nonspecific behavior disorders; in about 90 percent of the cases these are of minor degree. Bridge[6] graphically described as epileptic child's experience: He is abruptly seized with a sense of imminent doom. He loses consciousness, and then presently awakens with concerned people all around him. They tell him nothing has happened, but they begin to treat him differently. He is viewed as an object of special concern with a new diet, daily medications, and tests which clearly and ominously isolate him from his friends.

Deviance

Families react to this sudden illness as a major trauma. This is generally followed by an admixture of hopeful talk about how these things can be controlled nowadays. There are oscillations of anxiety about the reports of tests interwoven with their own knowledge of the stigma of epilepsy and the sense of hereditary guilt. Inevitably, there is much questioning to determine who on which side of the family has been known to have had seizures, and whether there was mental illness, feeblemindedness, or unfavorable genetic loading of any type. The specific inquiry keeps the subliminal sense of guilt going, always stimulated by the new quality of pained alertness which parents acquire when they know another seizure may come at any time. In their fantasies, the child may fall, break a bone, seriously injure himself, develop *status*, or at least soil himself, shame them publicly, and be a badge of familial defect in the public eye. A typical example of the reactions of modern, informed parents is reported by Kvaraceus and Hayes;[2] it appears in a collection of reports by parents on their handicapped children. One mother of an epileptic girl reports pseudonymously that she rarely uses the word epilepsy, even though she takes pains to keep her child active in school and socializing appropriately. She will describe the hazards of seizures and tell the parents of other children what to do if her child has a seizure while visiting, but refrains from using the term.

As in a number of complex medical and psychosocial problems, the parents are often forced to become experts. They need to find sympathetic professionals who have a congruent view of what is needed for their child, and they also need to be on the alert for side effects, changes in symptoms, the influence of altered dosages, and problems in community and school socialization. In their situation, there are few opportunities for seeing a seizure disorder as anything but threatening and negative, and possibly hazardous to the self-esteem of the whole family;[4] they must therefore come to grips with a stigma.[14] Many variations exist in the way parents strive to get complete control over the seizures and to agitate for responsive care. However, underlying much of the troublesome fractiousness reported in dealing with these families is their state of "chronic sorrow."[21] They live with a child who has a threatening condition which objectively, and usually permanently, darkens their lives. Good conservative medical care will often dictate keeping the child on medications for three years after the last observed seizure, so the threat is prolonged.

Western culture is not tolerant of deviance. In this instance the deviance is defined by long tradition as well as by the mass media. Throughout the Western world, the expectations of disease patterns involve a strong wish to cover up and hide difficulties and handicaps. The public wishes to be helpful and simultaneously fears to confront the full nature of the problem. This ambivalence shapes the way in which families and children with seizure disorders disclose their epilepsy. Kleck[18] showed how carefully the patients watched to see how the bystander would receive the information. They tell a little at a time, they tell certain people and not others, and, as time passes and people seem friendly, the whole picture will be released. Sometimes this occurs through rumor and indiscretion; parents themselves disagree about how much information to reveal. In a study by Goldin and Margolin,[16] most parents favored disclosure, but one quarter did not want to reveal the information. While the majority of epileptic children attend regular schools, teachers are quite fearful of having them in class; this often sets the tone for the rest of the students. Douglas[9] expounds the sociological view, that *deviance* is defined by the normal community (just as normality and abnormality are necessary poles because each is necessary to comprehend the other). In addition to the professional categorization of epilepsy, this social response adds to the aura of mystery surrounding it. While Hippocrates' designation of the "sacred disease" or the "falling sickness" 2,500 years ago is not now widespread, the threat of sudden helplessness permeates the popular view of epileptic children today. It still has some mystical quality. Only with the introduction of bromides in the nineteenth century were the aspect of mystery surrounding the disease along with its implication of demonic possession clearly diminished. There is widespread realistic knowledge that the last few decades have produced significantly improved medications for seizure control. This has brought with it new optimism and hope, and allowed the morbid pessimism and apprehension about dealing with families with epilepsy to decrease. The familial aspect of the disease contributes another negative sense of concern. Finesilver[11] notes that until quite recently many states had eugenic marriage laws which prohibited or severely restricted marriage by epileptics. Sterilization laws exist in some states, although they are rarely implemented. These legal anachronisms operate against the acceptance of epileptics and incline cultural attitudes against them. The U.S. Department of Labor[25] confirms this with data which demonstrates that the vocational placement of epileptics is among that most difficult of any group. The practical and necessary restrictions on licensing epileptics to drive also play a role in shaping the image of this illness.

Manifestations of Emotional Disturbance

In view of the above, it is clear that misapprehension over protectedness, real and imaginary threats to the child, the stigma of being retarded, and the anticipation of deteriorating intellectually pose serious problems for the child. All epileptic children are cast into a special role. This makes it harder for them to deal with the normal developmental phases in a flexible way. Because the majority of seizure disorders begin in the first decade of life, the disability can be expected to be a lifelong problem. This is true whether or not the seizures disappear (as they often will). As with most chronic childhood syndromes, the greatest obstacle to the rehabilitation of such children is the associated snarl of emotional problems that includes depression, apathy, and a sense of inferiority.[20, 1] This central theme of vague inadequacy and dyscontrol over one's life space pervades the child's experience. Adlerian psychology has long offered a felicitious way to understand the problem of the epileptic. The patient needs to find a means of achieving mastery over his organic or psychologic inferiority. Of course, Adler saw this as the germ of all neurosis; indeed, he regarded the human condition itself as one vulnerable to organ inferiority. With the child who has fits, it becomes a vital issue.

For the epileptic child many problems persist which nonetheless remain vague. Ervin[10] estimates that many children with petit mal who manifest few overt seizures may be "turned off" 20 to 30 percent of the time by unconscious seizure activity without being aware of it. As a result, their school performance may suffer without the organic nature of the issue ever becoming defined. Additionally, the dosages of phenytoin (Dilantin), primidone (Mysoline), bromides, or barbiturates given to control grand mal seizures become a continued load upon the child's state of consciousness; it is not easy to judge this in a subtle manner. The gross overdosing that produces a sluggish, dozing child is one end of the spectrum. On the other end are the many children who do seem to tolerate large doses very well and appear alert. Nonetheless, it is likely that they have to put forth extra effort to achieve normal levels of concentration. Paradoxically such altered states of consciousness have received very little attention from psychologists at a time when other means of altering levels of awareness are the targets of enormous amounts of focused study. The determinants are very different. The researches on most forms of sleep, dream states, and meditation are trying to explore the heightened awareness of the individual, while the epileptic usually suffers from diminished alertness alongside pathological sensory phenomena.[23] (Dysphoric odors, sounds, or changes in lighting are often enough the harbinger of another spell.) It is very likely that ego constriction will accompany these preoccupations and incline many epileptic children to withdraw from the outer world, the school environment, and the social scene. The fantasies of such children are commonly concerned with issues of control. These are often revealed on psychological testing. One thirteen-year-old boy with partially controlled seizures of both grand and petit mal types and an IQ of 117 (which he used inconsistently in school) had fantasies of demonic possession as a way of wishing this would control his actual disorder. For this boy, and for others with adequate academic skills, the sublimations that can be achieved in school are the best road to ultimate good adaptation and social competence.

There are two general groups of behavior difficulties which are manifested by children with seizures. Those of most concern to the psychiatrist are the struggles to maintain some sense of integrity and mastery over a disease which is the absolute epitome of dyscontrol. Another group of symptoms in children is related to the actual seizures themselves. This involves the postictal confusion, the headaches and weakness which follow, as well as the sense of shame over publicly unacceptable behavior, shaking, thrashing, and losing sphincter control. Additionally, for patients with uncontrollable seizures, there may be intellectual deterioration plus a shift and increase in the number and type of ictal symptoms. As these phenomena are part of a mixed psychosomatic unity, it is clear that they cannot be separated. Livingston[19] believes that psychological factors such as anxiety and tension are the commonest precipitants of seizures in children; other authors have stressed the need for children with seizure problems to be active and occupied as a way of deflecting seizures. Ford[12] alleges that in the essential epilepsies, alterations of personality frequently develop. And he feels that the personality change is manifested before there is any reduction of intelligence. He recounts that fractiousness, squabbling with peers, disobedience, and unreasonableness in school and home occur before there is a fall in learning performance. He also feels that the frequency and severity of seizures do not always parallel these changes.

The Body Schema

This constantly changing and dynamic configuration of inner and outer concepts and stimuli goes through a developmental process. Schilder's work[22] on the development of the body image is reminiscent of Piaget, with three stages suggested in the development of the body image: (1) egocentrism; (2) socialization; and (3) complete objectivity. For the child who has an epileptic aura, unusual visual stimuli, buzzing, sudden ungovernable affects, headache, and muscular aching all surrounding seizure activity, the configuration of his body image must have very personal and unique significance which one does not often have a chance to examine in the course of hospital consultation. Anna Freud[13] has written about the redistribution of libido in illness, a redistribution which is so dramatic in epilepsy.

For the psychiatrist, his most effective work lies in helping the child maintain a worthwhile self-image. The body image described by Schilder always included a *social* body schema as well, indicating that the child's self-concept was much affected by how he perceived other people to see him. For the epileptic child, the self-system is always under threat, and is likely to constrict the body image considerably. The disease does not usually add physical distortions of the body image, but a child's sense of reliance on his body and his feeling of competence are forever under the threat of an unpredictable seizure. His self-image is endangered, and he can be socially stigmatized by public announcement of his disease. Some patients adopt various assertive ways of handling these inferiority feelings. One boy of eleven had had seizures for two years; he was elaborately concerned about dressing in a neat and stylish way, while he simultaneously criticized his mother's poor speech, his father's casual dress, and his

sister's foul mouth, all to make himself feel less aberrant. In school, where his problem was public knowledge, he would occasionally pretend a grand mal seizure, as if by this combination of clowning and assertiveness he achieved a counterphobic victory over his disability.

Children who fall and break bones and who are bruised and scarred by their spells show the impact of the defect on their body image. It has become visible and public, and they and their families are very much ashamed. They often lie or disguise what has happened in order to take the onus off epilepsy as the cause of their trouble. For children with the common overgrowth of their gums due to phenytoin, similar feelings of embarrassment pervade their dental care and restrict social smiling.

Care of the Child with Seizures

A variety of physicians manage epileptic children. Some are seen by neurologists, some by pediatric neurologists, some by family doctors, and some by pediatricians. Psychiatrists tend to become involved in the cases which present complicated problems of adjustment or diagnosis, or where questions of psychosis, brain damage, or sexual misconduct are prominent. Many pediatricians will follow the uncomplicated epileptic child themselves, including his behavioral management. Unless there is a worsening of seizures, they refer the child to a pediatric neurologist once a year. Deutsch and Weiner[8] see the objectives of psychotherapy with the epileptic child as the removal of upsetting factors in his life, giving him support with normal developmental tasks, and providing "reconditioning" to help the child accept his limitations. Framed in this way, these objectives should be acceptable, common sense, office management goals for nonpsychiatric physicians. What becomes rapidly more difficult is to focus on the matrix of problems facing the child and his family in school and community. Goldin and Margolin[16] corroborated the established view that young children with epilepsy who have pathological family relations also fare badly in their relations with peers, at school, and in recreational settings. The psychiatrist needs to involve himself in the family dynamics of the problem. He needs to see how the siblings are interacting, how ashamed they are of the patient, and how evasive they are about dealing with him. Is there active hostility toward the patient? Is he the recipient of unique treatment in his family because he is given a special place by his parents or excluded by his siblings? Does he live an isolated existence within the family as well as within his school and neighborhood? The psychiatric consultant should be able to help make plans for the school, the physician, or the clinic for the long-term care of a child with seizure disorders. He should be able to outline a plan of management with clear, concise goals for dealing with the withdrawn child. Many years ago, Brosin[7] noted that these patients have a defect in their egos which interferes with adaptation. They have lost their sense of security and their sense of completeness. This makes them turn inward in an attempt to compensate themselves through self-loving and self-protectiveness. In effect, they withdraw libido from the outside world. This process of contraction and constriction must be regarded as a family mechanism which the medical caretaker needs to guide. He can seek to do this by means of personal interaction with the family, or with the help of a nurse clinician, caseworker, or psychotherapist. Sometimes, it is best for the family doctor and psychiatrist to sit down with the whole family in order to review the situation. The current trend toward genetic counseling is foisting much statistical data upon families who are unable to hear or comprehend this information. Thus, a number of family members may have abnormal EEGs, there may be an epileptic daughter with petit mal, and a grandfather who has had seizures. Such families need to be supported emotionally and given information adjusted to their level of anxiety and comprehension. Genetic counseling that has not been skillfully managed has produced vague medical declarations which sound like harsh and decisive predictions, and which frighten parents about the future of the epileptic vocationally and academically. There are facts which need frequent restatement if a family is even to begin to hear them, let alone assimilate them.

For some epileptic children, direct formal psychotherapy is necessary. This follows the usual child psychiatry model. However, the therapist had best keep informed about the medical status of the disease and know as much as possible about side effects of the medications. Indeed, he must remain alert to minor behavioral symptoms evolving in the therapy hours which are due to organic disease and not to personality problems. With the emphasis on navigating the child toward better adaptation, the therapist can work at the resolution of neurotic conflict and the maintenance of hope. He can guide the maladapted epileptic toward better self-esteem, and a less narcissistic position. Sometimes he can enable the child to have fewer seizures by operating affectively in a pattern that is at once smoother and less desperate.

Guidance for teachers is important. The local and national organizations for epileptics and their families provide valuable services, as do many rehabilitation facilities. For latency-age and older children with seizure disorders, homogenous short-term group therapy has been very useful. It has enabled patients and their families to share problems and affects which enable them to function better and to manage their sense of stigma better.

The untreated child is much more prone to uncontrollable seizures and more likely to develop an isolated and introverted life style. This carries with it many attendant handicaps in terms of social competence and personal unhappiness. The opportunities to prevent suffering and to produce socially and economically more effective adults are enormous.

REFERENCES

1. Adler, A., *The Practice and Theory of Individual Psychology*, Harcourt Brace, New York, 1927.
2. Andrews, J., "We Learned to Live with Epilepsy," in Kvaraceus, W. C., and Hayes, E. N. (Eds), *If Your Child Is Handicapped*, pp. 356–364, Porter Sargent, Boston, 1969.
3. Bakwin, H., and Bakwin, R., *Behavior Disorders in Children*, W. B. Saunders Co., Philadelphia, 1972.
4. Bernstein, N. R. (Ed.), *Diminished People*, Little, Brown and Co., Boston, 1970.
5. Brain, R., *Diseases of the Nervous System*, 5th Ed., Oxford University Press, London, 1956.
6. Bridge, E. M., *Epilepsy and Convulsive Disorders in Children*, McGraw-Hill, New York, 1949.
7. Brosin, H., "Contributions of Psychoanalysis to the Study of Organic Cerebral Disorders," in Alexander, F., and Ross, H. (Eds.), *Dynamic Psychiatry*, pp. 211–254, University of Chicago Press, Chicago, 1952.
8. Deutsch, L., and Weiner, L., "Children with Epilepsy: Emotional Problems and Treatment," *American Journal of Orthopsychiatry, 18*:65–73, 1948.
9. Douglas, J. D., *Deviance and Respectability: The Social Construction of Moral Meanings*, Basic Books, New York, 1970.
10. Ervin, F., "Organic Brain Syndromes Associated with Epilepsy," in Freedman, A. M., Kaplan, H. I., and Sadock, B., *Modern Synopsis of Comprehensive Textbook of Psychiatry*, 2nd ed., pp. 1138–1157, Williams and Wilkins, Baltimore, 1976.
11. Finesilver, S. G., "Legal Aspects of Epilepsy," in

Wright, G. N., *Epilepsy Rehabilitation*, pp. 51–65, Little, Brown and Co., 1974.

12. FORD, F., *Diseases of the Nervous System*, Charles C Thomas, 1966.

13. FREUD, A., "The Role of Bodily Illness in the Mental Life of Children," in Eissler, R. S., et al. (Eds.), *The Psychoanalytic Study of the Child*, vol. 7, pp. 69–81, International Universities Press, New York, 1952.

14. GOFFMAN, E., *Stigma: Notes on the Management of Spoiled Identity*, Prentice-Hall, Englewood Cliffs, N.J., 1963.

15. GOLDIN, G., et al., *Rehabilitation of the Young Epileptic*, D. C. Heath, Lexington, Mass., 1971.

16. GOLDIN, G., and MARGOLIN, R. J., "The Psychosocial Aspects of Epilepsy," in Goldin, G., et al., *Rehabilitation of the Young Epileptic*, p. 66, Prentice-Hall, Englewood Cliffs, N.J., 1963.

17. HURLEY, R., *Poverty and Mental Retardation: A Causal Relation*, Random House, New York, 1969.

18. KLECK, R., *Self-disclosure Patterns Among Epileptics*, Dartmouth College, Hanover, New Hampshire, 1968.

19. LIVINGSTON, S., "General Principles of Antiepileptic Drug Therapy," *Clinical Pediatrics*, 2:233, 1963.

20. MCDANIEL, J., *Physical Disability and Human Behavior*, Pergamon Press, Elmsford, New York, 1969.

21. OLSHANSKY, S., "Chronic Sorrow: A Response to Having a Mentally Defective Child," *Social Casework*, April, 1962.

22. SCHILDER, P., *The Image and Appearance of the Human Body*, International Universities Press, New York, 1950.

23. TART, C. T. (Ed.), *Altered States of Consciousness*, John Wiley, New York, 1969.

24. TIZARD, B., "The Personality of Epileptics—A Discussion of the Evidence," *Psychological Bulletin*, 59: 196, 1962.

25. U.S. Department of Labor, "Workmen's Compensation and the Physically Handicapped Worker," Bulletin No. 234, Washington, D.C., Bureau of Labor Standards, 1961.

52 / The Child with Congenital Heart Disease

Leonard M. Linde, Nancy M. Klein, and Peggy B. Leavitt

Introduction

In the last two decades, great progress has been made in the diagnosis and treatment of heart disease in children. Refinement of clinical methods of diagnosis, development of heart catheterization, angiocardiographic techniques, and, more recently, echocardiography parallel advances in medicine's ability to affect the natural history of heart disease by cardiac surgery. Psychological and developmental studies of children with heart disease have not kept pace with other medical advances. In this chapter, current knowledge and approaches to these underemphasized areas will be reviewed. However, because of their bearing on the psychological development of the child and on the reaction of the family, clinical history and physical state will initially be briefly discussed. A second section will summarize the present literature dealing with psychological and psychiatric factors in congenital heart disease. Finally, an approach to dealing with the emotional problems associated with hospitalization, heart catheterization, and cardiac surgery, will be presented.

Physical Factors

Approximately seven babies in a thousand live births are born with congenital heart disease (CHD). Many of these neonates have very severe cardiac anomalies, and die in the first few weeks of life; others die before the end of the first year. These conditions include many for which no satisfactory surgical approach has yet been developed. After infancy, congenital cardiac diseases can be classified physiologically according to pulmonary blood flow (normal, increased, or decreased), and clinically as to the presence or absence of cyanosis. These methods of classification also have psychological import as the symptoms in the various groups may differ. Children with increased pulmonary blood flow due to atrial septal defect, ventricular septal defect, and patent ductus arteriosus are all acyanotic, and may suffer from episodes of congestive heart failure and pneumonia. In contrast, cyanotic children with decreased pulmonary blood flow usually suffer most from fatigue, delay in motor development, and a more obvious state of handicap which increases with age. In both groups, frequent hospitalizations may affect emotional development. The body reacts to cyanotic heart disease with polycythemia, and this in turn may lead to cerebrovascular accident and hemiplegia. All children with right-to-left shunts are susceptible to cerebral embolism or brain abscess; these are the serious complications of cyanotic congenital cardiac disease.

Growth retardation often accompanies CHD.[10] This retardation is more marked for weight than for height, more prominent with cyanosis, and more severe in those whose heart disease is part of a syndrome associated with a chromosomal disorder. Growth retardation is usually more severe in males, and frequently proportional to the degree of hemodynamic abnormality. Children with cyanotic congenital heart disease often show delayed pubescence, implying endocrine or central nervous system derangement. Puberty in these children may begin as much as three to four years after the expected age. This is similar to the delay in the pubescence of normal children who grow up in the Peruvian Andes as compared to their compatriots living at sea level. There may be a relation to arterial oxygen tension or, as has been suggested, the fact that puberty may begin when these children reach the height age for a normal twelve- to thirteen-year-old, rather than in relation to their chronologic age.

Psychological Studies

Rapid development of more sophisticated surgical techniques may presently allow for the correction of complicated lesions in the early stages of infancy; ultimately, this may eliminate congenital heart disease as a chronic illness. Psychological investigations are relatively recent, and most studies deal with cardiac problems in relations to diagnostic and surgical procedures—cardiac catheterization and open heart surgery—rather than as an ongoing, long-term disease. The focus has shifted from the problems of the child as a chronic invalid to problems of the child and his family in coping with the diagnostic and surgical procedures.[2, 1] Nonetheless, the child with CHD still must be considered handicapped for whatever period of time the lesion remains uncorrected. Indeed, in view of complicated family interaction, the lesion is seldom so minor that it does not impede the child in some fashion. Not only the disease process but hospitalization and surgical procedures may result in impairment of intellectual function and emotional stability.[2]

Cooper[4] stresses the need for understanding the struggle of the child with congenital heart disease from birth onward. From the beginning, the infant may have a harder time coping with anxiety-provoking situations and achieving normal emotional development. His development involves difficulty with feeding, shortness of breath, limited energy, and a disturbed parent-child relationship. At each stage of growth, new problems may make the struggle to cope progressively more difficult than the corresponding efforts of normal children.

Parents are often concerned that children with congenital heart disease may suffer deleterious effects on intellectual functioning secondary to suboptimal cerebral oxygenation. In a study of intellectual function,[12, 16] children with CHD scored lower than normal children. These lower scores were evident in the first three years of life, and were more marked in cyanotic children. However, intellectual testing in the first three years of life by such methods as the Gesell and Cattell rely heavily on gross motor functioning. Children with cardiac disease may have impaired physical capacity which limits their responsiveness and ability to perform physical activities and to develop gross motor skills. In such children, a better estimate of ultimate intellectual capacity can be obtained from their adaptive and social behavior.

In older children with heart disease, both cyanotic and acyanotic children had IQ scores which fell within the normal range (although on a statistical basis, mean scores were at the lower end). Factors which may be responsible include altered or limited environmental experiences, such as decreased social contacts, numerous hospitalizations, and deficits in school experience. However, subclinical nervous system lesions cannot be ruled out. In the handicapped child, especially the cyanotic infant, it is particularly important for the physician to avoid basing a conclusion of deficient IQ on deficits in gross motor performance.

Since the child is born with the defect, his ways of handling his problems are inextricably interwoven with, and influenced by, those of the mother. Studies indicate that the child perceives himself and his illness in the light of his mother's anxiety, or lack of it, and reacts accordingly. The child whose mother overestimates the severity of the illness sees his defect as affecting his life more than does the child whose mother perceives the illness more appropriately.[15] In one study,[13] the child's anxiety correlated closely with maternal anxiety, regardless of the severity of the heart condition. This stood in contrast to the physician's estimate of the physical incapacity, which very closely correlated with other clinical measures of limitation in the children. The conclusion was that poor adjustment of the cardiac child related more to maternal anxiety than to the actual degree of incapacity. Landtman[8, 9] also found no significant correlation between the severity of the heart disease and the mother-child relationship; he did find, however, that behavioral disorders among children with CHD were closely related to the degree of maternal indulgence.

The arousal of guilt, when the mother first learns of her child's defect, seems to be a universal reaction. How the mother deals with this initially and how she continues to do so will affect her child's attitudes and ability to cope. Overprotection appears to be a very common neurotic reaction, and can interfere in a major way with the child's emotional and intellectual development. The child's place in the family, his relationship with his siblings and peers, and his performance at school are all influenced by parental attitudes and the way the parents handle his illness.[13] In one study,[17] denial was the most prominent defense. Some parents withdrew from the child defensively, while others described difficulties involving themselves with the child from the time of diagnosis. One reaction to this feeling was overprotection. Parents often displace their anxiety to concerns about minor or inappropriate facets of their child's disease. Some parents demonstrated anticipatory mourning, as evidenced by their inability to leave the child in the hospital, their increased worry about his crying, or their overinvolvement in minute details of the hospitalization. Other parents reacted to the same stresses by inability to deal with the child or themselves. They withdrew completely from the hospitalized child, from the medical situation, and from their own emotions. The expression of deep feelings about death was avoided by most parents. Anger with the sick child was not overt, but most parents showed anger which they had difficulty in channeling. Some expressed anger with God, fate, or with themselves. Unconscious anger appeared to exaggerate parental guilt. Occasionally, these diffuse angry feelings surfaced in connection with medical personnel. The parents wanted an omnipotent doctor and an omnipotent staff who knew all the answers and made no mistakes. When it was apparent that this goal could not be obtained, parents developed hostility to the doctor and to the rest of the medical staff. Frequently, they failed to comply completely with the prescribed therapeutic regimen.

Group therapy sessions could be useful, particularly with the parents of younger children with heart disease. Such an approach might help parents to become more conscious of their defenses and feelings. This can be painful, but might help parents be fairer to themselves, to the child, and to the doctor.

A much more immediate and threatening situation is that of the child with an implanted pacemaker. The pacemaker is necessary for the treatment of complete heart block, either on a congenital basis or secondary to cardiac surgery. Galdston[5] observed a group of such parents and children. They were able to function and to cope with the continual stressful situations through the parents' use of a trio of defenses: (1) identification with the medical attitude; (2) intellectualization; and (3) denial of affect, accompanied by a triad of mutual faith: of the child and his parent, the parent and the doctor, and the doctor in the future.

The problem of communication between parents and physicians can be an important factor in the management of congenital heart disease.[2] Socioeconomic factors can be significant here, since lower-class families are more likely to receive distorted messages. This may be due to their reluctance to ask questions. In general, all parents will tend to respond to instructions on how to protect the child more than to instructions allowing the child unrestricted activities.

Since children tend not to be verbal, analysis of children's drawings has been used as a research and therapeutic tool.[7, 6, 18] Children with congenital heart disease tended to draw themselves as smaller than normal children would, suggesting that accompanying their actual physical disability, they have a constricted view of their bodies, a limited physical self-concept.[6] A seven-year-old girl consistently drew a hole in the tree in the House-Tree-Person test,[18] possibly indicating the hole in her heart. A preliminary study of children's drawings of their hearts before and after surgery indicated that childen aged five through twelve years knew that there had been something wrong with their hearts.[7] The images were not necessarily anatomical. Although the drawings indicated that something had been made better, their concepts often differed from what had been told them by parents and doctors.

When directly questioned, children tend to deny any anxiety about their hearts, and there are many instances where parents have not been able, or have not wanted, to tell their child about this disability. The great impact of the physician's diagnosis is all too plain. It is indicated by one study in which an initial diagnosis of heart disease, later disproven, resulted in prolonged physical and emotional disability. This persisted even after the diagnosis of cardiac nondisease was established and transmitted to the family and the child.[3, 15]

A Program of Preparation
for Hospitalization and Procedures

Noshpitz[14] has pointed out the varying psychological problems faced by children hospitalized at different ages. In the one-year-old child, separation from the parent is the most threatening factor, and this can be helped greatly by a rooming-in program. In the two-year-old child, the hospitalization and medical procedures may be perceived as a loss of love or anger on the part of the parent. Again, rooming-in and parental reassurance can be very helpful here. In the child who is four or five years of age, the procedures and various invasions of his body provoke castration anxiety. Here, a careful explanation of the forthcoming procedure, emphasizing that the tubes and wires are all temporary and will be removed and stressing that the child will leave the hospital intact but with his heart repaired, can be of great help to the child.

If a rooming-in program is not available, frequent visiting can help reduce posthospitalization psychological problems. Because the frightened child expresses his problems by crying and by difficult behavior associated with the parents' visit, some hospital staff incorrectly feel that parental visits should be limited. Fortunately, this outmoded approach has been changed in most pediatric units.

Familiarization and education regarding the unknown reduces anxiety and fear, builds trust, and provides a basis for coping.[11] Play is the child's natural and symbolic way of working through problems, tension, and anxiety, and provides an avenue for mastery. It has become evident that hospitalization can be a traumatic experience that impairs healthy personality development. In response to this, some hospitals are recognizing the need for therapeutic play programs and employing methods of preparing children for hospitalization and medical procedures. The therapeutic play program is set up in a similar fashion to a quality, open-class, multi-aged nursery school. It is staffed with professional child development specialists. Educational and play equipment appropriate for children from infancy to age twelve is available. Ideally, adolescents have their own room and special equipment available to them. These programs allow children to develop a trusting relationship with a child development specialist, to be themselves in a safe and trusting atmosphere, to master aspects of hospitalization, and to continue in their developmental processes. Certified school teachers are often a part of the program. Among the methods for preparing children for hospitalization are individual, family, or group prehospitalization tours, which help the child and his parents to become familiar with the hospital. Some hospitals offer puppet shows, video tapes, and films about the hospital environment and medical procedures.

All of this allows a child and his family the opportunity to understand, master, and successfully cope with the various emotional problems concerning heart disease. This includes surgery and hospitalization. These are vital to the treatment of children with CHD. The authors are committed to helping children and their families work through the many emotional disturbances that may develop. Very effective methods for accomplishing this have been developed, and have proved to be successful. Some emotional problems can be prevented and others worked with. If severe emotional disturbances are detected, referral for psychiatric help can be made.

To provide an intervention program, the work of many professionals needs to be closely coordinated. These professionals include cardiologist, surgeon, social worker, teacher, the child development specialist, and nurses. They become closely involved with the family in a variety of ways.

The relationship of the child and the family begins with the first visit to the cardiologist's office. An appropriately simple explanation of the diagnosis is made. If hospitalization will be required, an explanation is made of the need and nature of the contemplated procedures. Eventually, the child and the parents will need to become familiar with the hospital environment and the people they will encounter. The physician's role includes parent education. Preparation must be child-oriented, and include many things which seem minor to the physician, such as the fact that the child will have to undress in the hospital, will have to use a bedpan, will have blood tests and, during and after the operation, will have multiple tubes inserted. It is important to emphasize the temporary nature of these insults to the body.[14]

When the cardiologist determines that hospitalization is necessary, he instructs the parents to contact the child development specialist. A prehospitalization tour is arranged. If the parents are particularly anxious, prior to the tour it may be necessary for them to have a conference with the child development specialist or social worker. Ideally, the prehospitalization tour is individualized for each family. The child and his parents are introduced to the social worker and to a nurse. They are shown the location of the child's bed and the toilet, and places for personal belongings, eating, medical treatment, and for playing. Many details and developmental factors can then be discussed to help the family prepare for the hospitalization. Parents are advised to bring their child's own pajamas, slippers, favorite toys, blanket, and whatever else would make the child more comfortable. In the authors' experience, a policy of rooming-in has proved very successful in decreasing postoperative psychological complications.

Before a cardiac catheterization, operation, or other procedure, the child and his parents will take part in the play and educational therapy program. This is conducted by the child development specialist in a special highly innovative therapy room. This little room is separate from the play room. Here there is a range of play equipment, each item carefully selected to help children learn about their impending procedure through concrete miniature hospital equipment and actual medical supplies. There are also other media, such as miniature people, furniture, animals, blocks, paints, clay, etc., to give the child an opportunity to work through his feelings, experiences, and fantasies by means of play.

Parents are very anxious when their children are hospitalized, and they are therefore invited to the first play and educational therapy session. Hearing a simple explanation of their child's impending operation or medical procedure can relieve some of their own anxieties. Seeing the child begin to cope and understand also eases some of the stress. A trustful relationship is established between the child and the child development specialist, and the parents and the child development specialist. More than that, the relationship between the child and his parents is often strengthened.

After the child has undergone surgery, follow-up play therapy sessions allow the child opportunities to play and work through his feelings and experiences. The child development specialist is able to perceive the child's fantasies and feelings and to clarify them when appropriate. Parents are encouraged to call the social worker or child development specialist after hospitalization, particularly when they need support and guidance in handling their child at home. At times, developmental problems occur, or other difficulties appear, which make it necessary for the child to come back for play therapy even after discharge from the hospital.

Conclusion

As with all life-threatening illnesses, CHD exerts diffuse effect, not only on the affected child, but on the entire family. Knowledge of the developmental pattern of children with chronic disease may help the physician prevent nonorganic pathology in the patient and his family. In this chapter, some of the physical factors and psychological and psychiatric aspects of children with CHD have been presented. Methods of preparation for hospitalization and procedures were outlined.

REFERENCES

1. AISENBERG, R. B., et al., "Psychological Impact of Cardiac Catheterization," *Pediatrics*, 51(6):1051–1060, 1973.

2. AUER, E. T., et al., "Congenital Heart Disease and Childhood Adjustment," *Psychiatry in Medicine*, 2:23–42, 1971.

3. BERGMAN, A. B., and STAMM, S. J., "The Morbidity of Cardiac Nondisease in School Children," *New England Journal of Medicine*, 276:1008–1013, 1967.

4. COOPER, H., "Psychological Aspects of Congenital Heart Disease," *South African Medical Journal*, 33(17):349–357, 1959.

5. GALDSTON, R., and GAMBLE, W. J., "On Borrowed Time: Observations on Children with Implanted Cardiac Pacemakers and Their Families," *American Journal of Psychiatry*, 126(1):142–146, 1969.

6. GREEN, M., and LEVITT, E. E., "Construction of Body Image in Children with Congenital Heart Disease," *Pediatrics*, 29:438–445, 1962.

7. LANDTMAN, B., "Ideas of Children with Congenital Heart Disease About their Heart," *Giornale Italiano di Cardiologia*, 3(3):399–409, 1973.

8. ———, VALANNE, E. H., and AUKEE, M., "Emotional Implications of Heart Disease," *Annales Paeditriae Fenniae*, 14:1–27, 1968.

9. LANDTMAN, B., et al., "Psychosomatic Behavior of Children with Congenital Heart Disease," *Annales Paeditriae Fenniae*, Suppl. 15 to vol. 6, pp. 1–162, 1960.

10. LINDE, L. M., et al., "Growth in Children with Congenital Heart Disease," *Journal of Pediatrics, 70(3):* 413–419, 1967.

11. LINDE, L. M., and LINDE, S. D., "Emotional Factors of Pediatric Patients in Cardiac Surgery," *American Operating Room Nurse's Journal, 18(1):*95–99, 1973.

12. LINDE, L. M., RASOF, B., and DUNN, O. J., "Mental Development in Congenital Heart Disease," *Journal of Pediatrics, 71(2):*198–203, 1967.

13. ———, and RABB, E., "Attitudinal Factors in Congenital Heart Disease," *Pediatrics, 38(1):*92–103, 1966.

14. NOSHPITZ, J., *Hospitalization of the Child and Preparation for Surgery*, personal communication, 1972.

15. OFFORD, D. R., et al., "Perceived and Actual Severity of Congenital Heart Disease and Effect on Family Life," *Psychosomatics, 13(6):*391–401, 1972.

16. RASOF, B., LINDE, L. M., and DUNN, O. J., "Intellectual Development in Children with Congenital Heart Disease," *Child Development, 38(4):*1043–1053, 1967.

17. ROSANSKY, G., and LINDE, L. M., "Psychiatric Study of Parents of Children with Cyanotic Congenital Heart Disease," *Pediatrics, 48(3):*450–451, 1971.

18. TOKER, E., "Psychiatric Aspects of Cardiac Surgery in a Child," *Journal of the American Academy of Child Psychiatry,* 10:156–162, 1971.

53 / The Child with Diabetes Mellitus

David R. Leaverton

Unique Characteristics of the Child with Diabetes

The child's diabetes is often discovered when there is an onset of vague lethargy, overeating, overdrinking, excessive urination, and possibly a slight fever; these usually culminate in dehydration, ketoacidosis, and possibly coma. This critical state which has no visible cause is perplexing both to the child and his parents; inevitably it has a profound effect on their adaptation. The visual evidence of sugar in the urine-testing tube confronts both parent and child with a concrete demonstration of the abnormality; it thus becomes an early focus of attention. The injections of insulin may have to be given more than once daily in an effort to bring the child's metabolism into balance. For most children and parents this is both painful and difficult. Dietary restrictions become burdensome since gratification through food is a way of life for most children. The fact that the condition persists without improvement, that it is sometimes life-threatening, and that it may indeed have frequent complications puts enormous stress on the family system, especially on the mother-child interaction.

Approximately 1 in 600 of the children under eighteen in the United States have diabetes.[12] Recent studies indicate that the incidence is increasing. The mean age of onset is between ten and twelve years, although diabetes has been diagnosed in newborns.[11] Perhaps 20 percent will have a "remission" phase when insulin will not be required. This may last a few days to a few months. This event may confuse the child and the parents and provide a basis for "magical thinking" that the disease has been cured.

The role heredity plays in the etiology of diabetes is poorly understood. Only one-third of children have a family history of diabetes. Accusation, "genetic blame" by spouse and relatives, as well as parental guilt and self-blame are often extremely important factors which affect the management of the child's illness.

There are currently more than one hundred articles in the literature about the emotional aspects of juvenile diabetes. The role of stress as an etiologic factor is still being debated.[8] There is little argument that emotions profoundly influence the diet, insulin dosage, exercise, and other aspects of management. Vascular abnormalities lead to many long-term complications of the disease, including progressive retinal changes which can produce blindness, kidney disease, and possibly death during coma. Many children with diabetes can expect to have their normal life span shortened by one-third. There is much debate, with little agreement, about whether or not better management (less sugar in the urine) reduces the complications. Short-term complications include insulin shock and ketoacidosis.

Insulin shock (hypoglycemia) occurs when the child receives too much insulin compared with his food intake and exercise. This most frequent preventable complication is a distressing and frightening experience for child and parent. It often occurs when the parent, the doctor, or the child is trying to achieve less sugar in the urine as a hedge against future long-term complications. Children who are anxiety-ridden with chronic depression are especially susceptible to increased insulin; a vicious cycle of increased insulin with no change in the urine sugar or acetone may then occur. The child becomes pale, confused, and shaky; he may lose consciousness, and can even have a convulsion. Permanent brain damage can follow, and appears to correlate with the duration and severity of the hypoglycemia. In order to avoid this, sugar in some form is often kept available by those around the child. Because the first manifestations of these symptoms are difficult to interpret, the child may manipulate those around him (teachers, relatives, friends) to receive desired food. The anxiety generated in those involved with the child characteristically reaches high levels.

Don, age three, had had diabetes since ten months. His mother was unable to respond to the crying of Jerry, her second son, age one, because Don would not eat if Jerry received more attention. Whenever she picked up Jerry during an illness, Don would stop eating. This difficult situation caused an overinvolvement with the diabetic child, since mother was panicky about preventing low blood sugar in Don.

Ketoacidosis occurs when there is insufficient insulin available in the child's body for use in sugar metabolism. This may happen when the child receives too little insulin, has an infection, and/or is stressed by psychologic events. Children are frequently hospitalized if they vomit, become too dehydrated, develop abnormal blood chemistry findings, and/or frighten their parents with refusal of food or drink. Coping with another illness, such as a cold, diarrhea, or influenza, adds additional stress which parents may not respond to quickly enough if they feel ambivalent about their child.

Robin, age seven, would frequently respond with vomiting if her mother left her too long to visit relatives or friends. Her mother (who projected onto Robin the anger she felt toward herself and her own mother) would be so anxious when she returned from these visits that she would forget to give the child her insulin. This led to frequent hospitalizations for Robin. On one such occasion, there was delay in receiving care, and Robin became so dehydrated that she had a mini-stroke and lost control of one side of her body for a week.

For the parent, diabetes is a heavy burden. It takes extra money, time, and patience to deal with the diabetic child. Costs for insulin, physicians,

laboratory tests, and hospitalization account for a significant portion (5 percent) of the family's income. There are many varieties of parental response to the burden.[11, 1, 6]

Often they feel guilty and become excessively permissive. They overindulge the child in material ways as well as behaviorally. This leads to a child who is filled with self-pity; who takes advantage of his parents; who commits dietary, insulin, and urine-testing indiscretions; and who, all in all, behaves badly. The result is a child in poor chemical balance who is both self-destructive and/or depressed.

The parent finds many ways to express his excessive anxiety and fear. There may be constant warnings and threats about the dangers of the disease, resulting in a frightened child who is dependent and passive. Although such a child may achieve good chemical balance, his individuality and personality may be distorted with the subsequent appearance of paranoia and submissiveness. The parent may become overprotective. This may mount to such an extent that in sheer self-defense the child rebels with ensuing conscious avoidance of necessary health maintenance duties. The result again is poor chemical balance. A perfectionistic, controlling, and punitive parental attitude may result in an obsessively regimented life. This is then mirrored in the child by a pattern of compulsive behavior. Rigid control can be achieved in this way but this in turn can lead to inflexibility in the face of life stresses.

Suzanne, age thirteen, was found to have diabetes at age eleven. She was meticulous in her appearance, and outwardly seemed to be well adjusted to her diabetes. However, when she wanted to go camping with her friends in the mountains, she was afraid to use toilets other than her own.

Where the parent is angry and resentful, both parent and child may deny their feelings, as well as the need for control of diet, insulin, exercise, and urine testing. A chronic state of chemical inbalance often follows.

Randy, age fourteen, was found to have diabetes at age two. When Randy was eight, his parents responded by separation but did not divorce. Father blamed mother for Randy's diabetes. Randy stole cars and skipped school for several years. Judges were lenient with him because of his diabetes, and his mother infantilized him. During his puberty, their conflict became overwhelming with verbal and physical assaults everyday occurrences. This minority Chicano family was characterized by machismo, in that the males acted out anger through antisocial acts. Suicide threats and attempts by mother and Randy became commonplace. Often, Randy refused to take his insulin, and his control was very erratic.

Less frequently, parents accept the child's "imperfection" and become relaxed and tolerant. They are able to cope with regression when the child needs support without encouraging too much dependence. They facilitate expression of the child's true feelings of frustration and help the child subliminate his energies into acceptable behavior.

The Child's Developmental Coping Experiences

Infants and toddlers with diabetes present special problems for parents. Urine collections, the child's refusal to eat, and the recurrent painful injections which the parents may be afraid to give create excessive parental anxiety which the child often incorporates as a way of life.

Eddie was ten months old when his mother noted that he was lethargic, took his bottle poorly, and was wetting very frequently. At the same time there were none of the usual signs of illness. Eddie's father usually played golf on the weekends leaving the mother alone with the child. Nor did he support her when she expressed concern about Eddie's condition. She was afraid to call her physician because the child showed none of the familiar signs of illness to which she could point. Meanwhile, the child became more and more lethargic. She picked him up, rocked him, and cried helplessly, feeling at the same time that her worry was unnecessary. When she took him to the physician the next day, the diagnosis was made in the office. A phone call was made to father, but he did not come to the hospital until he had finished his day at work. His excessive use of denial and the mother's immense concern eventually led to their marriage ending in divorce. The mother became overly involved with Eddie; she cried each time she had to give him an injection of insulin. Later, when he became enuretic, encopretic, and stole food, psychotherapy was sought.

This infant developed a symptom (enuresis) which is commonly associated with anger toward the parent. Many of these children learn to have temper tantrums at will. At best, they cannot understand why their parent has to hurt them. In addition, they are more prone to insulin shock if the parent or the physician tries to maintain a sugar-free urine level. The irritability that manifests itself with hypoglycemia may teach the child to become manipulative in order to get a food reward. It has been demonstrated that older siblings of these children often become jealous. They resent the child with diabetes because of the special treatment he receives.[2]

In the child, this overinvolvement may take the form of an increased fear of strangers and distrust of adults. Many parents of diabetic children, at all stages of development, tend to be secretive about their child's handicap. Young children often distort the cause of their illness and attribute it to the environment. Thus, a child with diabetes may feel that he has to take shots because he "ate too much candy."

When the young child begins preschool or kindergarten, the parents face a new task. A new caretaker must be entrusted with their "secret," and with the management of this child about whom they have such strong feelings. Increased separation anxiety is common, and some parents delay enrolling these children in school until they are older. Nor are these fears altogether groundless. School brings its own hazards. Stigmatizing may begin when the teacher or principal shows fear or anxiety about the child's management.

Terrylyn was six and her recently divorced mother was attempting to become self-sufficient by attending nursing school. The child's diabetes had been diagnosed when she was four. With the mother at school, Terrylyn missed her presence. For her part, mother resented the feelings of constantly being tied down. She showed open hostility to Terrylyn and fought with her over food intake. Terrylyn would refuse to eat breakfast. This prevented mother from getting off to her nursing classes since she was afraid that Terrylyn would have another hypoglycemic reaction at school. Whenever such a reaction occurred, it would disrupt mother's classes even more seriously because she would have to go to daughter's school to deal with the teacher's and principal's anxiety. Terrylyn missed a great deal of school; she became school phobic; and a vicious cycle was set up. Only after much education and support could mother send the child to school without having her finish breakfast. Much support and intervention were necessary for school personnel to be comfortable in changing the cycle. In play therapy, Terrylyn repeatedly played mother, doctor, and nurse with the need to act out frequent injections, punishment, intravenous tubes, and forced feedings.

It is not uncommon for mothers who manage a diabetic child to begin nurses' training, thus providing them the defense of intellectualization. The young child masters his anxiety through play and fantasy. He may enact a special operation to repair the defective pancreas which is felt to be missing or only partially there; some children talk of removal of a bad part of themselves. The stress of painful injections seems to accentuate the need to be a "good or bad" child. An excess craving for sweets or a complete denial of such a desire is often present. The young child with diabetes is more apt to be aggressive because he can get away with it without limit-setting, whereas another child could not. Should the initial school adjustment be positive, it may continue long enough to provide gratifying rewards for cognitive mastery. The child may then be able to sublimate his resentment and anger about the fact that his requirements for life are different. This adaptation leads to enhanced ego development.

The latency child's performance at school is a key to his adaptation. This depends a great deal on whether he is still having frequent hypoglycemic attacks and frequent hospitalizations for ketoacidosis. It is also important that the family be able to support the child without the stigmatizing effects of insisting on special diets, requiring special exercise programs, and taking special precautions to refrigerate insulin on trips (when this is really unnecessary, since insulin is quite stable except under extreme changes in temperature). The child's anger about having to do urine checks is often directed at the parents with each reminder from them.

Robbie was nine and had diabetes diagnosed at two years of age. His mother still weighed his portions of food, bought special ice cream labeled "diabetic," and restricted his sugar intake. Meanwhile, his brother, Frank, was allowed to choose his own diet. Mother asked Robbie to do laps around the house in wintertime for exercise, whereas his brother did not have to meet this requirement. Robbie attempted to run away frequently. His kinetic family drawing showed him isolated from the rest of his family. Although his achievement in school was excellent on tests, he was repeatedly taken to see the principal for stealing from lunches and urinating on the walls of the restroom. The physician made a number of suggestions to lessen the stigma for this child. However, it took several months of psychotherapy before Robbie's mother was able to become more flexible around mealtimes. Individual psychotherapy for Robbie himself was slower going, and there was frequent acting out. School became the one place where Robbie felt accepted. He was given accelerated tasks there which he dispatched readily.

The most common resentment of the child with diabetes is the diet. This may be so because restricting types of food lets out the secret and singles out the child as different.

Much more is written about the adolescent's emotional response to diabetes than about the younger child's reactions.[7, 4, 10] The metabolic changes associated with growth have profound effects on the endocrine system. But the task of achieving independence from the family may be more important to consider. The usual fantasies of future work, marriage, and procreation are complicated for the child who has been told that diabetes is an inherited disease. To be the subject of "special" treatment in regard to driver's licenses, scholarship programs, and job opportunities is often traumatic in and of itself. Fears and anxieties about sexual information add to the stress of knowing that one's body is chemically different. Moreover, in this "era of drug abuse," the child who "shoots up" with a syringe may have particular concerns about being similar to the drug addict.

With greater peer pressures for conformity, the dietary needs become an even more important area of conflict. This is compounded by parental secretiveness—the child may be asked to keep his illness concealed. The resultant double bind may then cause increased anxiety and subsequent acidosis. Case reports of self-destructive behavior are numerous,[7, 4] and excessive recourse is made to denial and magical thinking. Some examples of this are forgetting to take insulin during exams, going off to sleep-away camp without insulin, running away to test one's body, and using muscle-building exercises with barbells to show no need for daily injections. When this denial becomes conscious and deliberate, it indicates a very severe degree of psychopathology.

Psychologic Profile

Four different personality patterns (with mixtures) have been documented: (1) dependent, passive, and submissive; (2) self-destructive and depressive; (3) angry and rebellious; and (4) obsessive and compulsive.

This list is not meant to be inclusive and is a summation of many studies done in many different ways. There is no longer a question of the degree of intelligence in children with diabetes; large-scale studies have shown that as a group, they are average.

Body Image Disturbances at Different Levels of Development

Draw-a-person exercises (from table 53.1) show a highly significant difference ($p < .01$) in how many bodies are included when compared with controls matched for age, sex, race, and social class. This large-scale study included children seven through fifteen, with a mean age of twelve. Thus denial of the body in human figure drawings is all too evident.

TABLE 53–1

Draw-a-Person and the Child with Diabetes
(10 day pretest/posttest interval at camp)

Child Group	Heads Only	Bodies Only	Total
Pretest with diabetes	37	62	99
Posttest with diabetes	40	59	99
Pretest control	19	83	102
Posttest control	13	85	98

Early, the child's self-concept may be distorted through an overinvolvement with the parent(s). He may feel somewhat special with all the attention from health personnel. If this becomes a way of life, it can contribute to recurrent hospitalization and somatizing.

Later when the child has the cognitive ability to understand that he is unique, he usually devalues himself. This is especially true if stigmatizing events occur at school in the presence of his peers.

Diabetes often has profound effects on interpersonal relationships. Pity, sympathy, or suspicion are common from peers and other parents, with the result that distortion of relationships easily occurs. It is not unusual for other parents and children to be frightened about the contagiousness of diabetes, i.e., in respect to slumber parties and overnights.

In a society without an extended family, such interactions with peers are of immense importance. Children, even very young ones, are often forced to take responsibility for interpreting urine results, measuring, and injecting insulin in order to meet their parents' need for less involvement.

At any age, the relationship between the child with diabetes and the physician is important. The child who is having trouble with his parents may look to the physician as a special resource. Should the similarities between the physician and the parent be too great, then the transfer of feelings onto the physician with resulting rebellion against authority will further serve to isolate the child and his feelings.[6, 3, 5]

Specific Defenses Against the Handicap

As shown from table 53.1, the child's use of denial may be incorporated into his self-concept. When the family helps the child to avoid athletics, rigorous vacations, or occupations involving physi-

cal labor, identity formation may be distorted. Life insurance is often difficult to obtain. Family planning may revolve around the child's "disability."

These events serve to reinforce the "sick role." Regression is seen whenever children are hospitalized or kept from school. Occasionally children are asked to identify with successful adult role models with diabetes. Athletes who have coped successfully are frequently cited, and reaction-formation is fostered. This may reach psychotic proportions, such as the child exercising with barbells with the fantasy of ridding his body of diabetes.

Perhaps the early questions clinicians raised about the intelligence of children with diabetes occurred because of these children's overconcern with the need to use intellectual skills; in their world, the mastery of physical skills was seen as an unrealistic expectation. The use of intellectualization is still a common way for children to cope with the anger, fear, and resentment that derive from living with diabetes. Some children will discuss their condition as though their illness was exclusively their "parents' problem." This use of displacement may reach absurd levels. Projection of the child's anger onto the parents is common.

Programs to Reduce Psychopathological Effects of Diabetes

Over the past few years, most physicians concerned with juvenile diabetes have gradually liberalized dietary restrictions to make them more realistic. This is sensible; there has never been any proof that the diabetic child's hunger-appetite regulatory mechanism is different from that of children without diabetes. However, this liberalization has often coincided with overzealousness in asking the child to take responsibility for his disease at an inappropriately early age. Pediatricians, nurses, mothers, camp personnel, and others often urge that dietary management and insulin dosage changes should be regulated by the child. This may occur when the child's cognitive development does not allow for the abstract thought necessary to understand what is needed to achieve chemical balance.

Summer camps for children with diabetes are common; indeed, they are to be found in almost every state. There has been no controlled study, however, to prove their efficacy. Perhaps they further reinforce the child's concept of abnormality and prevent the necessary changes in policies of regular summer camps to allow children with diabetes to attend. Most of the diabetic camps have scholarships for children who need financial aid; certainly they provide the experience of seeing the different ways in which other children cope. For the children with overprotective parents, it may provide their only opportunity to observe alternative ways of living. None the less, more flexibility in regular summer camps might be even more desirable; it would allow the child with diabetes to see his normal peers in action.

These children are often referred to medical centers where pediatric endocrinologists consult with the child's physician. Many of these sub-specialty clinics have excellent teaching programs utilizing dieticians, clinical nurse specialists, social workers, psychologists, and psychiatrists, who develop special talents in relating to children with diabetes. However, this interdisciplinary work can only be as good as the communication and co-operation among the disciplines. Moreover, if distance makes travel time excessive, the necessary personal relationship is lost and the child may then become more alienated rather than less. When the various trainees rotate to other services, meaningful relationships may be lost at a time when continuity of care for these children is most essential.

Individual and group psychotherapy have both been reported to be effective.[11, 1, 4] The referral rate depends in part on the level of trust established between the physician and psychotherapist.

Local diabetes associations are sometimes oriented toward maturity-onset diabetes and may be of benefit to only a few parents. Literature sent to parents stressing the complications of long-term diabetes may be especially frightening to the parents of a newly diagnosed child. Sometimes these organizations provide parent groups and parent-to-parent counseling efforts which can be supportive to new parents.

School personnel are becoming more sophisticated about diabetes and, with support, can work out individual programs that do not stigmatize the child in the classroom. The noon urine check, as well as the midmorning and midafternoon snacks, are rarely necessary. If they are prescribed, they need to be handled judiciously by the teacher. If they are not threatened, school nurses can help by informing teachers about the realistic needs of the child with diabetes.

Perhaps the most crucial point at which a program could be effective in reducing potential psychopathological effects is during the initial diagnostic period. The meaning of the disease to the parents and child is often obscured by hospital personnel working too hard to teach all aspects of case management during the initial stay. If they were to work slowly, observe, and listen to what impact this condition is having on the child and his family, many future episodes of hypoglycemia, coma, and hospitalization could be avoided. Age-appropriate behavior needs to be stressed and possible psychologic complications predicted so they may be prevented. Some families need to be referred for counseling immediately rather than later; there are many failures of parental management that result from ambivalence about accepting the child's defect. Parental handling of genetic blame is an excellent example of where a sensitive mental health professional can assess family dynamics and intervene appropriately. Initial psychosocial intervention has rarely been tried, but the financial benefits of avoiding future hospitalizations, school phobia with regression, and self-destructive behavior would easily make such a program feasible.

Prognosis With and Without Intervention

It is common to hear case reports of children who are hospitalized with diabetes more than fifty times in a few years. Under closer scrutiny, family crises are almost always the primary precipitating causes. This is a dramatic example:

Jean, a seventeen-year-old girl, had had diabetes since age eight. She was the first of four children born to married first cousins. In family sessions, the second child, a boy, was observed to be the "spitting image" of his father. The third child, a girl, was also diabetic. The last child was mentally retarded. Jean was hospitalized more than sixty times over a four-year period. The parents frequently dropped her off at the emergency room after a family argument. Family dynamics involved the mother who was devalued by the father because of his own insecurity. His attacks on her competence had led to depression and a mental hospital stay several years previously. Over the following years, she was repeatedly "scapegoated" about this by father and son. This occurred even though father changed jobs frequently while mother provided the family's major income through steady employment. Any expression of tenderness was actively avoided by this father, who laughed off all display of emotions.

Jean's hospitalizations were routinized by the hospital medical staff and she received much secondary gain. She acquired many supportive friends despite such behavior as injecting insulin into her pillow. Despite her hospitalizations, Jean maintained her school work, while her sister, Judy, was delinquent and school phobic. Yet Judy did not often manifest ketoacidosis severe enough to necessitate hospitalization.

It was difficult for this family to see any relationship between family strife and Jean's recurrent hospital admissions. When Jean saved her money and applied for college, her father and brother teased her. Their devaluation of her wish to excell academically was a severe stress. This led to impulsive behavior on her part. In order to gain independence, she took a job as a waitress in a sandwich shop. She worked too hard, became overtired, and had difficulty with school. Ultimately, despite valiant efforts by the chief pediatric resident to help her avoid hospitalization, she was left in the emergency room by her father. Gradually, the pediatric housestaff began to change their practice of routine admission, and instead treated her in the emergency room for a few hours. Slowly, with support both in the emergency room and in family psychotherapy, she was able to cope with family stress without the need for frequent hospitalizations.

Suicidal attempts by insulin underdosing and overdosing are also common. This is especially true during adolescence and early adulthood when the first complications sometimes appear. The results of present research studies, where adequate controls have been used, indicate that more than one-third of children with diabetes have severe emotional problems.* Mothers of these children have been found to be significantly emotionally ill.[9] Families are reported to be under enough stress to account for increased separation both before and after the diabetes is diagnosed.[8, 2] No prospective study has been reported in which families genetically vulnerable to diabetes were observed for patterns of emotional development before the onset of the child's illness. Since there has been no controlled study done proving the effectiveness of counseling, the prognosis with intervention cannot be said to be necessarily improved. However, many individual case reports indicate psychosocial intervention was of benefit.[11, 1, 4]

* See references 11, 1, 6, 10, 3, and 9.

REFERENCES

1. BRUCH, H., "Physiologic and Psychologic Interrelationships in Diabetes in Children," *Psychosomatic Medicine, 11*:200–210, 1949.

2. CRAIN, A. J., SUSSMAN, M. B., and WEIL, W. B., "Effects of a Diabetic Child on Marital Integration and Related Measures of Family Functioning," *Journal of Health and Human Behavior, 7*:122–127, 1966.

3. KOSKI, M., "The Coping Processes in Childhood Diabetes," *Acta Paediatrica Scandinavica, 198*:9–56, 1969.

4. ROSEN, H., and LIDZ, T., "Emotional Factors in the Precipitation of Recurrent Diabetic Acidosis," *Psychosomatic Medicine, 11*:211–215, 1949.

5. SAYED, A. J., and LEAVERTON, D. R., "Kinetic-Family-Drawings of Children with Diabetes," *Child Psychiatry and Human Development, 5*:40–50, 1974.

6. SCHIFF, L. J., "Emotional Problems of Diabetic Children and Their Parents," *Psychosomatics, 5*:362–364, 1964.

7. STEARNS, S., "Self-destructive Behavior in Young Patients with Diabetes Mellitus," *Diabetes, 8*:379–382, 1959.

8. STEIN, S. P., and CHARLES, E., "Emotional Factors in Juvenile Diabetes Mellitus: A Study of Early Life Experience of Adolescent Diabetics," *American Journal of Psychiatry, 128(5–8)*:700–704, 1971.

9. STERKY, G., "Family Background and State of Mental Health in a Group of Diabetic School Children," *Acta Paediatrica Scandinavica, 52*:377–390, 1963.

10. SWIFT, C. R., SEIDMAN, F. L., and STEIN, H., "Adjustment Problems in Juvenile Diabetes," *Psychosomatic Medicine, 29*:555–571, 1967.

11. VANDEN BERGH, R. L., "Emotional Aspects," in Sussman, K. E., *Juvenile-Type Diabetes and Its Complications*, pp. 411–438, Charles C Thomas, Springfield, Ill., 1971.

12. WHITE, P., "Childhood Diabetes: Its Course and Influence on the Second and Third Generation," *Diabetes, 9*:345–355, 1960.

54 / The Dialysis Patient

John P. Kemph and Joel P. Zrull

The child dialysis patient presents some of the same problems as those commonly encountered in patients with other forms of chronic illness, particularly patients with renal failure. The restriction of behavior, the isolation, the limitation of the potential for cognitive development, the dependency, the depression, and the fear of death are all common to chronic illness. Chronic fatigue, anorexia, vomiting, inhibited growth, convulsions, and transient psychosis are some of the specific symptoms and signs of the uremic syndrome.[38]

The etiology of renal failure in children varies considerably. In some there has been warning of severe illness through repeated episodes of acute glomerulonephritis or pyelonephritis with fever and toxicity or obstructive uropathy. However, often the onset is insidious with symptoms of apathy and anorexia; unless a urinalysis is performed, the diagnosis may not be made for months or even years after the onset of chronic glomerulonephritis.

A fifteen-year-old girl developed nausea and vomiting, convulsive seizures and hallucinations. At that point she was first found to have end stage renal disease with very little kidney function. A careful review of her history indicated that she had probably first developed renal disease when she was ten years old. At that time her activity level decreased considerably over a period of several months. Where she had previously been motorically very active, eager to play with friends, and interested in school, she became less interested in sports and school, was slow to arise in the morning and easily fatigued. Her parents brought this to the attention of the family doctor who, after a physical exam without laboratory studies, attributed the change to normal preadolescent maturation. The parents stated that several times during the next few years they sought help from physicians but the diagnosis was not made until flagrant symptoms developed and she was referred to the university hospital.

Unfortunately, this is not an uncommon history in areas where patients are not provided with a routine urinalysis. Usually however, the diagnosis is known and the condition treated, but the disease often progresses inexorably to renal failure.

Then the patient and his family are informed about three alternatives—chronic dialysis, kidney transplant, or coma and death. Very few refuse both dialysis and transplant, and, in any case, a period of dialysis is usually required in preparation for transplant. Therefore, the majority of patients with renal failure receive dialysis on a temporary or permanent basis.

In general, these are two major forms of dialysis, peritoneal and hemodialysis. Regardless of which procedure is used, the children should be prepared for it by a dialogue during which what is going to happen is clearly explained in concrete terms. If they know what to expect, they tolerate the procedure much better without painful surprises. Although peritoneal dialysis may be the only form of treatment available in some instances, it is certainly the least desirable, particularly with children. The hypertonic solution introduced into the peritoneal cavity to remove fluid and high levels of urea, creatinine, sodium, potassium, etc., is sometimes irritating to the peritoneum; this, coupled with distension of the abdominal cavity, is painful. Furthermore, this prolonged distension gives rise to fantasies of body distortion and destruction. Most children respond to this treatment by fighting against those administering it, but some lie quietly allowing the dialysis to proceed. Usually, however, although they do not object forcefully, they are very frightened.

While lying qietly in bed during peritoneal dialysis, a nine-year-old girl shared with her doctor that she was very scared by the procedure but that her mother's talking with her while it was going on made it tolerable.

Hemodialysis is the most commonly used form of dialysis and is relatively asymptomatic. Cannulae can be inserted either subcutaneously or protruding from the skin surface. Some children and adolescents may utilize denial fairly effectively to avoid experiencing fantasies of body mutilation in association with the insertion of cannulae and the subsequent dialysis, while others will express such fantasies verbally.

During the first few times that the child is connected to the dialysis machine, great care should be taken to explain what is being done (to the extent that the child wishes to know). Children tend to be more fearful if they are not knowledgeable about the procedure. On rare occasions a child will not cooperate at all and, out of fear, physically resist the treatment. Removing the fear then becomes a life-saving task. Several patients have responded favorably to an approach that gave them considerable autonomy and control over the procedure, once they were familiar with it. They enjoy showing the physicians, technicians, nurses, and relatives what the machine will accomplish for them as they connect their cannulae to it (always under supervision). Medical students assigned to attend dialysis patients have been creative in finding ways to interest children in their own dialysis.

Another common reason for children to resist dialysis is denial of illness. If they don't get dialysis they can more easily deny their illness.

A thirteen-year-old boy who had been treated extensively and repeatedly for chronic glomerulonephritis was finally left with very little kidney function. He agreed to an out-patient program of dialysis two or three times a week (the number depending upon weekly laboratory test results). He and his parents frequently missed treatments, "forgetting" what days he was assigned to dialysis. It was evident that taking such treatment reminded him of sickness. After trying a variety of techniques, the dialysis team became partially successful by rewarding him for riding his bicycle to the hospital early in the morning; they played his favorite games with him while he was attached to the apparatus. He later stated that he was often not aware of being dialyzed. He further stated that he could "forget" that he was sick most of the time he was being treated.

The child on dialysis for several hours a day, two to five days a week, may adapt well by utilizing the time to learn through reading or school work. If a hospital school is available, the teachers can keep him at grade level or above. Usually, creative measures are required to keep the child or adolescent interested in learning. In many dialysis units, the physiological technology far surpasses the sociopsychoeducational technology and supports. The most frequent complications of dialysis are social and psychological; not the least of these are active and passive suicide (the patient either kills himself or allows himself to die). Yet much less creative work is being done to provide emotional supports to the patients and staff who spend much of their lives in a dialysis unit than is devoted to the management of the pathophysiology.

The Pediatric Dialysis Team

Although adults have survived by this means since the early 1960s,[1] the child on dialysis is a relative newcomer to the medical psychiatric scene.[41]

Most dialysis programs begin by treating adults and adolescents with no special programs for children. Therefore, initially, children in need are usually placed in adult dialysis units where personnel have little training or experience in working with the young. The authors have worked in three university hospital dialysis units where this has been done; it is their observation that children are not well attended to in such programs. Nurses and technical personnel who work with adults are usually unable to understand children's behavior, and are therefore unable to provide appropriate emotional support and structure. Children in adult units require specific child workers and pediatric nurses, and, when possible, a milieu team of educator, occupational therapist, child psychiatrist, and social worker.

A brief history of the development of the pediatric dialysis team at one center will exemplify this approach. The first few children with renal failure treated at the center were dialyzed in the adult unit. During unit meetings, heated discussions about the children occurred, with much dissension expressed about the staff's approach to the children while they were on the machine. There were varying opinions among the staff. Some proposed a firm, strict set of rules, others permissiveness, while still others expressed anxiety about exposing children to this psychologically traumatic procedure. A few openly expressed anger at already having too much work; now they had to give extra time to meet children's demands! The pediatric nephrologist and child psychiatrist were unable to provide sufficient time during periods of dialysis to reassure both patients and staff, and the dissension continued. An immature, frightened eleven-year-old girl produced a crisis when she screamed and ran away from the dialysis staff when she was being prepared for treatment. After several unsuccessful attempts, the staff and the child's mother used coercion. The child submitted to the procedure, and then cried unceasingly during the many hours on dialysis. Nor did the child's behavior change much during the next several procedures. At this point the adult dialysis team and hospital administration agreed to support a pediatric dialysis unit. First a pediatric nurse, a social worker, and a dietitian were attached to the pediatric nephrologist and child psychiatrist to form the team. After a few days of explanation to the child and mother, a warm relationship was established with the nurse, and the child became completely cooperative. However, the prolonged periods of dialysis become boring. The patient and mother (who remained with her throughout) both became disenchanted and discouraged, and the child became apathetic and depressed.

It was learned that the patient was four years behind grade level in reading. A specialist in reading was therefore requested to join the team to stimulate further interest in reading and other forms of learning. This educator also provided educational therapy, an individualized educational program devised to meet the cognitive and emotional needs of the specific child. In working with this child, the academic, psychological, and physical aspects of her functioning were taken into consideration. A detailed description of the educational therapist's role is described elsewhere.[37] Finally, an occupational therapist was utilized to teach the child to sew and to develop skills in several crafts. This attempt to involve the child in as many normal activities as possible served to minimize problems of depression, withdrawal, negativism, anger, and aggressive behavior.

More space and several additional machines were obtained and a four-bed pediatric dialysis unit was established. Initially the child psychiatrist's role was to provide psychotherapy to the children and counseling for the parents and staff. As the team became a functioning unit, one of the staff who worked in the unit tended to form a closer working relationship with a particular child. At this point the child psychiatrist became the consultant to the staff member, giving less time to direct contact with the child. Eventually each staff member had responsibility for specific patients with support from other staff.

An important function of the child psychiatrist was to review these close relationships between patient and staff. Some staff would invite the patients to their homes and behave as parents or benefactors. Similarly, patients or their relatives might become too dependent on the staff member, where this was tolerated by the staff. The child psychiatrist met with some of the staff each week and periodically with the entire staff to review these relationships. His mission was to minimize overdependency and jealousy and to enhance an esprit de corps among the team members by giving them support and recognition as a special group. Theirs was the heroic task two to five times a week of helping the same terminally ill children and families cope with prolongation of life.

Most centers recognize the need to manage the children undergoing dialysis from a broader perspective than that of the nephrologist alone. Teams of personnel including the pediatric nephrologist, nurse, dietitian, social worker, child psychologist, and/or child psychiatrist and educational therapist (or teacher) are all vital in their input to treatment. As with other teams working with specific life-threatening disease entities, they often undergo an evolution and develop a team character and cohesiveness.[41] This serves to meet the multiplicity of problems confronting the child, his family, and the dialysis unit itself. The members of the team are able to support each other in what is an emotionally stressful task.

Psychological Effects

The psychodynamics of children on dialysis are similar to those of adults, but the child's normally dependent state and ongoing development produce variations. The child frequently views his illness as a retaliation for being bad; he may also implicate other causative factors.[30] Frequently, the child feels guilt in relationship to his illness. Because he is in the process of growing up, the child may particularly resent the enforced regression and dependency induced by the recurrent periods of hospitalization. The child's activity level may be curtailed, and his freedom to discharge energy and aggression limited; this will tend to precipitate a depressive state. It leads to fewer associations with peers and serves to accentuate a sense of differentness. Chronic illness, and the "serious" atmosphere created by caring for the child afflicted with it, bring a heightened concern over death. In the nature of things, this is a stress with which the child must cope. This in itself may lead to chronic anxiety and depression.

Those conditions are specific to renal disease and cause unique problems for the child who is a potential dialysis patient. Edema evokes body image concerns. Because his growth may be retarded,[15] the child wonders whether he will ever grow up. His recurrent clouded sensorium and hallucinatory experiences make the sensitive child or youth wonder if he is "going crazy." The anxiety induced by anorexia with subsequent vomiting and nausea lead the child to feel deprived or that his life is threatened. Special diets simply add to the deprivation that the child or youth may feel. If convulsions occur with the renal disease, they only add to the insecurity and fear of death.

The family is affected by their lack of knowledge regarding renal disease. Since dialysis is not universally available, most are vaguely acquainted with the difficulty of obtaining adequate care.

They observe the changes in body configuration, and also have some awareness of the psychologic and behavioral aspects of their child's condition. All of this encourages anxiety and guilt, and leads to frustrations which may be directed toward the physician and/or the team involved with the child's care.

Initially, at least, dialysis itself is a threatening, restrictive, and often painful process. An operative procedure introduces the experience since an arterial venous fistula or shunt must be provided, which may be painful.[5] The child is then restricted for several hours two to five times weekly as the dialysis is performed. During this time he is attached to the machine vital to his life. Maintaining integrity as an individual while directly and mechanically associated with the dialyzer becomes difficult.[32] Body image is severely disturbed, and, when coupled with the psychological effects of the uremic condition, serious distortions of reality relationships can result. This can be further enhanced by the comparative isolation of the child during dialysis. Growth itself may be compromised by the necessarily stringent diet which must accompany dialysis. Taken together with the potential problems of sexual maturation, this can produce many adverse developmental experiences.

The family of the child with renal illness faces many of the same emotional stresses known to those of other chronically ill children. The concern over the well-being and life of the child can lead parents to engage in overprotective and overindulgent behavior. Guilt can accentuate such attitudes. At the same time, the parents' exposure to prolonged continuation of specialized care often results in a sense of helplessness. This may bring parents to a state of chronic anxiety; ultimately they will reject the child. For their part, siblings too can resent the special treatment and attention afforded the sick child, which may lead to rejection at their hands.

The family, of course, can feel relief when the child is first accepted for dialysis.[41] Over time, however, the ongoing commitment to the two- to five-time-per-week procedure often becomes intolerable. Mothers are most often enlisted to help dialyze the child, producing a potential challenge to the father's need or desire to be involved. Paternal resentment can arise over not being included, as can maternal resentment over the convenient absence of the father from the process. Under certain circumstances, home dialysis is possible. However, this puts the mother into a very demanding role which may result in further anxiety and resentment. For families who are in a state of disruption prior to the dialysis, the stress is enhanced by the demands of the process. Many families experienced additional stress because of the financial drain on their income or savings. Since Federal aid and third-party payers have accepted this burden, it is now felt less by families. On the other hand, if a family were intact and functioning well, this is likely to continue in the face of dialysis.[34]

With the assistance of a skilled team, children and adolescents can overcome the initial fear and nausea; and the other discomforts of hemodialysis. Inevitably however, the quality of life is altered significantly. Their sense of helpless dependency is heightened by frequent prolonged procedures, and doubts are raised both when they see their peers repeatedly in a moribund state, and by their own diminished physical capacities.[23] Even in an ideal pediatric dialysis program, children and adolescents along with their close relatives tend to become recurrently depressed and anxious. This may lead to acting out with the hemodialysis staff[25] in order to fulfill unconscious needs for punishment, revenge and salvation.

Renal Transplantation

After reviewing the problems encountered in dialysis, it is not surprising to find many families turning with great optimism to kidney transplant as a treatment modality.

This process is initiated by looking for a donor; the child is usually aware of what is being considered. If it is to be a live related donor, the child often knows about the risk to the donor. If a cadaver donor is sought, the child must wait for a possible transplant. He tends to develop unrealistic expectations of what it would do for him. In the face of transplant, the child once again encounters a surgical procedure with the accompanying fear of loss of body integrity. More than that, even though nonfunctional, loss of his own kidneys is sometimes feared as a last decisive step from which there is no return. Finally the transplant takes place and the family anxiously waits for the new kidney to begin to function. This means an agonizing several days to two weeks until functioning occurs. If the kidney fails to function, the family of the patient and the donor become predictably furious at the transplant team.[24] If the kidney functions well, all the people concerned are relieved to the point of euphoria. This then is followed by fear of future rejection of the kidney, and of further procedures if that happens. This in turn is complicated by the feelings that the child experiences if rejection takes place: Did he do something wrong that caused this? Was he bad in some way? Did he "waste" a family member's kidney?

Efforts at preserving a kidney which is being rejected include the use of immunosuppressive drugs. This usually results in body changes—for instance, moon face and excess weight gain. If the transplant does succeed, it usually leads to a longer, fuller life. In those children and their families where there has been a presurgery history of instability, psychiatric complications are greater.

Throughout the course of the uremic syndrome, hemodialysis, and transplantation, these patients are vulnerable to sudden changes in physical status which confront them with the dire implications of their state. Ultimately, most of them recognize that they live on borrowed time. A youth may feel that with the restriction and pain of dialysis, or the possible multiple transplant operations, life is undesirable. Consciously or unconsciously he may then wish for death.[36]

In sum, the major stress that a family first encounters when their child is approaching transplantation is the search for a donor suitable to provide the child with a kidney.[35] Often this is a family member, although if it is a minor, medico-legal complications could ensue.[35] Most parents willingly offer their kidney for the child. However, this is not done without great concern, both over their own integrity, and also over whether or not it will remain successfully transplanted. If it is rejected, the donor may experience guilt and often resentment over the rejection. During the post-operative period parents usually become over-protective; they often require some direction in helping to rehabilitate the child. When the transplant is successful, the ability of the family to adjust correlates with the family's previous history of stability.[27]

Psychotherapy

The shifts in family interrelationships and the repetitive episodes of depression experienced by children and adolescents warrant the inclusion of a child psychiatrist on both the dialysis and kidney transplant teams.[22, 21, 20] The best solution to the dilemma of the child or adolescent with renal failure is a renal transplant from an identical twin. Even in this relatively ideal situation, there is considerable family disturbance created by the uremic syndrome, dialysis, and transplant.[22, 21] In other cases of this syndrome, the common concern is total loss of kidney function with no available treatment. The resultant realistic fear of dying may be conscious or unconscious, but it is always present in these patients. The authors have provided psychotherapy for children and adolescents with renal failure, dialysis, and kidney transplant; they have found that a supportive approach is essential to prevent anxiety, depression, and suicide, to treat severe emotional disturbances when they develop, and to allow these patients their best performance.[22, 21, 20] The most effective psychotherapeutic approach consisted of supporting the patient's expression of anger and guilt regarding his illness and its medical management, and condoning the exploration of his feelings about his illness and various treatments. The child psychiatrist can encourage the patient to recognize, understand, and express his shifting moods of euphoria, guilt, anxiety, and depression.

REFERENCES

1. Abram, H. S., Zwany, R. V., and Johnson, H. K., "Physicians' Attitudes Toward Organ Donation, *Southern Medical Journal, 68(4):*443–446, 1975.

2. Ahart, S. M., "The Problem of Cadaver Kidney Transplantation in Children Today, As Seen by a Parent and Kidney Donor," *Transplantation Proceedings, 5(2):*1073–1075, 1973.

3. ———, "Survival by Machine: The Psychological Stress of Chronic Hemodialysis," *Psychiatry in Medicine, 1(1):*27–51, 1970.

4. Bernstein, D. M., and Simmons, R. G., "The Adolescent Kidney Donor: The Right to Give," *American Journal of Psychiatry, 131(12):*1338–1343, 1974.

5. Cameron, J. S., "The Treatment of Chronic Renal Failure in Children by Regular Dialysis and by Transplantation," *Nephron, 11(2):*221–251, 1973.

6. Christopherson, L. K., and Gonda, T. A., "Patterns of Grief: End-Stage Renal Failure and Kidney Transplantations," *Transplantation Proceedings, 5(2):*1051–1057, 1973.

7. Committee on Dialysis and Transplantation, American Society of Pediatric Nephrology and the National Kidney Foundation, "Hemodialysis and Renal Transplantation in Children, The Role of the Pediatric Nephrology Team," *Pediatrics, 53(6):*864–866, 1974.

8. De Nour, A. K., "Role and Reactions of Psychiatrists in Chronic Hemodialysis Programs," *Psychiatry in Medicine, 4(1):*63–76, 1973.

9. ———, and Czakes, J. W., "Professional Team Opinion and Personal Bias: A Study of a Chronic Hemodialysis Unit Team," *Journal of Chronic Diseases, 24(9):*533–541, 1971.

10. De Shazo, C. V., et al., "Results of Renal Transplantation in 100 Children," *Surgery, 76(3):*461–468, 1974.

11. Drotar, D., "The Treatment of a Severe Anxiety Reaction in an Adolescent Boy Following Renal Transplantation," *Journal of the American Academy of Child Psychiatry, 14(3):*451–461, 1975.

12. Eisenbroth, R. M., et al., "Service Meetings in a Renal Transplant Unit, an Unused Adjunct to Total Patient Care," *Psychiatry in Medicine, 1(1):*53–59, 1970.

13. Fine, R. N., and Grushkin, C. M., "Hemodialysis and Renal Transplantation in Children," *Clinical Nephrology, 1(4):*243–256, 1973.

14. Glick, I. D., Goldfield, M. D., and Kornat, P. J., "Recognition and Management of Psychosis Associated with Hemodialysis," *California Medicine, 119(5):*56–59, 1973.

15. Grushkin, C. M., and Fine, R. N., "Growth in Children Following Renal Transplantation," *American Journal of Diseases of Children, 125:*514–516, 1973.

16. Haybury, B., "A Prospective Study of Patients in Chronic Hemodialysis—III, Pediatric Value of Intelligence, Cognitive Deficit and Ego Defense Structures in Rehabilitation," *Journal of Psychosomatic Research, 18(3):*151–160, 1974.

17. Holliday, Chantler, and Holliday, M. A., "Growth in Children with Renal Disease with Particular Reference to the Effects of Calorie Malnutrition: A Review," *Clinical Nephrology, 1(7):*230–232, 1973.

18. *Journal of the American Medical Association,* Editorial, "Emotional Stresses of Patient—Physician Encounters," *223(9):*1037–1038, 1973.

19. Kaye, R., Leight, H., and Stranch, B., "The Role of the Liaison Psychiatrist in a Hemodialysis Program: A Case Study," *Psychiatry in Medicine, 4(3):*313–321, 1973.

20. Kemph, J. P., "Psychotherapy with Donors and Recipients of Kidney Transplants," *Seminars in Psychiatry, 3(1):*145–158, 1971.

21. ———, "Psychotherapy with Identical Twins with Kidney Transplant," in Proceedings of the Fifth World Congress of Psychiatry, *Excerpta Medica,* Symposium 31, 1287–1290, 1971.

22. ———, "Psychotherapy with Patients Receiving Kidney Transplant," *American Journal of Psychiatry, 124(5):*623–629, 1967.

23. ———, "Renal Failure, Artificial Kidney and Kidney Transplant," *American Journal of Psychiatry, 122(11):*1270–1274, 1966.

24. ———, Bermann, E. A., and Coppolillo, H. P., "Kidney Transplant and Shifts in Family Dynamics," *American Journal of Psychiatry, 125(11):*1485–1490, 1969.

25. Kemph, J. P., and Hertel, R. K., "Psychologic Effects of Kidney Transplantation," *Psychosomatic Medicine, 31:*607–618, 1969.

26. Korsch, B. M., et al., "Long Term Follow-up on Kidney Transplant Patients and Their Families," *Proceedings of the European Dialysis Association, 9:*359–363, 1972.

27. Korsch, B. M., Negrete, V. F., and Gardner, J. E., "Kidney Transplantation in Children: Psychological Follow-up Study on Child and Family," *Pediatrics, 83(3):*399–408, 1973.

28. Levy, N. B., et al., "Panel: Living or Dying, Adaptation to Hemodialysis," in Levy, N. B. (Ed.), *Living or Dying: Adaptation to Hemodialysis,* Charles C Thomas, Springfield, Ill., 1974.

29. Lewis, M., "Kidney Donation by a 7 Year Old Identical Twin Child," *Journal of the American Academy of Child Psychiatry, 13(2):*221–245, 1974.

30. Mattsson, A., "Long Term Physical Illness in Childhood: A Challenge to Psychological Adaptation," *Pediatrics, 50(5):*801–811, 1972.

31. Moore, G. L., "Nursing Response to the Long Term Dialysis Patient," *Nephron, 9(4):*193–199, 1972.

32. Neff, S. A., "Autonomy Concerns of a Child on Dialysis," *Maternal-Child Nursing Journal, 4(2):*101–106, 1975.

33. Raimboult, G., "Psychological Aspects of Chronic Renal Failure and Hemodialysis," *Nephron, 11:*242–260, 1973.

34. Sampson, T. F., "The Child in Renal Failure," *Journal of American Academy of Child Psychiatry, 14(3):*462–476, 1975.

35. Santiago-Delpin, E. A., Simmons, R. L., and Simmons, R. G., "Medico-Legal Management of the Juvenile Kidney Donor," *Transplantation Proceedings, 6(4):*441–445, 1974.

36. Schowalter, J. E., Ferholt, S. B., and Munn, N. M., "The Adolescents' Decision to Die," *Pediatrics, 51(1):*97–103, 1973.

37. Schultz, M. T., McVicar, M. I., and Kemph, J. P., "Treatment of the Emotional and Cognitive Deficits of the Child Receiving Hemodialysis," in Levy, N. B. (Ed.), *Living or Dying: Adaptation to Hemodialysis,* pp. 62–73, Charles C. Thomas, Springfield, Ill., 1974.

38. Scribner, B. H., et al., "The Technique of Continuous Hemodialysis," *Transactions of the American Society for Artificial Internal Organs, 6:*88, 1960.

39. Simmons, R. G., and Klein, S. D., "Family Noncommunication: The Search for Kidney Donors," *American Journal of Psychiatry, 129(6):*687–692, 1972.

40. Viederman, M., "Adaptive and Maladaptive Regression in Hemodialysis," *Psychiatry, 37(1):*68–77, 1974.

41. Wolters, W. H. G., Beuckamp, A. L. M., and Donchewolck, R., "Experiences in the Development of a Hemodialysis Center for Children," *Journal of Psychosomatic Research, 17(4):*226, 1973.

42. Zarinsky, I., "Psychological Problems of Kidney Transplanted Adolescents," *Adolescence, 10(37):*101–107, 1975.

55 / The Child with Severe Burns

Norman R. Bernstein

Character of the Handicap: The Social Matrix of the Problem

There are several major factors in severe burn injuries. The United States now has the highest incidence of home fires in the world. This is very largely related to wooden home construction, the widespread use of plastic materials, flammable fabrics, and the aging of the cities with their worn and crumbling electrical and heating systems. Several million burns occur annually, and several hundred thousand people require medical care. At least 12,000 people die annually of burns, of which a large number are children. There are accidental burns, there are childhood firesetters, there are pyromaniacs and arsonists, and there are child abusers who burn children. Arson is the most rapidly growing crime in the country, with a strong economic motive behind it. Children can be hired to set old stores on fire, and businessmen often find it expedient to ignite a building for the insurance rather than go through bankruptcy proceedings. Incendiary fires, known or suspected, had increased to 114,000 incidents by 1974, a rise of 237 percent over a ten-year period. This is the greatest increase on record and closely parallels the unemployment and bankruptcy figures.[8] It goes beyond the incidents of firesetting in homes and forests caused by childhood incendiarism. More than half a billion dollars were lost in 1974 from intentional and suspicious fires. Studies in the ego psychology of firesetting children have revealed fascinating psychodynamic data, but these children are a small fraction of the miscreants. In fact, technically, the distinction might be drawn between the neurotic firesetting child and the arsonist who fraudulently or maliciously burns property. This contrasts with incendiaries, who deliberately set fires.

The fascination with fire is profoundly human. The many fears and counterphobic games played with fires, flammable chemicals, and open furnaces and stoves exist worldwide. Macht and Mack[10] underscored the complexity of firesetting dynamics, and the varied meanings of this behavior for these patients. Some of the injuries children receive offer grim hints, making one ponder how many are part of child-abuse syndromes. Self-immolation for political reasons or derangement is rare, but in warfare, many children have been burned by the widespread use of napalm and other incendiary bombs. Levin[8] distinguishes solitary firesetting, group firesetting, arson for profit by psychopaths, and patterns of firesetting for revenge. None of these factors include the retarded, who apparently account for a substantial part of the burn-injured population. They are variously the dupes who set fires for pay, uncomprehending experimenters with flammables, and passive victims of the activities of others. On the basis of studies in a variety of countries, it is generally agreed that burn injuries, like other traumata, are much more likely to occur in those disturbed families which are called accidentprone. However, once the injury has been a burn, and not a fall or a poisoning, the nature of the course for the family and the child will be influenced by the particulars of the disease, and the complex workings of medical technology and the health care system.

The Burned Child's Coping at Different Levels of Development

STAGES OF THE BURN INJURY

While the social context in which burn injuries occur is clearly of enormous complexity, the final common pathway in a severe burn imposes catastrophic trauma upon the child and his family. The nature of burn injuries prefigures much of the care: surgical excision, isolation to manage bacterial contamination and infection control, and a long series of treatments and procedures which go on for years.

The Emergency. When a burned child is brought to the emergency room, he is often in surgical shock as well as psychological shock, and the people around him are usually disorganized, traumatized, and overwhelmed. Often the home has been lost, the catastrophe may have ruined the family financially, and other people may have died in the disaster. All of these obtrude upon the family from the outset. Abruptly, a physically healthy child is turned into a critically ill patient. The child has no comprehension of what has occurred. He may have been transported to a burn center directly, or he may even have passed through one or two hospitals and emergency rooms before being moved to a burn center. There is a great deal of concern on the part of the medical specialists about the massive technical challenges of acute surgical burn care, and with children, adult surgeons may not be well informed about the special management of fluid balance problems.

Fantasies. The enormous range of stimuli involved in burn injuries touch the varied levels of personality structure for children of all ages. While some theorists have stressed that for the child there is little distinction between the seriousness of the illness and the child's castration fears, it does appear that where the traumata are sufficiently massive, they will produce a greater primitivity in response. The burned child has fantasies of abandonment, mutilation, and generalized concerns about destruction. Some of the most compliant and overtly pleasant children have the wildest and most monstrous undercurrents in their imagery. Two Vietnamese children had been brought to this country and remained here for several years. They always demonstrated the most exquisite politeness and cooperation, without any irrational conduct. At ages nine and eleven, during their play periods they compulsively drew bombs, burning houses, and airplanes, in direct connection with their personal experience. Another child, with marked chest scarring but a very attractive puckish demeanor, never talked of his nightmares filled with pursuing monsters that recurred so often at home. Children who have lost relatives had nightmares, night terrors, and vivid recollections of these departed individuals as part of the mourning process that interwove with other aspects of their care. Misinterpretation of the purposes of their various treatments was uneven and often dramatic, varying from calm and realistic acceptance of pain, to wild and abrupt battling against restraints, anesthesia, injections, or even the placement of grafts. It was as if the barrier against more primitive material in the unconscious was abruptly torn through. Anesthesia was an area in which staff members often did not appreciate the pictures of being drowned, killed,

abandoned, or suffocated which the children produced. Many youngsters shared common recollections of the terror of being taken to the operating room and subsequently having illusions, and postoperative confusional states with ghosts, TV monsters, or transmuted images of their doctors and nurses interwoven into nightmarish scenarios of being chased and tormented. Over time, the general trend was a shift from the primary process mechanisms of the early traumatic stage toward conscious material; however, sporadic recrudescences of primitive material would occur for eighteen months afterward. Many patients fantasize themselves looking intact and healthy over and over for years.

Symptoms: Acute Reactions. Most people familiar with minor household burns and scalds focus upon the acute pain. In third-degree burns where the skin is completely lost, there is a different feeling of pain which is more diffuse, and sometimes the patients are so obtunded by shock as to seem dulled to acute pain. This is partially due to the pain sensors in the skin being completely burned off. But usually there is a combination of second- and third-degree burns in different areas so that pain is not absent. Some patients lose consciousness, and this may even be some protection against the horrors of being rushed into surgery, debrided, given anesthesia, placed in isolation, and swathed in bandages or blackened by silver nitrate poured on the wounds to prevent infection. During the first two weeks, disorientation is often present, along with confusional states, and intermittent and variable delirium. The children thrash, vomit, void, and have diarrhea. Speech often decomposes and serious regression occurs. In severely burned children who have marked anoxia or problems of inhalation, there is often widespread neurological dysfunction, paralysis, dysarthria, dulling of consciousness, amnesia, and even coma. The first issues are survival and the treatment of shock. With the passing of weeks, this changes into a struggle against infection, in particular against invasion by protozoans of low virulence. These are organisms to which healthy children would be resistant, but which the burn patient may not be able to fend off. The family is often swept out of the way while the intensive care of the child is pursued in order to save his life. With third-degree burns which extend over 50 percent of the body the hazard to life is great, and persistent.

Adaptations. As the weeks pass, there is greater communication between the patients, their families, and the caretaking staff. The focus begins to shift toward longer-term issues. However, the burn patient is subjected to many trips to the operating room and many anesthetics, further debridement, amputations, replacement of airways, and grafting. This may mean taking skin from one part of the body and reimplanting it at the burn site, or it may involve placing cadaver skin on the burn site as a nidus for epithelialization. Or skin may be taken from parents and other relatives who are anti-genetically suitable. Transfusions, antibiotics, and the technical aspects of medicine dominate everything.

The mastery of acute trauma produces the gamut of symptoms of toxic psychosis, including illusions, confusional states, disorientation, and delusions. Striking regression may occur in speech and excretory control, along with the hallucinatory symptoms of sensory deprivation. Physical agitation, interspersed with lapses into immobility, are common in these children. The emergence of primary process unconscious material, in nightmares, persecutory images, and the traumatic reworking of the burn incident is all too common, with children crying out that they remember the fire, or sobbing about a lost relative or friend. Denial occurs prominently with latency-age and adolescent burn patients, either in relation to the extent of the injury or in connection with the emotional problems associated with it. This is usually inconsistent and obviously an attempt to manage the constant threat of emotional flooding. Tremendous ego constriction is forced on the child by the massive multiple traumata which must be managed, and children will often focus upon the food, the operating room, or father's next visit. Some children will become obsessed with cleaning their ears, shifting their head positions, having their hair combed, having ribbons put in their hair, or sucking and chewing. Emotional instability is a constant issue, with tearfulness, crotchetiness, feeble threats to kill people who started the fires, and lapses into weepiness and desolation.

Depression. In addition to the physiological depletion depression that is so prevalent in the third month or so of hospitalization, there are episodes of loss of hope, along with overreactions to minor comments by passersby, to delay of surgical reconstruction, or to a minor change in visitation. Flashbacks of the original episode and mourning reactions bob up as much as two years after the injury. The childrens' feelings of sadness are related to the complex dynamics of their distorted body image processes; as a result they are frequently not verbalized. This is tied to the difficulty most individuals express in giving good

verbal descriptions of themselves, but it also connects to the attempts of the burn patient to deny, repress, and suppress negative affects, and evade the sense of despair. Additionally, burn injuries concentrate among households of the poor, disturbed, and uneducated where verbal expression of emotion is not well mastered.

After seven or eight weeks in the hospital the threat to survival is usually reduced and the focus shifts toward other problems. Patients with severe burns are generally feeding problems. The nurses are under intense pressure to make them eat in order to provide the protein for skin and wound healing; the children feel exhausted and irritable, and are often resistant and cantankerous. In the face of the multitude of manipulations forced upon them, not eating is often the one area in which they can manifest any control. Commonly, struggles over nutrition highlight the intermediate phase of care, and are shadowed by depression. Children appear somewhat more resistant to the depression which is almost universal in adult burns, and regression is more apparent. However, after several helpless and vitiating months in the hospital, weeping, hopelessness, psychomotor retardation, loss of appetite, questions about death, dying, amputation, and concerns about the loss of siblings, friends, and home begin to color the course of psychological reaction. Repeated surgical procedures do not diminish the fear of dying in surgery. Additionally, there is more articulation of the guilt felt by the children and questions about what happened to property. Who else was injured? Are people angry with them? Should they be punished for their presence at the fire or for misdeeds involved in causing the fire? Survivor's guilt may surface at this point. Insurance questions begin to circulate in the staff and family, and add to the question of locating the cause of the fire; for the children this may serve only to underline the question of culpability.

Patterns of Mastery. As the child progresses, he is taken to the physical therapy tanks for exercise and debridement of his wounds. This is a painful and often difficult time for all, with screams, physical resistence, and enormous fearfulness on the part of the child about seeing parts of himself float off in the water.[5] In effect, he is forced to shift from passivity to activity. Each phase of progress tends to produce spurts of anxiety and oppositional behavior from the children. They fear moving in the tanks, they are both eager and anxious about coming out of the bacteria-control isolation units in which they have often spent so many weeks Some are fearful about the initial efforts to get up and walk, to sit in a chair, to go to the bathroom on their own, and to start working with the ward teacher or becoming more active with the recreational therapist. Overall, with the increase of physiological healing there is psychological progress, uneven as it may be.

Concern about appearance pops up from the first. This is most striking when the child begins to move about the ward, to look at other children, and to talk in groups or in private sessions with other patients or nurses; it is especially notable on the evening shift where time seems to make this more feasible. More questions about long-term scarring appear. Some children play one "expert" against another, asking mother, father, night nurse, pediatrician, surgical resident, or plastic surgeon serially about discharge dates and long-term outcomes, struggling to absorb these reports while trying to enjoy the interplay between reporters.

Returning home and returning to school present both hopes and threats. Some children like to go out on trips with the staff as first experiments in enlarging their social orbits, and they face the stares, the shock, and the shame of being disfigured and deformed. For many, even though their scars are covered, the burn injuries lead to orthopedic problems, with deformed hands, bent backs, and limited motion in hips and knees. But they often go out with an arm bandaged as well, and a goodly number have facial scars which are destructive to their social acceptability and hence particularly upsetting. Often they go home for visits and return to the hospital. Generally they go home before going back to school. Every step is marked by apprehension about social rejection.

After discharge, the severely burned child is usually fated to have long-term medical contacts. Scars contract and have to be surgically released. Multiple procedures are required to permit growth and to perform the multiple interventions necessary for reconstructive and plastic surgery. The most significant issues in the ability of a child to manage what has befallen him lie in three areas. These are: his own ego and its strength, the supportive structure of the family, and the school and community response to his injury. In each area, the balance is one of active over passive forces, of the efforts at reaching toward predominating over the tendencies to contract and flinch away. If the child reaches out to people and becomes active he will move ahead. If the family can surmount its shame and guilt, it can put aside some of its other problems in order to support the child and his program of care. Given this, he will be strengthened in his efforts to cope with catastrophe. When teachers, neighbors, peers, and classmates can reach toward the child and keep calling him on the phone, sending cards, and providing homework, visits, and encouragement, then the child can progress more normally.

Overall Psychological Profile. Woodward and Jackson[13] reported that 80 percent of children were described by their parents as emotionally upset one year after a burn hospitalization. In a control series, 10 percent were described as disturbed. These children face major developmental and social burdens throughout their growing up. For them, rehabilitation involves a constant revision of their self-concept, and always in a way that deviates from the normal. Since this occurs at the same time they are attempting to navigate the normal stages of personality unfolding, serious deviations are inevitable.

Enormous amounts of energy go into meeting each successive stress and trauma. Along with all this, some ego restriction generally occurs. Some children move quickly into the sick role and stick there, permanently deviant. Others are more flexible and begin to enlarge their life activities between operations and surgical procedures. The more able they are to become involved in school and hobbies, the better the outlook. Those who can return to sports, who will go swimming in spite of scars, who are scrappy and sharp-tongued, seem to fare better by being on the side of active coping. Many burned children come from disturbed homes, however, and they continue to bear the stigmata of the preexisting household pathology. By the same token, those children who have held strongly to religious beliefs have found them of much help. The development of special burn units has offered technical advantages to the doctors, but the children are often eager to be among other children on pediatric services, and parents often feel this keenly. There is a balancing effect here which works out in multifarious ways for individual children and their families. When they return for further care to burn units they can see their old friends and the parents can share experiences with each other, but they are part of a stigmatized group. On the other hand, if they go to more general settings, they will not be as well accepted with their visible scars, nor will they have people with specialized knowledge about burn care and physical therapy of burns to deal with them. At the same time, the problem of stigma and its management is decreased.

The most general issue to be kept clearly in mind is that for burned children the scale of progress is one of years rather than months. In order to see the movement forward as the children develop, those who observe their progress have to measure it in such long-range terms. Gradually, the boys and girls who are preschool remain "cute" to people for a long time, and, during latency, they still can have the protection of being small children. When they reach adolescence they are under great social pressure to be part of a group and to be competent, attractive, and participant; at this point the peer group is also most critical. If the parents are ready for this, the children can be given a great deal of support during the difficult times.

In adolescence there is the inevitable recrudescence of erotic feelings, and rapid shifting, attempts at intellectualizing problems, and dealing with object love.[4] With this, the handicapped burn patient is under particularly heavy pressure from within and without. Obsessive masturbation is not exceptional, but heterosexual activity has usually been restricted to peer patients in the hospital. The sad reality is that these children are not acceptable in the ordinary adolescent world. The nearer the defects are to the face, the more difficult it appears to be for these children to find social acceptance and the approbation of people they esteem in their peer group. For many, adolescence is a time of anguish, social failure, withdrawal, suicidal ruminations, and, for an undefined percentage, *social death*.[9] This refers to the dissolution of most social bonds, with the development of a closeted existence and avoidance of almost all public exposure. Many reports of suicidal threats are made by parents, nursing, and rehabilitative staffs, and suicide has been anecdotally reported after adolescence. In fact, however, few authenticated cases have been recorded. This may be due to the withdrawal phenomenon; with no professional to care for them, little is known about the ultimate fate of many burn patients.

With the high incidence of disturbed families producing burn accidents and injuries, the responses of families may roughly be placed in two categories: the intact, stable families of greater economic means who tend to be middle class, and the larger group of multiproblem families who show such varied responses. In the case of an intact middle-class family where the child is burned in a true accident, there is still a great deal of guilt to be managed. These families may take years to struggle with their guilt and the stigma they feel about being seen with their handicapped child. Nonetheless, they are usually quite reliable about visiting the hospital, bringing the children back to physical therapy, and scheduling ongoing care. As they articulate readily with the middle-class staff orientation, they are likely to be viewed as "good parents." Their pattern is characteristic. They involve themselves in the socially useful and mutually supporting burn prevention groups, and they help with volunteer work in the hospital. They lobby for flame-retardant clothing and they function as intermediaries with schools. However, their inner grief goes on interminably, and they engage in a struggle analagous to that of the patient over placing blame. They may do this even when they were not present at the accident, or in no way related. If, for example, they had planned to refurbish the house but had not done it when the fire occurred, their guilt is multiplied.

For the multiproblem family, a different series of events ensues, and the helplessness of the parent or parents is striking. In the beginning, all families share a common myth, that burns are "surface" injuries. After all, most have only experienced sunburn or minor scalds that healed regardless of treatment and did not leave scars. These fantasies, which may be retained for years, are ways in which the families maintain hope. They return over many summers for further reconstructive surgery to improve the appearance of their children and seem totally unable to hear the realistic predictions of the doctors about their children's appearance. Overall, this appears to be a useful way of protecting themselves and their children. Both troubled and stable families may be caught up in the need to give skin for their children. They are asked quite literally to donate parts of themselves to be placed on the burns of their offspring. This offers them both a hope of healing and a chance for guilt expiation. The broken families are more likely to be suspected of child abuse, and are less persuasive in their explanations about the injury. This seems to be true whether or not insurance and court pressures focus upon these issues. Poor people with burned children have all the expectable problems of becoming confused about hospital visitation hours, transportation arrangements, payments, and the like; they are often absent during visitation hours. This tends to produce moralistic reactions from the nurses and doctors about their being inadequate parents. It takes time to understand how overwhelmed, despairing, and paralyzed many of these parents feel, especially when they are mothers who have been abandoned by their husbands. They require much more outreach effort and sustained friendliness from the caretakers to keep them going through the long haul of medical care for burn victims.

Characteristically, the staff reaction breaks down into several different patterns. In Pasnau's book, *Consultation-Liaison Psychiatry*,[11] surgeons are described as the "warrior cult" of medicine and emphasis is placed on the mechanistic and emotionally controlled aspects of this group of doctors. Clearly this is variable, and individual surgeons form relationships with burned children that last for decades. Nevertheless, the general surgeon deals mostly with the acute and technical problems; the pediatrician, who has more of a relationship with the family, deals with the metabolic issues and more of the patient's feelings and his long-term school planning. Within this framework, the plastic and cosmetic surgeon falls somewhere in between, in that he tends to have long-term relations based upon the many procedures and revisions of procedures that are required. Social workers, psychiatrists, and psychologists clearly focus upon the feelings and the social issues; in fact, however, many mental health people avoid any work in these settings. Their empathetic availability makes them vulnerable; they are concerned over being flooded by their own feelings, or they suspect they have little to offer in the face of these physical tragedies. The nurses and physical therapists have the most intimate and sustained relationships with these patients, and they are under the most stress in early stages of treatment. Their concern over becoming attached to dying and permanently handicapped children forces them to consider their own competence; they must inflict more pain in performing this work than they would in most other settings. To add to their burdens, they are usually young women who are particularly concerned about physical appearance and the issues of their own attractiveness. Above all, they put in long days in close contact with the patients and their families, and have the least authority in the health care decision making. Nightmares, insomnia, and rapid job turnover are endemic phenomena in some burn units. There are others, however, built around a cadre of strong leaders and with sufficient psychological support which have been able to maintain staff for years. Some of these front-line workers retreat into a fixed focus technique; they use the same mechanisms of intellectualization and distancing as do the doctors, but this is very much a minority.

Body Image Disturbances of the Burned Child at Different Levels of Development

EFFECTS ON SELF-CONCEPT

As burn injuries are in their very nature destructive to the body surface, they are important to the onlookers of the patient at all ages. Infants with large burned areas are painful for their mothers and interfere with the abilities of these mothers to touch, to hold, to diaper them comfortably and with easy affectionate exchanges. The burned baby then faces a more complex world of altered body communication, which generally acts to damp down spontaneity and is often heavily larded with the guilt of the mother. As the child becomes more active, he is likely to become aware of the fact that his scars or dressings are frightening or attention-getting from other children. Four-year-olds seem to handle this well, and the children can often absorb the special attention without feeling it is only negative, especially if the staff and the family are encouraging and don't overreact. Once the child gets to school and has to dress or undress and face the responses of others, the scar usually becomes a handicap. It is a painful and embarrassing feature of which the child is ashamed; often the feeling is strong enough to keep him from going swimming and participating in overnight visits. Indeed, sometimes the child feels ashamed even when the scars are quite readily concealed. In toto the scars are a burden for the self-concept: To be sure, they are a burden which many people handle well, but only under the rarest circumstance do they become an acceptable aspect of the body image. Confidence must be sought in other areas.

EFFECTS ON INTERPERSONAL RELATIONSHIPS

The social body image has been described as encompassing the ways in which one thinks of himself in relation to other people. The child feels small near the teacher, the adolescent girl is horrified by one pimple when she stands close to her dancing partner, and the handicapped person is aware of his special relation to his audience when he walks or talks. With the burned child considerable thought goes into covering scars, walking to hide a contracture, and not getting too close when people may show horror at a hand with ropy keloids, deformity, and limited movement. He learns a repertoire of body language that differs from the normal-appearing individual. With all people, the body image comprises a changing series of phenomena, both conscious and unconscious; these keep shifting with the relationship between people, and with their tension states. Some children learn to get across the limits of their scars and their self-acceptance quickly, and this makes it possible to deal with them more easily. Some learn very quickly to tell a bystander who has not even spoken "I was burned in an accident" so they can move on to a different phase of the relationship. The more assertive styles appear to be overwhelmingly more adaptive.

The crucial balance appears to be between the ability to deny enough to maintain self-acceptance, and the tendency to distort the response to reality. It is of the essence to maintain awareness of the necessary degree of reality, while not focusing upon it excessively. A variety of ways of using the voice, facial expressions, gestures, postures, and movements enter into the individual's pattern of handling interpersonal issues. Humor is easier for adults with disfigurements, though there is a boisterous style which is fundamentally counterphobic which some children use energetically to force themselves into social situations. Buffoonery is one part of it; exaggerated flirtatiousness and sometimes regressive coyness are also used.

Specific Defenses Against the Handicap

The management of damaged identity formation is central to the problem of dealing with the handicap. Denial in fantasy works for children whose handicaps are minor, but in the area of burns, it has been noted that often a minor scar is harder to deal with than a major one. This is because the major defect *forces* the issue unambiguously, while the minor one makes the individual struggle with his own sensitivities and his variable awareness of the responses of the people around him; these in turn are protean, varying from acceptance to frozen horror. The self-concept of the individual who copes successfully comes partly from other sources and partly from the realistic satisfaction of having transcended the handicap. For many, this is a rather brittle success which requires the child to keep forcing himself into new social situations to prove repeatedly that he really is acceptable. It is essential to appreciate

the potential for new social traumata when the child is rejected by people who are afraid of him, and who treat him as an object rather than as a child. Extra psychic energy must constantly be kept in reserve for being abruptly converted into a frightful thing in social situations. The potential for frightening people remains, and it is like a racial issue or social prejudice which lingers in the background but can suddenly be mentioned, shock everyone, and overwhelm a social situation. Therefore, the socially active child must always remain hyperalert, while the passive, withdrawing child can too readily withdraw into himself in order to evade social contacts and their threats entirely. Ultimately, such youngsters become the closet people or socially dead patients that Macgregor[9] described.

Programs to Reduce the Effects of the Handicap

The direct care of patients may involve medication for the delirium; hypnosis for failure to eat or to cooperate with the physical therapy; milieu management; short-term psychotherapy for grief reactions; and longer-term therapy where the conventional indications for psychotherapy exist. The most useful deployment of psychiatric time is in the liaison role. In particular, the psychiatrist needs to keep up a pattern of continuing support for the nursing staff and for the treatment team in general. This begins at that early stage where delirium and delusional symptoms need to be explained to the staff. The psychiatrist not only explains behavior by notes in the chart, but meets regularly with the treatment staff. Any efforts of the liaison psychiatrist to get into action the moment the patient is admitted are likely to prove ineffective. A medical history is needed, and the intensive-care situation must develop with a crisis orientation. The stunned state of the parents, confused about all the staff maneuverings and unable to sort out who does what, preclude much useful psychiatric intervention. After a few days, however, the psychiatrist should be able to do selected assessments of the children and families. He can begin to establish his role in sedating parents, tranquilizing children, and helping with the pain medications; most of all, he should help in planning. This is done in meetings with surgical residents, pediatric house officers, nurses, burn technicians, school teachers, play ladies, practical nurses, and other ancillary personnel, preferably in regularly scheduled staff meetings. The psychiatrist should supervise and/or consult with the social workers who run the parent groups. He should either run patient groups that are so helpful in enabling these children to share their negative affects or counsel those who lead them. Overall, he should concentrate on watching the social system of the burn unit or burn ward. In this way he can support the individual relationships which nurses, aides, and house staff build with patients. Experience has demonstrated that these special affinities are the crux of the supportive relations between patients and staff members; these provide the long-term support which forms the bridge to the outside world and keeps the rehabilitative effort functioning. Throughout this, the psychiatrist needs to explain to the patients and the families that they are not sick, but that exploration of their feelings is part of the treatment plan to help in the long-range adjustment. This is long-term work, and in consulting with these families and their schools, caseworkers, and doctors, the psychiatrist should have a perspective of years.

PSYCHOPHARMACOLOGIC AGENTS

One of the problems specific to burn care is the plethora of staff who may prescribe drugs. There is a combination of frequent anesthetics such as codeine, morphine, meperidine (Demerol), and acetaminophen (Tylenol) for pain, mixed in with special medications to stimulate appetite, plus a variety of drugs to reduce anxiety. All this makes it particularly desirable for the psychiatrist to monitor the psychoactive drugs that are given. In response to the multiplicity of agents foisted upon them, children will often become agitated and then be hard to rouse. This is particularly likely when the staff is not composed of pediatric surgeons, and overreacts to the crying and the agitation of the children. Drug studies with children have many methodologic problems. The following material, based on the pooling of interdisciplinary burn ward experiences, is intended to serve as a clinical guide.

1. Barbiturates should not be used except as anticonvulsant medication.
2. An effort should be made to use *one* agent and push it for effect. The need for specific pain and sleeping medicine can be reduced almost three-fourths by utilizing diazepam, meprobamate, and chlorpromazine. One advantage of using tranquilizers is that they do not usually produce the escalation problems so common with narcotics and sleeping pills.
   Diazepam (Valium): 2mg/kg/24 hours.
   Meprobamate (Miltown): 10mg/kg/24 hours with dosage increased as necessary to achieve results in children six years or older.
   Chlorpromazine (Thorazine): 2mg/kg/24 hours can help with the hallucinosis of delirium and intense agitation. It also appears helpful in temperature control in children whose homeostatic functions are impaired through the loss of large skin areas.

For pain, some stress has been laid upon treating the anxiety element and avoiding narcotics. When the anxiety is clinically evident, it should be treated. But when in doubt, it is best to use pain medications, as the drug-dependence problem with burned children is quite manageable in the hospital setting. In brief, active pain relief early will reduce problems of anxiety later. When one medication is insufficient, some patients do require both a tranquilizer and an analgesic. But all agents should be kept to a minimum, and the relations with the various staff members should be invoked as much as possible to manage feelings of distress.

ESTABLISHMENT OF A NETWORK OF CARE

The visible damage which causes strangers to reject a patient are exactly the opposite of neurotic feelings of unworthiness; they cannot be treated as if they were neurotic symptoms. The people who deal with the burned child should have a team approach. This hackneyed phrase really means that there is a consistent perspective in the ongoing care directed toward the burned child and his family. The defect must be acknowledged, but not dwelt upon. All members of the system should be so articulated as to communicate with each other readily. The physical therapist who learns of a child's refusal to go to gym should be quick to tell the social worker or psychologist. There are few secrets in these situations because of the long-term nature of the care. (There may indeed be family secrets related to insurance claims about the cause of the injury; this too needs a consistent attitude from the caretaking team.) For many of these children, a special nurse, a recreation therapist, or a play lady may have the strongest affective tie to the child; this should not be fought over, with the psychiatrist or psychologist feeling touchy about their prerogatives. In fact, the mental health professional often does better to serve as a consultant to the staff in their handling of these children with minimal direct therapy. Again this is dictated by the fact that there is not a conflict to be resolved, but a deficit or a cicatrix to be borne.

The Association for Prevention of Burn Injuries in Children is an organization which provides mutual support. Fire departments are frequently interested. Sports figures and entertainers are often willing to visit these children. All this is encouraged. Some older children have collected essays, poems, pictures, and handicrafts and made calendars. Staff members in all professional groups need to write these patients and their parents after their departure. These are many nursing and rehabilitation student projects which involve keeping contact with old patients; whatever scientific merit they may have, their patient care potential is great. Mental health workers are more likely to "distance" these patients and not make such relationships. Individual surgeons, and especially plastic surgeons, have contacts which last for years; sometimes they provide these linkages even though they never talk explicitly about the emotional situation. The doctor's secretary may be the bridge. The more open and shared this work of ego maintenance can be, the better off the patient will be, and the more supported and supporting will be their families.

Parent groups have been informative and provide the feeling of mutual understanding and acceptance that is vital for some families; for others, however, this can be appalling; they need to "go it alone." These are parents for whom active work in fire prevention or in influencing legislation may be a very helpful way of dealing with their feelings. Sometimes individual therapy is indicated for parents who need to deal with their guilt and shame about the child before they can function more appropriately as parents. With the staff, the focus of the psychiatrist's consulting work is to help them accept the bitterness, hostility, and passive resistence of burn patients and their families toward the world in general and toward medical care in particular.

Prognosis Without Interventions Compared to Outcome With Adequate Help

Outcome studies are unsatisfactory in the area of burns because of the huge numbers of unknown and unstudied cases. It is clear that many individuals who receive no help nevertheless overcome their problems and proceed to live full lives. These are more likely to be children whose handicaps do not involve orthopedic sequelae and whose scars can be covered. Some courageous individuals with greater handicaps but with strong family and economic support available do progress to self-realization. However, it appears that the majority of children, especially those with facial scarring, who do not have psychological support from teachers, friends, relatives, and professionals particularly during adolescence, become lost. They turn into closeted creatures who hide from the world, and who in effect suffer death in life. Their misery, which is at best a depleted apathy, can assume the proportions of intense agony, and oftimes suicidal despair. At the other end of the scale, unfortunately, there are people who receive a great deal of intervention and who do not succeed in taking hold of any kind of tolerable life existence. Woodward and Jackson[13] found that 80 percent of children in hospitals for serious burns were disturbed one year after leaving the hospital but other later workers[2] have been able to reduce this to 20 percent, and this shift should be changed further with adequate care.

REFERENCES

1. BERNSTEIN, N. R., "Medical Tragedies in Facial Burn Disfigurement," *Psychiatric Annals, 10*:31–49, 1976.
2. ———, *Emotional Care of the Facially Burned and Disfigured*, Little, Brown and Co., Boston, 1976.
3. ———, "Management of Burned Children with the Aid of Hypnosis," *Journal of Child Psychology, 4*:93–98, 1963.
4. FREUD, A., "Instinctual Anxiety During Puberty," in *The Writings of Anna Freud*, vol. 2, *The Ego and The Mechanisms of Defense*, International Universities Press, New York, 1936, Revised ed., 1966.
5. GALDSTON, R., "The Burning and Healing of Children," *Psychiatry, 35*:57, 1972.
6. JABALEY, M. E., et al., "The Burned Child," in Debuskey, Matthew (Ed.), *The Chronically Ill Child and His Family*, pp. 89–110, Charles C Thomas, Springfield, Ill., 1970.
7. KING, L. J., "Managing Emotional Reactions to Chronic Medical Illness," *Medical World News, 17*:8, 1976.
8. LEVIN, B., "Psychological Characteristics of Firesetters," *Fire Journal, 70*:36, 1976.

9. MACGREGOR, F. C., et al. (Eds.), *Facial Deformities and Plastic Surgery: A Psychosocial Study*, Charles C Thomas, Springfield, Ill., 1953.

10. MACHT, L. B., and MACK, J. E., "The Firesetter Syndrome," *Psychiatry, 31:*277, 1968.

11. PASNAU, ROBERT (Ed.), *Consultation-Liaison Psychiatry*, Grune & Stratton, New York, 1975.

12. SOLNIT, A., and PRIEL, B., "Psychological Reactions to Facial and Hand Burns in Young Men," in Eissler, R. S., et al. (Eds.), *The Psychoanalytic Study of the Child*, vol. 30, pp. 549–566, Yale University Press, New Haven, 1975.

13. WOODWARD, J., and JACKSON, D., "Emotional Reactions in Burned Children and Their Mothers," *British Journal of Plastic Surgery, 13:*316–324, 1961.

56 / The Child with Ambiguous Genitalia

John Money and Viola G. Lewis

For the purposes of this chapter, the term genital ambiguity includes not only hermaphroditism in the conventional sense but also such conditions as microphallus, epispadias, vaginal atresia, and third-degree hypospadias with undescended testes. There are, in addition, some birth defects of the sex organs which might not present in a form so obviously ambiguous as an enlarged clitoris or a hypospadiac microphallus; nonetheless, they may be subjectively experienced by the patient as a genital ambiguity.

There is no register of any type of birth defect in the United States. As a result, both the frequency and incidence of their occurrence are unknown. It is, however, safe to conjecture at one extreme an incidence of no fewer than 1 in 5,000 live births and at the other, no more than 1 in 1,000.

Current medical and surgical knowledge and technology do not justify optimism about making severely defective male genitals adequate. Irrespective of gonadal and genetic sex, chromosomal and gonadal males born with a clitorine penis (the most typical genital ambiguity), microphallus, or agenesis of the penis should always be assigned and rehabilitated as girls. If the affected child is assigned and reared as a male, phallic repair may not even permit urination in the standing position, much less adequate genital function in coitus. To attempt surgical conversion of such children into full masculinity requires many hospitalizations and many years, with results that all too often end in disappointment and possible psychopathology. Despite many hours of counseling, the prognosis for a successful sex life cannot be guaranteed.

By contrast, chromosomal and gonadal males born with ambiguous genitalia who are sex assigned and rehabilitated as girls face relatively few hospitalizations and, ultimately, a more positive prognosis. Assignment as a girl is compatible with differentiation of a feminine gender identity and role. The good results of feminizing surgery serve at once to reinforce the child's femininity for the parents; her feminine gender identity for herself; and the achievement of a decent future sex life.

In the case of the chromosomal and gonadal hermaphroditic female with ambiguous genitals, the neonatal appearance may be indistinguishable from that of ambiguity in chromosomal and gonadal males. It is also possible for a female hermaphrodite to be born with a fully formed penis and empty scrotum. No matter how masculine the external genitalia, however, it is relatively easy to get a good result with feminizing surgery. Therefore, when the diagnosis of female hermaphroditism is accurately established neonatally, it is feasible to make the sex assignment female and to undertake surgical and hormonal rehabilitation procedures accordingly.

Masculinization of chromosomally female fetuses occurs chiefly in two syndromes, the adrenogenital syndrome and the syndrome of progestin-induced hermaphroditism. Since exogenous progestins which may masculinize the fetus are no longer prescribed to pregnant women (to prevent loss of the pregnancy), the latter syndrome is not being considered here. In the adrenogenital syndrome, however, a difficult decision may have to be made. This arises when a newborn chromosomal female is diagnosed as having the syndrome with genitalia so masculinized that the baby has a fully formed penis complete with a penile urethra and empty scrotum. Prenatal masculinization affects not only the external genitalia but also the developing nervous system. Developmentally, this prenatal androgen effect on the nervous system is manifested as tomboyism. The combination of masculinized external genitalia and masculinized nervous system makes it feasible for a chromosomal female with the adrenogenital syndrome and complete penis to be assigned and rehabilitated as a male.

Tomboyism is not a matter of absolute difference. It refers, rather, to the level or threshold of sexually dimorphic behavior. There are few imperative, nonoptional role differences that are bona fide sexual. For females, these are menstruation, gestation, and lactation; for males, impregnation. Most behaviorally dimorphic sex differences are, in fact, sex-coded and optional. They are the products of cultural history, even though in times past, they may have been secondarily derived from nonoptional sex differences.

In the case of males, there is no autonym for tomboyism in girls, except stigmatizing terms, like sissy or effeminate. Tomboyism, and its male counterpart, are both global entities which can be subdivided into behavioral components which are sex-shared, but threshold-dimorphic. They are subject to a variable degree of sexual dimorphism, that is, of male/female difference. On the basis of combined animal-experimental and human-clinical evidence, this behavioral dimorphism is inferred to be the product of prenatal hormonal programming. Examples are:

1. General kinesis, as in vigorous outdoor energy expenditure
2. Competitive rivalry and dominance assertion
3. Roaming and territorial mapping (which may ultimately be related to spatial and mathematical skills)
4. Defense of the troop against predators
5. Defense of the young against harm
6. Nesting or housing the young
7. Parental caretaking

None of these forms of behavior belongs exclusively to either sex; nor is it preordained that there is an absolute sex difference in the level of the threshold that must be transcended before the behavior manifests itself. On the contrary, there is overlap between the sexes, sometimes of considerable degree.

Not all sex differences in behavior include an element of prenatal hormonal programming. Some are optional in the sense that they are the product of historical and cultural stereotyping. They are referred to as sex-coded. Nature has preordained for the human species that such sex-coded roles will be programmed into the system postnatally; the child learns them as one learns a native language. That is why in cases of borderline sex-organ ambiguity one has the option with regard to sex of assignment. Indeed, in cases where there is a severe defect in somatic and anatomic male differentiation the physician has full freedom to contradict the gonadal and chromosomal sex.

Some people raise the question of fertility when the assigned sex contradicts the gonadal sex. In cases of gonadal male hermaphroditism, this is actually not an issue. The widespread rule is infertility. Rightly or wrongly, the issue of fertility is often used as the clinical criterion. Based on this, adrenogenital female hermaphrodites conventionally have been neonatally assigned as girls, despite the prediction of tomboyism in their subsequent behavioral development, and despite the size of the phallic organ.

Prenatal disposition inclines a child either to masculine or feminine dimorphism of behavior. This can become programmed into a postnatal differentiation that is either masculine, feminine, or ambivalent. The two principles operating in the postnatal phase of differentiation are identification and complementation. Usually, though not exclusively, the same-sexed parent is the identification model, and the other parent the complementation model. Ideally, they both agree on the boundaries of what constitutes sexual dimorphism of behavior, regardless of whether these boundaries contain traditional stereotypes or avant-garde nonstereotypes. Ambiguity is then avoided. Peer modeling becomes important after infancy.

There is a first step in counseling parents with regard to the prognosis for their newborn child of uncertain sex. With the aid of diagrams, one teaches them about embryonic sexual differentiation from the neutral state to a state of sexual dimorphism. In this context it can be explained that their child was born with the sex organs unfinished. The second step is to teach the parents about the principles of identification and complementation, thresholds, and the similarities between the sexes. This is input information. A good counseling session also requires equal time for output from the parents. For future documentation, it is invaluable to make a parent-dictated summary at the end of a session. Only if the parents have the opportunity to express their version of what was said does the doctor know how to gauge their degree of understanding.

One of the things that concerns parents is what to tell other children in the family about what has happened to an erstwhile baby brother or sister. Siblings will be reassured by seeing the baby's repaired genitalia. They will also need reassurance that they will not become candidates for similar surgery. They need not have their sex reassigned. This information can be tied in with their sex education, with the help of the professional's advice and guidance. It is well worth the time and effort, for it prevents future problems for both the siblings and the patient. In view of the space limitations here, a reader confronted with detailed problems in case management is advised to check the references at the end of this chapter.

One experience that children born with ambiguous genitalia share in common is repeated hospital visits. In this respect they are not different from children who have continued hospital visits for chronic illnesses. Children's reactions to hospital visits, procedures, and admission run the gamut from resignation and fear to outrage. In general, children's reactions reflect those of their parents. Outrage, when it occurs, is particularly in evidence during the late childhood through teenage years. Repeated genital examinations create a special problem, especially when unfamiliar personnel in training are brought in as onlookers.

Annual medico-psychologic followup visits are indicated for preventive purposes. In many instances of sexual ambiguity, children will need pharmacologic treatment with injections or pills. They will need psychologic followup to insure that they are developing in a healthy way, and not feeling freaky. Those children who need lifelong maintenance medication (for example, estrogen, testosterone, or cortisone) need to be given an explanation of why they have to keep on taking it. They do not always remember the explanation. It is therefore necessary to repeat and update the information, gearing it to the level of the child's comprehension and understanding. This may continue even into the patient's teenage years.

Aphoristically, hormones can be likened to pure food extracts rather than to drugs. For many children, this similarity takes away the stigma of disease and/or freakishness. Here one has a partial guarantee against noncompliance and denial of illness, especially during the teens.

The fact that a patient takes medication is one of the aspects of the medical history and present condition that may need to be explained casually to friends, or, more technically, to professionals. For this purpose, rehearsal of explanatory words and phrases proves invaluable. For the same reason, rehearsal of explanations for possible hospitalizations is indicated. Explanations usually do not follow a formula; they have to be tailor-made for the person and situation. In the case of the adrenogenital syndrome, for example, the patient may even have to rehearse how to defy a doctor who tries to withdraw medication with cortisone. In this syndrome it is necessary to double the cortisone dosage in the face of any kind of physical stress. The majority of patients register with Medic-Alert so that in case of emergency, essential information as to their diagnosis, prognosis, and treatment can be transmitted from this source to any doctor or hospital in the country. The patient who registers with Medic-Alert always wears a special bracelet or necklace that will permit any examining physician to identify the syndrome and its treatment.

In talking with a patient (or parent) about a prognosis, probability statements are always preferable to prophecies. Prophecies may be wrong, or they may fail to allow for tomorrow's medical discovery. Worse, however, they close the door of hope. For example, a prophecy that one will be unable to have children creates an outlook that is as bleak as it is false. The truth may be that one is only unable to create a pregnancy. The infertile can always have children, either by adoption or by means of the "sperm bank." The statement of probability rather than a prophecy of infertility allows the young patient to rehearse a future which will include marriage and family.

Children with a history of birth defect of the sex organs are not necessarily in greater need of high-quality sex education than are their normal siblings. Good sex education, however, is imperative if they are to be guaranteed a satisfying recreational sex life and good parenthood. When sex education is done by a professional, it is beneficial to talk with the parents and child separately, sharing with the parent the materials which will be used with the children. The individual interviews can then be followed by a conference session including both parents, doctors, and patient, so that all can share the new knowledge. The joint session encourages the family to make sex an open-minded topic of conversation in the home.

Early in the teens, patients need the vocabulary and concepts of self-disclosure to use with their prospective marriage partners. They also need the counsel that the best time for such explanations is only after marriage is being discussed, and not early in a love affair which might not last. Also, by adolescence, sex education can be extended to include genetic counseling. This is important in those cases in which genetic transmission is a legitimate concern of either the patient, the patient's siblings, or more distant relatives (depending on the diagnosis).

In the authors' experience, severe behavioral pathology and/or other forms of psychopathology encountered in children with ambiguous genitalia usually correlate with family psychosocial pathology. In some instances, pathology in the family is secondary to traumatic transmission of diagnostic information to the patient or, earlier in life, to the parents. If the parents are undergoing marital or sexual discord which affects all family members, the birth of a child with a defect of the genital organs may intensify these problems. Nonadept professionals and parents sow the seeds of future difficulties by corner-cutting or withholding explanations in the mistaken belief that they are "sparing the patient."

Even potentially traumatic information can be made in a diplomatic fashion. For example, a girl does not want to hear that she was born with testes, and the doctor should speak of sex glands or of gonads. Likewise, the same girl will assimilate more easily the concept that one of her chromosomes has short arms rather than that it is Y, and male. If she has been diplomatically prepared at an early stage of counseling, eventually the same girl will not be traumatized, even if she reads in her medical file the raw (and not meticulously accurate) statements about her chromosomal and gonadal status.

The wise professional develops a complete lexicon of nontraumatic terms and explanations—not only for patients but also for parents. The doctor who does good counseling from birth onward is a good agent of preventive care. In the event of preventive failure, two imperatives ensue. The first is to provide individual psychotherapy. The second is to maneuver a way to discuss in the open the patient's covert diagnostic self-knowledge which otherwise remains unmentionable, and exerts its traumatizing influence in secret. With good therapy, but better still with good preventive counseling, the rehabilitative prognosis in cases of ambiguity or other birth defects of sex organs is entirely satisfactory.

REFERENCES

1. Money, J., "Sex Education and Infertility Counseling in Various Endocrine Related Syndromes: The Juvenile and Adolescent Years," in Gardner, L. I. (Ed.), *Endocrine and Genetic Diseases of Childhood and Adolescence*, 2nd ed., W. B. Saunders, Philadelphia, 1975.

2. ———, "Psychologic Counseling: Hermaphroditism," in Gardner, L. I. (Ed.), *Endocrine and Genetic Diseases of Childhood and Adolescence*, 2nd ed., W. B. Saunders, Philadelphia, 1975.

3. ———, "Phyletic and Idiosyncratic Determinants of Gender Identity," *Danish Medical Bulletin, 19*:259–264, 1972.

4. ———, "Identification and Complementation in the Differentiation of Gender Identity," *Danish Medical Bulletin, 19*:265–268, 1972.

5. ———, *Sex Errors of the Body: Dilemmas, Education, Counseling*, Johns Hopkins University Press, Baltimore, 1968.

57 / The Dying Child

Michael B. Rothenberg

Introduction

Not much more than 125 years ago, in Victorian England, one of the most popular books written for children was called *The Peep of Day*.[4] Death of children was a favorite topic in these books, and the manner in which it was usually presented is typified by the following passage:

When a little child, who loves God, falls sick, and is going to die, God says to the angels, "Go and fetch that little child's soul up to Heaven." Then the angels fly down, the little darling shuts its eyes, it lays its head on its mother's bosom, its breath stops;—the child is dead. Where is its soul? The angels are carrying it up to Heaven.

How happy the child is now! Its pain is over; it is quite good; it is bright like an angel. It holds a harp in its hand, and begins to sing a sweet song of praise to God. Its little body is put into a grave and turns into dust. One day God will make its body alive again.

Dear children, will you pray to God to send his angels to fetch your souls when you die?[4] [p. 33]

Today, very few of even the most religious families would choose to present the subject of death to their children in this manner. However, the author chose to quote this passage to help the reader better understand how much progress has been made during the past century and a quarter in understanding the dying child—and just how much remains to be accomplished.

The recent wave of interest in the subject of death and dying, including the dying child, has been expressed in numerous professional and lay articles and books, as well as through the mass media. On one hand, this is encouraging, but on the other it leaves one concerned. As is so often the case, this sudden increase of interest in a long taboo topic may result in the topic's becoming a fad, and presently, as the fad dies down, a loss of interest will follow.

Only if the understanding of the dying child is anchored firmly in a developmental base, and is accompanied by an understanding of the professional's own emotional responses to the dying child and his family (covered elsewhere in this chapter) can the field hope to make substantive and permanent progress.

A Developmental Approach

Table 57–1 represents a schematic outline developed by Townes[9] that attempts to place children's concepts of life and death into a developmental framework. The dotted arrows in the lower part of the table were added by the author to represent the gradual transition of concepts from one developmental phase to another.

In order better to be able to appreciate this data, it is important to keep in mind that the processes of growth and development involve completing innumerable physical, intellectual, emotional, and social tasks. Among their many other purposes, these serve to make the child or adolescent progressively more independent of his caretakers. One must further recall that serious illness, and, certainly, the awareness of impending death (on whatever level that awareness exists) present major obstacles to every one of these developmental tasks. Only then is one prepared to

understand the common reactions of the dying child or adolescent.

The author has found it helpful to think of the reactions of the dying child in terms of four major emotional responses, all of which are present to some extent in every child dealing with this experience (and, for that matter, to some extent in every family member and health care provider associated with the dying child). Some years ago, a group of students gave these reactions an acronym, "the FAGS syndrome."[6] The letters stand for fear, anger, guilt, and sadness. Each of these reactions merits study in some detail and in relation to developmental process.

There are many things which the dying child fears, but three of these fears appear most commonly: fear of separation, fear of pain, and fear of mutilation. Which of these is feared most depends on the child's age, his previous experience with illnesses (his own and others'), and the family's cultural and religious values and belief systems. Referring back to Townes's conception in table 57–1, it is clear that the preschool-age child, without an understanding of the irreversibility of death or an ability to appreciate the specific meaning of pathophysiology, will have his sense of fear focused primarily on separation from his mother or other primary caretaker. The school-age child can manage only a primitive concept of pathophysiology and lacks an understanding of the irreversibility of death. He tends to concretize and anthropomorphize in order better to control the often frightening larger world into which he has been thrust from the embrace of his family. Hence, since he conceives of death as a man or a humanoid type of monster, he will tend to focus on fears of mutilation and pain. The adolescent, on the other hand, has a greater understanding of pathophysiology and can appreciate death as an irreversible biological process. Hence, in western society, he will most often react with fear that is focused on separation both from meaningful individuals and from important activities. In other cultures, and in some subcultures in this society, as Townes's schematic outline suggests, in the face of the knowledge of his own imminent death, the adolescent's overt reaction may be one of indifference or even familiarity.

The amount of anger expressed by the dying child and the manner in which he chooses to express it are determined far more by the child's family and cultural background than by age-specific developmental factors. Clearly, the child who has been permitted to express anger openly in his own family constellation will find it a good

TABLE 57–1

*A Comparison of Stage Theories of Development and Their Relationship to
Concepts of Life and Death and to Mourning Processes*

Theorists	Approximate Age in Years			
	0–2	2–7	7–11	11–18
Piaget	sensorimotor	preoperational	concrete oper-ations	formal opera-tions
Heider	Global asso-ciation	global asso-ciation	extended com-mission	careless, purposive, and justified com-mission
Kohlberg	self-other	negativism, identification	identification	independence
Freud	oral	oral-anal-phallic	latency	genital
Sullivan	self-other	reality-fantasy	authority, intimacy	symbolic, genital
Erikson	trust	autonomy, initiative	industry	identity, intimacy
Existential	present	present	present	past and present

	Life, Death, and Mourning			
Life	no concept	activity	movement, spontaneous movement	growth
Death	no concept	temporary	a man	a biological process
Attitude toward Death	separation anxiety	.........................>	fear of mutilation	fear, indiffer-ence, or famil-iarity
Mourning	protest, despair, & denial	....	........................>	protest, des-pair, & detach-ment

NOTE: Reprinted by permission of Brenda D. Townes, Ph.D., unpublished manuscript, University of Washington School of Medicine.

deal easier to do so in the hospital. This will be true even in the face of what is usually a very repressive institutional attitude.

A teenage boy from a socioeconomically dis-advantaged but hard-working and upwardly striv-ing family was dying of leukemia. As death approached in the hospital, he became severely depressed and began to pick and tear at the skin of his hands and forearms until he bled.[7] At that point, a pediatrician who was oriented toward comprehensive care verbalized his anger for him. The youngster thereupon stopped tearing at his skin. Even though it was extremely difficult for him to verbalize his anger directly, he became brighter and more communicative. In contrast to this is the reaction of another dying teenage boy in the terminal phase of cystic fibrosis. At the time, the hospital chaplain was not trained in comprehensive care issues or in pastoral counsel-ing. He told the boy that when he died he would go to heaven, where he would no longer have cystic fibrosis and where he would no longer have difficulty breathing. The boy listened to the chaplain's words with an intense expression of anger in his eyes and his face and burst out, "But I don't *want* to die!" It was only when this young-ster was spoken to later by his comprehensive-care–oriented pediatrician[2] that he was able fully to ventilate just how furious he was. He had a full intellectual understanding of the nature of his illness. Nonetheless he was angry at his parents and at all of the health care providers around him for not finding some way miraculously to cure him. Kliman[3] describes a nearly five-year-old boy who was dying of leukemia and whose anger was turned against himself; this was expressed in two of the child's original songs: "If I were an orange I'd eat me" and "If I were a tooth I'd scrunch me."

It seems generally true that where anger goes, especially nonrational anger, guilt is never very far behind. The younger child is normally involved in a good deal of magical thinking. In the face of great stress, he is especially prone to imagining or even to drawing conclusions about why it's all happening. Often he is sure that the painful procedures and the toxic side effects of certain medications, indeed the illness itself, are a punishment for real or imagined errors ("sins") of omission or commission. While this is most prominent in the preschool or early school-age child, it is by no means absent in the older child and the adolescent—any more than it is absent entirely in dying adults!

Since guilt is an unpleasant feeling, it is common to develop anger at the person who makes one feel guilty. Thus, the dying child initially feels anger at his parents and the health care providers for not preventing his illness or at least making him well; then he becomes guilty about these angry feelings; and finally he becomes secondarily angry at these same people because they have made him feel guilty. Thus, a vicious cycle of guilt and anger is rapidly established, and, like a simple, cybernetic positive feedback system, this chain reaction spirals rapidly toward greater and greater intensity.

The author has found it terribly important to remind himself regularly that, while those who survive must deal with the sadness of losing one person who dies, the dying person must deal with the sadness of the impending loss of everyone and everything in his world. This is a difficult task for most adults, even those who are dying at an advanced age and after highly productive lives; for the child or adolescent who has barely begun to touch all of life's treasures, it is an awesome task indeed.

A special note is called for here concerning the issue of depression. Pediatricians and other health care providers working with dying children often ask the child psychiatrist consultant how to differentiate the dying child's sadness from acute or chronic depression. Depression and sadness may both entail the sense of real or imagined loss of an emotionally important person or object, but they can be distinguished by the striking degree of psychomotor retardation in the former as compared with the latter. (One may here leave aside states of agitated depression which are unusual in children and particularly rare in dying children.) With all due respect to the volumes that have been written on the subject of depression, in this context it seems that the most critical point to remember is that, in contrast to sadness, depression always involves held-back anger. This is what makes the clinical detection of depression in the dying patient so critical, for it is the release of that anger that will provide the definitive treatment for the depression.

One final note is necessary before proceeding to the question of a treatment approach to the dying child. Solnit[8] pointed out more than ten years ago

that a more systematic investigation of a child's psychological reactions to his own dying will have to take into account the adults' tendency not to perceive the dying child's behavioral and verbal communications about his own fears because of the anxiety evoked in the adult by the dying child. [p. 273]

Despite increased professional and lay interest in death and dying in recent years, Solnit's concern is as valid today as it was when he initially expressed it, and it applies as much to the other reactions of the dying child which have just been described as it does to the reaction of fear.

Treatment

If the "FAGS syndrome" is dealt with on an appropriate developmental level, the dying child can live relatively comfortably from moment to moment, receiving and giving pleasure from his parental and medical caretakers. Specifically, a three-step process has been found to be most helpful in responding to the psychosocial needs of the dying child.

First, the patient must be assessed thoroughly: what is his developmental status in each of the four major areas of growth and development—physical, intellectual, emotional, and social; what are his strengths and weaknesses in each of these areas, and how is the terminal illness affecting the child's developmental processes; what is the patient's family background, with particular reference to health history, and to what extent do family members appear capable of functioning as "therapeutic allies" with the health care providers in meeting the child's needs?

The second step involves dealing with each aspect of the patient's FAGS syndrome. One primary health care provider should be designated who will continue to deal with the FAGS syndrome as it reappears, in a variety of ways, during the course of the patient's illness.

The third step involves regular repetition of the first two steps, i.e., reassessment of the patient's total status as it is affected both by the course of the illness and the patient's growth and development. This implies further clarification and working through of the misconceptions and misunderstandings that continue to arise, and of the FAGS syndrome as it reasserts itself with each new medical crisis.

It should be clear that what is involved here is a form of crisis intervention which closely follows classical crisis theory and which can provide the same kinds of highly effective interventions which crisis states often uniquely make possible.

This is also an area in which the use of classical, psychodynamic therapeutic play can be extremely effective. For the preschool and young school-age child, play is normally the most effective method of achieving mastery over all types of obstacles. Hence, management of the child should include the use of dolls representing a variety of health care providers and furnishings which can represent various settings within the hospital. These will provide an opportunity for the expression of the entire spectrum of affective responses (all of the FAGS syndrome, for example) which the child is experiencing. For example, a seven-year-old boy was being prepared for his second open-heart surgery procedure.[1] He played out the role of the surgeon operating on a "patient" whom he had made out of clay. In the course of this, he was able to express his fear that this procedure would be as unsuccessful as the first one had been, and that he would die. For the young-child psychiatric consultant who worked on this case, his own unresolved anxiety about the possibility of the child's death interfered with his efforts. He could not assist the child's natural tendency to undergo a working-through process in his play.

Work with the dying child or adolescent provides frequent opportunity for the use of what the author has called "the third-person technique."[6] There is a high level of intensity to the anxiety experienced by the patient, his family, and many of the health care providers in his environment. Because of this, when dealing with a terminal illness, the older child or adolescent who otherwise might be far more articulate is often inarticulate to the point of being mute. Here, the child psychiatric consultant is challenged to engage in a good deal more activity than that to which he may be accustomed. Specifically, it has been tremendously useful to verbalize for the child or adolescent, using a third-person approach. Thus, one might say something like, "Lots of times, kids

in your situation find themselves beginning to wonder whether they will ever get well. Does that make any sense to you?" This gives the patient three options: He may opt in and respond that it not only makes sense but indeed represents exactly what he's been thinking and feeling; he may opt out by denying that such a possibility makes any sense at all; or, he may choose a middle ground in which he acknowledges that such a possibility makes sense, but goes on to say that it doesn't apply to him. Repeated "third-person sessions," focused on the specific details of the child's clinical course, give the patient regular opportunities to change his option. Most important, the initial verbalization of the most anxiety-producing words, thoughts, and feelings (for example, "Lots of times, kids who have just been through a crisis like yours find themselves beginning to wonder if they're going to die.") makes it clear to the patient that the *doctor* is willing and able to talk about the patient's most intense fears and other feelings. Thus, when the patient is psychologically ready, he knows to whom he can turn for help in working through these feelings.[7]

"The Last Day of April"[5] is the title of a pamphlet written by Nancy Roach and published by the California Division of the American Cancer Society in San Francisco in 1974. Three years after the diagnosis was made, Mr. and Mrs. Roach's daughter, Erin, died of leukemia at the age of five and one-half. The entire pamphlet is an extraordinary expression of the needs and reactions of the dying child, and a response to those needs which may be held out as a goal for everyone who works with dying children. Following Erin's death, her mother wrote the following untitled poem, which ends the pamphlet and which seems to provide a fitting conclusion for this chapter.*

> Come little one
> Let us share your pain
> And comfort you.
>
> We will try to match your strength
> Meet the challenge
> And grow with you.
>
> We'll speak to you of things you fear
> And so do we—
> So hard and yet so good.
>
> To share our thoughts
> And see you unafraid
> Know we've conquered fear—
>
>> to love you
>> to see your pain
>> to watch you die

* Reprinted by permission of the author.

We have seen our circle full
Our final April end
And felt the deepest sorrow known.

Your life, tho' brief, was rich and full—
You taught us love
Helped us grow.

REFERENCES

1. CLINE, F. W., and ROTHENBERG, M. B., "Preparation of a Child for Major Surgery," *Journal of the American Academy of Child Psychiatry, 13(1):*78–94, 1974.

2. GOULD, R. C., and ROTHENBERG, M. B., "The Chronically Ill Child Facing Death—How Can the Pediatrician Help?," *Clinical Pediatrics, 12(7):*381–383, 1973.

3. KLIMAN, G., *Psychological Emergencies of Childhood*, Grune & Stratton, New York, 1968.

4. MORTIMER, F. L., *The Peep of Day, or, A Series of the Earliest Religious Instruction the Infant Mind is Capable of Receiving*, Thomas Hatchard, London, 1859.

5. ROACH, N., "The Last Day of April," California Division of the American Cancer Society, San Francisco, 1974.

6. ROTHENBERG, M. B., "Reactions of Children to Illness and Hospitalization," in Smith, D. W., and Marshall, R. E. (Eds.), *Introduction to Clinical Pediatrics*, 2nd ed., pp. 22–25, W. B. Saunders, Philadelphia, 1972.

7. ———, "Reactions of Those Who Treat Children with Cancer," *Pediatrics, 40:*507–510, 1967.

8. SOLNIT, A. J., and PROVENCE, S., *Modern Perspectives in Child Development*, International Universities Press, New York, 1963.

9. TOWNES, B. D., "Piaget's Theory of Child Development," in Marshall, R. E., and Smith, D. W. (Eds.), *Pediatrics Synopsis*, pp. J1–J5, Department of Pediatrics, University of Washington, Seattle, 1970.

Selected Bibliography for Additional Reading

ALEXANDER, I. E., and ALDERSTEIN, A. M., "Affective Responses to the Concept of Death in a Population of Children and Early Adolescents," *Journal of Genetic Psychology, 93:*167–177, 1958.

BURTON, L., "Tolerating the Intolerable—The Problems Facing Parents and Children Following Diagnosis," in Burton, L. (Ed.), *Care of the Child Facing Death*, pp. 16–38, Routledge & Keagan Paul, London, 1974.

EASSON, W. M., *The Dying Child*, Charles C Thomas, Springfield, Ill., 1970.

GREEN, M., "Care of the Dying Child," *Pediatrics, 40(3):*492–498, 1967.

KASTENBAUM, R., "Time and Death in Adolescence," in Feifel, H. (Ed.), *The Meaning of Death*, pp. 99–113, McGraw-Hill, New York, 1959.

LEE, V., *The Magic Moth*, Seabury Press, New York, 1972. (To be read to and by children.)

MAURER, A., "Adolescent Attitudes Toward Death," *Journal of Genetic Psychology, 105:*75–90, 1964.

MITCHELL, M. E., *The Child's Attitude to Death*, Schocken Books, New York, 1967.

MORRISEY, J. R., "Death Anxiety in Children with a Fatal Illness," *American Journal of Psychiatry, 18:*600–615, 1964.

NAGY, M. H., "The Child's View of Death," *Journal of Genetic Psychology, 73:*3–27, 1948. Reprinted in *The Meaning of Death*, (Ed.), Feifel, H., McGraw-Hill, New York, 1959.

NATTERSON, J. M., and KNUDSON, A. G., "Children and Their Mothers: Observations Concerning the Fear of Death in Fatally Ill Children," *Psychosomatic Medicine, 22:*456–465, 1960.

OREMLAND, E. K., and OREMLAND, J. D., *The Effects of Hospitalization on Children*, Charles C Thomas, Springfield, Ill., 1973.

PIAGET, J., *The Construction of Reality in the Child*, Basic Books, New York, 1954.

SAFIER, G., "A Study in Relationships Between the Life and Death Concepts in Children," *Journal of Genetic Psychology, 105:*283–294, 1964.

VERNICK, J., and KARON, M., "Who's Afraid of Death on a Leukemia Ward?," *American Journal of Diseases of Children, 109(5):*393–397, 1965.

VIORST, J., *The Tenth Good Thing About Barney*, Atheneum Press, New York, 1971. (To be read to and by children.)

YUDKIN, S., "Children and Death," *Lancet, 1:*37–41, 1967.

WOLF, A. W. M., *Helping Your Child to Understand Death*, Child Study Press, New York, 1973.

WOLFF, S., *Children Under Stress*, Penguin, London, 1969.

SECTION III

Assessment

Richard L. Cohen / Editor

The editor of Section 3 expresses his deepest gratitude to the many individuals whose suggestions and generous cooperation contributed to the development of his section. If it is not self-evident that Dr. Joseph Noshpitz was a constant wellspring of empathic encouragement and wise guidance, this must be underscored. Special thanks go to Mildred Kutner Cohen, M.S., M.Ed., whose patience during the preparation of the manuscript and thoughtful proofreading of several drafts proved to be of major importance; to Mrs. Anita Marks who labored meticulously through draft after draft and proved to be a diplomatic but firm shepherdess with our several contributors; and to Ms. Janet Elkind who also worked so hard to produce quality typescripts for the publisher.

RICHARD L. COHEN

PART A

The Approach to Assessment

58 / Basic Concepts

Richard L. Cohen

Introduction

This section is concerned with the diagnostic assessment of the child. In keeping with the general usage in the Handbook, the term *child* will be used for the entire developmental spectrum from conception through adolescence.* Perhaps the approach to this area that will be employed here is best illustrated by an oft-told story.

A consulting electrical engineer submitted a $1,000 statement for his services to the manager of a hydroelectric dam. In questioning the size of the bill, the manager noted that the engineer had spent only fifteen minutes on the site in correcting a power failure. Under the circumstances, did the statement not seem exorbitant? Perhaps the engineer could clarify matters by itemizing the statement? Indeed, replied the engineer, this was a most reasonable request. His statement now read:

1. Replacement of defective terminal $ 5.00
2. Knowing which terminal to replace   995.00

                                           $1,000.00

The point of the tale need not be labored. The fact is that, as professionals, child psychiatrists tend to be somewhat prone to underplay the vital importance of proper and thorough assessment.

---

* Please note that, for convenience, the child or patient is consistently referred to as male. In like vein, the mother is assumed usually to be the primary caretaker although it is recognized that this may not always be the case. Similarly, the clinician is also frequently referred to in the male gender. Such usage is for the purpose of achieving a smoother style for the reader and is not meant to convey a sexist attitude.

They are sometimes inclined to attribute more glamor to the techniques of treatment; perhaps even to assume that any child who presents with a "problem" must automatically require their therapeutic services; and that diagnostic data will inevitably emerge as the treatment process unfolds. This is, at best, a wasteful use of professional (and patient) time. At worst, it can be dangerous and potentially harmful to a child and family whose real difficulty may emerge only after weeks or months of "treatment" have proven ineffective.

A child may present with loss of interest in food and with accompanying weight loss. The question becomes: is he suffering from a hysterical conversion reaction, a hypothalamic tumor, a masked depression, incipient anorexia nervosa, a phobic reaction, or some other pathology?

Is the child who presents with unpredictable, violent temper outbursts suffering from a seizure state, an adjustment reaction of adolescence, a character disorder, an expanding intracranial lesion, or some other pathology?

Is the child who presents with increased irritability, emotional lability, and a sleep disorder suffering from a depression, an anxiety reaction, thyrotoxicosis, hypoparathyroidism, or some other syndrome?

The answers to these questions can only be arrived at through an orderly and disciplined thinking process. Nosology in child psychiatry is still in its formative stages and the art of "diagnosis" outreaches the science by several lengths. (The reader is encouraged to study Section B of

Volume II on diagnosis in conjunction with this section on assessment. They are of a complementary nature.)

Nevertheless, there is a great deal that has been learned about evaluation of the child and his family. Except under the most dire circumstances (the usual rules of risk to life, limb, property, or the human spirit apply here), there is little excuse to proceed with any kind of intervention without first carrying out an appropriate evaluation.

The pressures of clinical practice, the demands of referring sources, or the unrealistic expectations of parents (or, often enough, all three) may help to create an atmosphere in which rapid decisions, simple answers, and swift action seem inescapable. A recent report of the Group for the Advancement of Psychiatry[5] addresses itself to this issue cogently:

The relationship between this latter kind of treatment planning and that based on the exchange of more complete information in a more formal manner should be kept in mind. A plan is being evolved but in sequence; it is evident from the beginning that planning will take place in steps. It is not hard to decide what takes precedence in the face of assaultive behavior, suicidal attempts and acute anxiety. The treatment plan answers the immediate need. Hopefully, the first step is taken as the beginning of a continuing plan and not as an end in itself. The ability to move on, with patient and family, to another step may reflect the skill of the planner. Action is not substituted for thought; the connection has to be made between thought and action, but the process is an accelerated one and a difference is made between practical short-term goals and longer-term planning.

It is probable that emergency planning represents a debased form of planning. The tendency is toward action, action within a closed system not offering many alternatives to planner, family or patient. Thus it is an accelerated planning process and the nature of the plan is determined in large part by the nature of the immediate situation. A number of planners may be involved; their skills lie in an instant recognition of the bare bones of the situation so that their actions will be appropriate.

Psychiatric emergencies arise in all families. However, they occur most often in the public eye for the disorganized poor, who move through life in a series of thumps and bumps, who gravitate without feelings of shame to hospital and police station. The recurrent emergency, for one family member or another, interfaces with more thoughtful approaches and becomes part of life style for family and for planner. The constant struggle to stabilize the situation takes the place of other planning and its momentum often carries family and child away from more complete treatment planning. [pp. 636–637]*

Perhaps it is important to state even more directly that many "crises" or "emergencies" in

child psychiatric practice are simply reflections of the life style of the family involved. The clinician may be diverted from his efforts at performing a careful step-wise assessment because of the life style of the family and its ability to suck helping resources into the vortex of its circular activity. If this happens, then the clinician runs a high risk of becoming part of the problem rather than part of the solution.

The frame of reference or context in which the assessment of a child takes place is of central importance. It matters as much as the skills and techniques of the clinician performing it. That context includes several dimensions.

PURPOSE OF THE ASSESSMENT

The purpose will influence how and what is done. Among the many reasons for performing an assessment are:

1. The need to help a disturbed child and/or a distressed family. To do this requires the selection of an appropriate modality of intervention. If treatment is indicated, at least the initial phases must be planned. Basic to any such undertaking, however, is the need for a comprehensive study of the child and family. There is no way to help without finding out what is wrong, and how best to right it. Assessment is the process of doing this.
2. The wish to help a community. This sometimes begets a need for triage, or at least for a rapid decision about disposition.
3. The need to screen large numbers of children who may be at risk for morbidity because they belong to a particular target population (for example, the offspring of drug abusers or the survivors of a natural disaster). Screening is a specialized form of assessment and diagnosis. This handbook contains a comprehensive section on prevention. The reader is referred to the topical headings of that section for detailed recommendations on screening procedures for specific at-risk target populations.
4. The need for "another opinion" requested by some individual or caretaking system (pediatrician, school, juvenile court, etc.). The referral source may already have considerable data about the child but cannot solve the problem and feels the need for input from an expert in the behavioral sciences.
5. A variety of special needs including follow-up studies, monitoring the status of patients who are in some form of long-term or chronic care, and meeting the requirements of a particular investigative project. (See chapter 83.)

In this section, the emphasis will fall on the differential use of evaluation techniques and the importance of tailoring each assessment to the purpose(s) for which the effort is being carried out.

---

* Reprinted by permission from *Psychopathological Disorders in Childhood—A Proposed Classification.* © 1966 by Group for the Advancement of Psychiatry.

QUESTION OF IDEOLOGY OR SCHOOL OF THOUGHT

It is important to acknowledge that child psychiatry does not yet boast a set of generally accepted operational premises from which most clinical practice can flow. There is no unifying theory of normal and abnormal behavior. As a result, there is inadequate consensus as to what kinds of data are most relevant to the clinical evaluation of a child. Thus, adherents of family systems theory will tend to give highest priority to information which clarifies the child's interaction with other family members and differentiates his role within the family system. Child psychiatrists who place particular emphasis on social and community systems will strive to understand the child's behavior primarily in relation to the sociocultural, economic, and political forces which are impinging upon him. Child psychoanalysts place high priority on data which delineate the substrate of the child's instinctual drives, the character of his interpersonal relationships, and the modes by which his drives seek expression at various stages of psychosexual development. Advocates of learning theory tend to study the child's repertoire of patterned responses to environmental signals. Child psychiatrists with a strong biologic orientation seek clinical information that would help explain behavior on a neurophysiologic or orthomolecular basis.

Certainly, there is value in having a clinical "position" to which one adheres. It assists in maintaining an orderly approach to one's work and in communicating with one's colleagues. However, in a field where "all the votes are not in yet," a clearly defined position may also operate as a perceptual or cognitive screening device to exclude those data which are not consonant with the clinician's bias. Self-fulfilling prophecies are not acceptable substitutes for the application of inductive reasoning.

The family therapist who does not conduct an intensive clinical examination of the child need not be burdened with awareness of the child's overwhelming intrapsychic conflict. The behavior therapist who does not take a detailed developmental history also does not have to struggle with the possible significance of the child's prolonged hyperthermia leading to convulsions at age eight months. The pharmacotherapist who does not inquire into the family's emotional support system need not be concerned that the patient's mother is in intense conflict with her own mother and has recently lost her closest friend in a fatal accident.

There is an impressive amount of selective inattention imposed on the diagnostic process because of the clinician's choice of orientation. Inevitably, once this first "data screening process" has taken place, then the choice of management options becomes similarly narrowed to a few favored techniques. Thus, in an otherwise excellent paper in which she rightly berates her colleagues for not performing thorough and multidimensional evaluations of their child psychiatric patients, McDonald[11] then goes on to say: "A recommendation must be a logical outgrowth of the diagnostic assessment. *It must be directed to relief of conflict.*" [Italics added.]

The above statement, taken within its fuller context, appears to mean that, whatever the problem, whatever the diagnosis and whatever its etiology, the treatment of choice must involve some effort to resolve intrapsychic conflict in the child! There is no intent here to single out this particular author. Similar examples are to be found among authors who overemphasize constitutional factors or behavioral perspectives. Indeed, it appears today that in child psychiatric circles generally this procrustean bed clinical style is the rule rather than the exception.

In sum, then, child psychiatry cannot lay justifiable claim to being one of the academic subdisciplines of medicine until it develops an assessment design which allows proper bench marks for measuring subsequent change, if any.

SEARCH FOR PATHOLOGY

Medical education (and, to a lesser extent, education in the other helping professions) rewards the identifier and delineator of disease. High accolades go to the "discoverer" of a new disease; there may even be a Nobel Prize for the special person who finds a "cure" for that new disease. On the other hand, health, as such, is a desired state, a goal to be attained but on the whole one that generates little scientific curiosity. Yet, an objective assessment of any individual (whether patient or not) depends on a balanced weighing of liabilities ("disease") against assets ("health").

At the end of a long and difficult diagnostic process, the clinician should not find himself the proud possessor of an accurate diagnosis and a specific choice of treatment modality, and withal be ignorant of the strengths in the child and the family. He may then be faced with the other half of the assessment that he should have been conducting all along, which he is now forced to perform it in a very hasty and imperfect manner.

A reliable indicator that this exclusively disease-oriented assessment has occurred becomes evident when the clinician starts musing: "Well, let's see now, what have we got to work with here?" It is only a slight oversimplification to state that it is the deficits (or problems) in a case that indicate the need for intervention. It is the number and quality of assets (or evidences of health) that influence the odds for the success of that intervention! This area of study of the patient and family will receive considerable emphasis in succeeding parts of this section.

Risks of Labeling. A collateral issue to this matter of psychiatry's tendency to be overoccupied with pathology has arisen during the past decade. Many professionals, parents, consumer interest groups, and child advocates have expressed mounting concern over the evils of "labeling" children.* This indeed is a serious problem. The use of screening procedures which have been poorly standardized is common practice in many well child settings and school systems. The use of testing instruments standardized on one cultural subgroup and then unthinkingly administered to another is another practice which until recently has gone unchallenged. It is still common to find that a label has been arbitrarily affixed to a child and made part of his record in order to facilitate his acceptance into a particular program. Since there appears to be no other alternative (so goes the thinking) this will get him some kind of assistance. Unfortunately, not only is the child unlikely to receive the help he needs, but the label will usually become a permanent stigma with which he must cope for the rest of his youth, perhaps of his life.

A partial listing of topics in this handbook to which the reader is referred for further information includes: the black child; the chicano child; the poverty child; the child with a congenital deformity; the child with Minimal Brain Dysfunction; the retarded child; classification of child psychiatric disorders; learning disorders; the school's role in identification impact of insurance and third-party payments; psychometric and projective testing; child advocacy; impact of consumerism; the rights of the child; changing status of civil rights and minority groups; changing issues and homosexuality; the effects of the juvenile justice system; professional standards review organizations.

A brief perusal of this listing should convince the reader that this is indeed a pervasive issue

* See references 2, 7, 8, 12, 14, and 18.

which cannot be brushed aside. The capricious use of "tags" or "markers" applied to children is a dehumanizing procedure. It reflects not only a reductionistic view concerning disability in childhood but often an overly expedient approach to case management. In the long term, this is counterproductive because it treats the child as only a casualty, not a child, and often results in euphemistic referrals to programs poorly suited to his overall needs.

Constant caution must be exerted by the clinician in assigning a "diagnosis" to a child to avoid engaging in this process of expedient labeling. A diagnosis is not a child. It is simply clinical shorthand to indicate the presence of a constellation of behavioral phenomena requiring further assessment and management.

VALUE OF ACTION-ORIENTED ASSESSMENT

A useful test for the significance of diagnostic data is the degree to which it leads decisively to a given course of action. This is particularly important in the practice of child psychiatry where one-to-one relationships between a discrete diagnostic label and a proven treatment of choice rarely exist. If there are, for example, ten treatment modalities available for a behaviorally disordered child in a given setting or community (for example, group psychotherapy, individual psychotherapy, pharmacotherapy, psychoeducational intervention, family therapy, child analysis, inpatient, or residential care, etc.) then, from the outset, the data should be collected and organized logically to point to which form of management is indicated. If the first choice is for some reason not available, then the second choice should be clearly indicated, and so on. Current utilization review procedures, to say nothing of plain common sense, make it incumbent on every clinician to relate the diagnostic facts to a clear treatment plan.

Sometimes the outcomes of a study are labyrinthine and exhaustively detailed descriptions of behavior, or family history, or psychodynamics which, taken in sum, do not facilitate the clinical decision-making process. Such a development suggests that the clinician has indulged in the luxury of a wasteful "fishing expedition" or is an undisciplined thinker.[1, 13, 15]

In summary, then, it is important to give proper emphasis to the diagnostic process. To be sure, bona fide crises *do* sometimes occur and require expeditious intervention before all the conventional information has been collected. As a rule, however, the diagnostic process is likely to proceed most productively if the following precepts are borne in mind:

1. Relate the evaluation to the purpose for which a diagnostic opinion is being requested.
2. Avoid the temptation to screen out certain kinds of diagnostic information which may be rank ordered into a comparatively low category in a particular clinician's belief system.
3. Pay as much attention to assets in the child and his environment as to evidences of pathology or deficit.
4. Design the diagnostic sequence so that it facilitates the clinical decision-making process with respect to differential use of treatment modalities.

The Clinical Team

Central to any consideration of the diagnostic process in child psychiatry is the much belabored question of the "team approach." The traditional triad of child psychiatrist, clinical psychologist, and psychiatric social worker had its beginnings in the child guidance movement during the first quarter of the twentieth century. The newfound skills in measuring intellectual capacity developed by Binet and Simon and later introduced into the United States separately by Terman and by Goddard made the psychologist a "natural" for membership on the newly forming teams. The early predecessors of today's psychiatric social workers were intimately familiar with the home environment and family structure of children; this made them an obvious choice to round out the triad.

For the next forty years, this team was able to evaluate and treat the various types of disorders in children who were being referred for attention. Unfortunately, a quality of ritual and stereotypy crept into this arrangement. During recent years, there has been a strong counterreaction to this traditional configuration with its elaborately demarcated areas of professional turf. It has not proven flexible enough to meet many types of problems. Economically, in the cost-conscious world of the 1970s, the numerous meetings implied in the very word *teamwork* are often wasteful of expensive staff time. The identification of new diagnostic and treatment modalities has expanded the universe of necessary knowledge and skills far beyond the capabilities of such a tripartite team.

Obviously, the standard diagnostic team must either be expanded from a triad to an as yet unidentified set (a quintet? an octet? a minyan?) on a routine basis, or there must be a shift to some other rationale for orchestrating the appropriate team skills on a case by case basis. This "score" must be dictated by several factors: the needs of each case, the purpose of the evaluation, and what is considered to be adequate data for decision making prior to the use of different treatment modalities. It would seem that today the direction of the field is toward the flexible rather than the uniformly structured team approach.

The child psychiatrist has no special corner on all, or even on most, of the skills needed. His combined background in biological and psychological medicine probably puts him in the most advantageous position to review all the available information on a given patient. He can then raise the unanswered questions (and assist further in arriving at the answers) which should be addressed before the book is closed on the evaluation. These questions can be the principal guidelines for deciding which additional skills, disciplines, and procedures need to be included as a part of the team process.

Has the manner in which the child handled a crayon or walked across the office suggested the need for a pediatric neurology consultation or a psychoeducational study—or both? Does the combination of the child's perinatal history and the incidence of certain types of mental retardation in the extended family history indicate the need for a comprehensive genetic and/or endocrine workup? Would a structured home visit answer some puzzling questions about the family dynamics? Would observing the child in a hospital for twenty-four hours add enough depth to his developmental profile to allow for more definitive treatment planning? Where reports from different sources yield conflicting data concerning the child's peer group adjustment, would direct observation of the child in his classroom setting clarify the matter?

Clearly, the legion of medical specialists, behavioral and laboratory scientists, developmental specialists, nurses, social workers, educational specialists, and paraprofessionals required today in order to perform a truly comprehensive study of a child cannot be assembled into a permanent, stable "team" as a part of one clinic or organization. Their talents have to be brokered (usually by a child psychiatrist) and, in the aggregate, they are most likely to be found in a university medical center. This is not to suggest that children cannot be well evaluated in other settings. However, it does suggest that the more complex the case, the more likely it is that the highly specialized talents needed will cluster around the psychiatric-pediatric-neurologic axis typical of academic medical settings.

In the real world, the talents and skills brought to bear on a case are often determined by happenstance—or by the child's presenting complaint (Kanner's "ticket of admission"). The term "happenstance" refers primarily to the identity and belief system of the first "gatekeeper" who perceives some problem in the child. If this happens to be a pediatrician, family physician, or well-child clinic, then the child is likely to be referred to the health system in the community. If it happens to be an agency social worker, then the team will be marshalled from the welfare or correctional system. If a teacher, then the "special education department" of the school system may be involved. If an "outreach" worker in a community mental health center satellite clinic, then the patient will encounter the mental health and mental retardation system.

Eventually, the child with, let us say, delayed speech development, may be sent to the speech clinic of a children's hospital (because he has "a communication disorder"); a foster home (because he is "emotionally deprived and understimulated"); a special education class (because he has a "learning disability"); or a child guidance clinic (because he is "emotionally disturbed").

Obviously there is much here that is dubious. Whatever the setting, it falls to the primary clinician who "inherits" this case to elicit the proper information, or, if he cannot, to assemble the right professionals to do so. Some systems facilitate this kind of individually tailored team approach and some, unfortunately, do not.

In a good many instances, the skills of a single, experienced clinician (or a beginner under competent supervision) are perfectly adequate to evaluate a case, particularly if the clinic, hospital, or agency has a good, uniform clinical data system.

At times, however, more than one clinician is desirable, not only because a wide spectrum of clinical subspecialization is dictated by the nature of the case, but for other technical reasons. There is a certain group of cases where experience indicates that at least two clinicians ought always to be assigned, even for the purposes of assessment. These are situations where the initial data suggest any one or a combination of the following conditions:

1. The presence of a behaviorally disordered child in a "multiproblem family" overstressed by a number of environmental contingencies (for example, serious health problems, financial decompensation, multigenerational conflicts, etc.) which include inadequate kinship or social supports.
2. A parent or parents who present with significant and gross emotional problems of their own, including passive-dependent personalities.
3. Problems with adolescents where complex issues of confidentiality may arise and where there may be value in providing a separate and "private" working relationship for the patient.
4. Occasionally, the clinician may be confronted with an adolescent patient who is considered sufficiently paranoid and assaultive to make it advisable to have more than one clinician present and participating in the evaluation.

In any of these circumstances, if he must, a tenacious and resourceful clinician *can* function successfully as a solo diagnostician. Many private practitioners do so routinely. However, in cases of these types, the complexity and the dimensions of the work load are more easily borne by a team of clinicians who divide the work collaboratively.

Other considerations may enter into the assignments for diagnostic purposes. The educational and training needs of a facility may dictate that various types of clinicians in training be assigned to several types of cases. Moreover, in order to provide them with the broadest possible experience, this is always arranged both on a solo and team basis. So long as no basic tenet of sound clinical practice is violated, this seems entirely justifiable.

Human Development as the Basic Science for Assessment

In evaluating child/patients, it is of critical importance to bear in mind that:

1. Childhood is a period when dependency is a natural and expected state. (To say the least, this makes for a major modification in the professional contract with the "patient.")
2. Behavioral (and, therefore, clinical) phenomena tend to reflect developmental level. In adults, it is more common for clusters of symptoms and signs to point to disease entities. (This mandates a modified body of knowledge and diagnostic skills.)
3. The child is in a constant state of flux (when compared to adulthood where increments of change are generally more gradual). (This has a major impact on treatment planning.)

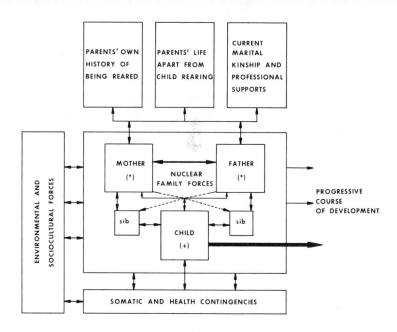

FIGURE 58–1

An Interactional Model of Development.

* Nature of behavior and degree of investment of primary caretakers in rearing this child.
† Idiosyncratic nature of child's endowments.

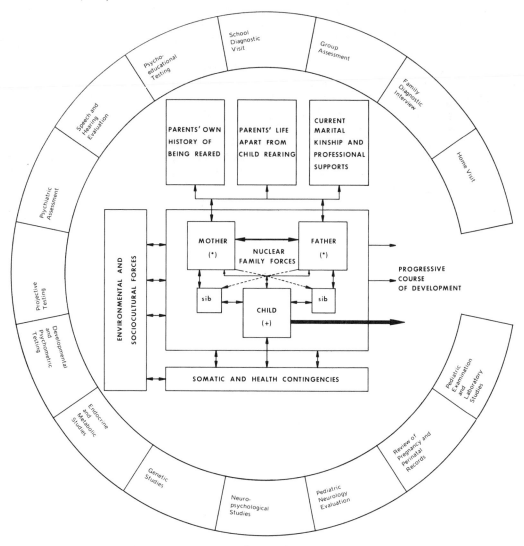

FIGURE 58–2

These are cogent and compelling reasons to think about the child referred for clinical attention in the broadest possible developmental framework. Even for the child psychiatry researcher whose basic purposes are investigative, exclusively nosological approaches prove to be self-limiting, overly simplistic, and not likely to generate new conceptual approaches.[17, 19]

However, in choosing the developmental framework within which to do one's clinical assessments, one is still left with many dilemmas. Currently, there are some acceptable, even excellent schemata available for evaluating clinical information from children, codifying it and using it to formulate a treatment plan.*

The practicing clinician once more finds himself in a position where he cannot wait for all of the votes to be in. Either he must proceed with a specific system which he finds most meaningful and convenient, or he can resort to some hybrid system which he has worked out on an idiosyncratic basis and in which he attempts to combine the desirable features of several schemata. It is foolish to pretend that the state of the science is more advanced than this, but it is incumbent on each practitioner not to make the cacaphony of opinion even more confusing by ignoring what work has been done and by resorting to systems which clearly cannot be supported in developmental investigation.

As noted, there is no single, unifying theory of human development now accepted in the field; nor is there any one system of classification and diagnostic formulation generally agreed upon by professionals. Nevertheless, whichever developmental

format the clinician uses as a structure for his diagnostic work, it should embody a clear and obvious system (and a very practical, down-to-earth methodology for making judgments) that can relate the goals of development to the clinical picture in the child. Stated most simply, if the goals of all human development have something to do with achieving ever-increasing levels of organization and integration leading to: (1) growing capacity for autonomous function and self-care; and (2) growing capacity for socially cooperative behavior and participation in significant human relationships—then, in relation to these two broad goals, there should be no major difficulties in correlating the child's clinical symptomatology with his progression or lack of it at various developmental levels.

In the course of teaching, figures 58–1 and 58–2 have been found useful as a kind of tree or skeleton on which to hang all of the clinical data which is consistent with the above theoretical constructs. They represent a mechanism into which all this information can be fed (whether collected through historical sources, clinical observation, laboratory studies, etc.), and from which a reasonably comprehensive picture of the factors influencing developmental outcome in the child can be formulated. Moreover, this approach has the additional advantage of not requiring the attachment of value systems to various philosophies or schools of thought. Best of all, however, it lends itself to an action-oriented treatment plan in that it generally points up those areas of strength and resource which can serve as building blocks for treatment, and those areas of deficit or negative influence which require shaping, modification, or elimination.

* See references 3, 4, 6, 9, 10, and 16.

REFERENCES

1. BEISER, H. R., "Psychiatric Diagnostic Interviews With Children," *Journal of the American Academy of Child Psychiatry*, 1:656–670, 1962.
2. DEUTSCH, M., "Happenings on the Way Back to the Forum: Social Science, IQ and Race Differences Revisited," *Harvard Educational Review*, 39:523–557, 1969.
3. FREUD, A., "The Concept of Developmental Lines," in Eissler, R. S., et al. (Eds.), *The Psychoanalytic Study of the Child*, vol. 18, pp. 245–265, International Universities Press, New York, 1963.
4. ———, "Assessment of Childhood Disturbances," in Eissler, R. S., et al. (Eds.), *The Psychoanalytic Study of the Child*, vol. 17, pp. 149–158, International Universities Press, New York, 1962.
5. Group for the Advancement of Psychiatry, "From Diagnosis to Treatment: An Approach to Treatment Planning for the Emotionally Disturbed Child," vol. 8, Report no. 87, pp. 636–637, 1973.

6. ———, "Psychopathological Disorders of Childhood," vol. 4, Report no. 62, pp. 175–199, 1966.
7. HETZNECKER, W., and FORMAN, M. A., *On Behalf of Children*, Grune & Stratton, New York, 1974.
8. HOBBS, N., *The Future of Children: Categories, Labels, and Their Consequences*, Jossey-Bass, San Francisco, 1975.
9. KLEIN, B., and MORDOCK, J., "A Guide to Differentiated Developmental Diagnosis with a Case Demonstrating Its Use," *Child Psychiatry and Human Development*, 5:242–253, 1975.
10. KNOBLOCH, H., and PASAMANICK, B. (Eds.), *Gesell and Amatruda's Developmental Diagnosis*, 3rd ed., Harper & Row, New York, 1974.
11. McDONALD, M., "The Psychiatric Evaluation of Children," *Journal of the American Academy of Child Psychiatry*, 4:569–612, 1965.
12. MacMILLAN, D. L., JONES, R. L., and ALOIA, G. F.,

"The Mentally Retarded Label: A Theoretical Analysis and Review of Research," *American Journal of Mental Deficiency,* 79:241–261, 1974.

13. MARKS, P. A., *An Assessment of the Diagnostic Process in a Child Guidance Clinic, Psychological Monographs,* vol. 4, No. 4, 1961.

14. MURPHY, J. M., "Psychiatric Labeling in Cross-Cultural Perspective," *Science,* 191:1019–1028, 1976.

15. REYNOLDS, M. C., "A Crisis in Evaluation," *Exceptional Children,* 32:387–395, 1966.

16. RUTTER, M., et al., "A Tri-Axial Classification of Mental Disorders in Childhood," *Journal of Child Psychology and Psychiatry,* 10:41–61, 1969.

17. SANTOSTEFANO, S., "Beyond Nosology: Diagnosis From the Viewpoint of Development," in Rie, H. E. (Ed.), *Perspectives in Child Psychopathology,* Aldine-Atherton, Chicago, 1971.

18. SOLNIT, A., "The Risks of Screening," *Pediatrics, 57:* 646–647, 1976.

19. SPITZER, R., and SHEEHY, M., "DSM-III: A Classification System in Development," *Psychiatric Annals,* 6:102–109, 1976.

59 / History Taking

Richard L. Cohen

Anamnesis in Child Psychiatry

The issue of anamnesis in child psychiatric practice is a surprisingly controversial one.

The literature on this subject is extensive and varied. Essentially, it falls into four categories:

1. Some clinicians do not separate "history taking" from "therapy" and contend that the relevant history can only evolve during the course of treatment.
2. Others* hold that history taking in child psychiatry is such an unreliable process that the data so obtained cannot be safely used for making clinical judgment about the child or for planning treatment strategies.
3. Still others † express positive attitudes toward the history taking process but may not offer a specific structure or format for obtaining the desired information.
4. Finally, there is a group ‡ of clinicians who contend that rigorous history taking is necessary and desirable, and who present structured or semistructured formats for conducting such interviews.

It is this last position which is held by this author. The objections outlined by the clinicians in the first two groups have much merit and should not be discounted. Nonetheless, it has been the experience of most clinicians that there is a better alternative; that an hour or two properly organized and properly invested in methodical and sensitive history taking can be indispensable

in understanding the nature of the child's disorder, the resources available for correcting it, and the modes of action indicated in the future.

In part, this depends on the development of a specific attitude about history taking.[13, 14] If it is viewed as a routine and stereotyped form of clinical drudgery, this attitude will communicate itself to the adults being interviewed. It will surely be reflected in the quantity and quality of data elicited; and in any case, it is not likely to be helpful to the outcome of the diagnostic study. If, on the other hand, it can be viewed each time as a new opportunity for exploration and discovery; if it can be experienced as an exciting interchange, even an adventure, this too will be communicated quickly and with appropriate outcome. Kanner[8] sums up a lifetime of work with families and children when he describes the history taking process as one which

. . . is not a cut-and-dried technique but a thrilling experience had by two people. The interviewer is in the process of recording a human document as rich and unique as any piece of fiction could possibly be; the person interviewed is in the process of telling not just a story but his or her story which gains in color and luster to the extent to which interest, understanding and empathy are sensed. [p. 193]

Many modern works that deal with the evaluation or examination of the child psychiatric patient do not appear to agree with Kanner. In general, there is a shockingly small amount of attention paid to the history-taking process and to the relevant techniques, interview flow, and content associated with collecting information from primary caretakers. There are probably

* See references 6, 11, 12, 15, 17, and 18.
† See references 2, 9, 10, and 19.
‡ See references 3, 4, 5, 7, 8, and 16.

numerous reasons for this. It is undoubtedly true that much information collected retrospectively proves on later examination to be either not very useful, highly inaccurate, or pure fantasy.

But this does not invalidate the history-taking process. The individuals who have been in daily contact with the child during his growing years are the primary reservoir of useful information. The task is to elicit this information in as reliable a form as possible, as quickly as possible, and in a fashion designed to facilitate clinical decision making. There are no tricks or gimmicks in this process. It does take a certain commitment of time and energy on the part of both the clinician and the parents, but in most instances, the potential rewards more than warrant this investment.

Under these conditions, one could easily expect either a paucity of information, or data which was so unreliable as to be unworthy of the time committed to the process by any of the participants. The parents will either withhold or censor information which they consider to be unacceptable; the interviewer will screen out data unrelated to his unverbalized personal agenda; the parents may feel disorganized, or like "subjects" in a poll-taking effort by a marketing organization; or they may see the questions as irrelevant and unrelated to their purpose in seeking help. If any or all of these conditions are present in the interview situation, one can depend on the presence of serious deficits or inaccuracies in the material collected.

Factors Influencing History Taking

A host of factors will influence the amount and quality of data derived from parent interviewing. They include:

1. Capacity for accurate recall on the part of the interviewee which, in turn, depends on the level of investment in child care and child rearing at the periods of time in the child's life under discussion.
2. Factors operating in the interview which may enhance or interfere with the quality of trust between clinician and parent.
3. The clinician's skill in facilitating recall, in using the interview as an organizing experience for the parent, and in maintaining sufficient structure and discipline that the data elicited is relevant to the task at hand.

Under the most adverse circumstances, one could conceive of an interview situation in which caretakers who were only loosely affiliated with the child are being asked for information of which they have only partial knowledge; where there is a marked disparity in sociocultural backgrounds, value systems, and belief systems between clinician and parents; where the parents are experiencing marked anxiety, depression, or some other disorganizing affect which is interfering with their capacity to attend to the interview; where the interviewer is relating himself either to the affective components of the interview exclusively, or, conversely, is pressing the parents only for "hard" facts rather than feelings or attitudes; and, moreover, where the interviewer is pursuing a symptom-oriented, totally child-focused format in which the circumstances surrounding the child's behavior do not emerge.

Means of Improving an Interview

These deficits and inaccuracies *can* be reduced to a minimum by adhering to certain basic principles about interviewing. These have little to do with child psychiatry as a discipline; they may in fact have little or nothing to do with any of the helping professions as such. Interviewing is a sophisticated and complex skill which must be mastered by a good many professionals as a part of their basic skills. It is equivalent to playing in a string quartet or in any similar joint human effort involving highly integrated intercommunication. It can never be mastered entirely; indeed it must be "worked at" throughout one's professional life in order to maintain at least a minimal level of proficiency.

First, there are some guidelines which must be borne in mind in order to set the tone for the interview, maintain a high level of quality of response, and insure a maximum level of relevance on the part of parents. These include:

1. It should be emphasized to the parents that the interviewer is as much interested in their and their child's strengths and in the positive resources of the family as he is in their problems. When questions are asked about a given area such as school, play, friends, work habits, etc., it should be made clear how important it is for the interviewer to get a *balanced* picture of the situation. The examiner is concerned with the child as a person, not simply as a bearer of problems. Almost all parents seek help with an underlying sense of guilt, frustration, and failure. This approach has the effect of getting the parents to think about their positive resources as well, and thus encourages them to reduce their defensive posture. They need to have their atten-

tion drawn to their strengths, and to their successes. This is best achieved not through flattery or "conning," but through their own careful examination of the life experience of the child and his growth and development. It is critical that this be done in a way which is not overly focused on failure and on their sense of inadequacy.

2. The parents should have a clear explanation of the purpose of the interview. It is important to go into some detail about the areas of content which will be covered, the order in which they will be covered, the order in which they will be taken up, and the reasons for this. They must understand that questions about the format of the interview and its structure are very much in order. If parents have other types of questions at the outset, the clinician should respond to them supportively and within the limits of the available data. Again, this has the effect of reducing defensiveness and reassuring them that they will be participating in a joint task rather than having a procedure performed upon them. This increases their sense of mastery and their feeling of involvement and responsibility for what happens to the child. For most parents, it also increases the quality of their participation. They begin to view the interview situation as a kind of positive challenge in which they are there to assist the clinician in problem solving and planning. On a technical basis, this also assists in the conduct of the interview since this initial explanation provides a "baseline" to which the interviewer can turn repeatedly as parents stray from the basic flow of the session. The precise nature of the explanation recommended in this interview will be discussed in chapter 60.

3. Depending on the level of education, sophistication, and probable intelligence of the parent or parents being interviewed, it may be important from time to time to explain the relevance of a given question or topic as this arises. This is particularly true when covering areas that have to do with parental experience or background. In general, parents will participate more fully at these points if they can perceive the connection between parental preparation for child bearing and child rearing, and the outcome of development. This can be put into simple, direct terms.

4. It is important to emphasize descriptions of behavior. The interpretations and judgments that parents make should, of course, be accepted when they are made, but the interviewer does not settle for them. The individual temperaments of the parents, their threshholds of stimulation, and their biases about particular kinds of behavior will necessarily introduce a great many value judgments into the descriptions they offer. Such statements as "He is very active" should be accepted and then responded to with requests for specific illustrations. In general, even after such a request for a more detailed picture of the behavior, parents will continue to assure the interviewer that they know whereof they speak. It may require a certain persistence to hold some parents to the task of describing the child in a variety of settings during the day. There is ample evidence that one parent may view a given child as very active, while another parent may describe a different child with an objectively lower level of activity (as measured by an independent observer) as even more active. It is just this kind of variability that has disillusioned clinicians about developmental interviewing. It is particularly important to get specific descriptions from prior periods of development. There is, in fact, no other way to get directly observed data about the child under those circumstances.

5. The task of facilitating parental recall without asking leading questions is a formidable one, but most interviewers will experience increasing degrees of gratification as they work at this. The tactful pursuit of veins of information can sometimes lead to mother lodes of developmental ore that afford a special kind of accompanying excitement to both interviewer and parent. This experience often results in genuine and useful insight. It is not helpful to ask a parent, "What was Johnny like when he was two years old?" Many parents will either confabulate, deny any memory of specific events or occurrences or simply state that there were no problems. Incidentally, this last statement will arise frequently during developmental interviews and should be confronted directly with the reminder that this is not specifically a search for problems so much as an attempt to understand the parents' experience in-depth while rearing the child. Constructive recall is more likely to occur if the parent can be helped to identify his own "milestones" in the family's developmental history. There are illnesses, geographic moves, deaths, separations, promotions, etc. If it is important to know what Johnny was like when he was two years old, approximate the date when Johnny was two and make an effort to find out what the family's experience was like during that time. The mother may say, "Oh, yes, in 1970 we moved into a new house and had all kinds of trouble with the heating system." At this point one can say to the mother, "Can you remember what Johnny was like around the time you moved into your new house? Did the heating problems affect his care?" Most of the time she will indeed remember something. Further support and stimulation of her associative processes will presently bring forth much more data.

6. Successful developmental interviewing depends, in part, on maintaining a consistent balance between empathy and discipline. Interviews that are constantly peppered with the question "How did you feel about that?" are likely to produce a sense in the parent that the interviewer is interested and concerned; in the long run, however, they may not result in a great deal of useful information. On the other hand, the pursuit of a rigidly structured format which is aimed only at eliciting specific descriptions of child behavior or reactions also has risks. There is a strong possibility that the parent will perceive the interview not as part of a helping process but as some sort of sterile laboratory technique.

There is no easy formula for maintaining this balance. Like most other aspects of good interviewing, it must be constantly worked at and refined. Despite years of experience, no interviewer should ever feel overconfident about being able to maintain this balance.

7. Very early in the interview, the clinician should make an assessment of the degree of difference between his own sociocultural background and that of the parents. Marked degrees of difference should alert the interviewer to be particularly attuned to avoiding value judgments. Indeed, until he has made a careful investigation of accepted norms in the family's subculture, he should be especially wary of making assumptions about how atypical or deviant the child's behavior might be. Of course, dangers exist as well when the difference in the sociocultural backgrounds of clinician and parents is minimal. Here the possibilities exist for overidentification with or another kind of stereotyping of parents. During the interview, countertransference phenomena stemming either from the interviewer's own experience in being reared, his own ethical system, or his own current life style are likely to make their presence felt frequently. It takes a high level of vigilance and discipline to cope with such responses, to make allowances for them, and to insure that they do not impinge unduly on the parents.[1] Such attitudes can result in either rejecting or seductive postures toward the parents, and thus act to shape parental responses. It is difficult enough to deal with parental stereotypes (for example, the clinician as stern judge, as all-knowing expert, as magician, as cold parent surrogate, etc.) which they themselves bring into helping situations. This will be explored later in more detail. However, it is worth noting once again that the greater the disparity in sociocultural background between parent and interviewer, the more likely that parental styles in dealing with the interviewer may interfere with fulfilling the purpose of the encounter and its successful completion. For example, at the extremes, the very poor or the very rich often represent particular red flags for interviewers. It is a matter of experience that parents from each of these subgroups tend to deal with the real or assumed power of professional people by ingenious maneuvers that have stood the test of time.

8. Of greatest importance is the acceptance of a strong developmental framework for conducting one's clinical practice. This should become instinctive, and should be evident from the first clinical contact. The entire interview can and should be conducted within the framework of a basic grasp on normal development. (See Section I.) The manner in which all these phenomena can be related to each other will be described. In general, however, *all* questions and all responses should be related to the basic issues of how the child grew. It does not help to think in terms of a separate "health history," "social history," "educational history," "parent history," etc. The interviewer's questions should be framed within a context which clarifies for the participants how the flow of the interview is progressing at any given moment, how it is related to the overall concept of the child's development, and how this will help the parent think about what he or she can do for the child. The impact of this kind of approach is to reduce parental defensiveness to a minimum and to maximize parental participation. In a sense, it begins the treatment process at once, but in a way that is safe. Almost from the outset, it serves as an organizing experience for the parent; under proper circumstances, parental understanding and parental coping often increase without any other intervention from the clinician.

In summary, then, the interviewer should:

Indicate a balanced interest in the child's strengths and weaknesses.

Include the parent at the outset in setting up the plan for conducting the interview.

Be able to demonstrate the relevance of all areas of inquiry to the purpose for which the parent is seeking help.

Emphasize specific descriptions of behavior in a wide variety of experiences and settings.

Broaden his repertoire of techniques for facilitating parental recall without the use of leading questions. Most important here is that the family has a developmental history of its own. Recall will improve if the child's development is associated with family changes, events, and experiences.

Strive for a consistent balance between empathy and discipline in the interview with the foreknowledge that this is a goal to be sought for, but never fully attained.

Be patricularly alert to interview artifacts that may arise either from marked similarities or marked disparities in the sociocultural background of clinician and parents.

Attempt to relate all areas of inquiry to their significance for the eventual outcome of developmental status in the child.

Several mental health facilities have found it useful to ask parents to complete an "application form" or initial information form prior to the first clinical contact. It is only appropriate to use this kind of information in instances where the clinical problem is not an emergency or of highly urgent nature.

Its principal advantages lie in its potential to save some time in the interview; to assist parents in organizing their thoughts prior to the first clinical contact; and (when accompanied by a signed release form) to allow the clinician to begin collecting information about the child more rapidly (thus accelerating the assessment process).

FIGURE 59–1

APPLICATION INFORMATION FORM

Your answers to the following questions will help us to better understand the problems for which you are seeking help. Your answers to these questions are regarded as confidential information, as is any other information you may give the Center. Please write or print clearly. You need not give lengthy answers, but if more space is needed, use the back of the form or attach extra sheets. A return envelope is enclosed for your convenience.

Child's Name: _____ Boy: _____ Girl: _____

Date and
Place of Birth: _____ Age: _____ Religion: _____

Address: _____ Telephone No.: _____
(zip code)

Township or Borough (if any): _____

Father's Name: _____ Date of Birth: _____

Living? _____ At home? _____ Nationality Background: _____ Religion: _____

Education: Years Completed: _____ Degrees Obtained: _____

Employer: _____ Occupation: _____

Mother's Maiden Name: _____ Date of Birth: _____
(first)   (last)

Living? _____ At home? _____ Nationality Background: _____ Religion: _____

Education: Years Completed: _____ Degrees Obtained: _____

Employer: _____ Occupation: _____

Date and Place of Marriage: _____

Previous Marriages: _____

List below your other children in order of birth (living or dead):

	Name	Birthdate	School Grade or Occupation
1.			
2.			
3.			
4.			
5.			

	Others Living in Home	Age	Relationship or Status in Home
1.			
2.			
3.			

1. *What school does the child attend?*
   a.   Grade? _____   b.   Name of Principal: _____
   c.   Name of Teacher: _____

2. *Has your child ever changed schools?*

Name and Address of Other Schools	Attended (date) from	to	Grades

3. *Has your child had difficulties in school in relation to:* his studies, his behavior, his relationship with teacher, his principal, his classmates?

FIGURE 59-1—*Continued*

4. *From what source did you learn of the Center?*
5. *What events or circumstances prompted you to call the Center at this time?*
6. *Describe what you believe has caused the difficulties your child is having.*
7. *What has the family done to try to help the child with these problems?*
8. *Have you sought professional help before?* From whom and for what? Was it helpful? (Examples of professional help might be: a social agency such as Family and Children's Service: a hospital such as Children's Hospital, a psychologist who might have tested the child at school or elsewhere, a child psychiatrist in private practice).
9. *History of Growth and Development.*

   a. Describe difficulties of pregnancy and delivery:
   b. In which month of pregnancy was the child born?
   c. What was the birth weight?
   d. At what age did the child accomplish the following? Were there any problems associated with them which concerned you?
      (1) Weaning
      (2) Sitting
      (3) Walking
      (4) Talking
      (5) Eating without help
      (6) Toilet Training: Bowel: _____ Bladder: _____
   e. Has the child ever had any difficulties with: (describe)
      (1) Coordination (tieing shoes, riding bike, jumping rope, etc.)
      (2) Hearing
      (3) Vision
      (4) Sleeping
      (5) Eating

      Has the child had trouble getting along with: (describe)
      (1) Brothers and sisters
      (2) Either or both parents
      (3) Other children

10. *Describe any family difficulties or events which were upsetting* (such as: deaths of family members or close relatives, moves, prolonged absences of a parent, illness of a parent, financial problems, etc.).
11. *Have you or other members of the family had difficulties, either physical or emotional?*
12. *When did the child last have a physical examination?*

    a. Date: _____ Results: _____
    b. Who is his physician? (please give name and address.)
    c. Is he now receiving treatment?
    d. List below serious illnesses, accidents, or operations which the child has had. Give the date of the illness or injury, and if the child was hospitalized give the name of the hospital, approximate length of stay, the attending physician.

13. *In what way do you believe the Center can be of help to you? Do any of the following ways express your opinion?*

    a. _____By helping us.
    b. _____By telling us what is wrong with our child.
    c. _____By telling us what to expect from our child.
    d. _____By telling us how to handle our child.
    e. _____By telling us what we have done wrong with our child.
    f. _____By telling us to understand our child.
    g. _____By helping us to understand ourselves and our child.

FIGURE 59–1 (*Continued*)

14. *Are both parents in agreement regarding the child's need for help?* Please describe.

15. *Were the questions answered by:*

Mother _____

Father _____

Both _____

Signed _____

_____ Date _____
(Parent or Parents)

PLEASE COMPLETE AND RETURN WITH THIS FORM THE INFORMATION PERMISSION.

See figure 59–1 for an example of one such form which has been in use for several years.

Usually, several contacts are required with the family and child in order to complete a thorough assessment. Depending on the nature of the case, these may include developmental interviews, physical and psychiatric examinations of the child, family interviews, contacts with the child in a school setting, and others.

There is no universally accepted format in the field which dictates the order and flow of these clinical contacts. Many clinicians prefer to "open" with a contact with one or both parents during which a developmental history can be taken. Some prefer to examine the child directly before collecting other data. Still others elect to see the entire family first (see chapter 75).

Although the question of sequence is a significant one (because this may affect the way relationships are formed and may influence the context in which information is uncovered), it is probably not of critical importance.

There is more than one correct way to assemble the relevant information. Through experience, clinicians tend to arrive at a modus operandi with which they are comfortable.

The description of the assessment process in the next chapter is predicated on a sequence which has wide acceptance. Although it allows for flexibility, in general, the sequence is: (1) initial contact, inquiry or application for service; (2) developmental interview; (3) direct psychiatric and physical examination of the child; (4) specialized examinations; and (5) interpretation conference with family and, when indicated, with referral source.

REFERENCES

1. ADAMS, P. L., and MCDONALD, N. P., "Clinical Cooling Out of Poor People," *American Journal of Orthopsychiatry, 38*:457–463, 1968.
2. CRAMER, J. B., "Psychiatric Examination of the Child," in Freedman, A. M., Kaplan, H. I., and Sadock, B. J. (Eds.), *Comprehensive Textbook of Psychiatry,* vol. 2, pp. 2055–2060, Williams and Wilkins Co., Baltimore, 1975.
3. FINCH, S. M., *Fundamentals of Child Psychiatry,* W. W. Norton and Company, New York, 1960.
4. GOODMAN, J. D., and SOURS, J. A., *The Child Mental Status Examination,* Basic Books, New York, 1967.
5. Group for the Advancement of Psychiatry, "The Diagnostic Process in Child Psychiatry," vol. 3, Report No. 38, 1957.
6. HAGGARD, E. A., BREKSTAD, A., and SKARD, A. G., "On the Reliability of the Anamnestic Interview," *Journal of Abnormal and Social Psychology, 61*:311–318, 1960.
7. JENKINS, R. L., "Diagnosis and Nomenclature in Child Psychiatry," in Jenkins, R. L., and Harms, E. (Eds.), *Understanding Disturbed Children,* pp. 45–60, Special Child Publications, Seattle, 1976.

8. KANNER, L., *Child Psychiatry,* Charles C Thomas, Springfield, Ill., 1957.
9. LOOFF, D. H., *Getting to Know the Troubled Child,* University of Tennessee Press, Knoxville, 1976.
10. LOURIE, R., and RIEGER, R., "Psychiatric and Psychological Examination of Children," in Arieti, S. (Ed.), *American Handbook of Psychiatry,* vol. 2, pp. 3–36, Basic Books, New York, 1974.
11. MEDNICK, S. A., SHAFFER, J. B. P., "Mothers' Retrospective Reports in Child Rearing Research, *American Journal of Orthopsychiatry, 32*:457–461, 1962.
12. ROBBINS, L. C., "The Accuracy of Parental Recall of Aspects of Child Development and Child Rearing Practices," *Journal of Abnormal and Social Psychology, 66*:261–270, 1963.
13. ROSE, J. A., "Psychologic Responsibilities of Medical Practice with Children," *The Pennsylvania Medical Journal, 63*:1473–1481, 1960.
14. ———, "The Psychological Aspect of Pediatric Practice," *Quarterly Journal of Child Behavior, 1*:140–149, 1949.

15. SHAW, C. R., *The Psychiatric Disorders of Childhood*, Appleton-Century-Crofts, New York, 1966.

16. SIMMONS, J. E., *Psychiatric Examination of Children*, Lea & Febiger, Philadelphia, 1974.

17. WENAR, C., "The Reliability of Developmental Histories," *Psychosomatic Medicine, 25*:505–509, 1963.

18. ———, and COULTER, J. B., "A Reliability Study of Developmental Histories," *Child Development, 33*:453–462, 1962.

19. WERKMAN, S., "The Psychiatric Diagnostic Interview With Children," *American Journal of Orthopsychiatry, 35*:764–771, 1965.

60 / The Developmental Interview

Richard L. Cohen

Means of Making the Interview Most Productive

The material which follows is largely paraphrased from the Instruction Manual which is used currently with trainees in the Division of Child Psychiatry at the University of Pittsburgh.* It forms the basis for a developmental practicum and for the introduction to clinical practice which are taught simultaneously in the first year of training.

This interview tends to be most productive and most effective when it is:

1. Carried out with the primary caretaker of the child (or the person who was the primary caretaker for most of the child's life). Adopted children [1] may present special problems in diagnosis and treatment. (See also chapter 36 concerning the adopted child.)
2. Carried out as early in the clinical process as possible—preferably as the first step.
3. Conducted with the primary caretaker alone. If the spouse or mate is present, some very useful information may be gleaned, but experience has indicated that the basic flow and rhythm of the interview is usually altered in a fundamental way.

* The approach embodied in this interview was first conceived by Dr. John A. Rose at the Philadelphia Child Guidance Clinic in the late 1950s. Since that time, it has been tested and revised through use with several "generations" of child psychiatry residents and fellows at the Universities of Pennsylvania, Nebraska, and Pittsburgh respectively. The author gratefully acknowledges the original work of Dr. Rose and the many contributions of his colleagues in the development and use of the interview as an educational and clinical tool. Among these colleagues, Doctors Meyer Sonis, Isobel Rigg, Ora Smith, Henry Cecil, Edward Beitenman, and Peter Henderson have been especially valuable.

In some instances, there are antecedent problems operating in relation to the mother which may tend to alter the progress of the interview. In previous contacts with professionals some mothers have felt deeply criticized, and they find it difficult to discuss the current behavior of the child. Other mothers are actually so detached from the child at this point that the very distance creates interviewing problems. In some instances, the mother or primary caretaker is so emotionally disturbed, so disorganized, or so dissociated that, on initial contact, conducting anything like a usual interview is virtually impossible. Adoptive mothers or mothers of children whose health and viability were highly threatened in the perinatal period present some very special problems. These require specific knowledge on the part of the interviewer in order to keep the interview "working." Other mothers experience their principal distress in connection with a person other than the child for whom they are ostensibly seeking help; in such instances it is often most difficult to hold them to the specific task of the diagnostic process.

In general, however, if appropriate discipline is maintained by the interviewer, the initial interview with the mother should be able to cover the necessary areas in adequate detail. Approximately ninety minutes (more or less depending on the age of the child) is usually required. The interview should never be conducted as if it were a simple chronological reporting of developmental sequences or milestones like beads on a string. These milestones of child development are important in terms of what else was going on with the child, with the mother, and with the family life situation at any given time.

Factors to Be Considered in the Interview

DISCUSSION OF PRECIPITATING SITUATIONS

The interview is usually opened by inquiring into the events which are perceived by the primary caretaker as having resulted in her seeking advice. If there is some aspect of the presenting situation that has in it any hint of emergency, it is critical that this be immediately identified and reacted to appropriately. It is also of value to know from the beginning if there are major contingencies which have put the family under unusual stress. Reality pressures, especially those that have come up recently, may make it difficult for the mother to adhere to the overall purpose of the interview.

Where it is clear that the work can proceed in its usual form, the interview is explained to the mother as the beginning step in a process of mutual evaluation. Its purpose is to enable the mother and the professional(s) to see more clearly what is needed for the child, and it is understood that this may lead to a decision to go further with additional clinical service. It should be stated early that it is unlikely that any direct conclusions or advice can be communicated as the result of one clinical contact. (In fact, if the interview is successful, the mother will begin to draw many correct conclusions herself and alter her management of the child without direct professional advice.)

It is very important to convey to the mother that the interviewer wishes to understand the mother's experience in rearing this child in the context of what was happening in her life and in the family's life during that epoch. It should be impressed upon her that she has the opportunity to discuss anything which she might feel is important. At the same time, there is an advantage in discussing things in a sequential way because whatever comes up will be reviewed in the light of the march of developmental events. It is essential to convey the importance the interviewer attaches to understanding things as the mother saw them; indeed, the interviewer's ability to serve her well (or even to know what service is needed) is dependent upon how clearly she can describe things as she saw them at the time they were occurring.

EXPLORATION OF CURRENT LIFE SITUATION

Having encouraged the mother to identify the immediate reasons for coming, and having explained the purpose of the diagnostic process, one should then try to obtain a general overview of the current life situation of the mother, family, and child. This is intended to identify any major problems of pressing importance and to sort out those issues which will later be discussed both more intensively and more extensively. The suggested dimensions of this exploration are as follows:

1. The age, physical size, and appearance of the child and identification of any major handicaps which may be present; a brief résumé of the child's behavior and general development; an account of his significant social relationships; and the identification of major problems in health or in behavioral disorganization.
2. The constitution of the family group, their ages, who lives at home; in general, a description of the current life circumstances of the family in terms of housing conditions, extended family, neighbors, and neighborhood.

DESCRIPTION OF THE INTERACTIONAL EXPERIENCE IN REARING THIS CHILD

The mother then is urged to go back in time to the beginning of her relationship with this child and to give an account of the various periods of the child's development almost to the present. In effect, mother is asked to relive each major life situation requiring adaptive behavior on her part. These experiences are reviewed in the context of what else was happening with the child, the mother, father, and other children, and with the family situation at the particular time.

The mother's attention is turned to the beginning of her relationship with this child, including timing and circumstances of conception. Emphasis is placed on importance of mother's life circumstances at the time she became pregnant, and she is asked to reflect on how the pregnancy fitted into events which were occurring at that time. The questions put to mother should be designed to elicit how both mother and child adapted to change; these include changes originating in the biological processes, from life situations which exerted adaptive pressures, and from the social behavior of others which called for particular response patterns. In relation to conception and pregnancy, for instance, one would want to know about the mother's initial reaction upon learning she had conceived, and any changes in this reaction as the pregnancy advanced. Of particular moment is the mother's perception of the marital and kinship system in terms of support or conflict. Similarly, complications of pregnancy, of the mother's health, or any perceived threats to the fetus should be noted. Contingencies that arise at the neonatal period are significant to the extent that they affect the mother's capacity for beginning caretaking. This review of the mother's reaction to conception and her experiences during pregnancy and the neonatal period is intended to throw light on her pattern of adaptation in the face of stress, change, and crisis.

From this point, the interviewing should be directed stepwise forward in time through the vicissitudes of the child's development from birth to the present. An effort should be made to obtain samples of both the mother's and the child's behavior at suitable intervals during growth.

The mother will have her own timetable of important life events by which she establishes the point at which particular changes occurred. These events are different for different families. Very few people keep time by months or years. Instead, it is usual to find that each individual creates a pattern of longitudinal chronology composed of births, deaths, operations, accidents, separations, illnesses, school changes, moves, etc. It is important to map these accurately.

Mothers will usually recall rather vividly the conditions which prevailed when a new infant was introduced into the home and family; a little later, they become vague about the concurrence between the age of the child and other events. It is important to locate the mother's milestones and then find out what else was going on with the family at that time. *Her memory about the child's behavior and development is likely to be most acute in terms of her own idiosyncratic milestones.* Patience and persistence are necessary; one must weave back and forth in time in order to place contemporary events in their correct context.

For instance, a mother may describe a period of concern about the child's behavior without in any way relating it to a move the family made, to the birth of another child, to a loss of the father's job, or to her own mother's coming to live with the family.

A detailed description of the child's behavior during infancy may reveal information about the child's constitutional endowment and pattern of responsivity to stimuli. Behavioral descriptions which illustrate the infant's position on the regularity-irregularity continuum, his threshhold to stimulation, his level of distractibility, his activity level, his reaction to the introduction of new experiences such as the bath or new food, all are especially valuable in pinpointing specific factors in the child's constitution. They reveal also what kind of start in life mother and child had together and whether there was any basic "mismatch" between the quality of the child's behavior and the mother's image of what she wanted to see in her infant. Every mother faces such child-rearing tasks as guidance, supervision, and limit setting. As the child grows, its capacities mature and mother is continually responding to ever more complex behavior. This is the time when beginning trends in the child's behavior may indicate problems in social cooperation and autonomous self-organization.

When mother is seeking service for an older child, it is often difficult for her to recall events in early child rearing. However, through skillful use of the mother's milestones, it will usually be possible to recapture adequate samples of the child's behavior at varying intervals of his development.

MOTHER'S EXPERIENCE IN BEING REARED

When the course of the mother's description of the child's development has arrived almost to the present, the flow of the interview should be directed to her own experience in being reared. It is important to interject this new direction just at this point in the flow because the mother has begun to gain an overall perspective about her child-rearing behavior. She should then be guided to review her recollection of the major milestones of her own development. The milestones most frequently identified by mothers are:

1. Beginning school and early school attendance
2. Onset of menarche
3. Adolescent social and sexual experience
4. Work experience, if any
5. Experience leading to the selection of a mate and beginning of marriage

It is natural to begin to find some relationship (whether positive or negative) between the way one is rearing a child and the way in which one was reared. A striking parallel often becomes evident between the difficulties a mother may have had in being reared and the difficulties she may be having or has had in rearing a child. It is important to note such parallelism when it exists. However, it is equally important not to be drawn into extensive discussions at this early stage of diagnosis by the mother's guilt about the current problem.

This phase of the interviewing requires the greatest skill and discipline on the part of the interviewer. It is important not to be caught up by deeply conflicted or neurotic aspects of the mother's past, especially in relation to her own mother. The focus of the interview should continue to be directed toward the mother's reason for coming in the first place, and on her own preparation for caretaking.

REVIEW OF CURRENT SITUATION

In the course of discussing her own history, the mother will presently approach more recent events. In contrast to the brief exploration of the current situation that was entered into early in the diagnostic interview, at this point a more detailed and precise description of the current behavior of the child is in order along with a review of the collective forces impinging upon the child and the family.

The interviewer seeks descriptions of the child's behavior in a wide variety of typical daily situations, along with an account of the mother's way of coping with the child. In effect, one is taking a "day history." This may be done quite literally by beginning with information about how the child typically awakens in the morning, what he does to make his presence known to the family, how the family reacts to this, etc. It continues with descriptions of the child's behavior around self-care and in performing assigned tasks; his social behavior with parents, siblings, and peers; his self-chosen activities and interests; and his responses in situations of success and frustration. Another important area is school behavior. This is approached in terms of how he acts when he is away from home, his behavior toward school authority and demands, his social relationships with peers, how he handles competitive peer-group situations, and how he deals with academic subjects. His way of coping with unusual situations such as moving, illness, trips on vacations, and so on, may graphically illustrate the nature of his adaptive efforts.

Other important aspects of the current situation are: the mother's patterns of response to her marital and kinship systems; her recourse to them as sources of support or of conflict; and the child's behavior in relation to the father and other members of the family. This line of inquiry is intended to throw light on the mother's sense of the significant relationships in the family. In particular, does she perceive them as helping or hindering her rear this particular child?

Along with the account of the mother's life, it is essential to obtain descriptions of the father, of his behavior, and what his pattern of development is with the family. Many factors must be explored: his interest in his child, in the other children, the amount of responsibility he takes for caretaking, his behavior as a mate, his investment in earning a living, and his involvement in the home as against outside activities. In order to grasp what is significant about the family constellation and dynamics, it is essential to obtain as many descriptions as possible of discrete episodes of the father's behavior and the mother's responses.

Similarly, it is useful to have examples of the mother's involvement with her own mother, in-laws, or other close members of the extended family. Illustrative material would include: her dependence on any significant members of the family for warmth, approval, and counsel; her dependence on them in terms of help with the child; and the conflict she may experience because of their claim on the husband for his loyalty and/or a special relationship.

The other children are viewed in the context of whether they are rewarding to the mother or are sources of stress, and the effect this has on the care of the child in question. One would especially want to know about the existence of handicapped, defective, or emotionally disturbed children who might make unusual demands and cause the expenditure of considerable emotional energy.

Finally, in the course of learning about a typical day for the mother, child, and family, there should also emerge some idea of the mother's sources of gratification, if any, outside of home and child rearing. Ultimately, these may prove to be assets in that they provide a sense of well-being and make mother's life more full. Or they may turn out to be liabilities which detract and interfere with her capacity to provide for the needs of the child under consideration. In either case, some picture of her activities outside of the family should be elicited.

Conclusions

To recapitulate briefly, the sequence of the initial interview with the mother or primary caretaker is as follows.

1. First, a brief exploration of the facts of immediate significance and the circumstances leading the family to seek professional assistance. Some explanation is offered concerning the purpose and nature of the initial interviewing process.

2. This is followed by an initial survey of the current life situation. At this point, one seeks to identify the significant factors related to the mother's and child's behavior in their current interaction and to note matters and issues which will later be discussed intensively and extensively.

3. A careful history is taken of the rearing of the child beginning with conception, pregnancy, and delivery. The neonatal period is reviewed, followed by interval periods of infancy care, young child care, and so on up almost to the present. The focus is upon the adaptive behavior of the mother and child and what else was happening with the family at the time; much use is made of the mother's chronological landmarks. This inquiry is built around a strong emphasis on an interactional model.

4. The exploration turns to the mother's own experience in being reared, with special emphasis on her adaptive behavior at maturational milestones. This leads up to and through marital choice, and brings the family in time almost to the present.

5. Finally, the current rearing experience with this child and his present behavior are reviewed. This includes patterns of the mother's and child's ongoing interaction; marital and kinship relationships as supports or stresses; and trends in mother's life situation apart from child rearing —family, personal strivings, and the impingement of other reality demands.

REFERENCES

1. OFFORD, D. R., APONTE, J. F., and CROSS, L. A., "Presenting Symptomatology of Adopted Children," *Archives of General Psychiatry*, 20:110–116, 1969.

PART B

Direct Examination of the Child

61 / The Clinical Examination

Richard L. Cohen

Generalizations Applicable to the Diagnostic Process

Direct clinical examination of the child is ordinarily conducted on a one-to-one basis in the office and/or playroom. However, depending on the nature of the problem, the needs for additional information, and the orientation of the clinician, this procedure can be supplemented by observations of the child in a group (of other patients), with his entire family, in school, at home, or, if necessary, even in an inpatient psychiatric service. Descriptions of these techniques are included below. Obviously, the procedures for evaluation of an infant, a school-age child, and an adolescent will vary considerably. Therefore, the principles of direct clinical examination will be described successively during three broad epochs of development: (1) the infant and young toddler, (2) the preschool and school-age child, and (3) the preadolescent and adolescent.

There are several generalizations which in some measure apply to diagnostic efforts during *all* of these developmental periods, and these should be considered first.

Much is written about communicating with the child "at his level." If one would like to observe this in its most degrading and humiliating form, both for adult and child, one need only tune in the television set some afternoon around four or five P.M. and watch the local version of "Freddie the Clown" or whoever has been employed to cajole, bribe, and patronize the local preschoolers to press their parents for a variety of junk foods, useless toys, and inane movies. This may be tolerable to children or even attractive. Coming in the form of electronically transmitted images of adults who have no real meaning in their lives, it can be considered entertainment.

Any flesh-and-blood adult who would behave in this way, particularly if it were someone with the authority and dependency gratifying stature of a clinician, could only produce a combination of hostility and anxiety in the child. Children do not need adults to behave toward them in a childlike fashion in order to "communicate." What most children need and can do rather quickly is to develop a sense of trust. They need to feel that the adult in question understands something about what it is like to be a child and can translate verbal and nonverbal messages into adult responses and signals; that the child indeed is being heard; and that even those parts of him which are "bad," painful, or ego-dystonic are accepted without criticism or judgment. On the other hand, it is scarcely helpful to the child if "behaving like an adult" means stuffiness, a high premium on maintaining one's dignity, or even an expectation that the child adultomorphize himself in order to make the interview more comfortable for the clinician.

On balance, in working with children, a certain humility is in order. No matter how experienced and how unflappable the clinician may feel about

505

his work, when he enters a new diagnostic situation, he may depend on being confronted with novel and puzzling configurations of behavior. Poise, presence, and flexibility are constantly in order, along with a readiness to improvise modifications of techniques which have been painfully learned, carefully husbanded, and often enough taught proudly to students. The next child who walks into the office is likely to be the "exception" to the rule one has just expounded.

One must never forget that, with the possible exception of the older adolescent, virtually all of this group of patients appears in the office not of their own volition but through a decision-making process implemented by parents or guardians. Inevitably, this has some effect on the "contract." Even though there may be no open opposition to participating in the process, the child ordinarily does not understand why he is in the clinician's office, what is expected of him, or whether it will have any significant impact on decisions which are made about him in the future. The clinician himself is at best only partially aware of the events leading up to the referral, and is sometimes totally ignorant of what the child has been told about the sessions. Moreover, this all takes on rather special and new meaning in the light of present-day developments in the area of the rights of minorities. There is a large constituency in the United States which views children as a minority, and there is a growing body of legal precedents which is making the problem of maintaining privacy and confidentiality for the child very complicated. In the instance of the child-patient, the so-called "contract" between clinician and patient must be tailor-made. With advancing age, and legal and social maturity, the rights of the child to maintain a certain level of privacy apart from his parents and guardians must be weighed very carefully against the potential advantages that may accrue for all involved when there is a process of open communication.

Child psychiatry is a medical discipline. The important technical questions about who may or may not perform physical evaluations of the child should be decided individually in each office, clinic, or hospital. There is mounting evidence that many children present themselves with multiple health problems (most of which are interactive with their behavioral states), that many have had inadequate or defective health care, that modern methods of electronic fetal monitoring were not available when most of our current patient population was born, and that the most common single presenting complaint in outpatient child psychiatric settings has to do with some form of difficulty in a school setting. Moreover, there is the basic medical responsibility involved in any setting which assigns its clients the legal status of "patient." All this makes mandatory an adequate overview of the child's physical status. This includes the current state of his central nervous system.

Although some portions of the diagnostic process may lend themselves to the use of a structured protocol, most of the "format" or "structure" must be carried around inside the examiner's head. The opportunity for spontaneous use of the time and, where appropriate, of play materials, is an indispensable part of the process. The information gained from the clinician's observations can later be assembled into an organized format. Many formats have been proposed and most are quite adequate. The outline of a particularly useful one will follow.

It is important to remember that the kinds of observations the clinician makes are influenced by his choice of approach. A strictly psychopathologic (or nosologic) approach results in a search for specific traits or diagnostic markers that will narrow down clinical decisions to a fixed set of syndromes. Even "developmental diagnosis" in the more literal sense of the word (as used, for instance, by Knoblock and Pasamanick[2] for determining the "integrity and functional maturity of the child's nervous system") may be quite useful and appropriate with infants and toddlers (see chapter 62) and still not be applicable in older children. Whatever approach is used, there should be room in the interview for the child to demonstrate verbally and behaviorally the range and quality of his assets.

Throughout this work, much will be made of the importance to children of nonverbal communication and play. Play, however, is not the *sine qua non* of diagnostic interviewing. Some children cannot or do not play during interviews. The essence of the matter is that if the clinician's theoretical framework is broad enough, whatever the child does can be of diagnostic value. Elaborate physical setups boasting hundreds of dollars' worth of toys may avail nothing with a child who is very atypically developed, or who is depressed, or comes from an extremely deprived background. The focus of the child's attention may prove to be a piece of string found in a corner of the room, a passing bread truck which can be viewed from the window, or the sounds of a conversation in the hallway. This then becomes the "content area" around which he may choose to have some interchange with the interviewer. In fact, play can be misused or used quite defensively in an hour, much in the same way that an adult might resort to verbalization as evasion or coverup. Meaningless, stereotyped, repetitive types of play may be encountered which really serve as smoke screens. A child may choose play as a distancing defense in order to deal with fears of invasiveness by intimacy with or loss of control toward the examiner. The problem then becomes that the child is not so much avoiding play as evading relationship. Like the analytic patient who fills his hour with one dream after another, he blocks out meaningful interchange with the clinician.

Countertransference problems with children are common and unavoidable. It is the responsibility of the clinician to deal with these at his own conscious level and to make allowance for them in the interview. There is much evidence to indicate that upper-middle-class children who are verbal, physically attractive, and intelligent are not only "easy" to examine, they tend to be the preferred patients and the best "teaching cases." Nonverbal children, children who act out destructively in the office or who are messy and abusive; children who are slow intellectually; and those who represent minority groups (perhaps other than one's own) present special problems in an interview.[1] Although it helps to know as much about the subcultures of the child as possible, this is not enough. Each clinician must be responsible for identifying the kinds of behavior in children which he finds most provocative. These tend to awaken once again perhaps only partially resolved past conflicts of his own, or may represent varieties of behavior against which he himself is only marginally defended. Performing diagnostic evaluations on those particular children constitutes each clinician's own private little purgatory. Perhaps it is helpful to know that all of one's colleagues are laden with similar burdens of countertransference. The clinician who feels he cannot deal with these should avoid such children, refer them to other colleagues, or ask to be reassigned to another case.

Observation, interviewing, and evaluation of children may not always take place in what Redl[4, 5] refers to as the "pressurized cabin" of the professional office. It may frequently need to occur in the less structured and controlled settings of classroom, pediatric ward, detention center, nursery school, or even the child's living room.

Under these circumstances (many of which are described later), it is useful for the clinician to be familiar with Redl's concepts of the "marginal interview" or the "life space interview."

Although Redl primarily emphasized the therapeutic value of such contacts (either as "emotional first aid" or as "exploitation of life events"), their diagnostic implications seem self-evident.

The clinician will find that developing skills in understanding a child's behavior against the backdrop and within the context of his many life situations is an indispensable asset.

Health History and
Physical Examination

There has existed for many years a controversy concerning the advisability (or permissibility) of the child psychiatrist's performing a physical examination on his child patient. As early as 1929, Levy had developed a schema for performing physical examinations as a part of the psychiatric examination. This approach involves explaining to, discussing with, and questioning of the patient during each step of the process. Levy[3] believed that this revealed material about body image, self-concept, fantasy life, etc., that might not otherwise be accessible.

There are many equally prominent clinicians who take a polar opposite position. Ekstein,* for instance, states that the child psychiatrist should *never* examine a child physically, especially if there is any possibility that he may be the child's clinician for ongoing treatment.

Between these rather extreme positions, one finds many modified approaches. Obviously, no authoritative statement (which truly represents the field) can be made at this time.

In any event, the more cogent issue concerns the kind and extent of data required for an accurate assessment, not the identity or discipline of the individual performing the examinations.

If the child has had adequate health care in the past, most if not all of the necessary data about the child's physical state will be readily obtainable from pediatrician, family physician, or other resource. This should be requested and carefully reviewed by the responsible child psychiatrist on the team. If it is not considered adequate for diagnostic purposes, or if the physical examina-

* R. Ekstein, "Notes on the Teaching and Learning of Child Psychotherapy within a Child Guidance Setting," *Bulletin of the Reiss-Davis Clinic,* 3:68–81, 1966.

tion and routine laboratory studies have not been performed within the last few months, then if at all possible, these should be carried out under the auspices of the mental health program now responsible for the child. The complex nature of developmental problems, learning disabilities, psychophysiologic disorders, and acute and chronic brain syndromes makes mandatory a minimal baseline of physical studies for each child. From these, an appropriate medical decision can be made about any possible need for further more sophisticated studies.

Whether or not the child psychiatrist performs the physical examination himself, he should approach all clinical contacts with the patient from the posture and with the discipline of a physician. By direct inspection of the child and by observation of his solitary and interactive play, it is possible to collect a large amount of relevant data about the child's physical status.

The following observations regarding general physical characteristics can be made as a matter of course (clearly, some of these overlap with several aspects of the mental status examination):

1. Nutritional state and personal hygiene.
2. Size for age; body fat distribution.
3. Posture and gait.
4. Physical deformities (including head size and shape, limbs, digits).
5. Vasomotor responses.
6. Contusions, lacerations, scars, eczema, acne, phlebitis, needle tracks.
7. Tics, choreo-athetoid movements, or other involuntary mannerisms.
8. Presence of odors (feces, urine, cannabis, etc.)
9. Presence of secondary characteristics.
10. Handedness.

One can similarly make the following observations about head and facial characteristics:

1. Head size and symmetry.
2. Facial symmetry and expression; muscle weakness.
3. Hair distribution.
4. Eyes, including set and slant, pupil size and reactivity, sclera, presence of strabismus, ptosis, nystagmus.
5. Gross estimate of visual and auditory acuity.
6. Structure of nasal and external ear cartilage.
7. Size of tongue and structure of teeth.
8. Breath odor.

The above listing is not complete but is intended only to remind the physician of the wealth of data that is available to the alert diagnostician without any "laying on of hands."

Beyond the usual urinalysis, hemoglobin, and white cell count (and perhaps serology), no laboratory examinations should be considered "routine." Most are costly for the child. Many specialized studies may prove to be necessary. Decisions concerning these should be made on an individual case basis.

A detailed health history is also necessary for thorough assessment. It is recommended that the portion of this material which is collected from the parents (in contrast to that collected from other health caretakers), be incorporated as a part of the developmental history. In this way, illnesses, hospitalizations, surgical procedures, etc., can be understood in the total context of the child's development. It becomes more possible to evaluate the impact on the child's coping mechanisms, the effects of socially isolating and physically limiting disorders which may have occurred at critical periods for the child. The human support system is also more easily evaluated since the illness can be viewed against the backdrop of other life events which were transpiring concurrently in the family.

REFERENCES

1. COATES, B., "White Adult Behavior Toward Black and White Children," *Child Development, 43:*143–154, 1972.

2. KNOBLOCH, H., and PASAMANICK, B. (Eds.), *Gesell and Amatruda's Developmental Diagnosis,* 3rd. ed., Harper & Row, New York, 1974.

3. LEVY, D., "The Physiologic and Psychiatric Examination," *American Journal of Psychiatry, 86:*121–194, 1929.

4. REDL, F., "The Concept of a 'Therapeutic Milieu,'" *American Journal of Orthopsychiatry, 19:*721–736, 1959.

5. ———, "The Life Space Interview: Strategy and Techniques of the Life Space Interview," *American Journal of Orthopsychiatry, 19:*1–18, 1959.

62 / Examination of the Infant and Toddler

Joseph Marcus

The task of assessment of the infant or very young child presents the examiner with the need for acquiring special skills. The developmental history-taking process is essentially similar for all ages. However, with children in this age group, data on the pregnancy, perinatal, and postnatal periods should be particularly sharp in focus and will always have a major bearing on how the examination of the child is conducted and how the various findings may be weighted.

This chapter details the assessment of the infant and young child.

—RLC

Introduction

In recent years, child psychiatrists have become ever more aware that they have a role to play in the examination and treatment of the infant and young child. In fact, this role may begin during pregnancy and the newborn period. The direction seems to be toward an emergent "Infant Psychiatry."

This shift in interest has grown out of increasing knowledge about the individual differences among infants, and the contribution that these differences make to the child's own development. These play a role as well in the developing interactional patterns between him and his surroundings. There has been a steady increase in knowledge about specific deficits, vulnerabilities, and developmental deviations, and in the refinement of methods for treating such deficits.

The infant is an *individual* with particular qualities; he differs in his own unique way from the rest of the universe of infants. This individuality may be a combination of congenital temperamental qualities, the status of his neurophysiological development, his inborn physiological adaptation mechanisms, and his general physical condition and appearance. All these make him the person that he is; they affect the manner in which he elicits responses from the environment and how he reacts to that environment. Many of the ways in which the infant affects his environment have been reviewed by Lewis and Rosenblum.[16]

For instance, he may be a fairly large, robust child, moderately active, with attractive physical features, a high level of awareness, and a tendency toward much spontaneous nonsocial smiling. Such a child can evoke very positive reactions from the mother and other caretakers; he can be easy to handle, and may become a principal actor in a newly developing loving, playful relationship.

On the other hand, the infant may be small and scrawny, possibly limp and inactive, with a tendency toward irritability and much given to crying. His muscle tonus may be tense and he may be hard to cuddle. There may be one or two physical anomalies which mother might find repulsive. His general behavior, particularly his noncuddliness, can be felt by a new, inexperienced mother as some form of rejection. It may make her feel frustrated, unhappy, and perhaps even fearful of this new infant.

Certainly the life histories of the two infants described here and their interactions with the world around them, particularly with their immediate caretakers, are likely to be very different. It falls well within the scope of the responsibilities of psychiatrists or other professionals (pediatricians, nurses, and other caretaking personnel—whom the psychiatrists should feel responsible for teaching and guiding) to make proper assessments of the infant, the mother, and the interactions between them. This may be necessary in order to help the newly developing relationship to flourish in a positive way and to provide the infant with the environment most likely to facilitate his development.

It is accepted as axiomatic that the development of the behavioral system in the infant and child proceeds in an orderly fashion. If, then, one identifies different behavioral patterns and defines them, they can each become a subject for assessment or diagnosis. Gesell and Amatruda[14] were pioneers in conceptualizing and describing this orderly process of development. They defined and carefully observed five fields of behavior: adaptive behavior, gross motor behavior, fine motor behavior, language behavior, and personal-social behavior. For them, these five areas formed the basic fabric of the behavioral repertoire of the developing child. The manner in which these areas developed was, in their view, an indicator of normal, deviant, or retarded development of the neurophysiological system.

Techniques for Examining the Newborn

SOME GENERAL CONSIDERATIONS

The focus of this material is the clinical appraisal of a child by a child psychiatrist or an allied professional. However, either the psychiatrist or psychologist may be involved in carrying out research on infants, and some reference will therefore be made to issues involved in examining babies in the framework of research as well as of clinical practice.

Ethical issues must be one of the primary considerations which enter into the planning and execution of examinations of newborns and infants. The examiner must develop every aspect of his experimental setting and procedures in such a way that he can honestly assure the person who is to give informed consent that the assessment procedure involves a very low probability of risk for the infant. This means not only that the examination procedure per se must not be invasive or harmful, but also that the general hygienic conditions of the laboratory or examining room and of the personnel involved must be high. One must check that the instruments which may be in contact with or used by the infant will be such that the infant cannot harm himself with them.

Anyone who is involved in examining infants, including the physician, should be screened for communicable diseases and should watch his daily stated health. For instance, incipient colds and sore throats should be a reason for canceling an examination. The obvious requirements have to be met as well; all personnel must wash their hands between the examination of every infant, and clean the objects or equipment with which the infant will come in contact.

Another ethical matter relates to the information given to the parent or guardian following the participation of an infant in the research project or following the clinical examination. If the examination is a clinical one, the decision as to what to tell the caretaker will be made within that framework. If the examination is for research purposes, one must be cognizant of the fact that the mother may have agreed to participate for any one of many reasons. It is important for all personnel working in this realm to be aware of this possibility and to be careful not to add to the caretaker's fears. It is often advisable to make additional clinical or supportive services available to mothers who do participate in an infant research project.

THE PHYSICAL SETTING FOR THE EXAMINATION OF NEWBORNS

In order to make a proper assessment of the neurological functioning and behavioral responses of the newborn, it is necessary to spend a considerable amount of time, under the best possible conditions, in a planned and careful interaction with the baby. It is advisable to have a separate examining room where one can obtain a high degree of control over the environment. The examiner must be able to define those reactions of the neonate which are specific to the stimuli which he is providing; hence, all important stimuli such as outside noise, temperature changes, and light conditions must be under his control. Temperature should be similar to that in the newborn nursery and warm enough to allow the infant to be comfortable when undressed. Light should be subdued, and, to the extent possible, extraneous noise should be excluded. Since considerable time must be spent examining the infant, it is best not to be under the feet of the busy nursing staff and in the hubbub of a full infant nursery. The infant himself should be examined under conditions which will best allow for his participation in the exam. The optimal time to see the infant is approximately an hour or so following the last feeding, so that hunger and irritability will not interfere. An initial observation at such a time will usually reveal that he is comfortably asleep. However, he should be capable of gradually being brought into an alert state.

All of the previous warnings regarding hygienic conditions must be particularly emphasized with newborns, and no person should examine such a baby who has not been trained in the necessary care.

If the examination is to include specialized procedures such as sleep studies, sucking studies, and so on, special arrangements are necessary. A description of such procedures is, however, beyond the scope of this chapter.

THE PHYSICAL SETTING FOR THE EXAMINATION OF OLDER INFANTS AND TODDLERS

As the child grows older, his ability to focus on specific stimuli increases, and the needs of a specialized examination room become somewhat less stringent. At that point, a good developmental evaluation demands only minor adaptations of the conventional furniture seen in the examining room of a well-baby clinic, an office, or even a home. Again, it is important that there be a separate room, as it is impossible to examine a child in a busy clinic with many other children around. One must always remember that surroundings are not to be taken for granted or overlooked. Even though the child's ability to focus on particular stimuli has improved with age, numerous aspects of the environment will continue to have stimulus value.

The minimal physical requirements are usually a free, flat surface on which the child can be placed to test his postural and gross motor capacities, and some restricted surface—a small testing table—on which various objects may be placed that will be used to elicit his reactions and to test his adaptive and fine motor behaviors. At earlier ages, the child can be provided with a low portable desk similar to a bed tray; at later ages, a nursery-size chair and table can be placed on the floor. (See figure 62–1.)

Both the physical setting for examining young children and the examination procedures to be used have been carefully described by Gesell and Amatruda; the newest edition of their textbook[14] will provide a good basic guide to anyone interested in the assessment of infants and toddlers. Illustrations and excerpts from their work are included here. It is suggested that anyone who wishes to become proficient at these examinations make full use of the basic text itself.

The materials for use in examining the development of the young child are a series of simple objects. (See figure 62–2.) Since the child uses such objects as play materials, they constitute control devices for eliciting behavior patterns which are specific to the child's developmental stage. These include such items as wooden cubes, pellets which can be put into a bottle, bells, and a ball.

PHYSICAL SETTING FOR THE EXAMINATION OF PARENT-INFANT INTERACTION

It was noted before that part of the assessment which is often made of the developing child deals with his reactions to his own caretaker. The interaction between the child and the caretaker can, of course, be observed in all situations. Pathological behavior of exceptional degree will probably manifest itself in most situations, whether in the physician's office or on a home visit. Much can be learned about the infant's reaction to the stimuli that he receives from the mother, and mother's reaction to the stimuli which she receives from the infant in these naturalistic types of observational settings. However, it is also possible to observe the dyadic interactions in more standardized settings unencumbered by the physical presence of the observer. Thus, particularly in research work, it is advisable to have available an observation room with a one-way screen where there is a feeling of relative nonintrusion, and where, in effect, the mother can be alone with her baby. Such observation rooms should be designed to make for a sense of relaxation so that the mother feels comfortable, and there should not be too many extraneous stimuli, such as decorations and so on. The examiner should be able to see as well as hear and, if possible, arrangements can be made for videotaping such observations for use in more exacting research studies.

SPECIFIC EXAMINATION PROCEDURES

Examination of the Newborn. As a basis for understanding the behavior of a newborn, one must first obtain a thorough medical assessment. This is usually carried out by the neonatologist; it is necessary for understanding the effects of disturbances which may have resulted from intrauterine influences or genetic disease. The assessment of the infant's neurological status has been described by various authors. One of the more sensitive and flexible examinations which is much used and recommended is that of Prechtl.* Some child psychiatrists might wish to familiarize themselves with this examination, in which case it is recommended that they make careful use of the manual written by Prechtl. The newborn's maturity at birth (i.e., gestational age) is usually assessed by the methods of Gruenwald,[12] Dubowitz et al.,[9] Lubchenko,[18] and others. The general medical and nutritional status should of course be observed, and it is in place to look for various minor physical anomalies which may be related to possible minimal brain damage.[25]

The child psychiatrist is likely to be principally interested in assessing the child's temperamental individualities, his reactivity to the environment, and his social responsiveness. The examiner should attempt to obtain a general feel for the capa-

---

* Prechtl, H. F. R., "The Neurological Examination of the Full-term Newborn Infant," *Clinics in Developmental Medicine*, vol. 63, Heinemann, London, 1977.

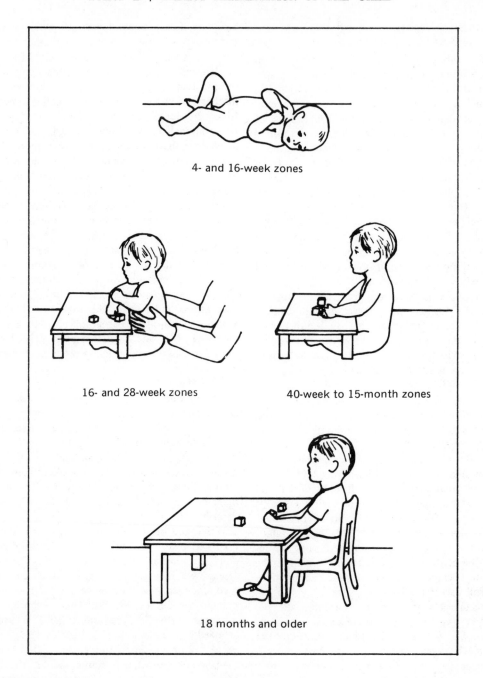

4- and 16-week zones

16- and 28-week zones

40-week to 15-month zones

18 months and older

FIGURE 62–1

Examination Arrangements Adapted to Advancing Grades of Postural Maturity: Supine, Supported Sitting, Free Sitting, and Chair Sitting

NOTE: Reprinted by permission of the publisher from *Gesell and Amatruda's Developmental Diagnosis*, 3rd ed., ed. H. Knobloch and B. Pasamanick (New York: Harper & Row, 1974), pp. 20–21. © 1974 by Harper & Row.

bilities of the child and his adaptability in dealing with his environment. He would want to know what things distinguish this particular infant from other infants, and how the infant orients toward stimuli, how capable are his homeostatic mechanisms, how irritable is he, and how social. To do

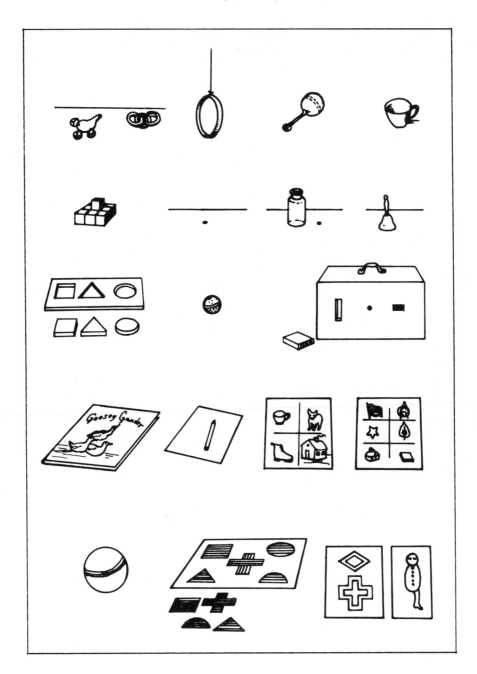

FIGURE 62–2

Examination materials: Catbells and tricolored rings, dangling ring, rattle, cup, cubes, pellet, pellet and bottle, bell, formboard and three blocks, small ball, performance box with square block, picture book, paper and crayon, picture cards, large ball, color forms, double diamond and cross, incomplete man.

NOTE: Reprinted by permission of the publisher from *Gesell and Amatruda's Developmental Diagnosis*, 3rd ed., ed. H. Knobloch and B. Pasamanick (New York: Harper & Row, 1974), pp. 20–21. © 1974 by Harper & Row.

this he must seek a sensitive interaction with that infant and, hopefully, experience something of what the mother experiences in interacting with her baby.

The best available outline of such an examination has been developed by Berry Brazelton[4] in collaboration with a number of other people. Together they have devised a sensitive and fairly standardized examination procedure, which is based on a set of specific steps for handling the infant. In addition to this, the examination includes various scales which provide dimensions for evaluation. Some psychological methodologists who seek strictly reliable "tests" still question the use of these scales. At the same time, there is no doubt that anyone who goes through this procedure with a newborn will gain an excellent feeling for his capabilities and, what one might call his "personality."

When testing an infant, a prime consideration is the state of his consciousness, or what has come to be called "state." State depends upon various physiological variables, such as hunger, nutrition, state of hydration, and time within the infant's wake/sleep cycle. Varying patterns of state, as well as the amount of movement from one state to another, appear to be relevant characteristics which differentiate between different infants.

There are six states to be considered, two of sleep and four of wakefulness. They may be summarized as follows. (See figures 62–3 to 62–7.)

SLEEP STATES

1. Deep sleep with regular breathing, eyes closed, no spontaneous activity except startles or jerky movements at quite regular intervals; external stimuli produce startles with some delay; suppression of startles is rapid; and state changes are less likely than from other states. No eye movements (figure 62–3).
2. Light sleep with eyes closed; rapid eye movements can be observed under closed lids; low activity level is present with random movements and startles or startle equivalents; movements are likely to be smoother and more monitored than in State 1; the baby responds to internal and external stimuli with startle equivalents, often with a resulting change of state. Respirations are irregular, sucking movements occur on and off (figure 62–4).

AWAKE STATES

1. Drowsy or semi-dozing; eyes may be open or closed, eyelids fluttering; activity level variable, with interspersed, mild startles from time to time; the baby is reactive to sensory stimuli, but the response is often delayed; state change after stimulation is frequently noted (figures 62–5.1 and 62–5.2).

2. Alert, with bright look; seems to focus attention on source of stimulation, such as an object to be sucked, or a visual or auditory stimulus; impinging stimuli may break through, but with some delay in response. Motor activity is at a minimum (figure 62–6).
3. Eyes are open; considerable motor activity is present with thrusting movements of the extremities, and even a few spontaneous startles; the baby is reactive to external stimulation with an increase in startles or motor activity, but discrete reactions are difficult to distinguish because of the general high energy level.
4. Crying; characterized by intense crying which is difficult to break through with stimulation (figure 62–7).

When the examination begins, the infant's basic state is noted for a period of about two minutes, and during the whole examination, which usually takes twenty to thirty minutes, careful note should be taken about the number of changes and types of changes in the infant's state.

The items which are involved in assessing the newborn include the following.

1. Response Decrement to Light
2. Response Decrement to Rattle
3. Response Decrement to Bell
4. Response Decrement to Pinprick
5. Orientation Response-Inanimate Visual
6. Orientation Response-Inanimate Auditory
7. Orientation-Animate Visual
8. Orientation-Animate Auditory
9. Orientation-Animate Visual and Auditory
10. Alertness
11. General Tonus
12. Motor Maturity
13. Pull-to-Sit
14. Cuddliness
15. Defensive Movements
16. Consolability with Intervention
17. Peak of Excitement
18. Rapidity of Buildup
19. Irritability
20. Activity
21. Tremulousness
22. Amount of Startle During Exam
23. Lability of Skin Color
24. Lability of States
25. Self-quieting Activity
26. Hand to Mouth Facility
27. Smiles

An examination of this type (described by Brazelton) can be considered the mainstay of the behavioral assessment of the newborn. However, there are a number of additional types of observations and testing techniques which have been used and are sometimes of special value. One of the foremost is the testing of the child's sucking behavior.[15] Kron and others have also described sucking behavior and found it to be highly related to neural functioning in the newborn.

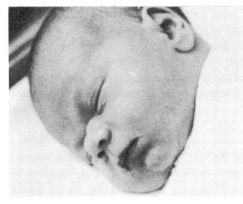

FIGURE 62-3

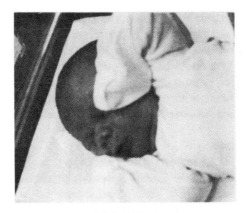

FIGURE 62-4

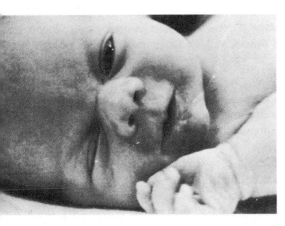

FIGURE 62-5.1

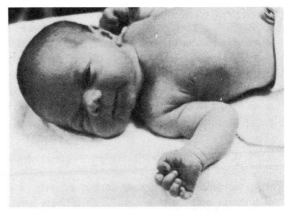

FIGURE 62-5.2

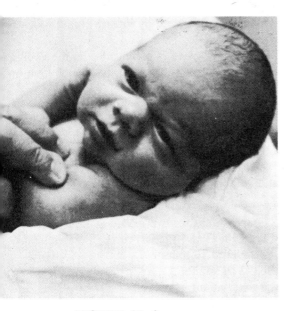

FIGURE 62-6

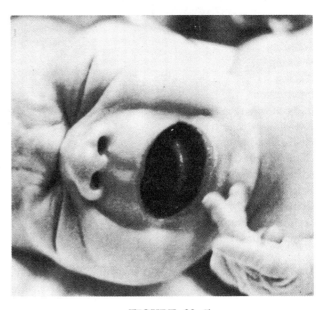

FIGURE 62-7

SOURCE: Reprinted by permission of the publisher from *A Neo-Natal Assessment Scale, Clinics in Developmental Medicine,* vol 50, ed. T. B. Brazelton (Philadelphia: Lippincott, 1973) pp. 6–7.

Other specialized techniques which are principally used for research involve the polygraphic study of sleep state[21, 22] and examination of autonomic reactivity.[17]

Examination of the Infant
(1-18 months)

MOTOR, ADAPTIVE, LANGUAGE, AND PERSONAL-SOCIAL BEHAVIOR

The examination of the growing and developing infant in terms of the behavioral characteristics representing his adaptive, motor, language, and social development was most clearly set out in the pioneering observations of Gesell and Amatruda.

The original work of Gesell and Amatruda has recently been reviewed and brought up to date in the third edition of their classic book, *Developmental Diagnosis*,[14] edited by two specialists in the field, Hilda Knobloch and Benjamin Pasamanick. Anyone interested in gaining a clearer understanding of developmental issues and examination procedures during infancy should use this book as a manual. Here an outline of the basic procedures will be given. Another standard examination which is in wide use today was developed by Nancy Bayley; the Bayley Scales can be learned from her manual.[2]

The Gesell and Bayley scales are based on an extended examination of the child, which usually takes anywhere from thirty minutes to an hour. Any child suspected of having some developmental deviancy merits such a careful assessment. Attempts have been made to devise screening tests which can be done in less time and can be administered by public health nurses or even by paraprofessionals. These abbreviated studies are intended only as winnowing devices to try to identify the deviant youngsters in large populations of children and refer them for closer, more thorough assessment. The most commonly used screening device in the United States is the Denver Developmental Screening Test.[10] (See figure 62–8.)

It is worth stressing again that infants do develop at different rates and there is certainly a natural range within which any given infant will arrive at a particular developmental stage. However, certain key ages have been picked for testing; these are 4, 16, 28, 40, and 52 weeks, and 18 months. Gesell felt that these were integrative periods which present major shifts in focus in the centers of behavioral organization. The basic developmental sequences are summarized in figures 62–9.1 through 62–9.6

The examinations, as described by the authors, are to be found in their book, *Gesell and Amatruda's Developmental Diagnosis*.[14] The diagrams which they have developed and which appeared originally in their text are in a measure self-explanatory. They are included here to give the reader a sense of how these studies are conducted at the various levels of development. (See figures 62-10.1 through 62-15.12.)

VISUAL ATTENTION

The ability of a young child to attend to a specific stimulus seems to be of diagnostic significance. Problems of attention are certainly seen in various pathological situations, such as minimal brain dysfunction. Examination of attention in the young infant may thus prove to be helpful to the clinician as well as to the researcher. Admittedly, at the time that this chapter is being written, very little work has been done regarding clinical use of attention, but considering the rapid development in the field of developmental testing, it would seem appropriate at least to mention these examinations briefly. Infants are usually presented with certain specific visual stimuli, such as complex patterns or pictures of the human face, and the amount of time which the individual infant concentrates on looking at this visual stimulus is recorded. The physical setup for such an examination can vary from something relatively simple to be used for finding gross differences, to quite sophisticated situations used in research.[13]

COGNITIVE DEVELOPMENT

The developmental quotients which result from infant testing are based largely on motor development and adaptive social behavior. It is important to keep in mind that these quotients do not show very high correlations with later examinations of IQ. Without going into all of the problematics of testing and the theories regarding IQ assessments, it would seem relevant to mention that several developmental psychologists feel that later intellectual capacities are directly related to early development of the various cognitive functionings. Accordingly, they have attempted to devise tests and scales which are oriented to this parameter of development. The views of these authors are based primarily on the research and theoretical framework of Piaget. They conceive of psychological development as an elaboration of cognitive structures which also have motivational and emo-

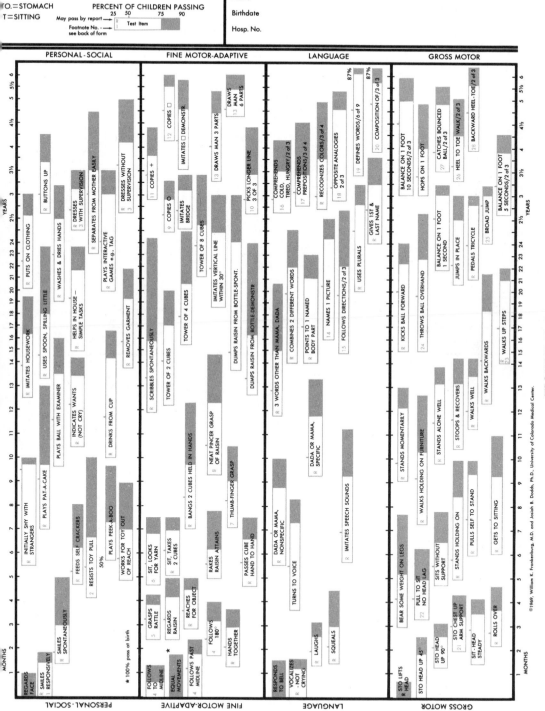

FIGURE 62–8

NOTE: Reprinted by permission of the publisher from "The Denver Developmental Screening Test," by W. K. Frankenburg and J. B. Dodds in *Journal of Pediatrics*, vol. 71, 1967, p. 185.

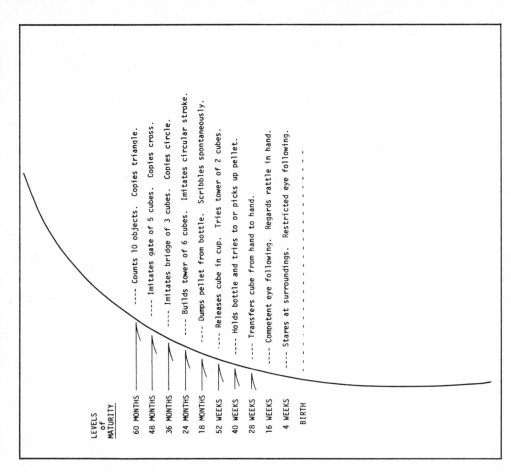

FIGURE 62-9.2

Developmental sequences of adaptive behavior.

To determine how the infant exploits the environment we present him with a variety of simple objects. The small one-inch cubes serve not only to test motor coordination, but also reveal the child's capacity to put his motor equipment to constructive and adaptive ends. The cube tests create an objective opportunity for the examiner to observe adaptivity in action—motor coordination combined with judgment. Such tests illustrate the principles which also underlie the de-

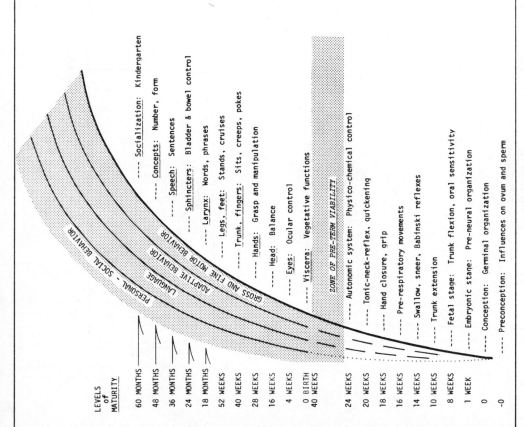

FIGURE 62-9.1

The development of behavior in the five major fields.

NOTE: Figures 62-9.1, 62-9.2, 62-9.3, 62-9.4, 62-9.5, 62-9.6 reprinted by permission of the publisher from *Gesell and Amatruda's Developmental Diagnosis*, 3rd ed., ed. H. Knobloch and B. Pasamanick (New York: Harper & Row, 1974), pp. 9-14, 20-21, 29-31, 39-41, 51-53,

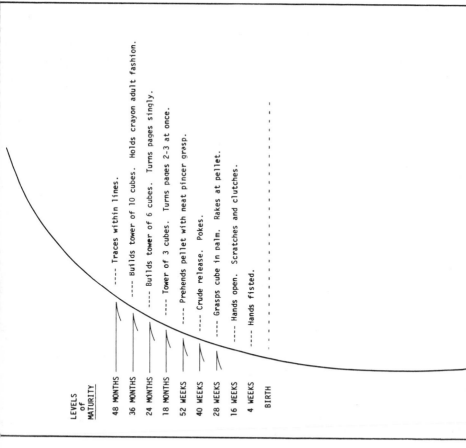

LEVELS
of
MATURITY

48 MONTHS ——— ---- Traces within lines.

36 MONTHS ——— ---- Builds tower of 10 cubes. Holds crayon adult fashion.

24 MONTHS ——— ---- Builds tower of 6 cubes. Turns pages singly.

18 MONTHS ——— ---- Tower of 3 cubes. Turns pages 2-3 at once.

52 WEEKS ——— ---- Prehends pellet with neat pincer grasp.

40 WEEKS ——— ---- Crude release. Pokes.

28 WEEKS ——— ---- Grasps cube in palm. Rakes at pellet.

16 WEEKS ——— ---- Hands open. Scratches and clutches.

4 WEEKS ——— ---- Hands fisted.

BIRTH ------------

FIGURE 62-9.4

Developmental sequences of fine motor behavior.

Fine motor control is evaluated by using small objects such as cubes, pellet, and string to elicit patterns of varying degrees of manual control.

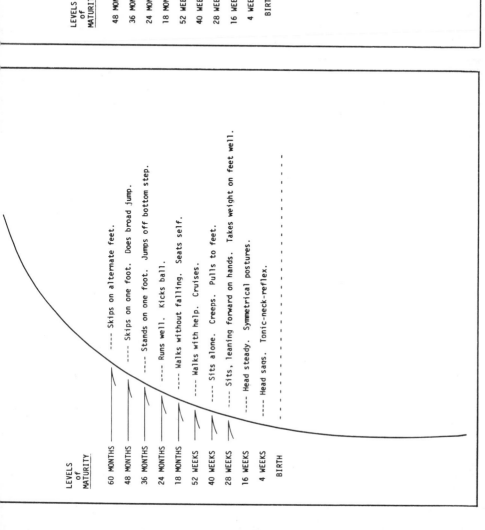

LEVELS
of
MATURITY

60 MONTHS ——— ---- Skips on alternate feet.

48 MONTHS ——— ---- Skips on one foot. Does broad jump.

36 MONTHS ——— ---- Stands on one foot. Jumps off bottom step.

24 MONTHS ——— ---- Runs well. Kicks ball.

18 MONTHS ——— ---- Walks without falling. Seats self.

52 WEEKS ——— ---- Walks with help. Cruises.

40 WEEKS ——— ---- Sits alone. Creeps. Pulls to feet.

28 WEEKS ——— ---- Sits, leaning forward on hands. Takes weight on feet well.

16 WEEKS ——— ---- Head steady. Symmetrical postures.

4 WEEKS ——— ---- Head sags. Tonic-neck-reflex.

BIRTH ------------

FIGURE 62-9.3

Developmental sequences of gross motor behavior.

To ascertain the maturity of postural control, we institute formal postural tests which reveal the repertoire of the infant's behavior: supine, prone, sitting, and standing.

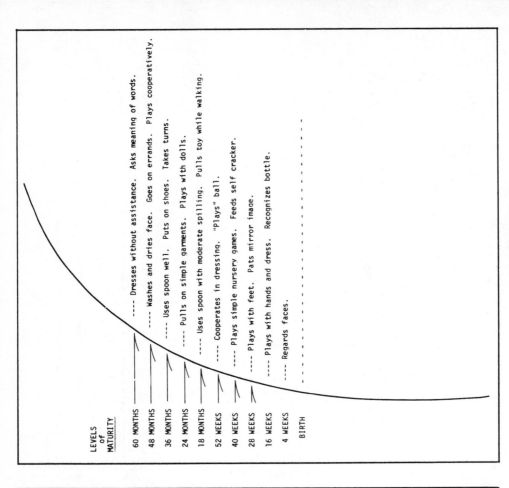

FIGURE 62-9.5

Developmental sequences of language behavior.

LEVELS of MATURITY

60 MONTHS —— Speaks without infantile articulation. Asks "Why?"

48 MONTHS —— Uses conjunctions. Understands prepositions.

36 MONTHS —— Talks in sentences. Answers simple questions

24 MONTHS —— Uses phrases. Understands simple directions.

18 MONTHS —— Jargons. Recognizes pictures.

52 WEEKS —— Says 2 or more words. Recognizes objects by name.

40 WEEKS —— Says one word. Imitates sounds.

28 WEEKS —— Vocalizes to toys. Makes single consonant syllables.

16 WEEKS —— Coos. Laughs. Vocalizes socially.

4 WEEKS —— Small throaty sounds. Heeds bell.

BIRTH

Language maturity is estimated in terms of articulation, vocabulary, adaptive use and comprehension. During the course of a developmental examination, both spontaneous and responsive language behavior is observed. Valuable supplementary information also is secured by questioning the adult familiar with the child's everyday behavior at home.

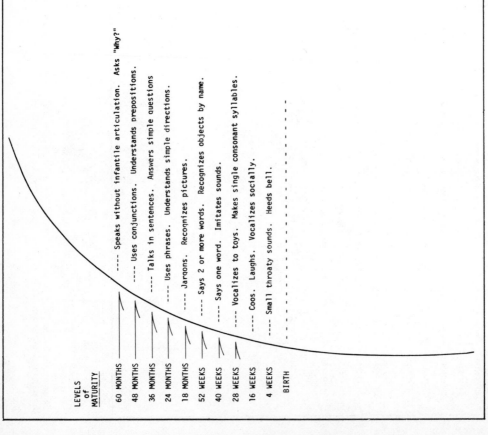

FIGURE 62-9.6

Developmental sequences of personal-social behavior.

LEVELS of MATURITY

60 MONTHS —— Dresses without assistance. Asks meaning of words.

48 MONTHS —— Washes and dries face. Goes on errands. Plays cooperatively.

36 MONTHS —— Uses spoon well. Puts on shoes. Takes turns.

24 MONTHS —— Pulls on simple garments. Plays with dolls.

18 MONTHS —— Uses spoon with moderate spilling. Pulls toy while walking.

52 WEEKS —— Cooperates in dressing. "Plays" ball.

40 WEEKS —— Plays simple nursery games. Feeds self cracker.

28 WEEKS —— Plays with feet. Pats mirror image.

16 WEEKS —— Plays with hands and dress. Recognizes bottle.

4 WEEKS —— Regards faces.

BIRTH

Personal-social behavior is greatly affected by the temperament of the child and by the behavior of the parents or others by whom he is reared. The range of individual variation is wide. Nevertheless, maturity factors and the degree of intactness of the central nervous system play a role in the socialization of the child. His social conduct is ascertained by incidental observation and by inquiry. The chart illustrates types of behavior which may be considered in evalu-

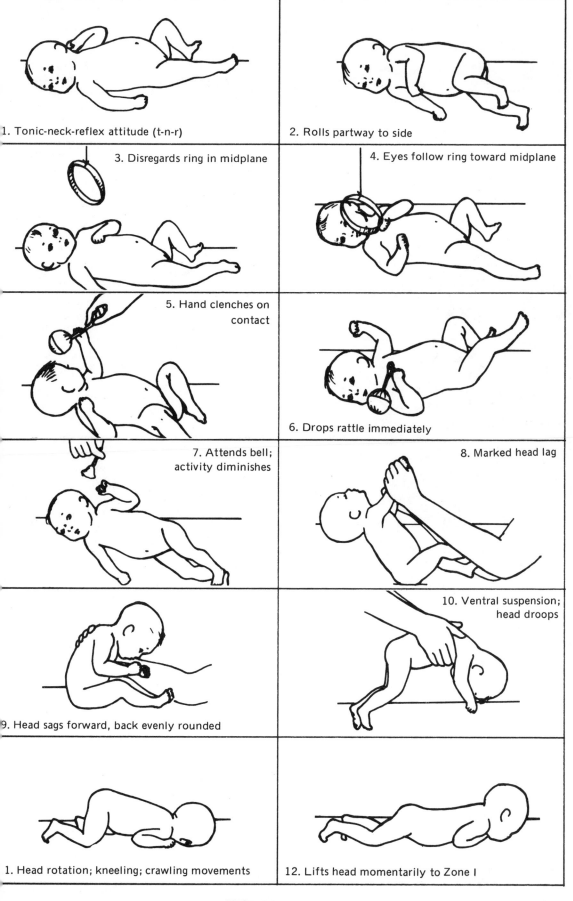

1. Tonic-neck-reflex attitude (t-n-r)

2. Rolls partway to side

3. Disregards ring in midplane

4. Eyes follow ring toward midplane

5. Hand clenches on contact

6. Drops rattle immediately

7. Attends bell; activity diminishes

8. Marked head lag

9. Head sags forward, back evenly rounded

10. Ventral suspension; head droops

11. Head rotation; kneeling; crawling movements

12. Lifts head momentarily to Zone I

FIGURE 62–10
Four Weeks or Less

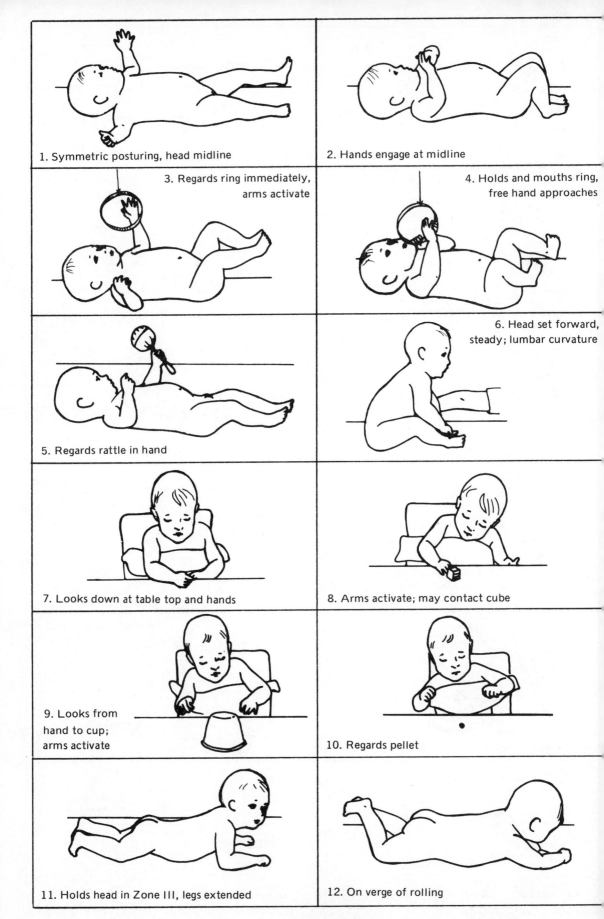

1. Symmetric posturing, head midline

2. Hands engage at midline

3. Regards ring immediately, arms activate

4. Holds and mouths ring, free hand approaches

5. Regards rattle in hand

6. Head set forward, steady; lumbar curvature

7. Looks down at table top and hands

8. Arms activate; may contact cube

9. Looks from hand to cup; arms activate

10. Regards pellet

11. Holds head in Zone III, legs extended

12. On verge of rolling

FIGURE 62–11
Sixteen Weeks

1. Transfers cube

2. Holds 2 cubes more than momentarily

3. Rakes at pellet

4. Bangs bell

5. Transfers and mouths bell

6. Regards image; pats glass

7. Sits momentarily leaning on hands

8. Sustains large fraction of weight; bounces

9. Lifts head

10. Transfers ring

11. Reaches with one hand

12. Feet to mouth

FIGURE 62–12
Twenty-eight Weeks

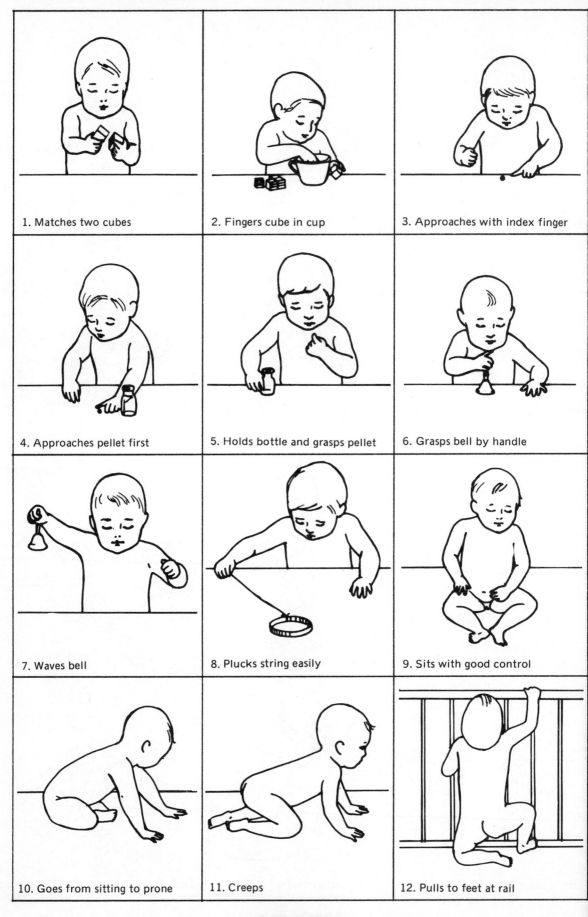

1. Matches two cubes

2. Fingers cube in cup

3. Approaches with index finger

4. Approaches pellet first

5. Holds bottle and grasps pellet

6. Grasps bell by handle

7. Waves bell

8. Plucks string easily

9. Sits with good control

10. Goes from sitting to prone

11. Creeps

12. Pulls to feet at rail

FIGURE 62–13
Forty Weeks

1. Applies cube on cube without release

2. Attempts tower; it falls

3. Releases one cube into cup after demonstration

4. Gives toy on request

5. Tries to insert pellet

6. Pellet falls outside bottle

7. Dangles ring by string

8. Looks selectively at round hole

9. May cast ball imitatively

10. Offers ball to mirror image

11. Walks when only one hand is held

12. Walks when only one hand is held

FIGURE 62–14
Fifty-two Weeks

1. Walks alone, seldom falls

2. Seats self in small chair

3. Turns pages two or three at a time

4. Builds tower of three

5. Fills cup with cubes

6. Dumps pellet from bottle

7. Imitates stroke

8. Identifies one picture

9. Hurls ball in standing

10. On command puts ball on chair

11. Walks into ball

12. Pulls toy

FIGURE 62–15
Eighteen Months

tional significance. The scales which are coming into use are those of Uzgiris and Hunt.[24] These authors have developed the following five scales:

Scale 1: The development of visual pursuit and the permanence of objects.
Scale 2: The development of means for obtaining desired environmental events.
Scale 3: The development of vocal imitation and the development of gestural imitation.
Scale 4: The development of operational causality.
Scale 5: The construction of object relations in space.
Scale 6: The development of schemes for relating to objects.

The reader interested in the details and the administration of such a test is referred to the basic description of these tests in *Assessment in Infancy* by Uzgiris and Hunt.

EXAMINATION OF TEMPERAMENT

The work of Thomas, Chess, and Birch has clearly illustrated the developmental role played by each infant's individual differences and temperamental qualities.[23] These determine the infant's interaction with the environment, the degree of consonance or dissonance between the infant and the environment, and the effect of this on the infant's behavior. It is, therefore, very much in place for the psychiatrist to make an assessment of the temperamental qualities of the infant. The information needed to evaluate these qualities can be elicited through careful questioning of parents and other caretakers. The behavioral reactions of the infant are surveyed in all types of activities, such as eating, sleeping, approaching new situations, bathing, and so on. A description of the temperamental characteristics and detailed methodology of questioning parents in order to elicit the specific type of information needed are described in the book of Thomas, Chess, and Birch.[23] While the specific research methodology involved in the search for temperamental information is rather lengthy, any clinician familiar with this area can easily get a good "feel" for the infant through some general questioning of the caretakers. Carey[6, 7] has worked out a questionnaire which can easily be filled in by parents or can be used by clinicians as a guideline to tap this information.

ASSESSMENT OF THE ENVIRONMENT AND THE INFANT'S EMOTIONAL ATTACHMENTS

As has been stressed over and over again, the development of a child is the result of a dynamic interaction between that child and his environ-ment. It is therefore vital to have a good picture of the world in which the child is growing up. There is no available methodology for describing that world which can be outlined here. However, various researchers, such as Greenberg and Hurley,[11] have tried to work out specific scales for such things as parental behavior and parental attitudes.

Ainsworth and Wittig[1] developed a structured observation situation to assess infant attachment behavior at the age of one year. The spontaneous behavior of the child is observed in eight "scenes" in which he is with mother, is left by mother, is with a stranger, etc. The behaviors are classified as proximity-seeking; proximity and interaction-avoiding; contact-maintaining; contact and inter-action-resisting; search; crying; and exploratory locomotion. These behaviors have been found to be sensitive criteria for the assessment of discrimination and selective responses of the infant towards his environment. However, all such "laboratory observations" should be complemented with a home visit where the infant and his caretaker can be seen in their natural setting.

Bettye Caldwell[5] has also described a scale for the assessment of the amount of stimulation which the child is receiving from his environment. It is useful in estimating the degree of deprivation which the infant may be experiencing.

SIGNS OF DISTURBED DEVELOPMENT

One may also look at the child in terms of function—thus, in the different areas of daily functioning, such as sleeping, eating, relating to other people, etc., he either is or is not behaving appropriately. To look at it another way, one might say that the examiner should look for "symptoms" of malfunctioning in the emotional sphere. One should try to assess the child's feelings and emotional development.

There are many symptoms which have been described to be pathognomonic of certain emotional conditions. This may well be so. However, one should constantly keep in mind many of the other basic qualities which have been discussed so far, such as the child's potentialities, his basic neuro-integrative status, and his temperament. Some of the classic symptoms of emotional malfunctioning, such as excessive activity, have often been found to belong to the area of temperament. Thus, the clinician must be careful to distinguish that which is primary and constitutional, from that which is secondary and reactive. It is necessary to assess and sort out those behaviors that are basically neurophysiological from those which are symptomatological (i.e., adaptive behaviors used to solve conflicts, in the psychoanalytic sense). Both are highly relevant to understanding the young child and require careful elucidation.

The Table 62–1 lists some of the common "symptoms" or maladaptive behaviors often seen in infants. The list is certainly not inclusive, nor is it meaningful in terms of etiology. Rather, it is intended only to guide the reader in looking for signs of malfunctioning. An understanding of the child's overall functioning will result only from a full assessment of all the various factors along with a careful consideration of their interactions.

Lois Murphy[19] has made an attempt to systematize the evaluation of all the items whose assessment has been described in this section. Her Vulnerability Inventory can be used as a theoretical framework within which the anamnestic, observational, and examination data can be ar-

Table 62–1

*Some Signs of Disturbance
in the First 18 Months of Life*

Tremors, flaccidity. Hypertension of muscles, stiffness, uncuddliness. Strange or unusual posturing.
Eating disturbances. Chronic vomiting, spitting, gagging, refusal of food, refusal to swallow.
Colic.
Sleep disturbances, excessive sleep, difficulty falling asleep.
Oversensitivity to stimuli, irritability, marked sensitivity to being handled.
Eczema.
Excessive crying, screaming, temper tantrums.
Poor affective responses, blank, or unchanging sad, or empty facial expression. Lack of approach behavior to mother or others, withdrawal, lack of interpersonal play. Lack of smiling.
Lack of vocal responsiveness. General lack of responsiveness to environment.
Hyperactivity and destructive activity.
Low frustration tolerance.
Negativistic behavior.
Excessive thumb sucking, finger chewing, biting, pica, teeth grinding, hitting, scratching, throwing, head banging, breath holding.
Fecal eating or smearing.
Anxiety. Fear of strangers with withdrawal. Fear of animals, strange places. Panic attacks.

---

ranged. This would be the first step in formulating a multifactorial diagnosis and an inclusive intervention plan. It is important that assessment aim at identifying strengths and capabilities as well as vulnerabilities; the child psychiatrist should do everything to help the family and the child capitalize upon those strengths to ensure optimal growth and development.

Conclusion

A few concluding remarks: The assessment of the newborn and infant is an essential procedure. It will provide the child psychiatrist with information that may be of untold value in helping shape the optimal conditions for a particular child's development. It may also provide the researcher with the baseline knowledge necessary for longitudinal studies of child development. However, development is a dynamic process influenced by multiple factors; and care must be taken that the conclusions derived from the initial assessment are limited to statements with a solid scientific basis. The predictive value of the currently available tools is still somewhat uncertain. In particular, the relationship between global behavior in infancy and specific behaviors in later life (such as performing well on some IQ test) is tenuous. The child psychiatrist should train himself to use the abundant information he can gain about the infant and his environment in a useful and careful way. If he does so, he may gain both important insights and valuable new objective knowledge, as well as provide excellent care to a mother-infant couple in need of his help. Ultimately, he will have a rewarding experience for himself.

Finally, it is necessary to stress that the whole field of the study of infant behaviors is a rapidly developing one. What has been outlined in this section is a mere sampling of what seem today to be some of the more useful clinical methods for assessing the newborn, the infant, and their environments. New methods will undoubtedly be forthcoming, and both students and practicing child psychiatrists should attempt to follow these developments.

REFERENCES

1. Ainsworth, M. D. S., and Wittig, B. A., Attachment and Exploratory Behavior of One-Year-Olds in a Strange Situation," in Foss, B. M. (Ed.), *Determinants of Infant Behavior*, vol. 4, pp. 111–136, Metheun, New York, 1969.
2. Bayley, N., *Bayley Scales of Infant Development—Manual*, The Psychological Corporation, New York, 1969.
3. Birch, H., and Gussow, G. D., *Disadvantaged Children*, Grune & Stratton, New York, 1970.
4. Brazelton, T. B. (Ed.), *A Neonatal Assessment Scale*, Clinics in Developmental Medicine, vol. 50, Heinemann, London, 1973.
5. Caldwell, B. M., "The Home Observation and Measurement of Environment (H.O.M.E.) Inventory," unpublished; available through Dr. Caldwell at the Center for Early Development and Education, 814 Sherman, Little Rock, Arkansas, 1973.
6. Carey, W. B., "Clinical Applications of Infant Temperament Measurements," *Journal of Pediatrics, 81:* 823–828, 1972.
7. ———, "A Simplified Method for Measuring Infant Temperament," *Journal of Pediatrics,* 77:188–194, 1970.
8. Cattell, P., *The Measurement of Intelligence in Infants and Young Children*, The Psychological Corporation, New York, 1947.
9. Dubowitz, L. M., Dubowitz, V., and Goldberg, C., "Clinical Assessment of Gestational Age in the Newborn Infant," *Journal of Pediatrics,* 77:1, 1970.
10. Frankenburg, W. K., and Dodds, J. B., "The Denver Developmental Screening Test," *Journal of Pediatrics,* 71:181–191, 1967.
11. Greenberg, N. H., and Hurley, J., "The Maternal Personality Inventory," in Hellmuth, J. (Ed.), *The Exceptional Infant,* vol. 2, pp. 128–151, Brunner-Mazel, New York, 1971.
12. Grvenwald, P., "Growth of the Human Fetus: I. Normal Growth and Its Variations," *American Journal of Obstetrics and Gynecology,* 94:1112–1119, 1966.
13. Horowitz, F. D., "Infant Attention and Discrimination: Methodological and Substantive Issues," in Horowitz, F. D. (Ed.), *Visual Attention, Auditory Stimulation and Language Discrimination in Young Infants,* vol. 39, nos.

5–6, pp. 1–15, University of Chicago Press, Chicago, 1974.
14. Knobloch, H., and Pasamanick, B. (Eds.), *Gesell and Amatruda's Developmental Diagnosis,* 3rd ed., Harper & Row, New York, 1974.
15. Kron, R. E., Stein, M., and Goddard, K. E., "A Method of Measuring Sucking Behavior in Newborn Infants," *Psychosomatic Medicine,* 25:181–191, 1963.
16. Lewis, M., and Rosenblum, L. A. (Eds.), *The Effect of the Infant on Its Caregiver,* John Wiley, New York, 1974.
17. Lipton, E. L., Steinschneider, A., and Richmond, J. B., "The Autonomic Nervous System in Early Life," *New England Journal of Medicine,* 273:147–154, 201–208, 1965.
18. Lubchenco, L. O., "Assessment of Gestational Age and Development at Birth," *Pediatric Clinics of North America,* 17:125, 1970.
19. Murphy, L. B., "The Vulnerability Inventory," in Chandler, C. A., Lourie, R. S., and Peters, A. Dettuff (Eds.), *Early Child Care: The New Perspectives,* pp. 364–372, Atherton Press, New York, 1968.
20. Parmalee, A., et al., "Maturation of EEG Activity During Sleep in Premature Infants," *Electroencephalography and Clinical Neurophysiology,* 24:319–329, 1968.
21. Prechtl, H., et al., "Polygraphic Studies of the Full-term Newborn," in Bax, M. C., and MacKeith, R. C. (Eds.), *Clinics in Developmental Medicine,* vol. 27, pp. 1–40, Heinemann, London, 1968.
22. Schulte, F., Hinze, G., and Schrempf, G., "Maternal Toxemia, Fetal Malnutrition and Bioelectric Brain Activity of the Newborn," *Neuropaediatrie,* 2:439–460, 1971.
23. Thomas, A., Chess, S., and Birch, H., *Temperament and Behavior Disorders in Children,* New York University Press, New York, 1968.
24. Uzgiris, I. C., and Hunt, J. McV., *Assessment in Infancy,* University of Illinois Press, Urbana, 1975.
25. Waldrop, M. F., and Halverson, L. F., "Minor Physical Anomalies and Hyperactive Behavior in Young Children," in Hellmuth, J. (Ed.), *The Exceptional Infant,* vol. 2, pp. 343–380, Brunner-Mazel, New York, 1971.

63 / Examination of the Preschool and School-age Child

Richard L. Cohen

Suggested Space and Equipment

For a workmanlike performance, the correct tools are necessary. The space and equipment recommended for diagnostic interviews with preschool and school-age children need not be extensive or elaborate; on the other hand, the particular needs of this age group require certain special adaptations. Where the situation is at all flexible, the same type of space and equipment can be used for both preschoolers and school-age children.

Some clinicians prefer a "playroom" specifically set up for this purpose and apart from the regular office space. Others would rather set aside a corner or a portion of their office which can be demarcated with bookcases or dividers; this serves as a space clearly earmarked for children's spontaneous movement and play. There should be a variety of chairs of different sizes, with some of the furniture designed to fit small children. The floor should be made either of asphalt tile, which is easily cleaned, or of some other hard, nonabsorbent material. Expensive paintings, bric-a-brac, or other valuables should be excluded from this part of the office. It is wise to have cabinets which can be locked; it is then possible to expose overactive or very low threshold children to a few specific objects or games on a selective basis.

Running water and sandboxes are best confined to a formal playroom situation and to the subsection of an office. Considering the havoc that may be wrought by hyperaggressive or messy children, and the high cost of maintaining order and cleanliness in what is basically an office setting, their value for short-term diagnostic work is at best dubious.

Clinicians differ, to some degree, on the issue of number and diversity of playthings with which an examining or therapy room should be stocked. Some prefer a few very simple toys and attempt to keep the interviews mainly verbal and interactive. Others may provide scores of playthings in the expectation that these will enable almost any child to select some object or activity with which he may be comfortable.

Most assume a more intermediate position and contend that it is more important to have a modest number of well-chosen items than to have a large smorgasbord. Too much choice can be a little bewildering to some children, and may interfere with the child's ability to concentrate on a smaller range of appropriate activities.

The most useful items include:

1. A variety of writing and drawing materials. (Useful for observing sensory-motor integration, perception, body image, mood, range of intellectual functioning, fantasy life, family dynamics, use of symbols, etc.)
2. A selection of human figures (of several occupations, ages, sex, race, etc.), hand puppets, animals (wild and domestic), along with some form of playhouse which includes furniture and other housekeeping equipment. (This is useful for making observations on the child's understanding of family dynamics, ego ideals, social role identity, ego defensive structure, fantasy life, etc.)
3. A collection of vehicles such as trucks, planes, cars, etc., is important. (Children use these to express aggressive fantasies, social role identity, and object relatedness.)
4. A variety of games and puzzles is necessary. The materials should cover a wide span of developmental periods from approximately thirty months to twelve years. They can include both games of skill and chance and games which do and others which do not emphasize competitive activity. Time-consuming games like card games should be avoided since the need to "finish the game" will often extend them beyond the period when useful observations can be made. (Again, these lend themselves to observations of the level of sensory-motor integration, concept formation, ethical structure, self-image, ego defenses, level of intellectual functioning, the manner in which child handles both success and failure, etc.)
5. Materials for fabrication and construction; for example, blocks, tinker toys, etc., are desirable. (These are useful for observing object relatedness, sensory-motor integration, spatial orientation, conceptual thinking, etc.)
6. "Communicaton" instruments such as toy telephones are important. The clinician's own dictating equipment or tape recorder may be invaluable with older children; it allows them to speak into an impersonal instrument without having to confront the clinician directly. (These measure articulation and maturity of speech and allow for the expression of mood, fantasy life, and even insight.)
7. Toy guns and other weapons will be improvised by the children in any case and are best supplied. (They allow access to aggressive fantasies particularly where the child views them as solutions to interpersonal difficulties.)
8. The matter of candy or other edibles requires a note. Many clinicians do use food both during the diagnostic and treatment phases (in the latter instance, food usually assumes very different significance).[5] During diagnosis, sweets are probably best used sparingly but are often useful in work with: very young children; very primitive, regressed children; or children from extremely deprived backgrounds.

A modest selection from the above categories will meet the needs of both preschoolers and school-age children. The availabilty of such attractive and physically safe objects will often facilitate the interchange of the examination, and will help many kinds of children to communicate useful information.

Preparation of the Child for the Interview

The importance of this preparation is hard to overestimate.[1] A great deal of valuable clinical time can be wasted if the child is brought for an examination with no preparation, or with preparation that has been deceptive and inappropriate.

Parents will naturally have some anxiety about bringing a young child for psychiatric evaluation. In part, at least, that anxiety can be tempered by the clinician by means of some anticipatory counseling and by offering some guidelines about constructive preparation of the child. This preparation can be a regular part of the history-taking sessions with the parents and should come toward the end of an interview in which next steps are being discussed.

Nine times out of ten, the child is not even aware of the fact that the parents have already consulted a child psychiatrist. This is because the parents are either experiencing a high level of anxiety and defensiveness about the move, or are simply nonplussed about what to tell the child.

In working with parents about this, it is important to avoid formula or cookbook approaches. A good way to begin is to ask first whether the child knows that the parents have consulted someone for professional help. The most common answer is no. Where appropriate, the clinician should then indicate that the next step will require a direct interview with the child. What had the parent or parents thought they might tell the child about this? Again, it is best to solicit responses from the parents first. This in itself is an important diagnostic step; the parents' answer often reveals a great deal about their own feelings toward seeking help, about what they fear is really wrong with the child, and about the struggles with guilt, inadequacy, or hostility they may be going through in the course of taking this step.

If the parental response seems to be sound, constructive, and geared to the developmental level of the child, they then need only the support and reassurance to continue with this line of thinking. Most commonly, the response is not, or the parent will "draw a blank" and ask for help. It is then important to stress that "honesty is the best policy." Both parents should be encouraged first to take the child aside. This is particularly important if there are other children in the house and privacy is an issue. In most cases, the relevant matters have come up many times in the past, at home or in school, and have been discussed previously. In speaking with the child, the parents should refer to these events, and explain their own concerns about the child in language which is meaningful and nonaccusatory. They should tell the child that they have made many efforts to understand what is wrong and to help him but that they have not felt entirely successful in doing so. Now they are seeking the help of a doctor who has a particular interest in children who are having some problem in ———— (and here the parent can be more specific, relating the purpose of the interview to the nature of the difficulties which the child is having). If the child has expressed "un-happiness" or discomfort in some area, this should be referred to by the parents.

The timing of this explanation is rather important. For very young children, it should precede the diagnostic session by no more than twenty-four hours. For older children, several days' notice is desirable. In both instances, this permits the child to think about it, to ask questions, and to get as much clarification as possible. Many parents will not be able to provide much help here because they themselves are so uncertain about what will happen to the child once he gets to the office. They tend to fall back on stereotypes and to reassure the child that this is "a worry doctor" or "talking doctor" who doesn't wear a white coat, or examine you physically, or give you shots. This is probably as much as can be hoped for from any given parent; the chances are, however, that these are not particularly useful statements. Their net effect is to emphasize what will not happen, and to set this doctor apart from others. In fact, the etiology of the child's disordered behavior is very uncertain at this point and all kinds of physical procedures may indeed turn out to be necessary and may be ordered by this doctor before the diagnostic work is complete.

The child should be told that he will have one or more sessions with this doctor. The purpose is to give the doctor a chance to get to know him as well as possible and to understand as much as he can about what he is good at and what he is having some trouble with. When the doctor understands enough, he will try to help the parents (and school, etc.) to help the child cope with these matters in a more satisfying way.

The imparting of this information by the parents should be done in a firm, supportive, and unequivocal fashion. It is not appropriate for the child to be making choices or decisions about whether he will participate in such an evaluation. Where it is anticipated that the child will openly oppose such a move, the parents can be instructed to say to the child, in effect, "Look, you are expected to go. We have an appointment on such and such a date. We will be taking you at that time. What you do when you get inside the office with the doctor—whether you tell him anything or do anything else when you get there—that part of it is your business and is between you and the doctor. No one can force you to use the time in a certain way. All we can do as your parents is provide this opportunity and, in our opinion, this is necessary now."

During this preparatory period, the clinician should also be trying to collect as much collateral information about the child as possible (with, of course, parental permission). This can be obtained from schools, pediatricians, or other health agencies; it is often appropriate to request the child's birth record. Perusal of this information as it arrives may even result in some modification of the "game plan" and give rise to a request for other evaluations or studies prior to the initial psychiatric examination. This is a matter of individual judgment on the part of each clinician.

Since the school represents such a rich resource for useful data, it is particularly important to request information about the child in a form which: (1) is meaningful and understandable to educators; (2) communicates a sense of respect and understanding about behavior which is best observed and measured in a school setting; and (3) requires a minimal amount of "paper work" in view of the other heavy demands on educators. Many facilities have developed standard instruments for such a purpose. For an example of an instrument which has proved useful, see figure 63–1.

Finally, the child's response to the knowledge that he is coming for a psychiatric examination may be so atypical or so unexpected as to be shocking to the parents; it too may provide new insights or useful information. The parents should be instructed that if anything new or different arises in the course of preparing the child for the examination, this information should be telephoned in ahead of time. It is important data and

FIGURE 63–1

SCHOOL QUESTIONNAIRE

To the teacher: *The intent of this questionnaire is to obtain information about the child from your perspective. Your time in completing this questionnaire is appreciated.*

Date: _____

Child's Name: _____ Grade: _____
            (Last)   (First)   (Middle)

Birthdate: _____ Age: _____

Parents: _____ Address: _____ Phone: _____

Teacher: (Mr. Ms. Dr.) _____

Principal: (Mr. Ms. Dr.) _____

School: _____ Phone: _____
    (Name of School)   (Address)   (District)

I. *GENERAL CLASSROOM INFORMATION*

1. Number of children in class: _____
2. Is this a special or ungraded class? ( ) Yes ( ) No
   If yes, briefly describe type of child in it:
3. Are you the child's primary teacher? ( ) Yes ( ) No
   If no, specify:
4. How long have you known the child? _____
5. Compared to most classes of this grade, this child's class as a whole is:
   ( ) Faster ( ) Average ( ) Slower

II. *ACADEMIC PERFORMANCE*

1. In comparison with *other children in the class*, the child's general level of achievement is:

   ( ) Far Above Average
   ( ) Above Average
   ( ) Average
   ( ) Below Average
   ( ) Far Below Others in Class

FIGURE 63–1 (*Continued*)

2. How does the child compare with other children in the class in each of the following areas?

	Upper ¼	Middle ½	Lower ¼
Reading	( )	( )	( )
Arithmetic	( )	( )	( )
Spelling	( )	( )	( )
Oral expression	( )	( )	( )
Written expression	( )	( )	( )
Social Studies	( )	( )	( )
Science	( )	( )	( )
Art	( )	( )	( )
Music	( )	( )	( )
Physical Education	( )	( )	( )

3. Has there been any change in academic or social behavior in the past six months?
( ) Yes   ( ) No
If yes, briefly describe:

4. Have there been any notable changes in academic or social behavior during the entire school career?   ( ) Yes   ( ) No
If yes, briefly describe:

5. Tests administered: (Please disregard this item if testing information will be sent under separate cover.)

   a. Date _____

   b. Test _____

   c. Result(s) _____

III. *BEHAVIORAL CHECKLIST*

This section contains statements which describe various child behaviors. Check the column which is appropriate. As you make each rating, judge the child in comparison with other children of the same sex and age.

Motivation and Attitude	Much less than most children	Less	Slightly less	Slightly more	More	Much more than most children
1. Shows concern with academic progress.						
2. Feels he can make progress academically.						
3. Feels he can learn to control behavior.						
4. Respects class rules and routines.						
5. Feels rewarded by acquisition of skills.						
6. Finds completing tasks rewarding.						
7. Feels rewarded by attention and praise.						
8. Feels rewarded by tangible rewards (candy, etc.)						
9. Has positive attitude toward self.						
10. Has realistic view of abilities and disabilities.						

Comments:

FIGURE 63–1 (*Continued*)

Behavior in the Classroom

	Much less than most children	Less	Slightly less	Slightly more	More	Much more than most children
1. Has self control.						
2. Is hyperactive in class.						
3. Destroys/damages property.						
4. Is disruptive in class.						
5. Is impulsive.						
6. Has to be excluded from classroom.						
7. Daydreams.						
8. Becomes angry.						
9. Tolerates frustration.						
10. Becomes upset by changes in routine.						
11. Provokes other children.						

Comments:

Task-Related Classroom Performance

	Much less than most children	Less	Slightly less	Slightly more	More	Much more than most children
1. Completes assignments.						
2. Accepts responsibility for performance.						
3. Work is sloppy.						
4. Performance is commensurate with ability.						
5. Deals effectively with academic failures.						
6. Exhibits motor difficulties.						
7. Exhibits visual perception difficulties.						
8. Exhibits auditory perception difficulties.						
9. Has fine motor coordination appropriate to age.						
10. Expresses interest in wide variety of subjects.						
11. Is flexible in learning tasks.						
12. Follows instructions.						
13. Retains material learned.						
14. Moves from one task to another easily.						
15. Accepts constructive criticism and correction of work.						
16. Concern about correctness of work interferes with work performance.						
17. Attends to task until completion.						
18. Has confidence in learning new tasks.						
19. Works independently.						
20. Is distracted by extraneous stimuli.						

Comments:

Adult Relationships

	Much less than most children	Less	Slightly less	Slightly more	More	Much more than most children
1. Trusts adults.						
2. Tries to manipulate adults.						
3. Is dependent upon adults.						
4. Avoids closeness to adults of same sex.						
5. Avoids closeness to adults of opposite sex.						
6. Ues adults well in working through problems.						

Comments:

FIGURE 63–1 (*Continued*)

Peer Relationships	Much less than most children	Less	Slightly less	Slightly more	More	Much more than most children
1. Relates successfully with peers.						
2. Gets into fights.						
3. Is considerate of needs of peers.						
4. Deals effectively with competitive situations.						
5. Shares with peers.						
6. Demonstrates positive leadership qualities.						
7. Is sought out by peers.						
8. Gains peer attention in a negative way.						
9. Is isolated by peers.						
10. Isolates self from peers.						
11. Is openly rejected by peers.						
12. Is manipulated by peers.						
13. Participates in peer group activities.						

Comments:

IV. GENERAL DESCRIPTION

Please describe the child. Include examples of typical classroom behavior and any special circumstances that influence his social adjustment.

Signature_____

NOTE: The contributions of Robin Barack, M.Ed., Vivian T. Harway, Ph.D., Anne Bowes, Ph.D., and Virginia Fargione, M.S.W. (Pittsburgh Child Guidance Center) in developing this questionnaire are gratefully acknowledged.

may assist the clinician substantially in facilitating the initial phase of the examination or in handling some of the child's resistance more expeditiously.

Conduct of the Examination

There are innumerable formats and outlines for the clinical examination of a child. Many of these are excellent and serve the purpose admirably. Each clinician or setting needs to choose a basic format which makes sense in terms of its particular spirit, is comfortable for all concerned, and fits well within the overall conceptual framework in which the group operates. The findings which arise from such a study are used for many purposes. Thus, reports to governmental sources, funding agencies, and other financial and service entities involve certain kinds of information. On the other hand, information of quite different character may be required for selecting treatment options and for the initial phases of treatment planning. In any case, it is most important that the data should indicate possible need for other kinds of studies prior to making a decision.

The direct examination of the child may be divided into four steps: (1) initial contact, (2) beginning phase of interview, (3) body of the interview, and (4) termination.

These will be discussed in sequence. Throughout, the purpose is to acquire data concerning the child's developmental level, constitutional endowment, defenses and other coping mechanisms, interpersonal skills, capacity for communication, and other similar information. This will be combined with data obtained from parents and other sources to flesh out as complete a picture of the child as possible. The reader is once more referred to the diagram in figure 58–1. The developmental interview is aimed at collecting information in almost all of the parameters represented in that schema. The function of the direct examination is to explore, through the senses of a trained observer, various aspects of the child's current functioning. This will not only add facts which others have not been trained to look for but will serve as an additional reliability check on many observations by other significant adults in the child's life.

This usually occurs in a waiting room or antechamber. Regardless of the age of the child, at the time of the first contact, the clinician should go to the waiting room, greet the adult(s) accompanying the child, and then turn rather quickly to the child. If the parents do not introduce the doctor promptly, then he should do so himself in a pleasant, brief, and casual way. At this point, he should state that he and the child are now going off to his office (or whatever designation seems appropriate), and that they will be there for x minutes, after which they will return to the waiting room to the parents.

The doctor should then move in an anticipatory way in the direction of his office, clearly communicating to the child an expectation to follow. With very young children, handholding or a hand on the shoulder may be appropriate.

At this point, the child will be particularly alert to parental cues. If there is marked ambivalence in the parent about separation from the child or about the whole diagnostic process, this will be communicated by body movements and facial expression. In any event, the child will respond to such signals with fussing, resistance, or open opposition.

In the face of this, the clinician should continue to reassure the child and to indicate calmly and firmly that he is to accompany him to the office. It is now of critical importance to observe whatever parental behavior occurs. Parents may suddenly "go limp." They may remove their attention from the child and direct it to the clinician either with explanations such as, "You see—this is the way he is, this is what we were talking about." Or, the communication (verbal or nonverbal) may be, "You're the expert. Let's see what you can do about this." It is important here for the clinician to indicate both by word and deed that the decision to bring the child was a parental one and that the responsibility for remanding the child into the temporary charge of the clinician is also a parental one.

When there are serious problems about separation, rapid waiting-room decisions need to be made. These problems arise frequently. If the child is very young, it may be wise to start the interview a little early so that the parent accompanies the child to the office and is present for the first several minutes of the examination. This can even be explained to the child ahead of time so that he is prepared for it. With older children, if a "scene" is developing in the waiting room, if the child is experiencing some panic on separation, and if the clinician does not see adequate parental support to separate, it is then better to bring mother and child to the office together. The separation can then be handled in a more graduated and controlled fashion. Generally, the child will come to the office easily if the mother comes along.

Once both are in the office, it becomes possible to discuss more openly what the child may be afraid of. As a rule, the anxiety derives from concern with mother, or the child may fear that some painful or mutilating procedure awaits him in the office. Occasionally, the fear is ersatz, and is used by the child as a countercontrol measure against the responsible adults.

Whatever the case, it is easier to make decisions in the office than it is in the waiting room. The child should be given an opportunity to explore the office physically so that it becomes less frightening and unknown; the mother should once more be encouraged to repeat that she will be present and available in the waiting room at the completion of the examination. This procedure may take approximately ten minutes; having gone through it, the clinician should then indicate to the mother that she may depart. Where it is clinically appropriate, firm but gentle physical restraint of the child may be employed at this point. As a rule, not only is this not harmful to the diagnostic process, but, on the contrary, it is often reassuring to the child. Many a child becomes overwhelmed in the face of family behavior which endows him with enormous power to control events and which encourages unrealistic feelings of omnipotence.

One final word about the waiting room. Because of the potential richness of material that may arise from waiting-room observations of children and parents, many clinicians have attempted to formalize or structure these into a protocol to be filled out by the receptionist while the family is waiting for the appointment. Although there is no doubt about the value of such material, to collect it in a serious way presents a few problems which need consideration. First, in a busy outpatient clinic, group practice, or hospital, where there may be as many as ten or twelve families waiting for appointments at any moment, it is impractical for someone with receptionist duties to attempt to make and record these types of observations, especially if she is expected to attend to the responsibilities for maintaining telephone coverage, scheduling of appointments, etc. If one introduces a separate individual, such as some type of paraprofessional or child development worker to make these observations, the role of that person in the waiting room needs to be clarified to the parents. For many families, the failure to do so and to explain that observations of behavior and family interaction are being recorded may raise important ethical considerations. There may be legal implications as well.

THE PSYCHIATRIC EXAMINATION OF THE CHILD: THE INITIAL PHASE

A good deal of basic observation is done at the time of the initial contact, during transit to the playroom, and in the course of the first few minutes of the appointment.

The child's overall appearance is generally quite informative. Children who are "dressed to the teeth" as if going to church or to a fancy party have probably also been misinformed about the nature of the appointment. They may very well have been instructed to be on their best behavior, to put their best foot forward, be "nice to the doctor," "do everything the doctor tells you," etc. Children who are "underdressed" in the sense that they give the appearance of having been plucked from a game of street hockey with dirty faces and hands, messy or torn clothing obviously intended for rough play, may also be coming to the appointment totally unprepared. This can occur despite the best efforts of the clinician. Poor personal hygiene does not, of course, necessarily mean lack of preparation; however, it may represent the general state of care of this child and reveal something about the child's prevailing mood and self-image.

A good deal of a gross neurologic examination can be accomplished through careful observation of the child during the early phases of the interview. Most of the rest of it can be worked in during other aspects of the examination without actually having to "lay hands on the child." Gait, station, gross motor coordination, sensorimotor integration, speech articulation, hearing, extraocular movements, handedness, many aspects of sensory perception, sensorium, the presence of tremors, tics, and other involuntary movements can be observed very easily and should be recorded as a part of the examination.

There is no "safe" formula for initiating the interaction with the child. A great deal depends on the patient's developmental level and his relative comfort or discomfort with new settings, particularly professional offices. Sometimes, it is counterproductive to ask a child why he has come or what the problem is. This kind of query is not well handled by most preschool and school-age children. Some older children and most adolescents may be aware that the examiner has met with his parents and that they have explained in detail what "the problem" is. Second, his capacity to verbalize his concerns, particularly in a framework which would be meaningful to the examiner, may become possible only after a climate of trust and comfort has eventually been established.

If the clinician feels it is important to have the child talk about the reasons for his coming, it is generally wise to ask what his parents have told him about the appointment. Even this kind of question generally meets with a perfunctory and superficial response. If the child does respond in a substantive way, this presents a good point of departure for further interaction. If, on the other hand, the child responds in a way that reveals gross distortions, this too can be addressed. Nine times out of ten, however, the child will give a nonsubstantive answer which leaves the examiner in a position of having either to push or to change the subject.

In many instances, matters tend to proceed more smoothly if no initial mention of the problem is attempted. Some children whose temperament is "high approach" or whose activity levels and curiosity lead them to be quite exploratory may immediately plunge into the office and its contents, fingering objects, asking questions, or selecting a specific game or toy to use with almost no introduction. Most children, however, will "lay back" and wait for the examiner to set the ground rules.

Nor should he hesitate to do so. As always, these "ground rules" need to be couched in terms appropriate to the developmental level of the child. Unless the examiner has prior knowledge that this is a very active and destructive child, little needs to be said about protecting the child, the examiner, and the property in the office from any harm. Some youngsters do need this caveat, but it is not wise to use it unless there is some indication of its appropriateness. Otherwise, it takes on the dimensions of admonishing a child "not to put that bean up your nose."

Rather, it is important to emphasize the positive. The examiner should indicate that the time will be used for the doctor to get to know the child as well as possible and to understand him.

They both know that the child has been brought here out of some worry about how he is doing at home or in school. It is therefore most important for the doctor to understand clearly how the child feels about this, what he is good at, what he is having trouble with, what he is interested in, and so on. This understanding can come about by talking, by the child's playing alone if he wishes to with any of the toys in the room, or by playing with the doctor if he would prefer that. He does not have to do anything or talk about anything special if he has some reason not to. In other words, it is important to communicate to the child early that this procedure is not being done to him but *with* him, that he will have some choices to make, and that his own integrity and freedom of choice as an individual will not be violated either through force or by deception.

On pages 542–546 there will be some consideration given to those children who, despite the best efforts of the examiner, still have great difficulty in using the time constructively or in developing any interaction with the examiner.

Frequently, it is productive to solicit questions from the child concerning his understanding about who and what the examiner is. Distortions and stereotypes may be identified (special teacher, law enforcement agent, etc.) and dealt with directly. More subtle questions may emerge if the examiner is obviously pregnant, a member of a racial minority, or physically handicapped. Material derived in this way is highly specific to the interpersonal situation at hand; it may provide easy access to the child's fantasy life and to areas which are emotionally charged or seriously conflict laden.

THE BODY OF THE INTERVIEW

It is important to distinguish between the *manner* in which clinical observations of a child are conducted and the *format* in which those observations are recorded. As is the case in developmental history taking, both the manner and format should be designed to assist in the clinical decision-making process.

Some clinicians find it useful to adapt the more traditional mental status examination (originally designed for adults) to children. For purposes of completeness, the outline of one form of child psychiatric mental status examination follows.

1. *General Appearance:* Include such items as size relative to age, general activity level, personal hygiene and dress, nutritional state, etc.
2. *Mood:* Include such items as prevailing mood, if any, appropriateness of affective response to verbalization or play, rapid or unpredictable mood swings, etc.
3. *Thought Processes:* Include such items as abstract thinking, fantasy themes, dreams, capacity to calculate and problem solve, self-identity, general fund of information, etc.
4. *Capacity for Communication:* Include such items as presence of communicative speech, speed and flow of speech, articulation, intonation, syntax, pronominal usage, mannerisms of speech, use of nonverbal modes for communcation, etc.
5. *Motility, Coordination, and Sensorimotor Integration:* Include such items as posture and gait, gross and fine motor activity, capacity to convert visual and auditory signals into appropriate motor responses and vice versa, etc.
6. *Ego Defenses and Coping Mechanisms:* Include such items as most common defenses employed including specific illustrations, response to novel stimuli or demands, approach or avoidance behavior, etc.
7. *Ethical Structure:* Include such items as expressed ideals, judgments concerning acceptable social behavior, degree to which value system is internalized, apparent rigidity or flexibility of superego, etc.
8. *Summary and Conclusions:* Include an integrated picture of the salient, contributory findings and follow with a diagnosis or differential diagnosis.

Several other outlines for mental status examinations have been described and are in daily use. For more detailed discussion of their application, the reader is referred to Goodman and Sours[3] and to Simmons.[9]

Many clinicians consider the mental status examination less useful with children than adults. It is viewed as reductionistic in nature and tending to lead to diagnostic labels rather than functional, developmentally based formulations.

For those who are inclined to approach clinical problems more from this functional or adaptive position (in contrast to a more phenomenologic one), the following format may be useful.

Data indicating the child's level of autonomous functioning relative to his developmental and chronologic age.

The child's approach to novel situations is exemplified by his response to the entire experience of the examination itself, the clinician, the physical setting, etc. A wide range of responses is possible. This may from freezing panic or withdrawal, through "high approach" behavior, constructive curiosity and exploration and meaningful use of the time spent with the examiner, to physical invasiveness and destructive manipulation of everything in sight.

The very nature of the initial diagnostic interview makes it a perfect laboratory for observing the child's coping capacity and his ability to incorporate new stimuli and "process" them; for understanding his modes of problem-solving behavior; for getting a picture of his level of exploratory and curiosity-gratifying behavior; and for obtaining a surprisingly informative picture of certain constitutional or temperamental characteristics such as approach patterns, threshholds to stimulation, frustration tolerance, attention span, etc.

Children obsessed with sameness may seek to meet each new situation as if it is an analogue of some previously known and comfortable situation which had already been understood and mastered. Under such circumstances, stereotypy may appear or even a noticeable amount of autoerotic stimulation in the face of flooding anxiety.

The intellectually limited or brain-damaged child may also tend to show stereotypy in new situations; when it appears, brain damage should always be suspected.

When a child needs to face a novel task in a new environment without customary family supports, a broad range of ego defenses may be mustered and brought into play within the first five minutes of the appointment. At this point they may emerge in much bolder relief than they will appear later when the examiner may be less threatening and the environment more familiar.

Object relationships and object differentiation.

This area, considered in its broadest sense, covers a multitude of functions and behaviors. A great deal can be learned from the manner in which the child differentiates the clinician's role from that of the parents' or the school's role. What does he understand about the setting in which he is being seen? What are his actual perceptions of the physical environment and the use of the objects in it? This may vary over so wide a range that at one end, there is the child who clings to mother and eats the crayon with which he is asked to draw, while at the other, a sophisticated and discriminatory judgment is present about the role of a mental health worker and the production of a well-organized, witty, and communicative crayon drawing. This realm of observation is extremely important; it may reveal very primitive ego defects, perceptual problems, and distortions in social role discrimination over the full spectrum of development from infancy through adolescence.

Behavior pertaining to self-care, self- and body-image and sex role.

How clear is the child about his or her own sexual identity? What can be learned about the child's overall self-image, particularly in the face of success or failure? Is the child harboring fears of mutilation or annihilation? What can be learned about the child's attitudes toward self by way of dress, personal hygiene, body movements and posture, voice projection, and prevailing mood? Are there gross signs of self-destructive behavior?

Self-inhibitory or self-regulatory functions.

What is the capacity of the child for age appropriate impulse control? Are there manifestations that bowel and bladder control are inappropriate for age? Is baseline motor activity beyond the normal range? What stimulates increased activity? What decreases it? Are there tantrums, gross or bizarre motor signs, or any seizure manifestations?

Quality and content of thought processes.

What can be told grossly about the child's level of intellectual functioning? What can be determined about the child's fantasies? Can the child label them as fantasies? Is the child goal directed or are associations loose? What is the capacity for abstract thinking? Capacity to calculate and carry out other formal operations? Is general fund of knowledge appropriate?

Observations concerning attainment of socially cooperative behavior. The manner in which the child relates to adult authority figures or dependency gratifying figures. What is known of peer group relationships? What kinds of demands does the child place on adults (parents, receptionist, examiner, etc.)? How does he respond to requests for socially conforming behavior, or for the performance of a specific task? To what degree is social interaction self-initiated? During the entire examination, it is likely to be examiner-initiated, but there is plenty of room for the child's own interest in social exchange to express itself. Careful consideration must be given to the determinants of this process.

A special note concerning mood or affect should be recorded here. Caution should be exercised concerning judgments about the child's mood in an interview situation. Most commonly, one is observing the child's affective response to the examiner and the general office "climate." Of course, grossly inappropriate affect or extreme mood swings are worthy of note, but reliable information concerning the child's *prevailing* mood and his responses to different life situations is best obtained by careful interviewing of parents, teachers, and other family members.

One final comment in relation to the area of "socially cooperative behavior" concerns the function of interpersonal communication. Although much of this may occur nonverbally, the *capacity* for communicative speech is one of paramount importance. The amount, spontaneity and flow of speech should be recorded. Speech mannerisms, problems with articulation, speech dysrhythmias (such as stuttering), dysphonics (for example, problems with pitch or loudness) etc., may be indications of interference with central nervous functioning, auditory reception, maturational lags, or functional difficulties in interpersonal relationships. However, since most speech is employed for interpersonal communication, in the course of the examination it is logical to view it within that context.

What can be learned of the child's ethical structure?

Is this age appropriate? Is the need for impulse gratification handled in a sociopathic fashion? How does the child handle the formal structure of competitive games? What is the nature of the identification process which has occurred with significant adults (either care givers or idealized persons)? Is the child expressing neurotic guilt? What is the child's understanding of his family structure, extended kinship system, sibships, and the role of peers in his life?

The basic premise of this approach is that the overall purposes of "normal" human development include two major goals: the gradual arrival at autonomous functioning, and the stepwise achievement of socially cooperative behavior at increasingly sophisticated and organized levels of functioning. This format should not be regarded as a mental status examination or an outline for case formulation. It is rather a way of thinking about a child within a developmental framework.

The examiner should be making constant mental reference to the interactional diagram presented in figure 63–1.

Not all of the factors impinging on the child can be elicited by means of the developmental interview or through the direct clinical examination. In fact, the direct clinical examination may be the least reliable source of such information. It is, however, the prime context for studying outcome behavior. This then needs to be related back to the knowledge gleaned about the various historical factors which have been interacting with the child's constitutional endowment and level of central nervous system functioning during his entire life.

In truth, even the most expert clinical psychiatric examination is but a thin "slice of life." For the diagnostician, a certain amount of humility combined with a quality of "looseness" and quick

adaptability to the unexpected are especially precious assets.

In the early years of the child guidance clinics, diagnostic work generally proceeded at a leisurely pace. This was the accepted, even the approved style of work. Today, cost effectiveness and mounting pressures for service have altered the approach to the pace of effort in a fundamental way. At present, a time-limited and brief diagnostic period is obligatory in all but the most complicated situations.

Some Techniques for Eliciting Data

There is some difference of opinion concerning whether diagnostic hours should be structured or unstructured. Many clinicians have designed structured or semi-structured sessions for specific purposes.* In this regard, every clinician will eventually develop his own style. The usual compromise is a combination in which some of the time with the child is spent in a fairly unstructured way, while the remaining time is used selectively to introduce certain structured tasks or activities that seem most likely to elicit the desired information. Some of these more structured techniques are herein described.

USE OF GRAPHIC MATERIALS

Probably the most simple and useful tasks have to do with writing or drawing.[3] This provides access to the study of many complex functions. As a rule, this is quite revealing in relation to the child's affect, thought processes, and fantasy life. Again, body image concepts, family dynamics, and the child's attitudes toward sexuality and aggression are often most easily observed through the use of various art media to obtain graphic representations. There is an enormous body of literature (see chapter 66) which will assist the reader in understanding the administration and interpretation of art techniques in work with children. This is a helpful technique, and merits study. It is the kind of procedure from which a good bit of "mileage" can be extracted during a diagnostic interview. For many a child, this is an area of interest or expertise, and the child may spontaneously offer to draw or write. If not, at

* See references 2, 6, 7, 8, and 9.

some time during the interview, the child should be requested to do so and provided with a choice of materials. If the child resists or refuses, he should be encouraged to proceed and reassured that "This is not school, no one is grading you or concerned about how well you do—this is just another way of our getting acquainted and being able to express ourselves freely." Most children will respond to support and encouragement. If time is limited, it is well to give the child a specific drawing task. The most instructive one is human figure drawing. Again, many children will resist this and offer to draw something else, saying "I cannot draw people." A compromise can then be reached and the child given an opportunity to draw something else first that he feels he is good at before he takes on the more difficult task of drawing a person. Given a choice, what the child will usually draw first is some special interest area which he has picked up from reading or television (for example, space ships, some aspect of sports, or a battle scene). It is likely to be a fairly stereotyped production, one that he has done many times before. He may also reproduce something he has done recently in school. If the child glibly tosses off a drawing that has a stylized appearance and that demanded little concentration and effort, it is probably of little value for diagnostic purposes. In effect, he is tossing a "bone to the dog" who is insisting on some artistic effort.

The way in which the child reproduces human figures is almost always revealing. An occasional child has artistic talent and may even have had some art instruction. Again, this becomes quickly apparent and represents an excellent departure point for discussion and for expressions of interest and reward from the examiner.

Some children apologize for their work both before beginning and after the entire effort is complete. This again tells a good deal about their self-image and their sense of anticipatory failure.

The child's use of or avoidance of colors is noteworthy. It is important to observe the order in which drawing is approached and the way in which the available space is used. These often tell a great deal about the child's goal directedness, sense of spatial orientation, perceptual fields, sensory-motor integration, and other key areas of central nervous system functioning.

It is worthwhile always to indicate that the child should draw a person rather than a boy or a girl, or some other designation which includes sexual identity. The child should be free to choose the gender of his figure and then to demonstrate graphically how he perceives sexual differentiation in body characteristics, dress, etc. Having drawn a person, he should be asked to talk about it. What kind of person is this, what sex, what age, is this a real person or an imaginary one; if it is imaginary, can he make up a story about the character? Grossly distorted figures, or figures which are dismembered or have major body parts missing should be carefully noted. The decision as to whether to discuss this openly in the interview needs to be made on the basis of the child's level of anxiety at that point in the examination.

The child should then be asked to draw a figure of the sex opposite to the one he selected first. This often meets with more resistance, but again the child is likely to respond to support and reassurance. The child's imagery concerning sexual differentiation will be quickly revealed in the new drawing. The inquiry indicated above can then be repeated.

There are any number of possible modifications and amplifications of this procedure. The child can be asked to draw his family, or his house or school. Each of these drawings potentially represents a gold mine of information in terms of the child's internalized image of these figures or objects. It can also provide a stimulus for further interaction between examiner and patient.

The child who draws his family and leaves himself out, or omits some other family member, or draws one family member significantly apart from the rest of the family; or who draws himself much smaller or much larger relative to the manner in which he ought to be compared to his siblings and parents; or who draws a family scene in which there is either considerable isolation, interaction, overt aggression, or other "family business" taking place, is in each instance again presenting the examiner with an important tool for further exploration.

It is always wise to give the child an opportunity to draw something he would like to. On the other hand, he should be discouraged from grinding out obviously ritualized drawings which have the same quality as perseverative speech.

USE OF DRAMA AND STORYTELLING

Certain children do not volunteer substantive information about their thought processes and fantasy life. In such instances, it is often possible to structure an interaction for which they, in effect, write the scenario. This can be accomplished using puppets, human doll figures, animals, toy soldiers, or other toys. The clinician must be sufficiently imaginative to stimulate the child to respond; sensitive enough to suggest areas which are, for this child, emotionally charged; and cautious enough to design a situation in which the child will be free to avoid direct confrontation with his own problems (if he must) while still communicating important material about his inner life.

For instance, there may be reason to suspect that the child is experiencing a sense of isolation from or abandonment by his family. The examiner may then suggest a play in which the parents and siblings are all busily occupied and one child is in his room alone or watching TV. The child can then be encouraged to develop a "story line," to verbalize the dialogue going on between family members and to express what they may be thinking about each other.

Or, the examiner may have cause to suspect that the child has serious problems either expressing or inhibiting aggression. To explore this one need simply suggest a scene of family conflict or a battlefield scene, and then observe how the child deals with the aggressive interactions inherent in the situation.

Using this type of technique, the possibilities are really unlimited. The clinician may suggest that the child make up a story about a picture he has drawn. The clinician may engage in some role playing using toys with assigned roles of parent, teacher, policeman, etc.

USE OF GAMES AND PUZZLES

The clinician may select one or more games or puzzles which he knows require certain types of abstract thinking and a particular level of problem solving. These are also useful for studying the child's attention span, persistence, and frustration tolerance.

Competitive games are useful for gaining more knowledge about the child's self-esteem and his mode of relating to adults in authority. Games and puzzles are especially revealing (when carefully selected for this purpose) about central nervous system functioning. Children who are reported to have academic problems should be asked to perform tasks which examine their spatial orientation, capacity to follow directions, and their ability to handle operations in sequence and to translate auditory or visual cues into motor tasks.

USE OF OTHER TECHNIQUES AND MATERIALS

In similar fashion, it is feasible to engage the child in many structured activities which will assist the examiner in eliciting the information necessary to complete his examination. These may involve either the use of other materials (for example, building blocks, modeling clay, rubber-tipped darts, ring toss, etc.) or some structured interaction with the examiner ("Simon Says," guessing the identity of sounds, etc.).

In any case, the examiner must constantly be moving through a problem-solving process in which he is using developmentally appropriate play activities to assist the patient in communicating the relevant data necessary for clinical decision making.

Needs for Special Techniques

Some types of children present a greater challenge to the examiner than others. Examples of four such types will be described.

THE NONVERBAL CHILD

The mute or nonverbal child requires special attention. Although, as has already been indicated, much of what is learned about every patient is through nonverbal behavior, it is still very useful to be able to speak with a child.

Of particular concern here is the child who, from the history, is known to possess formal speech unlike the infant or the older child with very primitive development who has not acquired language skills, but who, for some reason, cannot or will not speak to the examiner.

Silence during the early part of an interview is not uncommon; as a rule it is caused by excessive anxiety related to the separation from mother, the strangeness of the office, and uncertainty concerning the purpose and outcome of the examination.

In such instances techniques should be invoked which gradually titrate the intensity of interaction. These start from a relatively distant level, and lead to a pattern of gradually increasing closeness. This may permit the child sufficient comfort to begin to communicate or to interact without undue anxiety. When the child continues to have difficulty, there is no need for the examiner himself to panic. The entire session can be carried out in a nonverbal form. Admittedly, this is not easy, but much of the information which cannot be acquired through verbal interchange may be obtained in other ways at considerably less cost to everyone.

Indeed, nonverbal techniques are often the most successful. With young children who are very anxious, it is often possible to catch them up in a process of parallel play. Two sets of blocks, two sets of drawing materials, or two sets of animal figures may be set up on the play table. The examiner then begins to use one set. Eye contact should be avoided, and there should be no expressed expectation that the child follow suit. Very frequently, however, so long as it is clear that verbal interaction is not required, the child will start to use these materials.

After several minutes of this parallel play, it may then become possible to begin interacting— not with the child directly but with his play materials. Again, direct confrontation should be avoided. If building blocks are being used, an extension may be developed which begins to connect with something the child is building. An animal may wander into his "pasture" and begin to come into physical (or verbal) contact with the child's animals. For the mute or extremely frightened child, this is by far the safest kind of interaction possible, and it is so indirect, and so displaced from one-to-one confrontation with the examiner, that the youngster may begin to risk experimenting with it.

Some less frightened children may be able to engage in interactive play at once although again, without verbalization. A game of tic tac toe, Old Maid, or checkers may be acceptable, and long before a word is spoken, it may begin to reveal a great deal about the child's personality structure and central nervous system functioning.

At some point, the examiner may proceed to speak while making it very clear that he is not talking directly to the child but to some imaginary third party. Again, no response is requested, but the child's verbal expressions, such as they are, his body language and his nonverbal vocalizations will usually be most instructive. The examiner may strike up a conversation with a stuffed figure or puppet which he begins to talk to about some neutral subject (sometimes it is best to do this jokingly, and with a smile in one's voice, sometimes not). Or, in a nonthreatening way, he may initiate a conversation about the child in question emphasizing positive aspects and dropping small hints to indicate that he already knows something about the child, about both his strengths and his problems. With some children, this can turn into a game in which they communicate briefly with the imaginary presence or with the inanimate object without ever directly addressing the examiner.

With other children, the inferred threat from the examiner must be buffered. If appropriate distancing mechanisms are introduced to do this, more direct communication can then take place. There are children who would otherwise be totally blocked, but who are able to communicate if they can whisper down a long tube, or through the sleeve of their coat. It is particularly helpful if the examiner whispers gently first and expresses something which is not affectively charged for the child, or even something of a humorous nature (although never, never at the child's expense). A pair of toy telephones can be especially helpful at this juncture, and should always be in the playroom. One can always resort to the electronic distancing device of the dictating machine or tape recorder. When direct verbal interchange is impossible for them, some children are able to leave whispered messages on this impersonal piece of equipment, or even to respond to messages from the examiner. They become so fascinated with and caught up in the technology of the instrument that the interpersonal issues which keep them from speaking recede, at least temporarily, into the background.

None of these approaches is intended to serve as a mode for diagnosing mutism. These are merely diagnostic maneuvers for facilitating communication with the child who enters an interview with the express intent of not communicating at all.

THE SYMBIOTIC OR EXCESSIVELY DEPENDENT CHILD

As indicated earlier in this chapter, some children will resist separation from the mother in the waiting room and will do so in a very manipulative, countercontrolling way. At times, this merely reflects the child's understanding of the parent's intense ambivalence about bringing him to professional attention in the first place. However, this is not the type of youngster being considered here. Again, from his previous knowledge of the developmental history, the examiner will have had some sense of what the difficulty might be. He may be dealing with a youngster where separation and individuation issues between mother and patient are significantly unresolved; when they are together, each experiences a sense of both partial individual identity and fused collective identity. When any separation has to be faced, this then brings on a flood of anxiety bordering on terror. Where the clinician has some anticipatory hint of this state of affairs, it is not incumbent on him to prove either to himself or anyone else that he can pry this dyad apart in his waiting room or in his office.

This part of the diagnosis is often the easiest one to make. The real task may then become to find out what the child is capable of doing in spite of his symbiotic state, and what coping mechanisms are available to him.

Once it is clear that separation will produce only a frozen, nonfunctioning child and a panicked, nonsupportive mother (the usual parent involved), then the mother's aid should be enlisted for the conduct of the examination. Both child and mother should be brought into the office together and given support and reassurance. Certain joint tasks can be explained to the parent, who can participate actively in a number of ways. She can play with the child, organize competitive games, they can draw or paint together, and she can interact with the child verbally in such a way as to enable him to expose his understanding of his family relationships, his concerns about himself, the fears of separation, the nature of demands on mother, etc. If at the outset he were seen alone, this wealth of information could never have been "extracted" from the child. If the diagnostic process can be prolonged, the examiner may wish to experiment with brief periods of separation. These can presently be extended in time in order to test out the child's capacities to function autonomously. Again, these are probably more easily determined with careful history taking and are more germane to the treatment process which may come later. They may be diagnostic luxuries which are not fundamental to dispositional decisions.

THE EXCESSIVELY DEPRIVED OR POVERTY CHILD

Here, one is not dealing merely with the issue of differences in sociocultural background between examiner and patient. As indicated previously, the examiner always needs to be acutely aware of such differences and prepared to make allowances for them. Such differences, however, do not necessarily imply marked deprivation; the child whose parents are third generation multimillionaires may also be culturally very much different from the interviewer. Here the concern is with the child who has experienced prolonged, chronic material and emotional deprivation.

First: The most obvious demand on the examiner is usually to cope with the child's way of expressing himself. The youngster's verbal and other communication skills are likely to be quite different from those with which the examiner is familiar. Most of these children come from rather disorganized, crisis-ridden environments in which there is small value placed on verbal skills and little expectation that needs expressed through words will be gratified or will lead to some easing of the child's level of discomfort.

Second: A large percentage of these children come from environments in which they are very understimulated. It is therefore particularly important to be able to control the level of stimulation in the hour especially with respect to visually attractive games, play objects, or edibles. A few objects which may be inviting to the child should be made available to him (preferably things which may be at least partially familiar to him through watching television commercials or other visual media). This is less likely to produce overstimulation along with its inevitable further disorganization.

Third: For many examiners, countertransference problems may become particularly troublesome. Because of the child's obvious deprivation, one may be plagued by overwhelming impulses to "give" to the child in an open-ended, nonexpectant fashion. This may also be accompanied by the examiner feeling frustration, hopelessness, and a sense that, no matter what the "diagnosis" or what intervention is planned, the child represents a bottomless pit. Or, worse yet, the feeling can be that this is an intrinsically damaged child for whom no level of compensation or corrective experience will serve, for whom there is no reasonable chance of getting his developmental process "back on the track" again. It is most important for the examiner to récognize and accept these feelings when they arise, and to learn how then to proceed in as balanced, open-ended, and objective a fashion as possible. Throughout, he is searching for the child's strengths and his potential for further growth and development.

Fourth: Important diagnostic cues come when the child demonstrates some capacity for object relatedness, when he indicates an ability to "use" the experience even if only briefly and superficially. Many deprived children approach new situations with such an intense need to be given to (materially, they have lost all trust that significant adults would seek to make them feel good by giving to them emotionally) that the interaction may soon devolve into a physical struggle. The child insists that he be given a specific toy or some other object that has caught his eye. He will want to be given this permanently; it is his to take home with him. If the examiner does not comply, he will fill the air with oaths and vows to bring it back (he never does) if that is the coin required to obtain it. Should the examiner permit it, the entire session may be wasted in an empty dialogue about what the child may or may not "have." In the child's struggle to extract some object from the examiner, he will resort to many ploys. He may become extremely flattering and complimentary about the examiner's person, the office, and "how nice everything is." He may finger a whole succession of objects constantly exclaiming about their uniqueness and beauty. He will constantly repeat that this is new to him, that he has nothing like this and that he would give anything to own such a toy.

There are a few maneuvers that may be helpful in getting the interaction away from this kind of demand for material giving. The examiner may offer the child some candy or a soft drink and thereby establish himself as a giving kind of person. He may have a box of small, expendable toys of the Cracker Jack prize variety which tend to be more symbolic. More often than not, however, this is really not effective. The child may even communicate his own sense of worthlessness and depression by relinquishing his demand for an object which he sees as materially valuable, and shifting to a demand for something senseless and worthless.

He may retrieve a dried-up ball point pen from the wastebasket and ask poignantly whether he can take this home. This is dangerous ground for the examiner. Under no circumstances should the child's sense of being a piece of human flotsam be reinforced by giving him a worthless object which has already been discarded. If necessary, he should be confronted with this directly. The examiner can feel free to say that he values people too much to give them junk or trash or worthless objects. He likes children and thinks too well of them (including this one) to give them something of that kind.

The final test of the child's potential often boils down to a confrontation in which the examiner says, in effect: "Look, there is no point to giving you any of these toys. You have been sitting here for thirty minutes and you have not used a single one of them. It seems that you aren't able to use them here in the office. What point is there to giving them to you to take home with you when you can't even enjoy them here? Why don't you pick out a toy that you like the best and let's have some fun with it while you are here in the office?" This is a direct confrontation of the child's incapacity to enjoy himself because he is caught up in a never-ending struggle to extract symbols of material value from the adult environment. The question is, to what extent can he appreciate his own sense of capacity, and is there any potential left in him to trust the dependency gratifying resources in adults. It is for this reason that such a confrontation often stands the best chance of providing prognostic clues concerning the child's availability for change, and the degree of early damage to his ego development.

HYPERACTIVE AND/OR DESTRUCTIVE CHILDREN

Again, it is important to avoid power struggles with these children. These boil down simply to questions of who has the most physical strength or the most tenacity. From the descriptions given by the parents and the school, the examiner will often have reason to expect behavior that is extremely active and destructive. Quite frequently, this turns out not to be true. The child simply does not exhibit this pattern where there is a one-to-one relationship with an adult in an office situation. Indeed, in a first office interview, where the child has the uninterrupted and undivided attention of the examiner, more often than not the problem behavior will not be observed. In considering what kind of limit setting needs to be introduced, it is therefore especially important to take one's own reading of the child's level of activity and aggressiveness. Alarmed by ominous reports, an examiner may invoke all sorts of limits and prohibitions at the outset before the child's office behavior has really indicated any need for these. The prophecy may well produce its own fulfillment.

Although in clinical practice hyperactivity and destructiveness frequently accompany one another, this is by no means universally true. It is quite important to determine whether the child's activity level does indeed possess a component of aggressive behavior directed against person or property. For the diagnostician, hyperactivity in itself presents a less serious technical problem than does marked antisocial behavior in the office.

In terms of management:

First: As with the understimulated child, it is important to have a good bit of control over the physical environment and the amount of stimulation to which the child will be exposed. The examiner needs to have ways of grading or titrating the number and kinds of stimuli to which the child is exposed at any moment. If he does, children with very low threshholds to stimulation will be easier to observe in the office, and their behavior will be easier to measure and record. This may require locks on some cabinets and a fair amount of prior planning (based on the developmental interview) concerning what kinds of experiences or objects it is best to begin with.

Destructiveness or stealing needs to be confronted quickly, firmly, and unequivocally. The child must be told that these are unacceptable forms of behavior and that the clinician will do whatever is necessary to limit them. Occasionally, this may involve a gentle, enveloping kind of physical restraint in which the child is simply held close and "swathed" by the examiner. Any form of grasp (on the arms, legs, or any body part) which is painful to the child is contraindicated. If the examiner can use his larger body to contain the youngster in an enveloping maneuver, this may even be soothing and quieting. Where even this measure of control is of no avail, and the child persists in defying reasonable limits, he should know that (albeit unwillingly and as a last resort) termination of the session will be resorted to.

Second: The use of the examiner's voice in a steady, reassuring but persistent fashion is often helpful. Constant verbal rewards for observing the rules along with a good bit of support and reassurance are often helpful.

Third: It is important to test out the child's limits for attending to a particular task. Once this is done and the child's attention span is found to be very brief, then that information should be acted upon. For example, the session can be broken up into very small segments so that the child's attention is constantly being redirected to new and interesting subjects or activities. The child should not be led toward extended involvement in any one undertaking.

Fourth: At points where the examiner sees the first signs of the child's attention beginning to lag, some anticipatory direction can be very helpful. With this type of child, this may even include dividing the diagnostic examination into a number of much shorter sessions. If the interviews are reduced to fifteen or twenty minutes each rather than kept to the customary fifty minutes or one hour, they may be much more productive.

Terminating the Interview

Terminating the interview is an important aspect to consider. Toward the end of the meeting it is important to give the child some "notice" that the allotted time is drawing to a close. This will afford him a sense of having some control over

the termination process, and will help handle any separation affects that may be involved. The child can also be asked to clean up any play materials which were in use, or to assist the examiner in doing so. The child's reaction to this kind of expectation and this sort of task is often a very revealing aspect of the diagnostic process. If the examiner does not expect to see the child again, this should be clearly stated and the child offered an opportunity to say good-bye. If the matter of further contacts is unclear, then this too should be stated directly, and the child given to understand that at this point matters will have to be left open-ended.

If further interviews are obviously necessary, or some specialized diagnostic procedure is indicated, then this should be explained to the child as carefully as possible, and he should be given an opportunity to ask questions. It should also be made clear that his parents will need to know about this and that this will require their support and permission as well.

Any problem the child has around ending the interview or separating from the examiner should be carefully noted. The very child who may have involved his parent in a power struggle which led to all sorts of difficulties about coming to the office or beginning the hour may now involve the examiner in a similar struggle over who has the authority to set limits to the interview. Or the child may cling tenaciously to a toy which has attracted his attention, demanding to take it with him. He may stall and ask for only a few more minutes to complete a task or a drawing or a bridge he is building. Some flexibility is needed here if the few more minutes would really make a difference. Often, these delaying tactics are symptomatic of the child's repertoire of defenses for dealing with his own feelings of insecurity, inadequacy, and smallness. Again, bribes, threats, or unrealistic inducements to leave the examining room and rejoin the parents are contraindicated. Firm direction delivered in a relatively neutral but supportive way is usually effective. Sometimes this must be accompanied by a clear demonstration that the examiner is terminating the interview. Simply putting play objects away, putting the examining room in order, and beginning to leave the office and enter the corridor are usually enough to make it clear to the child that remaining behind would be a hollow show of power.

Particularly with young children, it is important to accompany the child physically back to his parents and to "deliver" him personally into the parents' custody. This literal transfer is symbolically important to many children, particularly to those who fear that they might be abandoned or relinquished by their parents and given over to some professional authority. The next steps in the process should then be explained to the parents in the waiting room within earshot of the child. Obviously, this should have been preceded by appropriate consultation with one's colleagues.

Many parents are indeed anxious about the examination and its results. It is therefore not uncommon for the examiner to be pressed in the waiting room for detailed information. The parents are likely to ask how the examination went, what conclusions can be drawn, and what "first aid" recommendations the examiner may wish to make in order to ease their distress with the child. This must be handled with discretion and without giving the parents the feeling that they are being dismissed or put off. No secret confabs or tête-à-têtes should be conducted in the waiting room while the child sits off in a corner, not privy to the discussion, but knowing only too well that he is being talked about. Parents should be firmly but gently informed that the child's interview was satisfactory (an explanation for this term can be given later). The examiner should explain that these situations are too complex, that too much is involved both for family and child to attempt oversimplified comments in a waiting room situation. There needs to be a proper opportunity for discussion, for questions and for answers, and this needs an adequate site and time. Most parents are not put off by this kind of approach. At the same time, the examiner should be particularly alert to the possibility of resentment at this point, and, if he senses that it is occurring, it should be handled in the subsequent interpretation interview with the parents.

REFERENCES

1. ABLER, B. S., and NEWTON, J. R., "The Diagnostic Evaluation on a Child Psychiatry Outpatient Service From the Perspectives of Parents and Staff," *Journal of Clinical Psychology,* 26:384–386, 1970.
2. BERSOFF, D. N., and GRIEGER, R. M., "An Interview Model for the Psychosituational Assessment of Children's Behavior," *American Journal of Orthopsychiatry,* 41:483–493, 1971.
3. DiREO, J. H., *Children's Drawings as Diagnostic Aids,* Brunner-Mazel, New York, 1973.
4. GOODMAN, J. D., and SOURS, J. A., *The Child Mental Status Examination,* Basic Books, New York, 1967.
5. HAWORTH, M. R., and KELLER, M. J., "The Use of Food in the Diagnosis and Therapy of Emotionally Disturbed Children," *Journal of the American Academy of Child Psychiatry,* 1:548–563, 1962.
6. HERJANIC, B., and CAMPBELL, J. W., "Differentiating Psychiatrically Disturbed Children on the Basis of a Structured Interview," Paper presented at Annual Meeting, American Academy of Child Psychiatry, St. Louis, Missouri, 1975.
7. JABODA, H., and GOLDFARB, W., "Use of a Standard Observation for the Psychological Evaluation of Non-Speaking Children," *American Journal of Orthopsychiatry,* 27:745–753, 1957.
8. SILVER, A. A., HAGIN, R. A., DeVITO, E., "A Search Battery for Scanning Kindergarten Children for Potential Learning Disability," *Journal of the American Academy of Child Psychiatry,* 15:224–239, 1976.
9. SILVER, L., "The Playroom Diagnostic Evaluation of Children With Neurologically Based Learning Disabilities," *Journal of the American Academy of Child Psychiatry,* 15:240–256, 1976.
10. SIMMONS, J. E., *Psychiatric Examination of Children,* Lea & Febiger, Philadelphia, 1974.

64 / Special Considerations in the Examination of Adolescents

Richard L. Cohen

The Approach to Adolescents

Much of the preceding chapter applies very directly to interviewing adolescents. However, to achieve optimal diagnostic effectiveness, the particular developmental characteristics of this epoch usually necessitate the introduction of some additional approaches.

Inevitably, the evaluation of adolescents tends to be more like the formal, adult mental status examination. In most instances, however, it is a mistake to assume that the adult examination can simply be superimposed on the adolescent.

There is a mercurial quality to many adolescents; their mood swings are unpredictable, and their defenses relatively loose and variable. They have a tendency to regress briefly and then to reorganize and reintegrate for brief periods of time during which they display very adequate functioning. These qualities should make the examiner extremely cautious about drawing conclusions from brief, time-limited examinations. The appearance of bizarre fantasies or marked feelings of depression and self-negation may not warrant the kind of serious prognostic label that similar findings would justify at the age of twenty-five or thirty-five years. Conversely, the fourteen-year-old girl on a "hunger strike" or displaying marked "fears" of going to school could be displaying the incipient signs of a grave psychotic process; whereas at age six, these same symptoms ordinarily do not carry with them serious prognostic implications, and may indeed respond to relatively simple interventive techniques.

The Professional Contact

For the adolescent, it is often important to set up the diagnostic process in a different way. Much depends on the nature of the initial contact with the parents or the referral source. If the adolescent appears to be reasonably well integrated, even if he is involved in some serious family conflict, it may be desirable to see the youngster first before the parents are interviewed. The communication to everyone concerned is that because of his developmental level, a higher level of involvement, participation, and responsibility is automatically being assigned to the patient. Of course, the diagnostic process can and should remain family-oriented. This is simply a question of shifting the focus slightly because of the age of the patient. In some instances, it may even be wise to suggest that the patient call for the first appointment himself and set up the time and date with the examiner. For some patients, this may be rather anxiety producing. However, it carries clear implications that the patient will not be left out of the decision-making process and will have "first crack" at the examiner; this also makes it more reassuring. Parents, in turn, may indeed be threatened by this process. They will need support and the reassurance that they will have a full and complete opportunity to communicate with the examiner, to give historical information, to ask questions, and to have final veto power in relation to the decision-making process.

The decision concerning whether the adolescent will be included in the final "interpretation conference" with the parents is one that can be delayed until much more information is available. One needs to ascertain whether such a conference is likely to be a working meeting or an unproductive confrontation. In the latter instance, it is usually desirable to set up an independent interpretation conference with the adolescent. More than that, the whole question of confidentiality must be considered in a new light. The six-year-old should not be reassured blithely that what he tells the clinician will be held in confidence. It may be true that he will not be quoted directly; but he does need to know that his parents will be given to understand the significance of what has transpired in the diagnostic session(s). With the adolescent, much more clear-cut guarantees of privacy are usually desirable. The clinician must here walk a fine line; at some later point he will indeed be expected to interpret his findings and his conclusions to the parents. Barring serious threats to life and limb and barring grossly illegal acts on the part of the adolescent, it is not necessary to quote directly or to share material of a sensitive nature with the parents. The adolescent needs to know this in unequivocal terms. He also needs to know that he can stop the interview at any point and reiterate with the examiner that some particular material is especially sensitive or confidential and must remain between them. On the other hand, the examiner must reserve the right to suggest to the adolescent that, in the best interests of everyone involved, certain things should be shared with the parents. When this is the case and it is mutually agreed upon, it is best if it comes from the adolescent himself. The clinician can be present to mediate or to buffer the process if it seems particularly difficult. If the clinician feels strongly about this, and gives enough rational explanation and enough emotional support, it is usually possible to convince the adolescent to share the information.

Variations in Interview Content

Most adolescents who come to a mental health setting in the 1970s are knowledgeable and sophisticated (in the popular sense) about psychiatric practice and the work of mental health clinicians. Few factual explanations are necessary. However, there is a more subtle, underlying process characteristic of adolescence which is often silently present. It is probably safe to say that all adolescents experience bizarre and ego-dystonic thought processes from time to time. Their own tendencies toward identity diffusion in the face of such ideation lead to understandable fears of being or going "crazy." For the adolescent who appears in the office of a child psychiatrist, these fears may surge up with marked intensity. For some patients, these will be dealt with through marked denial or heroic reaction formations. As he evaluates the patient, the diagnostician must be constantly alert and responsive to this process. This is far more important than any pedantic explanations of interview technique, the nature of the examination, or what psychiatrists do for a living. For some adolescents, firm, gentle reassurance is sufficient along with a clear, simple statement that no assumptions are being made and that the adolescent will have the full opportunity to tell the facts as he sees them. Youngsters whose defenses are looser may tend to use the diagnostic experience either as a self-fulfilling prophecy that they are indeed "crazy," or as a contest with the examiner in which their main task is to prove that they are "normal" (and, often enough, that he is the crazy one).

The examiner's style, tone, and overall attitude about adolescent development will make a difference, if not immediately, then eventually.

In the face of the stormy affect which the adolescent may be experiencing, a steady, matter of fact, low-key, dignified, and respectful posture on the part of the examiner is, in itself, reassuring and stabilizing. When adolescents can contact an adult who is not "thrown" by the bizarre, unacceptable, and uncomfortable inner life they may be experiencing, for the most part they begin to feel accepted, less different, more at ease, and, very soon, able to identify with that adult. The youth's constant underlying fear of the loss of impulse control is much allayed by the fact that the adult is not fearful of his impulse life; indeed, he indicates that when and if necessary in the office, he will lend his ego to the management of those impulses.

In general, "hip" or street language, unless it has entered the general vernacular of the culture, is unnecessary, and may be viewed by the adolescent as an effort on the part of the examiner to curry favor or to impress him. On the other hand, it is usually important and valuable to be able to demonstrate some understanding of the current adolescent scene. A passable knowledge of the music which is now in vogue and of some of the artists currently being idealized by that age

group is often an open sesame to dialogue with an adolescent. At least superficial knowledge of the sports scene, particularly some of the sports less identified with middle-aged spectators (for example, motorcycling) communicates to the youngster a sense of genuine interest in adolescent life.

The whole matter of history taking is modifiable with the adolescent. With the young child, history taking is generally noninformative and useful only for entrée into the little one's fantasy life. Spending some time on the adolescent's retrospective view of his own development, on the life cycle of his family together with the crucial milestones he has experienced, is usually a worthwhile process. Later it becomes even more informative when the opportunity arises to compare it with a similar history derived from the parents.

The discussion of sexual experience demands special mention. Except for the clearly delinquent and character-disordered adolescent (who will often discuss sexual material freely and in a derogatory or offhand way), most teenagers have considerable difficulty in discussing this sort of subject matter with a strange adult. If the diagnostic process is more prolonged, an appropriate opportunity for this is more likely to arise. In a one contact interview, it is usually unwise to introduce clearly sexually oriented questions unless the patient initiates such a discussion. With girls, it is sometimes possible to introduce this material by asking rather neutral questions about menarche, current menstrual cycle, and any related symptoms or health problems. This may lead naturally into a discussion of the youngster's sexual experience. One must assume that all adolescents are sexually conflicted, are struggling with impulses that are controlled either inadequately or excessively, and that this is anxiety producing for them. To inquire into the intimate details of this material during a short diagnostic process is not likely to be very helpful and may well be viewed by the adolescent as invasive and voyeuristic.

Nonverbal Communication

The adolescent does not necessarily do best in an entirely verbal interview.

For many youngsters, the introduction of art materials and other age-appropriate media assists in the communication process. It can reduce anxiety and permit the sharing of sensitive material without direct confrontation. Most adolescents have a natural tendency to experience some measure of regression in the face of marked anxiety; this might well be expected to appear during a psychiatric interview. If the office setup permits, it is often desirable to bring the adolescent into the part of the room which is clearly adult-oriented but within view of the "child" area with its games, toys, art materials, etc. Many an adolescent looks for support or permission to become involved with some of the play materials; the examiner must observe carefully during the interview to see if such an interest is present. If the youth is clearly having communication problems, and if he is showing some disorganization in the face of his anxiety, he may even need to be encouraged to engage in play. There are many adolescents who, given nonjudgmental and non-accusatory "permission," have been able to use the play table or even sit on the floor, building with tinker toys or using clay. In the course of this there was a noticeable improvement in their capacity for interchange with the examiner. This productive activity not only acts to sublimate and therefore to reduce unproductive anxiety, but, perhaps of even more importance, it communicates to the patient a continuing comfort with and acceptance of the infantile and primitive impulses which are so much a part of adolescence.

Two Areas of Special Concern

Although the diagnosis and management of both drug abuse and potential suicide in adolescents are dealt with at length in sections of this text, a special note is indicated here. Drug abuse and suicide are discussed here in association with each other because they are in fact so frequently associated in adolescent behavior.

Many suicides are, of course, "accidental" or semi-intentional, and result from drug overdoses. The automobile, too, is frequently associated with adolescent risk taking so that in this age group, a large percentage of traffic fatalities are probably related to preconscious self-destructive behavior.

For these and many other reasons, it is not possible to collect very reliable epidemiologic data on the incidence of suicide. Equally unreliable are the so-called "predictors" or "indicators" which will alert the clinician to the adolescents who are most likely to attempt suicide. We must conclude that suicide is not a specific clinical entity. It is more likely to be an "end-point behavior" resulting

from a decision on the patient's part that no other solution will resolve his dilemma.

Despite these methodologic limitations, the possibility of suicidal attempts should remain high on the "suspected list" for any clinician evaluating a seriously disturbed adolescent.

Although almost any event may serve as a trigger mechanism for adolescent suicidal behavior, the clinician should be particularly alert in the face of any one or any combination of the following:

1. Sudden or precipitant alienation from parents in the absence of other emotionally supportive human relationships.
2. Real or imagined rejection by a peer (of either sex) whose relationship has been highly valued; or by a peer group in which membership was experienced as secure.
3. A significant failure (usually either athletic or academic) involving "public" exposure.
4. Major family disruption or dissolution (usually involving the parental marriage) especially if the patient implicates himself as a reason for that disruption.

No implication is intended that the above list approaches completeness. Only clinical alertness can ferret out possible precipitating events in any individual case.

These factors become more ominous when they occur in the presence of:

1. A long-standing history of the use of maladaptive coping mechanisms in the adolescent (for example, frequent runaways, truancy, stealing, etc.).
2. A history of accident proneness.
3. Social isolation which has recently become more prominent.
4. Drug or alcohol abuse.

Affective state in adolescence is a notoriously poor prognosticator for self-destructive behavior. Suicidal attempts may occur in the absence of any clear-cut signs of depression.

Similarly, there is no prototype for the adolescent substance abuser. The clinician should become familiar with these signs which are presumptive of the presence of the various depressants, stimulants, and hallucinogens currently in vogue in his community. Signs of withdrawal from these substances are often more reliable diagnostic cues concerning abuse, and the clinician should be particularly alert to these.

Certainly, the presence of myosis, needle tracks, phlebitis, marked alterations in mood or alertness, or the characteristic odor of marijuana (resembling that of dried hay) clinging to the patient should prompt the clinician to probe more carefully for a history of substance abuse.

65 / Note on Concluding the Psychiatric Examination and Planning Next Steps

Richard L. Cohen

As the allotted time for the psychiatric examination comes to an end, the examiner must make several rather rapid decisions. If he is conducting a "solo" evaluation, then his decision-making process is entirely an individual one. However, if there is a team involved, he will need to confer with his colleagues before making any final plans about the next steps.

These "next steps" are basically of three types:

1. Further direct examination of the child is required because not enough information was elicited in the time available; or, given additional time, there is a reasonable possibility that the child's defenses will loosen sufficiently to allow better communication.
2. There are indications that other specialized types of examinations or consultations are necessary in order to complete the evaluation. However, these need to be conducted by disciplines not immediately available within the current team.
3. Enough information has been collected for decision-making purposes. The clinician and his colleagues should now conduct an interpretative interview with the parents or guardians in which they share findings and make recommendations.

If the team has decided that there is enough information to give feedback to the parents (and child), and to the referral source, if appropriate, then it is simply a matter of setting up a time for such a session. The question of who should be present at such an interpretation conference requires careful consideration.

On the other hand, the clinician may decide that he needs further time with the child. Such a possibility should have been made known to the parents during their initial contact with the examiner, and at this point, the matter can be explained briefly.

Lastly, there is the question of requesting further, more specialized types of examinations. These may take many forms; here too, however, the process tends to lend itself to three alternatives, although these are most certainly not mutually exclusive and the examiner may have justifiable reasons for pursuing several parallel examinations. These options fall into the following types:

1. Projective and/or psychometric testing.
2. Examinations designed to study some aspect of central nervous system functioning in more focused detail.
3. Some procedure designed to explore the child's interpersonal relationships more directly (including family and/or peer group relationships).

PART C
Special Diagnostic Techniques

Introduction

It seems appropriate at this point to interrupt the account of the direct diagnostic examination of the child and family in order to introduce certain more specialized material. These include descriptions and explanations by a variety of experts of the use of various types of diagnostic modalities. To be sure, in some instances, a given specialized procedure of this sort may be carried out by a team member who is customarily found in a children's mental health facility (for example, clinical psychologist, psychiatric social worker, or psychoeducational specialist). In many instances, however, the examination needs to be conducted elsewhere by an outside consultant with whom ongoing working relationships permit frequent collaboration and communication.

In any case, the examiner should have a definite reason for requesting these specialized examinations and should be able to explain it both to parents and child (particularly if the child is old enough). He needs to describe not only what will happen in the examination, but what additional information he is hoping to secure with these techniques. Parents will sense quickly enough if the examiner is merely going on a "fishing" expedition. They will perceive either that he is at something of a loss to understand what is going on with the child, or that it is his style to cast a wide net hoping in a compulsive fashion to collect all available information whether or not it is useful or relevant. In any case, they will soon begin to lose confidence and the effect of much excellent work that has already been performed may be lost.

The Psychological Examination

EXAMINATIONS DESIGNED TO STUDY SOME
ASPECT OF CENTRAL NERVOUS SYSTEM
FUNCTIONING IN MORE FOCUSED DETAIL

Any number of factors may suggest to the examiner the need for more extensive neurologic, neuropsychological, genetic, or endocrine studies of the child. (See chapters 67–73.) Some sequence of historical events or health contingencies, or some current constellation of signs and symptoms may be enough. Any one of them may lead to the possibility that a hitherto unidentified central nervous system deficit is adversely influencing the child's current level of functioning. There may be a suspicion of: (1) a constitutional deficit; (2) some post-infectious, toxic, or degenerative syndrome which at this point may not be active; or (3) a process which is currently active or even progressive.

Only a high index of suspicion will lead the examiner to pursue such leads carefully. If his background and orientation tend to make him want to explain all disordered behavior on the basis of intrapsychic or interpersonal phenomena, then it is unlikely that such leads will be pursued. The following represents some examples of "red flags" which should lead any diagnostician to take a closer look at the degree of intactness and integrity of the child's central nervous system.

1. Any history of severe toxic or infectious states accompanied by prolonged hyperthermia, stupor, coma, or convulsions, especially during the first twelve or eighteen months of life.
2. Any phenomena suggesting a seizure state, particularly temporal lobe epilepsy, which is notorious for its tendency to be masked by behavioral or emotional symptoms (such as hallucinatory phenomena, anxiety, irritability, aggressive behavior, hyperactivity, bizarre sensations).
3. Any observations (including the clinician's own made during the regular psychiatric examination) suggesting the possible presence of perceptual or perceptual-motor difficulties, problems with coordination, possible presence of vertigo, visual difficulties, etc.
4. A history of the possible ingestion of toxic substances (in particular, the presence of pica should alert the clinician to this).
5. "Unexplained" problems in school in the face

of a normal or superior intellectual endowment. This becomes particularly suspicious when the problems are of a relatively specific nature (for example some form of dyslexia). This may have been identified by the clinician during his examination as he has watched the child read or write, it may be part of a summary received from the school, or it may have come up in previous psychological testing in terms of an unspecified perceptual-motor or "data-processing" difficulty.

6. *A birth history which suggests severe perinatal insult (for example, a five-minute Apgar of five or less; a history of serious problems in resuscitation; a history of respiratory distress syndrome; the presence of fetal distress as revealed by electronic monitoring (where the tracings show extreme variability or late deceleration).*

7. *The presence of the so-called MBD diathesis (hyperactivity, short attention span, impulsivity, poor self-image, peer relationship problems, etc.).*

8. *Suspected mental retardation of either primary (biological) or secondary (environmental) character which may not have been identified by previous examinations. This can be masked by better than average social skills in the child or by a family which has been overfunctioning for the child.*

The above represents only a smattering of the kinds of findings which should alert the examiner that more intensive study should be considered.

—RLC

---

66 / Psychometric and Projective Techniques

Max G. Magnussen

This chapter deals with the clinical application of the psychological examination. It addresses the issues and problems in the use of psychological assessment in the interdisciplinary psychodiagnostic process. The primary focus is on commonly used psychological tests for the assessment of intelligence and personality of children and adolescents.

The chapter provides information on indications for referral for psychological testing and indicates the kind of data one may expect from the testing. Basic technical concepts in psychological evaluation are presented and test administration issues are discussed. The use of psychological reports in clinical practice is covered. Current issues and attacks on tests are reviewed.

There are many techniques available for the clinical examination of children from infancy through adolescence. This presentation is not intended as an exhaustive or comprehensive review of this realm. For the reader who seeks more detailed information in a given area, a compilation of supplementary references has been inserted at the end of this chapter.

—RLC

Introduction to Psychological Tests

In contrast to the clinical interview and observation (which have been reviewed earlier), psychological tests are usually more highly structured procedures. In fact, clinical psychological tests are interviews which differ largely on the dimension of unstructured compared to structured approaches. The more highly structured test procedures clearly specify, and limit, the number and kinds of materials available. Specific verbal instructions are given and clearly defined problem situations are presented for the child's solution.

Clinical psychological tests also vary among themselves on the unstructured-structured dimension. The Rorschach Test, for example, is much less structured than the Wechsler Intelligence Scale for Children (WISC).

Although all tests provide a relatively standardized situation in which the child's behavior can be observed, two broad classifications are generally made: psychometric and projective techniques. The psychometric techniques focus on the measurement of intelligence; the projective techniques on the assessment of personality. Highly structured tests of personality do exist; however, most of these are group tests used for screening and identifying children and adolescents in need of more comprehensive evaluation. Additionally, they tend to suffer from limited reliability and validity. Such an approach is to be commended, but further investigation and research on the tests are needed. Two examples of structured tests of personality are the Institute for Personality and Ability Testing (IPAT) Children's Personality Questionnaire and the California Test of Personality.

The psychometric techniques are more highly structured than projective techniques. With psychometric approaches, a large assortment of specific items are presented which cover a composite of abilities and one may earn a pass or fail score. This serves as the highly structured condition. Projective techniques, on the other hand, tend to provide a relatively ambiguous stimulus situation (such as inkblots, pictures, or stories) which, optimally, will enable the child to reveal individuality of functioning.

Prior to using tests in the evaluation of children, it is imperative to evaluate fully the purposes of psychodiagnosis.

PURPOSES OF DIAGNOSIS

The clinical psychiatric literature suggests four purposes for psychological diagnosis: (1) to discover etiology; (2) to describe a cluster of symptoms; (3) to plan treatment; and (4) to predict the course of illness.[28, 9] Clinicians who refer children for psychological evaluation should therefore be clear about the purposes of the referral.

In clinical practice, these four goals of diagnosis are probably overlapping and interdigitating functions of an evaluation process. Although the purposes of diagnosis may be intertwined, clinicians should be specific about what questions they are asking of the assessment method(s). The importance of making explicit to the clinician and the referral source the reason for diagnosis cannot be emphasized too strongly.

To be useful, an assessment should suggest differential action on the part of child mental health personnel which can be employed in behalf of the patient. The value of any effort to establish a valid and accurate diagnosis depends, at least in part, upon how well this is done.

It is evident that there are many legitimate purposes for diagnosis. Cole and Magnussen[8] focus on disposition and action as the ultimate criteria. They point out that a major assumption underlies any case study and that is, that the categorization of information about an individual will enable the professional to utilize his skills and clinical facilities in a way that will lead to problem solution. It is their thesis that most diagnostic procedures are only loosely related, if at all, to disposition and treatment. It is emphasized that

the ultimate criteria for a meaningful clinical study of a patient rests with the ability to distinguish among a number of dispositions, one disposition which will lead to action resulting in better handling of whatever problem exists, and not necessarily the accuracy with which labels can be applied or agree with someone else . . . (pp. 539–540)

Hence, the usefulness of any information depends directly upon how well it helps in making treatment decisions.

However, whether the purpose of diagnosis is selection of treatment or assignment of a diagnosis, the research literature suggests that relatively limited clinical information may be sufficient.

Several studies* have investigated accuracy of prediction as a function of varying amounts of information. In these, it was found that the amount of data available to the judge is not related to the accuracy of his judgments.

Guaron[17] asked psychiatrists to make diagnoses utilizing information which was contained in independent case history categories. It was found that out of the forty pieces of information requested, there were only ten necessary and sufficient pieces required to make a diagnosis. The categories which psychiatrists reported as helpful to them in decision making did not correspond to those which were actually employed. The major data utilized in reaching their decisions were the clinical impressions of the patient as provided in the mental status categories.

Gottheil et al.[14] studied the psychiatric decision to recommend discharge or retention of a soldier in the armed forces. In the course of this, they reviewed the contribution that specific items of intake information made to this process. It was found that the interview alone had determined the judges' decisions. Moreover, despite the fact that the information from the face-to-face interaction was crucial, it could not be specified by the interviewers.

This suggests that in diagnostic practice, minimal clinical information is often utilized to make various decisions. One of the early tasks for the child clinician thus becomes that of identifying what is the minimal information necessary to arrive directly at a treatment decision or for any other purpose of diagnosis.

When to Refer for Clinical Psychological Appraisal

In the course of a referral, there should be an explicit statement of what specific questions are to be answered, and the reasons for the psychological examinations. The choice between collecting maximal wide range versus minimal critical information reenters the scene. Precise formulation helps the evaluator focus on the essential aspects of the problem and avoid irrelevancies and digressions.

It is unrealistic to expect that the clinical decision maker will always be able to formulate the

* See references 34, 19, 38, 43, 13, 29, and 36.

referral questions in a clear, concise, and precise manner. Here a competent clinical child phychologist can be of help in consulting on a referral question and in specifying what clinical information and tests can best answer the questions. A skilled and well-trained clinical child psychologist will be equipped to analyze the appropriate questions and referral context and then select the appropriate data or specific tests to analyze the problem.

In some cases test data may not be necessary. Demographic data, parental information, clinical observations, or interview items may answer the questions.

Levine[20] deals in an action-oriented framework with "why and when to test." In making a choice between whether to employ clinical interview or formal psychological testing to answer the diagnostic questions, it is necessary to refer back to the "payoff load" of tests. In other words, one must determine the utility of tests for their consumers.

At this juncture, a look at the general advantages and disadvantages of tests is indicated. What is their potential?

WHAT TESTS CAN AND CANNOT DO

In some instances, formal testing for specific purposes can provide a relatively controlled, standardized sample of behavior. This saves a great deal of time and is more efficient than repeated clinical interviews and history-taking methods. Again, because of reliability and validity problems, it is important to contrast and compare test results with clinical data from several other sources.

For the diagnostic purpose of determining etiology, some of the projective tests, such as the Rorschach and Children's Apperception Test (CAT), are capable of sampling personality dynamics. They are especially likely to illuminate the child's perceptions of authority representatives, parental figures, the environment, and significant others. In any of these areas, test results might discover origins and sources of possible disturbance. Psychometric tests are capable of providing information on the level and quality (i.e., the manner in which the child approaches and handles tasks) of intellectual functioning. Where certain intellectual functions are arrested, either generally or specifically, the distinction between retardation and specific learning disability must be explored. The intactness of perceptual-motor functions and the possible influence of neurobiologic factors on

their functioning may be assessed. In general, the level and quality of development as expressed in test results may point toward etiological considerations.

Formal tests can contribute to diagnostic classification. The level of tested intellectual functioning is one major factor in diagnosing mental retardation. The quality of intellectual functioning can be of diagnostic significance for classifying childhood schizophrenia, learning disabilities, neurological impairment, delinquency, and neurotic disorders.

Projective test findings are capable of contributing to the differential diagnosis of psychoneurotic, psychotic, and characterological conditions. Certain projective and objective measurement methods may help predict the course of disorders. Data on competencies, strengths, flexibilities, and the potential for change and growth in development may be discovered and related directly to prognostic predictions.

The choice of treatment modality can be influenced by the quality, level, degree, and areas of dysfunction and strength that can be culled from both projective and psychometric tests.

To best answer the clinical inquiries, precise formulation of the referral and diagnostic questions permits more specific selection of tests and collection of data. Many reliability and validity issues arise in the course of answering referral questions. To best deal with them, the selection of optimal combinations of tests (batteries) is a procedure of considerable importance.

REFERRAL QUESTIONS

The questions formulated in referrals will affect the quality of psychological reports. In general, it is highly likely that vague and nonspecific referral questions will beget similar kinds of psychological reports. For instance, referral questions that simply ask for "intelligence testing," "an IQ," or "projective tests" are too global to provide direction or focus for the psychologist's clinical examination or reporting of results. A better approach than to ask for "intelligence testing" would be to state the reasons (treatment planning, school placement, questions as to perceptual-motor functioning, thinking disturbances, etc.) for requesting an intellectual evaluation. This kind of input can assist all parties involved in obtaining more useful and technically sound information from a psychological assessment.

Test Administration Issues

Many factors have relevance in the context of test administration. The different types of tests and the different age levels of children provide special test administration issues. Broadly outlined, the factors to be considered include the examinee, the examiner, and the interaction that occurs in the social-psychological context of the clinical examination.

EXAMINEE FACTORS

In order to consider the test findings in proper perspective, the examiner would need to know the physical status of the subject. Factors such as malnutrition, fatigue, ill health, use of certain medication, etc., may have an influence on the examinee's test responses. The current psychological status of the examinee and the nature of activities or events preceding the test may affect the findings. For example, even the order in which tests have been presented within the examinational context may influence results. Magnussen[21] provides data which suggests that the sequence of the individual tests as they are given in the course of a battery can exert a significant influence on the productivity of certain content in the Rorschach Test. More specifically, subjects who were administered tests emphasizing animal drawings and animal stories (CAT) prior to being given the Rorschach produced significantly more animal content than the control group.

In terms of the performance proper, the "set" of the examinee is of considerable importance. An important aspect of this set is the way the child is prepared for examination by the parents and the referring professional. The need to deal with the subject's individual concerns about the testing plus the kinds of sets provided by the parents and the referring professional person can make the examiner's task doubly difficult. To control the examinee's set within the testing context requires both standardization procedures and clinical sensitivity to different developmental levels and conditions.

In tests of a child's abilities, the underlying assumption is that he is functioning at his optimal level. In order to be appropriately compared on the ability measured, it is assumed that each individual is doing his best. The motivational and emotional variables that must be clinically noted and/or controlled are thoroughly covered by Anastasi.[4, 5]

EXAMINER FACTORS

The examiner functions in the individual clinical assessment process include establishment of rapport, eliciting involvement in the tasks, focusing attention on the procedures, sustaining concentration on the tests, and striving to obtain optimal performances from the patient. Each developmental level of the child and each kind of clinical measurement require different "loadings" on these examiner functions.

Masling[24, 25] reviews the literature on the examiner and situational variables that influence the clinical findings. Rosenthal[31, 32] enumerates the experimenter variables that have effects in the outcome of behavioral investigation. Although the clinical assessment and research functions are different, many of the behavioral and examiner (or experimenter) characteristics have a similar impact on the performance of the subject. Gardner[12] deals with the therapist variables that are important in the psychotherapeutic approach to the resistant child. In essence, clinicians performing either diagnostic, research, or treatment functions with individuals have found that appearance, social status, age, sex, interpersonal warmth, responsiveness, self-assuredness, and firmness significantly affected subject performance. Verbal and nonverbal behavior of the examiner has been found to influence Rorschach productivity in studies by Magnussen[22] and Gross.[16] These two studies independently found that verbal reinforcement (for example, the examiner's saying "Uh huh" following a response) and the nonverbal reinforcement (for example, head nodding after a reply) increase the frequency of the preselected responses in the Rorschach test situation. In addition, the findings suggest that the verbal stimulus is no more effective than the nonverbal stimulus in terms of increasing reinforced responses. These extremely subtle influences significantly increased specific Rorschach content. The importance of examiner awareness of his/her behavior and its influence upon the examiner-subject interaction and test interpretation is of importance in many different clinical functions. Situational factors include context of the room and location of examination (school, laboratory, detention center, etc.). These variables have been demonstrated to influence test findings in significant ways.

EXAMINER-EXAMINEE INTERACTION

It is the interaction between examiner and examinee and context variables that provide the broad conceptual framework by which one understands the ingredients of the diagnostic testing process. As one example, the examiner's professional status and interpersonal warmth may have a differential effect on examinees with different kinds of interpersonal difficulties. The effect may also be modified by the characteristics of the context in which the assessment took place. Rosenthal[31] has summarized a number of studies bearing on clinician expectancy effects in the use of clinical assessment techniques. Racial examiner effects have been reviewed by Sattler.[35] Tuma and McGraw[40] reveal examiner sex differences as influencing Rorschach productivity. Once again, the social-psychological aspects of the relationship between the examiner's data collection and the subject and setting suggests high relevance in consideration of the interactions effects.

Basic Technical Concepts in Psychological Evaluation

How can the usefulness of a test be evaluated? To be most useful a measurement instrument should be standardized on a large group of subjects representative of those for whom it is intended. The instruments used in measurement must be checked for their validity, reliability, and objectivity. That is, they must measure what they purport to measure, give consistent results if repeated, and give the same result when scored by different persons. The characteristics of validity, reliability, and objectivity are most readily achieved in psychological tests such as those designed to measure intelligence. Before a formal test is actually used in determining the intellectual functions of children, a number of conditions must be met. There is a systematic and empirical period of "testing the tests" to determine their applicability in particular situations.

STANDARDIZATION

This concept refers to the establishment of uniform conditions for administering a test and uniform methods of interpreting test findings. A large number of individuals are tested in an identical manner to provide norms with which to compare any individual test score. The intention of standardization is to make certain that the particular characteristic of the patient is the sole variable being measured, to the exclusion of other factors. Extreme care is taken to insure proper standardization of testing procedures and conditions. The examiner's manual for a particular test specifies the uniform directions to be delivered to every child, the precise demonstrations, the exact procedures, etc. The psychologist strives to keep motivation high and to minimize distractions and fatigue. If such conditions are maintained for one group and not another, the test scores may reflect motivational or other differences in addition to the ability differences which it is supposed to measure.

Measurement of ability is a relative matter. Individual test scores are used on an ordinal scale. An ordinal scale ranks scores in order. Single test scores must be interpreted in relationship to the scores of other children. This is a relative rather than an absolute measure. It is for this reason that a test constructor must give the test to a large number of children. The sample to which it is administered is the standardization group. The various scores obtained by the children in this sample are identified as the test norms. These norms provide the average score and reveal the degree of variability present in the scores. There are many ways to report norms, and clinical psychologists can use statistical procedures to convert from one kind of norm to another. Basically, one aspires to obtain a large distribution of scores. On a frequency distribution, one plots the scores corresponding to the variability (standard deviation), above and below the measure of central tendency. It is possible, then, to report scores in standard deviations, cumulative percentiles, standard scores, and, sometimes, by all of these methods. Age norms are typically provided when the test is to be utilized for people of heterogenous ages. They are usually omitted if the test is used for a relatively homogenous group, for example, children from five to seven. Norms may be provided for any other classification of children that may be relevant, for example, for grade in school, sex, or race. It is always essential to be aware of the exact characteristics of the standardization sample. In order to interpret test results accurately, it is mandatory that our standardization norms represent the kind of children with whom it is fair and appropriate to compare a child's score. If the standardization sample is not at least several hundred, norms may be inappropriate (too high or too low) as a condition of chance in the selection of the standardization group. It is easy to see that standardization and interpretation of individual test results is closely related to normative data.

557

NORMS

A single test score has no meaning by itself. These scores are known as raw scores. A raw score assumes significance only when compared with a distribution of scores made by a large number of other individuals who have taken the same test. Such distributions are called norms. An example of one kind of norm is the mental age norm in which an individual child's score on an intelligence test is compared to the average score obtained by children of different ages. A psychological test has no preselected or arbitrary pass-fail score. This test must be given to a large number of people who form a representative sample of the population for which the test is designed. The scores obtained by this sample provide the test norms. Test manuals should provide the users of tests with this information on the size and characteristics of the normative sample. The psychologist must be aware of these standardization variables and be able to evaluate their adequacy and applicability to the children who are to be assessed.

Different tests purported to measure the same function may provide different scores for any single individual child. This may be related to differences in the characteristics of the samples (age, socioeconomic status, cultural variables, etc.) on which the different examinations have been standardized. Therefore, it is essential that for the testing of any individual the name of the test that was administered be specified. A similar situation exists pertaining to norms and standardization when clinicians are evaluating by the interview method. What the clinician observes and hears in an interview or observation is not valuable until it is compared and interpreted in terms of other children of similar age, sex, developmental level, condition, background, and situational context. It is in the process of collecting clinical norms that some of the most glaring inadequacies in interviewing and observations can be made. The clinician develops a set of "internal norms" based on clinical interviews of a wide variety of children with different strengths, problems, and developmental levels. The comparison of the individual child with other children previously interviewed or observed is an "inside of the head" clinical sampling task. The purposes of the interview, such as identifying deviancy, capacity to profit from intervention, etc., require the clinician to compare the individual against sets of "internal norms." Furthermore, the clinician does not always confront each clinical subject with the same standardized set of questions delivered in a uniform manner. As a consequence, the clinician is not always certain if the response made by the patient is due to the variation in approach or other factors. This makes collection of systematic, objective "clinical norms" exceedingly difficult, if not impossible.

VALIDITY

When tests are used for diagnostic purposes, an essential characteristic is their validity. Reliability refers to consistency of measurement. Validity pertains to the degree to which the test measures that which it was designed to measure. A test may be highly reliable but still not valid. A thermometer, for example, may give consistent readings but it is certainly not a valid instrument for measuring specific gravity. Validity in psychological measurement concerns itself with the relationships of a test to other data about the individual. A systematic study of the relationships makes it possible to determine what the instrument measures and to what degree it correlates with an independent criterion.

Why are some tests valid and others not? One of the reasons must be that valid tests are those which measure the kinds of abilities and characteristics actually needed in real-life functioning. This exceedingly important technical property of a test—validity—leads to differing viewpoints in terms of the practical use of diagnostic psychological tests. In keeping with any viewpoint, it is always essential to know the purpose for which the test has specified validity. In conventional classification, tests may possess content validity, criterion-related validity, or construct validity, or any combination of these.[5]

The criterion in content validity is the degree of accuracy and completeness that test items sample the content function that is being assessed.

Criterion-related validity involves correlation of a test score with an external criterion. To measure validity, two scores are required for each individual. One of these scores is the test score. The other score is some measure of what it is that the test is purported to be measuring. The latter measure is termed a criterion. A coefficient of correlation between the test scores and the criterion measure scores is computed. This provides a validity coefficient and provides information about how valid a given test is for a given purpose. The higher the positive correlation, the better the prediction that can be made from the test to the criterion. The coefficient of correlation is conventionally designated *r*. Such an *r* varies between perfect positive correlation (r = +1.00) and perfect negative correlation (r = −1.00). Lack of relationship is designated r = .00. Both extremes in the direction of high positive and high negative correlations can be equally predictive.

Construct validity is a generalized, all-inclusive kind of validity. Its use generally deals with research refutation, verification of theoretical constructs, or experimental hypotheses concerning human behavior.

VALIDITY IN TERMS OF CLINICAL DECISION MAKING

Validity is an extremely critical factor. The clinician is repeatedly confronted with this concept. In applied clinical practice, validity coefficients of relatively low magnitude are often useful for making predictions for specified purposes. In striving to make predictions for the individual case, however, it is usually impossible to obtain validity coefficients of the high absolute value that remain as a standard for large normative samples.

Further practical issues in applied contexts have resulted in expanded definitions of validity. It is important to review some of these broadened notions pertaining to validity.

In the conventional orientation toward validity in assessment, the general goal of testing is interpreted as involving the prediction of human behavior. Typically, the purpose of a test is to forecast nontest behavior. Test validity considerations, such as construct and criterion validity, refer to some measurable aspect of the child, and the criterion for test validation is viewed as involving the behavior of the individual tested. F+% in a Rorschach analysis, for example, is viewed as having validity as a clinical concept when it refers to some demonstrable behavior, perhaps labeled "perceptual accuracy." Gough[15] states that the primary evaluation of an assessment technique identifies the criteria that are principally relevant to the test; how well the technique predicts what it seeks to predict; measures what it purports to measure; or defines what it is intended to define. An implicit rule is that assessment techniques predict, measure, or define some aspect of human behavior.

In contrast to independent verification of the predictions of an assessment in the traditional validation procedure, dispositional assessment suggests that treatment procedures are evaluated *in addition* to the usual procedures of scientific validation. The question of the value of tests, when considered in their practical use, becomes not "Does the test correlate with a criterion?" or "Does the test accord with a nomological net?" Instead, the question becomes "Does the use of the test improve the success of the decision-making process?" either by making it more efficient, less costly, more accurate, more rational, or more clinically relevant.

Levine[20] raises these issues and his conclusion is that the clinical-actuarial controversy is academic since most of the research in that area is irrelevant to decision making. His polarized position is that much of the research on test validity is not relevant to the practical use of psychological tests. His contention is that the demonstrations that psychological tests do not agree with psychiatric diagnoses and that psychologists can identify diagnostic classifications from test falls into the irrelevant category. This notion may hold for clinical decision making, but if one purpose of assessment is diagnostic classification, the typical procedure of validity has some degree of utility.

Just as the clinical-statistical controversy is present in varying degrees, there are also arguments about construct validity and the definition of validity from the clinical decision-making point of reference. Development of psychological tests which measure complex clinical-social-psychological variables is obviously difficult. Similarly, research on whether psychological testing improves the payoff function in a decision-making orientation is exceedingly difficult. The struggles with idiographic or single individual and nomothetic or normative assessment for specific purposes provides a tremendous technical and conceptual challenge. It is easy to discern that validity is an extremely essential characteristic, but differing views exist on this subject in the area of assessment. The critical question pertaining to validity is "Does the test measure what it is supposed to measure?"

RELIABILITY

In simplest terms, reliability refers to the degree to which the test measures something consistently. If an intelligence test yielded an IQ of 125 for an individual one day and an IQ of 75 the next, the test would be highly unreliable. The question asked of reliability is "Does the test generally rank the individuals in approximately the same way each time it is administered?" Prior to actual use in clinical practice, psychological tests are evaluated for reliability. One of the methods is by the test-retest method, which involves giving the same test to the same individuals at two different times. Sometimes two equivalent forms of a test are developed, both given to the same individuals and the reliability determined.

In addition to retest and equivalent form methods for computing reliability, there are the split-half and Kuder-Richardson techniques. The statistical method of correlation is used in answering the reliability question. The resulting statistical correlation is called the reliability coefficient. Test designers strive to achieve test reliabilities above 90 but often reliabilities in the 60s or 70s are useful, depending on the purpose of prediction. Tests which are too short are often unreliable, as are many tests which do not use objectively determined scores. It is in this area that projective tests provide special difficulties for scorer reliability. Examiner reliability is another possible source of variance that is typically addressed by providing highly standardized procedures for administration and manuals with precise instructions for scoring.

Developmental Range of Psychological Tests for Children and Youth

The child psychologist has available an array of measurement instruments which cover a broad developmental range. A sampling of the commonly used intelligence tests that are frequently given at each developmental level follows.

Based on convention, infant tests usually cover the first eighteen months of life. The bulk of these examinations are controlled observations of sensorimotor development. Preschool tests typically cover the ages of eighteen to sixty months. The child at these ages can sit, walk, communicate by language, manipulate objects, and interact in an interpersonal process. The procedures therefore are more varied and provide broader samplings of developmental behaviors. Examples of commonly used sets of methods at the infant and preschool level are the Gesell and Amatruda Developmental Schedules. The Gesell Schedules extend from the age of four weeks to six years. These schedules reflect the fine line between observations and standardized tests. The examinations are essentially an elaboration and refinement of the qualitative observation commonly conducted by pediatricians. Most of the items are made on the

observations of the child's behavioral development in the motor, language, adaptive, and personal-social areas. The parent provides the examiner with supplemental information to compare with the norms in the four areas.

The Cattell Infant Intelligence Scale samples an age range from three to thirty months. Uzgiris and Hunt,[41] inspired by Piaget's writings on infant intelligence, devised seven scales to survey an age range from one through twenty months. The scales assess visual pursuit and permanence of objects, development of means for obtaining desired environmental events, development of gestural imitation, development of vocal imitation, development of operational causality, the construction of object relations in space and the development of schemes for relating to objects. This is an ordinal measurement device and the approach is being researched.

The Bayley Scales of Infant Development cover a range in age from two through thirty months. These scales are designed to provide a tripartite basis for evaluation (sensory-perceptual motor, social and objective orientations) of the child's developmental status.

Beyond the developmental level of infancy and into preschool and school-age stages of growth, commonly utilized measures of intelligence include the Stanford-Binet Intelligence Scale (Form L-M, ages two years and over), Wechsler Intelligence Scale for Children (WISC) (ages five to fifteen years), and Wechsler Intelligence Scale for Children—Revised (WISC-R) (ages six through sixteen years).

Projective techniques which are commonly used to measure personality traits at different developmental levels include the Children's Apperception Test (CAT) (ages three to ten years), the Rorschach, with norms established by Ames et al.[1, 2, 3] (two to sixteen years), Rosenzweig Picture Frustration Study: Form for Children (ages four through thirteen years), and the Thematic Apperception Test (TAT) (four years and beyond).

CHILDREN'S INTELLIGENCE TESTS

Intelligence tests are psychometric devices which, in practice, consist of sets of standardized questions and tasks that are used to assess a child's potential for purposive and functional behavior. There are several definitions of intelligence. In general, however, psychologists distinguish between ability (quality and level of actual performance) and capacity (potential ability or "trainability"). When psychologists speak of potential intelligence of a child, their interpretations are based under two categories: (1) test scatter and (2) measures of intellectual deterioration. Test scatter involves both intertest patterns and intratest variability of performances. It is possible with the point-type scales (Wechsler's tests) to interpret intratest scatter on the basis of the ordinal relationship of passes and fails within the same subtest. For example, if a child passes many of the difficult items and misses most of the easier questions in a subtest and, therefore, obtains a generally low total score, the question might be raised concerning potential intelligence. Similarly, intertest scatter and indices of deterioration for a variety of diagnostic classifications have been proposed; however, the research findings on these different factors have been inconclusive and contradictory. It is debatable whether intelligence tests measure capacity. The notion that intelligence tests are measures of current functioning of the child appears more defensible.

Even though "intelligence" tests are comprised of measures of several primary mental abilities, it is most common to find expression in terms of general intelligence, expressed as an IQ. The intelligence quotient is based on a ratio between an individual's mental and chronological ages and thus, purportedly, shows rate of mental growth.

Many earlier studies suggested the relative constancy of the IQ, that is, an individual's IQ tendency to remain relatively stable unless environmental factors changed markedly. In recent decades, research has demonstrated that the IQ is an unstable index and that it is vulnerable to environmental influences, especially in the case of children. In order to assess the predictability and stability of intelligence, accuracy of determination of a child's relative standing to the general population can be increased by repeated individual testing over a reasonable time frame. This further supports the position that intelligence tests are best considered as a measure of *current* functioning.

Intelligence is distributed among the population in a normal distribution curve, with about half the population falling in the "average" range from 90 to 109. Mentally retarded children and youth can be classified on intellectual measures, with various subclassifications that reflect severity, from IQ's ranging from 0 to 70. Around IQ 70 there is a band of doubt where some individuals must be considered "borderline"—that is, incapable of conducting their own affairs adequately because of low intelligence—where others are not. It must be emphasized that mental deficiency or retarda-

tion is diagnosed by a number of historic, clinical, and social criteria. Intelligence test results are only part of the diagnostic material. At the other end of the intellectual scale, one finds the mentally gifted. Once again, additional criteria are necessary in determining this characteristic.

Rabin and McKinney[30] provide reviews of empirical findings with intelligence tests and several nosological groupings of psychopathology. Imperfect as the current psychiatric diagnostic categories are, they are the nosological schemes with which the psychologist must cope. Inferences from intelligence tests are made through parallelisms between test responses and the symptom clusters of the traditional classifications. For example, the terms "brain damage" and "organicity" are very vague and complex. Under this category, especially with children, one finds variable diffuseness of damage, different localization of structural insults, a variety of diseases, many disorders of different degrees of chronicity, nonstatic status (in the sense that improvement and/or degeneration may occur).

The wide variety of patterns in "brain-damaged" children challenges the psychologists to locate the differential effects upon intellectual functioning. The implications for the sampling of patients in the research of the test patterns of scatter and deterioration are obvious. Inconsistent findings in many studies are therefore common. In clinical practice, where clinicians encounter many kinds of "organicity," it is impossible to find universal indices of scatter or deterioration. In some clinical instances, organically damaged children may demonstrate poorer functioning on memory items and the performance scales of the WISC.

In comparing research and application findings, some support seems to suggest that patients with lesions of the right cerebral hemisphere show a lower performance level on intelligence tests and relatively intact verbal level functioning. In left hemisphere damage, the verbal performance is lowered in comparison to the more intact performance scales. A review of scatter on the WISC suggests that the intertest difference between verbal and performance scales is approximately as far as current findings have consistently evolved.

With children, the conclusiveness of intratest variability is very uncertain. Clinicians must depend a great deal upon clinical experiences and hunches. However, the human instrument—the psychologist—and the psychometric instrument—the intelligence test—can be useful in the differential diagnostic process. Science and clinical "art" often combine in the area of diagnostic application.

The characteristics of validity, reliability, and objectivity are most readily achieved in psychological tests such as those developed to measure intelligence. The Stanford-Binet is very widely used because it correlates so well with grades in school. Hence, it is helpful in predicting a child's school progress and planning for curriculum. It is limited in that it is predominantly a test of verbal intelligence and is standardized only on nonclinic children. Therefore, for a child who does not come from an English-speaking home or for a hard-of-hearing child, the Stanford-Binet often does not provide an accurate measurement.

Thus, it has been necessary to develop certain tests called performance tests in which motor and/or visual reactions are substituted for verbal reactions. Sometimes even the instructions are given without the use of speech. The Wechsler Intelligence Scale for Children combines the verbal and performance tests into one test designed to measure intelligence. The test is constructed in two parts, verbal and performance.

The WISC differs from the Stanford-Binet in that it abandons the concept of mental age. This concept has been found to have certain deficiencies in testing older children. The finding is that the mental age concept is not a very useful one above the age of thirteen. Up to thirteen years of age, it is not difficult to find tests that can be passed by a higher age group while being failed by those one year younger. This is the age differentiation technique by which most infant, preschool and early elementary school-age intelligence tests have been validated. The construct of intelligence is that some functions demonstrate progressive improvement as the child matures and develops with advancing age. After approximately age thirteen, the gain in scores per year is so minimal that differentiating mental age scales cannot be easily constructed.

Without such tests, it is not feasible to continue mental age scales. In order to maintain the mental age concept and the IQ above age thirteen, arbitrary scoring devices must be used. As a certain intellectual developmental level is reached around adolescence, it is more appropriate to compare scores of an individual with results earned by others of a similar age. The Wechsler Preschool and Primary Scale of Intelligence (WPPSI), the WISC, the WISC-R (the children's intelligence measures) and the Wechsler Adult Intelligence Scale (WAIS) (adolescent and adult measures) are computed by comparing individual test performances with the scores earned by others of similar age groups only. The individual score represents relative intelligence at a particular age in relationship to peers.

McClelland[23] offers an alternative approach to the traditional notions of general intelligence and the technical characteristics of tests. He advocates criterion sampling. That is, placing in tests real-life samples from the criterion that are actually possessed by those with proficient behavior. McClelland elaborates on life-outcome criteria in both theoretical and practical application terms to challenge the ingrown world of traditional intelligence testing. He advocates very eloquently the need to test for competence rather than for "intelligence."

The importance of the various cognitive tests, language tests, and behavioral assessment approaches must be kept in mind. Other sections of this volume discuss these strategies.

PROJECTIVE TECHNIQUES

Some structured personality inventories have fixed alternatives for responding, so that the subject must reply by making a choice among ready-made answers. Projective tests are more ambiguous and less highly structured. The replies the subject can give are freer. Because the subject produces more of his own replies, the person is said to project his "personality" through them. Hence, the name "projective" techniques. The subject is presented with a standardized set of ambiguous or neutral stimuli—pictures or inkblots which have no definite meaning but may be interpreted in various ways—and is allowed to interpret freely what is "seen" in them. Thus the subject may project into each stimulus presented some special, private meaning.

Projective techniques are difficult to slant or bias because there are no obviously "right" or "wrong" answers. Although the tests are hard to slant, a major limitation is that the psychologist must rely to a large extent upon subjective judgment in scoring and interpretation. Even though objective standards have been established for scoring responses and norms have been established for some tests, much clinical skill is required on the part of the examiner.

Earlier mention has been made of the issues and problems with the interview and the social-psychological context involving examiner, examinee, and situational variable interactions. These identical issues also highly influence the interpretation of data from projective techniques. The chief deficit of the projective techniques is their equivocal validity status. Studies of the Rorschach and TAT generally reveal that the methods cannot predict the validity criteria within a satisfactory level of statistical probability. This burden of questionable validity must remain until it can be established operationally what kinds of moods, conflicts, etc., contribute to what specific kinds of behaviors under what conditions. Perhaps, if this could be defined, some of the projective devices might assist in the prediction of behavior. For the present, projective methods simply provide a clinical impression of the child's subjective "set" at a given moment in time.

Regardless of how projective techniques are scored or interpreted, they yield a degree of subjective measure of "personality"—primarily impressions of dominant moods, frustrations, conflicts, and of modes of perception. In this sense, projective methods are little more than standardized interviews. Similar to less standardized interviews, their usefulness depends on the skill of the professional who administers them and interprets them. Once again, reliance and comparison with many sources of information is important for use of the projective technique in the diagnostic function.

Inkblot Method. The *Rorschach*, one of the oldest projective methods, makes use of a series of inkblots. The technique is frequently called the "inkblot test." This method often provides the skilled psycho-diagnostician with clinical information which cannot be elicited as quickly or specifically by clinical interviews. Ames et al.[2] provides updated and enlarged norms over previous contributions.[1, 3] This new sample offers increased comparison data for children and adolescent protocols. Exner[10] integrates the features of the numerous approaches to the Rorschach and provides the major postulates necessary for clinical use of the technique. The approach is used mostly as an extension of the interview. In the strictest technical sense, the Rorschach is not a test. Its dubious reliability and validity place the method closer to an interview than a test.

Picture Story Tests. An adaptation of the Thematic Apperception Test, a technique that consists of a series of pictures of people, is the *Children's Apperception Test* (CAT). The CAT is comprised of a series of pictures of animals. Bellak[7] published a volume that deals particularly with the TAT, CAT, and SAT (Senior Apperception Technique), and that focuses on the clinical application and use of these projective methods. In this work, we see the progression of methods of assessment provided on a developmental continuum from childhood, adulthood, to the aged.

The TAT is interpreted by noting recurring themes in the stories: the characteristic needs and frustrations of the hero; the relationships of the hero to peers; to parents or authority or to members of the opposite sex; and the perception of the world. Also noted are the overall emotional tenor of the stories, whether bland, overly optimistic, depressed, angry, violent, or destructive.

The CAT is designed with an implicit, if not explicit, assumption of a psychoanalytic developmental orientation. Pictures of animals depicting problems of feeding, toilet-training, and parent-child interactions are used as stimuli to produce fantasy behavior. The Blacky Pictures comprise a series of cartoons depicting a dog. This approach is explicitly based on a psychoanalytic, psychosexual developmental theory. The CAT, TAT, SAT, and the Blacky Pictures all suffer the deficiencies of the Rorschach in regard to validity and reliability.

Mundy[27] provides the distinction of projective techniques which require verbal responses (examples are the Rorschach and CAT) and projectives that elicit motor behavior (drawings, Bender Visual-Motor Gestalt, as examples). Thus, children who may have difficulties with one or the other modality of behavior can be assessed via different methods of projective testing.

In comparison with tests of intelligence, projective techniques in general are much less satisfactory in terms of the basic technical essentials of reliability, validity, and norms. It is for these reasons that in the area of personality assessment a multiinformational approach is extremely important. Information achieved from projective tests should be augmented and verified from such sources as interviews and clinical observations of the child, reports from parents and teachers, developmental histories, and other relevant behavioral observations.

Mundy[27] reviews the difficulties of administration, scoring, interpretation, and prediction encountered in the use of projective techniques. Clinicians who value actuarial or statistical prediction refute the projective methods as inconclusive (at best). Those clinicians who demand that the test predict future behavior in a direct fashion reject the value of these methods. A balanced view suggests that most experienced clinicians in the child clinical area supplement idiographic methods of assessment with nomothetic procedures.

The effectiveness of any kind of clinical technique cannot be evaluated in isolation or independent of the expertise of the clinician prividing the application.

GROUP TESTS

It is exceedingly difficult to make predictions about the individual through any diagnostic or measurement technique that is currently available. Correspondingly, group tests are severely handicapped in terms of making predictions about the individual. In fact, it must be emphasized that group tests are specifically designed for rapid mass screening and for identifying children in need of further assessment. Group intelligence tests are useful when a crude estimate of intellectual level serves the purpose and in situations where more sophisticated evaluations are not obtainable. In comparison to the individual clinical instruments, one loses, with the group methods, the improved essential test factors, work methods, social and emotional behavior, and qualitative aspects of the individual child's behavior. Furthermore, one can never be certain of the maintenance of the individual child's motivation and attention to the tasks. Anastasi[4] provides data on group tests to prepare users to evaluate them and to interpret the test results correctly.

Use of Psychological Reports

Psychological reports can be useful in developing diagnostic formulations and treatment planning for the child.

The practical clinical use of psychological reports must include the interpreting of psychological findings to the parent and/or child, either directly by the clinical child psychologist as primary or consulting clinician or by a clinician of another discipline. In some cases, teachers and other caregivers need to have "feedback" of findings in order to manage or assist the child in their respective roles. The clinical skill involved in translating psychological findings into practical usefulness for the patient, parents, primary clinician, and other significant persons dealing with the child patient is of the utmost importance.

At the present time, there is much attention being given to the rights of the child and the parents to clinical information. Without delving into this body of issues and the definitions of "in the best interests" of the child, it may be sufficient to remind the reader that clinicians must make judgments on interpretation of findings and use of findings in behalf of the patient. In each clinical case, it is the responsibility of the evaluating clinician to translate into practical, useful terms the findings which facilitate the functioning of the child. Without the benefits of practical and meaningful application to assist the patient, clinical examination findings or reports are relatively useless to assist the patient. Diagnostic classification that does not eventuate into providing direction or application for the patient, generally is useless assessment information for this purpose.

Some of the psychological data can be used to provide actuarial predictions.[26] It is important to recognize that in speaking of an actuarial prediction, the reference is to a method of statistically combining data to make a decision or prediction. As for clinical prediction, clinical judgment is still part of actuarial prediction.[37] It is in this area of clinical decision making that clinical and actuarial methods are combined and hopefully provide intervention strategies.

INTERPRETATION OF TEST RESULTS

In the interpretation of the findings to the parents and/or child, it is the role of the primary clinician, regardless of discipline, to process and combine what information is to be shared for the benefits of the patient in his/her development. (See chapter 78, "Interpretation Conference.") If the findings are to be interpreted to the family by a team, preparation on the part of the codiagnosticians in making the interpretation session most productive is an essential for success in outcome. Certainly, within the context and content of the interpretation session, the diagnostic and treatment process are ideally intertwined. The factor of compartmentalizing into two different areas the functions of diagnosis and treatment, rather than in treating these two areas as one basic process, occasionally provides difficulties to those demanding scientific precision in the assessment function. In clinical practice it is difficult to provide services that are helpful if these functions are perceived and implemented as two markedly different and relatively independent roles.

Within the context of the interpretation of results to the parents and the patient, the mutual opportunity to share, explore, confirm, reject, expand, or modify the findings and recommendations should be provided for all concerned parties.

A brief case vignette in which a clinical child psychologist and a child psychiatrist interpreted the findings from the two sources of examination data is offered as an illustration of such a parental conference.

The child was a ten-year-old male who was referred by the parents with complaints of "academic underachievement—getting all B's and no A's, few friends, and socially and emotionally more like an eight-year-old." The father was a physician, mother, a medical librarian. An eighteen-year-old daughter was a student at Dartmouth.

The child psychiatrist obtained a developmental history from the parents, and interviewed and observed the child in a play session. The child was referred for psychological assessment with specific questions being asked about his intellectual functioning and developmental level.

The parents, child, and two diagnosticians were present at the session dealing with the interpretation of findings. The psychologist shared the clinical findings concerning the intellectual level as related to the concerns about receiving B's—or "underachieving." The level and quality of intellectual functioning in this instance suggested that the child was functioning at his ability level. The parents immediately questioned the precision, accuracy of the findings, the credentials of the psychologist, and searched for actual raw scores and exact bits of data. The parental reaction offered the psychologist the chance to observe, point out this reaction, and bring the parents to discussion of whether this behavior was part of the problem that needed to be identified and worked upon. The psychologist was able to directly inform the child of his level of intellectual and academic competence. He could serve the child as an ally and encourage him to talk about his reactions to the current set of interchanges and his perceptions of his own problems and assets. In sequence, the psychological findings were presented and openly contrasted and compared (differences and similarities) with the psychiatrist's impressions of the parents and the child. In this particular case, the two professionals could complement, support, and facilitate movement in understanding of the problems and in a redefinition of difficulties. They could also provide an opportunity to test skills in resolution on the part of the three family members. Since clinical case illustrations are offered to document a point, this one was selected as a brief example in which the interview set in motion the initial steps toward accepting and entering into parental counseling and therapy for the child.

Current Issues and Attacks on Tests

A brief overview has been given of the issues of so-called "culture-fair" and "culture-free" tests and the criticisms of testing.

For several decades, in the course of measuring both intelligence and personality, findings have been presented that demonstrate differences among children who come from different home backgrounds, subcultures, and cultures. Differences were found in socioeconomic levels, urban and rural contexts and minority groups.[6] In general, it is not surprising that these differences are found to be based on antecedent conditions and living environments. However, in order to interpret any such differences, one must carefully assess the normative and standardization information. In the attempt to develop culture-fair and culture-free tests, professional attention has come to focus ever more sharply in this direction.

It appears that in recent years, intelligence and ability testing have borne the brunt of the widespread critique. This is probably because of the extensive group ability and intelligence testing employed by schools. The findings were often used to make significant educational decisions about children. On the other hand, individual intelligence testing and personality assessment have not received the same massive public concern and attention. Undoubtedly, this is due to the fact that they are used largely for clinical and diagnostic purposes. As a result, far fewer children are involved. In the 1960s and early 1970s, along with the many other social, political, and economic changes occurring in the United States, psychological testing came under serious attack. The occasional burning of tests and the widespread preoccupation about their use, misuse, and abuse stimulated much consumer and professional concern. Legal suits were instituted which alleged that minority-group children were improperly placed in special classes on the basis of biased tests. As an example, a lawsuit in California (*Diana* v. *California State Board of Education*) was settled with the judgment that several thousand Mexican-American students were given allegedly culturally unfair intelligence tests in English instead of Spanish.

Jensen[18] published a disturbing paper in which

he reported that using both traditional intelligence tests and culture-free tests, he had found that blacks on the average scored 10 to 20 points below whites in intelligence. The response was immediate and intense. Civil rights leaders and many professionals labelled Jensen a racist. Racists utilized his results to justify their prejudice and bigotry. Fincher[11] does not deem these findings to be psychologically important. His stance is that in a complex society, it has never been demonstrated that a 15-point difference in intelligence, as measured by IQ, has an significant functional relationship to performance. He stresses that IQ has a proven value only in predicting how well students will perform in conventional schools. He argues that there is no evidence that people with IQ's 15 points higher than others function better at work or in complex societal contexts. As pointed out in a review by Wade,[42] the entire controversy continues to broaden. Suspicion of scientific fraud has been leveled at the late Cyril Burt, whose studies have been underpinnings for the hereditarian positions of Jensen and Herrnstein.

Conclusions

Despite the limitations of intelligence tests, their usefulness in the hands of a well-trained clinical child psychologist seem to this writer to require the following perspectives:

1. Decisions about any child's intellectual status require supplementary and confirmatory data from several significant sources.
2. Tests cannot be overvalued and used as sole sources of information for decision making, or totally undervalued and abandoned because of their obvious defects.
3. A well-trained and conscientious clinical child psychologist can detect when the test is or is not appropriate for the specific purpose of the examination.
4. The test's validity for specific purposes suggests whether cultural variables should be included or eliminated.

Sources for Specific Areas of Interest

For more details on:

1. Introductions to the uses of testing in clinical practice, but not exclusively focused on the developmental periods examined in the present volume:
    GOLDMAN, L., *Using Tests in Counselling*, Appleton-Century-Crofts, New York, 1961.
    WOODY, R. H., and WOODY, J. V., *Clinical As-*

sessment in Counselling and Psychotherapy, Appleton-Century-Crofts, New York, 1972.
2. Comprehensive and detailed technical information about existing and new intelligence and projective tests (individual and group):
    ANASTASI, A., *Psychological Testing*, 4th ed., Macmillan, New York, 1975.
    ———, "Psychological Testing of Children," in Freedman, A. M., and Kaplan, H. I. (Eds.), *The Child: His Psychological and Cultural Development*, vol. 1, chap. 7, *Normal Development and Psychological Assessment*, Athenum, New York, 1972.
    BUROS, O. K., (Ed.), *Tests in Print, II,* Gryphon Press, Highland Park, N.J., 1974.
    ———, *The Seventh Mental Measurements Yearbook*, Gryphon Press, Highland Park, N. J., 1972.
    GOLDMAN, B. A., and SAUNDERS, J. L., *Directory of Unpublished Experimental Mental Measures*, vol. 1, Behavioral Publications, New York, 1974.
3. Specific clinical application of psychological tests:
    EXNER, J. E., JR., *The Rorschach: A Comprehensive System*, Wiley, New York, 1974. The volume strives to integrate the features of the numerous approaches to the Rorschach and provides the major postulates necessary for clinical use of the technique.
    HALPERN, F., *A Clinical Approach to Children's Rorschachs*, Grune & Stratton, New York, 1953. This book focuses on Rorschach test findings on children.
    LEVITT, E. E., and TRUUMAA, A., *The Rorschach Technique with Children and Adolescents*, Grune & Stratton, New York, 1972. This book provides norms for quantifiable Rorschach factors and a method to form a basis for general interpretation of child and adolescent records.
    MUNDY, J., "The Use of Projective Techniques with Children," in Wolman, B. B. (Ed.), *Manual of Child Psychopathology*, chap. 25, McGraw-Hill, New York, 1972. This chapter provides a review of the clinical use of projective techniques and presents the difficulties in the application of the procedures.
    POTKAY, C. R., *The Rorschach Clinicians: A New Research Approach and its Application*, Grune & Stratton, New York, 1971. A compilation of studies which translates clinical theory into experimental designs and systematic methodologies. The emphasis is on need to offer interpretations based on empirical studies.
    RABIN, A. I., "Diagnostic Use of Intelligence Tests," in Wolman, B. B., *Handbook of Clinical Psychology*, chap. 19, McGraw-Hill, New York, 1965. The author reviews the application of intelligence tests in the diagnostic procedure.
    ———, and McKINNEY, J. P., "Intelligence Tests and Childhood Psychopathology," in Wolman, B. B., (Ed.), *Manual of Child Psychopathology*, chap. 24, McGraw-Hill, New York, 1972. This chapter deals with the effects of

chronic conditions upon intellectual functions as manifested on standardized intelligence measures. The patterns are related to deviation in the developmental process and disorders of childhood. Reviews of empirical findings with intelligence tests and several nosological groupings of psychopathology are offered.

——, and HAWORTH, M., (Eds.), *Projective Techniques with Children*, Grune & Stratton, New York, 1960. This edited volume provides a series of chapters that address theoretical rationale for specific tests, administration, scoring, interpretation, research, and clinical case vignettes.

4. The controversies and questions as to whether intelligence and achievement tests should be discontinued or continued in use with minority children:

ANASTASI, A., "Cultural Differentials in Test Performance," in Freedman, A. M., and Kaplan, H. I., (Eds.), *The Child: His Psychological and Cultural Development*, vol. 1, *Normal Development and Psychological Assessment*, pp. 149–150, Anthenum, New York, 1972.

PADILLA, A. M., and RUIZ, R. A., "Personality Assessment and Test Interpretation of Mexican-Americans: A Critique," *Journal of Personality Assessment*, 39(2):103–109, 1975. This journal article provides a current review

and several recommendations for increasing the efficiency of assessment techniques for use with this minority group of children.

WILLIAMS, G. J., and GORDON, S., (Eds.), part 5 in *Clinical Child Psychology, Current Practice and Future Perspectives*, Behavioral Publication, New York, 1974. Presentations pertaining to continuance and discontinuance of testing.

5. Theoretical and technical considerations in measurement:

CRONBACH, L. J., and GLESSER, G. C., *Psychological Tests and Personnel Decisions*, 2nd ed. University of Illinois Press, Urbana, Ill., 1965. This textbook provides a theory of measurement in which the value of a test depends on the decision problems for which tests are used as well as the predictive accuracy of an instrument.

KLINE, P., (Ed.), *New Approaches in Psychological Measurement*, John Wiley, London, 1974. An edited book that contains several contributions that aspire to either equate validity with "usefulness" or emphasize behavior criterions rather than traditional test validity. Many of the conventional technical considerations in both intelligence and projective testing are confronted by posing alternative models—including decision-making approaches.

REFERENCES

1. AMES, L. B., et al., *Child Rorschach Responses: Developmental Trends from Two to Ten Years*, Hoeber Medical Division, Harper & Row, New York, 1952.

2. AMES, L. B., et al., *Child Rorschach Responses: Developmental Trends from Two to Ten Years*, Brunner-Mazel, New York, 1974.

3. AMES, L. B., METRAUX, R. W., and WALKER, R. N., *Adolescent Rorschach Responses: Developmental Trends from Ten to Sixteen Years*, Hoeber Medical Division, Harper & Row, New York, 1959.

4. ANASTASI, A., *Psychological Testing*, 4th ed., Macmillan, New York, 1975.

5. ——, "Psychological Testing of Children" in Freedman, A. M., and Kaplan, H. I. (Eds.), *The Child: His Psychological and Cultural Development*, vol. 1, *Normal Development and Psychological Assessment*, Anthenum, New York, 1972.

6. ——, *Differential Psychology*, Macmillan, New York, 1958.

7. BELLAK, L., *The T.A.T., C.A.T., and S.A.T. in Clinical Use*, Grune & Stratton, New York, 1975.

8. COLE, J. K., and MAGNUSSEN, M. G., "Where the Action Is," *Journal of Consulting Psychology*, 30:539–543, 1966.

9. ENGLISH, O. S., and FINCH, S. M., *Introduction to Psychiatry*, Norton, New York, 1957.

10. EXNER, J. E., JR., *The Rorschach: A Comprehensive System*, John Wiley, New York, 1974.

11. FINCHER, J., *Human Intelligence*, Basic Books, New York, 1976.

12. GARDNER, R. A., *Psychotherapeutic Approaches to the Resistant Child*, Aronson, New York, 1975.

13. GOLDEN, M., "Some Effects of Combining Psychological Tests on Clinical Inferences," *Journal of Consulting Psychology*, 28:440–446, 1964.

14. GOTTHEIL, E., KRAMER, M., and HURVICH, M. S.,

"Intake Procedures and Psychiatric Decisions," *Comprehensive Psychiatry*, 7:207–215, 1966.

15. GOUGH, H. G., and HEILBURN, A. B., *The Adjective Check List Manual*, Palo Alto Co., Consulting Psychologists Press, Palo Alto, California, 1965.

16. GROSS, L. R., "Effects of Verbal and Nonverbal Reinforcement in the Rorschach," *Journal of Consulting Psychology*, 23:66–68, 1959.

17. GUARON, E. F., and DICKINSON, J. K., "Diagnostic Decision Making in Psychiatry Information Usage," *Archives of General Psychiatry*, 14:225–232, 1966.

18. JENSEN, A., "How Much Can We Boost IQ and Scholastic Achievement?" *Harvard Educational Review*, 39(1):1–123, 1969.

19. KOSTLAN, A., "A Method for the Empirical Study of Psychodiagnosis," *Journal of Consulting Psychology*, 18:83–88, 1954.

20. LEVINE, D., "Why and When to Test: The Social Context of Psychological Testing," in Rabin, A. I. (Ed.), *Projective Techniques in Personality Assessment, A Modern Introduction*, Spinger, New York, 1968.

21. MAGNUSSEN, M. G., "Effect of Test Order Upon Children's Rorschach Animal Content," *Journal of Projective Techniques*, 16(2):41–43, 1967.

22. ——, "Verbal and Nonverbal Reinforces in the Rorschach Situation," *Journal of Clinical Psychology*, 16(2):167–169, 1960.

23. McCLELLAND, D. C., "Testing for Competence Rather than for 'Intelligence,'" in Chess, S., and Thomas, A. (Eds.), *Annual Progress in Child Psychiatry and Child Development*, Brunner-Mazel, New York, 1974.

24. MASLING, J., "Role-related Behavior of the Subject and Psychologist and Its Effects Upon Psychological Data," in Levine, D. (Ed.), *Nebraska Symposium on Motivation*, vol. 14, University of Nebraska Press, Lincoln, Nebraska, 1966.

25. ———, "The Influence of Situational and Interpersonal Variables in Project Testing," *Psychology Bulletin, 57:*65, 1960.

26. MEEHL, P. E., *Clinical vs. Statistical Prediction*, Minneapolis University at Minnesota Press, Minneapolis, 1954.

27. MUNDY, J., "The Use of Projective Techniques with Children," in Wolman, B. B. (Ed.), *Manual of Child Psychopathology*, McGraw-Hill, New York, 1972.

28. NOYES, A. P., and KOLB, L. C., *Modern Clinical Psychiatry*, 6th ed., W. B. Saunders, Philadelphia, 1963.

29. OSKAMP, S., "Overconfidence in Case-Study Judgments," *Journal of Consulting Psychology, 29:*261–265, 1965.

30. RABIN, A. I., and McKINNEY, J. P., "Intelligence Tests and Childhood Psychopathology," in Wolman, B. B. (Ed.), *Manual of Child Psychopathology*, McGraw-Hill, New York, 1972.

31. ROSENTHAL, R., "Unintended Effects of the Clinician in Clinical Interaction: A Taxonomy and a Review of Clinician Expectancy Effects," *Australian Journal of Psychology, 21:*1–20, 1969.

32. ———, *Experimenter Effects in Behavioral Research*, Appleton-Century-Crofts, New York, 1966.

33. ———, and ROSNOW, R. L. (Eds.), *Artifact in Behavioral Research*, Academic Press, New York, 1969.

34. SARBIN, T., "Contribution of the Study of Actuarial and Independent Methods of Prediction," *American Journal of Sociology, 48:*593–602, 1942.

35. SATTLER, I. M., "Racial 'Experimenter Effects' in Experimentation, Testing, Interviewing and Psychotherapy," *Psychological Bulletin, 73:*137–160, 1970.

36. SCHWARTZ, M. L., "Validity and Reliability in Clinical Judgments of C-V-S Protocols as a Function of Amount of Information and Diagnostic Category," *Psychological Report, 20:*767–774, 1967.

37. SINES, J. O., "Actuarial vs. Clinical Prediction in Psychopathology," *British Journal of Psychiatry, 116:* 129–144, 1970.

38. SINES, L. K., "The Relative Contribution of Four Kinds of Data to Accuracy in Personality Assessment," *Journal of Consulting Psychology, 23:*483–495, 1959.

39. SNYDERMAN, B. B., et al., CDC Forms A, B, C, D, and E, Copyright: Pittsburgh Child Guidance Center Clinical Data System, 1975.

40. TUMA, J. M., and McGRAW, R. K., "Influences of Examiner Differences on Rorschach Productivity in Children," *Journal of Personality Assessment, 39(4):*362–368, 1975.

41. UZGIRIS, I. C., and HUNT, J. McV., *Assessment in Infancy: Ordinal Scales of Psychological Development*, University of Illinois Press, Urbana, 1975.

42. WADE, N., "IQ and Heredity: Suspicion of Fraud Beclouds Classic Equipment," *Science, 194(4268):*916–919, 1976.

43. WEISS, J. H., "Effect of Professional Training and Amount of Accuracy of Information on Behavioral Prediction," *Journal of Consulting Psychology, 27:*257–262, 1963.

67 / Principles of the Neurological Examination

Marcel Kinsbourne

In general, the first order of additional exploration that is likely to be needed is a pediatric neurological examination. Ordinarily, this can be performed on a simple level during the course of a regular psychiatric evaluation by observing various related functions (as described above). However, if necessary, every child psychiatrist should be himself prepared to perform a pediatric neurological examination; indeed it is desirable that he carry out the initial examination directly. Where such an examination reveals the possible presence of a definitive neurologic syndrome, additional expert opinion should be sought through neurologic consultation. The capricious and indiscriminate ordering of EEG's as a kind of screening device or short cut should be scrupulously avoided.

In the following chapter, the procedure for carrying out such an examination is described in some detail.

—RLC

The neurological examination in young children does not differ in principle from that prescribed for adults in any textbook of general neurology. It does differ radically in the manner in which it is conducted, and it also differs with respect to the particular signs that are emphasized.

Suggestions for Conducting a Neurological Examination in a Young Child

In virtually every instance, in conducting the examination, the general neurologist can take the complete cooperation of the adult patient for granted. The young child, however, is less cooperative of course. Therefore, the younger the child, the more the clinician must behave in such a manner as to elicit and maintain the child's cooperation. He must also program the sequence of observations so that the first observations are those least likely to disturb the child and thus render him temporarily unexaminable. At all points in time, the possibility must be firmly kept in mind that the opportunity for examination may abruptly cease.

The younger the child, the less effective it is to conduct one's examination under conditions of exhortation and command. This applies not only to the clinician but also to the parent, who should not be allowed to intervene with frequent exhortations of "Do what the doctor tells you" or complaints, "Why can't you ever behave?" The clinician should determine in his own mind whether the parent is effective in setting limits with this child. If so, the physician should take advantage of that help. If not, he should politely but firmly assume that role.

Because of the child's previously established fears and stereotypes about the consequences of a visit to the doctor's office, the clinician should take pains to render the scene as everyday and unclinical as is consistent with the demands of the situation. One should refrain from wearing a white coat or prominently displaying instruments such as a stethoscope. A male physician should remove his jacket, and he may wish to contribute to an atmosphere of relaxation by abstaining from wearing a necktie. The customary clutter of metallic paraphernalia is best kept out of sight. A mild degree of disorder in the office (somewhere short of chaos) is advantageous for making the child feel at home. Children's artwork pinned to the wall and a few simple toys scattered around contribute to the desired informal atmosphere.

When a young child comes in held by, or holding hands with the parent, the clinician should not make an immediate effort to separate them or to permit the parent to detach from the child. Such action might lead to a collapse of the whole situation at its very beginning. The parent should be asked to take a seat and continue to hold the child, hold hands with the child, or have the child sit nearby (unless it is clearly within the range of the child's own wishes to detach at this early stage). In the first instance, the clinician may speak either to the parent or the child, depending on the situation. In any case, the answers to several questions can be determined from a distance.

1. What is the child's level of consciousness and awareness?
2. Is the child awake?

3. Is the child alertly looking around or subdued, apathetic, or bordering on the somnolent?
4. Specifically, is the child's alertness punctuated by momentary lapses of consciousness, apparent through a second or two of arrested movement, with perhaps a momentary turning of the eyes upward and outward.
5. Are there any manifestations of involuntary twitching, of tremor, or of a dystonic posturing of any limb or of the head and neck?

As observation continues, it becomes possible to note whether the child fails to use any limb or fails to turn head, or eyes, or both in one direction or the other.

If the child plays spontaneously or otherwise manipulates objects, it becomes possible to observe his coordination from a distance. Similarly, should the child spontaneously walk around, the gait can be observed. Otherwise the clinician may now approach the child cautiously, staying at about the same level as the child and taking care not to loom over his head, and not yet attempt to separate the child from the parent. The examiner may then offer the child a toy or some other small object, and observe how the youngster picks it up. Are the hand and arm movements smooth, subject to a continuous tremor, or punctuated by irregular myoclonic jerking? As the arm approaches the target is there a terminal tremor, with a lateral shaking of increasing amplitude closer to the target? Does the child pick up the item using a proper pincer grip between index finger and thumb or do the other fingers compulsively flex in sympathy? As the child picks up the object, do the arm and hand rotate into abnormal pronation, and do the fingers fan out and extend notably on the ulnar side? This series of observations is made separately with each of the two arms. If necessary, one should fill the hand that was first used with some other large object so that if the child wishes to keep holding it he must use the other hand to pick up what is offered. Then one can begin to test the strength of these movements by offering slight resistance on each side to further picking up.

Observe the child's ability to move the eyes by holding an attractive object, such as a doll, to the right, to the left, up, and down, so that the child's eyes follow and any limitation of eye movement, disturbance of gaze, or nystagmus is thus revealed. Show the child a flashlight, let him handle it, then obliquely illuminate each pupil to test the reactions. Engage the child in conversation, make him smile, and observe the movement of the mouth for asymmetry and the possibility of a unilateral facial paresis. The examiner may then protrude his tongue and coax the child to do likewise, noting the direction of the tongue's protusion and the presence on its surface of areas of wasting or fasciculation. The child's perception of the whispered voice, in each ear, should then be tested. Examination of the mouth and pharynx should be delayed as this is liable to impair cooperation for the rest of examination.

At this stage, the child may be ready to separate from the parent sufficiently to walk, run, jump, and hop on one or another leg. An attempt should be made to present these actions as fun or games. If the child is reluctant to walk, then he can be induced to do so by having the parent take a few steps away, whereupon he will invariably follow. The gait is observed for its steadiness. Is it widely based? Is it high stepping, or asymmetrical with perhaps a footdrop on one's side?

Only after everything has been observed that can be observed from a distance should the examination proceed. If one is then successful in securing the child's voluntary cooperation, it is appropriate to have the child lie down for the rest of the examination. In fact, even the reflexes may be elicited while the child is sitting on the parent's lap, with arms and legs dangling free. Again, if the child is fearful, the tendon hammer should first be given to him to play with. Then, the child can be engaged in the game of guessing "whether the leg will jump" when the tendon hammer is applied. The eliciting of the planter response is not usually much appreciated by the child, but an attempt can be made to maintain good humor by presenting it as a way of tickling.

When the child then does lie down, it becomes possible to examine the abdominal reflexes and, incidentally, to examine chest and abdomen in ways not relevant to the neurological examination but still often necessary in relation to problems he presents. Any muscular wasting, and, in particular, any asymmetry of the body can be observed. This asymmetry may affect the skull with, for example, flattening on one side (most commonly this is frontally located and known as frontal recession). The shape of the skull is, in general, inspected. Is the skull abnormally large or small? Are the fontanelles still open after the age of eighteen months, or were they already closed before the age of one year? Is the skull unduly narrow and compensatorily extended in the sagital plane (dolichocephaly), or is it unduly broad and telescoped in the sagital plane (brachycephaly)? If so, the examiner should gently feel the coronal and sagittal sutures for premature fusion, as in any of the variants of craniosynostosis. Any facial asym-

metry coincident with limitation of the size of the cranial cavity on the same side should be noted. The skull should be percussed to elicit the possible presence of a "crack-pot" note.

The comparative length of the arms and of the legs (by lining up the anterior superior spines and the internal malleoli) should be noted. The size of the two palms and the size of the soles of the feet should also be compared. By such means one can detect hemiatrophy, which is a relative underdevelopment of one side of the body, customarily contralateral to a congenital lateralized cerebral lesion.

Having the child lie so as to expose his back, the examiner should inspect in particular for any irregularity or curvature of the spine and any dimple, pouch, tuft of hair, or midline discoloration, particularly in the lumbar area.

Only at the very end of the examination should any attempt be made to perform those maneuvers which are almost certain to upset most young children and thus make physical restraint necessary. These are examination of the internal auditory canal, the mouth, and the pharynx, and viewing of the eye grounds. In fact, unless the clinician is exceptionally fortunate in eliciting cooperation, at best the latter maneuver will often be unsuccessful in a young child. If this part of the examination is crucial, it may have to be performed with dilated pupils or even under an anesthetic.

The sensory examination is usually quite limited in young children, since it requires a type of cooperation that is not usually forthcoming. Fortunately, it is uncommon for the exact detailed pattern of sensory loss to be of crucial diagnostic import. However, as a minimum, the visual fields should be roughly examined by confrontation. If the child is not cooperating verbally, a sudden threat motion to one or the other side of the visual field may reveal the failure to blink, and thus the presence of a lateralized field defect. Where sensory evaluation involves testing for the preservation of the sense of pain, the usual method is by means of pin-prick. Again, this is best left until near the end of the examination, because the child's cooperation will thereafter be less readily available.

Indications for Securing Pediatric Neurology Consultation

The mental health professional should seek child neurology consultation if he (1) suspects the presence of an organic disease of the nervous system, (2) has elicited signs which lend themselves to ambiguous interpretation (for example, whether they represent the presence of a neurological disorder or a functional one), (3) has not been successful in eliciting the child's cooperation to the extent required to perform a satisfactory examination of the nervous system.

SEIZURE STATES

With regard to children who present primarily with behavioral disorders, the most frequent question that arises which might require consultation involves the possible presence of an atypical seizure disorder. Do the child's periodic outbursts of temper tantrums, or periodic states of confusion represent, respectively, a recurring temporal lobe seizure state or the incidence of multiple minor epileptic (petit mal) episodes? Do the child's complaints of a strange epigastric burning sensation, an evil taste in his mouth, or an apparently spontaneous visual manifestation represent the aura of a temporal lobe attack? Are his unaccountable states of fear, or feelings either of inappropriate strangeness or familiarity temporal epileptic manifestations? Was his unaccountable behavior in wandering off for several hours a psychomotor fugue? Are his recurrent stereotypic nightmares based on a similar abnormality?

Many times such questions can only be resolved by an attempt at controlling the manifestations in question with anticonvulsant medication as a therapeutic test. Prior to this, an electroencephalogram should always be performed. The therapeutic test itself is best done by the neurologist who can judge the accuracy of the anticonvulsant regime instituted.

DECLINING INTELLECTUAL CAPACITY

Another frequent reason for referral is the observation of a declining intellectual capability. For example, a child repeatedly tested by standard psychometric instruments shows a descending IQ; at the same time, corresponding complaints, particularly from the teacher, reveal declining school performance. Is this due to psychogenic factors, or is the child subject to some form of progressive cerebral degeneration? There are types that sometimes present primarily with initial intellectual decline (such as metachromatic leukodystrophy, sudanophilic cerebral sclerosis, or subacute sclerosing panencephalitis). Is the intellectual decline related to the chronic ingestion of some poison, such as lead? Is this an epileptic child, in which case the IQ might be declining because of the repeated concussion involved in the initial falling component of a major epileptic fit? Or, perhaps the decline is apparent rather than real, and related to anticonvulsant medication effect. Or, are minor inhibitory seizures so frequent that the child's attention is continually punctured by momentary unconsciousness, thus precluding him from following any consecutive train of thought?

DIFFERENTIAL DIAGNOSIS OF HYSTERIA

There are a subset of symptoms that are ambiguous in import and susceptible to either a neurological or psychiatric interpretation; among them are a variety of common manifestations of hysteria. Prominent among these are hyperventilation "seizures," unsteadiness of gait, and hysterical blindness or deafness. The detection of hysterical (or simulated) sensorimotor deficit is usually quite a simple task for the pediatric neurologist. He will rely on auditory or visual observations (for example, eye blink to a loud sound, or optokinetic nystagmus elicited by rotating a striped drum) which reveal that the relevant channel is in fact not closed. A hysterically deranged gait or stance will fail to conform in certain respects to the various known postural or locomotor abnormalities. For instance, there are patients who for functional reasons sway and threaten to fall after standing with eyes closed. With eyes open, however, and looking straight up, they will usually stand steadily. From the point of view of visual cues to insure bodily stability, they might as well close their eyes for all the use it is to look up.

But it is also easy to make the converse mistake and ascribe an unfamiliar organic manifestation to hysteria or malingering. For instance, ataxia due to a midline cerebellar lesion (so-called "vermis-ataxia") produces a wide based wildly staggering gait without coincident ataxia of any limb. This is often mistakenly regarded as functional. The same is true of the dystonias. These variable distortions of bodily posture are closely linked to a child's emotional state (although caused by structural brain damage at the level of the basal ganglia). They are much accentuated by self-consciousness and embarrassment and hence, during examination, they will often be extreme. Yet they are virtually absent when the patient is back in his room and believes himself to be alone. This behavior may suggest a functional condition, but actually is inherent in the nature of the neurophysiological disorder. Again, virtually all involuntary movement ceases during sleep. Such arrest of involuntary movement is therefore fully consistent with an organic diagnosis.

An important differential decision is the one between real seizures and simulated seizures. That difference can be particularly difficult to discern because usually the person who simulates seizures has also experienced genuine epileptic fits. Suspicion should be aroused by the following state of affairs: a person keeps reporting fits in the face of increasing anticonvulsant dosage, seems to have them primarily in public settings, yet manages not to hurt himself when he falls. The situation becomes particularly difficult when an occasional patient deliberately injures himself to make the report of seizure more convincing.

When the seizure occurs in the clinician's presence, he can at times observe circumstances, such as a random thrashing around, that do not in fact occur during a genuine major seizure. Also, he can use suggestion by making remarks within context of the ostensibly unconscious patient, of the order of "within fifteen seconds, his arms will stiffen and extend straight forward." The situation is most difficult when there is only a history to go on; in such a case the wider experience of the neurologist is particularly useful.

A special case of functionally triggered seizures is the hyperventilation episode. The patient, usually a female adolescent, breathes heavily and regularly up to a point at which itching or tingling of fingers and around the mouth, and forced supination of the wrist with semiflexed fingers, is followed by a true lapse of consciousness. A history of heavy breathing before the attack is very indicative. The episode can then be simulated by instructing the patient to breathe heavily and regularly on the examination couch. When a simulation is successful, it is relatively easy to stop further such events by forceful reassurance. The clinician is then free to focus on the dynamic factors that precipitated the abnormal behavior.

The differentiation between hysteria and neurological pathology is a crucial indication for pediatric neurology consultation. This is important not only to avoid misdiagnosing organic disease, but also in order to avoid consolidating hysterical manifestation by shrouding it in the mystique of elaborate nonproductive medical investigation.

Additional Investigative Techniques Available

Further information about neurological disorder may be obtained from four main sources. These are (1) cellular and chemical analysis of the cerebral spinal fluid, (2) electrophysiological recordings at relevant levels of the nervous system (typically electroencephalography, electromyography, and the measurement of conduction velocities along peripheral nerves), (3) neuroradiological investigations, and (4) analysis of biopsy specimens.

Two properties of the cerebrospinal fluid are revealing with respect to neurological disease. These are its pressure relationships and its composition.

CEREBRAL SPINAL FLUID

Pressure Relationships. Except in the very youngest children, the central nervous system is encased in a space of limited capacity. The swelling of any part of the central nervous system will therefore raise the pressure of the fluid that surrounds it. Obstruction to flow will similarly raise its pressure proximal to the site of obstruction. Therefore, a generally raised cerebrospinal fluid pressure indicates local or general brain swelling whereas failure of pressure relationships to change on compression of neck veins indicates a block to the circulation of fluid at that spinal level. Compression of the neck veins raises intracranial pressure by engorging the intracranial venous circulation; the failure of this maneuver to increase the flow of cerebrospinal fluid through a lumbar puncture needle suggests a blockage of flow between the intracranial cavity and the location of the needle.

Where there exists substantially raised intracranial pressure due to a space-occupying lesion, it is to be hoped that this fact be inferred from the history (for example, pressure headaches exacerbated by coughing, sneezing, or straining at stool) and the presence of vomiting, the presence of papilledema, or typical radiological findings. Under these circumstances, a spinal tap is contraindicated, as an acute lowering of pressure in the spinal space might lead to a sudden displacement downward of the brain stem, jamming it into the foramen magnum. This carries with it the danger of compression of brain stem vasomotor and respiratory centers and, subsequently, collapse of blood pressure and respiratory arrest.

Cerebrospinal Fluid Composition. The composition of the cerebrospinal fluid reflects both the chemical status of the central nervous system and the dynamics of the flow of the fluid.

In cases of inflammation of the brain, spinal cord, or its meninges, inflammatory cells will be found in the cerebrospinal fluid. With bacterial infection, these will be more likely polymorphonuclear; with viral infections, lymphocytic. Various inflammatory and degenerative disorders of the central nervous system are reflected in an increased level of cerebrospinal fluid protein. Some acute bacterial infections result in the lowering of cerebrospinal fluid sugar content. Various allergic and autoimmune phenomena may change the relative composition of the different fractions of cerebrospinal fluid protein, with typical rises at various points in the gammaglobulin spectrum.

Stagnation of the spinal fluid, for instance below a block, will in time result in progressive rise in the protein content of the fluid.

ELECTROPHYSIOLOGICAL RECORDINGS

Electrophysiological recordings may be taken from the convexity of the scalp (therefore indirectly from the brain), from certain peripheral nerves, and from voluntary muscle.

The *electroencephalogram* (EEG) offers the opportunity of noting disturbances of the customary spectrum of brain-related rhythms. These disturbances may be diffuse or local.

Diffuse or widespread EEG abnormalities often take the form of a slowing of the dominant rhythms. When these are mild and of long standing, a relative immaturity of brain development is suggested. When they are severe, widespread damage to the brain is suggested. A general acceleration of brain rhythms occurs as a side effect of barbiturate intake. The normal rhythms may be completely missing when brain death has occurred or replaced by chaotic arrhythmic changes uncorrelated across leads (as in "hypsarrhythmia," a severe epileptic variant in infants). In addition to the normal rhythms, there may be abnormal rhythmic discharge or episodic spike wave forms representing subclinical or clinically apparent epileptic disturbances. When concentrated in one part of the area from which the recording is taken, this may localize the epileptogenic lesion.

The various stages of sleep are readily identifiable from the EEG. By its use, sleep stages or pathological sleep, as in narcolepsy, can be differentiated from coma at its various levels. Certain adjunctive procedures extend the range of usefulness of the EEG. These are drug administration and the presentation of stimuli while recording. For instance, the barbiturate-related quick rhythms may be missing over an area of damaged brain and their absence is then of diagnostic import. Some other drugs are used as provocative agents to reveal otherwise obscure epileptic tendencies.

Stroboscopic stimulation is able to drive the dominant posterior 8 to 13 per second alpha rhythm. Visual and auditory stimulation give rise to so-called evoked potential changes over the scalp adjacent to the primary receiving areas for these modalities. The appearance of such potentials guarantees integrity of the conducting pathways at least up to the first cortical relay for the modality.

The EEG does not identify the part of the brain currently active in the course of an individual's mental processes. Nor does it facilitate the appraisal of intelligence or other cognitive abilities. While an abnormal EEG can be helpful, as discussed above, it is rarely possible to conclude *anything* from *absence* of abnormality from the EEG. In particular, a normal EEG does not invalidate a clinically based diagnosis of epilepsy.

The measurement of conduction velocity of impulses along peripheral nerves gives an estimate of the integrity of the larger, faster-conducting nerve fibers. In certain neuropathies, the rate of this conduction will be diminished because the larger fibers may be selectively destroyed by the pathological process. If a peripheral nerve is stimulated and the elicited muscle twitch recorded, then it is possible to evaluate the efficiency of transmission across the neuromuscular junction. In myasthenia, a constant nerve stimulus is met with a diminishing amplitude of muscular response.

Electrical recording from muscle, if it yields an abnormality, is primarily capable of distinguishing between a weakness due to failure of innervation of the muscle (neurogenic) and one due to muscular disease proper (myogenic). The recording electrode picks up the activity of individual clusters of muscle fibers supplied by a single nerve fiber, the motor unit. In neurogenic problems, the number of motor units is diminished but the surviving motor units are normal as regards the configuration of their potentials. In contrast, in myogenic disorders the motor units are generally affected. All will show diminished amplitude and otherwise distorted potentials.

Neuroradiology. X-rays of the *skull* will reveal abnormalities in shape, notably pathological enlargement (hyrocephalus) or pathologically small size (microcephaly). They will also indicate whether some sutures may be selectively prematurely fused causing the distortions of the skull configuration characteristic of craniostenosis. Intracranial calcification and ‘abnormal vascular markings may give clues to particular types of pathology. Raised intercranial pressure has its own characteristic effects detectable by plain skull x-rays.

The nervous system can be further examined by the use of air or other contrast materials to outline the periphery of intercranial structures, by opacifying blood vessels which supply these structures, and by two more recent methods, brain scan and computerized axial tomography (CAT).

Air encephalography consists in the injection of air into the meningeal space. The air outlines neural structures, revealing either an expansion of normally occurring spaces as in brain atrophies, or "filling defects" where abnormal matter (such as tumor material) may have encroached upon a naturally occurring cavity. The use of opaque materials, such as myodil, is particularly useful in the investigation of the contour of the spinal cord and sometimes also during the process of ventriculography. In *arteriography*, an opaque dye injected into the arterial system, most commonly the carotid artery, enables a section of the cerebral circulation to be visualized. Here an arterial segment may be missing from view, indicating an obstruction; be expanded, indicating a pathological dilatation; or be distorted in its path, indicating pressure on it from abnormal material somewhere along its course.

In *brain scanning* radioactive material is administered and picked up by Geiger counter from the convexity of the skull. It is capable of revealing highly vascular tumors and malformations through the appearance of increased radioactive uptake.

The CAT technique is a recent and versatile procedure. It is an extension of plain skull radiography in which fine contrast between intracranial tissue densities are brought into view so that the normal anatomy and distortions of that anatomy at various levels of the central nervous system may be discerned.

Biopsy. A definitive diagnosis may sometimes demand the acquisition of some of the actual tissue under investigation. Muscle biopsy is virtually indispensable as a diagnostic step in disease of muscle. Inflammatory or degenerative changes of various kinds become apparent. Biopsy of strips of peripheral nerve or autonomic nerve plexus at times confirms the diagnosis of a neuropathy. Brain biopsy is rarely justifiable in the patient's interest, as it mainly applies to brain degenerations which are at present incurable. Occasionally, it may be justifiable when the child is already severely disabled and genetic counseling is a crucial issue.

---

68 / Neuropsychological Assessment

Maureen Dennis

The more recent development of the field of pediatric neuropsychology has seen the development of techniques aimed at performing more precise measurements of central nervous system functioning. Any aspects of the history, psychiatric, psychometric, or neurologic findings which suggest that this type of study of discrete CNS functions may add clarity to the diagnostic picture in the child should bring the potential contribution of the neuropsychologist to mind.

Many of the indications for and uses of a neuropsychological study of the child are described in the following chapter.

—RLC

A neuropsychological assessment is an analysis of behavior performed with the aim of providing a precise description of the child's cognitive functioning. The purpose of this chapter is to indicate the kinds of questions which can be answered by such an assessment, and to draw attention to the behaviors which, because of their aberrant quality or impaired development, provide the impetus for testing.

General Aspects of Testing

Neuropsychological testing involves taking samples of behavior in controlled situations and then making decisions about whether or not the observed behaviors deviate from expectation. This conceptualization presupposes that there are available, first, test techniques sufficiently sensitive to measure each of the behaviors under consideration; and, second, a definition of expected performance for the task in question.

The decision-making process of a neuropsychological assessment is done in successive stages. The first set of decisions concern the *level* at which a particular behavioral function is operating; the second involves the *configuration or pattern* of skills that make up the overall function; and the third relates to the *processes* that underlie the skill itself.

To evaluate the level, pattern, and underlying processes of the child's behavior, it is necessary to have a set of rules by which the various decisions can be made. Judgments about level of function involve application of the simplest rules. The IQ measure, for example, is itself a standard score defining performance in relation to normal levels, so mental or intellectual impairment is decided upon by reference to the level of intelligence test score. Less attention has been directed towards decision making about ability patterns, partly because interpretation of score configurations is a more complex task than evaluation of single scores. Still less concern has been given to interpretation of the processes by which tasks are performed. An analysis of process, however, is the explicit or implicit goal of a neuropsychological assessment. A child's impairment is understood fully only when its dimensions are understood sufficiently to bring the deficit under experimental control, i.e., to make it appear or disappear by manipulating the processing the child is required to perform.

Decision making about behavior elicited by a test requires a clear understanding of expected or normal performance. For a child, this will change with age so that (in contrast to the case in adults) there must be a series of definitions of normal performance linked to successive developmental levels. The art in child assessment is to separate effects due to cognitive impairment from those that reflect normal but immature function.

Immaturity itself is often the object of investigation. A minority of children are referred to a neuropsychologist for evaluation of demonstrable central nervous system lesions. The presenting symptom in many instances is failure to acquire certain cognitive skills at the expected rate. Most children with problems of development can be labeled as neurologically intact in the sense that they do not show the pathological signs that commonly signal neurological disorder. Yet their behavior is abnormal, not because of its intrinsic pathology, but rather because it is inappropriate for age. Normal cognitive functioning involves age-appropriate developmental attainments, not just an absence of pathological signs on the classical neurological examination. It is the neuropsychological assessment, with its analysis of the levels, patterns, and processes of behavioral functioning, which answers questions about cognitive development.

The Neuropsychological Assessment

GENERAL COGNITIVE ABILITY

The beginning of a neuropsychological test session is typically an intelligence test. The reason for this is that specific impairments cannot be interpreted without reference to the overall level of cognitive development—immature language in a child with an IQ of 40, for example, does not have the same meaning as it would in a child of normal intelligence.

The Wechsler IQ tests (WISC, WISC-R) will be considered in light of the aforementioned general considerations. The first clinical decision to be made concerns the child's level of intellectual function. The IQ score itself expresses the ratio of test performance to that of age peers, but interpretation of IQ level can be extended by placing the IQ score in defined categories[7, 6] or by assigning it a percentile rank.[4]

Analysis of intellectual level must be carried further. Consider two children with Full Scale IQs of 99 and 100, respectively. On the basis of these scores, it would be noted that the children are intellectually normal and not different from each other. The Full Scale IQ is the mean of two types of functions, one (Verbal IQ) reflecting language use and understanding, the other (Performance IQ) expressing visuo-perceptual and manipulative skills. Suppose that the normal and similar IQ scores of 99 and 100 were composed of Verbal IQs of 112 and 89, and Performance IQs of 87 and 100, respectively. The overall score in each instance would represent above-average function in one area and below-average performance in the other. The Full Scale IQ measure may express divergent levels of cognitive function.

How is a decision made about the meaning of a discrepancy between Verbal IQ and Performance IQ? Decision making about what constitutes a genuine difference in functioning between the two areas involves two statistical questions. First, is the observed difference *abnormal* (i.e., so large that it occurs infrequently in a population of normal children)? Second, is the observed difference *reliable* (i.e., larger than that variability known to arise from errors of measurement in the tests)? The statistical reference point for the first question is the percentage of normal children showing the observed Verbal IQ-Performance IQ discrepancy; for the second, it is the test error.[3] Both questions can be answered by consulting the appropriate tables.* It might be noted that the issues which will lead the neuropsychologist to stress a "normative" or "test error" decision for a given discrepancy are partly pragmatic. For example, a reliable difference between Verbal IQ and Performance IQ may be clinically significant for diagnosis or remediation in a given child, even though it is not abnormal in terms of how often it would occur in a population of normal children.

The next stage of analysis of IQ information concerns the patterning of the scaled scores in the Verbal IQ and Performance IQ measures. The question to be answered is whether variability across subtests is a significant attribute of the test performances. One technique for evaluating the significance of variations in subtest patterning in the WISC and WISC-R is the Rhodes scatter profile.[4, 5] This summarizes performance on each individual subtest and shows graphically how much each one differs (and whether or not it differs significantly) from the child's overall level of performance on the test. Configurations can be evaluated separately for Full Scale, Verbal, and Performance scales. The value of such a procedure is that it objectifies decision making about the scatter of subtest scores.

The patterning *within* a given WISC or WISC-R scale is a dimension of performance separate from the previously-discussed variation *between* Verbal and Performance scales. Figure 68–1 illustrates this point.

The graphs show the Rhodes WISC-R scatter profiles for six children on both Verbal and Performance scales. Each circled subtest varies significantly from the child's own level of performance on that scale. Note that three of the children show statistically significant discrepancies between Verbal IQ and Performance IQ scores and three do not; and also that, within each group of three, one shows no within-scale variation, another shows variation on one scale but not the other, while the third performs diversely on both scales. In terms of Full Scale, Verbal IQ, and

Performance IQ measures, some of the children appear to be more similar to each other than they prove to be on the basis of figure 68–1. A pattern analysis, then, provides information that is not derivable from Verbal IQ, Performance IQ, Full Scale IQ or discrepancy measures.

The intelligence test still has not yielded all the diagnostic information it contains. The next stage of analysis is that of process. Although there is usually one correct response for a given test item, incorrect responses are quite varied. The child's errors often reveal the nature of the impaired processing that underlies failure on the test.

Figure 68–2 represents the attempts of eight children to assemble four blocks to match a seen target with a time limit of forty-five seconds. Each failed the task and obtained a score of 0. Looking at the group's incorrect productions, it is apparent that the processing failures are diverse. The type of impaired process in each instance can be characterized. Since some errors represent a more fundamental or more extensive processing disorder, the children might even be rank-ordered in terms of severity of impairment.

The failure of Subject 1 is easily understood, since he was defeated only by time constraints. To bring his functioning under experimental control, it would be necessary only to allow more time for the test item. The remaining children did not succeed in producing a target response. Were they unable to generate or to produce correct mental targets? To settle this question and extend understanding of their impairments, the children might next be asked to select the correct block construction from among a set containing both correct and incorrect exemplars (for example, 7). The study of process would continue in this manner until the nature of the impairment was judged to be understood.

At this point in the assessment, provided that patterns and processes as well as summary scores have been studied, the path that more specific or experimental investigations will take is usually evident. These more specialized neuropsychological functions will next be considered.

SPECIALIZED NEUROPHYCHOLOGICAL ASSESSMENT

The first task for a neuropsychologist planning a detailed assessment is to categorize the child to be assessed into one of three groups. In the first are children old enough to have acquired an adultlike competence in the areas to be investigated. In the second are those who, at some

---

* See references 6 and 2.

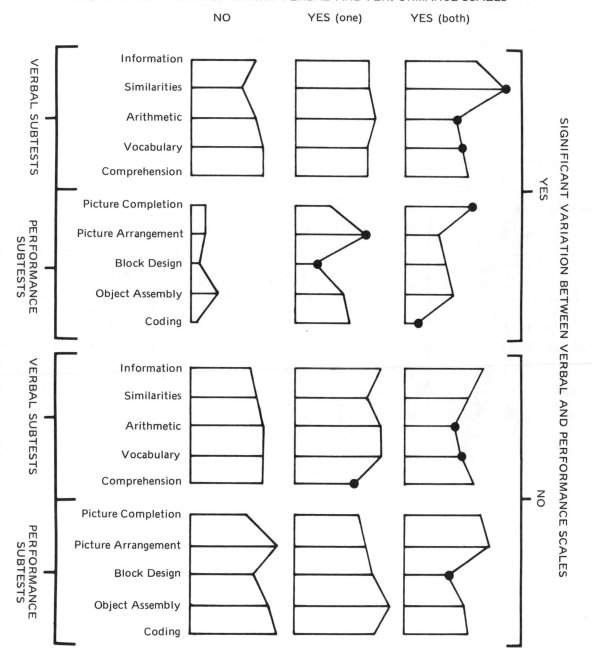

FIGURE 68–1

Patterning of subtest performance of 6 children using Rhodes scatter analysis data.[4]
Variability within the scales (circled vs. noncircled subtests) is a separate aspect of test
performance from variability between scales (left vs. right sides of the page).

IMPAIRED PROCESS

 TARGET (45″)		Visuo-motor Speed	Figure-ground Relationships	Spatial Orientation	Figural Relationships	Basic Constructional Praxis
SUBJECT 1.	 (50″)	YES	NO	NO	NO	NO
2.	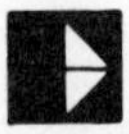 (44″)	NO	YES	NO	NO	NO
3.	 (24″)	NO	NO	YES	NO	NO
4.	 (21″)	NO	NO	YES	?	NO
5.	 (25″)	NO	NO	NO	YES	NO
6.	 (11″)	NO	NO	YES	YES	NO
7.	 (32″)	NO	NO	YES	YES	NO
8.	 (40″)	?	?	?	?	YES

FIGURE 68–2

The unsuccessful attempts of eight children to assemble four blocks to form a target design from the WISC-R Block Design test.[2] The failures represent impairments in different underlying processes.

defined point in development, have sustained a trauma causing disruption of the smooth functioning of the behavioral skill in question. Although these children are not fully mature, we can pinpoint the ontogenetic stage at which functioning began to be impaired. Children in the third group have sustained no obvious insult or trauma but do not appear to be acquiring the behavioral competence appropriate to their chronological age.

The issues for investigation are obviously different in the three types, so the test procedures will vary accordingly. For children of the first group, issues of behavioral acquisition are not relevant to the diagnostic question because their development in the tested area is substantially complete. It can sometimes be informative to describe performance of these children in terms of the developmental age to which the impaired skill has deteriorated. For the most part, however, the test techniques will be those that ordinarily assess mature function. A behavioral analysis of the children in the second and third groups involves a thorough understanding of the stages of normal acquisition of the skills to be tested, as well as possession of a set of techniques able to assess these stages. Consider a five-year-old girl referred for assessment of speech and language following a head injury. The child's language system was organized differently from that of an adult before the accident, so it is meaningless to ask whether measures of adult language performance could have expressed the effects of the trauma. The issue is not whether the child is scorable on adult neuropsychological tests.

She may or may not be so. It is, instead, whether measures of adult function reflect normal or abnormal immature language in any meaningful manner. The proper diagnostic question here concerns the presence or absence of deviations from the speech and language of normal five-year-old children.

Examples of different problems in the assessment of specific skills (sensory motor, language, and visuo-spatial) will next be considered.

Sensory-motor Capacities. Case SD is a sixteen-year-old boy whose cognitive and physical development had been uneventful until the three months before hospital admission, during which time he had several episodes of excessive sleep (twenty-two out of twenty-four hours). The EEG was normal, but a cerebral angiogram noted a right cerebello-pontine abnormality either of congenital or of more recent origin. One section of the neuropsychological assessment focused on sensory-motor function. Sensitivity to pressure was normal in each hand, and (as expected in a right-hander), the sensory threshold of the left hand was slightly lower than that of the right. Tactile identification and naming were intact in both hands. General static coordination was proficient for age, and SD had no trouble in performing the fifteen- to sixteen-year tests for this function (for example, balancing on one leg with the sole of the other foot held against the knee, eyes closed). Dynamic coordination of the hands was also normal. He had difficulty with the more complex synkinesis tests, but it was observed that he failed because of associated movements and not because of any dystaxia or dysmetria. On standard rapid alternating movement tests, there was no dysdiadocho-cinesia. SD was easily able to maintain a volitional posture against displacement without any abnormal rebound oscillation. It was concluded that the tested sensory and motor functions were those of a normal sixteen-year-old.

Case DR presented at the age of six for investigation of an ataxia of one year's duration. The motor assessment was directed toward establishing the developmental levels of the various motor functions. General static coordination was below age three; for example, DR could not advance one foot in front of the other or balance on tip-toe. Dynamic coordination of the body was extremely impaired, and he could not hop or jump. Dynamic coordination of the hands was at a four-to-five-year level—DR could throw a ball through a target and touch the point of his nose with eyes closed. Motor speed involving the hands corresponded to the five-year level. The capacity

to make simultaneous voluntary movements was also at a five-year level—DR was able to describe circles with both index fingers simultaneously. Some associated movement (for example, a conjugate gaze to the left while clenching teeth) was present on the six-year, but not four- or five-year, tests for synkinesis. It was concluded that whole body coordination, both static and dynamic, was significantly impaired, while fine motor skills and motor differentiation were preserved at the age level of the onset of the ataxia. Educational planning was then based on the fact that DR's ataxia had occasioned a selective and not generalized disruption of motor function.

Case JE was investigated at the age of nine for precocious puberty. On neurological investigation no abnormality was detected, and visual fields, sensory and motor function were intact. The EEG was normal. An air encephalogram showed a congenital absence of the middle and posterior regions of the corpus callosum. He was seen at the age of fourteen for a neuropsychological investigation. Tactile sensitivity and motor strength proved to be intact in each hand. However, certain aspects of sensory and motor competence did not seem to have been acquired. He had a within-hand, bilaterally evident, sensory defect—the individual fingers could be discriminated from each other but finger interrelationships were not perceived accurately. JE was also extremely poor for age in the ability to perform independent finger movements. Abduction of the fingers of one hand was accompanied by gross movement of the other fingers of the moving hand, as well as of the other hand. It was concluded that JE showed sensory and motor immaturities of development but no sensory-motor impairment of the kind associated with cortical lesions.

Sensory and motor function in Case SD was normal and mature before the onset of the behavioral disruption, so the issue for investigation and the test procedures were those appropriate to adults. Testing, nevertheless, involved an investigation of processes as well as scores. A failure on the fifteen-to-sixteen-year synkinesis test, for example, could have been due to associated movement or to dysmetria and dystaxia. Clarification of the process underlying failure was an important part of the diagnostic task because each type of impairment bore a different relationship to the underlying cerebral pathology.

Development of motor function in Case DR had been normal until age five, when a seemingly progressive lesion occurred. The issue for assessment, as well as for remediation and educational planning, concerned relative development levels—had the ataxia disrupted motor functions uniformly, or were some more spared than others?

Sensory and motor function in Case JE appeared aberrant principally because of his age. Each of the impairments he showed is part of a regular developmental process—children below the age of seven have difficulty in discriminating finger relationships and in making independent finger movements. What was abnormal about JE was that he had failed to acquire these aspects of differentiated sensory and motor control by the age of fourteen. Since he did not show sensory loss or motor weakness, his sensory-motor status was described as immature rather than impaired. Immaturity and impairment, of course, may be equally disruptive to the smooth operation of a behavioral skill.

Language, Oral and Written. Case BC was normal until the age of twelve, when she developed a sudden right hemiparesis and global aphasia. Computerized axial tomography showed decreased density in the left fronto-temporal area; cerebral arteriogram revealed occlusion of the left middle cerebral artery. One week after the onset of the stroke, speech was moderately dysarthric, with vowels prolonged and plosives imprecise, but BC was able to give biographical information, produce simple sentences, and define simple words. Neuropsychological assessment of language at this time revealed a variety of problems. Naming to visual confrontation and description of object use had deteriorated below a six-year level and responses showed circumlocution, semantic (*comb* for *brush*) and phonemic (*nome* for *comb*) paraphasias. BC was unable to name any object placed in the right hand. Tactile naming with the left hand was somewhat better, but there were still some anomic errors (*flashlight* for *light bulb; egg lifter* for *eggbeater*). Other aspects of language expression were also disordered. Comprehension was intact at the level of the single word but impaired for longer, nonredundant commands. Written language functions were all three years above oral language skills. It was concluded that BC's stroke had caused a deterioration of her oral language functions, both expressive and receptive, to a level somewhat below that of a six-year-old. Written language abilities had also been impaired, albeit much less severely.

Case TM sustained a head injury at the age of seven, and since then reported a progressive difficulty with school work. He was evaluated at the age of eleven for oral and written language competence. Visual confrontation naming was at a seven-year level. TM had difficulty in generating names for common objects. He approached these tasks by means of successive approximations, for example, naming a paper clip, he said, ". . . a pin . . . a pin clip . . . a paper-pin . . . a clip . . ."; naming a jar, he said, ". . . a container, a glass whatever . . ." Although he was unable to label common objects, he had no difficulty in describing the use and function of the same objects. Sentence repetition, at a six-year level, was quite poor, with many neologisms and paraphasic substitutions: "The iron was quite hot" was repeated as "The arms quelt fot"; "The paper was under the chair" was repeated as "The people were under the tree." The tendency to reverse phonemes was also evident when TM was asked to repeat single words. Word fluency was quite constricted, and the ability to construct sentences from simple words was quite impaired. The comprehension of nonredundant oral commands was extremely poor for age. Verbal memory was generally age-appropriate. Interestingly, most basic written language functions (oral reading of sentences, reading names and sentences for meaning, visual-graphic naming, writing names and sentences to dictation) were quite intact. TM thus presented as a boy with impairment in three areas of oral language: naming to visual confrontation, phoneme production, and sentence comprehension. His ability to perform written language operations was better than his oral language.

Case LR developed normally until the age of four, when she suddenly began to talk less and less, pointing to objects instead of calling them by name. At this time, she had episodes of eye flutter behind closed lids. An EEG was very abnormal with seizure activity appearing to arise centrally. An audiogram was normal. At the time of the neuropsychological assessment some weeks after the onset of the problem, LR produced no spontaneous speech, tending to avoid verbal interactions and reacting to vocalization with distress or aggression. Three questions were posed of LR (assuming that she could hear): (1) did sound have representational qualities? (2) did she have the conceptualization abilities appropriate to her age? and (3) how well developed were her nonverbal skills? The first question was answered in the affirmative, since LR consistently identified the origin of tape-recorded sounds (for example, hearing a tape recording of a horse neighing, she reliably chose a picture of a horse in a four-choice display). Print also appeared to have some representational function—in copying letters, LR was noted to transfer the lower-case *f* of the model into a capital *F* in her copy. The answer to the second question also appeared to be affirmative, since LR could sort plastic tokens of the basis of color and shape. No clear answer could be given to the third question. Although LR did perform some constructional tasks at a three-year-old level, she refused to attempt the more difficult items. It was concluded that she displayed an acquired aphasia due to a disorder of central language function. Throughout the disturbance, sounds and print had continued to have a representational function while speech had not.

Case KE was referred for neuropsychological assessment of language following temporal lobectomy for a seizure disorder beginning at the age of seven. He was quite anomic to visual confrontation, being unable to generate names for objects as simple as brushes and ashtrays. His errors tended to be verbal paraphasias (*comb* for *brush*) or associative paraphasias (*the cigarette . . . the case* for *ashtray*). Asked to describe the use of simple objects, he was somewhat better, although descriptions were oblique rather than direct. Tactile naming was poor in both hands, but tactile-visual matching with the same objects was proficient, indicating that a language problem rather than a sensory-discriminative disorder was involved. KE's errors, further, were obviously anomic ones (feeling a plate, he said, "You use it when you are eating . . . I forget the name of it"). KE's speech was quite fluent. Although able to produce all the phonemes of English, he had problems in reauditorizing the sequence of heard phonemes. As a result, sentence repetition was very poor. Sentence construction was also impaired, and KE attempted this task by means of successive approximations. When asked to make a sentence of the two words "boy" and "snow," for example, he said, "Snowman . . . boy . . . snow . . . the snow where the boy stand . . . it snowed where the boy was standing." Comprehension was generally at a higher age level than expressive language skills. KE was totally unable to manage the simplest tasks involving written language. He could not name letters or read simple words, silently or orally; he appeared to have no comprehension of written words; he could not produce even an approximation to the phonemic-graphemic rules of English. Testing indicated that these problems were not due to discriminative visual difficulties or to dyspraxia— KE was able to match letters (although he could not name them), and he could copy correctly sentences he was unable to read or write. KE thus presented as a boy with a moderate problem in expressive language, and a fundamental alexia and

agraphia evident even on the level of the single letter. The process underlying the written language impairment was an inability to perform auditory-visual associations between the sounds and symbols of English.

Case GT was a boy of fourteen who had experienced difficulty in reading since beginning school. The impaired speech articulation that he showed in spontaneous speech was also apparent when imitating phoneme sequences—his mimicry involved continual phoneme substitutions (*b* for *l, p* for *t*) and additional or irrelevant phonemes. Although able to analyze words into their component parts, he could not blend sounds to form words. The cross-modal aspects of written language were intact, and GT had no difficulty in establishing associations between visual symbols and phonemes. When the task was to translate phonemes into graphemes, and graphemes into phonemes, however, he was significantly impaired. It was concluded that GT had a fairly basic problem in speech articulation which interfered with his capacity to read and spell. The speech articulation defect meant that, when required to reauditorize internally what was heard, the resultant version was incorrect. GT was then forced to use his own impaired reauditorized version as the basis for further translation into visual representations. In short, he appeared to be writing down his own misarticulations.

Each of the aforementioned five cases presented for investigation of language function, but both the nature and the origin of the language impairment differed. In order for the assessment to address itself directly to the child's impairment, it was necessary that the test techniques be varied according to the presenting problem.

Although LR, TM, and BC all showed acquired language disorders, the nature of the investigation was different in each case. The issue for LR was whether she possessed sufficient internal language to be retrained with conventional oral techniques, or whether sound and speech retained so little representational function that a visual language system such as manual signing was indicated. Since she had no functional language or speech, the test techniques were tailor-made for her problem. TM and BC could be given almost identical tests, despite the fact that they presented with different problems—in TM's case, a failure to develop certain language skills; in BC's, a loss of previously acquired normal language competence.

Disorders of written language are a common problem in children, but such impairments have no single cause. The same symptom of poor reading and spelling in KE and GT reflected underlying problems in, respectively, the formation of auditory-visual associations and the production of correct speech output. The assessment must include a task analysis of reading and spelling if the underlying process responsible for the written language impairment is to be isolated.

Language can be modulated by oral or written processes, and the level of function of the two sets of skills may be either correlated or dissociated. The relatively good preservation of written language in BC and TM served to highlight their severe disruption of oral language; in KE, written language was the more disturbed of the two; while in GT, the written language impairment was related to (and, indeed, appeared to be a consequence of) disordered verbal output. It is evident that oral and written language must be assessed both separately and in relation to each other.

Visuo-Spatial Ability. Case DR presented at the age of fifteen with a three-month history of facial weakness and headaches. Investigations revealed a large cystic lesion involving the right frontal lobe. The neuropsychological examination noted a variety of problems in visuo-spatial function. DR showed a clear constructional apraxia. Not only was the overall level of performance on constructional tasks low in relation to age expectation, but responses were inverted, rotated and lacking in clear figure-ground limits. Perceptual closure was also poor, and DR could not identify serially fragmented pictures of common objects. The capacity to orient through a visual maze had deteriorated to an eight-year-old level. Topographic spatial confusion was evident on several tasks, with an inability to discriminate the left and right sides of space. It was concluded that DR had sustained a disruption of a wide variety of visuo-spatial skills.

Case JC suffered a head injury at the age of five, after which she showed a progressive deterioration in school performance. On neuropsychological testing, she displayed great difficulty with constructional praxis tests and her models were rotated in space or inverted. She had inordinate trouble in creating the bare outlines of a figure. More specialized tests clarified the source of these problems. Eye-hand coordination was well developed in relation to age, and form constancy was at an age-appropriate level. The capacity to discriminate figure from ground was significantly impaired, and the capacity to identify spatial relationships and spatial position were also four years retarded for JC's mental and chronological

age. Visually guided route finding on mazes was normal for age. JC showed a selective set of problems in visuo-spatial function.

Both of the preceding cases presented with a general difficulty in manipulating visual space and they are similarly impaired on three-dimensional praxis tests. However, the other visuo-spatial skills which correlated with the impairment were different in the two cases—in DR, almost all aspects of visuo-perceptual skill had deteriorated but in JC, the impairment was considerably more specific. Performance on tests of related functions may suggest different interpretations of the same test scores. The necessity of testing correlated capacities is clear if one considers that eye-hand coordination problems will also cause difficulty on visuo-spatial tests requiring praxis. Only by evaluating a set of correlated skills can the specificity of a visuo-spatial disorder be assessed.

When Has the Goal of Testing Been Reached?

The aim of a neuropsychological assessment is a clear description of the capacities that are aberrant and the impaired processing that underlies them. Providing such a description involves not the administration of a uniform set of tests to all children regardless of age or presenting complaint but rather the use of a series of clues to focus the behavioral investigation. The indications for referral are usually clues of the first level—behaviors that suddenly appeared abnormal in relation to the child's history or which were not acquired at the expected times in the developmental schedule. Using these preliminary clues, the next task is to observe the child's behavior in situations which require different kinds of behavioral skills. The IQ test provides a useful means of noting the abilities of the child in twelve different contexts, and results from this test will usually provide second-level clues to indicate the specific aspects of processing to be studied. Understanding cognitive impairment must involve a flexible application of investigative tools—in some cases, the use of the same test to study different problems; in others, the use of different tests to clarify the meaning of similar presenting symptoms.

When should an assessment be terminated? Ideally, not before the behavioral description is complete enough to allow manipulative understanding of the child's impairment, i.e., the ability to make the disorder appear or disappear by changing the set task in some critical aspect. A fringe benefit of continuing the assessment to this stage is that the component of behavior critical to remediation will have been pinpointed. The remedial task, in fact, involves taking the critical aspect of processing and giving control of it back to the child, either by retraining specific skills or by teaching compensatory strategies.

Acknowledgment

The author is supported by a Research Scholarship from the Ontario Mental Health Foundation. The patients were referred for assessment by Drs. H. J. Hoffman, R. P. Humphreys, and K. L. Meloff of the Hospital for Sick Children.

REFERENCES

1. BORTNER, M., and BIRCH, H. G., "Perception and Perceptual-Motor Dissociation in Cerebral Palsied Children," *Journal of Nervous and Mental Disease, 130:*49, 1960.
2. FIELD, J. G., "Two Types of Tables for Use With Wechsler's Intelligence Scales," *Journal of Clinical Psychology, 16:*3, 1960.
3. PAYNE, R. W., and JONES, H. G., "Statistics for the Investigation of Individual Cases," *Journal of Clinical Psychology, 13:*115, 1957.
4. RHODES, F., *Manual for the WISC-R Scatter Profile,*
Educational and Industrial Testing Service, San Diego, 1975.
5. ———, *Manual for the Rhodes WISC Scatter Profile,* Educational and Industrial Testing Service, San Diego, 1969.
6. WECHSLER, D., *Manual for the Wechsler Intelligence Scale for Children—Revised,* The Psychological Corporation, New York, 1974.
7. ———, *Manual for the Wechsler Intelligence Scale for Children,* The Psychological Corporation, New York, 1949.

---

69 / Psychoeducational Assessment

Vivian Thackaberry Harway

The examinations customarily administered by a clinical psychologist and a neuropsychologist have been outlined previously. There are, however, any number of "indicators" which may suggest the need for more intensive study, especially in the psychoeducational area. If there is any reason to suspect that the child has a specific learning disability, the assistance of a special educator trained in diagnostic techniques is often invaluable. Such a specialist has available an armamentarium of techniques for identifying specific areas of deficits in the child's perception, processing, integration, or expression of information which may be missed by other approaches.

In the following material, some of these procedures are outlined in detail.

—RLC

Introduction

The child with a learning disorder may present a complex problem in differential diagnosis to the child psychiatrist. The failure to achieve expected levels of academic success may be particularly baffling because by definition, the learning disabled child has average or better learning potential. He is prevented from fully realizing this potential by the interference of disorders in the ability to attend, to understand, or to "process" written or spoken communication, or to express himself appropriately in words, gestures, writing, or pictures. He may thus have imperfect ability to listen, think, speak, read, write, spell, or do arithmetic, although basically normal in sensorimotor functioning. This paraphrasing of the most commonly accepted definition of Learning Disability (see Appendix 1, p. 592) stresses the obvious point that Learning Disability is first and foremost an educational concept. Yet, for the school-age child, success in educational attainment is a primary developmental task. The child's sense of adequacy and acceptability as a person, and his sense of his own worthiness in the eyes of others, especially in terms of his parents' expectations, is inextricably tied to school performance.

It is estimated by the Department of Health, Education and Welfare that between 10 and 12 million children in the United States are faced with the problem of learning disability in one form or another. It is found in every stratum of our society. It is insidious because it is often concealed behind its secondary effects. The same processes which produce a baffling failure to learn in specific areas can also produce behavior which can be irritating and annoying to people whom the child wants most to please and be close to. It is very common to find these children described as lazy, interfering, unpopular with peers, inattentive, impulsive, procrastinating, non-conforming to group standards, or worse, by those who try to deal with them on a day-to-day basis.

In the basic process of assessment, it is important that these behavioral side effects be noted, but they must be separated from the primary areas of learning weakness and significant areas of learning strengths must be pinpointed. The aim of psychoeducational assessment is to determine the nature of the learning disturbance and to use this information in plotting strategies of educational intervention, so that the spiral of learning problem ⟶ failure ⟶ behavior which interferes with attitudes toward learning ⟶ further failure ⟶ increasingly negative view of self as learner may be broken.

In this chapter, the learning disabled child will be described in terms of how he or she would appear to the child psychiatrist. The functioning of the L.D. child in basic academic skill areas will be described in comparison to normal expectations, and some simple formal and informal screening instruments which might be available to the child psychiatrist to help determine which children require further psychoeducational study will be noted. The process of individual psychoeducational assessment will be described, and the implications of such assessment for individualized educational programming will be discussed.

What Are the Characteristics of the L.D. Child?

Although most authors refer to ten basic characteristics of learning disability (see Appendix 2, p. 592), these traits are not mutually exclusive. For purposes of our discussion, they may be grouped into five major descriptive categories, and the "learning disabled" child may be considered to show one or several of the following:

1. Academic lags: (1) in important skill areas in the older child; (2) in the basic "readiness" skill areas for the younger child.
2. These lags are usually associated with a history of uneven developmental rate in language, motor, and self-help areas. (Often this unevenness may be expressed as what appeared to be marked acceleration in one area, language especially.)
3. Often mentioned and yet most difficult to typify are hyperactivity and variability in attention span.
4. Difficulty in processing information within a sensory modality and/or across modalities.

Academic Lags

READING

Normal Expectations. For many children, particularly children in the early years, it is difficult to determine if academic lags truly exist since they are at the beginning of exposure to formal academic training. By the time the child is nine years old, such lags may be clearly demonstrated by objective measures such as performance on standardized achievement tests, used by almost all school districts, or by classroom grades. By then effective remediation is much more difficult to initiate. A lag of two years is judged to be severe in a child above nine years of age and a lag of one-and-a-half years is judged to be severe between seven and nine years.[2] Although this may be reflected in achievement test performance, and the child psychiatrist should request such scores from the school district, it is well to have a brief acquaintance with reading expectations for the younger child so that some estimate of functional lag may be made which might help determine if further, more intensive study would be indicated.

By the end of kindergarten, a child should know by sight and sound the letters of the alphabet.

He should be interested in books and able to attend to the stories and details of books designed for this age child, such as the numerous books in the "I Can Read" series pioneered by Dr. Seuss (Theodore Geisel). Whether the school which the child attends emphasizes the phonics approach, the "whole word" approach, or as in most settings today, a judicious combination of both, by the end of second grade the child should be able to deal with vowel and consonant sounds, consonant clusters, prefixes and suffixes, and punctuation marks. Many children founder on the shoals of "auditory-visual integration." They can recognize individual letters, but they have difficulty associating the sounds of a group of letters with the sound patterns of familiar words. They may have problems in hearing the sounds in spoken words or in decoding sounds in printed words. (For example, a seven-year-old girl who was trying to write the word "bad" asked the author, "How do you write an *ah*?" She could make the auditory analysis but did not have a firm association of sound with letter form.)

At third grade and beyond, the emphasis is on the further development of language arts and comprehension. Instruction in spelling, grammar, writing, speaking, and listening is integrated and overlapping. By fourth grade or nine years old, most children should be fairly independent in word-attack skills, and their greater appreciation of logical sequence makes them seek out stories with more complicated plot lines. At this level, children are capable of creating a synopsis of what they read.

Brief Formal Measures of Achievement in Basic Reading Skills Areas. The Wide Range Achievement Test[25] is useful, in addition to scores on standardized Group Achievement tests, since it offers a short, reliable assessment of functioning in reading, math, and spelling, over a range from kindergarten to college levels. The reading test consists of a list of words graded as to difficulty level. It evaluates reading skills in the absence of sentence context.

The Gray Oral Reading Test[20] presents the child with a series of paragraphs graded in difficulty from the preprimer level through Adult reading skills (Grade 14+). Although it basically reveals problems with the mechanics of reading, it is also possible to infer some measure of reading comprehension. It demonstrates quickly the kinds of problems the child is having with reading and whether the child tends to rely more on word recognition or has developed some awareness of auditory-visual integration.

Informal Measures. Have the child relate an event or tell a story—note if the sequences follow a logical order, note if the syntax is appropriate (tenses of verbs, normality of word order), note the sentence length, use of adjectives, and richness of vocabulary.

Reversals. There is a very common tendency on the part of some children to reverse words in reading—*was* for *saw, pot* for *top*, etc.—but by second grade, regardless of the reading approach used with them, they should have overcome this tendency. A simple test of persistent reversal tendencies is to hand the child a card with these words typed on it and say, "Read these words as fast as you can . . . hurry!"

Test words: pal, even, no, saw, raw, ten, tar, won, pot, rats, naps, tops, read, lap, keep.

ARITHMETIC

Normal Expectations. Success in mathematical functioning is dependent upon a variety of skills including visual and auditory memory, the ability to perceive spatial relationships, the ability to generalize, to discriminate between forms, and the ability to visualize quantities in the presence of a symbolic representation of them, a printed or written number. Most typically the normal child begins arithmetic instruction with counting, enumeration, and sequencing. They then learn to read numbers and to associate numbers with concrete representations of quantities. They learn to group numbers and to manipulate quantities. There are many different approaches to teaching children basic mathematics skills, and these become more divergent as the child proceeds up the academic ladder. However, it is a fairly reasonable assumption that by the end of second grade, the child would have had some exposure to numbers and number sequencing, and can manipulate one-digit and some two-digit numbers in simple addition and subtraction, and is familiar with common instruments of measurement and terms of number usage.

Lags in arithmetic function may be associated with other learning problems, notably disturbances in visual spatial organization, left-right confusion, and poor perceptual-motor integration.

Brief Formal and Informal Measures of Achievement in Mathematics. For the older child a two-year lag in arithmetic function on standardized achievement tests is considered severe. For the younger child the Wide Range Achievement Test Arithmetic subtests may provide a useful screening tool, or the informal series of screening questions below adapted from standard educational measures[13, 14, 36] may prove helpful as a guide to suggest possible problems in arithmetic readiness in five- to seven-year olds.

1. *Number Sequence*
   (Beginning First Grade)
   When I say 1, 2, 3, 4 . . . what comes next?
   What number is left out? 1-2-3-4-5-7-8-9?
   What number is left out? 100-200-300-400-600.
   (Beginning Second Grade)
   When I say 5, 10, 15, 20 . . . what comes next?
   When I say 2, 4, 6, 8 . . . what comes next?
   What number is left out? 10-20-30-50-60.

2. *Reading Numbers*
   (Beginning First Grade)
   Read these numbers for me: 5, 8, 9.
   (Beginning Second Grade)
   Read these numbers for me: 21, 34, 47.

3. *Uses of Numbers in Problem Solving*
   (Beginning First Grade)
   Bob had 5 pennies. He spent 1 penny. How many pennies did he have left?
   Mary had 2 cents. Her aunt gave her 3 cents. How many cents did she have in all?
   How many 5-cent candy bars can you buy for a dime?
   (Beginning Second Grade)
   Jimmy is 4 years old. His sister is 1 year younger. How old is she?
   John has 20 pennies. He wants twice as many. How many does he want?
   Carol was invited to a 3 o'clock party. She got there at 3:30. Was she early or late?

4. *Familiarity with Instruments and Units of Measurement*
   (Beginning First Grade)
   What is the thing we use to tell what time it is?
   What is the thing we use to find how long a room is?
   What is the thing we use to tell the day of the month?
   How many cents in a nickel?
   (Beginning Second Grade)
   What is the thing we use to tell how warm or cold a room is?
   What is the thing we use to tell how heavy a child is?
   How many cents in a dime?
   How many nickles make a dime?
   How many days does it take to make a week?

5. *Familiarity with Common Usage*
   (Beginning First Grade)
   If I cut an apple in half, how many pieces will I have?
   How many things is a pair of things?
   When is your birthday?
   (Beginning Second Grade)
   How many things make a dozen?

SPELLING

Normal Expectations. Spelling is a very sensitive indicator of language disabilities since there are fewer methods of compensation for the dis-

ability. Although poor readers are almost always poor spellers, it is not unusual to find a spelling disability in the absence of reading problems. Success in spelling involves visual and auditory analysis and visual sequentialization and integration all performed simultaneously.

Brief Formal and Informal Achievement Measures. The Wide Range Achievement Test contains a useful list of words arranged in order of difficulty for screening possible spelling problems. However, a list of "nonsense" words is often helpful in revealing areas of process difficulties such as awareness of vowel and consonant sounds and blending. Such a list might include such syllables as: fis, hin, sut, jav, tope, duts, sult.

WRITING

Normal Expectations. Written language is the last language skill acquired and is achieved only when all the preceding levels have been established. Success in writing is a complex amalgam of motor skills involved in the grasp of writing utensil and maintaining paper position, perceptual skills involved in perception of letter shape patterns and letter-word sequencing patterns, and cognitive-automatic integration. Typically in American schools, the young child learns to print first, using the "ball and stick" method, and later transfers (around third grade) to cursive writing. This transfer process is difficult for some children. The printing method is taught first with the rationale that it most resembles what the child is working with in reading. However, children who encounter developmental lags in right-left orientation, and who tend to have prolongation of tendencies toward reversal, find these tendencies intensified in handwriting, and their confusion is often compounded. For children with strong tendencies toward reversals, early instruction in cursive writing is quite helpful and can help in reading difficulty—it seems to provide a different framework for viewing letter-word relationships and also provides the child with a writing task which has rhythm and flow and provides fewer directional choice points.

Informal Assessment. Formal handwriting scales abound, but informal handwriting samples, obtained by the child psychiatrist, can be valuable indicators of illegibility, taking too much time to shape letters, poor spacing and organization, and tendencies toward reversal or rotations. Asking the child to write his name, or short sentences such as "See the bad dog. He bit the big boy," and phrases such as "big pig" can often be helpful.

Uneven Developmental History

In the family and developmental histories of children at risk for learning disorder, a number of factors may appear with some degree of regularity. Most children with learning disabilities are boys. Bryant and McLoughlin,[6] in their review of variables associated with learning problems, report that the ratio of boys to girls reported across incidence studies is 4:1. There is often a family history of learning difficulties, especially problems in developing reading skills. Sometimes, but not always, there is a history of prenatal or perinatal distress. High risk of a learning difficulty has been associated with such conditions as toxemia, prenatal bleeding, low birth weight, anoxia at birth, poor maternal nutrition, long-term maternal emotional stress, poor early mother-child interaction, and impoverishment of early learning environment.

In their infancy and preschool years learning disabled children are often described by their parents as having been active and restless and "into everything." They may have been early walkers who were unintentionally oblivious to the destructive impact of their attempts to ambulate on household objects and the property of others. Conversely, they may also be described as having lagged in motor development, but shown precocious language development. Such children are often described as having used their language facility to express negativism, stubbornness, defiance, etc. Sometimes the early-walking child is described as clumsy and poorly coordinated in later motor behavior, or wide differences in fine and gross motor functioning may be described in preschool years. Lags in development of self-help skills associated with dressing are often reported. Limited interest in coloring, cutting with scissors, pasting, and playing with puzzles and blocks are noted in preschool settings, as well as problems conforming to group behavioral standards at story hour or rest time. Compared to siblings, parents often describe a child with learning difficulties as having been more impulsive, less easy to control, more given to dramatic release of emotion, and more clinging and demanding of emotional reassurance, and thus difficult to deal with in ways that encourage autonomous, independent functioning.

In giving a history, parents will more often than not describe negative, trying behaviors. Irregularities and inconsistencies in behaviors will be the rule, rather than the exception. These are conditions which put a severe strain on the family unit.

However, a subtle element of parent behavior that is often present in families with a child with learning disorder, as compared to parents with a child with a primary behavior disorder, is that the former are often baffled, hurt, confused, but they have tried to adapt, and they recognize the child's efforts to conform to expectations, even when these efforts are not successful. Despite the strains, the general attitude toward the child is positive and accepting.

HYPERACTIVITY AND VARIABILITY
IN ATTENTION

These two characteristics are frequently thought of as interrelated. Obviously the child who cannot sit still will have a harder time attending to a task. Conversely, the child whose attention is constantly drawn by sights and sounds apart from the designated task (i.e., who has difficulty screening out competing visual and auditory stimuli) will have a difficult time sitting still. The child's attention will be fleeting; it will dart away and move back. This will give a fragmented quality to his perceptual organization of the particular learning experience. It is as though the experience were viewed as a reflection in a broken mirror so that different elements are perceived in different spatial relationship to one another.

These are characteristics most often attributed to the learning disabled child by parents, teachers, and learning disability specialists, yet with the least validity. They are often subjective judgments at best. Children vary in activity levels—when does activity become hyperactivity? The general thrust of recent research in this area[30, 32] is that children vary in activity level depending on the situation and the task and their expectation of success or failure, and that distractibility does not necessarily accompany high activity level.

Another group of researchers have focused on the possible relationships between hyperactivity, poor performance on tests of attention span and impulsivity, and brain dysfunction. Stimulant drugs have been found to increase ability to focus attention and thus limit hyperactivity to some degree. This is supposed to be the result of activation of dysfunctional neural pathways in the reticular system.[12] Even the most neurologically oriented of such researchers are often unclear and unidimensional in defining "hyperactivity" and report that only certain types of hyperkinesis, characterized by excessive fidgetiness and impulsivity, react well to amphetamine therapy.[9, 34]

Recent studies comparing rates of learning of

hyperactive and normal children, matched for age and intellectual level,[15, 29] resulted in the finding that hyperactive and normal children learn at similar rates under conditions of constant reinforcement, but normal children were able to learn more rapidly under conditions of partial reinforcement. This suggests that hyperactive children may perhaps have a lowered threshhold for the frustration of nonreward and may tend to give up sooner. This finding is similar to the common occurrence in clinical practice of seeing a child described as "extremely hyperactive" in a classroom situation remain fairly calm and "on task" for up to two hours in a one-to-one situation with a reassuring and consistently reinforcing adult figure. "Hyperactivity" thus may be a reactive component of the learning disabled child, a result of anxieties generated by repeated experiences of failure, expectations of not achieving, and feelings of having "let down" important figures in their young lives. Certainly, it is clear that there is no clear-cut isomorphic relationship between learning dysfunction and activity level. It is extremely important to determine by questioning and observation *when* the child becomes more active, and how such activity manifests itself. This kind of careful questioning can have important consequences for planning effective intervention.

By the same token, disturbances in attention, in alertness, ability to focus attention on an appropriate stimulus, and watchfulness can be noted in the child's everyday life in problems in understanding and following directions, in memorizing material, and determining what behaviors should be repeated in problem solving. This also varies with the situation and the motivational level of the child. Problems in attention may increase when the amount of stimulation around the child increases. Particularly for the young child, there seems to be difficulty in screening out irrelevant stimuli and focusing on the most important aspect of the situation, while everything else becomes background. Difficulty in shifting attention is also noted in some children. Problems of hyperactivity and distractibility are often highly responsive to environmental management, both at home and in the school. Children who manifest such behavior function best in highly structured situations where stimulus input is well controlled.

PROBLEMS IN PROCESSING INFORMATION

"Processing" refers to the child's ability to organize, give meaning to, and generalize from sensorimotor experiences. Problems in this function may be manifest in myriad ways, depending on the age, ability level, and environmental situation of the child. We may roughly group them into problems in spatial awareness, problems in co-ordination across sensory modalities, and problems in conceptualization.

Problems in spatial awareness are usually thought of in terms of reversals or rotations in reading or writing, but they show up at much earlier developmental stages as difficulties in dealing with preschool puzzles, avoiding playing with blocks, problems in learning to ride a bike, skip rope, climb trees, fasten buttons, and tie shoes. In primary-grade pupils, human figure drawings may show poor concepts of body organization. The "tadpole" man (head, with legs and arms) of the three-and-a-half- to four-year-old child may persist into ages five to seven, or parts are out of proportion, and necks or shoulders may be omitted. In their drawings of people, such children frequently minimally comply with instructions and then verbally elaborate and embellish their productions. For the older child (eight and above), the figure may possess a number of sophisticated additions in terms of body parts, such as nostrils, pupils of the eyes, lids and lashes, clothing details, but be poorly organized and differentiated, and resemble, in terms of organizational maturity, the drawing of a much younger child. Handedness in children with learning problems is often not clearly established until past age six. Even when there is a clear-cut hard preference, the child (above age six) may have difficulty in orienting himself directionally in space, and the command "Touch your right ear with your left thumb" may produce confusion. This is also seen in attempts to coordinate movement with visual pursuit. It is not unusual to find children with problems in spatial orientation who have difficulty with batting, catching, shooting baskets, etc., although they may excel at swimming or football where judgments of distance and direction do not require such accuracy. In the older school-age child, spatial problems may persist in difficulties in dealing with maps and problems in conceptualizing two-dimensional images representing three-dimensional space. These older children seem to have problems reading diagrams, copying material from blackboards, etc., and it is not unusual for them to avoid the mania for model building of the school-age child, or if they do succumb to the craze, to construct models without following the diagrams, following their own idea and kinesthetic impressions of what this three-dimensional car, airplane, or animal might look like.

Tasks which are purely visual (for example, pictorial identification, matching, letter recognition) seem fairly easy for some children, and tasks that are purely auditory in nature (vocabulary recognition, auditory memory, auditory-verbal reasoning) may pose little challenge for others. They encounter difficulty when they must coordinate the information that comes to them from different sensory impressions, for example, the shape of the letter *a* with the short vowel sound *a*. At a more mature level, they may have difficulty combining their knowledge of a word like "bird," for example, with the combination and blending of letter sounds which make it up.

Sometimes there are problems in coordinating impressions within a sensory modality. All children have to learn and develop an appreciation for the logical sequence of sounds in a word or words in a sentence. For children with processing problems, the *logical* arrangement of sounds, words, or ideas may present a very frustrating problem in communication. In speaking to children, the clinician should be alert for such common expressive errors as *aminal* (animal), *pisketti* (spaghetti), *platsic* (plastic), or "It looks me like . . ." for "It looks to me like," a confusion of tenses and concepts in narration. Another example of the latter is a very bright nine-year-old girl's attempt to say that she used to have a pet cat but it was lost: "I haved a now kitty but him got losted." In the visual-motor sphere this may be noted in children whose spoken language is impeccable, but who write *wrok* for *work*, or *spot* for *stop* or *pruple* for *purple*, and who have problems recognizing their error on later inspection.

Conceptually the clinician may note that the child has difficulty in grasping and working with basic conceptual relationships, such as time, space, dates, family relationships, etc. The child may be slow to develop categorizing skills or may show gaps in general knowledge which suggest a concrete appreciation of the environment. He may not know his own birthday, for example, even after school entrance, when such events become major causes for celebration. Learning to tell time is often quite difficult without concrete representational aids; the common terms for the passage of time and representations of past, present, and future time are poorly comprehended. Once he learns something in one sense, it is difficult to conceptualize it in another sense. (For example: the author's office may be reached from the lobby by elevator, or up one flight of stairs. For many children, it is difficult for them to conceptualize that the lobby will indeed be reached by descending the stairs, if they left it by ascending the elevator. They express surprise when they find that the stairs reach the same place.)

When to Refer for More Intensive Assessment

To briefly sum up, a child with learning problems may appear to a child psychiatrist as a child who shows significant lags in acquisition of basic learning skills on formal academic measures and informal office screening and interview. The child's history suggests lags in some areas of development or at least developmental rates which are not consistent in all areas, and may also reveal early problems in development of self-help skills, communication skills, and ability to respond to parental suggestions and commands. There may be evidence of increased activity and distractability in different situations. There also may be, as the child encounters more and more challenges to abstract and symbolic functioning, increasing evidence of problems in development of self-help skills, comacross sensory modalities, dealing with spatial orientation, and conceptualizing and logical thought. If on the basis of the interview, review of school material, and informal screening, problems in one or several of these areas are indicated, further intensive individual study utilizing a battery of psychoeducational tests is indicated. Such study will help determine areas of strengths and weaknesses, and help plan programs geared toward helping the child to realize his fullest learning potential while minimizing the corrosive effects of failure on the self-image.

The purpose of assessment is to find out what factors are interfering with the child's learning functioning, and to suggest more effective educational approaches based upon this information. Although some direct remedial suggestions may be expected, it is also helpful to recommend ways in which the child's strong areas may best be utilized to reinforce and in some instances, to compensate for areas of weakness. Myklebust[26] has called this approach "teaching to strengths." Psychoeducational assessment may also yield information about the severity of the disorder and thus the most appropriate educational setting within which effective remedial intervention might take place. There is increasing concern at the present time among educators and clinicians that the child receive special educational inputs in "the least restrictive setting," i.e. the setting which most closely resembles that planned for nonspecial pupils, and yet still meets the child's needs. Another purpose of psychoeducational assessment is to determine the impact of educational and social failure on the child and the family, and to suggest appropriate therapeutic inputs if necessary.

The Process of Psychoeducational Assessment

The concept of selecting an appropriate "battery" of tests to answer the questions posed by the referring clinician has been described by Magnussen (see chapter 66). When a primary learning disorder is suspected, the battery of tests usually consists of:

1. Developmental and family history.
2. A test of general abilities.
3. Tests of specific perceptual functioning.
4. More intensive study of areas of academic weakness.
5. Tests of personality functioning.

For material on developmental and family history taking, the reader is referred to chapter 59. Tests of general abilities and specific patterning of responses of children with neuropsychological disorders on the Wechsler Intelligence Scale for Children[36] are discussed in chapters 66 and 68.

We will now briefly consider some of the more widely used instruments for assessing perceptual and perceptual-motor functioning and the kinds of information which each scale might yield.

PERCEPTUAL TESTS

Tests of perceptual and perceptual-motor functioning may be roughly classified as follows.

Tests of Visual-Motor Perception. These tests for the most part yield information about visual perceptual analysis, visual processing, visual-motor integration, spatial orientation, motor coordination, and visual sequencing in children at different stages of perceptual development.

1. The Frostig Developmental Test of Visual Perception[16] for children aged four through eight.
2. The Bender Motor Gestalt Test[2]—useful for all ages from four through adult.
3. The Developmental Test of Visual-Motor Integration[1] for preschool and school-age children.

4. Rutgers Drawing Test[35] for school-age children.
5. Benton Visual Retention Test[3]—this test is particularly sensitive to possible problems of spatial orientation and visual sequencing in the older child.
6. Raven Progressive Matrices Test[31]—this gives an excellent insight into visual perceptual functioning in the absence of a motor response in children from five-and-a-half to nine-and-a-half years old. It is truly culture free, and is presently being restandardized on an international population.[33]

Tests of Auditory-Verbal Perceptual Functioning. These tests assess auditory verbal processing and integration, and help to determine the extent to which language difficulties are present and if so, whether these difficulties tend to cluster in expressive, receptive, or associative areas, or may involve combinations of these. Three widely used tests of this type are:

1. Lindamood Auditory Conceptualization Test.[28]
2. Wepman Auditory Discrimination Test.[37]
3. Goldman-Fristoe-Woodcock Test of Auditory Discrimination.[18]

Tests of Combined Auditory and Visual Perceptual Functioning. These tests almost constitute "batteries" in and of themselves. They are often used to pinpoint possible problem areas which may then be studied in more detail by tests geared to specific functions.

1. Illinois Test of Psycholinguistic Abilities,[27] popularly known as the ITPA. This highly respected test measures auditory and visual aspects of children's language functioning (p. 3–9) at expressive, receptive, associative, and automatic levels. It is particularly useful in helping to pinpoint areas which may require remediation.
2. Meeting Street School Screening Test.[21] This is helpful in determining school readiness at the preschool level.
3. Slingerland Screening Tests for Identifying Children with Specific Language Disability.[33]

TESTS OF ACADEMIC ACHIEVEMENT

It is a rare public or private school which does not carry out periodic testing of academic achievement, using one of the many fine nationally standardized group instruments available to educators. The results of this achievement testing can and should be made available to the clinician, as a valuable indicator of a school child's academic functioning relative to representative peer groups. In addition, it is desirable to do individual diagnostic study in specific academic subject areas to assess not just areas of difficulty, but the nature of the problem within an area. Such diagnostic educational study is essential if meaningful educational programs are to be planned for individual children. Some of the more widely used individual tests of achievement are:

1. Peabody Individual Achievement Test[10] (a broad-spectrum diagnostic test of basic academic areas).
2. Durrell Analysis of Reading Difficulty.[11]
3. Gates-McKillop Reading Diagnostic Tests.[17]
4. Key Math Diagnostic Arithmetic Test.[8]

PERSONALITY TESTS

Projective testing, using such tests as the Rorschach Test or Structured Diagnostic Play Interview, is often an essential part of the test battery. These and other related tests represent standardized observations of the child's characteristic manner of dealing with new and relatively unstructured situations, and the nature of the personality defenses called into play to cope with the interpersonal challenge such situations present. They are helpful in determining the extent to which emotional factors may interfere with the child's ability to fully utilize his intellectual and perceptual skills in coping with his day-to-day life experiences. They are helpful too in providing indications for intervention at an individual, or perhaps at a family, level to help remedy patterns of unproductive emotional interaction.

INTERPRETATION AND INTERVENTION

Interpretation of the results of the tests which constitute the psychoeducational battery will help to determine the extent to which there is impairment of learning efficiency, and the extent to which specialized interventions need to be instituted in educational programming. Should such interventions be indicated, they would take several forms, depending on the age of the child, the nature and severity of the learning dysfunction, and to some degree also on the resources offered by the specific community.

It is axiomatic that the younger the child at the time of the assessment, the less drastic the educational intervention that might be indicated. The child who is just beginning to be exposed to training in basic learning skills will have a more satisfying and less stressful experience if remedial inputs are initiated at the beginning of his educational career than will the child who has experienced failure, and who also most probably has to unlearn inefficient habits and approaches to learning tasks.

When specialized programs for learning disabled children were first organized in the early 1960s, it was considered necessary to isolate these children from their peers and to spend long hours in perceptual retraining and controlled stimulus presentation. With increased understanding of the nature of learning difficulties in children and vastly improved techniques of individual assessment there has come the realization that each learning disabled child needs an individually planned program, based on his unique pattern of learning and his perceptual and emotional strengths and weaknesses. There is also the presumption that, given appropriate remedial intervention, the learning disabled child may one day be able to function in a regular classroom setting, with little or no supportive services. Thus, the original concept of isolation of children with learning problems has given way to the concept of "mainstreaming" children as soon as they achieve equal competence with their peers in prescribed academic areas. Most school districts which offer specialized services to learning disabled children offer a "self-contained" classroom program of individualized instruction for children with severe and more generalized learning problems, and "resource rooms" where children may spend specified amounts of time receiving intensive remedial instruction in areas prescribed by psychoeducational assessment, while spending the remainder of the school day with their peers. The "resource room" also serves as a useful bridge between the self-contained classroom and the regular class. Many school districts further foster "mainstreaming" by employing Learning Disabilities Specialists who consult directly with classroom teachers about the specialized academic needs of children in regular classroom settings, and provide teachers with specialized materials, suggest more individualized teaching methods, and generally function to help individual children to adjust to classroom demands without leaving the group.

For the older learning disabled child, the most usual pattern of services is the resource room, where individualized instruction may take the form of intensive subject-matter tutoring. This approach is appropriate for many junior high and high school level learning problems. However, there are many young people at this level whose learning problems have gone undiagnosed for a variety of social or community reasons. For these young people the resource room constitutes a "Band-Aid" at best. There is a need for intensive remedial intervention at the intermediate and secondary levels to help those young people whose needs were unrecognized or unmet when they were younger, before they drop out in response to continued frustration and failure.

The child psychiatrist increasingly encounters children who are not happy in school, who are unhappy with themselves because they fail to achieve up to their own or other's expectations, and who mask their unhappiness behind an "I don't care" and "I hate school" attitude. It is important that the child psychiatrist be sensitive to the signs of learning disability in children, so that potential difficulties may be unearthed at an early age and effective intervention procedures instituted.

Appendix I

Specific Learning Disabilities, as defined in the Education of the Handicapped Act (Title VI, P.L. 91–230, Parts 121–121j):

"Children with specific learning disabilities" means those children who have a disorder in one or more of the basic psychological processes involved in understanding or in using language spoken or written, which disorder may manifest itself in imperfect ability to listen, think, speak, read, write, spell, or do mathematical calculations.

Such disorders include such conditions as perceptual handicaps, brain injury, minimal brain dysfunction, dyslexia, and developmental aphasia. Such term does not include children who have learning problems which are primarily the result of visual, hearing, or motor handicaps, of mental retardation, of emotional disturbance,[7] or of environmental disadvantage.

Appendix II

The ten most cited characteristics of learning disabilities are:[7]

1. Hyperactivity.
2. Perceptual-motor impairment.
3. Emotional lability.
4. General coordination deficits.
5. Disorders of attention (short attention span, distractibility, presentation).
6. Impulsivity.
7. Disorders of memory and thinking.
8. Specific learning disabilities: reading, arithmetic, writing, spelling.
9. Disorders of speech and hearing.
10. Equivocal neurological signs and electroencephalographic irregularities.

REFERENCES

1. BEERY, K. E., *Developmental Test of Visual-Motor Integration*, Ages 2–15, Follett Publishing Co., Chicago, 1967.
2. BENDER, L., *Bender Motor Gestalt Test*, American Orthopsychiatric Association, New York, 1946.
3. BENTON, A. L., *The Revised Visual Retention Test*, The Psychological Corporation, New York, 1963.
4. BRYAN, TANIS H., and BRYAN, J. H., *Understanding Learning Disabilities*, Alfred Publishing Co., Port Washington, N.Y., 1975.
5. BRYANT, N. D., and KASS, CORRINE E., *Leadership Training Institute in Learning Disabilities*, Dept. of Special Education, University of Arizona; and Program Devel. Branch, Bureau of Education for the Handicapped, U.S. Office of Education, vol. 1, 1972.
6. BRYANT, N. D., and McLOUGHLIN, J. A., "Subject Variables: Definition, Incidence, Characteristics and Correlates," *Leadership Training Institute in Learning Disabilities*, Bureau of Education for the Handicapped, U.S. Office of Education, vol. 1, 1972.
7. CLEMENTS, S. D., "Minimal Brain Dysfunction in Children, Phase I," NINDB Mimeograph, U.S. Dept. of Health, Education and Welfare, Washington, D.C., 1966.
8. CONNOLLY, J., NACHTMAN, W., and PRITCHETT, E., *Key Math Diagnostic Arithmetic Test*, American Guidance Service, Circle Pines, Minn., 1976.
9. DENKLA, M. B., "Research Needs in Learning Disabilities: A Neurologist's Point of View," *Journal of Learning Disabilities*, 6:441–450, 1973.
10. DUNN, L. M., and MARKWARDT, F. C., *Peabody Individual Achievement Test*, Ages 5–18, American Guidance Service, 1970.
11. DURRELL, D. D., *Durrell Analysis of Reading Difficulty*, Harcourt Brace and World, New York, 1955.
12. DYKMAN, R. A., et al., "Specific Learning Disabilities: An Attentional Deficit Syndrome," in Myklebust, H. R. (Ed.), *Progress in Learning Disabilities*, vol. 2, pp. 55–93, Grune & Stratton, New York, 1971.
13. EDGINGTON, RUTH, *Helping Children with Reading Disability*, Developmental Learning Materials, Chicago, 1968.
14. EDGINGTON, RUTH, *Educational Screening Evaluation*, Child Study Center, University of Arkansas Medical Center, Little Rock, 1968.
15. FREIBERGS, V., and DOUGLAS, J. I., "Concept Learning in Hyperactive and Normal Children," *Journal of Abnormal Psychology*, 74:388–395, 1969.
16. FROSTIG, MARIANNE, *Developmental Test of Visual Perception*, Consulting Psychologists Press, Palo Alto, California, 1966.
17. GATES, A. I., and McKILLOP, ANNE S., *Gates-McKillop Reading Diagnostic Tests*, Teachers College Press, Columbia University, New York, 1962.
18. GOLDMAN, R., FRISTOE, M., and WOODCOCK, R. W., *Goldman-Fristoe-Woodcock Test of Auditory Discrimination*, American Guidance Service, Circle Pines, Minn., 1970.
19. GOLICK, M., *A Parents' Guide to Learning Problems*, Quebec Assoc. for Children with Learning Disabilities, Montreal, 1970.

20. GRAY, W. S., *Gray Oral Reading Tests*, Bobbs-Merrill, New York, 1967.

21. HAINSWORTH, P. K., and SIQUELAND, MARIAN L., *Meeting Street School Screening Test*, Ages 5.0–6.11, Crippled Children and Adults of Rhode Island, 1969.

22. HALLAHAN, D. P., and CRUICKSHANK, W. M., *Psychoeducational Foundations of Learning Disabilities*, Prentice-Hall, Englewood Cliffs, N.J., 1973.

23. HARWAY, VIVIAN T., "Parent Counseling, An Overview," in Arena, J., and Lawson, S. (Eds.), *Meeting Total Needs of Learning Disabled Children: Selected Papers on Learning Disabilities*, Seventh Annual International Conference of the Association for Children with Learning Disabilities, Academic Quarterly Press, San Rafael, Calif., 1971.

24. ———, *Psychological Assessment of the Learning Disabled Child: A Guide for Parents*, Association for Children with Learning Disabilities, Pittsburgh, 1971.

25. JASTAK, J. R., and JASTAK, S. R., *Wide Range Achievement Test, Manual and Test Blanks*, Guidance Associates, Wilmington, Del., 1965.

26. JOHNSON, DORIS J., and MYKLEBUST, H. R., *Learning Disabilities, Educational Principles and Practices*, Grune & Stratton, New York, 1967.

27. KIRK, S. A., McCARTHY, J. J., and KIRK, WINIFRED D., *Illinois Test of Psycholinguistic Abilities*, University of Illinois Press, Urbana, 1968.

28. LINDAMOOD, C. H., and LINDAMOOD, PATRICIA C., *Lindamood Auditory Conceptualization Test*, Teaching Resources Corporation, Boston, 1971.

29. PALKES, H., STEWART, M., and FREEDMAN, J., "Improvement in Maze Performance of Hyperactive Boys as a Function of Verbal-Training Procedures," *Journal of Special Education*, 5:337–342, 1971.

30. POPE, LILLIE, "Motor Activity in Brain-Injured Children," *American Journal of Orthopsychiatry*, 40:783–794, 1970.

31. RAVEN, J. C., *The Coloured Progressive Matrices Test*, The Psychological Corporation, New York, 1960.

32. SCHULMAN, J. L., KASPAR, J. C., and THRONE, F. M., *Brain Damage and Behavior*, Charles C Thomas, Springfield, Ill., 1965.

33. SLINGERLAND, BETH H., *Slingerland Screening Tests for Identifying Children with Specific Language Disability*, Educators Publishing Service, Cambridge, Mass., 1970.

34. SOLOMONS, G., "Guidelines on the Use and Medical Effects of Psychostimulant Drugs in Therapy," *Journal of Learning Disabilities*, 4:420–475, 1971.

35. STARR, ANNA SPEISMAN, *The Rutgers Drawing Test Form (A + B)*, Available from Anna S. Starr, Ph.D., 126 Montgomery Street, Highland Park, N.J. 08904, 1974.

36. WECHSLER, D., *Wechsler Intelligence Scale for Children—Revised*, The Psychological Corporation, New York, 1974.

37. WEPMAN, J. M., *Auditory Discrimination Test*, Ages 5–8, Language Research Associates, Chicago, 1973.

70 / Note on Speech and Hearing Evaluation

Richard L. Cohen

The special functions of speech and hearing are complex in their development and require highly specialized personnel for their accurate evaluation. The child psychiatric clinician should be aware of the most frequent indicators for referral for such evaluation. If he entertains any doubt concerning the status of the child's equipment for language reception and expression, or his ability to use such equipment effectively, the clinician should not hesitate to request this evaluation.

There is no need for specialized screening procedures in order to identify those children who require referral for speech and hearing evaluation. During the regular child psychiatric examination, careful attention to the child's apparent auditory receptiveness and to the form and quality of his speech should provide adequate data for this purpose.

Careful review of the developmental history and reports of classroom activity should also provide valuable cues. A distinction should be made between language problems and speech disability. *Language* generally refers to the more central process of decoding the encoding symbols. *Speech* generally connotes the more peripheral process of expression and communication of those symbols. Thus, for example, aphasia may be considered a disorder of language, while stuttering is a disorder of speech.

Disorders of hearing, language, and speech may occur separately or in combination in the same child, and may be either of organic or functional origin.

Because of his medical background, the child psychiatrist will be rather more familiar with disorders of hearing and language. Speech disorders represent a less familiar area. Therefore, the following schema may be helpful in conceptualizing an approach to early identification and possible need for referral to a speech pathologist.

1. *Speech delay or significant immaturity in speech for chronological age:* It is important to distinguish between those delays which involve difficulties in abstract thinking and the acquisition of a symbol system (language) from those where the difficulties lie in sound and word for-

mation. The latter are often related to neuro-muscular coordination (speech).

2. *Articulation disorders:* For example, defects in speech may involve an inability to pronounce certain consonants, such as "*r*" and "*l*," or the child may omit certain sounds which he cannot articulate. Speech may be garbled without any central defect in language formation.

3. *Phonation disorders:* For example, excessive nasality or hoarseness.

4. *Fluency disorders:* For example, repetition of sounds or phrases, silent stoppages of sound with accessory body movements.

Any significant occurrence of the above should result in a request for a speech evaluation. Ordinarily, this should be accompanied by an assessment by a competent audiologist.

A fuller delineation of these syndromes will be found in Volume II.

---

71 / Genetic Laboratory Studies

R. Rodney Howell and Charleen M. Moore

The sciences of genetics and pediatric endocrinology have been adding steadily to our knowledge of constitutional and developmental disorders in children which may be evidenced either in developmental lags, mental retardation, or serious behavioral disorders. It is not recommended that these techniques be used lightly or capriciously. They are often expensive, extended in nature, and require considerable time both for collaboration with the specialists involved and for subsequent explanation and interpretation to the family.

This and the following chapter delineate the scope of application of such tests, the indications for their differential use, and their significance for current practice with developmentally handicapped children. It is suggested that, unless the child psychiatrist has a reasonable working knowledge of the use of these diagnostic procedures himself, he provide (or insist that there be provided) an opportunity for the parents to have full discussion with the geneticist or endocrinologist. This can either be arranged independently, or take place as part of the interpretation conference, during which the findings are outlined for the parents.

—RLC

Introduction

Genetic disorders, single gene and chromosomal, are commonly present in the 10 to 25 percent of mentally retarded patients who have IQ's below 50. This stands in contrast to the findings with retarded patients whose IQ's fall in the range of 50 to 70 and in contrast as well to psychotic patients. In the latter two groups, it is uncommon for the disorder to have single gene or chromosomal basis.[25] Many of the psychoses indicate a polygenic mode of inheritance with a familial tendency but with no distinctly Mendelizing pattern.

To determine whether a disorder has a genetic basis, the clinician should keep several points in mind. First, a detailed family history should be obtained. If other family members are affected or multiple spontaneous abortions have occurred, a dominant, recessive, or X-linked Mendelian inheritance pattern or a chromosomal disorder may be indicated. Second, to diagnose a genetic disorder properly, a detailed physical examination is extremely important. Very minor physical abnormalities, when grouped together, may suggest a specific syndrome. Third, there are many laboratory tests, some very simple and others quite sophisticated, which are of absolute necessity in determining the exact nature of a given metabolic or chromosomal disorder. Often, this is the only way to identify both the affected individuals and the carriers for these disorders. In many instances, physical examination alone will not identify the problem, and one must rely on these laboratory tests for the exact diagnosis. This is critical, for without an absolutely specific diagnosis, counseling cannot be done.

There are important considerations in genetic disease, not only for the patient but for his parents and relatives as well. In many cases, if the disease is identified sufficiently early, a proper diet can be instituted and much, if not all, of the mental retardation associated with the disorder can be eliminated, as in, for example, phenylketonuria.[11] There are a number of disorders in which the recurrence risk is very high; parents should be aware of this in order to plan future pregnancies. Precise genetic counseling can aid not only the parents but other relatives who may also be at risk. In certain instances, even carriers for a recessive disease can be identified accurately; as a result, such families may know they are at risk for a given disorder before an affected child is born. This risk can be reduced in certain instances through the use of prenatal diagnosis (amniocentesis).[17, 22] This test can identify fetuses with certain metabolic disorders and all chromosomal abnormalities; it is of importance to the older mother and to parents who are carriers for particular metabolic or chromosomal abnormalities.

Laboratory Tests for Genetic Disorders

Specialized laboratory tests used in the genetic evaluation of the child are, in general, quite time-consuming and expensive. It is, therefore, important for the physician to be selective in the use of these tests and to take advantage of the less expensive screening tests[36] which are more easily performed.

For questionable genetic disorders there are two types of laboratory screening tests available: a battery of urinary tests for metabolic disorders, and a buccal smear for abnormal numbers (aneuploidies) of the sex chromosomes. At present, no screening test exists for aneuploidies of the non-sex chromosomes (autosomes).

Screening Tests for Metabolic Disorders

When an inborn error of metabolism is suspected, one can use a battery of screening tests. These are simple methods of detecting alterations in the biochemical composition of plasma and of urine.[2, 28, 29, 36] A characteristic battery is given in table 71–1 with a list of the inborn errors which give positive results. The great value of these tests as screening devices is that they are simple, rapid, and inexpensive to run and that they are non-specific, i.e., they are positive for many different substances, including drugs and medications. Thus, with relatively few tests, large numbers of individuals can be screened at small cost, and many disorders can be detected.

Most of these tests involve a simple color change; when the reaction is positive, the urine changes to red, green, blue, or grey. An example of a very nonspecific test which can give a positive reaction in many disorders is the ferric chloride test.[36] (See table 71–1.) This usually indicates the presence of α-keto acids, although certain drugs and other metabolites may also give positive reactions. The ferric chloride test is useful in studying undiagnosed mental retardation. This is, in part, due to the fact that some untreated phenylketonuric (PKU) patients may function in the dull normal range of intelligence. Untreated women have an extremely high risk of delivering mentally retarded children with intrauterine growth retardation and, possibly, structural abnormalities, such as congenital heart disease.[12]

Other noteworthy characteristics to observe when screening for genetic disease[36] are odor, color, and the presence of crystals in the urine. Many odors are characteristic and sometimes almost diagnostic. A classic example is maple syrup urine disease. In this disorder, the urine has the distinctive odor of maple syrup. Certain rare conditions can change the color of the urine or be associated with urinary crystals. (Examples of these are also given in table 71–1.)

In most states, screening of newborns for certain inborn errors is required by law. The number of mandatory screening tests is increasing steadily. The widely used Guthrie test[9] is specific for phenylalanine and is used as a screening test for PKU. Modifications of the Guthrie test permit screening for many metabolites.

Identification of the Specific Metabolic Disorder

When a screening test is positive, it only indicates the general metabolic pathway along which the defect may be present. In order to determine the exact error, other more elaborate and expensive tests must be performed. One of the most widely used specific tests is chromatography of the amino acids in urine or serum.[16, 31, 32] This is a valuable

TABLE 71–1

Urinary Screening Tests and Inherited Errors of Metabolism Which Give Positive Results

Test	Compounds Which Are Responsible	Inborn Error of Metabolism*
Benedict's Test (Clinitest®)	Reducing Substances	Galactosemia (transferase deficiency) Galactosemia (galatokinase deficiency) Fructose intolerance Fructosuria, essential Pentosuria Lactosuria
Dinitrophenylhydrazine	α-Keto Acids	Maple syrup urine disease Oasthouse disease Phenylketonuria Pyruvic acidemia Tyrosinemia
Toluidine Blue Spot Test Acid Albumin	Mucopolysaccharides	Hurler syndrome Hunter syndrome Sanfilippo syndrome Morquio syndrome Scheie syndrome Maroteaux-Lamy syndrome
Nitroprusside	Cystine/Homocystine	Cystinuria Homocystinuria β-Mercaptolactate-cystine disulfiduria
Ferric Chloride	α-Keto Acids	Alcaptonuria Formiminotransferase deficiency syndrome Histidinemia Maple syrup urine disease Oasthouse disease Phenylketonuria Tyrosinemia Tyrosinosis (Medes disease)
Guthrie Test† (Bacterial Inhibition Assay)	Phenylalanine	Phenylketonuria Hyperphenylaninemia
Odor		
Musty odor	Phenylacetic acid	Phenylketonuria
Maple syrup or burned sugar	Branched chain α-Keto acids	Maple syrup urine disease
Cheesy or sweaty feet	Isovaleric acid	Isovaleric acidemia
Oasthouse or brewery	α-Hydroxybutyric acid	Oasthouse disease
Oasthouse	α-Hydroxybutyric acid	Methionine malabsorption
Rancid butter or rotten cabbage	α-Keto-γ-methiol butyric acid	Hypermethioninemia
Sweaty feet	Butyric and hexanoic acids	Butyric/hexanoic acidemia
Stale fish	Trimethylamine	Trimethylaminuria
Crystals		
Fine spindles	Orotic acid	Orotic aciduria
Various forms	Uric acid	Lesch-Nyhan syndrome
Hexagonal	Cystine	Cystinuria
Lemon-shaped	Xanthine	Xanthinuria
Feathery	Tyrosine	Tyrosinemia
Ditetragonal pyramid crystals	Calcium oxalate	Hyperoxaluria
Color		
Red	Myoglobin, hemoglobin	McArdle's disease, Paroxysmal nocturnal hemoglobinuria
Blue	Indican	Tryptophan malabsorption
Darkens on standing (when alkaline)	Homogentisic acid	Alcaptonuria

* Many drugs give positive reactions. For details, see Thomas, G. H., and Howell, R. R., *Selected Screening Tests for Genetic Metabolic Diseases*, Year Book Medical Publishers, Inc., Chicago, 1973.
† Can be modified to react specifically with other metabolites.

technique in the evaluation of patients with developmental abnormalities because: (1) many disorders can be identified from one test; (2) mental retardation is an important feature in many of the aminoacidopathies; and (3) the clinical diagnosis is difficult because there are usually only non-specific clinical characteristics which are present.

Using sophisticated experimental tools, forty different sugars in the urine or blood can now be identified.[13] The importance in man of many of these sugars is unknown. Identification of these sugars can, therefore, be a valuable research tool as well as a diagnostic tool in many of the genetic disorders. A similar experimental identification instrument is the ultraviolet light analyzer which distinguishes about 150 compounds in normal urine.[1]

Through the use of these sophisticated instruments, genetic disorders such as homocystinuria can be rapidly and accurately identified and managed. In the classic form of homocystinuria, there is a deficiency or absence of the enzyme cystathionine synthase, resulting in an increase in the urinary concentration of homocystine. If early diagnosis is made with institution of a diet containing low concentrations of cystine and homocystine and, in some cases, increased amounts of vitamin B_{12}, many of the major problems associated with this disorder, including mental retardation, may be reduced.[11]

In many disorders one can examine the specific enzyme which is affected. One series of enzymes which can be examined directly and which is of considerable importance is the battery of lysosomal enzymes. These are absent or defective in many storage disorders. Currently, over fifteen lysosomal enzyme deficiencies are recognized in man.

BUCCAL SMEAR

The only screening test available for chromosome disorders is the buccal smear.[18, 21, 24] It is a rapid, easily done, and inexpensive way to determine the number of X and Y chromosomes present. It will not, however, detect abnormalities in any of the autosomes (the non sex chromosomes). The buccal smear is obtained by gently scraping the buccal mucosa with the edge of a tongue depressor or spatula, spreading the loose epithelial cells on a clean microscope slide, and immediately placing the slide in a fixative of 95 percent ethyl alcohol. The cells should not be allowed to dry before placing them in the alcohol since this destroys the morphology of the cells. A control slide obtained from a normal female is usually taken at the same time.

The slides are stained by two methods. A chromatin stain is used for detecting the presence of Barr bodies (for the number of X chromosomes), and a fluorescent dye is used in the detection of Y bodies (for the number of Y chromosomes). According to the Lyon hypothesis,[15] only one X chromosome is active in any diploid cell. The other X chromosomes, regardless of number, are inactive. At interphase, each inactive X forms a very darkly staining oval mass, the Barr body, which is usually located at the nuclear membrane. Thus, the number of X chromosomes can be quickly determined by the number of Barr bodies present, this number being one more than the number of Barr bodies per cell. Normal females (46,XX) have two X chromosomes per cell; therefore, the interphase cells contain one Barr body per cell. This is observable in about 20 to 40 percent of the interphase cells.[18, 21] Normal males (46,XY) have a single X per cell; therefore, the interphase cells do not contain a Barr body. Patients with aneuploidies of the sex chromosomes have abnormal numbers of Barr bodies. For example, females with Turner's syndrome who have a single X in the chromosomal complement do not have Barr bodies. In contrast to this, males with a 47,XXY karyotype (Klinefelter's syndrome) have a single Barr body per interphase cell. Differences in size of the Barr body, either larger or smaller than normal, indicate abnormalities of the structure of the X chromosome which, in many cases, also produce Turner's syndrome.

Recently developed methodology has improved the study of the male (Y) chromosome.[24] A fluorescent dye such as quinicrine mustard deeply stains the distal portion of the long arm of the Y. This can be seen as a very bright spot in the interphase nucleus (Y body). The number of Y bodies per cell is equivalent to the number of Y chromosomes. Thus, a normal male has one Y body per cell, while a normal female has none.

In a few hours after the buccal smear is received, the laboratory can determine the number of X and Y chromosomes present. If the results are inconsistent with the phenotypic sex of the individual, i.e., what sex the patient appears to be clinically, then a complete chromosomal study should be done; the buccal smear should never be used for the final diagnosis.

CHROMOSOMAL ANALYSIS

If abnormalities of the autosomes are suspected, a complete karyotype analysis is necessary. Karyotype studies of the chromosomes are usually derived from blood samples, since this is one of the easiest tissues to obtain. However, these studies can also be done using cultured fibroblasts obtained from various sites such as skin and liver, from bone marrow aspirates, or from cultured amniotic fluid cells. In contrast to the buccal smear, karyotype analysis takes about two or three weeks to complete, requires more expertise in interpretation, and is more expensive.

There are usually 46 chromosomes per cell in the normal individual. These include the sex chromosomes, 2 X's in females, a single X and Y in males, and 22 pairs of autosomes. These are arranged according to the classification set by the Chicago[5] and Paris[23] conventions. Basically, the 46 chromosomes are divided into seven groups, A to G, according to their structure; within the groups, they are ranged from largest to smallest.

New staining procedures, for example, G- and Q-banding,[3, 7] give even greater detail by producing unique banding patterns for each pair of chromosomes. (See figure 71–1.) Very small deletions, additions, or rearrangements which are not observable by standard staining methods can be identified by these banding techniques. As a result, accurate identification of each chromosome within the basic group is now possible.

In certain chromosomal disorders an entire chromosome is extra or missing. The sex chromosome aneuploidies include missing X chromosomes or additional X's and Y's. These patients may present with learning difficulties—for example, patients with Turner's syndrome who have problems with spatial concepts and math;[33] with educational difficulties—for example, patients with Klinefelter's syndrome who are in the dull or

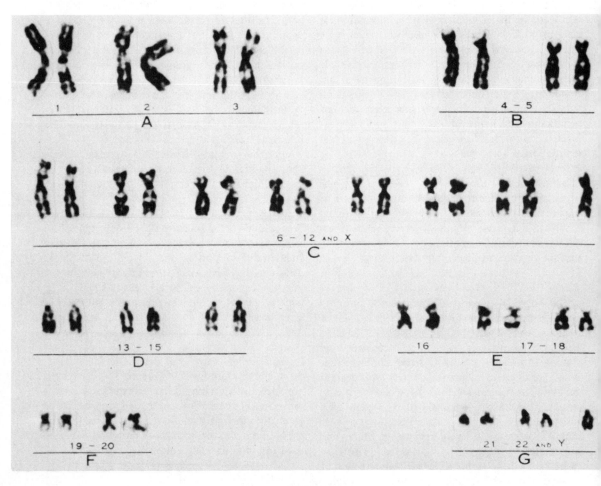

FIGURE 71–1

Karyotype of a normal male stained to show G-bands. Each pair of homologs has a unique banding pattern which allows accurate identification of each chromosome.

borderline IQ range;[6, 19] with psychoses—for example, 47,XXX women who have an increased tendency toward schizophrenia or other psychoses;[14, 20] with behavior problems—for example, 47,XXY men who were thought to have a tendency toward aggressive behavior (there is strong disagreement at the present time concerning this;[30]) or with severe mental retardation—for example, 48,XXXX females or 48,XXXY males.[14, 20]

The common autosomal aneuploidies include the trisomies of chromosomes 21, 18, and 13. Rarely, other trisomies are observed as trisomies 8 and 9. Patients with trisomy 18 or trisomy 13 are usually seen in the early months of life since the life expectancy for these individuals is extremely short. However, patients with trisomy 21 (mongolism or Down's syndrome) have a life expectancy of about sixty years and may present with severe mental retardation and, in rare, instances, with behavior problems.[35] Patients with trisomy 8 or trisomy 9 are usually moderately retarded and need very special schooling to attain their full potential.[4, 10]

In other disorders only a small portion of a chromosome is additional or missing. Cri-du-chat syndrome, a disorder caused by the deletion of the short arms of one of the number 5 chromosomes, and cat eye syndrome, a disorder caused by the presence of a small, extra metacentric chromosome, are examples. Both lead to profound retardation.[34]

INCREASED RISK OF CHROMOSOMAL DISORDERS

In the majority of cases, chromosomal abnormalities are sporadic and the chance of their recurrence in the same family is small. There are two exceptions to this: One occurs in the case of advanced maternal age, and the second in the case of balanced translocation carriers.

When maternal age increases, there is a significant increase in the risk of producing a trisomic child. For example, when a woman is twenty, her chances of having a child with Down's syndrome is 1 in 2,300; as the same woman approaches forty, he chances have increased to 1 in 100; and as she approaches forty-five, they are 1 in 40.[25, 27] (See figure 71-2.)

Also, there are individuals who are themselves normal, but who have chromosomes in a rearranged form. The genetic material present is proper in amount, but different in structural form. This is referred to as a balanced translocation and the affected individuals are called translocation carriers. The most common of these is a D/D

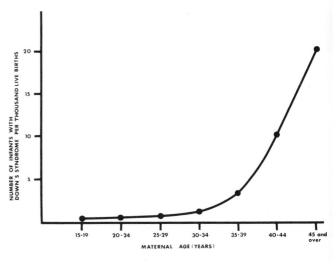

FIGURE 71-2
Incidence of Down's syndrome (mongolism) as a function of maternal age.

translocation in which two D group chromosomes have bcome attached to each other. These individuals are at high risk for transmitting these translocation chromosomes to their offspring in an unbalanced form, such as in a trisomic or a monosomic condition (the latter usually resulting in spontaneous abortion).[8]

AMINOCENTESIS (PRENATAL DIAGNOSIS)

For these two situations and also for any parents who have had a chromosomally abnormal child, there is a way to reduce the risk. This involves monitoring each pregnancy for chromosomal abnormalities through the use of aminocentesis.[17, 22] In many of the metabolic disorders in which the biochemical defect has been identified, prenatal diagnosis is of special value in detecting an affected fetus.

Amniocentesis is performed by inserting a needle into the amniotic sac transabdominally, and withdrawing about 20 cc. of amniotic fluid. Fetal cells which are floating in the fluid can be cultured in the laboratory under very strict conditions. Since it takes three to five weeks to culture an adequate number of cells for analysis, the timing of the test is of extreme importance. It is usually done between the fourteenth and sixteenth weeks of pregnancy. There is adequate time then to grow the cells, time for a second tap if the first is unsuccessful, and time to terminate the pregnancy if an abnormal fetus is detected. If an experienced physician is performing the amniocentesis, there is only a very slight risk associated with this procedure. The complications include possible infection, spontaneous abortion, or injury to the fetus. Since a slight risk is involved, the test is recommended only for those pregnancies in which a significant chance of an abnormal fetus is known to exist. It is important to point out that amniocentesis cannot be done to ensure a "normal" baby; it can only exclude specific defects for which the family is at risk.

At the present time, there is no known treatment for many of these conditions. If an affected fetus is found, the only alternative one can offer the parents is termination of the pregnancy. Should the parents be unwilling to consider this in any case, amniocentesis would be contraindicated. This test has been of outstanding benefit to parents with a high risk of having a child with a chromosomal or metabolic disorder. Before the test was available, many of them would not have considered having offspring on their own. Amnio-

centesis reduces their risk to that of any average couple, and allows these parents the option of having their own children.

Conclusion

Laboratory tests for genetic disease can, therefore, be simple or elaborate. These are quite valuable in making an accurate diagnosis of a genetic disease. This is important not only in the management of the patient but also in providing counseling for the patient's parents or relatives. Early diagnosis is essential in many disorders in order to initiate a certain diet or to establish realistic goals and educational plans to achieve the patient's highest potential. In many cases, accurate diagnosis also makes it possible to reduce the risks of this problem recurring in the family. When a genetic disease is suspected, the help of an experienced geneticist with sophisticated laboratory backup is essential.

REFERENCES

1. BAVICH, J. M., and HOWELL, R. R., "Ultraviolet-absorbing Compounds in the Urine of Normal Newborns and Young Children," *Clinical Chemistry, 16:*702, 1970.

2. BOGGS, D. E., "Detection of Inborn Errors of Metabolism," *Critical Reviews in Clinical Laboratory Sciences, 2:*529, 1971.

3. CASPERSSON, T., ZECH, L., and JOHANSSON, C., "Analysis of the Human Metaphase Chromosome Set by Aid of DNA-Binding Fluorescent Agents," *Experimental Cell Research, 62:*490, 1970.

4. CASSIDY, S. B., et al., "The Trisomy 8 Syndrome Defined from Fifteen Published Cases Identified by Chromosome Banding Pattern, Including a Personal Observation," *Pediatrics, 56:*826–831, 1975.

5. Chicago Conference, "Standardization in Human Cytogenetics," *Birth Defects: Original Article Series, 12(2),* The National Foundation, New York, 1966.

6. COURT BROWN, W. M., HARNDEN, D. G., and JACOBS, P. A., "Abnormalities of the Sex Chromosome Compliment in Man," Medical Research Council, Special Report Series No. 305, Her Majesty's Stationery Office, London, 1964.

7. DRETS, M. E., and SHAW, M. W., "Specific Banding Patterns of Human Chromosomes," *Proceedings of the National Academy of Science* (U.S.), 68:2073, 1971.

8. DUTRILLAUX, B., and LEJEUNE, J., "Étude de la Descendance des Individus Porteurs d'une Translocation t (DqDq)," *Annales de Génétique, 13:*11, 1970.

9. GUTHRIE, R., and MURPHY, W. H., "Micro-biologic Screening Procedures for Detection of Inborn Errors of Metabolism in the Newborn Infant," in Bickle, H., Hudson, R. P., and Wolf, L. (Eds.), *Phenylketonuria and Some Other Inborn Errors of Amino Acid Metabolism Biochemistry, Genetics, Diagnosis, and Therapy,* p. 132, Thieme, Stuttgart, 1971.

10. HASLAM, R. H. A., et al., "Trisomy 9 Mosaicism

with Multiple Congenital Anomalies," *Journal of Medical Genetics, 10:*180, 1973.

11. HOLTZMAN, N. A., "Dietary Treatment of Inborn Errors of Metabolism," *Annual Review of Medicine, 21:*335, 1970.

12. HOWELL, R. R., and STEVENSON, R. E., "The Offspring of Phenylketonuric Women," *Social Biology, 18:*19, 1971.

13. JOLLEY, R. L., and FREEMAN, M.L., "Automated Carbohydrate Analysis of Physiological Fluids," *Clinical Chemistry, 14:*538, 1968.

14. KIDD, C. B., KNOX, R. S., and MANTLE, D. J., "A Psychiatric Investigation of Triple-X Chromosome Females," *British Journal of Psychiatry, 109:*90, 1963.

15. LYON, M. F., "Gene Action in the X-Chromosome of the Mouse," *Nature* (London), 190:372, 1961.

16. MABRY, C. C., "High Voltage Electrophoresis," *Critical Reviews in Clinical Laboratory Sciences, 1:*135, 1970.

17. MILUNSKY, A., et al., "Prenatal Genetic Diagnosis," *New England Journal of Medicine, 283:*1370, 1970.

18. MITTWOCH, U., "Sex Chromatin," *Journal of Medical Genetics, 1:*50, 1964.

19. MONEY, J., "Two Cytogenetic Syndromes, Psychologic Comparisons. I. Intelligence and Specific-Factor Quotients," *Journal of Psychiatric Research, 2:*223, 1964.

20. ———, and HIRSCH, S., "Chromosome Anomalies, Mental Deficiency and Schizophrenia: A Study of Triple X and Triple X/Y Chromosomes in Five Patients and Their Families," *Archives of General Psychiatry, 8:*242, 1963.

21. MOORE, K. L., and BARR, M. L., "Smears from the Oral Mucosa in the Detection of Chromosomal Sex," *Lancet, 2:*57, 1955.

22. NADLER, H. L., "Prenatal Detection of Genetic Defects," *Journal of Pediatrics, 74:*132, 1969.

23. Paris Conference, "Standardization in Human Cytogenetics," *Birth Defects: Original Article Series, 8(7):*, The National Foundation, New York, 1972.

24. PEARSON, P. L., BOBROW, M., and VOSKA, C. G., "Technique for Identifying Y Chromosomes in Human Interphase Nuclei," *Nature* (London), *226:*78, 1970.

25. PENROSE, L. S., *The Biology of Mental Defect*, 2nd ed., Grune & Stratton, New York, 1963.

26. ———, "Mongolism," *British Medical Bulletin, 17:*184, 1961.

27. ———, and SMITH, G. F., *Down's Anomaly*, Churchill, London, 1966.

28. PERRY, T. L., HANSEN, S., and MACDOUGALL, L., "Urinary Screening Tests in the Prevention of Mental Deficiency," *Canadian Medical Association Journal, 95:*89, 1966.

29. RENUART, A. W., "Screening for Inborn Errors of Metabolism Associated with Mental Deficiency or Neurologic Disorders or Both," *New England Journal of Medicine,* 274:384, 1966.

30. Report of the XYY Chromosomal Abnormality,

Publication No. 2103, U.S. National Institute of Mental Health, Center for Studies of Crime and Delinquency, Chevy Chase, Maryland, 1970.

31. SAIFER, A., "Rapid Screening Methods for the Detection of Inherited and Acquired Aminoacidopathies," *Advances in Clinical Chemistry, 14:*145, 1971.

32. SCRIVER, C. R., DAVIES, E., and CULLEN, A. M., "Application of a Simple Micromethod to the Screening of Plasma for a Variety of Aminoacidopathies," *Lancet, 2:*230, 1964.

33. SHAFFER, J. W., "A Specific Cognitive Deficit Observed in Gonadal Aplasia (Turner's Syndrome)," *Journal of Clinical Psychology, 18:*403, 1962.

34. SMITH, D. W., *Recognizable Patterns of Human Malformation*, W. B. Saunders, Philadelphia, 1970.

35. ———, and WILSON, A. A., *The Child with Down's Syndrome (Mongolism)*, W. B. Saunders, Philadelphia, 1973.

36. THOMAS, G. H., and HOWELL, R. R., *Selected Screening Tests for Genetic Metabolic Diseases*, Year Book Medical Publishers, Chicago, 1973.

72 / Endocrinology

Dorothy J. Becker and Allan L. Drash

Introduction

The field of pediatric endocrinology encompasses those diseases and disorders occurring in childhood which result from either a deficiency or excess of one or more hormones. In addition, there are disorders of the timing of endocrine function such as early or delayed sexual function. Growth disorders of all types and etiologies may be referred to the endocrinologist for evaluation and diagnosis. Examples would include hypopituitarism, hypothyroidism, genetic short stature, a variety of bone disorders such as achondroplasia, chromosomal disorders such as Turner's syndrome and Mongolism, other chronic diseases such as chronic renal disease, malabsorption, and a variety of other disorders that affect the rate of linear growth and maturation. Alterations in the development of the internal and external genitalia, which may result from a variety of genetic alterations in gonadal function, obviously also belong in the sphere of the pediatric endocrinologist.

The disorders of energy metabolism including diabetes mellitus, hypoglycemia, obesity, and anorexia frequently are referred to the pediatric endocrinologist for diagnosis and management. In addition, many of the classical pediatric syndromes as well as the undiagnosed or undiagnosable "funny-looking kid syndrome," particularly if the children are short and/or mentally retarded, are eventually evaluated in an endocrine clinic.

In clinical practice, therefore, the pediatric endocrinologist is responsible for a broad range of pediatric problems which may extend far beyond the borders of classical endocrinology, but which may be referred for exclusion of possible underlying endocrine involvement. It is with this broad range of clinical problems that the following discussion is concerned.

Normal Physiology

Knowledge of the physiologic control of the endocrine system is important in the understanding of the pathogenesis of endocrine disorders and the tests used in their diagnosis. Using sophisticated techniques, mainly radioimmunoassays, competitive protein-binding assays, radioreceptor assays, and occasionally bioassays, one can now measure most circulating hormones from the target endocrine glands, many of the pituitary hormones, and some of the hypothalamic releasing hormones. As a general principle, single measurements (i.e., of one blood sample) rarely reflect the status of a specific hormone, with the notable exception of the thyroid hormones. However, a single blood or urine test may be useful as a screen for endocrine disease. More frequently, it is necessary to perform serial blood sampling to measure normal hypothalamically induced fluctuations (often associated with sleep cycles), or employ stimulatory or suppression tests based on known control of hormone homeostasis.

Control of hormone secretion from the hypothalamus and all the endocrine glands is based primarily on feedback systems with intermittent alterations in response to environmental and metabolic demands mediated by the nervous system, energy metabolites, and other hormones. For easier understanding, one can divide the endocrine system into three major homeostatic subsystems. These are depicted in a very simplified form in figures 72–1, 72–2, and 72–3. It is important to realize that these three systems are intimately interrelated though the mechanisms by which they interact are not yet fully elucidated.

The most complex system is the hypothalamo-pituitary-target endocrine gland system. Neural stimuli, which include those due to emotion, stress, and sleep, from the cerebral cortex and others from lower centers of the brain, in particular the midbrain nuclei, reach the hypothalamus via neurotransmitters. The best documented of these are dopamine, epinephrine, and serotonin. The hypothalamus secretes a number of releasing hormones and inhibitory hormones which stimulate or suppress the production of trophic hormones from the pituitary. Only two hypothalamic releasing hormones have been synthesized and assayed. These are (1) TRH, which stimulates both thyroid-stimulating hormone (TSH) and prolactin secretion from the pituitary, and (2) GnRH, which causes release of LH and FSH from the pituitary. Corticotropin-releasing factor is shown by bioassay to stimulate ACTH, and it possibly affects melanin-stimulating hormone also.

A growth hormone release inhibitory factor or somatostatin has now been synthesized and can be measured. It not only inhibits GH secretion, but in pharmacologic amounts also inhibits TSH, prolactin, insulin, glucagon, and gastrin secretion. Its exact function is, therefore, at present questionable, especially as it is widely distributed in the brain (as is TRH) and also in the stomach,

duodenum, and pancreas. The major control of prolactin, which is tonically secreted by the pituitary, seems to be prolactin inhibitory factor (PIF) from the hypothalamus. There is also probably an MSH inhibitory factor.

No hypothalamic controlling hormones for antidiuretic hormone (ADH) and oxytocin are known, but their output is associated with the release of the protein carriers neurophysin 1 and 2. The release of ADH seems to be triggered via osmoreceptors in the hypothalamus. ADH controls water excretion in the distal tubules of the kidney, and serum osmolality is an integral part of its feedback system. Each of the pituitary-trophic hormones acts on a target endocrine organ which produces hormones which feed back at both the pituitary and hypothalamic levels. GH has direct effects on energy homeostasis, particularly blood glucose and lipid metabolism. Its effect on growth of cells, particularly skeletal growth, is indirect by stimulating the release of somatomedin from the liver. It is this substance, at present difficult to quantitate accurately, which mediates growth at cartilage level.

Pituitary secretion of TSH allows release of thyroxine (T_4) and triiodothyronine (T_3) from the thyroid and is in turn controlled by the blood levels of these hormones. The same applies to ACTH, which stimulates cortisol, adrenal androgens, and to a lesser extent, aldosterone secretion from the adrenal cortex. Although ACTH does have a role in the control of aldosterone output, the major control of aldosterone is via the renin angiotensin system. Renin is secreted by the juxtaglomerular apparatus of the kidney in response to changes of electrolytes and blood volume. In the male, LH primarily stimulates testosterone secretion from the testis and FSH controls spermatogenesis. In the female, LH and FSH are necessary for estrogen and progesterone secretion and ovulation. The feedback control of LH and FSH by the sex hormones seems to be the most complex. Although many functions are postulated for prolactin, the only well-documented ones are its synergistic role in breast development and lactation.

The second system is that of energy homeostasis (i.e., the utilization, storage, and production of glucose, lipid, and amino acid metabolism). Ingested food is digested in the gut, where it stimulates secretion of gut hormones, such as gastrin, which stimulates hydrochloric acid secretion in the stomach, cholecystokinin-pancreozymin, "gut glucagon," and gastrointestinal inhibitory polypeptide. These hormones together with the

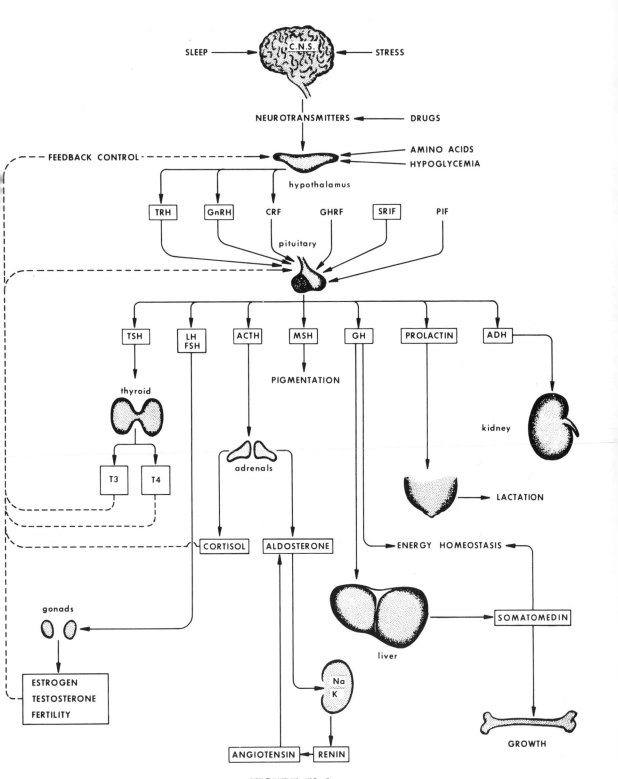

FIGURE 72–1

Hypothalamo-Pituitary-target organ system. Hormones in squares can be measured by available assays.

TRH = Thyrotropin Releasing Hormones
GnRH = Gonadotropin Releasing Hormones
CRF = Corticotropin Releasing Factor
GHRF = Growth Hormone Releasing Factor
SRIF = Somatostatin Inhibitory Factor
PIF = Prolactin Inhibitory Factor

ADH = Antidiuretic Hormone
LH = Luteinizing Hormone
FSH = Follicular Stimulating Hormone
ACTH = Adrenocorticotropic Hormone
GH = Growth Hormone
MSH = Melanin Stimulating Hormone

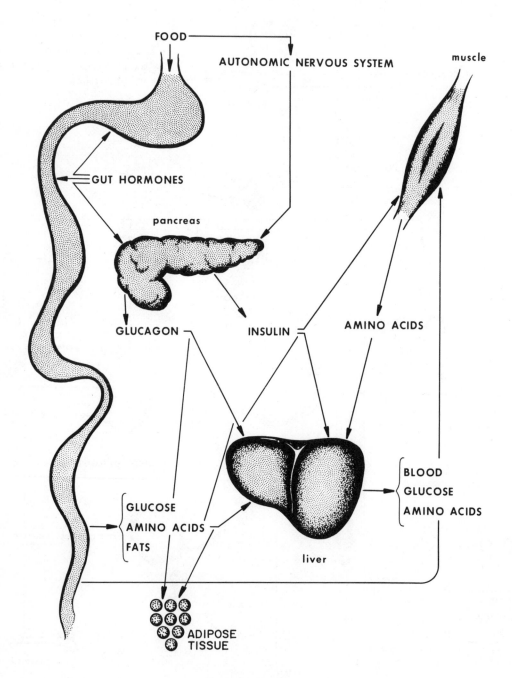

FIGURE 72–2
Energy homeostosis—very simplified.

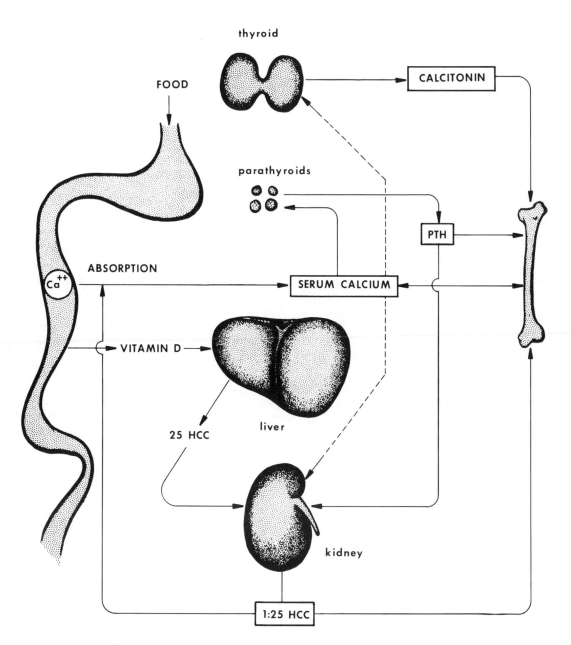

FIGURE 72–3
Calcium Homeostosis.

absorbed glucose and amino acids stimulate secretion of insulin and glucagon from the pancreas, which in turn control glucose, lipid, and amino acid uptake by the liver and their utilization in the periphery. Insulin and glucagon control glycogen formation and its breakdown to glucose and also gluconeogenesis from amino acids. Growth hormone, cortisol, and catecholamines also have important roles in energy homeostasis.

The third system is that controlling calcium and phosphate homeostasis and bone metabolism. It is well known that parathormone (PTH from the parathyroids) controls blood levels of calcium by affecting its absorption from the gut, uptake and turnover in bone, and exchange in the proximal tubule of the kidneys. We have been aware of the effect of vitamin D on calcium metabolism working in conjunction with PTH for many years. Recent work has shown that vitamin D is a prohormone which is converted by the liver to 25-hydroxycholecalciferol, which in turn is activated by the kidneys to form 1,25 dihydroxycholecalciferol. It is 1,25 dihydroxycholecalciferol which has the major action on calcium absorption from the gut and mineralization of osteoid in bone.

All three endocrine systems are affected by stimuli from the autonomic system either directly or via output of adrenalin and noradrenalin from the adrenal medulla.

CONTROL OF GROWTH

Physical, intellectual, and emotional growth is the dominant feature characterizing childhood from the neonatal period through adolescence. The overall control mechanisms for the growth process are primarily under the influence of the endocrine system. Normal physical growth depends upon the availability of an adequate supply of all basic foodstuffs including calories, carbohydrates, fat, protein, vitamins, and minerals and an intact gastrointestinal system for absorption. Growth—that is, increase in organ or body size—occurs by the combination of cell multiplication and cell enlargement (i.e., hyperplasia and hypertrophy).

The endocrine system is involved in the absorption of nutrients from the gastrointestinal tract; the control of the rate of synthesis, storage, and retrieval of energy substrate; modification of the cell permeability to allow for changes in the uptake of amino acids, glucose, etc.; and direct influence upon the growth and multiplication of cells. Growth may be disturbed by any chronic disease or loss of nutrients due to gastrointestinal malabsorption or diabetes mellitus; or by the abnormal

dissipation of nutrients which may occur in thyrotoxicosis or pheochromocytoma. Impairment of basic growth processes may occur in chronic acidosis.

A proper integration of changes in concentration levels and timing over the total period of childhood and adolescence is necessary if a normal growth process is to be achieved. Apparently, the hormones of primary importance during gestation and during the first two years of life are the thyroid hormones T_4 and T_3 and insulin. Sometime during the first two years of life, growth hormone becomes an essential factor in normal growth. It continues to be of great importance through adolescence. At adolescence, the sex steroids become of great importance, producing the growth spurt of adolescence and leading eventually to the closure of epiphysis and completion of growth. Testosterone, produced by the male testes, is a particularly potent growth promoter accounting for the greater growth spurt in males than females and for the eventual greater adult height in males than females. The timing of adolescence and ultimate adult height are genetically predetermined but may be altered by a variety of environmental factors including intrauterine disorders, gestational age, birth weight, nutrition, chronic disease, and brain damage.

SEX DIFFERENTIATION

Under normal circumstances, the chromosomal makeup of the individual determines the phenotypic classification of the individual. The normal chromosomal complement is 46 chromosomes made up of 44 autosomes and 2 sex chromosomes. The normal female has 2 X chromosomes, while the normal male has an X and a Y chromosome. Early intrauterine sex development is comparable for both males and females. Differentiation along male lines results from the action of two factors elaborated from the fetal testes. Mullerian inhibitory factor, probably a polypeptide, supresses Mullerian or female internal organs, while testosterone stimulates the development of the Wolffian system leading to normal male sex organs and differentiation to male external genitalia. In the absence of these two hormones from the fetal testes, the fetus will differentiate along female lines regardless of the chromosomal sex. Pathological production of excessive amounts of androgens or malelike hormones in the developing female fetus, such as occurs in the virilizing adrenogenital syndrome, will allow virilization, resulting in the birth of a genetic female infant with either sexual ambiguity or apparent complete masculinization.

Psychosexual differentiation or gender identity is determined primarily by the appearance of the external genitalia and the sex of rearing. Gender identity is firmly imprinted by eighteen months to two years and fully differentiated by three-and-a-half to four-and-a-half years of age. Fetal and neonatal androgen exposure produce some behavioral characteristics but do not influence gender identity significantly. The absence of androgen, rather than the presence of estrogen, produces a more feminine type personality prior to adolescence. At adolescence, the previously formed sexual identity is further potentiated by the action of sex hormones inducing secondary sexual characteristics.

PUBERTY AND ADOLESCENCE

Puberty is a period of very rapid physical, sexual, and emotional change associated with dramatic alterations of the hypothalamo-pituitary-gonadal axis and increased output of adrenal androgens. It is a hormonally induced period of physical change with concomitant psychological adjustment. Some, but not all, of the behavioral changes during adolescence may be influenced by the effects of androgens on the brain, but emotional maturity usually occurs with sexual maturity.

The exact trigger for the onset of these hormonal changes is poorly understood. The time of onset of puberty is variable, and may occur between eight and a half and thirteen years in girls and nine and a half and fourteen years in boys. However, it may be quite normal, though psychologically disturbing, for adolescence to start at seventeen to nineteen years. Variability of the onset of puberty is probably associated with (1) nutrition—obese children are sexually advanced and thin, short children often delayed, (2) genetic factors, (3) physical and emotional stress, (4) race, and (5) chronic disease, such as sickle-cell anemia and inflammatory bowel disease.

As shown in figure 72–4, it appears that the hypothalamic gonadostat prepubertally is highly sensitive to the small amounts of estrogens and androgens; thus only small amounts of LH and FSH are secreted. With the onset of adolescence,

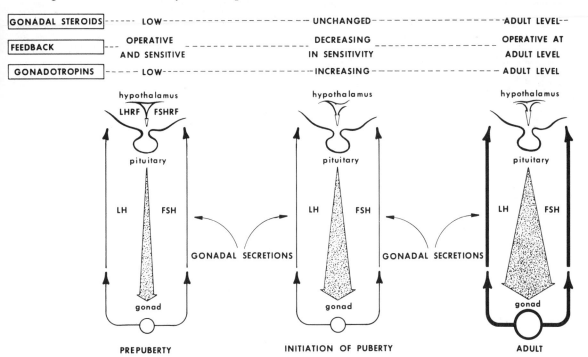

FIGURE 72–4

Schematic diagram of the progressive change in gonadotropin secretion which results from a decrease in hypothalamic sensitivity to gonadal steroids.

NOTE: Reprinted by permission of the authors and publisher from Reiter, E, and Root, A., "Hormonal Changes of Adolescence," *Medical Clinics of North America*, 59(6):1300, 1975.

the sensitivity of this gonadostat decreases, resulting in a greater output of LH and FSH and resultant increased secretion of androgens or estrogens. Eventually a new steady state is achieved. In the female, after a few years, cycling is superimposed on this resulting in ovulation.

The first sign of adolescence in the female is usually breast enlargement, followed shortly by the development of sex hair secondary to adrenal androgen secretion. In males, testosterone first causes scrotal changes and penile enlargement and later the development of sex hair. Sexual maturation has been classified into five stages by Tanner based on breast development, genital maturation, and pubic hair. Tanner Stage I is prepuberty; Stage II, early puberty; Stage III, midpuberty; Stage IV, late puberty; and Stage V, sexual maturity.

A percentage of normal males may, for undetermined reasons, develop greater than usual gynecomastia during adolescence. This usually regresses spontaneously, disappearing after one to two years. If severe, or if it produces significant psychological disturbances, it should be corrected surgically. It does not imply femininity.

THE CENTRAL NERVOUS SYSTEM AND THE DEVELOPING CHILD

Normal intellectual and emotional growth are dependent upon multiplication and growth of central neurons, induced by adequate nutrition and biochemical and emotional environmental stimulation. This is seen clinically as an appropriate increase in head size. Intellectual and emotional growth usually progress simultaneously with physical growth and may be disturbed when there is an abnormality of the latter. There is accumulating evidence that brain maturation, learning, and memory are directly influenced by hormones. The role of thyroid hormone in normal maturation and multiplication of brain cells in utero and in the neonatal period is the best known. Recently, studies in both rats and humans suggest that ACTH, MSH, and vasopressin are important in the development of learning ability and memory retention. Fetal exposure to excessive amounts of hormones, particularly androgens, is thought to stimulate behavior patterns such as aggressiveness, achievement orientation, and "tomboyism." At adolescence and in adult life, the sex hormones influence sex drive. There is less definite evidence for a role of estrogens and progesterone in human behavior apart from producing a feeling of well-being.

It is therefore interesting that receptor sites for estrogens, but none for androgens, have been documented in the hypothalamic cell nuclei. It has been suggested that testosterone must be aromatized to estrogen before becoming effective in the brain. Prolactin is known to influence migration and breeding habits in birds, but as yet no definite effect on human behavior is documented. There is speculation about the possible direct effects of some of the hypothalamic-releasing hormones on human behavior. There is controversial evidence for a mood-altering role of thyroid releasing hormone (TRH) which is actually distributed throughout the brain. In hypophysectomized rats, gonadotrophin-releasing hormone (GnRH) induces sex behavior. Somatostatin, the factor known to inhibit growth hormone and most other pituitary and pancreatic hormone secretion, is widely distributed in the brain and also in the upper gastrointestinal tract and pancreas, and is reported to decrease physical activity in rats and monkeys. One may conclude that these and other hormones play a vital role in CNS function and behavioral patterns throughout life.

Endocrine Disorders Causing Psychosocial Problems

SHORT STATURE

Children with abnormalities of physical growth constitute the largest proportion of referrals to the pediatric endocrinologist. Only a small proportion of such referrals for short stature are due to classical endocrine dysfunction. (See table 72–1.) This group of patients may be generally classified as follows.

1. Genetic short stature with or without associated physical stigmata.
2. Constitutional delay in growth and maturation.
3. Skeletal diseases.
4. Chromosomal abnormalities.
5. Chronic nonendocrine diseases.
6. Diseases of the endocrine system.

A specific diagnosis can be made in most cases. A careful history and physical examination with selected appropriate blood tests will usually rule in or out chronic diseases such as renal disease, congenital heart disease, chronic inflammatory bowel disease, etc. Radiological evaluation of the

TABLE 72–1

Causes of Short Stature in Children

I. *Systemic Disease*
  CNS: With or without mental retardation
  Cardiovascular: Congenital heart disease
  Rheumatic heart disease
  Respiratory: Asthma
  Chronic lung disease
  Renal: Chronic renal failure
  Tubular acidosis
  Nephrogenic diabetes insipidus
  Gastrointestinal: Malabsorption syndromes
  Regional ileitis
  Hematologic: Chronic anemias
  Skeletal: Rickets
  Osteochondrodystrophies
  Epiphyseal and metaphyseal dysplasias
  Spine disorders
  Metabolic: Inborn errors of metabolism

II. *Primordial Dwarfism*
  Dwarfism without associated anomalies
  Dwarfism with congenital abnormalities
  ("syndromes")
  Intrauterine infection
  Small for gestational age

III. *Genetic*
  Familial short stature
  Chromosomal disorders—trisomies
  gonadal dysgenesis

IV. *Constitutional Short Stature*

V. *Endocrine Disorders*
  Primary hypothyroidism
  Organic hypopituitarism
  Idiopathic hypopituitarism
  Isolated growth hormone deficiency
  Familial hypopituitarism
  Psychosocial dwarfism
  Excessive androgen or estrogen with early
  epiphyseal fusion
  —congenital adrenal hyperplasia
  —precocious puberty
  Glucocorticoid excess
  Insulin deficiency
  Pseudo and Pseudopseudo hypoparathyroidism
  Prader-Willi syndrome

skeletal system will allow diagnosis of the common skeletal disorders such as achondroplastic dwarfism. Specific physical stigmata should lead to proper diagnosis of conditions such as Mongolism, a mucopolysaccharide disorder, etc. X-rays of the wrist for bone maturation is a simple, relatively inexpensive, and highly important initial study to obtain in the evaluation of the child with short stature. If the child's bone age is comparable to his chronological age, then a diagnosis of genetic short stature is substantiated and there is little or nothing that can be done therapeutically to in-

crease the ultimate adult height of such a child. On the other hand, if the child has a significant retardation in bone age when compared with chronological age, then the possibility for future growth is great, depending, of course, upon the underlying diagnosis. Retarded bone maturation is characteristically seen in hypopituitarism, hypothyroidism, malnutrition, chronic disease, and in constitutional slow growth and short stature.

In children with sexual precocity of whatever cause, growth during the early years of life is excessive, as is the rate of maturation. However, because of the sex hormone excess, epiphyseal maturation is advanced, the bones fuse early, and these children terminate growth several years in advance of the normal. Consequently, they may be significantly reduced in ultimate adult height.

Hypopituitarism. Hypopituitarism causes short stature resulting from growth hormone deficiency. In such patients, growth hormone may be the only anterior pituitary hormone deficient or there may be multiple hormone deficiencies such as TSH, ACTH, and gonadotropin deficiency associated with growth hormone absence. Anterior pituitary deficiency may result from a defect in the anterior pituitary itself or a primary abnormality in the hypothalamus or in the hypothalamic pituitary feedback control mechanism. Hypopituitarism may be familial or sporadic. It may be associated with identifiable CNS pathology or, in the more usual case, be referred to as idiopathic hypopituitarism because of inability to identify the specific reason for pituitary deficiency.

A common syndrome of particular interest associated with hypopituitarism is septo-optic dysplasia. This condition includes hypothalamic hypoplasia, optic nerve hypoplasia, and agenesis of the septum pellucidum and/or corpus callosum. Tumors of the pituitary, or more commonly, hypothalamus, most often a craniopharyngioma, can produce hypopituitarism and may present at any time during childhood. In the presence of CNS tumors, the most frequent clinical symptoms (in addition to those of hormonal deficiency) include increased intracranial pressure, personality changes, decrease in peripheral vision, and radiological changes of the skull demonstrating erosion of the pituitary fossa or calcification of the tumor. These radiological signs may not appear for many years. Consequently, the absence of clinical and/or radiological evidence of organic pathology cannot completely rule out the presence of a tumor in a child with apparent idiopathic hypopituitarism. The presence of both anterior and posterior pituitary deficiency strongly suggests either tumor development or histiocytosis X as the underlying factor.

Children with growth hormone deficiency are classically short with truncal obesity and immature facial features. The marked delay in bone age corresponds to their delayed height age. Additionally, they may have signs of mild hypothyroidism when there is TSH deficiency. Hypoglycemia may be a significant problem in the younger child with hypopituitarism but usually resolves spontaneously as the child increases in age and body weight. Chronic fatigue may be an expression of ACTH and cortisol deficiency. The absence of secondary sexual development in the adolescent years when appropriate physical growth is achieved suggests that gonadotropic hormones are deficient. Hypopituitarism should be suspected in the child with extreme short stature and delay in bone maturation, assuming specific systemic disease has been excluded. Such patients should be referred to an endocrinologist for complete evaluation of pituitary function including growth hormone, thyroid, adrenal hormones and, if of adolescent age, gonadotropin and sex steroid analysis.

The therapy of such patients should be directed toward the specific deficiencies. Unfortunately, growth hormone is in extremely limited supply and is available in the United States through the NIH only for research purposes. Consequently, many children with clearly documented hypopituitarism have not been able to receive the therapeutic benefit of HGH. Hopefully, a synthetic preparation will eventually be available or the supply of HGH will be increased. In the absence of HGH the use of mild anabolic steroids such as oxandralone (Anavar) may be of some definite benefit.

Those children who have documented deficiency of TSH and/or ACTH should receive replacement therapy with thyroxine and cortisone. However, very careful monitoring of the dosage must be carried out in order to prevent potential further loss of growth. Treatment with sex steroids to induce pubertal changes is usually delayed until late adolescence or until acceptable or the best possible growth has been achieved, as sex steroids will rapidly close the epiphyses and prevent further growth.

Although children with hypopituitarism, excluding those with brain damage secondary to tumors and/or neurosurgery, are of normal intelligence, their achievement in the academic situation, in social interaction, and in the job market is frequently not up to full potential. This is related to the emotional handicaps associated with poor growth and retardation of secondary sexual development. Psychological counseling is regularly needed in such individuals.

Primary Hypothyroidism. The presence of thyroid hormone in optimal amounts is essential for normal physical and intellectual growth. Thyroid hormone deficiency results in marked impairment of growth. Hypothyroidism may occur in the newborn period, when the physical features only occasionally lead to the diagnosis of cretinism. Unfortunately, the classical clinical signs usually are not obvious until two to three months of age. These infants may have either congenital goitrous cretinism or athyreosis. Such infants, unless diagnosed early and treated adequately, are left with a high degree of irreversible brain damage.

The mechanism of brain damage appears to be thyroid deficiency mediated interference with RNA replication in the central nervous system leading to decrease in size of the CNS neurons, axons, and dendrites. In rats made hypothyroid in utero, there is a delay of cerebellar differentiation and transient decrease in cell number which can be reversed to normal with early and appropriate thyroid therapy. In humans, the prognosis for a normal IQ is relatively good if thyroid replacement is initiated before three months of age. However, in some patients there is a slow increase in IQ following several years of therapy. Intelligence in such children may, but does not necessarily, correlate with signs of neurological deficit.

The development of hypothyroidism in the older child or adult is nearly always the end result of a chronic autoimmune inflammatory process of the thyroid gland called Hashimoto's thyroiditis. Permanent brain damage does not result if hypothyroidism develops after brain growth is complete, that is, sometime between eighteen and twenty-four months of life. However, hypothyroidism at any age does produce such CNS symptoms as lethargy, depression, sleepiness, irritability, and poor academic performance. Delayed linear growth associated with delayed bone maturation is characteristic. If hypothyroidism develops during adolescent years, the progression of adolescent maturation is impaired.

A diagnosis of hypothyroidism should be suspected in any patient with marked delay in physical growth associated with bone age delay; immature body proportions; skin which is cold, dry, pale, and sometimes slightly yellow due to an increase in carotene pigment; anemia; and delayed reflexes. Diagnosis of primary hypothyroidism is substantiated by the finding of a T_4 blood concentration which is low and TSH which is high. In the older child, serum cholesterol concentration may also be quite elevated.

Replacement therapy with thyroid hormones will reverse all the physical stigmata of this condition except for brain damage if this has occurred early in infancy. The rate of catchup growth may be extremely dramatic, but it may not be complete if the condition has been long-standing with treatment started near puberty.

Gonadal Dysgenesis or Turner's Syndrome. This syndrome is a chromosomal disease occurring in phenotypic females with short stature and other specific physical stigmata. The classical patient has a chromosomal karyotype of 45 XO (i.e., there is the loss of one of the X chromosomes). Other chromosomal patterns described with similar physical features include mosaics in which some cells have the normal XX components while other cells have the XO genetic component. The X′ (prime) isochromosome X patients may have only short stature without other physical stigmata.

The physical features of Turner's syndrome include short stature, webbed neck, low hairline, characteristic relatively unattractive facies, broad shield chest with hypoplastic nipples, hypoplastic finger- and toenails, increased carrying angle of the arms, short fourth metacarpals, increased number of pigmented nevi, and congenital heart disease. The great majority of these girls have either no ovarian tissue or streak ovaries. Consequently, they do not develop secondary sexual characteristics except for slight pubic hair growth. Turner's syndrome, in infant girls, was formerly referred to as the Bonnevie-Ullrich syndrome, characterized by edema of the hands and feet and redundant folds of skin of the neck.

Referral of such patients to the pediatric endocrinologist may occur at any time because of short stature, but more commonly occurs in the adolescent age group because of the combination of short stature and absence of adolescent development. This diagnosis should be considered in any girl with sexual delay and short stature. The diagnosis is made by a buccal smear with Barr body count (normally 20 to 40 percent) either greatly reduced or 0 (i.e., the count one would expect to see in a normal male). Confirmation of the diagnosis, if necessary, can be obtained by study of chromosomal karyotype. During the pubertal age group, these girls have an increase in the circulating levels of LH and FSH due to the absence of ovarian hormone secretion.

The measured IQ in most girls with Turner's syndrome is within the normal range. However, many of them have a specific cognitive defect with special problems in space-form conceptualization. This is manifest in school, particularly in subjects related to the field of mathematics. These girls may need special education counseling due to this learning disability. In addition, they usually need psychological support because of the combined problem of short stature and absence of sexual development. Their ultimate height is between 54 and 58 inches. Therapy has little effect upon the ultimate adult height. Treatment with oxandralone (Anavar) prepubertally may result in some gain in height over bone age. The patients will eventually need replacement therapy with estrogen which will result in breast development, increase in sexual hair growth, and establishment of menstrual periods. As a general rule, estrogen therapy should be delayed as long as is psychologically reasonable in order to ensure as much linear growth as possible before epiphyseal closure.

Noonan's syndrome is a condition which shares many of the clinical features of Turner's syndrome without a detectable abnormality in the chromosomal karyotype. The condition, when it occurs in males, is associated with short stature, sexual infantilism, hypospadias, and cryptorchidism, as well as the other physical features of Turner's syndrome. The boys, however, have a normal XY karyotype. Pulmonary stenosis is commonly associated.

Adrenogenital Syndrome or Congenital Adrenal Hyperplasia. This is a genetic disease with autosomal recessive transmission, involving the deficiency of one of the enzymes involved in steroid metabolism of the adrenal cortex. There are five types (figure 72–5) of which 21-hydroxylase deficiency is the commonest. There is a block in the formation of 11-desoxycortisol (compound s) and, therefore, also cortisol, from 17-OH progesterone. About 50 percent of these children have the salt-losing form with failure of formation of 11-desoxycortiosterone and thus aldosterone. Deyhdration, hyponatremia, and acidosis, therefore, may result in a life-threatening situation prior to diagnosis. In the absence of cortisol, there is an increased secretion of ACTH, which in turn increases the output of adrenal androgens.

This stimulus occurs in utero and results in varying degrees of virilism in the female baby at birth, with ambiguous or malelike genitalia, or a large and/or pigmented phallus in the male. If there is no salt loss, the diagnosis may readily be missed, particularly in a boy. Continued stimulation by the excessively secreted adrenal androgens

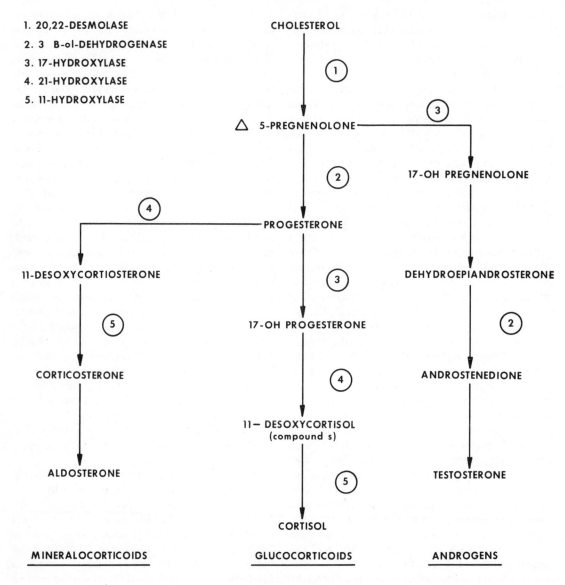

1. 20,22-DESMOLASE
2. 3 B-ol-DEHYDROGENASE
3. 17-HYDROXYLASE
4. 21-HYDROXYLASE
5. 11-HYDROXYLASE

FIGURE 72–5
Enzymatic deficiencies in congenital adrenal hyperplasia.

will occur with initial rapid linear and osseous growth acceleration. Later, early puberty with premature closure of the epiphyses results in cessation of growth with ultimate short stature.

Control of this condition is difficult even with early diagnosis. These children must adjust to taking medication, usually three times every day of their lives, with fairly accurate timing and increased dosage during stress. Dose of replacement steroid is titrated against growth velocity and urinary output of 17-ketosteroids and degree of salt loss (the latter controlled with fludrocortisone acetate [Florinef]). Despite treatment with apparently adequate doses of cortisone to turn off increased ACTH and androgen secretion, many patients are ultimately short, probably due to incomplete compliance. Excess steroids, while controlling virilization, will also produce short stature with delayed bone age and a Cushingoid appearance. Muscularity and virilization with amenorrhea in poorly controlled girls is usually more of a burden than their height, as will be discussed later.

Isosexual Precocious Puberty. Idiopathic precocious puberty is more common in girls than boys. For some reason, the trigger for the onset of puberty occurs early. Precocious puberty may be due to an organic CNS lesion or a sex-hormone-secreting tumor of a gonad. This is the commonest cause in boys. In both sexes there is a rapid growth spurt with concomitant advance of bone age leading to premature closure of the epiphyses. Thus final height is less than the genetic potential. Therapy is aimed at removal of the cause if this is due to a tumor. Unfortunately, CNS tumors are difficult to handle. At present there is little effective hormonal therapy to treat the idiopathic type. Medroxyprogesterone was formerly used with little success. There are reports of success with an antiandrogen, cyproterone acetate, which is not yet available in the United States.

Glucocorticoid Excess. The commonest cause of this problem in childhood is high-dose steroid therapy for chronic illness such as asthma, collagenosis, and ulcerative colitis. The systemic disease alone may retard growth. This is compounded by the antagonistic effect of steroids on somatomedin action. The children often also show the features of steroid excess (i.e., moon face, buffalo hump, bruising, truncal obesity, muscular wasting, and the development of striae). Aseptic necrosis of the hip is a severe complication as are osteoporosis and diabetes. These side effects are usually reversible if steroid dosage is decreased. Unfortunately, the severity of the underlying illness rarely allows this. There has been some success in stimulating growth with oxandralone (Anavar) (a weak androgen that has greater effects on linear growth than epiphyseal closure).

Cushing's syndrome is unusual in childhood and its commonest cause is adrenal carcinoma, particularly when it occurs in infancy. Less often it results from adrenal adenoma and hyperplasia. The latter may be idiopathic, of hypothalamic origin, or due to a pituitary tumor. There is an excessive output of glucocorticoids and androgens causing the previously mentioned features of glucocorticoid excess, plus varying degrees of virilization. The degree of short stature, which may, with obesity, be the presenting symptom, depends on the proportions of cortisone and androgens secreted. There is usually catchup growth with the removal of the excessive steroid source, unless this includes removal of the pituitary and/or pituitary irradiation with loss of growth hormone and often other pituitary hormones.

Pseudo- and Pseudo-pseudo Hypoparathyroidism. Children with these conditions may present because of short stature and obesity. These problems may be superseded by the associated mental retardation. The characteristic features of pseudo-hypoparathyroidism are round face, short extremities, short fourth and fifth metacarpals, calcification of the subcutaneous tissues and basal ganglia, and sometimes cataracts and osteoporosis. Serum calcium is low with the chemical abnormalities of primary hypoparathyroidism except that PTH levels are normal. The renal tubules are unresponsive to the action of PTH. Pseudo-pseudo hypoparathyroidism has the same physical features, but normal biochemistry. Both have short stature as part of the genetic rather than endocrine abnormality. The diagnosis is mainly a clinical and radiological one; pseudo-hypoparathyroidism is diagnosed by a low serum calcium, high phosphorous, and often high alkaline phosphates.

SEXUAL ABNORMALITIES

Sexual Abnormalities. This is the area where the collaboration of a psychiatrist is usually vital. Problems are due to delay or failure to develop endogenous puberty and subsequent infertility, virilization in girls, or poorly established gender identity due to sexual ambiguity or underdeveloped genitalia. In the case of ambiguous genitalia, the sex of rearing and first appearance of the external genitalia determine psychosexual identity. As mentioned previously, gender identity is not chromosomally or hormonally controlled. Ambivalence about sex identity is usually related to abnormal appearance of the genitalia or ambivalence in the minds of the parents. It is vital to assign a sex to a child according to the adequacy of the external genitalia as sexually functional organs and not according to chromosomal sex. If the penis is too small for adequate function, it is always easier to construct female than male genitalia. Such XY females can live a very normal sexual life, including the attainment of orgasm. If there is firm sex assignment by two years of age, these individuals do not have a greater propensity to become transexuals or homosexuals. However, they will have to contend with infertility and adoption of a family. The very difficult problem of what to tell these patients, when and how, has been discussed at length by Dr. John Money in various publications.*

Congenital Adrenal Hyperplasia. This condition has already been discussed. Psychological problems are centered mainly around short stature in boys. However, adolescents with inadequate therapy may develop small testicular tumors due to hyperplasia of adrenal rest tissue or have suppression of

* See the list of suggested readings.

testicular function and poor fertility. These defects are reversible by adequate therapy. There is a small group of genetic females severely virilized at birth and brought up as males—particularly where the diagnosis is missed. Penile size is rarely adequate and they have varying degrees of hypospadias and an empty scrotum. The severest form (i.e., with complete virilization) may only present at puberty with short stature and "bleeding" through the urinary tract, which is actually menstruation. They require removal of the female internal organs and testicular prosthesis.

These individuals, with and without plastic surgery to the genitalia, function as psychologically and sexually normal but infertile males. More often the penis is too small and the hypospadias too severe to be amenable to plastic surgery; thus sexual function is impaired. This syndrome is the commonest cause of pseudohermaphroditism in girls. Girls are usually virilized at birth and thus more easily recognized and diagnosed. The clitoris is enlarged to variable degrees and the perineum is closed to form a urogenital sinus. They may also have urinary tract defects.

It is important that the ambiguous genitalia be assessed in the neonatal period and sex assignment be made as soon as possible, as was discussed earlier. Plastic surgery in one or more stages will normalize the female genitalia. If medication is taken regularly, these girls will grow into normal adolescence with a normal prognosis for marriage and pregnancy. Inadequate therapy may result in virilization with hirsutism, amenorrhea, and poor breast development. It has been shown in two studies that these girls often have the personalities associated with intrauterine androgen exposure, but this is within the norms of society.

Hermaphroditism. Hermaphroditism refers to the presence or apparent presence of both male and female sex structures in the same individual. The term "true hermaphroditism" refers to individuals who have documentation of the presence of both ovarian and testicular tissue. There may be ovo-testes bilaterally, or an ovary on one side and testis on the other. In most reported cases true hermaphrodites have an XX chromosomal karyotype. However, XX/XY and XY patterns, as well as a number of other mosaic patterns, have been described. The external genital configuration in such individuals may be either female, male, or ambiguous.

The term "male pseudohermaphroditism" refers to a condition in which the patient is a genetic male (i.e., whose chromosomal complement is 46 XY), who has testicular tissue, and who has either ambiguity of external genitalia or female external genital configuration. Female pseudohermaphroditism is a condition in which the patient has 46 XX chromosomal complement, normal ovaries, but also ambiguity or marked virilization of the external genitalia.

Female Pseudohermaphroditism. The most common cause of female pseudohermaphroditism is the adrenogenital syndrome. In this condition, during intrauterine development of the fetal adrenal structure produces excessive amounts of androgens, stimulating external genital development along male lines. Consequently, at birth, these girls have varying degrees of virilization of the external genitalia with labioscrotal fusion and clitoral enlargement. As discussed earlier, the condition is diagnosed by the finding of elevated ketosteroids in urine. The condition is treated by replacement therapy with cortisone and with surgical correction of the sexual ambiguity. The internal sex organs in these patients are normal.

Other causes of female pseudohermaphroditism include maternal ingestion of androgens or progestins during pregnancy and ovarian or adrenal tumors producing androgens during the course of pregnancy in either the mother or fetus.

Male Pseudohermaphroditism. There are five known possible enzymatic defects in testosterone synthesis which will result in varying degrees of incomplete virilization. The most common form of male pseudohermaphroditism is the condition known as testicular feminization. This is a familial condition resulting from tissue unresponsiveness to endogenous or exogenous androgens. These patients are usually considered to be perfectly normal females because their external genital configuration is that of a normal female. The diagnosis may be made by the finding of lumps in the inguinal area, which frequently are diagnosed as inguinal hernias. These individuals usually feminize (i.e., breast tissue appears spontaneously at puberty). However, the internal sex organs are incomplete, the vagina is usually short, and there is little or no uterine development. Consequently, there is primary amenorrhea. In addition, sexual hair growth is minimal.

One of the more completely understood forms of male pseudohermaphroditism is deficiency of the enzyme 5 alpha reductase. Such patients are unable to convert testosterone to its more active substrate, dihydrotestosterone. They have incomplete virilization or ambiguity of the external genitalia at birth but virilize at puberty. In all of the types of male pseudohermaphroditism, the virilization of the internal and external genitalia is variable. In all infants with sexual ambiguity at birth, a definitive etiologic diagnosis should be made as rapidly as possible and a decision regarding sex rearing established. As a general rule, all genetic females (i.e., infants with a 46 XX karyotype and the presence of ovaries) should be reared as females. The virilized external genitalia should be surgically corrected. On the other hand, genetic males with or without adequate testicular development should be reared as females if the penis is incompletely developed for adequate sexual functioning. Vaginal construction can be carried out at an appropriate age and estrogen therapy will lead to breast development.

Mixed Gonadal Dysgenesis. These patients are phenotypic females who have a karyotype of XO/XY mosaic, who usually have a streak gonad on one side, a dysgenetic testis on the other, ambiguous genitalia, and often some features of Turner's syndrome. They usually do best as females with estrogen supplementation at puberty. They are infertile and often short. The presence of a Y chromosome increases the risk of a gonadoblastoma and the gonads should be removed.

Turner's Syndrome (see "Short Stature," pages 608–613). Girls with Turner's syndrome develop a small amount of pubic hair but usually will not progress spontaneously into adolescence. Estrogen replacement therapy is needed, and this is usually deferred as long as possible in order to maximize linear growth before bone closure. After establishing uterine maturation with continuous estrogen administration, these patients should be treated with cyclic estrogen or a combination of estrogen and progesterone to induce menstruation. Because of the absence of functioning ovaries, the patients are almost always infertile. However, marriage and perfectly normal sexual responsiveness is possible with estrogen therapy. Many patients benefit from psychological counseling regarding their problems with short stature and absent sexual development. In addition, education guidance may be necessary.

Klinefelter's Syndrome. These are males with an extra X chromosome (i.e., 47 XXY or a mosaic). They may present because of delayed or absent puberty. Even prior to puberty, they are usually tall and have an increased arm span which becomes more marked when they reach the adolescent age due to failure of closure of the epiphyses. Testicular size may be initially normal but becomes smaller than normal in adulthood. These patients are infertile and have normal or somewhat decreased testosterone levels, an elevated LH and FSH, and a positive buccal smear.

They are probably more vulnerable to emotional disorders than their peers (i.e., apart from the psychological trauma of hypogonadism).

Delayed Puberty. Delay in the normal timing of secondary sexual development is a common cause for concern in both adolescent-age males and females. In a great majority of such individuals, the delay is a physiologic rather than pathologic one. That is, evaluation of such individuals does not lead to the definition of specific endocrine disease, and such patients eventually establish normal sexual maturation leading to perfectly normal adult sexual status.

A very common form of delayed maturation is that referred to as constitutional delay in growth and development. These patients, almost always boys, give a history of short stature (at or below the third percentile for height) since preschool days. At adolescence, they have no secondary sexual development and show a further slowdown in linear growth compared to their peers. Commonly, the fathers of these boys give a similar developmental history.

Emotional problems in these cases may be intense and require active psychological guidance. In such cases, treatment with testosterone for a period of a few months may also be very helpful in hastening both growth and maturation and helping improve the patient's body image. There are also a variety of specific causes for delayed adolescence including hypopituitarism, primary gonadal disease, hypothalamic disease, hypothyroidism, and other chronic systemic diseases, as was discussed previously.

Precocious Puberty. The onset of sexual maturation prior to nine years of age is generally considered to be below the range of normal distribution. This is seen more commonly in girls than boys and, in the United States, in black children more frequently than white. Premature sexual development may occur at any time from birth until adolescence, but it is most commonly observed in the age range from six to eight years. Because of the presence of sex hormones at an early age, one of the characteristic physical features of these children is rapid physical growth so that they are initially larger than their peers with eventual short stature due to premature epiphyseal closure. In addition, secondary sexual characteristics appear early, with increase in physical strength and in body maturation. Emotional problems may appear in such patients and/or their families. These children are usually treated as if they are considerably older; consequently, expectations are placed upon them which they are not mature enough to handle. Guidance of the patient, the family, and the school system is usually necessary. There is currently no medical therapy available which is effective in interrupting early sexual development. An androgen antagonist, cyproterone acetate, has been used with some effectiveness in Europe.

DIABETES MELLITUS

Juvenile-onset diabetes mellitus is a very common endocrine disease occurring in approximately 1 in 600 normal children. The condition results from a deficiency of the production of insulin by the pancreas. It appears to have a genetic component with environmental factors such as virus infections possibly playing a major role in the expression of the disease. In the absence of insulin, the patients develop hyperglycemia leading to polyuria, polydypsia, and polyphagia. If the diagnosis is not established, diabetic ketoacidosis, a life-threatening condition, will supervene. The therapy of children with diabetes mellitus invariably includes the administration of insulin by injection on a daily basis. In addition, the use of diets with decreased proportions of free sugar and saturated fats is important. Hypoglcyemia is an everpresent danger in children with diabetes mellitus. It is likely to occur if the insulin dose administered is excessive, if the caloric intake is inadequate, or the energy expenditure by way of exercise is increased.

The course of diabetes includes a high probability that the individual will eventually develop one or more of the so-called "diabetic complications" which include vascular damage, strokes, blindness, and neuropathy. There is increasing evidence that there is a relationship between the adequacy of metabolic management and the eventual development of diabetic complications. Inability to completely control the metabolic aspects of diabetes is frustrating to the family, the patient, and the physician. Excessive attempts to achieve normality are almost invariably associated with highly rigid systems of management, carrying with them psychological hazards as well as increased likelihood of hypoglycemia. Repeated or severe episodes of hypoglycemia undoubtedly cause neurological damage, while mild or infrequent episodes usually do not produce apparent neurologic deficit.

The child with diabetes mellitus is highly likely to develop significant psychological problems associated with the disease, particularly during the adolescent years. Ideally, all such patients and their families should have the benefit of psychological counseling of a preventive nature. This is rarely possible. Therefore, psychiatric intervention on a crisis basis is the more likely outcome.

Endocrine Disorders Presenting as Psychiatric Disturbances

THYROTOXICOSIS OR GRAVE'S DISEASE

Thyrotoxicosis is not uncommon in childhood and often presents with behavioral disturbances, deterioration of school work with decreased attention span, anxiety, emotional lability, sleep disturbance, and fatigue. A tremor with deterioration of handwriting is very common. Appetite is usually excellent. The weight loss, classical of adult hyperthyroidism, is seen less often in children. In fact, they may sometimes actually gain weight if appetite increases to the extent that they eat more calories than they use. Diarrhea is also not very common although there is usually some increase in stools. Palpitations are also a less common complaint than in adults. Thus the clinical picture is very much like an anxiety state, but it can be differentiated by careful examination. Children with thyrotoxicosis usually have a growth spurt and advanced bone age with poor or appropriate but, rarely, excessive, weight gain. There is often some proptosis with lid lag and usually tachycardia with hot sweaty hands and a fine tremor of the outstretched fingers. Thyromegaly is usual in childhood and may have an associated bruit. A blood test showing a raised T_4 confirms the diagnosis. If this is normal and the diagnosis is still suspect, T_3 should be measured by immunoassay to exclude T_3 toxicosis, a condition in which the gland preferentially secretes T_3. This is apparently rare in children.

The usual treatment is the use of antithyroid drugs such as propylthiouracil for two or more years to block T_3 and T_4 production, with or without coverage with thyroxine. Surgery is indicated if there is drug sensitivity or failure to achieve control, usually due to lack of compliance. The behavior and school problems usually abate with resolution of the disease. Patients must be evaluated at regular intervals for recurrence of the condition. Thyrotoxicosis may rarely be caused by a thyroid adenoma presenting as a solitary thyroid nodule on examination and hot nodule on scan. The treatment of choice for this is surgery in childhood. In both situations, many of the symptoms which are mediated by catecholamines may be relieved by propranolol.

HYPOTHYROIDISM
(see "Short Stature," pages 608–613)

If chronic, this presents as short stature. However, the first features may be fatigue, depression, and poor school performance. In milder cases, the children may do very well at school as they do not have the energy to play and they do their homework instead. They may have problems with deteriorating school work and uncontrolled physical energy during the first months of therapy, as they "go wild" with their newly found energy.

GLUCOCORTICOID EXCESS
(see "Short Stature," pages 608–613)

Cushing's disease may present with psychiatric disorders, as it does in adults. Depression is common, and patients may even become psychotic. Other symptoms encountered are difficulty in concentration, irritability, insomnia, and sometimes paranoid delusions. Exogenous steroid excess, by contrast, causes euphoria. The differences between endogenous and exogenous steroid excess may be associated with the presence or absence of excessive ACTH secretion as part of the syndrome.

PITUITARY OR HYPOTHALAMIC TUMOR

These patients, particularly those with craniopharyngiomas, may present with personality changes. This is compounded by symptoms associated with their hormonal disturbances. The more posterior the tumor extends into the diencephalon, the more likely they are to have psychological and weight alterations as their presenting symptoms.

ADDISON'S DISEASE

These patients may present with apathy, depression, and fatigue. They may even develop an organic psychosis with memory deficit and clouding of consciousness. Anorexia, vomiting, and weight loss are usual and often present a picture similar to anorexia nervosa. There is an interesting increased sensitivity to taste, smell, and hearing and a decreased threshold for the taste of salt. They may have symptoms of hypoglycemia, postural hypotension, and salt craving. Examina-

tion reveals increased pigmentation particularly of scars, nipples, palmar creases, and gum margins and decreased sex hair. Hypotension is a danger, as is electrolyte disturbance with low sodium and high potassium. Random plasma cortisol and urinary 17-hydroxysteroids are low and do not increase with ACTH stimulation. There is also urinary salt loss. Treatment involves replacement with cortisone and a mineralcorticoid (usually fludrocortisone acetate [Florinef]).

HYPOGLYCEMIA

Hypoglycemia is not a specific diagnosis but is rather a biochemical state. In the older child or adult, the documentation of a blood glucose below 40 mg. percent in association with symptoms usually leads to a diagnosis of hypoglycemia. It is then necessary to carry out appropriate studies in order to determine the underlying etiology.

The excessive fall in blood glucose results in a diminution in the delivery of glucose, an essential CNS nutrient, to the brain. The body's response to this is characterized by two phenomena. The first is the stress response mediated by epinephrine release. This includes the subjective sensation of anxiety, nervousness, hunger, and headache with abdominal pain and nausea and, less commonly, vomiting. Physiological response includes tachycardia, sweating, pallor, and hypertension.

If the blood glucose concentration continues to fall, the second set of responses will begin to occur as there develops gross nutritional impairment to the CNS. This includes confusion, bizarre behavior, lack of comprehension, physical violence, abnormal eye movements, progressing to convulsions, and coma.

It would appear that brief episodes of hypoglycemia probably do not result in permanent brain damage. However, severe prolonged hypoglycemia or recurrent hypoglycemia, particularly when initially occurring in the child under one year of age, is highly likely to lead to permanent, irreversible brain damage. Mental retardation and behavioral disturbances may be seen with recurrent hypoglycemia. Episodic, irrational behavior should lead to the suspicion of hypoglycemia. Acute anxiety occurring a few hours after meals or disorientation relieved by food ingestion should also bring this diagnosis to mind.

Hypoglycemia may be part of the expression of a variety of disease states in childhood. This would include hyperinsulinism, such as may result from islet cell adenoma or nesidioblastosis (islet cell hyperplasia); deficiency of growth hormone, cortisone, epinephrine, or glucagon; chronic liver disease such as the glycogen storage diseases; fructose and galactose intolerance; or leucine sensitivity. The child with documented hypoglycemia should be fully evaluated in order to ascertain the basic underlying pathology. Therapy should then be directed toward this specific abnormality rather than the problem of glucose regulation.

HYPOPARATHYROIDISM

The most common form of hypoparathyroidism is autoimmune destruction of parathyroid glands. This may occur singularly or in association with autoimmune damage of other endocrine glands such as adrenal, thyroid, ovaries, and pancreas. The second most common form of hypoparathyroidism is that occurring accidentally during surgical thyroidectomy. Pseudoparathyroidism has been discussed under short stature. The presenting feature of the first two forms is usually a "pins and needles" sensation of the hands, cramps, carpopedal spasm, or frank tetany due to hypocalcemia. The patients may have a severe convulsive disorder as the presenting feature in infancy and childhood.

In idiopathic hypoparathyroidism about one-third of the patients have intellectual impairment. Others may have emotional lability, anxiety, irritability, and depression. Symptoms are usually reversible by therapy unless there has been organic brain damage. Mental retardation in pseudohypoparathyroidism is often only partially reversible when the serum calcium is restored to normal. Hypocalcemia manifests clinically with a positive Chvostek and/or Trosseau's sign. Serum calcium is low, less than 8 mg. percent, on repeated occasions, as is serum PTH in primary and surgical hypoparathyroidism. PTH is usually high in the pseudo form.

Diagnosis is confirmed by a PTH infusion test, measuring serum or urine cyclic AMP or urine phosphate. Treatment is difficult to regulate and consists of oral calcium and vitamin D.

HYPERCALCEMIA

Causes of this disorder are hyperparathyroidism, usually due to a parathyroid adenoma, excessive ingestion of vitamin D, renal failure, or the idiopathic hypercalcemic syndrome of infancy. The latter is characterized by a pixie face and pulmonary vascular stenosis. Presenting features are bone pain, abdominal pain, polyuria, and thirst. However, hypercalcemia may first manifest with mental symptoms ranging from mental retardation to memory impairment, confusion, depression, delusions, or loss of consciousness. The diagnosis is confirmed if repeated serum levels of calcium (blood taken without a cuff) are over 13 mg. percent in the absence of dehydration.

PHEOCHROMOCYTOMA

This condition is extremely rare and presents with episodes of catecholamine-induced acute anxiety, sweating, and hypertension. Diagnosis is suspected by finding hypertension during these episodes or paroxysmally without symptoms.

PRADER-WILLI SYNDROME

This is a syndrome of hypotonia, hyperphagia, and hypogonadism. These children, usually with short stature, present because of behavior disturbances centered around their enormous appetite and mental retardation. They are grossly obese with characteristic facies, small hands and feet, and hypogonadism with cryptorchidism and a micropenis. Glucose intolerance develops later during adolescence or adulthood. They have a characteristic history of feeding difficulties and hypotonia in the newborn period.

Endocrine Disorders Caused by Psychiatric Disturbances

OBESITY

The majority of obese people are overweight due to overeating and underactivity. Overeating is thought to be a manifestation of emotional disturbances. Obesity, in turn, causes further psychological problems. Endocrine disorders causing obesity are rare and can usually be excluded by physical exam. These include Cushing's syndrome, Prader-Willi syndrome, pseudohypoparathyroidism, and Lawrence-Moon-Biedl syndrome with hypogonadism, mental retardation, polydactaly, and retinitis pigmentosa. Occasionally a hypothalamic tumor may cause obesity with short stature and hypogonadism.

Children with exogenous obesity, by contrast, usually are tall for their age and have early puberty. The initial impression of micropenis in the obese male is dispelled by pushing back the pubic fat pad. Obesity itself causes endocrine changes (i.e., hyperinsulinism sometimes with glucose intolerance, decreased GH response to stimulation, and increased urinary steroids). These are reversible with weight loss, but in females rapid weight change is often followed by a period of amenorrhea.

Successful long-term treatment is notoriously difficult to achieve. Obesity under two years of age associated with overfeeding causes cellular hyperplasia and is reversible with dieting. After this age, increasing fat mass is due to cellular hypertrophy and is more difficult to reverse. It has been shown that people without a tendency to obesity, if force fed, reach a maximum weight and stay there, whereas obese people continue to gain. Thus, there is much to this syndrome which remains unclear. Anorectic drugs are rarely of any real use in therapy, and the only treatment involves decreasing caloric intake and increasing utilization with exercise.

ANOREXIA NERVOSA

This condition occurs most often in adolescent girls who were occasionally previously somewhat obese. It consists of willful restriction of food intake and a distorted body image. There is progressive weight loss with eventual cachexia, the appearance of lanugo hair, and, in females, breast atrophy. Endocrine abnormalities, which are reversible, are similar to those found in both childhood and adult protein-calorie malnutrition. GH levels are high, insulin is decreased, serum cortisol is high, and thyroid hormones normal or decreased. If the onset is during the growing age, growth may be stunted and puberty delayed. Postpubertal girls develop amenorrhea, associated low LH and decreased LH response to LRH. The same clinical features and endocrine abnormalities occur in organic hypothalamic disorders such as the diencephalic syndrome, and it may sometimes be difficult to differentiate these conditions.

PSYCHOSOCIAL DWARFISM

Children with this diagnosis have been labeled as having emotional deprivation, failure to thrive, or deprivation dwarfism. They come from a stressful home environment, often due to a broken marriage, an alcoholic father, and a mother with a character disorder or extreme dependency. Why one or two children of the family should react to this circumstance differently from the others is not clearly understood. There are frequently, but by no means always, features of child abuse and malnutrition in these children. However, many children present merely with short stature with normal or slightly decreased or even increased weight for height and give the clinical picture of GH deficiency. On closer examination, it becomes clear that they have retardation of intellectual, emotional, and motor development and delay in expressive language development together with growth retardation, and some may even be thought to be autistic. Classical features in the history include: (1) polyphagia with food stealing even from garbage cans and gorging to the extent that their abdomen bloats and they vomit, only to eat again; (2) polydypsia with drinking from drains and toilet bowl; (3) encopresis and enuresis; (4) sleep disturbance accompanied by wandering around the house and streets at night; (5) retarded speech and shyness, but also temper tantrums and difficulty with peer relationships. Despite their enormous food intake and bulky stools, there is no evidence of malabsorption. Apparently, the absorbed calories are used for purposes other than growth.

Extensive endocrine evaluation may reveal findings compatible with organic hypopituitarism with GH and ACTH deficiency and delayed bone age. However, there is some evidence that GH may be high in children under three years of age. Immediately upon removal from the stressful environment, there is usually a dramatic and rapid increase of weight and height and head circumference. In some, there is radiological evidence of splitting of the sutures on skull X-ray, presumably due to brain growth. There is equally dramatic change in their personality and speech capacity. Endocrine abnormalities usually return to normal within weeks. Presumably, there is growth failure because of GH deficiency. The mechanism by which emotional factors block GH is not known. It has been suggested that abnormal sleep habits may prevent GH release during sleep. However, it has been shown that sleep patterns may be normal with no GH release.

If intervention occurs at an early age, the prognosis is favorable with no external intervention other than a good home. Unfortunately, this is not always possible to achieve.

PSYCHOGENIC WATER DRINKING

Diabetes insipidus is a condition resulting from the inability to concentrate the urine adequately, resulting in excessive loss of water. The urine volume may be several liters of very dilute concentration each 24 hours. The organic form of diabetes insipidus includes (1) disorders of the hypothalamus or posterior pituitary resulting in deficient production of vasopressin (ADH) or (2) nephrogenic diabetes insipidus, a genetic condition caused by a lack of responsiveness of the renal tubules to endogenous ADH.

Psychogenic water drinking is a psychological condition characterized by extraordinary intake of water without the stimulus of thirst and with consequent large and frequent urinary output. Some investigators theorize that the self-induction of mild hyponatremia is either pleasurable or of some other emotional benefit to these patients. Frequently, they are obese. Because of the excessive water intake, a relative resistance to the action of ADH may be induced, complicating the diagnostic and therapeutic setting.

The diagnosis is best made by a careful dehydration test (Miller and Moses) checking weight loss, serum sodium, and urine osmolality hourly to assess renal concentration capacity. When the urine osmolality no longer increases, pitressin is administered. In the patient with psychogenic water drinking, urine osmolality is quite low at the beginning of the test but there is a slow prolonged increase in urine concentration while the serum sodium concentration remains within normal limits. If pitressin is administered before the urine osmolality plateaus, it has minimal effect. By contrast, pitressin will increase urine concentration in central organic diabetes insipidus.

Drugs Causing Endocrine Disturbances

Most drugs used in psychiatric practice affect the neurotransmitters and therefore probably affect the hypothalamo-pituitary axis. The ones of greatest clinical importance are the amphetamines and methylphenidate (Ritalin), which may cause growth retardation possibly by inhibition of GH secretion. Phenothiazines and antidepressants stimulate prolactin secretion and in estrogenized girls can cause galactorrhea.

Conclusion

The child psychiatrist plays a vital role as a collaborator for the pediatric endocrinologist. It is important that the former have a clear understanding of the patient's condition in order to elucidate the problem and to replace unfounded fears with reality. Under ideal circumstances, the child with endocrine or related disease and his family should be the recipient of care from a well-organized, integrated team which would include the referring physician, pediatric endocrinologist, psychologist, psychiatric social worker, and psychiatrist. Rarely is this optimal situation achieved.

As an alternate approach, an identification of those children most likely to need joint supervision by the child psychiatrist and pediatric endocrinologist may prove useful. Drs. John Money and Anke Ehrhardt's work have led to a greater understanding of the psychiatric aspects of pediatric endocrinology.

Children with growth problems, most particularly those with significant retardation in linear growth, probably represent the most frequent situation that will lead to psychological disturbance and should have the benefit of endocrine evaluation. Therapy directed toward growth stimulation may greatly enhance the child's emotional adjustment while, conversely, psychological counseling may improve a child's ability to accept his short stature in a situation that is not amenable to significant therapeutic response.

An area of special interest involves those children who have very significant variations in the timing of sexual maturation. The child with sexual precocity and, possibly even more so, the parents of the child with sexual precocity need psychological guidance and counseling. Boys with the combined problem of short stature and delay in sexual maturation may have very serious psychological manifestations including withdrawal, depression, and suicidal tendencies. While hormonal therapy is invariably effective in the stimulation of growth and maturation, counseling may be highly appropriate in addition. The girl with sexual delay, as in Turner's syndrome, will benefit from mutual attention by the psychiatrist and endocrinologist. Patients with gender identity problems on an obvious organic basis, such as sexual ambiguity, should have the benefit of a complete endocrine workup and extensive psychiatric therapy based on the etiology of the problem. Children with diabetes mellitus commonly have emotional problems of varying severity. Inadequate metabolic control may contribute to the emotional problems and vice versa.

It is necessary to realize that, even in childhood, endocrine disorders may present first as behavior or emotional disturbances. The child with excessive nervousness and anxiety or behavior problems and poor school performance should bring to the psychiatrist's mind the possibility of thyrotoxicosis, pheochromocytoma, hypercalcemia, or recurrent hypoglycemia. Suspicion of the existence of these disorders is raised by taking an appropriate history supported by a physical examination. If a metabolic disturbance is considered, these patients should be referred to an endocrinologist for a thorough evaluation.

SUGGESTED READINGS

Adolescent Medicine, The Medical Clinics of North America, *59(6)*, 1975.

ALSEVER, R. N., and GOTLIN, R. W., *Handbook of Endocrine Tests in Adults and Children*, Year Book Medical Publishers, Chicago, 1975.

Disorders of Puberty, Clinics in Endocrinology and Metabolism, *4(1)*, 1975.

GARDNER, L. I. (Ed.), *Endocrine and Genetic Diseases of Childhood and Adolescence*, 2nd ed., W. B. Saunders, Philadelphia, 1975.

GRUMBACH, M. M., GRAVE, G. D., and MAYER, F. E. (Eds.), *Control of the Onset of Puberty*, John Wiley, New York, 1974.

LEVINE, S. (Ed.), *Hormones and Behavior*, Academic Press, New York, 1972.

MONEY, J., *Psychologic Aspects of Endocrine and Genetic Disease in Children. Endocrine and Genetic Diseases of Childhood*, Gardner, L. I. (Ed.), W. B. Saunders, Philadelphia, 1975.

———, and EHRHARDT, A., *Man and Woman, Boy and Girl: The Differentiation and Dimorphism of Gender Identity from Conception to Maturity*, Johns Hopkins University Press, Baltimore, 1972.

WILLIAMS, R. H. (Ed.), *Textbook of Endocrinology*, W. B. Saunders, Philadelphia, 1974.

73 / Note on Organic Brain Syndromes

Richard L. Cohen

Because of the relative confusion about and lack of conformity among terms and diagnostic categories, it is important to say a few words about the significance of so-called "acute" and "chronic" brain syndromes. In the past, it has not been typical for children with these conditions to be part of the everyday office practice of child psychiatry. Most such patients attended clinics, institutions for the retarded, or developmental clinics operated by pediatric hospitals. Due largely to advances in neonatology, the availability of treatment for metabolic and endocrine disorders, and advances in pediatric surgery, the percentage of these children in the general population is probably increasing. This may be influencing the increase in the relative numbers of such patients who are coming to child psychiatrists. The growing relationship of child psychiatric programs to community mental health and its catchment area approach tends to draw in a much wider and more general type of child population. This means that more of these children are being referred to mental health programs for diagnosis and care.

This population falls well within the scope of child psychiatric practice. The responsibilities of the child psychiatrist for such patients cannot and should not be avoided or assigned to others.

In summary: GAP[1] has the following to say concerning acute brain syndromes:

. . . they may also be subclinical . . . with subtle disturbance in awareness or mildly stuporous states, withdrawn behavior, or irrational fears. Perceptual motor difficulties may persist for some time even if complete recovery occurs rendering the child more vulnerable to learning difficulties upon return to school in the absence of persistent brain damage.

Preexisting or underlying psychotic, psychoneurotic, or personality disorders may be made more manifest after such insults to the central nervous system while reactive disorders or later developmental deviations in cognitive or other areas may result from their impact and reverberations . . . [pp. 264–65]

Concerning chronic brain syndrome, GAP[1] has the following to say:

. . . Many children with chronic brain syndrome are not significantly retarded in intellectual development; they often show significant learning difficulties, however, and they function at a mentally retarded level with psychological and social factors playing a contributory role . . . [p. 266]

REFERENCE

1. Group for the Advancement of Psychiatry, Committee on Child Psychiatry, *Psychopathological Disorders in Childhood: Theoretical Considerations and a Proposed* *Classification*, vol. 6, no. 62, Group for the Advancement of Psychiatry, New York, 1966.

---

74 / Note on Special Procedures for Assessing Familial Group and Other Interpersonal Dynamics

Richard L. Cohen

This is an appropriate point to mention that many diagnosticians do not consider some of the following procedures "special."

Most child psychiatrists are family oriented or family centered in their clinical practice. A minority, however, diagnose and treat childhood disorders almost exclusively by means of family-centered techniques. Since this does not represent the usual practice in the field, it is not presented here as a routine procedure. There are other procedures such as home visits, observation of the child in school, and group diagnostic procedures (that is, adding the child to an existing, ongoing, open-ended patient group for the purpose of diagnostic study) which in some settings may be considered rather "routine." But the field, in general, does not perform such studies as standard operating procedure. In the hands of many practitioners these are powerful diagnostic techniques. Some, indeed, such as family diagnostic interviews, are by now the subject of a massive literature. It is of interest that much of this writing is not child oriented. Historically, diagnostic procedures with families have not evolved in a form which identifies the child as a discrete and specific individual, nor have they developed methods which help to understand the child's development in relation to the overall family matrix. There are some exceptions, however. Child psychiatrists have been hard at work developing such an approach, and one example of this thinking will be presented within this section.

In such a clinic, the diagnostic family interview involving children is carried out not only on a routine basis but as the initial step in the diagnostic process. Whether or not this is the usual practice in any given setting, there is much to be learned from the basic concepts and principles outlined by such a practitioner.

Often, the decision to employ a family diagnostic interview is made selectively, or differentially. Before considering the procedures to be described, perhaps it would be useful to state some of the more common indications for the use of such an interview on a selective basis. One indication arises when the nature of the family structure and dynamics has not emerged clearly from other types of interactions with the child and parents. There are a number of sequences that should alert the examiner to the possible need for a family diagnostic interview. Thus, having examined the status of the child's development, he may be left with significant questions about the relationship between it and the overt, stated child-rearing practices of the family, the apparent resources (or deficits) for child rearing, the mechanisms for decision making in the family (particularly with respect to the care of the children) and the way in which the adults in the family have their affectional needs gratified.

There are three general "categories" of families which make family interviewing particularly rewarding and informative.

SEVERAL TYPES OF PATHOLOGICALLY ORGANIZED AND DYSFUNCTIONAL FAMILIES

Scapegoating. Although this phenomenon can usually be identified by appropriate developmental interviewing, at times the nature of the unconscious conspiracy against the identified patient is such that it can only be recognized through direct observation. Most often, of course, it is the most vulnerable member of the family (the identified patient) who is being scapegoated despite apparent efforts to support, protect, and reassure him. This may occur in many subtle forms which can best be identified by observing the family interaction.

The "Symbiotic" Family. This is more easily recognized in the case of younger children. With adolescents, or when the symbiotic relationships involve two adults in the family, this may quickly come to light during a relatively brief family interview as the very presence of the examiner begins to threaten the family equilibrium.

The Power-oriented/Litigious/Paranoid Family. In this situation, there is usually one very dominant parent. This individual may "go along" with the decision to seek aid for a child while carefully and often unconsciously sabotaging all efforts either to clarify the nature of how decisions are made in the family or what the source of disturbance may be. Such people are usually surrounded by an aura of unlisted telephone numbers, references to attorneys, cameras, tape recorders, and multiple crises involving real or imagined offenses by neighbors, school teachers, welfare workers, and others. On individual interview, this parent may appear to be entirley reasonable, comfortable, and in some ways the strongest and healthiest family member. Within the context of the family interaction, what may be observed rather quickly is a process of oppressive tyranny in which the other family members by nonverbal compact agree to organize themselves in such a way as to maintain the sanity and social acceptability of their most deviant member.

FAMILIES WHOSE SOCIOCULTURAL BACKGROUND
DIFFERS IN A MAJOR WAY FROM THAT OF THE
MAJORITY OF CLINICAL TEAM MEMBERS

Many of these issues were discussed previously in relation to the individual examination of the child. However, some of the diagnostic pitfalls may not be encountered until the family is seen as a unit. There are two common examples which come up in clinical practice in large urban areas. These involve:

The Very Wealthy, Influential, and Powerful Family (the VIP Family). The examiner should be alerted to the possible need for a family diagnostic interview when it becomes difficult to have much contact with the parents because they are constantly traveling for social, political, or business activities which make them unavailable. During the interviews with the child, this is confirmed by a review of the life style of the family. Also, the receipt of expensive gifts, telephone calls from political figures who may have some control over funding the clinical facility involved, offers of special favors or social invitations to important events—all of these should indicate the possibility that this family's style for achieving a desired outcome involves much manipulation and, often, subtle contempt for those individuals at the other end of the process.[2] During the diagnostic sessions, it is not important to attempt to change this although one should certainly not become a party to it. The important issue is to determine to what degree these practices have entered into child rearing. They may be playing an important part both in what the child has learned about dealing with significant others and how the child has organized his own defensive structure to deal with the unpleasant, the unwanted, or the uncomfortable aspects of learning, achievement, and human relationships.

Conversely, serious diagnostic problems arise as well with those at the opposite end of the socioeconomic spectrum. This is not so strange, for here it is critical to learn techniques for manipulating others and for extracting that which is desired from an essentially ungiving environment.

In both of the preceding instances, the basic diagnostic issue is that the professional is dealing with an interactive system that has developed coping strategies for manipulating perceived power in social institutions. These modes of dealing with the environment may have become very significant forces in the child's life; unfortunately, they may also jam or disguise certain aspects of the diagnostic process.

THE DISORGANIZED OR MARKEDLY
DEPRIVED FAMILY

Perhaps one might view this as a subset of the aforementioned type of family at the low end of the socioeconomic spectrum. Diagnostically, however, there are important differences. This type of family tends to be much more alienated. Its members experience a sense of powerlessness and harbor deep doubts that *any* solutions to problems may exist at all, either in themselves or in the environment. Indeed, they are convinced that their problems and value systems cannot and will not be understood. In many ways, these situations present the most difficult diagnostic problems.[1] One approach that is often helpful is to have within the team at least one member of each of the various minority groups in the community. Such a "bridging" person may attempt to "translate" and help to interpret for his colleagues the sometimes meaningless, often infuriating and frustrating behavior of the alienated family. The opportunity to view the family as a group, even though it may be disorganized and chaotic, often tends to make this much more real for the middle-class or upper middle-class clinician. Where it is especially helpful is the assist it can give to his efforts to understand the impact of this family experience on the child's development.

With the above as a general introduction to the subject, it is now useful to consider a more explicit statement of family diagnostic interview.

REFERENCES

1. SCHIFF, M., and KALTER, N., "The Multi-Problem Family Presents in a Children's Outpatient Psychiatric Clinic," *Child Psychiatry and Human Development*, 6:233–243, 1976.

2. STONE, M. H., "Treating the Wealthy and Their Children," *International Journal of Child Psychiatry*, 1: 15–46, 1972.

75 / A Child-centered Family Diagnostic Interview

Alberto C. Serrano

Introduction

The *family* diagnostic interview can play a major role in evaluating the identified child. Its structure can best be presented by describing a typical, step-by-step interview showing not only the "how to," but the "why." However, the preparation, construction, and interpretation of such an interview must be understood within a total perspective. The description of the procedure is the most direct path to delineating this orientation: In diagnostic assessment and in establishing a base for treatment, it is most helpful for the clinician to interview the child with emotional and behavioral difficulties in the context of his family.[9]

The complexities of emotional, behavioral, and learning disorders cannot be explained by a single theoretical model or in terms of a unique etiology. The members of the traditional orthopsychiatric team divided up the family, and each studied his aspect of the case separately. This often resulted in a failure to integrate theoretical concepts, or to explain how symptoms emerge.[3] To study those symptoms in isolation is to miss the opportunity of understanding them in the transactional context in which they most often appear.[4]

In the course of a family diagnostic interview, the child can be observed as a part of a whole. Such an approach begins to underline his individual rights as a human being.[10] He is recognized not just as "the problem;" he is a component within a larger context.[4] Although his symptoms are frequently a reflection of family dysfunctions, typically the child is neither victim nor victimizer.

To see the child and family interact provides the diagnostician with "here and now" information and insight. It is within the basic social matrix of the family that the child is developing, learning to feel, to think, and to perceive the world around him; it is from this source that he draws his instrumental and emotional support. The symptoms of his difficulties appear most commonly in the context of his everyday family life; he is affecting the family and it is affecting him continuously.

When he works this way, the diagnostician has the opportunity to see many of the complaint behaviors in *statu nascendi*. He can observe how each member of the family interacts with the others. These observations provide the most relevant information in the ecological context in which the symptoms appear. Observations about the physical appearance of the family members, sitting positions assumed around the room, and all verbal and nonverbal behaviors during the session provide invaluable insight. Additionally, it is possible to begin assessing which symptoms may relate to family interactions and to extrafamilial transactions, in contrast to more purely intrapsychic difficulties in the child and in family members.[1]

When we include the child with his family in the *initial* interview, an additional benefit may accrue: The child may become aware that he has not been previously discussed with the therapist and "judged," and that his individual rights are respected.

The Need to Clarify the Clinician's Role and that of the Family Before the Diagnostic Interview

For the first family session, the invitation is extended to those members who live together. This includes the younger children[10] and any other relatives or significant others who play a relevant role and who are willing to participate in the interview. It is important to explain that all members of the family are invited because their help is needed in order to understand the problem. A positive approach is presented to solving mutual concerns. Each member's individuality and his role in relationship to the problem will be recognized.

Resistance to participate in a family session is likely to occur. It is often necessary to reassure everyone that the "well" siblings will not be contaminated by the experience, but will have the opportunity to participate in solving a problem that inevitably affects them. When resistance is encountered, it is useful for a therapist to make a phone call explaining the procedure and describing what will be an information gathering, non-accusatory experience. A reluctant father will often respond positively to a call from a male staff member.[5]

In the phrasing of the invitation, it is important to create the least additional pressure on the referred child. The emphasis should be that the interview is a joint effort to solve a problem of mutual concern. This facilitates the other members of the family engaging in therapeutic work, and reduces the tendency for them to feel threatened, used, or discarded.

Some Unique Aspects of the Clinician's Role and Attitude in Interviewing Families

It is hard enough to learn how to diagnose and treat individuals. When clinicians undertake family assessment, their roles become more complicated. Usually, the family in distress has authorized them to examine only their "problem child." It is tempting for the beginner to try to diagnose parental pathology or to point at other aspects of individual and family dysfunction on the basis of fragmented information or hearsay. While the troubled child is the initial key concern, we should equally be committed to the understanding of his basic social context. Should we fail to do this, we may be unwittingly reinforcing further "scapegoating" of him.

There is another hazard in store for the clinician: Facing an entire family is frequently intimidating. It is a natural group with a past, present, and future—with powerful interlocking relationships and loyalties. Frequently, the family sees the referral symptoms as alien to the family economy even though, on subsequent clinical observation, they may be recognized to be stabilizing. Often, family members project the blame for the problem on the referred patient, or on extrafamilial causes or may blame themselves or each other. In order to gain trust, the clinicians should be participant observers while remaining respectful of existing family and individual boundaries and defenses.[5]

It is important to learn to become comfortable with the sheer numbers involved and with the pressures to give quick solutions or to act as a referee. It is very important to be flexible with procedures; to retain a sense of humor and to use it wisely; and above all, to have the courage to maintain objectivity as the family exposes itself and pressures to arrive at simple solutions increase.

The Advantages of the Use of a Clinical Team

It is characteristic of work with families that the complexities that arise from the need to understand more than one individual make this an extremely difficult task for a single clinician. The multiple transferential problems encountered under these circumstances can be dealt with far more readily by the use of multiple clinicians. Teams may include psychiatrists, psychologists, social workers, nurses, and/or other professionals and paraprofessionals, depending on clinical and training needs.

The team approach is most frequently used as a model for training, with a senior clinician being paired with a trainee and acting as a model and a "live supervisor."[6] The use of a team provides a "stereoscopic view" of the family and lends opportunity for a division of labor while the clinicians have an opportunity to monitor each other. One clinician "acts as a triangulating agent between the other one and the family."[8] An ideal team that offers a climate of smooth collaboration can provide a model of openness, respect, and comradeship.

It is of special value for children and adolescents to witness adults who are able to deal openly and honestly with their feelings and who, in their agreements and disagreements, recognize and respect individual differences and opinions.

The intent is to create an atmosphere of openness, informality, freedom, and permissiveness, while maintaining firm boundaries. The ideal office should provide a "living room atmosphere," including comfortable chairs and a small sofa. For younger children, soft toys, a pad and crayons should be available.

From the time family members walk into the room, they will demonstrate a wide range of telling verbal and nonverbal behaviors. Clothing, appearance, attitude, posture, seating arrangement, gestures, eye contact, initial family alignments, physical and emotional closeness and distances are but a few of them. Who looks sad, angry, afraid, indifferent, apathetic, or happy? Where does the identified patient sit? What is his attitude? Are his behaviors age typical in terms of his physical, emotional, intellectual development, and sociocultural status? How does he relate verbally and nonverbally with each family member? And to the interviewer? It will be most useful to notice the differences with individual interviews. What about parents and siblings? Is any significant member absent?

The following sequence was observed within five minutes of a first interview and illustrates the quick flow of transactions.

Tom, age eight, was brought to the clinic with complaints of immature behavior, extreme jealousy of younger brother, and enuresis. As the family enters the office, Tom sat on a sofa very close to his mother.

Father chose a chair opposite to them while John, the four-year-old brother, moved around the room freely and provoked Tom verbally and physically. As Tom responded with similar behaviors, his father became tense, explaining that John's conduct was playful and cute. Tom, on the other hand, was accused of being too harsh, lacking a sense of humor, and of being immature. At this point, mother started to cry and blamed herself for having overprotected Tom. Father then sank in his chair looking tired, discouraged and started to talk about his long working hours.

Structuring the Family Diagnostic Interview

During the brief social phase of welcome and introductions, it is useful to structure the experience by explaining to everyone present an outline of the diagnostic plan. For most families, it is a new experience to meet as a group with relative strangers to discuss personal problems openly. Everyone is likely feeling tense and uncomfortable.

Usually, at least one-and-a-half to two hours are needed for an initial family assessment.[5] This will provide enough time for an opening family conference (of about forty-five minutes) to be followed by conjoint and individual sessions. An individual interview with the referred patient is most useful but it may be scheduled for a different time. It is useful to spend at least a few minutes in a closing family session to summarize preliminary findings and recommendations for further care.

In guiding the initial conference, the interviewers must recognize the boundaries of authority, of role, and of function within the family matrix, with particular emphasis on the identified patient's role in the family politics.

Much tact and caution should be exerted in the course of exploring what and how much the family members are willing to reveal in front of each other. The index child is probably accustomed to having difficulties discussed "behind his back" or "over his head." Encouraging the family to discuss what they perceive to be the problem areas in his presence may be a novel experience for him; often it is a reassuring one.

Alice, a seventeen-year-old girl with a history of drug abuse, immature behavior, and suicidal tendencies initially resisted a first meeting with her parents and younger siblings. At the outset, the family blamed her for all their unhappiness. Soon further exploration revealed long-standing marital difficulties and the presence of disturbed behaviors in several family members. These could not be explained solely as reactive to Alice's pathology. While this mobilized considerable anxiety and discomfort in the family. Alice experienced surprise and reassurance. She knew that she was not the only "sick" one, but now it was out in the open.

After some initial reluctance, most families open up and start defining their complaints. Typically, as this interactional phase begins, one of the parents will become the spokesperson. Sometimes, that person finds it difficult to speak, not only in front of the index child, but with other children who may allegedly be unaware of the situation. This parent can be reassured that there will be opportunities for confidential discussion; at the same time, openness is to be encouraged and all family members should be invited to interact, and help to define problem areas. Participating siblings and significant others often reveal crucial material.

Mary was Alice's fifteen-year-old sister and the "well sibling." She was described as sensitive, bright, conforming, helpful to family, teachers and friends. She was said to be happy, strong, successful, mature, and having no problems. Mary revealed long-standing feelings of depression, anger, and frustration. She stated that for years she had covered for mother in housekeeping activities while the latter spent considerable time doing volunteer work in church and civic organizations. Meanwhile, she reported that father would be isolated and read voraciously in his room. The younger sibs depended on Mary for meals, clothing, tutoring, discipline, and most parental responsibilities. Much to the shock and dismay of her parents, Mary announced in tears her plan to move away from home. Alice's problems seemed less unique now that other aspects of family disorganization became more manifest.

It is important to keep in mind that as the family discusses the problem, the index child will be on the "hot seat."

When the interviewer invites the family to present the problem, it is typical for a parent to become the spokesperson and to recite all of the "charges" against the nominal patient. He already knows that the family would not be seeking help if it were not for him. At this point it is helpful to redirect the dialogue to other members in the expectation of opening up more information about structure and function of the family. When it is obvious that the family is "ganging up" against the index child, the clinicians need to be alert to provide support for the child. He should be assured that the clinicians are interested in hearing his views in front of his family, but that he will also have a chance to discuss them in a separate individual session. It is important to convey the idea that while dealing initially with the symptoms presented by one family member, the clinicians are also interested in all aspects of family structure and functioning.

Younger children often express themselves mostly in play and action, which adds a most useful dimension.[10]

Suzy, age twelve and the oldest of four, was described by her mother as selfish, undependable, and rebellious. During the session, Jimmy, who was about one year old, fell off a low chair and started to cry. Mother continued on the same subject while Jimmy called on Suzy, who quickly responded by taking good care of him. Further exploration revealed that this was not an unusual behavior. Without Jimmy and the presence of the five- and eight-year-old siblings, this relevant information may have been missed.

What generally emerges is the gradual unfolding of historical material as a result of the family-clinician interaction. This process is preferred to any attempt to obtain a formal chronological history.

Presently, a more open expression of feelings begins to take place, thus increasing the tension. The clinicians can then witness how each member deals with emotions, and recognize family and individual patterns of defense against anxiety. As defenses soften, one gets a clearer picture of the role of the index patient and the significance of his symptoms in the context of the family structure and function. His individual developmental uniqueness can be seen in better perspective. It is often possible to obtain enough background history from the parents to explain their ability or inability to provide adaptive support at the appropriate developmental phases. How able was this family to provide the basic instrumental and emotional tools to facilitate mastery over developmental phases? How were individuation and differentiation handled by each member? Areas of fixation, arrest, and regression can now begin to be recognized. These may be more prominent in the index patient but can now be noticed in other family members as well. Conflicts between family members now become manifest.[7]

It is useful to look at the family as a basic social system with three subsystems: (1) parent-child; (2) marital; and (3) sibling. In three-generation families we need to add two more subsystems: (4) grandparent-parent; and (5) grandparent-grandchild. To recognize functional and dysfunctional patterns in each of the subsystems is of great significance. While chaotic, disorganized families frequently present deficits in many areas, most families are functional in one or more of the subsystems. Symptoms are likely to be prominent primarily in one area, typically in parent-child relationships or marital relationships.

Discrepancies, incongruities, and new historical data soon shed further light on the referring problem. Care should be exerted not to extend too rapidly the focus of intervention beyond the family's level of readiness to engage with the team in the helping process. Since the family, typically, comes because one of its children presents behavioral, emotional, and/or learning difficulties, it may want help "just for that."

As other problem areas start emerging, intervention should reflect respect, concern, openness, curiosity, and some humor, although never at the family's expense. Team members become facilitators, go-betweens.[11] They help bridge differences between family members. They must continue checking with each other all the while to share impressions and feelings.

Side-taking, confrontation, and interpretations should be reserved for later intervention. Paraphrasing Ackerman, tickling the family defenses can be a most effective means of exploring their readiness to mobilize healthier adaptive patterns and of assessing treatment potential.[4]

Frequently, the child and other family members will find that the pressure of the discussion becomes unbearable, and will start to cry or to express feelings openly. Many emotions unfold including anger, sadness, guilt, confusion, tenderness, excitement, and often a fear of loss of control. Often this triggers some active confrontation among the other family members as well. Parents may take polarized positions attacking or defending the index child. Alliances and coalitions along or across generational and/or gender lines may become manifest. Frequently, family secrets are revealed. At the same time, existing and potentially healthy adaptive resources often start to be recognized.

When an initial family session has lasted about forty-five minutes to one hour, it then usually reaches a point when problem areas are more clearly defined, and tension is sufficiently mobilized to facilitate considerable catharsis later in individual interviews.

It is very useful to follow the initial family interview by separate interviews with the index child and the other family members.

The index child has seen the interviewer being fair to all parties, giving each a chance to communicate openly without focusing on him and without being judgmental. Knowing that what the therapist knows is not all hearsay encourages him to be more open and gives the doctor more credibility. Often the child is observed to behave at a different developmental level compared to that which he demonstrated in his interaction with his family.

John, a ten-year-old child, was described as immature, playful, and enuretic. He was a chubby, overanxious boy who talked in a childish, whiny voice in the presence of his parents and siblings. In the individual session, he was calmer, and could discuss self, family, and school and was able to function as a developmentally mature, bright ten-year-old boy. He seemed interested in assuming responsibility for his enuresis and asked about possible treatment.

The individual interview with the referred patient serves several purposes. It meets one of the requirements for a formal diagnostic evaluation. It also provides the child with a private opportunity to discuss his views about the problems. Confidentiality is an important issue. The clinician should use a careful balance of clinical judgment, tact, and honesty in order to protect individual trust, while maintaining the integrity of the family. As a conseqeunce, considerable energy should be deployed to encourage the patient to share selective information with family members. This will facilitate bridging communication gaps, furthering possible avenues for negotiation. Trust in the therapist can be maintained as he attempts to avoid creating new family splits. The discretion and clinical judgment of senior team members often provides a model for less experienced clinicians.[6]

Individual interviews with parents and siblings, and other separate conferences for various boundary considerations, are arranged for according to family structure and the team's impressions. Often it is useful to see siblings together before seeing the index patient in a separate interview.

Closing the Family
Diagnostic Interview

At this point, convergence of views should have developed, with the integration of information gathered from various sessions, along with the intake data and reports from referring sources, school, and family physician. Clinicians may meet by themselves or with a supervisor consultant. In sharing impressions, feelings, and recommendations, it is typical for the less experienced clinicians to be overwhelmed by the overload of information obtained verbally and nonverbally in their contacts with the family. They regularly get "sucked into" the powerful dynamic forces of the family and identify themselves with different members, often with the symptomatic child. Examination of the countertransference typically produces a "gut awareness" that is most useful in the effort to understand clearly how the dynamic equilibrium of the family affects all its members. The manner in which the index patient contributes through deviant behaviors to the maintenance of the disturbed equilibrium also needs emphasis.

A young trainee recommended at the conference that the parents be confronted with the "normality" of their fifteen-year-old girl's behavior and the need to grant her more freedom. She had discussed with him that all she wanted was freedom from an arbitrary and restrictive father. The resident was identifying with the girl before recognizing the following: (1) mother admitted that she had undercut discipline for years covering up for the children for fear of her husband's reaction; (2) the girl, by her own admission, has been drinking heavily, had used several drugs, and was sexually active with a number of older boys.

The girl's discussion of her deviant behaviors provided some excitement for mother's monotony and kept father actively involved with the family even if it was only as a policeman or a rescuer. The father admitted that had he not felt that his presence was essential to provide some discipline, he would have left the family a long time ago.

When the diagnostic team meets again with the family, one of the major tasks is to find ways of negotiating change. This is best done through family members who may be more willing to break the now predictable patterns. It is crucial to assess their readiness and willingness to change before moving into a treatment phase. Strengths and weaknesses in the family structure and in the functioning of its members are now more clearly understood. The referral symptoms now have gained multidimensional significance. Scapegoating mechanisms are more obvious. It may become evident to key family members that the initial contract in which they brought one individual to be changed was inappropriate. This awareness may evoke feelings of depression and guilt, with family members taking turns at blaming themselves. The significance of historical and environmental factors acquires a better perspective.

After participating for almost two hours of significant interaction with the team, the family members have typically experienced a new awareness of their difficulties in the climate of respect, honesty, and openness. The symptoms they brought have become more understandable and are frequently "owned" by several or by most family members. This does not apply of course to those cases where a key family member suppresses essential information, hides some agenda not uncovered until it is too late, or engages in dishonest manipulations while intimidating other family members. In such a case, the cautious use of confrontation and interpretation is indicated and may precipitate a crisis of therapeutic value.

It is wise to hold a team debriefing shortly after the family leaves. This serves the purpose of diagnostic clarification, mutual support after a difficult encounter, discussion of team interaction and of family and individual dynamics with senior consultants and supervisors. It should clarify the planning for further diagnostic work, treatment, or disposition.[5]

A major question in assessing a child's behavioral and emotional problems is to determine to what extent the findings represent purely intrapsychic phenomena and to what extent they are interpersonal and relate to the child's family ecosystem.[3]

Henry, a black seven-year-old boy, was brought to attention because of immaturity and slow developmental progress. In his family, the "role" which was asigned to him was that of "baby." He was fulfilling it admirably. While it might have been tempting to blame the parents for reinforcing immature behavior, it was important to recognize the active participation of the child, including his temperament, the presence of developmental lags, and perceptual deficits.

Additionally, the family interview helps to clarify the ways in which the family reacts not only to a particular index child but also to the other siblings. How sensitive are the parents to the basic developmental needs of the children or of a "different" child? Do they expect him to think and perform beyond his developmental level? Or on the other hand, do they "baby talk," underestimating their children's capacity to reason and will for themselves or state their own feelings?

Some Final Remarks

The family diagnostic interview provides a framework for the correlation of the events of family growth and individual development at each stage of the life cycle.[7] While "thinking family" is most useful, clinicians must bear in mind that they must not limit their competence to family intervention techniques. Proficiency and flexibility in the use of a full range of diagnostic and treatment approaches is mandatory in child psychiatric practice.

REFERENCES

1. Ackerman, N., "Family Psychotherapy and Psychoanalysis: The Implications of Difference," in Ackerman, N. (Ed.), *Family Process*, pp. 5–18, Basic Books, New York, 1970.
2. ———, "Family Therapy," in Arieti, S. (Ed.), *American Handbook of Psychiatry*, vol. 3, pp. 201–210, Basic Books, New York, 1966.
3. Auerswald, E., "Interdisciplinary Versus Ecological Approach," in Ackerman, N. (Ed.), *Family Process*, pp. 235–248, Basic Books, New York, 1970.
4. Framo, J., "Symptoms From a Family Transactional View Point," in Sager, C. J., and Kaplan, H. S. (Eds.), *Progress in Group and Family Therapy*, pp. 271–308, Brunner-Mazel, New York, 1972.
5. Serrano, A., "Multiple Impact Therapy with Families—Current Practical Applications," in Hardy, R. E., and Cull, J. G. (Eds.), *Techniques and Approaches in Marital and Family Counseling*, pp. 143–158, Charles C Thomas, Springfield, Ill., 1974.
6. Serrano, A., "Introducing Medical Students to a Family Psychiatry Orientation," published in Proceedings of the Nathan Ackerman Memorial Conference, Cumana, Venezuela, Family Process Editorial Board, 1974.
7. ———, et al., "Adolescent Maladjustment and Family Dynamics," *American Journal of Psychiatry*, 118(10):897–901, 1962.
8. Whitaker, C., and Napier, A., "A Conversation About Cotherapy," in Farber, A., Mendelshon, M., and Napier, A. (Eds.), *The Book of Family Therapy*, pp. 480–506, Science House, New York, 1972.
9. Williams, F., "Family Therapy," in Marmor, J. (Ed.), *Modern Psychoanalysis*, pp. 387–406, Basic Books, New York, 1968.
10. Zilbach, J., Bergel, E., and Gass, C., "The Role of the Young Child in Family Therapy," in Sager, C. J., and Kaplan, H. S. (Eds.), *Progress in Group and Family Therapy*, pp. 385–399, Brunner-Mazel, New York, 1972.
11. Zuk, G., *Family Therapy: A Triadic-Based Approach*, Behavioral Publications, New York, 1971.

76 / Note on Other Diagnostic Settings

Richard L. Cohen

The Home Visit

This, of course, is a modification of the family diagnostic interview. The rationale clinical technique for conducting the child psychiatric home visit have been well described by Freeman.[2]

Freeman's contribution should be reviewed in the original but its salient points will be outlined here.

There is no question that a home visit consumes much time (particularly because it always involves travel). However, when used selectively, it may eventually conserve time because it may disclose important data difficult or impossible to obtain through other procedures.

According to Freeman, the most frequent indications for a diagnostic home visit include:

1. Examination of the very young child who may regress markedly in a hospital or clinic setting.
2. Examination of a child whose fearfulness or uncontrollable behavior in the office may make reliable observations very difficult.
3. Persistent parental reports that the child "is very different at home" (for example, the child may be reported as quite verbal at home but mute in the office).
4. Examination of a child with a major physical disability.
5. Examination of one or more (usually older) siblings who either refuse or cannot participate in office visits for some reason.
6. Observation of a very complex and/or atypical family system (for example, index family may live with a part of a more extended kinship system in the latter's home).

Contraindications to home visiting may exist either when prohibitive travel is involved, or when parents are excessively suspicious and view the visit as invasive of privacy.

Salient issues involved in clinical technique emphasized by Freeman include:

1. Proper preparation of the family and the identified child patient.
2. Rational discussion of fee involved for professional time extended.
3. Realistic allotment of time needed to conduct the observations.
4. Avoidance of participation by more than two clinicians.
5. Timing of session to ensure availability of all family members.
6. Avoidance of on-site note taking.
7. Dealing soundly with offers of food and meals.
8. Use of the opportunity to observe directly child-rearing practices, sleeping and play arrange-

ments, other sources of family stress or reward, etc.

Finally, the home visit will often provide an opportunity for the family to demonstrate its strengths and its resources. For many families this is more difficult in the rather artificial and problem-oriented environment of the clinic or hospital.[4]

Group Diagnostic Procedures

A child may be observed in a variety of groups, but the use of patient groups for diagnostic purposes with children has not had an extensive overview in the literature. Nonetheless, use of group diagnostic procedures is worthy of mention. As early as 1965, Churchill[1] was reporting the use of group diagnostic techniques in a child guidance clinic with interesting results. Understandably, the logistical problems of assembling the "right" group of children in time and place, and the amount of preparatory work which always goes into forming, organizing, and physically providing the necessary environment for the group, make it a procedure which may be too cumbersome for most settings.

In the procedure described by Churchill, comparatively little emphasis is placed on an analysis of group process. The group merely provides the milieu "in which pertinent observations can be made," and the primary concern is the individual within the group. The goal of such a diagnostic group is to evaluate problems of each member as they present themselves in relation to their peers. These groups were established with no more than six children usually within two years of age of each other and of the same sex. It was felt that a by-product of the diagnostic group procedure was to give the resistant child a greater sense of acceptance by the clinic. Much emphasis was placed on preparation of the child and family. The usual procedure involved four diagnostic contacts each with its own format rather carefully structured. The information gathered was descriptive and impressionistic in nature with the emphasis on: (1) relationship of each child to the group; (2) relationship to the adult conducting the interviews; and (3) evidence of the child's knowledge and use of social skills. The literature continues to be rather sparse in this area but it does seem a promising one and merits further investigation.

The Use of Hospitalization for Diagnostic Purposes

The admission of a child to a psychiatric inpatient setting or residential treatment center is always a move to be pondered carefully. On occasion, this option may be turned to in the service of completing a diagnostic study. Although there are a great variety of indications and uses for institutionalizing a child, the major indications for hospitalizing a child for diagnostic purposes are listed briefly here. For a fuller discussion of the theoretical issues involved, the reader is referred to an excellent paper by Rose and Sonis.[3]

Specifically, one should give serious consideration to brief hospitalization as a means of clarifying a child's diagnostic picture when one or more of the following conditions obtain:

1. There are instances when even careful history taking, examination of the child, and the use of family diagnostic interviews are not enough. They leave the examiner with significant questions concerning the impact of the family's current dynamics on the clinical picture presented by the child. Another way of stating this is that there is something about the child's role in the family's emotional economy that continues to remain obscure. When this occurs, it may be possible to clarify the answers to these questions only by removing the child temporarily from the family context, and then observing both child and family under these altered circumstances. There is an additional advantage to be gained from following this course. One can study the child in a novel environment, a setting which does not respond to him in the modes to which he has become adjusted.

2. Occasionally the various reports concerning the nature of a child's behavior and adjustment are altogether diverse, incompatible, and conflicting (these may even include impressions collected during the child's current diagnostic assessment). It may be concluded that diagnosis is impossible without an extended opportunity for reliable observation. This in turn leads to a decision to place the child in a more controlled and structured environment where he can be observed by several trained clinicians over a twenty-four-hour cycle for several days.

3. Following a period of therapeutic trial on a given modality (or several modalities) of treatment, it becomes clear that significant progress is not being made. The clinician may conclude either that the treatment requires "fine tuning," or that there is some reason to question the original choice of modality. This is often the case in the use of psychoactive agents. Sometimes there is reason to suspect that the medication is not being administered according to

directions. A brief period of hospitalization may then be warranted in order to "stabilize" the patient, to adjust the treatment efforts, and to reassess the original treatment decision. Since the treatment is ordinarily administered on an ambulatory basis without hospitalization, the use of the inpatient setting is primarily for assessment purposes.

REFERENCES

1. Churchill, S. R., "Social Group Work: A Diagnostic Tool in Child Guidance," *American Journal of Orthopsychiatry, 35:*581–588, 1965.

2. Freeman, R. D., "The Home Visit in Child Psychiatry: Its Usefulness in Diagnosis and Training," *Journal of the American Academy of Child Psychiatry, 6:*276–294, 1967.

3. Rose, J. A., and Sonis, M., "The Use of Separation as a Diagnostic Measure in the Parent-Child Emotional Crises," *American Journal of Psychiatry, 116:*409–415, 1959.

4. Tearney, A. I., "Nursing Assessments—Screening for Developmental Problems. I. Home Visit as Related to a Diagnostic Clinical Evaluation," in Krajcek, M. J., and Tearney, A. I. (Eds.), *Detection of Developmental Problems in Children,* pp. 1–5, University Park Press, Baltimore, 1977.

PART D

Case Formulation and Management

77 / Case Formulation and Treatment Planning

Richard L. Cohen

The precursor of all science is magic. It is therefore not surprising that the prehistory of treatment planning in child psychiatry is steeped in irrational appraisals and unrealistic expectations of what moral, educational or religious measures might accomplish. The first logical step to treatment planning is adequate diagnostic evaluation and historically the same causal connection holds. It was only after the child had been recognized as a psychological entity in himself and prone to a wide spectrum of psychological disturbances that subsequent therapeutic strategies could be envisaged and brought into action. . . .[4] [pp. 531–532]

Introduction

The above quotation is drawn from what is probably still the most complete and definitive effort to analyze the case-formulation and treatment-planning process in child psychiatry. This 140-page monograph published by the Group for the Advancement of Psychiatry in 1973 is recommended to all students of this field for careful study and critical thought. Although one may differ with it in detail, in sum it remains the most careful and thorough approach to this most intricate step in the total diagnostic process. The subsequent discussion will make frequent reference to this monograph.

Again, the consideration of this area requires mention of the now-familiar caveat. The clinician's identification with a specific ideology or with one highly favored treatment modality can act as a potentially limiting and constraining as-

pect to his freedom of choice.[1, 3, 5, 6] For instance, if one begins the formulation process with the bias or assumption that the child has no emotional life separate from the adults who care for him and that his behavior can be understood and changed only within the "family system," then a systems approach to management based on some variation of family therapy is almost a foregone conclusion. Conversely, if the treatment of choice for a child is almost always assumed to be the resolution of internalized conflict, then this will slant the priorities for treatment in the direction of individual psychotherapy.

Case formulation and treatment planning are a ritualistic sham if one does not begin from a polytherapeutic position. In fact, in the modern practice of child psychiatry, there are at least a dozen or fifteen "modalities" of treatment which can be employed judiciously, singly or in combination, with a reasonable expectation of helping. Again, to quote from the 1973 GAP Report:[4]

Differential treatment planning consists of selecting, in order of priority, curative, corrective, ameliorative or palliative approaches to a child patient, his family and when needed, his extended environment . . . [p. 546]

The indications for each modality of treatment are included in volume 3 of this handbook which should be considered a companion piece to this effort at explaining formulation and treatment planning.

When that "special moment" arrives which leads the clinician(s) to conclude that there are now enough objective data with which to formulate diagnostic judgments and make recommendations, then a careful and deliberate cognitive exercise must ensue. In order to formulate and to make recommendations, obviously, one does not need to know everything. Indeed, a good part of the information collected may not necessarily be relevant to decision making and recommendations. However, this is usually apparent only after the fact. The information is not useless; it simply does not need to be included in this part of the process. Later in the course of actually carrying out the treatment, it may prove to be extremely valuable. In any event (just as there are therapeutic aspects to the diagnostic process[7] for many families), the diagnostic process does not stop with the inception of therapy. One must always assume that new data will appear as the treatment process proceeds. Optimally, these will impinge on the "internal guidance system" and lead to adjustments, fine tuning, and subsequent modifications which will keep the treatment process "on course."

TEAM DYNAMICS

Volumes have been written about the dynamics of team interactions in child psychiatry.[2, 9] These dynamics are always at work, but they come into play with particular intensity during the decision-making process. Once more, the reader is referred to GAP Report No. 87 for a well thought-out examination of this team process.*

Much can be said in favor of democratization of the team process. This implies an adequate opportunity for *real* input from all those clinicians who have been in contact with the child and family. Clearly, their various disciplines and skills are invaluable and provide the broad repertoire of capabilities necessary in many situations. Much can also be said for a system that assigns final authority to one clinician with whom the "buck stops." Needless to say, the effectiveness of any team system in carrying out a diagnostic process is a function of many things. It reflects the soundness of the administrative organization within which it is structured, as well as the members and their sense of mutual respect for each other. No team process is productive when the narcissistic needs of one or more team members interferes with the deliberate and careful winnowing of information within a previously agreed-upon format for arriving at definitive recommendations.

* See chap. 5, "Dynamics of Small Group Planning," pp. 560–571.

There are many systems that can be effective. The constituency of the team needs more to be determined by the needs of the case than the table of organization of the mental health facility where the family is being seen.

The Diagnosis and Treatment Plan

As a rule, a diagnosis is "made" and a formulation is constructed on several levels. In part, this relates to the original purpose of the diagnostic workup. Usually, however, both the diagnosis and the "action plan" need each to be thought out on at least two levels.

DIAGNOSIS

A nosological diagnosis needs little justification. It is not only required, but desirable. It is important for communication within the team, between facilities, and for public health purposes. Although it condenses too much and involves many oversimplifications, its very shorthand is an important aspect of conducting professional practice.

A dynamic/developmental formulation is essential both for an understanding of the needs of the child and family and for the development of a treatment plan. Only rarely are treatment plans tied to diagnostic labels.

TREATMENT PLAN

In the best of all possible worlds, for each case there would no doubt be some ideal or highly desirable treatment plan which might be carried out. Sometimes, this would require basic changes in the character structure of the parents, as well as alterations in the economic, social, and political forces at work within the institution involved and within the community. Ultimately it goes beyond the realm of the merely ideal and enters into the kingdom of the grossly unrealistic.

In brief, the actual or real treatment plan finally agreed upon is, in the nature of things, a compromise. This is true whether it is happening in the mind of the solo clinician or among team members. This end product of the balancing of needs and possibilities is then communicated to the patient and his family, and to the referral sources.

Reduced to its most simple terms, one hopes to

emerge from the formulation process with reasonable answers to the following questions:

1. What, if anything, is wrong?
2. What are the resources available within the child, in the family, and in the community that could be mobilized to address the problem(s)?
3. What course of action should be recommended to each?

To answer these questions, however, the clinician needs a conceptual framework into which he can place all of the pertinent and useful data he has collected. Many such formats exist. It is more important to choose one that is sensible, comprehensive, and with which the clinician can be consistent and comfortable than it is to attempt to find the universally satisfactory format with which all could agree. If the developmental frame of reference is accepted as basic, then it should constantly be referred to in constructing the final framework.

In his excellent monograph on examination of the child, Simmons[8] suggests the following:

1. How sick or impaired is this child?
2. In what areas of his functioning is his impairment manifested and in what areas does he function well?
3. Is there any past or present evidence that the central nervous system is not functionally intact?
4. What psychosocial factors in his past life have probably contributed to the problem?
5. Which psychosocial factors in his current life continue to contribute to his problem or are apt to be an impediment to recovery?
6. Which of the factors under questions (2), (3), (4), and (5) is it imperative to change in order for improvement to occur?
7. Are there factors under questions (2), (3), (4), and (5) which are perhaps not essential for change in the child's presenting symptoms, but which the clinician would desire to change for the general well-being of the child?
8. What methods, if any, can be used to effect the desired changes noted under questions (6) and (7)?

Other equally sensible and useful approaches are available in the literature.

The format recommended here is not represented as unique or original; it has borrowed from many important contributors, including Simmons. However, it does seek to be sufficiently broad to cover almost all situations. In particular, it provides the kind of agenda that compels the team's attention to the decision-making process. To illustrate the way the outline works, case material will be presented from a specific diagnostic workup. Hopefully, this will demonstrate how the material may be pulled together in a concise and organized fashion.

The Diagnostic Outline

1. A demographic summary which highlights socioeconomic factors, family structure, and the child's ordinal position in the family and other related factors.
2. The *functional* description of the difficulties which the child is presenting to himself or to his environment.
3. Contributory information concerning the nature of the child's constitutional endowment (temperamental characteristics, congenital abnormalities, intellectual functioning, etc.).
4. Past and current contributory health and other contingencies (if there are multiple contingencies, a life/time flow chart is often helpful at this point).
5. Family, kinship, and social support systems indicating both assets and liabilities.
6. In the light of the child's chronological age and development stage, a listing of his major functional assets and liabilities (for example, self-care, cognition, task performance, problem solving, social skills, etc.). This should include a statement about where he may be significantly "off the track" with respect to anticipated developmental status. In other words, the salient findings of the mental status examination would be noted in this section.
7. In the event that significant dysfunctioning or developmental lags are identified, a compilation should be made which lists the most important priorities for stimulating, modifying, or supporting development in order to arrive at more modal levels.
8. A description of any significant difference between the priorities identified for change by the family and those listed above. If there are, can these be reconciled?
9. The method(s) of choice for most expeditiously effecting the above changes.
10. An attempt to identify the resources necessary to effect these changes, either within the current treatment facility or elsewhere in the community. If not immediately available, are they obtainable anywhere within reason?
11. In the event that the most desirable resources are not available, a suggestion for an acceptable contingency treatment plan.
12. Differential diagnosis.
13. Outlook or prognosis.

To illustrate the manner in which such a formulation outline may be used in practice, table 77–1 is presented. Obviously, no single case can encompass all of the advantages and disadvantages of a particular approach. The format may need to be modified for various clinical settings and for cases which present special or unusual features.

The discipline involved in completing this kind of formulation for each case is in fact a rewarding educational exercise for all concerned. More than that, it tends to provide some guarantees

TABLE 77–1

1. A demographic summary which highlights socio-economic factors, family structure, and the child's ordinal position in the family and other related factors.

Harry L. is an eight-year-old, white Roman Catholic boy, the middle of three children. There is a ten-year-old sister and a brother who is five. Mother is twenty-nine, a housewife, and father is thirty-two, in partnership with his uncle. They own and operate a supermarket. Family lives in the suburbs of a large urban area. Family is in the upper middle-income bracket. They own their home and each child has his own bedroom. Harry attends an all-white public elementary school where he is currently repeating second grade. Father completed two years of college and dropped out to enter military service, completing a tour of duty in Vietnam. Mother completed one year of college and dropped out to marry and raise a family.

2. The *functional* description of the difficulties which the child is presenting to himself or his environment.

Patient referred for evaluation and disposition by family physician with the following complaints:
1. Though intelligence appears above average, Harry is failing in most second-grade subjects for the second time.
2. School attendance is sporadic, with the absences apparently related to a series of vague somatic complaints and multiple family crises.
3. He is described as very restless, fidgety, and impulsive.
4. There has been frequent stealing, mostly noted at home; rarely in school.
5. He displays immature speech, and is hard to understand when excited.
6. Marked sibling rivalry is present accompanied by both verbal and physical abuse.
7. Peer relationships are deteriorating because of aggressive behavior and impulsivity.
8. Atypical eating habits. May skip a meal, then eat excessively; many food fads; "carbohydrate hunger" (can eat two-pound box of candy and then ask for ice cream); eats large amounts of powdered soap mix without water.

3. Contributory information concerning the nature of the child's constitutional endowment (temperamental characteristics, congenital abnormalities, intellectual functioning, etc.).

Harry was born weighing 2,945 grams; after a 39-week gestation; his length was 19½ inches. The 1 minute Apgar was 8 and 5 minute Apgar was 10. Pregnancy described as medically uneventful, but extremely stressful for mother because of family and marital problems. Mother states she was in "a constant turmoil" and fears this had a bad effect on the fetus. Baby described as very active and "unpredictable." Always has had low threshhold to stimulation. Prevailing mood, cranky and irritable. Easily frustrated and very distractible.

He cannot grade responses, and appears non-reactive to emotionally charged situations or over-reacts.

Psychometric testing reveals a high normal IQ of 108 (FS) with a verbal quotient of 111 and a performance quotient of 105 (Bellevue-Weschler Test). This score was attained only with constant support and encouragement by examiner because Harry was so easily frustrated.

Psychoeducational evaluation reveals no signs of specific learning disability but rather a generalized deficit in all academic areas (for example, calculation, number concepts, reading comprehension, etc.). The conclusion of the examiner was that Harry had almost "none of the tools required for second-grade performance."

636

TABLE 77-1 (*Continued*)

4. Past and current contributory health and other contingencies (here a life/time flow chart is often helpful if there are multiple contingencies).

Physical examination and routine laboratory findings have been and are currently well within normal limits. No history of serious illnesses or operations. Though child terrifies parents by getting into medications and playing with dangerous tools, has never had an accident. Possible metabolic disorder (suggested by abnormal carbohydrate intake) investigated through pediatric endocrinology consultation. All findings negative.

Family physician placed Harry on methylphenidate 5 mg. t.i.d. eight months ago without noticeable change in behavior or school performance.

5. Family, kinship and social support system indicating both assets and liabilities.

Intact family with mother present and assuming primary caretaking role since patient's birth. Mother reared by natural parents. Paternal grandparents killed in auto accident when father was ten. He was then reared by aunt and uncle (with whom he is now in a business partnership). Parents are very inconsistent with Harry, vacillating between excessive permissiveness and harsh discipline and deprivation (latest threat is to put him up for adoption). Although there is an extensive kinship system on both sides of the family, this has not been supportive of child rearing. There is strong antagonism by mother toward father's family and vice versa. Mother sees father's family as "closed and clannish"; also she suspects them to be dishonest in business dealings. Feels that uncle has cheated father and exploited him in supermarket operation. Father decided to enter this business shortly after conception of Harry; this caused major crisis in marriage. Constitutional characteristics of patient were interpreted by mother to mean that Harry would be antisocial, unreasonable, and "mean" like father's family. These same traits led father and his relatives to predict that Harry would be slow and underachieving like mother's family. Through entire eight years of patient's life, parents have been receiving "advice" from both families concerning how best to "cope" with Harry. Most of it has been contradictory and unrelated to this child's actual needs.

6. Taking into consideration the child's chronological age and developmental stage, what are his major functional assets and liabilities (for example, self-care, cognition, task performance, problem solving, social skills, etc.). This should include a statement concerning in which of these areas he may be significantly "off the track" with respect to anticipated developmental status.

1. When confronted with a novel situation, Harry's initial response is to expect to be overwhelmed. He handles this either with regression or bravado.
2. He tends to select out some special aspect of the environment as potentially attacking, and focuses his efforts on evading or "tricking." He is usually so preoccupied with this that he cannot absorb the total gestalt of a situation and appears flighty or intellectually dull.
3. Harry's understanding of the diagnostic interviews was that he was bad, stole things, lied, and hit people; and that his parents expected the examiner to "do something about it."
4. Self-concept is poorly differentiated and that which *is* defined is seen as defective ("rotten").
5. Inanimate objects are perceived appropriately and used with age-appropriate skills.
6. Temperamental characteristics have been described. In one-to-one interaction with an adult, activity level decreases and attention span is moderately longer.
7. Mood variable and unpredictable, ranging rapidly from depression to elation.
8. Fantasy life largely occupied by thoughts of

TABLE 77–1 (*Continued*)

violent aggressive behavior toward adults, with impunity for the perpetrator. Often the "helpless" child acts as an agent provocateur tricking adults into attacking each other.

9. Much impulsive behavior, often non-goal directed.
10. Views self as inferior to peers; tends to buy acceptance with material gifts or attempts to impress them ("our plane was hijacked when we were coming back from Florida"; "Jerry Lewis is spending the weekend at our house").
11. Speech indicates excellent capacity for symbol use, good syntax, but very immature with respect to articulation.
12. Ethical concepts quite immature; all wrong-doing should be summarily punished by extreme measures. No distinction between minor infractions and capital offenses.

Projective testing: Confirms the above clinical observations emphasizing Harry's "preoccupation" with the dysphonic and the devaluated. Associations never portray real people but witches, skeletons, etc. Testing results "not typical of a child with sensory-perceptual deficits despite his apparent hyperkinesis."

7. In the event that significant dysfunctioning or developmental lags are identified in the above area, what are considered the most important priorities for stimulating, modifying or supporting development toward more modal levels?

1. Patient's prevailing dysphoria and defective self-image require prompt attention.
2. Capacity for self-organization, impulse control, attending and grading of responses should be high priority.
3. Patient needs a wider repertoire of defenses, especially capacity for identification with authoritative, dependency gratifying adults.
4. Cognitive skills require age-appropriate maturation.
5. Speech is also not age-appropriate and requires corrective attention.

8. Is there evidence that there is a significant difference from the above in the priorities identified for change by the family? If so, can these be reconciled?

First priority for mother appears to be conformity with (her) social norms and assurance that Harry will not prove to be the "bad seed" she has anticipated from birth on.

First priority for father appears to be more socially acceptable aggression and achievement by Harry. Father's basic concern is that patient is "slow" and "will never accomplish anything." Only a therapeutic trial will answer questions concerning possible compatibility of parental goals.

9. What would be the method(s) of choice for most expeditiously effecting the above changes?

This case requires a complex team approach including: individual psychotherapy for the child; intensive parental (perhaps leading to marital) counseling; if feasible, the above should be combined with family therapy sessions. The use of pharmacotherapy should be reexplored. Dosage of methylphenidate may have been too low or incorrectly timed. If this medication is not effective, dextroamphetamine or pemoline should be tried. A special education class with a one to four or five teacher-pupil ratio is required; teacher should be certified to work with "socially and emotionally maladjusted"; this child has a general educational deficit. Corrective speech therapy is indicated.

10. Can resources to effect these changes be identified within the current treatment facility? Elsewhere in the community? Anywhere within reason?

All of the above resources are available within reasonable distance from family's residence.

TABLE 77–1 (*Continued*)

11. What would represent an acceptable contingency treatment plan in the event that the most desirable resources are not available?	Although all resources are available, parents may not be ready or able to participate in the management plan described above. In that event, residential treatment for Harry would be an acceptable alternative.
12. Differential Diagnosis.	1. Character Disorder of Childhood 2. Depression of Childhood 3. Borderline Psychotic Reaction 4. Hyperkinetic Syndrome 5. Learning Disability, Generalized 6. Speech Disorder, Dysartheria
13. Outlook or Prognosis.	Probably only fair with treatment. In the absence of intensive intervention, poor.

that treatment facilities are being differentially employed and that the clinician and his colleagues are not falling into automatic or stereotyped responses to certain symptom complexes.

Changes Which May Occur During Diagnostic Process

A few concluding remarks are in order at this point. First, it sometimes happens that, in the course of a diagnostic study, marked changes occur in the symptom picture. When this does occur, the clinician should not assume that such sudden symptom improvement or even apparent return to health is necessarily dubious. It does not always represent the classical "flight into health" engendered by a heightening and reorganizing of defenses. Sometimes, there are genuine therapeutic effects that flow from the diagnostic process itself. For some families who are not very disordered or disorganized, the "simple" process of reexamining the development of the child and all of the factors which have fed into it proves very insightful; without any direct intervention on the clinician's part, it provides them with a sense of inner direction and purpose which they previously

lacked. In this connection, GAP Report No. 87 remarks:[4]

> The planner must constantly bear in mind that whatever one does for a patient—whether it is giving him an appointment, listening to his complaints, evaluating him or planning his treatment—is likely to improve his general contact with the world at large and bring about some improvement in his behavior or functioning. . . . [p. 548]

When a mother has worked very hard on participating in the kind of developmental interview described above, it is not an uncommon experience for her to tell the examiner that she is feeling better about the child, has a much clearer understanding which she can now articulate of what needs to be done, and is not requesting any additional professional assistance at this time.

Conversely, there are families for whom unrealistically prolonged diagnostic planning processes or extended periods on the waiting list may prove antitherapeutic. Several studies indicate that a significant number of children and families either improve or do not change at all on the waiting list, but as many as a quarter may be expected to worsen significantly. At times, overextended resources may make these delays unavoidable. It is important, however, not to contribute to the delay by allowing team dialectics to go on for weeks prior to arriving at a definitive plan.

REFERENCES

1. BAHN, A. K., CHANDLER, C. A., and EISENBERG, L., "Diagnostic Characteristics Related to Services in Psychiatric Clinics for Children," *Milbank Memorial Fund Quarterly*, 40:289–318, 1962.

2. CUNNINGHAM, J. M., "Problems of Communication in Scientific and Professional Disciplines," *American Journal of Orthopsychiatry*, 22:445–456, 1952.

3. FREEMAN, R. D., "The Home Visit in Child Psychi-

atry: Its Usefulness in Diagnosis and Training," *Journal of the American Academy of Child Psychiatry, 6:*276–294, 1967.

4. Group for the Advancement of Psychiatry, *From Diagnosis to Treatment: An Approach to Treatment Planning for the Emotionally Disturbed Child,* vol. 8, Report No. 87, 1973.

5. KURTZ, R. M., WEECK, A. A., and DIZENHUZ, J. M., "Decision Making as to Type of Treatment in a Child Psychiatry Clinic," *American Journal of Orthopsychiatry,* 40:795–805, 1970.

6. LESSING, E. E., and SCHILLING, F. H., "Relationship Between Treatment Selection Variables and Treatment Outcome in a Child Guidance Clinic," *Journal of the American Academy of Child Psychiatry, 5:*313–348, 1966.

7. MEYERS, H. L., "The Therapeutic Function of the Diagnostic Process," *Bulletin of the Menninger Clinic, 10:*9–19, 1956.

8. SIMMONS, J. E., *Psychiatric Examination of Children,* Lea & Febiger, Philadelphia, 1974.

9. STAVER, N., and LaFORGE, E., "Intake as a Conflict Area in Clinic Function," *Journal of the American Academy of Child Psychiatry, 14:*589–599, 1975.

---

78 / Interpretation Conference and Communication with Referral Sources

Richard L. Cohen

The ingredients of the study as they have been described in the preceding chapters may appear extremely complex and all too long. It is in the nature of some cases brought for diagnosis that this is truly unavoidable. In most situations, much of the necessary information can be collected from referring sources ahead of time, and the developmental interview and examination of the child can be managed rather quickly. After the interviews are complete, unless specialized studies are indicated, there is little excuse for not getting to the interpretation conference with the family within a matter of a few days or, at the most, a few weeks. The more extended the team, the more cumbersome and awkward the decision-making process may be; nonetheless, it is the responsibility of the clinicians to avoid prolonged delays.

If possible, both parents should attend the conference. Awkward situations may arise if parents are divorced or separated. In a surprising number of instances, however, it is possible to bring parents together physically for a joint interview. A realistic (and not guilt-producing) appeal is made to them in the name of clear communication, the need for open and honest participation by both parents in planning for the child's future, and the importance of having both parties present when questions are asked by the other parent. Unfortunately, there are situations in which it is impossible for both parents to be together. When they are both still significant factors in the child's life, it may be necessary to conduct separate interpretation interviews.

The issue of whether the child should be present and participate in such an interview should be discussed by the team. Unless there are clear contraindications, adolescents are routinely included. With younger children, individual decisions must be made based on the child's capacity to participate in a joint session, his level of verbal skills, and his capacity for conceptualization.

The question of staff representation at an interpretation conference with parents is relatively simple, but here, too, there are a few caveats to bear in mind. Parents should not be overwhelmed by a covey of high-powered professionals. Even though a sizable team has been involved in the assessment, it is usually enough to have present the clinician who had the primary contacts with the parents and the one who did the psychiatric evaluation of the child. Exceptions to this occur when there are findings of a highly technical or specialized nature which lie beyond the general areas of knowledge of the two primary clinicians. This might occur in the event of unusual electroencephalographic findings, biochemical studies, or neuropsychological findings which emerged in the course of investigating a learning disability. Even so, it may be best to have this "specialist" present for only part of the interpretation interview, not the entire session. It is most important to have the child's primary clinician present and not to assume that the parent's clinician can present and interpret all of the findings. Even if this is technically true, most parents need the experience of interacting directly with the clinician who examined the child. They need to know firsthand that this is an interested, committed, and empathic person who seeks basically to support them. He is not an adversary, nor is he allied with a hostile or alienated child (who may even have misrepresented the clinician following his examination—a not uncommon occurrence). The surprising readiness of some parents to accept statements from the child that "Dr. Jones thinks you ought to get off my back" (or similar attributions) should be borne in mind; indeed, they should be sought out actively during the conference and dealt with sensitively.

Usually, one interpretation session is adequate although it is difficult to plan its length exactly. In most instances, the amount of time which needs to be spent in interpreting findings and communicating recommendations is not so much a function of the complexity of the case or the child's clinical picture. It tends rather to reflect the level of overall family dynamics, parental resistances and defenses, and the degree of flexibility or rigidity of parental personality structure.

The goals of the interpretation conference should be few in number. Indeed, in most instances, they are self-evident. These include:

1. The achievement of genuine understanding on the part of the parents concerning the nature and significance of the findings which have been uncovered in the assessment process. One should not expect their grasp to be complete, or comprehensive, or laden with insight; but they should expect to achieve at least the beginnings of this process.
2. The identification of parental resistances and defenses should continue (this work would ordinarily have been initiated during other parts of the assessment). If the recommendations for management seriously threaten family homeostasis, these defenses are likely to come into bolder relief as the interview proceeds. It is, of course, not enough merely to identify these resistances and defenses. The clinicians must begin to come to grips with them in the session (with direct confrontation as a last resort) because implementation of the treatment plan is not likely to occur without this.
3. The achievement of some commonality of purpose. There is often considerable lip service given to this during the early parts of the assessment before the true dimensions of the problem emerge. Toward the end of the assessment process, commonality of purpose is put to the acid test. The parents who have come only to have the child's behavior altered, or his impulse life laundered, or his IQ raised 40 points may not have been able to give voice to this intent

until the final act of this diagnostic drama. The beginning of this commonality cannot occur during the interpretation conference. It must have its roots in the first contact or first telephone call. All communications and all actions must be aimed at conveying a supportive posture to the parents, one in which they can see the clinicians as individuals that they can enlist in problem solving, and, perhaps most important of all, as individuals who have the ability to comprehend the nature of their experience in rearing this child, and what it is like to live with him currently. Such a stance cannot be achieved by a process of conning, or seduction, or inappropriate reinforcement of behavior which is tension reducing for the parents but disruptive for the child. The process reaches its peak in the interpretation conference. The parents are presented with a *tentative* plan for management (with the understanding that it is not finalized). It is made clear that their input into it, their reactions to it, and their final veto over it are all basic to the process. The older child must be included actively as well, must participate in the decision making, and must have some conviction about the soundness of the actual plan.

The content of the interview: In the nature of things, this must vary widely. It is important to remember that parents who have waited anxiously for "results" need clear and unequivocal statements about the findings (even though the conclusions may be all too unequivocal). It is unwise to attempt to use the interpretation conference as an experience in which the solutions to problems will be "extracted" from parents by some open-ended, nondirective technique. Rogerian interviewing has its proper place. The interpretation conference is not that place.

If the assessment process has been a relatively protracted one or there are indications that rapid changes are taking place, it is usually wise to begin the conference by asking the parents whether there are any new developments, whether any additional information has come up which they have not shared previously, and whether they can tell anything about the child's responses to his own examination(s). Although this is sometimes nonproductive, in a surprising number of instances the parents will come up with information that is most informative. The child's verbal responses to his own sessions may add a previously unavailable dimension to the diagnostic picture. The parents may have observed a marked symptomatic change in the child since his professional contacts (which they perceive either as marked improvement or worsening of symptoms). Some major change in the family may have occurred which alters the support system considerably.

Clinicians may be shocked or amazed to find that the parents have already made other arrangements for the child (for example, a total change of school setting or the introduction of parallel arrangement for testing). They may represent this most innocently as an expression of their parental responsibility for the child by manipulating his environment, or by "getting another set of opinions." No clinican should come to the end of an interpretation conference only to find that other intervening life events have descended upon the family or have been introduced by the family actively without his knowledge, so that now many of his recommendations are either irrelevant or untimely. If humanly possible, such information should be elicited at the beginning of the interview.

Having proceeded thus far, the clinicians should then *summarize* the important information they have elicited about the child both from the patient directly (without quoting him) and from collateral sources; and they should summarize their understanding of the significance of the material collected from the parents in the developmental interview (without extensive parroting back of historical sequences).

It is most important to avoid diagnostic labels, technical jargon, exact numerical values (whether of intelligence quotients or laboratory studies), or other similar information which can have little genuine value to the parents and which runs the risk of being misused or fed into some as yet unidentified defensive system to create greater problems later. Parents who press for such technical information should not find the clinicians readily and passively acquiescent; on the other hand, it is foolish to engage in power struggles over such details. It is important to clarify with the parents what they want the information for, what they plan to do with it, how they will use it, and of what help it will be to them. It is important to stop frequently along the way and invite questions since parents may have difficulty in assimilating all of the information at one sitting; amid the welter of information that is being exchanged, they may forget the most significant questions of all.

For most parents, the most meaningful information is usually couched in developmental terms which do not need to be technical or highly sophisticated. For example, children between the ages of three and five are always struggling for the achievement of certain developmental gains. The clinical picture which the child is presenting is invariably related to partial or total failure in the mastery of these developmental tasks. In simple direct terms the parents need to know what the child is struggling with and, to the best of the clinician's knowledge at the time, what factors (be they constitutional, intrapsychic, intrafamilial, societal, etc.) may be interfering with successful mastery and gratification. It is this kind of language that best sets the stage for the development of a treatment plan. Moreover, it helps parents clarify in understandable terms how they may participate directly in altering the balance of stresses that surrounds the child.

All along the way, the presentation of findings should be peppered with a due recognition of the strengths in the child and in the family. This needs to be done without fawning or sugar coating but with a clear communication to the parents that the early professed interest in both assets *and* liabilities has been a real one, and that these have been taken into consideration both in establishing the diagnosis and in formulating recommendations. The importance of this latter point cannot be overemphasized too strongly. Almost all parents coming for aid with their children are defensive, sensitive, and guilty. Extreme caution needs to be exercised to avoid shaming, exposing, or devaluing parental investment in the child.

Generally, about midway through the session, it is inevitable that the parents will inquire what can be done about the situation; what are the recommendations of the clinicians and, in effect, "Where do we go from here?" To be sure, they must have a full opportunity to make their own suggestions and to react to recommendations. However, if the clinicians have done their homework properly, they should have no hesitation in tying their "treatment plan" to the information they have already shared with the parents concerning the child's developmental status.

Often, it is at this point that the interview assumes its full dynamic force. It is important to remember that only about 40 percent of prescriptions written by physicians are ever filled. Some studies suggest that of the 40 percent which are filled, even fewer are administered in the form and according to the routine the physician directed. One could speculate endlessly about the significance of this information; in sum, it is probably safe to say that no treatment plan is likely to be carried out very effectively unless the parents "take possession of it."

To quote from the GAP Report No. 87:[2]

. . . Resistance to the reception of the message can arise from lack of clarity or empathy in the sending, or as we more often expect, it can arise as the receivers defend themselves against the message whose import they fear. . . . The planner must believe that the treatment plan belongs to the family and that an effort is being made to give it over to them. . . . The planner can only advise—the family can consent, demur or confiscate. The planner's message may be received as sent or it may be lost, stolen, strayed or received with distortion. [p. 589]

It is not unusual for parents to press for absolute answers and clear-cut specific directions. In some cases, it is possible to make *some* definitive statements and to give *some* directions. When such luxuries do exist, they should by all means be enjoyed. For instance, in certain hyperkinetic syndromes, the use of certain kinds of psychoactive drugs is clearly indicated. To be sure, this does not encompass all of the problem; it is not a total solution. However, it is important, definitive, and clear-cut; the parents are given specific directions on how to handle the medication with the child and with the school; they are told what kinds of side effects or adverse reactions to watch for and what to do about these. This kind of assertion of medical knowledge is comforting to the parents, and not unrealistic. However, it is not the usual state of affairs. More often than not, no absolute statements can be made about etiology, management strategies, prognosis, or length of treatment. Whatever is said in these areas usually carries with it a number of qualifying phrases which, to say the least, the parents are likely to find disconcerting. However, it is better to support them in their anxiety than it is to allay the anxiety artificially with cookbook answers. The GAP monograph states eloquently:[2]

. . . The less there is to say, the more important it is not to say too much. This is an axiom and as useful as most axioms. The more confused the facts, the less clear the alternatives, the simpler the presentation must be. However obvious this may be, it is difficult for the most experienced of planners to remain silent while a family cries for absolutes and an end to the balance between "on the one hand—and on the other." The more serious the pathology, the simpler the central facts should be made. The seriousness of the pathology can be stated at once and then dealt with descriptively, or the implications of an initial statement can be developed gradually over several sessions. . . . [p. 595]

The following case illustrations may be of some assistance. They do not necessarily portray the most typical situations encountered during an interpretation conference; however, they arise with sufficient frequency as to warrant a state of heightened alertness on the part of the clinician. In the nature of things, individual countertransference phenomena will make any given interpretation conference much more difficult for some clinicians than for others. However, the following four "types" seem to pose difficulties for most, and illustrate some of the finer nuances of conducting such conferences successfully.

PARENTS WHO ARE "SHOPPING"

Often, prior to the interpretation interview, one or both parents will have given several cues that they approach the assessment with a fixed set of biases concerning the nature of the child's difficulty. Equally often, they will have kept secret their previous contacts with other mental health professionals or medical specialists (justifying this behavior on the basis of their wish to acquire yet one more "independent judgment"). If in fact the original assessment left them in doubt, or without confidence in the professional skills of the initial examiner, there is nothing amiss with parents seeking one or more independent judgments about a child. Indeed, they might be remiss if they failed to do this, and this obviously is not the issue. What is most characteristic of the "shopper," however, is not the search for an independent judgment; what he is seeking is a judgment which confirms his own conclusions about the child. And this despite any facts which may be uncovered as the assessment progresses. Unless the present clinician wishes to join what may be rather a long line of prior, fruitless clinical contacts, he should assume that it is not enough simply to render one more independent judgment. The fixed and rigid nature of the parental attitudes and judgments about the cause and nature of the child's difficulty should arouse suspicion that the "shopping syndrome" is present. The clinician must then take some steps to deal with this cycle. With some parents, it is effective simply to ask directly whether they have had previous contacts with mental health clinicians about which they were perhaps dissatisfied and haven't spoken. It is not necessary to push them for names, dates, or results. These may be entirely irrelevant to the basic issues. If they can simply acknowledge that they are shopping and that they have been dissatisfied, then the door is open for consideration of the reasons for their discontent. At this point, it is important to shift the interview away from what is wrong with the child and "what the answers are," and to get some definitive understanding with the parents about why they have felt so unsatisfied in the past with professional help and what it would take to reassure them. A very common response is for parents to indicate that they themselves have not been listened to by previous clinicians, and that they are not convinced that their own input has had any particular impact. On the other hand, one may be dealing with a very pathologically organized family (see chapter 74, p. 622) which may need to maintain the child in a "sick" position for the preservation of the existing family equilibrium.

In this instance, it is not so much that the family has not been "listened to" but that it cannot "listen." A variety of defensive forces operating both intrapsychically and within the interpersonal system of the family may make it virtually impossible for them to perceive and to integrate the facts being presented to them about their child.

Where the stresses are internal, the most common defense patterns resorted to involve denial and projection; and where they are experienced among family members, the responses are scapegoating and pseudomutuality. Therefore, professional judgments concerning the causes of the child's problems and the steps necessary for change may be so threatening to the family homeostasis that shopping is inevitable. This should be recognized, but no interpretations which are too directly confronting should be given the parents. Recommendations which require cataclysmic changes in the way the family is organized without allowing for a slow step-by-step process are simply not clinically realistic; indeed, they may actually strengthen the shopping tendency rather than bring it to rest.

It is necessary to get the family to identify clearly its own set of priorities (both in relation to the child and to itself) and to see whether these are "compatible" with the priorities arrived at clinically. They do not need to be identical, only compatible.

Perhaps the most common reason for shopping, unfortunately, is that the parental "questions" about the child have not yet really been heard. Clinicians have been responding to the overt inquiries rather than the secret questions which the parents are either not able to verbalize because of their anxiety or because they are only preconscious.

FAMILIES CONTAINING A "VULNERABLE" CHILD

Green and Solnit[1] have described the "vulnerable child syndrome" in the following manner. The "vulnerable" child has previously experienced some life-threatening illness (later experience indicates that it is only necessary for the parents to have perceived a life threat even if this were not based in medical fact). This past life-threatening situation "attaches" itself to many of the subsequent developmental vicissitudes. Mother and child come to anticipate failure particularly in the achievement of developmental advances. The child senses the mother's belief in his vulnerability, accepts this distorted image, and uses physical symptoms to displace the threat of death to a particular part of the body. Both mother and child become fearful of separation (hence, growth) which is interpreted as dangerous.

This syndrome presents the interpretation conference with particular problems. Here the clinicians are often struggling with a basic motivational problem in the parents. In these situations, all expectation for positive outcome of development has been lost. Instead, there is a pervasive fear of lack of intactness. The parents see the child in terms of basic, innate weakness or defect which makes him particularly vulnerable to stress or change. Such phenomena are all too characteristic of treatment in child psychiatry.[3] Here one is not dealing with some disparity in priorities or goals (as is often the case with the shopping family), but with a conviction that somehow, within himself, the child lacks any capacity for growth or development. The clinician can essay simple reassurance (perhaps repeated once or twice in different variations); he can state that earlier real or perceived insults to the child's health or development at some early stage of life have not left him permanently damaged or inherently weak and vulnerable. If the parents do not respond, then one is justified in assuming that constant repetition of this reassurance will be worthless; that irritation and abruptness will compound the problem; and that the basic outcome will depend on whether parental images and expectations about the child can be altered.

PARENTS WHO ARE PROFESSIONALS

As used here, the term "professionals" refers to one of the so-called helping professions. There are frequent situations where one or both parents are actively employed in working with children and youth in one of the health, education, or welfare career fields. In many instances, this does not present a particular problem but is actually an asset. The parents' sophistication is higher, communication is easier, and they are less defended against the basic concept of working with behavioral and developmental problems in children. When problems do arise, it is usually because parents attempt to substitute their own knowledge system for that of the clinician. They have difficulty shifting roles as they enter the office. With many such parents, a gentle reminder often delivered in a light, humorous vein is quite sufficient. A statement such as "Oh, oh, there you go again playing musical chairs with me; I guess it's tough to switch hats when you know so much about this kind of work yourself" may be quite helpful.

Sometimes, however, it is necessary to be more direct and more firm. The clinician must make it clear that he will not engage in any contest with the parents to determine who "knows more" about the field or even who "knows more" about the particular child in question. As he is with all parents, he is there simply to be of support and assistance, not to "take over."

A surprising number of clinicians overestimate the expertise and knowledge of the professional parent. This can lead to assumptions which cause the clinician to omit or skim over areas which should in fact be discussed in detail. Careful cues must be taken from the parents about how much they need to know or in how much detail they wish to discuss a given area. A certain amount of face-saving behavior is to be expected, and is, indeed, perfectly normal. The professional parent must feel free to indicate what he wants attention directed to in the interpretation conference. Some will admit openly that, despite their expertise, they are bewildered by the current situation and want to be treated like any other parents.

DIVORCED, SEPARATED, OR ALIENATED PARENTS

Certain aspects of this problem have been discussed (chapter 40) in the review of history taking. Those comments will not be repeated here. The interpretation conference, however, raises a few additional issues which are worthy of note.

By the time of the conference, the clinician should have a reasonably clear idea about the differences between the parents (particularly with respect to *this* child). Earlier, these may have been important in the etiology of the child's disorder; now they are critical for planning. The fact that the two parents have incompatible goals for the child must be discussed openly, and the implications of this state of affairs for the child's future development faced directly. Parents need some assistance to "put themselves in the child's shoes"; it is hard for them to understand what it must be like to receive such discordant and incompatible

signals from one's parents about what is acceptable behavior and how one should act. The clinician must avoid becoming a referee or arbitrator of parental differences. To enter into such a pattern would lead him inevitably into an ersatz marriage-counseling role which is inconsistent with the original "contract" established at the outset of the assessment.

Separated or divorced parents will almost always attempt to press the clinicians to "take sides." If one parent is in fact perceived as much more emotionally healthy than the other, there may be a considerable temptation to do so. This is a most dubious procedure. The alienation of either parent by the clinical team may result in total sabotage of the treatment plan; regardless of its original value, this is likely to render it useless.

It is frequently desirable to have the child present for part of the interpretation conference. Often enough, the child is able to verbalize his confusion and conflict to the parents more directly and with more emotional impact than the clinicians could possibly convey. However, the child should *not* be put in the position of having to speak for the clinicians, do their work for them, or become the focal point of conflict in the interview. In the final analysis, the basic issues revolve around one critical question: Despite the conflicts that may continue to exist between the parents, is there enough commonality and overlap of investment and interest in the child to provide a basis for mutual planning for him? If the clinicians hold to this "negotiating base" courageously, and with enough tenacity, then it is possible to set up an effective system of communication between the parents and to implement an effective treatment plan.

Unsophisticated parents may need a great deal of careful detailed explanation about whatever treatment modalities are recommended. At best, these are complex. They may range from simple parental counseling (without direct involvement of the child) to intensive pharmacologic treatment, inpatient (milieu) care, outpatient psychotherapy, family therapy, and other major treatment modalities. Considerable time and effort may have to be invested in answering their questions about what they may expect from such experiences. In addition, the clinicians must anticipate and discuss issues on the basis of already existing knowledge about the family dynamics, parental concerns about the child, and the nature of resources and assets in the family. Even so, it can be expected that only part of this will be heard and that the questions may need to be answered anew, and the various problems dealt with again and again as the treatment program progresses.

One final caveat about the interpretation conference. It sometimes happens that even prior to the assessment, the clinicians know that they cannot be involved in any ongoing treatment. This may come about for many reasons; there may be conflicting time commitments, this may not be their function within the facility, or there may be some other reason. In any case, it is of vital importance to make this explicit at the outset. Some parents may elect to seek assistance elsewhere because they feel continuity of care is important. In any event, it is rather jarring for parents to learn in an interpretation conference that ongoing treatment is indicated for the child and family, but that a whole new set of clinicians will have to be introduced to carry this out. Even though this may be standard operating procedure, it is important to remember that attachments have been developed, transferences exist, some trust and confidence have been developed. In the face of this, such a relevation on the part of the clinicians can easily lead to a sense of abandonment.

Communication With Referral Source

Responsible clinicians respect their sources of patient referrals. This implies not only an acknowledgment early in the diagnostic process (together with a request for whatever additional data gathering may be necessary from the referral source), but *substantive* feedback as well. Family physicians, well-child clinics, school counselors, social welfare agencies, probation officers, and others may each require different kinds of feedback. The referring source may even have been involved at some point in planning the treatment recommendations. If the case is to be referred back to that resource, it is particularly important to include the referring person in the decision making before speaking to the parents in terms of any commitments.

One caveat is important here. Referral sources should not be included actively in planning conferences without the knowledge and permission of the parents or there may indeed be a serious breach of confidentiality. In communicating with referral sources, the whole issue of confidentiality becomes a bilateral matter. This actually proves to be the case in a large percentage of instances.

At the least, this can cause the clinicians some embarrassment; thus they may have used terminology that the parents perceive to be accusatory or derogatory; or they may have shared information with the referral source which was not previously clarified with the parents. At worst, serious damage can be done to professional relationships, and a child in dire need of care may be lost in the shuffle.

Essentially, the letter sent back to referral sources should contain a brief summary of the pertinent findings and a thumbnail sketch of the treatment plan proposed to the parents. If the referral source is to become an active partner in the treatment program or is to assume a major responsibility within it, then a more detailed statement is necessary. The letter should offer the suggestion of explanatory telephone conversations to follow, or of one or more face-to-face meetings if there are additional questions.

Confidentiality laws and the legal rights to privacy vary from state to state. Each clinician should be intimately familiar with the statutes governing such communications in the area where he practices.

The common complaint heard from referral sources is that they have little followup or feedback. Again and again the story is that for years they have been sending disturbed or developmentally disordered children to a certain clinician or a certain facility but it ended there. After that they have not been able to learn much about what happens to the children. Feedback communications serve many purposes. The obvious one is to share pertinent information about the patient. Less evident, but not less important, is the need gradually to educate the referral source about child psychiatry and its related disciplines, and about the agent or agency to which the referrals are being made. Inevitably, this will influence the "quality" of referrals (in the sense that they will become more and more relevant to the service offered). More than that, however, it will affect the quantity and quality of clinical information which accompanies the referral. This important by-product of the educational process will gradually be arrived at over a period of time. Many educational and welfare facilities use their interaction with a mental health practitioner as a kind of staff development process. As a result of these interactions, the sophistication of their own staffs increases and, presently, out of the continuous process of development of their knowledge and skills, the less complex and difficult cases can be cared for without referral.

REFERENCES

1. GREEN, M., and SOLNIT, A. J., "Reactions to the Threatened Loss of a Child: A Vulnerable Child Syndrome," Pediatric Management of the Dying Child, Part 2, *Pediatrics, 34:*58–66, 1964.

2. Group for the Advancement of Psychiatry, *From Diagnosis to Treatment: An Approach to Treatment Planning for the Emotionally Disturbed Child*, vol. 8, Report No. 87, 1973.

3. ROSE, J. A., "The Prevention of Mothering Breakdown Associated With Physical Abnormalities of the Infant," in Caplan, G. (Ed.), *Prevention of Mental Disorders in Children*, pp. 265–282, Basic Books, New York, 1961.

PART E
Special Applications

79 / Direct Consultation on a Pediatric Service

John B. Reinhart

Not infrequently, the child psychiatrist is confronted with the need to evaluate the mental and developmental status of the child who has been hospitalized on a pediatric ward or in a pediatric general hospital. This requires major modifications in many of the principles and techniques which have already been outlined. In particular, it demands the acceptance of a different set of goals for the evaluation (note chapter 58, "Purposes of the Assessment").

—RLC

Child psychiatrists and other behavioral scientists who work in pediatric settings must be aware of the dichotomies that exist in philosophy of care. The focus of attention varies between the extremes diagrammed here:

Body	Mind
Organ—Laboratory	Patient as a Person
Technique	Process
Crisis	Continuity
Action—RX	Listen—Observe
Cure	Care
Life vs. Death	Living vs. Existence
	Quality of Life
Individual Patient	Patient in a Family

The pediatric setting, particularly in the inpatient and emergency room areas, tends to stress those activities on the left side of the diagram; the child psychiatrist and his colleagues tend to stress those on the right. When the child psychia-

trist consults in a children's hospital, he must therefore adapt to a setting where attention is weighted toward the critical care of a child with organic problems, and where immediate answers are sought for extremely complicated questions.

Requests for psychiatric consultation on pediatric patients depend on the ability of the pediatrician or pediatric surgical specialist to be aware of and sensitive to the need for psychiatric appraisal, and the availability of the child psychiatrist for consultation. Just as beauty is in the eye of the beholder, so also is the need for psychiatric intervention. Some years ago, the American Academy of Pediatrics conducted a survey in an effort to determine the role of psychological factors in patients coming to pediatricians' or general practitioners' offices. It revealed that the incidence was reported from 0 to over 90 percent depending on the physician's sensitivity.

In another survey of routine admissions to a pediatric hospital, it was found that at least 50 percent of children admitted came in for psychosocial reasons. But only 10 percent of those admitted had requests for psychological evaluation during the hospitalization. As child psychiatrists and pediatricians learn to communicate with each other, and as medical education tends to stress the importance of psychosocial factors in all patients, the hope for the future is that truly comprehensive care will be available for all patients. Of all the medical specialties, pediatrics is perhaps the most aware and interested in the fact that a child lives in a family and that there is a mutual interaction between that child and his family. Pediatricians can accept the fact that psychosocial factors influence the way a child behaves, psychologically as well as physically. However, the millennium has not been reached and child psychiatrists continue to be aware of the ambivalence many physicians feel toward psychological problems.

The child psychiatrist cannot afford to "lose his cool" and became frustrated under these circumstances. He must accept the fact that other physicians may not be as sensitive or as interested in these aspects of care as he is. At the same time, he must be willing to adapt to the pediatric situation. One must often interview a child or parent on a busy ward or in an emergency room. Equipment, such as toys to facilitate communication, may not be available, and ingenuity is essential. One must be able to respond to emergency situations—as seen by one's colleagues— just as other medical specialists do, and not expect to be specially treated. When it is possible for members of a behavioral science team to be easily available on pediatric wards or clinics, it facilitates communication between ward personnel, physicians, and patients and their families. Ideally, the child psychiatrist's office should be in the hospital and he or she should be easily available to the wards. Tours of the wards, lunch times with staff, and attendance at other pediatric staff meetings makes it possible for pediatricians and house staff to communicate about patients and their needs for consultation. "Out of sight is out of mind" is a rule that governs pediatric consultation services. When a psychiatrist can meet the needs of the physician and his patients, even though complete satisfaction is seldom possible, progress becomes possible. The gradual education of the physician about what behavioral scientists can and cannot do will then proceed.

The role of a psychiatric consultant has been defined as that of a person who should be "of practical assistance in a total evaluation and furtherance of treatment of any given patient."[*] Consultation is an exchange between one physician requesting some form of help and another who seeks to extend it. The consultation process has three phases: (1) the reception of the request for consultation; (2) the gathering of information; and (3) the communication of the consultant's findings.

Among the most common reasons for psychiatric consultation are: (1) when uncertainty exists about the diagnosis and about whether psychological and social factors play a part; (2) the presence of gross problems such as hallucinations or bizarre behavior; (3) "unusual behavior" on the patient's part which makes his care difficult and upsets the attending nurses and physicians; (4) some difficulty in the doctor-patient-family relationship; (5) the family's or the child's specific request for psychological help. Ideally, the physician requesting psychiatric consultation should communicate with the psychiatrist about the reason for the request; in fact, this is seldom done. For many years, medical specialists have made repeated attempts to find the perfect form to be filled out in order to determine what the referring physician had in mind when he requested the consultation. In the busy hospital setting this turns out to be a very difficult thing to do. If the physician requesting the consultation has the interest and takes the time to write a brief note about why the consultation is desired, the psychiatrist's work is much easier to accomplish. The request merely to see "the new patient on ward four" or "that boy for whom we have been unable to find a cause for his abdominal pain" is much harder to honor in any useful way. Consultations are sometimes requested for "emergencies" which turn out on inspection to be less urgent; in fact, true emergencies are relatively few. Yet requests for consultation need to be responded to within twenty-four hours, or, at the latest, forty-eight hours. If not, the patient is all too likely to be discharged or the referring physician to lose interest, or both. A brief contact may be enough to determine if the problem can be postponed and the consultation done on an outpatient basis.

Following are a few case vignettes which will illustrate several of the points.

CASE 1

Susan, age four, was experiencing her sixth hospital admission for vomiting. On her fourth hospitalization she had had a laparotomy which did not explain the vomiting episodes. A history was taken which revealed the fact that the mother had had long-standing anxiety about her ability to rear this particular child. In spite of the many hospitalizations and procedures, the etiology of the child's symptoms remained unexplained. The psychiatrist was able to suggest to the family that the illness was a functional one, and could

* M. R. Kaufman, "The Role of the Psychiatrist in a General Hospital," *Psychiatric Quarterly,* 27:367–381, 1953.

be treated if the child's and the family's anxiety could be allayed. After a rather difficult two weeks for the parents, particularly the mother, with many telephone calls, reassurance, and offers to rehospitalize the child if parents were too anxious to cope with the situation, gradual improvement was obtained.

Pediatricians have much more difficulty in making a functional diagnosis than does the psychiatrist. It is part of psychiatric training to understand and work with psychological factors which contribute to or exaggerate physical complaints. When a pediatrician and a child psychiatrist can collaborate well, comprehensive care is easily afforded.

CASE 2

A patient with anorexia nervosa was being managed on the pediatric ward without difficulty. However, as the evaluation proceeded, the child became more anxious. One evening she removed a bowel movement from her pants and spread it on her house officer's shirt. This strange behavior so upset the house officer that he called the psychiatrist at eleven o'clock in the evening. Because of the house officer's panic, the patient had to be transferred to a psychiatric ward. Unusual behavior or symptoms such as hallucinations or delirium tend to cause more anxiety for medically oriented physicians than psychiatrists. And the converse is true—the psychiatrist is usually more upset by bleeding and other physical symptoms than are most of his medical colleagues. The child psychiatrist in the pediatric setting must help his pediatric colleagues deal with behavioral symptoms and his own psychiatric colleagues deal with their anxieties about physical symptoms.

CASE 3

A nursing conference was requested because of nurses' concerns that an adolescent boy knew he had leukemia. The physician had not talked with him about this matter. The house officer caring for the young man was invited to the nursing conference, the matter was discussed, but there was considerable resistance on the young physician's part to talk with the boy about his illness. However, that evening he did spend three hours talking with the boy and, the next day, the patient was much more comfortable on the ward, much less surly, and much more cooperative.

On a subsequent admission, this patient had arachnoiditis, severe edema, and pain in his feet, probably due to his Vincristine therapy. Many medications, nerve blocks, electro-stimulation, and other procedures were of no avail in treating the boy's painful feet. A new house officer, in an informal hallway consultation, asked about the use of hypnosis to relieve the boy's pain. When he was asked what he knew about the family or the boy's previous history, he was not very knowledgeable. It was suggested to this young house officer that the boy needed a psychiatric consultation in order to assist him in understanding the subjective aspects of the pain. However, the following day, the boy was discharged from the hospital.

Nurses later reported that, by coincidence, the patient was moved from a single room in the hall to a ward near another boy with an orthopedic deformity. The latter was a very aggressive child and became involved in trying to interest the leukemic patient in doing something with him. Initially, the adolescent was angry about the boy's intrusiveness. However, within a matter of hours, he began to be more pleasant, much less of a nursing problem, and his pain diminished. Though the pediatric house officer in the first instance was resistant to talking with his patient, given time he did the appropriate thing and the patient improved. On the second hospitalization, the house officer sensed that there might be emotional factors contributing to the picture, but for multiple reasons did not get a psychiatric consultation. A request for magic, that is, hypnosis, was sought as a quick answer to a most complicated problem, and when this help was not quickly forthcoming, the patient was discharged.

CASE 4

An adolescent male was admitted with symptoms of abdominal distress. An x-ray of the abdomen was taken and a pencil was seen in the area of the rectum. This could not be reached by proctoscopy, and a laparotomy was done, the pencil removed, and a colostomy constructed.

The surgeon, recognizing the boy's need for psychiatric evaluation, requested a psychiatric consultation. The psychiatrist went to the ward to see the young man, but before he had proceeded with his interview more than a few minutes, received notice from the ward nurse that the patient's father wished to stop him from talking with the boy. He talked with the father, who was irate, and the father was referred to the surgeon who had requested the consultation.

It is always wise to be certain that the patient as well as the family knows that a psychiatric consultation has been requested. If, at the onset of the interview, the child or the family professes not to know, it is wise to ask how they feel about such a matter. If there is any objection, it is best not to continue with the consultation but to refer them back to the attending physician. In this particular case, the family's defensiveness about psychiatric intervention was tremendous. Though the surgeon as well as the psychiatrist thoroughly recognized the need for psychiatric involvement, the family was adamant about this not being done.

Whether the child is an infant or an adolescent, the actual interview differs from other examinations of children only in that the setting is the hospital ward. The patient may or may not be physically ill. Depending on circumstances, it may be possible to review the hospital chart, speak to the head nurse or other nursing staff interested in the case, and talk with physicians who have initiated the request for consultation. If the family is available, it is wise to contact them, to ascertain whether they are aware that a psychiatric consultation has been requested, and to find out what their feelings and thoughts are about this. Many times the request is made without the family's knowledge, or they have been informed in only the most vague way. Occasionally, a family may be quite upset to hear that their child has been asked to see a psychiatrist and may object to this. In such instances, the psychiatrist should not see the patient and should refer the family back to the attending physician for further discussion.

When the consultation proceeds, sometimes the patient can be seen in the psychiatrist's office. As a rule, however, the press of time, the inconvenience, and the fact that the child's illness prevents his being moved may require that the interview take place at the bedside. Once the meeting is underway, "everything is grist for the mill," and the behavior of the child with a new adult, another physician, and his dependence or independence of his parents (should they be there) are all data to be noted. One may proceed in many ways. One good way is for the doctor to identify himself by name and to ask whether or not the patient's physician had told him of the visit. Often, this did not occur, and the psychiatric consultation is a surprise not only to parents, but to patient as well. The patient can then be told that the physician is a psychiatrist and asked whether or not he knows what a psychiatrist is. Where the usual answer, "I don't know," is forthcoming, the patient asked to guess what that specialty is all about. Younger patients may be told of a young man who, after a consultation, said, "Now I know

what a psychiatrist is, he's a worry doctor." Pursuing this, the doctor explains that he would like to know if there are any worries which might have caused this patient to have his particular symptom or to have led his parents or his physician to want to have him talk to a psychiatrist. No matter what his age, a brief history should be taken from the patient, touching on how he became ill, why he came to the hospital, what his experiences were prior to the hospitalization, and his ideas as to what might be wrong with him. A history taken from the child may reveal that he is able to identify all of his brothers and sisters except one, that he may talk only about one or the other parent, or other noteworthy observations. If the problem is one of pain, the patient may be asked to describe it or point to it with a finger. He can be given materials and asked to "draw the pain." He may be asked what worries he believes could possibly cause this, and whether or not he would be interested in seeing a psychiatrist or people who work with him in the future after he leaves the hospital.

Where it seems appropriate, a brief neurological examination can be done to confirm previous neurological findings. Mental status can be examined to determine reality orientation or depth of consciousness; and simple intellectual exams or drawing (draw-a-person, house-tree-person) tests may be given. In pre- and postoperative disturbances which affect the body image, the house-tree-person drawings are of great value; the patient can even do this alone in his room and the drawings picked up at a later time.

If the consultation is done on the ward, nurses in training, medical students, and house officers (particularly those caring for the patient) may be welcome to observe these examinations. As a rule, this does not interfere with the examination to any great degree; it is moreover a valuable teaching method and a basis for discussion with those in training. As the residents and interns gain experience and become involved in the examination of the patient, it is possible for the examiner to sit back, to become an observer, and to obtain further data about the patient's ability to interact that does not emerge as readily in the one-to-one interview.

Ideally, it is valuable to be able to see the parents, if only briefly, at the time the child is seen on the ward. As a rule, one does not have the luxury of the time one might have in a psychiatric clinic or in a private office. Nor does one have the easy availability of the social worker, psychologist, and other colleagues at the time of the consultation. These colleagues can, however, be introduced, at least in concept, and arrangements made with the family for further examination on another day, or after the patient is discharged from the hospital. From his standpoint, the psychiatrist will usually be able to give some idea about the seriousness of the problem at this point, and the degree to which psychiatric treatment is likely to be of help. At the same time, he has the opportunity to ascertain the family's ability to understand and to accept psychological explanations of the child's illness and symptomatology.

When the parents are not available, the psychiatrist must depend on the attending physicians or the ward personnel to inform the family about the psychiatric opinion. Again, ideally, a face-to-face discussion of the problem with the attending physicians is of the greatest value. If this is not possible, then telephone conversation may suffice. In any case, a note concerning the consultation must always be written in the patient's chart. Obviously, this must be done with circumspection. On the one hand, if they wish to be understood, psychiatrists simply should not use psychiatric jargon. Most physicians have not had training in this area and will quickly disregard an abstruse and incomprehensible statement. On the other, they must also remember that the medical chart is available to some nonmedical people and that some sense of privacy must be preserved. It is enough to document the presence of "family problems"; the details of interaction between parents need not be described in the open medical chart.

The referring physician wants to know: (1) Does the consultant believe that psychological factors are involved in this case? (2) How serious a problem is it? (3) Is this something that the physician can handle himself, or does it need referral for more complicated treatment? Ideally, something can be said about prognosis. Where possible, there should be a statment about whether or not medications are necessary, or what change in the medical management of the patient is recommended from a psychiatric standpoint. Consultation notes should not be long, for the longer the note, the more likely it is that it will not be read. Where it is reasonable to make definite statements about the nature of the condition and its management, this should be done. Sometimes, however, additional investigation will be necessary. For instance, should psychological testing or further interviews with the parents or child be indicated, this should be indicated and responsibility for such investigation assumed. A telephone call to the physician attending to the patient or communication by way of chart or hospital personnel will usually suffice until more complete notes can be dictated to the referring physician.

In addition to the ward psychiatric interview with the child and with the parents, a consultant in a pediatric hospital should make a special effort to talk with nurses caring for the child or with other personnel on the ward. Any ward aides, dietitians, play and recreation personnel, or teachers who have had contact with the patient will have made pertinent and useful observations. Nursing notes can be of extreme value. The regularity of visits, especially with infants and young children, comments about the parents' behavior in interaction with the nursing staff, and notes about the child's behavior are rich sources of data. Their import can be crucial in formulating recommendations. Typically, nurses will have had a great deal of experience with large numbers of children of that specific age on their wards, and they will have no difficulty in telling the psychiatrist whether or not the child falls within the range of what they consider to be "normal behavior."

Ideally, every pediatric ward should have an assigned social worker who spends a good deal of time directly on the ward, and who maintains an active liaison with the nurses and house officers. Such a person will have a great deal of information; often enough, it is the social worker who suggests the need for psychiatric consultation. There are hospitals where, over the years, the plan is to assign social workers with psychiatric background to medical wards and specialty areas; in this way, psychosocial factors can be considered in the care of all patients. After the patient has been seen in consultation, such social workers can be involved in the continuity of care and help to the patient. They can support his family, and assist the attending physician in getting these patients to other facilities for further psychiatric diagnosis and/or treatment.

The nurse specialist is a pediatric nurse who has training at a Master's level in child development. She is an extremely valuable person in general, and may be of special help in this area. She is trained to make intensive observations of diagnostic import and to continue on with a therapeutic program within the hospital. Such assistance is particularly valuable on surgical wards around such problems as amputations, iliostomies, correction of scoliosis, or other surgical procedures which involve change in body image. These highly trained personnel also render valuable aid in the management of children who have chronic physical illness or disability such as leukemia, cystic fibrosis, or diabetes.

Once a consultation has been completed, it is important to remember that the patient "belongs to the attending physician and not to the consultant." If a recommendation is made for further psychiatric intervention in the form of extended diagnostic work or treatment, its implementation is still a decision that the attending physician must make. If he does agree, then it is he who should communicate this to the child and family. How this is done will therefore depend on the approach of that specific physician. Often, he will say to the psychiatrist, "I thought all along that this was a psychological problem and if they need help for it, please talk with them and make arrangements." This is a clear-cut instruction that a transfer has been considered and is accepted. Many times, where there are very real organic problems such as cystic fibrosis, diabetes, or severe renal disease, the physician may want the psychiatrist to take care only of those problems secondary to that illness while he continues to pay attention to the primary organic aspects of the problem. At times, the pediatrician is aware of psychological difficulties, such as arise with the oppositional diabetic or the asthmatic with frequent hospitalizations. He suspects they may be important and wants confirmation of his suspicions along with help either in continuing to care for the patient or in making a decision as to referral. Sometimes the physician has exhausted all possibilities and is baffled. He does not really feel that psychological factors are important, but wishes to be certain. He may even hope that the psychiatrist will uncover something of real importance so that he can take over the responsibility for care. On occasion, there are obvious psychological phenomena which the physician is certain he does not want to deal with and would like to refer immediately to the psychiatrist. Physicians tend to be most uncomfortable with behavioral symptoms, and it is there that some of their greatest errors are made. Luckily, they are seldom of life-and-death importance; but studies indicate that psychosocial problems are the most difficult for young house staff in particular to respond to, to diagnose, and to manage.

Physicians will tell their patients, "I want you to see the dermatologist about this skin rash"; regarding psychiatric referral, however, they will say, "Would you be willing to see a psychiatrist about this?" Psychiatric referral or request for consultation is greatly influenced by the pediatrician's attitude. He is in a critical spot for influencing the attitudes of the patients about the need for psychiatric consultation and can be most helpful. If he truly believes that the mind does influence the body and that human behavior can be understood and explained, he will be able to make a rational explanation to a child and his family about the need for investigation of this particular area. If his feelings about psychiatry, its reasonableness, and its value are at best mixed, he will communicate this to his patients as well.

In summary, psychiatric consultation is one area where the pediatrician and the child psychiatrist must find ways to communicate with each other. It is never a question of who can do what better, but rather who is more appropriate to be the attending physician. Sometimes both can be involved in care with continuing collaboration and communication. Consultation is a two-way street. Pediatricians and child psychiatrists have much to give and to receive from each other. Many patients and their families can have adequate care of the psychological aspects of illness quite appropriately handled by their pediatrician if he is inclined to do so. Some patients may need more intensive psychological management. The pediatrician may not have the time or the expertise to do so. There are things the child psychiatrist knows that can help the pediatrician in his practice. Sorting out this spectrum of problems is the function of consultation. Interpretation of the consultant's findings to the patient and family can and should be done by the physician; indeed, it is particularly appropriate that the pediatrician interpret the psychiatric consultation to the family just as he does other consultations. Psychiatric problems are not diagnosed by exclusion, and the findings of an abnormal laboratory test does not mean that psychological factors are not important in any particular case. For patients to receive truly comprehensive care, the interaction of mind and body, child and family, and family and social milieu need to be examined both by the pediatrician and the child psychiatrist.

REFERENCES

1. AWARD, G. A., and POZNANSKI, E. O., "Psychiatric Consultations in a Pediatric Hospital," *American Journal of Psychiatry, 132(9)*:915–918, 1975.
2. BOLIAN, G., "Psychiatric Consultation within a Community of Sick Children: Lessons from a Children's Hospital," *Journal of the American Academy of Child Psychiatry, 10*:293–307, 1971.
3. FINEMAN, A., "Introduction of Psychiatry to a Surgical Service," Presented at a workshop on Psychiatric Teaching Programs in Pediatric Settings, American Orthopedic Association, Chicago, March 19, 1957.
4. GARDNER, G. E., "The Establishment of Child Psychiatry Programs in a Children's Hospital," *American Journal of Orthopsychiatry, 28*:523–533, 1958.
5. LANGFORD, W. S., "The Child in the Pediatric Hospital: Adaptation to Illness and Hospitalization," *American Journal of Orthopsychiatry, 31*:668–684, 1961.
6. LIPOWSKI, Z. J., "Review of Consultation Psychiatry and Psychosomatic Medicine, I. General Principles, *Psychosomatic Medicine, 29*:153–171, 1967.
7. ———, "Review of Consultation Psychiatry and Psychosomatic Medicine. II. Clinical Aspects," *Psychosomatic Medicine, 29*:201–224, 1967.
8. ———, "Review of Consultation Psychiatry and Psychosomatic Medicine. III. Theoretical Issues, *Psychosomatic Medicine, 30*:395–422, 1968.
9. MONNELLY, E., JANZITO, B., and STEWART, M., "Psychiatric Consultation in a Children's Hospital," *American Journal of Psychiatry, 130*:789–790, 1973.
10. NUFFIELD, E. J., and REINHART, J. B., "Child Psychiatric-Pediatric Liaison" (unpublished).
11. PRUGH, D. G., "Investigations Dealing with the Reactions of Children and Families to Hospitalization: Problems and Potentialities," in Caplan, G., *Emotional Problems of Early Childhood*, pp. 307–321, Basic Books, New York, 1955.
12. SCHOWALTER, J. E., and SOLNIT, A. J., "Child Psychiatry Consultation in a General Hospital Emergency Room," *Journal of the American Academy of Child Psychiatry, 5*:534–551, 1966.
13. WILSON, J. A., "Joint Pediatric and Psychiatric Care of the Hospitalized Child," *American Journal of Orthopsychiatry, 28*:539–546, 1958.

80 / Note on Special Considerations in Evaluation of a Child in Connection with Court Proceedings

Richard L. Cohen

The child psychiatrist is often asked to evaluate children and to make recommendations to a court where the future status of the child is under adjudication. Although the general principles and practices previously outlined continue to be valid, they must frequently be adapted to the particular circumstances of each case. Usually, whether physically present in the court or represented only through his written report, the child psychiatrist is functioning as an expert witness. This role, together with the fact that his findings may be used to assist in making many decisions (of a nonclinical nature) which may affect the child's life, impose special responsibilities on the clinician.

The expertise of the child psychiatrist is most likely to be sought in one or more of four circumstances:

1. One or both parents may be suspected of child abuse, neglect, or exploitation.
2. Divorced or separated parents are in conflict concerning the custody of the child.
3. There is question of whether the severity of mental illness in a child warrants psychiatric hospitalization or some other type of institutionalization.
4. A child has committed one or more antisocial acts and the court needs consultation in arriving at the plan most likely to result in rehabilitation.[1]

Guidelines for Performing Evaluations

The following guidelines may be of assistance to child psychiatric clinicians in performing evaluations which will be employed in court.

It is valuable to have a working knowledge of the local court system where one is practicing. Rules of operation and jurisdictional scope vary widely. In large urban areas where there may be juvenile courts, family courts, domestic relations courts, and others, it is valuable to understand why certain cases are being considered within a given jurisdiction. This may influence the kinds of information considered most valuable in a particular case.

Correlatively, a simple working knowledge of the law(s) governing the case at hand is invaluable (for example, child abuse legislation). This will assist the clinician in making recommendations which are legally enforceable by the court.

Whenever possible, the clinician should arrange to represent the court rather than either "side." This may help to avoid prolonged polemics by contesting counsel with each selecting experts who may present a point of view favorable to its case. This does not preclude the court from procuring several opinions (which may be in some disagreement). It does make it more possible for the court to sort out the facts and act on its best judgment.

Because of the pressures imposed by court calendars, there may be frequent requests for reports within an unrealistically short period of time. Yet most cases referred are very complex and do not lend themselves to rapid or simplistic diagnostic procedures. In order to do justice to the child and other interested parties, it is often advisable to request that sufficient time be allowed to perform the evaluation carefully and thoroughly. Considerable firmness may be necessary on the part of the clinician in having this request implemented. However, judges will generally respond to such a request if it is accompanied by adequate explanation in terms that make it unequivocally clear that the child psychiatrist possesses no magic formulas to resolve these situations where the rights of the child, family, and society may be in conflict. In fact, the clinician may well explain the various procedures which may be necessary even to arrive at partial "answers" together with some estimate of the time required to perform these.

Over time, it is quite valuable to develop working relationships with personnel of the court, detention facility, child welfare service, and protective shelter. They can be of inestimable assistance in facilitating an evaluation and in supplying observational data which might otherwise be unavailable.

At times, adult psychiatric facilities may have been requested to evaluate one or both parents involved (often without the knowledge of the child clinician). Inquiries should be made concerning this on a routine basis. If such evaluation is planned or is in process, permission should be obtained to communicate with the involved clinician(s). Otherwise, the child psychiatrist may discover that he has expressed a judgment concerning the resources of a given family to rear the child in question while the adult facility has performed an adult mental status examination and reported to the court that the parents are not mentally ill. This discordant process can only be confusing to the court and may result in irrelevant or even illogical judgments.

When the evaluation has been completed, the clinician should: (1) limit his conclusions strictly to the data available; (2) avoid legal or quasi-legal judgments; (3) indicate several possible dispositions, rank-ordering them with respect to their desirability ranging from optimal to minimally acceptable; (4) be particularly careful to relate his report to the original purpose of the court's request.

REFERENCE

1. LEWIS, D. O., "Diagnostic Evaluation of the Juvenile Offender: Toward the Clarification of Often Overlooked Psychopathology," *Child Psychiatry and Human Development,* 6:198–213, 1976.

81 / Note on Automated Systems, Minimal Clinical Data Systems, and Computer-assisted Diagnostic Systems

Richard L. Cohen

Most of what has been described previously in this section on assessment may be categorized as "optimal" or even "maximal" clinical data collection. Hopefully, all of the data is seen as useful and pertinent; at the same time, no effort has been made to limit or confine the clinician to certain very specific items in an effort to "economize" on the diagnostic process, or to force the clinical thinking into a decision tree type of model. For training and education purposes, particularly, such a maximal data system is desirable. It exposes the trainee in an orderly fashion to the broadest possible spectrum of developmental forces or determinants, and it protects against the tendency toward stereotypy which can make clinical practice a numbing, assembly-line kind of experience.

Nevertheless, in large, busy clinical settings where much of the daily practice needs to be carried out in the most efficient possible manner and where educational goals may not necessarily rank as first priority (or even a high priority), there has been a long-felt need for a "minimal clinical data system" which is both valid and reliable. In the field of child psychiatry, several such systems are being developed. Each has its advantages and disadvantages.

The term "minimal" is here used to refer to a certain principle: that it is possible to begin with a spectrum of all the known and available treatment models in child psychiatry and to work backward from them. In this way, one can define a series of uniform standardized data forms. These are based on the minimum clinical criteria required to document the choice of each form of management.

Clearly, all such systems lend themselves rather easily to computerization. Data retrieval is relatively simple, and there are manifold possibilities for performing complex statistical procedures. Thus one can readily search for relationships between the presence of, let us say, a given constellation of symptoms and a variety of treatment models and the nature of the outcome. However, there is a sizable gap between this type of minimal clinical data system where the data is computer-ized for use in program planning and clinical investigation and the technologically more advanced concept of "computerized diagnosis."[1, 2] At the present time, there is no reliable system for computerized diagnosis in child psychiatry. (This would imply a capacity to feed previously prescribed data items into the computer with immediate feedback, in terms of both the nature of the child's clinical problem and a specific and well-differentiated treatment plan.) The fact is that the complex needs of such a diagnostic and treatment-planning process simply outstrip current technology.

One reason for this is that the computer lends itself very well to linear or sequential processing of data rather than to associative, lateral processes (which is the way most clinicians think). Computers are oriented to numeric logic. At this point in the art and science of child psychiatry, the "good" clinician must tolerate much ambiguity. In considering a case, he must be prepared to communicate dialetically with his fellow team members and with referral sources and consultants before a final "diagnosis" can be arrived at and a treatment plan evolved. The arrival at a conclusion through a process of exchange is altogether characteristic of clinical work, and most difficult to computerize.

Computers can now be programmed to screen electrocardiograms, chest x-rays, and even some highly standardized behavioral or attitudinal profiles like the Minnesota Multiphase Personality Inventory (MMPI). On the whole, however, the application of computers to the clinical decision-making process remains a fuzzy area. There are some innovative systems employed in individual research centers for highly specific purposes; these would be hard to replicate in clinical practice. It is even difficult to get reliability between the research centers where these systems are employed.

In addition, on one level or another, a whole array of indirectly related "systems data" is usually involved. While not really part of the immediate clinical decision-making process, it nonetheless impinges on the way the case is ultimately managed. Whether they think this out in a formal and logical fashion or not, most clinicians who are the gatekeepers (usually the senior diagnosticians attached to a clinical service) are constantly considering such questions as:

1. Who will accept this kind of referral?
2. What kind of "label" should I give it to make it most acceptable or most appropriate to the program I really want to refer it to?
3. How many such referrals have they taken from me recently—am I wearing out my welcome?
4. How many days of reimbursable care does this patient have left this year?
5. Is this case going to end up in court?
6. What do I know about the judgment of the referring source?

When it becomes possible to feed this kind of information into computers, the field will come considerably closer to having a practical and workable automated approach to disposition. The linear and numeric thinking process of the present-day computer is a distinct and formidable obstacle to including it as a full partner in the diagnostic process.

With these limitations in mind, there remain many advantages to the use of a minimal clinical data system in a large, complex child mental health facility. One such system is described in chapter 82.

Serious consideration should be given to the use of this or similar systems. The advantages are obvious: The more economical use of staff time, the possibility of more comprehensive and coherent communication (both internally and between clinical facilities) and, perhaps most important of all, the provision of a data base for *convincing* clinical investigation in the area of treatment outcome.

REFERENCES

1. Coddington, R. D., and King, T. L., "Automated History Taking in Child Psychiatry," *American Journal of Psychiatry, 129*:276–282, 1972.

2. Dow, J. T., "Designing Computer Software for Information Systems in Psychiatry," *Computers and Biomedical Research, 8*:538–559, 1975.

82 / Standardized Data Collection

Barbara Snyderman, Max G. Magnussen, and Peter B. Henderson

Introduction

We now turn to an examination of a method of recording information obtained in the course of assessment: the standardized data collection instrument. Such instruments, which can either supplement or replace written reports, typically consist of checklists or questionnaires on which information about the patient is recorded. The use of such a standardized record-keeping system, if adopted by an agency or hospital, ensures that all data considered essential is collected, regardless of the training, theoretical preference, or experience of the clinicians involved with the case. More importantly, such a record-keeping system provides uniform, comparable, and retrievable data on all patients.

A common clinical data base is the essential underpinning for many purposes. The information can be directed to such uses as peer review, program planning, program evaluation, clinical management, training, and clinical research. Finally, standardized evaluation systems lend themselves to automation. That is, computer technology can be used for the recording, storing, processing, retrieving, and analyzing of clinical information.

There are certainly concerns voiced regarding the use of standardized and automated data systems. Clinicians may fear that the categorization is too constraining, or that the patient is depersonalized, or that the thinking of the clinician becomes too fixed. In addition, many clinicians are intimidated by computers.[21]

However, there are major advantages to an automated data processing system. Such a method

657

provides for a centralized, systematized, and easily accessible data base which manual systems cannot provide. With increased emphasis on accountability, it becomes more important to have such a data base. Since for many, the advantages far outweigh the limitations, many institutions during the last decade have turned to automation for handling psychiatric records.[2]*

There are many excellent examples of automated information systems for use with adult psychiatric populations. Highly developed systems are in use, for example, at The Institute of Living in Hartford[4, 6] and at the Missouri Institute of Psychiatry.[25] At least one system, the Multi-State Information System based at Rockland State Hospital, New York, involves participation by a number of facilities and state departments of mental health across the country.[6, 3, 13] The U.S. Army is served by the Computer Support in Military Psychiatry (COMPSY) project.[18] Kupfer and Detre[14] collect and computerize data for purposes of diagnostic formulation, treatment planning, and estimate of prognosis.

All of these information systems are designed to collect data on adult populations. As we have seen in previous chapters, evaluation of children involves collection of different kinds of data than evaluation of adults: Data must be collected not only about the child's problems, but about such areas as the child's mastery of developmental tasks, his functioning in school, and the parental management of and relationship with the child. Data systems designed to record assessment of adults, in other words, are not applicable to children.

A Clinical Data System for Child
Mental Health Facilities

A standardized information system for child psychiatric services has been developed at the Pittsburgh Child Guidance Center.[17, 27] The assessment portion of the Clinical Data for Children (CDC) system consists of a set of forms on which are recorded the pertinent clinical information collected during the intake and diagnostic evaluation of the child and his family. Although easily supplemented by other materials if desired,

the forms are designed to replace the narrative summaries which traditionally constitute the clinical record.

PHILOSOPHY OF THE CDC SYSTEM

Clinicians who develop a standardized information system must face the issue of what data to include in that system. What information is essential to collect and record on every case? The answer must depend upon one's definition of the purposes for which data is being collected.

In developing the system reported here, the purpose of collecting data has been defined in terms of the decisions that have to be made. The clinical process has been viewed as a series of steps, with each step ending when decisions are made regarding case management.

The first such step is the intake period, which ends when sufficient information has been gathered to decide on such issues as acceptance of the case for evaluation and the urgency of the case. The data that must be collected during the intake period, then, becomes defined as that data needed in order to make those decisions.

The next step in the clinical process is the evaluation or assessment period, which ends with decisions regarding what form of treatment, if any, will be recommended. The primary purpose of the evaluation thus becomes defined in terms of decisions that must be made regarding treatment. Many other authors share the view that the purpose of diagnostic evaluation can best be defined as the selection of a treatment plan.*

A second position taken in developing the CDC system is that minimal rather than maximal data should be included in the assessment portion of the data system. The literature suggests that the amount of data available to a clinician is not related to the accuracy of clinical judgments.† Many studies suggest that, providing the basic required information is available, relatively limited information may be optimal.‡ In some cases, more information may be necessary to carry out treatment once the treatment decision has been made. If so, this would become another stage of information collection.

DEVELOPMENT OF THE INSTRUMENT

Having taken the position that the data system should include the information necessary for decision making, the authors developed a model

---

* American Psychiatric Association Task Force on Automation and Data Processing, *Task Force Report 3: Automation and Data Processing in Psychiatry*, Elmer A. Garderner, Chairman, Washington, D.C., 1970.

* See references 10, 31, 28, 1, and 25.
† See references 24, 33, 8, 20, and 23.
‡ See references 7, 5, 9, 32, 29, and 30.

by means of which such data would be identified.[11] For the evaluation sections, the process was that of first identifying all possible treatment recommendations (for example, individual therapy, family therapy, group therapy, psychopharmacological therapy, no therapy, etc.). For each of these types of treatment, a set of rules or assumptions was developed, hypothesizing how clinicians decide to recommend that particular form of treatment. The data required in order to apply these rules became the information to be included in the data system.

By this method, the authors of the system identified what were considered to be the minimal data necessary to collect during the intake and evaluation process. At the same time, a number of testable hypotheses were being generated. That is, there are specific predictions with respect to the relationship of items in the data system to the selection of the various treatment modalities. These predictions will be tested empirically when sufficient data have been collected.

DESCRIPTION OF THE CDC SYSTEM

The intake and evaluation portions of the data system consist of a series of forms called CDC (Clinical Data for Children) Scales. These forms represent the basic evaluation packet which is included in the records of all cases seen for evaluation. A brief description of these forms follows.

CDC-A: Intake Data. Form A covers the intake period—the interval between the initial referral of a family to the clinic and the assignment of that family to one or more clinicians for evaluation. The questions in this form collect the information necessary to make the decisions which are made at the end of the intake period: (1) whether or not the family will be accepted for evaluation; (2) if accepted, the urgency of assignment for evaluation; (3) if accepted, whether there are any particular skills required of the clinician doing the evaluation; (4) which agencies should be contacted for information. Procedures used to obtain information for Form A will vary; information may be obtained in a referral telephone call, through a face-to-face intake interview, through an application form completed by a parent, through information from a referral source, or some combination of these sources.

CDC-B: Child Evaluation. Form B, to be completed by the clinician responsible for the evaluation of the child, consists of questions regarding the referred child. The answers to these questions are obtained through interviews with the child and through whatever other methods may be necessary in any particular case: information from parents or other informants, psychological testing, school reports, etc. Again, the items which have been included in CDC-B bear a hypothesized relationship to decisions about possible treatment for the child.

CDC-C: Parent Evaluation. An integral part of the diagnostic assessment of a child is an evaluation of the family system of which that child is a part. Form C is designed to record such information and is to be completed by the clinician responsible for evaluation of the parents and family. The information will be obtained primarily through interviews with parents and/or families and observation of their interactions with each other and with the referred child. Questions are designed to elicit information which will enable decisions to be made about the need for treatment, the family's potential to use treatment, and the kind of treatment indicated, if any.

CDC-D: Clinical Process Data. The section on clinical process data covers details concerning how and by whom the answers to the questions in the evaluation sections (CDC-B and CDC-C) were obtained. In addition, other factors are included which are not related specifically to the patient but which may have a bearing on the treatment decision. Many of the items in this section were included on the basis of research which suggests that treatment decisions may be influenced in part by factors not related directly to the patient, but related to the clinician and the setting in which the evaluation is done. Thus, for example, the professional discipline of the clinician has been demonstrated to be correlated with choice of treatment.[12, 19, 22] Additionally, it seems possible that such factors as waiting lists, training needs, or nonavailability in the community of a certain kind of treatment all may affect decisions.

CDC-E: Decision-making Meeting. This section provides a format for recording the decision-making conference, including recommendations for treatment (or no treatment) and goals for treatment. This section represents the end point of the evaluation process. In addition to kind of treatment recommended, there are some "clinical process" items included, such as the kind of decision-making meeting held, the personnel involved, whether or not there was disagreement about the decision, and factors in addition to case material which entered into the decision. Again, the justification for including this kind of information lies in the intention to assess the influence of these various factors on clinical decision making.

Several supplemental forms have recently been developed and should be considered "working versions" of the CDC system—revisions will be made after they have been in use for some time. The use of these supplemental forms depends upon the specific needs of a case.

CDC-B 1: Developmental History. The basic evaluation package does not include a formal developmental history. B-1 provides a form for recording this information, should the evaluating clinician wish to include it. B-1 may also be completed during the treatment process, since developmental information is usually useful in the course of therapy.

CDC-B 2: The Physician's Report. This form can be used to record any medical information obtained from a child's physician.

CDC-B 3: Medical History Interview. For cases where a physical examination is part of an evaluation process, a medical history interview is also conducted and form B-3 is available for recording the data.

CDC-B 4: Summary Results of Physical Examination and Physical Laboratory Tests. If a physical examination is part of the evaluation process, CDC-B 4 provides easy retrievability of the findings of the examination and laboratory tests.

FORMAT OF ITEMS IN CDC-B AND CDC-C

The two forms CDC-B and CDC-C, the child and parent evaluation sections, comprise the bulk of the evaluation package. These sections contain the basic information about the child and family which will be used to make decisions regarding treatment.

A word about the construction or format of the individual questions is necessary. Each item consists of a stem question and a list of subitems under it.

For example, see table 82–1. The two questions from CDC-B therein contained relate to depression in the child.

As illustrated in the two questions in table 82–1, the stem questions of the items in the data system are phased in such a way that the questions can be answered yes or no, with a "yes" answer indicating that this is a problem area for the child.

The subitems serve several purposes, as demonstrated in the examples above. First, subitems provide an operational definition of the stem

TABLE 82–1

Questions from CDC–B

7. Does the child show any behavioral signs of depression?
   Yes_____   No_____
   If yes, indicate signs of depression, describe, and include source:
   _____Saddened facial expression_____
   _____Crying_____
   _____Pattern of speech (e.g., subdued)_____
   _____Reduction in bodily movement_____
   _____Child verbalizes feelings of depression (e.g., sad, lonely)

   _____Other behavioral indicators (specify)_____

8. Can depression be inferred from other indicators?
   Yes_____   No_____
   If yes, indicate, describe, and include source:
   _____Artistic expressions or creations depict themes of depression
   _____Child's stories are depressed in content_____
   _____Psychological test data_____
   _____Impairment of physiological functioning (e.g., sleep patterns)

   _____Impairment of academic functioning_____
   _____Impairment of social functioning_____
   _____Other (specify)_____

NOTE: The tables in this chapter are reprinted by permission of the Pittsburgh Child Guidance Center, Pittsburgh, Pa.

question: behavioral signs of depression are considered to include saddened facial expression, crying, etc. Subitems are phrased, wherever it is feasible, in terms that are behaviorally observable or capable of behavioral description. It is recognized, however, that inference is unavoidable when making judgments about such constructs as anxiety and depression. Where a judgment is to be based on inference, an attempt has been made in the forms to specify that, as in question eight of table 82–1.

A second purpose served by the subitems is that of giving an indication of the severity of the problem. Where possible, subitems are listed roughly from least to more severe; thus, the items checked represent an indication of the severity of the problem.

Finally, through the subitems a picture of the child and family emerges. Each subitem has a line or space available for brief, narrative information, thus allowing the clinician to provide further clarification and description. It is here that the clinician completing the form fills in the data that describe the child and family being evaluated. A request is also made for identification of the source of the information regarding the subitem. It is important to identify the source of the information so that outcome data from the same source can be compared with this assessment.

The format of the CDC system allows the forms to be used in the traditional manner of a narrative chart. That is, the forms contain descriptive information which can be kept in a file and read by clinicians or consultants. The fact that they are in a format which allows for computerization does not mean that computerization is required. However, by translating the data into an automated system, a clinic can increase its capacity to provide information about its patient population. Such information may be needed for administrative and other purposes and can facilitate research regarding the clinical process.

Clinical Case Examples

In order to illustrate the content of this Clinical Data System, the use of the forms, and the way the information collected leads to decisions, two clinical examples are presented.

The cases were selected by computer. In order to illustrate the decision-making use of the forms, it was decided to select two children of similar age and similar referral complaints for whom, after evaluation, the treatment recommendations differed. The information collected during the assessment process and recorded on the forms could then be examined to demonstrate how the data collected on each case led to different decisions despite the initial appearance of similarity of the two cases. With the aid of computer printouts of referral data and treatment recommendations, two elementary school-age boys were selected. For both boys, the referral problems had been coded by the intake worker as "behavior problems in school," "anxiety," and "interpersonal difficulties." The recommendation in one case after the evaluation was completed was for individual therapy for the referred child with collaborative therapy for mother. For the other case, the recommendation was for family therapy.

As the information collected on these two case examples is presented, the reader should get a clearer picture of the clinical utilization of the forms.

CDC-A: INTAKE INFORMATION

The information in CDC-A will serve to introduce the two cases. Selected questions from form A will be presented in tables with the answers, for each of the two cases presented side by side. Table 82–2 gives the first comparison.

The preceding questions, selected from among the twenty-six questions in CDC-A, describe two third-grade boys with school and interpersonal difficulties. In an earlier section, the decisions made after the intake period were identified. CDC-A ends with a series of questions which constitute a record of those decisions. This allows consideration of the manner in which the information collected on the two cases led to making the intake decisions on each case.

The first decision (to be made by a senior clinician) is whether or not the case should be accepted for evaluation. The decision for both the case examples was to accept them—referral problems were deemed appropriate to an outpatient clinic (and also both patients lived in the geographic area served by the clinic).

The second decision is reflected in the following item, which was answered differently for the two cases. (See table 82–3.)

Case 1 was seen by the clinician responsible for the decision as a routine referral. Case 2, on the other hand, was identified as needing immediate assignment for evaluation because it is important that a school refusal of recent onset be seen

TABLE 82–2

Case 1	Case 2
3. Age at time of referral: 9 years	3. Age at time of referral: 8 years
4. Sex: Male	4. Sex: Male
5. Race: White	5. Race: White
11. Family Composition:	11. Family Composition:

Case 1 — 11. Family Composition:

Relationship or Role	Age
Stepfather	24
Mother	30
Sister	11
Patient	9
Half-brother	5
Half-brother	3

Case 2 — 11. Family Composition:

Relationship or Role	Age
Father (Separated)	36
Mother	33
Brother	14
Sister	12
Patient	8

Case 1

12. Grade: 3

16. Referring Problems:
Briefly describe referring problems and estimate duration:
(1) Behavior problems at school, approximately three years;
(2) Difficulty relating to peer group;
(3) Speech sometimes difficult to understand.
Note: School problems seem to have gotten worse since child's biological father, whom he sees intermittently, had open heart surgery for the second time, approximately one year prior to referral.

22. Are there, or have there been significant physical or mental problems within the referred child's family?

__X__Yes _____No

If yes, describe briefly the nature of the problem:
(1) Natural father has had congenital heart disease with two open heart operations, both successful; most recent one occurred a year prior to referral.

Case 2

12. Grade: 3

16. Referring Problems:
Briefly describe referring problems and estimate duration:
(1) School refusal, onset within last two weeks;
(2) Child cries easily and frequently, approximately last six months;
(3) Fighting with friends—had been able to maintain friendships until about six months ago;
(4) Behavior out of control, getting worse for past six months.
Note: School refusal followed incident of father beating up mother in front of child.

22. Are there, or have there been significant physical or mental problems within the referred child's family?

__X__Yes _____No

If yes, describe briefly the nature of the problem:
(1) Mother seen two and three years ago at community mental health clinic for depression, related to concerns around recent separation.
(2) Sister seen four years ago at same community mental health center for problems related to sleep disorder, nightmares, and anxiety. Referral sources for case was the community mental health center where mother and sister had been seen.

TABLE 82–3

Case 1	Case 2
Urgency of Assignment	Urgency of Assignment
_____Immediate	__X__Immediate (Turmoil in home; school refusal)
_____Preferential	_____Preferential
__X__Routine	_____Routine
_____Other	_____Other

TABLE 82-4

---

3. Is further child psychiatric attention required?

_____Yes   _____No

If yes, indicate which of the following is needed:

_____Psychiatrist to be directly involved in the evaluation (specify)

_____Psychiatrist to be consulted prior to diagnostic conference

_____Psychiatrist to chair conference_____

_____Other (specify)_____

_____4. Comments_____

Date reviewed_____Signature of Psychiatrist_____

---

quickly. Case 2 was viewed as a short-term or acute situation, while Case 1 was considered more long-term or chronic.

The third class of decisions made after intake is the kinds of clinicians that need to be involved in the evaluation. One aspect of this is the degree of medical input required. A child psychiatrist reviews the data from CDC-A and answers the questions in table 82-4.

Another point of medical review occurs after a physical examination (CDC B-4) and Medical History Interview (CDC B-3) are conducted by a pediatric nurse-practitioner. The child psychiatrist then answers the question in table 82-5.

In both cases, the reviewing psychiatrist saw no necessity for further child psychiatric or medical involvement. The clinicians making the assignment for evaluation also saw no reason to specify the discipline of the clinicians who would do the evaluation. Case 1 was assigned to a staff psychologist who did both child and parent evaluations; Case 2 was assigned to a psychology intern for child evaluation and a staff social worker for parent evaluation.

Finally, the information in CDC-A is used to determine what sources need to be contacted for information about the child. In both these cases,

it was decided that school information would be needed. In Case 2, in addition, information would be obtained from the community mental health center which was the referring agency.

CDC-B: CHILD EVALUATION

Form CDC-B consists of thirty-three questions regarding the referred child. All of the data that will be reported in this section on the two case examples was recorded on Form B. Rather than reproduce all questions, however, much of the data will be summarized narratively, with a few questions reproduced for illustrative purposes. The data discussed is primarily that which seemed important to the clinicians in making a treatment decision.

Neither child was seen to have impaired contact with reality, nor any evidence of a thought disorder. The question related to speech disturbance is reproduced in table 82-6. As in all questions reproduced in this chapter, the X's indicate which items the clinician checked, and the comments in parentheses are the explanatory material written by the clinician.

We thus have learned the nature of child 1's speech problems and the fact that his difficulties are exacerbated by stress.

On the questions regarding depression, the child in Case 1 was judged not to be depressed on any of the indicators. The boy in Case 2 was not seen in the interview as depressed; however, a behavioral sign of depression was frequent crying reported by mother. Depression was also inferred on the basis of psychological test data. In projective testing, he idealized a happy, peaceful, and comfortable home life.

Neither boy was seen as having suicidal tendencies.

TABLE 82-5

---

2. Is further medical attention required?

_____Yes   _____No

If yes, indicate which of the following is needed:

_____Neurological examination_____

_____Special laboratory tests (specify)_____

_____Pediatric consultation_____

_____Referral (specify)_____

_____Other (specify)_____

TABLE 82–6

Case 1	Case 2
6. Does the child have a notable speech disturbance? __X__Yes _____No If yes, indicate nature of disturbance and describe: __X__Child lisps _____Child stutters __X__Poor enunciation for age (Mother says problem becomes worse when child is upset or anxious) _____Garbled speech _____Child is mute _____Other	6. Does the child have a notable speech disturbance? _____Yes __X__No If yes, indicate nature of disturbance and describe: _____Child lisps _____Child stutters _____Poor enunciation for age _____Garbled speech _____Child is mute _____Other

TABLE 82–7

Case 1	Case 2
10. Does child show any behavioral signs of anxiety? __X__Yes _____No If yes, indicate signs, describe, and include source: __X__Tense or rigid motor behavior (at times) _____Physiological signs __X__Child's verbalizations (worried about father being hospitalized and about having to go to the hospital himself some day) __X__Phobic behavior _____Avoidance of expected developmental experiences _____Ritualistic thoughts or behaviors _____Other	10. Does child show any behavioral signs of anxiety? __X__Yes _____No If yes, indicate signs, describe, and include source: _____Tense or rigid motor behavior _____Physiological signs _____Child's verbalizations __X__Phobic behavior (Crying, refusal to go to school several mornings. Reported by mother, sibs. Child claims he was ill.) _____Avoidance of expected developmental experiences _____Ritualistic thoughts or behaviors _____Other
11. Can anxiety be inferred from other indicators? __X__Yes _____No If yes, indicate, describe, and include source: _____Major denials of anxiousness _____Artistic expressions or creations __X__Child's stories (long discussion of illness and accidents witnessed) __X__Psychological test results (TAT) __X__Impairment of academic functioning (inattentive) __X__Impairment of social functioning (fearful of most adult relationships; overinvested in relationship with natural father) _____Other	11. Can anxiety be inferred from other indicators? _____Yes __X__No If yes, indicate, describe, and include source: _____Major denials of anxiousness _____Artistic expressions of creations _____Child's stories _____Psychological test results _____Impairment of academic functioning _____Impairment of social functioning _____Other

The questions on anxiety will be reproduced in table 82–7. They are illustrative of how the subitems reveal differences between the two boys, although both are judged as anxious.

On the basis of the data thus far, the reader can probably deduce which child was judged to be a candidate for individual psychotherapy. The anxiety described in Case 1 is far more pervasive, and interferes with the child's functioning to a far greater extent than in Case 2.

On a question regarding hyperactivity, Child 1 was described as overactive only in specific situations, notably when discussing natural father's illness. Child 2 was not seen as hyperactive.

Both children were seen as having difficulties in impulse control. Subitems checked for Child 1 were "tantrums" and "aggressive behavior." For Child 2, impulse control problems were also manifested by aggressive behavior. The clinician described frequent fighting with siblings and occasional outbursts with friends.

Child 1 was not seen as having feelings of inadequacy. Child 2 was seen as having such feelings in that he feels powerless against aggressive attacks of older siblings.

For assessment of intellectual ability, the WISC-R was administered to both boys. Child 1 obtained a score indicating average intelligence (Full Scale IQ = 102); Child 2 obtained a score in the superior range (Full Scale IQ = 126). Child 1 revealed some sensorimotor difficulties on the Bender Visual-Motor Gestalt test and on the WISC Block Design. No signs of cognitive dysfunction were found for Child 2.

Neither child was reported to be having difficulties in academic achievement. Other difficulties in school are reported in table 82–8.

From this item we see that, although the referral code had included school-related problems for both boys, the problem in Case 2 was a school refusal, and no behavior problems *in* school are reported. Again we see evidence that the disturbance for Child 1 is a more pervasive one, leading the clinician to recommend individual therapy.

Another question in which subitems reveal a difference between the two youngsters regards difficulties in peer relationships. Both boys are described as having some difficulty in this area, but Child 1 is seen as overly aggressive and as requiring structure and supervision to function with peers.

On the question regarding difficulties with parents, again the answer was yes for both boys, but again the particular subitems checked revealed important differences between them. Child 1 was described by mother as difficult to handle for a few days after a visit to natural father. Child 2 was described as having a conflict-laden relationship with both parents. The clinician noted that "each parent plays the children against the spouse." Here is perhaps the first hint of why the clinicians ultimately decided to recommend family therapy in Case 2. Most of the data that leads to a family therapy recommendation emerges in the Parent Evaluation section.

A final question on motivation gives further data that leads to the recommendation for individual therapy for Child 1. He was seen as motivated to change—he recognized his problematic behavior, enjoyed the evaluation sessions, and was willing to talk during the sessions, even about anxiety-producing topics. Child 2 was described as not motivated to change or to participate in treatment. The clinician noted that the

TABLE 82–8

Case 1	Case 2
22. Is the child having significant difficulties in school in areas *other* than academic achievement?	22. Is the child having significant difficulties in school in areas *other* than academic achievement?
__X__Yes _____No	_____Yes __X__No
If yes, indicate, describe, and include source:	If yes, indicate, describe, and include source:
__X__Behavior problems (Inattentive and preoccupied at times, according to teacher)	_____Behavior problems
_____Problems with school authorities	_____Problems with school authorities
__X__Peer group problems specific to the academic situation (teacher states he disrupts others to get attention)	_____Peer group problems specific to the academic situation
_____Other	_____Other

child had returned to school after the first interview and did not see himself as needing treatment.

Child 1 emerges as a child whose difficulties are relatively long-standing and are severe enough to permeate several areas of functioning. For such a child, particularly one who is motivated, individual psychotherapy is deemed appropriate. Child 2, on the other hand, emerges as one who, while unhappy and presenting significant symptoms, seems mostly to be reacting to turmoil and conflict in the home. The clinician has therefore judged that individual therapy would not be the treatment of choice for him.

Other kinds of interventions have also, implicitly or explicitly, been ruled out for both boys by the data in CDC-B. Thus, for example, neither presents problems severe enough to warrant residential treatment, and neither presents the characteristics of the children for whom psychopharmacological interventions are consistently recommended. By the time CDC-B has been completed, then, a number of recommendations can be made by the clinician.

The final questions in CDC-B ask the child clinician for a suggested diagnosis, using the nomenclature of the APA Revised Diagnostic and Statistical Manual,* and a suggested treatment plan

* Committee on Nomenclature and Statistics of the American Psychiatric Association, *Diagnostic and Statistical Manual of Mental Disorders*, 2nd ed. (DSM II), American Psychiatric Association, Washington, D. C., 1968.

for the child. These recommendations are not final—the final decisions regarding diagnosis and recommended treatment are made jointly at a conference (summarized in CDC-E) attended by all clinicians involved with the case and a conference chairman.

For Child 1, the clinician suggested a diagnosis of "Adjustment Reaction of Childhood" and recommended individual therapy for the child. For Child 2, the clinician deferred a recommendation regarding diagnosis. The treatment recommendation was family therapy, with the following explanatory note: "Problems revolve around family interaction—not internalized in child."

CDC-C: PARENT EVALUATION

Form CDC-C consists of twenty-nine questions regarding the parents and family. The information collected covers the parental management of and relationship with the referred child and the characteristics of the family interaction. This form is completed by the clinician assigned to evaluate the parents and family. In solo evaluations (as in Case 1), CDC-B and CDC-C would both be completed by the individual performing the total evaluation.

The responses to the questions in CDC-C should provide the information necessary to decide if parents or family members should be included in

TABLE 82–9

Case 1	Case 2
6. Has the family sought help because of concerns about a particular child?	6. Has the family sought help because of concerns about a particular child?
__X__ Yes _____No	__X__ Yes _____No
If yes, list problems and duration:	If yes, list problems and duration:
(School has been concerned about referred child for three years and has made repeated referrals. Mother did not follow through until she was told child would be put in special class if she did not get outside help.)	(Child refused to go to school several times within past two weeks. Crying and aggressive behavior for about six months.)
7. Has the family sought help because of concerns about family or marital functioning?	7. Has the family sought help because of concerns about family or marital functioning?
_____Yes __X__No	__X__ Yes _____No
If yes, list problems:	If yes, list problems:
(Though mother initially denied family difficulties, she became freer during the evaluation to discuss marital problems. She reported that stepfather is a drug abuser and an alcoholic, that she had recently tried to get him into a drug abuse program and, when he refused, she had initiated a separation.)	(Child seems to be the calling card for the family. Critical issues seem to be: divorce pending; general level of anxiety, anger, and chaos in the family; and the fact that the children are caught between two hostile parents.)

TABLE 82–10

Case 1	Case 2

8. Are parents overly involved with the referred child?

_____ Yes __X__ No

If yes, indicate and describe:

Other
Mo Fa *Adult*

— — _____ Overconcern for child's safety and health

— — _____ Speak for child

— — _____ Confuses child's needs with own

— — _____ Other

Parental behavior toward siblings

_____ Check if parents are also overinvolved with siblings

9. Are parents underinvolved or uninvolved with referred child?

_____ Yes __X__ No

If yes, indicate and describe:

Other
Mo Fa *Adult*

— — _____ Child often left untended

— — _____ Physical care is lacking

— — _____ Lack of interest in child's activities

— — _____ Other forms of parental uninvolvement

Parental behavior towards siblings

_____ Check is parents are also underinvolved with siblings

12. Are there parental problems in child management? (e.g., child does not behave in ways they would like child to behave)

__X__ Yes _____ No

If yes, indicate areas of problem and describe:

Other   (Natural
Mo Fa *Adult*   Father)

— — __X__ Do not set limits firmly enough

— — _____ Expects too much compliance

— — _____ Overly punitive

— — _____ Do not encourage desired behavior

— — _____ One parent undermines efforts on the part of the other spouse

_X_ — _____ Other difficulties in child management (has difficulty managing referred child for two or three days after he returns from a visit to his father; feels this is because father places no restrictions on him at all)

Parental behavior toward siblings

_____ Check if parents also have difficulty managing siblings

---

8. Are parents overly involved with the referred child?

__X__ Yes _____ No

If yes, indicate and describe:

Other
Mo Fa *Adult*

— — _____ Overconcern for child's safety and health

— — _____ Speak for child

_X_ _X_ _____ Confuses child's needs with own (both parents interpret child's needs in light of their own)

— — _____ Other

Parental behavor toward siblings

__X__ Check if parents are also overinvolved with siblings

9. Are parents underinvolved or uninvolved with referred child?

__X__ Yes _____ No

If yes, indicate and describe:

Other
Mo Fa *Adult*

— — _____ Child often left untended

— — _____ Physical care is lacking

— — _____ Lack of interest in child's activities

_X_ — _____ Other forms of parental uninvolvement (general uninvolvement regarding time spent with all of her children—capacity to relate to their needs when mother is overwhelmed with her own problems seems to be an issue. The interest on her part seems there, but not the energy or feeling of reward)

Parental behavior toward siblings

__X__ Check if parents are also underinvolved with siblings

12. Are there parental problems in child management? (e.g., child does not behave in ways they would like child to behave)

__X__ Yes _____ No

If yes, indicate areas of problem and describe:

Other
Mo Fa *Adult*

_X_ — _____ Do not set limits firmly enough

— — _____ Expect too much compliance

— — _____ Overly punitive

— — _____ Do not encourage desired behavior

— — _____ One parent undermines efforts on the part of the other spouse

— _X_ _____ Other difficulties in child management (he denies any difficulties, though children express great fear of him)

Parental behavior toward siblings

__X__ Check if parents also have difficulty managing siblings a treatment program and, if so, what form of treatment. Among the treatment recommendations that can be considered are parent counseling (defined as work with parents with the specific goal of facilitating the development of a given child patient), family therapy (defined as an intervention whose primary emphasis is on changing family interactions), or individual treatment with one or both parents.

The answers given to selected questions in the two sample cases are given in table 82–9.

From the information in table 82–9, it seems clear that both family situations are troubled. The question thus becomes one of judging what form of intervention might be of most help to each of the two families.

The next series of questions relate to parental management of the referred child. (See table 82–10.)

With the exception of mother's feeling that Child 1's visits to natural father are followed by some difficulty, the questions in table 82–10 do not reveal significant difficulties in Case 1. On the other hand, the parents in Case 2 *are* seen to have significant problems in relating to and managing the referred child and their other children.

In some instances, the difficulties reported on these questions relating to child-rearing practices suggest that parents need help in learning more effective techniques of child rearing. This is particularly so when parents demonstrate child-rearing difficulties with all their children, not just the referred child. In such cases, parent counselling might be a treatment recommendation. In Case 2, however, the clinician's comments seem to suggest that the difficulties in child management are related more to family conflicts than to lack of knowledge or skill on the part of the parents. This interpretation would lead more to a recommendation for family therapy.

The questions in CDC-C presented in table 82–11 relate to the characteristics of family interaction. The answers given further define the difficulties being experienced within the two families.

Question 16 in table 82–11 provides an interesting contrast between the two families. Both families are said to have problems in communication, but the subitem answers reveal important differences between them. In Case 1, the fact that mother has not told the children about the separation suggests that she has difficulty in dealing with anxiety-laden material. This may be one reason the clinician recommended therapy for

her. In Case 2, question 16 reveals the degree to which the children are enmeshed in the parental difficulties, suggesting the advisability of a family therapy approach.

In other questions, Family 1 was thought to function as a closed system (i.e., relatively inaccessible to outside influences). Evidence for this judgment was that mother has little contact with her family of origin, rarely goes out, has few friends, and has been resistant to referrals for help in the past. This data both bespeaks the need for help and suggests the possibility of resistance to it. Family 2 was not seen as a closed system.

Both families were judged to be lacking in flexibility in dealing with new or changing situations. The clinician commented regarding Case 2 that intense unmet needs and emotional problems in all family members makes flexibility within the system difficult.

The remaining questions in CDC-C are designed to assess the families' potential to profit from therapy themselves and to support therapy for the child. Three such questions are presented in table 82–12.

From the three questions presented in table 82–12, we see that in both cases, the clinician saw some evidence that mother would be able to profit from therapy and would support the recommendations. Differences in approach are also suggested by the responses to these questions. The mother in Case 1 is primarily focused on coping with her own depression and with an alcoholic and drug-addicted husband, while in Case 2, the focus is more on the whole family.

To summarize the impressions from CDC-C, we see two families with a number of similarities. In both families, the father has recently left the home; both have been struggling with the stress preceding and accompanying such a separation. In neither family is the father willing to be involved in treatment.

In spite of the similarities, there are also major differences. In Case 1, the mother emerges as an isolated and depressed person who has had two unsuccessful marriages and who has difficulty dealing with anxiety-arousing material. In Case 2, the predominant impression is of a chaotic and conflicted situation involving all three children.

Based on the evaluation, the clinician in Case 1 recommended individual therapy for mother, commenting on her need for a supportive relationship. In Case 2, the recommendation was for family therapy initially, with mother and all three children participating. The clinician suggested that, follow-

TABLE 82–11

Case 1	Case 2
16. Are there problems in communication among family members?	16. Are there problems in communication among family members?
__X__ Yes _____ No	__X__ Yes _____ No
If yes, indicate and describe problems and family members involved:	If yes, indicate and describe problems and family members involved:
__X__ Too little communication (mother has not told children about separation; says father is away on business)	_____ Too little communication
_____ Communication unclear	__X__ Communication unclear (distorted by anger)
_____ Contradictory communications	__X__ Contradictory communications
_____ Communication between members of a family carried out through a third family member	__X__ Communication between members of family carried out through a third family member (parents communicate to each other through children and use children to convey their anger)
_____ Communication level inappropriately high —"enmeshed system"	__X__ Communication level inappropriately high —"enmeshed system"
_____ Other communication problems	_____ Other communication problems
17. Are there significant conflicts within the family?	17. Are there significant conflicts within the family?
__X__ Yes _____ No	__X__ Yes _____ No
If yes, indicate areas of conflict:	If yes, indicate areas of conflict:
_____ Child management	__X__ Child management
_____ Financial problems	_____ Financial Problems
_____ Sexual difficulties	_____ Sexual difficulties
_____ Parent-child conflicts	__X__ Parent-child conflicts
_____ Excessive sibling rivalry	__X__ Excessive sibling rivalry (between referred child and sister; other child withdraws)
__X__ Marital difficulties (stepfather is in and out of the home periodically, even though mother considers them separated)	__X__ Marital difficulties (arguments over divorce settlement, possible custody battle)
If yes above, indicate manifestations of the conflict, and briefly describe:	If yes above, indicate manifestations of the conflict, and briefly describe:
__X__ Arguments (between mother and stepfather whenever stepfather is in the home)	__X__ Arguments (between referred child and sister; between mother and all three children)
__X__ Physical fights (child has witnessed stepfather hitting mother)	__X__ Physical fights (mother provokes father with explosive anger; father has beaten her up)
_____ Other	_____ Other

ing the period of family therapy with the children involved, it might be appropriate to continue for a period of therapy with mother alone.

CDC-D: CLINICAL PROCESS DATA

CDC-D consists of ten questions about the clinicians who performed the evaluation and about the nature of the evaluation sessions. This information is collected primarily for research and statistical purposes. With this information available on all cases, the impact of clinician variables (for example, discipline, experience level, theoretical preference) on treatment recommendations can be assessed. In addition, data is made available for administrative purposes on the number of sessions and techniques used in all evaluations.

The questions in table 82–13 provide information on the form of the evaluation in the two case examples.

Some of the characteristics of the clinicians involved in the two cases have been noted. Evaluation of Case 1 was conducted entirely by a staff psychologist. Evaluation of Case 2 was

TABLE 82–12

Case 1	Case 2

24. Did parents experience the evaluation as meaningful?

   X Yes   No

If yes, indicate in what ways and describe briefly:

		Other	
Mo	Fa	Adult	
—	—	———	Developed an increased understanding of child's problem
—	—	———	Developed an increased understanding of family interactions
—	—	———	Modified their behavior toward each other
—	—	———	Modified management of child
—	—	———	Expressed positive reactions about sessions or clinicians
X	—	———	Other evidence that evaluation was meaningful to parents (mother became less resistant to discussing family problem, and less focused on referred child alone as "her only problem")

26. Would parents support treatment of child if it were recommended?

   X Yes   No

If yes, indicate evidence and describe:

		Other	
Mo	Fa	Adult	
X	—	———	Believe child needs help (mother only, father is opposed)
X	—	———	Believe child can be helped by treatment
—	—	———	Would be willing to provide transportation
—	—	———	Other evidence of parental support

27. Would parents be motivated to participate in treatment themselves if it were recommended?

   X Yes   No

If yes, indicate evidence and describe:

		Other	
Mo	Fa	Adult	
—	—	———	Are seeking help in child management
—	—	———	Believe that changes in child can occur in relation to changes in themselves
X	—	———	Would like to change some of the ways family members relate to each other (mother is seeking help for marital problems but husband refused treatment)
X	—	———	Willing to come for future appointments (mother, who reports being depressed at times, has made references to the idea of treatment for herself but is threatened by the prospect)
—	—	———	Other

---

24. Did parents experience the evaluation as meaningful?

   X Yes   No

If yes, indicate in what ways and describe briefly:

		Other	
Mo	Fa	Adult	
X	—	———	Developed an increased understanding of child's problem
X	—	———	Developed an increased understanding of family interactions
—	—	———	Modified their behavior toward each other
—	—	———	Modified management of child
—	—	———	Expressed positive reactions about sessions or clinicians
X	—	———	Other evidence that evaluation was meaningful to parents (mother requested continuation of family meeting even when enough diagnostic material had already obviously been obtained)

26. Would parents support treatment of child if it were recommended?

   X Yes   No

If yes, indicate evidence and describe:

		Other	
Mo	Fa	Adult	
X	—	———	Believe child needs help (mother only, father does not)
X	—	———	Believe child can be helped by treatment
X	—	———	Would be willing to provide transportation
X	—	———	Other evidence (mother has brought in all children even when they were resistant; father sees treatment, except for his wife, as inappropriate and is encouraging resistance in the referred child)

27. Would parents be motivated to participate in treatment themselves if it were recommended?

   X Yes   No

If yes, indicate evidence and describe:

		Other	
Mo	Fa	Adult	
X	—	———	Are seeking help in child management
X	—	———	Believe that changes in child can occur in relation to changes in themselves
X	—	———	Would like to change some of the ways family members relate to each other
X	—	———	Willing to come for future appointments (father came in alone for one evaluation appointment. He refused to participate in a family session and will not participate in treatment)
—	—	———	Other

TABLE 82–13

Case 1	Case 2
2. Number and dates of contacts during evaluation (include interviews and all specialized sessions): *Number of Sessions* __4__ Child alone __4__ Mother alone _____ Father alone _____ Parents together _____ Family—total group _____ Other	2. Number and dates of contacts during evaluation (include interviews and all specialized sessions): *Number of Sessions* __5__ Child alone __5__ Mother alone __1__ Father alone _____ Parents together __1__ Family—total group _____ Other
3. Which of the following techniques were used in this evaluation? __X__ Interview __X__ Psychological testing _____ Educational evaluation _____ Expressive arts evaluation _____ Neurological screening _____ Other (specify)	3. Which of the following techniques were used in this evaluation? __X__ Interview __X__ Psychological testing _____ Educational evaluation _____ Expressive arts evaluation _____ Neurological screening _____ Other (specify)

conducted by a psychology intern; parents in Case 2 were seen by a staff social worker.

Further data about the clinicians is provided by the questions in table 82–14.

Question 7 in CDC-D asks for similar data about the parent clinician. In Case 1, it was the same person. In Case 2, the clinician was also a white female. She has had five to ten years of clinical experience, and described her theoretical preference as eclectic.

If clinician characteristics had a significant impact on the recommendations in the two cases under discussion, it is not obvious from the above data. This sort of judgment is an empirical question which will be investigated. For example, a hundred cases evaluated by clinicians of one discipline could be compared with a hundred cases evaluated by clinicians of another discipline to determine if recommendations differ systematically. The expectation of the authors is that clusters of clinician variables will be related to treatment recommended. That is, it is predicted that the "belief system" of the clinician is related to clinical judgments and decisions in some systematic way.

CDC-E: DECISION-MAKING MEETING

The concluding phase of the evaluation process is a conference attended by the clinicians involved in the case and by one or more chairmen/

consultants. At this meeting, the case is discussed and recommendations regarding treatment are made. As will be seen, recommendations for treatment include a formulation of the goals of treatment.

CDC-E, which consists of twelve questions, represents the record of that conference. Answers to selected questions from the two sample cases will be presented.

The conference on Case 1 was co-chaired by a child psychiatrist and a social worker, and attended by the psychologist who had served as the child and parent clinician. The chairman of the conference on Case 2 was a social worker; both clinicians (psychologist and social worker) involved in the evaluation participated.

One of the decisions that must be made at the conference is that of the diagnosis of the referred child. The data system is not primarily aimed at selecting a diagnostic category for the child. Nevertheless, for statistical and administrative purposes, it is common practice to classify the patient population according to diagnostic categories identified in the APA Diagnostic and Statistical Manual (DSM II). A diagnosis of record is therefore required.

In both the case examples, the diagnosis assigned was "307.1 Adjustment Reaction of Childhood." The authors feel obliged to record some disagreement with this diagnosis for Child 1. In view of the length and severity of the child's

TABLE 82–14

Case 1	Case 2

6. Identifying characteristics of child clinician
  Number of years of clinical experience
  _____ Less than two years
  __X__ Two to less than five years
  _____ Five to less than ten years
  _____ Ten years or more
      Theoretical Preference(s)
  __X__ Learning theory
  _____ Psychoanalytic theory
  _____ Developmental theory
  _____ Family-interactional theory
  _____ Gestalt theory
  _____ Eclectic
  _____ Other (specify)
      Sex
  _____ Male
  __X__ Female
      Race
  __X__ White
  _____ Black
  _____ Oriental
  _____ Other (specify)
	6. Identifying characteristics of child clinician
	  Number of years of clinical experience
	  _____ Less than two years
	  __X__ Two to less than five years
	  _____ Five to less than ten years
	  _____ Ten years or more
	      Theoretical Preference(s)
	  _____ Learning Theory
	  _____ Psychoanalytic theory
	  _____ Developmental theory
	  _____ Family-interactional theory
	  _____ Gestalt theory
	  __X__ Eclectic
	  _____ Other (specify)
	      Sex
	  _____ Male
	  __X__ Female
	      Race
	  __X__ White
	  _____ Black
	  _____ Oriental
	  _____ Other (specify)

symptoms, a diagnosis such as "308.2 Behavior Disorder of Childhood—Overanxious Reaction" would seem more appropriate. However, the fact that the two children received the same diagnosis but different treatment recommendations is a good illustration of the point made earlier that there is often little or no relationship between diagnosis and treatment. The specific diagnosis used in these cases is reminiscent of the position taken by Kessler[13] that a diagnosis of "Adjustment Reaction of Childhood" is more a matter of form than of significance.

With respect to treatment recommendations, in both cases the recommendations which had been made by the evaluating clinicians were accepted. For Case 1, the recommendation was for individual therapy for the referred child and individual therapy for mother. In Case 2, the recommendation was for family therapy, initially to include mother and three children. It was also suggested that after a course of family therapy with the children participating, a period of working with mother alone might be considered.

The question in table 82–15 covers the suggested goals of treatment.

The question on problems and goals is designed to provide a framework for therapy and is the beginning of a basis for judging future therapeutic progress. Subsequent to the time these two cases were evaluated, the question on goals was revised and expanded. The intent has been to focus more specifically on goals and to summarize the assets derived from the evaluation as well as the problems. Although this question was not available to the clinicians involved in these evaluations, a sample of how the clinicians in the conference on Case 1 *might have* formulated one goal for the mother is provided to illustrate the revised question.

Case 1

4. Goals for Parent/Family

Goal 1: Support attempts at independent functioning for separated mother, through establishment of trust relationship with an individual therapist.

Problems: List parent/family problems that will improve if this goal is attained.

1. Mother is relatively socially isolated, noncommunicative, and has no current family or social supports upon whom she can depend, nor with whom she can communicate.

2. Mother's difficulty in accepting and discussing

TABLE 82–15

Case 1	Case 2
4. List the problems evident in the completed evaluation. Where possible, indicate recommendations for treatment goals and potential methods of intervention.	4. List the problems evident in the completed evaluation. Where possible, indicate recommendations for treatment goals and potential methods of intervention.
Referred Child	*Referred Child*
Problems: excessive fears, preoccupation disrupts functioning	*Problems:* stress reaction to insecure, chaotic home environment
Goals: provide opportunity to discuss concerns and ventilate feelings	*Goals:* provide support in family therapy; help child "de-triangulate" himself from marital conflicts
Parents	*Parents*
Problems: mother's feeling of inadequacy; inability to function independently; emotional unavailability to child	*Problems:* constant fighting, using children against each other, allowing children to witness violent confrontations
Goals: initial goal to help mother accept the idea of individual therapy; establish trusting relationship with mother and support attempts at independent functioning	*Goals:* make mother aware of how she creates problems for children; support mother in accepting separation and divorce
Others:	*Others:*
Problems:	*Problems:* siblings experience same chaotic environment as referred child
Goals:	*Goals:* supportive counseling through family therapy; help siblings to avoid being used as pawns in parental conflicts

the marital problems and separation has led to increased tension in the home and rendered her emotionally unavailable to her children.

Assets to be utilized in achieving this goal:

Individual: Mother has in many ways been an adequate mother to her children; potential for improved functioning is also indicated by the fact that constructive changes began to occur during the evaluation.

Family: Referred child is willing to talk about problems and would support mother's dealing with her difficulties.

Community: Potential assets in the community will have to be explored; mother does have relatives in the community and a neighbor who occasionally watches the children. These people might become sources of support and of social diversion.

Comments (e.g., short-term goals, interventions and strategies to be used):

Help mother become able to discuss the marital difficulties and separation with her children.

It is anticipated that the revised format will help to provide the basis for conceptualizing and recording therapy in terms of goals to be attained. Since therapy is a process of building on assets as well as relieving problems, it was felt to be important to focus on assets as well as problems in formulating goals.

The final question in CDC-E deals with predictions. For the two sample cases, the responses were as presented in table 82–16.

In both cases, the child's prognosis with treatment was judged to be good.

Conclusion

It must be obvious from the two examples given that it is unlikely that there will be simple relationships between any one data item and any one treatment modality. To take one example, it might be predicted that the presence of anxiety in a child would be related to the selection of individual therapy. However, most children referred to mental health centers are seen as anxious—of a sample of 148 children evaluated at the Pittsburgh Child Guidance Center in 1975, 114 or 77 percent were described as anxious. As in our two case examples, it is not the simple presence or absence of anxiety, but rather the manifestations and severity of anxiety that, in combination with many other factors, lead to decisions about treatment.

Perhaps the most important conclusion is that, whether or not a standardized data collection

TABLE 82–16

Case 1	Case 2
10. Predictions:	10. Predictions:

Length of Treatment	*Length of Treatment*
_____ Less than three months	__X__ Less than three months
_____ Three months to less than six months	_____ Three months to less than six months
_____ Six months to less than nine months	_____ Six months to less than nine months
__X__ Nine months to less than one year (for child)	_____ Nine months to less than one year
__X__ One year or more (for mother)	_____ One year or more
_____ Other (specify)	__X__ Other (specify) (contract may then be renegotiated if additional work with mother alone is indicated)

Prognosis with Treatment	*Prognosis with Treatment*
__X__ Good	__X__ Good
_____ Fair	_____ Fair
_____ Poor	_____ Poor
_____ Other (specify)	_____ Other (specify)

Prognosis without Treatment	*Prognosis without Treatment*
_____ Good	_____ Good
_____ Fair	_____ Fair
__X__ Poor	__X__ Poor
_____ Other (specify)	_____ Other (specify)

instrument is used, evaluation of children and families is never a routine or simplistic process.

ACKNOWLEDGMENTS

This project has been partially supported by grants from the Buhl Foundation of Pittsburgh and by corporate contributions through the Neighborhood Assistance Act.

We wish to thank our colleagues who have worked with us on various phases of the project: Juergen Homann, M.D.; Patricia J. Devroude, M.P.H.; Neil D. Rosenblum, Ph.D.; Carolyn M. Hiltner, M.S.W.; Zaven Khachaturian, Ph.D.; and Norberto A. Rodriguez, M.D. We are also grateful to the administration and staff of the Pittsburgh Child Guidance Center, who have been most supportive of our work.

REFERENCES

1. COLE, J. K., and MAGNUSSEN, M. G., "Where the Action Is," *Journal of Consulting Psychology, 30:*539–543, 1966.
2. CRAWFORD, J. L., MORGAN, D. W., and GIANTURCO, D. T. (Eds.), *Progress in Mental Health Information Systems: Computer Applications*, Ballinger Publishing Co., Cambridge, Mass., 1974.
3. CURRAN, W. J., et al., "Protection of Privacy and Confidentiality," *Science, 182:*797–802, 1973.
4. DONNELLY, J., ROSENBERG, M., and FLEESON, W. P., "The Evolution of the Mental Status—Past and Future," *American Journal of Psychiatry, 126(7):*997–1002, 1970.
5. GAURON, E. J., and DICKINSON, J. K., "Diagnostic Decision Making in Psychiatry. Information Usage," *Archives of General Psychiatry, 14:*225–232, 1966.
6. GLUECK, B. C., and STROEBEL, C. F., "The Computer and the Clinical Decision Process II," *American Journal of Psychiatry*, Suppl., *125:*2–7, 1969.

7. GOLDBERG, L. R., "Simple Models or Simple Processes? Some Research on Clinical Judgments," *American Psychologist, 23:*483–496, 1968.
8. GOLDEN, M., "Some Effects of Combining Psychological Tests on Clinical Inferences," *Journal of Consulting Psychology, 28:*440–446, 1964.
9. GOTTHEIL, E., KRAMER, M., and HURVICH, M. D., "Intake Procedures and Psychiatric Decisions," *Comprehensive Psychiatry, 7:*207–215, 1966.
10. HADLEY, J. M., *Clinical and Counseling Psychology*, Knopf, New York, 1958.
11. HENDERSON, P. B., et al., "A Clinical Decision-Making Model for Child Psychiatric Intervention Selection," *Psychological Reports, 37:*923–934, 1975.
12. KATZ, M. M., COLE, J. O., and LOWERY, H. A., "Studies of the Diagnostic Process: The Influence of Symptom Perception, Past Experience, and Ethnic Background on Diagnostic Decisions," *American Journal of Psychiatry, 125:*937–947, 1969.

13. Kessler, J. W., *Psychopathology of Childhood*, Prentice-Hall, Englewood Cliffs, N.J., 1966.

14. Kupfer, D. J., and Detre, T. P., "Development and Application of the KDS-1 in Inpatient and Outpatient Settings," *Psychological Reports*, 29:607–617, 1971.

15. Laska, E., "The Multi-State Information System," in Crawford, J. L., Morgan, D. W., and Gianturco, D. T. (Eds.), *Progress in Mental Health Information Systems: Computer Applications*, vol. 1, Ballinger Publishing Co., Cambridge, Mass., 1974.

16. ———, et al., "The Multi-State Information System," *Evaluation*, 66–71, 1972.

17. Magnussen, M. G., et al., *Clinical Data Forms A, B, C, D, and E*, Copyright: Pittsburgh Child Guidance Center Clinical Data System, 1974.

18. Morgan, D. W., and Frenkel, S. I., "Computer Support in Military Psychiatry," in Crawford, J. L., Morgan, D. W., and Gianturco, D. T. (Eds.), *Progress in Mental Health Information Systems: Computer Applications*, Ballinger Publishing Co., Cambridge, Mass., 1974.

19. Nathan, P. E., et al., "Thirty-Two Observers and One Patient: A Study of Diagnostic Reliability," *Journal of Clinical Psychology*, 25:9–15, 1969.

20. Oskamp, S., "Overconfidence in Case-Study Judgments," *Journal of Consulting Psychology*, 29:261–265, 1965.

21. Reznikoff, M., Holland, C. H., and Stroebel, C. F., "Attitudes Toward Computers Among Employees of a Psychiatric Hospital," *Hospital and Community Psychiatry*, 19:419–425, 1968.

22. Russ, S. W., "Treatment Decisions as a Function of Clinical Assessment Procedures." Ph.D. Dissertation, University of Pittsburgh, 1970.

23. Schwartz, M. L., "Validity and Reliability in Clinical Judgments of C-V-S Protocols as a Function of Amount of Information and Diagnostic Category," *Psychological Reports*, 20:767–774, 1967.

24. Sines, L. K., "The Relative Contribution of Four Kinds of Data to Accuracy in Personality Assessment," *Journal of Consulting Psychology*, 23:483, 495, 1959.

25. Sletten, I. W., and Ulett, G. A., "The Present Status of Automation in a State Psychiatric System," *Psychiatric Annals*, 2:42–57, 1972.

26. ———, and Evenson, R. C., "PSRO's in Psychiatry: Problems and Opportunities," Paper presented at the Annual American Psychiatric Association Meeting, 1974.

27. Snyderman, B. B., et al., *CDC Forms A, B, C, D, and E*, Copyright: Pittsburgh Child Guidance Center Clinical Data System, December 1975.

28. Sundberg, N. D., and Tyler, L. E., *Clinical Psychology*, Appleton-Century-Crofts, New York, 1962.

29. Taft, R., "Multiple Methods of Personality Assessment," *Psychological Bulletin*, 56:333–352, 1959.

30. ———, "The Ability to Judge People," *Psychological Bulletin*, 51:1–25, 1955.

31. Wallen, R. W., *Clinical Psychology: The Study of Persons*, McGraw-Hill, New York, 1956.

32. Webster, E. C., *Decision Making in the Employment Interview*, McGill University Press, Montreal, 1967.

33. Weiss, J. H., "Effect of Professional Training and Amount of Accuracy of Information on Behavioral Prediction," *Journal of Consulting Psychology*, 27:257–262, 1963.

83 / Rating Scales

C. Keith Conners

There is a special area of practice in child psychiatry that calls for the use of standardized rating scales. A variety of these instruments have been developed by many investigators. Those scientists with a particular interest in clinical psychopharmacology research with children have often led the way in this process. In fact, the need for other kinds of longitudinally oriented checklists and outcome scales reaches into many areas of study. Sometimes these techniques must be adapted to general clinical use, but as a rule they are designed to focus in on a particular aspect of treatment outcome or disease process.

The present state of the art and science in this area is well described in the following contribution.

—RLC

Introduction

In the attempt to describe and measure behavior, rating scales are assessment techniques with a venerable history. Their modern origin is commonly ascribed to Sir Francis Galton who developed scales for evaluating the vividness of imagery.[15] Guilford[17] notes that as early as 1828, the religious group of New Harmony in Indiana used ratings of such traits as judgment, imagination, reflection, memory, perception, excitability, courage, and strength. While generally acknowledged to be instruments fraught with methodologic pitfalls and multiple sources of error, rating scales seem to have a particular attraction to the psychiatric observer. In recent years, a great many sophisticated and varied instruments have been developed for use in psychiatric diagnosis, treatment, and research. For example, in 1968, Lyerly and Abbott[25] compiled an annotated monograph of nineteen scales widely used in adult psychiatric studies between 1950 and 1964. The fact that five of the nineteen scales were specifically directed toward the phenomena of depression suggests that the new emergence of antidepressant drugs and associated research gave strong impetus to the development of such instruments.

More recently, there have been continued attempts to develop sophisticated batteries of measures for assessing change in psychotherapy[37] or in drug studies.[11] It appears that the need for specific instruments of evaluation comes to the fore in research as questions become more focused and therapies more specific. The same trend has begun, though at a much slower rate, in child psychiatry. Despite their limitations, it is likely that rating scales will presently become central among methods for the assessment of behavior in child psychiatry. One reason for this probably lies in the compatibility of this technique with the practitioner's basic clinical approach: His skills are usually applied to integrating and synthesizing many bits of information into molar patterns; discrete behaviors are usually of interest only insofar as they reveal larger configurations of functions of the individual. In this sense, the clinical process is usually regarded as "ipsative" rather than "normative," and molar rather than molecular; it is thus particularly compatible with instruments designed for recording judgments or higher-order concepts in contrast to discrete behaviors. Henry Murray (the inventor of the Thematic Apperception Test) took note of this issue in his seminal *Explorations in Personality* in 1938:[27]

Some psychologists may prefer to limit themselves to the study of one kind of episode. For instance, they may study the responses of a great number of individuals to a specific situation. They may attempt to discover what changes in their situation bring about important changes in response. But, since every response is partially determined by the after-effects of previous experiences, the psychologist will never fully understand an episode if he abstracts it from ontogeny, the developmental history of the individual. [p. 3]

He goes on to distinguish between short motor units of behavior (actones) and units related to some adaptive goal of the organism and its environmental demands (thema). This developmental point of view both recognizes the contextual meaning of behaviors and their "global" quality. Such a point of view is likely to be shared by most child psychiatric workers, and is easily adapted to the use of rating scale techniques.

However, this point of view often pits the "lumpers" against the "splitters." It is thus likely to lead to a dispute between two kinds of observers. On the one hand is the behaviorally oriented scientist who requires that terms be carefully operationalized by rigorous procedures having specific, usually molecular, units of behavior as their referents. On the other are the more global assessments made by those who deal with higher order abstractions; these are often not easily referable to discrete behaviors. The behaviorist is likely to view rating methods as "soft" and mushy, while the psychiatrist is likely to view the behavioral methods (for example, direct time-sampling) as cumbersome, reductionistic, and basically invalid. The busy clinician then either eschews measurement altogether, viewing it as unfeasible or irrelevant, while the researcher dismisses most global ratings as unreliable. Actually, it appears that the behaviorist is usually more preoccupied with issues of *reliability* of instrumentation, while the psychiatrist is usually more attuned to issues of *validity* (or meaningfulness or relevance).

In any case, it seems clear that as child psychiatry moves more from the prescientific stages of being an art (albeit a subtle one) to that of an applied science, and particularly, as it becomes more conscious of the responsibility to evaluate its treatments, document its diagnoses, and operationalize its concepts, instruments such as rating scales will become ever more necessary. This trend also seems to be tied to the emergence of a variety of alternative therapeutic interventions such as pharmacotherapy, family or group methods, biofeedback, school consultation, etc. Each of these must ultimately justify its cost in terms of documented success. Moreover, child psychiatry, being a long-term, developmentally oriented discipline par excellence, must continue to develop careful long-term followup of its patients across wide spans of time. Here the rating scale will certainly continue to serve as a basic means of documentation.

Finally, psychiatry is a discipline requiring the use and evaluation of multiple sources of data. Information from the child, the parents, peers, relatives, and direct observation must all be taken into account before the main work of diagnostic synthesis and treatment planning can begin. Once this process has been initiated, these same sources are often called upon to provide information regarding the child's changing status, the fluctuation of his symptoms and moods, side effects of therapy, relationships with others, academic and social function, etc. Systematic recording of such data can aid record keeping, the monitoring of treatment, the formulation of research hypotheses, and the evaluation of outcomes for groups of patients according to different reference points. In many cases, neither the child's behavior as observed in the office nor the mother's impressionistic comments are sufficient to judge the efficacy of therapy or to monitor the complex fluctuations of development over time.

The purpose of the present chapter is to acquaint the reader with some of the recent developments in the use of rating scales in the context of psychiatric assessment and treatment. The chapter will illustrate some of the commonly used scales along with their advantages and disadvantages, and will touch upon the major methodologic issues involved. However, a complete discussion of methodology is beyond the scope of this presentation. Chapter 66 recommends appropriate sources for the practitioner who desires to become acquainted with the details of scale construction, validation, and interpretation. By presenting several available instruments, it is hoped that practitioners and researchers alike will move in the direction of the development of tools appropriate to the nature of the subject matter. Too often the psychiatrist has been asked to rely upon tools that are alien to the style, level of analysis, and type of process germane to his particular field. It is the development of instruments specifically appropriate to the field of inquiry known as child psychiatry that alone can guarantee scientific progress and the refinement of clinical skills.

Ratings Made by Psychiatrists

It is remarkable that virtually no empirical studies have been made which utilize the child psychiatrist's *interview* as a source of data for making diagnostic judgments. The landmark in the field was the 1968 study by Rutter and Graham,[31] who noted that only the study by Sherwin et al.[33] reports reliability and validity information regarding the psychiatric examination of the child. Fortunately, both studies appear to provide reassurance that ratings of the examination can be both reliable and valid. Rutter and Graham's standardized semi-structured half-hour interview procedure showed reasonably good inter-rater and test-retest reliability, as well as concurrent validity (agreement with parent-teacher judgments of psychiatric illness, and with diagnoses made by psychiatrists). They note that ratings of affect, especially sadness, were somewhat unreliable although they were still valid.

Of particular interest to psychiatrists should be their finding that:

. . . it was striking that some of the most global and inferential items were at least as reliable (as well as being more useful) than some of the specific and apparently objective pieces of behavior. For example, the overall rating of psychiatric abnormality and the rating on "emotional responsiveness" were both more reliable than "startle" or "muscular tension" or "tremulousness." . . . Whatever the explanation, it is clear from this study, as from many others . . . that concern with finer and finer units of behavior does not necessarily lead to greater reliability. Nor are inferential items necessarily unreliable. [p. 574]

It is always possible to make items more reliable by careful definitions and by training judges. There is a real question, however, whether such exercises are meaningful or necessary beyond a certain point. (This excludes the most specialized research contexts.)

A modified version of the Rutter-Graham ratings has been adopted by the NIMH Early Clinical Drug Evaluation Unit (ECDEU) for use in drug studies and psychopharmacologic screening with children (see Appendix). Recent work by D. Englehardt at Downstate Medical Center in New York City (unpublished) has shown the usefulness of these ratings in plotting developmental trends for severely disturbed children, and in establishing drug-development interactions. The value of such an instrument in research studies is obvious; it allows the investigator to specify objectively the characteristics of a patient sample, and to follow changes over time.

Ratings by psychiatrists of parent interviews are apparently somewhat more problematical than direct interviews with the child. This is so because mothers tend to be unreliable across interview sessions. In their report of the reliability and validity of the parent interview, Graham and Rutter[16] observed that items dealing with the relationship of the mother to the child, or peer and sibling relationships, were relatively unreliable. This was true as well for items requiring some inference (such as the child's feeling miserable, having a stomachache). These stood in contrast

CLINICAL GLOBAL IMPRESSIONS

INSTRUCTIONS: *Mark these items on General Scoring Sheet coded 01.*

Complete Item 1 —SEVERITY OF ILLNESS at the initial and subsequent assessments. Items 2 and 3 may be omitted at the initial assessment by marking 0 — "Not Assessed".

Mark on the left half of the scoring sheet on rows 38 — 41.

ROW NO.	CLINICAL GLOBAL IMPRESSIONS
38	**1. SEVERITY OF ILLNESS** Considering your total clinical experience with this particular population, how mentally ill is the patient at this time? 0 = Not assessed 4 = Moderately ill 1 = Normal, not at all ill 5 = Markedly ill 2 = Borderline mentally ill 6 = Severely ill 3 = Mildly ill 7 = Among the most extremely ill patients

---

> *THE NEXT TWO ITEMS MAY BE OMITTED AT THE INITIAL ASSESSMENT BY MARKING "NOT ASSESSED" FOR BOTH ITEMS*

ROW NO.	
39	**2. GLOBAL IMPROVEMENT** — Rate total improvement whether or not, in your judgment, it is due entirely to drug treatment. Compared to his condition at admission to the project, how much has he changed? 0 = Not assessed 4 = No change 1 = Very much improved 5 = Minimally worse 2 = Much improved 6 = Much worse 3 = Minimally improved 7 = Very much worse
40 & 41	**3. EFFICACY INDEX** — Rate this item on the basis of DRUG EFFECT ONLY. Select the terms which best describe the degrees of therapeutic effect and side effects and record the number in the box where the two items intersect. EXAMPLE: Therapeutic effect is rated as "Moderate" and side effects are judged "Do not significantly interfere with patient's functioning". Record 06 in rows 40 and 41.

THERAPEUTIC EFFECT	SIDE EFFECTS			
	None	Do not significantly interfere with patient's functioning	Significantly interferes with patient's functioning	Outweighs therapeutic effect
MARKED — Vast improvement. Complete or nearly complete remission of all symptoms	01	02	03	04
MODERATE — Decided improvement. Partial remission of symptoms	05	06	07	08
MINIMAL — Slight improvement which doesn't alter status of care of patient	09	10	11	12
UNCHANGED OR WORSE	13	14	15	16
Not Assessed = 00				

FIGURE 83–1

A simple global improvement and efficiency scale from the ECDEU battery.

NOTE: Reprinted by permission of the publisher from NIMH, "Children's ECDEU Battery," *Psychopharmacology Bulletin, Special Issue*, 9:196–239, 1973.

to such specific items as bedwetting, stealing, and temper tantrums. On the other hand, ratings were obtained from direct interviews on general emotional factors such as tension in the home, dissatisfaction, warmth, and hostility. With careful training, clear-cut criteria, and standardized interview procedures, these have been shown to be capable of highly reliable and valid measurement.[5]

Surprisingly, a simple global rating of the degree of severity of the overall problem, or the degree of improvement after psychiatric interviews or treatment has often been found to be both reliable and sensitive. An illustration of a combination of an improvement *rating* and *side effects* scale for drug studies from the ECDEU battery is shown in figure 83–1.

Ratings Made by Teachers

For students of child development, teachers have long been an important source of information. Cattell and Coan[7] gave the teachers of 198 first- and second-grade pupils a thirty-eight item trait list of bipolar items. This list was compiled to include the major markers from factor analytic work as well as "useful indicators of personality disturbance." Although their methods allowed them to identify some fifteen separate factors, the more usual result of such investigations was that found by Peterson.[29] He discerned two major factors with similar items—conduct disturbance and personality disturbance. Using 427 cases at a child

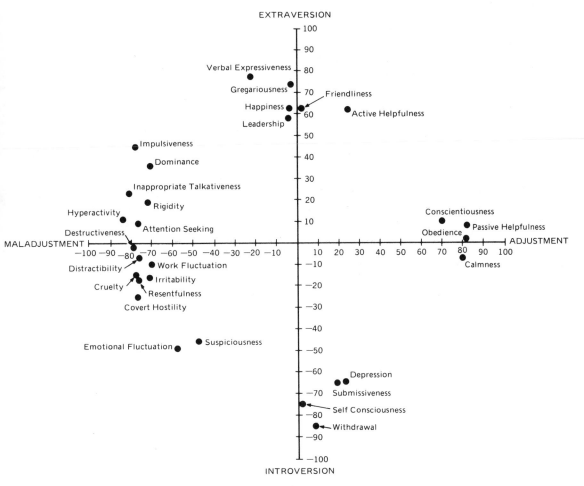

FIGURE 83–2

A two-dimensional "circumplex" for ordering a variety of traits derived from teachers' ratings of behavior in school children.

NOTE: Reprinted by permission of the author from Schaeffer, E., "Development of Heirarchical Configurational Models for Parent Behavior and Child Behavior," in J. P. Hill (Ed.), *Minnesota Symposia on Child Psychiatry*, vol. 5, pp. 130–161, University of Minnesota Press, Minneapolis, 1971.

guidance clinic, they selected the fifty-eight most common symptoms. These were then presented to teachers of 831 kindergarten through sixth-grade pupils for rating. Inter-rater reliabilities were about 0.77 for the two major factors. Subsequent work by Quay[30] and many others has shown that these two major dimensions of behavior show up repeatedly in symptom-oriented scales rated by teachers.

Careful work by Shaeffer[32] and colleagues at the Laboratory of Psychology of the National Institute of Mental Health has demonstrated that a very large pool of behavioral items rated by teachers tends to reduce to two orthogonal (uncorrelated) dimensions. The various items organize as a "circumplex" (i.e., the item clusters tend to be arranged in a meaningful way around a circle with the two major axes as coordinates). The bewildering array of symptoms and overt behaviors potentially ratable by teachers or other significant figures in the child's life can be conceptually ordered as two basic dimensions, one roughly equivalent to an inhibited-uninhibited, and the other to an adjustment-maladjustment dimension. Empirically then, it is possible to identify four distinct groups represented by the combination of the extreme ends of each dimension.

A carefully standardized multi-factor teacher scale with a good manual and easy format for teacher use is the Devereux Elementary School Behavior Rating Scale.[35] This scale provides factor scores in eleven different areas, with normative data available on 809 children from kindergarten through the sixth grade. A similar scale has been developed by the same authors for adolescents.

A thirty-nine item questionnaire was originally designed by Eisenberg and colleagues at Johns Hopkins Hospital for psychopharmacologic experiments. This has since been factor-analyzed by Conners[13] and is part of the ECDEU battery. It has now been widely used in drug studies[23] and norms have been developed.[33] Again, the most useful factors are the conduct-disturbance factor, the tension-anxiety factor, and the hyperactivity factor.

For certain hyperactive school-age children, pharmacotherapy is occasionally an appropriate modality of treatment. In those cases where the child is an outpatient, which is most often the case, a simple method of following the child's progress in school is to use the ten-item abbreviated school questionnaire. This has been adapted from the longer thirty-nine item version developed by this author.[11] Figure 83–3 presents data showing results of increasing dosages on the total score from the teachers scale as well as a global

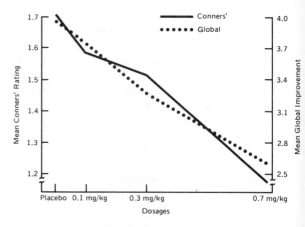

FIGURE 83–3

Data showing dose-response effect of drug in simple ten-item scale for measuring change in hyperactive children.

NOTE: Reprinted by permission of the publisher from Sprague, R. L., and Sleater, E. K., "Effects of Psychopharmacologic Agents on Learning Disorders," *Pediatric Clinics of North America*, 20(3):719–735, 1973.

clinical estimate of improvement. The scale, shown in the Appendix, is also embedded in a parent rating scale. This makes it possible to monitor the same symptoms as the parents see them during the course of treatment. During the early stages of treatment, the sensitivity of the scale to pharmacologic effects makes it very useful in the process of dosage titration. This holds true despite its apparent simplicity. Obviously, additional information must supplement these reports, but they serve a useful adjunctive role in treatment and research.

Using a modification of the Pittsburgh Adjustment Survey, Miller[26] extracted five factors from a pool of ninty-four items. He standardized them on a sample of normal children who were representative of the school population in IQ and socioeconomic status. Over 5,000 were involved. This scale might be quite useful to mental health workers. It is particularly appropriate in screening programs where large numbers of children are to be rated in connection with plans for the delivery of mental health services.

Recent years have seen an increasing concern over the question of accurate, early identification of mental disturbances in children. One of the more controversial issues involves the early recognition of the MBD syndrome or hyperactive behavior disturbances. Bell, Waldrop, and Weller[2] have developed a very useful screening scale for use by teachers in identifying preschool hyperactivity. The scale is an eleven-point roster to be applied during daily observations of children over a one-month period. Various categories are rated such as "frenetic play," "inability to delay," and "nomadic play." A factor-scoring system is based upon normative data from which one may compute a total hyperactivity score and a total "withdrawal" score. The instrument should be useful for following children over time and detecting changes due to interventions. If a preschool child were referred for psychiatric appraisal, collecting such data could substantially clarify the diagnostic process. It provides "hard" data based on a carefully developed instrument which has been standardized for normal children.

A related area for the psychiatrist is the evaluation of learning disorders in children. Obviously, the data provided by teachers is crucial in arriving at a complete description of the child's academic style and learning deficits. Increasingly, the psychiatrist is called upon to assist the teacher in developing a comprehensive program for such children; of necessity, this undertaking involves academic, social, and psychologic dimensions. One instrument that has proved useful for this purpose is the Myklebust scale.[28] This is a twenty-four item anchored scale grouped into four areas: auditory comprehension and learning; spoken language; orientation in time, space, and relationship; and behavior and motor functions. The scale was used in a study involving 2,767 third and fourth graders with identified learning problems. For children with known or suspected learning disabilities, this scale provides the teacher with an organized way of communicating information to the psychiatrist. The data that emerges is appropriate for developing specific forms of intervention.

Blunden, Spring, and Greenberg[3] developed a Classroom Behavior Inventory (CBI) and carried out extensive validation of this instrument using 320 kindergarten boys. The scale uses ten categories of behavior associated with the hyperkinetic syndrome. There are four individual items each rated on a four-point scale ("not at all like the child"—1 point to "very much like the child" —4 points). A factor analysis showed that restlessness, impulsivity, distractibility, low concentration, and low perseverance loaded highly on factor I. Cheerfulness, social participation, and verbal expression loaded on factor II, while irritability and resentfulness loaded on factor III. The fourth factor was uninterpretable.

Concurrent validity was measured by comparing the CBI with direct time-sampling in the classroom. To accomplish this, fifteen-second intervals were utilized over a fifteen-minute period three times a week. Thus, each subject had forty-five minutes of direct observation. Inter-observer agreement ranged from 71 percent to 78 percent.

The results were striking. Only one of the CBI scales (impulsiveness) actually correlated significantly with its directly observed counterpart ($r = .50$). Of the forty-nine correlations in the matrix, only nine were significant; six of those were correlations of the direct observations with teacher's ratings of impulsiveness. It appeared that teachers made global judgments as to whether or not children had behavior disorders. Moreover, on eight of ten teachers' *ratings*, there were significant differences, while only one of the *direct* observation scores differentiated the two groups (impulsiveness).

The authors suggest that either the low stability of the directly observed behaviors from the forty-five minute sample or limited inter-teacher reliabilities could have attenuated the correspondence of the two data sets. They also suggest that the teachers may in fact have been using only one "real" dimension—impulsiveness. However, one might equally well argue that the teachers' ratings were valid and that of the directly observed behaviors invalid. This could have come about because of their highly context-specific, unrepresentative nature.

Ratings Made by Parents

There is usefulness, as well as limitation, to the way parents report their children's symptoms. Both are illustrated by the careful study of Novick et al.* of the Deviant Behavior Inventory (DBI). This inventory of 237 symptoms is given to parents to sort independently into true, false, and not-sure categories. The study investigated the extent to which parents either omit symptoms that others report are present, or include symptoms that independent study reveals are absent. The authors conclude that "it is apparent from our findings that despite all efforts to minimize the error due to false endorsements by reporters, the residual error is of such magnitude as to seriously question the value of any behavioral assessment which does not take this into account." In other words, parental reports of symptoms must be viewed with caution.

Despite its limitations, however, this type of instrument serves a useful screening function. It covers virtually all areas of symptomatology of

* Novick, J., et al., "Ascertaining Deviant Behavior in Children," *Journal of Consulting Psychology*, 30:230–238, 1966.

relevance to the eight- to twelve-year-old age range. In particular, it can serve the psychiatrist well by pointing to relevant areas of inquiry, insuring comprehensive coverage of symptoms, and highlighting target behaviors for intervention and followup.

Studies of ratings of behavior made by parents or other adults have been valuable in identifying the major clusters of symptomatology found in middle childhood. Jenkins and Hewitt[21] were among the first to use this method; they rated traits identified from the case records of 500 children rated on ninety symptoms. Jenkins[20] subsequently identified five clusters which he labeled: "shy-seclusive," "overanxious-neurotic," "hyperactivity with poor concentration," "undomesticated," and "socialized delinquent." These clusters appeared to fall into two broad categories of inhibited and aggressive behavior similar to the two dimensions of "conduct disorder" and "personality disorder" described by Peterson,[29] Quay,[30] Dreger et al.,[14] and Borgatta and Fanshel.[4] This latter study produced twelve factors: defiance, unsocialized, tension-anxiety, lack of affection, infantilism, overcleanliness, sex precociousness, sex inhibition, learning difficulty, likeability, and responsibility. A second-order factor analysis produced six factors including an "acting out" factor, developmental immaturity, inhibited behavior, learning disorder, and sociable-responsible.

Spivack and Spotts* at the Devereux Foundation have developed an excellent anchored rating scale for nonprofessionals with good norms. It covers ninety-seven items in seventeen subscales. Like the Devereux Teachers' Scale, it is easy to use and score, includes a broad range of psychopathology, and has good standardization. The Missouri Children's Behavior Checklist[34] is a similar seventy-item, yes-no symptom list with factors of aggression, inhibition, activity level, sleep disturbance, somatization, and sociability. The scale has good demonstrated reliability with agreements between parents ranging from 53 to 94 percent. Validity studies of clinic vs. control subjects showed significant discrimination for all factors except somatization and sleep disturbance (the latter are apparently such common transient disturbances in childhood that they are poor discriminators).

This author[12] has developed a ninety-three item parent symptom checklist. It was factor-analyzed on 316 clinic patients between six and fourteen years of age, and on 367 normal controls of the

same age matched for social class and race. Twenty-four symptom categories such as problems of sleep, learning, and sociability were factored; they produced six principal components: aggressive conduct disturbance, anxious-inhibited, antisocial, enuresis-encopresis, psychosomatic, and anxious-immature. Discriminant function analysis showed that factor scores classified 83 percent of controls and 70 percent of clinic patients correctly. In 77 and 74 percent of cases, respectively, neurotic and hyperkinetic children were accurately identified. This scale is appropriate for typical outpatient samples, but it is not designed for symptoms relating to severe psychopathology such as hallucinations, withdrawal from reality, autistic behaviors, etc.

In general, these longer symptom inventories aid in obtaining a comprehensive description of the patient from the parent's point of view. Although they must be used with caution, they have proved to be both moderately reliable and valid. However, they are too long for another purpose, namely, wide-scale screening and early identification of psychiatric disturbance. The latter problem has been thoroughly investigated in an extension of the Manhattan Study by Langner et al.[24] In the 2,034 children sampled, a thirty-five item score correlated 0.82 with psychiatric impairment. Such scales could be usefully employed in community surveys to identify the most likely beneficiaries of mental health services, to provide epidemiologic indices for intervention strategies, and to screen large school populations using only parent data.

Ratings of Inpatients

Inpatient measurement of psychiatric disturbance presents somewhat different problems than those emerging from outpatient samples. As a rule, the symptoms to be observed are more severe. In addition, multiple observers are often available. Since multiple raters may disagree, this presents both an advantage and a possible source of confusion. More than that, the child is seen out of his usual context. There are behavioral changes induced by the hospitalization and the separation from family and familiar surroundings. Together, these are likely to confound any attempt to establish the "true" behavior pattern.

The Children's Behavior Inventory (CBI) is a 139-item yes-no scale with items grouped according to age-appropriateness.[6] The items are rationally grouped into categories of vegetative function, appearance and mannerisms, speech and voice, emotional display, socialization, and thought proc-

---

* Spivack, G., and Spotts, J., *The Devereux Child Behavior Scale*, Devereux Foundation, Devon, Pa., 1965.

esses. Relatively speaking, the scale items are directly observable. After the child has been observed over some specified interval, they are rated as present or absent. Thus, the child may be interacting with ward personnel who later record the presence/absence of symptoms which are developmentally inappropriate. This author has used the scale in an inpatient setting with considerable benefit. A one-hour period of observation during the lunch and dinner hours was used by morning and evening nursing staff as the basis for separate ratings. There are certain problems concerning the representative character of any particular time of day selected for observations. In general, however, reliability is better if a standard situation is used in the same environmental surroundings in order to minimize variability.

Data from such observations can serve to spe-cify diurnal variations in behavior, changes over time during hospitalization, and response to specific therapies. One example is shown in figure 83–4 which presents observations made on a twelve-year-old psychotic youngster who was thought to be either severely depressed or a borderline schizophrenic. Clinical impressions suggested that the child was somewhat improved on imipramine; the observations of nursing staff, however, indicate that, if anything, the child became more lethargic and angry on the antidepressant. It was also felt that the trial of a potent phenothiazine was of benefit, and the data from the CBI appear to support this judgment. However, it is interesting to note that neither anger nor lethargy are grossly impaired in this child, and neither shows a dramatic change with drug therapy. Such observations are extremely useful in

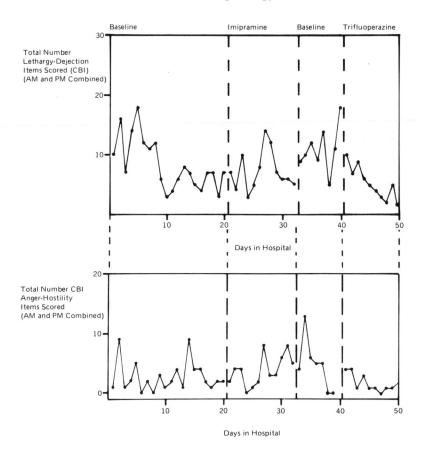

FIGURE 83–4

Use of the CBI for following hospital course. Only items relating to lethargy-dejection and anger-hostility from the scale are plotted here. An apparent clinical effect of imipramine is not substantiated by the data, which tend to show better effect from trifluoperazine (Stelazine). Data recorded by nurses trained to good degree of reliability.

SOURCE: NIMH, "Children's ECDEU Battery," *Pharmacotherapy Bulletin, Special Issue, 9:196–239, 1973.*

giving balance to the clinical decisions made about children. Investigators have repeatedly experienced the difficulty of making such decisions from impressionistic data alone, and have witnessed considerable disagreements among ward staff when everyone uses his own vocabulary, different periods of observation, or a different focus of symptomatology. A running record of reliably observed behaviors kept in a graphic form becomes an invaluable tool for measuring the impact of hospital practice upon disturbed children.

The Children's Pathology Index (CPI)[1] is a scale for inpatient observation of children that has received careful study. As described by the authors, the CPI:

> . . . consists of 38 categories each describing some type of disturbed function, behavior, attitude, relationship or emotional response. Each category contains five descriptive statements ordered from best adjustment (assigned a rank of 5) to worst adjustment (assigned a rank of 1). Each statement appears by itself, printed on a piece of paper 4¼" by 2". The five statements and a numbered title sheet are stapled together to form a booklet. The 38 booklets together make up the instrument and are presented in numerical order. . . . The rater's task is to select from each of the 38 booklets the statement that most typically describes the child. [p. 353]

The ranking of statements was verified by using six trained judges and computing coefficients of concordance, which ranged from 1.0 to 0.67. Twenty-two reached 0.9 or better, and all but five were at the 0.8 or better level. A factor analysis of the instrument produced four factors. The four factors—disturbed behavior toward adults, neurotic constriction, destructive behavior, and disturbed self-perception—appear to be similar to dimensions found on several other instruments; in particular, as noted above, the conduct disorder and anxiety factors seem to be constant dimensions of most instruments.

Reliabilities were computed using four raters, twenty-eight days apart and forty-two days apart. The twenty-eight day reliabilities were 0.85, 0.40, 0.79, and 0.79 for the four factors respectively; and the forty-two day reliabilities were 0.75, 0.72, 0.79, and 0.88.

Concurrent validity was investigated by comparing time samples of aggressive behavior with the factor I scores. A correlation of 0.59 was obtained. A biserial correlation of 0.82 was obtained between factor I scores and psychiatrists' discharge prognosis for community adjustment. This means, of course, that the psychiatrist simply felt that more aggressive children would adjust poorly. The actual patient status at eighteen months after discharge was significantly associated with all four factors. This assessment utilized categories of institutionalized, remaining in the community, and remaining in the community without significant difficulty. To what extent these findings reflect the self-fulfilling prophecy of the psychiatric discharge prognosis and recommendation is unclear. But it is noteworthy that most of the effects are accounted for by the difference between the hospitalized and the nonhospitalized children—a result compatible with this hypothesis. If the psychiatrist both made a prognosis and assigned the children to other institutions, this would not reflect true independent predictive validity of the instrument. A further study showed that in a comparison of four similar institutions, the CPI did not show significant interinstitutional profile differences. While this finding may imply the "universality" of the instrument as suggested by the authors, it could also be due to its insensitivity.

There are many direct observational procedures appropriate for measuring behavior changes in inpatient settings. As a rule, these require more intensive training of staff, and are more cumbersome. Time must be taken out from regular duties to obtain the observations as well as to summarize and graph them. But these methods have the invaluable asset of measuring behaviors specifically defined for the child or setting. These methods have been summarized in detail in two excellent chapters by Mann and Doke in a recent work by Hersen and Bellack.[19]

Further Reading

This chapter has attempted to present the rationale for the use of rating scales in child psychiatry, and to present some of the more useful scales available to the clinician or researcher. However, most workers will find that no single package of instruments suits the needs of different kinds of observers working with diverse patient groups with a wide array of developmental and social characteristics in a variety of settings. One is then faced with the prospect of either devising one's own scales for a particular purpose or uncovering the right scale from a voluminous literature.

Chapter 66 in this volume by Magnussen covers basic issues of reliability and validity and refers the reader to appropriate general texts on testing and measurement. The chapter on rating scales by Guilford in his 1954 text[18] is still one of the best introductions to the basic issues of scale construction, format, error of measurement, and standardization. A more advanced discussion may be found in Cattell and Warburton.[8] (These authors, incidentally, make an important point by arguing that test parameters of universality, efficiency, and utility are more important in test construction than the more usual reliability and validity issues.) The discussion by Lyerly and Abbott[25] of adult psychiatric rating scales, though dated, has an excellent review of reliability issues, such as percent agreement versus correlation coefficients. Johnson and Bommarito[22] have put together a useful compendium of tests and measurements in child development. The latter may be supplemented by Chun, Cobb, and French's "Measures for Psychological Assessment"[10] which contains a complete cross-indexed guide to 3,000 original sources. Comrey, Backer, and Glaser's final report of their NIMH-supported study of a taxonomy of data-collecting devices has been published as "A Sourcebook for Mental Health Measures."[9] It incorporates abstracts of over 1,100 measuring instruments, many not readily known from the usual sources. The 1973 *Psychopharmacology Bulletin*'s Special Issue on Children contains many valuable scales, including most described in this chapter, plus excellent discussions on diagnosis, measurement of side effects, laboratory studies, and other issues related to conducting drug studies with children. A complete package of rating scales in use by the ECDEU for children and adults is available from U.S. Government Printing Office as DHEW Publication No. (ADM) 76-338, 1976.

CHILDREN'S PSYCHIATRIC RATING SCALE

C
P
R
S

INSTRUCTIONS: *Insert General Scoring Sheet, Form 50, and Code 01 under Sheet Number.*

Rate the first 28 items exclusively on the basis of direct observation during the interview.

Rate the last 34 items (29–63) on the basis of the child's verbal report of occurrence at the time of the interview or during the past seven days. Do not use any other data, but that obtained in the interview with the child.

Mark all rows consecutively — do not skip any rows. Each row is numbered on the scoring sheet and also on the page with the item to facilitate marking on the correct row.

USE A NO. 2 LEAD PENCIL. BE SURE TO MAKE MARKS HEAVY AND DARK. ERASE COMPLETELY ANY MARKS YOU WISH TO CHANGE.

NOT AS-SESSED	NOT PRESENT	VERY MILD	MILD	MODER-ATE	MODER-ATELY SEVERE	SEVERE	EX-TREMELY SEVERE		NOT AS-SESSED	NOT PRESENT	VERY MILD	MILD	MODER-ATE	MODER-ATELY SEVERE	SEVERE	EX-TREMELY SEVERE

Mark on right half of scoring sheet on row specified — ROW NO.

Item	ROW NO.
1. **TENSION** *(Do not include fidgetiness)* Musculature appears taut, strained or tense. Fingers clothing, clenches jaws, grips arms of chair, hands tremulous.	1
2. **UNDERPRODUCTIVE SPEECH** *(Rate amount of speech only, not rate or relevance)* Fails to answer questions, monosyllabic, has to be pushed to get an answer, doesn't elaborate, blocked.	2
3. **FIDGETINESS** *(Do not include tics)* Wriggles, squirms, moves or shifts restlessly in chair.	3
4. **HYPERACTIVITY** Has difficulty sitting in chair, gets up, moves fast, vigorously, impulsive bursts of locomotion. Exclude slow ambling even if constant. In rating degree of overactivity, consider the ease with which the hyperactivity can be controlled.	4
5. **HYPOACTIVITY** Few or no spontaneous movements. Sluggish. Movements are slowed, feeble or labored. Requires prompting for initiation of motor movements. Long latencies of appropriate motor behavior.	5
6. **DISTRACTIBILITY** Distracted by usually minor, irrelevant stimuli. Shifts from one topic to another. Interrupts thought or action abruptly.	6
7. **ABNORMAL OBJECT RELATIONSHIPS** Autistic use of objects with disregard for usual function. Stereotyped and repetitive sequences or fragments of play. Aimless behavior without organizing goal idea.	7
8. **WITHDRAWAL** Oblivious of examiner, preoccupied. Facial expression and behavior do not respond directly to examiner. Attention focus is oblique and vague in direction, with avoidance of eye contact. Responses are very delayed and require forceful stimuli. *(The fact that the child may have peculiar interest in examiner, such as obsessive interest in parts of body or clothing does not preclude a rating of withdrawal).*	8
9. **OVERCOMPLIANT** Goes along with whatever examiner says in a passive fashion, even contradicting self. Does not assert self in a reasonable manner.	9
10. **NEGATIVE, UNCOOPERATIVE** Active opposition and resistance to examiner's initiative *(differs from withdrawal and oblique avoidance).* Guarded, evasive replies, teasing, manipulative or hostile refusal to cooperate. Child may remain silent in passive aggressive fashion.	10
11. **ANGRY AFFECT** Irritable, touchy, erupts easily – shouts angrily, screams at examiner, overtly and directly hostile.	11

Continue marking on right half of scoring sheet on row specified — ROW NO.

Item	ROW NO.
12. **SILLY AFFECT** Clowning, inappropriately giddy, playful, silly behavior.	12
13. **CONFUSION** Confused, bewildered, perplexed in behavior or verbal expression.	13
14. **DISORIENTATION** Child is unaware of identity of surroundings after being told where he is. Not aware of time discriminations. Doesn't know age or surname.	14
15. **CLINGING BEHAVIOR** Clinging, in physical and verbal behavior with the examiner. Seeks physical contact; demands constant direction.	15
16. **UNSPONTANEOUS RELATION TO EXAMINER** Responds to examiner, but does not initiate social or verbal overtures, nor sustain conversation once begun. Lacks spontaneity. Restricted.	16
17. **SUSPICIOUS AFFECT** Expresses concern about the intent of the examination. Questions instructions and good will of interviewer.	17
18. **DEPRESSED DEMEANOR** Exhibits a dejection, depression in mood. Looks sad. Seems to be in a state of painful dejection.	18
19. **BLUNTED AFFECT** Restricted range and intensity of emotional expressions; blank or fixed facial expression, monotonous voice.	19
20. **LABILITY OF AFFECT** Can suddenly vary from calm to silly to sullen mood, to screaming, crying, loud complaining.	20
21. **PRESSURE OF SPEECH** Speech is hurried, accelerated, pushed, difficult to interrupt.	21
22. **LEVEL OF SPEECH DEVELOPMENT** *(Do not include diction, rate of speech, or relevance of speech)* From age-appropriate (1) to severely retarded (7) speech development. Using your clinical judgment of verbal I.Q., estimate the level of speech development (in percent) in relation to verbal I.Q. 1 = Over 90% 2 = 76 – 90% 3 = 61 – 75% 4 = 46 – 60% 5 = 31 – 45% 6 = 15 – 30% 7 = Less than 15%	22
23. **STUTTERING**	23
24. **LOW VOICE** Voice weak, mumbling, whispering, almost inaudible.	24
25. **LOUD VOICE** Voice loud, boisterous, shouting.	25

APPENDIX

Copy of ECDEU Children's Psychiatric Rating Scale.

NOTE: Reprinted by permission of the publisher from NIMH, "Children's ECDEU Battery," *Psychopharmacology Bulletin, Special Issue,* 9:196-239, 1973.

CHILDREN'S PSYCHIATRIC RATING SCALE

		ROW NO.
Continue marking on right half of scoring sheet on row specified		
26.	**MISPRONUNCIATIONS**	26
	Lisping, mispronounces letters such as r, s, l, etc. Unclear speech.	
27.	**OTHER SPEECH DEVIANCE**	27
	Echolalia; question-like melody; neologisms; sentences fragmented, unusual syntax.	
28.	**RHYTHMIC MOTIONS (STEREOTYPE)**	28
	Rocking, whirling, head banging; rolling; repetitive jumping, hand movements, athetoid, twiddling, arm flapping.	
	RATE THE FOLLOWING 34 ITEMS ON THE BASIS OF THE CHILD'S VERBAL REPORT OF OCCURRENCE AT THE TIME OF THE INTERVIEW OR DURING THE PAST 7 DAYS. DO NOT USE ANY OTHER DATA BUT THAT OBTAINED IN INTERVIEW WITH THE CHILD.	
29.	**EXPRESSED FEELINGS OF INFERIORITY**	29
	Describes feelings of inadequacy, inferiority, self-deprecating, self-belittling.	
30.	**EXPRESSED FEELINGS OF GRANDIOSITY**	30
	Exaggerates own value, boasting. Unduly pleased with own achievement. Says he is much better than others. Distorted sense of own capacity.	
31.	**PHYSICAL COMPLAINTS**	31
	Somatic complaints of headaches, stomach aches, dizziness, not feeling well, etc. *(do not include fatigue).*	
32.	**OBESITY**	32
	Judge from child's appearance from normal physical appearance to severe obesity.	
33.	**OTHER EATING PROBLEMS**	33
	Picky, fussy, many dislikes, extremely restricted diet, peculiar food tastes.	
34.	**SEPARATION ANXIETY**	34
	Ease with which child separates from mother or other significant people. Extent of observed or reported anxiety (by child) experienced by child when separated from mother or other significant people.	
35.	**DEPRESSION**	35
	Admits feeling sad, lonely, feels like crying, expresses a despondent or despairing attitude. Difficulty in anticipating success and enjoyment.	
36.	**EUPHORIA – ELATION**	36
	States he feels terrific, great, elevation of mood, hypomanic state. "This is the best of all possible worlds." Feels elated and wonderful. Nothing is impossible.	
37.	**LACK OF ENERGY**	37
	States he feels sluggish, fatigued. Everything is too much. Weary and feels unable to make slightest effort. *(Do not infer from motor retardation or expressed indifference).*	

When you have completed this page (item 41), turn all pages on this side and continue with text (item 42) on page R1

		ROW NO.
38.	**PREOCCUPATION WITH TOPICS OF ANXIETY**	38
	Says he has nervous or scary feelings, concerns, apprehension, fears. Says he worries about failure or other mishaps, thinks about something happening to self or parents- illness, injury, death, loss or separation.	
39.	**PREOCCUPATION WITH DEPRESSIVE TOPICS**	39
	Preoccupied with feelings of inadequacy and inferiority. Expresses feeling that nothing can turn out all right. Preoccupied with feelings of uselessness, futility, and possibly guilt. Suicidal preoccupation.	
40.	**SUICIDAL ATTEMPTS**	40
	0 = Not assessed	
	1 = None	
	2 = Suicidal threat	
	3 = One minor gesture without danger	
	4 = A couple or several minor gestures without danger	
	5 = Dangerous gesture	
	6 = Infliction of life threatening damage to self	
	7 = Several life threatening attempts	
41.	**FEARS AND PHOBIAS**	41
	Irrational morbid fears of specific objects, person, or situations, which, if extreme, lead to avoidance behavior. Rate 6 or 7 only when fear is so severe it leads to phobic avoidance.	

APPENDIX (*continued*)

CHILDREN'S PSYCHIATRIC RATING SCALE

ROW NO.		Mark on left half of scoring sheet on row specified
1	42.	**COMPULSIVE ACTS** Acts or "habits" which are regarded as unreasonable by the child, such as, counting, checking, rituals, excessive orderliness, and cleanliness.
2	43.	**NERVOUS HABITS AND MANNERISMS** Stereotyped movements; rituals which are not perceived as irrational. Facial tics or mannerisms. Biting nails, fingers, cuticles. Sucking of objects or body parts *(thumb, fingers, hair, etc.);* Picking on skin, scabs, nose, twisting hair.
3	44.	**OBSESSIVE THINKING** Inability to "turn off" repetitive thought. Preoccupation, ruminations about abstract problems or personal matters.
4	45.	**SOLITARY INTERESTS** Interested in activities which require little if any peer interaction, such as stamp collecting, movie going, reading, school work, solitary activities.
5	46.	**LACK OF PEER INTERACTION** Isolated from other children. Has no friends or cannot name current close friend nor describe participation in play with peers. Lacks interest in peers.
6	47.	**GANG ACTIVITY** Joins in antisocial activities along with a group of children *(fighting, trouble making, stealing)* as a cooperating group against others.
7	48.	**FIGHTING WITH PEERS** Says he frequently gets into fights — beats up other kids or gets beaten up. Says he has a bad temper.
	49.	**BULLY** Says he's always the leader, winner; or says he teases, bullies children; pushes children around; threatens them.
9	50.	**TEMPER OUTBURSTS** Admits to feeling angry, irritable, touchy, admits he has a temper.
10	51.	**SCAPEGOAT** Says he's picked on, teased, left out or pushed around, and bullied by other children. May be called "sissy" or "baby".
11	52.	**LYING** Contradicts self in ways indicative of effort to hide the truth. Reports telling tall stories, fibs, or admits he's accused of telling lies.
12	53.	**EXPLOITATIVE RELATIONSHIPS** Interested in other people insofar as he can get something out of it. Callous and calculating in interpersonal activities.

ROW NO.		Continue marking on left half of scoring sheet on row specified
13	54.	**INABILITY TO FALL ASLEEP** Child reports a long time to fall asleep after going to bed. 1 = Not present 5 = 46 to 60 min. 2 = 10 to 15 min. 6 = 60 to 90 min. 3 = 16 to 30 min. 7 = Over 90 min. 4 = 31 to 45 min.
14	55.	**OTHER SLEEP DIFFICULTIES** Nightmares, early morning awakening, sleep walking, interrupted sleep.
15	56.	**BEDWETTING** Rating is for frequency of bedwetting for past 7 nights 1 = None 4 = 3 times 7 = 6 to 7 times 2 = One time 5 = 4 times 3 = 2 times 6 = 5 times
16	57.	**IDEAS OF REFERENCE** People are looking at him, following him, staring, etc. Malevolent intent is not necessary but may occur.
17	58.	**PERSECUTORY** Feels people have it in for him, try to hurt him. In the extreme rating, the thinking has a delusional quality in that the belief is impervious to change, rational arguments, or corrective experiences.
18	59.	**OTHER THINKING DISORDERS** Irrelevant speech; or incoherent speech; or loose associations.
19	60.	**DELUSIONS** Delusional beliefs or convictions besides paranoia (58), i.e. believes has introjected persons or objects in his body, has a mission, is some other person or character, has unusual powers; is guilty of some event.
20	61.	**HALLUCINATIONS** The overall rating is a frequency rating reflecting the constancy of the experience: 1 = Not present 5 = 4 to 5 times 2 = Once 6 = 5 to 6 times 3 = 2 times 7 = Daily recurrent phenomenon 4 = 3 times
21	62.	**PECULIAR FANTASIES** Morbid or bizarre fantasies and pre-occupations, peculiar body sensations, disturbances of body image experiences *(not figure drawings);* preoccupation with flying, supernatural influences, sadism, masochism.
22	63.	**LACK OF INSIGHT** Is convinced of the reality of hallucinations or fantasies.

APPENDIX *(continued)*

REFERENCES

1. ALDERTON, H., and HODDINOTT, B., "The Children's Pathology Index," *Canadian Psychiatric Association Journal, 13:*353–361, 1968.

2. BELL, R., WALDROP, M., and WELLER, G., "A Rating System for the Assessment of Hyperactive and Withdrawn Children in Preschool Samples," *American Journal of Orthopsychiatry, 42:*23–24, 1972.

3. BLUNDEN, D., SPRING, C., and GREENBERG, L., "Validation of the Classroom Behavior Inventory," *Journal of Consulting and Clinical Psychology, 42:*84–88, 1974.

4. BORGATTA, E. F., and FANSHEL, D., *Behavioral Characteristics of Children Known to Psychiatric Outpatient Clinics,* Child Welfare League of America, 1965.

5. BROWN, G. W., and RUTTER, M., "The Measurement of Family Activities and Relationships: A Methodological Study," *Human Relations, 19:*241–263, 1966.

6. BURDOCK, E. L., and HARDESTY, A. S., "A Children's Behavior Diagnostic Inventory," *Annals of the New York Academy of Sciences, 105:*890–896, 1964.

7. CATTELL, R., and COAN, R. W., "Child Personality Structure as Revealed by Teachers' Behavior Ratings," *Journal of Clinical Psychology, 13:*315–327, 1957.

8. CATTELL, R. B., and WARBURTON, F. W., *Objective Personality and Motivation Tests: A Theoretical Introduction and Practical Compendium,* University of Illinois Press, Urbana, 1967.

9. COMREY, A., BACKER, T., and GLASER, E., *A Sourcebook for Mental Health Measures,* Human Interaction Research Institute, Los Angeles, Calif., 1973.

10. CHUN, KI-TAEK, COBB, S., and FRENCH, J. R. P., *Measures for Psychological Assessment: A Guide to 3000 Original Sources and Their Applications,* Survey Research Center of the Institute for Social Research, University of Michigan, Ann Arbor, 1975.

11. CONNERS, C. K., "Rating Scales for Use in Drug Studies with Children," *Psychopharmacology Bulletin,* Special Issue on Children, NIMH, 1973.

12. ———, "Symptom Patterns in Hyperkinetic, Neurotic and Normal Children," *Child Development, 41:*667–682, 1970.

13. ———, "A Teacher Rating Scale for Use in Drug Studies with Children," *American Journal of Psychiatry, 126:*884–888, 1969.

14. DREGER, R. M., et al., "Behavioral Classification Project," *Journal of Consulting Psychology, 28:*1–13, 1964.

15. GALTON, F., *Memories of My Life,* Methuen, London, 1908.

16. GRAHAM, P., and RUTTER, M., "The Reliability and Validity of the Psychiatric Assessment of the Child: II. Interview with the Parent," *British Journal of Psychiatry, 114:*581–592, 1968.

17. GUILFORD, J. P., *Personality,* McGraw-Hill, New York, 1959.

18. ———, *Psychometric Methods,* 2nd ed., McGraw-Hill, New York, 1954.

19. HERSEN, M., and BELLACK, A. (Eds.), *Behavioral Assessment: A Practical Handbook,* Pergamon Press, New York, 1976.

20. JENKINS, R., "Psychiatric Syndromes in Children and their Relation to Family Background," *American Journal of Orthopsychiatry, 36:*450–457, 1966.

21. ———, and HEWITT, L., "Types of Personality Encountered in Child Guidance Clinics," *American Journal of Orthopsychiatry, 14:*84–94, 1944.

22. JOHNSON, O. G., and BOMMARITO, J. W., *Tests and Measurements in Child Development: A Handbook,* Jossey-Bass, San Francisco, 1971.

23. KUPIETZ, S., BIALER, I., and WINSBERG, B. G., "A Behavior Rating Scale for Assessing Improvement in Behaviorally Deviant Children: A Preliminary Investigation," *American Journal of Psychiatry, 128:*1432, 1972.

24. LANGNER, T. S., et al., "A Screening Inventory for Assessing Psychiatric Impairment in Children 6 to 18" *Journal of Consulting and Clinical Psychology, 44:*286–296, 1976.

25. LYERLY, S. B., and ABBOTT, P. S., *Handbook of Psychiatric Rating Scales (1950–1964),* NIMH, PHS Service Bulletin No. 1495, 1968.

26. MILLER, L. C., "School Behavior Checklist: An Inventory of Deviant Behavior for Elementary School Children," *Journal of Consulting and Clinical Psychology, 38:*134–144, 1973.

27. MURRAY, H. A., *Explorations in Personality,* Oxford University Press, New York, 1938.

28. MYKLEBUST, H., *The Pupil Rating Scale: Screening for Learning Disabilities,* Grune & Stratton, 1971.

29. PETERSON, D. R., "Behavior Problems of Middle Childhood," *Journal of Consulting Psychology, 25:*205–209, 1961.

30. QUAY, H. C., "Personality Dimensions in Delinquent Males as Inferred from the Factor Analysis of Behavior Ratings," *Journal of Research in Crime and Delinquency, 1:*33–37, 1964.

31. RUTTER, M., and GRAHAM, P., "The Reliability and Validity of the Psychiatric Assessment of the Child: I. Interview with the Child," *British Journal of Psychiatry, 3:*563–579, 1968.

32. SHAEFFER, E., Personal communication, 1976.

33. SHERWIN, A. C., et al., "Determination of Psychiatric Impairment in Children," *Journal of Nervous and Mental Disease, 141:*333–341, 1965.

34. SINES, J. O., et al., "Identification of Clinically Relevant Dimensions of Children's Behavior," *Journal of Consulting and Clinical Psychology, 33:*728–734, 1969.

35. SPIVACK, G., and LEVINE, M., "The Devereux Child Behavior Rating Scales: A Study of Symptom Behaviors in Latency Age Atypical Children," *American Journal of Mental Deficiency, 68:*700–717, 1964.

36. SPRAGUE, R. L., and SLEATOR, E. K., "Effects of Psychopharmacologic Agents on Learning Disorders," *Pediatric Clinics of North America, 38:*134–144, 1973.

37. WASKOW, E., and PARLOFF, M. B. (Eds.), *Psychotherapy Change Measures,* DHEW Publication No. (ADM) 74–120, 1975.

38. WERRY, J. S., SPRAGUE, R. L., and COHEN, M. N., "Conner's Teacher Scale for Use in Drug Studies with Children—An Empirical Study," *Journal of Abnormal Child Psychology, 3:*217–229, 1975.

Editor's Epilogue

A personal comment by the editor may not be out of place in closing. Perhaps such a comment is best represented as a "trade secret."

In perspective, the most difficult clinical tasks usually involve accurate assessment. Treatment obstacles often arise because assessment has been casual, nonrigorous, or carried out as an afterthought (during the 1940s a common house officer joke was "put the patient on penicillin and if he is not better in forty-eight hours, do a physical").

The highly valued intercession of the consultant most often involves his capacity and skill to ask the questions and observe the behavior which others have ignored or devalued. Having done so, he is in a position to impress his colleagues and students with his wisdom and his ability to suggest management options not considered previously. His carefully guarded secret is that he took the time and trouble to complete what was very likely an incomplete assessment.

The following two bibliographic lists may help the reader who would engage the minds of the many colleagues who have pondered the issues of assessment in years past.

—RLC

SUGGESTED ADDITIONAL READING

REFERENCES OF SIGNIFICANT HISTORICAL INTEREST

BAKER, H. J., and TRAPHAGEN, V., *The Diagnosis and Treatment of Behavior Problem Children*, Macmillan, New York, 1937.

BAKWIN, H., and BAKWIN, R. M., *Psychologic Care During Infancy and Childhood*, D. Appleton-Century Co., New York, 1942.

BROWN, S., and POTTER, H. W., *Psychiatric Study of Problem Children*, New York State Hospital Press, Utica, 1930.

CONN, J. H., "The Play Interview: A Method of Studying Children's Attitudes," *American Journal of Diseases of Children*, 58:1199–1214, 1939.

DARWIN, C., "A Biographical Sketch of an Infant," *Mind*, 2:285–294, 1877.

FREUD, A., "Indications for Child Analysis," in Eissler, R. S., et al. (Eds.), *The Psychoanalytic Study of the Child*, vol. 1, pp. 127–149, International Universities Press, New York, 1945.

GRACE, H. K., *The Development of a Child Psychiatric Treatment Program*, John Wiley, New York, 1974.

Institute for Juvenile Research, *Child Guidance Procedures*, D. Appleton-Century Co., New York, 1937.

LEVY, D. M., "Use of Play Technique as an Experimental Procedure," *American Journal of Orthopsychiatry*, 3:266–277, 1933.

LOUITT, W. S., *Clinical Psychology*, Harper and Brothers, New York, 1947.

Menninger Foundation, *Disturbed Children*, Jossey-Bass, San Francisco, 1969.

MOODIE, W., *The Doctor and the Difficult Child*, Commonwealth Fund, New York, 1947.

ROSE, J. A., "The Factors Affecting Maternal Adaptation in Cases of Blood Group Incompatibility Between Adult and Offspring," *Acta Paedopsychiatrica*, 29:211–212, 1954.

———, and SONIS, M., "The Use of Separation as a Diagnostic Measure in the Parent-Child Emotional Crisis," *American Journal of Psychiatry*, 116:409–415, 1959.

SAYLES, M., *Child Guidance Cases*, Commonwealth Fund, New York, 1932.

SCHULMAN, J. L., *Management of Emotional Disorders in Pediatric Practice*, Year Book Medical Publishers, Chicago, 1967.

SHIRLEY, H. F., *Pediatric Psychiatry*, Harvard University Press, Cambridge, 1963.

WITMER, H., *Psychiatric Interviews with Children*, Harvard University Press, Cambridge, 1946.

OTHER SOURCES

ARNOLO, EUGENE, and SWELTZER, DONALD J., "Behavior Checklist Factor Analysis for Children and Adolescents," *Archives of General Psychiatry*, 30:799–804, 1974.

BENDER, L., *Child Psychiatric Techniques*, Charles C Thomas, Springfield, Ill., 1952.

BRIM, O. G., "Macro-Structural Influences on Child Development and the Need for Childhood Social Indicators," *American Journal of Orthopsychiatry, 45:*516–524, 1975.

BUCKLE, D., and LEBOVICI, S., *Child Guidance Centers,* World Health Organization, Geneva, 1960.

CHESS, S., *An Introduction to Child Psychiatry,* Grune & Stratton, New York, 1959.

Committee on Child Health, *Services for Children with Emotional Disturbances,* The American Public Health Association, Inc., New York, 1961.

DICKIE, J., and BAGUR, J., "Considerations for the Study of Language in Young Low-Income Minority Group Children," *Merrill-Palmer Quarterly, 18:*25–38, 1972.

FORNESS, S. R., and ESVELDT, M. A., "Classroom Observation of Children Referred to a Child Psychiatric Clinic," *Journal of the American Academy of Child Psychiatry, 13:*335–343, 1974.

HELPER, MALCOLM M., "Parental Evaluations of Children and Children's Self-Evaluations," *Journal of Abnormal and Social Psychology, 56:*86–99, 1958.

HARING, N. G., and RIDGEWAY, R. W., "Early Identification of Children With Learning Disabilities," *Exceptional Children, 33:*387–395, 1967.

KESSLER, J. W., *Psychopathology of Childhood,* Prentice-Hall, Englewood Cliffs, N.J., 1966.

KUGELMASS, I. N., *The Autistic Child,* Charles C Thomas, Springfield, Ill., 1970.

LAYMAN, E. M., and LOURIE, R. S., "Waiting Room Observation as a Technique of Analysis of Communication Behavior in Children and Their Parents," in Hoch, P., and Zubin, J. (Eds.), *Psychopathology of Communication,* pp. 247–249, Grune & Stratton, New York, 1957.

MOUSTAKAS, C., SIGEL, I., and SHALOCK, H., "The Measurement and Analysis of Child-Adult Interaction," *Child Development, 27:*109–134, 1956.

O'LEARY, K. D., "Assessment of Psychopathology in Children," in Quay, H. C., and Werry, J. S. (Eds.), *Psychopathological Disorders of Childhood,* p. 259, John Wiley, New York, 1972.

ROBERTS, J., and BAIRD, J. T., *Parent Ratings of Behavioral Patterns of Children,* U.S. National Center for Health Statistics, Rockville, Md., U.S. Government Printing Office, 1971.

RUTTER, M., and GRAHAM, P., "The Reliability and Validity of the Psychiatric Assessment of the Child, I: Interview with the Child," *British Journal of Psychiatry, 114:*563–579, 1968.

SENN, M. J., and SOLNIT, A. J., *Problems in Child Behavior and Development,* Lea & Febiger, Philadelphia, 1968.

SHAPIRO, M. I., "Psychiatric Examination of the Child," *Mental Hygiene, 43:*32–39, 1959.

SILVER, A., et al., "A Search Battery for Scanning Kindergarten Children for Potential Learning Disability," *Journal of the American Academy of Child Psychiatry, 15:*224–239, 1976.

SILVER, L. B., "The Playroom Diagnostic Evaluation of Children with Neurologically Based Learning Disabilities," *Journal of the American Academy of Child Psychiatry, 16:*240–256, 1976.

SODDY, K., *Clinical Child Psychiatry,* Williams and Wilkins, Baltimore, 1960.

STAVER, N., and LaFORGE, E., "Intake as an Area of Conflict in Clinic Function," *Journal of the American Academy of Child Psychiatry, 14:*589–599, 1975.

YARROW, L. J., "Interviewing Children," in Mussen, P. N. (Ed.), *Handbook of Research Methods in Child Development,* pp. 561–602, John Wiley, New York, 1960.

NAME INDEX

Abbott, P. S., 676, 685
Ackerman, N., 628
Adams, P. L., 283–290
Adelson, E., 136
Adelson, J., 218, 220, 221, 223
Adler, A., 389, 399, 444
Ainsworth, M. D. S., 92, 527
Allnutt, B.-L., 373–378
Altshuler, K., 142
Amatruda, C. S., 116, 511, 516, 560
Ames, L. B., 563
Anastasi, A., 556, 566, 567
Anders, T., 79, 82
Anderson, J., 262
Andrews, T. F., 77
Anthony, E. J., 6
Anthony, J., 222
Ardon, M. S., 222
Arlow, J., 391
Aserinsky, E., 78
Attneave, C. L., 239–248

Babcock, C. G., 303
Babcock, D. G., 249
Bach, G. R., 365
Bach, J. C., 384
Bach, J. S., 384
Bach, W. F., 384
Backer, T., 685
Baird, D., 19
Baker, S. L., 312
Baksin, H., 442
Balikov, H., 413–420
Bardwick, Jr., 221
Barnett, C., 94
Barron, D. H., 15, 16
Barry, H., 392
Barry, H., Jr., 392
Barten, S., 82
Bateson, M., 136
Baumrind, D., 214
Bayley, N., 160, 175, 516, 560
Beebe, B., 136
Becker, E., 364
Becker, D. J., 601–621
Bekoff, M., 76
Bell, A., 152
Bell, R., 680
Bell, R. Q., 83, 84, 85, 95
Bell, S., 92
Bell, S. M., 108

Bellack, A., 684
Bellak, L., 563
Bender, L., 590
Benton, A. L., 590
Benjamin, J. D., 8, 67, 91, 97, 114, 117, 154
Berger, A. C., 222
Berger, H., 63
Bergman, A., 136, 174
Berkmann, T., 428
Berlin, I. N., 308
Berlin, R., 308
Bernal, J. F., 90
Bernard, J., 221
Bernstein, B., 130
Bernstein, N. R., 441–447, 465–474
Bernstine, R., 17
Bertalanffy, L. von, 73
Bibring, G. L., 20
Biles, M., 19
Biller, H. B., 365, 366
Billingsley, A., 249, 251
Birch, H. G., 308, 527
Birns, B., 82, 83, 84
Birtschnell, J., 392
Black, R., 91
Block, J., 223, 224
Bloom, L., 139
Blos, P., 200
Blunden, D., 681
Boek, R. D., 215
Bond, E. K., 85, 86
Borgatta, E. F., 682
Borge, G. F., 392
Borkowski, W., 17
Bornstein, B., 186, 187
Borow, H., 220
Bower, T. G. R., 158
Bowlby, J., 6, 93, 94, 107, 108, 154, 373, 374, 375, 376
Boyle, R. P., 220
Brasel, K. E., 426
Braungart, R. G., 224
Brazelton, T. B., 20, 74, 77, 80–81, 82, 96, 136, 137, 514
Brennan, M., 17
Bridge, E. M., 442
Bronfenbrenner, U., 214
Brosin, H., 446
Broverman, I. K., 221
Brown, C., 253
Brown, R., 170
Bruner, J., 132, 133, 141, 158, 168, 169
Brunswick, A., 215

Bryant, N. D., 587
Burlingham, D., 148, 414, 415, 416, 417
Buros, O. K., 566
Burt, C., 566
Buxbaum, E., 141
Bynum, T. W., 217

Cain, A. C., 414
Caldwell, B. M., 527
Call, J. D., 3–10, 83, 184–190, 233–236
Callahan, D., 273
Cannon, M. S., 251
Capparell, H. V., 388
Carlin, J. E., 290–300
Carlsmith, L., 366
Carlson, R., 219, 220
Carmichael, L., 16, 72
Carpenter, G., 91, 92, 109
Castaneda, A., 262
Castillo, F. G., 257–263
Cattell, R. B., 679, 685
Cazden, C., 130
Cellini, B., 383
Cellini, G., 383
Chase, M., 76, 77
Chess, S., 6, 11, 527
Cheyne, J. A., 423
Chomsky, N., 131–132, 134, 141
Chun, K.-T., 685
Church, J., 320
Churchill, S. R., 631
Clark, K. B., 252, 253, 256
Clark, R. A., 388
Clark-Stewart, A., 170
Clifton, R. K., 88
Clothier, F., 344
Coan, R. W., 679
Cobb, S., 685
Cobbs, P. M., 256
Cohen, D. J., 22–62
Cohen, J., 409
Cohen, L. B., 89
Cohen, R. L., 485–508, 529–553, 593–594, 621–624, 630–647, 654–657
Cole, J. K., 554
Coleman, J., 220, 249, 250
Coles, R., 252
Colombel, G., 393–396

Comrey, A., 685
Condon, W. S., 96, 109, 129
Conel, J. L., 76
Conners, C. K., 675–686
Cooper, H., 448
Cox, C., 329
Crick, F., 25, 26
Crumley, F. E., 312
Cunningham, M. R., 6

Dahlström, A., 40, 41, 43
Darnauer, P. F., 311
Darwin, C., 5, 370
Davis, B., 17
Davis, E. B., 249, 251, 252, 254
Davis, M., 16
Dayton, G. L., Jr., 86
Denisova, M., 78
Dennis, M., 574–583
Deutsch, C. P., 302
Deutsch, H., 200, 345, 367
Deutsch, L., 445
Devine, G., 273
Dickens, C., 352, 367
Dijkstra, J., 84
Dittrichova, Jr., 85
Dizenhuz, I. M., 278–382
Doke, L. A., 684
Dore, J., 133
Douglas, J. D., 443
Douglass, F., 248–249
Douvan, E., 218, 220, 221
Drash, A. L., 601–621
Dreger, R. M., 682
Dreyfus-Brisac, C., 65, 82
Drillien, C. M., 19
Drucker, J., 157–164
Dubowitz, L. M., 511
Dulit, E., 217
Durrell, D. D., 591

Eckstein, R., 507
Edelheit, H., 139, 140
Edington, G., 397–406
Ehrhardt, A. A., 151, 620
Eibl-Eibesfeldt, I., 107
Eiduson, B. T., 343, 369, 406–412

SUBJECT INDEX

Abandonment fears: blind child and, 417; severely-burned child and, 466; street child and, 301

Abstract thinking: adolescent, 235; black child and, 252; development from two and one-half to four years in, 168; development at ten years for, 198–199; intellectually superior children in, 328, 330; Jewish child and, 179; talented child and, 334–335

Accidents: adolescent suicide and, 550; child amputee and, 427; eight to ten year olds and, 191

Accommodation, 158, 216

Acculturation: American Indian child, 246; Puerto Rican child, 264

Acetaminophen, 472

Acetylcholine (ACh): anticholinergic agents and, 50; cholinergic neurons in mapping of, 42; diet and, 44; hypothalamic, 52; neurotransmission with, 30, 37–38; tricyclic antidepressants and, 48

Acetylcholine-sterase (AChE), 38

Achievement orientation, in commune-reared child, 408, 409

Achondroplasia, 20, 601

Acting out: adolescent, 210, 211, 223; adopted child and, 346; American Indian child and, 246; Jewish child and, 280; military child and, 314; only child and, 391, 398; Puerto Rican child and, 269; street child and, 305, 307

Activity: basic rest-activity cycle (BRAC) and, 79; bowel patterning of, 122; individual differences in levels of, 82, 83; macrorhythms of, 73

Adaptation: accommodation in, 158; adolescent, 227; androgeny as sexual identity and, 221; assimilation in, 158; birth process and, 80; black child and, 249; Chicano child and, 261; child behavior and, 430–431; chronically ill child and, 435; clinical examination of infant for, 516; commune-reared child and, 409, 411; definitions of normal in, 4; development from two and one-half to four years and, 175–176; discovery of genital differences and, 150–151; divorce and, 379; foster child and, 350; infant mortality rate and, 108; Jewish

child and, 276–277, 280, 281; late latency period and, 187; later psychopathology and, 4; military child and, 314, 315; mother-infant relationship and, 74; neuroendocrine response to stress and, 59; newborn, 73; only child and, 391; overseas child and, 317; Piagetian theory on, 158; Puerto Rican child and, 264, 266; refugee child and, 297; rich child and, 324; seizure disorder child and, 446; severely-burned child and, 466–467, 471; social conception of normal and, 3; street child and, 302, 306, 307

Addison's disease, 617

Adenine, 26

Adenosine triphosphate (ATP), 33

Adenyl cyclase, 53

Adenylate cyclase, 34, 39

Adolescence: adopted child in, 344, 346; American Indian child in, 245–246; anxiety and intrapsychic change during, 233–236; anxiety associated with physical development during, 209; asthmatic child and, 439; beautiful child and, 339, 340; black child and, 250, 253, 255; Catholic child and, 272, 274; child amputee in, 428, 429; children of famous people and, 384, 387; chronically ill child and, 433–434, 435; clinical examination during, 506, 547–553; cognitive development in, 216–217; commune-reared child and, 410; congenital heart disease child and, 450; deaf child and, 424, 425; developmental study of male adolescents in, 224–228; development from thirteen to sixteen years for, 205–213; development from sixteen to nineteen years for, 213–223; dialysis patient and, 460, 463; divorce and, 380; dying child and, 478, 480; EEG rhythms before, 70; endocrine system and changes during, 606, 607–608; family diagnostic interview and, 623, 626; fantasies and depersonalization in, 211; fatherless child in, 360–361, 363–364, 365, 366, 368; foster child in, 349, 350, 351, 353; hormones and, 215; initiation rites during, 278; intellectually superior child

and, 331, 332; Jewish child and, 278–279; military child and, 310, 311, 312, 313, 315; of mother, 502; motherless child and, 375; need for further research into, 229–230; only child in, 390–391, 398; overseas child in, 318, 320; physical development during, 205–207; physical maturation and psychosocial characteristics in, 215–216; physiological growth during, 214–216; psychological changes during, 209–212; psychosocial development during, 217–224; Puerto Rican child in, 265, 267, 268–269, 270; puppy love in, 234; reproductive changes during, 207–209; self-concept, cognitive abilities, and self-esteem in, 211–212; severly-burned child in, 469; sex differences in height in, 214–215; sex reassignment and, 476; Southeast Asian refugee child and, 293; stages of Erikson's life-cycle theory and, 217–223; street child and, 304–305, 307; suicide during, 550; symbiotic family and, 623; "third person technique" in therapy in, 481; twins in, 394, 395; use of term, 206; WASP child in, 284, 286, 288; younger boy with older sister during, 403; younger girl with older sister in, 405

Adopted child, 342–348; American Indian child as, 245; characteristics that define, 342; coping behavior in, 346; cultural reactions to, 345; developmental interview in history taking for, 500; developmental levels and, 342–344; distribution of, 342; emotional disturbances in, 345–346; family reactions to, 344–345; fantasies of, 346; handicapped child as, 347; refugee child as, 292, 299; reunion with biological parents and, 343; revocability of, 347; sex reassignment and, 476; social structures needed by, 346–347; transracial, 345

Adrenal hyperplasia, 613–614

Adrenocorticosteroids, 54

Adrenocorticotrophic hormone (ACTH), 206

696

amputee and, 431, 432; children of divorce and, 382; chronically ill child and, 436; dialysis patient and, 460, 461; dying child and, 481; military child and, 310, 311, 312; Southeast Asian refugee child and, 294–300; street child and, 306, 308; WASP child and, 285

Child rearing practices: American Indian, 242; beautiful child and, 338; Catholic child and, 272, 275; Chicano child and, 258–260; child development views and, 5, 9; commune-reared child and, 407–408; Jewish child and, 277, 280, 281; Puerto Rican child and, 264–265, 267; street child and, 302, 305; youngest child in, 400

Children's Apperception Test (CAT), 560; limitations of, 555; use of, 563

Children's Behavior Inventory (CBI), 682–683

Children's Pathology Index (CPI), 684

Choline, 38

Choline acetylase, 58

Choline acetyltransferase (CAT), 38

Chlorpromazine, 472

Chromaffin cells, 44

Chromatography of amino acids, 595–596

Chromosomal disorders, 433; amniocentesis for, 599–600; heart disease associated with, 448; translocation carriers in, 599

Chromosomes: autosomal chromosomes in, 24; buccal smear test for, 597; cytogenetics in study of, 23; dominant, 24; embryological malformations and, 14; fertilization and, 11; karyotype analysis of, 597–599; recessive, 24; sex chromosomes and, 24

Chronically ill child, 432–436; characteristics of, 432–433; coping style of, 435–436; cultural reactions to, 434; developmental levels of, 433–434; diabetic child and, 452–458; dialysis patient and, 459–464; emotional disturbances in, 434–435; familial reactions and, 434; magnitude of problem of, 433; social structures for, 436; vulnerable child syndrome in, 644

Church: blacks and, 249, 256; Puerto Ricans and, 269

Class: adolescence and, 227; fatherless child and, 362; future-orientation and, 218; prenatal developmental differences and, 19; Puerto Rican child and, 265;

self-esteem and, 219; WASP child and, 284–285

Classical conditioning: childhood development theories and, 6; effects before and after two months of age for, 75; newborn, 88, 89

Classroom Behavior Inventory (CBI), 681

Climbing behavior: development from three to five years in, 178; differentiation and, 153

Clinging behavior: as attachment behavior, 93, 107; fear of strangers and, 166; as schema, 107

Clinical Data for Children (CDC) system, 658–674

Clinical psychologists, on assessment team, 489

Clitoris: adolescent development of, 209; ambiguous genitalia in children and, 474; development from three to five years and, 180, 181; oedipal constellation and sensations in, 185; at puberty, 201

Codeine, 472

Codon, 27

Cognitive development: adolescent, 212, 216–217, 218; blind child and, 413, 418; Chicano child and, 262; Chomsky's model of language and, 132; clinical examination of infant for, 516; development from two to four weeks for, 110; development from six to twelve months for, 116–117; deaf child and, 421, 423; development during second year and, 157–158; development from ten to thirteen years and, 202; development from sixteen to nineteen years and, 212, 216–217, 218; diabetic child and, 455, 456; foster child and, 353; Jewish child and, 277; language development and, 159; latency period, 188; limitations in, before age of four, 169–170; linguistic structures related to, 128; measurement and evaluation of, 159–161; mental representations capable of being evoked and, 176–177; motherless child and, 377; neuropsychological assessment of, 575–582; phobic responses during second year and, 166; physiological maturation and, 229; Piagetian language acquisition and, 134, 158–159; preverbal roots of language and, 137; psychiatric examination of child for, 538, 539; sensorimotor theory on, 73; speech acts and, 133; street child and, 302, 308

Cognitive theories, 107–108; child-

hood development theories and, 6; deaf child in, 422; physical development and cognitive development in, 216

College students: adolescents as, 220; American Indian child as, 246; black, 254; Jewish child in, 281; pregnancies among, 222; research on, 230; sexual behavior of, 221; student activists among, 224; time- and future-orientation of, 218

College Board Aptitude Tests, 366

Commune-reared child, 406–412; child-rearing practices of commune and, 407–408; coping behavior of, 411; definition of, 406–407; demographic characteristics of, 408; economic factors and, 411; social structures for, 411–412; "two-world" gap in, 409

Communication: American Indian customs governing, 243; blind child and, 414, 419; deaf child and, 422–423, 424, 426; development from six to twelve months and, 115–116; distinction between language, speech and, 129; divorce and, 378; language system of, 128; No gesture in, 68–69; nonverbal, see Nonverbal communication; preverbal, 165; psychiatric examination of child for, 538; symbiotic, 171 symbolization and, 161–162

Competency: development at nine years and, 194; newborn research into, 74

Competitiveness and competition: fatherless child and, 359; foster child and, 351, 352; only child and, 398; siblings and, 397; twins and, 395; younger girl with older sister in, 404

Compulsive behavior: Catholic child and, 272; diabetic child and, 455; Jewish child and, 279

Computers: in diagnostic systems, 656–657; standardized data collection in, 657–675

Computer Support in Military Psychiatry (COMPSY), 658

Concept formation: language acquisition and, 140–141; motherless child and, 374; no gesture in, 69; twins and, 395

Conditioning: language acquisition and, 131; newborn, 74, 88–89

Confidentiality: middle child and, 400; referral sources and, 646; treatment of child of famous parents and, 387

Conflict: adolescent, 210; asthmatic child and, 438; developmental process and, 9; divorce and, 379; foster child and, 352, 353;